Although aging is not without problems, older adults can age successfully by adopting strategies and behaviors for optimal aging.

Development in Late Adulthood

Physical (Chapter 14)

Average life expectancy has increa_____des. Genes and environment affect longevity.

Endurance, vision, and hearing _____l declines after age 70 in many people.

The risk of cardiovascular disease (e.g., heart attack, stroke, hypertension) increases with age. However, risks are affected by lifestyle, and overall death rates from these diseases have declined in recent decades.

Older adults suffer shortness of breath and have increased risk of chronic obstructive pulmonary disorder (COPD). Emphysema and asthma are two common forms of COPD.

Sleep disturbances as well as cancer risk increase with age.

Biological Theories of Aging	
Programmed cell death	Aging is biologically or genetically programmed.
Wear-and-tear	Aging is caused by the body's systems wearing out.
Cellular	Processes within cells cause buildup of harmful substances or cell deterioration and damage over time.

© Lynn Morales/Alamy

Cognitive (Chapter 14)

Age differences in attention tasks depend on the level of difficulty. On easy tasks, older and younger adults have few differences; on difficult tasks, younger adults do better.

Older adults' psychomotor speed is slower than that of young adults. Practice, task expertise, and being physically fit lessen the amount of slowing.

Working memory typically declines with age. Older adults usually do worse on tests of episodic recall; recognition tasks are less affected by age. Semantic memory and implicit memory are affected little by aging. Memory aids can help older adults compensate.

Contrary to popular belief, wisdom is correlated with life experience, not age. After early middle age, creativity declines with increasing age, but an individual's creative peak varies across disciplines and occupations.

Socioemotional (Chapter 14)

Rates of depression are reduced from young adulthood to old age, and symptoms vary by age. Treatment for older adults includes medication, behavior therapy, and cognitive therapy.

Anxiety disorders increase in older adulthood due to loss of health, relocation stress, isolation, and fear of losing independence. Medication and psychotherapy are effective treatments.

© ALAN ODDIE/Photo Edit

Dementia causes severe cognitive impairment. Alzheimer's disease is the most common form of irreversible dementia and is fatal. Various interventions can improve the patient's quality of life.

Development in Early Childhood

Physical (Chapter 3)

Children grow steadily taller and heavier during the preschool years, but their bodies are top heavy because growth of the head and trunk outpaces growth of the legs.

During these years, nerve cells continue to acquire myelin, a natural insulator that allows them to transmit information more rapidly. At the same time, synapses that are unused are gradually eliminated.

Preschoolers' brains are very flexible (called *brain plasticity*) and can sometimes completely recover from injuries as healthy neurons take over from damaged neurons.

Fine motor control becomes more developed, and preschoolers can dress and feed themselves fairly efficiently.

Cognitive (Chapter 4)

Preschoolers mentally group objects (schemes) based on functional or conceptual relationships. Schemes change based on new experiences.

Vygotsky proposed that children learn best when they collaborate with others who are more skilled. Vygotsky's ideas include the *zone of proximal development, scaffolding,* and *private speech.*

Preschool children can remember events they experienced more than 1 year previously, although they are impressionable as to what others suggest they may have experienced.

Preschoolers adjust their speech to fit the listener's needs. By age 3, sentences of 10 or more words are common.

Piaget's Four Stages of Thinking	
0-2 years	Sensorimotor thinking
2-7 years	Preoperational thinking
7-11 years	Concrete operations
11 years up	Formal operations

Socioemotional (Chapter 5)

Erikson's theory proposes three stages for infancy through the preschool years, in which the child must resolve crises for psychosocial growth: *trust vs. mistrust* (0–1 year), *autonomy vs. shame and doubt* (1–3 years), and *initiative vs. guilt* (3–5).

Prosocial behavior (e.g., helping, sharing) is more likely when children are empathetic, feel responsible for the person in distress, feel they have the necessary skills, feel happy, and perceive that the costs of helping are small.

Children gradually learn that gender is stable over time and cannot be changed. Children begin to learn gender-typical behavior by observing members of their own sex.

As children grow, they become better skilled at cooperation and at regulating their emotions.

The first 5 years of life are profoundly influential for all children. The events of these early years initiate and direct a lifelong developmental journey.

Infant Development

Physical (Chapter 3)

Newborns are born with a set of reflexes that enable them to get nutrients for growth (e.g., rooting and sucking reflexes), protect them from dangers (e.g., eye blink and withdrawal reflexes), and are the foundation of larger patterns of motor activity (e.g., stepping reflex).

Infants typically double their birth weight by 3 months, and triple it by 1 year.

Learning to walk requires integrating many motor skills and perceptual cues; most children walk unassisted by 15 months of age.

Infants' hand control increases rapidly in the first year; handedness is established by age 2.

Infants begin to recognize themselves in the mirror by about 15 months of age. Self-awareness is established by age 2.

Infants' brains grow rapidly and the neurons become more efficient.

Infants' Sensory Abilities	
Smell	Recognize familiar odors
Taste	Differentiate sweet, salty, sour, bitter
Touch	Sensitive to touch; likely feel pain
Hearing	Hear pitches in the range of human speech
Sight	See colors and perceive depth

Cognitive (Chapter 4)

Infants mentally group objects (called *schemes*) based on the actions they can perform on them. Schemes change constantly as a result of an infant's new experiences.

At about 18 months of age, infants fully understand object permanence.

Infants prefer infant-directed speech, which is slower and has greater variation in pitch and volume.

Many infants begin to talk at about 1 year, although they appear to understand others' speech before they speak themselves. Soon after learning to talk, children begin to speak in two-word sentences, called telegraphic speech.

Socioemotional (Chapter 5)

Bowlby argued that children who form an attachment to an adult are more likely to survive, and infant behaviors (e.g., crying, clinging, sucking, and smiling) are likely to elicit caregiving.

By about 6 to 7 months of age, most infants designate their first attachment figure (usually their mother); attachments to others soon follow. Basic emotions (e.g., joy, anger, fear) emerge in the first year of life. Complex emotions (e.g., guilt, embarrassment, pride) emerge between 18 and 24 months.

Parallel play begins at about 12 to 15 months of age, followed by *simple social play*. By age 2, *cooperative play* emerges.

Types of Attachments	
Secure	Infants have complete trust in mother
Disorganized	Infants don't understand mother's absence
Avoidant	Infants ignore mother
Resistant	Infants seem angry with mother

Three Factors That Contribute to Wisdom	
Factor	**Trait**
General personal condition	Mental ability
Specific expertise condition	Practice or mentoring
Facilitative life context	Education or leadership experience

Older adults' life satisfaction is strongly related to the number and quality of their friendships. Sibling relationships are important in old age.

Socioemotional (Chapters 15, 16)

Erikson proposed that older adults struggle between *integrity versus despair,* primarily through a life review.

Whether older adults achieve subjective well-being depends on hardiness, chronic illness, marital status, social network, and stress.

Older adults use religion and spiritual support more often than any other strategy to cope with problems. Older adults who are committed to their faith have better physical and mental health.

Two Theories of Psychosocial Aging	
Continuity Theory	Older adults cope with daily life by applying familiar strategies based on past experience to maintain internal and external structures.
Competence and Environmental Press Theory	Older adults adapt optimally when there is a balance between their ability to cope and the level of environmental demands placed on them.

Most people retire by choice, although some are forced to because of health problems or job loss. Financial security, good health, and friends are correlated with satisfaction with retirement. Most retirees maintain their health, friendships, and activity levels.

Long-term marriages tend to be happy until one partner develops serious health problems. Caring for a spouse considerably strains the relationship.

Abuse and neglect of older adults is an increasing problem. Most perpetrators are family members.

Older adults are less anxious about death and deal with it better than any other age group.

Dealing with grief can take 1 to 2 years; unexpected death is usually more difficult to handle. Normal grief reactions include sorrow, sadness, denial, disbelief, guilt, and anniversary reactions.

The death of one's partner is a deeply personal loss.

The number of U.S. single parents is increasing. Financially, single mothers are typically worse off than single fathers.

Development in Middle Adulthood

Physical (Chapter 13)

Wrinkles, gray hair, and weight gain appear in middle age. Bone density declines with age, especially in women; severe bone loss may result in *osteoporosis*. Arthritis often begins in late middle age: *Osteoarthritis*, the most common form of arthritis, is a wear-and-tear disease caused by injury or overuse of joints in the hands, knees, hips, and spine; *rheumatoid arthritis* is a less common but more destructive disease of the joints.

Most middle-aged adults continue to have active sex lives.

Menopause occurs in women in the 40s or early 50s, and physical changes may affect sexual response. Menopausal hormone therapy (MHT) is a controversial treatment for menopausal symptoms.

Although sperm production declines with age, men are still able to father a child in middle age or later adulthood. Prostate cancer becomes more likely in middle age.

Regular aerobic exercise slows physiological aging, reduces psychological stress, and improves cardiovascular health and overall fitness.

Middle-aged people report the highest levels of stress. Stress results when people perceive a situation as taxing their resources; daily hassles are viewed as the primary source of stress.

Cognitive (Chapter 13)

Practical intelligence is maintained in middle age and does not significantly decline until late life.

People become experts in select areas, and expertise usually peaks in middle adulthood. Experts are more flexible thinkers than novices and can skip steps in solving problems.

Middle-aged adults need practical connections and a rationale for learning and are more motivated by internal factors.

Socioemotional (Chapters 11, 12, 13)

As the length of time a couple has been together increases, commitment also increases while passion and intimacy decrease.

Marital satisfaction ebbs and flows over time but often improves after children leave home. Being flexible and adaptable leads to happier marriages.

Gender and ethnicity play important roles in shaping people's occupational lives. People's personalities and preferences also factor heavily into career choices.

Erikson believed middle-aged adults become more concerned with helping younger people achieve than with getting ahead themselves—a shift in priorities he labeled *generativity*. Middle-aged mothers tend to adopt the role of kin-keepers to maintain family traditions and link generations.

Occupational Choice and Development Theories	
Holland's personality-type theory	People choose occupations that optimize the fit between their individual traits and their occupational interests.
Super's developmental view	People adapt to an occupational role, in which there are five stages: implementation, establishment, maintenance, deceleration, and retirement.
Social cognitive career theory	People choose a career based on self-efficacy, outcome expectations, interest, choice goals, supports, and barriers.

Occupation is a key part of a person's identity. Although most people work to earn a living, a key by-product is the possibility of personal growth.

Childhood and adolescence are times of remarkable change: At the beginning of childhood, children are still dependent on parents, rarely venture far from home, and their futures are uncertain. By the end of adolescence, they are largely independent, often travel widely, and have goals for their adult years.

During the elementary- and middle-school years, some children are much taller than average and others much shorter.

Development in Middle Childhood

Physical (Chapter 6)

School-aged children grow at a steady pace; most increases in height come from the legs, not the trunk.

Motor skills continue to improve as strength and dexterity increase. Boys tend to excel in motor skills requiring strength; girls excel in fine motor skills and those requiring flexibility and balance.

Many U.S. elementary school children are not physically fit, mainly because they are inactive.

Participation in sports improves motor skills and helps children learn social skills and use emerging cognitive skills.

Cognitive (Chapter 6)

From about ages 7 to 11, children are in Piaget's *concrete operational stage,* in which they become less egocentric, realize that appearances can be deceiving, and acquire mental operations.

At about age 11, school-aged children begin *formal operational thinking,* in which they can think hypothetically, reason abstractly, and use deductive reasoning.

Children begin to use memory strategies at about 7 to 8 years of age and learn to self-monitor the effectiveness of their memory strategies.

Major theories of intelligence include Carroll's hierarchical view, Gardner's theory of multiple intelligences, and Sternberg's theory of successful intelligence.

Children with learning disabilities have normal intelligence but struggle to master specific academic subjects.

Although giftedness used to be defined by IQ, today giftedness is more broadly defined to include exceptional talent in specific areas.

Socioemotional (Chapter 7)

Two key factors in parent–child relationships are parental warmth and control.

Punishment is most effective when it is immediate, consistent, explained, and administered by a caring parent.

School-aged friendships are based on loyalty, trust, and intimacy. Friends are usually similar in age, race, and attitudes. Older children and adolescents often form cliques.

Types of Parenting Styles	
Authoritarian	High control, little warmth
Authoritative	Medium control, lots of warmth
Indulgent–permissive	Little control, lots of warmth
Resistant	Little control, little warmth

Young adulthood lays the foundation for development changes people experience throughout their adult lives. In many respects, middle adulthood is the prime of life.

Development in Young Adulthood

Physical (Chapter 10)

Young adults are at the peak of the physical functioning for strength, muscle development, coordination, dexterity, and sensory acuity. Most of these abilities begin declining in middle age.

Overall health is at its peak, and death from disease is relatively rare. Accidents are the leading cause of death among adults ages 25–44.

Lifestyle factors that negatively affect health include smoking, alcohol abuse, and poor nutrition.

Socioeconomic status and level of education can affect an individual's health.

A healthy lifestyle in young adulthood reduces the chances of chronic disease later in life.

AP Photo/Mark Baker

Cognitive (Chapter 10)

Most modern theories of intelligence recognize that there is no single type of intelligence. Some aspects of intelligence improve and some decline during adulthood.

Primary mental abilities are intellectual abilities that can be studied as groups of related skills (e.g., memory). These skills improve until the early 40s, then begin to decline in the 50s.

Fluid intelligence consists of abilities related to flexible and adaptive thinking. These skills tend to decline during adulthood.

Crystallized intelligence reflects knowledge acquired through life experience and education in a particular culture. These skills improve during adulthood until late life.

Neuroscience research indicates that important brain development continues into young adulthood, involving important connections between emotion and thinking.

In their early 20s, individuals become capable of *postformal thought*, progressing from believing that there is only one right way of thinking and acting to accepting the fact that there are multiple approaches.

Socioemotional (Chapter 11)

According to Erikson, the major task for young adults is dealing with the psychosocial conflict of *intimacy versus isolation*. A key component of intimacy is a clear sense of identity.

Young adults have more friendships than other age groups, and women have more close friends than men. Men base friendships on shared interests, while women base friendships on emotional sharing.

Gay, lesbian, and heterosexual relationships all have similar issues. Lesbian couples tend to be more egalitarian.

Marital satisfaction declines in general through middle age, for couples both with children and without.

© Michael Goldman/Getty Images

Mate selection and marriage are most successful when there are shared values, goals, and interests.

Sternberg's Three Key Components of Love	
Passion	Intense physiological desire for someone
Intimacy	Sharing one's thoughts and actions with someone
Commitment	Staying with someone through good and bad times

Development in Adolescence

Physical (Chapter 8)

Puberty includes physical growth and sexual maturation. Girls typically begin puberty 2 years ahead of boys, at about age 10.

The timing of puberty is strongly influenced by genetics, health, nutrition, and (for girls) social environment. Early maturation tends to be harmful for girls but beneficial for boys.

Adolescents are very concerned with appearance. Many American teens are overweight, which increases the likelihood of being unpopular and having low self-esteem and future medical problems.

Due to cultural norms idealizing thinness, some teens (90% females, 10% males) develop eating disorders. Individuals with anorexia refuse to eat and irrationally fear becoming overweight; those with bulimia alternate between binge eating and purging.

Participation in sports improves physical fitness, self-esteem, and teaches initiative and teamwork.

Cognitive (Chapter 8)

Cognitive changes in adolescence are not as rapid as in childhood. Adolescents' cognitive processes are like adults' in terms of working memory, processing speed, content knowledge, and ability to identify task-appropriate strategies.

Although capable of adultlike cognition, teens may revert to simpler thinking. Their beliefs can blind them to more sophisticated thought processes.

Theories of What Drives Moral Reasoning	
Kohlberg	Moral reasoning is rooted in justice. One progresses sequentially through *preconventional*, *conventional*, and *postconventional* levels.
Gilligan	Moral reasoning is rooted in caring.

Most high school students hold part-time jobs. Working more than 15 hours per week can be detrimental.

Socioemotional (Chapter 9)

Adolescents seek to find an identity by experimenting with different roles, and they are more likely to achieve a well-defined sense of self when parents encourage discussion and autonomy.

Teens who achieve an ethnic identity tend to have higher self-esteem and do better in school.

Self-esteem often drops when children begin middle school or junior high. Self-esteem is linked to adolescents' actual competence in domains they value and how their parents and peers view them.

As teens become more independent, parents treat them more like equals. Most adolescents love and feel loved by their parents, seek their advice, and embrace their values.

Romantic relationships emerge in mid-adolescence. By the end of high school, about two-thirds of U.S. teens have had intercourse. Because many teens do not use contraceptives, STDs and pregnancy are common consequences of adolescent sexual behavior.

Many adolescents drink alcohol regularly. Parents, peers, and stress influence whether adolescents drink and smoke.

By late adolescence, 25% of adolescent girls and 10% of adolescent boys are depressed. Medication and improving social skills can help.

Many youth briefly engage in minor criminal acts, but only about 5% engage in *life-course persistent antisocial behavior*. Several factors contribute to antisocial behavior: biology, cognitive processes, family, and poverty.

Romantic relationships emerge in mid-adolescence.

ESSENTIALS OF
Human Development

A Life-Span View

ESSENTIALS OF
Human Development
A Life-Span View

Robert V. Kail
Purdue University

John C. Cavanaugh
Pennsylvania State System of Higher Education

WADSWORTH
CENGAGE Learning·

Australia · Brazil · Japan · Korea · Mexico · Singapore · Spain · United Kingdom · United States

WADSWORTH
CENGAGE Learning·

Essentials of Human Development:
A Life-Span View
Robert V. Kail and John C. Cavanaugh

Publisher: Jon-David Hague

Executive Editor: Jaime Perkins

Senior Developmental Editor: Kristin Makarewycz

Assistant Editor: Paige Leeds

Editorial Assistant: Audrey Espey

Senior Media Editor: Mary Noel

Senior Brand Manager: Elisabeth Rhoden

Market Development Manager: Christine Sosa

Program Manager: Adrienne Saperstein

Content Project Manager: Charlene Carpentier

Senior Art Director: Vernon T. Boes

Manufacturing Planner: Karen Hunt

Rights Acquisitions Specialist: Tom McDonough

Production Service and Composition: Graphic World Inc.

Photo Researcher: Roman Barnes

Text Researcher: Isabel Saraiva

Copy Editor: Graphic World Inc.

Text Designer: Lisa Delgado

Cover Designer: Paula Goldstein

Cover Image: John Lund/Getty Images; Shutterstock

For product information and technology assistance, contact us at
Cengage Learning Customer & Sales Support, 1-800-354-9706.
For permission to use material from this text or product,
submit all requests online at **www.cengage.com/permissions.**
Further permissions questions can be e-mailed to
permissionrequest@cengage.com.

Library of Congress Control Number: 2012942042

Student Edition:

ISBN-13: 978-1-133-94344-0

ISBN-10: 1-133-94344-6

Loose-Leaf Edition:

ISBN-13: 978-1-285-08968-3

ISBN-10: 1-285-08968-5

Wadsworth
20 Davis Drive
Belmont, CA 94002-3098
USA

Cengage Learning is a leading provider of customized learning solutions with office locations around the globe, including Singapore, the United Kingdom, Australia, Mexico, Brazil, and Japan. Locate your local office at **www.cengage.com/global.**

Cengage Learning products are represented in Canada by Nelson Education, Ltd.

To learn more about Wadsworth visit **www.cengage.com/Wadsworth**

Purchase any of our products at your local college store or at our preferred online store **www.CengageBrain.com.**

Printed in Canada

1   2   3   4   5   6   7   16   15   14   13   12

To Dea and Chris

About the Authors

ROBERT V. KAIL is Distinguished Professor of Psychological Sciences at Purdue University. His undergraduate degree is from Ohio Wesleyan University, and his Ph.D. is from the University of Michigan. Kail is editor of *Psychological Science,* the flagship journal of the Association for Psychological Science, and is the incoming editor of *Child Development Perspectives.* He received the McCandless Young Scientist Award from the American Psychological Association, was named the Distinguished Sesquicentennial Alumnus in Psychology by Ohio Wesleyan University, and is a fellow of the Association for Psychological Science. Kail has also written *Children and Their Development.* His research focuses on cognitive development during childhood and adolescence. Away from the office, he enjoys photography and working out.

JOHN C. CAVANAUGH is Chancellor of the Pennsylvania State System of Higher Education. He received his undergraduate degree from the University of Delaware and his Ph.D. from the University of Notre Dame. Cavanaugh is a fellow of the American Psychological Association (APA), the Association for Psychological Science, and the Gerontological Society of America, and he has served as president of the Adult Development and Aging Division (Division 20) of the APA. Cavanaugh has also written (with the late Fredda Blanchard-Fields) *Adult Development and Aging.* His research interests in gerontology concern family caregiving as well as the role of beliefs in older adults' cognitive performance. For enjoyment, he backpacks, writes poetry, and, while eating chocolate, ponders the relative administrative abilities of James T. Kirk, Jean-Luc Picard, Kathryn Janeway, Benjamin Sisko, and Jonathan Archer.

Brief Contents

Contents

Blue Jean Images/Glow Images

3 Tools for Exploring the World: Physical, Perceptual, and Motor Development 63

© age fotostock/SuperStock

PART 2 School-Age Children and Adolescents 155

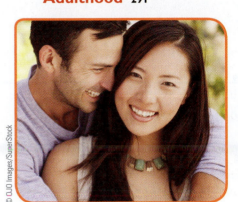

© OJO Images/SuperStock

Yellow Dog Productions/Getty Images

Preface

Human development is the most fascinating and most complex science there is. Describing how people change (and how they stay the same) over their lives requires a multidisciplinary approach to fully capture the richness of the physical, intellectual, and social dimensions of development. Instructors often find it challenging to cover human development in the typical semester-long course. Consequently, we have created a focused text that emphasizes the essential, defining features of modern research and theory in human development. Specifically, *Essentials of Human Development: A Life-Span View* fills the need for a shorter text that provides the following:

- A streamlined, readable account of human development across the life span
- Conceptual foundations that enable students to become educated and critical interpreters of developmental information
- An introduction to research and to the application of that research to important issues in life span development

ORGANIZATION

A Modified Chronological Approach

Some human development texts take a chronological approach (focusing on functioning at specific stages of the life span, such as infancy, adolescence, and middle adulthood), but others use a topical approach (following a specific aspect of development, such as personality, throughout the life span). Both approaches have their merits, so we have combined them in a way that captures the best aspects of both. The overall organization of the text is chronological: We trace development from conception through late life in sequential order and dedicate several chapters to topical issues pertaining to particular points in the life span (infancy and early childhood, adolescence, young adulthood, middle adulthood, and late life).

But because the developmental continuity of such topics as social and cognitive development gets lost with narrowly defined, artificial age-stage divisions, we dedicate some chapters to tracing their development over larger segments of the life span. These chapters provide a more coherent description of important developmental changes, emphasize that development is not easily divided into "slices," and provide students with understandable explanations of developmental theories.

Balanced Coverage of the Entire Life Span

A primary difference between *Essentials of Human Development: A Life-Span View* and similar texts is that this book provides a richer and more complete description of adult development and aging. Following the introductory chapter, the remaining 15 chapters of the text are evenly divided among childhood, adolescence, adulthood, and aging. This balanced treatment reflects not only the rapid emergence of adult development and aging as a major emphasis in the science of human development but also a recognition that roughly three-fourths of a person's life occurs beyond adolescence.

As a reflection of our modified chronological approach, *Essentials of Human Development: A Life-Span View* is divided into four main parts. After an introduction to the science of human development (Chapter 1), Part 1 includes a discussion of the biological foundations of life (Chapter 2) and development during infancy and early childhood (Chapters 3 to 5). Part 2 focuses on development during middle childhood and adolescence (Chapters 6 to 9). Part 3 (Chapters 10 to 13) focuses on young and middle adulthood. Part 4 examines late adulthood (Chapters 14 and 15) and concludes with a consideration of dying and bereavement (Chapter 16).

CONTENT AND APPROACH

Biopsychosocial Emphasis

Our text provides comprehensive, up-to-date coverage of research and theory from conception to old age and death. We explicitly adopt the biopsychosocial framework as an organizing theme, describing it in depth in Chapter 1, and then integrating it throughout the text—often in combination with other developmental theories.

An Engaging Personal Style

On several occasions, we communicate our personal involvement with the issues being discussed by providing examples from our experiences as illustrations of how human development plays itself out in people's lives. In addition, every major section of a chapter opens with a short vignette, helping personalize a concept before it is discussed. Other rich examples are integrated throughout the text narrative and showcased in the Real People feature in nearly every chapter.

Emphasis on Inclusiveness

In content coverage, in the personalized examples used, and in the photos displayed, we emphasize diversity—within the United States and around the world—in ethnicity, gender, race, age, ability, and sexual orientation.

Appreciation of the Diverse Career Goals of Students

Students often study human development because they're pursuing a career related to health and human sciences, be it as a nurse, physician, educator, psychologist, social worker, or speech–language therapist. These students are often eager to see how human development research can allow them to work more effectively with future patients, students, or clients. Consequently, *Essentials of Human Development: A Life-Span View* emphasizes the application of human development research across diverse professional settings. *Human Development in Action* features (in the margins) encourage students to imagine themselves in a specific professional setting and to apply knowledge of human development to a specific problem. Similarly, *Apply* questions at the end of every section ask students to use material presented in that section to solve a problem facing a professional in the health and human sciences. Thus, this book consistently underscores the utility of research and theory in human development for improving the human condition.

PEDAGOGICAL FEATURES

Among the most important aspects of *Essentials of Human Development: A Life-Span View* is its exceptional integration of pedagogical features, designed to help students maximize their learning. Features that are normally set apart are woven seamlessly into the narrative. This unrivaled integration is meant to help students stay focused on a seamless presentation of human development across the life span.

- **SPOTLIGHT ON RESEARCH** features emphasize a fuller understanding of the science and scope of life-span development.

- **REAL PEOPLE APPLYING HUMAN DEVELOPMENT** features illustrate the everyday applications of life-span development issues.
- **LINKING RESEARCH TO LIFE** features show how findings from research can be used to improve human development throughout the life span.
- *Learning Objectives,* followed by brief *vignettes,* open the major sections in each chapter. Each major section is numbered for easy assignment and to help students visually organize the material.
- **HUMAN DEVELOPMENT IN ACTION** questions in the margins encourage application of research to real problems in professional settings.
- *Test Yourself* questions at the end of major sections reinforce key concepts discussed in the section.
- A bulleted *Summary,* organized around the chapter's learning objectives within each major section, ends each chapter.

In sum, we believe that our integrated pedagogical system gives students all the tools they need to comprehend the material and study for tests.

SUPPLEMENTARY MATERIALS

Instructor's Resource Manual

ISBN: 978-1-285-41739-4
Instructor's Resource Manual by Rebecca Fraser-Thill of Bates College contains resources designed to streamline and maximize the effectiveness of course preparation. The contents include chapter overviews and outlines, learning objectives, critical thinking discussion questions, instructional goals, lecture expanders, video recommendations, and handouts.

Test Bank

ISBN: 978-1-285-41734-9
Test Bank by Jason Spiegelman of Community College of Baltimore County contains multiple-choice, completion, true-or-false, and essay questions with sample answers for each chapter.

Psychology CourseMate

Cengage Learning's Psychology CourseMate brings course concepts to life with interactive learning, study, and exam preparation tools that support the printed textbook. CourseMate contains an interactive eBook, flashcards, quizzes, videos, suggested websites, and more—as well as EngagementTracker, a first-of-its-kind tool that monitors student engagement in the course. The accompanying instructor website, available through login.cengage.com, offers access to password-protected resources such as an electronic version of the instructor's manual, test bank files, and Microsoft® Power-Point® slides. CourseMate can be bundled with the student text. Contact your Cengage sales representative for information on getting access to CourseMate.

PowerLecture with ExamView®

This one-stop digital library and presentation tool includes preassembled Microsoft PowerPoint lecture slides. In addition to a full instructor's manual and test bank files, PowerLecture includes ExamView testing software with all test items from the printed *Test Bank* in electronic format, enabling you to create customized tests in print or online. This tool puts all of your media resources in one place, including an image library with graphics from the printed book and videos.

WebTutor™ on Blackboard and WebCT

Jump-start your course with customizable, rich, text-specific content within your Course Management System. Whether you want to Web enable your class or put an entire course online, WebTutor delivers. WebTutor offers an array of resources, such as access to the eBook, flashcards, quizzes, videos, suggested websites, and more.

ACKNOWLEDGMENTS

Textbook authors do not produce books on their own. We owe a debt of thanks to many people who helped take this project from a first draft to a bound book. Thanks to Jim Brace-Thompson, for his enthusiasm, good humor, and sage advice at the beginning of this project; to Jaime Perkins for taking the reins and guiding this first edition; to Kristin Makarewycz, for providing helpful feedback as we revised; to Mary Noel for her work on the book's media; to Paige Leeds and Jessica Alderman for their attention to a host of details; and to Charlene Carpentier for shepherding the book through production. We also thank Vernon Boes for directing the book's design and Christine Sosa and Molly Felz in marketing for their contributions to the book. We are grateful to Cassie Carey at Graphic World for keeping everything on track. We also thank Karen Hunt, Roman Barnes, Tom McDonough, Isabel Saraiva, and Lisa Delgado.

Reviewers

We also thank the many reviewers who generously gave their time and effort to help us sharpen our thinking about human development and, in doing so, shape the development of this text:

EILEEN ACHORN
University of Texas, San Antonio

ERSKINE AUSBROOKS
Dyersburg State Community College

JENNIFER BAGGERLY
University of North Texas

SONIA BELL
Prince George's Community College

JENEL CAVAZOS
Cameron University

LINDA COTE-REILLY
Marymount University

MARK EVANS
Tarrant County College, Northwest

KENNETH FOSTER
Texas Woman's University

ALLISON FROM
Spalding University

SHANNON HALE
Northwestern State University, Natchitoches

ANIKA HUNTER
Prince George's Community College

JOANNA KEY
Gwinnett Technical College

DON KNOX
Midwestern State University

NANCY LOMAN
California State University, Channel Islands

GERI LOTZE
Virginia Commonwealth University

CHRIS MACDONALD
Indiana State University

JENNIFER MUSKAT
Plymouth State University

IAN PAYTON
Bethune Cookman University

PAMELA PEREZ
Brandman University

JEAN POPPEI
The Sage Colleges

CYNTHIA REED
Tarrant County College, Northwest

ROBERT REED
Tarrant County College, Northwest

JENNIFER SHAW
Northwestern State University, Natchitoches

JAMES SNOWDEN
Midwestern State University

COURTNEY STEIN
Colby-Sawyer College

DEIRDRE THOMPSON
Howard University

TIM VANDERGAST
William Patterson University

KITTIE M. WEBER
New England College

STEVE WISECARVER
Lord Fairfax Community College

To the Student

Essentials of Human Development: A Life-Span View is written with you, the student, in mind. In the next few pages, we describe several features of the book that make it easier for you to learn. Please don't skip this material; it will save you time in the long run.

Learning and Study Aids

Each chapter includes several distinctive features to help you learn the material and organize your studying:

- Each chapter opens with a detailed outline and an overview of the main topics.
- Each major section within a chapter begins with a set of learning objectives. There is also a brief vignette introducing one of the topics to be covered in that section and providing an example of the developmental issues people face.
- When key terms are introduced in the text, they appear in bold, orange type and are defined in the margins. This should make key terms easy to find and learn.
- Key developmental theories are introduced in Chapter 1 and are referred to throughout the text.
- *Human Development in Action* questions appear in the margins. These are designed to help you apply information from the text to problems that you might encounter as a professional in health, human sciences, or education.
- The end of each section includes a feature called *Test Yourself,* which will help you check your knowledge of major ideas you just read about. The *Test Yourself* questions serve two purposes. First, they give you a chance to spot-check your understanding of the material. Second, the questions relate the material you just read to other facts, theories, or the biopsychosocial framework you read about earlier.
- Text features that expand or highlight a specific topic are integrated with the rest of the material. This book includes the following three features, each identified by a distinctive icon:
  - **SPOTLIGHT ON RESEARCH** features elaborate on specific research studies discussed in the text and provide more details on the design and methods used.
  - **REAL PEOPLE: APPLYING HUMAN DEVELOPMENT** features present case studies that illustrate how issues in human development discussed in the chapter are manifested in the lives of real people.
  - **LINKING RESEARCH TO LIFE** features show how findings from research relate directly to real issues or problems facing people at different phases in their lives.
- The end of each chapter includes two special study tools. A *Summary,* organized by learning objective within major section headings, provides a review of the key ideas in the chapter. Next is a list of *Key Terms* that appear in the chapter.

We strongly encourage you to take advantage of these learning and study aids as you read the book. We also left room in the margins for you to make notes on the material so that you can more easily integrate the text with your class and lecture material.

Tips on How to Use This Book

Your instructor will probably assign about one chapter per week. Don't try to read an entire chapter in one sitting. Instead, on the first day, preview the chapter. Read the introduction and notice how the chapter fits into the entire book; next, page through the chapter, reading the learning objectives, vignettes, and major headings. Also read the italicized sentences and the boldfaced terms. Your goal is to get a general overview of the entire chapter—a sense of what it's all about.

Now you're ready to begin reading. Go to the first major section and preview it again, reminding yourself of the topics covered. Then start to read. As you read, think about what you're reading. Every few paragraphs, stop briefly. Try to summarize the main ideas in your own words, ask yourself whether the ideas describe your experiences or those of others you know, or tell a friend about something interesting in the material. In other words, read actively—get involved in what you're reading. Don't just stare glassy-eyed at the page!

Continue this pattern—reading, summarizing, and thinking—until you finish the section. Then answer the *Test Yourself* questions to determine how well you've learned what you've read. If you've followed the read–summarize–think cycle as you worked your way through the section, you should be able to answer most of the questions.

The next time you sit down to read (preferably the next day), start by reviewing the second major section. Then complete it with the read–summarize–think cycle. Repeat this procedure for all major sections.

When you've finished the last major section, wait a day or two and then review each major section. Pay careful attention to the italicized sentences, the boldfaced terms, and the *Test Yourself* questions. Also, use the study aids at the end of the chapter to help you integrate the ideas in the chapters.

With this approach, it should take several 30- to 45-minute study sessions to complete each chapter. Don't be tempted to rush through an entire chapter in a single session. Research consistently shows that you learn more effectively by having daily (or nearly daily) study sessions devoted to both reviewing familiar material and taking on a relatively small amount of new material.

Terminology

A few words about terminology before we embark. Certain terms are used to refer to different periods of the life span. Although you may already be familiar with the terms, here we clarify how they are used in this text. The following terms refer to a specific range of ages:

> *Newborn:* birth to 1 month
> *Infant:* 1 month to 1 year
> *Toddler:* 1 to 2 years
> *Preschooler:* 2 to 6 years
> *School-age child:* 6 to 12 years
> *Adolescent:* 12 to 20 years
> *Young adult:* 20 to 40 years
> *Middle-aged adult:* 40 to 60 years
> *Young-older adult:* 60 to 80 years
> *Old-old adult:* 80 years and beyond

Sometimes, for variety, we use other terms that are less tied to specific ages, such as babies, youngsters, and older adults. However, you will be able to determine the specific ages from the context.

Organization

To organize the material into meaningful segments across the life span, *Essentials of Human Development: A Life-Span View* is divided into four parts: Prenatal Development, Infancy, and Early Childhood; School-Age Children and Adolescents; Young and Middle Adulthood; and Late Adulthood. We believe this organization achieves two major goals. First, it divides the life span in ways that relate to the divisions encountered in everyday life. Second, it enables us to provide a more complete account of adulthood than other books do.

Because some developmental issues pertain only to a specific point in the life span, some chapters are organized around specific ages. Overall, the text begins with conception and proceeds through childhood, adolescence, adulthood, and old age to death. But because some developmental processes unfold over longer periods, some chapters are organized around specific topics.

Part 1 covers prenatal development, infancy, and early childhood. Here we see how genetic inheritance operates and how the prenatal environment affects a person's future development. During the first 2 years of life, the rate of change in both motor and perceptual arenas is amazing. How young children acquire language and begin to think about their world is as intriguing as it is rapid. Early childhood also marks the emergence of social relationships, as well as an understanding of gender roles and identity. By the end of this period, a child is reasonably proficient as a thinker, uses language in sophisticated ways, and is ready for the major transition into formal education.

Part 2 covers the years from elementary school through high school. In middle childhood and adolescence, the cognitive skills formed earlier in life evolve to adult-like levels in many areas. Family and peer relationships expand. During adolescence, there is increased attention to work and sexuality emerges. The young person begins to learn how to face difficult issues in life. By the end of this period, a person is on the verge of legal adulthood. The typical individual uses logic and has been introduced to most issues that adults face.

Part 3 covers young adulthood and middle age. During this period, most people achieve their most advanced modes of thinking, reach peak physical performance, form intimate relationships, start families of their own, begin and advance within their occupations, balance many conflicting roles, and begin to confront aging. Over these years, many people go from breaking away from their families to having their children break away from them. Relationships with parents are redefined, and the pressures of being caught between the younger and the older generations are felt. By the end of this period, most people have shifted focus from time since birth to time until death.

Part 4 covers the last decades of life. The biological, physical, cognitive, and social changes associated with aging become apparent. Although many changes reflect decline, many other aspects of old age represent positive elements: wisdom, retirement, friendships, and family relationships. We conclude this section, and the text, with a discussion of the end of life. Through our consideration of death, you will gain additional insights into the meaning of life and human development.

We hope the organization and learning features of the text are helpful to you—making it easier for you to learn about human development. After all, this book tells the story of people's lives, and understanding the story is what it's all about.

Neuroscience Index

Diversity Index

Note: Page numbers in *italic* type indicate figures, illustrations, or tables.

The Study of Human Development

1

Jeanne Calment was one of the most important people to have ever lived. Her achievement was not made in any profession. When she died in 1996 at an age of 122 years and 164 days, she set the world record for the longest verified human life span. Jeanne lived her whole life in Arles, France. She met Vincent Van Gogh and experienced the invention of the lightbulb, automobiles, airplanes, space travel, computers, and all sorts of everyday conveniences. Jeanne was extraordinarily healthy her whole life, hardly ever being ill. She was also active; she learned fencing when she was 85, and she was still riding a bicycle at age 100. She lived on her own until she was 110. Shortly before her 121st birthday, Music Disc released *Time's Mistress,* a CD of Jeanne speaking over a background of rap and hip-hop music.

Do you ever wonder what your life span will be? Do you ever think about how you changed from being a young child to the person you are now? Or what you might experience over the next few years or decades? Take a moment and think about your life. Make a note to yourself about—or share with someone else—your fondest memories from childhood or the events and people who have most influenced you. Also make a note about what you think you might experience during the rest of your life. (Then, many years from now, retrieve it and see whether you were right.)

Jeanne Calment experienced many changes in society during her 122-year life span.

3

In this course, you will have the opportunity to ask some of life's most basic questions: How did your life begin? How did you go from a single cell—about the size of the period at the end of a sentence in this text—to the fully grown, complex adult person you are today? Will you be the same or different by the time you reach late life? How do you influence other people's lives? How do they influence yours? How do the various roles you may have throughout life—child, teenager, partner, spouse, parent, worker, grandparent—shape your development? How will you deal with your own and others' deaths?

These are examples of the questions that create the scientific foundation of **human development***, the multidisciplinary study of how people change and how they remain the same over time.* Answering these questions requires us to draw on theories and research in the physical and social sciences. The science of human development reflects the complexity and uniqueness of each person and each person's experiences, as well as commonalities and patterns across people.

In this chapter, we go over the basics: theories, common issues and influences on development, and methods developmentalists use to make discoveries.

1.1 Thinking About Development

LEARNING OBJECTIVES

- What fundamental issues of development have scholars addressed throughout history?
- What are the basic forces in the biopsychosocial framework? How does the timing of these forces affect their impact?
- How does neuroscience enhance our understanding of human development?

Javier Suarez smiled broadly as he held his newborn grandson for the first time. So many thoughts rushed into his mind—What would Ricardo experience growing up? Would the poor neighborhood they live in prevent him from reaching his potential? Would the family genes for good health be passed on? How would Ricardo's life growing up as a Latino in the United States be different from Javier's own experiences in Mexico?

human development
the multidisciplinary study of how people change and how they remain the same over time

Like many grandparents, Javier wonders what the future holds for his grandson. The questions he asks relate to general issues of human development that have intrigued philosophers and scientists for centuries. Let's see what these issues are.

Recurring Issues in Human Development

What factors have shaped your life until now? Your genetic heritage, your family or neighborhood, the suddenness of some changes in your life and the gradualness of others, and the culture or cultures in which you grew up or now live might be among the influences. Everyone's life is shaped by a complex set of factors.

Your speculations capture three pairs of fundamental characteristics of human development: nature and nurture, continuity and discontinuity, and universal and context-specific development. A person's development is a blend of these characteristics; for example, some of your characteristics remain the same through life (continuity), and others change (discontinuity). Let's examine each pair of characteristics.

Nature and Nurture

Think for a minute about a particular feature that you and several people in your family have, such as intelligence, good looks, or a friendly and outgoing personality. Why is this feature so prevalent? Did you inherit it? Or is it mainly because of where and how you were brought up? *Answers to these questions illustrate different positions on the* **nature–nurture issue**, *which involves the degree to which genetic or hereditary influences (nature) and experiential or environmental influences (nurture) determine the kind of person you are.* The key point is that development is always shaped by both.

A major aim of human development research is to understand how heredity and environment jointly determine development. For Javier, the new grandparent at the opening of this section, it means his grandson's development will be shaped both by the genes he inherited and by the experiences he will have.

Continuity and Discontinuity

Do you think that you've changed little since you were a young child? This view suggests continuity in development: once a person begins down a particular developmental path—for example, toward friendliness or intelligence—he or she tends to stay on that path throughout life, other things being equal.

Another view—that development is not continuous—is illustrated in a *Hi and Lois* cartoon. Sweet and cooperative Trixie has become assertive and demanding. In this view, people can change from one developmental path to another, perhaps several times in their lives.

nature–nurture issue
the degree to which genetic or hereditary influences (nature) and experiential or environmental influences (nurture) determine the kind of person you are

Hi and Lois

Hi and Lois. Reprinted with permission of King Features Syndicate.

*The **continuity–discontinuity issue** concerns whether a particular developmental phenomenon represents a smooth progression throughout the life span (continuity) or a series of abrupt shifts (discontinuity).* Throughout this book, you will find examples of developmental changes that represent continuities and others that are discontinuities.

Universal and Context-Specific Development

In some cities in Brazil, 10- to 12-year-olds sell fruit and candy to pedestrians and passengers on buses, even though they have little formal education (Saxe, 1988). In contrast, 10- to 12-year-olds in the United States attend school to learn the arithmetic needed to handle money. Can one theory explain development in both groups of children? *The **universal versus context-specific development issue** concerns whether there is just one path of development or several paths.*

Some theorists argue that, despite what look like differences in development, most people worldwide follow a similar developmental path. The alternative view argues that human development is inextricably intertwined with the context within which it occurs. In this view, a person's development is a product of complex interaction with the environment, and that interaction is not fundamentally the same in all environments. Each environment has its own set of unique procedures that shape development.

Basic Forces in Human Development: The Biopsychosocial Framework

When trying to explain why people develop as they do, scientists usually consider four interactive forces that affect development:

- *Biological forces* that include all genetic and health-related factors
- *Psychological forces* that include all internal cognitive, emotional, perceptual, and personality factors
- *Sociocultural forces* that include interpersonal, societal, cultural, and ethnic factors
- *Life-cycle forces* that reflect differences in how the same event affects people of different ages

Each person is a unique combination of these forces. To see why each force is important, think about a mother deciding whether she should breast-feed her infant. Her decision is based on biological variables (e.g., the quality and amount of milk she produces), her attitudes about the virtues of breast-feeding, the influences of other people (e.g., the father), and her cultural traditions about appropriate ways to feed infants. In addition, her decision reflects her age and stage of life. Only by focusing on all of these forces can we have a complete view of the mother's decision.

*A useful way to organize the biological, psychological, and sociocultural forces on human development is with the **biopsychosocial framework**.* As you can see in Figure 1.1, the biopsychosocial framework emphasizes that each of the forces interacts with the others to make up development. Let's look at the different elements of the biopsychosocial model in more detail.

Biological Forces: Genetics and Health

Prenatal development, brain maturation, puberty, and menopause are examples of biological forces determined by our genetic code. But biological forces also include the effects of lifestyle factors, such as diet and exercise. Collectively, biological forces can be viewed as providing the raw material necessary and as setting the boundary conditions for development.

Psychological Forces: Known by Our Behavior

Psychological forces seem familiar because they are the ones used most often to describe the characteristics of a person. For example, think about how you describe

continuity–discontinuity issue
whether a particular developmental phenomenon represents a smooth progression throughout the life span (continuity) or a series of abrupt shifts (discontinuity)

universal versus context-specific development issue
whether there is just one path of development or several paths

biopsychosocial framework
a useful way to organize the biological, psychological, and sociocultural forces on human development

FIGURE 1.1

FIGURE 1.1

The biopsychosocial framework shows that human development results from interacting forces.

yourself to others: intelligent, honest, self-confident, and so on. Concepts like these reflect psychological forces.

In general, psychological forces are all internal cognitive, emotional, personality, perceptual, and related factors that influence behavior. Much of what we discuss throughout this text reflects psychological forces.

Sociocultural Forces: Race, Ethnicity, and Culture

People develop in the world, not in a vacuum. To understand human development, we need to view an individual's development as part of a larger system in which no individual part can act without influencing all other aspects of the system. This larger system includes an individual's parents, children, and siblings, as well as important people outside the family, such as friends, teachers, and co-workers. The system also includes institutions that influence development, such as schools, television, and the workplace. At a broader level, the society in which a person grows up plays a key role.

All of these people and institutions fit together to form a person's culture: the knowledge, attitudes, and behavior associated with a group of people. Culture can be linked to a particular country or people (e.g., French culture), to a specific point in time (e.g., popular culture of the 2000s), or to groups of individuals who maintain specific, identifiable cultural traditions (e.g., African Americans). Knowing the culture from which a person comes provides some general information about important influences that become manifest throughout the life span.

The culture in which you grow up influences how you experience life.

Life-Cycle Forces: Timing Is Everything

Consider the following two females. Jacqui, a 32-year-old, has been happily married for 6 years. She and her husband have a steady income. They decide to start a family, and a month later Jacqui learns she is pregnant. Jenny, a 14-year-old, lives in the same neighborhood as Jacqui. She has been sexually active for about 6 months but is not in a stable relationship. After missing her period, Jenny takes a pregnancy test and discovers that she is pregnant.

Although both Jacqui and Jenny have become pregnant, the outcome of each pregnancy will certainly be affected by factors in each woman's situation, such as her age, her financial situation, and the extent of her social support systems. The example illustrates life-cycle forces: The same event can have different effects depending on when it happens in a person's life.

Developmental forces are valuable in helping us understand how people's lives unfold. Lena Horne's (1917–2010) life is a great example. At the age of 2, she was on the cover of the magazine of the National Association for the Advancement of Colored People (NAACP); her paternal grandmother, Cora Calhoun Horne, was an early member of the NAACP. When she went to Hollywood in 1941 to sing in a nightclub, blacks were not allowed to live in that city. When her neighbors found out she was going to live in an apartment that a white man had initially rented and turned over to her, it took Humphrey Bogart to defend her rights to the community.

Lena broke many barriers in her career by signing a long-term contract with MGM and through her subsequent fame and great success as a jazz singer. In the 1960s she became very active in the civil rights movement. In 1981 she won a Tony Award for her one-woman show *Lena Horne: The Lady and Her Music.*

The combined influence of developmental forces is evident in Lena's life. Her mother had a career on the stage in Harlem, and her paternal grandparents were active in the NAACP. Growing up in New York in the 1920s and 1930s exposed her to opportunities, such as at the famous Cotton Club, that would not have been available in a small town. The psychological impact of discrimination, due to the sociocultural environment of the times, influenced her to fight for civil rights for all African Americans. And she was still singing and recording into the 1990s, which gave her the chance to influence several generations of people.

Looking back on her life when she was 80, Lena said: "My identity is very clear to me now. I am a black woman. I'm free. I no longer have to be a 'credit.' I don't have to be a symbol to anybody; I don't have to be a first to anybody. I don't have to be an imitation of a white woman that Hollywood sort of hoped I'd become. I'm me, and I'm like nobody else."

Photo by Dave Allocca / DMI / Time Life Pictures / Getty Images

Lena Horne

The Forces Interact

We've described the four forces in the biopsychosocial framework as if they were independent, but in reality each force shapes the others. No aspect of human development can be fully understood by examining the forces in isolation. All four must be considered in interaction. You'll see later in this chapter that integration across the major forces of the biopsychosocial framework is one criterion by which the adequacy of a developmental theory can be judged.

Combining the four developmental forces gives a view of human development that encompasses the life span yet appreciates the unique aspects of each phase of life. One way to see this is to look back on life from the perspective of old age. Lena Horne, discussed in the Real People feature, is a good example of this.

Neuroscience: A Window Into Human Development

Understanding that the four developmental forces interact is one thing. But what if you could actually see these forces interact? That's what is possible in the field of neuroscience. *Applied to human development,* **neuroscience** *is the study of the brain and nervous system, especially in terms of brain–behavior relationships.* Neuroscientists use a variety of methods to study brain-behavior relationships, from molecular analyses of individual brain cells to sophisticated brain imaging techniques.

Neuroscientific approaches are being applied to a range of issues in human development, especially those involving memory, reasoning, and emotion (Blanchard-Fields, 2010). For example, neuroscientists are beginning to unlock relationships among developmental changes in specific regions of the brain to explain well-known developmental phenomena, such as adolescents' tendency to engage in risky behavior and older adults' short-term memory problems.

neuroscience
the study of the brain and nervous system, especially in terms of brain–behavior relationships

Neuroscience brings an important perspective to human development that reveals interactions among biological, psychological, sociocultural, and life-cycle forces, allowing a better understanding of how each person is a unique expression of these forces.

Test Yourself

Recall

1. The nature–nurture issue involves the degree to which _____ and environment influence human development.

2. Azar remarked that her 14-year-old son is incredibly shy and has been so ever since he was a baby. This illustrates the _____ of development.

3. _____ forces include genetic and health factors.

4. Neuroscience examines _____ relationships.

Interpret

- How does the biopsychosocial framework provide insight into the recurring issues of development (nature–nurture, continuity–discontinuity, and universal–context-specific)?

- How would you explain criminal behavior and suggest ways to prevent it from both a nature and a nurture perspective?

Apply

- How does your life experience reflect the four developmental forces?

- How does understanding the forces underlying human development help you interpret people's behavior in your workplace?

1.2 Developmental Theories

LEARNING OBJECTIVES

- What is a developmental theory?
- How do psychodynamic theories account for development?
- What is the focus of the learning theories of development?
- How do cognitive-developmental theories explain changes in thinking?
- What are the main points in the ecological and systems approach?
- What are the major tenets of the life-span and the life-course theories?

Marcus has just graduated from high school, first in his class. For his proud mother, Betty, this is a time to reflect on her son's past and to ponder his future. Marcus has always been a happy, easygoing child—a joy to rear. And he's constantly been interested in learning. Betty wonders why he is so perpetually good natured and so curious. If she knew the secret, she likes to say with a laugh, she could write a best-selling book and be a guest on *The Colbert Report.*

To answer Betty's questions about her son's growth, developmental researchers need a theory of his development. Theories are essential because they provide the whys for development. *In human development, a* **theory** *is an organized set of ideas that is designed to explain development.* For example, suppose two of your friends wonder why their baby cries often. Maybe the baby cries because she's hungry; maybe she cries to get her parents to hold her; maybe she cries because she's simply a cranky, unhappy baby. Each of these explanations is a simple theory: It tries to explain why the baby cries so much. Actual theories in human development are more complicated, but the purpose is the same—to explain behavior and development.

theory
an organized set of ideas that is designed to explain development

There are no truly comprehensive theories of human development to guide research (Newman & Newman, 2007). Instead, five general perspectives influence current research: psychodynamic theory; learning theory; cognitive developmental

Erikson's Eight Stages of Psychosocial Development

Stage	Age	Challenge
Basic trust vs. mistrust	Birth to 1 year	To develop a sense that the world is a safe, "good" place
Autonomy vs. shame and doubt	1 to 3 years	To realize that one is an independent person who can make decisions and doubt
Initiative vs. guilt	3 to 6 years	To develop the ability to try new things and to handle failure
Industry vs. inferiority	6 years to adolescence	To learn basic skills and to work with others
Identity vs. identity confusion	Adolescence	To develop a lasting, integrated sense of self
Intimacy vs. isolation	Young adulthood	To commit to another in a loving relationship
Generativity vs. stagnation	Middle adulthood	To contribute to younger people through childrearing, child care, or other productive work
Integrity vs. despair	Late life	To view one's life as satisfactory and worth living

Copyright © Cengage Learning 2010

theory; ecological and systems theory; and theories involving the life-span perspective, selective optimization with compensation, and the life-course perspective. Let's consider each approach briefly.

Psychodynamic Theory

Psychodynamic theories *hold that development is largely determined by how well people resolve conflicts they face at different ages.* This perspective traces its roots to Sigmund Freud's theory that personality emerges from conflicts that children experience between what they want to do and what society wants them to do. Erik Erikson (1902–1994) elaborated on this idea in proposing his psychosocial theory, which was the first comprehensive life-span theory and remains an important theoretical framework.

Erikson's Theory

In his **psychosocial theory**, *Erikson proposed that personality development is determined by the interaction of an internal maturational plan and external societal demands.* He proposed that the life cycle is composed of eight stages (shown in Table 1.1) and that the order of the stages is biologically fixed. The name of each stage reflects the challenge people face at a particular age. Challenges are met through a combination of inner psychological influences and outer social influences. When challenges are met successfully, people are well prepared to meet the challenge of the next stage.

The sequence of stages in Erikson's theory is based on the **epigenetic principle**, *which means that each psychosocial strength has its own period of particular importance.* The eight stages represent the order of this ascendancy. It takes a lifetime to acquire all of the psychosocial strengths. Moreover, later stages are built on the foundation laid in previous stages.

Learning Theory

In contrast to the psychodynamic theory, the learning theory concentrates on how learning influences a person's behavior. This perspective emphasizes the role of experience, examining whether a person's behavior is rewarded or punished. This perspective also emphasizes that people learn from watching others around them. Two influential theories in this perspective are behaviorism and social learning theory.

Behaviorism

B. F. Skinner (1904–1990) pioneered the study of behaviorism, in which the consequences of a behavior determine whether a behavior is repeated in the future. Skinner showed that two kinds of consequences were especially influential. *A* **reinforcement**

© Bettmann/Corbis

Erik Erikson

psychodynamic theories
theories proposing that development is largely determined by how well people resolve conflicts they face at different ages

psychosocial theory
Erikson's proposal that personality development is determined by the interaction of an internal maturational plan and external societal demands

epigenetic principle
in Erikson's theory, the idea that each psychosocial strength has its own period of particular importance

reinforcement
a consequence that increase the future likelihood of the behavior that it follows

B. F. Skinner

HUMAN DEVELOPMENT in action

If you were an elementary-school teacher, how would understanding behaviorism help you understand the behavior of the students in your class?

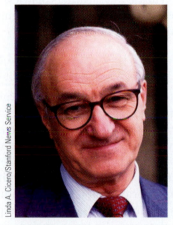

Albert Bandura

punishment
a consequence that decreases the future likelihood of the behavior that it follows

imitation or observational learning
learning that occurs by simply watching how others behave

self-efficacy
people's beliefs about their own abilities and talents

is a consequence that increases the future likelihood of the behavior that it follows. Positive reinforcement consists of giving a reward such as chocolate, gold stars, or paychecks to increase the likelihood of a previous behavior. A father who wants to encourage his daughter to help with chores may reinforce her with praise, food treats, or money whenever she cleans her room. Negative reinforcement consists of rewarding people by taking away unpleasant things. The same father could use negative reinforcement by saying that whenever his daughter cleans her room she doesn't have to wash the dishes or fold laundry.

A **punishment** *is a consequence that decreases the future likelihood of the behavior that it follows.* Punishment suppresses a behavior either by adding something aversive or by withholding a pleasant event. Should the daughter fail to clean her room, the father may punish her by nagging (adding something aversive) or by not allowing her to watch television (withholding a pleasant event).

Social Learning Theory

Reinforcement and punishment are powerful, but people sometimes learn by simply watching those around them, which is known as **imitation or observational learning**. For example, imitation occurs when a school-age child offers to help an older adult carry groceries because she's seen her parents do the same.

Imitation is not simply mimicry. And people do not always imitate what they see around them. People are more likely to imitate someone if the person they see is popular, smart, or talented and to imitate a behavior when they see it rewarded rather than punished. Findings like these imply that imitation is more complex than mimicry. People look to others for information about appropriate behavior.

Albert Bandura (1925–) based his social cognitive theory on this more complex view of reward, punishment, and imitation. Bandura's theory is "cognitive" because he believes people actively try to understand what goes on in their world; the theory is "social" because, along with reinforcement and punishment, what other people do is an important source of information about the world.

Bandura also argues that experience gives people a sense of **self-efficacy**, *which refers to people's beliefs about their own abilities and talents.* Self-efficacy beliefs help determine when people will imitate others. A child who sees himself as untalented athletically, for example, will not try to imitate LeBron James dunking a basketball, even though James is obviously talented and popular. Thus, whether an individual imitates others depends on who the other person is, on whether that person's behavior is rewarded, and on the individual's beliefs about his or her own abilities.

Cognitive-Developmental Theory

Another way to approach development is to focus on thought processes and the construction of knowledge. In the cognitive-developmental theory, the key is how people think and how thinking changes over time. Three distinct approaches have developed: Piaget's theory, information-processing theory, and Vygotsky's theory.

Piaget's Theory

Jean Piaget (1896–1980), who was the most influential developmental psychologist of the 20th century, believed that throughout infancy, childhood, and adolescence youngsters want to understand the workings of both the physical and the social world. When children try to comprehend their world, Piaget argued, they act like scientists, creating theories about the physical and social worlds. Children try to weave all they know about objects and people into complete theories, which are tested daily by experience because their theories lead them to expect certain things to happen. As with scientific theories, when a predicted event occurs, a child's belief in her theory grows stronger. When the predicted event does not occur, the child must revise her theory.

Piaget's Four Stages of Cognitive Development

Stage	Age	Characteristics
Sensorimotor	Birth to 2 years	Infant's knowledge of the world is based on senses and motor skills; by the end of the period, child uses mental representation
Preoperational thought	2 to 6 years	Child learns how to use symbols such as words and numbers to represent aspects of the world but relates to the world only through his or her perspective
Concrete operational thought	7 years to early adolescence	Child understands and applies logical operations to experiences provided they are focused on the here and now
Formal operational thought	Adolescence and beyond	Adolescent or adult thinks abstractly, deals with hypothetical situations, and speculates about what may be possible

© Bettmann/Corbis

Jean Piaget

Piaget also believed children revise their theories radically at a few critical points in development. These changes are so fundamental that the revised theory is, in many respects, a new theory. Piaget claimed that these changes occur three times in development: once around 2 years of age, a second time around age 7, and a third time just before adolescence. These changes mean that children go through four distinct stages in cognitive development. Each stage represents a fundamental change in how children understand and organize their environment, and each stage is characterized by more sophisticated types of reasoning. For example, the first or sensorimotor stage begins at birth and lasts until about 2 years of age. As the name implies, sensorimotor thinking refers to an infant constructing knowledge through sensory and motor skills. This stage and the three later stages are shown in Table 1.2.

Piaget's theory has had an enormous influence on how developmentalists and practitioners think about cognitive development. The theory has been applied in many ways—from the creation of discovery learning toys for children to the ways teachers plan lessons. Piaget also had his critics. In Chapter 10, we show how some have argued that cognitive development does not stop with adolescence but continues well into adulthood.

Information-Processing Theory

Information-processing theorists draw heavily on how computers work to explain thinking and how it develops through childhood and adolescence. *Just as computers consist of both hardware (disk drives, central processing unit, etc.) and software (the programs they run),* **information-processing theory** *proposes that human cognition consists of mental hardware and mental software.* Mental hardware refers to cognitive structures, including different memories where information is stored. Mental software includes organized sets of cognitive processes that enable people to complete specific tasks, such as reading a sentence, playing a video game, or hitting a baseball. For example, an information-processing psychologist would say that, for a student to do well on an exam, she must encode the information as she studies, store it in memory, and then retrieve the necessary information during the test.

Dorling Kindersley/Getty Images

Information-processing theory helps explain how this boy learns, stores, and retrieves information so that he can pass the exam he is studying for.

information-processing theory
a theory proposing that human cognition consists of mental hardware and mental software

According to information-processing psychologists, developmental changes in thinking reflect better mental hardware and mental software in older children and adolescents than in younger children. For example, older children typically solve math word problems better than younger children because they have greater memory capacity to store the facts in the problem and because their methods for performing arithmetic operations are more efficient. And, as we show in Chapter 14, deterioration of mental hardware—along with declines in the mental software—helps explain declines in cognitive skill associated with aging.

Lev Vygotsky

Vygotsky's Theory

Lev Vygotsky (1896–1934) was one of the first theorists to emphasize the influence of children's sociocultural context on their thinking. Vygotsky believed that, because all societies want children to acquire essential cultural values and skills, every aspect of a child's development must be considered against this backdrop. For example, most parents in the United States want their children to work hard in school and be admitted to college because earning a degree is one of the keys to finding a good job. However, in Mali (an African country), Bambara parents want their children to learn to farm, herd animals such as cattle and goats, gather food such as honey, and hunt because these skills are key to survival in their environment. Vygotsky viewed development as an apprenticeship in which children develop as they work with skilled adults, including teachers and parents.

Ecological and Systems Perspective

Most developmentalists agree that environment is an important force in many aspects of development. However, only ecological theories have focused on the complexities of environments and their links to development. *In* **ecological theory**, *human development is inseparable from the environmental contexts in which a person develops.* The ecological approach proposes that all aspects of development are interconnected, so no aspect of development can be isolated from others and understood independently. An ecological theorist would emphasize that to understand why adolescents behave as they do, we need to consider the many systems that influence them, including parents, peers, teachers, television, the neighborhood, and social policy.

We consider two examples of the ecological and systems approach: Bronfenbrenner's theory and the competence–environmental press framework.

Bronfenbrenner's Theory

The best-known proponent of the ecological approach was Urie Bronfenbrenner (1917–2005), who proposed that the developing person is embedded in a series of complex and interactive systems (Bronfenbrenner, 1979, 1989, 1995). Bronfenbrenner divided environment into the four levels shown in Figure 1.2: the microsystem, the mesosystem, the exosystem, and the macrosystem.

At any point in life, the **microsystem** *consists of the people and objects in an individual's immediate environment.* These are the people closest to a child, such as parents, siblings, or adults and children in a day-care setting. Microsystems strongly influence development.

Microsystems themselves are connected to create the mesosystem. *The* **mesosystem** *provides connections across microsystems, because what happens in one microsystem is likely to influence others.* Perhaps you've found that if you have a stressful day at work or school, then you're often grouchy at home, which shows connections between the microsystems of home and work.

The **exosystem** *refers to the social settings that a person may not experience firsthand but that still influence development.* For example, changes in government policy regarding welfare may mean that poor children have less opportunity for enriched preschool experiences. Although the influence of the exosystem is no more than secondhand, its effects on human development can be quite strong.

The broadest environmental context is the **macrosystem**, *the cultures and subcultures in which the microsystem, mesosystem, and exosystem are embedded.* Members of these cultural groups share a common identity, a common heritage, and common values. The macrosystem evolves over time; each successive generation may develop in a unique macrosystem.

Bronfenbrenner's ecological theory emphasizes the many levels of influence on human development. People are affected directly by family members and friends and indirectly by social systems, such as neighborhoods and religious institutions—which, in turn, are affected by the beliefs and heritage of a culture.

Urie Bronfenbrenner

ecological theory
a theory based on the idea that human development is inseparable from the environmental contexts in which a person develops

microsystem
the people and objects in an individual's immediate environment

mesosystem
provides connections across microsystems

exosystem
the social settings that a person may not experience firsthand but that still influence development

macrosystem
the cultures and subcultures in which the microsystem, mesosystem, and exosystem are embedded

FIGURE 1.2

Bronfenbrenner's ecological theory emphasizing interaction across systems in which people operate.

Source: Kopp, Claire B./Krakow, Joanne B., The child: Development in Social Context, 1st Edition, © 1982, p. 648. Adapted by permission of Pearson Education, Inc., Upper Saddle River, NJ.

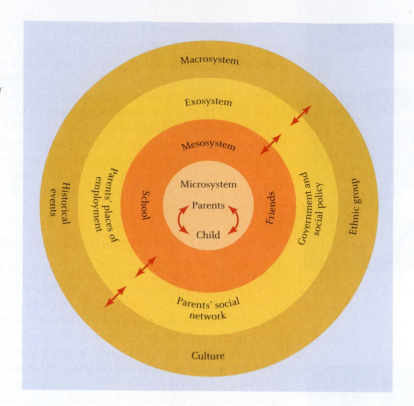

Competence–Environmental Press Theory

Another view of the influence of environments on human development comes from M. Powell Lawton's (1923–2001) and Lucille Nahemow's (1933–2000) competence–environmental press theory (Lawton and Nahemow, 1973). *According to this theory, people adapt most effectively when there is a good match between their* **competence**, *or abilities, and the* **environmental press**, *or demands put on them by the environment.* As with Bronfenbrenner's theory, competence–environmental press theory emphasizes that to understand people's functioning, it is essential to understand the systems in which they live.

Lifelong Development Perspective

Most theories of human development that we have considered so far pay little attention to the adult years of the life span. However, modern perspectives emphasize the importance of viewing human development as a lifelong process.

Life-Span Perspective and Selective Optimization With Compensation

competence
a person's abilities

environmental press
the demands put on an individual by the environment

life-span perspective
the view that human development is multiply determined and cannot be understood within the scope of a single framework

What would it be like to try to understand your best friend without knowing anything about his or her life? We cannot understand adults' experiences without appreciating their childhood and adolescence. Placing adults' lives in this broader context is what the life-span perspective does.

According to the **life-span perspective**, *human development is multiply determined and cannot be understood within the scope of a single framework.* The basic premise is that aging is a lifelong process of growing up and growing old, beginning with conception and ending with death. No single period of a person's life (e.g., child-

Paul Baltes

hood, adolescence, or middle age) can be understood apart from its origins and its consequences. To understand a specific period, we must know what came before and what is likely to come afterward (Riley, 1979). In addition, how someone's life is played out is affected by social, environmental, and historical change. Thus, the experiences of one generation may not be the same as those of another.

Paul Baltes (1939–2006) and his colleagues propose four features that are central to the life-span perspective (Baltes & Smith, 2003):

- *Multidirectionality.* Development involves both growth and decline; as people grow in one area, they may decline in another and at different rates.

- *Plasticity.* Capacity is not predetermined. Many skills can be learned or improved with practice, even in late life.

- *Historical context.* People develop within a particular set of circumstances determined by the historical time in which they are born and the culture in which they grow up.

- *Multiple causation.* Development results from the biological, psychological, sociocultural, and life-cycle forces that we mentioned previously.

Taken together, successful adaptation to aging occurs through interaction of three processes: selection, compensation, and optimization (Baltes, 1997; Baltes, Lindenberger, & Staudinger, 2006). Selection processes choose goals, life domains, and life tasks, whereas optimization and compensation are concerned with maintaining or enhancing chosen goals. *The basic assumption of the* **selective optimization with compensation model** *is that the three processes form a system of behavioral action that generates and regulates development and aging.*

As people mature and grow old, they select from a range of possibilities or opportunities. Selection can involve the continuation of previous goals on a lesser scale or the substitution of new goals, and it may be either proactive or reactive.

Compensation occurs when people's skills have decreased so that they no longer function well in a particular domain. When they compensate, they search for an alternative way to accomplish the goal; for example, if an injury reduces a person's ability to drive, then she might compensate by taking the bus. Thus, compensation differs from selection in that the task or goal is maintained—although other means are used to achieve it.

Optimization involves finding the best match possible between resources (biological, psychological, and sociocultural) and desired goals. Because people cannot achieve optimal outcomes in everything, development becomes a dynamic process of selecting the right goals and compensating when possible to help maximize the odds of achieving them.

Life-Course Perspective

The **life-course perspective** *describes the ways in which various generations experience the biological, psychological, and sociocultural forces of development in their respective historical contexts.* Specifically, it lets researchers examine the effects of historical time on how people create their lives (Dannefer & Miklowski, 2006; Hareven, 1995, 2001; Mayer, 2009). A key feature of the life-course perspective is the dynamic interplay between individual and society.

Research from the life-course perspective has clearly shown that major life transitions, such as marriage, childbearing, starting and ending a career, and completing an education, occur at different ages across people and generations. Research has also shown that life transitions are more continuous and multidirectional than previously thought. Finally, research shows that the various domains of people's lives are highly interdependent; for example, the decision to have a child is often made in the context of where the parents are in career and education.

Overall, life-span and life-course theories have drawn attention to the role of aging in the broader context of human development, even though they have yet to reach

selective optimization with compensation model
the model in which three processes (selection, optimization, and compensation) form a system of behavioral action that generates and regulates development and aging

life-course perspective
the ways in which various generations experience the biological, psychological, and sociocultural forces of development in their respective historical contexts

Theoretical Perspectives on Human Development

Theory	Examples	Main Idea	Force Emphases in Biopsychosocial Framework	Positions on Developmental Issues
Psychodynamic	Psychosocial theory (Erikson)	Personality develops through sequence of stages	Psychological, sociocultural, and life cycle crucial; less emphasis on biological	Nature–nurture interaction, discontinuity, universal sequence of stages but context-specific differences in rate
Learning	Behaviorism (Skinner) Social learning theory (Bandura)	Consequences determine repetition of behaviors People learn through modeling and observing	In both theories, major emphasis on sociocultural, some on biological and psychological, little recognition of life cycle	In both theories, strongly nurture, continuity, universal principles of learning
Cognitive Developmental	Piaget's theory	Thinking develops in a sequence of stages	Main emphasis on biological and sociocultural forces, less on psychological, little on life cycle	Strongly nature, discontinuity, universal sequence of stages
	Information-processing theory	Thought develops by increases in efficiency at handling information	Emphasis on biological and psychological, less on sociocultural and life cycle	Nature–nurture interaction, continuity, context-specific differences in universal structures
	Vygotsky's theory	Development is influenced by culture	Emphasis on psychological and sociocultural forces	Nature–nurture interaction, continuity, context-specific differences
Ecological and Systems	Bronfenbrenner's theory	Developing person is embedded in a series of interacting systems	Main emphasis on sociocultural, some on psychological and life cycle, little on biological	Nature–nurture interaction, continuity, context-specific differences
	Competence– environmental press (Lawton and Nahemow)	Adaptation is optimal when ability and demands are in balance	Strong emphasis on biological, psychological, and sociocultural; moderate on life cycle	Nature–nurture interaction, continuity, context-specific differences
Life Span and Selective Optimization With Compensation	Baltes's proposals	Development is multiply determined, goals are optimized	Strong emphasis on the interactions of all four forces; cannot consider any in isolation	Nature–nurture interaction, continuity and discontinuity, context-specific differences
Life Course	Life-course theory	Life-course transitions are decreasingly tied to age, continuity increases over time, specific life paths across domains are interdependent	Strong emphasis on psychological, sociocultural, and life cycle; less on biological	Nature–nurture interaction, continuity and discontinuity, context-specific differences

their full explanatory potential (Mayer, 2009). These theories have played a major role in conceptualizing adulthood and have greatly influenced the research we consider in Chapters 10 through 15.

The Big Picture

As summarized in Table 1.3, each of the theories provides ways of explaining how the biological, psychological, sociocultural, and life-cycle forces create human development. Because no single theory provides a complete explanation of all aspects of development, we must rely on this biopsychosocial framework to help piece together an account based on different theories.

Test Yourself

Recall

1. _____ organize knowledge to provide testable explanations of human behaviors and the ways in which they change over time.
2. The _____ theory proposes that personality development is determined by the interaction of an internal maturational plan and external societal demands.
3. According to social learning theory, people learn from reinforcements, from punishments, and through _____.
4. Piaget's theory and Vygotsky's theory are examples of the _____ perspective.
5. According to Bronfenbrenner, development occurs in the context of the _____, mesosystem, exosystem, and macrosystem.
6. A belief that human development is characterized by multidirectionality and plasticity is fundamental to the _____ perspective.

Interpret

- How are the information-processing theory and Piaget's theory similar? How are they different?
- How does a life-span perspective take a different view of human development compared to that of a theory that only focuses on childhood or adolescence?

Apply

- Using three developmental theories, explain how LeBron James or Beyoncé achieved success.
- How could you use theories of human development to help you at your job?

1.3 Doing Developmental Research

LEARNING OBJECTIVES

- How do scientists measure topics of interest in studying human development?
- What research designs are used to study human development?
- What ethical procedures must researchers follow?
- How do investigators communicate results from research studies?
- How does research affect public policy?

Leah and Joan are both mothers of 10-year-old boys. Their sons have many friends, but the basis for the friendships is not obvious to the mothers. Leah believes "opposites attract"—children form friendships with peers who have complementary interests and abilities. Joan doubts this; her son seems to seek out other boys who are near clones of himself in terms of interests and abilities.

Suppose Leah and Joan ask you to settle their argument. Leah believes complementary children are more often friends, whereas Joan believes similar children are more often friends. You know that research could show whose ideas are supported under which circumstances, but how? Let's see what steps a developmental researcher would take.

Measurement in Human Development Research

The first step in doing developmental research is deciding how to measure the topic or behavior of interest, choosing from among four approaches: observing systematically, using tasks to sample behavior, asking people for self-reports, and taking physiological measures.

Systematic Observation

As the name implies, **systematic observation** *involves watching people and carefully recording what they do or say.* Two forms of systematic observation are common. *In* **naturalistic observation***, people are observed as they behave spontaneously in a real-life situation.* **Structured observations** *differ from naturalistic observations in that the researcher creates a setting that is likely to bring out the behavior of interest.*

Structured observations are valuable in enabling researchers to observe behavior or behaviors that would otherwise be difficult to study. But there are limits as well. Researchers must be careful that their method does not make the behavior they are observing unnatural or unrealistic.

Sampling Behavior With Tasks

When investigators can't observe a behavior directly, another popular alternative is to create tasks that are thought to sample the behavior of interest. An example is shown in Figure 1.3. To study the ability to recognize emotions, the child has been asked to look at the photographs and point to the face that looks happy. A child's answers on this sort of task are useful in determining his or her ability to recognize emotions. This approach is popular and convenient. However, there is a potential problem with it: the task may not provide a realistic sample of the behavior of interest. For example, asking children to judge emotions from photographs may not be valid, because it underestimates what they do in real life. Can you think of reasons this might be the case? We mention several reasons on page 26 just before the chapter summary.

Self-Reports

Self-reporting represents a special case of using tasks to measure people's behavior. **Self-reports** *are people's answers to questions about the topic of interest.* When questions are posed in written form, the self-report is a questionnaire; when questions are posed orally, the self-report is an interview. Either way, questions are created that probe different aspects of the topic of interest.

Self-reports are useful because they can lead directly to information on the topic of interest. They are also relatively convenient, particularly when they can be administered to groups of participants or online.

However, self-reports are not always a good measure of people's behavior, because people may not remember past events accurately or may be biased in their responses (because some answers are more socially acceptable than others). As long as investigators remain aware of these potential shortcomings, self-report can be a valuable tool for research in human development.

HUMAN DEVELOPMENT in action

If you were an adult protective services caseworker, what would be the relative advantages of systematic observation, sampling behavior with tasks, and self-reports?

systematic observation
watching people and carefully recording what they do or say

naturalistic observation
a technique in which people are observed as they behave spontaneously in some real-life situation

structured observations
the researcher creates a setting that is likely to elicit the behavior of interest

self-reports
people's answers to questions about the topic of interest

FIGURE 1.3
In this example of sampling behavior with tasks, the child is to select the face that looks happy.

© Cengage Learning 2010

Measuring Behaviors of Interest in Human Development Research

Method	Strength	Weakness
Systematic Observation		
Naturalistic observation	Captures people's behavior in its natural setting	Difficult to use with behaviors that are rare or that typically occur in private settings
Structured observation	Can be used to study behaviors that are rare or that typically occur in private settings	May be invalid if the structured setting distorts the behavior
Sampling Behavior With Tasks	Convenient—can be used to study most behaviors	May be invalid if the task does not sample behavior as it occurs naturally
Self-Reports	Convenient—can be used to study most behaviors	May be invalid because people answer incorrectly (due to either forgetting or response bias)
Physiological Measures	Provide a more direct measure of underlying behavior	Highly specific in what is measured and thus cannot be applied broadly

Copyright © Cengage Learning 2010

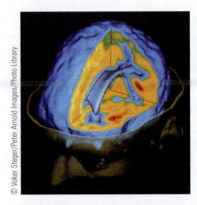

© Voker Steger/Peter Arnold Images/Photo Library

FIGURE 1.4

Brain imaging techniques provide a physiological measure that helps researchers understand brain–behavior relationships.

Physiological Measures

One less common but potentially powerful form of measurement is measuring people's physiological responses. Earlier, we saw that brain activity is used in neuroscience research to track certain behaviors, such as memory. Brain imaging techniques, like the one shown in Figure 1.4, are among the ways researchers accomplish this. Another measure is heart rate, which often slows down when people are paying close attention to something interesting. As another example, the hormone cortisol is often secreted in response to stress.

Physiological measures are usually specialized—they focus on a particular aspect of a person's behavior (memory, attention, and stress in the examples). What's more, they're often used with other behaviorally oriented methods. A researcher studying stress might observe several people for overt signs of stress; ask parents, partners, or friends to rate the target people's stress; and measure cortisol in the target people's saliva. If all three measures lead to the same conclusions about stress, then the researcher can be more confident about the conclusions.

The strengths and weaknesses of the four approaches to measurement are summarized in Table 1.4.

Reliability and Validity

After researchers choose a method, they must show that it is both reliable and valid. *The **reliability** of a measure is the extent to which it provides a consistent index of a characteristic.* A measure of friendship, for example, is reliable if it gives a consistent estimate of a person's friendship network each time researchers administer it. But reliability isn't enough. A measure must also be valid to be useful in research.

*The **validity** of a measure refers to whether it really measures what researchers think it measures.* For example, a measure of friendship is valid if it actually measures friendship and not, for example, popularity. Validity is often established by showing that the measure in question is closely related to another measure that is known to be valid.

Representative Sampling

Valid measures also depend on the people who are tested. *Researchers are usually interested in broad groups of people called **populations***. Examples of populations would be all American 7-year-olds or all African American grandparents. *Virtually all studies include only a **sample** of people, which is a subset of the population.* Researchers must take care that their sample is representative of the population of interest, because an

reliability
the extent to which a measure provides a consistent index of a characteristic

validity
the extent to which a measure actually assesses what researchers think it assesses

populations
broad groups of people that are of interest to researchers

sample
a subset of the population

unrepresentative sample can lead to invalid conclusions. For example, if a study of friendship in older adults tested only people who had no siblings, you would probably decide that this sample is not representative of the population of older adults and question the validity of its results.

General Designs for Research

Having selected a way to measure the topic or behavior of interest, researchers must next embed this measure in a research design that yields useful, relevant results. Human development researchers rely on two primary designs in their work: correlational studies and experimental studies.

Correlational Studies

In a **correlational study**, *investigators look at relations between variables as they exist naturally in the world.* Imagine a researcher who wants to test the idea that smarter people have more friends. To find out, the researcher would measure two variables for each person, the number of friends that the person has and the person's intelligence, and then see whether the two variables are related.

The results of a correlational study are usually measured by calculating a **correlation coefficient**, *which expresses the strength and direction of a relation between two variables.* Correlations can range from −1.0 to 1.0. The correlation coefficient reflects one of three possible relationships—in our example, between intelligence and number of friends:

- People's intelligence is unrelated to the number of friends they have, reflected in a correlation of 0.

- People who are smart tend to have more friends than people who are not as smart. That is, more intelligence is associated with having more friends. In this case, the variables are positively related, so the correlation is between 0 and 1.

- People who are smart tend to have fewer friends than people who are not as smart. That is, more intelligence is associated with having fewer friends. In this case, the variables are negatively related, so the correlation is between −1 and 0.

In interpreting a correlation coefficient, the sign and the size of the correlation are both important. The sign indicates the direction of the relation between variables: a positive sign means that larger values of one variable are associated with larger values of the second variable, but a negative sign means that larger values of one variable are associated with smaller values of the second variable.

The size or strength of a relation is measured by how much the correlation differs from 0, either positively or negatively. A correlation of .9 between intelligence and number of friends would indicate a very strong relation. If instead the correlation were only .3, then the link between intelligence and number of friends would be relatively weak. Similarly, a correlation of −.9 would indicate a strong negative relation between intelligence and number of friends, whereas a correlation of −.3 would indicate a weak negative relation.

A correlational study can determine whether variables are related, but it doesn't address the question of cause and effect between the variables. For example, suppose the correlation between intelligence and number of friends is .7, which indicates that smarter people have more friends than people who are not as smart. This correlation has three possible interpretations, shown in Figure 1.5: (1) being smart causes people to have more friends; (2) having more friends causes people to be smarter; or (3) neither variable causes the other but instead both intelligence and number of friends are caused by a third variable (e.g., parents who are supportive) that was not measured in the study. Any of these interpretations could be true, and they cannot be distinguished in a correlational study. Investigators who wish to track down causes must resort to a different design, called an experimental study.

correlational study
an investigation that looks at relations between variables as they exist naturally in the world

correlation coefficient
an expression of the strength and direction of a relation between two variables

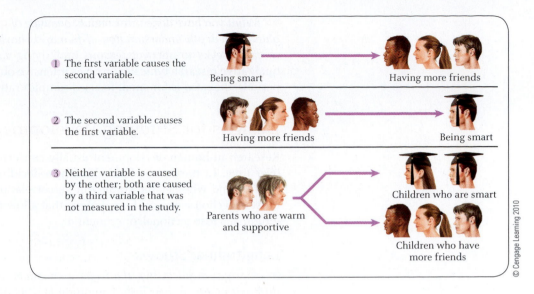

① The first variable causes the second variable.
Being smart → Having more friends

② The second variable causes the first variable.
Having more friends → Being smart

③ Neither variable is caused by the other; both are caused by a third variable that was not measured in the study.
Parents who are warm and supportive → Children who are smart / Children who have more friends

© Cengage Learning 2010

Experimental Studies

An **experiment** *is a systematic way of manipulating the key factor or factors that the investigator thinks causes a particular behavior. The factor being manipulated is called the* **independent variable**; *the behavior being observed is called the* **dependent variable**. In human development, an experiment requires the investigator to begin with one or more independent variables (usually different conditions, treatments, or interventions) that are thought to affect the behavior of interest. People are then assigned randomly to conditions that differ in the amount of the independent variable they are given. Finally, an appropriate measure (the dependent variable) is taken of all participants to see whether the treatment or treatments had the expected effect. Because each person has an equal chance of being assigned to each treatment condition (the definition of random assignment), differences among the conditions are attributed to the differential treatment people received in the experiment.

Suppose that a scientist believes that older adults' driving is more accident prone when they are talking on a cell phone. To test this hypothesis, older adults would come to the laboratory, where they would simulate driving from point A to point B on a simulator. The drive is the same except that, based on random assignment, some participants talk on a cell phone during the drive but others do not. If driving is more hazardous in the cell phone condition than in the no phone condition, this would provide strong evidence that talking on a cell phone while driving causes people to drive less safely.

Human development researchers usually conduct experiments in laboratory-like settings, because this allows better control over the variables that may influence the outcome of the research. Thus, a shortcoming of laboratory experiments is that the behavior of interest is not studied in its natural setting. Consequently, there is always the potential problem that the results may be invalid because they are artificial—specific to the laboratory setting and not representative of the behavior in the real world.

experiment
a systematic way of manipulating the key factor or factors that the investigator thinks causes a particular behavior

independent variable
the factor being manipulated

dependent variable
the behavior being observed

Qualitative Studies

Suppose you live near a children's playground. Each day, you watch the children play various games with one another and on the swings and slides. Because you are interested in learning more about how children go about playing, you decide to watch more carefully. With the parents' permission, you record video of the children's play each day for several weeks. You then watch the videos and notice whether there are specific patterns that emerge.

What you have done is to conduct one type of **qualitative research**, *which involves gaining in-depth understanding of human behavior and what governs it.* Qualitative research seeks to uncover reasons underlying various aspects of behavior. Because qualitative research typically involves intensive observation of behavior over extended periods, the need is for small focused samples rather than large random samples.

Designs for Studying Development

Research in human development usually concerns differences or changes that occur over time. In these cases—in addition to deciding how to measure the behavior of interest and whether the study will be correlational or experimental—investigators must also choose one of three designs that allow them to examine development: longitudinal, cross-sectional, or sequential.

Longitudinal Studies

In a **longitudinal study**, *the same individuals are observed or tested repeatedly at different points in their lives.* Longitudinal research is the most direct way to identify change and is the only way to answer questions about the stability or instability of behavior: Will a regular exercise program begun in middle age have benefits in later life? Does people's satisfaction with their life remain the same or change across adulthood? Such questions can be explored only by testing people at one point in their development and then retesting them later.

The Spotlight on Research feature describes a longitudinal study that focuses on the stability of life satisfaction during adulthood.

The longitudinal approach has disadvantages that frequently offset its strengths. One is cost: Keeping up with a large sample of individuals can be expensive. A related problem is the need to keep the sample together throughout the research; some may move, some die, and some stop responding. Even when the sample remains constant, taking the same test many times may make people "test wise." Because of these and other problems with the longitudinal method, human development researchers often use cross-sectional studies instead.

Cross-Sectional Studies

In a **cross-sectional study**, *developmental differences are identified by testing people of different ages.* Development is charted by noting the differences between individuals of different ages at the same point in calendar time. The cross-sectional approach avoids the problems of repeated testing and the costs of tracking a sample over time. But cross-sectional research has weaknesses. Because people are tested only once, we learn nothing about the continuity of development. Consequently, we cannot tell whether an aggressive 14-year-old remains aggressive at age 30 because the person would be tested either at age 14 or at age 30 but not at both.

Cross-sectional studies are also affected by **cohort effects**, *meaning that differences between age groups (cohorts) may reflect environmental events instead of developmental processes.* A cross-sectional study assumes that, when the older people were younger, they resembled the people in the younger age group. This isn't always true (e.g., today's young adults have access to more sophisticated technology than did today's older adults when they were younger), and this fact—rather than difference in age—may be responsible for differences between the groups.

Sequential Studies

Some researchers use another, more complex research approach, called a **sequential design**, *that is based on both cross-sectional and longitudinal designs.* Basically, a

---

qualitative research
a method that involves gaining in-depth understanding of human behavior and what governs it

longitudinal study
a research design in which the same individuals are observed or tested repeatedly at different points in their lives

cross-sectional study
a study in which developmental differences are identified by testing people of different ages

cohort effects
problems with cross-sectional designs in which differences between age groups (cohorts) may result as easily from environmental events as from developmental processes

sequential design
a developmental research design based on cross-sectional and longitudinal designs

Stability and Change in Life Satisfaction

Who were the investigators, and what was the aim of the study?

Frank Fujita and Ed Diener (2005) were interested in learning whether life satisfaction stays the same or changes across adulthood. So they compared measures of life satisfaction to physiological and demographic data over a 17-year period.

How did the investigators measure the topic of interest?

Life satisfaction was measured by self-ratings to the question "How happy are you at present with your life as a whole?" from 0 (totally unhappy) to 10 (totally happy). In addition, measures of height, weight, body mass index (BMI), systolic and diastolic blood pressure, income, and personality were obtained.

Who were the participants in the study?

The participants were 3,608 Germans (1,709 males and 1,899 females) who had answered a question about life satisfaction every year from 1984 to 2000 as part of the German Socio-Economic Panel study. They were born between 1902 and 1968.

What was the design of the study?

The study used a longitudinal design, with assessments conducted annually.

Were there ethical concerns with the study?

All participants were provided information about the purpose of the study and the tests they would take. Each participant provided informed consent.

What were the study results?

Figure 1.6 shows correlations between successive measurements. Variables such as height, weight, and BMI are stable—they are consistent from one measurement to the next, as shown by the strong positive correlations (nearly 1.0). In contrast, blood pressure, personality traits, income, and—most important—life satisfaction are less stable. And these factors show greater change as the time between measurements increases.

What did the investigators conclude?

Fujita and Diener argued that life satisfaction is somewhat stable but can vary over time. This is important, particularly for people whose life satisfaction may be low; there is the chance that things could improve.

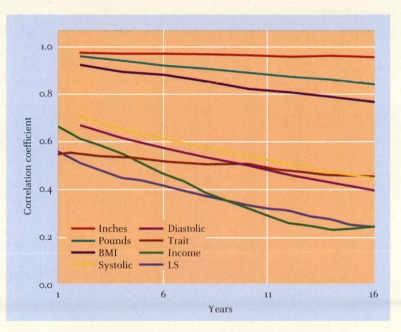

FIGURE 1.6

In this study, overall life satisfaction showed some decrease over a 17-year period compared to height, weight, BMI, and personality but was less stable over time than personality.

From Fujita, F., & Diener, E. (2005). Life satisfaction set point stability and change. Journal of Personality and Social Psychology, 88(1), p. 161. Copyright © 2005 by the American Psychological Association.

What converging evidence would strengthen the investigators' conclusions?

Because the sample included only German adults, it would be necessary to study people from other cultures to find out whether the results generalize cross-culturally.

 Go to Psychology CourseMate at **www.cengagebrain.com** to enhance your understanding of this research.

---

sequential design begins with a simple cross-sectional or longitudinal design. At some regular interval, the researcher then adds more cross-sectional or longitudinal studies, resulting in a sequence of these studies. For example, a researcher might begin with a cross-sectional study comparing 20-year-olds with 70-year-olds and then decide to test both groups at 5-year intervals (when the groups are 25 and 75 years old, respectively). This provides useful evidence about continuity of development without being as time consuming as a longitudinal study.

Table 1.5 summarizes the strengths and weaknesses of the general research designs and the developmental designs.

● TABLE 1.5

Designs Used in Human Development Research

Type of Design	Main Idea	Strength	Weakness
General Designs			
Correlational	Observe variables as they exist in the world and determine their relations	Behavior is measured as it occurs naturally	Cannot determine cause and effect
Experimental	Manipulate an independent variable and determine the effect on a dependent variable	Control of variables allows conclusions about cause and effect	Work is often laboratory based, which can be artificial
Developmental Designs			
Longitudinal	Test one group of people repeatedly as they develop	Only way to chart an individual's development and look at the stability of behavior over time	Expensive, participants drop out, and repeated testing can distort performance
Cross-sectional	Test people of different ages at the same time	Convenient—solves all problems associated with longitudinal studies	Cannot study stability of behavior; cohort effects complicate interpretation of differences between groups
Sequential	Test multiple groups of people over time, based on either multiple longitudinal or cross-sectional designs	Best way to address limitations of single longitudinal and cross-sectional designs	Very expensive and time consuming; may not completely solve limitations of longitudinal and cross-sectional designs

Copyright © Cengage Learning 2010

Informed consent is a necessary aspect of any research effort in human development.

© Amy Etra / Photo Edit

Conducting Research Ethically

In choosing a good research design, scientists must determine that their methods are ethical and do not violate the rights of people who participate. To verify that every research project incorporates these protections, local panels of experts and community representatives review proposed studies before any data are collected. Only with the approval of this panel can scientists begin their study. If the review panel objects to some aspects of the proposed study, then the researcher must revise those aspects and present them anew for the panel's approval.

Additionally, each participant must be informed about what the research entails, what procedures they will experience, and any risks that they may be exposed to. Typically, this information is provided in an informed consent document that the participant, or the participant's parent or legal guardian if the participant is a minor or cannot give consent for themselves, signs.

Communicating Research Results

When the study is complete and the data have been analyzed, researchers write a report that describes what they did and why, their results, and the meaning or meanings behind their results. The researchers submit the report to one of several scientific journals that specialize in human development research (e.g., *Child Development, Developmental Psychology, Psychology and Aging,* or *The Journals of Gerontology*). If the journal editor accepts the report, then it appears in the journal, where other human development researchers can learn of the results.

These reports of research are the basis for the information we present in this book. We cite relevant reports in the format of names in parentheses, followed by a date, like this:

(Smith & Jones, 2012)

This indicates the authors of the research report and the year in which it was published. By looking in the Reference section at the end of the book, which is organized alphabetically by the first author's last name, you can find the title of the article and the journal in which it was published.

Applying Research Results: Social Policy

Research on human development has a strong influence on policy makers and politicians. For example, every state in the United States and many countries around the world have laws against child abuse and laws that govern child labor practices. Some states in the United States are changing the way older drivers are screened when they renew their driver's licenses. Human development research played a role in the establishing of such laws and regulations.

Other examples of how developmental research affects social policy include the elimination of mandatory retirement, the Americans with Disabilities Act, many educational reform laws, and indices courts use to decide whether an adolescent offender should be tried as a juvenile or as an adult. Clearly, the research done by developmentalists influences many aspects of daily life that are governed by laws and societal rules.

At several points in this text, we describe important connections between human development research and social policy. As you will see, these connections are broad ranging and include areas that you may even take for granted. For example, lead-based paint can no longer be used in the United States, mainly because research by developmentalists showed that infants and young children who were exposed to lead-based paint (and who sometimes ate paint chips as they flaked off) suffered brain damage and learning problems. Research on human development not only provides many insights into what makes people tick but also can provide ways to improve quality of life. The Linking Research to Life feature at the end of each chapter provides examples of how research is translated into public policy or public debate.

Test Yourself

Recall

1. In _____, people are observed as they behave spontaneously in a real-life setting.

2. A _____ is a group of individuals thought to be representative of some larger population of interest.

3. The _____ variable is measured in an experiment to evaluate the impact of the variable that was manipulated.

4. Problems of longitudinal studies include the length of time to complete the work, loss of research participants over time, and _____.

5. Human development researchers must submit their plans for research to a review panel that determines whether the research _____.

Interpret

• How could a longitudinal design be used to test Piaget's theory?

• Why are longitudinal data needed for research on new medications?

Apply

• While at work, you notice that some people advance faster in their careers than others. How could you determine what factors might be responsible for or related to such success?

• How could you evaluate whether a government program has the desired outcomes?

Recall answers: (1) naturalistic observation, (2) sample, (3) dependent, (4) influence of repeated testing on a person's performance, (5) preserves the rights of research participants

Linking **Research to life** • STEM CELL RESEARCH

Imagine you were unable to walk because of a severe spinal cord injury received in an accident. Imagine further that there was a possible cure: inducing the damaged nerve cells in your spine to regenerate, thereby enabling you to walk again. Would you support every effort possible to ensure that this research was pursued, especially if you knew that there were positive outcomes in research (Nistor et al., 2005) on other animal species? But what if you knew also that applying this research to humans would require using stem cells from human embryos? Would that affect your opinion about the research?

Research on regeneration of nerve cells and for treatment of other diseases—such as Alzheimer's disease, leukemia, and Parkinson's disease—could be revolutionized through the use of stem cells. Researchers such as Hans Keirstead, co-director of the Sue and Bill Gross Stem Cell Research Center at the University of California at Irvine, believe that stem cell research represents the future for medical treatment breakthroughs. His lab developed the first treatment for spinal cord injuries based on human stem cells approved by the U.S. Food and Drug Administration in 2009.

Stem cells *are unspecialized human or animal cells that can produce mature specialized body cells and can replicate themselves.* There are two basic types of stem cells: embryonic and "adult." Embryonic stem cells are derived from a blastocyst, which is a young embryo that contains 200 to 250 cells and is shaped like a hollow sphere (see Chapter 2 for more information on embryos). The stem cells themselves are the cells in the blastocyst that ultimately would develop into a person or animal. Adult stem cells are derived from the umbilical cord and placenta or from blood, bone marrow, skin, and other tissues.

Medical researchers are interested in using stem cells to repair or replace damaged body tissues, because stem cells are less likely than other foreign cells to be rejected by the immune system when they are implanted in the body. (Tissue and organ rejection is a major problem following transplant surgery, for example.) Embryonic stem cells have the capacity to develop into every type of tissue found in the human body. Stem cells have been used experimentally to form the blood-making cells of the bone marrow, as well as heart, blood vessel, muscle, and insulin-producing tissue. Embryonic germ line cells have been used to help paralyzed mice regain some of their ability to move. Since the 1990s, umbilical cord blood stem cells have been used to treat heart and other defects in children who have rare metabolic diseases and to treat children with certain anemias and leukemias. Stem cell research has also produced several positive results regarding Parkinson's disease.

Even though stem cell research holds much promise and has already been shown to be effective in treating some conditions, it is extremely controversial. The George W. Bush administration restricted federally funded research to certain existing colonies of embryonic stem cells, pointing out that creating additional embryonic stem cells involves the destruction of human embryos, which advocates of the restrictions considered wrong. But proponents of the research argue that most embryonic stem cells used in research are left over from fertility clinics and are destined to be destroyed anyway. The Obama administration moved to ease restrictions through an executive order in 2009, which many researchers thought settled the issue. However, a federal judge overturned that in 2010, ruling that the previous restrictions regarding federal funding of research were still in effect. Clearly, the legal and political aspects of stem cell research remain far from settled.

The relationship between research and social policy regarding stem cells is also informed by individuals such as Stephen Bellamy, a scientist and Anglican theologian/ethicist (Lako, Trounson, & Daher, 2010). Bellamy distinguishes among various approaches to both reproduction and research, arguing that there is no one stance that applies equally to all situations.

For more information about stem cell research, the related controversies, and the U.S. government's policy, check the websites at the National Institutes of Health and the American Association for the Advancement of Science. What do you think should be done?

© Cengage Learning 2010

Problems With Using Photographs to Measure Understanding of Emotions

On page 18, we invited you to consider why asking children to judge emotions from photos may not be valid. Children's judgments of the emotions depicted in photographs may be less accurate than they would be in real life, because in real life (1) facial features are usually moving—not still, as in photographs—and movement may be one of the clues children naturally use to judge emotions; (2) facial expressions are often accompanied by sounds, and children use both sight and sound to judge emotions; and (3) children most often judge facial expressions of people they know (parents, siblings, peers, teachers, etc.), and knowing the "usual" appearance of a face may help children judge emotions accurately.

stem cells
unspecialized human or animal cells that can produce mature specialized body cells and can replicate themselves

Summary

1.1 Thinking About Development

What fundamental issues of development have scholars addressed throughout history?

- Three main issues are prominent in the study of human development. The nature–nurture issue involves the degree to which genetics and environment influence human development. In general, theorists and researchers view nature and nurture as mutually interactive influences; development is always shaped by both. The continuity–discontinuity issue concerns whether the same explanations (continuity) or different explanations (discontinuity) must be used to justify changes in people over time. In the issue of universal versus context-specific development, the question is whether development follows the same general path in all people or fundamentally depends on the sociocultural context.

What are the basic forces in the biopsychosocial framework? How does the timing of these forces affect their impact?

- Development is based on the combined impact of four primary forces.

- Biological forces include all genetic and health-related factors that affect development. Many of these biological forces are determined by our genetic code.

- Psychological forces include all internal cognitive, emotional, perceptual, and personality factors that influence development. Collectively, psychological forces explain the most noticeable differences among people.

- Sociocultural forces include interpersonal, societal, cultural, and ethnic factors that affect development. Culture consists of the knowledge, attitudes, and behavior associated with a group of people. Overall, sociocultural forces provide the context or backdrop for development.

- Life-cycle forces provide a context for understanding how people perceive their current situation and its effects on them.

- The biopsychosocial framework emphasizes that the four forces are mutually interactive; development cannot be understood by examining the forces in isolation. Furthermore, the same event can have different effects, depending on when it happens.

How does neuroscience enhance our understanding of human development?

- Neuroscience is the study of the brain and the nervous system, especially in terms of brain–behavior relationships. Identifying patterns of brain activity helps demonstrate how developmental forces interact.

1.2 Developmental Theories

What is a developmental theory?

- Developmental theories organize knowledge so as to provide testable explanations of human behaviors and the ways in which they change over time. Current approaches to developmental theory focus on specific aspects of behavior. At present, there is no single unified theory of human development.

How do psychodynamic theories account for development?

- Psychodynamic theories propose that development is primarily determined by the way people deal with conflicts they face at different ages. Erikson proposed a theory of psychosocial development, consisting of eight universal stages, each characterized by a particular challenge.

What is the focus of the learning theories of development?

- The learning theory focuses on the development of observable behavior. Behaviorism is based on the notions of reinforcement and punishment. Social learning theory proposes that people learn by observing others.

How do cognitive-developmental theories explain changes in thinking?

- The cognitive-developmental theory focuses on thought processes. Piaget proposed a four-stage universal sequence based on the notion that, throughout development, people create their own theories to explain how the world works. According to information-processing theory, people deal with information like a computer does; development consists of increased efficiency in handling information. Vygotsky emphasized the influence of culture on development.

What are the main points in the ecological and systems approach?

- Bronfenbrenner proposed that development occurs in the context of several interconnected systems of increasing complexity. The competence–environmental press theory postulates that there is a "best fit" between a person's abilities and the demands placed on that person by the environment.

What are the major tenets of the life-span and life-course theories?

- According to the life-span perspective, human development is characterized by multidirectionality, plasticity, historical context, and multiple causation. All four developmental forces are critical.

- Selective optimization with compensation refers to the developmental trends to focus a person's efforts and abilities in successively fewer domains as that individual ages and to acquire ways to compensate for normative losses.

- The life-course perspective refers to understanding human development within the context of the historical period in which a generation develops, which creates unique sets of experiences.

1.3 Doing Developmental Research

How do scientists measure topics of interest in studying human development?

- Research typically begins by determining how to measure the topic of interest. Systematic observation involves recording people's behavior as it takes place, in either a natural environment (naturalistic observation) or a structured setting (structured observation). Researchers sometimes create tasks to obtain samples of behavior. In self-reports, people answer questions posed by the experimenter. Physiological measures provide a way to examine body–behavior relationships.

- Researchers must determine that their measures are reliable and valid; they must also obtain a sample representative of some larger population.

What research designs are used to study human development?

- In correlational studies, investigators examine relations between variables as they occur naturally. This relation is often measured by a correlation coefficient, which can vary from −1 (strong inverse relation) to 0 (no relation) to +1 (strong positive relation). Correlational studies cannot determine cause and effect, so researchers do experimental studies, in which an independent variable is manipulated and the impact of this manipulation on a dependent variable is recorded. Experimental studies allow conclusions about cause and effect, but the required strict control of other variables often makes the situation artificial. The best approach is to use both experimental and correlational studies to provide converging evidence. Qualitative research permits in-depth analysis of behavior.

- To study development, some researchers use a longitudinal design in which the same people are observed repeatedly as they age. This approach provides evidence concerning patterns of an individual's development but has several shortcomings: It is time consuming, some people drop out of the project, and repeated testing can affect performance.

- An alternative, the cross-sectional design, involves testing people of different ages. This design avoids the problems of the longitudinal design but provides no information about stability of behavior. Also, what appear to be age differences may be cohort effects. Because neither design is problem free, the best approach involves using both to provide converging evidence.

- Sequential designs are based on multiple longitudinal or cross-sectional designs.

What ethical procedures must researchers follow?

- Planning research involves selecting methods that preserve the rights of research participants. This includes providing informed consent.

How do investigators communicate results from research studies?

- Once research data are collected and analyzed, investigators publish the results in scientific outlets such as journals and books. Such results form the foundation of knowledge about human development.

How does research affect public policy?

- Research results are sometimes used to inform and shape public policy. Controversial topics such as stem cell research also form the basis for public policy in terms of what types of research are permitted.

Key Terms

human development 4
nature–nurture issue 5
continuity–discontinuity issue 6
universal versus context-specific development issue 6
biopsychosocial framework 6
neuroscience 8
theory 9
psychodynamic theories 10
psychosocial theory 10
epigenetic principle 10

reinforcement 10
punishment 11
imitation or observational learning 11
self-efficacy 11
information-processing theory 12
ecological theory 13
microsystem 13
mesosystem 13
exosystem 13
macrosystem 13
competence 14

environmental press 14
life-span perspective 14
selective optimization with compensation model 15
life-course perspective 15
systematic observation 18
naturalistic observation 18
structured observations 18
self-reports 18
reliability 19
validity 19

Online Resources

Go to CengageBrain.com to access Psychology CourseMate, where you will find an interactive eBook, flashcards, quizzes, videos, websites, and more.

Biological Foundations

Heredity, Prenatal Development, and Birth

2

If you ask parents to name the most memorable experiences of their lives, many immediately mention the events associated with the birth of their children. For parents, pregnancy and birth evoke awe and wonder.

The period before birth is the foundation for all human development and the focus of this chapter. In the first section, you'll see the merger of heredity material from egg and sperm cells that marks the onset of pregnancy. The second section of the chapter traces the events that transform sperm and egg into a living, breathing human. In the third section, we talk about some problems that can occur during predevelopment. The last section focuses on labor, delivery, and the newborn baby.

LEARNING OBJECTIVES

- What are chromosomes and genes? How do they carry hereditary information?

- How is children's heredity influenced by their environment?

Leslie and Glenn are excited at the thought of starting a family. But they're also nervous because Leslie's grandfather had sickle-cell disease and died when he was a young adult. Leslie is terrified that her baby may inherit the disease that killed her grandfather. She and Glenn wish that someone could reassure them that their baby will be okay.

How can we reassure Leslie and Glenn? When a person has sickle-cell disease, the red blood cells that carry oxygen are long and curved like a sickle. These stiff, misshapen cells cannot pass through small capillaries, so oxygen cannot reach all parts of the body. The trapped sickle cells also block the way of white blood cells that are the body's natural defense against bacteria. As a result, many people with sickle-cell disease—including Leslie's grandfather and many other African Americans, who are particularly prone to this disease—die before the age of 20.

Sickle-cell disease is inherited and, because Leslie's grandfather had the disorder, it runs in her family. Will Leslie's baby inherit the disease? To answer this question, we need to examine the mechanisms of heredity.

Mechanisms of Heredity

chromosomes
threadlike structures in the nuclei of cells that contain genetic material

autosomes
the first 22 pairs of chromosomes

sex chromosomes
the 23rd pair of chromosomes, which determines the sex of the child

At conception, egg and sperm create a new organism that incorporates characteristics of each parent. *Each egg and sperm cell has 23* **chromosomes**, *threadlike structures that contain genetic material.* When a sperm penetrates an egg, their chromosomes combine to produce 23 pairs of chromosomes. *The first 22 pairs of chromosomes are called* **autosomes**. *The 23rd pair determines the sex of the child, so these are called* **sex chromosomes**. When the 23rd pair consists of an X and a Y chromosome, the result is a boy; two X chromosomes produce a girl.

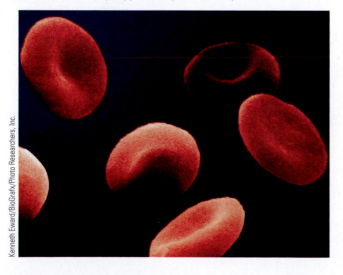

Red blood cells carry oxygen throughout the body.

Kenneth Eward/BioGrafx/Photo Researchers, Inc.

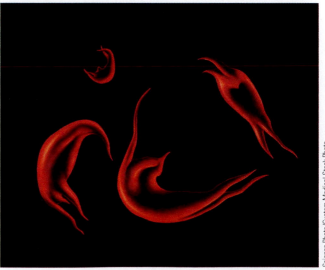

Sickle-shaped blood cells associated with sickle-cell disease cannot pass through the body's smallest blood vessels.

Science Photo/Custom Medical Stock Photo

Each chromosome consists of one molecule of **deoxyribonucleic acid**—*DNA for short*—*that is the biochemical basis of heredity*. To understand the structure of DNA, imagine four colors of beads placed on two strings. The strings complement each other precisely: Wherever a red bead appears on one string, a blue bead appears on the other; wherever a green bead appears on one string, a yellow one appears on the other. DNA is organized this way, except that the four colors of beads are four chemical compounds known as nucleotide bases: adenine, thymine, guanine, and cytosine. The strings, which are made up of phosphates and sugars, wrap around each other to create the double helix shown in Figure 2.1.

The order in which the chemical "beads" appear is a code that causes cells to create specific amino acids, proteins, and enzymes—important biological building blocks. For example, three consecutive thymine "beads" is the instruction to create the amino acid phenylalanine. *Each group of compounds that provides a specific set of biochemical instructions is a* **gene**. Thus, genes are the functional units of heredity because they determine the production of chemical substances that are the basis for all human characteristics and abilities.

Altogether, a person's 46 chromosomes include roughly 25,000 genes (Pennisi, 2005). Most genes are the same for all people—fewer than 1% of genes cause differences among people (Human Genome Project, 2003). Through biochemical

deoxyribonucleic acid (DNA)
the molecule that composes one chromosome, making it the biochemical basis of heredity

gene
a group of compounds that provides a specific set of biochemical instructions

FIGURE 2.1

DNA is organized in a double helix, with strands of phosphates and sugars linked by chemical compounds (adenine, thymine, guanine, cytosine).

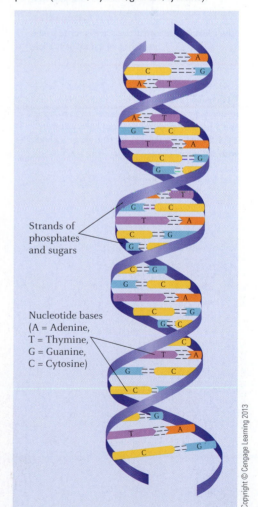

Strands of phosphates and sugars

Nucleotide bases
(A = Adenine,
T = Thymine,
G = Guanine,
C = Cytosine)

Copyright © Cengage Learning 2013

Humans have 23 pairs of chromosomes, including 22 pairs of autosomes and 1 pair of sex chromosomes.

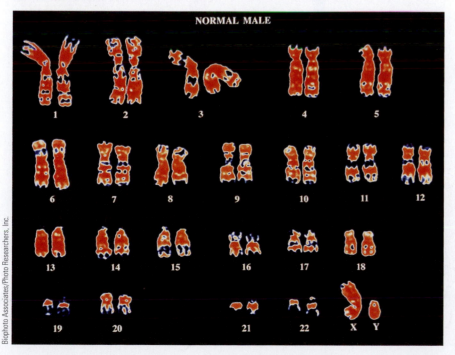

NORMAL MALE

1 2 3 4 5
6 7 8 9 10 11 12
13 14 15 16 17 18
19 20 21 22 X Y

Biophoto Associates/Photo Researchers, Inc.

instructions that are coded in DNA, genes regulate the development of all human characteristics and abilities. *The complete set of genes that makes up a person's heredity is the person's* **genotype**. *Genetic instructions, with environmental influences, produce a* **phenotype**, *an individual's physical, behavioral, and psychological features.*

How do genetic instructions produce the misshapen red blood cells of sickle-cell disease? *Genes come in different forms that are known as* **alleles**. With red blood cells, for example, one allele has instructions for normal red blood cells; another has instructions for sickle-shaped red blood cells. *The alleles in the pair of chromosomes are sometimes the same, which is known as being* **homozygous**. *The alleles sometimes differ, which is known as being* **heterozygous**. Leslie's baby would be homozygous if it had two alleles for normal cells or two alleles for sickle-shaped cells. The baby would be heterozygous if it had one allele of each type.

How does a genotype produce a phenotype? When a person is homozygous, the alleles are the same and have the same chemical instructions, which typically yield the phenotype. If Leslie's baby had two alleles for normal red blood cells, then the baby would be almost guaranteed to have normal cells. If, instead, the baby had two alleles for sickle-shaped cells, then it would almost certainly suffer from the disease.

When a person is heterozygous, the process is more complex. *Often one allele is* **dominant**, *which means that its chemical instructions are followed while those of the other,* **recessive** *allele are ignored.* In sickle-cell disease, the allele for normal cells is dominant and the allele for sickle-shaped cells is recessive. This is good news for Leslie: As long as either she or Glenn contributes the allele for normal red blood cells, their baby will not develop sickle-cell disease.

Figure 2.2 summarizes what you've learned about sickle-cell disease: *A* denotes the allele for normal blood cells, and *a* denotes the allele for sickle-shaped cells. Only if Leslie's baby inherits two recessive alleles for sickle-shaped cells is it likely to develop

genotype
the complete set of genes that makes up a person's heredity

phenotype
physical, behavioral, and psychological features that result from the interaction between an individual's genes and the environment

alleles
variations of genes

homozygous
alleles in a pair of chromosomes that are the same

heterozygous
alleles in a pair of chromosomes that differ from each other

dominant
the allele whose chemical instructions are followed

recessive
the allele whose instructions are ignored in the presence of a dominant allele

FIGURE 2.2

In single-gene inheritance, a heterozygous father and a heterozygous mother can have a healthy child, a child with the sickle-cell trait, or a child with sickle-cell disease.

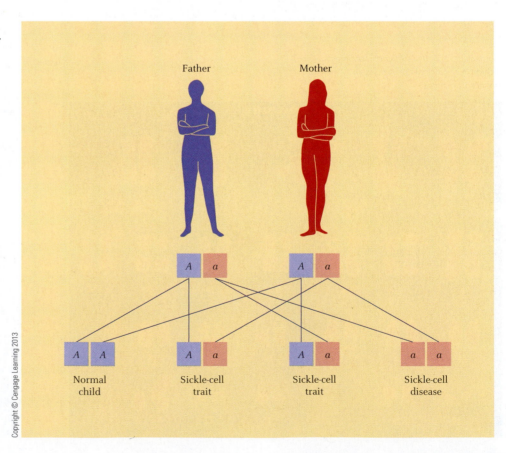

● TABLE 2.1
Common Phenotypes Associated With Single Pairs of Genes

Dominant Phenotype	Recessive Phenotype
Curly hair	Straight hair
Normal hair	Pattern baldness (men)
Dark hair	Blond hair
Thick lips	Thin lips
Cheek dimples	No dimples
Normal hearing	Some types of deafness
Normal vision	Nearsightedness
Farsightedness	Normal vision
Normal color vision	Red–green color blindness
Type A blood	Type O blood
Type B blood	Type O blood
Rh-positive blood	Rh-negative blood

SOURCE: McKusick, 1995.

HUMAN DEVELOPMENT in action

Imaging that you are a licensed nurse practioner. Your patient is a young woman whose father has cystic fibrosis, an inherited disease in which the lungs fill with mucous, making breathing difficult. Cystic fibrosis is caused by a recessive gene, and your patient wonders whether her baby will inherit the disease. What would you tell her?

Children with Down syndrome typically have upward slanting eyes with a fold over the eyelid, a flattened facial profile, and a smaller-than-average nose and mouth.

iStockphoto.com/Diloute

sickle-cell disease. But this is unlikely: No one in Glenn's family has had sickle-cell disease, so he almost certainly has two alleles for normal blood cells.

The simple genetic mechanism responsible for sickle-cell disease—a single gene pair with one dominant allele and one recessive allele—is also responsible for numerous other common traits, as shown in Table 2.1. In each instance, individuals with the recessive phenotype have two recessive alleles, one from each parent. Individuals with the dominant phenotype have at least one dominant allele.

Sometimes individuals do not receive 46 chromosomes because a sperm or egg cell has more or fewer than the usual 23 chromosomes. In this case, development is always disturbed. The best example is Down syndrome, which is usually caused by an extra 21st chromosome. People with Down syndrome have almond-shaped eyes and a fold over the eyelid. Their head, neck, and nose are usually smaller than normal. During the first several months of life, development of babies with Down syndrome seems to be normal. Thereafter, their mental and behavioral development begins to lag behind the average child's. For example, a child with Down syndrome might first sit up without help around 1 year, walk at 2 years, and talk at 3 years, reaching each of these developmental milestones months or even years behind children without Down syndrome. By childhood, most aspects of cognitive and social development are seriously delayed.

The odds that a woman will bear a child with Down syndrome increase markedly as she gets older, from about 1 in 1,000 during her 20s to 1 in 50 during her 40s. Why? A woman's eggs have been in her ovaries since her own prenatal development. Eggs may deteriorate over time as part of aging or because an older woman has a longer history of exposure to hazards in the environment that may damage her eggs (e.g., X-rays).

Abnormal sex chromosomes can also disrupt development. Table 2.2 lists four disorders associated with atypical numbers of X and Y chromosomes. There are no disorders consisting solely of Y chromosomes. The presence of an X chromosome appears to be necessary for life.

Common Disorders Associated With the Sex Chromosomes

Disorder	Sex Chromosomes	Frequency	Characteristics
Klinefelter's syndrome	XXY	1 in 500 male births	Tall, small testicles, sterile, below-normal intelligence, passive
XYY complement	XYY	1 in 1,000 male births	Tall, some individuals apparently have below-normal intelligence
Turner's syndrome	X	1 in 2,500 to 5,000 female births	Short, limited development of secondary sex characteristics, problems perceiving spatial relations
XXX syndrome	XXX	1 in 500 to 1,200 female births	Normal stature but delayed motor and language development

Heredity, Environment, and Development

Traits controlled by single genes are usually either–or phenotypes. A person has either normal color vision or red–green color blindness; a person's blood either clots normally or does not. In contrast, most important behavioral and psychological characteristics are not of an either–or nature; rather, a range of outcomes is possible. Take extraversion as an example. You probably know some extremely outgoing individuals (extroverts) and a few intensely shy people (introverts), but most people fall between these two extremes. The result is a distribution of individuals ranging from extreme introversion at one end to extreme extroversion at the other.

Many behavioral and psychological characteristics are distributed in this fashion, including intelligence and many aspects of personality. *When phenotypes reflect the combined activity of many separate genes, the pattern is known as* **polygenic inheritance**. Because so many genes are involved in polygenic inheritance, we usually cannot trace the effects of each gene. But we can use a hypothetical example to show how many genes work together to produce a behavioral phenotype that spans a continuum. Suppose that four pairs of genes contribute to extroversion, that the allele for extroversion is dominant, and that the total amount of extroversion is simply the sum of the dominant alleles. Using uppercase letters to represent dominant alleles and lowercase letters to represent recessive alleles, the four gene pairs would be Aa, Bb, Cc, and Dd.

These four pairs of genes produce 81 different genotypes and nine distinct phenotypes. For example, a person with the genotype AABBCCDD has eight alleles for extroversion. A person with the genotype aabbccdd has no alleles for extroversion. All other genotypes involve some combination of dominant and recessive alleles, so these are associated with phenotypes representing intermediate levels of extroversion. This example is hypothetical, but it shows how several genes working together can produce a continuum of phenotypes. Something like our example is probably involved in the inheritance of many human behavioral traits, except that many more pairs of genes are involved. What's more, environment influences phenotype.

If many behavioral phenotypes involve countless genes, how can we unravel the influence of heredity? Twins and adopted children provide important clues. In twin studies, researchers compare identical and fraternal twins. *Identical twins are called* **monozygotic twins** *because they come from a single fertilized egg that splits in two.* Because identical twins come from the same fertilized egg, the same genes control their body structure, height, and facial features, which explains why identical twins look alike. *In contrast, fraternal or* **dizygotic twins** *come from two separate eggs fertilized by two separate sperm.* Genetically, fraternal twins are just like any other siblings—on average, about half their genes are the same. In twin studies, scientists compare identical and fraternal twins: When identical twins are more alike than are fraternal twins, this implicates heredity (Phelps, Davis, & Schartz, 1997).

A similar logic is used in adoption studies, in which adopted children are compared with their biological parents and their adoptive parents. Because biological

polygenic inheritance
phenotypes are the result of the combined activity of many separate genes

monozygotic twins
the result of a single fertilized egg splitting to form two new individuals; also called identical twins

dizygotic twins
the result of two separate eggs fertilized by two sperm; also called fraternal twins

iStockphoto.com/Noriko Cooper

Identical twins are called monozygotic twins because they came from a single fertilized egg that split in two; consequently, they have identical genes.

parents provide their child's genes but adoptive parents provide the child's environment, if a behavior has important genetic roots, then adopted children should behave more like their biological parents than like their adoptive parents.

Throughout this book, you'll encounter many instances that show the interactive influences of heredity and environment on human development. In the next few pages, however, we want to mention some general principles of heredity–environment interactions.

Paths From Genes to Behavior

How do genes work together—for example, to make some people brighter than others and some more outgoing than others? The specific paths from genes to behavior are largely uncharted (Meaney, 2010), but some general properties are known.

■ *Heredity and environment interact dynamically throughout development.* A traditional view is that heredity provides the clay of life and experience does the sculpting, but this is too simple: genes and environments constantly interact to produce phenotypes throughout a person's development (Meaney, 2010; Rutter, 2007). Although we often think that a certain genotype necessarily leads to a phenotype, the path from genotype to phenotype is massively more complicated and less direct than this. A more accurate description would be that a genotype leads to a phenotype only if the environment "cooperates" in the usual manner.

A good example of this genotype–phenotype link is seen in the disease phenylketonuria (PKU for short). PKU is a homozygous recessive trait in which phenylalanine accumulates in the child's body, damaging the nervous system and leading to retarded mental development. Phenylalanine is abundant in many foods that many children eat—meat, chicken, eggs, cheese, and so on—so the environment usually provides the input (phenylalanine) necessary for the phenotype (PKU) to emerge. However, the biochemical basis for PKU was discovered in the 20th century, and now newborns are tested for the disorder. Infants who have the genotype for the disease are immediately placed on a diet that limits phenylalanine and the disease does not appear; their nervous system develops normally. In more general terms, a genotype is expressed differently (no disease) when exposed to a different environment (one lacking phenylalanine).

The effect can work in the other direction too: People's experiences can help determine how and when genes are activated. For instance, teenage girls begin to menstruate at a younger age if they've had a stressful childhood (Belsky, Houts, & Fearon, 2010). The exact pathway of influence is unknown (though it probably involves the hormones that are triggered by stress and those that initiate ovulation), but this is a clear case in which the environment advances the genes that regulate the developmental clock (Ellis, 2004).

PKU and the onset of menstruation show intimate connections between nature and nurture in human development. At a biological level, genes always operate in a cellular environment, which can be influenced by a host of broader environmental factors (e.g., hormones triggered by a child's experiences). In the analogy of sculpting clay, new and different forms of genetic clay are constantly being added to the sculpture, leading to resculpting by the environment, which causes more clay to be added, and the cycle continues. Hereditary clay and environmental sculpting are continuously interweaving and influencing each other.

■ *Genes can influence the kind of environment to which a person is exposed.* In other words, nature helps determine the kind of nurturing that a child receives (Scarr, 1992; Scarr & McCartney, 1983). A person's genotype can lead others to respond in a specific way. For example, imagine someone who is bright and outgoing as a

Ben and Matt Kail were born 25 months apart. Even as a young baby, Ben was always a "people person." He relished contact with other people and preferred play that involved others. From the beginning, Matt was different. He was more withdrawn and was quite happy to play alone. When they entered school, Ben enjoyed increasing the scope of his friendships; Matt liked all the activities that were available and barely noticed the new faces. As Ben and Matt grew, they consistently sought environments that fit their differing needs for social stimulation. Ben was involved in team sports and enjoyed helping others. Matt took art and photography classes and was happy working at his computer. Though brothers, Ben and Matt are quite dissimilar in terms of their sociability, a characteristic known to have important genetic components (Braungart et al., 1992) and this genetic difference led them to choose different niches.

Children who are outgoing often like to be with other people and deliberately seek them; this is an example of niche-picking.

Children's experiences within a family typically make them different from one another, not alike.

niche-picking
the process of deliberately seeking environments that are compatible with one's genetic makeup

nonshared environmental influences
forces within a family that make siblings different from one another

result, in part, of her genes. As a child, she may receive plenty of attention and encouragement from teachers. In contrast, someone who is not as bright and is more withdrawn (again, due in part to heredity) may be easily overlooked by teachers. In addition, as children become more independent with age, they actively seek environments that fit their genetic makeup. Children who are bright may actively seek peers, adults, and activities that strengthen their intellectual development. Similarly, people who are outgoing may seek the company of other people, particularly extroverts like themselves. *This process of deliberately seeking environments that fit one's heredity is called* **niche-picking**. Niche-picking is first seen in childhood and becomes more common as children grow older and can control their environments. The Real People feature shows niche-picking in action.

■ *Environmental influences typically make children within a family different.* Traditionally, scientists thought some parenting practices were more effective than others, and parents who used these effective practices were believed to have children who are, on average, better off than children of parents who don't use these practices. This view leads to a simple prediction: Children within a family should be similar, because they receive the same type of effective (or ineffective) parenting. However, behavioral genetic studies show that siblings are not greatly alike in their cognitive and social development (Plomin & Spinath, 2004).

Does this mean that family environment is not important? No. *These findings point to the importance of* **nonshared environmental influences**, *the forces within a family that make children different from one another.* The family environment usually affects each child in a unique way, which makes siblings differ. Each child is likely to have different experiences in daily family life. For example, parents may be more affectionate with one child than with another, punish one child more than another, or have higher expectations for one child than for another. All these contrasting parental influences tend to make siblings different, not alike (Liang & Eley, 2005). Family environments are important, but families actually create multiple unique environments, one for each person in the family.

Much of what we have said about genes, environment, and development is summarized in Figure 2.3 (Lytton, 2000). Parents are the source of children's genes and, at least for young children, the primary source of children's experiences. Children's genes also influence the experiences they have and the impact of those experiences on them. However, to capture the idea of nonshared environmental influences, we would need

FIGURE 2.3

Parents influence their children by providing genes and by providing experiences; children's genes and their environments work together to shape development.

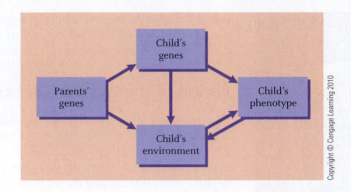

Copyright © Cengage Learning 2010

a separate diagram for each child, reflecting that parents provide unique genes and a unique family environment for each of their offspring.

Most of this book explains the links among nature, nurture, and development. We can first see the interaction of nature and nurture during prenatal development, which we examine in the next section of this chapter.

Test Yourself

Recall

1. The first 22 pairs of chromosomes are called _____.
2. _____ reflects the combined activity of a number of distinct genes.
3. Individuals with _____ have an extra 21st chromosome, usually inherited from the mother.
4. Nonshared environmental influences tend to make siblings _____.

Interpret

- Explain how niche-picking shows the interaction between heredity and environment.
- Describe how polygenic inheritance could help shape a child's intelligence.

Apply

- Leslie and Glenn are already charting their baby's life course. Leslie has always loved to sing and is confident that her baby will be a fantastic musician. Glenn is a pilot and is just as confident that his child will share his love of flying. What advice might a developmental psychologist give to Leslie and Glenn about factors they are ignoring?
- How does niche-picking help explain your academic interests, your hobbies, and your friendships?

Recall answers: (1) autosomes, (2) Polygenic inheritance, (3) Down syndrome, (4) different from one another

---

2.2 From Conception to Birth

LEARNING OBJECTIVES

- What happens to a fertilized egg in the first 2 weeks after conception?
- When do body structures and internal organs emerge in prenatal development?
- When do body systems begin to function well enough to support life?

Eun Jung has just learned that she is pregnant with her first child. Like many other parents-to-be, she and her husband, Kinam, are ecstatic. They're eager to visit Eun Jung's obstetrician to learn more about the normal timetable of events during pregnancy.

prenatal development
the many changes that turn a fertilized egg into a newborn human

Prenatal development begins when a sperm successfully fertilizes an egg. *The many changes that transform the fertilized egg into a newborn human constitute* **prenatal development**. Prenatal development takes an average of 38 weeks, which are divided

CHAPTER 2: BIOLOGICAL FOUNDATIONS | **41**

into three periods: the period of the zygote, the period of the embryo, and the period of the fetus.* Each period gets its name from the term used to describe the baby-to-be at that point in its prenatal development.

Period of the Zygote (Weeks 1 and 2)

The teaspoon of seminal fluid produced during an ejaculation contains 200 million to 500 million sperm, but only a few hundred complete the 6- or 7-inch journey to the Fallopian tubes. Here, an egg arrives monthly, hours after it is released by an ovary. If an egg is present, many sperm simultaneously begin to burrow their way through the cluster of nurturing cells that surround the egg. When one sperm finally penetrates the cellular wall of the egg, chemical changes block all other sperm. Then the nuclei of the egg and the sperm fuse, and the two independent sets of 23 chromosomes are interchanged. The development of a new human is under way!

Fertilization begins the period of the **zygote**, *the technical term for the fertilized egg.* This period ends when the zygote implants itself in the wall of the uterus. During these 2 weeks, the zygote grows rapidly through cell division (see Figure 2.4). The zygote travels down the Fallopian tube toward the uterus and divides for the first time; it then continues to do so every 12 hours.

After about 4 days, the zygote includes about 100 cells and resembles a hollow ball. *A small cluster of cells near the center of the zygote, the* **germ disc**, *will eventually develop into the baby.* The outer layer of cells will form a number of structures that provide a life-support system throughout prenatal development. *For example, the layer of cells closest to the uterus will become the* **placenta**, *a structure through which nutrients and wastes are exchanged between the pregnant woman and the developing organism.* By the end of the first week, the zygote reaches the uterus. *The next step is*

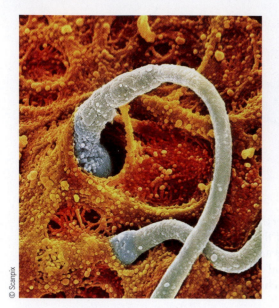

Fertilization begins when sperm cells burrow their way through the outer layers of an egg cell. In this photo, the tails of two sperm can be seen, but one sperm has burrowed so deeply that the head is barely visible.

zygote
the fertilized egg

germ disc
small cluster of cells near the center of the zygote that will eventually develop into a baby

placenta
a structure through which nutrients and wastes are exchanged between the pregnant woman and the developing child

*Perhaps you've heard that pregnancy lasts 40 weeks and wonder why we say prenatal development lasts 38 weeks. The reason is that the 40 weeks of pregnancy are measured from the start of a woman's last menstrual period, which typically is about 2 weeks before conception.

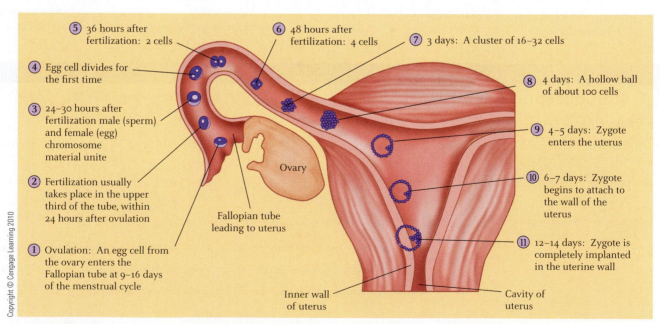

⑤ 36 hours after fertilization: 2 cells
④ Egg cell divides for the first time
③ 24–30 hours after fertilization male (sperm) and female (egg) chromosome material unite
② Fertilization usually takes place in the upper third of the tube, within 24 hours after ovulation
① Ovulation: An egg cell from the ovary enters the Fallopian tube at 9–16 days of the menstrual cycle
⑥ 48 hours after fertilization: 4 cells
⑦ 3 days: A cluster of 16–32 cells
⑧ 4 days: A hollow ball of about 100 cells
⑨ 4–5 days: Zygote enters the uterus
⑩ 6–7 days: Zygote begins to attach to the wall of the uterus
⑪ 12–14 days: Zygote is completely implanted in the uterine wall
Ovary
Fallopian tube leading to uterus
Inner wall of uterus
Cavity of uterus

FIGURE 2.4
The period of the zygote spans 14 days, beginning with fertilization of the egg in the Fallopian tube and ending with implantation of the fertilized egg in the wall of the uterus.

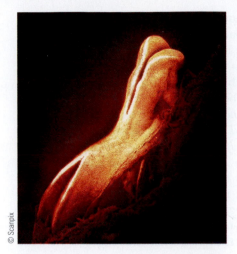

At 3 weeks after conception, the fertilized egg is about 2 millimeters long and resembles a salamander.

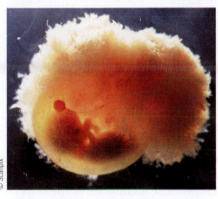

At 8 weeks after conception, near the end of the period of the embryo, the fertilized egg is recognizable as a baby-to-be.

implantation, *in which the zygote burrows into the uterine wall and establishes connections with a woman's blood vessels.* Implantation triggers hormonal changes that prevent menstruation, letting the woman know that she has conceived.

Implantation and differentiation of cells mark the end of the period of the zygote. Sheltered in the uterus, the zygote is well prepared for the remaining 36 weeks of the marvelous trek leading to birth.

Period of the Embryo (Weeks 3–8)

Once the zygote is embedded in the uterine wall, it is called an **embryo***.* This new period typically begins the third week after conception and lasts until the end of the eighth week. During this period, body structures and internal organs develop rapidly. The 3-week-old embryo is about 2 millimeters long and looks like a salamander. However, growth and specialization proceed so quickly that an 8-week-old embryo looks human, with eyes, arms, and legs. The brain and the nervous system are developing rapidly, and the heart has been beating for nearly a month. Yet because it is only an inch long and weighs but a fraction of an ounce, the embryo is too small for the pregnant woman to feel it.

The embryo's environment is shown in Figure 2.5. *The embryo rests in a sac called the* **amnion***, which is filled with* **amniotic fluid** *that cushions the embryo and maintains a constant temperature.* The embryo is linked to the pregnant woman via the placenta and the umbilical cord. *The* **umbilical cord** *houses blood vessels that join the embryo to the placenta.* In the placenta, the blood vessels from the umbilical cord run close to the pregnant woman's blood vessels but aren't connected to them. The proximity of the blood vessels allows nutrients, oxygen, vitamins, and waste products to be exchanged between mother-to-be and embryo.

Period of the Fetus (Weeks 9–38)

The final and longest phase of prenatal development, the **period of the fetus***, begins at the ninth week and ends at birth.* During this period, the fetus becomes larger and its bodily systems begin to work. The increase in size is remarkable. At the beginning of this period, the fetus weighs less than an ounce, but in the last 5 months of pregnancy, it will gain an additional 7 or 8 pounds before birth.

implantation
the zygote burrows into the uterine wall and establishes connections with a woman's blood vessels

embryo
the term given to the zygote after it is completely implanted in the uterine wall

amnion
the inner sac in which the developing child rests

amniotic fluid
the fluid that surrounds the fetus

umbilical cord
the structure containing veins and arteries that connects the developing child to the placenta

period of the fetus
the longest period of prenatal development, extending from the 9th until the 38th week after conception

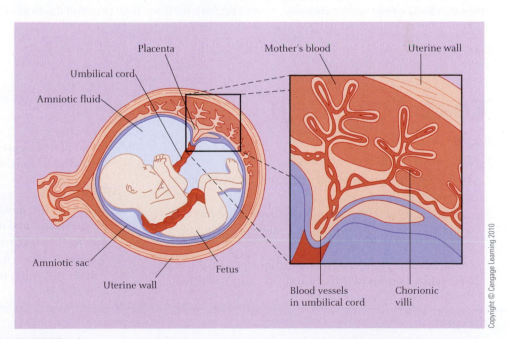

FIGURE 2.5
The fetus is wrapped in the amniotic sac and connected to the mother-to-be through the umbilical cord.

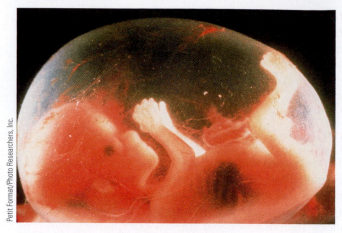

Petit Format/Photo Researchers, Inc.

At 22–28 weeks after conception, the fetus has achieved the age of viability, meaning that it has a chance of surviving if born prematurely.

HUMAN DEVELOPMENT in action

Suppose you're a nurse caring for a baby born 26 weeks after conception. Describe the main challenges that the baby faces.

age of viability
the age, typically 22–28 weeks after conception, at which a fetus can survive if born because most of its bodily systems function adequately

During the fetal period, the finishing touches are placed on many systems essential to human life, such as respiration, digestion, and vision. For example, by the start of the fetal period, the brain has distinct structures and has begun to regulate body functions. During the period of the fetus, all regions of the brain grow (we describe this in detail on pages 73–74). *With these and other rapid changes, by 22–28 weeks after conception, most systems function well enough that a fetus born at this time has a chance of surviving if born, which is why this age range is called the* **age of viability**. By this age, the fetus looks babylike, but babies born this early have trouble breathing because their lungs are not yet mature; in addition, they don't regulate their body temperature well because they lack body fat that provides insulation. With modern neonatal intensive care, infants born this early can survive, but they face other challenges, as we'll see later in this chapter.

During the fetal period, the fetus starts to behave (Joseph, 2000). The delicate movements that were barely noticeable at 4 months are now obvious. The fetus is a budding gymnast and kickboxer rolled into one. It punches or kicks and turns somersaults (DiPietro et al., 2004). These bursts of activity are followed by times of stillness as regular activity cycles emerge.

Another sign of growing behavioral maturity is that the senses work. There's not much to see in the uterus (imagine being in a cave with a flashlight that has a weak battery), but there are sounds galore. The fetus can hear the pregnant woman's heart beating and can hear her food digesting. More important, the fetus can hear her speak and can hear others speak to her (Lecanuet, Granier-Deferre, & Busnel, 1995). And there are tastes: As the fetus swallows amniotic fluid, it responds to different flavors in the fluid.

What's more, infants remember these sensory experiences after birth. For example, they recognize foods that the mother-to-be ate frequently in pregnancy (Mennella, Jagnow, & Beauchamp, 2001). Thus, Eun Jung's obstetrician, mentioned at the start of this section, will tell her that prenatal development typically leaves the fetus remarkably well prepared for independent living as a newborn baby. Unfortunately, not all babies arrive well prepared. Sometimes their prenatal development is disrupted. In the next section, we'll see how prenatal development can go awry.

Test Yourself

Recall

1. The period of the zygote ends _____.
2. Body structures and internal organs are created during the period of the _____.
3. _____ is called the age of viability because this is when most body systems function well enough to support life.
4. In the last few months of prenatal development, the fetus has regular periods of activity and _____, which are the first signs of fetal behavior.

Interpret

- Compare the events of prenatal development that precede the age of viability with those that follow it.

- What period of prenatal development is described as the "growth and finishing" stage? Why?

Apply

- In the last few months before birth, the fetus has some basic perceptual and motor skills. What are the advantages of having these skills in place months before they're needed?

- A woman who is 8 months pregnant wonders if her fetus can see, hear, and taste. What would a health care professional tell her?

Recall answers: (1) 2 weeks after conception (when the zygote is completely implanted in the wall of the uterus), (2) embryo, (3) Between 22 and 28 weeks, (4) the senses work

LEARNING OBJECTIVES

- How is prenatal development influenced by a pregnant woman's age, her nutrition, and the stress she experiences?

- How can diseases, drugs, and environmental hazards affect prenatal development?

- What general principles affect the ways that prenatal development can be harmed?

- How can prenatal development be monitored? Can abnormal prenatal development be corrected?

Chloe was 2 months pregnant at her first prenatal checkup. As her appointment drew near, she began a list of questions to ask her obstetrician. "I use my cell phone a lot. Is radiation from the phone harmful to my baby?" "At night my husband and I have a glass of wine to help unwind from the stress of the day. Is light drinking like this okay?" "I'm 38. I know older women give birth to babies with mental retardation more often. Can I know if my baby will be mentally retarded?"

Each of Chloe's questions concerns harm to her baby-to-be. She worries about the safety of her cell phone, about her nightly glass of wine, and about her age. Chloe's concerns are well founded. Many factors influence the course of prenatal development, and they are the focus of this section.

General Risk Factors

As the name implies, general risk factors can have widespread effects on prenatal development. Scientists have identified three types: nutrition, stress, and a pregnant woman's age.

Nutrition

The mother-to-be is the developing child's sole source of nutrition, so a balanced diet that includes foods from each of the five major food groups is vital. Most pregnant women need to increase their intake of calories by about 10 to 20% to meet the needs of prenatal development. What's more, pregnant women need to consume proteins, vitamins, and minerals that are essential for normal prenatal development. When a pregnant woman does not provide adequate nourishment, her infant may be born prematurely and be underweight. Inadequate nourishment during the last few months of pregnancy can particularly affect the nervous system, because this is a time of rapid brain growth. Finally, babies who do not receive adequate nourishment are vulnerable to illness (Morgane et al., 1993).

Stress

Does a pregnant woman's mood affect the zygote, embryo, or fetus in her uterus? Is a harried office worker more likely to give birth to an irritable baby? These questions address the impact on prenatal development of chronic stress, which refers to a person's physical and psychological responses to threatening or challenging situations. Women who report greater anxiety during pregnancy more often give birth early or have babies who weigh less than average (Copper et al., 1996; Paarlberg et al., 1995). What's more, when women are anxious throughout pregnancy, their children are less able to pay attention as infants and more prone to behavioral problems as preschoolers (Huizink et al., 2002; O'Connor et al., 2002). Similar results emerge in studies of pregnant women exposed to disasters, such as the September 11 attacks on the World

© 2011 Terra Images/Jupiter Images

When pregnant women experience chronic stress, they're more likely to give birth early or have smaller babies; this may be because women who are stressed are more likely to smoke or drink and less likely to rest, exercise, and eat properly.

© Beyond Fotomedia/Alamy

For teenage mothers and their babies, life is often a struggle because the mothers are unable to complete their education and often live in poverty.

Trade Center: their children's physical and behavioral development is affected (Engel et al., 2005; Laplante et al., 2004).

Increased stress can harm prenatal development in several ways. First, when a pregnant woman experiences stress, her body secretes hormones that reduce the flow of oxygen to the fetus (Monk et al., 2000). Second, stress can weaken a pregnant woman's immune system, making her more susceptible to illness (Cohen & Williamson, 1991). Third, pregnant women under stress are more likely to smoke or drink alcohol and are less likely to rest, exercise, and eat properly (DiPietro et al., 2004).

These results apply to women who experience prolonged, extreme stress. Virtually all women sometimes become anxious or upset while pregnant. Occasional, relatively mild anxiety during pregnancy is not thought to be harmful.

A Pregnant Woman's Age

Traditionally, the 20s were thought to be the prime childbearing years. In fact, compared to women in their 20s, teenage women are more likely to have problems during pregnancy, labor, and delivery. This is largely because pregnant teenagers are more likely to be economically disadvantaged and to lack good prenatal care—either because they are unaware of the need for it or because they cannot afford it (Turley, 2003). Nevertheless, even when a teenager receives adequate prenatal care and gives birth to a healthy baby, all is not rosy. Children of teenage mothers generally do less well in school and more frequently have behavioral problems (D'Onofrio et al., 2009; Fergusson & Woodward, 2000). The problems of teenage motherhood—incomplete education, poverty, and marital difficulties—affect the child's later development (Moore & Brooks-Gunn, 2002).

Not all teenage mothers and their infants follow this dismal life course. Some teenage mothers finish school, find good jobs, and have happy marriages; their children do well in school, academically and socially. These "success stories" are more likely when teenage moms live with a relative—typically, the child's grandmother (Gordon, Chase-Lansdale, & Brooks-Gunn, 2004). However, teenage pregnancies with "happy endings" are the exception; for most teenage mothers and their children, life is a struggle.

Today's American woman is waiting longer than ever to have her first child (Hamilton, Martin, & Ventura, 2010), which has consequences: women in their 30s are less fertile than they were in their 20s and are more prone to miscarriage (Dunson, Colombo, & Baird, 2002). Also, women in their 40s are more liable to give birth to babies with Down syndrome. As mothers, however, older women are quite effective. For example, they are able to provide the sort of sensitive, responsive caregiving that promotes a child's development (Bornstein et al., 2006).

In general, then, prenatal development is most likely to proceed normally when women are between 20 and 35 years of age, are healthy and eat right, get good health care, and lead lives that are free of chronic stress. But even in these optimal cases, prenatal development can be disrupted, as we'll see in the next section.

Teratogens: Drugs, Diseases, and Environmental Hazards

In the late 1950s, many pregnant women in Germany took thalidomide, a drug that helped them sleep. Soon, however, came reports that many of these women were giving birth to babies with deformed arms, legs, hands, or fingers. *Thalidomide is a powerful*

Teratogenic Drugs and Their Consequences

Drug	Potential Consequences
Alcohol	FAS, cognitive deficits, heart damage, retarded growth
Aspirin	Deficits in intelligence, attention, and motor skills
Caffeine	Lower birth weight, decreased muscle tone
Cocaine and heroin	Retarded growth, irritability in newborns
Marijuana	Lower birth weight, less motor control
Nicotine	Retarded growth, possible cognitive impairments

When pregnant women drink large amounts of alcohol, their children often have FAS; they tend to have a small head and a thin upper lip, as well as retarded mental development.

teratogen
an agent that causes abnormal prenatal development

fetal alcohol spectrum disorder
a disorder affecting babies whose mothers consumed large amounts of alcohol while they were pregnant

teratogen, *an agent that causes abnormal prenatal development.* Ultimately, more than 7,000 babies worldwide were harmed before thalidomide was withdrawn from the market (Kolberg, 1999).

Prompted by the thalidomide disaster, scientists identified many drugs, diseases, and environmental hazards as teratogens.

Drugs

Thalidomide illustrates the harm that drugs can cause during prenatal development. Table 2.3 lists several drugs that are known teratogens. Most drugs in the list are familiar (e.g., alcohol and aspirin) but present special dangers during pregnancy (Behnke & Eyler, 1993). For example, the nicotine in cigarette smoke constricts blood vessels and thus reduces the oxygen and nutrients that can reach the fetus by means of the placenta. Therefore, pregnant women who smoke are more likely to miscarry and to bear children who are smaller than average at birth (Cnattingius, 2004; Ernst, Moolchan, & Robinson, 2001). And, as such children develop, they are more likely to show signs of impaired attention, language, and cognitive skills (Brennan et al., 2002; Wakschlag et al., 2006). Finally, even secondhand smoke harms the fetus: When pregnant women don't smoke but fathers do, babies tend to be smaller at birth (Friedman & Polifka, 1996).

Alcohol also carries serious risk. *Pregnant women who regularly consume quantities of alcoholic beverages may give birth to babies with* **fetal alcohol spectrum disorder**. The most extreme form, fetal alcohol syndrome (FAS), is found in pregnant women who are heavy recreational drinkers—that is, women who drink 5 ounces or more of alcohol a few times each week (Jacobson & Jacobson, 2000; Lee, Mattson, & Riley, 2004). Children with FAS usually grow more slowly than normal, have heart problems and misshapen faces, and have serious attentional, cognitive, and behavioral problems (e.g., Howell et al., 2006; Sokol, Delaney-Black, & Nordstrom, 2003).

Is there any amount of drinking that's safe during pregnancy? Maybe, but scientists have yet to determine one. This inconclusiveness stems from two factors. First, drinking is often estimated from women's responses to interviews or questionnaires, which may be inaccurate. Second, any safe level of consumption is probably not the same for all women. Based on their health and heredity, some women may be able to consume more alcohol safely than others. These factors

© David Young-Wolff/Photo Edit

TABLE 2.4

Teratogenic Diseases and Their Consequences

Disease	Potential Consequences
AIDS	Frequent infections, neurological disorders, death
Chicken pox	Spontaneous abortion, developmental delays, mental retardation
Chlamydia	Premature birth, low birth weight, eye inflammation
Cytomegalovirus	Deafness, blindness, abnormally small head, mental retardation
Genital herpes	Encephalitis, enlarged spleen, improper blood clotting
Rubella (German measles)	Mental retardation; damage to eyes, ears, and heart
Syphilis	Damage to the central nervous system, teeth, and bones
Toxoplasmosis	Damage to eye and brain, learning disabilities

make it impossible to offer guaranteed statements about safe levels of alcohol or any other drug. For this reason, the best policy is for women to avoid all drugs throughout pregnancy.

Diseases

Sometimes women become ill while pregnant. Most diseases, such as colds and many strains of the flu, do not affect the fetus. However, some bacterial and viral infections can be quite harmful; several are listed in Table 2.4. The only way to guarantee that these diseases will not harm prenatal development is for a woman to be sure that she does not contract them either before or during her pregnancy. Medicines that may help treat a woman after she has become ill do not prevent the disease from damaging the fetus.

Environmental Hazards

As a by-product of life in an industrialized world, people are often exposed to toxins in food and in the air. Chemicals associated with industrial waste are the most common form of environmental teratogens. The quantity involved is usually minute; however, as with drugs, amounts that go unnoticed in an adult can cause serious damage to the fetus.

Several environmental hazards that are known teratogens are listed in Table 2.5. You may be wondering about one ubiquitous feature of modern environments that doesn't appear in Table 2.5: cell phones. Is a pregnant woman's cell phone usage hazardous to the health of her fetus? The radiofrequency radiation that cell phones generate has sometimes been linked to health risks in adults (e.g., cancer), but the findings are inconsistent (National Radiological Protection Board, 2004; Verschaeve, 2009). More research is needed to know whether a cell phone is a risk during pregnancy. One way in which cell phones represent a huge health risk for pregnant women is talking while driving, which reduces a driver's performance to the level seen by drunk drivers (Strayer, Drews, & Crouch, 2006). So, while we wait for research to provide more information, the best advice for a pregnant woman is to keep a cell phone at a distance when it's not being used and never use it while driving.

Environmental teratogens are treacherous because people are unaware of their presence in the environment, which makes it more difficult for a pregnant woman to protect herself from them. The best advice is for a pregnant woman to be particularly careful about the foods she eats and the air she breathes. Be sure that all foods are cleaned thoroughly to rid them of insecticides. Try to avoid convenience foods, which often contain many chemical additives. Stay away from air that's been contaminated

TABLE 2.5

Environmental Teratogens and Their Consequences

Hazard	Potential Consequences
Lead	Mental retardation
Mercury	Retarded growth, mental retardation, cerebral palsy
PCBs	Impaired memory and verbal skills
X-rays	Retarded growth, leukemia, mental retardation

Copyright © Cengage Learning 2010

by household products such as cleansers, paint strippers, and fertilizers. Finally, because environmental teratogens continue to increase, check with a health care provider to learn whether other materials should be avoided.

How Teratogens Influence Prenatal Development

Scientists have identified five important general principles about how teratogens usually work (Hogge, 1990; Jacobson & Jacobson, 2000; Vorhees & Mollnow, 1987).

- *The impact of a teratogen depends on the genotype of the organism.* A substance may be harmful to one species but not to another. For example, thalidomide was safe when tested on pregnant rats, yet when pregnant women took the same drug in comparable doses, many had children with deformed limbs.

- *The impact of teratogens changes over the course of prenatal development.* Figure 2.6 shows how the consequences of teratogens differ for the periods

FIGURE 2.6

The effects of a teratogen on an unborn child depend on the stage of prenatal development.

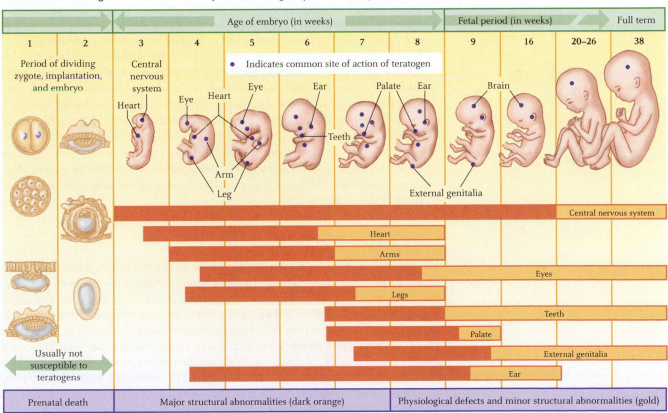

Source: This article was published in *Before We Are Born*, Fourth Edition, by K. L. Moore and T. V. N. Persaud, p. 130. Copyright © 1993 W. B. Saunders. Reprinted with permission.

of the zygote, embryo, and fetus. During the period of the zygote, exposure to teratogens usually results in spontaneous abortion of the fertilized egg. During the period of the embryo, exposure to teratogens produces major defects in bodily structure. For instance, women who took thalidomide during the period of the embryo had babies with ill-formed or missing limbs, and women who contract rubella during the period of the embryo have babies with heart defects. During the period of the fetus, exposure to teratogens either produces minor defects in bodily structure or causes body systems to function improperly. For example, when women drink large quantities of alcohol during this period, the fetus develops fewer brain cells.

Even within the different periods of prenatal development, developing body parts and systems are more vulnerable at some times than others. The dark orange shading in the chart indicates a time of maximum vulnerability; gold shading indicates a time when the developing organism is less vulnerable. The heart, for example, is most sensitive to teratogens during the first half of the embryonic period. Exposure to teratogens before this time rarely produces heart damage, and exposure after this time results in relatively mild damage.

■ *Each teratogen affects a specific aspect (or aspects) of prenatal development.* Teratogens do not harm all body systems; instead, damage is selective. For example, when women contract rubella, their babies often have problems with their eyes, ears, and heart but have normal limbs.

■ *The impact of teratogens depends on the dose.* Just as a single drop of oil won't pollute a lake, small doses of teratogens may not harm the fetus. In general, the greater the exposure, the greater the risk for damage (Adams, 1999). An implication of this principle is that researchers should be able to determine safe levels for a teratogen. In reality, this is extremely difficult because sensitivity to teratogens is not the same for all people (and it's not practical to establish separate safe amounts for each person). Hence, the safest rule is zero exposure to teratogens.

■ *Damage from teratogens is not always evident at birth but may appear later in life.* In the case of malformed limbs or babies born addicted to cocaine, the effects of a teratogen are obvious immediately. Sometimes, however, the damage from a teratogen becomes evident only later in life. To illustrate, between 1947 and 1971, many pregnant women took the drug diethylstilbestrol (DES) to prevent miscarriages. Their babies were apparently normal at birth. As adults, however, daughters of women who took DES are more likely to have breast cancer or a rare cancer of the vagina. And they sometimes have abnormalities in their reproductive tract that make it difficult to become pregnant. Sons of women who took DES are at risk for testicular abnormalities and testicular cancer (National Cancer Institute, 2006). In this case, the impact of the teratogen is not evident until decades after birth.

The Real World of Prenatal Risk

We have discussed risk factors individually as if each factor were the only potential threat to prenatal development. In reality, many infants are exposed to multiple general risks and multiple teratogens. Pregnant women who drink alcohol often smoke and drink coffee (Haslam & Lawrence, 2004). Pregnant women who are under stress often drink alcohol and may self-medicate with aspirin or other over-the-counter drugs. Many of these same women live in poverty, which means they may have inadequate nutrition and receive minimal medical care during pregnancy. When all risks are combined, prenatal development is rarely optimal (Yumoto, Jacobson, & Jacobson, 2008).

This pattern explains why it's often challenging for human development researchers to determine the harm associated with individual teratogens. Cocaine is a perfect example. You may remember stories about "crack babies" and their developmental problems, but the jury is still out on the issue of cocaine as a teratogen (Jones, 2006). Some investigators (e.g., Bennett, Bendersky, & Lewis, 2008; Dennis et al., 2006) find harmful effects, but others (e.g., Brown et al., 2004; Frank et al., 2001) argue that most effects attributed to cocaine stem from concurrent smoking and drinking by parents and to the inadequate parenting that their children receive. Similarly, harmful effects attributed to smoking during pregnancy may arise because pregnant women who smoke are more likely to be less educated and to have a history of psychological problems, including antisocial behavior (D'Onofrio et al., 2010).

Findings like these don't mean that pregnant women should feel free to light up (or, for that matter, to shoot up). Instead, they highlight the difficulties involved in determining the harm associated with a single risk factor (e.g., smoking) when it usually occurs with many other risk factors (e.g., inadequate parenting and continued exposure to smoke after birth).

Prenatal Diagnosis and Treatment

Parents-to-be hope for a healthy baby, and advances in technology mean that parents can have a better idea of whether their baby is developing normally.

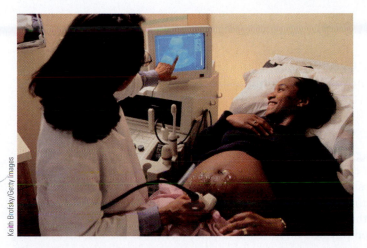

Keith Brofsky/Getty Images

A standard part of prenatal care is ultrasound, in which sound waves generate an image of the fetus that shows its position in the uterus.

Prenatal Diagnosis

Traditionally, obstetricians tracked prenatal development by feeling the size and position of the fetus through a woman's abdomen. This technique was not very precise and couldn't be done until the fetus was large enough to feel. Today, however, several techniques have revolutionized the ability to monitor prenatal growth. *A standard part of prenatal care in the United States is* **ultrasound**, *in which sound waves are used to generate a picture of the fetus*. In this procedure, a tool about the size of a hair dryer is rubbed over the woman's abdomen, and the image appears on a nearby computer monitor. The pictures generated are grainy, and it takes an expert's eye to distinguish what's what. Ultrasound pictures are quite useful for determining the position of the fetus within the uterus and, 16–20 weeks after conception, its sex. Ultrasound is also helpful in detecting twins or triplets, as well as gross physical deformities.

For pregnancies in which a genetic disorder is suspected, two other techniques are valuable because they provide a sample of fetal cells that can be analyzed. *In* **amniocentesis**, *a needle is inserted through the pregnant woman's abdomen to obtain a sample of the amniotic fluid that surrounds the fetus.* The fluid contains skin cells that can be grown in a laboratory dish and then analyzed to determine the genotype of the fetus.

A procedure that can be used earlier in pregnancy is **chorionic villus sampling** (CVS) in which a sample of tissue is obtained from part of the placenta. This procedure can be used within 9–12 weeks after conception, much earlier than amniocentesis.

Results are returned from the lab in about 2 weeks following amniocentesis and in 7 to 10 days following CVS. (The wait is longer for amniocentesis because genetic material can't be evaluated until enough cells have reproduced for analysis.) With the samples obtained from either technique, roughly 200 genetic disorders, including Down syndrome, can be detected. These procedures are virtually free of errors but come at a price: Miscarriages are slightly—1 or 2%—more likely

ultrasound
a prenatal diagnostic technique that uses sound waves to generate an image of the fetus

amniocentesis
a prenatal diagnostic technique that uses a syringe to withdraw a sample of amniotic fluid through the pregnant woman's abdomen

chorionic villus sampling (CVS)
a prenatal diagnostic technique that involves taking a sample of tissue from the chorion

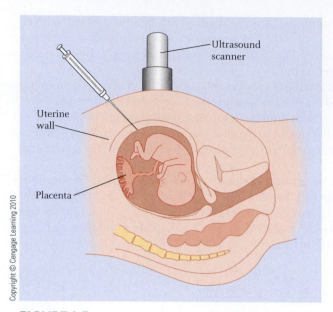

FIGURE 2.7

In amniocentesis, a sample of fetal cells is extracted from the fluid in the amniotic sac.

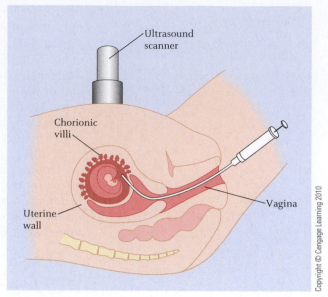

FIGURE 2.8

In CVS, fetal cells are extracted from the placenta.

after amniocentesis or CVS (Wilson, 2000). A woman must decide whether the information gained from either procedure justifies the slightly increased risks of a possible miscarriage.

Fetal Medicine

When diagnostic testing indicates abnormal prenatal development, some problems can be treated (Rodeck & Whittle, 2009). *A new field called* **fetal medicine** *is concerned with treating prenatal problems before birth.* One approach is to treat disorders medically by administering drugs or hormones to the fetus. For example, in fetal hypothyroidism, the fetal thyroid gland does not produce enough hormones. This can lead to retarded physical and mental development, but the disorder can be treated by injecting the necessary hormones directly into the amniotic cavity, resulting in normal growth.

Another way to correct prenatal problems is fetal surgery (Warner, Altimier, & Crombleholme, 2007). For instance, spina bifida can be corrected with fetal surgery in the seventh or eighth month of pregnancy. Surgeons cut through the pregnant woman's abdominal wall to expose the fetus and then cut through the fetal abdominal wall; the spinal cord is repaired, and the fetus is returned to the uterus. However, the procedure is far from foolproof: The best techniques and the ideal times to use them are still unknown (Adzick, 2010).

Yet another approach is genetic engineering, in which defective genes are replaced by synthetic normal genes. Take sickle-cell disease as an example. Recall from page 36 that when a baby inherits the recessive allele for sickle-cell disease from both parents, the child has misshaped red blood cells that can't pass through capillaries. In theory, it should be possible to take a sample of cells from the fetus and replace the recessive genes with dominant genes. These "repaired" cells would then multiply and cause normal red blood cells to be produced (David & Rodeck, 2009). As with fetal surgery, however, translating idea into practice is challenging. Researchers are still studying these techniques with mice and sheep, and there have been some successful applications with older children (Coutelle et al., 2005; Maguire et al., 2009). However, routine use of this method in fetal medicine is still years away.

Suppose that you're a health care professional meeting with Chloe from the section-opening vignette. Return to her questions (page 45) and answer them for her.

fetal medicine
a field of medicine concerned with treating prenatal problems before birth

Test Yourself

Recall

1. General risk factors in pregnancy include a woman's nutrition, _____, and her age.
2. _____ are some of the most dangerous teratogens because a pregnant woman is often unaware of their presence.
3. During the period of the zygote, exposure to a teratogen typically results in _____.
4. Two techniques used to determine whether a fetus has a hereditary disorder are amniocentesis and _____.

Interpret

- Explain how the impact of a teratogen changes over the course of prenatal development.
- What general risk factors can affect prenatal development?

Apply

- Imagine that you are 42-years-old and pregnant. Would you want to have amniocentesis or CVS to determine the genotype of the fetus?
- A pregnant woman reluctant to give up her morning cup of coffee and nightly glass of wine says, "I drink so little coffee and wine that it couldn't possibly hurt my baby." If you were a health care professional, what would you say to her?

Recall answers: (1) prolonged stress, (2) Environmental hazards, (3) spontaneous abortion of the fertilized egg, (4) CVS

2.4 Labor and Delivery

LEARNING OBJECTIVES

- What are the stages of labor and delivery?
- What are "natural" ways of coping with the pain of childbirth?
- What adjustments do parents face after a baby's birth?
- What are some complications that can occur during birth?
- What contributes to infant mortality in developed and least developed countries?

Dominique is 6 months pregnant; soon she and her partner will begin childbirth classes at the local hospital. She is relieved that the classes are finally starting, because this means that pregnancy is nearly over. But all the talk she has heard about "breathing exercises" and "coaching" sounds mysterious to her. Dominique wonders what's involved and how the classes will help her during labor and delivery.

As women like Dominique near the end of pregnancy, their sleeping and breathing become more difficult, they tire more rapidly, and their legs and feet swell. Women look forward to birth, both to relieve their discomfort and to see their baby. In this section, you'll see the steps involved in birth, review approaches to childbirth, and look at problems that can arise. Along the way, we look at classes like those Dominique will take and the exercises that she'll learn.

Stages of Labor and Delivery

Labor is an appropriate name for childbirth, which is the most intense, prolonged physical effort that humans experience. Labor and delivery are usually divided into the three stages shown in Figure 2.9.

- In stage 1, which may last from 12 to 24 hours for a first birth, the uterus starts to contract. The first contractions are weak and irregular. Gradually, they become stronger and more rhythmic, enlarging the cervix (the opening from the uterus to the vagina) to approximately 10 centimeters.

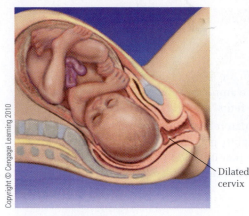
Stage 1

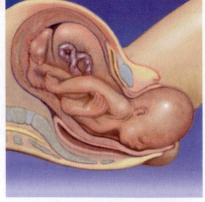
Stage 2

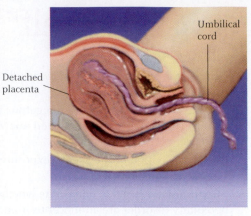
Umbilical cord

Detached placenta

Stage 3

Copyright © Cengage Learning 2010

FIGURE 2.9
Labor and delivery include three stages, beginning when the uterus contracts and ending when the placenta is expelled.

- In stage 2, the baby passes through the cervix and enters the vagina. The pregnant woman helps push the baby along by contracting muscles in her abdomen. Within about an hour, the baby is delivered.

- In stage 3, which lasts only minutes, the mother-to-be pushes a few more times to expel the placenta (also called the afterbirth).

The times given for each of the stages are only approximations; the actual times vary greatly. For most women, labor with their second and subsequent children is more rapid.

Approaches to Childbirth

In the middle of the 20th century, two European physicians—Grantly Dick-Read (1890–1959) and Ferdinand Lamaze (1891–1957)—revolutionized approaches to childbirth (Dick-Read, 1959; Lamaze, 1958). Labor and delivery had become elaborate medical procedures with components that were often unnecessary and that frequently left women afraid of giving birth. These physicians argued for a more "natural" or prepared approach to childbirth, viewing labor and delivery as life events to be celebrated rather than medical procedures to be endured.

Today, many varieties of prepared childbirth are available; most share some fundamental beliefs. One ingredient is a view that birth is more likely to be problem free and rewarding when mothers and fathers understand what's happening during pregnancy, labor, and delivery. Consequently, prepared childbirth means going to classes to learn basic facts about pregnancy and childbirth.

A second ingredient is that natural methods of dealing with pain are emphasized over medication. Anesthetized women can't use their abdominal muscles to push the baby through the birth canal, which means that potentially risky mechanical devices are needed to pull the baby through the birth canal (Johanson et al., 1993). Also, pain-reducing drugs cross the placenta and can affect the baby, making it withdrawn or irritable for days or even weeks (Brazelton, Nugent, & Lester, 1987; Ransjoe-Arvidson et al., 2001). These effects go away, but they may give the new mother the impression that she has a difficult baby. It is best, therefore, to minimize the use of pain-relieving drugs during birth.

Relaxation is the key to reducing birth pain without drugs, because pain often feels greater when a person is tense. Pregnant women learn to minimize pain by relaxing through deep breathing or by visualizing a reassuring, pleasant scene or experience.

A third common element of prepared childbirth is to involve a supportive "coach" (e.g., father-to-be or friend) who attends childbirth classes with the mother-to-be and learns techniques for coping with pain. During labor and delivery, the coach helps the woman use the techniques and offers support and encouragement. This preparation and support is effective in reducing the amount of medication that women like Dominique from the vignette take during labor (Maimburg et al., 2010).

HUMAN DEVELOPMENT in action
A 24-year-old who is pregnant for the first time thinks that childbirth preparation classes seem like a waste of time. As a health care professional, what would you say to convince her that these classes are worthwhile?

During childbirth preparation classes, pregnant women learn exercises that help them relax and reduce the pain associated with childbirth.

Adjusting to Parenthood

The time immediately after birth involves adjustments for parents. A woman experiences many physical changes after birth. Her breasts begin to produce milk, her uterus becomes smaller, and levels of female hormones drop. Parents must also adjust psychologically. They reorganize old routines, particularly for first-born children, to fit the young baby's sleep–wake cycle. In the process, fathers sometimes feel left out when mothers devote most of their attention to the baby.

Roughly half of new mothers find that their initial excitement gives way to irritation, resentment, and crying spells—the so-called baby blues. These feelings usually last a week or two and probably reflect both the stress of caring for a new baby and the woman's body returning to its nonpregnant state (Brockington, 1996). For 10 to 15% of new mothers, however, irritability continues for months and is often accompanied by feelings of low self-worth, disturbed sleep, poor appetite, and apathy—a condition known as postpartum depression. Women with postpartum depression don't talk to or cuddle their new babies, and they are less effective in handling feeding and sleep (Field, 2010). When postpartum depression persists over years, children's development is affected (Wachs, Black, & Engle, 2009).

Thus, postpartum depression is a serious condition; if a mom's depression doesn't lift after a few weeks, she should seek help. Home visits by trained health care professionals can be valuable by showing a mother better ways to cope with the changes that accompany the new baby. Visitors also provide emotional support, and they can refer the mother to other resources in the community. Finally, one simple way to reduce the risk of postpartum depression is breast-feeding. A mom who breast-feeds is less likely to become depressed, perhaps because breast-feeding releases hormones that act as antidepressants (Gagliardi, 2005).

Birth Complications

When women are not healthy or don't receive adequate prenatal care, problems can surface during labor and delivery. (Of course, even healthy women can have problems, but not as often.) The more common birth complications are listed in Table 2.6.

Some of these complications, such as a prolapsed umbilical cord, are dangerous because they can disrupt the flow of blood through the umbilical cord. *If this flow of blood is disrupted, then infants do not receive adequate oxygen, a condition known as* **hypoxia**. Hypoxia is serious because it can lead to mental retardation or death (Hogan et al., 2006).

The hazards are birth complications that extend beyond the newborn period: When babies experience many birth complications, they are at risk for becoming aggressive or violent and for developing schizophrenia (Cannon et al., 2000; de Haan et al., 2006).

hypoxia

a birth complication in which umbilical blood flow is disrupted and the infant does not receive adequate oxygen

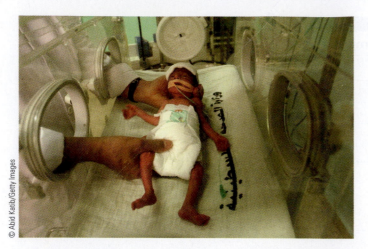

Low birth weight babies often survive, but their cognitive and motor development usually are delayed.

This is particularly true for newborns with birth complications who later experience family adversity, such as living in poverty (Arseneault et al., 2002).

Problems also arise when babies are born too early or too small. Normally, a baby spends about 38 weeks developing before being born. *Babies born before the 36th week are called* **preterm (premature)**. In the first year or so, preterm infants often lag behind full-term infants in many facets of development. However, by 2 or 3 years of age, such differences have vanished, and most preterm infants develop normally (Greenberg & Crnic, 1988).

Prospects are usually not as bright for babies who are "small for date." These infants are most often born to women who smoke or drink alcohol frequently during pregnancy or who do not eat enough nutritious food (Chomitz, Cheung, & Lieberman, 1995). *Newborns who weigh 2,500 grams (5.5 pounds) or less are said to have* **low birth weight***; newborns weighing less than 1,500 grams (3.3 pounds) are said to have* **very low birth weight***; and those weighing less than 1,000 grams (2.2 pounds) are said to have* **extremely low birth weight***.*

Babies with very or extremely low birth weight do not fare well. Many do not survive, and those who live often lag behind in the development of intellectual and motor skills (Kavsek & Bornstein, 2010). These impaired cognitive processes are shown in the Spotlight on Research feature.

The odds are better for newborns who weigh more than 1,500 grams. Most survive, and their prospects are better if they receive appropriate care. Small-for-date babies are typically placed in special, sealed beds where temperature and air quality are regulated carefully. They often receive auditory stimulation (e.g., a tape recording of soothing music or their mother's voice) or visual stimulation provided from a mobile placed over the bed. Infants also receive tactile stimulation from daily "massages." These forms of stimulation foster physical and cognitive development in small-for-date babies (Field & Diego, 2010).

This special care should continue when infants leave the hospital for home. Consequently, intervention programs for small-for-date babies typically include training programs in which parents learn how to respond appropriately to their child's behaviors. For example, they are taught the signs that a baby is in distress, overstimulated, or ready to interact. In addition, children are enrolled in high-quality childcare centers where the curriculum is coordinated with parent training. This sensitive care promotes development in low birth weight babies; for example, sometimes they catch up to full-term infants in terms of cognitive development (Hill, Brooks-Gunn, & Waldfogel, 2003).

preterm (premature)
babies born before the 36th week after conception

low birth weight
newborns who weigh less than 2,500 grams (5.5 pounds)

very low birth weight
newborns who weigh less than 1,500 grams (3.3 pounds)

extremely low birth weight
newborns who weigh less than 1,000 grams (2.2 pounds)

infant mortality rate
the percentage of infants who die before their first birthday

Long-term positive outcomes for these infants depend critically on providing a supportive and stimulating home environment. Unfortunately, not all at-risk babies have optimal experiences. Many receive inadequate medical care because their families live in poverty. Others experience stress and disorder in their family life. For these low birth weight babies, development is usually delayed and sometimes permanently diminished. When biological and sociocultural forces are both harmful—low birth weight plus inadequate medical care or family stress—the prognosis for babies is grim. The message to parents of low birth weight newborns is clear: Do not despair, because excellent caregiving can compensate for all but the most severe birth problems (Werner, 1994; Werner & Smith, 1992).

Infant Mortality

Tragically, many babies around the world do not survive. **Infant mortality rate** *is defined as the percentage of infants who die before their first birthday.* Figure 2.11 shows infant mortality rates for 15 developed nations and for 15 of the least

Impaired Cognitive Functions in Low Birth Weight Babies

Who were the investigators, and what was the aim of the study?
Cognitive development is often delayed in low birth weight babies. Susan Rose and her colleagues (2009) hoped to understand whether memory developed normally in such children.

How did the investigators measure the topic of interest?
Memory is an essential skill, because it allows us to benefit from past experiences. Rose and her colleagues measured children's memory in several ways, including an imitation task in which an experimenter demonstrated a brief sequence of novel events, such as making a gong from two posts, a base, and a metal plate. After a brief delay, children were given the parts and encouraged to reproduce what they'd seen.

Who were the participants in the study?
The sample included 144 full-term babies who weighed at least 2,500 grams at birth and 59 babies born prematurely who weighed, on average, about 1,100 grams at birth. The memory tasks were administered when children were 2-year-olds and again when they were 3-year-olds.

What was the design of the study?
The study was correlational because the investigators were interested in the relation that existed naturally between two variables: birth weight and memory skill. The study was longitudinal because children were tested twice: at 2 and at 3 years of age.

Were there ethical concerns with the study?
No. The study posed no known risks to children. The investigators obtained permission from the parents for the children to participate.

What were the results?
The graph in Figure 2.10 shows the percentage of actions in each event that children successfully imitated. Memory improves substantially between 2 and 3 years. Nevertheless, at each age, children who had been born prematurely imitated a smaller percentage of events than did children born after a full term.

What did the investigators conclude?
Low birth weight impairs basic cognitive processes—in this case, memory—and during the toddler years, there's no evidence that

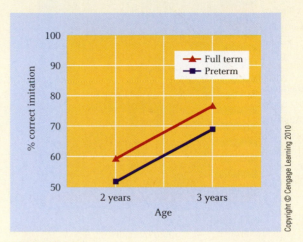

Copyright © Cengage Learning 2010

FIGURE 2.10
At both 2 and 3 years, preterm children remember less than full-term children do.

children born prematurely catch up: They're just as far behind at age 3 as at age 2.

What converging evidence would strengthen these conclusions?
The results show that low birth weight affects children's memory. More convincing would be additional longitudinal results showing that low birth weight children with impaired basic skills are more likely to be diagnosed with a learning disability, more likely to repeat a grade, or less likely to graduate from high school.

 Go to Psychology CourseMate at **www.cengagebrain.com** to enhance your understanding of this research.

developed countries. Not surprisingly, risks to infants are far greater in the least developed nations (United Nations Children's Fund, 2007). Among developed nations, the United States ranks near the bottom. Why? The United States has more babies with low birth weight than virtually all other developed countries, and we've already seen that low birth weight places an infant at risk. Low birth weight can usually be prevented when a pregnant woman gets regular prenatal care, but many pregnant women in the United States receive inadequate or no prenatal care (Cohen, Martinez, & Ward, 2010). Virtually all countries that rank ahead of the United States provide complete prenatal care at little or no cost. Many of these countries also provide for a paid leave of absence for pregnant women (Organisation for Economic Co-operation and Development, 2006).

In least developed countries, inadequate prenatal care is common and mothers often have inadequate nutrition. After birth, infants in these countries face the

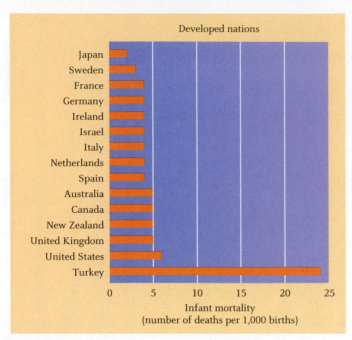

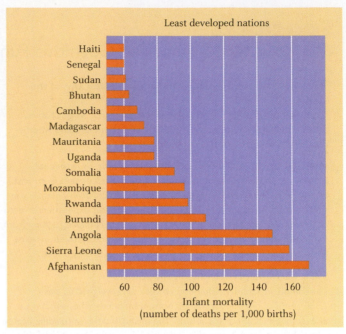

FIGURE 2.11

The infant mortality rate in the world's least developed countries is much higher than in developed countries.

Data from The state of the world's children, 2008, by United Nations Children's Fund. Copyright © United Nations Children's Fund 2007.

twin challenges of receiving adequate nutrition and avoiding disease. However, with improved prenatal care and improved health care and nutrition for infants, the global infant mortality rate has been cut in half since 1990 (United Nations Children's Fund, 2007). With continued improvements in such care, the main challenges for infants worldwide will be walking, talking, and bonding with parents—not sheer survival.

Test Yourself

Recall

1. In the third stage of labor and delivery, the _____ is delivered.

2. Two problems with using anesthesia during labor are that a woman can't use her abdominal muscles to help push the baby down the birth canal and _____.

3. When the supply of oxygen to the fetus is disrupted because the umbilical cord is squeezed shut, _____ results.

Interpret

- Explain why some at-risk newborns develop normally but others do not.

- Describe the main events of the three stages of labor and delivery.

Apply

- A friend of yours has just given birth 6 weeks prematurely. The baby is average size for a baby born prematurely and seems to be faring well, but your friend is concerned nonetheless. What could you say to reassure your friend?

- Lynn gave birth 10 days ago and now spends much of her day crying and resenting her husband's absence. She is so weepy and overwhelmed that she is considering giving her baby up for adoption. How might a social worker counsel Lynn?"

Recall answers: (1) placenta, (2) the pain-relieving medication crosses the placenta and affects the baby, (3) hypoxia

More than 30 years ago, Louise Brown captured the world's attention as the first test-tube baby—conceived in a petri dish instead of in her mother-to-be's body. Today, this reproductive technology is no longer experimental; it is used more than 140,000 times annually by American women and produces more than 55,000 babies each year (Centers for Disease Control and Prevention, 2007a). Many new techniques are available to couples who cannot conceive a child through sexual intercourse. *The best-known technique,* **in vitro fertilization**, *involves mixing sperm and eggs together in a petri dish and then placing several fertilized eggs in the woman's uterus, with the hope that they will become implanted in the uterine wall.* Other methods include injecting many sperm directly into the Fallopian tubes or a single sperm directly into an egg.

The sperm and eggs usually come from the prospective parents, but sometimes they are provided by donors. Typically, the fertilized eggs are placed in the uterus of the prospective mother, but sometimes they are placed in the uterus of a surrogate mother who carries the baby to term. This means that a baby could have as many as five "parents": the man and woman who provided the sperm and eggs; the surrogate mother who carried the baby; and the mother and father who rear the baby.

New reproductive techniques offer hope for couples who have long wanted a child, and studies of the first generation of children conceived via these techniques indicate that their social and emotional development is normal (Golombok et al., 2004; MacCallum, Golombok, & Brinsden, 2007). But there are difficulties as well. Only about one third of attempts at in vitro fertilization succeed. What's more, when a woman becomes pregnant, she is more likely to have twins or triplets because multiple eggs are transferred to increase the odds that at least one fertilized egg implants in the woman's uterus. (An extreme example of this would be "Octomom," a woman who had octuplets following in vitro fertilization.) She is also at greater risk for giving birth to a baby with low birth weight or birth defects. Finally, the procedure is expensive—the average cost in the United States of a single cycle of treatment is between $10,000 and $15,000—and often is not covered by health insurance.

These problems emphasize that, although technology has increased the alternatives for infertile couples, pregnancy on demand is still in the realm of science fiction. At the same time, the new technologies have led to much controversy because of some complex ethical issues associated with their use. One concerns the prospective parents' right to select particular egg and sperm cells; another involves who should be able to use this technology.

Pick Your Egg and Sperm Cells From a Catalog

Until recently, prospective parents knew nothing about egg and sperm donors. Today, however, they are sometimes able to select eggs and sperm based on physical and psychological characteristics of the donors, including appearance and race. Some claim that such prospective parents have a right to be fully informed about the person who provides the genetic material for their baby. *Others argue that this amounts to* **eugenics**, *which is the effort to improve the human species by allowing only certain people to mate and pass along their genes to subsequent generations.*

Available to All

Most couples who use in vitro fertilization are in their 30s and 40s, but a number of older women have begun to use the technology. Many of these women cannot conceive naturally because they have gone through menopause and no longer ovulate. Some argue that it is unfair to a child to have parents who may not live until the child reaches adulthood. Others point out that people are living longer and that middle-age (or older) adults make better parents. (We discuss this issue in more depth in Chapter 13.)

What do you think? Should prospective parents be allowed to browse a catalog with photos and biographies of prospective donors? Should new reproductive technologies be available to all, regardless of age?

in vitro fertilization
the process by which sperm and an egg are mixed in a petri dish to create a zygote, which is then placed in a woman's uterus

eugenics
the effort to improve the human species by letting only people whose characteristics are valued by a society mate and pass along their genes

Summary

2.1 In the Beginning: 23 Pairs of Chromosomes

What are chromosomes and genes? How do they carry hereditary information?

- At conception, the 23 chromosomes in the sperm merge with the 23 chromosomes in the egg. Each chromosome is one molecule of DNA; a section of DNA that provides specific biochemical instructions is called a gene.

- All of a person's genes make up a genotype; the phenotype refers to the physical, behavioral, and psychological characteristics that develop when the genotype is exposed to a specific environment.

- Different forms of the same gene are called alleles. A person who inherits the same alleles on a pair of chromosomes is homozygous; in this case, the biochemical instructions of the alleles are followed. A person who inherits different alleles is heterozygous; in this case, the instructions of the dominant allele are followed and those of the recessive allele are ignored.

- Sometimes fertilized eggs do not have 46 chromosomes. Such an exception is Down syndrome, in which individuals usually have an extra 21st chromosome. Down syndrome individuals have a distinctive appearance and are mentally retarded.

How is children's heredity influenced by their environment?

- Behavioral and psychological phenotypes (e.g., intelligence and aspects of personality) often involve polygenic inheritance. In polygenic inheritance, the phenotype reflects the combined activity of many distinct genes. Polygenic inheritance has been examined traditionally by studying twins and adopted children.

- The impact of heredity on a child's development depends on the environment in which the genetic instructions are carried out, and these heredity–environment interactions occur throughout a child's life. A child's genotype can affect the kinds of experiences the child has; children and adolescents often actively seek environments related to their genetic makeup. Family environments affect siblings differently (nonshared environmental influence); parents provide a unique environment for each child in the family.

2.2 From Conception to Birth

What happens to a fertilized egg in the first 2 weeks after conception?

- The first period of prenatal development lasts 2 weeks. It begins when the egg is fertilized by the sperm in the Fallopian tube and ends when the fertilized egg has implanted itself in the wall of the uterus. By the end of this period, cells have begun to differentiate.

When do body structures and internal organs emerge in prenatal development?

- The second period of prenatal development begins 2 weeks after conception and ends 8 weeks after. This is a period of rapid growth in which most major body structures are created.

When do body systems begin to function well enough to support life?

- The third period of prenatal development begins 9 weeks after conception and lasts until birth. The highlights of this period are a remarkable increase in the size of the fetus and changes in body systems that are necessary for life. By 7 months, most body systems function well enough to support life.

2.3 Influences on Prenatal Development

How is prenatal development influenced by a pregnant woman's age, her nutrition, and the stress she experiences?

- A pregnant woman's age can affect prenatal development. Teenagers often have problem pregnancies, mainly because they rarely receive adequate prenatal care. After age 35, pregnant women are more likely to have a miscarriage or to give birth to a child with mental retardation. Prenatal development can also be harmed if a pregnant woman has inadequate nutrition or experiences considerable stress.

How can diseases, drugs, and environmental hazards affect prenatal development?

- Teratogens are agents that can cause abnormal prenatal development. Many drugs that adults take are teratogens. For most drugs, scientists have not established amounts that can be consumed safely during pregnancy.

- Several diseases are teratogens. Only by avoiding these diseases can a pregnant woman and her fetus escape their harmful consequences.

- Environmental teratogens are particularly dangerous because a pregnant woman may not know that these substances are present in the environment.

What general principles affect the ways that prenatal development can be harmed?

- The impact of teratogens depends on the genotype of the organism, the period of prenatal development when the organism is exposed to the teratogen, and the amount of exposure. Sometimes the effect of a teratogen is not evident until later in life.

How can prenatal development be monitored? Can abnormal prenatal development be corrected?

- A common component of prenatal care is ultrasound, which uses sound waves to generate a picture of the fetus. This picture can be used to determine the position of the fetus, its sex, and whether there are gross physical deformities.

- When genetic disorders are suspected, amniocentesis and CVS are used to determine the genotype of the fetus.

- Fetal medicine is a new field in which problems of prenatal development are corrected medically via surgery or genetic engineering.

2.4 Labor and Delivery

What are the stages of labor and delivery?

- Labor and delivery consist of three stages. In stage 1, the muscles of the uterus contract. The contractions, which are weak at first and gradually become stronger, cause the cervix to enlarge. In stage 2, the baby moves through the birth canal. In stage 3, the placenta is delivered.

What are "natural" ways of coping with the pain of childbirth?

- Natural or prepared childbirth is based on the assumption that parents should understand what takes place during pregnancy and birth. In natural childbirth, women learn to cope with pain through relaxation, imagery, and the help of a supportive coach.

What adjustments do parents face after a baby's birth?

- Following the birth of a child, a woman's body changes physiologically (e.g., her breasts fill with milk). Both parents also adjust psychologically, and sometimes fathers feel left out. After giving birth, some women experience postpartum depression: they are irritable, have poor appetite and disturbed sleep, and are apathetic.

What are some complications that can occur during birth?

- During labor and delivery, the flow of blood to the fetus can be disrupted because the umbilical cord is squeezed shut. This causes hypoxia, a lack of oxygen to the fetus. Some babies are born prematurely, and others are small for date. Preterm babies develop more slowly at first but catch up by 2 or 3 years of age. Small-for-date babies often do not fare well, particularly if they weigh less than 1,500 grams at birth and if their environment is stressful.

What contributes to infant mortality in developed and least developed countries?

- Infant mortality is relatively high in many countries around the world, primarily because of inadequate care before birth and disease and inadequate nutrition after birth.

Key Terms

chromosomes 34
autosomes 34
sex chromosomes 34
deoxyribonucleic acid (DNA) 35
gene 35
genotype 36
phenotype 36
alleles 36
homozygous 36
heterozygous 36
dominant 36
recessive 36
polygenic inheritance 38
monozygotic twins 38

dizygotic twins 38
niche-picking 40
nonshared environmental influences 40
prenatal development 41
zygote 42
germ disc 42
placenta 42
implantation 43
embryo 43
amnion 43
amniotic fluid 43
umbilical cord 43
period of the fetus 43
age of viability 44

teratogen 47
fetal alcohol spectrum disorder 47
ultrasound 51
amniocentesis 51
chorionic villus sampling (CVS) 51
fetal medicine 52
hypoxia 55
preterm (premature) 56
low birth weight 56
very low birth weight 56
extremely low birth weight 56
infant mortality rate 56
in vitro fertilization 59
eugenics 59

Online Resources

Go to CengageBrain.com to access Psychology CourseMate, where you will find an interactive eBook, flashcards, quizzes, videos, websites, and more.

Tools for Exploring the World

3

Physical, Perceptual, and Motor Development

The changes that occur in the first few years after birth are incredible. In less than 2 years, an infant is transformed from a seemingly helpless newborn into a talking, walking, havoc-wreaking toddler. No changes at any other point in the life span come close to the drama and excitement of these early years.

In this chapter, our tour of these 2 years begins with the newborn and then moves to growth in the body and the brain. The third section of the chapter examines how babies learn to walk and to use their hands. In the fourth section, we examine changes in infants' sensory abilities that allow them to comprehend their world. In the last section, we look at how babies learn more about themselves and about others.

LEARNING OBJECTIVES

- How do reflexes help newborns interact with the world?
- How do we determine whether a baby is healthy?
- What behavioral states are common among newborns?
- What are different features of temperament?

Lisa and Steve, proud but exhausted parents, are astonished at how their lives revolve around 10-day-old Dan's eating and sleeping. Lisa feels as if she is feeding Dan around the clock. When Dan naps, Lisa thinks of many things she should do but usually naps herself because she is so tired. Steve wonders when Dan will start sleeping through the night so that he and Lisa can get a good night's sleep themselves.

The newborn baby that thrills parents like Lisa and Steve arrives covered with blood and vernix, a white-colored "wax" that protected the skin during prenatal development. The newborn has a beer belly and is bowlegged, and its head is temporarily distorted from its journey through the birth canal.

What can newborns like Dan do? We answer that question in this section and, as we do, see when Lisa and Steve can expect to get a full night's sleep.

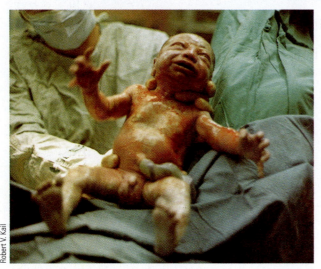

This newborn baby (Ben Kail at 20 seconds old) is covered with vernix and is bowlegged; his head is distorted from the journey down the birth canal.

The Newborn's Reflexes

*Newborns are well prepared to interact with their world because they are endowed with a rich set of **reflexes**, unlearned responses that are triggered by a specific form of stimulation.* Table 3.1 shows the variety of reflexes commonly found in newborn babies. Some reflexes help newborns get the nutrients they need to grow: The rooting and sucking reflexes ensure that the newborn can begin a new diet of life-sustaining milk. Other reflexes protect the newborn from danger in its environment. The eye blink, for example, helps newborns avoid unpleasant stimulation. Still other reflexes are the foundation for larger, voluntary patterns of motor activity. For example, the stepping reflex is a precursor to walking.

Reflexes also help reveal whether the newborn's nervous system is working properly. For example, infants with damage to the sciatic nerve do not show the withdrawal reflex. Similarly, many reflexes normally vanish during infancy; if they linger, this suggests a problem in the developing nervous system.

Assessing the Newborn

To assess a newborn's health, medical personnel often calculate an Apgar score, which measures five vital signs: breathing, heart rate, muscle tone, presence of reflexes, and skin tone. Each of the five vital signs receives a score of 0, 1, or 2, where 2 is the optimal score. For example, a newborn whose muscles are limp receives a 0; a baby who shows strong movements of arms and legs receives a 2. The five scores are added together, with a total score of 7 or more indicating a baby who is in good physical condition. A score of 4 to 6 means that the newborn needs special attention and care. A score of 3 or less signals a life-threatening situation that requires emergency medical care (Apgar, 1953).

reflexes
unlearned responses triggered by specific stimulation

Some Major Reflexes Found in Newborns

Name	Response	Age When Reflex Disappears	Significance
Babinski	A baby's toes fan out when the sole of the foot is stroked from heel to toe	8–12 months	Perhaps a remnant of evolution
Blink	A baby's eyes close in response to bright light or loud noise	Permanent	Protects the eyes
Moro	A baby throws its arms out and then inward (as if embracing) in response to loud noise or when its head falls	6 months	May help a baby cling to its mother
Palmar	A baby grasps an object placed in the palm of its hand	3–4 months	Precursor to voluntary grasping
Rooting	When a baby's cheek is stroked, it turns its head toward the stroking and opens its mouth	3–4 weeks (replaced by voluntary head turning)	Helps a baby find the nipple
Stepping	A baby who is held upright by an adult and is then moved forward begins to step rhythmically	2–3 months	Precursor to voluntary walking
Sucking	A baby sucks when an object is placed in its mouth	4 months (replaced by voluntary sucking)	Permits feeding
Withdrawal	A baby withdraws its foot when the sole is pricked with a pin	Permanent	Protects baby from unpleasant stimulation

© Cengage Learning 2010

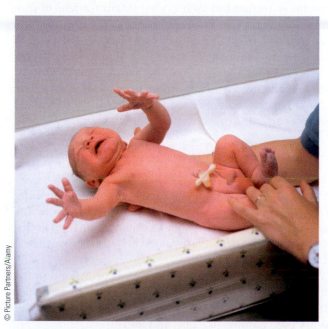

© Picture Partners/Alamy

Newborns exhibit the Moro reflex, opening their arms and then bringing them inward in response to loud noise or when their head falls.

For a comprehensive evaluation of the newborn's well-being, specialists sometimes administer the Neonatal Behavioral Assessment Scale, or NBAS for short (Brazelton & Nugent, 1995). The NBAS is used with newborns to 24-month-olds to provide a detailed portrait of the baby's behavioral repertoire. The scale includes 28 behavioral items (e.g., the baby's response to light, sound, and touch), along with 18 items that test reflexes. The baby's performance is used to evaluate the functioning of these four systems:

- *Autonomic,* the ability to control body functions such as breathing and temperature regulation
- *Motor,* the ability to control body movements and activity level
- *State,* the ability to maintain a state (e.g., staying alert or staying asleep)
- *Social,* the ability to interact with people

When administering the NBAS, examiners go to great lengths to bring out a baby's best performance. They do everything possible to make a baby feel comfortable and secure during testing. And if an infant does not at first succeed on an item, the examiner provides some assistance (Alberts, 2005).

The Newborn's States

alert inactivity
the state in which a baby is calm, with eyes open and attentive, and seems to be deliberately inspecting its environment

waking activity
the state in which a baby's eyes are open but seem unfocused while the arms or legs move in bursts of uncoordinated motion

crying
the state in which a baby cries vigorously, usually accompanied by agitated but uncoordinated movement

Newborns spend most of each day alternating among four states (St. James-Roberts & Plewis, 1996):

- **Alert inactivity**. *The baby is calm with eyes open and attentive; the baby seems to be deliberately inspecting its environment.*
- **Waking activity**. *The baby's eyes are open, but they seem unfocused; the arms or legs move in bursts of uncoordinated motion.*
- **Crying**. *The baby cries vigorously, usually accompanied by agitated but uncoordinated motion.*

In many countries worldwide, infants are wrapped tightly in blankets as a way to keep them soothed.

- ■ **Sleeping**. *The baby alternates from being still and breathing regularly to moving gently and breathing irregularly; eyes are closed throughout.*

Of these states, crying and sleeping have captured the attention of parents and researchers alike.

Crying

Newborns spend 2 to 3 hours each day crying or on the verge of crying, which comes in three forms (Snow, 1998). *A **basic cry** starts softly and gradually becomes more intense; it usually occurs when a baby is hungry or tired. A **mad cry** is a more intense version of a basic cry; and a **pain cry** begins with a sudden, long burst of crying followed by a long pause and gasping.* Thus, crying represents the newborn's first efforts to communicate. By crying, babies tell their parents that they are hungry or tired, angry or hurt.

Parents are naturally concerned when their baby cries, and they've developed little tricks to sooth a crying baby. Many Western parents lift a baby to the shoulder and walk or gently rock the baby. Sometimes they also sing lullabies, pat the baby's back, or give the baby a pacifier. Another useful technique is swaddling, in which an infant is wrapped tightly in a blanket. Swaddling is used in many cultures around the world, including Turkey and Peru, as well as by Native Americans. Swaddling provides warmth and tactile stimulation that usually works well to soothe a baby (Delaney, 2000).

Parents are sometimes reluctant to respond to their crying infant for fear of producing a baby who cries constantly. If, in fact, parents respond immediately every time their infant cries, the result may well be a fussy, whiny baby. Instead, parents need to consider why their infant is crying and the intensity of the crying. When a baby wakes during the night and cries quietly, a parent should allow the baby a chance to calm itself. However, when parents hear a loud noise from an infant's bedroom followed by a mad cry, they should respond immediately. Parents need to decide what the infant is trying to tell them and whether that warrants a quick response or whether they should let the baby soothe itself.

Sleeping

Crying may get parents' attention, but sleep is what newborns do more than anything else, sleeping 16 to 18 hours daily. Newborns typically go through a cycle of wakefulness and sleep about every 4 hours: they are awake for about an hour, sleep for 3 hours, and then repeat the cycle. When awake, infants regularly move between states of alert inactivity, waking activity, and crying.

As babies grow older, the sleep–wake cycle gradually begins to correspond to the day–night cycle (St. James-Roberts & Plewis, 1996). By 3 or 4 months, many babies sleep for 5 to 6 hours straight; by 6 months, many are sleeping for 10 to 12 hours at night, a major milestone for bleary-eyed parents like Lisa and Steve.

*Roughly half of newborns' sleep period is **irregular or rapid-eye-movement (REM) sleep**, a time when newborns move their arms and legs and their eyes may dart beneath their eyelids.* Brain waves register fast activity, the heart beats more rapidly, and breathing is more rapid. *In **regular (non-REM) sleep**, breathing, heart rate, and brain activity are steady and newborns lie quietly without the twitching associated with REM sleep.* REM sleep becomes less frequent as infants grow. By 4 months, 40% of sleep time is REM sleep. By the first birthday, REM sleep drops to 25%—not far from the adult average of 20% (Halpern, MacLean, & Baumeister, 1995).

Older children and adults dream during REM sleep, and brain waves during REM sleep resemble those of an alert, awake person. Consequently, many scientists believe that REM sleep provides stimulation for the brain that fosters growth in the nervous system (Halpern, MacLean, & Baumeister, 1995; Roffwarg, Muzio, & Dement, 1966).

HUMAN DEVELOPMENT in action

When Mary's 4-month-old son cries, she rushes to him immediately and does everything possible to console him. As a nurse practitioner, what would you say to Mary?

sleeping
the state in which a baby alternates from being still and breathing regularly to moving gently and breathing irregularly, with the eyes closed throughout

basic cry
a cry that starts softly, gradually becomes more intense, and is often heard when babies are hungry or tired

mad cry
a more intense version of a basic cry

pain cry
a cry that begins with a sudden long burst, followed by a long pause and gasping

irregular or rapid-eye-movement (REM) sleep
sleep in which an infant's eyes dart rapidly beneath the eyelids while the body is quite active

regular (non-REM) sleep
sleep in which heart rate, breathing, and brain activity are steady

From National Institute of Child Health and Development

FIGURE 3.1

This poster is one part of an effective campaign to reduce SIDS by encouraging parents to have their babies sleep on their backs.

sudden infant death syndrome (SIDS)
when a healthy baby dies suddenly for no apparent reason

temperament
a consistent style or pattern of behavior

Sudden Infant Death Syndrome

Many parents worry when their young baby sleeps. *In* **sudden infant death syndrome (SIDS)**, *a healthy baby dies suddenly for no apparent reason.* Approximately 1 to 3 of every 1,000 American babies dies from SIDS. Most are between 2 and 4 months of age (Wegman, 1994).

Scientists don't know the exact causes of SIDS, but one idea is that 2- to 4-month-old infants are particularly vulnerable to SIDS because many newborn reflexes wane during these months; thus, infants may not respond effectively when breathing becomes difficult. For example, they may not reflexively move their head away from a blanket or pillow that is smothering them (Lipsitt, 2003).

Researchers have also identified several risk factors associated with SIDS (Sahni, Fifer, & Myers, 2007). Babies are more vulnerable if they were born prematurely, they have low birth weight, and their parents smoke. SIDS is more likely when a baby sleeps on its stomach (face down) than when it sleeps on its back (face up). Finally, SIDS is more likely during winter, when babies sometimes become overheated from too many blankets and sleepwear that is too heavy (Carroll & Loughlin, 1994).

In 1992, based on mounting evidence that SIDS occurred more often when infants slept on their stomachs, the American Academy of Pediatrics (AAP) began advising parents to put babies to sleep on their backs or sides. In 1994 the AAP joined forces with the U.S. Public Health Service to launch a national program to educate parents about the dangers of SIDS and the importance of putting babies to sleep on their backs. The Back to Sleep campaign was widely publicized through brochures, posters like the one shown in Figure 3.1, and videos. Since the campaign began, far more infants are sleeping on their backs and the incidence of SIDS has dropped (Dwyer & Ponsonby, 2009). However, African American infants were still more likely to die from SIDS, apparently because they were more likely to be placed on their stomachs to sleep. Consequently, in the 21st century the National Institutes of Health has partnered with groups such as Women in the National Association for the Advancement of Colored People and the National Council of 100 Black Women to convey the Back to Sleep message to African American communities (National Institute of Child Health and Human Development, 2004). The message for all parents—particularly if their babies were premature or small for date—is to keep their babies away from smoke, to put them on their backs to sleep, and to avoid overdressing them or wrapping them too tightly in blankets (Willinger, 1995).

Temperament

So far, we've talked as if all babies are alike, but this isn't true. Some babies are quiet most of the time, but others cry often. Some infants respond warmly to strangers, while others seem shy. *These characteristics of infants indicate a consistent style or pattern of infant behavior, and collectively they define an infant's* **temperament**.

Scientists believe that temperament includes from two to six dimensions. For example, Rothbart (2007) proposed an influential theory of temperament that includes three dimensions:

■ *Surgency/extroversion* refers to the extent to which a child is generally happy, active, vocal, and regularly seeks interesting stimulation.

■ *Negative affect* refers to the extent to which a child is angry, fearful, frustrated, shy, and not easily soothed.

■ *Effortful control* refers to the extent to which a child can focus attention, is not readily distracted, and can inhibit responses.

These dimensions of temperament emerge in infancy and are related to dimensions of personality that are found in adolescence and adulthood (Gartstein, Knyazev,

Twin studies show the impact of heredity on temperament: If one identical twin is active, the other one usually is as well.

& Slobodskaya, 2005). Temperament is moderately stable throughout infancy, childhood, and adolescence (Janson & Mathiesen, 2008; Wachs & Bates, 2001). For example, newborns who cry under moderate stress tend, as 5-month-olds, to cry when they are placed in stressful situations (Stifter & Fox, 1990).

Hereditary and Environmental Contributions to Temperament

Most theories agree that temperament reflects both heredity and experience (Caspi, Roberts, & Shiner, 2005). For example, identical twins are more alike than fraternal twins in most aspects of temperament (Goldsmith, Pollak, & Davidson, 2008). However, the impact of heredity also depends on the temperamental dimension and the child's age. For example, negative affect is more influenced by heredity than are the other dimensions, and temperament in childhood is more influenced by heredity than is temperament in infancy (Wachs & Bates, 2001).

The environment also contributes to temperament. Infants are less emotional when parents are responsive (Gudmundson & Leerkes, 2012; Hane & Fox, 2006). Conversely, infants become increasingly fearful when their mothers are depressed (Gartstein et al., 2010). And some temperamental characteristics are more common in certain cultures than in others. For example, Asian babies tend to be less emotional than European American babies (Gartstein, Slobodskaya, & Kinsht, 2003; Kagan et al., 1994).

Test Yourself

Recall

1. Some reflexes help infants get necessary nutrients, other reflexes protect infants from danger, and still other reflexes _____.

2. An _____ is based on five vital functions and provides a quick indication of a newborn's physical health.

3. A baby lying calmly with its eyes open and focused is in a state of _____.

4. Newborns spend more time asleep than awake, and about half this sleep time is spent in _____, a time thought to foster growth in the central nervous system.

5. The campaign to reduce SIDS emphasizes that infants should _____.

6. Research on sources of temperament indicate that _____ both play a role.

Interpret

- Compare the Apgar scale and the NBAS as measures of a newborn baby's well-being.

- Newborns seem to be extremely well prepared to begin interacting with their environment. Which of the theories described in Chapter 1 predict such preparedness? Which do not?

Apply

- Your friend is amazed at how easily her newborn took to breast-feeding. Describe for her ways in which reflexes make young babies well prepared to interact with their environment.

- When 8-month-old Chantal gets upset, she cries long and hard. How might Chantal's pediatrician advise her parents on soothing her?"

Recall answers: (1) serve as the basis for later motor behaviors, (2) Apgar score, (3) alert inactivity, (4) REM sleep, (5) sleep on their backs, (6) heredity and environment

Physical Development

LEARNING OBJECTIVES

- How do height and weight change from birth to 2 years of age?

- What nutrients do young children need? How are they best provided?

- What are the consequences of malnutrition? How can it be treated?

- What are nerve cells? How are they organized in the brain?

- How does the brain develop? When does it begin to function?

While crossing the street, 4-year-old Martin was struck by a passing car. He was in a coma for a week but gradually became more alert. Now he seems to be aware of his surroundings. Needless to say, Martin's mother is grateful that he survived the accident, but she wonders what the future holds for her son.

For parents and children alike, physical growth is a topic of great interest and a source of pride. Parents marvel at the speed with which babies add pounds and inches, and 2-year-olds proudly proclaim, "I bigger now!" In this section, we examine some basic features of physical growth, see how the brain develops, and discover how the accident just mentioned affected Martin's development.

Growth of the Body

Growth is more rapid in infancy than during any other period after birth. Average heights and weights for young children are represented by the lines marked 50th percentile in Figure 3.2. Typically, infants double their birth weight by 3 months of age and triple it by their first birthday. This rate of growth is so rapid that, if continued throughout childhood, a typical 10-year-old boy would be nearly as long as a jumbo jet and weigh almost as much (McCall, 1979).

Infants are not simply scaled-down versions of adults. Compared to adolescents and adults, infants and young children look top-heavy because their heads and trunks are disproportionately large. As growth of the hips, legs, and feet catches up later in childhood, their bodies take on more adult proportions.

"You Are What You Eat": Nutrition and Growth

In a typical 2-month-old, roughly 40% of the body's energy is devoted to growth. Most of the remaining energy is used for basic bodily functions, such as digestion and respiration. A much smaller portion is consumed in physical activity.

Because growth requires so much high energy, young babies must consume an enormous number of calories relative to their body weight. A typical 12-pound 3-month-old, for example, should ingest about 600 calories daily, or about 50 calories per pound of body weight (compared to 15 to 20 calories per pound for adults).

Breast-feeding is the best way to ensure that babies get their nourishment. Human milk contains the proper amounts of carbohydrates, fats, protein, vitamins, and minerals for babies. Breast-feeding also has several other advantages compared to bottle-feeding (Dewey, 2001). First, breast-fed babies are ill less often because breast milk contains the mother's antibodies. Second, breast-fed babies are less prone to diarrhea and constipation. Third, breast-fed babies typically make the transition to solid foods more easily, apparently because they are accustomed to changes in the

FIGURE 3.2

Boys and girls grow taller and heavier from birth to 3 years of age, but the range of normal heights and weights is quite wide.

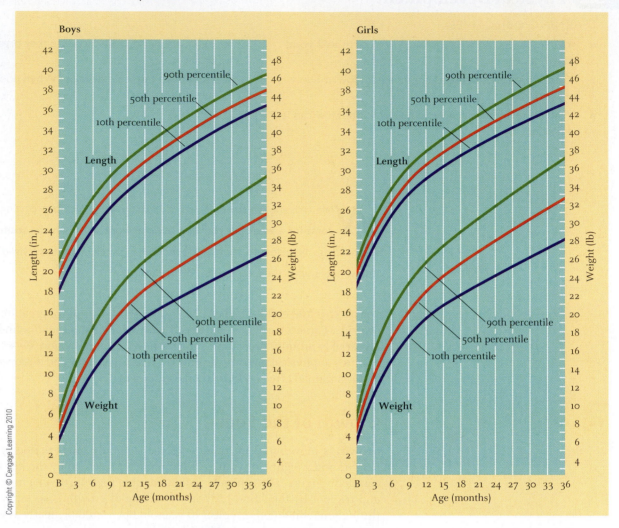

Copyright © Cengage Learning 2010

taste of breast milk that reflect a mother's diet. Fourth, breast milk cannot be contaminated, which is a significant problem in developing countries when formula is used to bottle-feed babies.

Because of these many advantages, the AAP recommends that children be breast-fed for the first year, with iron-enriched solid foods introduced gradually. Cereal is a good first semisolid food, followed by vegetables, fruits, and then meats. A good rule is to introduce only one food at a time. A 7-month-old having cheese for the first time, for instance, should have no other new foods for a few days. In this way, allergies that may develop can be linked to a particular food, making it easier to prevent recurrences.

The many benefits of breast-feeding do not mean that bottle-feeding is harmful. Formula, when prepared in sanitary conditions, provides generally the same nutrients as human milk, but it does not protect infants from disease. Even so, bottle-feeding has advantages of its own. A mother who cannot readily breast-feed can still enjoy the intimacy of feeding her baby, and other family members can participate in feeding. Breast- and bottle-fed babies are similar in physical and psychological development (Jansen, de Weerth, & Riksen-Walraven, 2008), so women in industrialized countries can choose either method and know that their babies' dietary needs are being met.

HUMAN DEVELOPMENT in action

Imagine that you're a social worker and one of your clients, the mother of a 2-month-old, is eager to stop breast-feeding because she thinks it's a hassle. What would you recommend to her?

In developing nations, bottle-feeding is potentially disastrous. Often, the only water available to prepare formula is contaminated, which causes infants to have chronic diarrhea, leading to dehydration and sometimes death. Or, in an effort to conserve valuable formula, parents may ignore instructions and use less formula than indicated when making milk; the resulting "weak" milk leads to malnutrition. For these reasons, the World Health Organization advocates breast-feeding as the primary source of nutrition for infants and toddlers in developing nations.

Growth slows by 2 years of age, so children need less to eat. This is also when many children become picky eaters, and toddlers and preschool children may find that foods they once ate willingly are now "yucky." Though such finickiness can be annoying, it may be adaptive for increasingly independent preschoolers. Because toddlers don't know what is safe to eat and what isn't, eating only familiar foods protects them from potential harm (Aldridge, Dovey, & Halford, 2009).

Toddlers and preschool children often become picky eaters. This can be annoying but should not concern parents.

Malnutrition

Worldwide, about one in four children under age 5 is **malnourished***, as indicated by being small for their age* (UNICEF, 2006). Nearly half of the world's undernourished children live in India, Bangladesh, and Pakistan (UNICEF, 2006), but malnutrition is regrettably common in industrialized countries too. Many American children growing up homeless and in poverty are malnourished. Approximately 10% of American households do not have adequate food (Nord, Andrews, & Carlson, 2007).

Malnourishment is especially damaging during infancy, because growth is so rapid during these years. By the school-age years, children with a history of infant malnutrition often have difficulty maintaining attention in school; they are easily distracted. Malnutrition during rapid periods of growth apparently damages the brain, affecting children's abilities to pay attention and learn (Laus et al., 2011; Morgane et al., 1993).

Malnutrition would seem to have a simple cure—an adequate diet—but this is not enough. Malnourished children are often quiet and express little interest in what goes on around them. These behaviors are adaptive in conserving limited energy (Ricciuti, 1993) but they often deprive youngsters of experiences that would further their development. For example, when lethargic children do not respond to parents' efforts to stimulate their development, this discourages parents from providing additional stimulation in the future. Over time, parents tend to provide fewer experiences that foster their children's development. The result is a self-perpetuating cycle in which malnourished children are forsaken by parents who feel as if they can do little to contribute to their children's growth. Thus, a biological influence (lethargy stemming from insufficient nourishment) causes a profound change in the experiences (parental teaching) that shape a child's development (Worobey, 2005).

To break the vicious cycle, children need an improved diet and parents must be taught how to foster their children's development. Programs that combine dietary supplements with parent training offer promise in treating malnutrition (Engle & Huffman, 2010). Children in these programs often catch up with their peers in physical and intellectual growth, showing that the best way to reduce the effect of malnutrition on psychological forces is by addressing both biological and sociocultural forces (Super, Herrera, & Mora, 1990).

Many children around the world are malnourished, such as these two in a Somali refugee camp.

malnourished
being small for age because of inadequate nutrition

neuron
a basic cellular unit of the brain and nervous system that specializes in receiving and transmitting information

cell body
the center of the neuron that keeps the neuron alive

The Emerging Nervous System

The physical changes we see as infants grow are impressive. Even more awe inspiring are changes involving the brain and the nervous system. Infants' feelings of hunger or pain, their smiles or laughs, and their efforts to sit upright or to hold a rattle all reflect the functioning of the brain and the rest of the emerging nervous system.

How does the brain accomplish these many tasks? To answer this question, we need to look at the organization of the brain. *The basic unit in the brain and the rest of the nervous system is the* **neuron***, a cell that specializes in receiving and transmitting information.* Neurons have the basic elements shown in Figure 3.3. *The* **cell body***, in*

FIGURE 3.3

A nerve cell includes dendrites that receive information, a cell body that has life-sustaining machinery, and for sending information, an axon that ends in terminal buttons.

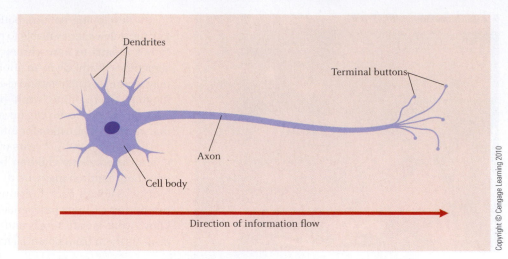

Dendrites

Terminal buttons

Axon

Cell body

Direction of information flow

dendrite

the end of the neuron that receives information, which looks like a tree with many branches

axon

a tubelike structure that emerges from the cell body and transmits information to other neurons

terminal buttons

small knobs at the end of the axon that release neurotransmitters

neurotransmitters

chemicals released by terminal buttons that allow neurons to communicate with one another

cerebral cortex

the wrinkled surface of the brain that regulates many functions that are distinctly human

hemispheres

right and left halves of the cortex

corpus callosum

a thick bundle of neurons that connects the brain's two hemispheres

frontal cortex

the brain region that regulates personality and goal-directed behavior

the center of the cell, contains the basic biological machinery that keeps the neuron alive. The receiving end of the neuron, the **dendrite***, looks like a tree with its many branches.* This structure allows one neuron to receive input from thousands of other neurons (Morgan & Gibson, 1991). *The tubelike structure that emerges from the other side of the cell body, the* **axon***, transmits information to other neurons. At the end of the axon are small knobs called* **terminal buttons***, which release chemicals. These chemicals, called* **neurotransmitters***, are the messengers that carry information to nearby neurons.*

About 50 billion to 100 billion neurons make up an adult's brain. *The wrinkled surface of the brain is the* **cerebral cortex***; made up of 10 billion neurons, the cortex regulates many functions that we think of as distinctly human. The cortex consists of left and right halves, called* **hemispheres***, which are linked by a thick bundle of neurons called the* **corpus callosum***.* The characteristics you value the most—your engaging personality, your way with words, or your uncanny knack for reading others' emotions—are all controlled by specific regions in the cortex (see Figure 3.4). *For example, your personality and your ability to make and carry out plans are largely centered in an area in the front of the cortex called (appropriately enough) the* **frontal cortex***.* For most people, the ability to produce and understand language is mainly housed in neurons in the left hemisphere of the cortex. When you recognize that others are happy or sad, neurons in your right hemisphere are usually at work.

FIGURE 3.4

The brain on the left, viewed from above, shows the left and right hemispheres. The brain on the right, viewed from the side, shows the major regions of the cortex and their primary functions.

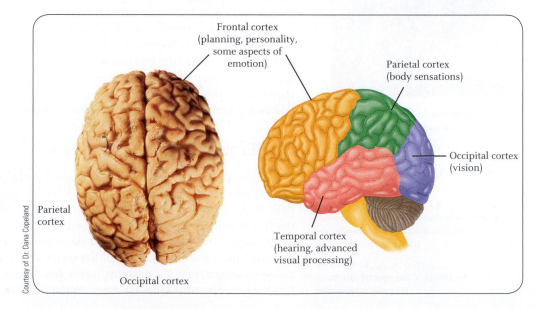

Courtesy of Dr. Dana Copeland

Frontal cortex
(planning, personality, some aspects of emotion)

Parietal cortex
(body sensations)

Occipital cortex
(vision)

Temporal cortex
(hearing, advanced visual processing)

Parietal cortex

Occipital cortex

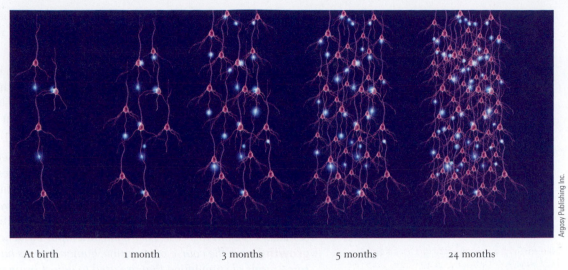

From birth to 2 years, neurons grow and create many new synapses with other neurons.

At birth   1 month   3 months   5 months   24 months

Emerging Brain Structures

The beginnings of the brain can be traced to the period of the zygote. *At roughly 3 weeks after conception, a group of cells form a flat structure known as the* **neural plate**. At 4 weeks, the neural plate folds to form a tube. When the ends of the tube fuse shut, neurons are produced in one small region of the neural tube. Production of neurons begins about 10 weeks after conception, and by 28 weeks the developing brain has virtually all the neurons it will ever have.

From the neuron-manufacturing site in the neural tube, neurons migrate to their final positions in the brain. The brain is built in stages: Neurons in the deepest layer are positioned first, followed by neurons in the second layer, continuing until all six layers of the mature brain are in place, at about 7 months after conception (Rakic, 1995). *In the fourth month of prenatal development, axons begin to acquire* **myelin**—*the fatty wrap that speeds neural transmission.* This process continues through infancy and into childhood and adolescence (Casaer, 1993).

In the months after birth, axons and dendrites grow longer, and, like a maturing tree, dendrites quickly sprout new limbs. As the number of dendrites increases, so does the number of synapses, reaching a peak around the first birthday. *Soon after, synapses disappear gradually, a phenomenon known as* **synaptic pruning**. Thus, beginning in infancy and continuing into early adolescence, the brain "downsizes," weeding synapses that aren't active (Webb, Monk, & Nelson, 2001).

Growth of a Specialized Brain

The mature brain is specialized, with psychological functions localized in particular areas, and scientists have identified some general principles that describe the brain's specialization as children develop:

■ *Specialization is evident early in development.* Many brain regions specialize early in infancy. For example, early specialization of the frontal cortex is shown by the finding that damage to this region in infancy results in impaired decision making and abnormal emotional responses (Anderson et al., 2001). Similarly, a newborn infant's left hemisphere generates more electrical activity in response to speech than does the right hemisphere (Molfese & Burger-Judisch, 1991), showing early specialization of the left hemisphere for language processing.

■ *Specialization takes two forms.* First, with development, the brain regions active during processing become more focused—like a thunderstorm that covers a huge region versus one that packs the same power in a smaller region (Durston et al., 2006). Second, the kinds of stimuli that trigger brain activity shift from being

neural plate
a flat group of cells present in prenatal development that becomes the brain and spinal cord

myelin
a fatty sheath that wraps around neurons and enables them to transmit information more rapidly

synaptic pruning
a gradual reduction in the number of synapses, beginning in infancy and continuing until early adolescence

general to specific (Johnson, Grossman, & Cohen Kadosh, 2009). For example, face processing becomes focused in a particular brain region and becomes tuned narrowly to faces (Scherf et al., 2007).

■ *Different brain systems specialize at different rates.* Brain regions involving basic sensory and perceptual processes specialize well before those regions necessary for higher order processes (Fox, Levitt, & Nelson, 2010). Similarly, some brain systems that are sensitive to reward reach maturity in adolescence, but the systems responsible for self-control aren't fully specialized until adulthood (Casey, Jones, & Somerville, 2011).

■ *Successful specialization requires stimulation from the environment.* The newborn's brain is equipped with preliminary neural pathways designed to perform certain functions. For example, the left hemisphere has some language pathways, and frontal cortex has some emotion-related pathways. However, completing the typical organization of the mature brain requires input from the environment (Greenough & Black, 1992). *In this case, environmental input influences **experience-expectant growth**—over the course of evolution, human infants have typically been exposed to some forms of stimulation that are used to adjust brain wiring, strengthening some circuits and eliminating others.* For example, under normal conditions, healthy human infants experience moving visual patterns (e.g., faces) and varied sounds (e.g., voices). Just as a newly planted seed depends on a water-filled environment for growth, a developing brain depends on environmental stimulation to fine-tune circuits for vision, hearing, and other systems (Black, 2003).

■ *The immature brain's lack of specialization confers a benefit—greater plasticity.* Remember Martin, the child in the vignette whose brain was damaged when he was struck by a car? His language skills were impaired after the accident. This was not surprising, because the left hemisphere of Martin's brain absorbed most of the force of the collision. But within several months, Martin had recovered his language skills. Apparently, other neurons took over language-related processing from the damaged neurons. This recovery of function is common—particularly for young children—and shows that the brain is plastic. In other words, young children often recover more skills after brain injury than older children and adults, apparently because functions are more easily reassigned in the young brain (Demir, Levine, & Goldin-Meadow, 2010; Stiles et al., 2005).

experience-expectant growth
the process by which the wiring of the brain is organized by experiences that are common to most humans

Test Yourself

Recall

1. Compared to older children and adults, an infant's head and trunk are _____.

2. Because of the high demands of growth, infants need _____ calories per pound than adults.

3. The most effective treatment for malnutrition combines improved diet and _____.

4. The _____ is the part of the neuron that contains the basic machinery to keep the cell alive.

5. By infancy, the frontal cortex is specialized for planning and the left hemisphere is specialized for _____.

6. A good example of brain plasticity is that although children with brain damage often have impaired cognitive processes, _____.

Interpret

• Compare growth of the brain before birth with growth of the brain after birth.

• In Chapter 2 we explained how polygenic inheritance is often involved when phenotypes form a continuum. Height is such a phenotype. Propose a simple polygenic model to explain how height might be inherited.

Apply

• How does malnutrition illustrate the influence on development of life-cycle forces in the biopsychosocial framework?

• Makayla believes that it's important to stimulate her baby's environment, and she exposes him to sights, sounds, and touches every day. Makayla's mom thinks that this is a waste of time; she says babies don't need stimulation until they can talk. What would Makayla's health care provider probably say to them?

Recall answers: (1) disproportionately large, (2) more, (3) parent training, (4) cell body, (5) language, (6) they often regain earlier skills over time

LEARNING OBJECTIVES

■ What skills are involved in learning to walk? When do infants master them?

■ How do infants learn to use their hands?

Nancy is 14 months old and a world-class crawler: She can go just about anywhere she wants on hands and knees, and she seems uninterested in learning to walk. Nancy's dad wonders whether he should be doing something to help Nancy progress beyond crawling. Deep down, he worries that perhaps he was negligent in not providing more exercise for Nancy when she was younger.

Do you remember what it was like to learn to type, to play a musical instrument, or to play a sport? *Each of these activities involves* **motor skills***: coordinated movements of the muscles and limbs.* Success demands that each movement be done in a precise way, in exactly the right sequence, and at exactly the right time. For example, in the few seconds that it takes you to type *human development,* if you don't move your fingers in exactly the correct sequence to the exact location on the keyboard, you might get *jinsj drveo;nrwnt.*

These activities are demanding for adults, but think about similar challenges for infants. *Infants must learn to move about in the world, to* **locomote**. At first unable to move independently, infants soon learn to crawl, to stand, and to walk. *Infants must also learn the* **fine motor skills** *associated with grasping, holding, and manipulating objects.* In the case of feeding, for example, infants progress from being fed by others, to holding a bottle, to feeding themselves with their fingers, to eating with utensils. In this section, we'll see how locomotion and fine motor skills develop and, as we do, we'll see whether Nancy's dad should worry about her lack of interest in walking.

Locomotion

Advances in posture and locomotion transform infants in little more than a year. By 7 months infants can sit alone, and by 10 months they can creep (see Figure 3.5). A typical 14-month-old is able to stand alone briefly and walk with assistance. Still, not all children walk at exactly the same age. Some walk before their first birthday; others—like Nancy, the world-class crawler in the vignette—take their first steps as late as 18 or 19 months of age. By 24 months, most children can climb steps, walk backward, and kick a ball.

According to **dynamic systems theory***, learning to walk involves many distinct skills that are organized and reorganized over time to meet goals.* For example, walking includes maintaining balance, moving limbs, perceiving the environment, and having a reason to move. Only by understanding each of these skills and how they are combined to allow movement in a specific situation can we understand walking (Thelen & Smith, 1998).

Posture and Balance

Maintaining an upright posture is fundamental to walking but difficult for young infants because their body is so top-heavy. Only with growth of the legs and muscles can infants maintain an upright posture (Thelen, Ulrich, & Jensen, 1989). Once infants can stand, they use visual cues and an inner-ear mechanism to adjust their balance and stay upright.

motor skills
coordinated movements of the muscles and limbs

locomotion
the ability to move around in the world

fine motor skills
body movements associated with grasping, holding, and manipulating objects

dynamic systems theory
the theory that views motor development as involving many distinct skills that are organized and reorganized over time to meet specific needs

FIGURE 3.5

Locomotor skills improve rapidly in the 15 months after birth, and progress can be measured by many developmental milestones.

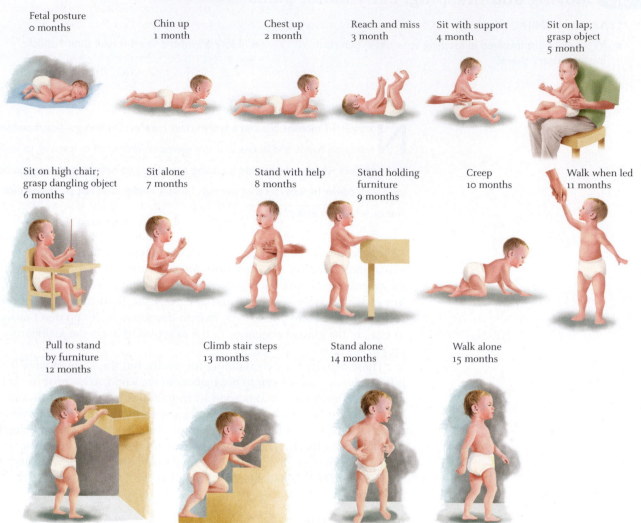

Fetal posture
0 months

Chin up
1 month

Chest up
2 month

Reach and miss
3 month

Sit with support
4 month

Sit on lap;
grasp object
5 month

Sit on high chair;
grasp dangling object
6 months

Sit alone
7 months

Stand with help
8 months

Stand holding
furniture
9 months

Creep
10 months

Walk when led
11 months

Pull to stand
by furniture
12 months

Climb stair steps
13 months

Stand alone
14 months

Walk alone
15 months

Based on Shirley, M.M. (1931). The first two years: A study of twenty-five babies. Vol. 1. *Postural and Locomotor Development*. Minneapolis: University of Minnesota Press and Bayley, N. (1969). *Bayley Scales of Infant Development*. SanAntonio, TX: Psychological Corp.

Balance must be relearned for sitting, crawling, walking, and other postures, because the body rotates around different points in each posture (e.g., the wrists for crawling versus the ankles for walking) and different muscle groups are used to generate compensating motions when infants begin to lose their balance. Once infants walk, they must adjust their posture further when they carry objects, which affect balance (Garciaguirre, Adolph, & Shrout, 2007). Infants must recalibrate the balance system as they take on each new posture, just as basketball players recalibrate their muscle movements when they move from dunking to shooting a three-pointer (Adolph, 2000, 2003).

Stepping

Another essential element of walking is moving the legs alternately, repeatedly transferring the weight of the body from one foot to the other. Children don't step spontaneously until approximately 10 months, because they must be able to stand in order to step. But if they are held upright by an adult and placed on a treadmill, 6- and 7-month-olds typically show the mature pattern of alternating steps on each leg. Apparently, the alternate stepping motion that is essential for walking is evident long before infants walk alone.

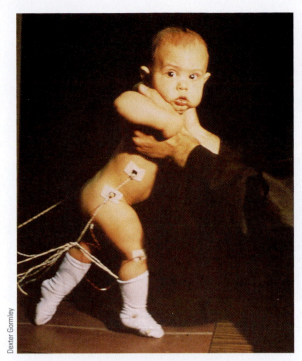

Infants are capable of stepping—moving the legs alternately—long before they can walk alone.

Locomotor skills develop rapidly in preschool children, making it possible for them to play vigorously.

differentiation
distinguishing and mastering individual motions

integration
linking individual motions into a coherent, coordinated whole

Environmental Cues

Many infants learn to walk in the safety of flat, uncluttered floors. But they soon discover that some surfaces are more conducive to walking than others. Infants use perceptual cues in their environment to judge whether a surface is suitable for walking. For example, they are more likely to cross a bridge when it's wide and has a rigid handrail than when it is narrow and has a wobbly handrail (Berger, Adolph, & Lobo, 2005).

Coordinating Skills

Dynamic systems theory emphasizes that learning to walk demands orchestration of many individual skills. Each component skill must first be mastered alone and then be integrated with the other skills (Werner, 1948). *That is, mastery of intricate motions requires both* **differentiation**, *or mastery of component skills, and* **integration**—*combining motions in proper sequence to form a coherent, working whole.* In the case of walking, not until 12 to 15 months of age have children mastered the component skills to be coordinated and so allow independent, unsupported walking.

Beyond Walking

Infants' first tentative steps soon become more refined: They take longer, straighter steps, and they begin to swing their arms (Ledebt, van Wieringen, & Savelsbergh, 2004). A few months later, children typically learn to run. Most 2-year-olds have a hurried walk instead of a true run; they move their legs stiffly (rather than bending them at the knees) and are not "airborne," as in true running. By 5 or 6 years, children run easily, quickly changing direction or speed.

Fine Motor Skills

A major accomplishment of infancy is skilled use of the hands (Bertenthal & Clifton, 1998). Newborns have little apparent control of their hands, but 1-year-olds are extraordinarily talented.

Reaching and Grasping

At about 4 months, infants can successfully reach for objects (Bertenthal & Clifton, 1998). These early reaches often look clumsy because infants don't move their arm and hand smoothly to the desired object. Instead, their hand moves a short distance, slows, then moves again in a slightly different direction—a process that's repeated until the hand finally contacts the object (McCarty & Ashmead, 1999). As infants grow, their reaches have fewer movements, though they are still not as continuous and smooth as reaches by older children and adults (Lee, Ranganathan, & Newell, 2011).

Grasping poses a different challenge from reaching: Now infants must coordinate movements of individual fingers to grab an object. Grasping also becomes more efficient during infancy. Most 4-month-olds use just their fingers to hold objects, wrapping objects tightly with them. Not until 7 or 8 months do most infants use their thumbs to hold objects (Siddiqui, 1995). At about this same age, infants begin to position their hands to make it easier to grasp an object. If trying to grasp a long, thin rod, for example, infants place their fingers perpendicular to the rod, which is the best position for grasping (Wentworth, Benson, & Haith, 2000).

Infants' growing control of each hand is accompanied by greater coordination of the two hands. Although 4-month-olds use both hands, their motions are not coordinated; each hand seems to have a mind of its own. Infants may hold a toy motionless

A typical 4-month-old grasps an object with fingers alone.

By age 5, fine motor skills are developed to a point at which most youngsters can dress themselves.

HUMAN DEVELOPMENT in action

Imagine you are a preschool teacher and your class includes 2- to 4-year-olds. When the class goes outside on a chilly day, how much will you need to help students as they put on their coats?

in one hand while shaking a rattle in the other. At roughly 5 to 6 months of age, infants can coordinate the motions of their hands so that each hand performs different actions that serve a common goal. A child might, for example, hold a toy animal in one hand and pet it with the other (Karniol, 1989).

As preschoolers, children become more dexterous and are able to make many precise and delicate movements with their hands and fingers. Greater fine motor skills mean that preschool children can begin to feed and clothe themselves. A 2- or 3-year-old, for example, can put on simple clothing and use zippers but not buttons; by 3 or 4 years, children can fasten buttons and take off their clothes when going to the bathroom; and most 5-year-olds can dress and undress themselves—except for tying shoes, which children typically master at about age 6.

All these actions illustrate the principles of differentiation and integration that were essential for locomotion. Development involves first mastering the separate elements and then assembling them into a smoothly functioning whole.

Handedness

When young babies reach for objects, they don't seem to prefer one hand over the other; they use their left and right hands interchangeably. By the first birthday, however, most youngsters are emergent right-handers. They use their left hand to steady the toy while the right hand manipulates the object. This early preference for one hand becomes stronger and more consistent during the preschool years and is well established by kindergarten (Marschik et al., 2008; Rönnqvist & Domellöff, 2006).

What determines whether children become left- or right-handed? Some scientists believe that a gene biases children toward right-handedness (Annett, 2008). But experience also contributes to handedness. Modern industrial cultures favor right-handedness. School desks, scissors, and can openers, for example, are designed for right-handed people. In the United States, elementary-school teachers at one time urged left-handed children to use their right hands. As this practice has diminished in the last 50 years, the percentage of left-handed children has risen steadily (Levy, 1976). Thus, handedness seems to have both hereditary and environmental influences.

Test Yourself

Recall

1. According to _____, motor development involves many distinct skills that are organized and reorganized over time, depending on task demands.

2. Skills important in learning to walk include maintaining upright posture and balance, stepping, and _____.

3. Akira uses both hands simultaneously, but not in a coordinated manner; each hand seems to be "doing its own thing." Akira is probably _____ months old.

4. Before the age of _____, children show no signs of handedness; they use their left and right hands interchangeably.

Interpret

- Compare and contrast the milestones of locomotor development in the first year with the fine motor milestones.

- How does learning to hop on one foot demonstrate differentiation and integration of motor skills?

Apply

- Describe how the mastery of a fine motor skill—such as learning to use a spoon or a crayon—illustrates the integration of biological, psychological, and sociocultural forces in the biopsychosocial framework.

- Suppose you're asked to teach preschool children some basic soccer skills. Based on what you know about the development of locomotion and fine motor skills, what could you expect to teach 3-year-olds?

Recall answers: (1) dynamic systems theory, (2) using perceptual information, (3) 4, (4) 1 year.

3.4 Coming to Know the World: Perception

LEARNING OBJECTIVES

- Are infants able to smell, to taste, and to experience pain? Can infants hear?

- How well can infants see? Can they see color and depth?

- How do infants coordinate information from different sensory modalities?

D arla is mesmerized by her newborn daughter, Olivia. Darla loves holding Olivia, talking to her, and simply watching her. Darla is certain that Olivia is coming to recognize her face and the sound of her voice. Darla's husband, Steve, thinks she is crazy: "Everyone knows that babies are born blind, and they probably can't hear much either." Darla doubts Steve and wishes someone could tell her the truth about Olivia's vision and hearing.

To answer Darla's questions, we need to define what it means for an infant to experience or sense the world. Humans have several sense organs, each receptive to a different kind of physical energy. For example, the retina at the back of the eye is sensitive to some types of electromagnetic energy, and sight is the result. The eardrum detects changes in air pressure, and hearing is the result. In each case, the sense organ translates the physical stimulus into nerve impulses that are sent to the brain. *The processes by which the brain receives, selects, modifies, and organizes these impulses are known as* **perception**.

Darla's questions are really about her newborn daughter's perceptual skills. In this section, we answer her questions by looking at how infants use different senses to experience the world.

Smelling, Tasting, Touching, and Hearing

perception
processes by which the brain receives, selects, modifies, and organizes incoming nerve impulses that are the result of physical stimulation

Newborns have a keen sense of smell. Infants respond positively to pleasant smells and negatively to unpleasant smells (Mennella & Beauchamp, 1997). They have a relaxed and contented facial expression when they smell honey, but they frown or turn away

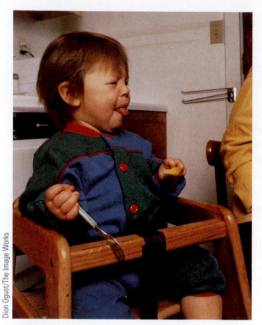

Infants and toddlers do not like bitter and sour tastes.

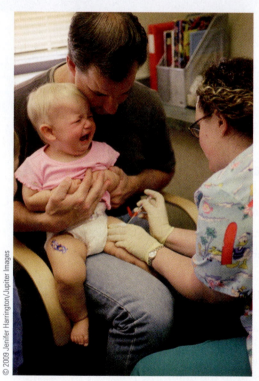

An infant's response to an inoculation—a distinctive facial expression, coupled with a distinctive cry—clearly suggests that the baby feels pain.

visual cliff

a glass-covered platform that appears to have a "shallow" side and a "deep" side and is used to study infants' depth perception

kinetic cues

cues to depth perception in which motion is used to estimate depth

when they smell rotten eggs. Young babies also recognize familiar odors, such as the smell of their mother's breast or her perfume (Porter & Winberg, 1999).

Newborns also have a highly developed sense of taste. They readily differentiate salty, sour, bitter, and sweet tastes (Rostenstein & Oster, 1997). Most infants seem to have a "sweet tooth." They react to sweet substances by smiling, sucking, and licking their lips (Steiner et al., 2001) but grimace when fed bitter or sour substances (Kaijura, Cowart, & Beauchamp, 1992).

Newborns are sensitive to touch. As we saw earlier in this chapter, many areas of the newborn's body respond reflexively when touched. What's more, babies' behavior in response to apparent pain-provoking stimuli suggests that they experience pain (Warnock & Sandrin, 2004). A painful stimulus elicits a unique high-pitched cry, increased heart rate, and movements of arms and legs (Craig et al., 1993; Goubet, Clifton, & Shah, 2001). Collectively, these signs suggest that babies experience pain.

Newborns typically respond to sounds in their surroundings. If a parent is quiet but then coughs, an infant may startle, blink its eyes, and move its arms or legs. Interestingly, infants best hear sounds that have pitches in the range of human speech: neither very high nor very low pitched. Infants can differentiate speech sounds, such as vowels from consonant sounds, and by 4 or 5 months they can recognize their name (Jusczyk, 1995; Mandel, Jusczyk, & Pisoni, 1995).

These perceptual skills are extraordinarily useful to newborns and young babies. For example, smell, touching, and hearing help them recognize their mothers. Early development of smell, taste, touch, and hearing prepares newborns and young babies to learn about the world.

Seeing

Infants spend much of their waking time looking around. Sometimes they seem to be generally scanning their environment, and sometimes they seem to be focusing on nearby objects. This behavior reflects a visual system—the eye, the optic nerve, and the brain—that is relatively well developed at birth. Newborns and 1-month-olds see at 20 feet what normal adults would see at 200 to 400 feet. But by the first birthday, an infant's acuity is essentially the same as that of an adult with normal vision (Kellman & Arterberry, 2006).

Not only do infants begin to see the world with greater acuity during the first year, they also begin to see it in color. Newborns and young babies can perceive few colors, but by 3 months they see the full range of colors (Kellman & Arterberry, 2006). Like adults, infants tend to see categories of color: they see the spectrum as a group of reds, a group of yellows, a group of greens, and the like (Dannemiller, 1998).

Depth

People see objects as having three dimensions: height, width, and depth. Height and width can be represented directly on the flat two-dimensional surface of the retina. In contrast, depth cannot be represented directly on this surface but must be inferred from perceptual processes.

The origins of depth perception were first studied in classic research by Gibson and Walk (1960). *In their work, babies were placed on a glass-covered platform, a device known as the* **visual cliff**. On one side of the platform, a checkerboard pattern appeared directly under the glass; on the other side, the pattern appeared several feet below the glass. The result was that the first side looked shallow but the other looked deep, like a cliff. When mothers tried to coax their infants across the deep or the shallow side, most babies willingly crosses the shallow side but not the deep side. Infants used the checkerboard to infer that one side was deep and therefore unsafe.

What cues allow infants to infer depth, on the visual cliff or anywhere? *Among the first are* **kinetic cues**, *in which motion is used to estimate depth. One such cue*

Infants avoid the "deep" side of the visual cliff, indicating that they perceive depth.

visual expansion

a kinetic cue to depth perception that is based an object filling an ever-greater proportion of the retina as it moves closer

motion parallax

a kinetic cue to depth perception based on nearby objects moving across our visual field faster than distant moving objects

is **visual expansion**, *which refers to an object filling an ever-greater proportion of the retina as it moves closer.* Visual expansion is why we flinch when someone unexpectedly tosses a ball toward us. *Another cue,* **motion parallax***, refers to nearby objects moving across our visual field faster than moving objects that are at a distance.* Motion parallax is in action when you look out the side window in a moving car: Trees next to the road move rapidly across the visual field, but mountains in the distance move slowly. Babies use these cues in the first weeks after birth; for example, a 1-month-old baby blinks if a moving object looks as if it's going to hit it in the face (Nánez & Yonas, 1994).

By 7 months, infants use another cue: **Retinal disparity** *occurs because the left and right eyes often see slightly different versions of the same scene.* Greater disparity in retinal images signifies that an object is close (Kellman & Arterberry, 2006).

Several cues for depth depend on the arrangement of objects in the environment. *These are sometimes called* **pictorial cues***, because they're the cues that artists use to convey depth in drawings and paintings.* Here are two examples of pictorial cues that 7-month-olds use to infer depth:

■ **Linear perspective**. *Parallel lines come together at a single point in the distance.* Thus, we use the space between the lines as a cue to distance. Consequently, we decide the tracks that are close together are farther away than the tracks that are far apart.

■ **Texture gradient**. *The texture of objects changes from coarse and distinct for nearby objects to finer and less distinct for distant objects.* For example, we judge that distinct flowers are close and that blurred ones are distant.

Linear perspective is one cue to depth: We interpret the railroad tracks that are close together as being more distant than the tracks that are far apart.

Texture gradient is used to infer depth: We interpret the distinct flowers as being closer than the flowers with the coarse texture.

Perceiving Objects

Perceptual processes enable us to interpret patterns of lines, textures, and colors as objects. That is, our perception creates an object from sensory stimulation. By 4 months, infants use a number of cues to determine which elements go together to form objects. One important cue is motion: Elements that move together are usually part of the same object (Kellman & Arterberry, 2006). For example, at the left of Figure 3.6, a pencil appears to be moving back and forth behind a colored square. If the square were removed, you would be surprised to see a pair of pencil stubs, as shown on the right side of the diagram. The common movement of the pencil's eraser and point leads us to believe that they're part of the same pencil. Young infants are also surprised by demonstrations like this, suggesting that they use common motion to identify objects (Amso & Johnson, 2006; Eizenman & Bertenthal, 1998).

Motion is just one clue to object unity. As you can see in Figure 3.7, infants more often group features together (i.e., believe they're part of the same object) when they're the same color, have the same texture, and their edges are aligned (Johnson, 2001).

Perceiving Faces

One object that's particularly important for infants is the human face. Some scientists argue that babies are innately attracted to stimuli that are facelike. The claim is that some aspect of the face—perhaps three high-contrast blobs close together—constitutes a distinctive stimulus that is readily recognized, even by newborns (Johnson, Grossman, & Farroni, 2008).

By 7 or 8 months, infants process faces in much the same way that adults do: as a configuration in which the internal elements (e.g., eyes, nose, and mouth) are arranged and spaced in a unique way. Younger infants, in contrast, often perceive faces as an independent collection of facial features; presumably, they have not yet learned that the arrangement and spacing of features is critical (Bhatt et al., 2005; Schwarzer, Zauner, & Jovanovic, 2007).

Through the first 6 months after birth, infants have a general prototype for a face—one that includes human and nonhuman faces (Pascalis, de Haan, & Nelson, 2002). However, between 6 and 12 months of age, infants fine-tune their prototype of a face so that it reflects those kinds of faces that are familiar in their environments (Bremner, 2011). In the Spotlight on Research feature, we'll see that this age-related

retinal disparity
a way of inferring depth based on differences in the retinal images in the left and right eyes

pictorial cues
cues to depth perception that are used to convey depth in drawings and paintings

linear perspective
a cue to depth perception based on parallel lines coming together at a single point in the distance

texture gradient
a perceptual cue to depth based on the texture of objects changing from coarse and distinct for nearby objects to finer and less distinct for distant objects

FIGURE 3.6

After infants have seen the pencil ends moving behind the square, they are surprised to see two pencils when the square is removed; this shows that babies use common motion as a way to determine what makes up an object.

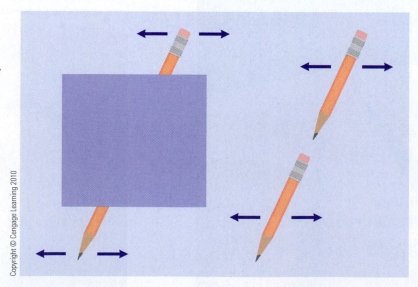

Copyright © Cengage Learning 2010

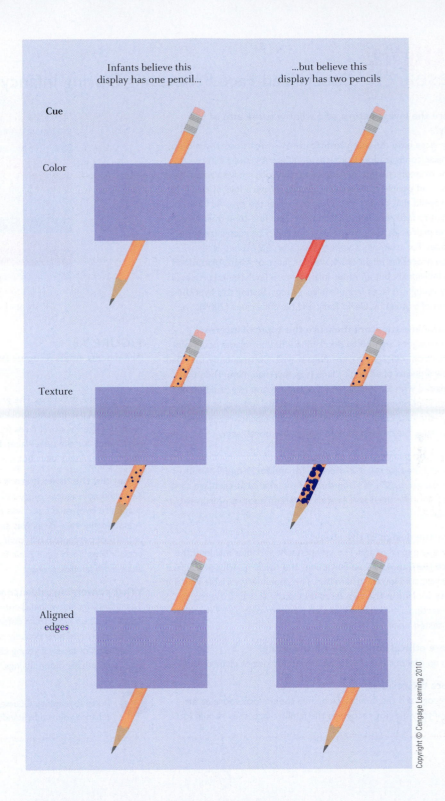

refinement of facial configurations results in a highly unusual outcome—3-month-olds outperform 9-month-olds.

The findings from the Spotlight on Research study suggest a crucial role for experience: Older infants' greater familiarity with faces leads to a more precise configuration of faces, one that includes faces of familiar racial and ethnic groups. This interpretation is supported by the finding that individuals born in Asia but adopted as infants by European parents recognize European faces better than Asian faces (Sangrigoli et al., 2005).

Specialized Face Processing During Infancy

Who were the investigators, and what was the aim of the study?

All human faces have the same basic features—eyes, nose, and mouth in the familiar configuration. But faces of different groups differ in their details. For example, people of African descent often have a relatively broad nose and people of Asian descent often have a fold of skin in the upper eyelid that covers the inner corner of the eye. As infants are exposed to faces in their environments and fine-tune their face-recognition processes, they might lose the ability to recognize some kinds of faces. For example, a young infant's broadly tuned face-recognition processes might work well for faces of Asian, African, and European individuals, but an older infant's more finely tuned processes might only recognize faces from familiar groups. Testing this hypothesis was the aim of a study by David Kelly and his colleagues (2009).

How did the investigators measure the topic of interest?

Kelly and colleagues wanted to determine whether infants could recognize faces from different groups equally well. Consequently, they had infants view a photo of an adult's face (e.g., an Asian man). Then that face was paired with a novel face of the same group (e.g., a different Asian man). Experimenters recorded participants' looking at the two faces—the expectation was that if the participants recognized the familiar face, they would look longer at the novel face.

Who were the participants in the study?

The study included forty-six 3-month-olds and forty-one 9-month-olds from Hangzhou, China. One third of the infants at each age saw Asian faces, another third saw African faces, and another third saw European faces.

What was the design of the study?

This study was experimental. The independent variables included the type of face (African, Asian, or European) and the familiarity of the face during the test trial (novel or familiar). The dependent variable was the participants' looking at the two faces during the test trial. The study was cross-sectional, because it included 3-month-olds and 9-month-olds, each tested once.

Were there ethical concerns with the study?

There was no obvious harm associated with looking at pictures of faces.

What were the results?

If infants recognized the familiar face, they should look more at the novel face; if they did not recognize the familiar face, they should look

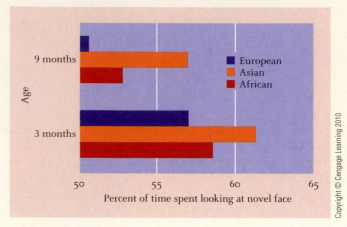

FIGURE 3.8

At 9 months, infants recognize faces only from their own racial groxup.

equally at the two faces. The graphs in Figure 3.8 show the percentage of time that participants looked at the novel face. The 3-month-olds looked longer at novel faces from all three groups (more than 50% preference for the novel face). In contrast, 9-month-olds looked longer at the novel Asian faces but not the novel African or European faces.

What did the investigators conclude?

Kelly and colleagues concluded that during the first year, "the ability to recognize own-race faces was retained, whereas the capacity to individuate other-race faces was simultaneously reduced, demonstrating a pattern of perceptual narrowing" (2009, p. 111). That is, from experience, infants finely tune their face-processing systems to include only faces from familiar groups.

What converging evidence would strengthen these conclusions?

These findings show that 3-month-olds' face processing systems work equally well on faces from different racial groups. The investigators could determine how broadly the system is tuned by studying infants' recognition of faces of young children and comparing the responses of infants who have older siblings with those who do not.

 Go to Psychology CourseMate at **www.cengagebrain.com** to enhance your understanding of this research.

Integrating Sensory Information

So far, we have discussed infants' sensory systems separately; however, most infant experiences are better described as multimedia events. For example, a nursing mother provides visual and taste cues to her baby. Infants readily perceive many of these relations, recognizing by sight an object that they have only touched previously (Sann & Streri, 2007). Similarly, babies can detect relations between information presented visually and auditorily. For example, babies look longer when an object's motion matches its sound (it makes higher-pitched sounds while rising but lower-pitched sounds while

A mother who breast-feeds provides her baby with a multimedia event: The baby sees, smells, hears, feels, and tastes her.

HUMAN DEVELOPMENT in action

Imagine that you're a pediatrician. Explain to Darla the many ways in which her baby's perceptual skills are sophisticated.

intersensory redundancy
being attuned to information presented simultaneously to different sensory modes

falling) than when it doesn't (Walker et al., 2010). Finally, they link their body movement to their perceptions of musical rhythm, giving new meaning to the phrase "feel the beat, baby!" (Gerry, Faux, & Trainor, 2010).

Traditionally, coordinating information from different senses (e.g., vision with hearing and vision with touch) was thought to be a challenging task for infants. But a new view is that cross-modal perception is easier for infants because regions in the brain devoted to sensory processing are not yet specialized in infancy. For example, regions in an adult's brain that respond only to visual stimuli respond to visual and auditory input in the infant's brain (Spector & Maurer, 2009). And *some researchers have argued that the infant's sensory systems are particularly attuned to* **intersensory redundancy**, *that is, to information that is presented simultaneously to different sensory modes* (Bahrick & Lickliter, 2002; Bahrick, Lickliter, & Flom, 2004). When an infant sees and hears the mother clapping (visual and auditory information), it focuses on the information conveyed to both senses and pays less attention to information that's only available in one sense, such as the color of the mother's nail polish or the sound of her humming along with the tune. Or the infant can learn that the mom's lips are chapped from seeing the flaking skin and by feeling the roughness as the mother kisses it. According to intersensory redundancy theory, it's as if infants follow the rule "Any information that's presented in multiple senses must be important, so pay attention to it" (Flom & Bahrick, 2007).

Integrating information from different senses is yet another variation on the theme that has dominated this chapter: Infants' sensory and perceptual skills are impressive. In short, like most infants, Darla's daughter (from the opening vignette) is exceptionally well prepared to begin making sense out of her environment.

Test Yourself

Recall

1. Infants respond negatively to substances that taste sour or _____.

2. Infants respond to _____ with a high-pitched cry that is hard to soothe.

3. Infants' hearing is best for sounds that have the pitch of _____.

4. At _____ of age, infants' acuity is like that of an adult with normal vision.

5. The term _____ refers to images of an object in the left and right eyes differing for nearby objects.

6. When elements consistently move together, infants decide that they are _____.

7. Infants readily integrate information from different senses, and their sensory systems seem to be particularly attuned to _____.

Interpret

- Compare the impact of nature and nurture on the development of infants' sensory and perceptual skills.

- Psychologists often refer to perceptual-motor skills, which implies that the two are closely related. Based on what you've learned in this chapter, how might motor skills influence perception? How could perception influence motor skills?

Apply

- Perceptual skills are quite refined at birth and mature rapidly. What evolutionary purposes are served by this rapid development?

- Six-month-old Sebastian often watches his mother type on a keyboard. She wonders how he knows that her fingers and the keyboard are not simply one big, unusual object. If you were a developmental psychologist, what would you say to her?

Recall answers: (1) bitter, (2) pain, (3) human speech, (4) 1 year, (5) retinal disparity, (6) part of the same object, (7) information presented redundantly to multiple senses

LEARNING OBJECTIVES

- When do children begin to realize that they exist?
- What are preschoolers' self-concepts like?

- When do preschool children begin to acquire a theory of mind?

When Ximena brushes her teeth, she puts her 20-month-old son, Christof, in an infant seat facing the bathroom mirror. She's been doing this for months, and Christof enjoys looking at the images in the mirror. Lately, he seems to pay special attention to his own reflection. Ximena thinks that sometimes Christof deliberately frowns or laughs just to see what he looks like. Is this possible, Ximena wonders, or is her imagination simply running wild?

As infants' physical, motor, and perceptual skills grow, they learn more about the world around them. As part of this learning, infants and toddlers begin to realize that they exist independently of other people and objects in the environment and that their existence continues over time. In this last section, you can see how children become self-aware and learn what Christof knows about himself.

Origins of Self-Concept

When do children begin to understand that they exist? Measuring the onset of this awareness is not easy. We can't simply ask a 3-year-old, "So, tell me, when did you first realize you existed and weren't just part of the furniture?" Investigators need a less direct approach, and a mirror offers one route. Babies sometimes touch the face in the mirror or wave at it, but none of their behaviors indicate that they recognize themselves in the mirror. Instead, babies act as if the face in the mirror is simply an interesting stimulus.

How would we know whether infants recognize themselves in a mirror? One clever approach is to have mothers place a red mark on their infant's nose; they do this surreptitiously, while wiping the baby's face. Then the infant is returned to the mirror. Many 1-year-olds touch the red mark on the mirror, showing that they notice the mark on the face in the mirror. By 15 months, however, an important change occurs: Babies see the red mark in the mirror, then reach up and touch their own noses. By age 2, virtually all children do this (Bullock & Lütkenhaus, 1990; Lewis & Brooks-Gunn, 1979). When these older children notice the red mark in the mirror, they understand that the funny-looking nose in the mirror is their own.

We don't need to rely solely on the mirror task to know that self-awareness emerges between 18 and 24 months. During this same period, toddlers look more at photographs of themselves than at photos of other children. They also refer to themselves by name or with a personal pronoun, such as *I* or *me,* and sometimes they know their age and their gender. These changes, which often occur together, suggest that self-awareness is well established in most children by age 2 (Lewis, 2011; Moore, 2007).

Once children fully understand that they exist, they begin to wonder who they are. When asked to describe themselves, preschoolers frequently mention physical characteristics ("I have blue eyes"), their preferences

Not until 15 to 18 months of age do babies recognize themselves in the mirror, which is an important step in becoming self-aware.

Pauline Breijer/Shutterstock.com

("I like spaghetti"), their competencies ("I can count to 50"), and their possessions ("I have a fire truck"). What these features have in common is a focus on a child's characteristics that are observable and concrete (Harter, 2006). As children enter school, their self-concepts become even more elaborate (Harter, 1994), changes that we'll explore in Chapter 9.

Theory of Mind

As youngsters gain more insights into themselves, they realize that people have thoughts, beliefs, and intentions and that these thoughts, beliefs, and intentions often cause people to behave as they do. Amazingly, even infants understand that people's behavior is often intentional—designed to achieve a goal. Imagine a father who says, "Where are the crackers?" in front of his 1-year-old daughter and then begins opening kitchen cabinets, moving some objects to look behind them. Finding the box of crackers, he says, "There they are!" If the infant understands intentionality, she then realizes how her father's actions (searching and moving objects) were related to the goal of finding the crackers.

Many clever experiments have revealed that 1-year-olds have this understanding of intentionality. In one study, infants observed an adult reaching over a barrier for a ball but failing to grasp it because the ball was just out of reach. Then the barrier was removed, and infants saw an adult using the same "over the barrier" reaching motion or reaching directly for the ball; in both cases, the adult grasped the ball. By 10 months, infants were surprised to see the adult relying on the over-the-barrier reach when it was no longer needed. In other words, with the barrier removed, infants expected to see the adult reach directly, because that was the best way to achieve the goal of getting the ball; they were surprised when the adult relied on the familiar but now unnecessary method of reaching (Brandone & Wellman, 2009).

From this early understanding of intentionality, young children's naive psychology expands rapidly. *Between 2 and 5 years of age, children develop a* **theory of mind**, *a naive understanding of the relations between mind and behavior.* In the earliest phase, 2-year-olds are aware of desires and often speak of their wants and likes, as in "Lemme see" or "I wanna sit." And they often link their desires to their behavior, such as "I happy there more cookies" (Wellman, 1993). Thus, by age 2, children understand that people have desires and that desires can cause behavior.

By about age 3, children clearly distinguish the mental world from the physical world. For example, if told about a girl who has a cookie and another who is thinking about a cookie, 3-year-olds know that only the first girl can see, touch, and eat her cookie (Harris et al., 1991). Most 3-year-olds also use "mental verbs" like *think, believe, remember,* and *forget,* which suggests that they have some understanding of different mental states (Bartsch & Wellman, 1995).

Not until 4 years of age do mental states take center stage in children's understanding of their actions and the actions of others. That is, by age 4, children understand that behavior is often based on a person's beliefs about events and situations, even when those beliefs are wrong. This developmental transformation is particularly evident when children are tested on false-belief tasks such as the one shown in Figure 3.9. In this story, the child being tested knows the ball is in the box, but Sally, the girl in the story, believes that the ball is still in the basket. Although 4-year-olds correctly say that Sally will look for the ball in the basket (i.e., will act on her false belief), most 3-year-olds claim that she will look for the ball in the box. The 4-year-olds understand that Sally's behavior is based on her beliefs even though her beliefs are incorrect (Wellman, Cross, & Watson, 2001). This general developmental pattern is evident in many cultures around the world (Callaghan et al., 2005; Liu et al., 2008).

This pattern signifies a fundamental change in children's understanding of the centrality of beliefs in a person's thinking about the world. By age 4, children "realize that people not only have thoughts and beliefs, but also that thoughts and beliefs are

theory of mind
ideas about connections among thoughts, beliefs, intentions, and behavior that create an intuitive understanding of the link between mind and behavior

This is Sally. Sally has a basket.

This is Anne. Anne has a box.

Sally puts her ball in her basket.

Sally goes out for a walk.

Anne takes the ball from the basket and puts it into the box.

Now Sally comes back. She wants to play with her ball. Where will she look for her ball?

Copyright © Cengage Learning 2010

FIGURE 3.9

In a false-belief task, most 3-year-olds say that Sally will look for the ball in the box, showing that they do not understand how people can act on their beliefs (where the ball is) even when those beliefs are wrong.

crucial to explaining why people do things; that is, actors' pursuits of their desires are inevitably shaped by their beliefs about the world" (Bartsch & Wellman, 1995, p. 144).

You can see preschool children's growing understanding of false belief in the Real People feature.

The early stages of children's theory of mind seem clear. But just how this happens is still debated. One view emphasizes the contribution of language, which develops rapidly during the same years that a theory of mind emerges (as we'll see in Chapter 4). Some scientists believe that children's language skills contribute to a theory of mind, perhaps reflecting the benefit of an expanding vocabulary that includes verbs describing mental states, such as *think, know,* and *believe* (Pascual et al., 2008).

A different view is that a child's theory of mind emerges from interactions with other people that provide insights into different mental states (Dunn & Brophy, 2005; Farrant, Maybery, & Fletcher, 2012). Through conversations with parents and older siblings that focus on other people's mental states, children learn facts of mental life, and this helps children see that others often have perspectives different from their own. In other words, when children frequently participate in conversations that focus on other people's moods, feelings, and intentions, they learn that people's behavior is based on their beliefs, regardless of the accuracy of those beliefs (Taumoepeau & Ruffman, 2008).

Test Yourself

Recall

1. Apparently children are first self-aware at age 2, because this is when they first recognize themselves in a mirror and in photographs and when they first use _____.

2. During the preschool years, children's self-concepts emphasize _____, physical characteristics, preferences, and competencies.

3. Unlike 4-year-olds, most 3-year-olds don't understand that other people's behavior is sometimes based on _____.

Interpret

• Compare and contrast different explanations for the growth of a theory of mind during the preschool years.

• Suppose you believe that a theory of mind develops faster when preschoolers spend time with other children. What sort of correlational study would you devise to test this hypothesis? How could you do an experimental study to test the same hypothesis?

Apply

• Self-concept emerges over the same months that toddlers show rapid gains in locomotor skills. How might changes in locomotor skills contribute to a toddler's emerging sense of self?

• Some toddlers seem reluctant to share their toys. How might you explain this behavior as linked to their emerging self-concept to preschool teachers?

Recall answers: (1) personal pronouns such as *I* and *me*, (2) possessions, (3) false beliefs

Preschoolers gradually recognize that people's behavior is sometimes guided by mistaken beliefs. We once witnessed an episode at a day-care center that documented this growing understanding. After lunch, Karen, a 2-year-old, saw ketchup on the floor and squealed, "Blood, blood!" Lonna, a 3-year-old, said in a disgusted tone, "It's not blood—it's ketchup." Then, Shenan, a 4-year-old, interjected, "Yeah, but Karen *thought* it was blood." A similar incident took place a few weeks later, on the day after Halloween. This time, Lonna put on a monster mask and scared Karen. When Karen began to cry, Lonna said, "Oh stop. It's just a mask." Shenan broke in again, saying, "You know it's just a mask. But she *thinks* it's a monster." In both cases, only Shenan understood that Karen's behavior was based on her beliefs (that the ketchup is blood and that the monster is real), even though her beliefs were false.

Linking Research to life • THEORY OF MIND IN CHILDREN WITH AUTISM

Autism is the most serious of a family of disorders known as autism spectrum disorder (ASD). Individuals with ASD acquire language later than usual, their speech often echoes what others say to them, they sometimes become intensely interested in objects (e.g., making the same actions with a toy repeatedly), they often seem uninterested in other people, and when they do interact, those exchanges are often awkward. Symptoms usually emerge early in life, typically by 18 to 24 months of age. Roughly 1 out of every 200 to 300 U.S. children is diagnosed with ASD; about 80% of them are boys (Mash & Wolfe, 2010). ASD is heritable, and many studies point to atypical brain functioning, perhaps due to abnormal levels of neurotransmitters (National Institute of Neurological Disorders and Stroke, 2009).

Children with ASD grasp false belief slowly, and this performance leads some researchers to conclude that the absence of a theory of mind—sometimes called "mindblindness" (Baron-Cohen, 1995)—is the defining characteristic of ASD (Tager-Flusberg, 2007). Other scientists aren't convinced. One idea emphasizes a focused processing style that is common in ASD. For example, children with ASD find hidden objects faster than typically developing children do (Joseph et al., 2009). But this emphasis on perceptual details usually comes at the expense of maintaining a coherent overall picture. Consequently, in social interactions, children with ASD may focus on one facet of another person's behavior (e.g., gestures) but ignore other verbal and nonverbal cues (e.g., speech, facial expressions, and body language) that collectively promote fluid interactions. Research to evaluate these claims is still ongoing; it's likely that the answers will indicate that multiple factors contribute to ASD.

ASD can't be cured. However, therapy can be used to improve language and social skills in children with autism. In addition, medications can be used to reduce some symptoms, such as repetitive behavior (National Institute of Neurological Disorders and Stroke, 2009). When ASD is diagnosed early and autistic children grow up in supportive, responsive environments and receive appropriate treatments, they can lead satisfying and productive lives.

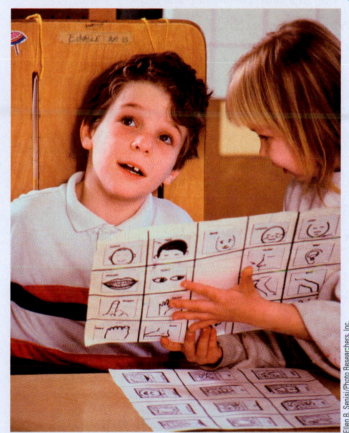

Ellen B. Senisi/Photo Researchers, Inc.

Children with autism master language later than usual and are often more interested in objects than in people.

Summary

3.1 The Newborn

How do reflexes help newborns interact with the world?

■ Babies are born with a number of reflexes. Some help them adjust to life outside of the uterus, some help protect them from danger, and some serve as the basis for later voluntary motor behavior.

How do we determine whether a baby is healthy?

■ The Apgar scale measures five vital signs to determine a newborn baby's physical well-being. The Neonatal Behavioral Assessment Scale provides a comprehensive evaluation of a baby's behavioral and physical status.

What behavioral states are common among newborns?

■ Newborns spend their day in one of four states: alert inactivity, waking activity, crying, and sleeping. A newborn's crying forms are a basic cry, a mad cry, and a pain cry. A popular way to calm a crying baby is to put it on the shoulder and rock the infant gently.

■ Newborns spend approximately two thirds of every day asleep and go through a complete sleep–wake cycle once every 4 hours. By 6 months, babies sleep most of the way through the night. Newborns spend about half of their time asleep in rapid-eye-movement sleep, an active form of sleep that may stimulate growth in the nervous system.

■ Some healthy babies die from sudden infant death syndrome (SIDS). Factors that contribute to SIDS are prematurity, low birth weight, and smoking. Also, babies are vulnerable to SIDS when they sleep on their stomach and when they are overheated. The goal of the Back to Sleep campaign is to prevent SIDS by encouraging parents to have infants sleep on their backs.

What are different features of temperament?

■ Temperament refers to a consistent style or pattern of infant behavior. Modern theories list two to six dimensions of temperament, such as extroversion and negative affect. Temperament is influenced both by heredity and by environment.

3.2 Physical Development

How do height and weight change from birth to 2 years of age?

■ Physical growth is particularly rapid during infancy. Infants and young children have disproportionately large heads and trunks.

What nutrients do young children need? How are they best provided?

■ Infants must consume a large number of calories relative to their body weight, primarily because of the energy required for growth. Breast-feeding and bottle-feeding both provide babies with adequate nutrition.

What are the consequences of malnutrition? How can it be treated?

■ Malnutrition is a worldwide problem that is particularly harmful during infancy, when growth is rapid. Treating malnutrition adequately requires improving children's diets and training their parents to provide stimulating environments.

What are nerve cells? How are they organized in the brain?

■ A nerve cell, called a neuron, includes a cell body, a dendrite, and an axon. The mature brain consists of billions of neurons, organized into nearly identical left and right hemispheres connected by the corpus callosum. The frontal cortex is associated with personality and goal-directed behavior; the left hemisphere of the cortex with language; and the right hemisphere of the cortex with nonverbal processes, such as perceiving emotions.

How does the brain develop? When does it begin to function?

■ Brain specialization is evident in infancy; further specialization involves more focused brain areas and narrowing of stimuli that trigger brain activity. Different systems specialize at different rates. Specialization depends upon stimulation from the environment. The relative lack of specialization in the immature brain makes it better able to recover from injury.

3.3 Moving and Grasping: Early Motor Skills

What skills are involved in learning to walk? When do infants master them?

■ Infants acquire a series of locomotor skills during their first year, culminating in walking soon after the first birthday. Learning to walk involves differentiating individual skills, such as maintaining balance and using the legs alternately, and then integrating these skills into a coherent whole.

How do infants learn to use their hands?

■ Infants first use only one hand at a time, then both hands independently, then both hands in common actions, and finally, at about 5 months of age, both hands in different actions with a common purpose.

■ Most people are right-handed, a preference that emerges after the first birthday and becomes well established during the preschool years. Handedness is determined by heredity but can be influenced by cultural values.

3.4 Coming to Know the World: Perception

Are infants able to smell, to taste, and to experience pain? Can infants hear?

- Newborns are able to smell, and some can recognize their mother's odor; they also taste, preferring sweet substances and responding negatively to bitter and sour tastes.

- Infants respond to touch. They probably experience pain, because their responses to painful stimuli are similar to those of older children.

- Babies can hear and distinguish different sounds.

How well can infants see? Can they see color and depth?

- A newborn's visual acuity is relatively poor, but 1-year-olds can see as well as an adult with normal vision. By 3 months, infants see the full range of colors.

- Infants are attracted to faces, and experience leads infants to form a face template based on faces they see often.

How do infants coordinate information from different sensory modalities?

- Infants coordinate information from different senses. They can recognize, by sight, an object they've felt previously. Infants are often particularly attentive to information presented redundantly to multiple senses.

3.5 Becoming Self-Aware

When do children begin to realize that they exist?

- Beginning at about 15 months, infants begin to recognize themselves in the mirror, which is one of the first signs of self-recognition. They also begin preferring to look at pictures of themselves and referring to themselves by name (or using personal pronouns).

What are preschoolers' self-concepts like?

- Preschoolers often define themselves in terms of observable characteristics, such as physical characteristics, preferences, competencies, and possessions.

When do preschool children begin to acquire a theory of mind?

- A theory of mind—which refers to a person's ideas about connections between thoughts and behavior—develops rapidly during the preschool years. Most 2-year-olds know that people have desires and that desires can cause behavior. By age 3, children distinguish the mental world from the physical world. By age 4, however, children understand that behavior is based on beliefs about the world, even when those beliefs are wrong. Children with autism have a limited theory of mind.

Key Terms

reflexes (64)
alert inactivity (65)
waking activity (65)
crying (65)
sleeping (66)
basic cry (66)
mad cry (66)
pain cry (66)
irregular or rapid-eye-movement (REM) sleep (66)
regular (non-REM) sleep (66)
sudden infant death syndrome (SIDS) (67)
temperament (67)
malnourished (71)
neuron (71)

cell body (71)
dendrite (72)
axon (72)
terminal buttons (72)
neurotransmitters (72)
cerebral cortex (72)
hemispheres (72)
corpus callosum (72)
frontal cortex (72)
neural plate (73)
myelin (73)
synaptic pruning (73)
experience-expectant growth (74)
motor skills (75)
locomotion (75)

fine motor skills (75)
dynamic systems theory (75)
differentiation (77)
integration (77)
perception (79)
visual cliff (80)
kinetic cues (80)
visual expansion (81)
motion parallax (81)
retinal disparity (82)
pictorial cues (82)
linear perspective (82)
texture gradient (82)
intersensory redundancy (85)
theory of mind (87)

Online Resources

Go to CengageBrain.com to access Psychology CourseMate, where you will find an interactive eBook, flashcards, quizzes, videos, websites, and more.

The Emergence of Thought and Language

Cognitive Development in Infancy and Early Childhood

On the TV show *Family Guy,* Stewie is a 1-year-old who can't stand his mother (Stewie: "Hey, mother, I come bearing a gift. I'll give you a hint. It's in my diaper and it's not a toaster.") and hopes to dominate the world. Much of the humor turns on the idea that babies have sophisticated thoughts that they can't express. But what thoughts really lurk in the mind of an infant who is not yet speaking? How does cognition develop during infancy and early childhood?

These questions provide the focus of this chapter. We begin with the first complete account of cognitive development, Jean Piaget's theory, as well as a later variant, core knowledge theories. The next two sections of the chapter concern alternative accounts of cognitive development: the information-processing perspective and Lev Vygotsky's theory. In the last section of this chapter, you'll see how children master their native language to express their thoughts.

LEARNING OBJECTIVES

- According to Piaget, how do schemes, assimilation, and accommodation provide the foundation for cognitive development?
- How does thinking become more advanced during the sensorimotor stage?

- What are the distinguishing characteristics of preoperational thinking?
- What are some criticisms of Piaget's theory?
- How have contemporary researchers extended Piaget's theory?

Three-year-old Jamila loves talking to her grandmother ("Gram") on the telephone. Sometimes these conversations are not successful, because Gram asks questions and Jamila replies by nodding or shaking her head. Jamila's dad has explained that Gram can't see her—that she needs to say "yes" or "no." But Jamila invariably returns to head nodding. Her dad can't see why such a bright and talkative child doesn't realize that such nodding is meaningless over the phone.

Why does Jamila insist on nodding her head when she's talking on the phone? As we'll see in a few pages, this behavior is typical for children in one of Piaget's four stages of thinking. We begin by describing some general features of Piaget's theory. We then examine his account of thinking during infancy and during the preschool years. Finally, we consider some alternative approaches prompted by criticisms of the theory.

Basic Principles of Cognitive Development

Piaget believed that children are naturally curious. They are like scientists creating theories about how the world works. Children's theories are often incomplete, but they're invaluable in making the world seem more predictable. *According to Piaget, children understand the world with* **schemes**, *psychological structures that organize experience.* Schemes are mental categories of related events, objects, and knowledge. During infancy, children group objects based on the actions they can perform on them. For example, infants suck and grasp, and they use these actions to create categories of objects that can be sucked and objects that can be grasped. After infancy, schemes are based on functional or conceptual relationships, not action. For example, preschoolers learn that forks, knives, and spoons form a functional category of "things I use to eat." Or they learn that dogs, cats, and goldfish form a conceptual category of "pets." Older children and adolescents add schemes based on abstract properties. For example, an adolescent might put fascism, racism, and sexism in a category of "ideologies I despise."

Assimilation and Accommodation

Schemes change constantly, adjusting to children's experiences. **Assimilation** *occurs when new experiences are readily incorporated into existing schemes.* Imagine a baby who has the familiar grasping scheme. She soon discovers that the grasping scheme also works on blocks and toy cars. Extending the existing grasping scheme to new objects illustrates assimilation. **Accommodation** *occurs when schemes are modified based on experience.* Soon the infant learns that some objects can only be lifted with two hands and that some can't be lifted. Changing the scheme so that it works for new objects (e.g., using two hands to grasp heavy objects) illustrates accommodation.

The Real People feature shows how accommodation and assimilation allow young children to understand their worlds.

schemes
according to Piaget, mental structures that organize information and regulate behavior

assimilation
according to Piaget, taking in information that is compatible with what is already known

accommodation
according to Piaget, changing existing knowledge based on new knowledge

When Ethan, an energetic 2½-year-old, first saw a monarch butterfly, his mother, Kat, told him, "Butterfly, butterfly; that's a butterfly, Ethan." A few minutes later, a zebra swallowtail butterfly landed on a nearby bush and Ethan shouted, "Butterfly, Mama, butterfly!" A bit later, a moth flew out of another bush; Ethan cried, "Butterfly, Mama, more butterfly!" As Kat told Ethan, "No, honey, that's a moth, not a butterfly," she marveled at how rapidly Ethan grasped new concepts with so little direction from her. How was this possible?

Piaget's explanation would be that when Kat named the monarch butterfly for Ethan, he formed a scheme, something like "Butterflies are bugs with big wings." The second butterfly differed in color but was still a bug with big wings, so it was readily *assimilated* into Ethan's new scheme for butterflies. However, when Ethan referred to the moth as a butterfly, Kat corrected him. Ethan was forced to *accommodate* to this new experience. He changed his scheme for butterflies to make it more precise: "Butterflies are bugs with thin bodies and big, colorful wings." He also created a new scheme, something like "A moth is a bug with a bigger body and plain wings." Accommodation and assimilation work together to help Ethan make sense of his experiences.

This baby will learn that many objects can be grasped easily with one hand—illustrating assimilation—but will also discover that bigger, heavier objects can be grasped only with two hands—illustrating accommodation.

Equilibration and Stages of Cognitive Development

Assimilation and accommodation are usually in balance, or equilibrium. Children find that many experiences are readily assimilated into their existing schemes but that they sometimes need to accommodate their schemes to adjust to new experiences. Periodically, however, this balance is upset, and a state of disequilibrium results. Children discover that their current schemes are not adequate because they are spending too much time accommodating and less time assimilating. *When disequilibrium occurs, children reorganize their schemes to return to a state of equilibrium, a process that Piaget called* **equilibration**. To restore the balance, current but outmoded ways of thinking are replaced by a qualitatively different, more advanced set of schemes.

One way to understand equilibration is to return to the metaphor of the child as a scientist. Sometimes scientists find that their theories contain critical flaws that can't be fixed simply by revising; instead, they must create a new theory that draws upon the older theory but differs fundamentally. For example, when the astronomer Copernicus realized that the earth-centered theory of the solar system was fundamentally wrong, his new theory built on the assumption that the sun is the center of the solar system. In much the same way, children periodically realize that their current theories seem to be wrong much of the time, so they abandon them in favor of more advanced ways of thinking.

According to Piaget, these revolutionary changes occur at approximately 2, 7, and 11 years of age, dividing cognitive development into four stages:

Stage	Age
Sensorimotor	Infancy (birth to 2 years)
Preoperational	Preschool and early-elementary-school years (2 to 6 years)
Concrete operational	Middle- and late-elementary-school years (7 to 11 years)
Formal operational	Adolescence and adulthood (11 years and up)

The ages listed are only approximate; some youngsters move through the periods more rapidly than others. But the only route to formal operations is through the first three stages; children cannot skip stages.

In the next few pages, we consider Piaget's first two stages. In Chapter 6, we return to Piaget's theory to examine the last two stages.

equilibration
according to Piaget, a process by which when disequilibrium occurs, children reorganize their schemes to return to a state of equilibrium

Sensorimotor Thinking

The **sensorimotor period**, *from birth to 2 years of age, is the first of Piaget's four stages.* In this stage, infants' thinking progresses along three important fronts.

Adapting to and Exploring the Environment

Newborns respond reflexively to many stimuli, but between 1 and 4 months of age, reflexes are first modified by experience. An infant may inadvertently touch his lips with his thumb, thereby initiating sucking and the pleasing sensations it produces. Later, the infant tries to re-create these sensations by guiding his thumb to his mouth. Sucking no longer occurs only in response to a nipple; instead, the infant has found a way to initiate sucking independently.

Eight months marks the onset of deliberate, intentional behavior. For the first time, the means and end of activities are distinct. If, for example, a father places his hand in front of a toy, an infant then moves his father's hand to play with the toy. The "moving the hand" scheme is used to achieve the goal of "grasping the toy." Using one action to achieve a goal is the first indication of purposeful behavior during infancy.

Beginning at about 12 months, infants become active experimenters. An infant may deliberately shake different objects, trying to discover which ones produce sounds. Or an infant may decide to drop different objects to see what happens. These actions represent a significant extension of intentional behavior; now babies repeat actions with different objects solely to see what happens.

When interesting toys are covered so that they can't be seen, young babies lose interest, as if "out of sight" means "out of existence."

Understanding Objects

Objects exist independently of our actions and thoughts toward them; they still exist when we close our eyes or wish they would go away. *The understanding that objects exist independently is* **object permanence**. Piaget claimed that infants lacked this understanding for much of the first year. Instead, for infants, objects exist only when in sight. If an attractive toy is placed near a baby and then covered with a cloth, 4- to 8-month-olds lose all interest in the object, as if the now-hidden object no longer exists: "out of sight, out of existence!"

Beginning at about 8 months, infants search for an object that an experimenter has covered with a cloth. Nevertheless, their understanding of object permanence remains incomplete, according to Piaget. If 8- to 10-month-olds see an object hidden under one container several times and then see it hidden under a second container, they usually reach for the toy under the first container. Piaget claimed that this shows infants' limited understanding of objects, because they do not distinguish the object from the actions they use to locate it, such as reaching for a particular container.

Piaget argued that not until approximately 18 months do infants have full understanding of object permanence. However, in a few pages, we'll see that infants know more about objects than Piaget claimed.

Using Symbols

By 18 months, most infants have begun to talk and gesture, evidence of their emerging capacity to use symbols. Words and gestures are symbols that stand for something else. When a baby waves, it's a symbol that's just as effective as saying "good-bye" to bid farewell. Children also begin to engage in pretend play, another use of symbols. A 20-month-old may move her hand back and forth in front of her mouth, pretending to brush her teeth.

In just 2 years, infants progress from reflexive responding to actively exploring their world, understanding objects, and using symbols. These remarkable achievements set the stage for preoperational thinking, which we examine next.

sensorimotor period
the first of Piaget's four stages of cognitive development, which lasts from birth to approximately 2 years

object permanence
the understanding, acquired in infancy, that objects exist independently

Preoperational Thinking

Once they have crossed into preoperational thinking, the power of symbols is available to young children. Harnessing this power is a lifelong process; preschoolers' efforts are tentative and sometimes incorrect (DeLoache, 1995). Piaget identified a number of characteristic shortcomings in preschoolers' symbolic skills. Let's look at three: egocentrism, centration, and appearance as reality (shown in Table 4.1).

Egocentrism

Preoperational children's view of the world is **egocentric**—*they believe others see the world exactly as they do.* Piaget's three-mountains problem demonstrates preoperational children's egocentrism (Piaget & Inhelder, 1956, chapter 8). Youngsters were seated at a table like the one shown in Figure 4.1 and asked to choose the photograph that corresponded to another person's view of the mountains. Preoperational youngsters usually picked the photograph that showed their own view of the mountains, apparently presuming that theirs is the only view, not one of many views. According to Piaget, only concrete operational children fully understand that all people do not experience an event in exactly the same way. Egocentrism explains why 3-year-old Jamila nods her head during phone conversations. Jamila assumes that because she knows her head is moving up and down (or side to side), her grandmother must be aware of it too.

Centration

A second characteristic of preoperational thinking is that children have the psychological equivalent of tunnel vision: They concentrate on one aspect of a problem but ignore other, equally relevant aspects. **Centration** *is Piaget's term for this narrowly focused thought that characterizes preoperational youngsters.*

Piaget demonstrated centration in his experiments involving conservation, shown in Figure 4.2. Each task begins with identical objects (or sets of objects). Then one of the objects (or sets) is transformed, and children are asked whether the objects are the same in terms of some important feature. For instance, in a problem involving conservation

egocentric
having difficulty in seeing the world from another's point of view, a characteristic typical of children in the preoperational period

centration
according to Piaget, a narrowly focused type of thought characteristic of preoperational children

FIGURE 4.1
Egocentrism: When asked to select the photograph that shows the mountains as the adult sees them, preschool children often select the photograph that shows how the mountains look to them.

Copyright © Cengage Learning 2010

Type of conservation	Starting configuration	Transformation	Final configuration
Liquid quantity	 Is there the same amount of water in each glass?	Pour water from one glass into a shorter, wider glass.	 Now is there the same amount of water in each glass, or does one glass have more?
Number	 Are there the same number of pennies in each row?	Stretch out the top row of pennies, push together the bottom row.	 Now are there the same number of pennies in each row, or does one row have more?
Length	 Are these sticks the same length?	Move one stick to the left and the other to the right.	 Now are the sticks the same length, or is one longer?
Mass	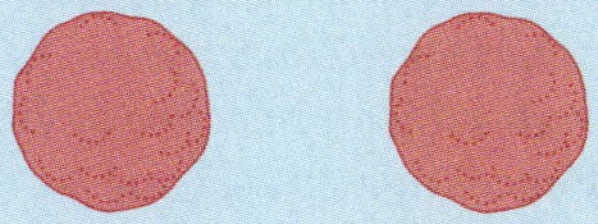 Does each ball have the same amount of clay?	Roll one ball so that it looks like a sausage.	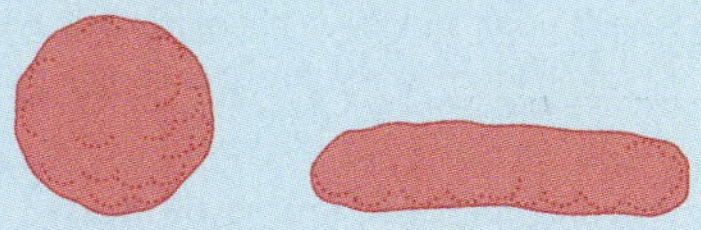 Now does each piece have the same amount of clay, or does one have more?
Area	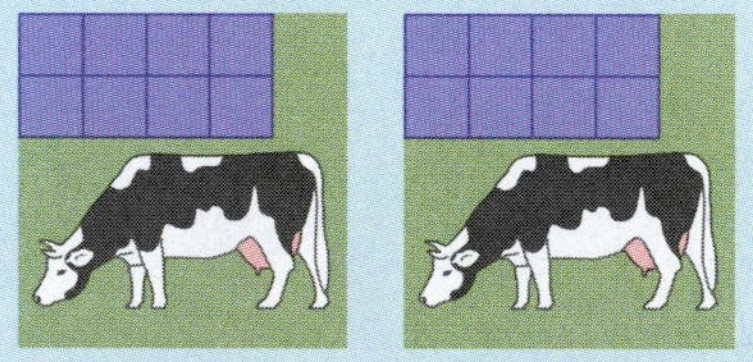 Does each cow have the same amount of grass to eat?	Spread out the squares in one field.	 Now does each cow have the same amount to eat, or does one cow have more?

Copyright © Cengage Learning 2010

FIGURE 4.2
Children in the preoperational stage of development typically have difficulty solving conservation problems, in which important features of an object (or objects) stay the same despite changes in physical appearance.

of liquid quantity, children are shown identical beakers filled with the same amount of juice. After children agree that the two beakers have the same amount, the juice is poured from one beaker into a taller, thinner beaker. The amount is unchanged, but preoperational children claim that the tall, thin beaker has more juice than the original beaker.

According to Piaget, preoperational children center on the level of the juice in the beaker. If the juice is higher after it is poured, preoperational children believe that there must be more juice now than before. Because preoperational thinking is characterized by centration, these youngsters ignore the change in the beaker's diameter that causes the change in the level of the juice. Thus, preoperational children's "centered" thinking means that they overlook other relevant parts of problems.

Characteristics of Preoperational Thinking

Characteristic	Definition	Example
Egocentrism	The child believes that all people see the world as he or she does	A child gestures during a telephone conversation, not realizing that the listener cannot see the gestures
Centration	The child focuses on one aspect of a problem or situation but ignores other relevant aspects	In conservation of liquid quantity, a child pays attention to the height of the liquid in the beaker but ignores the diameter of the beaker
Appearance as reality	The child assumes that an object really is what it appears to be	A child believes that a person smiling at another person is really happy, even though the other person is being mean

Copyright © Cengage Learning 2010

In conservation problems, preschool children typically do not believe that the quantity of a liquid remains the same when it is poured into a taller, more slender beaker.

Appearance as Reality

A final feature of preoperational thinking is that preschool children believe that an object's appearance tells what the object is really like. Consider the following examples in which appearances and reality conflict:

- A glass of milk looks brown when seen through sunglasses.

- A piece of hard rubber looks like food (e.g., like a piece of pizza).

- A boy is angry because a friend is being mean but smiles because he's afraid the friend will leave if he reveals his anger.

Older children and adults know that the milk looks brown, the object looks like food, and the boy looks happy but that the milk is actually white, the object is actually rubber, and the boy is actually angry. Preoperational children, however, confuse appearance and reality, thinking the milk is brown, the piece of rubber is edible, and the boy is happy.

Evaluating Piaget's Theory

Although Piaget's contributions to child development are legendary, some elements of his theory have held up better than others (Siegler & Alibali, 2005). The following are some common criticisms:

- *Piaget's theory underestimates cognitive competence in infants and young children and overestimates cognitive competence in adolescents.* By using tasks more sensitive than Piaget's, scientists have shown that infants and toddlers are more capable than expected based on Piaget's theory. For example, in a few pages we'll see that infants have much greater understanding of objects than Piaget believed. Paradoxically, Piaget overestimated cognitive skill in adolescents, whose reasoning is often not as sophisticated as expected by formal operational principles.

- *Piaget's theory is vague with respect to processes of change.* Many key components of the theory, such as accommodation and assimilation, are too vague to be tested scientifically. Consequently, scientists abandoned them in favor of other cognitive processes that could be evaluated more readily and hence could provide more convincing accounts of children's thinking.

- *Piaget's stage model does not account for variability in children's performance.* In Piaget's view, each stage has unique characteristics that leave their mark on everything a child does (e.g., egocentrism and centration in preoperational thinking). Consequently, children's performance on different tasks should be consistent. On conservation and three-mountains tasks, for instance, a 4-year-old should always respond in a preoperational way: He should say that the water is not the same after pouring and that another person sees the mountains the same way he does.

Instead, a child's thinking may be sophisticated in some domains but naive in others (Siegler, 1981). This inconsistency does not support Piaget's view that children's thinking always reflects the distinctive imprint of their current stage of cognitive development.

■ *Piaget's theory undervalues the influence of the sociocultural environment on cognitive development.* Piaget describes the child as a lone scientist, but in reality, a child's effort to understand the world is a social enterprise. Growing understanding of the world is profoundly influenced by interactions with family members, peers, and teachers, and it takes place against the backdrop of cultural values. Piaget did not ignore these social and cultural forces, but they are not prominent in his theory.

Due to these criticisms, researchers have attempted to round out our understanding of cognitive development using other theoretical perspectives that we discuss later in this chapter.

Extending Piaget's Account: Children's Naive Theories

In Piaget's view, children, like scientists, formulate theories about how the world works. Piaget described these theories as comprehensive in explaining a variety of phenomena—including objects, people, and morals, for example—within a common framework. More recent views retain the idea of children as theorists but propose that children, like real scientists, develop specialized theories about narrower areas. *For example, according to the* core knowledge hypothesis, *infants are born with rudimentary knowledge of the world, and this knowledge is elaborated based on children's experiences* (Spelke & Kinzler, 2007; Wellman & Gelman, 1998). Some of young children's first theories concern physics, psychology, and biology. That is, infants and toddlers rapidly develop theories that organize their knowledge about properties of objects, people, and living things (Wellman & Gelman, 1998).

We examined children's developing theory of mind in Chapter 3; in the next few pages, we look at children's naive theories of physics and biology.

Naive Physics

Scientists have long been interested in young children's understanding of objects, in part because Piaget claimed that such understanding develops slowly. However, by devising some clever procedures, other investigators have shown that babies understand objects earlier than Piaget claimed. Baillargeon (1987, 1994), for example, assessed object permanence by using a procedure in which infants first saw a silver screen that appeared to be rotating back and forth. After an infant became familiar with this display, one of two new displays was shown. In the "realistic" event, a red box appeared in a position behind the screen, making it impossible for the screen to rotate as far back as it had previously. Instead, the screen moved away from the infant until it made contact with the box then moved back toward the infant. In the "unrealistic" event, shown in Figure 4.3, the red box appeared but the screen continued to move as before. The screen moved away from the infant until it was flat then moved forward, again revealing the red box. The illusion was possible because the box dropped out of the way of the moving screen. However, from the infant's perspective, the box seemed to vanish behind the screen, only to reappear.

The disappearance and reappearance of the box violates the idea that objects exist permanently. Consequently, an infant who understands object permanence should be surprised by the unrealistic event and look at it longer. Baillargeon found that 4½-month-olds consistently looked longer at the unrealistic event than at the realistic event. Infants apparently thought that the unrealistic event was novel, just as we are surprised when an object vanishes from a magician's scarf.

core knowledge hypothesis
the theory that infants are born with rudimentary knowledge of the world, which is elaborated based on experiences

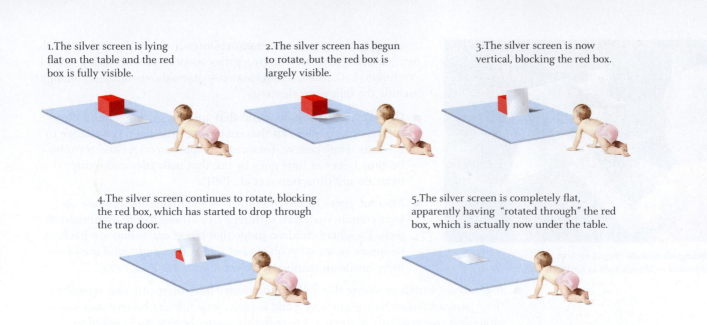

1. The silver screen is lying flat on the table and the red box is fully visible.

2. The silver screen has begun to rotate, but the red box is largely visible.

3. The silver screen is now vertical, blocking the red box.

4. The silver screen continues to rotate, blocking the red box, which has started to drop through the trap door.

5. The silver screen is completely flat, apparently having "rotated through" the red box, which is actually now under the table.

6. The silver screen is rotating back toward the infant but still blocks the red box.

7. The silver screen is again flat and the box fully visible to the infant.

FIGURE 4.3

Infants are surprised to see the silver screen rotate flat, which suggests that they understand the "permanence" of the red box.

Based on "Object permanence in 3½- and 4½-month-old infants," Developmental Psychology, Vol. 23, by R. Baillargeon, pp. 655–664. Copyright © American Psychological Association 1987.

Evidently, then, infants have some understanding of object permanence early in the first year of life.

Understanding that objects exist independently is just a start; objects have numerous other important properties, and infants know many of them. At 5 months, infants expect liquids but not solids to change shape as they're moved from one container to another (Hespos, Ferry, & Rips, 2009). By about 6 months, infants are surprised when an object that's released in midair doesn't fall, when an object remains stationary after being hit, or when an object passes through another solid object (Luo, Kaufman, & Baillargeon, 2009).

These amazing demonstrations show that the infant is an accomplished naive physicist (Hespos & vanMarle, 2012). The infant's theories are far from complete, because physical properties can be understood at many levels (Hood, Carey, & Prosada, 2000). Using gravity as an example, infants expect unsupported objects to fall, elementary-school children know they fall due to gravity, and physics students know the force of gravity equals the mass of an object times the acceleration caused by gravity. Obviously, infants do not understand objects at the level of physics students. However, they rapidly create a reasonably accurate theory of some basic properties of objects, which helps them predict how objects such as toys will act.

Naive Biology

Naive theories of biology begin in infancy, when youngsters first distinguish animate objects (e.g., people and insects) from inanimate objects (e.g., rocks and plants). Infants and toddlers use motion to identify animate objects, and by 12 to 15 months they have determined that animate objects are self-propelled, can move in irregular paths, and can act to achieve goals (Biro & Leslie, 2007; Rakison & Hahn, 2004).

Toddlers distinguish animate objects, such as goats, from inanimate objects, such as furniture and tools.

During the preschool years, children's naive theories of biology include many specific properties associated with living things (Wellman & Gelman, 1998). Many 4-year-olds' theories of biology include the following elements:

- *Growth.* Children understand that animals get bigger and physically more complex but that inanimate objects do not change in this way. They believe, for example, that sea otters and termites become larger as time goes by but that teakettles and teddy bears do not (Rosengren et al., 1991).

- *Internal parts.* Children know that the insides of animate objects contain materials different from those inside inanimate objects. Preschool children judge that blood and bones are likely to be inside an animate object but that cotton and metal are likely to be inside an inanimate object (Simons & Keil, 1995).

- *Inheritance.* Children realize that only living things have offspring that resemble their parents. Asked to explain why a dog is pink, preschoolers believe that some biological characteristic of the parents probably made the dog pink; asked to explain why a can is pink, preschoolers rely on mechanical causes (e.g., a worker used a machine) (Springer & Keil, 1991; Weissman & Kalish, 1999).

- *Healing.* Children understand that, when damaged, animate things heal by regrowth, whereas inanimate things must be fixed by humans. Preschoolers know that hair will grow back when cut from a child's head but must be repaired by a person when cut from a doll's head (Backscheider, Shatz, & Gelman, 1993).

Preschoolers' naive theories of biology aren't complete. Preschoolers don't know, for instance, that genes are the biological basis for inheritance (Springer & Keil, 1991). And, although preschoolers know that plants grow and heal, they don't fully understand that plants are living things (Margett & Witherington, 2011). Despite these limits, children's naive theories of biology, when joined with their naive theory of physics, provide powerful tools for making sense of their world and for understanding new experiences.

HUMAN DEVELOPMENT in action

As a developmental scientist, would you favor Piaget's account of young children's theories or the account provided by core knowledge theories?

Test Yourself

Recall

1. The term _____ refers to modification of schemes based on experience.

2. According to Piaget, _____ are psychological structures that organize experience.

3. Piaget believed that infants' understanding of objects could be summarized as _____.

4. By 18 months, most infants talk and gesture, which shows that they have the capacity _____.

5. One criticism of Piaget's theory is that it underestimates cognitive competence in _____.

6. Most 4-year-olds know that living things _____, have internal parts, resemble their parents, and heal when injured.

Interpret

- Piaget championed the view that children participate actively in their development. How do the sensorimotor child's contributions differ from the formal operational child's contributions?

- In Chapter 3, we traced the development of sensory, perceptual, and motor processes during infancy. How do those descriptions compare with Piaget's view of the sensorimotor period?

Apply

- Based on what you know about Piaget's theory, what would his position have been on the continuity–discontinuity issue discussed in Chapter 1?

- Children with low birth weight often have delayed intellectual development. As a health care professional, use Piaget's theory to describe the kinds of delays that might be expected.

Recall answers: (1) accommodation, (2) schemes, (3) "out of sight, out of existence," (4) to use symbols, (5) infants and young children, (6) grow

LEARNING OBJECTIVES

- What is the basis of the information-processing approach?
- How well do young children pay attention?
- What kinds of learning take place during infancy?

- Do infants and preschool children remember?
- What do infants and preschoolers know about numbers?

Infants (and older children) pay attention to loud stimuli at first but then ignore them if they aren't interesting or dangerous.

© Liu Jin/AFP/Getty Images

When Claire, a bubbly 3-year-old, is asked how old she'll be on her next birthday, she proudly says, "Four!" while holding up five fingers. Asked to count four objects, Claire almost always says, "1, 2, 6, 7. SEVEN!" Claire's older brothers find this funny, but her mother thinks that, obvious mistakes notwithstanding, Claire's behavior shows that she knows a lot about numbers and counting. But what, exactly, does Claire understand? That question has her mother stumped.

Today, many developmentalists borrow from computer science to formulate their ideas about human thinking and how it develops (Kail & Bisanz, 1992; Plunkett, 1996). As you should recall from Chapter 1, this approach is called information processing. In this section, we'll see what information processing has revealed about young children's thinking and, along the way, see what to make of Claire's counting.

General Principles of Information Processing

In the information-processing view, human thinking is based on both mental hardware and mental software. **Mental hardware** *refers to mental and neural structures that are built in and that allow the mind to operate.* **Mental software** *refers to mental "programs" that are the basis for performing particular tasks.* According to information-processing psychologists, as children develop, their mental software and mental hardware become more complex, more powerful, and more efficient.

In the next few pages, we look at the development of information-processing skills, beginning with attention.

Attention

mental hardware
mental and neural structures that are built in and that allow the mind to operate

mental software
mental "programs" that are the basis for performing particular tasks

attention
processes that determine which information is processed further by an individual

orienting response
an individual views a strong or unfamiliar stimulus, and changes in heart rate and brain-wave activity occur

habituation
becoming unresponsive to a stimulus that is presented repeatedly

Hannah was only 3-days-old and was often startled by the sounds of traffic outside her family's apartment. Hannah's parents worried that she might not get enough sleep. Yet within a few days, traffic sounds no longer disturbed Hannah; she slept blissfully. Why did traffic noise no longer bother her? *The key is* **attention**, *a process that determines which sensory information receives additional cognitive processing.*

Hannah's response was typical for infants, as well as for children and adolescents. *When presented with a strong or unfamiliar stimulus, an* **orienting response** *usually occurs: A person startles, fixes the eyes on the stimulus, and shows changes in heart rate and brain-wave activity.* Collectively, these responses indicate that the infant has noticed the stimulus. After repeated presentations of a stimulus, people recognize it as familiar, and the orienting response gradually disappears. **Habituation** *is the diminished response to a stimulus as it becomes more familiar.*

The orienting response and habituation are both useful to infants. Orienting makes infants aware of potentially important or dangerous events in the environment. Habituation keeps infants like Hannah from devoting too much energy to biologically nonsignificant events (Rovee-Collier, 1987).

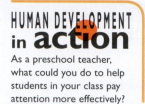
Preschool children gradually learn how to focus their attention but are more easily distracted by extraneous information than are older children and adults (Hatania & Smith, 2010). However, we can help children pay attention better. One straightforward approach is to make relevant information stand out. For example, closing a classroom door may not eliminate competing sounds and smells, but it makes them less noticeable. When preschoolers are working at a table or desk, we can remove objects that aren't needed. Another useful tactic is to remind children to pay attention to relevant information and to ignore the rest.

Learning

Infants are always learning. This learning can take several forms, including the just-discussed form of habituation, as well as classical conditioning, operant conditioning, and imitation.

Classical Conditioning

In **classical conditioning**, *a neutral stimulus elicits a response that was originally produced by another stimulus.* For example, infants suck reflexively when sugar water is placed in their mouth with a dropper; if a tone precedes the drops of sugar water, infants suck when they hear the tone (Lipsitt, 1990). The tone has been conditioned to produce sucking.

Classical conditioning is important because it gives infants a sense of order in their environment. Through classical conditioning, infants learn that a stimulus is a signal for what will happen next. A youngster may smile when she hears the family dog's collar because she knows the dog is coming to play with her. Or a toddler may frown when he hears water running in the bathroom because he realizes this means it's time for a bath.

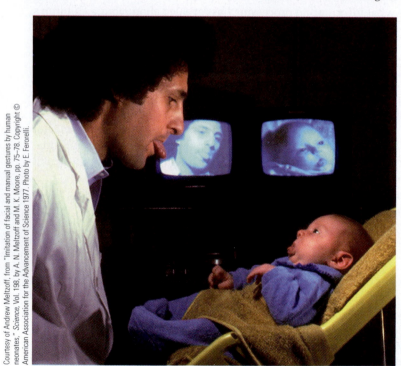

Courtesy of Andrew Meltzoff, from "Imitation of facial and manual gestures by human neonates," *Science*, Vol. 198, by A. N. Meltzoff and M. K. Moore, pp. 75–78. Copyright © American Association for the Advancement of Science 1977. Photo by E. Ferorelli.

Newborns imitate an adult's facial expressions.

Operant Conditioning

Operant conditioning *focuses on the relation between the consequences of behavior and the likelihood that the behavior will recur.* When a child's behavior leads to pleasant consequences, the child will probably behave similarly in the future; when the child's behavior leads to unpleasant consequences, the child will probably not repeat the behavior. When a baby smiles, an adult may hug the baby in return; this pleasing consequence makes the baby more likely to smile in the future. When a baby grabs a family heirloom, an adult may become angry and shout at the baby; these unpleasant consequences make the baby less likely to grab the heirloom in the future.

Imitation

Older children, adolescents, and young adults learn much simply by watching others behave. For example, children learn new sports moves by watching professional athletes, they learn how to pursue romantic relationships by watching TV, and they learn how to play new computer games by watching peers. Infants also are capable of imitation (Barr & Hayne, 1999). A 10-month-old may imitate an adult waving a finger back and forth or imitate another infant who knocks down a tower of blocks.

Even newborns imitate. Meltzoff and Moore (1989, 1994) found that 2- to 3-week-olds would stick out their tongue or open and close their mouth to match an adult's acts. Because the newborns' behavior is not novel—newborns are already capable of sticking out their tongue, as well as opening and closing their mouth—some researchers do not

classical conditioning
a form of learning that involves pairing a neutral stimulus and a response originally produced by another stimulus

operant conditioning
a form of learning in which reward and punishment determine the likelihood that a behavior will recur

consider this to be a "true" form of imitation (Anisfeld, 1991, 1996). This work may well be describing an early, limited form of imitation; over the course of the first year of life, infants are able to imitate a rapidly expanding range of behaviors.

Memory

Young babies remember events for days or even weeks at a time. To illustrate, if a ribbon from a mobile is attached to a 2- or 3-month-old's leg, the baby learns to kick to make the mobile move (Rovee-Collier, 1997, 1999). If the experimenter returns with the mobile a few days later, the infant still kicks. But if the experimenter returns several weeks later, the baby no longer kicks. However, reminding a baby—by moving the mobile without attaching the ribbon to the baby's foot—causes it to kick on its own. These experiments show three important features of memory in young babies: (1) an event from the past (kicking makes the mobile move) is remembered; (2) over time, the event is no longer recalled; and (3) a cue prompts a memory that seems to have been forgotten.

Memory improves rapidly in older infants and toddlers. Youngsters recall more of what they experience and remember it longer (Bauer & Lukowski, 2010; Pelphrey et al., 2004). These improvements in memory can be traced, in part, to growth in the brain regions that support memory (Bauer, 2007; Richmond & Nelson, 2007). On the one hand, the brain structures primarily responsible for the initial storage of information, including the hippocampus and amygdala, seem to develop early—by 6 months of age. On the other hand, the structure responsible for retrieving these stored memories, the prefrontal cortex, develops much later—into the 2nd year. Development of memory during the first 2 years therefore reflects growth in these two brain regions, shown in Figure 4.4.

FIGURE 4.4
The amygdala, hippocampus, and prefrontal cortex are brain structures that support memory.

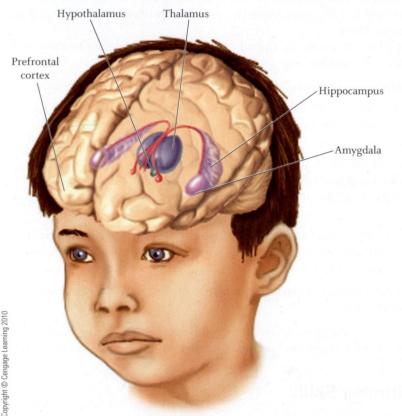

Hypothalamus   Thalamus

Prefrontal cortex

Hippocampus

Amygdala

autobiographical memory
memories of the significant events and experiences of someone's own life

Autobiographical Memory

Autobiographical memory *refers to people's memory of the significant events and experiences of their own lives.* Autobiographical memory is involved when you remember the name of your fourth-grade teacher or how you spent the summer after high-school graduation. Autobiographical memory is important because it helps people construct a personal life history and allows people to relate their experiences to others, creating socially shared memories (Bauer, 2006).

Autobiographical memory originates in the preschool years. According to one view (Fivush, 2011), autobiographical memory emerges gradually as children acquire some key skills. Infants and toddlers have the basic memory skills that enable them to remember past events. Layered on top of these memory skills during the preschool years are language skills and a child's sense of self. Language allows children to become conversational partners. After infants begin to talk, parents often converse with them about past and future events, particularly about personal experiences in their past and future. Parents may talk about what a child did today at day care or remind the child about what he or she will be doing during the coming weekend. Such conversations teach children the important features of events and how they are organized (Fivush, Reese, & Haden, 2006). Children's autobiographical memories are richer when parents talk about past events in detail and specifically when they encourage children to expand their description of past events by, for example, using open-ended questions (e.g., "Where did Mommy go last night?"). When parents use this conversational style

When parents talk with children about past or future events, this fosters their children's autobiographical memory.

with their preschool children, they have as young adolescents earlier memories of childhood (Jack et al., 2009).

How does an emergent sense of self contribute to autobiographical memory? During the first 2 years, infants rapidly acquire a sense that they exist independently in space and time. An emerging sense of self provides coherence and continuity to children's experience. Children realize that the self who went to the park a few days ago is the same self who is now at a birthday party and is the same self who will read a book with Dad before bedtime. The self provides a personal timeline and anchors a child's recall of the past (and anticipation of the future). In sum, a sense of self, language skills that enable children to converse with parents about past and future, and basic memory skills all contribute to the emergence of autobiographical memory in preschool children.

Preschoolers as Eyewitnesses

Research on children's autobiographical memory has played a central role in cases of suspected child abuse. When abuse is suspected, the victim is usually the sole witness. Consequently, to prosecute the alleged abuser, the child's testimony is needed. But preschoolers do not always provide reliable testimony, because they are particularly suggestible. When recalling past events, preschoolers are often confused about who did or said what; they frequently assume that they must have experienced something personally. Consequently, when preschool children are asked leading questions (e.g., "When the man touched you, did it hurt?"), this information is also stored in memory but without the source of the information. Because preschool children are not skilled at monitoring sources of information, they have trouble distinguishing what they actually experienced from what interviewers imply that they experienced (Ghetti, 2008).

Although preschoolers are easily misled, they can provide reliable testimony if interviewers follow these guidelines:

- Interview children as soon as possible after the event.

- Encourage children to tell the truth, to feel free to say "I don't know," and to correct interviewers when they say something that's incorrect.

- Start by asking children to describe the event in their own words ("Tell me what happened after school."), follow up with open-ended questions ("Can you tell me more about what happened while you were walking home?"), and minimize the use of specific questions (because they may suggest to children events that did not happen).

- Allow children to understand and feel comfortable in the interview format by beginning with a neutral event (e.g., a birthday party or holiday celebration) before moving to the event of interest.

- Ask questions that consider alternate explanations of the event (i.e., explanations that don't involve abuse).

Following guidelines like these fosters the conditions that lead young children to recall past events more accurately and thereby be better witnesses (Lamb et al., 2007).

Learning Number Skills

Powerful learning and memory skills allow infants and preschoolers to learn much about their worlds. This rapid growth is well illustrated by research on children's understanding of the concept of number. By five months, babies can distinguish two

FIGURE 4.5

FIGURE 4.5
Infants are surprised when they see objects added or removed but the original number of objects are still present when the screen is removed; this pattern suggests some basic understanding of addition and subtraction.

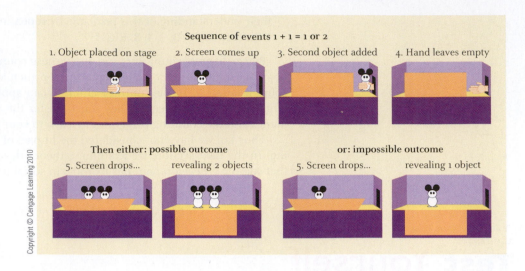

Copyright © Cengage Learning 2010

Sequence of events 1 + 1 = 1 or 2

1. Object placed on stage   2. Screen comes up   3. Second object added   4. Hand leaves empty

Then either: possible outcome

5. Screen drops...   revealing 2 objects

or: impossible outcome

5. Screen drops...   revealing 1 object

© Alan Oddie/PhotoEdit

By age 5, children have mastered the three counting principles and can apply them to large sets of objects.

objects from three and three objects from four (Cordes & Brannon, 2009; Wynn, 1996). Apparently, infants' perceptual processes enable them to distinguish differences in quantity. That is, just as colors (reds and blues) and shapes (triangles and squares) are basic perceptual properties, small quantities ("twoness" and "threeness") are as well.

What's more impressive, young babies can perform simple addition and subtraction. In experiments using the method shown in Figure 4.5, infants view a stage with one mouse. A screen hides the mouse, and then a hand appears with a second mouse, which is placed behind the screen. When the screen is removed, 5-month-olds look longer when this reveals one mouse than when two mice appear. Apparently, 5-month-olds expect that one mouse plus another mouse should equal two mice, and they look longer when this expectancy is violated (Wynn, 1992). Likewise, when the stage first has two mice and one of them is removed, infants are surprised when the screen is removed and two mice are still on the stage. These experiments only work with very small numbers, indicating that the means by which infants add and subtract are quite simple and not like the processes that older children use (Mix, Huttenlocher, & Levine, 2002).

Learning to Count

By 2 years of age, most youngsters know some number words and have begun to count. This counting, however, is usually full of mistakes. They might count "1, 2, 6, 7"—skipping 3, 4, and 5. Nevertheless, such counting reflects mastery of three basic principles of counting (Gelman & Meck, 1986):

one-to-one principle
a counting principle that states that there must be one and only one number name for each object counted

stable-order principle
a counting principle that states that number names must always be counted in the same order

cardinality principle
a counting principle in which the last number name denotes the number of objects being counted

- **One-to-one principle**. *There must be one and only one number name for each object that is counted.* A child who counts three objects as "1, 2, A" understands this principle, because the number of names matches the number of objects to be counted, even though the third name is a letter.

- **Stable-order principle**. *Number names must be counted in the same order.* A child who counts in the same sequence—for example, consistently counting four objects as "1, 2, 4, 5"—shows understanding of this principle.

- **Cardinality principle**. *The last number name differs from the previous ones in a counting sequence by denoting the number of objects.* Typically, 3-year-olds reveal

their understanding of this principle by repeating the last number name, often with emphasis: "1, 2, 4, 8. EIGHT!"

By age 5, most youngsters can apply these counting principles to as many as nine objects. Children's understanding of these principles does not mean that they always count accurately. To the contrary, children can apply all these principles consistently while counting incorrectly. They must master the conventional sequence of number names and the counting principles to learn to count accurately.

Thus far, we have not considered the impact of social context on children's thinking. In the next section, we examine a theory developed by Vygotsky, who believed that cognitive development has its roots in social interactions.

Test Yourself

Recall

1. One way to improve preschool children's attention is to make irrelevant stimuli _____ .

2. Four-month-old Tanya has forgotten that kicking moves a mobile. To remind her of the link between kicking and the mobile's movement, we could _____ .

3. Preschoolers may be particularly suggestible because they are less skilled at _____ .

4. When a child who is counting a set of objects repeats the last number, usually with emphasis, this indicates the child's understanding of the _____ principle of counting.

Interpret

- Do the developmental mechanisms in the information-processing perspective emphasize nature, nurture, or both? How?

- What roles might classical conditioning, operant conditioning, and imitation have in creating emotional bonds between infants and their parents?

Apply

- What should law-enforcement officials do to obtain reliable testimony from young children?

- Return to Claire, the 3-year-old in the vignette on page 103. What counting principles does she seem to have mastered?

Recall answers: (1) less noticeable, (2) let her view a moving mobile, (3) monitoring the sources of their memories, (4) cardinality

---

4.3 Mind and Culture: Vygotsky's Theory

LEARNING OBJECTIVES

- What is the zone of proximal development?

- Why is scaffolding a particularly effective way of teaching youngsters new concepts and skills?

- Why do children talk to themselves as they solve problems?

Victoria, a 4-year-old, enjoys solving jigsaw puzzles, coloring, and building towers with blocks. While busy with these activities, she often talks to herself. For example, as she was coloring a picture, she said, "Where's the red crayon? Stay inside the lines. Color the blocks blue." These remarks were not directed at anyone else; after all, Victoria was alone. Why did she say these things? What purpose did they serve?

Human development is often described as a journey that takes people along many paths. For Piaget and for information-processing psychologists, children make the journey alone. Other people (and culture in general) influence the direction that children take, but fundamentally the child is a solitary adventurer–explorer, boldly forging ahead. Vygotsky, a Russian psychologist, proposed a different account: Development is an apprenticeship in which children advance when they collaborate with others who are more skilled. According to Vygotsky (1934/1986), children make little headway on the developmental path when they walk alone; they progress when they walk hand in hand with an expert partner.

Vygotsky died of tuberculosis at the age of 37, so he never had the opportunity to provide a complete theory of cognitive development throughout childhood and adolescence (as Piaget did) or explain cognitive change in specific domains (as information-processing theorists do). However, many of his ideas are influential, largely because they fill in some gaps in the Piagetian and information-processing accounts. In the next few pages, we look at three of Vygotsky's most important contributions—the zone of proximal development, scaffolding, and private speech—and learn more about why Victoria talks to herself.

Young children can often accomplish far more with some adult guidance than they can accomplish alone; Vygotsky referred to this difference as the zone of proximal development.

© John Birdsall/The Image Works

The Zone of Proximal Development

Four-year-old Ian and his father often solve puzzles together. Although Ian does most of the work, his father encourages him, sometimes finds a piece that he needs, or shows Ian how to put parts together. When Ian tries to assemble the same puzzles by himself, he can rarely complete them. *The difference between what Ian can do with assistance and what he does alone defines his* **zone of proximal development**. That is, the zone is the area between the level of performance a child can achieve when working independently and a higher level of performance that is possible when working under the guidance of more skilled adults or peers (Wertsch & Tulviste, 1992). For example, elementary-school children are often asked to solve arithmetic story problems. Many youngsters have trouble with these problems, often because they simply don't know where to begin. By structuring the task for them—"first decide what you're supposed to figure out, then decide what information you're told in the problem"—teachers can help children accomplish what they cannot do by themselves. Thus, just as training wheels help children learn to ride a bike by allowing them to concentrate on certain aspects of bicycling, collaborators help children perform more effectively by providing structure, hints, and reminders.

The idea of a zone of proximal development follows naturally from Vygotsky's basic premise: Cognition develops first in a social setting and only gradually comes under the child's independent control. What factors aid this shift? This leads us to the second of Vygotsky's key contributions.

Scaffolding

zone of proximal development
the difference between what children can do with assistance and what they can do alone

scaffolding
a style in which teachers gauge the amount of assistance they offer to match the learner's needs

Master teachers often seem to know exactly when to offer help but otherwise let students work uninterrupted. **Scaffolding** *is a style in which teachers gauge the amount of assistance they offer to match the learner's needs.* Early in learning a new task, children know little, so teachers give much direct instruction about how to do a task. As the children catch on, teachers need to provide less direct instruction; they are more likely to be giving reminders.

Worldwide, parents attempt to scaffold their children's learning, but not always using the same methods. For example, mothers in the United States rely primarily on verbal instruction. Mothers in India and Guatemala use verbal instruction too, but they also rely on touches (e.g., nudging a child's elbow) or gaze (e.g., winking or staring) to guide their youngsters (Rogoff et al., 1993).

The defining characteristic of scaffolding—giving help but not more than is needed—clearly promotes learning (Cole, 2006). Youngsters do not learn readily when they are constantly told what to do or when they are simply left to struggle through a problem unaided. However, when teachers collaborate with them, allowing children to take on more of a task as they master its elements, they learn more effectively (van de Pol, Volman, & Beishuizen, 2010).

Carlos Caetano/Shutterstock.com

Young children often regulate their own behavior by talking to themselves.

private speech
a child's comments that are not intended for others but are designed instead to help regulate the child's behavior

Private Speech

Remember Victoria, the 4-year-old in the vignette who talked to herself as she colored? *Her behavior demonstrates* **private speech**: *comments that are not intended for others but are designed to help children regulate their own behavior* (Vygotsky, 1934/1986). Thus, Victoria's remarks are simply an effort to help herself color the picture.

Vygotsky viewed private speech as an intermediate step toward self-regulation of cognitive skills (Fernyhough, 2010). At first, children's behavior is regulated by speech from other people that is directed toward them. When youngsters first try to control their own behavior and thoughts without others present, they instruct themselves by speaking aloud. Private speech seems to be children's way of guiding themselves, of making sure that they do all required steps in solving a problem. Finally, as children gain ever greater skill, private speech becomes inner speech, which was Vygotsky's term for thought.

Thus, Vygotsky's work has characterized cognitive development not as a solitary undertaking but as a collaboration between expert and novice. His work reminds us of the importance of language, which we examine in detail in the last section of this chapter.

Test Yourself

Recall

1. The _____ is the difference between the level of performance youngsters can achieve with assistance and the level they can achieve alone.

2. The term _____ refers to a style in which teachers adjust their assistance to match a child's needs.

3. According to Vygotsky, _____ is an intermediate step between speech from others and inner speech.

Interpret

• How would scaffolding that's appropriate for infants differ from the scaffolding that's appropriate for preschool children?

• Vygotsky emphasized cognitive development as collaboration. How could such collaboration be included in Piaget's theory? In information processing?

Apply

• How would an information-processing psychologist explain why Ian (page 109) is more successful solving puzzles when his dad helps?

• How might a teacher explain the benefits of scaffolding to parents who think their child will learn more quickly if forced to do his homework entirely on his own?

Recall answers: (1) zone of proximal development, (2) scaffolding, (3) private speech

LEARNING OBJECTIVES

- When do infants first hear and make speech sounds?
- How do children learn new words and word meanings?
- How do young children learn grammar?
- How well do youngsters communicate?

Nabina is few weeks away from her first birthday. For the past month, she has seemed to understand much of her mother's speech. If her mom asks, "Where's Garfield?" (the family cat), Nabina scans the room and points toward Garfield. Yet Nabina's own speech is still gibberish: She "talks" constantly, but her mom can't understand a word of it. If Nabina apparently understands others' speech, why can't she speak herself?

An extraordinary human achievement occurs soon after the first birthday: Most children speak their first word, which is followed in the ensuing months by hundreds more. In reality, the first spoken words represent the climax of a year's worth of language growth. To tell the story of language acquisition properly and explain Nabina's seemingly strange behavior, we must begin with the months preceding the first words.

The Road to Speech

Perceiving Speech

Even newborn infants hear remarkably well (page 80) and the left hemisphere of a newborn's brain is sensitive to language (page 73). More importantly, infants can distinguish basic speech sounds. *The basic building blocks of language are* **phonemes**, *unique sounds that can be joined to create words.* Phonemes include consonant sounds, such as the sound of *t* in *toe* and *tap*, along with vowel sounds, such as the sound of *e* in *get* and *bed*. Infants can distinguish many of these sounds, differentiating some of them as early as 1 month after birth (Aslin, Jusczyk, & Pisoni, 1998).

THE IMPACT OF LANGUAGE EXPOSURE. Not all languages use the same set of phonemes; a distinction important in one language may be ignored in another. For example, French and Polish (unlike English) differentiate between nasal and nonnasal vowels. To hear the difference, say the word *rod*. Now repeat it, but holding your nose. The subtle difference between the two sounds illustrates a nonnasal vowel (the first version of *rod*) and a nasal one (the second version).

Because an infant might be exposed to any of the world's languages, it would be adaptive for young infants to be able to perceive a range of phonemes. Research shows that infants can distinguish phonemes that are not used in their native language. For example, Japanese does not distinguish the consonant sound of *r* in *rip* from the sound of *l* in *lip*, and Japanese adults trying to learn English have difficulty distinguishing these sounds. At about 6 to 8 months, Japanese and American infants distinguish these sounds equally well. However, by 10 to 12 months, perception of *r* and *l* improves for American infants—presumably because they hear these sounds frequently—but declines for Japanese babies (Kuhl et al., 2006).

Newborns apparently are biologically capable of hearing the entire range of phonemes in all languages worldwide, but as babies are more exposed to a particular language, they begin to notice only the linguistic distinctions that are meaningful in their own language (Maye, Weiss, & Aslin, 2008). Thus, specializing in one language apparently comes at the cost of making it more difficult to hear sounds in other languages

phonemes
unique sounds used to create words, making them the basic building blocks of language

(Best, 1995). In other words, just as greater exposure to human faces leads to a more refined notion of a human face (pages 82–84), exposure to language leads infants to a more refined notion of sounds that are important in their environment.

IDENTIFYING WORDS. Hearing individual phonemes is only the first step in perceiving speech. Infants need to identify recurring patterns of sounds—words. Imagine, for example, an infant overhearing this conversation between a parent and an older sibling:

Sibling: Jerry got a new *bike*.
Parent: Was his old *bike* broken?
Sibling: No. He saved his allowance to buy a new mountain *bike*.

When mothers and other adults talk to young children, they often use infant-directed speech, in which they speak slowly and with exaggerated changes in pitch and loudness.

An infant listening to this conversation hears *bike* three times. Can the infant learn from this experience? Yes. When 7- to 8-month-olds hear a word repeatedly in different sentences, they later pay more attention to this word than to words they haven't heard previously. Evidently, 7- and 8-month-olds can listen to sentences and recognize the sound patterns that they hear repeatedly (Houston & Jusczyk, 2003; Saffran, Aslin, & Newport, 1996).

In normal conversation, there are no silent gaps between words, so how do infants pick out words? Stress is one important clue. English contains many one-syllable words that are stressed and many two-syllable words that have a stressed syllable followed by an unstressed syllable (e.g., *dough'-nut, tooth'-paste, bas'-ket*). Infants pay more attention to stressed syllables than to unstressed syllables, which is a good strategy for identifying the beginnings of words (Mattys et al., 1999; Thiessen & Saffran, 2003). And infants learn words more readily when they appear at the beginning and end of sentences, probably because the brief pause between sentences makes it easier to identify first and last words (Seidl & Johnson, 2006).

Stress is not a foolproof sign. Many two-syllable words have stress on the second syllable (e.g., *gui-tar, sur-prise*), so infants need other methods to identify words in speech. One method is statistical. Infants notice syllables that go together frequently (Jusczyk, 2002). For example, in many studies, 8-month-olds heard the following sounds, which consisted of four three-syllable artificial words, said repeatedly in random order:

pa bi ku   go la tu   da ro pi   ti bu do   da ro pi   go la tu   pa bi ku   da ro pi . . .

We've underlined the words and inserted gaps between them so that you can see them more easily, but in the studies there were no breaks—just a steady flow of syllables for 3 minutes. Later, infants listened to these words less than to new words that were novel combinations of the same syllables. They had detected *pa bi ku, go la tu, da ro pi,* and *ti bu do* as familiar words because those syllables appeared together repeatedly (Aslin, Saffran, & Newport, 1998; Pelucci, Hay, & Saffran, 2009).

Parents (and other adults) often help infants master language sounds by talking in a distinctive style. *In* **infant-directed speech***, adults speak slowly and with exaggerated changes in pitch and loudness.* Adults speaking to infants often alternate between speaking softly and loudly and between high and low pitches, and their speech seems emotionally expressive (Liu, Tsao, & Kuhl, 2007; Trainor, Austin, & Desjardins, 2000).

Infant-directed speech may attract infants' attention because its slower pace and accentuated changes provide infants with more (and more salient) language clues (Cristia, 2010; Zhang et al., 2011). For example, infants can segment words more effectively when they hear them in infant-directed speech (Thiessen, Hill, & Saffran, 2005). In addition, infant-directed speech includes especially good examples of vowels (Kuhl et al., 1997), which may help infants learn to distinguish these sounds.

infant-directed speech
speech that adults use with infants that is slow, has exaggerated changes in pitch and volume, and is thought to aid language acquisition

Steps to Speech

Newborns and young babies make many sounds—they cry, burp, and sneeze. Language-based sounds don't appear immediately. *At 2 months, infants begin to produce vowel-like sounds, such as "ooooooo" or "ahhhhhh," a phenomenon known as* **cooing**. Sometimes infants become quite excited as they coo, perhaps reflecting the joy of simply playing with sounds.

After cooing comes **babbling**, *speechlike sounds that have no meaning*. A typical 6-month-old might say "dah" or "bah," utterances that sound like a single syllable consisting of a consonant and a vowel. Over the next few months, babbling becomes more elaborate as babies experiment with more complex speech sounds. Older infants sometimes repeat a sound, as in "bahbahbah," and begin to combine different sounds, such as "dahmahbah" (Hoff, 2009).

Babbling is not just mindless playing with sounds; it is a precursor to real speech. For example, at roughly 8 to 11 months, infants' babbling sounds more like real speech because infants stress some syllables and vary the pitch of their speech (Snow, 2006). In English declarative sentences, for example, pitch first rises and then falls toward the end of the sentence. In questions, however, the pitch is level and then rises toward the end of the question. Older babies' babbling reflects these patterns: Babies who are brought up by English-speaking parents have both the declarative and the question patterns of intonation in their babbling. Babies exposed to a language with different patterns of intonation, such as Japanese or French, reflect their language's intonation in their babbling (Levitt & Utman, 1992).

First Words and Many More

Recall that Nabina, the 1-year-old in the vignette, looks at the family cat when she hears its name. This phenomenon is common in 10- to 14-month-olds. They appear to understand what others say, even though their own speech is limited to advanced babbling (Fenson et al., 1994; Hoff-Ginsberg, 1997). Evidently, children have made the link between speech sounds and particular objects, even though they cannot yet manufacture the sounds themselves.

A few months later, most youngsters utter their first words. In many languages, those words are similar (Nelson, 1973; Tardif et al., 2008) and include terms for mother and father, greetings (*Hi, bye-bye*) as well as foods and toys (*juice, ball*). By age 2, most youngsters have a vocabulary of a few hundred words, and by age 6, a typical child's vocabulary includes more than 10,000 words (Bloom, 1998).

The Grand Insight: Words as Symbols

To make the transition from babbling to real speech, infants need to learn that particular sounds form words that can refer to objects, actions, and properties. Put another way, infants must recognize that words are symbols—entities that stand for other entities. Soon after the first birthday, children have formed concepts such as "round, bouncy things" or "furry things that bark" based on their experiences. With the insight that speech sounds can denote these concepts, infants begin to identify a word that goes with each concept (Reich, 1986).

Children use symbols in other areas, not just in language. Gestures are symbols, and infants begin to gesture shortly before their first birthday (Goodwyn & Acredolo, 1993). Young children may smack their lips to indicate hunger or wave "bye-bye" when leaving. In these cases, gestures and words convey a message equally well.

What's What? Fast Mapping of Words

After children develop the insight that a word can symbolize an object or action, their vocabularies grow, slowly at first. A typical 15-month-old, for example, may learn two to three new words each week. However, at about 18 months, many children experience a naming explosion during which they learn new words more rapidly than before. Children now learn 10 or more new words each week (Fenson et al., 1994; McMurray, 2007).

cooing
early vowel-like sounds that babies produce

babbling
speechlike sounds that consist of vowel–consonant combinations and are common at about 6 months

One of the challenges for theories of language learning is to explain how children figure out that the parent's words refer to the object, not to its color or texture.

Most youngsters learn the proper meanings of simple words in just a few presentations, which is surprising because most words have many plausible meanings. *Children's ability to connect new words to referents so rapidly that they cannot be considering all possible meanings for the new word is termed* **fast mapping**. How can young children learn new words so rapidly? Many factors contribute (Hollich, Hirsh-Pasek, & Golinkoff, 2000).

JOINT ATTENTION. Parents encourage word learning by carefully watching what interests their children. When toddlers touch or look at an object, parents often label it for them. When a youngster points to a banana, a parent may say, "Banana, that's a banana." Toddlers are more likely to learn the name of an object or action when adults look at the object or action while saying its name (Liebal et al., 2009; Nurmsoo & Bloom, 2008). Thus, beginning in the toddler years, parents and children work together to create conditions that foster word learning: Parents label objects, and youngsters rely on adults' behavior to interpret the words they hear.

CONSTRAINTS ON WORD NAMES. Joint attention simplifies word learning for children, but the problem remains: How do toddlers know that *banana* refers to the object that they're touching, as opposed to their activity (touching) or to the object's color (yellow)? Young children follow several simple rules that limit their conclusions about what labels mean. A study by Au and Glusman (1990) shows how researchers have identified these rules. Preschoolers were shown a stuffed animal with pink horns that otherwise resembled a monkey and the experimenter called it a "mido." "Mido" was then repeated several times, always referring to the stuffed animal with pink horns. Later, these youngsters were asked to find a *theri* in a set of stuffed animals that included several *mido*. Children never picked a *mido;* instead, they selected other stuffed animals. Knowing that *mido* referred to monkeylike animals with pink horns, they decided that *theri* must refer to a different stuffed animal.

Apparently children were following this simple rule for learning new words:

■ If an unfamiliar word is heard in the presence of objects that already have names and objects that don't, the word refers to one of the objects that doesn't have a name.

Children use several other simple rules to identify word meanings (Hoff, 2009; Woodward & Markman, 1998):

■ A name refers to a whole object, not its parts or its relation to other objects, and refers not just to this particular object but to all objects of the same type (Wu, Mareschal, & Rakison, 2011). When a grandparent points to a stuffed animal and says "dinosaur," children conclude that *dinosaur* refers to the entire dinosaur, not just its ears or nose, and not to this specific dinosaur but to all dinosaurlike objects.

■ If an object already has a name and another name is presented, the new name denotes a subcategory of the original name. If the child who knows the meaning of *dinosaur* sees a brother point to another dinosaur and hears the brother say "T. rex," the child will conclude that *T. rex* is a special type of dinosaur.

■ Given many similar category members, a word applied consistently to only one of them is a proper noun. If a child who knows *dinosaur* sees that one of a group of dinosaurs is always called "Dino," the child will conclude that *Dino* is the dinosaur's name.

fast mapping

a child's connections between words and referents that are made so quickly that he or she cannot consider all possible meanings of the word

Rules like these make it possible for children like Nabina, the child in the vignette, to learn words rapidly, because they reduce the number of possible referents. A child being shown a flower follows these rules to decide that *flower* refers to the entire object, not its parts or the action of pointing to it.

SENTENCE CUES. Sentences also provide helpful clues to a word's meaning (Yuan & Fisher, 2009). For example, when a parent describes an event using familiar words but an unfamiliar verb, children often infer that the verb refers to the action performed by the subject of the sentence (Fisher, 1996; Woodward & Markman, 1998). When youngsters hear, "The man is juggling," they infer that *juggling* refers to the man's actions with the bowling pins, because they already know *man* and because *-ing* refers to ongoing actions.

COGNITIVE FACTORS. The naming explosion coincides with a time of rapid cognitive growth, and children's increased cognitive skill helps them learn new words. As children's thinking becomes more sophisticated and, in particular, as they start to have goals and intentions, language becomes a means to express those goals and to achieve them. Thus, intention provides children with an important motive to learn language—to help achieve their goals (Bloom & Tinker, 2001).

In addition, young children's improving attentional and perceptual skills promote word learning. Infants and young children spontaneously pay attention to an object's shape, and this helps them learn new words (Smith, 2000, 2009). Children first associate names with a single object: for example, *cup* is associated with a favorite sippy cup. As children encounter new cups, they hear the same words applied to similarly shaped objects and reach the conclusion that cups are cylinders with handles. With further experience, children derive an even more general rule: Objects that have the same shape have the same name. From this, children realize that paying attention to shape is an easy way to learn names. Consistent with this theory, the shape bias and the naming explosion typically occur at about the same time (Gershkoff-Stowe & Smith, 2004).

DEVELOPMENTAL CHANGE IN WORD LEARNING. Some of the word-learning tools described in the past few pages are particularly important at different ages (Hirsh-Pasek & Golinkoff, 2008). Before 18 months, children rely heavily on simple attentional processes (e.g., shape) to learn new words. But by 24 months, children also use language cues (e.g., constraints on names) and a speaker's social cues. At any age, infants and toddlers rely on a mixture of word-learning tools, but with age they gradually move away from attentional cues to language and social cues.

NAMING ERRORS. These rules for learning new words are not perfect; initial mappings of words onto meanings are often only partially correct (Hoff & Naigles, 2002). *A common mistake is* **underextension**, *defining a word too narrowly.* Using *car* to refer only to the family car and *ball* to a favorite toy ball are examples of underextension. *Between 1 and 3 years, children sometimes make the opposite error,* **overextension**, *defining a word too broadly.* Children may use *car* to also refer to buses and trucks or use *doggie* to refer to all four-legged animals.

Individual Differences in Word Learning

BILINGUALISM. Millions of American children grow up in bilingual households; these youngsters usually speak English and another language. When infants learn two languages simultaneously, they often progress somewhat slowly at first. They mix words from the two languages and are less skilled at using language-specific sounds to guide word learning (Fennell, Byers-Heinlein, & Werker, 2007). Soon, however, they separate the languages, and bilingual children reach most language milestones at about the same age as monolingual children (Pettito et al., 2001). When each language is considered separately, bilingual children often have somewhat smaller vocabularies than monolingual children (Umbel et al., 1992). However, because bilingual youngsters often know words in one language but not the other, their total vocabulary (i.e., words known in both languages plus words known in either language but not both) is greater than that of monolingual children.

Being bilingual also has some important advantages. Bilingual children better understand that words are simply arbitrary symbols. Bilingual youngsters, for instance, are more likely than monolingual children to understand that, as long as all English

underextension
when children define words more narrowly than adults do

overextension
when children define words more broadly than adults do

speakers agreed, *dog* could refer to cats and *cat* could refer to dogs (Bialystok, 1988; Campbell & Sais, 1995). And they are more skilled at switching back and forth between tasks and often are better able to inhibit inappropriate responses (Bialystok, 2010; Carlson & Meltzoff, 2008), perhaps reflecting their experience of switching between languages and inhibiting relevant words from the "other" language (e.g., when shown a photo of a dog and asked, "What's this?" preschoolers bilingual in French and English must respond "dog" while suppressing "chien").

WORD-LEARNING STYLES. As youngsters expand their vocabulary, they often adopt a distinctive style of learning language (Bates, Bretherton, & Snyder, 1988; Nelson, 1973). *Some children have a* **referential style***: Their vocabularies mainly consist of words that name objects, people, or actions.* For example, Rachel, a referential child, had 41 name words in her 50-word vocabulary but only 2 words for social interaction or questions. *Other children have an* **expressive style***: Their vocabularies include some names but also many social phrases that are used like a single word, such as "go away," "what'd you want?" and "I want it."* Elizabeth, an expressive child, had a more balanced vocabulary than did Rachel, with 14 words for social interactions and questions and 24 name words.

For children with referential emphasis, language is primarily an intellectual tool: a means of learning and talking about objects (Masur, 1995). In contrast, for children with expressive emphasis, language is more of a social tool: a way of enhancing interactions with others. Both of these functions—intellectual and social—are important functions of language, which explains why most children blend the referential and expressive styles of learning language.

Encouraging Language Growth

For children to expand their vocabularies, they need to hear others speak. Not surprisingly, then, children learn words more rapidly if their parents speak to them frequently (Huttenlocher et al., 1991; Roberts, Burchinal, & Durham, 1999). Sheer quantity of parental speech is not all that matters. Parents can foster word learning by naming objects that are the focus of a child's attention (Dunham, Dunham, & Curwin, 1993). During a walk, parents can label the objects—birds, plants, vehicles, and so on—that the child sees.

Parents are more effective than videos in teaching new words to their children.

referential style
a language-learning style of children whose vocabularies are dominated by names of objects, people, or actions

expressive style
a language-learning style of children whose vocabularies include many social phrases that are used like one word

Parents can also help children learn words by reading books with them, because such reading provides opportunities for children to learn new words. Asking children questions during reading also helps (Sénéchal, Thomas, & Monker, 1995), because it forces children to identify meanings of new words and practice saying them.

Video is a common part of the lives of infants and young children and helps preschoolers learn new words. For example, preschool children who regularly watch *Sesame Street* usually have larger vocabularies than preschoolers who watch *Sesame Street* only occasionally (Wright et al., 2001). Other programs that promote word learning are those that tell a story (e.g., *Thomas the Tank Engine*), as well as programs like *Blue's Clues* and *Dora the Explorer,* which directly ask questions of the viewer. And the benefits of these programs are greatest when preschoolers watch them with adults, in part because the video content becomes the focus of joint attention, as described on page 114. In contrast, most cartoons have no benefit for language learning (Linebarger & Vaala, 2010).

What about videos claiming that they promote word learning in infants? Most evidence suggests that before 18 months of age, infant-oriented videos (e.g., *Baby Einstein, Brainy Baby*) are not effective in promoting infants' word learning (Linebarger & Vaala, 2010). The Spotlight on Research feature describes a study reporting this sort of negative evidence.

Why do baby videos seem to have no benefit for infants' word learning? One reason is that these videos are "poorly designed, insufficient to support language processing,

Do Infants Learn Words From Watching Infant-Oriented Media?

Who were the investigators, and what was the aim of the study?
Although marketing and some testimonials suggest that infants expand their vocabulary from watching infant-oriented video, there's little experimental work on the issue. Consequently, Judy DeLoache and her colleagues (2010) conducted an experiment to determine the impact of exposure to infant-oriented videos on word learning.

How did the investigators measure the topic of interest?
DeLoache et al. created four conditions. In two of them, parents were given a commercially available DVD that was designed to teach new words to young children. The video includes 25 common objects, and each object is labeled three times (e.g., This is a *clock*). In both conditions, infants watched the video at home five times a week for four weeks. However, in one condition, they watched it with a parent; in another condition, they watched it alone (although the parent was usually in the same room). In a third condition, parents were given a list of the 25 words presented in the video and encouraged to teach the words to their infant "in whatever way seems natural to you" (p. 1571) over the same four-week period. Finally, in a control condition, infants were not exposed to the 25 words; instead, they were simply tested at the beginning and the end of the four-week period to determine which words they understood. Infants in the other three conditions were also tested in this manner: Infants were shown a replica of one of the objects shown in the video (e.g., a clock), along with a replica of an object not shown in the video (e.g., a fan); then, the experimenter asked infants to show the target object (e.g., "Can you show me the clock?").

Who were the participants in the study?
DeLoache and her colleagues tested 72 children who were 12 to 18 months old.

What was the design of the study?
This study was experimental: The independent variable was the nature of the infants' exposure to the 25 words in the video (video with parental interaction, video only, parental teaching, or no systematic exposure). The dependent variable was the percentage of times that the infants selected the correct replica. The study was not developmental (12- to 18-month-olds were tested just once), so it was neither cross-sectional nor longitudinal.

Were there ethical concerns with the study?
No. The task posed no danger to the infants.

What were the results?
Infants learned the most words when parents taught them directly. These infants learned about half of the words. In contrast, the infants in the remaining conditions (the two video conditions and the control condition) only learned about one third of the words. In other words, regular daily exposure to the 25 words through the video produced no greater word learning than incidental, casual exposure that took place in the control condition.

What did the investigators conclude?
The findings indicate that the video was ineffective in promoting word learning. In the words of DeLoache et al., "the degree to which babies actually learn from baby videos is negligible" (p. 1573).

What converging evidence would strengthen these conclusions?
DeLoache and her colleagues tested only a single video; extending the work to other DVDs would be useful. In addition, most of the infants came from middle-class homes; it would be important to determine whether these videos have any effectiveness in promoting language for infants from families with lower socioeconomic status.

 Go to Psychology CourseMate at **www.cengagebrain.com** to enhance your understanding of this research.

and developmentally inappropriate" (Linebarger & Vaala, 2010, p. 184). Another reason is that toddlers have difficulty relating what they see in the video to those objects and actions as experienced in their own lives (Troseth, Pierroutsakos, & DeLoache, 2004).

Research on video and on parents' influence points to a simple but powerful conclusion: Children are most likely to learn new words when they participate in activities that force them to understand the meanings of new words and use those new words.

Speaking in Sentences: Grammatical Development

Within months after children say their first words, they form simple two-word sentences. Such sentences are based on "formulas" that children figure out from their experiences (Braine, 1976; Radford, 1995). Armed with a few formulas, children can express an enormous variety of ideas:

Formula	Example
Actor + action	Mommy sleep, Timmy run
Action + object	Gimme cookie, throw ball
Possessor + possession	Kimmy pail, Maya shovel

FIGURE 4.6

When shown these two birds, young children usually refer to them as two *wugs*, spontaneously adding an *-s* to *wug* to make it plural.

Source: Berko, J. (1958). The child's learning of English morphology, Figure 1, pg. 154. Reprinted by permission of the author.

From Two Words to Complex Sentences

Children rapidly move beyond two-word sentences, first doing so by linking two-word statements together: "Rachel kick" and "Kick ball" become "Rachel kick ball." Even longer sentences soon follow; sentences with 10 or more words are common in 3-year-olds' speech. Yet such sentences often fall short of adults' standards of grammar. Youngsters say "He eating" rather than "He is eating" or "two cat" rather than "two cats." *This sort of speech is called* **telegraphic speech** *because like telegrams of days gone by, children's speech includes only words directly relevant to meaning.* A telegram's cost was based on the number of words. Consequently, telegrams were brief and to the point, containing only the important nouns, verbs, adjectives, and adverbs—much like children's two-word speech. *The missing elements,* **grammatical morphemes**, *are words or endings of words (e.g., -ing, -ed, or -s) that make a sentence grammatical.* During the preschool years, children gradually acquire the grammatical morphemes, first mastering those that express simple relations like *-ing*, which is used to denote that the action expressed by the verb is ongoing. More complex forms, such as appropriate use of the various forms of the verb *to be*, are mastered later (Peters, 1995).

Children's growing knowledge of grammatical rules was first demonstrated in a landmark study by Berko (1958), in which preschoolers were shown pictures of nonsense objects like the one in Figure 4.6. The experimenter labeled it, saying, "This is a wug." Then youngsters were shown pictures of two of the objects, and the experimenter said, "These are two . . . ." Most children spontaneously said "wugs." Because both the singular and plural forms of this word were novel for these youngsters, they could have generated the correct plural form only by applying the familiar rule of adding *-s*.

Children growing up in homes where English is spoken face the problem that their native tongue is highly irregular, with many exceptions to the rules. *Sometimes children apply rules to words that are exceptions to the rule, errors called* **overregularizations**. With plurals, for example, youngsters may incorrectly add an *-s* instead of using an irregular plural—two "mans" instead of two "men." With the past tense, children may add *-ed* instead of using an irregular past tense: "I goed home" instead of "I went home" (Marcus et al., 1992; Mervis & Johnson, 1991).

Thus, not only must children learn an extensive set of specific rules, they must also absorb—case by case—all exceptions. Despite the enormity of this task, most children have mastered the basics of their native tongue by the time they enter school. How do they do it? Biological, psychological, and sociocultural forces all contribute.

How Do Children Acquire Grammar?

THE BEHAVIORIST ANSWER. The simplest explanation for learning grammar is that children imitate the grammatical forms they hear. Skinner (1957) and other learning theorists once claimed that all aspects of language—sounds, words, grammar, and communication—are learned through imitation and reinforcement (Moerk, 2000; Whitehurst & Vasta, 1975).

Critics were quick to point to some flaws in this theory. One problem is that most of children's sentences are novel, which is difficult to explain in terms of simple imitation of adults' speech. For example, when children imitate adult sentences, they do not imitate adult grammar. In trying to repeat "I am drawing a picture," young children may say, "I draw picture." And linguists (e.g., Chomsky, 1957, 1995) argued that grammatical rules are far too complex for toddlers and preschoolers to infer them solely on the basis of speech that they hear.

THE LINGUISTIC ANSWER. Many scientists believe that children are born with mechanisms that simplify the task of learning grammar (Slobin, 1985). According to this view, children are born with brain circuits for inferring the grammar of their native language. Grammar itself is not built into the child's nervous system, but processes that guide the learning of grammar are. Many findings indirectly support this view:

■ If children are born with a "grammar-learning processor," then specific regions of the brain should be involved in learning grammar. As we discussed on page 73, the left hemisphere of the brain plays a critical role in understanding language.

telegraphic speech
speech used by young children that contains only words necessary to convey a message

grammatical morphemes
words or endings of words that make a sentence grammatical

overregularizations
grammatical usage that results from applying rules to words that are exceptions to the rule

- If learning grammar depends on specialized neural mechanisms that are unique to humans, then efforts to teach grammar to nonhumans should fail. Indeed, efforts to teach grammar to chimpanzees (the species closest to humans on the evolutionary ladder) show that they master just a handful of grammatical rules governing two-word speech, but only with massive effort that is unlike the preschool child's learning of grammar (Savage-Rumbaugh, 2001; Seyfarth & Cheney, 1996).

- The period from birth to about 12 years is a critical period for acquiring language generally and mastering grammar particularly. If children do not acquire language in this period, they never truly master language later (Newport, 1991; Rymer, 1993).

Although these findings are consistent with the idea that children have innate grammar-learning mechanisms, they do not prove the existence of such mechanisms. Consequently, scientists have continued to look for other explanations.

THE COGNITIVE ANSWER. Some theorists (Braine, 1992) believe that children learn grammar through powerful cognitive skills that help them rapidly detect regularities in their environment, including patterns in the speech they hear. It's as if children establish a huge spreadsheet that has the speech they've heard in one column and the context in which they heard it in another; periodically, they scan the columns looking for recurring patterns (Maratsos, 1998). For example, children might be confused the first time they hear -*s* added to the end of a familiar noun. However, as the database expands to include many instances of familiar nouns with an added -*s*, children discover that -*s* is always added to a noun when there are multiple instances of the object. Thus, they create the rule: noun + -*s* = plural. With this view, children learn language by searching for regularities across many examples that are stored in memory, not through an inborn grammar-learning device (Bannard & Matthews, 2008).

THE SOCIAL-INTERACTION ANSWER. The social-interaction approach complements the others in emphasizing that much language learning takes place in the context of interactions between children and adults, with both parties eager for better communication (Bloom & Tinker, 2001). Children have an ever-expanding repertoire of ideas and intentions that they wish to convey to others, and caring adults want to understand their children, so both parties work to improve language skills as a means toward better communication. Thus, improved communication is an incentive for children to master language and for adults to help them.

All sources described here—linguistic, cognitive, and social interaction—likely contribute to children's mastery of grammar. That is, children's learning of grammar involves some mechanisms specific to learning grammar, children actively seeking to identify regularities in their environment, and linguistically rich interactions between children and adults (MacWhinney, 1998).

One reason children master language is to communicate more effectively with their parents.

© Michael Hall Photography Pty Ltd/Corbis/Glow Images

Communicating With Others

When two preschoolers converse, they sometimes try to speak at the same time, their remarks may be rambling, and they neglect to listen to one another. These actions reveal three key elements necessary for effective oral communication (Grice, 1975):

- People should take turns, alternating as speaker and listener.

- When speaking, remarks should be clear from the listener's perspective.

- When listening, listeners should let speakers know if their remarks don't make sense.

Complete mastery of these elements is a lifelong pursuit, but youngsters grasp many basics of communication early in life.

Taking Turns

Many parents begin to encourage turn-taking long before infants have said their first words (Field & Widmayer, 1982):

Parent: Can you see the bird?
Infant: (cooing) Ooooh.
Parent: It *is* a pretty bird.
Infant: Ooooh.
Parent: You're right, it's a cardinal.

Soon after 1-year-olds begin to speak, parents encourage their youngsters to participate in conversational turn-taking. To help their children along, parents often carry both sides of the conversation to show how the roles of speaker and listener are alternated (Hoff, 2009):

Parent: (initiating conversation) What's Kendra eating?
Parent: (illustrating reply for child) She's eating a cookie.

Help of this sort is needed less often by age 2, when spontaneous turn-taking is common in conversations between youngsters and adults (Barton & Tomasello, 1991). By 3 years of age, children have progressed to the point that, when a listener fails to reply promptly, the child often repeats the remarks to elicit a response and keep the conversation moving (Garvey & Berninger, 1981).

Speaking Effectively

When do children first try to initiate communications with others? The first deliberate attempts to communicate typically emerge at 10 months: an infant may point, touch, or make noises to get an adult to do something (Golinkoff, 1993; Tomasello, Carpenter, & Liszkowski, 2007). The communication may be a bit primitive by adult standards, but it works for babies. After the first birthday, children begin to use speech to communicate and often initiate conversations with adults (Bloom et al., 1996). Toddlers' first conversations are about themselves, but their conversational scope expands rapidly to include objects in the environment (e.g., toys, food).

Consistently constructing clear messages is a fine art that young children have yet to master. By the preschool years, however, youngsters have made their initial attempts to calibrate messages, adjusting them to match the listener and the context. Preschool children give more elaborate messages to listeners who lack access to critical information than to listeners who have this information (Nadig & Sedivy, 2002; O'Neill, 1996). For example, a child describing where to find a toy gives more detailed directions to a listener whose eyes were covered when the toy was hidden. And if a word's meaning might be ambiguous in the context of the conversation (e.g., bat as an animal versus as a piece of sporting equipment), young children sometimes gesture to indicate the meaning (Kidd & Holler, 2009).

Before children can speak, they use gestures to communicate with others.

Listening Well

When a message is vague or confusing, listeners need to ask speakers to clarify it. Preschoolers do not always realize when a message is ambiguous. Told to find "the red toy," preschoolers may promptly select the red ball from a pile that includes a red toy car, a red block, and a red toy hammer, assuming that they know which toy the speaker had in mind (Beal & Belgrad, 1990). During the elementary-school years, youngsters gradually master the many elements involved in determining whether another person's message is consistent and clear (Ackerman, 1993).

TABLE 4.2

Major Milestones of Language Development

Age	Milestones
Birth to 1 year	Babies hear phonemes from birth. They begin to coo between 2 and 4 months and then begin to babble at about 6 months.
About the first birthday	Babies begin to talk and to gesture, showing they have begun to use symbols.
1 to 3 years	Vocabulary expands rapidly (due to fast mapping), particularly at about 18 months. Two-word sentences emerge in telegraphic speech at about 18 months, and more complex sentences are evident by 3 years. Turn-taking is evident in communication by 2 years.
3 to 5 years	Vocabulary continues to expand, grammatical morphemes are added, and children begin to adjust their speech to listeners. However, as listeners, they often ignore problems in messages they receive.

Copyright © Cengage Learning 2010

Improvement in communication skills is yet another astonishing accomplishment in language during the first 5 years of life; changes are summarized in Table 4.2. By the time children are ready to enter kindergarten, they use language with remarkable proficiency and are able to communicate with growing skill.

Test Yourself

Recall

1. _____ are fundamental sounds used to create words.

2. Infants' mastery of language sounds may be fostered by _____, in which adults speak slowly and exaggerate changes in pitch and loudness.

3. Older infants' babbling often includes _____, a pattern of rising and falling pitch that distinguishes statements from questions.

4. Youngsters with a(n) _____ style have early vocabularies dominated by words that are names and use language primarily as an intellectual tool.

5. Answers to the question, "How do children acquire grammar?" include linguistic, cognitive, and _____ influences.

6. When talking to listeners who lack critical information, preschoolers _____ .

Interpret

- How do the various explanations of grammatical development differ in their view of the child's role in mastering grammar?

- Compare Piaget's theory, Vygotsky's theory, and the information-processing approach in their emphasis on the role of language in cognitive development.

Apply

- According to Piaget's theory, preschoolers are egocentric. How should this egocentrism influence their ability to communicate? Are the findings we described on children's communication skills consistent with Piaget's view?

- How might a pediatrician advise a parent who is unsure whether raising a child in a bilingual household will benefit or delay the child's language development?

Recall answers: (1) Phonemes, (2) infant-directed speech, (3) intonation, (4) referential, (5) social-interaction, (6) provide more elaborate messages

Much research supports Piaget's view that children actively try to understand the world around them and organize their knowledge (Flavell, 1996), and this view has been a rich source of ideas about ways for teachers and parents to foster children's development. The theory identifies several specific conditions that promote cognitive growth:

- Cognitive growth occurs as children construct their understanding of the world, so the teacher's role is to create environments in which children can discover how the world works. A teacher shouldn't tell children how addition and subtraction are complementary but instead should help children discover the complementarity themselves.
- Children profit from experience only when they can interpret this experience with their current cognitive structures. The best teaching experiences, then, are just ahead of the children's current level of thinking. As youngsters begin to master basic addition, teachers and parents should not jump right to subtraction but instead should go to slightly more difficult addition problems.
- Cognitive growth can be particularly rapid when children discover inconsistencies and errors in their thinking. Teachers should encourage

According to Piaget's theory of cognitive development, children learn best by discovery.

children to look at the consistency of their thinking. If a child is making mistakes in borrowing on subtraction problems, a teacher should encourage the child to look at many errors to discover what he or she is doing wrong.

Summary

4.1 The Onset of Thinking: Piaget's Account

According to Piaget, how do schemes, assimilation, and accommodation provide the foundation for cognitive development?

- In Piaget's view, children construct their own understanding of the world by creating schemes, categories of related events, objects, and knowledge. Infants' schemes are based on actions, but older children's and adolescents' schemes are based on functional, conceptual, and abstract properties.

- Schemes change constantly. In assimilation, experiences are readily incorporated into existing schemes. In accommodation, experiences cause schemes to be modified.

- When accommodation becomes more common than assimilation, this signals that schemes are inadequate—so children reorganize them. This reorganization produces four phases of mental development from infancy through adulthood.

How does thinking become more advanced during the sensorimotor stage?

- The first 2 years of life constitute Piaget's sensorimotor period. Over these 2 years, infants begin to adapt to and explore their environment, understand objects, and learn to use symbols.

What are the distinguishing characteristics of preoperational thinking?

- From 2 to 7 years of age, children are in Piaget's preoperational period. Although now capable of using symbols, their thinking is limited by egocentrism—the inability to see the world from another's point of view. Preoperational children are also centered in their thinking and sometimes confuse appearance with reality.

What are some criticisms of Piaget's theory?

- Piaget's theory has been criticized for underestimating infants' and preschoolers' competence, being vague regarding processes of change, not accounting for variability in performance, and undervaluing the influence of the sociocultural environment.

How have contemporary researchers extended Piaget's theory?

- In contrast to Piaget's idea that children create a comprehensive theory that integrates all their knowledge, the modern view is that children are specialists who generate naive theories in particular domains, including physics and biology. Infants understand many properties of objects; they know how objects move, what happens when objects collide, and that objects fall when not supported.

■ Infants understand the difference between animate and inanimate objects. As preschoolers, children know that—unlike inanimate objects—animate objects grow, have distinct internal parts, resemble their parents, and repair through healing.

4.2 Information Processing During Infancy and Early Childhood

What is the basis of the information-processing approach?

■ According to the information-processing view, cognitive development involves changes in mental hardware and in mental software.

How well do young children pay attention?

■ Infants use habituation to filter unimportant stimuli. Compared to older children, preschoolers are less able to pay attention to task-relevant information. Their attention can be improved by making irrelevant stimuli less noticeable.

What kinds of learning take place during infancy?

■ Infants are capable of many forms of learning, including classical conditioning, operant conditioning, and imitation.

Do infants and preschool children remember?

■ Infants can remember and can be reminded of events they seem to have forgotten. Memory improves during infancy, reflecting growth of the brain. Autobiographical memory emerges in the preschool years, reflecting children's growing language skills and their sense of self.

■ Preschoolers sometimes testify in cases of child abuse. When questioned repeatedly, they often have difficulty distinguishing what they experienced from what others may suggest they have experienced. Inaccuracies of this sort can be minimized by following certain guidelines when interviewing children, such as interviewing them as soon as possible after the event.

What do infants and preschoolers know about numbers?

■ Infants are able to distinguish small quantities, such as "twoness" from "threeness." By 3 years of age, children can count small sets of objects and in so doing adhere to the one-to-one, stable-order, and cardinality principles.

4.3 Mind and Culture: Vygotsky's Theory

What is the zone of proximal development?

■ Vygotsky believed that cognition develops first in a social setting and only gradually comes under the child's independent control. The difference between what children can do with assistance and what they can do alone constitutes the zone of proximal development.

Why is scaffolding a particularly effective way of teaching youngsters new concepts and skills?

■ Control of cognitive skills is most readily transferred to the child through scaffolding, a teaching style in which teachers let children take on more of a task as they master its components. Scaffolding is common worldwide, but the specific techniques for scaffolding children's learning vary from one cultural setting to the next.

Why do children talk to themselves as they solve problems?

■ Private speech helps children regulate their behavior, and it represents an intermediate step in the transfer of control of thinking from others to the self.

4.4 Language

When do infants first hear and make speech sounds?

■ Phonemes are the basic units of sound from which words are constructed. Infants can hear phonemes soon after birth. They can even hear phonemes that are not used in their native language, but this ability diminishes after the first birthday.

■ Infant-directed speech is adults' speech to infants that is slower and has greater variation in pitch and loudness. Infants prefer infant-directed speech, perhaps because it gives them additional language clues.

■ Newborns' communication is limited to crying, but babies coo at about 3 months of age. Babbling soon follows, consisting of a single syllable; over several months, infants' babbling comes to include longer syllables, as well as intonation.

How do children learn new words and word meanings?

■ After a brief period in which children appear to understand others' speech but do not speak themselves, most infants begin to speak around the first birthday. The first use of words is triggered by the realization that words are symbols. Soon after, the child's vocabulary expands rapidly.

■ Most children learn the meanings of words too rapidly for them to consider all plausible meanings systematically. Instead, children use certain rules to determine the probable meanings of new words. The rules do not always yield the correct meaning. An underextension is a child's meaning that is narrower than an adult's meaning; an overextension is a child's meaning that is broader.

■ Bilingual children learn language readily and better understand the arbitrary nature of words. Some youngsters use a referential word-learning style that emphasizes words as names and that views language as an intellectual tool. Other children use an expressive style that emphasizes phrases and views language as a social tool.

- Children's vocabulary is stimulated by experience. Parents can foster the growth of vocabulary by speaking with children and reading to them. Video helps preschoolers learn new words but is ineffective with infants.

How do young children learn grammar?

- Soon after children begin to speak, they create two-word sentences that are derived from their experiences. Moving from two-word to more complex sentences involves adding grammatical morphemes. Mastery of grammatical morphemes involves learning not only rules but also exceptions to the rules.

- Behaviorists proposed that children acquire grammar through imitation, but that explanation is incorrect. Today's explanations come from three perspectives. The linguistic perspective emphasizes inborn mechanisms that allow children to infer the grammatical rules of their native language. The cognitive perspective emphasizes cognitive processes that allow children to find recurring patterns in the speech they hear. Finally, the social-interaction perspective emphasizes social interactions with adults in which both parties want improved communication.

How well do youngsters communicate?

- Parents encourage turn-taking even before infants begin to talk, and later they demonstrate both the speaker and the listener roles for their children. By 3 years of age, children spontaneously take turns and prompt one another to take their turn.

- Preschool children adjust their speech in a rudimentary fashion to fit the listener's needs. However, preschoolers are unlikely to identify ambiguities in another's speech; instead, they are likely to assume they knew what the speaker meant.

Key Terms

schemes (94)
assimilation (94)
accommodation (94)
equilibration (95)
sensorimotor period (96)
object permanence (96)
egocentric (97)
centration (97)
core knowledge hypothesis (100)
mental hardware (103)
mental software (103)
attention (103)

orienting response (103)
habituation (103)
classical conditioning (104)
operant conditioning (104)
autobiographical memory (105)
one-to-one principle (107)
stable-order principle (107)
cardinality principle (107)
zone of proximal development (109)
scaffolding (109)
private speech (110)
phonemes (111)

infant-directed speech (112)
cooing (113)
babbling (113)
fast mapping (114)
underextension (115)
overextension (115)
referential style (116)
expressive style (116)
telegraphic speech (118)
grammatical morphemes (118)
overregularizations (118)

Online Resources

Go to CengageBrain.com to access Psychology CourseMate, where you will find an interactive eBook, flashcards, quizzes, videos, websites, and more.

Entering the Social World

Socioemotional Development in Infancy and Early Childhood

Humans enjoy one another's company. Social relationships of all sorts—friends, lovers, spouses, parents and children, co-workers, and teammates—make our lives both interesting and satisfying.

In this chapter, we trace the origins of these social relationships. We begin with the first social relationship—the one between an infant and a parent. Such a relationship is full of emotions—happiness, satisfaction, anger, and guilt, to name just a few. In the second section, you'll see how children express different emotions and how they recognize others' emotions.

In the third section, you'll learn how children's social horizons expand beyond parents to include peers. As children's interactions with others become more wide ranging, they begin to learn about the social roles they are expected to play, including those associated with gender. We explore gender roles in the last section.

LEARNING OBJECTIVES

- What are Erikson's first three stages of psychosocial development?

- How do infants form emotional attachments to parents?
- What are the kinds of attachment relationships?

Even since Samantha was a newborn, Karen and Rick looked forward to dinner out together on Friday night. But recently they've had a problem. When they leave 8-month-old "Sam" with a sitter, she gets a frightened look on her face and begins to cry hysterically. Karen and Rick wonder whether Sam's behavior is normal and whether their Friday-night dinners are coming to an end.

The socioemotional relationship that develops between an infant and a parent (usually, but not necessarily, the mother) is special. This is a baby's first relationship, and scientists and parents believe it should be satisfying and trouble free to set the stage for later relationships. In this section, we look at the steps involved in creating the baby's first emotional relationship. Along the way, we see why 8-month-old Sam cries when Karen and Rick leave her with a sitter.

Erikson's Stages of Early Psychosocial Development

Some of our keenest insights into the nature of psychosocial development come from a theory proposed by Erik Erikson (1982). We first encountered Erikson's theory in Chapter 1; he describes development as a series of eight stages, each with a unique crisis for psychosocial growth. When a crisis is resolved successfully, an area of psychosocial strength is established. When the crisis is not resolved, that aspect of psychosocial development is stunted, which may limit the individual's ability to resolve future crises.

In Erikson's theory, infancy and the preschool years are represented by three stages, shown in Table 5.1.

Basic Trust Versus Mistrust

Erikson argues that a sense of trust in oneself and others is the foundation of human development. Newborns leave the warmth and security of the uterus for an unfamiliar world. If parents respond to their infant's needs consistently, the infant comes to trust and feel secure in the world. Of course, parents may not always reach a falling baby in time or may accidentally feed an infant food that is too hot. Erikson sees value in these experiences, because infants learn mistrust. *With a proper balance of trust and mistrust, infants can acquire* **hope**—*an openness to new experience tempered by wariness that discomfort or danger may arise.*

Autonomy Versus Shame and Doubt

Between 1 and 3 years of age, children understand that they can control their actions. With this understanding, children strive for autonomy, for independence from others. However, autonomy is counteracted by children's doubt that they can handle demanding situations and by shame that may result from failure. *A blend of autonomy, shame, and doubt gives rise to* **will**, *the knowledge that, within limits, youngsters can act on their world intentionally.*

hope
according to Erikson, an openness to new experience tempered by wariness that occurs when trust and mistrust are in balance

will
according to Erikson, a young child's understanding that he or she can act on the world intentionally, which occurs when autonomy, shame, and doubt are in balance

Erikson's First Three Stages of Psychosocial Development

Age	Stage or Crisis	Strength
Birth to 1 year	Basic trust vs. mistrust	Hope
1 to 3 years	Autonomy vs. shame and doubt	Will
3 to 6 years	Initiative vs. guilt	Purpose

© Cengage Learning 2010

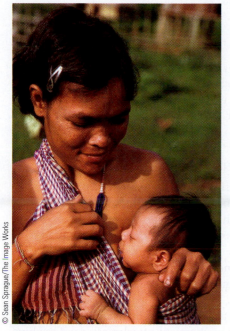

The parent–child attachment relationship is an evolutionary adaptation that helps infants survive.

Initiative Versus Guilt

Preschoolers start to explore the environment on their own, ask innumerable questions about the world, and imagine possibilities for themselves. But this initiative is moderated by guilt as children realize that their initiative may place them in conflict with others; they cannot pursue their ambitions with abandon. **Purpose** *is achieved with a balance between individual initiative and willingness to cooperate with others*.

In the next few pages, we concentrate on the first of Erikson's stages, or crises—the establishment of trust in the world—and look at the formation of bonds between infants and parents. (We return to subsequent stages in other chapters.)

The Growth of Attachment

An evolutionary perspective of early human relationships comes from Bowlby (1969, 1991). *According to Bowlby, children who form an* **attachment** *to an adult—that is, an enduring socioemotional relationship—are more likely to survive*. This person is usually the mother but need not be; the key is a strong emotional relationship with a responsive, caring person. Bowlby described four phases in the growth of attachment:

- *Preattachment* (birth to 6–8 weeks). Young babies rapidly learn to recognize their mother by smell and sound, which sets the stage for forging an attachment relationship (Hofer, 2006). What's more, evolution has endowed infants with many behaviors that elicit caregiving from an adult. When babies cry, smile, or gaze at a parent, the parent usually smiles back or holds the baby. Infants' behaviors and the responses they evoke in adults create an interactive system that is the first step in the formation of attachment relationships.

- *Attachment in the making* (6–8 weeks to 6–8 months). During these months, babies smile and laugh more often with the primary caregiver. And when babies are upset, they're more easily consoled by the primary caregiver. Babies are gradually identifying the primary caregiver as the person they can depend on when they're anxious or distressed.

- *True attachment* (6–8 to 18 months). By approximately 6 or 8 months, most infants have singled out the attachment figure—usually the mother. Infants trust their mother, who provides a stable socioemotional base. This is why infants like 8-month-old Sam from the vignette cry when separated from the attachment figure: they've lost their secure base.

- *Reciprocal relationships* (18 months on). Infants' growing cognitive and language skills allow them to act as true partners in the attachment relationship. They often take the initiative in interactions and begin to understand parents' feelings and goals.

Father–Infant Relationships

Attachment typically first develops between infants and their mother, but babies soon become attached to their father, too. Most fathers spend more time playing with their babies than taking care of them. And fathers emphasize physical play, whereas mothers

purpose
according to Erikson, a balance between individual initiative and willingness to cooperate with others

attachment
enduring socioemotional relationships between infants and their caregivers

Sequence of Events in the Strange Situation

1. An observer shows the experimental room to the mother and infant and then leaves the room.
2. The infant is allowed to explore the playroom for 3 minutes; the mother watches but does not participate.
3. A stranger enters the room, remains silent for 1 minute, talks to the baby for 1 minute, and then approaches the baby. The mother leaves unobtrusively.
4. The stranger does not play with the baby but attempts to comfort the baby if necessary.
5. After 3 minutes, the mother returns, greets, and consoles the baby.
6. When the baby has returned to play, the mother leaves again, this time saying "bye-bye" as she leaves.
7. The stranger attempts to calm and play with the baby.
8. After 3 minutes, the mother returns, and the stranger leaves.

© Cengage Learning 2010

When infants have an attachment relationship with their mother, they use her as a secure base from which to explore the environment.

spend more time reading and talking to babies, showing them toys, and playing quiet games (Paquette, 2004). Many infants prefer to play with their father but turn to their mother when distressed (Field, 1990).

Forms of Attachment

Attachment can take different forms, which were revealed by a procedure known as the Strange Situation (Ainsworth, 1978, 1993). Table 5.2 shows that the Strange Situation involves a series of episodes, each about 3 minutes long. The mother and infant enter an unfamiliar room filled with interesting toys. The mother leaves briefly, and then mother and baby are reunited. Meanwhile, the experimenter records the baby's response to separation and reunion.

Based on how the infant reacts to separation from—and reunion with—the mother, researchers have discovered four primary types of attachment relationships (Ainsworth, 1993; Thompson, 2006). One is a secure attachment, and three are types of insecure attachment (avoidant, resistant, and disorganized).

secure attachment
a relationship in which infants have come to trust and depend on their mothers

avoidant attachment
a relationship in which infants turn from their mothers when they are reunited following a brief separation

resistant attachment
a relationship in which, after a brief separation, infants want to be held but are difficult to console

disorganized (disoriented) attachment
a relationship in which infants don't seem to understand what's happening when they are separated and later reunited with their mothers

■ **Secure attachment**. *The baby may or may not cry when the mother leaves, but when she returns the baby wants to be with her—if the baby is crying, it stops.* Babies in this group seem to be saying, "I missed you terribly; I'm delighted to see you, but now that all is well, I'll get back to what I was doing." Approximately 60 to 65% of American babies have secure attachment relationships.

■ **Avoidant attachment**. *The baby is not upset when the mother leaves and, when she returns, may ignore her by looking or turning away.* Infants with an avoidant attachment look as if they're saying, "You left me *again*. I always have to take care of myself!" About 20% of American infants have an avoidant attachment relationship, which is one of three forms of insecure attachment.

■ **Resistant attachment**. *The baby is upset when the mother leaves, remains upset or even angry when she returns, and is difficult to console despite being held.* These babies seem to be telling the mother, "Why do you do this? I need you desperately, yet you just leave me without warning. I get so angry." About 10 to 15% of American babies have a resistant attachment relationship, which is another form of insecure attachment.

■ **Disorganized (disoriented) attachment**. *The baby seems confused when the mother leaves and when she returns, as if not really understanding what's happening.* The baby often behaves in contradictory ways, such as nearing the mother when she returns but not looking at her, as if wondering, "What's happening? I want you to be here, but you left and now you're back. I don't

When infants who have a resistant attachment relationship are reunited with the mother, they're typically tearful, angry, and difficult to console.

get what's going on!" About 5 to 10% of American babies have a disorganized attachment relationship, the last of the three kinds of insecure attachment.

Consequences of Attachment

As the first social relationship, infant–parent attachment lays the foundation for the infant's later social relationships (e.g., Waters & Cummings, 2000). Infants who experience the trust and compassion of a secure attachment develop into preschool children who interact confidently and successfully with their peers. For example, they have higher-quality friendships and fewer conflicts in their friendships than do children with insecure attachment relationships (McElwain, Booth-LaForce, & Wu, 2011). What's more, secure attachment in infancy is associated with more stable and higher-quality romantic relationships in adolescence (Collins, Welsh, & Furman, 2009). Finally, research consistently points to links between disorganized attachment and behavior problems involving anxiety, anger, and aggressive behavior (Fearon et al., 2010; Moss et al., 2006).

Of course, attachment is only the first of many steps along the long road of social development. Infants with insecure attachments are not forever damned, but this initial misstep can interfere with their social development. Consequently, we need to look at conditions that determine quality of attachment.

What Determines Quality of Attachment?

Because secure attachment is so important to a child's later development, researchers have tried to identify the factors involved. Undoubtedly, the most important is the interaction between parents and their babies (De Wolff & van IJzendoorn, 1997; Tomlinson, Cooper, & Murray, 2005). A secure attachment is most likely when parents respond to infants predictably and appropriately. For example, when the mother promptly responds to her baby's crying and reassures the baby, the mother's behavior evidently conveys that social interactions are predictable and satisfying. This behavior instills in infants the trust and confidence that are the hallmarks of secure attachment.

Why does predictable and responsive parenting promote secure attachment relationships? *Infants develop an* **internal working model**, *a set of expectations about parents' availability and responsiveness, both in general and in times of stress.* When parents are dependable and caring, babies come to trust them, knowing they can be relied on for comfort. That is, babies develop an internal working model in which they believe their parents are concerned about their needs and will try to meet them (Huth-Bocks et al., 2004; Thompson, 2000).

Temperament also influences the quality of attachment. Babies who fuss often and are difficult to console are more prone to insecure attachment, particularly when the mother is rigid and traditional (Mangelsdorf et al., 1990; Seifer et al., 1996). Rigid mothers do not adjust well to the often-erratic demands of their difficult babies; instead, they want the baby to adjust to them. This means that rigid mothers less often provide the responsive, sensitive care that leads to secure attachment.

Fortunately, even brief training for mothers of newborns can help them respond to their babies more effectively (Bakermans-Kranenburg, Van IJzendoorn, & Juffer, 2003). Mothers can be taught how to interact more sensitively, affectionately, and responsively, paving the way for secure attachment and the lifelong benefits associated with a positive internal working model of interpersonal relationships.

Perhaps the most important ingredient in fostering a secure attachment relationship is responding predictably and appropriately to an infant's needs.

internal working model
an infant's understanding of how responsive and dependable the mother is, which is thought to influence close relationships throughout the child's life

HUMAN DEVELOPMENT in action

As a health care professional, what advice would you give new parents so that their babies are likely to form a strong attachment relationship?

The formation of attachment illustrates the combined influence of the different components of the biopsychosocial framework. Many infant behaviors that elicit care-giving in adults—smiling and crying, for example—are biological in origin. When the caregiver is responsive to the infant (a sociocultural force), a secure attachment forms in which the infant trusts caregivers and knows that they can be relied on in stressful situations (a psychological force).

Test Yourself

Recall

1. _____ proposed that maturational and social factors come together to pose eight unique challenges for psychosocial growth during the life span.

2. Infants must balance trust and mistrust to achieve _____, openness to new experience that is coupled with awareness of possible danger.

3. By approximately _____ months of age, most infants have identified a special individual—usually the mother—as the attachment figure.

4. Joan, a 12-month-old, was separated from her mother for about 15 minutes. When they were reunited, Joan would not let her mother pick her up. When her mother approached, Joan would look the other way or toddle to another part of the room. This behavior suggests that Joan has a(n) _____ attachment relationship.

5. The most important factor in fostering a secure attachment relationship is _____.

6. Tim and Douglas, both 3-year-olds, rarely argue; when they disagree, one goes along with the other's ideas. The odds are good that both boys have _____ attachment relationships with their parents.

Interpret

- Compare the infant's contributions to the formation of mother–infant attachment with the mother's contributions.
- Based on Jean Piaget's description of infancy (pages 94–96), what cognitive skills might be important prerequisites for the formation of an attachment relationship?

Apply

- Based on what you know about the normal developmental timetable for the formation of mother–infant attachment, what would seem to be the optimal age range for children to be adopted?
- Imagine that you are a social worker with a client who is the mother of a 7-month-old. She wants to know whether her baby has a secure attachment relationship. How would you determine this?

Recall answers: (1) Erikson, (2) hope, (3) 7 or 8, (4) avoidant, (5) responding consistently and appropriately, (6) secure

---

5.2 Emerging Emotions

LEARNING OBJECTIVES

- At what age do children begin to express basic emotions?
- What are complex emotions? When do they develop?
- When do children begin to understand other people's emotions?
- How do children regulate their emotions?

Nicole is ecstatic that she is finally going to see her 7-month-old nephew, Claude. She rushes into the house and sweeps Claude from his crib with a big hug. After a brief, puzzled look, Claude bursts into angry tears and begins thrashing his arms and legs, as if saying to Nicole, "Who are you? What do you want? Put me down! Now!" Nicole quickly hands Claude to his mother, who is surprised by her baby's outburst and even more surprised that he continues to sob while she rocks him.

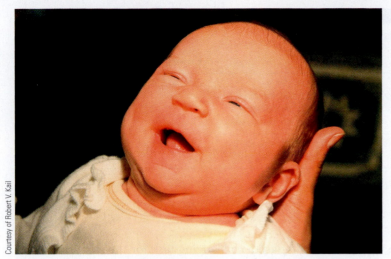

Courtesy of Robert V. Kail

Social smiles emerge at about 2 to 3 months, when infants smile in response to a human face.

This vignette illustrates three common emotions. Nicole's initial joy, Claude's anger, and his mother's surprise are familiar to all of us. In this section, we look at when children first express emotions, how children come to understand emotions in others, and finally, how children regulate their emotions. As we do, we'll learn why Claude reacted to Nicole as he did and how Nicole could have prevented Claude's outburst.

Experiencing and Expressing Emotions

The three emotions from the vignette—joy, anger, and fear—are considered "basic emotions," as are interest, disgust, distress, sadness, and surprise (Draghi-Lorenz, Reddy, & Costall, 2001). **Basic emotions** *are experienced by people worldwide, and each consists of three elements: a subjective feeling, a physiological change, and an overt behavior* (Izard, 2007).

According to one influential theory (Lewis, 2000), newborns experience only pleasure and distress. However, by 8 or 9 months of age, infants seem to experience all basic emotions. For example, joy emerges at about 2 or 3 months. *At this age* **social smiles** *first appear; infants smile when they see another human face.* Sometimes social smiling is accompanied by cooing, the early form of vocalization described in Chapter 4 (Sroufe & Waters, 1976). Smiling and cooing seem to be the infant's way of expressing pleasure at seeing another person. Sadness is also observed at about this age: Infants look sad, for example, when their mothers stop playing with them (Lewis, 2000).

Anger is one of the first negative emotions to emerge from generalized distress, typically between 4 and 6 months. Infants become angry, for example, if a favorite food or toy is taken away (Sullivan & Lewis, 2003). Older infants become angry when their attempts to achieve a goal are frustrated (Braungart-Rieker, Hill-Soderlund, & Karrass, 2010). For example, if a parent restrains an infant trying to pick up a toy, the guaranteed result is a very angry baby.

Like anger, fear emerges later in the first year. *At about 6 months, infants become wary in the presence of an unfamiliar adult, a reaction known as* **stranger wariness**. When a stranger approaches, a 6-month-old typically looks away and begins to fuss (Mangelsdorf, Shapiro, & Marzolf, 1995). If a grandmother picks up her grandchild without giving the infant a chance to warm to her, the outcome is as predictable as it was with Claude, the baby in the vignette who was frightened by his aunt: The baby cries, looks frightened, and reaches for someone familiar. Babies are less wary of strangers when they first talk with other adults and only gradually engage the baby (Mangelsdorf, 1992).

Wariness of strangers is adaptive because it emerges at the same time that children begin to master creeping and crawling (described on pages 75–77). Being wary of strangers provides a natural restraint against the tendency to wander away from familiar caregivers. However, as youngsters learn to interpret facial expressions and recognize when a person is friendly, their wariness of strangers declines.

Emergence of Complex Emotions

In addition to basic emotions such as joy and anger, people feel complex emotions such as pride, guilt, and embarrassment. Complex emotions don't surface until 18 to 24 months of age because they depend on the child having some understanding of the self, which typically occurs between 15 and 18 months (e.g., Lewis, 2000; Mascolo, Fischer, & Li, 2003). Children feel guilty or embarrassed, for example, when they've done something they know they shouldn't have done (Kochanska et al., 2002): A child who breaks a toy is thinking, "You told me to be careful. But I wasn't!" Similarly,

basic emotions
emotions experienced by humankind and that consist of three elements: a subjective feeling, a physiological change, and an overt behavior

social smiles
smiles that infants produce when they see a human face

stranger wariness
the first distinct signs of fear that emerge around 6 months of age when infants become wary in the presence of unfamiliar adults

TABLE 5.3

Infants' Expression of Emotions

Emotion Type	Definition	Emergent Age	Examples
Basic	Responses experienced by people worldwide that include a subjective feeling, a physiological response, and an overt behavior	Birth to 9 months	Happiness, anger, fear
Self-conscious	Responses to meeting or failing to meet expectations or standards	18 to 24 months	Pride, guilt, embarrassment

© Cengage Learning 2013

children feel pride when they accomplish a challenging task for the first time. Thus, children's growing understanding of themselves enables them to experience complex emotions like pride and guilt (Lewis, 2000).

The features of basic and self-conscious emotions are summarized in Table 5.3.

Later Developments

As children grow, they continue to experience basic and complex emotions, but different situations or events elicit these emotions. In the case of complex emotions, cognitive growth means that elementary-school children experience shame and guilt they would not have felt in similar situations when they were younger (Reimer, 1996). For example, unlike preschool children, many school-age children would be ashamed if they neglected to defend a classmate who had been wrongly accused of a theft.

Fear is another emotion that can be elicited in different ways, depending on a child's age. Many preschool children are afraid of the dark and of imaginary creatures. These fears typically diminish during the elementary-school years as children grow cognitively and better understand the difference between appearance and reality. Replacing these fears are concerns about school, health, and personal harm (Silverman, La Greca, & Wasserstein, 1995). Such worries are common and not a cause for concern in most children. In some youngsters, however, they become so extreme that they are overwhelming (Chorpita & Barlow, 1998). For example, a 7-year-old's worries about school would not be unusual unless her concern grew to the point that she refused to go to school.

Cultural Differences in Emotional Expression

Children worldwide express many of the same basic and complex emotions. However, cultures differ in the extent to which emotional expression is encouraged (Hess & Kirouac, 2000). In many Asian countries, for example, outward displays of emotion are discouraged in favor of emotional restraint (Camras et al., 2006). Cultures also differ in the events that trigger emotions, particularly complex emotions. For example, American elementary-school children often show pride at personal achievement, such as getting the highest grade on a test. In contrast, Asian elementary-school children are embarrassed by a public display of individual achievement but show great pride when their entire class is honored for an achievement (Lewis et al., 2010; Stevenson & Stigler, 1992).

Thus, culture can influence when and how much children express emotion. Of course, expressing emotion is only part of the developmental story. Children must also learn to recognize others' emotions, which is our next topic.

HUMAN DEVELOPMENT in action

Imagine that you're a clinical child psychologist. A neighbor worries that his preschool child is afraid of the dark. How would you advise him?

American children are often quite proud of personal achievement, but Asian children would be embarrassed by such a public display of individual accomplishments.

© David Young-Wolff/PhotoEdit

Recognizing and Using Others' Emotions

As early as 4 months, infants begin to distinguish facial expressions associated with different emotions. They can, for example, distinguish a happy, smiling face from a sad, frowning face (Bornstein & Arterberry, 2003; Montague & Walker-Andrews, 2001). What's more, like adults, infants are biased toward negative emotions: They attend more rapidly to faces depicting negative emotions (e.g., anger) and pay attention to them longer than emotionless or happy faces (LoBue & DeLoache, 2010; Peltola et al., 2008).

Not only can infants distinguish emotional expressions, but they also seem to understand those expressed emotions because they often match their emotions to other people's emotions. When happy mothers smile and talk in a pleasant voice, infants express happiness themselves. If mothers are angry or sad, infants become distressed too (Haviland & Lelwica, 1987; Montague & Walker-Andrews, 2001).

Also like adults, infants use others' emotions to direct their behavior. *Infants in an unfamiliar or ambiguous environment often look at their mother or father as if searching for cues to help them interpret the situation, a phenomenon known as* **social referencing**. As shown in Figure 5.1, if a parent looks afraid when shown a novel object, 12-month-olds are less likely to play with the toy than when a parent looks happy (Repacholi, 1998). Furthermore, an infant can use parents' facial expressions or vocal expressions alone to decide whether they want to explore an unfamiliar object (Mumme, Fernald, & Herrera, 1996). Thus, social referencing shows that infants are remarkably skilled in using the emotions of adults to help them direct their own behavior.

What experiences contribute to children's understanding of emotions? Not surprisingly, children learn about emotions when parents talk about feelings, explaining how they differ and the situations that elicit them (Brown & Dunn, 1996; Cervantes & Callanan, 1998). Also, a positive and rewarding relationship with parents and siblings is related to children's understanding of emotions (Brown & Dunn, 1996; Laible, 2011). The nature of this connection is still a mystery. One possibility is that, within positive parent–child and sibling relationships, people express a fuller range of emotions, do so more often, and are more willing to talk about why they feel as they do, providing children with more opportunities to learn about emotions.

Regulating Emotions

Adults often regulate emotions; for example, we routinely try to suppress fear (because we know there's no need to be afraid of the dark), anger (because we don't want to let a friend know how upset we are), and joy (because we don't want to seem like we're gloating over our good fortune).

As these examples illustrate, skillfully regulating emotions depends on cognitive processes like those described in Chapter 4 (Zelazo & Cunningham, 2007). Attention is an important part of emotion regulation: We can control emotions such as fear by diverting attention to other less emotional stimuli, thoughts, or feelings (Rothbart & Sheese, 2007; Watts, 2007). We can also use strategies to reappraise the meaning of an event (or of feelings or thoughts) so that it provokes less emotion (John & Gross, 2007).

social referencing
behavior in which infants in unfamiliar or ambiguous environments look at an adult for cues to help them interpret the situation

FIGURE 5.1
If parents seem frightened by an unfamiliar object, then babies are also wary or even afraid of it.

© Cengage Learning 2010

For example, a soccer player nervous about taking a penalty kick can reinterpret her state of physiological arousal as being "pumped up" instead of being "scared to death."

Emotion regulation clearly begins in infancy. By 4 to 6 months, infants use simple strategies to regulate their emotions (Buss & Goldsmith, 1998; Rothbart & Rueda, 2005). When something frightens or confuses infants—for example, a stranger or a mother who suddenly stops responding—they often look away. Frightened infants also move closer to a parent, another effective way of helping control their fear (Parritz, 1996). And by 24 months, a distressed toddler's face typically expresses sadness instead of fear or anger; apparently, by this age, a toddler has learned that a sad facial expression is the best way to get a mother's attention and support (Buss & Kiel, 2004).

Older children encounter a wider range of emotional situations, so it's fortunate they develop a number of new ways to regulate emotion (Eisenberg & Morris, 2002):

- Children begin to regulate their emotions and rely less on others to do this for them. A fearful child no longer runs to a parent but instead devises her own methods for dealing with fear (e.g., "I know the thunderstorm won't last long, and I'm safe inside the house").

- Children often rely on mental strategies to regulate emotions. For example, a child might reduce his disappointment at not receiving a much-expected gift by telling himself that he didn't really want the gift.

- Children accurately match the strategies for regulating emotion with the particular setting. For example, when faced with emotional situations that are unavoidable (e.g., a child must go to the dentist to have a cavity filled), children adjust to the situation (e.g., thinking of the positive consequences of treating the tooth) instead of trying to avoid it.

Collectively, these age-related trends give children tools for regulating emotions.

Unfortunately, not all children regulate their emotions well, and those who don't tend to have adjustment problems and problems interacting with peers (Eisenberg & Morris, 2002; Eisenberg et al., 2005). For example, when children are faced with a dispute over who gets to play with a toy, their unregulated anger can interfere with finding a mutually satisfying solution. Thus, ineffective regulation of emotions leads to more frequent conflicts with peers and, as a result, less satisfying peer relationships and less adaptive adjustment to school (Eisenberg et al., 2001; Olson et al., 2005).

Test Yourself

Recall

1. Basic emotions include a subjective feeling, a physiological change, and _____ .

2. The first detectable form of fear is _____, which emerges at about 6 months.

3. Wariness of strangers is adaptive because it emerges at about the same time that _____ .

4. Complex emotions, such as guilt and shame, emerge later than basic emotions because _____ .

5. In social referencing, infants use a parent's facial expression _____ .

6. Infants often control fear by looking away from a frightening event or by _____ .

Interpret

- How might an infant's ability to express emotions relate to the formation of attachment? How might this ability relate to the temperamental characteristics described on pages 67–68?

- Explain how the different forces in the biopsychosocial framework contribute to the development of basic and complex emotions.

Apply

- Your 15-month-old accidentally knocked an antique vase off a table, and it was smashed to bits. Would your baby feel embarrassed or guilty by her behavior?

- You are a child-care provider who is about to meet a potential client's 1-year-old for the first time. How should you behave so that the meeting is a success?

Recall answers: (1) an overt behavior, (2) wariness of strangers, (3) infants master creeping and crawling, (4) complex emotions require more advanced cognitive skills, (5) to direct their own behavior (e.g., deciding whether an unfamiliar situation is safe or frightening), (6) moving closer to a parent

LEARNING OBJECTIVES

■ When do youngsters first begin to play with one another? How does play change during infancy and the preschool years?

■ What determines whether children help one another?

Six-year-old Juan got his finger trapped in the DVD player when he tried to remove a disc. While he cried and cried, his 3-year-old brother, Antonio, and his 2-year-old sister, Carla, watched but did not help. Later, when their mother had soothed Juan and concluded that his finger was not injured, she worried about her younger children's reactions. In the face of their brother's obvious distress, why did Antonio and Carla do nothing?

Infants' initial interactions are with parents, but soon they begin to interact with other people, notably their peers. In this section, we trace the development of these interactions and learn why children like Antonio and Carla don't always help others.

The Joys of Play

Peer interactions begin surprisingly early in infancy. Two 6-month-olds together will look, smile, and point at each other. Over the next few months, infants laugh and babble when with other infants (Rubin, Bukowski, & Parker, 2006). *Soon after, children begin* **parallel play**, *in which each youngster plays alone but maintains a keen interest in what another is doing.* Two toddlers may each have a toy, but each will watch the other play too.

Beginning at roughly 15 to 18 months, toddlers no longer simply watch one another at play. *Instead, they engage in similar activities and talk or smile at one another, illustrating* **simple social play**. Play has become truly interactive (Howes & Matheson, 1992). An example of simple social play would be two 20-month-olds pushing toy cars along the floor, making "car sounds," and periodically trading cars.

Toward the second birthday, **cooperative play** *emerges: Now a distinct theme organizes children's play, and they take on special roles based on the theme.* They may play hide-and-seek and alternate the roles of hider and seeker, or they may have a tea party and take turns being the host and the guest (Parten, 1932).

In parallel play, children play independently but actively watch what other children are doing.

parallel play
when children play alone but are aware of and interested in what another child is doing

simple social play
play that begins at about 15 to 18 months and continues into toddlerhood, when talking and smiling at each other also occur

cooperative play
play that is organized around a theme, with each child taking on a different role, and that begins at about 2 years of age

Make-Believe

During the preschool years, cooperative play often takes the form of make-believe. Preschoolers have telephone conversations with imaginary partners or pretend to drink imaginary juice. In the early phases of make-believe, children rely on realistic props to support their play. While pretending to drink, younger preschoolers use a real cup; while pretending to drive a car, they use a toy steering wheel. In the later phases of make-believe, children no longer need realistic props; instead, they can imagine that a block is the cup or that a paper plate is the steering wheel. This gradual movement toward more abstract make-believe is possible because of cognitive growth that occurs during the preschool years (Striano, Tomasello, & Rochat, 2001).

Make-believe—a favorite of preschoolers everywhere—fosters cognitive development.

The first time that a parent pretends, this must be puzzling for toddlers. They probably wonder why mom is drinking from an empty glass or eating cereal from an empty bowl. But parents help toddlers make sense out of this behavior: When parents pretend, they typically look directly at the child and grin, as if to say, "This is just for fun—it's not real!" And toddlers return the smile, as if responding, "I get it! We're playing!" (Nishida & Lillard, 2007). When children are older, they usually tell play partners that they want to pretend ("Let's pretend") and then describe those aspects of reality that are being changed ("I'll be the pilot and this is my plane," referring to the couch). It's as if children mutually agree to enter a parallel universe that's governed by its own set of rules (Rakoczy, 2008; Weisberg & Bloom, 2009).

Make-believe play is not only entertaining—it also promotes cognitive development. Children who spend much time in make-believe play tend to be more advanced in language, memory, and reasoning (Bergen & Mauer, 2000). They also tend to have a more sophisticated understanding of other people's thoughts, beliefs, and feelings (Lindsey & Colwell, 2003).

Another benefit of make-believe is that it allows children to explore topics that frighten them. Children who are afraid of the dark may reassure a doll who is also afraid of the dark. By explaining to the doll why it need not be afraid, children come to understand and regulate their fear of darkness (Gottman, 1986).

For many preschool children, make-believe play involves imaginary companions. Children can usually describe their imaginary playmates in some detail, mentioning sex and age, as well as hair and eye color. Imaginary companions were once thought to be fairly rare, but many preschoolers, particularly firstborn and only children, report imaginary companions (Taylor et al., 2004). What's more, an imaginary companion is associated with many positive social characteristics (Gleason & Hohmann, 2006; Roby & Kidd, 2008): Preschoolers with imaginary friends tend to be more sociable and have more real friends than other preschoolers.

Solitary Play

At times throughout the preschool years, many children prefer to play alone. Should parents be worried? Usually, no. Solitary play comes in many forms, and most are normal—even healthy. Spending playtime alone coloring, solving puzzles, or assembling Legos is not a sign of maladjustment. Many youngsters enjoy solitary activities and, at other times, choose very social play.

However, some forms of solitary play are signs that children are uneasy interacting with others (Coplan et al., 2001; Harrist et al., 1997). One type of unhealthy solitary play is wandering aimlessly. Sometimes children go from one preschool activity center to the next, as if trying to decide what to do. But really they just keep wandering. Another unhealthy type of solitary play is hovering: A child stands near peers who are playing, watching them play but not participating. Over time, these behaviors do not bode well for youngsters (Coplan & Armer, 2007), so it's best for these youngsters to get professional help.

Gender Differences in Play

Between 2 and 3 years of age, children begin to prefer playing with same-sex peers (Martin & Fabes, 2001). Little boys play together with cars, and little girls play together with dolls. This preference increases during childhood, reaching a peak in preadolescence. This tendency for boys to play with boys and girls with girls has several distinctive features (Maccoby, 1998):

■ Children spontaneously select same-sex playmates; adult pressure is not necessary.

■ Children resist parents' efforts to get them to play with members of the opposite sex.

■ Children's reluctance to play with members of the opposite sex is obvious even in gender-neutral activities, such as playing tag or doing puzzles.

At about 2 or 3 years of age, boys and girls start to prefer playing with members of their own sex.

Why do boys and girls seem so attracted to same-sex play partners? One reason is that their styles of play differ. Boys prefer rough-and-tumble play and generally are more competitive and dominating in their interactions. In contrast, when girls play, they are more cooperative, prosocial, and conversation oriented (Rose & Rudolph, 2006). Boys don't enjoy the way that girls play, and girls find boys' play aversive (Maccoby, 1990, 1998).

Second, when girls and boys play together, girls do not readily influence boys. *Girls' interactions with one another are typically* **enabling actions**—*their actions and remarks tend to support others and sustain the interaction.* When drawing together, one girl might say to another, "Pretty picture" or "What do you want to do now?" *In contrast, boy's interactions are often* **constricting actions**—*one partner tries to emerge as the victor by threatening or contradicting the other, by exaggerating, and so on.* In the same drawing task, one boy might say to another, "My picture's better" or "Drawing is stupid—let's watch TV." When these styles are brought together, girls find their enabling style is ineffective with boys. The same subtle overtures that work with other girls have no impact on boys. Boys ignore girls' polite suggestions about what to do and ignore girls' efforts to resolve conflicts with discussion (Rose & Rudolph, 2006).

Early segregation of playmates by style of play means that boys learn primarily from boys and girls from girls. Over time, such social segregation by sex reinforces gender differences in play. When young boys spend most of their time playing with other boys, their play becomes more active and more aggressive. In contrast, when young girls spend most of their time playing with other girls, their play becomes less active and less aggressive (Martin & Fabes, 2001).

Parental Influence

Parents become involved in their preschool children's play in several ways (Parke & O'Neill, 2000):

- *Playmate.* Many parents enjoy the role of playmate (and many parents deserve an Oscar for their performances). They use the opportunity to scaffold their children's play (see page 109), often raising it to more sophisticated levels (Tamis-LeMonda & Bornstein, 1996). For example, if a toddler is stacking toy plates, a parent might help the child stack the plates (play at the same level) or might pretend to wash each plate (play at a more advanced level). When parents demonstrate more advanced forms of play, their children often play at the more advanced levels later (Lindsey & Mize, 2000).

- *Social director.* Many parents of young children arrange visits with peers, enroll children in activities (e.g., preschool programs), and take children to settings that attract young children (e.g., parks). This effort is worth it: Children whose parents provide them with frequent opportunities for peer interaction tend to get along better with their peers (Ladd & Pettit, 2002).

- *Coach.* Successful interactions are based on a host of skills, including how to initiate an interaction, make joint decisions, and resolve conflicts. When parents help their children acquire these skills, children tend to be more competent socially and to be more accepted by their peers (Parke et al., 2004). But there's a catch: The coaching needs to be constructive for children to benefit. Parent-coaches sometimes make suggestions that aren't clear or are even misguided. Bad coaching is worse than no coaching, because the former harms children's peer relations (Russell & Finnie, 1990).

enabling actions
individuals' actions and remarks that tend to support others and sustain the interaction

constricting actions
interactions in which one partner tries to emerge as the victor by threatening or contradicting the other

Parents influence their children's play in many ways, perhaps most importantly by mediating the disputes that arise when preschoolers play.

■ *Mediator.* When young children play, they often disagree, argue, and fight. However, children play more cooperatively and longer when parents are present to help iron out conflicts (Mize, Pettit, & Brown, 1995). When young children can't agree on what to play, a parent can negotiate a mutually acceptable activity. Here, too, parents scaffold their preschoolers' play, smoothing the interaction by providing some of the social skills that preschoolers lack.

In addition to these direct influences on children's play, parents influence children's play indirectly via the quality of the parent–child attachment relationship. When the parent–child relationship is of high quality and emotionally satisfying, children are encouraged to form relationships with other people.

Helping Others

Prosocial behavior *is any behavior that benefits another person.* Cooperation—that is, working together toward a common goal—is one form of prosocial behavior. Of course, cooperation often "works" because individuals gain more than they would by not cooperating. *In contrast,* **altruism** *is behavior that is driven by feelings of responsibility toward other people, such as helping and sharing, in which individuals do not benefit directly from their actions.* If two youngsters pool their funds to buy a candy bar to share, this is cooperative behavior. If one youngster gives half of her lunch to a peer who forgot his own, this is altruism.

Many scientists believe that humans are biologically predisposed to help, to share, to cooperate, and to be concerned for others (Hastings, Zahn-Waxler, & McShane, 2006). Basic acts of altruism can be seen by 18 months of age. When toddlers and preschoolers see other people who are obviously hurt or upset, they try to comfort such people by hugging or patting them (Zahn-Waxler et al., 1992). Apparently, at this early age, children recognize signs of distress. And if an adult is in obvious need of help—a teacher accidentally drops markers on the floor—most 18-month-olds spontaneously help, in this case by getting the markers (Warneken & Tomasello, 2006).

By 18 months of age, toddlers try to comfort others who are hurt or upset.

During the toddler and preschool years, children gradually begin to understand others' needs and learn appropriate altruistic responses (van der Mark, van IJzendoorn, & Bakermans-Kranenburg, 2002). When 3-year-old Alexis sees that her infant brother is crying because he's dropped his favorite bear, she retrieves it for him. These early attempts at altruistic behavior are limited because young children's knowledge of what they can do to help is modest. As youngsters acquire more strategies to help others, their preferred strategies become more adultlike (Eisenberg, Fabes, & Spinrad, 2006).

Let's look at some specific skills that set the stage for altruistic behaviors.

Skills Underlying Altruistic Behavior

Remember from Chapter 4 that preschool children are often egocentric, so they may not see the need for altruistic behavior. Youngsters who understand others' thoughts and feelings share better with others and help them more often (Strayer & Roberts, 2004; Vaish, Carpenter, & Tomasello, 2009). For example, young children might not share candy with a younger sibling because they cannot imagine how unhappy the sibling is without the candy. In contrast, school-age children can more easily take the sibling's point of view and are more inclined to share.

Related to understanding of another's feelings is **empathy**, *or experiencing another's feelings.* Children who deeply feel another individual's fear, disappointment, sorrow, or loneliness are more inclined to help that person than are children who do

prosocial behavior
any behavior that benefits another person

altruism
prosocial behavior such as helping and sharing in which the individual does not benefit directly from the behavior

empathy
experiencing another person's feelings

© Catchlight Visual Services/Alamy

When children can empathize with others who are sad or upset, they're more likely to offer to help.

not feel those emotions (Eisenberg, Fabes, & Spinrad, 2006; Malti et al., 2009). In other words, youngsters who are obviously distressed by what they are seeing are more likely to help if they can.

Situational Influences

Kind children occasionally disappoint us by being cruel, and children who are usually stingy sometimes surprise us by their generosity. Why? The setting helps determine whether children act altruistically:

- *Feelings of responsibility.* Children act altruistically when they feel responsible for the person in need. For example, children may help siblings and friends more often than strangers simply because they feel a direct responsibility for people they know well (Costin & Jones, 1992).

- *Feelings of competence.* Children act altruistically when they feel they have the skills to help the person in need. Suppose, for example, that a preschooler is growing increasingly upset because he can't figure out how a toy works. A peer unfamiliar with the toy is less likely to help, because the peer doesn't know what to do and could end up looking foolish (Peterson, 1983).

- *Mood.* Children act altruistically when they are happy or feeling successful but not when they are sad or feeling as if they have failed (Wentzel, Filisetti, & Looney, 2007). A preschool child who has just spent an exciting morning as the "leader" in nursery school is more inclined to share treats with siblings than is a preschooler who was punished by the teacher (Eisenberg, 2000).

- *Costs of altruism.* Children act altruistically when such actions entail few or modest sacrifices. A preschool child who was given a snack that she doesn't particularly like is more inclined to share it with others than one who was given her favorite food (Eisenberg & Shell, 1986).

Thus, children are most likely to help when they feel responsible for the person in need, have the needed skills, are happy, and believe they will give up little by helping. Thus, we can explain why Antonio and Carla, the children in the opening vignette, watched idly as their older brother cried. First, neither Antonio nor Carla may have felt responsible to help because with two children available to help, each child's feeling of individual responsibility is reduced and because younger children are less likely to feel responsible for an older sibling. Second, Antonio and Carla did not know how to use the DVD player. Consequently, they didn't feel competent to help because they didn't know how to help Juan remove his finger.

So far, we've seen that altruistic behavior is determined by children's skills (e.g., perspective taking) and by characteristics of situations (e.g., whether children feel competent to help in a particular situation). Whether children are altruistic is also determined by genetics and by socialization, our last two topics in this section.

HUMAN DEVELOPMENT in **action**

Suppose you are a kindergarten teacher and your students want to raise money for a gift for one of their classmates who is ill. Based on the information presented here, what advice can you give the children as they plan their fundraising?

The Contribution of Heredity

Genes affect prosocial behavior but do so indirectly, by influencing temperament. For example, children who are temperamentally less able to regulate their emotions (in part due to heredity) may help less often because they're so upset by another's distress that taking action is impossible (Eisenberg et al., 2007). Another temperamental influence is via inhibition (shyness). Children who are temperamentally shy are often reluctant to help others, particularly people they don't know well (Young, Fox, & Zahn-Waxler, 1999). Even though shy children realize that others need help and are upset by another person's apparent distress, their reticence keeps these feelings from being translated into action. Thus, in both cases, children are aware that others need help. But in the first instance they're too upset themselves to figure out how to help, and in the second instance they know how to help but are too inhibited to follow through.

Socialization of Altruism

Parents represent another influence on altruism; parents foster altruism in their children in several ways:

- *Modeling.* When children see adults helping and caring for others, they often imitate such prosocial behavior (Eisenberg et al., 2006). Parents are the models to whom children are most continuously exposed, so they exert a powerful influence. Parents who report frequent feelings of warmth and concern for others tend to have children who experience stronger feelings of empathy. When a mother is helpful and responsive, her children often imitate her by being cooperative, helpful, sharing, and less critical of others.

- *Disciplinary practices.* Children behave prosocially more often when their parents are warm and supportive, set guidelines, and provide feedback; in contrast, prosocial behavior is less common when parenting is harsh, is threatening, and includes frequent physical punishment (Asbury et al., 2003; Eisenberg & Fabes, 1998). Particularly important is parents' use of reasoning as a disciplinary tactic, with the goal of helping children see how their actions affect others. The Real People feature shows this practice in action.

- *Opportunities to behave prosocially.* Children and adolescents are more likely to act prosocially when they're routinely given the opportunity to help and cooperate with others (Choi, Johnson, & Johnson, 2011). At home, children can help with household tasks, such as cleaning and setting the table. Experiences like these help sensitize children to the needs of others and allow them to enjoy the satisfaction of helping (Grusec, Goodnow, & Cohen, 1996; McLellan & Youniss, 2003).

Thus, parents can foster altruism in their youngsters by behaving altruistically themselves, by using reasoning to discipline their children, and by encouraging their children to help at home and elsewhere. Situational factors also play a role, and altruism requires perspective taking and empathy. Combining these ingredients, we can give a general account of children's altruistic behavior. As children get older, their perspective-taking and empathic skills develop, which enables them to see and feel another's needs. Nonetheless, children are never altruistic (or, fortunately, nonaltruistic) all the time, because particular contexts affect altruistic behavior. These factors are summarized in Table 5.4.

real People   APPLYING HUMAN DEVELOPMENT
USING REASONING TO PROMOTE PROSOCIAL BEHAVIOR

Jim's 4-year-old daughter, Annie, was playing with a friend, Maurice. Annie asked Maurice if she could borrow his crayons. When Maurice refused, Annie pushed him aside and grabbed the crayons, which caused Maurice to cry. At this point, Jim returned the crayons to Maurice and had the following conversation with Annie:

Jim: Why did you take the crayons away from Maurice?

Annie: Because I wanted them.

Jim: How do you think he felt? Happy or sad?

Annie: I dunno.

Jim: I think that you know.

Annie: Okay. He was sad.

Jim: Would you like it if I took the crayons away from you? How would you feel?

Annie: I'd be mad. And sad too.

Jim: Well, that's how Maurice felt, and that's why you shouldn't just grab things away from people. It makes them angry and unhappy. Ask first, and if they say "no," then you *mustn't take them.*

Jim's approach is to reason with Annie to help her see how her actions affect others. He emphasizes the rights and needs of others, as well as the impact of one child's misbehavior on others. Repeated exposure to reasoning during discipline promotes children's ability to take another's perspective.

Factors Contributing to Children's Prosocial Behavior

General Category	Types of Influence	Children Are More Likely to Help When...
Skills	Perspective taking	they can take another person's point of view.
	Empathy	they feel another person's emotions.
Situational influences	Feelings of responsibility	they feel responsible to the person in need.
	Feelings of competence	they feel competent to help.
	Mood	they're in a good mood.
	Cost of altruism	the cost of prosocial behavior is small.
Heredity	Temperament	they're not shy and can control their emotions.
Parents' influences	Modeling	parents behave prosocially themselves.
	Discipline	parents reason with them.
	Opportunities	they practice at home and elsewhere.

© Cengage Learning 2013

Test Yourself

Recall

1. Toddlers often engage in _____ play, in which they play separately but look at one another and sometimes communicate verbally.

2. One of the advantages of _____ play is that children can explore topics that frighten them.

3. When girls interact, conflicts are typically resolved through _____ ; boys more often resort to intimidation.

4. _____ is the ability to understand and feel another person's emotions.

5. Situational influences on prosocial behavior include feelings of responsibility, feelings of competence, _____, and the costs associated with behaving prosocially.

6. Parents can foster altruism in their youngsters by behaving altruistically themselves, by using reasoning to discipline their children, and by _____.

Interpret

- Why must a full account of children's prosocial behavior include an emphasis on skills (e.g., empathy), as well as one on situations (e.g., whether a child feels responsible)?

- How might Piaget have explained the emergence of make-believe during the preschool years? How would Erikson explain it?

Apply

- Imagine you are a preschool teacher and the parents of one of your students ask how their preschool daughter could get along better with peers. What advice would you give them?

- Paula worries that her son Elliot is too selfish and wishes that he were more caring and compassionate. As a parent, what could Paula do to encourage Elliot to be more concerned about the welfare of others?

Recall answers: (1) parallel, (2) make-believe, (3) discussion and compromise, (4) Empathy, (5) mood, (6) providing children with opportunities to practice being altruistic

5.4 Gender Roles and Gender Identity

LEARNING OBJECTIVES

- What are our stereotypes about males and females? How well do they correspond to actual differences between boys and girls?

- How do young children learn gender roles?

- How are gender roles changing?

Meda and Perry want their 6-year-old daughter, Hope, to pick activities and friends based on her interests and abilities rather than on her gender. They have done their best to encourage gender-neutral values and behavior. Both are therefore astonished that Hope seems to be just like other 6-year-olds reared by conventional parents. Hope's close friends are all girls who love to play house or play with dolls. What's going wrong with Meda and Perry's plans for a gender-neutral girl?

Family and well-wishers are always eager to know the sex of a newborn. Why? Being a "boy" or "girl" is not simply a biological distinction. Instead, these terms are associated with distinct social roles. *Like a role in a play, a* social role *is a set of cultural guidelines as to how a person should behave, particularly with other people.* The roles associated with gender are among the first that children learn, starting in infancy. Youngsters rapidly learn about the behaviors that are assigned to males and females in their culture. At the same time, they begin to identify with one of these groups. As they do, they take on an identity as a boy or a girl.

In this section, you'll learn about the "female role" and the "male role" in North America today, and you'll discover why Meda and Perry are having so much trouble rearing a gender-neutral girl.

Images of Men and Women: Facts and Fantasy

All cultures have gender stereotypes—*beliefs and images about males and females that may or may not be true.* For example, many men and women believe that males are rational, active, independent, competitive, and aggressive. At the same time, many men and women claim that females are emotional, passive, dependent, sensitive, and gentle (Ruble, Martin, & Berenbaum, 2006).

Based on gender stereotypes, we expect males and females to act and feel in particular ways, and we respond to their behavior differently depending on their gender (Smith & Mackie, 2000). For example, if you saw a toddler playing with a doll, then you would probably assume that she is a girl, based on her taste in toys. Once we assume the child is a girl, our gender stereotypes lead to numerous inferences about behavior and personality.

Assuming a child is a girl leads to a host of other inferences about personality and behavior.

Learning Gender Stereotypes

Children don't live in a gender-neutral world for long. Although 12-month-old boys and girls look equally at gender-stereotyped toys, 18-month-olds do not: Girls look longer at pictures of dolls than pictures of trucks, but boys look longer at pictures of trucks (Serbin et al., 2001). By 4 years of age, children's knowledge of gender-stereotyped activities is extensive: They believe girls play hopscotch but boys play football, girls help bake cookies but boys take out the trash, and women feed babies but men chop wood (Gelman, Taylor, & Nguyen, 2004). They've also begun to learn about behaviors and traits that are stereotypically masculine or feminine. Preschoolers believe that boys are more often aggressive physically but that girls tend to be aggressive verbally (Giles & Heyman, 2005).

By the time children are ready to enter elementary school, they are well on their way to learning gender stereotypes. For example, 5-year-olds believe boys are strong and dominant and girls are emotional and gentle (Heyman & Legare, 2004). Children also learn that the traits and occupations associated with males tend to earn more money and have greater power than those associated with females (Weisgram, Bigler, & Liben, 2010).

Gender-Related Differences

So far we've only considered people's beliefs about differences between males and females, and many of them are false. Research reveals that males and females often do not differ in the ways specified by cultural stereotypes. What are the bona fide differences between males and females? In addition to the obvious anatomical differences, males are typically larger and stronger than females throughout most of the life span. As

social role
a set of cultural guidelines about how one should behave, especially with other people

gender stereotypes
beliefs and images about males and females that are not necessarily true

infants, boys are generally more active than girls, and this difference increases during childhood (Else-Quest et al., 2006; Saudino, 2009). However, girls typically have a lower mortality rate and are less susceptible to stress and disease (Zaslow & Hayes, 1986).

When it comes to social roles, activities for males tend to be more strenuous, involve more cooperation with others, and often require travel. Activities for females are usually less demanding physically, more solitary, and take place closer to home. This division of roles is much the same worldwide (Whiting & Edwards, 1988).

The extent of gender differences in the intellectual and psychosocial arenas remains uncertain. Research suggests differences between males and females in the following areas:

- *Verbal ability.* During the toddler years, girls typically have larger vocabularies than boys (Leaper & Smith, 2004). During elementary school and high school, most girls read, write, and spell better than boys, and more boys have reading and other language-related problems such as stuttering (Halpern et al., 2007; Wicks-Nelson & Israel, 2006).

- *Mathematics.* On math achievement tests, boys used to get higher scores, but that difference has diminished substantially over the past 25 years; now boys have a negligible advantage (Lindberg et al., 2010). This change apparently reflects efforts to encourage girls to pursue mathematics generally and to take more math courses specifically. Around the world, gender differences in math are negligible in countries where females have similar access to education, occupations, and political power as males, but gender differences remain where females are limited to traditionally feminine-stereotyped occupations that do not require math skills (Else-Quest, Hyde, & Linn, 2010).

- *Spatial ability.* On problems like those in Figure 5.2, which measure the ability to manipulate visual information mentally, you must decide which figures are rotated variants of the standard shown at the left. Males typically respond more rapidly and accurately than females, and these differences are observed in infancy (Halpern et al., 2007; Quinn & Liben, 2008).

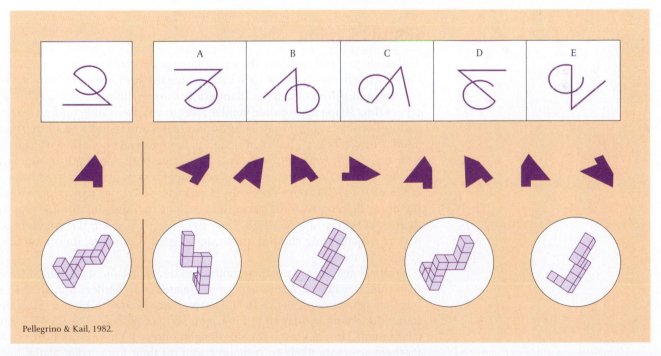

Pellegrino & Kail, 1982.

FIGURE 5.2
On spatial ability tasks, which involve visualizing information in different orientations, males tend to respond more rapidly and more accurately than females.
Source: R.J. Sternberg, Advances in the Psychology of Human Intelligence, Vol. 1, p.316. Advances in the psychology of human intelligence Copyright 1982 by TAYLOR & FRANCIS INFORMA UK LTD - JOURNALS. Reproduced with permission of TAYLOR & FRANCIS INFORMA UK LTD - JOURNALS in the format Textbook via Copyright Clearance Center.

- *Social influence.* Girls are more likely than boys to comply with the directions of adults (Maccoby & Jacklin, 1974). Girls and women are also more readily influenced by others in a variety of situations, particularly when they are under group pressure (Becker, 1986; Eagly, Karau, & Makhijani, 1995). However, these gender differences may simply reflect that females value group harmony more than males do and thus seem to give in to others (Miller, Danaher, & Forbes, 1986; Strough & Berg, 2000). For instance, at a meeting to plan a school function, girls are just as likely as boys to recognize the flaws in a bad idea, but girls are more willing to go along simply because they don't want the group to start arguing.

- *Aggression.* Boys are physically more aggressive than girls, and this is evident by 17 months of age (Baillargeon et al., 2007; Card et al., 2008). *In contrast, girls are more likely to resort to* **relational aggression**, *in which they try to hurt others by damaging their relationships with peers.* They may call children names, make fun of them, spread rumors about them, or pointedly ignore them (Ostrov & Godleski, 2010).

- *Emotional sensitivity.* Girls are often better able to express their emotions and interpret others' emotions (Hall & Halberstadt, 1981; Weinberg et al., 1999). For example, throughout infancy and childhood, girls identify facial expressions (e.g., a happy face versus a sad face) more accurately than boys do (McClure, 2000). And in their interactions with peers, girls are more empathic—they're better able to feel how other children and adolescents are feeling (Rose & Rudolph, 2006).

In most other intellectual and social domains, boys and girls are similar. When thinking about areas in which sex differences have been found, keep in mind that gender differences often depend on a person's experiences (Casey, 1996; Serbin, Powlishta, & Gulko, 1993). Also, gender differences may fluctuate over time, reflecting historical change in the contexts of childhood for boys and girls. Finally, each result just described refers to a difference in the average performance of boys and girls. These differences tend to be small, which means that they do not apply to all boys and all girls (Hyde, 2007). Many girls have greater spatial ability than some boys, and many boys are more susceptible to social influence than are some girls.

Gender Typing

According to social cognitive theory, children learn gender roles in much the same way they learn other social behaviors: by watching the world around them and learning the outcomes of different actions (Bandura & Bussey, 2004; Mischel, 1970). Parents and others thus shape appropriate gender roles in children, and children learn what their culture considers appropriate behavior for males and females by simply watching how adults and peers act. That is, although parents interact equally with sons and daughters, are equally warm to both, and encourage both sons and daughters to achieve, parents respond differently to sons and daughters in gender-related behavior (Lytton & Romney, 1991). Parents encourage daughters when they're playing with dolls, dressing up, or helping an adult but encourage sons in rough-and-tumble play and tolerate their mild aggression (Martin & Ross, 2005). As we'll see in the Spotlight on Research feature, when young children make stereotyped comments, their mothers usually go along with them.

Fathers are more likely than mothers to treat sons and daughters differently. More than mothers, fathers encourage gender-related play. Fathers punish their sons more, but they accept dependence in their daughters (Snow, Jacklin, & Maccoby, 1983). A father, for example, may urge his frightened young son to jump off a diving board ("Be a man!") but not insist that his daughter do so ("That's okay, honey"). Apparently, mothers are more likely to respond based on their knowledge of the needs of individual children, but fathers respond based on gender stereotypes. A mother responds to her son knowing that he's smart but unsure of himself; a father may respond based on what he thinks boys should be like.

relational aggression
aggression used to hurt others by undermining their social relationships

How Mothers Talk to Children About Gender

Who were the investigators, and what was the aim of the study?
Imagine a mother and her preschool son reading a picture book together. Seeing a picture of a girl catching a frog, he says, "Girls hate frogs!" Seeing a picture of a boy playing football, he exclaims, "Yes, Daniel and I like playing football!" When mothers hear children make gender-stereotyped statements like these, what do they do? Susan Gelman, Marianne Taylor, and Simone Nguyen (2004) conducted a study to answer this question.

How did the investigators measure the topic of interest?
Gelman and colleagues created books that included 16 pictures. Half of the pictures showed a person in a gender-stereotyped activity (e.g., a girl sewing, a man driving a truck); half showed a person in an activity that was counter to gender stereotypes (e.g., a boy baking, a woman fighting a fire). Mothers were asked to go through the picture book with the children, as they might do at home. They were not told about the investigators' interest in gender. Mothers and children were video-taped as they looked at the books.

Who were the participants in the study?
The study included 72 pairs of mothers and children: of the children, 24 were 2-year-olds, 24 were 4-year-olds, and 24 were 6-year-olds.

What was the design of the study?
This study was correlational because Gelman and colleagues were interested in the relations that existed naturally among a child's speech and a mother's reply to the child's speech, the child's age, and the child's sex. The study was cross-sectional because it included 2-year-olds, 4-year-olds, and 6-year-olds, each tested once.

Were there ethical concerns with the study?
No; most children enjoy reading picture books with parents.

What were the results?
First, the investigators determined the number of stereotyped statements that children made, including those that endorsed a stereotype—"Jackie and Sherry love to play with dolls!"—as well as those that deny a counterstereotype— "Boys aren't ballet dancers!" The 2-year-olds averaged about 24 of the statements; the 4- and 6-year-olds averaged about 30. Then the mother's response to stereotyped comments was classified in one of eight categories; we'll describe just three of the categories for simplicity:

- The mother *affirmed* her child's remark: "Yes, girls do like playing with dolls!"
- The mother *repeated* the child's remark as a question: "Are you sure boys aren't dancers?"
- The mother *negated* the child's remark: "Oh yes, boys *can* be dancers."

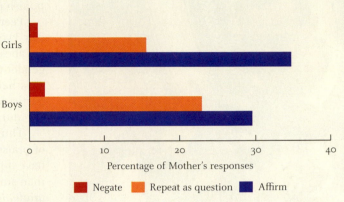

FIGURE 5.3
Mothers often affirm their children's stereotyped comments or repeat them as questions, but they rarely negate them.
Data from Gelman et al., 2004.

The percentage of times that mothers used each of these responses is shown in Figure 5.3. You can see that mothers agreed with their child's remarks about one third of the time. They almost never disagreed directly with their children: Fewer than 2% of mothers' comments fell in this category. But they did rephrase their children's statements as questions about 20% of the time, which is a subtle way for a mother to dispute her child. Overall, mothers' responses were similar for sons and daughters; they also were much the same for 2-, 4-, and 6-year-olds, so the data in the graphs are averaged across the three age groups.

What did the investigators conclude?
Gelman and colleagues concluded that "mothers are surprisingly accepting of children's stereotyping statements. Mothers rarely directly contradicted a child's gender stereotype statement, and in fact more often affirmed the child's stereotype than questioned it."

What converging evidence would strengthen these conclusions?
The mothers in this sample were well educated. It would be important to see whether mothers with less education respond in a similar fashion. In addition, it would be valuable to know the impact of a mother's reply on her child's gender stereotyping. When mothers question children's stereotyped statements, do children rethink their concepts? Or is this form of feedback too subtle to affect preschool children, particularly younger ones?

 Go to Psychology CourseMate at **www.cengagebrain.com** to enhance your understanding of this research.

Adults differ in their views on the relative rights and roles of males and females. Some have very traditional views, whereas others have more gender-neutral views. As you might expect, children's gender-related interests, attitudes, and self-concepts are more traditional when their parents have traditional views but are more gender neutral when their parents have nontraditional views (Crouter et al., 2007; Tenenbaum & Leaper, 2002).

Peers are also influential. By 3 years, most children's play shows the impact of gender stereotypes—boys prefer blocks and trucks, whereas girls prefer tea sets and dolls—and

Fathers are more likely than mothers to encourage their children's gender-related play.

youngsters are critical of peers who engage in gender-inappropriate play (Aspenlieder, 2009). This is particularly true of boys who like feminine toys or who choose feminine activities (Levy, Taylor, & Gelman, 1995). Once children learn rules about gender-typical play, they often harshly punish peers who violate those rules.

Peers influence gender roles in another way. We've seen that, by 2 or 3 years of age, children most often play with same-sex peers (Martin & Fabes, 2001). This early segregation of playmates based on a child's gender means that boys learn primarily from boys and girls from girls. This helps solidify a youngster's emerging sense of membership in a particular gender group and sharpens the contrast between their gender and the other gender.

Thus, through encouraging words, critical looks, and other forms of praise and punishment, other people influence boys and girls to behave differently (Jacobs & Eccles, 1992). However, children learn more than simply the specific behaviors associated with their gender. *A child gradually begins to identify with one group and to develop a **gender identity***—a sense of the self as a male or a female.

Gender Identity

If you were to listen to a typical conversation between two preschoolers, you might hear something like this:

Maria: When I grow up, I'm going to be a singer.
Juanita: When I grow up, I'm going to be a papa.
Maria: No, you can't be a papa—you'll be a mama.
Juanita: No, I wanna be a papa.
Maria: You can't be a papa. Only boys can be papas, and you're a girl!

Maria's understanding of gender is more developed than Juanita's. How can we explain these differences? According to Kohlberg (1966; Kohlberg & Ullian, 1974), children gradually develop a basic understanding that they are of either the female or the male sex. Gender then serves to organize many perceptions, attitudes, values, and behaviors. Full understanding of gender is said to develop gradually in three steps.

■ **Gender labeling**. *By age 2 or 3, children understand that they are either boys or girls and label themselves accordingly.*

■ **Gender stability**. *During the preschool years, children begin to understand that gender is stable: Boys become men and girls become women.* However, children in this stage may believe that a girl who wears her hair like a boy will become a boy and a boy who plays with dolls will become a girl (Fagot, 1985).

■ **Gender constancy**. *Between 4 and 7 years, most children understand that maleness and femaleness do not change over situations or according to personal wishes.* They understand that a child's sex is unaffected by the clothing a child wears or the toys a child likes.

Thus, Juanita and Maria both know that they're girls, but Maria has developed a greater sense of gender stability and gender constancy. According to Kohlberg's theory, children begin learning about gender roles after they have mastered gender constancy—that is, after they know that gender is fixed across time and situation.

Kohlberg's theory specifies when children begin learning about gender-appropriate behavior and activities but not how such learning takes place. A theory proposed by Martin (Martin et al., 1999; Martin & Ruble, 2004) addresses how children learn about gender (see Figure 5.4). *In **gender-schema theory**, children first decide whether an object, activity, or behavior is associated with females or males; then they use this information to decide whether they should learn more about the object, activity, or behavior.*

HUMAN DEVELOPMENT in action

As a preschool teacher, what would you think of the impact of same-sex classes (i.e., separate classes for boys and girls) on children's gender-related behaviors and stereotypes?

gender identity
a sense of oneself as male or female

gender labeling
young children's understanding that they are either boys or girls and naming of themselves accordingly

gender stability
the understanding in preschool children that boys become men and girls become women

gender constancy
the understanding that maleness and femaleness do not change over situations or personal wishes

gender-schema theory
a theory that states that children want to learn more about an activity only after first deciding whether it is masculine or feminine

FIGURE 5.4

According to gender-schema theory, children decide whether an object, activity, or behavior is for females or males before learning more about the objects, activities, or behaviors that are appropriate for their gender.

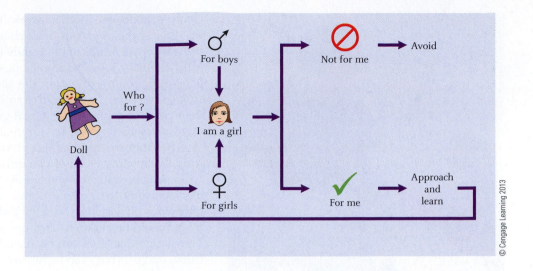

© Cengage Learning 2013

That is, once children know their gender, they pay attention primarily to experiences and events that are gender appropriate (Martin & Halverson, 1987). According to gender-schema theory, a preschool boy watching a group of girls playing in sand will decide that playing in sand is for girls and that, because he is a boy, playing in sand is not for him. Seeing a group of older boys playing football, he will decide that football is for boys and that, because he is a boy, football is acceptable and he should learn more about it.

According to gender-schema theory, after children understand gender, it's as if they see the world through special glasses that allow only gender-typical activities to be in focus (Liben & Bigler, 2002). For example, after children understand gender, their tastes in TV programs begin to shift along gender-specific lines (Luecke-Aleksa et al., 1995). In addition, they begin to use gender labels to evaluate toys and activities (Shutts, Banaji, & Spelke, 2010). This selective viewing of the world explains a great deal about children's learning of gender roles, but one final important element needs to be considered: biology.

Biological Influences

Biology also contributes to gender roles and gender identity. Men and women have performed vastly different roles for much of human history: Women were more invested in childrearing, and men were more invested in providing important resources (e.g., food and protection) for their offspring (Geary, 2002). In adapting to these roles, different traits and behaviors evolved for men and women. For example, men became more aggressive because that was adaptive in helping them ward off predators.

If gender roles are based in part on our evolutionary heritage, then behavior genetic research should show the impact of heredity on gender-role learning. Indeed, twin studies show a substantial hereditary impact on gender-role learning (Iervolino et al., 2005). The exact mechanism may be prenatal exposure to testosterone, which has a masculinizing influence on children's activities and interests (Hines, 2011).

Perhaps the most accurate conclusion to draw is that biology, the socializing influence of people and media, and the child's own efforts to understand gender-typical behavior all contribute to gender roles and differences. Recognizing the interactive nature of these influences on gender learning also enables us to better understand how gender roles are changing today, which we consider next.

Evolving Gender Roles

Gender roles are not etched in stone; they change with the times. In the United States, the range of acceptable roles for girls and boys and women and men has never been greater than today. For example, some fathers stay home to be primary caregivers for

© Tetra Images/Alamy

The range of roles acceptable today for men and women is very broad. Nevertheless, boys and girls still tend to have same-sex friends and to enjoy many sex-typed activities.

children, and some mothers work full time as sole support for the family. What is the impact of these changes on gender roles? Some insights come from the results of the Family Lifestyles Project (Weisner & Wilson-Mitchell, 1990), which examined families in which the adults were members of the counterculture of the 1960s and 1970s. Some of the families studied were deeply committed to living their own lives and to rearing their children without traditional gender stereotypes. In these families, men and women shared the household, financial, and child-care tasks.

The results of this project show that parents like Meda and Perry, from the opening vignette, can influence some aspects of gender stereotyping more readily than others. On the one hand, children in these families tend to have same-sex friends and to like sex-typed activities: The boys enjoy physical play, and the girls enjoy drawing and reading. On the other hand, the children have few stereotypes concerning occupations: They agree that girls can be president of the United States and drive trucks and that boys can be nurses and secretaries. They also have fewer sex-typed attitudes about the use of objects. They claim that boys and girls are equally likely to use an iron, a shovel, a hammer and nails, and a needle and thread.

Apparently, some features of gender roles and identities are more readily influenced by experience than others. This should not be surprising. Over the course of human history, it has been adaptive for women to be caring and nurturing because this increases the odds of a secure attachment and, ultimately, the survival of the infant. Men's responsibilities have included protecting the family unit from predators and hunting with other males, roles for which physical strength and aggressiveness are crucial. Circumstances of life in the 21st century are, of course, substantially different. Nevertheless, the cultural changes of the past few decades cannot erase hundreds of thousands of years of evolutionary history (Geary, 2002). We should not be surprised that boys and girls play differently, that girls tend to be more supportive in their interactions with others, and that boys are usually more aggressive physically.

Test Yourself

Recall

1. _____ are beliefs and images about males and females that may or may not be true.

2. Research on intellectual functioning and social behavior has revealed sex differences in verbal ability, _____, social influence, and aggression.

3. _____ may be particularly influential in teaching gender roles, because they more often treat sons and daughters differently.

4. According to Kohlberg's theory, understanding of gender includes gender labeling, gender stability, and _____.

5. Children studied in the Family Lifestyles Project, whose parents were members of the counterculture of the 1960s and 1970s, had traditional gender-related views toward friends and _____.

Interpret

- How do the different forces in the biopsychosocial framework contribute to the development of gender roles?

- How would different theories of cognitive development described in Chapter 4 explain the gender-related differences in cognitive skills described on page 145?

Apply

- What advice would you give to a mother who wants her daughter to grow to be gender free in her attitudes, beliefs, and aspirations?

- The women's liberation movement became a powerful social force in North America during the 1960s. Describe how a developmental psychologist might do research to determine whether the movement has changed the gender roles that children learn.

Recall answers: (1) Gender stereotypes, (2) spatial ability, (3) Fathers, (4) gender constancy, (5) preferred activities

Linking Research to life • ATTACHMENT AND CHILD CARE

Today, millions of infants and toddlers are cared for by someone other than their mother. Some are cared for in their own home by their father, a grandparent, or another relative. Others receive care in a provider's home; the provider is often a relative. Still others attend day-care or nursery-school programs. Parents and policy makers alike have been concerned about the impact of such care on children generally and on attachment specifically. Is there, for example, a maximum amount of time per week that infants should spend in care outside the home? Is there a minimum age below which infants should not be placed in care outside the home?

Research shows no overall effects of child-care experience on mother–infant attachment. In other words, a secure mother–infant attachment is just as likely regardless of the quality of child care, the amount of time the child spent in care, the age when the child began care, how frequently the parents changed child-care arrangements, or the type of child care (e.g., a child-care center or in the home with a nonrelative). However, insecure attachments are more common when less sensitive mothering is combined with low-quality or large amounts of child care (National Institute of Child Health and Human Development Early Child Care Research Network, 1997, 2001; Sagi et al., 2002).

Thus, parents can enroll their children in high-quality day-care programs with no fear of harmful consequences. When children are enrolled in high-quality day care, other factors (e.g., the type of child care or the amount of time the child spends in child care) typically do not affect the mother–child attachment relationship. When trying to find care for their children, parents should look for the following features (Burchinal et al., 2000; Lamb, 1999):

- A low ratio of children to caregivers
- Well-trained, experienced staff
- Low staff turnover
- Ample opportunities for educational and social stimulation
- Effective communication between parents and day-care workers concerning the general aims and routine functioning of the program

Centers that have well-trained, experienced staff caring for a relatively small number of children are more likely to provide good care, but the only way to know the quality of care with certainty is to see for yourself (Lamb, 1999).

Summary

5.1 Beginnings: Trust and Attachment

What are Erikson's first three stages of psychosocial development?

■ In Erikson's theory of psychosocial development, individuals face certain psychosocial crises at different stages in development. The crisis of infancy is to establish a balance between trust and mistrust of the world, producing hope; between 1 and 3 years of age, youngsters must blend autonomy, shame, and doubt to produce will; and between 3 and 6 years, initiative and guilt must be balanced to achieve purpose.

How do infants form emotional attachments to parents?

■ Attachment is an enduring socioemotional relationship between infant and parent. Bowlby's theory of attachment is rooted in evolutionary psychology and describes four stages in the development of attachment: preattachment, attachment in the making, true attachment, and reciprocal relationships.

What are the kinds of attachment relationships?

■ Research with the Strange Situation, in which infant and mother are separated briefly, reveals four primary forms of attachment. Most common is a secure attachment in which infants have complete trust in the mother. Less common are three types of attachment relationships in which this trust is lacking. In avoidant relationships, infants deal with the lack of trust by ignoring the mother; in resistant relationships, infants often seem angry with her; and in disorganized relationships, infants do not appear to understand the mother's absence.

■ Children who had secure attachment relationships during infancy often interact with their peers more readily and more skillfully. Secure attachment is most likely to occur when mothers respond sensitively and consistently to their infants' needs.

■ Responsive caregiving results in infants developing an internal working model that parents will try to meet their needs. Secure attachment can be harder to achieve when infants are temperamentally difficult.

5.2 Emerging Emotions

At what age do children begin to express basic emotions?

■ Basic emotions—which include joy, anger, and fear—emerge in the first year. Fear first appears in infancy as stranger wariness.

What are complex emotions? When do they develop?

- Complex emotions have an evaluative component and include guilt, embarrassment, and pride. They appear between 18 and 24 months and require more sophisticated cognitive skills than those involved with the basic emotions of happiness and fear. Cultures differ in the rules for expressing emotions and in the situations that elicit particular emotions.

When do children begin to understand other people's emotions?

- As early as 4 months, infants begin to recognize the emotions associated with different facial expressions. They use this information to help them evaluate unfamiliar situations. Beyond infancy, children learn more about the causes of different emotions.

How do children regulate their emotion?

- Infants use simple strategies to regulate emotions such as fear. As children grow, they become better skilled at regulating their emotions. Children who do not regulate emotions well tend to have problems interacting with others.

5.3 Interacting With Others

When do youngsters first begin to play with one another? How does play change during infancy and the preschool years?

- Even infants notice and respond to one another, but the first real interactions take the form of parallel play. in which toddlers play alone while watching each other. A few months later, simple social play emerges in which toddlers engage in similar activities and interact with one another. At about 2 years of age, cooperative play organized around a theme becomes common. Make-believe play is also common; in addition to being fun, it allows children to examine frightening topics. Most forms of solitary play are harmless.

What determines whether children help one another?

- Prosocial behaviors, such as helping or sharing, are more common in children who understand (by perspective taking) and experience (by empathy) another's feelings.

- Prosocial behavior is more likely when children feel responsible for the person in distress. Also, children help more often when they believe they have the skills needed, when they are feeling happy or successful, and when they perceive that the costs of helping are small.

- Prosocial behavior is influenced by heredity, probably through its impact on behavioral control (inhibition) and emotion regulation.

- Parents can foster altruism in their youngsters by behaving altruistically themselves, by using reasoning to discipline their children, and by encouraging their children to help at home and elsewhere.

5.4 Gender Roles and Gender Identity

What are our stereotypes about males and females? How well do they correspond to actual differences between boys and girls?

- Gender stereotypes are beliefs about males and females that are often used to make inferences about a person that are based solely on gender; children know many of these stereotypes by the time they enter elementary school.

- Studies of gender differences reveal that girls generally have greater verbal skill but that boys have greater spatial skill. Differences in math are negligible when females have access to education and occupations where math is valuable. Typically, girls are better able to interpret emotions and are more prone to social influence, but boys are more aggressive. These differences vary based on a number of factors, including the historical period.

How do young children learn gender roles?

- Parents treat sons and daughters similarly, except in sex-typed activities. Fathers may be particularly important in sex typing because they are more likely to treat sons and daughters differently.

- In Kohlberg's theory, children gradually learn that gender is stable over time and cannot be changed according to personal wishes. After children understand gender stability, they begin to learn gender-typical behavior. According to gender-schema theory, children learn about gender by paying attention to behaviors of members of their sex and ignoring behaviors of members of the other sex.

- Evolutionary developmental psychology reminds us that different roles for males and females caused different traits and behaviors to evolve for men and women. The idea that biology influences some aspects of gender roles is also supported by research on females exposed to male hormones during prenatal development.

How are gender roles changing?

- Gender roles have changed considerably in the past 50 years. However, studies of nontraditional families indicate that some components of gender stereotypes are more readily changed than others.

Key Terms

hope (128)
will (128)
purpose (129)
attachment (129)
secure attachment (130)
avoidant attachment (130)
resistant attachment (130)
disorganized (disoriented) attachment
    (130)
internal working model (131)

basic emotions (133)
social smiles (133)
stranger wariness (133)
social referencing (135)
parallel play (137)
simple social play (137)
cooperative play (137)
enabling actions (139)
constricting actions (139)
prosocial behavior (140)

altruism (140)
empathy (140)
social role (144)
gender stereotypes (144)
relational aggression (146)
gender identity (148)
gender labeling (148)
gender stability (148)
gender constancy (148)
gender-schema theory (148)

Online Resources

Go to CengageBrain.com to access Psychology CourseMate, where you will find an interactive eBook, flashcards, quizzes, videos, websites, and more.

© Fancy/Veer/Corbis/Glow Images

Off to School

Cognitive and Physical Development in Middle Childhood

Every fall, American 5- and 6-year-olds trot off to kindergarten, starting an educational journey that lasts 13 or more years. By journey's end, most children can read complete books and many have learned algebra and geometry. This mastery of complex academic skills is possible because of changes in children's thinking that are described in the first section of this chapter.

For most American schoolchildren, intelligence and aptitude tests are a common part of their educational travels. In the second and third sections, you'll see what tests measure and how they are used to identify schoolchildren with atypical or special needs. Next, we look at the ways in which students learn to read, write, and do math. In this section, you'll discover some practices that foster students' learning.

Finally, children's growing cognitive skills, when coupled with improved motor coordination, enable them to participate in sports. In the last section, we look at such participation and the physical changes that make it possible.

LEARNING OBJECTIVES

- What are the distinguishing characteristics of thought during Piaget's concrete-operational and formal-operational stages?

- How do children use strategies and monitoring to improve learning and remembering?

Adrian, a sixth grader in middle school, just took his first social studies test—and failed. He is shocked because he'd always received As and Bs in elementary school. Adrian realizes that glancing through the textbook chapter once before a test is probably not going to work in middle school, but he's not sure what he should be doing.

Adrian's cognitive skills far surpass those of the infants and toddlers that we examined in Chapter 4. In this section, we'll learn more about these skills, first from the perspective of Jean Piaget's theory and then by considering information processing.

More Sophisticated Thinking: Piaget's Version

Piaget's first two stages, sensorimotor and preoperational thinking, characterize infancy and the preschool years. In the next few pages, we describe the remaining two stages, the concrete-operational and formal-operational stages, which apply to school-age children and adolescents.

The Concrete-Operational Period

Preoperational children are egocentric, sometimes confuse appearance with reality, and are centered in their thinking. None of these limits applies to children in the concrete-operational stage, which extends from approximately 7 to 11 years. Egocentrism wanes as youngsters have more experiences with others who assert their perspectives on the world. The understanding that events can be interpreted in different ways leads to the realization that appearances can be deceiving. *Also, thought can be reversed, because school-age children have acquired* **mental operations**, *which are actions that can be performed on objects or ideas and that consistently yield a result.* Recall the conservation task from Chapter 4, in which liquid is transferred from one beaker to another of a different shape. In this task, concrete-operational children realize that the amount of liquid is the same after it has been poured into a different beaker—pointing out that the pouring can always be reversed.

Nevertheless, as the name implies, concrete-operational thinking is limited to the tangible and real, to the here and now. The concrete-operational youngster takes "an earthbound, concrete, practical-minded sort of problem-solving approach" (Flavell, 1985, p. 98). Thinking abstractly and hypothetically is acquired in the formal-operational period, as we'll see next.

The Formal-Operational Period

With the onset of the formal-operational period, which extends from roughly age 11 into adulthood, children and adolescents apply psychological operations to abstract entities; they are able to think hypothetically and reason abstractly (Siegler & Alibali, 2004).

To illustrate these differences, let's look at one of Piaget's experiments (Inhelder & Piaget, 1958). Children and adolescents were presented with several flasks, each containing what appeared to be a clear liquid. They were asked to find the combination of liquids

mental operations
cognitive actions that can be performed on objects or ideas

As a 15-year-old, Robert Kail delivered the *Indianapolis Star*. In 1965, the newspaper announced a contest for all newspaper carriers. The task was to list words that could be created from the letters contained in the words *safe race*. Whoever listed the most words would win two tickets to the Indianapolis 500 auto race.

Kail realized that this was a problem in combinatorial reasoning. All he needed to do was create all possible combinations of letters, then look them up. Following this procedure, he had to win (or, at worst, tie). So he created exhaustive lists of possible words, beginning with each of the letters individually, then trying all possible combinations of two letters,

and finally working his way up to all possible combinations of all eight letters (e.g., *scareefa scareeaf*). Then he looked up all those possible words in a dictionary. Weeks later, he had generated a list of 126 words. As predicted, a few months later, he learned that he had won the contest.

Concrete-operational thinkers often solve problems haphazardly, but formal-operational thinkers more often set up problems in abstract terms.

that would produce a blue liquid. A typical concrete-operational youngster plunges right in, mixing liquids from different flasks haphazardly. In contrast, formal-operational adolescents understand that the problem is not about pouring liquids but about combining elements until all possible combinations have been tested. So a teenager might mix liquid from the first flask with liquids from each of the other flasks. If none of those combinations produces a blue liquid, the teenager would conclude that the liquid in the first flask is not essential. The next step would be to mix the liquid in the second flask with each of the remaining liquids. Formal-operational thinkers continue in this manner until finding the critical combination that produces the blue liquid. Adolescents understand that solving the problem involves identifying possible combinations and then evaluating each one. This sort of adolescent combinatorial reasoning is illustrated in the Real People feature.

Adolescents' more sophisticated thinking is also shown in their ability to make appropriate conclusions from facts, which is known as **deductive reasoning**. Suppose we tell a person the following statement:

If you hit a glass with a hammer, the glass will break.

If you then tell the person, "You hit the glass with a hammer" he or she would conclude that "The glass will break," a conclusion that formal-operational adolescents do reach.

Concrete-operational youngsters sometimes reach this conclusion too—but based on their experience, not because the conclusion is logically necessary. To see the difference, imagine that the statement is now:

If you hit a glass with a feather, the glass will break.

Told "You hit the glass with a feather," the conclusion "the glass will break" follows just as logically as it did in the first example, but the conclusion goes against what experience tells us is true. Concrete-operational 10-year-olds resist reaching conclusions that are contrary to known facts, whereas formal-operational 15-year-olds often reach such conclusions (De Neys & Everaerts, 2008). Formal-operational teenagers understand that these problems are about abstractions that need not correspond to real-world relations. In contrast, concrete-operational youngsters reach conclusions based on their knowledge of the world.

Comments on Piaget's View

We mentioned in Chapter 4 some shortcomings in Piaget's theory (e.g., it overestimates cognitive competence in adolescents). Consequently, we need to consider other approaches; in the next few pages, we focus on the information-processing approach that we examined in Chapter 4.

deductive reasoning
a characteristic of formal-operational thought that involves drawing conclusions from facts

As children grow, they make more use of memory aids, such as taking notes.

HUMAN DEVELOPMENT in action

As a second-grade teacher, what strategies would your students be likely to use to help them learn words in a weekly spelling test?

organization
as applied to children's memory, a strategy in which information to be remembered is structured so that related information is placed together

elaboration
a memory strategy in which information is embellished to make it more memorable

metamemory
a person's informal understanding of memory, including the ability to diagnose memory problems accurately and to monitor the effectiveness of memory strategies

Information-Processing Strategies for Learning and Remembering

Information-processing psychologists focus on the means by which children store information in permanent memory and retrieve it when needed later. To illustrate, how do you try to learn the information in a textbook? If you're like many college students, you probably use some combination of highlighting key sentences, outlining chapters, taking notes, writing summaries, and testing yourself. These are all effective learning strategies that make it easier for you to store information permanently.

Children begin to use simple strategies fairly early. For example, 7- or 8-year-olds use rehearsal, a strategy of repetitively naming information that is to be remembered. As children grow older, they learn other memory strategies. *One memory strategy is* **organization**—*structuring information to be remembered so that related information is placed together.* For example, a sixth grader trying to remember major battles of the American Civil War could organize them geographically (e.g., Shiloh and Fort Donelson in Tennessee, Antietam and Monocacy in Maryland) or chronologically (e.g., Fort Sumter and First Manassas in 1861, Gettysburg and Vicksburg in 1863).

Another memory strategy is **elaboration**—*embellishing information to be remembered to make it more memorable.* To see elaboration in action, imagine a child who can't remember whether the second syllable of *rehearsal* is spelled *her* or *hear*. The child could remember the correct spelling by reminding himself that *rehearsal* is like *re-hear-ing*. Thus, thinking about the derivation of *rehearsal* makes it easier to remember how to spell it.

Finally, as children grow, they're more likely to use external aids to memory, such as making notes and writing down information on calendars so they won't forget future events (Eskritt & McLeod, 2008).

Metacognition

Just as there's not much value to a filled toolbox if you don't know how to use the tools, memory strategies aren't much good unless children know when to use them. For example, rehearsal is a great strategy for remembering phone numbers but lousy for remembering the plot of *Hamlet*. During the elementary-school years and adolescence, children gradually learn to identify different kinds of memory problems and the memory strategies most appropriate to each. For example, when reading a textbook or watching a television newscast, outlining or writing a summary are good strategies because they identify the main points and organize them. Children gradually become more skilled at selecting appropriate strategies, but even high-school students do not always use effective learning strategies when they should (Pressley & Hilden, 2006).

After children choose a memory strategy, they need to monitor its effectiveness to see whether it's working. If it's not, they need to begin anew, reanalyzing the memory task to select a better approach. If the strategy is working, they should determine the portion of the material they have not yet mastered and concentrate their efforts there. Monitoring improves gradually with age. For example, elementary-school children can accurately identify which material they have not yet learned, but they do not consistently focus their study efforts on this material (Bjorklund, 2005).

Diagnosing memory problems accurately and monitoring the effectiveness of memory strategies are two important elements of **metamemory**, *which refers to a child's intuitive understanding of memory.* That is, as children develop, they learn more about how memory operates and devise naive theories of memory that represent an extension of the theory of mind described on pages 87–88 (Lockl & Schneider, 2007). For example, children learn that memory is fallible (i.e., they sometimes forget) and that some types of memory tasks are easier than others. This growing knowledge of memory helps children use memory strategies more effectively, just as an experienced carpenter's accumulated knowledge of wood tells her when to use nails, screws, or glue to join two boards.

Children's growing understanding of memory is paralleled by their increased understanding of all cognitive processes. *Such knowledge and awareness of cognitive processes is called* **metacognitive knowledge**. Metacognitive knowledge grows rapidly during the elementary-school years: Children come to know much about perception, attention, intentions, knowledge, and thinking (Flavell, 2000; McCormick, 2003). For example, school-age children know that sometimes they deliberately direct their attention—as in searching for a parent's face in a crowd—but that sometimes events capture attention—as with an unexpected clap of thunder (Parault & Schwanenflugel, 2000).

Test Yourself

Recall

1. During Piaget's _____ stage, children are first able to represent objects mentally in different ways and to perform mental operations.

2. Hypothetical and deductive reasoning are characteristic of children in Piaget's _____ stage.

3. Children and adolescents often select a memory strategy after they have _____.

4. The term _____ refers to periodic evaluation of a strategy to determine whether it is working.

Interpret

- Do developmental improvements in memory strategies and metacognition emphasize nature, nurture, or both? How?

- Piaget and Erikson each proposed unique stages for ages 7 to 11 years. How similar are the stages they proposed? How do they differ?

Apply

- Formal-operational adolescents are able to reason abstractly. If you were a high-school science teacher, how might this ability help them conduct more sophisticated experiments?

- A 9-year-old is trying to figure out why a video game doesn't work. Describe how she's likely to troubleshoot the game.

Recall answers: (1) concrete-operational, (2) formal-operational, (3) determined the goal of the memory task, (4) monitoring

---

6.2 Aptitudes for School

LEARNING OBJECTIVES

- What is the nature of intelligence?
- What are intelligence tests like?
- How well do intelligence tests work?

- How do heredity and environment influence intelligence?
- How and why do test scores vary for different racial and ethnic groups?

Diana is an eager fourth-grade teacher who loves history but is frustrated when she teaches a unit on the Civil War. Although she's passionate about the subject, her enthusiasm is not contagious. Instead, her students' eyes glaze over and she can see young minds drifting off. Diana wishes there was a different way to teach this unit, one that would engage her students more effectively.

Before you read further, how would you define intelligence? Your definition probably includes the ability to reason logically, connect ideas, and solve real problems. You might mention verbal ability, meaning the ability to speak clearly and articulately. You might also mention social competence: for example, being interested in the world at large and being able to admit when you make a mistake (Sternberg & Kaufman, 1998).

metacognitive knowledge
a person's knowledge and awareness of cognitive processes

As you'll see in this section, many of these ideas about intelligence are included in theories of intelligence. You'll also see how intelligence tests were devised initially to assess individual differences in intellectual ability. Then we'll see how well tests work. Finally, we examine factors that influence intelligence.

Theories of Intelligence

More than 100 years ago, Spearman (1904) claimed that a general factor for intelligence, or *g*, is responsible for performance on all mental tests. Later, Thurstone and Thurstone (1941) acknowledged that a general factor operated in all tasks, but they emphasized more specific factors, such as word fluency, number proficiency, and reasoning. These views were reconciled in hierarchical theories of intelligence that include both general and specific components. Carroll (1993, 1996), for example, proposed the hierarchical theory with the three levels shown in Figure 6.1. At the top of the hierarchy is *g*, general intelligence. In the level underneath *g* are eight broad categories of intellectual skill, ranging from fluid intelligence to processing speed. Each ability in the second level is further divided into the skills listed in the third and most specific level. Crystallized intelligence, for example, includes understanding printed language, comprehending language, and knowing vocabulary.

Some critics argue that hierarchical theories are unsatisfactory because they ignore research and theory on cognitive development. One theory that addresses this criticism is Gardner's (1983, 2002, 2006) theory of multiple intelligences. Drawing on research in child development, studies of brain-damaged people, and studies of exceptionally talented people, Gardner identified the nine distinct intelligences shown in Table 6.1.

The first three intelligences in this list—linguistic, logical–mathematical, and spatial—are included in traditional theories of intelligence. The last six intelligences are not: Musical, bodily–kinesthetic, interpersonal, intrapersonal, naturalistic, and existential intelligences are unique to Gardner's theory. According to Gardner, Carlos Santana's wizardry on the guitar, Roger Federer's remarkable shots on the tennis court, and Oprah Winfrey's grace and charm in dealing with people are just as important in defining intelligence as is verbal or mathematical skill.

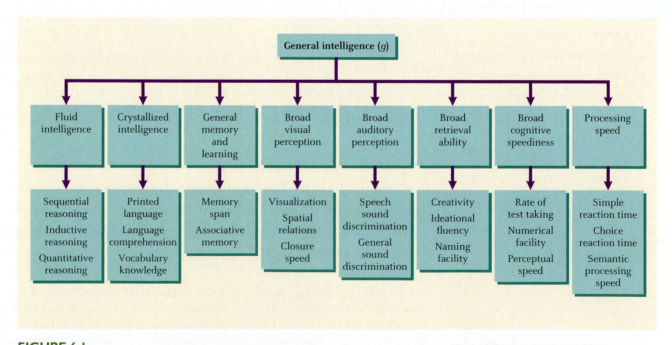

FIGURE 6.1

Hierarchical theories of intelligence have different levels that range from general intelligence (*g*) to specific skills.

From Human cognitive abilities: A survey of factor-analytic studies, by J. B. Carroll. Copyright © Cambridge University Press 1993.

TABLE 6.1

Nine Intelligences in Gardner's Theory of Multiple Intelligences

Type of Intelligence	Definition
Linguistic	Knowing the meanings of words, having the ability to use words to understand new ideas, and using language to convey ideas to others
Logical–mathematical	Understanding relations that exist among objects, actions, and ideas, as well as the logical or mathematical operations that can be performed on them
Spatial	Perceiving objects accurately and imagining in the "mind's eye" the appearance of an object before and after it has been transformed
Musical	Comprehending and producing sounds varying in pitch, rhythm, and emotional tone
Bodily–kinesthetic	Using one's body in highly differentiated ways, as dancers, craftspeople, and athletes do
Interpersonal	Identifying feelings, moods, motivations, and intentions in others
Intrapersonal	Understanding one's emotions and knowing one's strengths and weaknesses
Naturalistic	Understanding the natural world, distinguishing natural objects from artifacts, and grouping and labeling natural phenomena
Existential	Considering "ultimate" issues, such as the purpose of life and the nature of death

SOURCE: Gardner, 1983, 1999, 2002.

Prompted by Gardner's theory, researchers have examined other nontraditional aspects of intelligence. *One is* **emotional intelligence**, *which is the ability to use one's own and others' emotions effectively for solving problems and living happily.* One major model of emotional intelligence (Mayer, Salovey, & Caruso, 2008; Salovey & Grewal, 2005) includes perceiving emotions accurately (e.g., recognizing a happy face), understanding emotions (e.g., distinguishing happiness from ecstasy), and regulating one's emotions (e.g., hiding disappointment). People who are emotionally intelligent tend to have more satisfying interpersonal relationships, to have greater self-esteem, and to be more effective in the workplace (Chang, Sy, & Choi, 2012; Joseph & Newman, 2010).

Another modern theory, Sternberg's (1999, 2008) theory of successful intelligence, defines intelligence as using abilities skillfully to achieve personal goals. Goals can be short term (e.g., getting an A on a test) or longer term (e.g., having a successful career). In achieving personal goals, people use three kinds of abilities:

- **Analytic ability** *involves analyzing problems and generating different solutions.* Suppose a 12-year-old wants to download songs to her iPod, but something isn't working. Analytic intelligence is shown in considering different causes of the problem—maybe the iPod is broken, or maybe the software to download songs wasn't installed correctly.

- **Creative ability** *involves dealing adaptively with novel situations and problems.* Suppose our 12-year-old discovers her iPod is broken just as she's ready to leave on a daylong car trip. Lacking the time to buy a new player, creative intelligence is shown in dealing successfully with a novel goal: finding an enjoyable activity to pass the time on a long drive.

- **Practical ability** *involves knowing which solution or plan will work.* Problems can be solved in different ways, but often only solution is practical. Our 12-year-old may realize that the only way to figure out why her iPod isn't working is to surf the Internet: She doesn't want to ask for help because her parents wouldn't approve of many of the songs, and she doesn't want a sibling to know that she's downloading them anyway.

emotional intelligence
the ability to use one's own and others' emotions effectively for solving problems and living happily

analytic ability
in Sternberg's theory of successful intelligence, the ability to analyze problems and generate different solutions

creative ability
in Sternberg's theory of successful intelligence, the ability to deal adaptively with novel situations and problems

practical ability
in Sternberg's theory of successful intelligence, the ability to know which solutions to a problem are likely to work

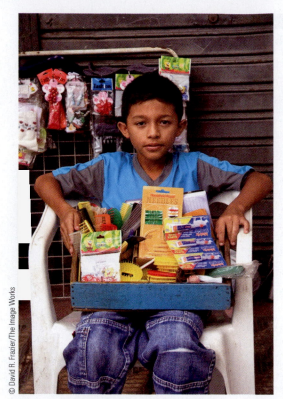

For street vendors in Brazil, successful intelligence involves sophisticated arithmetic operations for buying products, making change, and keeping track of sales.

Sternberg emphasizes that successful intelligence is revealed in people's pursuit of goals. Of course, these goals vary from one person to the next and, just as important, often vary in different cultural or ethnic groups. That is, intelligence is always partly defined by the demands of an environment or the cultural context. What is intelligent for children growing up in cities in North America may not be intelligent for children growing up in the Sahara desert, the Australian outback, or on a remote island in the Pacific Ocean. For example, in Brazil, many school-age boys sell candy and fruit to bus passengers and pedestrians. These children often cannot identify the numbers on paper money, yet they know how to purchase their goods from wholesale stores, make change for customers, and keep track of their sales (Saxe, 1988).

If the Brazilian vendors were given the tests that measure intelligence in American students, they would fare poorly. Does this mean they are less intelligent than American children? Of course not. The skills that are important to American conceptions of intelligence and assessed on our intelligence tests are less valued in these other cultures and so are not cultivated in the young. Each culture defines what it means to be intelligent, and the specialized computing skills of vendors are just as intelligent in their cultural settings as verbal skills are in American culture (Sternberg & Kaufman, 1998).

However intelligence is defined, individuals differ substantially in intellectual ability, and numerous tests have been devised to measure these differences. We examine the construction, properties, and limitations of these tests in the next section.

The Development of Intelligence Testing

In 1904, the Minister of Public Instruction in France asked two noted psychologists of the day, Alfred Binet and Theophile Simon, to devise a way of recognizing children who would have difficulty learning in school. Binet and Simon's approach was to select simple tasks that children of different ages should be able to do, such as naming colors, counting backward, and remembering numbers in order. They identified problems that typical 3-year-olds could solve, that typical 4-year-olds could solve, and so on. *Children's* **mental age**, *or* **MA**, *referred to the difficulty of the problems they could solve correctly.* A child of any chronological age (CA) who solved problems that the average 7-year-old could solve would have an MA of 7.

Binet and Simon used MA to distinguish "bright" from "dull" children. A bright child would have the MA of an older child—for example, a bright 6-year-old could have an MA of 9. A dull child would have the MA of a younger child—for example, a dull 6-year-old could have an MA of 4. Binet and Simon confirmed that bright children identified using their test did better in school than dull children.

The Stanford-Binet

Lewis Terman, of Stanford University, revised Binet and Simon's test substantially and published a version known as the Stanford-Binet test in 1916. *Terman described performance as an* **intelligence quotient**, *or* **IQ**, *which was the ratio of MA to CA, multiplied by 100:*

$$IQ = MA/CA \times 100$$

At any age, children who are perfectly average have an IQ score of 100, because their MA equals their CA. IQ can also be used to compare intelligence in children of different ages. A 4-year-old girl with an MA of 5 has an IQ score of 125 (5/4 × 100), as does an 8-year-old boy with an MA of 10 (10/8 × 100).

IQ scores are no longer computed as the ratio of MA to CA. Instead, children's IQ scores are determined by comparing their test performance to the average IQ score of other children their age. When children perform at the average for their age, their IQ

mental age (MA)

in intelligence testing, a measure of children's performance corresponding to the chronological age of those whose performance equals the child's

intelligence quotient (IQ)

a mathematical representation of how a person scores on an intelligence test in relation to how other people of the same age score

score is 100. Children who perform above the average have IQ scores greater than 100; children who perform below the average have IQ scores less than 100. Nevertheless, the concept of IQ as the ratio of MA to CA helped popularize the Stanford-Binet test.

Nearly 100 years later, the Stanford-Binet remains a popular test; the latest version was revised in 2003. Like the earlier versions, the modern Stanford-Binet test consists of various cognitive and motor tasks ranging from extremely easy to extremely difficult. The Stanford-Binet test, the Wechsler Intelligence Scale for Children IV (WISC-IV), and the Kaufman Assessment Battery for Children II are the primary individualized tests of intelligence in use today.

Do Tests Work?

If tests work, they should predict important outcomes in children's lives. That is, children who receive higher IQ scores should be more successful in school and after they leave school. In fact, IQ scores are remarkably powerful predictors of developmental outcomes. IQ scores predict school grades, scores on achievement tests, and number of years of education with correlations that are usually between .5 and .7 (Brody, 1992; Geary, 2005).

These correlations are far from perfect, which reminds us that some youngsters with high test scores do not excel in school and others with low test scores manage to get good grades. In fact, some researchers find that self-discipline predicts grades in school even better than IQ scores do (Duckworth & Seligman, 2005). In general, however, tests do a reasonable job of predicting school success.

Not only do intelligence scores predict success in school, but they also predict occupational success (Deary, Batty, & Gale, 2008; Judge, Klinger, & Simon, 2010). Individuals with higher IQ scores are more likely to hold high-paying, high-prestige positions within medicine, law, and engineering (Schmidt & Hunter, 1998), and among scientists with equal education, those with higher IQ scores have more patents and more articles published in scientific journals (Park, Lubinski, & Benbow, 2008). Even within a profession—among individuals who all have the same amount of education—IQ scores predict job performance and earnings, particularly for more complex jobs (Henderson, 2010; Schmidt & Hunter, 2004).

Hereditary and Environmental Factors

Following adoption, children's scores on intelligence tests tend to resemble the scores of their biological parents, not their adoptive parents, which shows the impact of heredity on intelligence.

In a typical U.S. elementary school, several first graders have IQ scores greater than 120 and a similar number have IQ scores in the low 80s. What accounts for the nearly 40-point difference in these youngsters' scores? Heredity's role is shown by test scores becoming more alike as siblings become more similar genetically (Bouchard, 2009). For example, fraternal twins' IQ scores are less similar than scores for identical twins. And adopted children's IQ scores usually resemble their biological parents' IQ scores more than their adoptive parents' IQ scores.

Yet environment is also crucial. For example, children with high test scores tend to come from homes that are well organized and have plenty of appropriate play materials (Bradley et al., 2001; Tamis-LeMonda et al., 2004).

The impact of environment on intelligence is also implicated by a dramatic rise in IQ test scores during the 20th century (Nisbett et al., 2012). For example, scores on the WISC increased by nearly 10 points over a 25-year period (Flynn, 1999). Heredity cannot account for such a rapid increase over a few decades. Consequently, the rise must reflect the impact of some

© Masterfile

High-quality preschool programs provide stimulating environments that can increase children's scores on intelligence tests and improve their school performance.

AP Photo/Mike Derer

aspect of environment, such as smaller, better-educated families with more leisure time (Daley et al., 2003; Dickens & Flynn, 2001).

The importance of a stimulating environment for intelligence is also demonstrated by intervention programs that prepare economically disadvantaged children for school, such as Head Start. These programs teach preschool youngsters basic school readiness skills and social skills and offer guidance to parents (Administration for Children and Families, 2010b; Campbell et al., 2001). When children participate in these enrichment programs, their test scores increase and school achievement improves (Ludwig & Phillips, 2007).

The Impact of Ethnicity and Socioeconomic Status

On many intelligence tests, ethnic groups differ in their average scores: Asian Americans tend to have the highest scores, followed by European Americans, Latino Americans, and African Americans (Hunt & Carlson, 2007). To a certain extent, these differences in test scores reflect group differences in socioeconomic status. Children from economically advantaged homes tend to have higher test scores than children from economically disadvantaged homes, and European American and Asian American families are more likely to be economically advantaged, whereas Latino American and African American families are more likely to be economically disadvantaged. Nevertheless, when children from comparable socioeconomic status are compared, group differences in IQ test scores are reduced but not eliminated (Magnuson & Duncan, 2006).

Because heredity helps determine a child's intelligence, does this mean that group differences in IQ scores reflect genetic differences among groups? No. Most researchers agree that there is no evidence that some ethnic groups have more "smart genes" than others. Instead, they believe that the environment is largely responsible for these differences (Bronfenbrenner & Morris, 2006; Neisser et al., 1996).

A popular analogy (Lewontin, 1976) demonstrates the thinking here. Imagine two kinds of corn: Each kind produces both short and tall plants, and height is known to be due to heredity. If one kind of corn grows in a good soil—plenty of water and nutrients—the mature plants will reach their genetically determined heights: some short, some tall. If the other kind of corn grows in poor soil, few of the plants will reach their full height, and overall the plants of this kind will be much shorter. Even though height is quite heritable for each type of corn, the difference in height between the two groups is due solely to the quality of the environment. Similarly, though IQ scores may be quite heritable for different groups, limited exposure to stimulating environments may mean that one group ends up with lower IQ scores overall (just as the plants growing in poor soil do not reach their full height).

If heredity is not involved, what is responsible for group differences in test scores? Three environmental influences contribute:

- *Experience with test contents.* Economically disadvantaged children are less likely to be familiar with test items, which generally assess knowledge based on middle-class experiences.

- *Test-taking skills.* Children from minority groups perform poorly because (1) their culture encourages children to solve problems in collaboration with others and discourages them from excelling as individuals or (2) they are wary of questions posed by unfamiliar adults and thus answer "I don't know" by default.

- *Stereotype threat.* When children from a minority group know that their group is thought to have below-average intelligence, this makes them anxious when taking IQ tests and they do poorly for fear of confirming the stereotype (Steele, 1997; Steele & Aronson, 1995).

Interpreting Test Scores

If all tests reflect cultural influences to at least some degree, how should we interpret test scores? Remember that tests assess successful adaptation to a particular cultural context. Most intelligence tests predict success in a school environment, which usually espouses middle-class values. Regardless of ethnic group, a child with a high test score has the intellectual skills needed for academic work based on middle-class values (Hunt & Carlson, 2007). A child with a low test score apparently lacks those skills. Does a low score mean that a child is destined to fail in school? No. It simply means that, based on the child's current skills, he or she is unlikely to do well. We know from intervention projects that improving children's skills improves their school performance.

By focusing on groups of people, it's easy to forget that individuals within these groups differ in intelligence. The average difference in IQ scores among various ethnic groups is relatively small compared to the entire range of scores for these groups (Sternberg, Grigorenko, & Kidd, 2005). All ethnic groups have some children with high IQ scores and others with low scores. In the next section, we look at children at the extremes of ability.

HUMAN DEVELOPMENT in action

As a school psychologist, you administer an IQ test to a 9-year-old and compute the child's score to be 90. When you report the result to the child's parents, they're upset and conclude that their child isn't "college material." What would you say to them?

Test Yourself

Recall

1. According to _____ theories, intelligence includes both general intelligence and more specific abilities, such as verbal and spatial skills.

2. Gardner's theory of multiple intelligences involves linguistic, logical–mathematical, and spatial intelligences, which are included in older theories, as well as musical, _____, interpersonal, intrapersonal, _____, and _____ intelligences.

3. According to Sternberg, successful intelligence depends on _____, creative, and practical abilities.

4. The impact of heredity on IQ scores is shown by (a) identical twins having similar IQ scores and (b) adopted children having IQ scores that are _____.

5. Evidence for the impact of environment on children's intelligence comes from studies of children's homes, historical change in IQ scores, and _____.

Interpret

- Compare and contrast the theories of intelligence in terms of the extent to which they integrate physical, cognitive, social, and emotional development.

- If Piaget were to create an intelligence test, how would it differ from the type of test Binet created?

Apply

- Suppose that a local government official proposes to end all funding for programs for disadvantaged preschool children. Imagine you are an administrator of such a program. Write a letter to this official in which you describe the value of these programs.

- Describe the analytic, creative, and practical abilities that might be involved in achieving the goal of graduating from college with honors.

Recall answers: (1) hierarchical, (2) bodily–kinesthetic, naturalistic, existential, (3) analytic, (4) more like their biological parents' scores than their adoptive parents' scores, (5) intervention programs

LEARNING OBJECTIVES

- What are the characteristics of gifted and creative children?
- What are different forms of disability?
- What are the distinguishing features of attention-deficit hyperactivity disorder?

Sanjit, a second grader, has taken two separate intelligence tests, and both times he had above-average scores. His parents took him to an ophthalmologist, who determined that his vision is fine. Nevertheless, Sanjit cannot read. Letters and words are as mysterious to him as Kanye West's music would be to Mozart. What is wrong?

Throughout history, societies have recognized children with unusual abilities and talents. We look at these extremes of human skill in this section and, as we do, understand why Sanjit can't read.

Gifted and Creative Children

Traditionally, giftedness was defined by an IQ score of 130 or greater. Today, however, definitions of giftedness are broader and include exceptional talent in an assortment of areas, such as art, music, creative writing, and dance (Reis & Renzulli, 2010; Winner, 2000).

However it's defined, exceptional talent has several prerequisites (Rathunde & Csikszentmihalyi, 1993):

- The child's love for the subject and overwhelming desire to master it
- Instruction, beginning at an early age, with inspiring and talented teachers
- Support and help from parents, who are committed to promoting their child's talent

In short, exceptional talent must be nurtured. Without encouragement and support from stimulating and challenging mentors, a youngster's talents will wither, not flourish. Talented children need a curriculum that is challenging and complex; they need teachers who know how to foster talent; and they need like-minded peers who stimulate their interests (Feldhusen, 1996).

FIGURE 6.2

One way to measure creativity is to determine how many original responses children can make to a specific stimulus.

Creativity

What is creativity, and how does it differ from intelligence? *Intelligence is associated with* **convergent thinking**, *which means using the information provided to determine a standard, correct answer. In contrast, creativity is linked to* **divergent thinking**, *in which the aim is not a single correct answer (often there isn't one) but instead to think in novel and unusual directions* (Callahan, 2000).

Divergent thinking is often measured by asking children to produce a large number of ideas in response to some specific stimulus (Kogan, 1983). Children might be asked to name different uses for a common object, such as a coat hanger. Or they might be given a page filled with circles and be asked to draw as many different pictures as they can, as shown in Figure 6.2. Both the number of responses and their originality are used to measure creativity.

Creativity, like giftedness, must be cultivated. Youngsters are more likely to be creative when their home and school environments value nonconformity and encourage children to be curious. And creativity can be enhanced by experiences that stimulate children to be flexible in their thinking and to explore alternatives (Starko, 1988).

As an elementary-school teacher, what could you do to promote your students' creativity?

convergent thinking
using information to arrive at one standard and correct answer

divergent thinking
thinking in novel and unusual directions

Children With Disability

"Little David" was the oldest of four children. He learned to sit only days before his first birthday, began to walk at 2 years, and said his first words as a 3-year-old. By age 5, David was far behind his age-mates developmentally. David had Down syndrome, a disorder described Chapter 2 that is caused by an extra 21st chromosome.

Children With Intellectual Disability

Down syndrome is an example of a condition that leads to **intellectual disability**, *which refers to substantial limitations in intellectual ability, as well as problems adapting to an environment, with both emerging before 18 years of age.* Limited intellectual skill is often defined as a score of 70 or less on an intelligence test such as the Stanford-Binet. Adaptive behavior includes conceptual skills important for successful adaptation (e.g., literacy and understanding money and time), social skills (e.g., interpersonal skill), and practical skills (e.g., personal grooming and occupational skills). Only people who are under 18, have problems adapting in these areas, and IQ scores of 70 or less are considered to have an intellectual disability (American Association on Intellectual and Developmental Disabilities Ad Hoc Committee on Terminology and Classification, 2010).*

Modern explanations pinpoint four factors that place individuals at risk for intellectual disability:

- Biomedical factors, including chromosomal disorders, malnutrition, and traumatic brain injury

- Social factors, such as poverty and impaired parent–child interactions

- Behavioral factors, such as child neglect or domestic violence

- Educational factors, including inadequate special education services

No individual factor in this list necessarily leads to intellectual disability. Instead, the risk for intellectual disability grows as more of these factors are present (American Association on Intellectual and Developmental Disabilities Ad Hoc Committee on Terminology and Classification, 2010). For example, the risk is great for a child with Down syndrome whose parents live in poverty and cannot take advantage of special education services.

Children With Learning Disability

A key element of the definition of intellectual disability is substantially below-average intelligence. In contrast, by definition children with learning disability have normal intelligence. *That is, children with* **learning disability** *(1) have difficulty mastering an academic subject, (2) have normal intelligence, and (3) are not suffering from other conditions that could explain poor performance, such as sensory impairment or inadequate instruction.*

In the United States, about 5% of school-age children are classified as learning disabled. The number of distinct disabilities is still debated, but most scientists agree that three are particularly common (Hulme & Snowling, 2009): difficulties in reading individual words, sometimes known as developmental dyslexia; difficulties understanding words that have been read successfully, called impaired reading comprehension; and difficulties in mathematics, termed mathematical learning disability or developmental dyscalculia.

Children with reading disabilities often have trouble associating sounds with letters.

intellectual disability
substantially below-average intelligence and problems adapting to an environment that emerge before the age of 18

learning disability
difficulty mastering at least one academic subject when a child has normal intelligence yet does not suffer other conditions that explain the poor performance

---

*Intellectual disability was long known as *mental retardation,* and much federal and state law in the United States still uses the latter term.

Understanding learning disabilities is complicated because each type has its own causes (Landerl et al., 2009) and thus requires its own treatment. For example, developmental dyslexia is the most common type of learning disability. Many children with this disorder have problems distinguishing sounds in written and oral language. For children with developmental dyslexia—like Sanjit (in the opening vignette)—distinguishing *bis* from *bep* or *bis* from *dis* is difficult; apparently the syllables all sound similar (Melby-Lervag, Lyster, & Hulme, 2012). The Spotlight on Research feature illustrates research that has examined this problem in detail.

Children with developmental dyslexia typically benefit from two kinds of instruction: training in phonological awareness—experiences that help them identify subtle but important differences in language sounds—and explicit instruction on the connections between letters and their sounds. With intensive instruction of this sort, youngsters with developmental dyslexia can read more effectively (Hulme & Snowling, 2009).

Children with impaired reading comprehension, another common learning disability, read individual words easily, but they understand far less of what they read. Asked to read a sentence such as "The man rode the bus to go to work," they do so easily, but they find it difficult to answer questions about what they've read (e.g., "What did the man ride?"). These problems seem to reflect limited spoken vocabulary (they simply know fewer words), as well as problems linking words in a sentence together to create coherent meaning (Hulme & Snowling, 2009). In other words, for these youngsters, impaired reading comprehension seems to be a by-product of impaired oral (spoken) language. Consistent with this view, these children understand more of what they read following extensive instruction in vocabulary and other language skills that are not specific to reading (P. J. Clarke et al., 2010).

A third common form of learning disability is mathematical learning disability. Roughly 5 to 10% of young children struggle with arithmetic instruction from the beginning. These youngsters progress slowly in their efforts to learn to count, to add, and to subtract; many are also diagnosed with reading difficulties. As they move into second and third grade (and beyond), these children often use inefficient methods

Spotlight on research — Phonological Representations in Children With Developmental Dyslexia

Who were the investigators, and what was the aim of the study?
Children with developmental dyslexia have difficulty with phonological processing, that is, with translating print into sound. Why? One idea is that phonological representations—knowledge about the sounds of words—may be less detailed or less precise in children who have a reading disability. For example, think about pairs of similar-sounding words such as *bit* and *bet* or *bud* and *bed*. In each pair, only the vowels distinguish the two words, and the vowels themselves sound similar. If children with dyslexia have less precise knowledge about vowel sounds, this could cause them to read more slowly and less accurately.

According to this hypothesis, developmental dyslexia is really a language-related disability and should be apparent when children use language sounds in nonreading tasks. Jennifer Bruno and her colleagues—Frank Manis, Patricia Keating, Anne Sperling, Jonathan Nakamoto, and Mark Seidenberg—(2007) tested this hypothesis by determining how well children with a reading disability recognized familiar words that were presented auditorily.

How did the investigators measure the topic of interest?
Familiar one-syllable words (e.g., *bone* and *boat*) were presented on audiotape, and children were asked to say what they were. What made the task difficult for children is that only a portion of the word was presented at a time, beginning with just the initial consonant and a small portion of the vowel. If children could not recognize the word on this initial presentation (most couldn't), the word was repeated with a bit more of the vowel presented. This process was repeated, adding more of the vowel and, later, the final consonant, until the child recognized the word. (This was possible because the experimenters recorded an adult saying each of the words and then used specially designed software that allowed them to edit each word so that a precise amount of vowel was presented.)

Who were the participants in the study?
Bruno and her colleagues tested 8- to 14-year-olds with a reading disability, along with 8- to 14-year-olds with normal reading skills.

What was the design of the study?
The study was both experimental and correlational. In the experimental part of the study, the independent variable was the type of consonant

Continued

Continued

sound that ended the word. Some words ended in stop consonants (*dot* and *seat*), some ended in lateral consonants (*coal*, *feel*), and some in nasal consonants (*cone*, *pan*). The dependent variable was how much of the word had to be presented before children recognized it. The study was also correlational because the investigators were interested in the relation between reading skill (reading disabled versus normal reading skill) and ease of recognizing words. The investigators did not look at age differences, so the study was neither longitudinal nor cross-sectional.

Were there ethical concerns with the study?
No. The tasks are frequently used in research, with no known risks.

What were the results?
The graph in Figure 6.3 shows what proportion of a word was presented before children recognized it. Words ending in stop consonants were easiest for both groups of readers—they recognized these words based on hearing just less than half of the word. Words ending in lateral and nasal consonants were more difficult—children needed to hear more of the word to recognize it—and this was particularly true for children with a reading disability.

What did the investigators conclude?
For words that end with lateral and nasal consonants, children with developmental dyslexia need to hear more of a word to recognize it. Bruno and colleagues suggest that this is because their phonological representations of these simple words in memory is less precise than are comparable representations in children with normal reading ability. The differences in the graph are small, but these small differences add up quickly when children repeatedly access the sounds of words during reading.

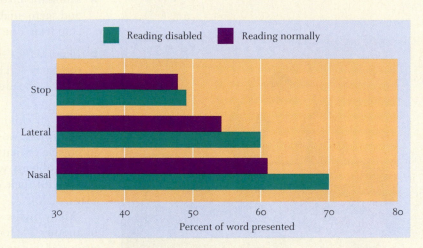

FIGURE 6.3

Children with a reading disability need to hear more of a word before they recognize it.
Data from Bruno et al., 2007.

What converging evidence would strengthen these conclusions?
This study focused on stop, lateral, and nasal consonants; it would be useful to extend this work to a broader range of vowel and consonant sounds. Doing so would allow researchers to generate a more complete profile of the phonological representations of children with developmental dyslexia.

 Go to Psychology CourseMate at **www.cengagebrain.com** to enhance your understanding of this research.

for computing solutions, for example, still using their fingers as third graders to solve problems such as 9 + 7 (Geary, 2005; Jordan, 2007).

We know far less about mathematical learning disability, largely because mathematics engages a broader set of skills than reading. Some scientists propose that the heart of the problem is a poorly developed number sense, which includes such skills as understanding and comparing quantities (e.g., 9 > 6) and representing quantity on a number line (Berch, 2005; Jordan, 2007). Another possibility is that youngsters with mathematical learning disability are impaired in counting and retrieving arithmetic facts from memory (Hulme & Snowling, 2009). Still others suggest that mathematical learning disability reflects problems in the basic cognitive processes that are used in doing arithmetic, such as working memory and processing speed (Geary et al., 2007).

Attention-Deficit Hyperactivity Disorder

About 3 to 5% of all school-age children are diagnosed with attention-deficit hyperactivity disorder—ADHD for short (Rapport, 1995). Boys outnumber girls by a 3:1 ratio (Wicks-Nelson & Israel, 2006). Three symptoms are at the heart of ADHD (American Psychiatric Association, 1994):

- *Hyperactivity.* Children with ADHD are unusually energetic, fidgety, and unable to keep still—especially when they need to limit their activity.

© Catherine Ledner/Getty Images

Children with ADHD are typically hyperactive, as well as being inattentive and impulsive.

■ *Inattention.* Youngsters with ADHD do not pay attention in class and seem unable to concentrate on schoolwork; instead, they skip from one task to another.

■ *Impulsivity.* Children with ADHD often act before thinking; they may run into a street before looking for traffic or interrupt others who are already speaking.

Not all children with ADHD show all these symptoms to the same degree. Most children with ADHD are hyperactive and either impulsive or inattentive (Barkley, 2003). Children with ADHD often have problems with academic performance, conduct, and getting along with their peers (Murray-Close et al., 2010; Stevens & Ward-Estes, 2006).

Many myths surround ADHD. Some concern causes. At one time or another, TV, food allergies, sugar, and poor home life have all been proposed as causes of ADHD, but research does not consistently support any of these theories (e.g., Wolraich et al., 1994). Instead, heredity is an important factor (Saudino & Plomin, 2007). In addition, prenatal exposure to alcohol and other drugs can place children at risk for ADHD (Milberger et al., 1997).

Another myth is that most children "grow out of" ADHD in adolescence or young adulthood. More than half of children diagnosed with ADHD have problems related to overactivity, inattention, and impulsivity as adolescents and young adults (Biederman et al., 2010). A final myth is that many healthy children are wrongly diagnosed with ADHD. The number of children diagnosed with ADHD increased substantially during the 1990s, but not because children were being routinely misdiagnosed; the increased numbers reflected growing awareness of ADHD and more frequent diagnoses of ADHD in girls and adolescents (Goldman et al., 1998).

Because ADHD affects academic and social success throughout childhood and adolescence, researchers have worked hard to find effective treatments. Children with ADHD often respond well to stimulant drugs such as Ritalin. It may seem odd that stimulants are given to children who are already overactive, but these drugs stimulate the parts of the brain that normally inhibit hyperactive and impulsive behavior. Thus, stimulants actually have a calming influence for many youngsters with ADHD, allowing them to focus their attention (Barkley, 2004).

Drug therapy is not the only approach: Psychosocial treatments are designed to improve children's cognitive and social skills; treatments often include home-based intervention and intensive summer programs (Richters et al., 1995). For example, children can be taught to remind themselves to read instructions before starting assignments. And they can be reinforced by others for inhibiting impulsive and hyperactive behavior (Barkley, 2004).

This variety of treatments led scientists to wonder which was the most effective. Consequently, in the mid-1990s, the Multimodal Treatment Study of Children With ADHD (for short, the MTA) was begun. Elementary-school children with ADHD were assigned to different treatment modes and received treatment for 14 months.

The initial results—obtained at the end of the 14 months of treatment—showed that medication alone was the best way to treat hyperactivity per se. However, for academic and social skills, as well as parent–child relations, medication plus psychosocial treatment was somewhat more effective than medication alone (MTA Cooperative Group, 1999). In contrast, in follow-up studies conducted 6 and 8 years after the 14-month treatment period ended, the treatment groups no longer differed and all groups fared worse than children without ADHD: Children with ADHD were more likely to be inattentive, hyperactive, and impulsive; they were more aggressive; and they were less likely to succeed in school (Molina et al., 2009).

For researchers, parents, and children with ADHD, these are disappointing results. Yet they point to an important conclusion, one with implications for policy: Several months of intensive treatment will not "cure" ADHD; instead, ADHD is perhaps better considered as a chronic condition, like diabetes or asthma, that requires ongoing monitoring and treatment (Hazell, 2009).

Test Yourself

Recall

1. A problem with defining giftedness solely in terms of IQ score is that _____.

2. Creativity is associated with _____ thinking, in which the goal is to think in novel and unusual directions.

3. Intellectual disability involves substantial limits in intellectual ability and _____ that emerge before 18 years of age.

4. Biomedical, social, _____, and educational factors place some children at risk for intellectual disability.

5. In developmental dyslexia, children have difficulty with _____.

6. Key symptoms of ADHD are overactivity, _____, and impulsivity.

7. The results of the MTA show that, in the short run, the best way to treat the full spectrum of symptoms of ADHD is through stimulant drugs combined with _____.

Interpret

- How might our definitions of giftedness and intellectual disability differ if they were based on Gardner's theory of multiple intelligences?

- How might Piaget have explained differences in intellectual functioning between children with intellectual disability and children without intellectual disability? How might an information-processing psychologist explain these differences?

Apply

- Leeni has a son who was recently diagnosed with ADHD and wants his doctor to prescribe stimulant medication to cure the disorder. What would his pediatrician tell her?

- A school psychologist told Ryan that his son has a reading disability. Ryan is concerned that this is just a politically correct way of saying that his son is stupid. Is he right?

Recall answers: (1) it excludes talents in areas such as art, music, and dance, (2) divergent, (3) problems adapting to the environment, (4) behavioral, (5) distinguishing language sounds, (6) inattentiveness, (7) psychosocial treatment that improves children's cognitive and social skills

---

Academic Skills

LEARNING OBJECTIVES

- What are the components of skilled reading?
- As children develop, how does their writing improve?
- How do arithmetic skills change during the elementary-school years?
- What are the hallmarks of effective schools and effective teachers?

Angelique is a fifth grader who loves to read. As a preschooler, Angelique's parents read Dr. Seuss stories to her, and she has progressed to the point where she can read (and understand) 400-page novels intended for teens. Her parents marvel at this accomplishment and wish they better understood the skills that were involved so that they could help Angelique's younger brother learn to read as well as his sister does.

Reading is a complex task, and learning to read well is a wonderful accomplishment. Much the same can be said for writing and math. We examine each of these academic skills in this section. As we do, you'll learn about the skills that underlie Angelique's mastery of reading. We end the section by looking at characteristics that make some schools and some teachers better than others.

Reading

Foundations of Reading Skill

English words are made up of individual letters, so children need to know their letters before they can learn to read. Children learn more about letters and word forms when they're frequently involved in literacy-related activities, such as reading with an adult, playing with magnetic letters, or trying to print simple words. Not surprisingly, children who develop their prereading skills by learning more about letters and word forms later learn to read more easily than their peers who know less (Levy et al., 2006; Treiman & Kessler, 2003).

A second essential skill is sensitivity to language sounds. *The ability to distinguish the sounds in spoken words is known as* **phonological awareness**. English words consist of syllables, and a syllable is made up of a vowel that's usually but not always accompanied by consonants. For example, *dust* includes the initial consonant *d*, the vowel *u*, and the final consonant cluster *st*. Phonological awareness is shown when children can decompose words in this manner by, for example, correctly answering "What's the first sound in *dust*?" or "*Dust* without the *d* sounds like what?" Phonological awareness is strongly related to success in learning to read: Children who readily identify different sounds in spoken words learn to read more readily than children who do not (Melby-Lervag, Lyster, & Hulme, 2012).

Learning to read in English is particularly challenging because English is incredibly inconsistent in the way that letters are pronounced (e.g., compare the sound of "a" in *bat, far, rake,* and *was*) and the way that sounds are spelled (e.g., the long "e" sound is the same in each of these spellings: *team, feet, piece, lady, receive,* and *magazine*). In contrast, many other languages—Greek, Finnish, German, Italian, Spanish, Dutch, and so on—are far more consistent, which simplifies the mapping of sounds to letters. In fact, children learn to read more rapidly in languages where letter–sound rules are more consistent, but phonological awareness remains the best predictor of reading success in many languages (Lervåg, Bråten, & Hulme, 2009; Ziegler et al., 2010).

If phonological skills are so essential, how can we help children master them? Reading to children is one approach that's fun for children and parents alike. When parents read stories, their children learn many language-related skills that prepare them for reading (Justice, Pullen, & Pence, 2008; Raikes et al., 2006). And the benefits are not limited to the first steps in learning to read but persist into the middle elementary-school years (Chow et al., 2008; Sénéchal & LeFevre, 2002).

Recognizing Words

At the beginning of reading, children sometimes learn to read a few words "by sight," but they have no understanding of the links between printed letters and the word's sound. However, the first step in true reading is learning to decode printed words by sounding out the letters in them: Beginning readers often say the sounds associated with each letter and then blend the sounds to produce a recognizable word. After a word has been sounded out a few times, it becomes a known word that can be read by retrieval directly from long-term memory: As the individual letters in a word are identified, long-term memory is searched to see whether there is a matching sequence of letters. After the child knows that the letters are, in sequence, *c-a-t*, for example, long-term memory is searched for a match and the child recognizes the word as *cat* (Rayner et al., 2001).

phonological awareness
the ability to hear the distinctive sounds of letters

Beginning readers usually rely heavily on "sounding out" a word.

Thus, from their first efforts to read, most children use retrieval for some words. From that point on, the general strategy is to try retrieval first and, if that fails, to sound out the word or ask a more skilled reader for help. With more experience, the child sounds out fewer words and retrieves more (Siegler, 1986). That is, by sounding out novel words, children increase their store of information about words in long-term memory that is required for direct retrieval (Cunningham et al., 2002; Share, 2008).

So far, word recognition may seem like a one-way street where readers first recognize letters and then recognize words. In reality, we know that information flows both ways: Readers constantly use context to help them recognize letters and words (Rayner et al., 2001). For example, when reading

The little girl's pet dog chased the cat.

most readers recognize *cat* rapidly because the preceding words lead them to expect the last word to be something "chaseable." Beginning and skilled readers both use sentence context like this to help them recognize words (Archer & Bryant, 2001; Kim & Goetz, 1994).

Comprehension

Once individual words are recognized, reading begins to have a lot in common with understanding speech. People understand a written sentence in much the same way as they understand spoken language (Oakhill & Cain, 2004).

As children gain more reading experience, they better comprehend what they read. Several factors contribute to this improved comprehension (Siegler & Alibali, 2004):

- *Children become more skilled at recognizing words, allowing effort to be devoted to comprehension* (Zinar, 2000). When children recognize words effortlessly, they can focus their efforts on deriving meaning from the whole sentence.

- *Children acquire more general knowledge of their physical, social, and psychological worlds.* This allows them to understand more of what they read (Ferreol-Barbey, Piolat, & Roussey, 2000). For example, even if 6-year-olds could recognize all of the words in a long sentence about an election, they would not fully comprehend the meaning of the passage because they lack the necessary knowledge of politics.

- *With experience, children use more appropriate reading strategies.* The goal of reading and the nature of the text influence reading. For example, reading a textbook requires attention to both the overall organization and the relation of details to that organization. Older, more experienced readers are better able to select a reading strategy that suits the material being read (Brown et al., 1996; Cain, 1999).

- *With experience, children better monitor their comprehension.* When readers don't grasp the meaning of a passage because it is difficult or confusing, they read it again (Baker, 1994). Try this sentence (adapted from Carpenter & Daneman, 1981): "The Midwest State Fishing Contest would draw fishermen from all around the region, including some of the best bass guitarists in Michigan." You probably interpreted *bass* as a fish, but this didn't make sense, so you reread the phrase to determine that *bass* refers to a type of guitar. Older readers are better able to realize that their understanding is not complete and take corrective action.

Writing

Though few of us end up being a Maya Angelou, a Sandra Cisneros, or a J. K. Rowling, most adults write, both at home and at work. The basics of good writing are remarkably straightforward, but writing skill develops only gradually during childhood, adolescence, and young adulthood. Research indicates that a number of factors contribute to improved writing as children develop (Adams, Treiman, & Pressley, 1998; Siegler & Alibali, 2004).

Knowledge About Topics

Writing is about telling "something" to others. With age, children have more to tell as they gain more knowledge about the world and incorporate this knowledge into their writing (Benton et al., 1995). For example, asked to write about a mayoral election, 8-year-olds are apt to describe it much like a popularity contest, but 12-year-olds more often describe it in terms of specific political issues.

POW

P Pick my idea

O Organize my notes

W Write and say more

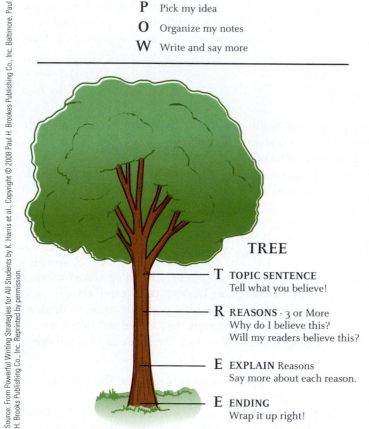

TREE

T TOPIC SENTENCE
Tell what you believe!

R REASONS - 3 or More
Why do I believe this?
Will my readers believe this?

E EXPLAIN Reasons
Say more about each reason.

E ENDING
Wrap it up right!

FIGURE 6.4
The POW + TREE strategy for good writing provides young writers with a general plan for writing (POW) and a structure for a paragraph (TREE).

knowledge-telling strategy
writing down information as it is retrieved from memory, a common practice for young writers

knowledge-transforming strategy
deciding what information to include and how best to organize it to convey a point

Organizing Writing

One difficult aspect of writing is organization, arranging all necessary information in a manner that readers find clear and interesting. Children and young adolescents organize their writing differently than do older adolescents and adults (Bereiter & Scardamalia, 1987). *Young writers often use a* **knowledge-telling strategy**, *writing down information on the topic as they retrieve it from memory.* For example, asked to write about the day's events at school, a second grader wrote:

> It is a rainy day. We hope the sun will shine. We got new spelling books. We had our pictures taken. We sang "Happy Birthday" to Barbara. (Waters, 1980, p. 155)

The story has no obvious structure. Apparently, the writer simply described each event as it came to mind.

Toward the end of the elementary-school years, children begin to use a **knowledge-transforming strategy**, *deciding what information to include and how best to organize it for the point they wish to convey to the reader.* This approach involves considering the purpose of writing (e.g., to inform, to persuade, or to entertain), and the information needed to achieve this purpose. It also involves considering the needs, interests, and knowledge of the anticipated audience.

Mechanical Requirements of Writing

Compared to speaking, writing is more difficult because we need to worry about spelling, punctuation, and forming the letters. These many mechanical aspects of writing are a special burden for young writers. For example, when youngsters are absorbed by the task of printing letters correctly, the quality of their writing usually suffers (Graham, Harris, & Fink, 2000; Olinghouse, 2008). As children master printed and cursive letters, they can pay more attention to other aspects of writing.

Fortunately, students can be taught to write better. When instruction focuses on the building blocks of effective writing—strategies for planning, drafting, and revising text—students' writing improves substantially (Graham & Perin, 2007; Tracy, Reid, & Graham, 2009). For example, one successful program for teaching writing—the Self-Regulated Strategy Development in Writing program—tells students that POW + TREE is a trick that good writers use. As you can see in Figure 6.4, POW provides young writers with a general plan for writing; TREE tells them how to organize their writing in a nicely structured paragraph (Harris et al., 2008).

HUMAN DEVELOPMENT in action

As a second-grade teacher, what are some of the main obstacles that your students face as beginning writers?

Mastering the full set of writing skills is a huge challenge, one that spans all of childhood, adolescence, and adulthood. Much the same can be said for mastering math skills, as we explain next.

Math Skills

In Chapter 4 we saw that preschoolers understand many principles underlying counting, even if they sometimes stumble over the mechanics of counting. By kindergarten, children have mastered counting and use this skill as the starting point for learning to add. For instance, suppose you ask a kindergartner to solve the following problem: "John had four oranges. Then Mary gave him two more oranges. How many oranges does John have now?" Many 5-year-old children solve the problem by counting. They first count out four fingers on one hand, then count out two more on the other. Finally, they count all six fingers on both hands. After children begin to receive formal arithmetic instruction in first grade, addition problems are less often solved by counting aloud or by counting fingers (Jordan et al., 2008). Instead, children add and subtract by counting mentally. That is, children act as if they are counting silently, beginning with the larger number and then adding on. By age 8 or 9, children have learned the addition tables so well that sums of the single-digit integers (from zero to nine) are facts that can be simply retrieved from memory (Ashcraft, 1982).

Arithmetic skills continue to improve as children move through elementary school. They become more proficient in addition and subtraction, learn multiplication and division, and move on to the more sophisticated mathematical concepts involved in algebra, geometry, trigonometry, and calculus.

© 2011 Purestock/Shutterstock.com

Young children often solve addition problems by counting, either on their fingers or in their head.

Effective Schools, Effective Teachers

U.S. schools differ along many dimensions, including their emphasis on academic goals and the involvement of parents. Teachers, too, differ in many ways, such as how they run their classrooms and how they teach. These and other variables affect student achievement, as you'll see in the next few pages. Let's begin with school-based influences.

School-Based Influences on Student Achievement

Some American schools are more successful than others, whether success is defined in terms of the percentage of students who are literate, graduate, or go to college. Why? Researchers (El Nokali, Bachman, & Votruba-Drzal, 2010; Good & Brophy, 2008; Hill & Taylor, 2004) have identified a number of characteristics of schools in which students typically succeed rather than fail:

- *Staff and students alike understand that academic excellence is the primary goal of the school and of every student in the school.* The school day emphasizes instruction, and students are recognized publicly for their academic accomplishments.

- *The school climate is safe and nurturant.* Students know that they can devote their energy to learning (instead of worrying about potential harm) and that the staff truly cares that they succeed.

- *Parents are involved.* In some cases, this may be through formal arrangements such as parent–teacher organizations. Or involvement may be informal: Parents may spend some time each week in school grading papers or tutoring a child.

© Michael J. Doolittle/The Image Works

In successful schools, the child's parents are involved—often as tutors.

Such involvement signals to both teachers and students that parents are committed to students' success.

■ *Progress of students, teachers, and programs is monitored.* The only way to know whether schools are succeeding is by measuring performance. Students, teachers, and programs need to be evaluated regularly, using objective measures that reflect academic goals.

In schools that follow these guidelines regularly, students usually succeed. Of course, on a daily basis, individual teachers have the most potential for impact. Let's see how teachers can influence their students' achievement.

Teacher-Based Influences on Student Achievement

In most schools, some teachers are highly sought after because their classes are successful: students learn, and the classroom climate is usually positive. What are the keys to the success of these master teachers? Research reveals that several factors are critical for students' achievement (Good & Brophy, 2008; Stevenson & Stigler, 1992; Walberg, 1995). Students tend to learn the most when teachers:

■ *Manage the classroom effectively so that they can devote most of their time to instruction.* When teachers spend a lot of time disciplining students or when students do not move smoothly from one class activity to the next, instructional time is wasted and students are apt to learn less.

■ *Believe they are responsible for their students' learning and that their students will learn when taught well.* When students don't understand a new topic, these teachers may repeat the original instruction (in case the student missed something) or create new instructions (in case the student heard everything but just didn't "get it"). These teachers keep plugging away because they feel at fault if students don't learn.

■ *Emphasize mastery of topics.* Teachers should introduce a topic and then give students many opportunities to understand, practice, and apply the topic. Just as you'd find it hard to go directly from driver's ed to driving a race car, students more often achieve when they grasp a new topic thoroughly and then gradually move to other, more advanced topics.

■ *Teach actively.* Effective teachers don't just talk or give students an endless stream of worksheets. Instead, they demonstrate topics concretely or have hands-on demonstrations for students. They also have students participate in class activities and encourage students to interact, generating ideas and solving problems together.

■ *Pay careful attention to pacing.* Teachers present material slowly enough so that students can understand a new concept but not so slowly that students get bored.

■ *Value tutoring.* Teachers work with students individually or in small groups so they can gear their instruction to each student's level and check each student's understanding. They also encourage peer tutoring, in which more capable students tutor less capable students. Children who are tutored by peers learn—and so do the tutors, because teaching helps tutors to organize their knowledge.

■ *Teach students techniques for monitoring and managing their own learning.* Students are more likely to achieve when they are taught how to recognize the aims of school tasks, as well as effective strategies (e.g., those described on pages 160–161) for achieving those aims.

Jordache/Shutterstock.com

Peer tutoring can be effective; both the tutored student and the tutor usually learn.

When teachers rely on most of these guidelines for effective teaching most of the time, their students generally learn the material and enjoy doing so (Good & Brophy, 1994; Stevenson & Stigler, 1992; Walberg, 1995).

Test Yourself

Recall

1. Important prereading skills include knowing letters and _____.

2. Beginning readers typically recognize words by sounding them out; with greater experience, readers are more likely able to _____.

3. Older and more experienced readers understand more of what they read because they read individual words more easily, they have more general knowledge of the world, they are more likely to use appropriate reading strategies, and _____.

4. Young elementary-school children typically use a _____ to organize their writing.

5. The simplest way of solving addition problems is to _____; the most advanced way is to retrieve sums from long-term memory.

6. In schools whose students usually succeed, academic excellence is a priority, the school is safe and nurturant, progress of students and teachers is monitored, and _____.

7. Effective teachers manage classrooms well, believe they are responsible for their students' learning, _____, teach actively, pay attention to pacing, value tutoring, and show children how to monitor their own learning.

Interpret

- Review the research on page 175 regarding factors associated with skilled reading comprehension. Which of these factors might also contribute to skilled writing?

- Would some of the ways to promote students' learning listed on page 178 be more appropriate for students in Piaget's concrete-operational stage? Would some be better for students in the formal-operational stage?

Apply

- Imagine two first graders. One can sound out many words and recognizes a rapidly growing set of words. The other has just mastered the letters of the alphabet and knows only a handful of letter–sound correspondences. How are these differences in reading skills likely to lead to different experiences in first grade?

- Your spouse has decided to run for the local school board on a platform emphasizing promoting student achievement. What specific instructional practices could your spouse recommend?

Recall answers: (1) sounds associated with each letter, (2) retrieve words from long-term memory, (3) they monitor their comprehension more effectively, (4) knowledge-telling strategy, (5) count on one's fingers, (6) parents are involved, (7) emphasize mastery of topics

6.5 Physical Development

LEARNING OBJECTIVES

- How much do school-age children grow?
- How do motor skills improve during the elementary-school years?
- Are American children physically fit?
- What are the consequences of participating in sports?

Miguel and Dan are 9-year-olds playing organized baseball for the first time. Miguel's coach is always upbeat. He constantly emphasizes the positive. When they lost a game 12 to 2, the coach complimented all the players on their play. In contrast, Dan's coach was livid when the team lost, and he was extremely critical of three players who made errors that contributed to the loss. Miguel thinks that baseball is great, but Dan can hardly wait for the season to be over.

During the elementary-school years, children steadily grow and their motor skills continue to improve. We trace these changes in the first two parts of this section. Then we'll see whether U.S. children are physically fit. We end the section by examining children's participation in sports and see how coaches like those in the vignette influence children in organized sports.

Growth

Physical growth during the elementary-school years continues at the steady pace established during the preschool years. From Figure 6.5, you can see that a typical 6-year-old weighs about 45 pounds and is 45 inches tall but grows to about 90 pounds and 60 inches by age 12. In other words, most children gain about 8 pounds and 2 to 3 inches per year. Many parents notice that their elementary-school children outgrow shoes and pants more rapidly than they outgrow sweaters, shirts, or jackets; this is because most of the increase in height comes from the legs, not the trunk.

Boys and girls are about the same size for most of these years (which is why they are combined in the figure), but girls are more likely than boys to enter puberty toward the end of the elementary-school years. Once girls enter puberty, they grow rapidly and become much bigger than the boys their age. (We have more to say about this in Chapter 8.) Thus, at ages 11 and 12, the average girl is about half an inch taller than the average boy.

To support this growth and to provide energy for their busy lives, school-age children need to eat more. Although preschool children need only consume about 1,500 to 1,700 calories per day, the average 7- to 10-year-old needs about 2,400 calories each day. The exact figure depends on the child's age and size and can range anywhere from roughly 1,700 to 3,300 calories daily.

As was true for preschool children, elementary-school children need a well-balanced diet. They should eat regularly from each of the major food groups: grains, vegetables, fruits, milk, meat, and beans. Too often children consume "empty" calories from sweets that have little nutritional value.

It's also important that school-age children eat breakfast. At this age, many children skip breakfast because they're too rushed in the morning. However, breakfast should provide about one fourth of a child's daily calories. When children don't

FIGURE 6.5

Height and weight increase steadily during the elementary-school years.

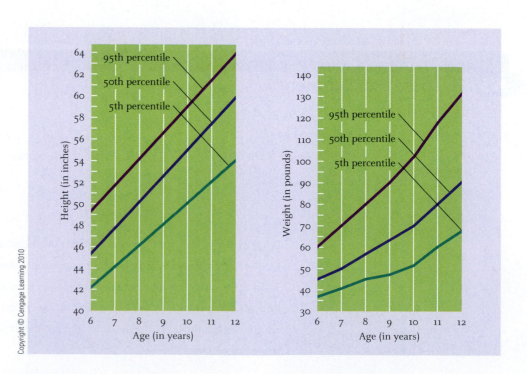

eat breakfast, they often have difficulty paying attention or remembering in school (Pollitt, 1995). Therefore, parents should organize their mornings so that their children have enough time for breakfast.

Development of Motor Skills

Elementary-school children's greater size and strength contribute to improved motor skills. During these years, children steadily run faster and jump farther. For example, Figure 6.6 shows how far a typical boy and girl can throw a ball and how far they can jump (in the standing long jump). By the time children are 11 years old, most can throw a ball at least three times farther than they could at age 6 and can jump nearly twice as far.

Fine motor skills also improve as children move through the elementary-school years. Children's greater dexterity is evident in a host of activities, ranging from typing, writing, and drawing to working on puzzles, playing the piano, and building model cars. Children gain greater control over their fingers and hands, making them nimbler. This greater fine motor coordination is obvious in children's handwriting.

Gender Differences in Motor Skills

In both gross and fine motor skills, there are gender differences in performance levels. Girls tend to excel in fine motor skills; their handwriting tends to be better than that of boys, for example. Girls also excel in gross motor skills that require flexibility and balance, such as tumbling. On gross motor skills that emphasize strength, boys usually have the advantage. Figure 6.6 shows that boys throw and jump farther than girls.

Some gender differences in gross motor skills that require strength reflect that, as children approach and enter puberty, girls' bodies have proportionately more fat and less muscle than do boys' bodies. This difference explains why, for example, boys can hang by their hands or arms from a bar much longer than girls can. However, for other gross motor skills, such as running, throwing, and catching, body composition is less important (Duff, Ericsson, & Baluch, 2007; Smoll & Schutz, 1990). In these cases, children's

FIGURE 6.6
Between 6 and 11 years, children's motor skills improve considerably.

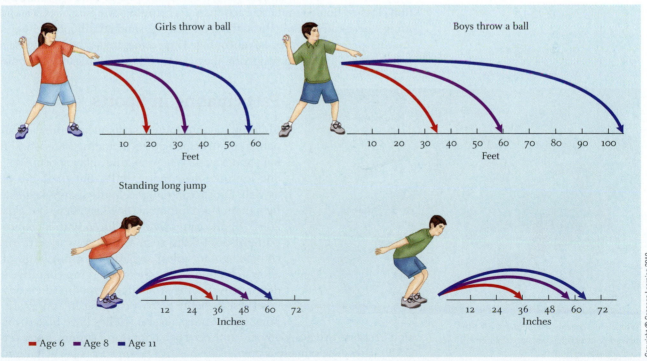

experience is crucial. During recess, elementary-school girls are more often found on a swing set, jumping rope, or perhaps talking quietly in a group; in contrast, boys are playing football or shooting baskets. Many girls and their parents believe that sports and physical fitness are less valuable for girls than boys. Consequently, girls spend less time in these sports and fitness-related activities than boys, depriving them of the opportunities to practice that are essential for developing motor skills (Fredricks & Eccles, 2005).

Physical Fitness

Being active physically has many benefits for children: it helps promote physical and mental growth and health (Best, 2010; Biddle & Asare, 2011; Hillman et al., 2009) and can help establish a lifelong pattern of exercise (Perkins et al., 2004). During the elementary-school years, most U.S. school-age children meet the current guidelines of being physically active at least 60 minutes daily (President's Council on Physical Fitness and Sports, 2004).

Unfortunately, when children are tested with a full battery of fitness tests, such as the mile run, pull-ups, and sit-ups, fewer than half usually meet standards for fitness on all tasks (Morrow, 2005). And, as we discuss in Chapter 8, obesity has reached epidemic proportions among American children and adolescents (U.S. Department of Health and Human Services, 2010).

Many factors contribute to low levels of fitness. In most schools, physical education classes meet only once or twice a week and are usually not required of high-school students (Johnston, Delva, & O'Malley, 2007). Even when students are in these classes, they spend a surprisingly large proportion of time—nearly half—standing around instead of exercising (Lowry et al., 2001; Parcel et al., 1989). Television and other sedentary leisure-time activities may contribute too. Youth who spend much time online or watching TV often tend to be less fit physically (Lobelo et al., 2009), but the nature of this relation remains poorly understood: Children glued to a TV or computer screen likely have fewer opportunities to exercise, but it might be that children in poor physical condition chose sedentary activities over exercise.

Many experts believe that U.S. schools should offer physical education more frequently each week. And many suggest that physical education classes should offer a range of activities in which all children can participate and that can be the foundation for a lifelong program of fitness (National Association for Sport and Physical Fitness, 2004). Thus, instead of emphasizing team sports such as touch football, physical education classes should emphasize activities like running, walking, racket sports, and swimming; these can be done throughout adolescence and adulthood—either alone or with another person. Families can encourage fitness too. Instead of spending an afternoon watching TV and eating popcorn, they can go biking, hiking, or swimming together.

When adult coaches encourage their team instead of criticizing mistakes, children are likely to enjoy playing sports.

Participating in Sports

Children's greater motor skills means they are able to participate in many team sports, including baseball, softball, basketball, and soccer. When children play sports, they get exercise and improve their motor skills. But there are other benefits as well. Sports can enhance participants' self-esteem and can help them learn initiative (Bowker, 2006; Donaldson & Ronan, 2006). Sports can provide children with a chance to learn important social skills, such as how to work effectively (often in complementary roles) as part of a group. And playing sports allows children to use their emerging cognitive skills as they devise new playing strategies or modify the rules of a game.

These benefits of participating in sports are balanced by potential hazards. Several studies have linked youth participation in sports to delinquent and antisocial behavior (e.g., Gardner, Roth, & Brooks-Gunn, 2009). However, outcomes are usually positive when sports participation is combined

HUMAN DEVELOPMENT in action

Imagine that you are a supervisor in your city's department of parks and recreation. You need to present a workshop to new coaches for a basketball program for first and second graders. What would you emphasize?

with participation in activities that involve adults, such as school, religious, or youth groups (Linver, Roth, & Brooks-Gunn, 2009; Zarrett et al., 2009). But these potential benefits hinge on the adults who are involved. When adult coaches like the one in the opening vignette encourage their players and emphasize skill development, children usually enjoy playing, often improve their skills, and increase their self-esteem (Coatsworth & Conroy, 2009). In contrast, when coaches emphasize winning over skill development and criticize or punish players for bad plays, children lose interest and stop playing (Bailey & Rasmussen, 1996; Smith & Smoll, 1996). And when adolescents find sports too stressful, they often get "burned out"—they lose interest and quit (Raedeke & Smith, 2004).

To encourage youth to participate, adults (and parents) need to have realistic expectations for children and coach positively, praising children instead of criticizing them. And they need to remember that children play games for recreation, which means they should have fun.

Test Yourself

Recall

1. Boys and girls grow at about the same rate during elementary-school years, but at the end of this period, girls _____ .

2. When children skip breakfast, _____ .

3. Boys typically have the advantage of gross motor skills that emphasize strength, but girls tend to have the advantage of _____ .

4. Children may lose interest in sports and quit playing if coaches _____ and criticize or punish players for mistakes.

Interpret

- Compare the profile of physical development shown in Figure 6.5 with Piaget's profile of cognitive development during these years.

- What cognitive and social skills make it possible for children to participate in organized sports?

Apply

- Imagine you are a third grade teacher and find that one of your students rarely eats breakfast. What might you say to the student's parents to encourage them to make time to provide breakfast for their child?

- Jessica and Tommy are 7-year-old fraternal twins who are talented soccer players and teammates. As they develop, how are gender-related differences in physical growth likely to affect their soccer careers?

Recall answers: (1) are more likely to enter puberty and grow rapidly, (2) they often have difficulty paying attention and remembering in school, (3) fine motor skills that emphasize dexterity, (4) emphasize winning over skill development

Linking Research to life • TEACHING USING THE THEORY OF MULTIPLE INTELLIGENCES

The theory of multiple intelligences has important implications for education. Gardner (1993, 1995) believes that schools should foster all intelligences, not just the traditional linguistic and logical–mathematical intelligences. Teachers should capitalize on the strongest intelligences of individual children. That is, teachers need to know a child's profile of intelligence—the child's strengths and weaknesses—and gear instruction to the strengths (Chen & Gardner, 2005). For example, Diana, the fourth-grade teacher in the opening vignette of Section 6.2, could help some of her students understand the Civil War by studying music of that period (musical intelligence). Other students might benefit by emphasis on maps that show the movement of armies in battle (spatial intelligence). Still others might profit from focusing on the experiences of African Americans living in the North and the South (interpersonal intelligence).

These guidelines do not mean that teachers should gear instruction solely to a child's strongest intelligence, pigeonholing youngsters as "numerical learners" or "spatial learners." Instead, whether the topic is the signing of the Declaration of Independence or Shakespeare's *Hamlet*, instruction should try to engage as many intelligences as possible (Gardner, 1999, 2002). The typical result is a richer understanding of the topic by all students.

Some American schools have enthusiastically embraced Gardner's ideas (1993). Are these schools better than those that have not? Educators in schools using the theory think so; they cite evidence that their students benefit in many ways (Kornhaber, Fierros, & Veenema, 2004). However, some critics are not yet convinced (Waterhouse, 2006). Only time (and more research) will tell.

Summary

6.1 Cognitive Development

What are the distinguishing characteristics of thought during Piaget's concrete-operational and formal-operational stages?

- In concrete operations, children are less egocentric than they were in the preoperational period, rarely confuse appearances with reality, and are able to reverse their thinking. Thinking at this stage is limited to the concrete and the real.

- With the onset of formal-operational thinking, adolescents can think hypothetically and reason abstractly. In deductive reasoning, they understand that conclusions are based on logic, not on experience.

How do children use strategies and monitoring to improve learning and remembering?

- Rehearsal and other memory strategies are used to store information in permanent memory and to retrieve it later. Children begin to rehearse at about age 7 or 8 and take up other strategies as they grow older.

- Effective use of strategies for learning and remembering begins with an analysis of the goals of a learning task. It also includes monitoring performance to determine whether the strategy is working. Collectively, these processes make up an important group of study skills.

6.2 Aptitudes for School

What is the nature of intelligence?

- Traditional approaches to intelligence include theories that describe intelligence as a general factor, as well as theories that include specific factors. Hierarchical theories include both general intelligence and various specific skills, such as verbal and spatial ability.

- Gardner's theory of multiple intelligences proposes nine distinct intelligences: linguistic, logical–mathematical, spatial, musical, bodily–kinesthetic, interpersonal, intrapersonal, naturalistic, and existential intelligence. Gardner's theory has stimulated research on nontraditional forms of intelligence, such as emotional intelligence.

- According to Sternberg, intelligence is defined as using abilities to achieve short- and long-term goals and depends on three abilities: analytic ability to analyze a problem and generate a solution, creative ability to deal adaptively with novel situations, and practical ability to know which solutions will work.

What are intelligence tests like?

- Binet created the first intelligence test to identify students who would have difficulty in school. Using this work,

Terman created the Stanford-Binet test in 1916; it remains an important intelligence test. The Stanford-Binet test introduced the concept of the intelligence quotient (IQ): MA/CA $\times$ 100.

How well do intelligence tests work?

- Intelligence tests are reasonably valid measures of achievement in school. They also predict people's performance in the workplace.

How do heredity and environment influence intelligence?

- Evidence for the impact of heredity on IQ scores comes from the findings that (1) siblings' IQ scores become more alike as siblings become more similar genetically and (2) adopted children's IQ scores are more like their biological parents' test scores than their adoptive parents' scores. Evidence for the impact of environment comes from the finding that children who live in responsive, well-organized home environments tend to have higher IQ scores, as do children who participate in intervention programs.

How and why do test scores vary for different racial and ethnic groups?

- There are substantial differences among ethnic groups in their average scores on IQ tests. These differences are attributed to the greater likelihood of Latino American and African American youth being economically disadvantaged and to tests assessing knowledge based on middle-class experiences. Stereotype threat and test-taking skills also contribute to group differences. Still, IQ scores remain valid predictors of school success because middle-class experience is often a prerequisite for school success.

6.3 Special Children, Special Needs

What are the characteristics of gifted and creative children?

- Traditionally, gifted children are those with high scores on IQ tests. Modern definitions of giftedness have been broadened to include exceptional talent in the arts. However defined, giftedness must be nurtured by parents and teachers alike.

- Creativity is associated with divergent thinking, in which the aim is to think in novel and unusual directions. Tests of divergent thinking can predict which children are most likely to be creative. Creativity can be fostered by experiences that encourage children to think flexibly and to explore alternatives.

What are the different forms of disability?

- Individuals with intellectual disability have IQ scores of 70 or lower and deficits in adaptive behavior. Biomedical, social, behavioral, and educational factors place children at risk for intellectual disability. Children with learning disability have normal intelligence but have difficulty mastering specific academic subjects. The most common learning disability is developmental dyslexia, which involves difficulty reading individual words because children haven't mastered language sounds.

What are the distinguishing features of attention-deficit hyperactivity disorder?

- Children with ADHD are distinguished by being hyperactive, inattentive, and impulsive. According to the Multimodal Treatment Study of Children With ADHD, treating ADHD with medication and psychosocial treatment is effective in the short run but does not cure children of the disorder.

6.4 Academic Skills

What are the components of skilled reading?

- Reading includes a number of component skills. Prereading skills include knowing letters and the sounds associated with them. Word recognition is the process of identifying a word. Beginning readers more often accomplish this by sounding out words; advanced readers more often retrieve a word from long-term memory. Comprehension, the act of extracting meaning from text, improves with age as a result of several factors: children recognize individual words more easily, they gain more world knowledge, they match their reading strategies to the goals of the reading task, and they are better able to monitor what they read.

As children develop, how does their writing improve?

- As children develop, their writing improves, which reflects several factors: They know more about the world and so have more to say, they use more effective ways of organizing their writing, and they master the mechanics of writing (e.g., handwriting and spelling).

How do arithmetic skills change during the elementary-school years?

- Children first add and subtract by counting, but soon they use more effective strategies, such as retrieving addition facts directly from memory.

What are the hallmarks of effective schools and effective teachers?

- Schools influence students' achievement in many ways. Students are most likely to achieve when their school

emphasizes academic excellence, has a safe and nurturing environment, monitors pupils' and teachers' progress, and encourages parents to be involved.

- Students achieve at higher levels when their teachers manage classrooms effectively, take responsibility for their students' learning, teach mastery of material, pace material well, value tutoring, and show children how to monitor their own learning.

6.5 Physical Development

How much do school-age children grow?

- Elementary-school children grow at a steady pace, but more so in the legs than in the trunk. Boys and girls tend to be about the same size for most of these years.

- Elementary-school children need approximately 2,400 calories daily, preferably drawn from each of the basic food groups. Children need to eat breakfast, a meal that should provide approximately one fourth of their daily calories. Without breakfast, children often have trouble concentrating in school.

How do motor skills develop during the elementary-school years?

- Fine and gross motor skills improve substantially over the elementary-school years, reflecting children's greater size and strength. Girls tend to excel in fine motor skills that emphasize dexterity, as well as in gross motor skills that require flexibility and balance; boys tend to excel in gross motor skills that emphasize strength. Although some of these differences reflect differences in body makeup, they also reflect differing cultural expectations regarding motor skills for boys and girls.

Are American children physically fit?

- Many American schoolchildren don't meet today's standards for being physically fit, and childhood obesity is a growing concern.

What are the consequences of participating in sports?

- Many school-age children participate in team sports. Benefits of participation include exercise, enhanced self-esteem, and improved social skills. But participation sometimes leads to antisocial behavior, and when adults are involved they sometimes overemphasize competition, which can turn "play" into "work."

Key Terms

mental operations (158)
deductive reasoning (159)
organization (160)
elaboration (160)
metamemory (160)
metacognitive knowledge (161)
emotional intelligence (163)

analytic ability (163)
creative ability (163)
practical ability (163)
mental age (MA) (164)
intelligence quotient (IQ) (164)
convergent thinking (168)
divergent thinking (168)

intellectual disability (169)
learning disability (169)
phonological awareness (174)
knowledge-telling strategy (176)
knowl edge-transforming strategy (176)

Online Resources

Go to CengageBrain.com to access Psychology CourseMate, where you will find an interactive eBook, flashcards, quizzes, videos, websites, and more.

Expanding Social Horizons

Socioemotional Development in Middle Childhood

Like all humans, since birth you have been learning to become a member of your culture. *Teaching children the values, roles, and behaviors of their culture—*socialization*—is a major goal of all peoples.* In most cultures, the task of socialization falls initially to parents. In the first section of this chapter, we see how parents set and try to enforce standards of behavior for their children. Other powerful forces soon contribute to socialization. In the second and third sections, you'll discover how peers and the media contribute to socialization. As children become socialized, they begin to understand more about other people. We examine this growing understanding in the last section.

LEARNING OBJECTIVES

- What are the primary dimensions of parenting?
- What determines how siblings get along? How do first-born, later-born, and only children differ?
- How do divorce and remarriage affect children?
- What factors lead children to be maltreated?

Tanya and Sheila, both sixth graders, wanted to go to a Miley Cyrus concert with two boys from their school. When Tanya asked whether she could go, her mom said, "No way!" Tanya replied defiantly, "Why not?" Her mother blew up: "Because I say so. That's why. Stop bugging me." Sheila wasn't allowed to go either. When she asked why, her mom said, "I just think that you're still too young to be dating. I don't mind your going to the concert. If you want to go just with Tanya, that would be fine. What do you think of that?"

The vignette illustrates what we all know from personal experience—parents go about childrearing in many ways. We study these approaches in this chapter and learn how Tanya and Sheila are likely to be affected by their mothers' styles of parenting.

Dimensions and Styles of Parenting

Parenting can be described in terms of general dimensions that are like personality traits, because they are stable aspects of parental behavior that hold across different situations (Holden & Miller, 1999). When viewed this way, two general dimensions of parental behavior emerge. One is the degree of warmth and responsiveness that parents show their children. At one end of the spectrum are parents who are openly warm and affectionate with their children. They are involved with them, respond to their emotional needs, and spend considerable time with them. At the other end of the spectrum are parents who are relatively uninvolved with their children and sometimes even hostile toward them. These parents often seem more focused on their own needs and interests than on those of their children. As you might expect, children benefit from warm and responsive parenting (Pettit, Bates, & Dodge, 1997; Zhou et al., 2002).

The second general dimension of parental behavior involves control. Some parents are dictatorial: They try to regulate every facet of their children's lives, like a puppeteer controlling a marionette. At the other extreme are parents who exert little or no control over their children: These children do whatever they want without asking their parents first or worrying about their parents' response. What's best for children is an intermediate amount of control, when parents set reasonable standards for their children's behavior, expect their children to meet those standards, and monitor their children's behavior by knowing where their children are, what they're doing, and with whom (Racz & McMahon, 2011).

	Parental control	
	High	Low
High	Authoritative	Permissive
Low	Authoritarian	Uninvolved

(Parental warmth — vertical axis)

FIGURE 7.1

Combining the two dimensions of parental behavior (warmth and control) creates four prototypical styles of parenting.

Parenting Styles

Combining the dimensions of warmth and control produces four prototypic styles of parenting, as shown in Figure 7.1 (Baumrind, 1975, 1991).

- **Authoritarian parenting** *combines high control with little warmth.* These parents lay down rules and expect them to be followed without discussion. Hard work, respect, and obedience are what authoritarian parents wish to cultivate in their children. This style is illustrated by Tanya's mother in the opening vignette. She feels no obligation to explain her decision.

socialization

teaching children the values, roles, and behaviors of their culture

authoritarian parenting

a style of parenting in which parents show high levels of control and low levels of warmth toward their children

Authoritative parents are warm and responsive with children and encourage discussion.

- **Authoritative parenting** *combines a fair degree of parental control with being warm and responsive to children.* Authoritative parents explain rules and encourage discussion. This style is exemplified by Sheila's mother in the opening vignette. Sheila's mother explained why she did not want the girls going to the concert with the boys and encouraged her daughter to discuss the issue with her.

- **Permissive parenting** *offers warmth and caring but little parental control.* These parents generally accept their children's behavior and punish them infrequently. An indulgent and permissive parent would readily agree to Tanya's or Sheila's request to go to the concert simply because it is something the child wants to do.

- **Uninvolved parenting** *provides neither warmth nor control.* Indifferent and uninvolved parents provide for their children's basic physical and emotional needs but little else. They try to minimize the amount of time spent with their children and avoid becoming emotionally involved with them. If Tanya's parents had this style, she might have simply gone to the concert without asking, knowing that her parents wouldn't care and would rather not be bothered.

Authoritative parenting is best for most children most of the time. Children with authoritative parents tend to have higher grades and are responsible, self-reliant, and friendly (Amato & Fowler, 2002; Aunola, Stattin, & Nurmi, 2000). In contrast, children with authoritarian parents often are unhappy, have low self-esteem, and frequently are overly aggressive (e.g., Silk et al., 2003; Zhou et al., 2008). Finally, children with permissive parents often are impulsive and have little self-control, whereas children with uninvolved parents often do poorly in school and are aggressive (Aunola, Stattin, & Nurmi, 2000; Barber & Olsen, 1997; Driscoll, Russell, & Crockett, 2008). Thus, children typically thrive with a parental style that combines control, warmth, and affection.

VARIATIONS ASSOCIATED WITH CULTURE AND SOCIOECONOMIC STATUS. The goal of helping children become contributing members of their culture is much the same worldwide (Whiting & Child, 1953), but views about the "proper" amount of warmth and the "proper" amount of control vary with particular cultures. European Americans want their children to be happy and self-reliant individuals, and they believe these goals are best achieved when parents are warm and exert moderate control (Goodnow, 1992). In many Asian and Latin American countries, however, individualism is less important than cooperation and collaboration (Okagaki & Sternberg, 1993; Wang, Pomerantz, & Chen, 2007). For example, Latino culture typically places greater emphasis on strong family ties and respecting the roles of all family members, particularly adults; these values lead parents to be more protective of their children and to set more rules for them (Halgunseth, Ispa, & Rudy, 2006). Thus, cultural values help specify appropriate ways for parents to interact with their offspring.

Parental styles also depend on parents' socioeconomic status. Within the United States, parents of lower socioeconomic status tend to be more controlling and more punitive—characteristics associated with the authoritarian parenting style—than are parents of higher socioeconomic status (Hoff-Ginsberg & Tardif, 1995). This difference may reflect educational differences that help define socioeconomic status. Parents of higher socioeconomic status are, by definition, more educated and consequently often see development as a more complex process requiring the more nuanced and child-friendly approach that marks authoritative parenting (Skinner, 1985).

Another contributing factor derives from a variable that defines socioeconomic status: income (Melby et al., 2008). Because of limited financial resources, parents of lower socioeconomic status often lead more stressful lives and are far more likely to live in neighborhoods where violence, drugs, and crime are commonplace. Thus, parents of lower socioeconomic status may be too stressed to invest the energy needed

authoritative parenting
a style of parenting in which parents use a moderate amount of control and are warm and responsive to their children

permissive parenting
a style of parenting that offers warmth and caring but little parental control over children

uninvolved parenting
a style of parenting that provides neither warmth nor control and that minimizes the amount of time parents spend with children

for authoritative parenting, and the authoritarian approach—with its emphasis on the child's immediate compliance—may protect children growing up in dangerous neighborhoods (Parke & Buriel, 1998).

As important as these dimensions and styles are for understanding parenting, there is more to effective childrearing, as we'll see in the next section.

Parental Behavior

Dimensions and styles are useful as general characterizations of parents, but they tell us little about how parents behave in specific situations and how these parental behaviors influence children's development. Put another way, what specific parental behaviors influence children? Researchers who study parents name three: direct instruction, modeling, and feedback.

Simon Winnall/Getty Images

Parents can use reinforcement to encourage their children to complete tasks that they don't enjoy, such as household chores.

direct instruction
telling a child what to do, when, and why

negative reinforcement trap
unwittingly reinforcing a behavior you want to discourage

DIRECT INSTRUCTION. Parents often tell their children what to do. But simply playing the role of drill sergeant and ordering children around—"Clean your room!" "Turn off the TV!"—is not effective. *A better approach is* **direct instruction**, *which involves telling a child what to do, when, and why.* Instead of just shouting, "Share your candy with your brother!" a parent should explain when and why it's important to share with a sibling. In other words, just as coaches help athletes master sports skills, parents can help their youngsters master social and emotional skills. Children who get this sort of parental "coaching" tend to be more socially skilled and, not surprisingly, get along better with their peers.

MODELING. Children learn a great deal from parents simply by watching them. The parents' modeling and the youngsters' observational learning lead to imitation, so children's behavior resembles the behavior they observe. Observational learning explains why parental behavior is often consistent from one generation to the next. When, for example, parents often use harsh physical punishment to discipline their children, these children will, when they are parents, follow suit (Bailey et al., 2009).

FEEDBACK. By giving feedback to their children, parents indicate whether a behavior is appropriate and should continue or is inappropriate and should stop. Feedback comes in two general forms. Reinforcement is any action that increases the likelihood of the response that it follows. Parents may use praise to reinforce a child's studying or give a reward for completing household chores. Punishment is any action that discourages the recurrence of the response that it follows. Parents may forbid children to watch television when they get poor grades in school or make children go to bed early for neglecting household chores.

Parents have been rewarding and punishing their children for centuries, but research has provided some surprising insights concerning these processes. *Parents often unwittingly reinforce the very behaviors they want to discourage, a situation called the* **negative reinforcement trap** (Patterson, 1980). The negative reinforcement trap occurs in three steps, most often between a mother and her son. In the first step, the mother tells her son to do something he doesn't want to do. She might tell him to clean up his room, to come inside while he's outdoors playing with friends, or to study instead of watching television. In the next step, the son responds with some behavior that most parents find intolerable, such as prolonged arguing or complaining. In the last step, the mother gives in—saying that the son needn't do as she told him initially—simply to get the son to stop the behavior that is so intolerable. The feedback to the son is that arguing (or complaining) works; the mother rewards that behavior by withdrawing the request that the son did not like.

An effective form of punishment is time-out, in which children sit alone briefly.

As for punishment, research shows that it works best when administered consistently, directly after the undesired behavior occurs, is accompanied by an explanation, and is delivered by someone with whom the child has a warm relationship. At the same time, punishment has some serious drawbacks. One is that punishment is primarily suppressive: Punished responses are stopped, but only temporarily if children do not learn new behaviors to replace those that were punished. For example, denying TV to brothers who are fighting stops the undesirable behavior, but fighting is likely to recur unless the boys learn new ways of solving their disputes.

A second drawback is that punishment can have undesirable side effects. Children become upset when they are being punished, which means they often miss the feedback that punishment is meant to convey. A child denied TV for misbehaving may become angry over the punishment itself and ignore why he's being punished. What's more, when children are punished physically, this often leads them to behave aggressively (Gershoff et al., 2010).

One method combines the best features of punishment while avoiding its shortcomings. *In* **time-out**, *a child who misbehaves must briefly sit alone in a quiet, unstimulating location.* Some parents have children sit alone in a bathroom; others have children sit in a corner of a room. Time-out is punishing because it interrupts the child's ongoing activity and isolates the child from other family members, toys, books, and generally, all forms of rewarding stimulation.

A time-out period usually lasts just a few minutes, which helps parents use the method consistently. During time-out, both parent and child typically calm down. Then, when time-out is over, a parent can talk with the child and explain why the punished behavior is objectionable and what the child should do instead.

Influences of the Marital System

We've seen that parents affect children directly through specific child-directed behaviors (e.g., reinforcement). But just as important are indirect influences. For example, when parents are constantly in conflict, children and adolescents often become anxious, withdrawn, and aggressive, and they're more prone to chronic diseases (Miller & Chen, 2010; Rhoades, 2008). Parental conflict affects children's development through three distinct mechanisms. First, seeing parents fight frightens children because it undermines a child's feeling that the family is stable (Sturge-Apple et al., 2008). Second, chronic conflict between parents often spills over into the parent–child relationship. A wife who frequently confronts her husband may adopt a similar ineffective style when interacting with her children (Cox, Paley, & Harter, 2001). Third, when parents invest time and energy fighting with each other, they're often too tired to invest themselves in high-quality parenting (Katz & Woodin, 2002).

However, when disagreements are handled constructively (e.g., through solution-oriented discussion) children respond positively. This strengthens their belief that their family is cohesive and able to withstand life's problems (Goeke-Moray et al., 2003).

Another indirect influence concerns parents' effectiveness as a parenting team. Just as a doubles tennis team won't win many matches if each player ignores the other, parenting is far less effective when each parent tries to "go it alone" instead of working with the other to achieve shared goals using methods that they both accept. When parents don't work together, when they compete, or when they limit each other's access to their children, problems can result; for example, children can become withdrawn (McHale et al., 2002).

Yet another indirect influence is work-related stress. Not surprisingly, when men and women lead stressful lives at work, they parent less effectively. Sometimes frazzled parents withdraw from family interactions. Over time, this gives the appearance that the parent is detached and uninterested, which makes children anxious and upset. And sometimes work-stressed parents are less accepting and less tolerant, leading to conflicts with their children (Crouter & Bumpus, 2001; Maggi et al., 2008).

time-out
a punishment that involves removing children who are misbehaving from a situation to a quiet, unstimulating environment

Children's Contributions: Reciprocal Influence

The family is a dynamic, interactive system with parents and children: Not only do parents influence children, but children help determine how their parents parent. By their behaviors, attitudes, and interests, children affect how their parents behave toward them. For example, parents respond differently to children based on their age. Parents become more reserved in their affection and gradually relinquish control as children develop cognitively (Shanahan et al., 2007). Mutual influence is also shown by children's temperament. A modest amount of parental control may work well with a moderately active young child who is eager to please adults but not with an active child who is less eager to please, in which case a parent may need to be more controlling and directive (Brody & Ge, 2001; Hastings & Rubin, 1999). Thus, influence is reciprocal: Children's behavior helps determine how parents treat them, and the resulting parental behavior influences children's behavior, which in turn causes parents to again change their behavior (Schermerhorn, Chow, & Cummings, 2010).

As time goes by, these reciprocal influences lead many families to adopt routine ways of interacting with each other. Some families end up functioning smoothly: Parents and children cooperate, anticipate each other's needs, and are generally happy. Unfortunately, other families end up troubled: Disagreements are common, parents spend much time trying unsuccessfully to control their defiant children, and everyone is often angry and upset. Still others are characterized by disengagement: Parents withdraw from each other and are not available to their children (Sturge-Apple, Davies, & Cummings, 2010). Over the long term, such troubled families do not fare well, so it's important that these negative reciprocal influences are nipped in the bud (Carrere & Gottman, 1999; Roche et al., 2011).

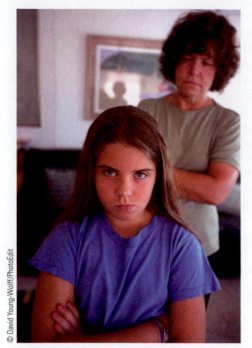

When children respond defiantly to discipline, parents often resort to harsher discipline in the future.

Siblings

For most of a year, all first-born children are only children. Some children remain "onlies" forever, but most get brothers and sisters. As the family acquires these new members, parent–child relationships become more complex. Parents can no longer focus on a single child but must adjust to the needs of multiple children. Just as important, siblings influence each other's development.

From the beginning, sibling relationships are complicated. Children usually are excited by the prospect of another child, but its arrival is often distressing because children must share parental attention and affection (Gottlieb & Mendelson, 1990). However, distress can be avoided if parents remain responsive to their older children's needs (Howe & Ross, 1990). One benefit of a sibling's birth is that fathers become more involved with their older children because mothers must devote more time to a newborn (Stewart et al., 1987).

Many older siblings enjoy helping their parents take care of a newborn. Older children play with the baby, console it, feed it, or change its diapers. In middle-class Western families, such caregiving often occurs in the context of play, with parents nearby. But in many developing nations, children—particularly girls—play an important role in providing care for their younger siblings (Zukow-Goldring, 2002). As the infant grows, interactions between siblings become more frequent and more complicated. Older siblings become a source of care and comfort for younger siblings when they are distressed or upset (Gass, Jenkins, & Dunn, 2007; Kim et al., 2007). Older siblings also serve as teachers for their younger siblings, teaching them to play games or how to cook simple foods (Maynard, 2002). Finally, when older children do well in school and are popular with peers, younger siblings often follow suit (Brody et al., 2003).

As time goes by, some siblings grow close, becoming best friends in ways that nonsiblings can never be. Other siblings constantly argue, compete, and overall, simply do not get along with each other. The basic pattern of sibling interaction seems to be established early in development and remains fairly stable (Kramer, 2010).

In many cultures, older siblings regularly provide care for younger siblings.

Why are some sibling relationships so filled with love and respect while others are dominated by jealousy and resentment? In general, sibling relations are more often warm and harmonious between siblings of the same sex (Dunn & Kendrick, 1981) and when neither sibling is too emotional (Brody, Stoneman, & McCoy, 1994). Age also matters: Sibling relationships generally improve as the younger child approaches adolescence, because siblings begin to perceive each other as equals (Buhrmester & Furman, 1990; Kim et al., 2006). And parents contribute: Siblings more often get along when they believe that parents have no "favorites" but treat all siblings fairly and when parents have a warm, harmonious relationship (Erel, Margolin, & John, 1998; McGuire & Shanahan, 2010).

Thus, parents can help reduce friction between siblings by being equally affectionate, responsive, and caring to all of their children and by caring for each other. At the same time, parents must realize that some dissension is natural in families, especially those with young boys and girls. Children's different interests lead to conflicts that youngsters cannot resolve because their social skills are limited.

Impact of Birth Order

First-born children are often "guinea pigs" for most parents, who have lots of enthusiasm but little practical experience rearing children. Parents typically have high expectations for their first-borns and are both more affectionate and more punitive toward them. As more children arrive, most parents become more adept at their roles, having learned "the tricks of the trade" from earlier children. With later-born children, parents have more realistic expectations and are more relaxed in their discipline (Baskett, 1985).

The different approaches that parents use with their first- and later-born children help explain differences that are commonly observed between these children. First-born children generally have higher scores on intelligence tests and are more likely to go to college than their younger siblings. They are also more willing to conform to parents' and adults' requests. In contrast, perhaps because later-born children are less concerned about pleasing parents and adults, they are more popular with their peers and are more innovative (Beck, Burnet, & Vosper, 2006; Bjerkedal et al., 2007).

What about only children? According to conventional wisdom, parents dote on onlies, who therefore become selfish and egotistical. Is the folklore correct? No. Comparisons between only children and children with siblings often find no differences; when differences are found, the advantage usually goes to the only child (Falbo & Polit, 1986; Liu, Lin, & Chen, 2010). Only children are often more successful in school and have higher levels of intelligence, leadership, autonomy, and maturity than children with siblings (Falbo & Polit, 1986).

Although the folklore says that indulgent parenting causes only children to be selfish, in fact, only children are often smarter and more mature than children with siblings.

Divorce and Remarriage

Many children are distressed by their parents' divorce because it involves conflict between parents, separation from one of them, and economic hardship. Not surprisingly, in school achievement, conduct, adjustment, self-concept, and parent–child relations, children whose parents had divorced fare poorly compared to children from intact families (Amato, 2001; Lansford, 2009). As adults, children of divorce are more likely to experience conflict in their own marriages, to have negative attitudes toward marriage, to become depressed, and to become divorced themselves (Hetherington & Kelly, 2002; Segrin, Taylor, & Altman, 2005).

Divorce is more harmful when it occurs during childhood and adolescence than during the preschool or college years. Also, children who are temperamentally more emotional tend to be more affected by divorce (Lengua et al., 1999). And children suffer more when they are inclined to interpret events negatively: After a father forgets to take a child on a promised outing, the impact is greater on a child who believes the father didn't want to go and won't make similar plans again (Mazur et al., 1999).

The first year following a divorce is often rocky for parents and children alike. But beginning in the second year, most children start to adjust to their new circumstances (Hetherington & Kelly, 2002). Children adjust to divorce more readily if their divorced parents cooperate with each other, especially on disciplinary matters (Buchanan & Heiges, 2001). *In* **joint custody**, *both parents retain legal custody of the children.* Children benefit from joint custody if their parents get along (Bauserman, 2002).

Of course, many parents do not get along after a divorce, which eliminates joint custody as an option. Traditionally, mothers have been awarded custody; when this happens, children benefit when fathers remain involved in parenting (Fabricius & Luecken, 2007). In recent years fathers have increasingly often been given custody, especially of sons. This practice coincides with findings that children often adjust better when they live with same-sex parents: Boys often fare better with fathers and girls fare better with mothers (McLanahan, 1999). One reason boys are often better off with their fathers is that boys are likely to become involved in negative reinforcement traps (described on page 192) with their mothers. Another explanation is that both boys and girls may forge stronger emotional relationships with same-sex parents than with opposite-sex parents (Zimiles & Lee, 1991).

Reducing the Harm of Divorce

Parents can reduce divorce-related stress and help children adjust to their new life circumstances. Parents should explain together to children why they are divorcing and what their children can expect to happen to them. They should reassure children that they will always love them and always be their parents; parents must back up these words with actions by remaining involved in their children's lives despite the increased difficulty of doing so.

To help children deal with divorce, parents should not compete with each other for their children's love and attention; children adjust to divorce best when they maintain good relationships with both parents. Parents should neither take out their anger with each other on their children nor criticize their ex-spouse in front of the children. Finally, parents should not ask children to mediate disputes.

Following all these rules all the time is not easy. After all, divorce is stressful and painful for adults too. Fortunately, there are effective programs available that can help parents and children adjust to life following divorce. The Spotlight on Research feature describes one such program.

Blended Families

Following divorce, most children live in a single-parent household for about 5 years. However, more than two thirds of men and women eventually remarry (Sweeney, 2010). *The resulting unit, consisting of a biological parent, a stepparent, and children, is known as a* **blended family**. (Other terms for this family configuration are remarried family and reconstituted family.)

The most common form of blended family is a mother, her children, and a stepfather. Most stepfathers do not participate actively in childrearing and often seem reluctant to become involved (Clarke-Stewart & Brentano, 2005). Nevertheless, boys typically benefit from the presence of a stepfather, particularly when he is warm and involved. Preadolescent girls, however, do not adjust readily to their mother's remarriage, apparently because it disrupts the intimate relationship they have established with her (Visher, Visher, & Pasley, 2003).

These adjustments are more difficult when mothers of adolescents remarry. Adolescents do not adapt to the new family circumstances as easily as children do; they're more likely to challenge a stepfather's authority. And adjustment is more difficult when a stepfather brings his own biological children into the blended family. In such

HUMAN DEVELOPMENT in action

Imagine that you're a marriage and family therapist. Your clients, a young couple with three school-age children, have decided to divorce due to irreconcilable differences. What advice would you give them to help minimize the impact of their impending divorce on their children?

joint custody
when both parents retain legal custody of their children following divorce

blended family
a family consisting of a biological parent, a stepparent, and children

Evaluation of a Program to Help Parents and Children Adjust to Life After Divorce

Who were the investigators, and what was the aim of the study?
Divorce puts children at risk for reduced school achievement, behavior problems, and other less desirable outcomes. Clorinda Vélez, Sharlene Wolchik, Jenn-Yun Tein, and Irwin Sandler (2011) wanted to determine the benefits for children of an intervention program for mothers that focused primarily on the quality of the mother–child relationship and effective disciplinary methods.

How did the investigators measure the topic of interest?
Vélez and her colleagues assigned mothers to one of two conditions: in the intervention condition, mothers learned (1) ways to foster parent–child relationships and (2) effective disciplinary techniques. In the control condition, mothers were provided books that described how to adjust to divorce, as well as a reading guide. Mothers and children completed several questionnaires designed to measure parenting quality (defined here as being warm and communicating effectively). In addition, children completed questionnaires designed to measure whether they were coping effectively with divorce-related adjustment (e.g., being proactive in making changes, being optimistic).

Who were the participants in the study?
The study included 240 mothers who had been divorced within the previous 2 years and who had at least one child between 9 and 12 years of age. The mothers had not remarried and had no plans for doing so in the near future.

What was the design of the study?
This study was experimental because Vélez and her colleagues assigned mothers randomly to either an intervention condition or a control condition. The study was longitudinal because mothers and children were tested five times: prior to the experimental treatment, immediately after the treatment, and at 3-month, 6-month, and 6-year intervals after the treatment.

Were there ethical concerns with the study?
No; the questionnaires that parents and children completed were ones commonly used to study parent–child relationships and family interactions.

What were the results?
Correlations were computed between experimental conditions, relationship quality, and children's active coping. The results revealed that parent–child relationships were of higher quality when mothers participated in the intervention condition and that higher-quality relationships were associated with more active coping on the part of children. In other words, the intervention condition improved mother–child relationships and this improvement, in turn, resulted in children's use of more active coping to deal with their problems.

What did the investigators conclude?
Vélez and her colleagues concluded that, "by increasing one of children's most important interpersonal resources, mother–child relationship quality, the [intervention program] improved youth's coping efficacy and active coping" (p. 255). In other words, when children have a high-quality relationship with their mother—she is warm to them and communicates well with them—they are empowered to deal with the unique challenges they face as they adjust to life after their parents' divorce.

What converging evidence would strengthen these conclusions?
There are two limits to these findings. First, the children were all in middle childhood; it is unclear whether intervention would be equally effective with preschool children or with adolescents. Second, mothers and children were mainly middle class. Would intervention work as well with divorced women living in poverty, who face additional stresses and obstacles to effective parenting? Answering these questions would provide more convincing evidence of the effectiveness of intervention programs designed to help children and mothers adjust to life following divorce.

 Go to Psychology CourseMate at **www.cengagebrain.com** to enhance your understanding of this research.

families, parents sometimes favor their biological children over their stepchildren—they're more involved with and warmer toward their biological children. Such preferential treatment almost always leads to conflict and unhappiness (Dunn & Davies, 2001; Sweeney, 2010). Similarly, when the mother and stepfather argue, children usually side with their biological parent (Dunn, O'Connor, & Cheng, 2005).

The best strategy for stepfathers is to be interested in their new stepchildren but to avoid encroaching on established relationships. Newly remarried mothers must be careful that their enthusiasm for their new spouse does not come at the expense of time and affection for their children. Both parents and children need to have realistic expectations. The blended family can be successful, but it takes effort because of the complicated relationships, conflicting loyalties, and jealousies that usually exist (Sweeney, 2010; White & Gilbreth, 2001). Fortunately, programs are available to help members of blended families adjust to their new roles (Bullard et al., 2010). Such programs emphasize effective co-parenting (described on page 193) and, in particular, ways of dealing with behavior problems that children often display with stepparents. These programs result in fewer behavior problems and greater marital satisfaction.

Parent–Child Relationships Gone Awry: Child Maltreatment

The first time that 7-year-old Max came to school with bruises on his face, he explained to his teacher that he had fallen down the basement steps. When Max had similar bruises a few weeks later, his teacher contacted local authorities. It turned out that Max's mother thrashed him with a paddle for even minor misconduct; for serious transgressions, she made him sleep alone in a dark, unheated basement.

Maltreatment includes physical abuse involving assault that leads to injuries and sexual abuse involving fondling, intercourse, or other sexual behaviors. Another form of maltreatment is neglect, not giving children adequate food, clothing, or medical care. Children can also be harmed by psychological abuse—ridicule, rejection, and humiliation (Cicchetti & Toth, 2006; Wicks-Nelson & Israel, 2006). Nearly three quarters of a million children annually suffer maltreatment. About 75% are neglected, about 15% are abused physically, about 10% are abused sexually, and 5% are maltreated psychologically; some experience more than one type of maltreatment (U.S. Department of Health and Human Services, 2010a).

The prognosis for maltreated youngsters is not good. Some suffer permanent physical damage. Even when there is no lasting physical damage, children's social and emotional development is often disrupted. They tend to have poor relationships with peers, often because they are too aggressive (Appleyard, Yang, & Runyan, 2010; Cullerton-Sen et al., 2008). Their cognitive development and academic performance are also disturbed. Abused youngsters typically get lower grades in school, score lower on standardized achievement tests, and are more frequently retained in a grade rather than promoted. Also, school-related behavior problems (e.g., being disruptive in class) are common, in part because maltreated children are often socially unskilled and don't regulate their emotions well (Burack et al., 2006; Maughan & Cicchetti, 2002).

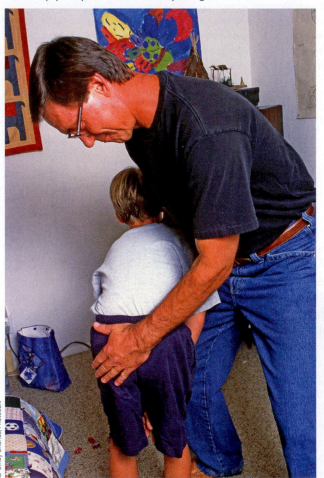

Child abuse is more common in societies that condone physical punishment such as spanking.

What Children Are At Risk for Maltreatment?

Many factors put some children at risk for abuse and protect others; the number and combination of factors determine whether the child is a likely target for abuse (Cicchetti & Toth, 2006). The most general category of contributing factors includes those dealing with cultural values and the social conditions in which parents rear their children. Many countries in Europe and Asia have strong cultural prohibitions against physical punishment. It simply isn't done and would be viewed in much the same way we would view an American parent who punished by not feeding the child for a few days. Countries that do not condone physical punishment tend to have lower rates of child maltreatment than the United States.

Poverty is also linked to maltreatment, in part because lack of money increases the stress of daily life (Duncan & Brooks-Gunn, 2000). When parents are worrying about whether they can buy groceries or pay rent, they are more likely to punish their children physically instead of making the extra effort to reason with them. Similarly, abuse is more common among military families when a soldier is deployed in a combat zone (Gibbs et al., 2007). In this case, maltreatment may be rooted in stress stemming from concern over the absent parent and temporary single parenthood.

Social isolation also contributes: Abuse is more likely when families are socially isolated from other relatives or neighbors. When a family lives in relative isolation, it deprives children of adults who could protect them and deprives parents of social support that would help them better deal with life's stresses (Coulton et al., 2007).

Focusing on families reveals several other factors that place children at risk. Maltreatment is more likely when parents were abused themselves as children, when parents use ineffective disciplinary techniques, and when parents' interactions with each other are often unpredictable, unsupportive, and unsatisfying for both husbands and wives (Berlin, Appleyard, & Dodge, 2011; Bugental & Happaney, 2004).

To place the last few pieces in the puzzle, we must look at the abused children themselves. Our earlier discussion of the reciprocal influence between parents and children should remind you that children may inadvertently, through their behavior, contribute to their own abuse. Infants and preschoolers are more often abused than older children, probably because they are less able to regulate aversive behaviors that may elicit abuse, such as excessive crying or whining (Sidebotham, Heron, & the Avon Longitudinal Study of Parents and Children Study Team, 2003).

For much the same reason, children who are frequently ill are more often abused. When children are sick, they're more likely to cry and whine, annoying parents. Also, a child's sickness increases burdens (and stress) on parents because of the need to provide medical care and to arrange for alternative child care (Rogosch et al., 1995). And stepchildren are at risk for abuse: Parents are less invested emotionally in their stepchildren, making them vulnerable to abuse (Daly & Wilson, 1996).

Thus, no single factor causes abuse. Instead, maltreatment becomes more likely when cultures condone physical punishment, parents lack effective skills for dealing with children, and a child's behavior is frequently aversive. In the Linking Research to Life feature on pages 212–213, we describe ways to prevent maltreatment.

Test Yourself

Recall

1. A(n) _____ parental style combines high control with low involvement.

2. Most children seem to benefit when parents rely on a(n) _____ style.

3. Parental behaviors that influence children include direct instruction, modeling (learning through observation), and _____.

4. With later-born children, parents often have more realistic expectations and are _____.

5. When mothers remarry, daughters do not adjust as readily as sons because _____.

6. Children are more likely to be abused when they are younger and when they are _____.

Interpret

- From a child's viewpoint, what are the pros and cons of a blended family?

- How can child maltreatment be explained in terms of the biological, psychological, and sociocultural forces in the biopsychosocial framework?

Apply

- When 10-year-old Dylan's family got a puppy, he agreed to walk it every day after school. But when his mom asks him to do this, he gets angry because he'd rather watch TV. They argue, then Dylan's mom gives up and walks the dog herself; Dylan goes back to watching TV. As a family therapist, what would you advise Dylan's mom to do to prevent these regular arguments?

- Calvin, age 8, and his younger sister, Hope, constantly argue and constantly compete for their parents' attention. Teenage sisters Melissa and Caroline love doing everything together and enjoy sharing clothes and secrets about their teen romances. Why might Calvin and Hope get along so poorly while Melissa and Caroline get along so well?

Recall answers: (1) authoritarian, (2) authoritative, (3) feedback (reward and punishment), (4) more relaxed in their discipline, (5) the remarriage disrupts an intimate mother–daughter relationship, (6) often ill

LEARNING OBJECTIVES

- What are the benefits of friendship?
- What are the important features of groups of children and adolescents? How do these groups influence individuals?

- Why are some children more popular than others? Why are some rejected?
- What are some effects of childhood aggression? Why are some children chronic victims of aggression?

Only 36 hours had passed since the campers arrived at Crab Orchard Summer Camp. Nevertheless, groups had already formed spontaneously based on the campers' interests: arts and crafts, hiking, and swimming. Within each group, leaders and followers had already emerged. This happens every year, but the staff is always astonished at how quickly a "social network" emerges at camp.

The groups that form as summer camps—as well as in schools and neighborhoods—represent one of the more complex forms of peer relationships: Many children are involved, and there are multiple relationships. We examine these kinds of interactions later in this section. Let's start by looking at a simpler social relationship, friendship.

Friendships

Over time, children develop special relationships with certain peers. **Friendship** *is a voluntary relationship between two people involving mutual liking.* The first friendships emerge at about 4 or 5 years of age when children select peers that they like and who are good playmates. As children develop, their friendships become more complex. For older elementary-school children (ages 8 to 11), mutual liking and shared activities are joined by features that are more psychological in nature: trust and assistance. At this age, children expect that they can depend on their friends—their friends will be nice to them, will keep their promises, and won't say mean things about them to others. Children also expect friends to step forward in times of need: A friend should willingly help with homework or willingly share a snack.

Adolescence adds another layer of complexity to friendships—intimacy. Friends now confide in one another, sharing personal thoughts and feelings. Teenagers reveal their excitement over a new romance or disappointment at not being cast in a school musical. Intimacy is more common in friendships among girls, who are more likely than boys to have one exclusive "best friend" (Markovits, Benenson, & Dolenszky, 2001). Because intimacy is at the core of their friendships, girls are also more likely to be concerned about the faithfulness of their friends and worry about being rejected (Benenson & Christakos, 2003; Poulin & Chan, 2010).

The emergence of intimacy in adolescent friendships means that friends also come to be seen as sources of social and emotional support. Elementary-school children generally rely on close family members—parents, siblings, and grandparents—as primary sources of support when they need help or are bothered by something. But adolescents turn to close friends instead. Because adolescent friends share intimate thoughts and feelings, they can provide support during emotional or stressful periods (del Valle, Bravo, & Lopez, 2010; Levitt, Guacci-Franco, & Levitt, 1993).

Who Are Friends?

friendship
a voluntary relationship between two people involving mutual liking

Most childhood friends are alike in age, gender, and race (Hamm, 2000; Mehta & Strough, 2009). Because friends are supposed to treat each other as equals, friendships

Childhood friends tend to be alike in age, race, and sex.

are rare between an older, more experienced child and a younger, less experienced child. Because children typically play with same-sex peers, boys and girls rarely become friends.

Friendships are more common between children from the same race or ethnic group than between those from different groups, reflecting racial segregation in American society. Friendships among children of different groups are more common when a child's school and neighborhood are ethnically diverse (Quillian & Campbell, 2003). Although cross-group friendships are uncommon, they are valuable: Children from majority groups typically form more positive attitudes toward a minority group following a friendship with a youth from that group (Feddes, Noack, & Rutland, 2009).

Childhood friends are usually alike not only in age, sex, and race but also in attitudes toward school, activities they enjoy, and plans for the future (Hamm, 2000; Schaefer et al., 2011). Children and adolescents befriend others who are similar to themselves, and as time passes, friends become more similar in their attitudes and values (Popp et al., 2008; Van Zalk et al., 2010). Nevertheless, friends are not photocopies of each other; friends are less similar, for example, than spouses or dizygotic twins (Rushton & Bons, 2005).

Quality and Consequences of Friendships

Some childhood friendships are long-lasting and satisfying, but others rapidly wear thin and end. What accounts for these differences in the quality and longevity of friendships? Sometimes friendships are brief because children lack the skills to sustain them (Jiao, 1999; Parker & Seal, 1996). As friends, they can't keep secrets or they're too bossy. Sometimes friendships end because, when conflicts arise, children are more concerned about their own interests and are unwilling to compromise or negotiate (Fonzi et al., 1997; Rose & Asher, 1999). And sometimes friendships end when children discover that their needs and interests aren't as similar as they thought initially (Gavin & Furman, 1996).

When youth have good friends, they're better able to cope with life's stresses.

When friendships endure, children benefit (Berndt & Murphy, 2002). Compared to children who lack friends, children with good friends have higher self-esteem, are less likely to be lonely and depressed, and more often act prosocially by sharing and cooperating with others (Burk & Laursen, 2005; Hartup & Stevens, 1999). Children with good friends cope better with life stresses, such as transitioning from elementary to middle or junior high school (Berndt & Keefe, 1995) or being rejected by peers (McDonald et al., 2010). The benefits of friendship are also long-lasting: Children who have friends have greater self-worth as young adults (Bagwell, Newcomb, & Bukowski, 1998).

Although children and adolescents benefit from their friends' support, there can be costs as well. *Sometimes friends spend much of their time together discussing each other's personal problems, which is known as* **co-rumination**. Girls do this more than boys (consistent with intimacy being more important to girls' friendships). Such co-rumination strengthens girls' friendships but also puts them at risk for greater depression and anxiety. In other words, when Avanti and Shruti spend day after day talking about problems with their parents and their schoolwork, they grow closer but more troubled (Brendgen et al., 2010; Rose, Carlson, & Waller, 2007).

There are other ways in which friendships can be hazardous (Bagwell, 2004). For example, when aggressive children are friends, they often encourage each other's aggressive behavior (Dishion, Poulin, & Burraston, 2001; Piehler & Dishion, 2007). Similarly, when teens engage in risky behavior (e.g., when they drink, smoke, or have sex), they often reinforce each other's risky behavior (Bot et al., 2005; Henry et al., 2007).

co-rumination
conversations about personal problems, common among adolescent girls

Groups

At the summer camp in the vignette, new campers form groups based on common interests. Groups are just as prevalent in American schools. "Jocks," "preps," "burnouts," "druggies," "nerds," and "brains"—you may remember these or similar terms referring to groups of older children and adolescents. During late childhood and early adolescence, the peer group becomes the focal point of social relationships for youth (Rubin, Bukowski, & Parker, 1998). *The starting point is often a* **clique**—*a small group of children or adolescents who are friends and tend to be similar in age, sex, race, and attitudes.* Members of a clique spend time together and often dress, talk, and act alike. *A* **crowd** *is a larger mixed-sex group of older children or adolescents who have similar values and attitudes and are known by a common label, such as jocks or nerds* (Brown & Klute, 2003).

Some crowds have more status than others. In many schools, jocks are the most prestigious crowd, whereas the burnouts are among the least prestigious. Students from high-status crowds tend to have greater self-esteem than those from low-status crowds (Sussman et al., 2007).

Why do some students become nerds while others join the burnouts? Adolescents' interests and abilities matter. Brighter students who enjoy school gravitate to the brain or nerd crowds, while athletically talented teens become part of the jock crowd (Prinstein & La Greca, 2004). Adolescents' crowds also reveal parents' influence. When parents practice authoritative parenting—they are warm but controlling—their children become involved with crowds that endorse adult standards of behavior (e.g., jocks, brains). But when parents' style is neglectful or permissive, their children are less likely to identify with adult standards of behavior and instead join crowds like druggies that disavow adult standards. This seems to be true of African, Asian, European, and Hispanic American children and their parents (Brown et al., 1993).

Group leaders tend to be those who have skills that are valuable to the group: Girl Scout patrol leaders, for example, tend to be goal oriented and to have good ideas.

Group Structure

Groups typically have a well-defined structure known as a **dominance hierarchy***, headed by a leader to whom all other members of the group defer.* Other members know their position in the hierarchy. They yield to members who are above them in the hierarchy and assert themselves over members who are below them. A dominance hierarchy is useful in reducing conflict within groups because members know their place.

What determines where members stand in the hierarchy? In groups of young boys, leaders are often physically intimidating (Hawley, 1999). Among girls and older boys, hierarchies are often based on individual traits that relate to the group's main function (Li et al., 2007). At Crab Orchard Summer Camp, for example, the leaders are most often the children with the greatest camping experience. Among Girl Scouts, girls chosen to be patrol leaders tend to be bright and goal oriented and to have new ideas (Edwards, 1994). Thus, leadership based on key skills is effective because it gives the greatest influence to those with the skills most important to the functioning of the group.

Peer Pressure

Groups establish norms—standards of behavior that apply to all group members—and may pressure members to conform to these norms. Such "peer pressure" is often characterized as an irresistible, harmful force. The stereotype is that teenagers exert enormous pressure on one another to behave antisocially. In reality, peer pressure is neither always powerful nor always evil. For example, most junior and senior high-school students resist peer pressure to behave in ways that are clearly antisocial, such as stealing (Brown, Lohr, & McClenahan, 1986), and such resistance increases from mid to late adolescence (Steinberg & Monahan, 2007). Peer pressure can be positive too; peers often urge one another to work hard in school, to participate in school activities such as trying out for a play or working on the yearbook, or to become involved in community action projects such as Habitat for Humanity (Kindermann, 2007; Molloy, Gest, & Rulison, 2011).

clique
a small group of friends who are similar in age, sex, race, and attitudes

crowd
a large group including many cliques that have similar attitudes and values

dominance hierarchy
the ordering of individuals within a group in which group members with lower status defer to those with greater status

Peers are most influential when one or more of the following conditions are present: (1) youth are younger and more socially anxious; (2) peers have high status; (3) peers are friends; and (4) standards for appropriate behavior are not clear-cut, as in tastes in music or clothing or standards for smoking and drinking (Anderson et al., 2011; Brechwald & Prinstein, 2011). For example, when 14-year-old Doug's best friend (who's one of the most popular kids in school) gets his hair cut like Justin Bieber, Doug may go along because he's young, the peer is popular and his friend, and there are no fixed standards for hairstyle. But when an unpopular kid that 18-year-old Kelly barely knows suggests to her that they go to the mall and shoplift some earrings, Kelly will resist because she's older, the peer is unpopular and not a friend, and norms for shoplifting are clear.

Popularity and Rejection

Most school classrooms include some truly popular children—they're liked by nearly everyone and peers are eager to be with them—as well as children disliked (sometimes intensely) by most classmates. Studies of popularity (Hymel et al., 2004) reveal that most children in elementary-school classrooms can be placed, fairly consistently, in one of these five categories:

- **Popular children** *are liked by many classmates.*

- **Rejected children** *are disliked by many classmates.*

- **Controversial children** *are both liked and disliked intensely by classmates.*

- **Average children** *are liked and disliked by some classmates but without the intensity found for popular, rejected, or controversial children.*

- **Neglected children** *are ignored by classmates.*

Of these categories, we know most about popular and rejected children. Each of these categories includes two subtypes. Most popular children are skilled academically and socially. They are good students who are usually friendly, cooperative, and helpful (Graziano, Keane, & Calkins, 2007; Rubin, Bukowski, & Parker, 2006; Véronneau et al., 2010). A smaller group of popular children includes physically aggressive boys who pick fights with peers and relationally aggressive girls who, like the Plastics in the film *Mean Girls,* thrive on manipulating social relationships. Although these youth are not particularly friendly, their antisocial behavior nevertheless apparently has a certain appeal to peers (Cillessen & Rose, 2005; Xie et al., 2006).

popular children
children who are liked by many classmates

rejected children
as applied to children's popularity, children who are disliked by many classmates

controversial children
as applied to children's popularity, children who are both liked and disliked intensely by classmates

average children
as applied to children's popularity, children who are liked and disliked by different classmates, but with relatively little intensity

neglected children
as applied to children's popularity, children who are ignored—neither liked nor disliked—by their classmates

Most popular children are good students and socially skilled: they tend to be friendly with and helpful to peers.

© MBI/Alamy

As for rejected children, many are overly aggressive, hyperactive, socially unskilled, and unable to regulate their emotions. These children are usually more hostile than popular aggressive children and seem to be aggressive for the sheer fun of it, which peers dislike, instead of using aggression as a means toward other ends, which peers may not like but grudgingly respect (Prinstein & Cillessen, 2003). Other rejected children are shy, withdrawn, timid, and not surprisingly, lonely (Asher & Paquette, 2003; Rubin, Coplan, & Bowker, 2009).

Causes and Consequences of Rejection

No one enjoys being rejected. For children, repeated peer rejection in childhood can have serious long-term consequences that are less often seen in other groups, including dropping out of school, committing juvenile offenses, and experiencing psychopathology (Ladd, 2006; Rubin, Bukowski, & Parker, 1998).

Peer rejection can be traced, at least in part, to the influences of parents (Ladd, 1998). As expected from social cognitive theory, children see how their parents respond in different social situations and often imitate these responses later. In particular, when parents typically respond to interpersonal conflict with intimidation or aggression, their children may imitate them, hampering the development of their social skills and making them less popular in the long run (Kawabata et al., 2011).

Parents also contribute to their children's social skills and popularity through their disciplinary practices. Inconsistent discipline—punishing a child for misbehaving one day and ignoring the same behavior the next—is associated with antisocial, aggressive behavior, paving the way for rejection. Consistent punishment that does not rely on power assertion but is tied to parental love and affection is more likely to promote social skills and, in the process, popularity (Dekovic & Janssens, 1992; Rubin, Stewart, & Chen, 1995).

Thus, the origins of rejection are clear: Socially awkward, aggressive children are often rejected because they rely on an aggressive interpersonal style, which can be traced to parenting. However, by teaching youngsters (and their parents) more effective ways of interacting with others, rejected children can learn skills that lead to peer acceptance and thereby avoid the long-term harm associated with being rejected (La Greca, 1993; Mize & Ladd, 1990).

Aggressive Children and Their Victims

By the time toddlers are old enough to play with one another, they show aggression. For example, 1- and 2-year-olds sometimes use physical aggression to resolve their conflicts (Dodge, Coie, & Lynam, 2006). *In* **instrumental aggression**, *a child uses aggression to achieve an explicit goal.* By the start of the elementary-school years, another form of aggression emerges (Coie et al., 1991). **Hostile aggression** *is unprovoked and is designed to intimidate, harass, or humiliate another child.* Hostile aggression is illustrated by a child who spontaneously says, "You're stupid!" and then kicks a classmate. A third form of aggression is relational aggression, in which children try to hurt others by undermining their social relationships (see Chapter 5). Examples would include telling friends to avoid a particular classmate or spreading malicious gossip (Crick et al., 2004).

Tendencies to behave aggressively are stable over time, particularly among children who are highly aggressive at a young age. For example, in a study involving more than 200 German preschool children (Asendorpf, Denissen, & van Anken, 2008), those children who were judged by teachers to be most aggressive were, as young adults, 12 times more likely than the least aggressive children to have been charged for criminal activity. And violent behavior in adulthood is not the only long-term outcome of childhood aggression; poor adjustment to high school (e.g., dropping out or failing a grade) and unemployment are others (Asendorpf et al, 2008; Ladd, 2003). Clearly, aggression is not simply a case of playful pushing and shoving that children always outgrow. To the contrary, a small minority of children who are highly aggressive develop into young adults who create havoc in society.

instrumental aggression
aggression used to achieve an explicit goal

hostile aggression
unprovoked aggression that seems to have the sole goal of intimidating, harassing, or humiliating another child

Children are likely to become chronic victims of aggression if they refuse to defend themselves.

Some youngsters are chronic targets of bullying, either through physical aggression (e.g., a child who is beat up daily on the playground) or through relational aggression (e.g., a child who is constantly the subject of rumors spread by classmates). Not surprisingly, when children are chronic victims of aggression, they're often lonely, anxious, and depressed; they dislike school; and they have low self-esteem (Ladd & Ladd, 1998; Rudolph, Troop-Gordon, & Flynn, 2009).

Why do some children suffer the sad fate of being victims? Some victims are aggressive themselves (Veenstra et al., 2005). These youngsters often overreact, are restless, and are easily irritated. Their aggressive peers soon learn that these children are easily baited. A group of children will, for example, insult or ridicule them, knowing that they will probably start a fight even though they are outnumbered. Other victims tend to be withdrawn and submissive. They are unwilling or unable to defend themselves from their peers' aggression, so they are usually referred to as passive victims (Guerra, Williams, & Sadek, 2011; Ladd & Ladd, 1998; Salmivalli & Isaacs, 2005). When attacked, they show obvious signs of distress and usually give in to their attackers, thereby rewarding the aggressive behavior. Thus, both aggressive and withdrawn submissive children end up as victims.

Victimized children can be taught ways of dealing with aggression: they can be encouraged to not respond in kind when insulted and to not show fear when threatened. In addition, increasing self-esteem can help. When attacked, children with low self-esteem may think, "I'm a loser and have to put up with this because I have no choice." Increasing children's self-esteem makes them less tolerant of personal attacks (Egan, Monson, & Perry, 1998). Another useful way to help victims is to foster their friendships with peers. When children have friends, they're not as likely to be victimized (Veenstra et al., 2010). Finally, the best solution is to prevent bullying and victimization altogether; an effective way to do this is to create a school climate in which bullying is not condoned and victims are supported by their peers (Kärnä et al., 2011).

Test Yourself

Recall

1. Friends are usually similar in age, sex, race, and _____.

2. As a group forms, a _____ typically emerges, with the leader at the top.

3. Peer pressure is most powerful when _____.

4. Popular children often share, cooperate, and are _____.

5. Rejected youngsters are more likely to drop out of school, to commit juvenile offenses, and _____.

6. Some children who are chronic victims of aggression overreact and are easily irritated; other chronic victims are _____.

Interpret

- How could developmental change in the nature of friendship be explained in terms of Jean Piaget's stages of intellectual development, discussed in Chapters 4 and 6?

- Chapter 5 described important differences in the ways that boys and girls interact with same-sex peers. How might these differences help explain why boys' and girls' dominance hierarchies differ?

Apply

- Jay is the least popular child in his class. Jay's mom is worried about his lack of popularity and wants to know what she can do to help her son. Jay's dad thinks that Jay's mom is upset over nothing—he argues that, like fame, popularity is fleeting and that Jay will turn out okay in the end. What advice might a school psychologist give to Jay's parents?

- Chris and Kathy worry that their son Brooks may get involved with the wrong crowd when he begins high school. How can they influence his choice of crowds?

Recall answers: (1) attitudes, (2) dominance hierarchy, (3) standards for appropriate behavior are vague, (4) socially skilled, (5) to experience psychopathology, (6) unwilling or unable to defend themselves

LEARNING OBJECTIVES

■ What is the impact of watching television on children's attitudes, behavior, and cognitive development?

■ How do children use computers at home?

After school, 7-year-old Roberto watches one action-adventure cartoon after another until dinner. Roberto's mother is disturbed by her son's constant TV viewing, particularly because of the amount of violence he sees. Her husband tells her to stop worrying: "Let him watch what he wants. It won't hurt him, and besides, it keeps him occupied."

In generations past, children learned their culture's values from parents, teachers, religious leaders, and print media. These sources of cultural knowledge are still with us, but they coexist with new technologies. Satellite TV, video game players, iPads, smart phones, and the Internet are some of the new forces that can potentially influence children's development. Two of these technologies—television and computers—are the focus of this section. As we look at their influence, we'll see whether Roberto's mother should be worried.

Television

The typical U.S. high-school graduate has watched 20,000 hours of TV—the equivalent of 2 full years of watching TV 24/7. No wonder social scientists and laypeople alike have come to see TV as an important contributor to the socialization of North American children.

It is hard to imagine that such massive viewing of TV would have no effect on children's behavior. Indeed, research consistently shows that TV is a powerful influence (Browne & Hamilton-Giachritsis, 2005; Huesmann, 2007). For example, children become more aggressive after viewing violence on television (Konijn, Bijvank, & Bushman, 2007), and children learn about gender stereotypes from TV (Huesmann, 2007). Thus, Roberto's mother should be concerned. Watching can also help children learn to be more generous and cooperative and to have greater self-control (Wilson, 2008). However, prosocial behaviors are portrayed on TV far less frequently than aggressive behaviors, so opportunities to learn the former from television are limited; we are far from harnessing the power of television for prosocial uses.

When children play violent video games, they often become more aggressive.

The biggest positive influence of TV on American children has been *Sesame Street*. Big Bird, Bert, Ernie, and their friends have been helping educate preschool children for more than 40 years. Remarkably, the time preschool children spend watching *Sesame Street* predicts their grades in high school and the amount of time they spend reading as adolescents (Anderson et al., 2001).

Today, *Sesame Street* is joined by programs designed to teach young children about language and reading skills *(Arthur, Martha Speaks)* and programs that teach basic science and math concepts *(Curious George, Sid the Science Kid)*. Programs like these (and older programs, such as *Electric Company* and *3-2-1 Contact*) show that the power of TV can be harnessed to help children learn important academic skills and useful social skills.

Television has its critics, who argue that the medium—independent of the content of programs—has harmful effects on children (Huston & Wright, 1998). One common criticism is that, because TV programs consist of many brief segments presented in rapid succession, children who watch a lot of TV develop short attention spans and have difficulty concentrating in school. Another concern is that because TV provides ready-made, simple-to-interpret images, children who watch a lot of TV become passive, lazy thinkers and become less creative.

As stated, neither of these criticisms is consistently supported by research (Huston & Wright, 1998). Increased TV viewing does not lead to reduced attention, greater impulsivity, reduced task persistence, or increased activity levels (Foster & Watkins, 2010). The content of TV programs can influence these dimensions of children's behavior—children who watch impulsive models behave more impulsively themselves—but TV per se does not harm children's ability to pay attention.

As for the criticism that TV viewing fosters lazy thinking and stifles creativity, the evidence is mixed. Many studies find no link between amount of TV viewing and creativity (e.g., Anderson et al., 2001). Some find a negative relation in which as children watch more TV, they tend to get lower scores on tests of creativity (Valkenburg & van der Voort, 1994, 1995). Researchers don't know why the negative effects aren't found more consistently, although one idea is that the effects depend on what programs children watch, not simply the amount of TV watched.

In general, then, the sheer amount of TV that children watch is not a powerful influence on development. Most of the impact of TV—for good or bad—comes through the content of TV programs that children watch.

Computers

Most American children and adolescents have computers at home, and they use them mainly to access the Internet. For example, they search the web for information for school assignments. However, a far more common use of computers, particularly for boys, is to play games online. Research reveals that computer games affect youth in much the same way that TV does—content matters. In other words, just as children and adolescents are influenced by the TV programs they watch, they're influenced by the content of the computer games they play. On the one hand, many games, including *Tetris* and *Star Fox,* emphasize perceptual–spatial skills, such as estimating the trajectory of a moving object and responding rapidly. When children play such games frequently, their spatial skills often improve (Subrahmanyam et al., 2001), as does their processing speed (Mackey et al., 2011). On the other hand, many popular games, such as *Manhunt* and *Grand Theft Auto,* are violent, with players killing game characters in extraordinarily gruesome ways. Just as exposure to televised violence can make children behave more aggressively, playing violent video games can make children more aggressive (Anderson et al., 2010). And a minority—roughly 10%—of youth get "hooked" on video games. They show many of the same symptoms associated with pathological gambling: Playing video games comes to dominate their lives, it provides a "high," and it leads to conflict with others (Gentile, 2009).

The other main use of home computers (and cell phones) is to communicate with peers, often through social networking sites such as Facebook. Many children and adolescents use the Internet (and other communication technologies) to maintain existing "real" social connections. Online communication seems to promote self-disclosure, which produces high-quality friendships and, in turn, well-being (Valkenburg & Jochen, 2009). Boys, in particular, benefit from online communication because self-disclosure is easier for them online than face to face (Valkenburg, Sumter, & Peter, 2011).

In many respects, new technologies have changed the how of childhood and adolescence but not the what. As with previous generations, children and adolescents still play games, connect with peers, and do homework. Technology like a home computer simply provides a different means for accomplishing these tasks.

HUMAN DEVELOPMENT in action

Imagine that you're a social worker. Plan a workshop for parents that shows the impact of computer use on children and adolescents.

Test Yourself

Recall

1. When children watch a lot of TV violence, they often become _____.

2. Contrary to popular criticisms, frequent TV viewing is not consistently related to reduced attention or to lack of _____.

3. Children use computers at home to do schoolwork, play games, and _____.

4. When children frequently play violent video games, they _____.

Interpret

- How might growth in cognitive development change the impact of TV viewing on children?

- Compare and contrast the ways in which TV viewing and web surfing might affect children's development.

Apply

- Suppose you work for the Federal Communications Communication, the U.S. agency that sets guidelines for TV programming. If you had the authority to write new regulations for children's TV programs, what shows would you encourage? What shows would you want to limit?

- Teenage Andy plays video games at least 3 hours daily and often argues with his parents about his game playing. They think he should spend more time studying, and they may be right: Andy's grades have slipped recently. Does Andy have signs of pathological game playing?

Recall answers: (1) more aggressive, (2) creativity, (3) communicate with friends, (4) often behave more aggressively

---

LEARNING OBJECTIVES

- As children develop, how do their descriptions of others change?

- How does understanding of others' thinking change as children develop?

- When and why do children develop prejudice toward others?

When 12-year-old Ian agreed to babysit his 5-year-old brother, Kyle, their mother reminded Ian to keep Kyle out of the basement because Kyle's birthday presents were there, unwrapped. But as soon as their mother left, Kyle wanted to go to the basement to ride his tricycle. When Ian told him no, Kyle burst into angry tears and shouted, "I'm gonna tell Mom that you were mean to me!" Ian wished he could explain to Kyle, but he knew that would just cause more trouble.

As children spend more time with other people, they begin to understand other people better. In this vignette, for example, Ian realizes why Kyle is angry, and he knows that if he gives in to Kyle now, his mother will be angry when she returns. Children's growing understanding of others is the focus of this section. We begin by looking at how children describe others and then examine their understanding of how others think. Finally, we'll see how children's recognition of different social groups can lead to prejudices.

Describing Others

As children develop, more sophisticated cognitive processes cause self-descriptions to become richer, more abstract, and more psychological. These same changes occur in children's descriptions of others. Children begin by describing other people in terms

Every few years, Tamsen was asked to describe a girl whom she liked a lot. Here's what she said as a 7-year-old:

> Vanessa is short. She has black hair and brown eyes. She uses a wheelchair because she can't walk. She's in my class. She has dolls like mine. She likes to sing and read.

Tamsen's description of Vanessa is probably not too different from the way she would have described herself: The emphasis is on concrete characteristics, such as Vanessa's appearance, possessions, and preferences. Contrast this with the following description, which Tamsen gave as a 10-year-old:

> Kate lives in my apartment building. She is a good reader and is also good at math and science. She's nice to everyone in our class. And she's very funny. Sometimes her jokes make me laugh so-o-o hard! She takes piano lessons and likes to play soccer.

Tamsen's account still includes concrete features, such as where Kate lives and what she likes to do. However, psychological traits are also evident: Tamsen describes Kate as nice and funny. By age 10, children move beyond the purely concrete and observable in describing others. During adolescence, descriptions become even more complex, as you can see in the following, from Tamsen as a 16-year-old:

> Jeannie is very understanding. Whenever anyone at school is upset, she's there to give a helping hand. Yet in private, Jeannie can say some really nasty things about people. But I know she'd never say that stuff if she thought people would hear it because she wouldn't want to hurt their feelings.

This description is more abstract: Tamsen now focuses on psychological traits like understanding and concern for others' feelings. It's also more integrated: Tamsen tries to explain how Jeannie can be both understanding and sarcastic.

Each of Tamsen's three descriptions is typical. As a 7-year-old, she emphasized concrete characteristics; as a 10-year-old, she began to include psychological traits; and as a 16-year-old, she tried to integrate traits to form a cohesive account.

of concrete features, such as behavior, and progress to describing them in terms of abstract traits (Barenboim, 1981; Livesley & Bromley, 1973). The Real People feature shows this progression in one child.

Research supports the trend to more abstract and richer psychological descriptions of others but indicates that young children's understanding of other people is more sophisticated than is suggested by their verbal descriptions of people they know (Heyman, 2009). Most 4- and 5-year-olds have begun to think about other people in terms of psychological traits, such as being smart, friendly, helpful, and shy. They can use behavioral examples to infer an underlying trait: Told about a child who won't share cookies or won't allow another child to play with a toy, 4- and 5-year-olds accurately describe the child as selfish. In addition, given information about a trait, they correctly predict future behavior: Told about a child who is shy, they believe that the child will not volunteer to help a puppeteer and will be quiet at a meal with many relatives (Liu, Gelman, & Wellman, 2007).

One idiosyncrasy of young children's descriptions of others is that they see others "through rose-colored glasses." Until about 10 years of age, children have a bias to look for positive traits, not negative traits, in others. Young children are willing to believe that someone is smart, friendly, or helpful (Boseovski, 2010, 2012).

Understanding What Others Think

Preschool children's thinking is egocentric—they have difficulty in seeing the world from another's view. As children move beyond the preschool years, though, they realize that others see the world differently, both literally and figuratively. For example, in the vignette, Ian knows why his little brother Kyle is angry: Kyle thinks that Ian is being bossy and mean. Ian understands that Kyle doesn't know there is a good reason he can't go to the basement.

Sophisticated understanding of how others think is achieved gradually throughout childhood and adolescence. According to a theory proposed by Selman, the development of perspective-taking skill progresses through the five stages shown in Table 7.1 (Selman, 1980, 1981).

To see the progression from stage to stage, imagine two boys arguing about what to do after school. One wants to go to a playground, and the other wants to watch TV. If the boys were 5-year-olds (undifferentiated stage), neither would understand why

Selman's Stages of Perspective Taking

Stage	Age	Characteristics
Undifferentiated	3 to 6 years	Children know that they and others can have different thoughts and feelings but often confuse the two.
Social-informational	4 to 9 years	Children know that perspectives differ because people have access to different information.
Self-reflective	7 to 12 years	Children can step into another's shoes and view themselves as others do; they know that others can do the same.
Third person	10 to 15 years	Children can step outside of the immediate situation to see how they and another person are viewed by a third person.
Societal	14 years to adult	Adolescents realize that a third-person perspective is influenced by broader personal, social, and cultural contexts.

© Cengage Learning 2013

the other wants to do something different. Their reasoning is simple: "If I want to go to the playground, you should too!"

During the early elementary-school years (social-informational stage), each child understands that the other wants to do something different, and they explain their differing views in terms of the other person lacking essential information. Their thinking would be along these lines: "I know that you want to watch TV, but if you knew what I knew, you'd want to go to the playground." By the late elementary-school years (self-reflective stage), the boys would understand that each wants to do something different, and they could "step into the other's shoes" to understand why: "I know you want to go to the playground because you haven't been there all week."

In early adolescence (third-person stage), the boys could step even farther apart and imagine how another person (e.g., a parent or teacher) could view the disagreement. Finally, in late adolescence (societal stage), the boys (now young men, really) could remove themselves even further and appreciate, for example, that many people would think it's silly to watch TV on a beautiful sunny day.

One of the benefits of a developing appreciation of others' thoughts and viewpoints is that it allows children to get along better with their peers. That is, children who can readily take another's perspective are typically well liked by their peers (FitzGerald & White, 2003; LeMare & Rubin, 1987). In the photo on this page, for example, the children with the soccer ball evidently recognized that the girl on the sideline wants to play, so they're inviting her to join them.

Socially skilled youth understand what others are thinking; in this case, they invite the girl on the sideline to join them.

Mere understanding does not guarantee good social behavior; sometimes children who understand what another child is thinking take advantage of that child. In general, however, greater understanding of others seems to promote positive interactions.

Prejudice

As children learn more about others, they discover that people belong to different social groups that are based on variables such as gender, ethnicity, and social class. By the preschool years, most children can identify people from different ethnic groups (Aboud, 1993). *Once children learn their membership in a specific group, they typically show* **prejudice***, a view of others, usually negative, that is based on their membership in a different group.* In young children, prejudice is not so much a negative view of others as it is an enhanced view of their own group. Preschool and kindergarten children attribute to their own group many positive traits, such as being friendly and smart, and few negative traits, such as being mean (Bigler, Jones, & Lobliner, 1997; Patterson

prejudice

a view of other people, usually negative, that is based on their membership in a specific group

& Bigler, 2006). And young children's negative views of other groups typically don't involve overt hostility; it's simply that other groups "come up short" when compared to their own group (Aboud, 2003).

As children move into the elementary-school years, their knowledge of racial stereotypes and prejudices increases steadily; by 10 or 11 years of age, most children are aware of broadly held racial stereotypes (Pauker, Ambady, & Apfelbaum, 2010). During these years, prejudice declines some, in part because children learn norms that discourage openly favoring their own group over others (Apfelbaum et al., 2008).

During early adolescence, prejudice sometimes increases again. This resurgence apparently reflects two processes (Black-Gutman & Hickson, 1996; Teichman, 2001). One is experiential: Exposed to the prejudices of those around them, children and adolescents internalize some of these views (Castelli, Zogmaister, & Tomelleri, 2009). A second process concerns adolescents' identity. In the search for identity (described on pages 240–242), adolescents' preferences for their own groups often intensify (Rutland, Killen, & Abrams, 2010). Thus, greater prejudice in older children and adolescents reflects a more positive view of their own group, as well as a more negative view of other groups. For example, Bob, a 14-year-old European American growing up in Arizona, becomes more prejudiced as he views his European American heritage more positively and acquires prejudicial attitudes toward Native Americans from his parents and peers.

Some scientists believe that bias and prejudice emerge naturally out of children's efforts to understand their social world (Bigler & Liben, 2007). Young children actively categorize animate and inanimate objects as they try to understand the world around them. As children's social horizons expand beyond their parents to include peers, they continue to categorize and try to decide how different groups of people "go together." They use perceptually salient features (e.g., race, gender, and age), as well as verbal labels that adults may apply to different groups (e.g., "Girls go to lunch first and then the boys eat"). After children have identified the salient features that define peers in their environment, they begin to classify people that they encounter along these dimensions. For example, Jacob is now seen as a white boy; Kalika is now seen as a black girl (Patterson & Bigler, 2006).

What can parents, teachers, and other adults do to rid children of prejudice? One way is to encourage friendly and constructive contacts among children from different groups. However, contact alone usually accomplishes little. Intergroup contact reduces prejudice only when the participating groups of children are equal in status, when the contact among groups involves pursuing common goals (not competing), and when parents and teachers support the goal of reducing prejudice (Cameron et al., 2006; Killen & McGlothlin, 2005). For example, adults might have children from different groups work together toward a common goal. In school, this might be a class project. In sports, it might be mastering a new skill. By working together, Gary starts to realize that Vic acts, thinks, and feels as he does simply because he's Vic, not because he's an Italian American.

Another useful approach is to ask children to play different roles (Davidson & Davidson, 1994; Tynes, 2007). They can be asked to imagine that—because of their race, ethnic background, or gender—they have been insulted verbally or not allowed to participate in special activities. A child might be asked to imagine that she can't go to a private swimming club because she's African American or that she wasn't invited to a party because she's Hispanic American. Afterward, children reflect on how they felt when prejudice and discrimination was directed at them. They're also asked to think about what would be fair: What should be done in situations like these?

A final strategy against prejudice involves education. In one study (Hughes, Bigler, & Levy, 2007), European American elementary-school children learned about the racism that famous African Americans experienced. For example, they learned that Jackie Robinson played for a team in the old Negro Leagues because the white people in charge of Major League Baseball wouldn't allow any African Americans to play. The

One effective way to reduce prejudice is for children from different races to work together toward a common goal, such as completing a class project.

© Ellen B. Senisi/The Image Works

HUMAN DEVELOPMENT in action

As an elementary-school teacher, what could you do to discourage prejudice in your students?

study also included a control group in which the biographies omitted the experiences of racism. When children learned about racism directed at African Americans, they had more positive attitudes toward African Americans.

From experiences like these, children and adolescents discover for themselves that a person's membership in a social group tells them little about that person. They learn instead that all children are different and that each person is a unique mix of experiences, skills, and values.

Test Yourself

Recall

1. When adolescents describe others, they usually _____.

2. In the most advanced stage of Selman's theory, adolescents _____.

3. Young adolescents often become more prejudiced, reflecting the views of those around them and _____.

Interpret

- Compare developmental change in children's descriptions of others with developmental change in children's self-concept (described on pages 86–87).

- How do Selman's stages of perspective taking correspond to Piaget's stages of cognitive development?

Apply

- Gracie can hardly wait for her cousin Andrew to arrive for a weeklong visit. Gracie knows that Andrew will want to go swimming right away because Gracie loves to swim. Based on this example, what stage of perspective taking is Gracie in? About how old is she?

- Carolina and Mikael were horrified when their 5-year-old daughter Marit announced, "Swedes are better than any other group." They fear that Marit is learning prejudice. As a family therapist, what would you say to reassure them?

Recall answers: (1) try to provide a cohesive, integrated account, (2) provide a third-person perspective on situations and recognize the influence of context on this perspective, (3) greater affiliation with their own group

Linking Research to life • PREVENTING CHILD MALTREATMENT

The complexity of child abuse dashes any hopes for a simple solution (Kelly, 2011). Because maltreatment is more apt to occur when several contributing factors are present, eradicating child maltreatment requires many approaches.

As one approach, American attitudes toward "acceptable" levels of punishment and poverty would have to change. American children will be abused as long as physical punishment is considered acceptable and effective and as long as poverty-stricken families live in chronic stress from simply trying to provide food and shelter. Parents also need counseling and training in parenting skills. Abuse will continue as long as parents remain ignorant of effective methods of parenting and discipline.

It would be naive to expect these changes to occur overnight. However, by focusing on some of the more manageable factors, the risk of maltreatment can be reduced. Social supports help. When parents know they can turn to other helpful adults for advice and reassurance,

Continued

Continued

they better manage the stresses of childrearing that might otherwise lead to abuse. Families can also be taught more effective ways of coping with situations that might otherwise trigger abuse (Wicks-Nelson & Israel, 2006). Through role-playing sessions, parents can learn the benefits of authoritative parenting and effective ways of using feedback and modeling to regulate children's behavior.

Providing social supports and teaching effective parenting are typically done when maltreatment and abuse have already occurred. Preventing maltreatment in the first place is more desirable and more cost effective. For prevention, one useful tool is familiar: early childhood intervention programs. That is, maltreatment and abuse can be cut in half when families participate for 2 or more years in intervention programs that include preschool education along with family support activities aimed at encouraging parents to become more involved in their children's education (Reynolds & Robertson, 2003). When parents participate in these programs, they become more committed to their children's education. This leads their children to be more successful in school, reducing a source of stress and enhancing parents' confidence in their childrearing skills, thereby reducing the risks of maltreatment.

Another successful approach focuses specifically on parenting skills in families where children are at risk for maltreatment. In one program (Bugental & Schwartz, 2009), mothers of infants at risk for abuse (due to medical problems at birth) participated in an extensive training program in which they learned to identify likely causes of recurring problems encountered while caring for their babies (e.g., problems associated with feeding, sleeping, crying). Then they were given help in devising methods to deal with those problems and in monitoring the effectiveness of the methods. When mothers participated in the program, they were less likely to use harsh punishment (a known risk factor for child maltreatment), and their children were less likely to suffer injuries at home (a common measure of parental neglect).

There are also effective programs targeting parents of older children who are at risk for maltreatment. One program, parent–child interaction therapy, focuses on helping parents (1) build warm and positive relationships with their children (2) develop reasonable expectations for their children and (3) use more effective disciplinary practices. When parents of at-risk children participate in this program, they report less stress, their behavior with their children becomes more positive (more praise and fewer commands), and critically, suspected abuse is reduced (Thomas & Zimmer-Gimbeck, 2011).

Summary

7.1 Family Relationships

What are the primary dimensions of parenting?

- One key factor in parent–child relationships is the degree of warmth that parents express: Children clearly benefit from warm, caring parents. A second factor is control, which is complicated because neither too much nor too little control is desirable.

- Taking into account both warmth and control, four prototypic parental styles emerge: Authoritarian parents are controlling but uninvolved; authoritative parents are fairly controlling but are also responsive to their children; permissive parents are loving but exert little control; and uninvolved parents are neither warm nor controlling. Authoritative parenting seems best for children in terms of both cognitive and social development, but there are important exceptions associated with culture and socioeconomic status.

- Parents influence development by direct instruction and coaching. In addition, parents serve as models for their children, who sometimes imitate parents' behavior directly. Parents also use feedback to influence children's behavior. Sometimes parents fall into the negative reinforcement trap, inadvertently reinforcing behaviors that they want to discourage.

- Punishment is effective when it is prompt, consistent, accompanied by an explanation, and delivered by a person with whom the child has a warm relationship. Punishment has limited value because it suppresses behaviors but does not eliminate them, and it often has side effects. Time-out is one useful form of punishment.

- Chronic conflict is harmful to children, but children can benefit when their parents solve problems constructively. Parenting is a team sport, but not all parents play well together because they may disagree in childrearing goals or parenting methods.

- Parenting is influenced by characteristics of children themselves. Children's age and temperament influence parental behavior.

What determines how siblings get along? How do first-born, later-born, and only children differ?

- The birth of a sibling can be stressful for children, particularly when they are still young and when parents ignore their needs. Siblings get along better when they are of the same sex, believe that parents treat them similarly, enter adolescence, and have parents who get along well.

- Parents have higher expectations for first-born children, which explains why such children are more intelligent and more likely to go to college than their younger siblings. Later-born children are more popular and more innovative. Contradicting folklore, only children are almost never worse off than children with siblings; in some respects (e.g., intelligence, achievement, and autonomy), they are often better off.

How do divorce and remarriage affect children?

- Divorce can harm children in a number of areas, ranging from school achievement to adjustment. Divorce is most harmful during childhood and adolescence, and when children are emotional and interpret events negatively. Children often benefit when parents have joint custody following divorce or when they live with the same-sex parent.

- Parents can reduce the harm of divorce by reassuring children of their ongoing love for them and by not competing with or criticizing each other.

- When a mother remarries, daughters sometimes have difficulty adjusting because the new stepfather encroaches on an intimate mother–daughter relationship.

What factors lead children to be maltreated?

- Children who are abused often lag behind age-mates in cognitive and social development. Factors that contribute to child abuse include poverty, social isolation, and a culture's views on violence. Parents who abuse their children were often neglected or abused themselves and tend to be unhappy, socially unskilled individuals. Younger or unhealthy children are more likely to be targets of abuse.

7.2 Peers

What are the benefits of friendship?

- Friendships among preschoolers are based on common interests and getting along well. As children grow, loyalty, trust, and intimacy become more important features in their friendships. Friends are usually similar in age, sex, race, and attitudes. Children with friends are more skilled socially and are better adjusted.

What are the important features of groups of children and adolescents? How do these groups influence individuals?

- Older children and adolescents often form cliques—small groups of like-minded individuals—that become part of a crowd. Some crowds have higher status than others, and members of higher-status crowds often have higher self-esteem than members of lower-status crowds.

- Common to most groups is a dominance hierarchy, a well-defined structure with a leader at the top. Physical power often determines the dominance hierarchy, particularly among boys. However, with older children and adolescents, dominance hierarchies are more often based on skills that are important to the group.

- Peer pressure is neither totally powerful nor totally evil. Groups influence individuals primarily in areas with unclear standards of behavior, such as tastes in music or clothing or standards concerning drinking, drug use, and sex.

Why are some children more popular than others? Why are some rejected?

- Most popular children are socially skilled. They often share with, cooperate with, and help others. A far smaller number of popular children use aggression to achieve their social goals.

- Some children are rejected by their peers because they are too aggressive. Others are rejected for being too timid or withdrawn. Repeated peer rejection often leads to school failure and behavioral problems.

What are some effects of childhood aggression? Why are some children chronic victims of aggression?

- Many highly aggressive children end up being violent and poorly adjusted as adults.

- Children who are chronic victims of aggression typically either overreact or refuse to defend themselves.

7.3 Electronic Media

What is the impact of watching television on children's attitudes, behavior, and cognitive development?

- TV programs can cause children to become more aggressive, to adopt gender stereotypes, and to act prosocially. Programs designed to foster children's cognitive skills, such as *Sesame Street,* are effective. Many criticisms about TV as a medium (e.g., it shortens children's attention span) are not supported by research.

How do children use computers at home?

- At home, children use computers for schoolwork, to communicate with friends via the Internet, and to play video games. They are influenced by the content of the games they play.

7.4 Understanding Others

As children develop, how do their descriptions of others change?

- Children's descriptions of others change in much the same way that children's descriptions of themselves change. During the early elementary-school years, descriptions emphasize concrete characteristics. In the late elementary-school years, they emphasize personality traits. In adolescence, they emphasize providing an integrated picture of others.

How does understanding of others' thinking change as children develop?

- According to Selman's theory, children's understanding of how others think progresses through five stages. In the first (undifferentiated) stage, children often confuse their own and another's view. In the last (societal) stage, adolescents can take a third-person perspective and know that this perspective is influenced by context.

When and why do children develop prejudice toward others?

■ Prejudice emerges in the preschool years, soon after children recognize different social groups. Prejudice often increases in early adolescence, reflecting exposure to prejudiced views of others and adolescents' greater affiliation with their own group as they seek an identity. Prejudice can be reduced with positive contact among groups, role playing, and greater knowledge of racism directed at minority groups.

Key Terms

socialization (190)
authoritarian parenting (190)
authoritative parenting (191)
permissive parenting (191)
uninvolved parenting (191)
direct instruction (192)
negative reinforcement trap (192)
time-out (193)

joint custody (196)
blended family (196)
friendship (200)
co-rumination (201)
clique (202)
crowd (202)
dominance hierarchy (202)
popular children (203)

rejected children (203)
controversial children (203)
average children (203)
neglected children (203)
instrumental aggression (204)
hostile aggression (204)
prejudice (210)

Online Resources

Go to CengageBrain.com to access Psychology CourseMate, where you will find an interactive eBook, flashcards, quizzes, videos, websites, and more.

Rites of Passage

Physical and Cognitive Development During Adolescence

At age 10, Michelle Wie became the youngest player to qualify for a professional golf tournament for adult players; at age 13, she won the U.S. Women's Amateur Public Links Championship; and at age 16, she became the youngest female golfer to make the cut in a professional golf tournament for men. Michelle's steady march to the top of her sport during her adolescence is remarkable, yet these years are times of profound changes for all adolescents. In this chapter, we examine the physical and cognitive developments that occur during adolescence. We begin by describing the important features of physical growth in the teenage years. Next, we examine the nature of information processing during adolescence. Finally, we'll see how adolescents reason about moral issues.

LEARNING OBJECTIVES

- What physical changes occur during adolescence that mark the transition to a mature young adult?

- What factors cause the physical changes associated with puberty?

- How do physical changes affect adolescents' psychological development?

Pete just celebrated his 15th birthday, but he saw no reason to celebrate. Although most of his friends have grown 6 inches in the past year, have a much larger penis and larger testicles, and mounds of pubic hair, Pete looks just as he did when he was 10 years old. He is embarrassed by his appearance, particularly in the locker room, where he looks like a little boy among men. "Won't I ever change?" he wonders.

The appearance of body hair, the emergence of breasts, and the enlargement of the penis and testicles are all signs that adolescence has arrived. Many teenagers take great satisfaction in these signs of maturity. Others, like Pete, worry as they wait for outward signs of adolescence.

In this section, we begin by describing the normal pattern of physical changes during adolescence and look at the mechanisms responsible for them. Then we'll discover the impact of these physical changes on adolescents' psychological functioning. As we do, we'll learn about the possible effects on Pete of maturing later than his peers.

Signs of Physical Maturation

Puberty *denotes two types of physical changes that mark the transition from childhood to young adulthood.* The first are bodily changes, including increases in height and weight, as well as changes in the body's fat and muscle content. The second concern sexual maturation, including change in the reproductive organs and the appearance of secondary sexual characteristics, such as facial and body hair and growth of the breasts.

Physical Growth

For physical growth, the elementary-school years represent the calm before the adolescent storm. Figure 8.1 shows that, in an average year, a typical 6- to 10-year-old gains about 5 to 7 pounds and grows 2 to 3 inches. In contrast, during the peak of the adolescent growth spurt, a girl may gain as much as 14 pounds in a year and a boy as much as 16 pounds (Tanner, 1970).

Girls typically start the growth spurt at about age 11, reach their peak rate of growth at about 12, and achieve mature stature at about 15. In contrast, boys start the growth spurt at about age 13, hit peak growth at about 14, and reach mature stature at about 17. This 2-year difference in the growth spurt can lead to awkward social interactions between 11- and 12-year-old boys and girls because the girls are often taller and look more mature than the boys.

Body parts don't all mature at the same rate. Instead, the head, hands, and feet usually begin to grow first, followed by growth in the arms and legs. The trunk and shoulders are the last to grow (Tanner, 1990). These differing growth rates cause an adolescent's body to look out of proportion—teens have a head and hands that are too big for the rest of their body. Fortunately, these imbalances don't last long as the later-developing parts catch up.

HUMAN DEVELOPMENT
in action

If you were a nurse, what would you look for as the first signs of puberty in boys and girls?

puberty

a collection of physical changes that mark the onset of adolescence, including a growth spurt and the growth of breasts or testes

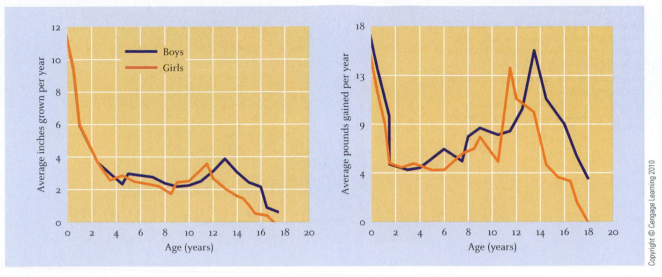

FIGURE 8.1

Children grow steadily taller and heavier until puberty, when they experience a rapid increase known as the adolescent growth spurt.

During the growth spurt, girls are often much taller than boys of the same age.

During the growth spurt, bones become longer and denser. In addition, muscle fibers become thicker and denser during adolescence, producing substantial increases in strength, particularly for boys (Smoll & Schutz, 1990). Body fat also increases during adolescence, but more rapidly in girls. Finally, heart and lung capacity increase more in adolescent boys than in adolescent girls. Together, these changes help explain why the typical adolescent boy is stronger, is quicker, and has greater endurance than the typical adolescent girl.

Brain Growth During Adolescence

At the beginning of adolescence, the brain is nearly full size, but it's still being fine tuned. Two features of brain development that begin early in life (discussed in Chapter 3) are nearly complete by adolescence: myelination, which is the acquisition of fatty insulation that makes neurons transmit information faster, and synaptic pruning, which is the weeding out of unnecessary connections between neurons (Ben Bashat et al., 2005; Toga, Thompson, & Sowell, 2006; Wozniak & Lim, 2006). These changes mean that different regions in the adolescent brain are well connected and information is rapidly conveyed between them, which allows adolescents to process information more efficiently than children.

Another distinguishing feature of the adolescent brain is that some brain regions reach maturity. Notably, the limbic system, which helps regulate experiences of reward, pleasure, and emotion, reaches maturity in early adolescence. In contrast, systems in the frontal cortex that are associated with deliberate control of behavior are still developing during adolescence (Bava & Tapert, 2010). As shown in Figure 8.2, because the reward- and pleasure-seeking systems are more mature than the systems for controlling behavior, the anticipated rewards and pleasure of risky behavior sometimes swamp the adolescent's ability to suppress the desire to engage in such activities (Sturman & Moghaddam, 2012).

Sexual Maturation

primary sex characteristics
physical signs of maturity that are directly linked to the reproductive organs

Not only do adolescents become taller and heavier, they also become mature sexually. *Sexual maturation includes change in* **primary sex characteristics**, *which refer to organs that are directly involved in reproduction.* These include the ovaries, uterus,

FIGURE 8.2

Adolescence is a vulnerable time because the reward- and pleasure-seeking centers of the brain (limbic system) mature more rapidly than the behavioral control systems (frontal cortex); the gap between the two systems is particularly great during adolescence.

Source: Casey et al., 2008, "The Adolescent Brain," **Annals of the New York Academy of Sciences,** 1124, Fig. 3, p. 116. Reprinted by permission of John Wiley & Sons.

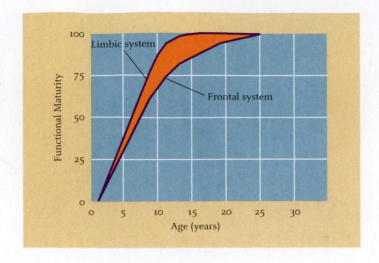

and vagina in girls and the scrotum, testes, and penis in boys. *Sexual maturation also includes changes in* **secondary sex characteristics**, *which are physical signs of maturity that are not directly linked to the reproductive organs.* These include the growth of breasts and the widening of the pelvis in girls, the appearance of facial hair and the broadening of shoulders in boys, and the appearance of body hair and changes in voice and skin in both boys and girls.

Changes in primary and secondary sexual characteristics occur in a predictable sequence for boys and for girls. For girls, puberty begins with growth of the breasts and the growth spurt, followed by the appearance of pubic hair. **Menarche**, *the onset of menstruation, typically occurs at about age 13.* Early menstrual cycles are usually irregular and without ovulation.

For boys, puberty usually commences with the growth of the testes and scrotum, followed by the appearance of pubic hair, start of the growth spurt, and growth of the penis. *At about age 13, most boys reach* **spermarche**, *the first spontaneous ejaculation of sperm-laden fluid.* Initial ejaculations often contain relatively few sperm; only later are there sufficient sperm to fertilize an egg (Chilman, 1983).

Mechanisms of Maturation

What causes the many physical changes that occur during puberty? The pituitary gland is the key player: It releases growth hormone and signals other glands to secrete hormones. During the early elementary-school years, the pituitary gland signals the adrenal glands to release androgens, initiating the biochemical changes that produce body hair. A few years later, girls' pituitary gland signals the ovaries to release estrogen, which causes the breasts to enlarge, female genitals to mature, and fat to accumulate. In boys, the pituitary gland signals the testes to release the androgen hormone testosterone, which causes the male genitals to mature and muscle mass to increase.

The timing of pubertal events is regulated, in part, by genetics. For example, a mother's age at menarche is related to her daughter's age at menarche (Belsky et al., 2007). However, these genetic forces are strongly influenced by environment, particularly an adolescent's nutrition and health. Puberty occurs earlier in adolescents who are well nourished and healthy than in adolescents who are not. For example, menarche occurs earlier in areas of the world where nutrition and health care are adequate, such as Western Europe and North America.

What may surprise you is that the social environment also influences the onset of puberty, at least for girls. Menarche occurs at younger ages in girls who experience

secondary sex characteristics
physical signs of maturity that are not directly linked to reproductive organs

menarche
the onset of menstruation

spermarche
the first spontaneous ejaculation of sperm

Young adolescents are often quite concerned about their appearance.

chronic stress or who are depressed (Belsky, Steinberg, & Draper, 1991; Moffit et al., 1992). For example, girls have their first menstrual period at a younger age when their mothers used harsh punishment with them as preschoolers and young children (Belsky et al., 2007). When young girls experience chronic socioemotional stress—their family life is harsh and they lack warm, supportive parents—the hormones elicited by this stress may help activate the hormones that trigger menarche.

Psychological Impact of Puberty

Of course, teenagers are well aware of the changes taking places in their bodies. Not surprisingly, some of these changes affect adolescents' psychological development.

Body Image

Compared to children and adults, adolescents are more concerned about their overall appearance. Many teenagers look in the mirror regularly, checking for signs of additional physical change. Generally, girls worry more than boys about appearance and are more likely to be dissatisfied with their appearance, particularly when appearance is a frequent topic of conversation with friends (Vander Wal & Thelen, 2000). Peers have relatively little influence on boys' satisfaction with their looks; instead, boys are unhappy with their appearance when they expect to have an idealized strong, muscular body but do not (Carlson Jones, 2004).

Moodiness

Adolescents are often thought to be extraordinarily moody, moving from joy to sadness to irritation to anger over the course of a morning or afternoon. And the source of teenage moodiness is often presumed to be the influx of hormones associated with puberty—"hormones running wild." Although adolescents are moodier than children or adults, this is not primarily due to hormones (Steinberg, 1999). Instead, mood shifts are associated with changes in activities and social settings (Csikszentmihalyi & Larson, 1984). Teens are more likely to report being in a good mood when with friends or when recreating; they tend to report being in a bad mood when in adult-regulated settings, such as school classrooms or at a part-time job. Because adolescents often change activities and social settings many times in a single day, they appear to be moodier than adults.

Because children enter puberty at different ages, early-maturing teens tower over their later-maturing age-mates.

Rate of Maturation

Although puberty begins at age 11 in the average girl and age 13 in the average boy, for many children puberty begins months or even years before or after these norms. An early-maturing boy might begin puberty at age 11, whereas a late-maturing boy might start at 15 or 16. An early-maturing girl might start puberty at age 9, a late-maturing girl could begin at 14 or 15.

Maturing early or late has different psychological consequences for boys and for girls. Early maturation can be harmful for girls. Girls who mature early often lack self-confidence, are less popular, are more likely to be depressed and have behavior problems, and are more likely to smoke and drink (Ge, Conger, & Elder, 2001; Harden & Mendle, 2012; Mendle, Turkheimer, & Emery, 2007). Early maturation can also have life-changing effects on early-maturing girls who are pressured into sex and become mothers while still teenagers: As adults, they typically have less prestigious, lower-paying jobs (Mendle, et al., 2007). These ill effects of early maturation tend to be stronger for European American and Latina girls than for African American girls (Cavanagh, 2004).

The good news is that the harmful effects of early maturation can be offset by other factors: For example, an early-maturing girl who has warm and supportive parents is less likely to suffer the potential harmful consequences of early maturation (Ge et al., 2002).

The findings for boys are more confusing. Some early studies suggested that early maturation benefits boys: they dated more often and had more positive feelings about their physical development and their athletic abilities (Simmons & Blyth, 1987). But other studies have supported the "off-time hypothesis" for boys. In this view, being early or late is stressful for boys, who strongly prefer to be "on time" in their physical development (Natsuaki, Biehl, & Ge, 2009).

Scientists cannot yet explain this bewildering pattern of results, but it's clear that the transition to puberty seems to have few long-lasting effects for boys. In contrast to what happens with girls, the effects associated with puberty and its timing vanish by young adulthood. When Pete, the late-maturing boy in the vignette, finally matures, others will treat him like an adult, and the few extra years of being treated like a child will not be harmful (Weichold & Silbereisen, 2005).

Test Yourself

Recall

1. Puberty refers to changes in height and weight, to changes in the body's fat and muscle contents, and to _____.

2. Girls tend to have their growth spurts about _____ earlier than boys.

3. During adolescent physical growth, boys have greater muscle growth than girls, acquire less _____, and have greater increases in heart and lung capacity.

4. Primary sex characteristics are organs directly related to reproduction, whereas secondary sex characteristics are _____.

5. Adolescents are moodier than children and adults primarily because _____.

6. Early maturation tends to be harmful to girls because _____.

Interpret

- Compare and contrast the impact of rate of maturation—that is, maturing early versus late—on boys and girls.

- Summarize the ways in which biology and experience interact to trigger the onset of puberty.

Apply

- Lindsey is a 13-year-old whose moods seem to shift in a split second. Her mother is convinced that this is due to the same surging hormones that are causing Lindsey to mature physically. As a pediatrician, what would you say to Lindsey's mom?

- Shelby showed the first signs of physical maturation at age 10. By 13, she'd caught the eye of many older boys in her school. Should Shelby's parents be concerned?

Recall answers: (1) sexual maturation, (2) 2 years, (3) fat, (4) physical signs of maturity that are not linked directly to reproductive organs, such as the appearance of body hair, (5) they change activities and social settings frequently, and their moods track these changes, (6) they are more likely to become involved in activities for which they are ill prepared, such as drinking and sex

---

8.2 Health

LEARNING OBJECTIVES

- What are the elements of a healthy diet for adolescents? Why do some adolescents have eating disorders?

- Do adolescents get enough exercise? What are the consequences of participating in sports in high school?

- What are common obstacles to healthy growth during adolescence?

Dana had just started the seventh grade and was eager to try out for the school football team. He was usually the star in football games played at recess or in gym class, but this was his first opportunity to play on an actual team—with a real helmet, jersey, pads, and everything—and he was jazzed! Dana's dad played football in high school and thought Dana could benefit from the experience. His mom wasn't so sure—she was afraid that he might get a serious injury.

Adolescence is a time of transition when it comes to health. Teens are less affected by the minor illnesses that would have kept them in bed as children, but they are at greater risk for harm from unhealthy and unsafe behaviors. In this section, we look at some factors essential to adolescent health and see whether Dana's mother should be worried about sports-related injuries.

Nutrition

The physical growth associated with puberty means that the body has special nutritional needs. A typical teenage girl should consume about 2,200 calories per day; a typical boy should consume about 2,700 calories. (The exact levels depend on a number of factors, including body composition, growth rate, and activity level.) Teenagers also need calcium for bone growth and iron to make extra hemoglobin, the matter in red blood cells that carries oxygen. Boys need additional hemoglobin because of their increased muscle mass; girls need hemoglobin to replace that lost during menstruation.

Unfortunately, although many U.S. teenagers consume enough calories each day, too much of their intake consists of fast food rather than well-balanced meals. The result of too many meals of burgers, french fries, and a shake is that teens may get inadequate iron or calcium and far too much sodium and fat. With inadequate iron, teens are often listless and moody; with inadequate calcium, bones may not develop fully, placing the person at risk later in life for osteoporosis.

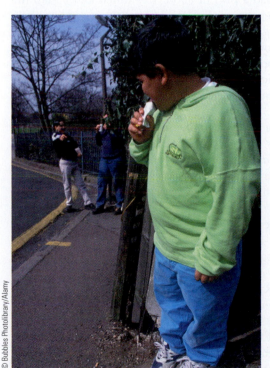

Childhood obesity has reached epidemic proportions in the United States.

body mass index (BMI)
an adjusted ratio of weight to height that is used to define *overweight*

basal metabolic rate
the speed at which the body consumes calories

Obesity

Many American children and adolescents are overweight. *The technical definition of* overweight *is based on the* **body mass index (BMI)***, which is an adjusted ratio of weight to height.* Children and adolescents who are in the upper 5% (very heavy for their height) are defined as being overweight. In the past 25 to 30 years, the number of overweight children has doubled and the number of overweight adolescents has tripled so that today roughly one child or adolescent out of six is overweight (U.S. Department of Health and Human Services, 2010b).

Overweight youngsters are often unpopular and have low self-esteem (Mustillo, Hendrix, & Schafer, 2012; Puhl & Latner, 2007). They are also at risk for many medical problems throughout life, including high blood pressure and diabetes, because the vast majority of overweight children and adolescents become overweight adults (U.S. Department of Health and Human Services, 2010b).

Heredity plays an important role in juvenile obesity. For example, in adoption studies, children's and adolescents' weight is related to the weight of their biological parents, not the weight of their adoptive parents (Stunkard et al., 1986). Genes may influence obesity by influencing a person's activity level. Being genetically more prone to inactivity makes it more difficult to burn off calories and easier to gain weight. *Heredity may also help set the* **basal metabolic rate***, the speed at which the body consumes calories.* Children and adolescents with a slower basal metabolic rate burn off calories less rapidly, making it easier for them to gain weight (Epstein & Cluss, 1986).

The environment is also influential. Television advertising, for example, encourages youth to eat tasty but fattening foods. Parents play a role too. They may inadvertently encourage obesity by emphasizing external eating signals—"finish what's on your plate!"—rather than internal cues, such as feelings of hunger. Thus, obese children and adolescents may overeat in part because they rely on external cues and disregard internal cues to stop (Coelho et al., 2009; Wansink & Sobal, 2007).

© Bubbles Photolibrary/Alamy

Adolescent girls with anorexia nervosa believe that they are overweight, and they refuse to eat.

Obese youth can lose weight. The most effective programs change obese children's eating habits, encourage them to become more active, and teach them to monitor their eating, exercise, and sedentary behavior. Goals are established in each area and parents are trained to help children meet these goals (Epstein et al., 2007; Foreyt & Goodrick, 1995). However, even after losing weight, many of these children remain overweight. Consequently, it's best to avoid becoming overweight and obesity in the first place through increased physical activity and good eating habits (U.S. Department of Health and Human Services, 2001).

Fast food is not the only risky diet common among adolescents. Many teenage girls worry about their weight and are attracted to the "lose 10 pounds in 2 weeks!" diets advertised on TV and in teen magazines. Many of these diets are unhealthy—they deprive youth of the many substances necessary for growth. Similarly, for philosophical or health reasons, many adolescents decide to eliminate meat from their diets. Vegetarian diets can be healthy for teens, but only when adolescents adjust the rest of their diet to assure that they have adequate sources of protein, calcium, and iron.

Other food-related problems common during adolescence are two eating disorders, anorexia and bulimia.

Anorexia and Bulimia

In 2006, Brazilian supermodel Ana Carolina Reston died of kidney failure just months after turning 21. At her death, she weighed less than 90 pounds and had a BMI of about 13—much lower than the BMI of 16 that is the benchmark for starvation. *Reston had* **anorexia nervosa***, a disorder marked by a persistent refusal to eat and an irrational fear of being overweight.* Individuals with anorexia nervosa have a grossly distorted image of their body and claim to be overweight despite being painfully thin (Wilson, Heffernan, & Black, 1996). Anorexia is a serious disorder, often leading to heart damage. Without treatment, as many as 15% of adolescents with anorexia die (Wang & Brownell, 2005).

A related eating disorder is bulimia nervosa. *Individuals with* **bulimia nervosa** *alternate between binge eating periods, when they eat uncontrollably, and purging through self-induced vomiting or use of laxatives.* The frequency of binge eating varies remarkably among people with bulimia nervosa, from a few times a week to more than 30 times a week. What's common to all is the feeling that they cannot stop eating (Mizes & Palermo, 1997).

Anorexia and bulimia primarily affect adolescent females, and many factors put teenage girls at risk for both disorders. Heredity matters, as do psychosocial factors such as a history of eating problems (e.g., being a picky eater), having negative self-esteem, or experiencing mood or anxiety disorders (Hutchinson, Rapee, & Taylor, 2010; Jacobi et al., 2004; Wojtowicz & von Ranson, 2012). However, the most important risk factor for adolescents is being overly concerned about their body and weight and having a history of dieting (George & Franko, 2010). Why do some teens become concerned about being thin? Peers and the media: Teenage girls worry about being overweight when they have friends who diet to stay thin and when they frequently watch TV shows that emphasize attractive, thin characters (Dohnt & Tiggemann, 2006; Paxton, Eisenberg, & Neumark-Sztainer, 2006).

Although eating disorders are far more common in girls, boys make up about 10% of diagnosed cases of eating disorders. Risk factors for boys include childhood obesity, low self-esteem, pressure from parents and peers to lose weight, and participating in sports that emphasize being lean (Ricciardelli & McCabe, 2004; Shoemaker & Furman, 2009).

Fortunately, programs can help protect teens from eating disorders (Stice & Shaw, 2004). The most effective programs are designed for at-risk youth, such as those who are

HUMAN DEVELOPMENT in action

Imagine that you are a social worker. Plan a workshop that would alert parents to the dangers and signs of eating disorders in their teenage daughters and sons.

anorexia nervosa
a persistent refusal to eat accompanied by an irrational fear of being overweight

bulimia nervosa
a disease in which people alternate between binge eating—periods when they eat uncontrollably—and purging through use of laxatives or self-induced vomiting

Track and field is now the most popular sport for adolescent American girls.

unhappy with their body. These programs teach youth new skills, such as how to resist social pressure to be thin, and work to change critical attitudes (e.g., ideals regarding thinness) and critical behaviors (e.g., dieting and overeating). For those teens affected by eating disorders, treatment is available: Like prevention programs, treatment typically focuses on modifying key attitudes and behaviors (Puhl & Brownell, 2005).

Physical Fitness

Being physically active promotes mental and physical health, both during adolescence and throughout adulthood. Individuals who regularly engage in physical activity reduce their risk for obesity, cancer, heart disease, diabetes, and psychological disorders, including depression and anxiety. "Regular activity" typically means exercising for 30 minutes, at least three times a week, at a pace that keeps an adolescent's heart rate at about 140 beats per minute (President's Council on Physical Fitness and Sports, 2004). Running, vigorous walking, swimming, aerobic dancing, biking, and cross-country skiing are all examples of activities that can provide this level of intensity.

Unfortunately, most adolescents rarely get enough exercise (Kann et al., 1995). For many high-school students, physical education classes provide the only regular opportunity for exercise, yet a minority of high-school students is enrolled in physical education and most who are enrolled do not attend daily.

Many teenagers get exercise by participating in organized sports. More than a million U.S. boys play high-school football. The next most popular sports for American boys are track and field, basketball, and baseball. For U.S. girls, the most popular sport is track and field; approximately half a million girls participate. The next most popular sports are basketball, volleyball, and fast-pitch softball (National Federation of State High School Associations, 2011).

Participating in sports has many benefits for youth. Sports can enhance participants' self-esteem and can help them learn initiative (Bowker, 2006; Donaldson & Ronan, 2006). Sports can also provide adolescents a chance to learn important social skills, such as how to work effectively as part of a group. At the same time, there are some potential costs. About 15% of high-school athletes will be injured and require some medical treatment. Fortunately, most of these injuries are not serious, involving mere bruises or strained muscles (Nelson, 1996). Dana's mom can rest easy; the odds are that her son won't be injured, and if he is, it won't be serious.

A more serious problem is the use of illegal drugs to improve performance (American Academy of Pediatrics, 2005). Some athletes use anabolic steroids—drugs that are chemically similar to the male hormone testosterone—to increase muscle size and strength and to promote more rapid recovery from injury. Approximately 2% of high-school students report having used anabolic steroids, with use more frequent in boys and in younger students (Dunn & White, 2011; vandenBerg, Neumark-Sztainer, & Wall, 2007). This is disturbing, because steroid use can damage the liver, reproductive system, skeleton, and cardiovascular system; in addition, use of anabolic steroids is associated with mood swings, aggression, and depression (Kanayama, Hudson, & Pope, 2008). Parents, coaches, and health professionals need to be sure that high-school athletes are aware of the dangers of steroids and should encourage youth to meet their athletic goals through methods that do not involve drug use (American Academy of Pediatrics, 2005).

Threats to Adolescent Well-Being

Every year, approximately 1 U.S. adolescent out of 1,000 dies. Figure 8.3 shows that for boys, most deaths are due to accidents involving motor vehicles or firearms. For European American and Asian American boys, motor vehicles are more deadly

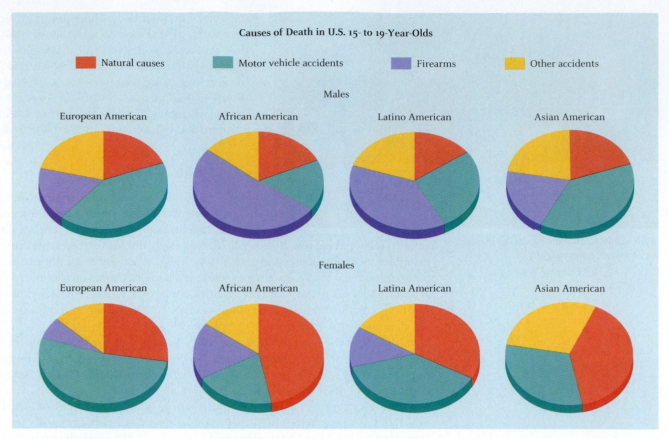

Causes of Death in U.S. 15- to 19-Year-Olds

■ Natural causes   ■ Motor vehicle accidents   ■ Firearms   ■ Other accidents

Males

European American   African American   Latino American   Asian American

Females

European American   African American   Latina American   Asian American

FIGURE 8.3

Adolescent boys are more likely than adolescent girls to die from accidents or use of firearms, and this is particularly true for African American, Asian American, and Latino American teenage boys.

From America's children: Key national indicators of well-being, by the Federal Interagency Forum on Child and Family Statistics. Copyright © U.S. Government Printing Office 2005.

than guns, but the reverse is true for African American boys. Among girls, most deaths are due to natural causes or accidents involving motor vehicles. For European American girls, motor vehicle accidents account for nearly half of all deaths; for African American girls, natural causes account for nearly half of all deaths; and for Latina American and Asian American girls, natural causes and motor vehicles account for about the same number of deaths (Federal Interagency Forum on Child and Family Statistics, 2005).

Sadly, many of these deaths are preventable. Deaths in automobile accidents are often linked to driving too fast, drinking alcohol, and not wearing seatbelts (U.S. Department of Health and Human Services, 1997). And deaths due to guns are often linked to easy access to firearms in the home: In far too many homes, firearms are stored loaded, unlocked, or both (Johnson et al., 2006).

Adolescent deaths from accidents can be explained, in part, because adolescents take risks that adults often find unacceptable (Nell, 2002). Teens drive cars recklessly, engage in unprotected sex, and sometimes use illegal and dangerous drugs (we discuss the latter behaviors more in Chapter 9). Surprisingly, adolescents vastly overestimate the actual likelihood of harm associated with many risky behaviors, such as drunk driving and unprotected sex (Millstein & Halpern-Felsher, 2002). But they believe that, as individuals, they are not likely to experience the harmful consequences of risky behaviors. In other words, driving drunk and having unprotected sex are viewed as dangerous, but only to others (Reyna & Farley, 2006).

In addition, adolescents find the rewards associated with risky behavior far more appealing than adults do—so much so that they're willing to ignore the risks. For many adolescents, the pleasure, excitement, and intimacy of sex far outweigh the risks of disease and pregnancy (Halpern-Felsher & Cauffman, 2001; Reyna & Farley, 2006), which reflects the maturity of the pleasure-seeking brain regions relative to those regions that control behavior (Somerville & Casey, 2010).

Test Yourself

Recall

1. An adolescent's diet should contain adequate calories, _____ , and iron.

2. Individuals with _____ alternate between binge eating and purging.

3. During adolescence, the most important risk factors for anorexia and bulimia are _____ .

4. Regular physical activity helps promote _____ and physical health.

5. Some teenage athletes use anabolic steroids to increase muscular strength and to _____ .

6. More teenage girls die from _____ than other causes.

7. Because they place greater emphasis on the _____ actions, adolescents make what adults think are risky decisions.

Interpret

- Distinguish the biological factors that contribute to obesity from the environmental factors.

- How does adolescent risk taking illustrate the idea that individuals help shape their own development?

Apply

- Many students in middle schools and high schools do not eat well-balanced meals and do not get enough exercise. What might a school nurse do to improve students' dietary and exercise habits?

- Fifteen-year-old Kara has decided to become a vegetarian. She insists that this won't be a burden at mealtimes because she'll just skip the meat and take bigger portions of everything else. What's the flaw in Kara's reasoning?

Recall answers: (1) calcium, (2) bulimia nervosa, (3) being overly concerned about one's body and a history of dieting, (4) mental health, (5) promote more rapid recovery from an injury, (6) natural causes or automobile accidents, (7) rewards associated with their

---

8.3 Information Processing During Adolescence

LEARNING OBJECTIVES

- How do working memory and processing speed change during adolescence?

- How do increases in content knowledge, strategies, and metacognitive skills influence adolescent cognition?

- What changes in problem solving and reasoning take place in adolescents?

Calvin, a 14-year-old, was an enigma to his mother, Crystal. On the one hand, Calvin's growing reasoning skills impressed her: He readily grasped technical discussions of her medical work and easily found loopholes in her explanations of why he wasn't allowed to do some things with his friends. On the other hand, sometimes Calvin was a real teenage "space cadet." Simple problem solving stumped him, or he made silly mistakes and got the wrong answer. Calvin didn't correspond to Crystal's image of the formal operational thinker that she remembered from her college human development class.

For information-processing theorists, adolescence is a gradual transitional period between the rapidly changing cognitive processes of childhood and the mature cognitive processes of young adulthood. Cognitive changes take place during adolescence, but they are small compared to those seen in childhood. We describe these changes in this section, and as we do, we'll see why adolescents like Crystal's son don't always think as effectively as they might.

FIGURE 8.4

Response time declines steadily during child-hood and reaches adultlike levels during middle adolescence.

Data from Kail (2004).

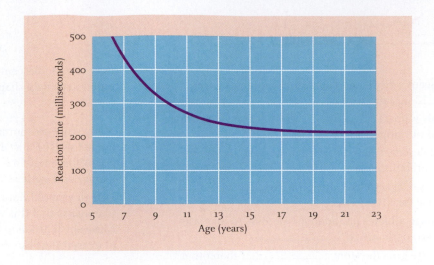

Working Memory and Processing Speed

Working memory is the site of ongoing cognitive processing, and processing speed is the speed with which individuals complete basic cognitive processes. Both of these capacities achieve adultlike levels during adolescence. Adolescents' working memory has about the same capacity as adults' working memory, which means that teenagers are better able than children to store information needed for ongoing cognitive processes. In addition, Figure 8.4 illustrates changes in processing speed, exemplified in this case by performance on a simple reaction-time task in which people press a button quickly in response to a visual stimulus. The time needed to respond drops steadily during childhood but reaches adult levels during adolescence. This pattern is found for a range of cognitive tasks: Adolescents process information about as quickly as young adults (Kail, 2004). Change in working memory and processing speed means that, compared to children, adolescents process information efficiently.

These changes in efficiency reflect the maturational changes to the brain that were described earlier (page 221). Increases in myelination during adolescence allow nerve impulses to travel more rapidly, which contributes to more rapid and more efficient information processing during this period (Dockstader et al., 2012; Schmithorst & Yuan, 2010).

Adolescents often have adultlike skills in some domains, such as using cell phones, which allows them to teach adults.

Courtesy of Robert V. Kail

Content Knowledge, Strategies, and Metacognitive Skill

As children move into adolescence, they acquire adultlike levels of knowledge and understanding in many domains. For example, many parents turn to their teens for help in learning to use fancy features on their smart phone. This increased knowledge is useful for its own sake, but it also has the indirect effect of enabling adolescents to learn, understand, and remember more of new experiences (Schneider & Bjorklund, 1998; Schneider & Pressley, 1997). Imagine two middle-school students—one a baseball expert, the other not—watching a baseball game. Compared to the novice, the adolescent expert would understand many nuances of the game and, later, remember more features of the game.

As their content knowledge increases, adolescents also become better skilled at identifying strategies appropriate for a specific task and then monitoring the chosen strategy to verify that it is working (Schneider & Pressley, 1997). For example, adolescents are more likely than children to outline and highlight information in a text. They are more likely to make lists of material they should study, and they more often embed these activities in a master study plan (e.g., a list of

Information Processing During Adolescence

Feature	State
Working memory and processing speed	Adolescents have adultlike working memory capacity and processing speed, enabling them to process information efficiently.
Content knowledge	Adolescents' greater knowledge of the world facilitates understanding and memory of new experiences.
Strategies and metacognition	Adolescents are better able to identify task-appropriate strategies and to monitor the effectiveness of those strategies.
Problem solving and reasoning	Adolescents often solve problems analytically by relying on mathematics or logic, and they are able to detect weaknesses in scientific evidence and logical arguments.

© Cengage Learning 2013

HUMAN DEVELOPMENT in action

Suppose you were an experienced fifth-grade teacher who's going to be teaching high school for the first time. What study skills could you expect from your new students that you wouldn't expect in fifth graders?

assignments, quizzes, and tests for a 2-week period). All these activities help adolescents learn more effectively and remember more accurately (Schneider & Pressley, 1997; Thomas et al., 1993).

Problem Solving and Reasoning

Adolescents typically solve problems more readily than children, in part because their approach is more sophisticated. Often children rely on heuristics, which are rules of thumb that do not guarantee a solution but are useful in solving a range of problems. Heuristics tend to be fast and require little effort. In contrast, adolescents are more likely to solve problems analytically—determining an answer mathematically or logically, depending on the nature of the problem (Stanovich, Toplak, & West, 2008). For example, in trying to decide which model of bicycle to buy, one solution—more common among children—involves a heuristic that relies on personal experience: Buy the bike that a friend says is best. The analytic solution—more common among adolescents—involves relying on statistical information: Buy the bike that's rated best by a large sample of buyers (Kokis et al., 2002).

Adolescents are also better skilled at finding weaknesses in arguments. In scientific reasoning, for example, adolescents recognize the hazards of making generalizations from extremely small samples. They would be wary of concluding that people from another country are particularly friendly based on meeting just two people from that country (Klaczynski & Lavallee, 2005). And, as we see in the Spotlight on Research feature, they can pinpoint certain kinds of flaws in logical arguments.

The ability to detect flawed arguments is yet another demonstration of improved information processing during adolescence, summarized in Table 8.1. Adolescents may not always use their skills effectively. Sometimes they resort to heuristics because they take less effort and are "good enough" for the problem. Also, sometimes adolescents' beliefs interfere with effective thinking: When evidence is inconsistent with adolescents' beliefs, they may dismiss the evidence as irrelevant or try to reinterpret the evidence to make it consistent with their beliefs (Klaczynski & Lavallee, 2005; Klaczynski & Narasimham, 1998). In other words, adolescents use their reasoning skills selectively, raising their standards to dismiss findings that threaten their beliefs and lowering them to admit findings compatible with their beliefs.

Findings like these tell us that Crystal, the mother in the opening vignette, should not be so perplexed by her son's seemingly erratic thinking: Adolescents (and adults, for that matter) do not always use the most powerful levels of thinking that they possess. The information-processing account of intellectual functioning during adolescence is a description of how children and adolescents can think, not how they always or even usually think.

Adolescents Can Identify Fallacies in Arguments

Who were the investigators, and what was the aim of the study?

In formal debates and informal conversations, people sometimes rely on irrelevant arguments. One of the most common is an ad hominem argument, in which someone attacks the person making a claim, not the claim itself. If one adolescent is arguing that *Grey's Anatomy* is the best TV show ever, a peer's ad hominem argument would be to say, "You only think that because your sister is a surgical intern." This statement may be true (the sister is an intern, and that's why the peer likes *Grey's Anatomy*), but it's irrelevant to the debate about the quality of the TV show. Michael Weinstock and his colleagues (2006) at Ben Gurion University of the Negev—Yair Neuman and Amnon Glassner (2006)—wanted to determine how well adolescents could identify reasoning fallacies like the ad hominem argument.

How did the investigators measure the topic of interest?

The researchers created brief scenarios involving a discussion between two individuals. In some scenarios, one person made an ad hominem argument. For example, in a scenario about the presence of living creatures elsewhere in the universe, an ad hominem argument involved saying that a person does not believe in life elsewhere because the person is unimaginative. Other scenarios involved ad populum arguments, which assert that a claim must be true because most people believe it to be true. In other words, this is "truth by popular vote." Finally, some scenarios involved ad ignorantiam arguments, which assert that a claim must be true because no one has shown that it's false: "There must be living creatures on other planets because nobody has proven that Earth is the only planet with living creatures." Other scenarios had no false arguments; participants read each scenario and were asked to identify any problems in the arguments.

Who were the participants in the study?

Weinstock and his colleagues tested fifty-three 13-year-olds, fifty-eight 15-year-olds, and eighty-two 17-year-olds. For simplicity, we just discuss the results for the youngest and oldest students.

What was the design of the study?

This study was experimental because Weinstock and his colleagues included two independent variables: the age of the participant and the nature of the false argument in the scenarios (ad hominem, ad populum, and ad ignorantiam). The dependent variable was the percentage of times that the students detected the flawed argument. The study was cross-sectional because 13-, 15-, and 17-year-olds were all tested at approximately the same time.

Were there ethical concerns with the study?

No. The scenarios involved topics that students were likely to encounter and discuss in daily life.

What were the results?

Figure 8.5 shows the percentage of false arguments detected at each age. Two patterns are evident. First, older adolescents were more likely

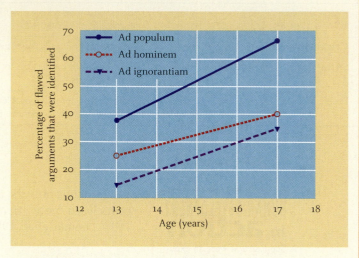

FIGURE 8.5

Older adolescents detect more flawed arguments; ad populum flaws are the easiest to detect, and ad ignorantiam flaws are the most difficult.
Data from Weinstock et al. (2006).

to detect each kind of flawed argument. Second, at both ages the ad populum arguments ("truth by popular vote") were easiest to detect while ad ignorantiam arguments were the most difficult. Most averages shown in the graph are below 50%, which means that adolescents miss more than half of the flawed arguments.

What did the investigators conclude?

Weinstock and his colleagues concluded that the ability to detect flawed arguments improves substantially during adolescence, although even the oldest adolescents in the sample were far from perfect in identifying the ad hominem and ad ignorantiam fallacies. The researchers suggested several reasons for the improvement, including greater experience with argumentation and improved metacognitive skills.

What converging evidence would strengthen these conclusions?

An obvious way to bolster these results would be to conduct a longitudinal study to see how these skills unfold over time for an individual. For example, the averages shown in Figure 8.5 indicate that ad populum fallacies were the easiest to detect and ad ignorantiam flaws were the hardest. A longitudinal study could confirm this sequence by showing that, as individuals develop, they first master the ad populum fallacy, then the ad hominem fallacy, and finally the ad ignorantiam fallacy.

 Go to Psychology CourseMate at **www.cengagebrain.com** to enhance your understanding of this research.

Test Yourself

Recall

1. According to information-processing theorists, adolescence is a time of important changes in working memory, processing speed, _____, strategies, and metacognition.

2. Information-processing theorists view adolescence as a time of _____.

3. When solving problems, children often rely on heuristics, but adolescents are more likely to solve problems _____.

4. When evidence is inconsistent with their beliefs, adolescents often _____.

Interpret

- The information-processing account of cognitive change in adolescents emphasizes working memory, knowledge, and strategies. How might each of these factors be influenced by nature? By nurture?

- Students typically are introduced to the study of complex topics such as philosophy and experimental science during adolescence. Explain how their maturing cognitive skills contribute to the study of these and other subject areas.

Apply

- Terry's scout troop wants to go camping. According to an article in the newspaper, Tall Trees State Park is one of the most popular in the state. But Terry's aunt camps at Rapid River State Park, and she thinks it's the best. If Terry is 8 years old, which park would she say is better?

- Alex, age 15, and his 9-year-old brother Tom love to play a video game that involves remembering targets and shooting quickly whenever they appear on the screen. Tom beats most of his friends, but he always loses to Alex. How would an information-processing psychologist explain Alex's ability to win constantly?

8.4 Reasoning About Moral Issues

LEARNING OBJECTIVES

- How do adolescents reason about moral issues?

- How do concern for justice and caring for other people contribute to moral reasoning?

Howard, the least popular boy in eighth grade, had been wrongly accused of stealing a sixth grader's iPod. Min-shen, another eighth grader, knew that Howard was innocent but said nothing to the school principal for fear of what his friends would say about siding with Howard. A few days later, when Min-shen's father heard about the incident, he was upset that his son had so little "moral fiber." Why hadn't Min-shen acted in the face of an injustice?

One day, two articles appeared in the local paper. The first described a 15-year-old girl who was badly burned while saving her younger brothers from a fire in their apartment. Her mother said she wasn't surprised by her daughter's actions because she had always been an extraordinarily caring person. The other article was about two 17-year-old boys who had beaten an elderly man to death. They had only planned to steal his wallet, but when he insulted them and tried to punch them, they became enraged.

Reading articles like these, you can't help but question why some teenagers act in ways that earn our deepest respect and admiration, whereas others earn our contempt, as well as our pity. And we wonder why Min-shen didn't tell the truth about the stolen iPod. To get some answers, we start with a prominent theory of moral reasoning.

Kohlberg's Theory of Moral Reasoning

The most influential account of moral development was proposed by Lawrence Kohlberg (1927–1987), who asked participants to respond to moral dilemmas like this:

> In Europe, a woman was near death from cancer. One drug might save her, a form of radium that a druggist in the same town had recently discovered. The druggist was charging $2,000, ten times what the drug cost him to make. The sick woman's husband, Heinz, went to everyone he knew to borrow the money, but he could only get together about half of what it cost. He told the druggist that his wife was dying and asked him to sell it cheaper or let him pay later. But the druggist said, "No." The husband got desperate and broke into the man's store to steal the drug for his wife. (1969, p. 379)

Thus, Heinz faces a moral dilemma in which there is no correct answer; all courses of action have desirable and undesirable features.

Kohlberg analyzed children's, adolescents', and adults' responses to a large number of such dilemmas and identified three levels of moral reasoning: preconventional, conventional, and postconventional. Each level is further subdivided into two stages. *At the* **preconventional level***, moral reasoning is based on external forces.* For most children, many adolescents, and some adults, moral reasoning is controlled almost exclusively by rewards and punishments. *Individuals in stage 1 moral reasoning assume an* **obedience orientation***, which means believing that authority figures know what is right and wrong.* Consequently, stage 1 individuals do what authorities say is right to avoid being punished. At this stage, one might argue that Heinz shouldn't steal the drug because an authority figure (e.g., parent or police officer) said he shouldn't do it. Alternatively, one might argue that he should steal the drug because he would get into trouble if he let his wife die.

In stage 2 of the preconventional level, people adopt an **instrumental orientation***, in which they look out for their own needs.* Stage 2 individuals are nice to others because they expect the favor to be returned in the future. Someone at this stage could justify stealing the drug because Heinz's wife might do something nice for Heinz in return. Or, they might argue that Heinz shouldn't steal the drug because it will create more problems for him.

At the **conventional level***, adolescents and adults look to society's norms for moral guidance.* In other words, people's reasoning is largely determined by others' expectations of them. *In stage 3, adolescents' and adults' moral reasoning is based on* **interpersonal norms***, the aim of which is to win the approval of other people by behaving as "good boys" and "good girls" would.* Stage 3 individuals might argue that Heinz shouldn't steal the drug because he must keep his reputation as an honest man or that he should steal the drug because no one would think negatively of him for trying to save his wife's life.

Stage 4 of the conventional level focuses on **social system morality***.* Here, adolescents and adults believe that social roles, expectations, and laws exist to maintain order within society and to promote the good of all people. Stage 4 individuals might reason that Heinz shouldn't steal the drug, even though his wife might die, because it is illegal and no one is above the law. Alternatively, they might claim that he should steal it to live up to his marriage vow of protecting his wife, even though he will face negative consequences for his theft.

At the **postconventional level***, moral reasoning is based on a personal moral code.* The emphasis is no longer on external forces like punishment, reward, or social roles. *In stage 5, people base their moral reasoning on a* **social contract***.* Adults agree that members of social groups adhere to a social contract because a common set of expectations and laws benefits all group members. However, if these expectations and laws no longer promote the welfare of individuals, they become invalid. Consequently, stage 5 individuals might reason that Heinz should steal the drug because social rules about property rights no longer benefit individuals' welfare. They could alternatively argue that he shouldn't steal it because it would create social anarchy.

preconventional level
the first level in Kohlberg's theory, in which moral reasoning is based on external forces

obedience orientation
a characteristic of Kohlberg's stage 1, in which moral reasoning is based on the belief that adults know what is right and wrong

instrumental orientation
a characteristic of Kohlberg's stage 2, in which moral reasoning is based on the aim of looking out for one's needs

conventional level
the second level in Kohlberg's theory, in which moral reasoning is based on society's norms

interpersonal norms
a characteristic of Kohlberg's stage 3, in which moral reasoning is based on winning the approval of others

social system morality
a characteristic of Kohlberg's stage 4, in which moral reasoning is based on maintenance of order in society

postconventional level
the third level in Kohlberg's theory, in which moral reasoning is based on a personal moral code

social contract
a characteristic of Kohlberg's stage 5, in which moral reasoning is based on the belief that laws are for the good of all members of society

In 1939, Oskar Schindler was an entrepreneur who made a great deal of money working for the Germans after they conquered Poland. Motivated at first strictly by the potential for personal profit, he opened—with few qualms—a factory in which he employed Jews as slave labor.

Schindler's company was quite successful. But as the war continued, Jewish citizens in Poland were rounded up and shipped to concentration camps or summarily executed. Schindler was deeply disturbed by this, and his attitudes began to change. His employees suggested that he give the Germans a list of workers essential to the factory's continued operation. The list protected employees because the plant's products were used in the war effort. No longer driven by profit, Schindler went to great lengths to preserve life: He created cover stories to support his claims that certain employees were essential and went to Auschwitz to rescue employees who were sent there despite being included on his lists.

Schindler's list saved many lives. He began the war at Kohlberg's preconventional level—where he was motivated solely by personal profit—but he ultimately moved to the postconventional level—where he was motivated by the higher principle of saving lives. It is at the postconventional level that heroes are made.

AP Photo/Peter Hillebrecht, File

During World War II, Schindler saved the lives of many Jews by adding their names to lists of employees who were essential for his factory's operation.

AP Photo/Bill Wolf

Teenagers who engage in moral behavior, such as participating in protest marches, often reason at high levels in Kohlberg's theory.

Finally, in stage 6 of the postconventional level, abstract principles such as justice, compassion, and equality form the basis of a personal code that may sometimes conflict with society's expectations and laws. Stage 6 individuals might argue that Heinz should steal the drug because saving a life takes precedence over everything, including the law. Or they might claim that Heinz's wife has a right to die and that he should not force his views on her by stealing and administering the drug.

This developmental sequence usually unfolds over many years, but sometimes it happens more dramatically, such as when individuals undergo a major transformation in their moral motivation. One noteworthy example of such a transformation was depicted in Steven Spielberg's Oscar-winning movie *Schindler's List,* as described in the Real People feature.

Support for Kohlberg's Theory

Kohlberg proposed that individuals move through the six stages of moral reasoning only in the order listed, and longitudinal studies show that individuals progress through each stage in sequence, with virtually no individual skipping stages (Colby et al., 1983). Further support for the theory is a link between moral reasoning and moral behavior: adolescents who defend their principles in difficult situations tend to be more advanced in Kohlberg's stages (Gibbs et al., 1986). Individuals at the advanced levels are compelled to action by their moral principles, but individuals at less advanced levels act only when such action is endorsed by external forces. This explains why Min-shen, the boy in the vignette, said nothing. Speaking out on behalf of the unpopular student won't lead to reward and violates social norms against "squealing" on friends. Consequently, an eighth grader—who is probably in the preconventional or conventional level of moral reasoning—lets the unpopular student be punished unfairly.

On some other features, Kohlberg's theory does not fare as well. Many critics note that Kohlberg's emphasis on individual rights and justice reflects traditional American culture and Judeo-Christian theology. Not all cultures and religions share

HUMAN DEVELOPMENT in action

As a pastor, you hope to recruit adolescents to participate in a mission trip during spring vacation to poverty stricken areas of Appalachia. What level of moral reasoning would you expect of students who volunteer?

this emphasis; the Hindu religion, for example, emphasizes duty and responsibility to others, not individual rights and justice (Simpson, 1974). Indeed, children and adults reared with traditional Hindu beliefs emphasize caring for others in their moral reasoning more than individuals brought up in the Judeo-Christian tradition. In the Heinz dilemma, for example, Hindu children and adolescents would urge Heinz to steal the drug because caring for others—especially family members—trumps everything else (Miller & Bersoff, 1992; Savani et al., 2011). Clearly, moral reasoning reflects the culture in which a person is reared.

Beyond Kohlberg's Theory

Findings like those described in the previous section indicate that Kohlberg's theory is most useful in understanding moral reasoning in cultures with Western philosophical and religious traditions. But researcher Carol Gilligan argued that Kohlberg's emphasis on justice applies more to males than to females, whose reasoning about moral issues is often rooted in concern for others (Gilligan, 1982; Gilligan & Attanucci, 1988). According to Gilligan, this "ethic of care" leads females to put priority on fulfilling obligations to other people and those obligations guide their moral decision making.

What does research tell us about the importance of justice and care in moral reasoning? And do females and males differ in the bases of their moral reasoning? Males tend to get slightly greater scores on problems that emphasize justice, whereas females tend to get slightly greater scores on problems that emphasize caring (Jaffee & Hyde, 2000). But the differences are small and do not indicate that moral reasoning by females is predominated by a concern with care and that moral reasoning by males is predominated by a concern with justice. Instead, girls and boys, as well as men and women, reason about moral issues similarly. Most people think about moral issues in terms of both justice and caring, depending on the nature of the moral dilemma and the context (Turiel, 2006).

Whether it is based on justice or care, most cultures and most parents want to encourage adolescents to think carefully about moral issues. In the Linking Research to Life feature, we consider what can be done to help adolescents develop more mature forms of moral reasoning.

According to Gilligan, moral reasoning is driven by the need to care for others.

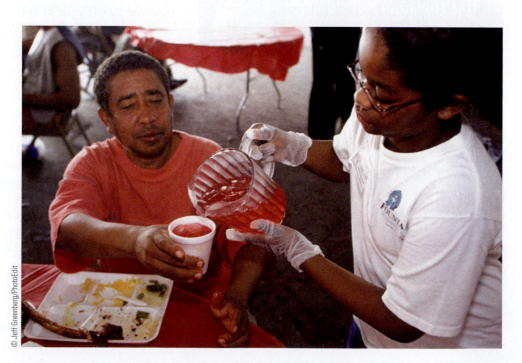

© Jeff Greenberg/PhotoEdit

Test Yourself

Recall

1. Kohlberg's theory includes the preconventional, conventional, and _____ levels.

2. For children and adolescents in the preconventional level, moral reasoning is strongly influenced by _____ .

3. Supporting Kohlberg's theory are findings that people progress through the stages in the predicted sequence and that _____ .

4. Gilligan's view of morality emphasizes _____ instead of justice.

5. When boys' and girls' moral reasoning is compared, the typical result is that _____ .

Interpret

- How similar is Jean Piaget's stage of formal operational thought to Kohlberg's stage of conventional moral reasoning?

- Research shows that people sometimes do not reason at the most advanced levels of which they are capable; instead, they revert to simpler, less mature levels. Might this happen in the realm of moral reasoning too? What factors might make it more likely for a person's moral reasoning to revert to a less sophisticated level?

Apply

- When Jing's younger brother forgot to bring his lunch to school, she readily shared her meal because her brother would now "owe her"—he would have to share his lunch if she forgot hers. As a developmental psychologist, how would you describe Jing's moral reasoning?

- Two teenagers found a $20 bill in Ms. Sherman's front yard. One teen thinks they should ask Ms. Sherman if it's hers. The other thinks they should use the money to buy flowers for a friend who broke her leg. What is the moral rationale supporting each course of action?

Recall answers: (1) postconventional, (2) reward or punishment, (3) more advanced moral reasoning is associated with moral action, (4) caring for others, (5) they differ little

Linking Research to life • PROMOTING MORAL REASONING

How can we teach adolescents more mature forms of moral reasoning or to aspire to moral heroism like that shown by Schindler? Sometimes simply being exposed to more advanced moral reasoning is sufficient to promote developmental change (Walker, 1980). Adolescents may notice, for example, that older friends do not wait to be rewarded to help others. Or a teenager may notice that respected peers take courageous positions regardless of the social consequences. Such experiences apparently cause adolescents to reevaluate their reasoning on moral issues and propel them toward more sophisticated thinking.

Discussion can be particularly effective in revealing shortcomings in moral reasoning (Berkowitz et al., 2006). When people reason about moral issues with others whose reasoning is at a higher level, the usual result is that individuals reasoning at lower levels improve. Adolescents' moral reasoning (and moral behavior) is also influenced by their involvement in religion. Adolescents who are more involved in religion have greater concern for others and place more emphasis on helping them (Youniss, McLellan, & Yates, 1999). An obvious explanation for this link is that religion provides moral beliefs and guidelines for adolescents. But participation in religion promotes moral reasoning in a second, less direct way. Involvement in a religious community connects teens to an extended network of caring peers and adults. From interacting with individuals in this network, earning their trust, and sharing their values, adolescents gain a sense of responsibility to and concern for others (King & Furrow, 2004).

Research findings such as these send an important message to parents: Discussion is probably the best way for parents to help their children think about moral issues in more mature terms (Walker & Taylor, 1991). Research consistently shows that mature moral reasoning comes about when adolescents are free to express their opinions on moral issues to their parents, who in turn express their opinions and thus expose their adolescent children to more mature moral reasoning (Hoffman, 1988, 1994).

Summary

8.1 Pubertal Changes

What physical changes occur during adolescence that mark the transition to a mature young adult?

- Puberty includes bodily changes in height and weight, as well as sexual maturation. Girls typically begin the growth spurt earlier than boys, who acquire more muscle, less fat, and greater heart and lung capacity. The brain communicates more effectively, and the frontal cortex continues to mature. Sexual maturation, which includes primary and secondary sex characteristics, occurs in predictable sequences for boys and girls.

What factors cause the physical changes associated with puberty?

- Pubertal changes take place when the pituitary gland signals the adrenal gland, ovaries, and testes to secrete hormones that initiate physical changes. The timing of puberty is influenced strongly by health, nutrition, and social environment; for example, puberty occurs earlier for girls who experience stress.

How do physical changes affect adolescents' psychological development?

- Pubertal changes affect adolescents' psychological functioning. Teens, particularly girls, become concerned about their appearance. Adolescents are moodier than children or adults primarily because their moods shift in response to frequent changes in activities and social setting. Early maturation tends to be harmful to girls.

8.2 Health

What are the elements of a healthy diet for adolescents? Why do some adolescents have eating disorders?

- For proper growth, teenagers need to consume adequate calories, calcium, and iron. Unfortunately, many teenagers do not eat properly and do not receive adequate nutrition.

- Anorexia and bulimia, eating disorders that typically affect adolescent girls, are characterized by an irrational fear of being overweight. Several factors contribute to these disorders, including heredity, a childhood history of eating problems, negative self-esteem, and a preoccupation with one's body and weight. Treatment and prevention programs emphasize changing adolescents' views toward thinness and their eating-related behaviors.

Do adolescents get enough exercise? What are the consequences of participating in sports in high school?

- Individuals who exercise regularly often have improved physical and mental health. Unfortunately, many high-school students do not get enough exercise.

- Millions of American boys and girls participate in sports. The benefits of participating in sports include improved physical fitness, enhanced self-esteem, and understanding about teamwork. The potential costs include injury and abuse of performance-enhancing drugs.

What are common obstacles to healthy growth during adolescence?

- Accidents involving automobiles or firearms are the most common cause of death in American teenagers. Adolescents often overestimate the harm of risky behavior in general, but they don't see themselves as being personally at risk and often place greater value on the rewards associated with risky behavior.

8.3 Information Processing During Adolescence

How do working memory and processing speed change during adolescence?

- Working memory increases in capacity, and processing speed becomes faster. Both achieve adultlike levels during adolescence.

How do increases in content knowledge, strategies, and metacognitive skills influence adolescent cognition?

- Content knowledge increases, even to expertlike levels in some domains. Strategies and metacognitive skills become more sophisticated.

What changes in problem solving and reasoning take place in adolescents?

- Adolescents often solve problems analytically, using mathematics or logic. They also acquire skill in detecting weaknesses in scientific evidence and in logical arguments.

8.4 Reasoning About Moral Issues

How do adolescents reason about moral issues?

- Kohlberg proposed that moral reasoning includes preconventional, conventional, and postconventional levels. Moral reasoning is first based on rewards and punishments and much later based on personal moral codes. However, not all cultures emphasize justice in moral reasoning. For instance, Hindu children emphasize caring for other people in their moral reasoning.

How do concern for justice and caring for other people contribute to moral reasoning?

- Gilligan proposed that females' moral reasoning is based on caring and responsibility for others, not justice. But other research does not support consistent sex differences in moral reasoning; instead, researchers have found that males and females both consider caring and justice in their moral judgments, depending on the situation.

Key Terms

puberty (218)
primary sex characteristics (219)
secondary sex characteristics (220)
menarche (220)
spermarche (220)
body mass index (BMI) (223)

basal metabolic rate (223)
anorexia nervosa (224)
bulimia nervosa (224)
preconventional level (232)
obedience orientation (232)
instrumental orientation (232)

conventional level (232)
interpersonal norms (232)
social system morality (232)
postconventional level (232)
social contract (232)

Online Resources

Go to CengageBrain.com to access Psychology CourseMate, where you will find an interactive eBook, flashcards, quizzes, videos, websites, and more.

SIGN UP TO VOTE TODAY!

Moving Into the Adult Social World

Socioemotional Development in Adolescence

You probably have vivid memories of your teenage years. Remember your high-school graduation, your first feelings of love and sexuality, your first day on the job when you couldn't do anything right, and countless arguments with your parents? Feelings of pride, accomplishment, embarrassment, and anger are common to adolescents, who are in transition from childhood to adulthood. This is when individuals grapple with their identity, many have their first experiences with love and sex, and some enter the world of work. In the first three sections of this chapter, we investigate these challenging developmental issues. Then we look at the special obstacles that sometimes make adolescence difficult to handle.

LEARNING OBJECTIVES

■ How do adolescents achieve an identity?

■ What are the stages and results of acquiring an ethnic identity?

■ How does self-esteem change in adolescence?

Dea was born in Seoul of Korean parents but was adopted by a Dutch couple in Michigan when she was 3 months old. Growing up, she considered herself a red-blooded American. In college, however, Dea realized that others saw her as an Asian American, an identity about which she had never given much thought. She began to wonder, "Who am I really? American? Dutch American? Asian American?"

Like Dea, do you sometimes wonder who you are? Self-concept refers to the attitudes, behaviors, and values that make a person unique. In adolescence, self-concept takes on special significance as individuals struggle to achieve an identity that will allow them to participate in the adult world. In this section, we'll learn more about how adolescents like Dea search for an identity.

The Search for Identity

According to Erik Erikson's (1968) theory, adolescents face a crisis between identity and role confusion. They must balance the desire to try out many possible selves and the need to select a single self. Adolescents who achieve a sense of identity are well prepared to face the next developmental challenge: establishing intimate relationships with others. In contrast, teenagers who are confused about their identity remain isolated and respond to others stereotypically.

Adolescents use the hypothetical reasoning skills of the formal operational stage to experiment with different selves and thus learn more about possible identities. Experimentation is often career oriented. Some adolescents may envision themselves as

As part of their search for an identity, adolescents often try on different roles, for example, imagining what life might be like as a rock star.

© Juice Images/Alamy

Identity Statuses

Status	Definition	Example
Diffusion	The individual is overwhelmed by the task of achieving an identity and does little to accomplish the task.	Larry hates the idea of deciding what to do with his future, so he spends most of his free time playing video games.
Foreclosure	The individual has a status determined by adults rather than by personal exploration.	For as long as she can remember, Sakura's parents have told her that she should be an attorney and join the family law firm. She plans to study prelaw in college, though she's never given the matter much thought.
Moratorium	The individual is examining different alternatives but has yet to find one that's satisfactory.	Brad enjoys almost all of his high-school classes. Some days he thinks it would be fun to be a chemist, some days he wants to be a novelist, and some days he'd like to be an elementary-school teacher. He thinks it's a little weird to change his mind so often, but he also enjoys thinking about different jobs.
Achievement	The individual has explored alternatives and has deliberately chosen a specific identity.	Throughout middle school, Efrat wanted to play in the WNBA. During 9th and 10th grades, she thought it would be cool to be a physician. In 11th grade, she took a computing course and everything finally "clicked"—she'd found her niche. She knew that she wanted to study computer science in college.

Adolescents often believe that others are constantly watching them, a phenomenon known as imaginary audience; as a result, they're often upset or embarrassed when they make obvious mistakes or blunders, such as spilling food or drink.

adolescent egocentrism
self-absorption that is characteristic of teenagers as they search for identity

imaginary audience
adolescents' feeling that their behavior is constantly being watched by their peers

personal fable
the attitude of many adolescents that their feelings and experiences are unique and have never before been experienced by anyone

illusion of invulnerability
adolescents' belief that misfortunes cannot happen to them

rock stars; others may imagine being professional athletes or best-selling novelists. Other testing is romantically oriented. Teens may fall in love and imagine living with the loved one. Still other exploration involves religious and political beliefs (Harre, 2007; King, Elder, & Whitbeck, 1997). Teens give different identities a trial run just as you might test-drive different cars before selecting one. By fantasizing about their future, adolescents begin to discover who they will be.

As adolescents strive to achieve an identity, they often progress through different phases or statuses, as shown in Table 9.1. Unlike Piaget's stages, these four phases do not necessarily occur in sequence. Most young adolescents are in states of diffusion or foreclosure, in which they are not exploring alternative identities. They are avoiding the crisis or have resolved it by taking on an identity suggested by others. However, as individuals move beyond early adolescence and into young adulthood and have more opportunity to explore alternative identities, achievement and moratorium become more common (Meeus et al., 2010).

During the search for identity, adolescents reveal a number of characteristic ways of thinking. *The self-absorption that marks the teenage search for identity is referred to as* **adolescent egocentrism** (Elkind, 1978). Unlike preschoolers, adolescents know that others have different perspectives on the world. Adolescents are simply more interested in their own feelings and experiences than in anyone else's experiences. In addition, as they search for an identity, many adolescents wrongly believe that they are the focus of others' thinking. A teen who spills food on herself may imagine that all her friends are thinking only about the stain on her blouse and how sloppy she is. *Many adolescents feel that they are actors watched constantly by their peers, a phenomenon known as the* **imaginary audience**.

Adolescent self-absorption is also demonstrated by the **personal fable**, *teenagers' tendency to believe that their experiences and feelings are unique and that no one has ever felt or thought as they do.* Whether the excitement of first love, the despair of a broken relationship, or the confusion of planning for the future, adolescents often believe they are the first to experience these feelings and that no one else could possibly understand their emotions (Elkind & Bowen, 1979). *Adolescents' belief in their uniqueness also contributes to an* **illusion of invulnerability**: *the belief that misfortune happens only to others.* Teens think they can have sex without becoming pregnant or

HUMAN DEVELOPMENT in action

As a high-school counselor, plan a presentation for parents that describes the unique features of adolescents' thinking.

contracting a sexually transmitted disease or that they can drive recklessly without being in an auto accident.

As adolescents make progress toward achieving an identity, adolescent egocentrism, imaginary audiences, personal fables, and the illusion of invulnerability become less common. What circumstances help adolescents achieve identity? Parents are influential (Marcia, 1980). When parents encourage discussion and recognize children's autonomy, their children are more likely to reach the achievement status because they undertake the personal experimentation that leads to identity. In contrast, when parents set rules with little justification and enforce them without explanation, children are more likely to remain in the foreclosure status. These teens are discouraged from experimenting personally; instead, their parents simply tell them what identity to adopt. Overall, adolescents are most likely to establish a well-defined identity in a family atmosphere in which parents encourage children to explore alternatives on their own but do not pressure or provide explicit direction (Missotten et al., 2011; Smits et al., 2010).

Beyond parents, peers are also influential. When adolescents have close friends that they trust, they feel more secure exploring alternatives (Meeus, Oosterwegel, & Vollebergh, 2002). The broader social context also contributes (Bosma & Kunnen, 2001). Exploration takes time and access to resources, which may not be available to adolescents living in poverty (e.g., they can't explore because they drop out of school to support themselves and their family). Finally, through their personality, adolescents may affect the ease with which they achieve an identity. Individuals who are more open to experience and are more agreeable (friendly, generous, and helpful) are more likely to achieve an identity (Crocetti et al., 2008).

Ethnic Identity

Roughly one third of the adolescents and young adults living in the United States are members of ethnic minority groups, including African, Asian, Latino, and Native Americans. *These individuals typically develop an* **ethnic identity**: *They feel they are part of their ethnic group and learn the special customs and traditions of their group's culture and heritage* (Phinney, 2005).

Achieving an ethnic identity seems to occur in three phases (Phinney, 1989, p. 44). Initially, adolescents have not examined their ethnic roots, often due to lack of interest. In the second phase, adolescents like Dea (from the vignette) begin to explore the personal impact of their ethnic heritage. A teenage Mexican American girl in this stage said, "I want to know what we do and how our culture is different from others. Going to festivals and cultural events helps me to learn more about my own culture and about myself" (Phinney, 1989, p. 44). Part of this phase involves learning cultural traditions; for example, many adolescents learn to prepare ethnic food.

In the third phase, individuals achieve a distinct ethnic self-concept. One Asian American adolescent explained his ethnic identification like this: "I have been born Filipino and am born to be Filipino. I'm here in America, and people of many different cultures are here, too. So I don't consider myself only Filipino, but also American" (Phinney, 1989, p. 44).

Adolescents benefit from a strong ethnic identity; they tend to have higher self-esteem, to enjoy their interactions with family and friends more, and to be happier (Mandara et al., 2009; Roberts et al., 1999). In addition, adolescents with a strong ethnic identity do better in school and are more likely to go to college than adolescents whose ethnic identities are weaker (Altschul, Oyserman, & Bybee, 2006; Chavous et al., 2003).

Part of the search for an ethnic identity involves learning cultural traditions, such as learning how to prepare foods associated with one's ethnic group.

© David Young-Wolff/PhotoEdit

ethnic identity
the feeling of belonging to a specific ethnic group

Self-Esteem in Adolescence

Self-esteem is normally high in preschool children but declines gradually during the early elementary-school years as children compare themselves to others. By the beginning of adolescence, self-esteem has usually stabilized—it neither increases nor decreases in these years (Harter, Whitesell, & Kowalski, 1992). However, self-esteem sometimes drops when children move from elementary to middle or junior high school (Twenge & Campbell, 2001). Apparently, when students from different elementary schools enter the same middle or junior high school, they know where they stand compared to their old elementary-school classmates but not compared to students from other elementary schools. Thus, peer comparisons begin anew, and self-esteem often suffers temporarily. As a new school becomes familiar and students gradually adjust to the new pecking order, self-esteem again increases.

These changes in overall level of self-esteem are accompanied by another important change: Self-esteem becomes more differentiated as children enter adolescence (Boivin, Vitaro, & Gagnon, 1992). Youth are able to evaluate themselves in more domains as they develop, and their evaluations in each domain are increasingly independent. For example, a 9-year-old may have high self-esteem in the academic, social, and physical domains, but a 15-year-old might have high self-esteem in the academic domain, moderate self-esteem in the social domain, and low self-esteem in the physical domain.

During adolescence, the social component of self-esteem becomes particularly well differentiated. Adolescents distinguish self-worth in many different social relationships. A teenager may, for example, feel positive about her relationships with her parents but believe that she's a loser in romantic relationships (Harter, Waters, & Whitesell, 1998).

Influences on Adolescents' Self-Esteem

What factors contribute to adolescents' self-esteem? First, children's and adolescents' self-esteem is greater when they are skilled in areas they value. In other words, interests, abilities, and self-concept are coupled. Children tend to like domains in which they do well, and their self-concepts reflect this (Denissen, Zarret, & Eccles, 2007). Mark, who likes and gets good grades in math, has a positive math self-concept: "I'm good at math and do well when I have to learn something new in math. And I'd probably like a job that involved math."

Children's and adolescents' self-worth is also influenced by how others view them. Parents matter—even to adolescents. Children are more likely to view themselves positively when their parents are affectionate toward them and involved with them (Lord, Eccles, & McCarthy, 1994; Ojanen & Perry, 2007). Parents' discipline also counts. Children with high self-esteem generally have parents who have reasonable expectations for their children and are willing to discuss rules and discipline with their children (Laible & Carlo, 2004). Parents who fail to set rules are, in effect, telling their children that they don't care—they don't value them enough to go to the trouble of creating rules and enforcing them.

Peers' views are important too. Children's and particularly adolescents' self-worth is greater when they believe that their peers think highly of them (Molloy, Ram, & Gest, 2011). Maddy's self-worth increases, for example, when she hears that Pedro, Matt, and Michael think she's the hottest girl in the eighth grade.

Thus, children's and adolescents' self-worth depends on whether they are competent at something they value and are valued by people who are important to them. By encouraging children to find their special talents and by being genuinely interested in their progress, parents and teachers can enhance the self-esteem of all students.

The Myth of Storm and Stress

According to novelists and filmmakers, the search for identity that we've just described is inherently a struggle, a time of storm and stress for adolescents. Although this view may make for best-selling novels and hit movies, in reality the rebellious teen is vastly overstated. Adolescents generally enjoy happy and satisfying relationships with their parents (Steinberg, 2001). Most teens love their parents and feel loved by them. And they embrace many of their parents' values and look to them for advice (Güngör & Bornstein, 2010; Offer et al., 1988).

Parent–child relations do change during adolescence. As teens become more independent, their relationships with their parents become more egalitarian. Parents must adjust to their children's growing sense of autonomy by treating them more like equals (Laursen & Collins, 1994). This growing independence means that teens spend less time with their parents, are less affectionate toward them, and argue more often with them about matters of style, taste, and freedom (Shanahan et al., 2007). Adolescents have more disagreements with parents, but these disputes are usually relatively mild—bickering, not all-out shouting matches—and usually concern personal choices (e.g., hairstyle, clothing). These changes are natural by-products of an evolving parent–child relationship in which the "child" is nearly a fully independent young adult (Steinberg & Silk, 2002).

Before you think that this portrait of parent–child relationships in adolescence is too good to be true, recognize that for a minority of families (roughly 25%), parent–child conflicts in adolescence are more serious and are associated with behavior problems in adolescents (van Doorn, Branje, & Meeus, 2008). These more harmful conflicts are more common among adolescents who don't regulate their emotions well (Eisenberg et al., 2008), and they often predate adolescence—as children, these adolescents were prone to conflict with their parents (Steinberg, 2001).

Test Yourself

Recall

1. According to Erikson, adolescents face a crisis between identity and _____.

2. The _____ status would describe an adolescent who has attained an identity based almost entirely on her parents' advice and urging.

3. _____ refers to adolescents sometimes believing that their lives are a performance, with their peers watching them constantly.

4. Adolescents are most likely to achieve an identity when parents _____.

5. In the second phase of achieving an ethnic identity, adolescents _____.

6. Self-esteem often drops when students enter middle or junior high school because young adolescents _____.

Interpret

- Although Piaget's theory of cognitive development was not concerned with identity formation, how might his theory explain why identity is a central issue in adolescence?

- How do parent–child relationships change in adolescence? Do these changes indicate a period of storm and stress?

Apply

- The Tran family immigrated to the United States from Vietnam. The mother and father want their two children to grow up appreciating their Vietnamese heritage but worry that a strong ethnic identity may not be good for their kids. As a social worker helping the Tran family adjust to life in the U.S., what advice would you give Mr. and Mrs. Tran about the impact of ethnic identity on children's development?

- Jenny thinks she might like to be an engineer, but she also enjoys dance. To help decide what path would be best for her, Jenny has completed some interest inventories and her guidance counselor has suggested colleges at which she could pursue both engineering and dance. Which of the four statuses best describes Jenny, at least as far as a possible occupation is concerned?

Recall answers: (1) role confusion, (2) foreclosure, (3) Imaginary audience, (4) encourage them to explore alternative identities but do not pressure them or provide direction, (5) start to explore the personal impact of their ethnic roots, (6) no longer know where they stand among their peers, so they must establish a new pecking order.

LEARNING OBJECTIVES

- Why do teenagers date?
- Why are some adolescents sexually active? Why do so few use contraceptives?
- What determines an adolescent's sexual orientation?
- What circumstances make dating violence especially likely?

For 6 months, 15-year-old Gretchen has been dating Jeff, a 17-year-old. She thinks she is truly in love and imagines being married to Jeff. They have had sex a few times, each time without contraception. It sometimes crosses Gretchen's mind that if she gets pregnant she could move into her own apartment and begin a family.

© 2008 Radius Images/Jupiter Images

Adolescent romantic relationships build on friendships and offer companionship, as well as an outlet for sexual exploration.

The fires of romantic relationships have long warmed the hearts of American adolescents. Often, as with Jeff and Gretchen, romance leads to sex. In this section, we explore adolescent dating and sexual behavior. As we do, you'll better understand Gretchen's reasons for having unprotected sex with Jeff.

Romantic Relationships

The social landscape adds a distinctive landmark in adolescence—romantic relationships. These are uncommon during elementary school, but by high school roughly two thirds of U.S. adolescents have had a romantic relationship within the previous 1½ years and most have been involved in a romance lasting nearly a year (Carver, Joyner, & Udry, 2003). Romantic relationships build on friendships. Like friends, romantic partners tend to be similar in popularity and physical attractiveness. And a best friendship serves both as a prototype for and a source of support during ups and downs of close relationships (Collins, Welsh, & Furman, 2009). What's more, romantic relationships change over time in ways that resemble changes in friendship: for younger adolescents, romantic relationships offer companionship (like that provided by a best friend) and an outlet for sexual exploration. For older adolescents, intimacy, trust, and support become important features of romantic relationships (Shulman & Kipnis, 2001).

It's tempting to dismiss teen romances as nothing more than "puppy love," but they are often developmentally significant (Collins et al., 2009). On the one hand, adolescents involved in a romantic relationship are often more self-confident and have higher self-esteem. And high-quality adolescent romances are associated with positive relationships during adulthood. On the other hand, adolescents in romantic relationships report more emotional upheaval and conflict (Joyner & Udry, 2000). In addition, early dating with many partners is associated with a host of problems in adolescence (e.g., drug use and lower grades) and is associated with less satisfying romantic relationships in adulthood (Collins, 2003).

Sexual Behavior

We've already seen that sexual exploration is an important feature of romantic relationships for younger adolescents. By the end of high school, about two thirds of American adolescents will have had intercourse at least once (Eaton et al., 2008). No single factor predicts adolescent sexual behavior. Instead, adolescents are more likely

TABLE 9.2

Features of STDs

Disease	U.S. Frequency	Symptoms	Complications
Caused by bacteria			
Chlamydia	3.3% of adolescent females and 0.7% of adolescent males	75% of women and 50% of men have no symptoms; sometimes abnormal discharge of pus from the vagina or penis, pain while urinating	Infections of the cervix and Fallopian tubes that can lead to infertility; rare in men
Gonorrhea	0.6% of adolescent females and 0.3% of adolescent males	Often no symptoms; pus discharged from the penis or vagina, pain associated with urination; for women, pain during intercourse; for men, swollen testicles	Pelvic inflammatory disease, a serious infection of the female reproductive tract that can lead to infertility; epididymitis, an infection of the testicles that can lead to infertility
Syphilis	About 4,000 cases annually among 15- to 24-year-olds	A sore, called a chancre, at the site of infection—usually the penis, vulva, or vagina	If left untreated, can damage internal organs such as the brain, nerves, eyes, heart, bones, and joints
Caused by virus			
Genital herpes	At least 45 million age 12 and older (roughly 1 in 5 adolescents and adults)	Itching, burning, or pain in the genital or anal area; sores on the mouth, penis, or vagina	Recurrent sores; pregnant women can pass the virus (which can be fatal to a newborn) to the baby during birth
Genital human papilloma virus	About 20 million	Usually no symptoms; sometimes genital warts, discharge from the penis or vagina	Usually goes away; in rare cases leads to cervical cancer
Hepatitis B	About 75,000 annually	Jaundice, fatigue, loss of appetite, abdominal pain	Death from chronic liver disease
HIV	About 40,000 diagnosed annually	Initially a flulike illness; later, enlarged lymph nodes, lack of energy, weight loss, frequent fevers	Loss of immune cells (AIDS), cancer, death

SOURCE: Centers for Disease Control and Prevention, 2007b, 2010b.

to be sexually active when they acquire (from parents and peers) permissive attitudes toward sex, when their parents don't monitor their behavior, when their peers approve and they believe their peers are also having sex, when they are more physically mature, and when they drink alcohol regularly (Belsky et al., 2010; Hipwell et al., 2010; Zimmer-Gembeck & Helfand, 2008).

Although a majority of boys and girls have sex at some point during adolescence, sexual activity has different meanings for boys and girls (Brooks-Gunn & Paikoff, 1993). Girls tend to describe their first sexual partner as "someone they love," but boys describe their first partner as a "casual date." In other words, for boys, sexual behavior is viewed as recreational and self-oriented; for girls, sexual behavior is viewed as romantic and is interpreted through their capacity to form intimate interpersonal relationships (Steinberg, 1999; Walsh et al., 2011).

Sexually Transmitted Diseases

Adolescent sexual activity is cause for concern because a number of diseases are transmitted from one person to another through sexual intercourse. Table 9.2 lists several of the most common types of sexually transmitted diseases (STDs). Some STDs, such as chlamydia and syphilis, are caused by bacteria; others, such as herpes and hepatitis B, are caused by a virus.

Several STDs can have serious complications if left untreated. Most are cured readily with antibiotics. In contrast, the prognosis is bleak for individuals who contract the human immunodeficiency virus (HIV), which typically leads to acquired immunodeficiency syndrome (AIDS). In people with AIDS, the immune system is no longer able to protect the body from infections, and they often die from one of these infections.

Teenage Pregnancy and Contraception

Adolescents' sexual behavior is also troubling because, among American adolescent girls who have ever had intercourse, approximately one in six becomes pregnant. The result is that nearly a half million babies are born to American teenagers annually. African American and Hispanic American adolescents are the most likely to become pregnant (Ventura et al., 2008).

Teenage mothers and their children usually face bleak futures. If this is the case, why do so many teens become pregnant? The answer is simple: Only about half of teenagers use contraception when they first have intercourse, and about 10% of teens who are sexually active do not use contraception. Those who do often use ineffective methods, such as withdrawal, or practice contraception inconsistently (Besharov & Gardiner, 1997; Kirby, 2001).

Why don't some sexually active teens use birth control consistently or correctly? Several factors contribute (Gordon, 1996). First, many adolescents are ignorant of basic facts of conception, and many believe that they are invulnerable—that only others become pregnant. Second, some teenagers do not know how to use or where to obtain contraceptives, and others are embarrassed to buy them (Ralph & Brindis, 2010). Third, for some adolescent girls, like Gretchen from the opening vignette, becoming pregnant is appealing (Phipps et al., 2008). They think having a child is a way to break away from parents, gain status as an independent-living adult, and have "someone to love them."

The best way to reduce adolescent sexual behavior and teen pregnancy is with comprehensive sex education programs (Kirby & Laris, 2009). These programs teach the biological aspects of sex and emphasize responsible sexual behavior or abstaining from premarital sex. They also include discussions of the pressures to become involved sexually and ways to respond to this pressure. A key element is that in role-playing sessions, students practice strategies for refusing to have sex. Youth who participate in programs like these are less likely to have intercourse; when they do have intercourse, they are more likely to use contraceptives. In contrast, there is little evidence that programs focusing solely on abstinence are effective in reducing sexual activity or encouraging contraceptive use.

HUMAN DEVELOPMENT in action

Suppose that you were a school nurse. What would you say to high-school freshmen about the hazards of adolescent sex and teenage pregnancy?

Sexual Orientation

For most adolescents, dating and romance involve members of the opposite sex. However, in early and midadolescence, roughly 15% of teens experience a period of sexual questioning, during which they sometimes report emotional and sexual attractions to members of their own sex (Carver, Egan, & Perry, 2004). For most adolescents, these experiences are simply a part of the larger process of role experimentation common to adolescence. However, about 5% of teenage boys and girls identify their sexual orientation as gay or lesbian (Rotherman-Borus & Langabeer, 2001).

The roots of sexual orientation are poorly understood, but modern theories suggest that attraction to same-sex individuals comes about differently in males and in females (Diamond, 2007). For males, genes and hormones may lead some boys to feel "different" during early adolescence; these feelings lead to an interest in gender-atypical activities and, later, attraction to other males. For females, the path to same-sex attraction is less predictable. Attraction to other females usually does not emerge until mid- or late adolescence and, in some cases, not until middle or old age. What's more, for many lesbian women, same-sex attraction grows out of deep feelings for a particular woman that, over time, extends to other females.

Gay and lesbian adolescents face many challenges. Their family and peer relationships are often disrupted, and they endure verbal and physical attacks (Heatherington & Lavner, 2008). Given these problems, it's not surprising that gay and lesbian youth often experience mental health problems (Toomey et al., 2010) and are at risk for substance abuse (Marshal et al., 2008). In recent years, social changes have helped gay and lesbian youth respond more effectively to these challenges, including more (and more visible) role models and more centers for gay and lesbian youth. These resources are making it easier for gay and lesbian youth to understand their sexual orientation and to cope with the many other demands of adolescence.

About 5% of adolescents identify themselves as gay or lesbian.

Dating Violence

As adolescents begin to explore romantic relationships and sex, many teens experience violence in dating, which can include physical violence (e.g., being hit or kicked), emotional violence (e.g., threats or bullying), or sexual violence (being forced to engage in sexual activity against one's will). Roughly 25% of adolescents report these experiences, and as you can imagine, these youth often don't do well in school and frequently have mental health and behavioral problems (Centers for Disease Control and Prevention, 2008).

Of the various kinds of dating violence, scientists know the most about factors that place adolescents at risk for sexual violence. One of the most important factors is drug and alcohol use: Heavy drinking usually impairs a female's ability to send a clear message regarding her intentions and makes males less able and less inclined to interpret such messages (Maurer & Robinson, 2008; Reyes et al., 2011). Females are also more at risk when they adhere to more traditional gender stereotypes, apparently because their view of the female gender role includes being relatively submissive to a male's desires (Foshee et al., 2004).

What factors make teenage boys likely to commit acts of violence? The Spotlight on Research feature has some answers.

Spotlight on research — Why Are Some Boys More Likely to Perpetrate Dating Violence?

Who were the investigators, and what was the aim of the study?
Vangie Foshee and her colleagues (2001) designed a study to determine why some teenage boys are more likely than others to perpetrate violence while on a date.

How did the investigators measure the topic of interest?
The investigators measured dating violence by asking teenage boys whether they had ever committed any of 18 violent acts while on a date, including hitting, choking, slapping, or kicking a partner or forcing a partner to have sex. In addition, several other questionnaires were created that measured factors that might make a boy more at risk for perpetrating dating violence, including peers' behaviors, other problem behaviors (e.g., drinking), and personal competencies (e.g., self-esteem, communication skills).

Who were the participants in the study?
The study included 576 boys in eighth and ninth grades who reported that they had begun dating.

What was the design of the study?
This study was correlational because the investigators were interested in the relations that existed naturally between boys' perpetration of violence and other variables that might be related to perpetration of violence. The study was longitudinal because adolescents were tested first in eighth or ninth grade and then a second time about 18 months later. For simplicity, we describe only the results from the first testing.

Were there ethical concerns with the study?
Yes. Violence is a sensitive topic, and the investigators were careful to be sure that they obtained consent from parents and adolescents and that the adolescents' responses were confidential.

What were the results?
Most boys said that they had never perpetrated dating violence. However, 10% said that they had used one of the milder forms (e.g., slapped,

pushed), and 4% said that they had used one of the more severe forms (e.g., choked, burned, assaulted with a gun or knife). Personal competence was not related to dating violence, but two factors were linked. One was alcohol use: Boys were 1.3 times more likely to perpetrate violence if they reported frequent use of alcohol. The second was having a friend who had perpetrated dating violence: Boys were 3.6 times more likely to perpetrate violence if they had a friend who had perpetrated violence.

What did the investigators conclude?
Some boys represent a greater risk for dating violence. Boys are more likely to perpetrate violence when they drink, which parallels the finding that girls are more likely to be victims when they drink. Drinking and dating are clearly an extremely dangerous mix. Second, boys more often perpetrate violence when they believe that their friends are doing the same. As we saw in Chapter 7, friends can be powerful forces for good or for bad.

What converging evidence would strengthen these conclusions?
The main limitation of the study concerns the source of the data—questionnaires completed by the boys themselves. The results hinge on the assumption that adolescent boys' reports are accurate, and there's good reason to doubt the accuracy of these reports. Clearly, some boys may be reluctant to admit that they've been violent on a date. These findings would be more compelling if there were converging information from another source about frequency of violence during dating. For example, boys and girls who are actively dating could each complete questionnaires, and researchers could compare the boy's responses to questions about perpetration of violence with the girl's responses to questions about being a victim.

 Go to Psychology CourseMate at **www.cengagebrain.com** to enhance your understanding of this research.

One effective program for reducing sexual violence is Safe Dates (Foshee & Langwick, 2004). Targeted for middle- and high-school students, the program features a brief play, 9-hour-long interactive sessions devoted to topics such as overcoming gender stereotypes and how to prevent sexual assault, and a poster contest. Teens who participate in Safe Date are less likely to be victims of sexual violence and are less likely to perpetrate it (Foshee et al., 2004).

Test Yourself

Recall

1. For younger adolescents, romantic relationships offer companionship and _____.

2. When parents do not approve of sex, their adolescent children are _____.

3. Adolescents often fail to use contraception because they are ignorant of the facts of conception, are attracted to becoming pregnant, and _____.

4. For some boys, the first step toward a gay sexual orientation occurs in early adolescence, when they feel different and are interested in gender-atypical activities; in contrast, for girls, the first step toward a lesbian sexual orientation often grows out of _____.

5. A girl is more likely to be a victim of sexual violence if she has been drinking and if she _____.

Interpret

- What factors lead boys to perpetrate dating violence? Would some of these be more likely in early, middle, and late adolescence?

- Some sexually active teenagers do not use contraceptives. How do the reasons for this failure show connections among cognitive, social, and emotional development?

Apply

- How might the stages of ethnic identity be used to describe the processes by which adolescents identify their sexual orientation as gay or lesbian?

- Harmony's 15-year-old son Brett has just begun dating. Harmony wonders if this represents an important developmental milestone. As a developmental psychologist, what would you tell her?

Recall answers: (1) an outlet for sexual exploration, (2) less likely to be active sexually, (3) don't know where to get contraceptives (or how to use them), (4) strong attraction to one particular female, (5) holds traditional views of gender roles

---

9.3 The World of Work

LEARNING OBJECTIVES

- How do adolescents select an occupation?

- What is the impact of part-time employment on adolescents?

When 15-year-old Aaron announced that he wanted an after-school job at the local supermarket, his mother was delighted, believing that he would learn much from the experience. Five months later, she had her doubts. Aaron had lost interest in school, and they argued constantly about how he spent his money.

"What do you want to be when you grow up?" Children are often asked this question in fun. Beginning in adolescence, however, it takes on special significance because work is such an important element of the adult life that is looming on the horizon. In this section, we'll see how adolescents begin to think about possible occupations. We also look at adolescents' first exposure to the world of work, which usually occurs in the form of part-time jobs like Aaron's.

In the specification stage of career development, adolescents try to learn more about different careers, sometimes by serving as an apprentice.

© Mark Richards/PhotoEdit

Career Development

In most developed nations, adolescence is a time when youth face the challenge of selecting a career. According to a theory proposed by Donald Super identity is a primary force in an adolescent's choice of a career (Super, 1976, 1980). *At about age 13 or 14, adolescents use their emerging identity as a source of ideas about careers, a process called* **crystallization**. Teenagers use their ideas about their own talents and interests to limit potential career prospects. A teenager who is extroverted and sociable may decide that working with people would be the career for him. Decisions are provisional, and adolescents experiment with hypothetical careers, trying to envision what each might be like.

At about age 18, adolescents enter a new phase. *During* **specification**, *individuals further limit their career possibilities by learning more about specific lines of work and by starting to obtain the training required for a specific job.* The extroverted teenager who wants to work with people may decide he's well suited for a career in sales. The teen who likes math may have learned more about careers and decided she'd like to be an accountant. Some teens may begin an apprenticeship as a way to learn a trade.

The end of the teenage years or the early 20s marks the beginning of the third phase. *During* **implementation**, *individuals enter the workforce and learn firsthand about jobs.* This is a time of learning about responsibility and productivity, of learning to get along with co-workers, and of altering lifestyle to accommodate work. This period is often unstable; individuals may change jobs frequently as they adjust to the reality of life in the workplace.

The Real People feature shows these three phases in one young woman's career development.

crystallization
the first phase in Super's theory of career development, in which adolescents use their emerging identities to form ideas about careers

specification
the second phase in Super's theory of career development, in which adolescents learn more about specific lines of work and begin training

implementation
the third phase in Super's theory of career development, in which individuals enter the workforce

---

real People
APPLYING HUMAN DEVELOPMENT
THE LIFE OF LYNNE: A DRAMA IN THREE ACTS

Act 1: Crystallization. In high school, Lynne was treasurer of several school organizations and found it satisfying to keep the financial records in order. By the end of her junior year, Lynne decided that she wanted to study business in college, a decision that fit with her good grades in English and math.

Act 2: Specification. Lynne was accepted into the business school of a state university.

She decided that accounting fit her skills and temperament, so this became her major. During the summers, she worked as a cashier at Target. This helped pay for college and gave her experience in the world of retail sales.

Act 3: Implementation. A few months after graduation, Lynne was offered a junior accounting position with Walmart. Her job required that she work Tuesday through Friday,

auditing Walmart stores in several nearby cities. Lynne liked the pay, the company car, the feeling of independence, and especially the pay. However, she often found it awkward to deal with store managers, many of whom were twice her age and rather intimidating. She was coming to the conclusion that there was more to a successful career as an accountant than simply having the numbers add up correctly.

Personality Types in Holland's Theory

Personality Type	Description	Careers
Realistic	Individuals enjoy physical labor and working with their hands; they like to solve concrete problems.	Mechanic, truck driver, construction worker
Investigative	Individuals are task oriented and enjoy thinking about abstract relations.	Scientist, technical writer
Social	Individuals are skilled verbally and interpersonally; they enjoy solving problems using these skills.	Teacher, counselor, social worker
Conventional	Individuals have verbal and quantitative skills that they like to apply to structured, well-defined tasks assigned to them by others.	Bank teller, payroll clerk, traffic manager
Enterprising	Individuals enjoy using their verbal skills in positions of power, status, and leadership.	Business executive, television producer, real estate agent
Artistic	Individuals enjoy expressing themselves through unstructured tasks.	Poet, musician, actor

Fuse/Getty Images

According to Holland's personality-type theory, people are satisfied with a job when it matches their personality; for example, adolescents with an enterprising personality type enjoy working in business because this allows them to use verbal skills in positions of leadership.

personality-type theory
the view proposed by Holland that people find their work fulfilling when the important features of a job or profession fit the worker's personality

The Life of Lynne illustrates the progressive refinement that takes place in a person's career development. An initial interest in math and finance led to a degree in business, which led to a job as an accountant, with its accompanying upsides and downsides.

Personality-Type Theory

Super's (1976, 1980) work helps explain how self-concept and career aspirations develop hand in hand, but his theory of vocational choice does not explain why particular individuals are attracted to a specific line of work. Explaining the match between people and occupations has been the aim of a theory devised by John Holland (1985, 1987, 1996). *According to Holland's* **personality-type theory**, *people find work fulfilling when the important features of a job or profession fit the worker's personality.* Holland identified six prototypic personalities that are relevant to the world of work. Each one is best suited to a specific set of occupations, as indicated in the right-hand column of Table 9.3. Remember, these are merely prototypes. Most people do not match any one personality type exactly. Instead, their work-related personalities are a blend of the six.

This model is useful in describing the career preferences of African, Asian, European, Native, and Latino American adolescents (Gupta, Tracey, & Gore, 2008). When people have jobs that match their personality type, they are more productive employees and have more stable career paths (Holland, 1996). For example, an enterprising youth is likely to be successful in business because he enjoys positions of power in which he can use his verbal skills.

There's more to job satisfaction than the match between personality type and important features of a job. Even when people are well matched to a job, some find the work more satisfying than others because of a host of factors, including pay, stress in the workplace, and frequency of conflicts between work and family obligations (Hammer et al., 2005). Nevertheless, the person–job match is a good place to start thinking about a vocation.

Combining Holland's work-related personality types with Super's theory of career development gives us a comprehensive picture of vocational growth. While Super's theory explains the developmental progression by which individuals translate general interests into a specific career, Holland's theory explains what makes a good match between specific interests and specific careers.

When adolescents work long hours in a part-time job, they often have trouble juggling the demands of work, school, and sleep.

© Digital Vision/Jupiter Images

Part-Time Employment

Today, about 25% of high-school freshmen have a part-time job, and about 75% of high-school seniors do (Bachman et al., 2011). About two thirds of these youth work in retail, and half of those working in retail are employed in the food and beverage industry (U.S. Department of Labor, 2000).

Most adults praise teens for working, believing that early exposure to the workplace teaches adolescents self-discipline, self-confidence, and important job skills (Snedeker, 1982). For most adolescents, however, the reality is quite different. Part-time work can be harmful, for several reasons.

- *School performance suffers.* When students work more than approximately 20 hours per week, they become less engaged in school and are less likely to be successful in college (Bachman et al., 2011; Monahan, Lee, & Steinberg, 2011).

- *Mental health and behavioral problems.* Adolescents who work long hours—more than 15 or 20 hours a week—are more likely to experience anxiety and depression, and their self-esteem often suffers. Many adolescents find themselves in jobs that are repetitive and boring but stressful, and such conditions undermine self-esteem and breed anxiety. Extensive part-time work frequently leads to substance abuse and frequent problem behavior, such as theft and cheating in school (Monahan et al., 2011).

- *Misleading affluence.* Working adolescents spend most of their earnings on themselves: to buy clothing, snack food, or cosmetics and to pay for entertainment. Few working teens set aside much of their income for future goals, such as a college education, or use it to contribute to their family's expenses (Shanahan et al., 1996b). Thus, for many teens the part-time work experience provides unrealistic expectations about how income can be allocated (Darling et al., 2006; Zhang, Cartmill, & Ferrence, 2008).

The message that emerges repeatedly from research on part-time employment is hardly encouraging. Like Aaron, the teenage boy in the vignette, adolescents who work long hours at part-time jobs do not benefit from the experience. However, part-time employment can be a good experience when students limit the number of hours of work. Most students could easily work 5 hours weekly without harm, and many could work 10 hours weekly. Also, part-time work can be valuable when adolescents have jobs that allow them to use their skills (e.g., bookkeeping, computing, or typing) and acquire new ones: their self-esteem is enhanced, and they learn from their work experience (Staff & Schulenberg, 2010; Vazsonyi & Snider, 2008). Yet another factor is how teens spend their earnings. When they save their money or

HUMAN DEVELOPMENT in action

Suppose that you are a high-school guidance counselor and have been asked to prepare a set of guidelines for students who want to work part time. What would you recommend?

use it to pay for clothes and school expenses, their parent–child relationships often improve (Shanahan et al., 1996a).

Finally, summer jobs typically do not involve conflict between work and school. Consequently, many of the harmful effects associated with part-time employment during the school year do not hold for summer employment. Such employment sometimes enhances adolescents' self-esteem, especially when they save part of their income for future plans (Marsh, 1991).

Test Yourself

Recall

1. During the _____ phase of vocational choice, adolescents learn more about specific lines of work and begin training.

2. Individuals with a(n) _____ personality type are best suited for a career as a teacher or counselor.

3. Adolescents who work extensively at part-time jobs during the school year often get lower grades, have behavior problems, and _____.

4. Part-time employment during the school year can be beneficial if adolescents limit the number of hours they work and _____.

Interpret

- Based on the description of Lynne's career, how would you describe continuity of vocational development during adolescence and young adulthood?

- How do the personality types in Holland's theory relate to the types of intelligence proposed by Howard Gardner, described in Chapter 6?

Apply

- Teenage Lee Ann is outgoing and talkative and gets along well with her peers. They often ask her advice about school and relationships, and she enjoys providing it. According to Holland's theory, what is Lee Ann's personality type? What careers would be a good match for her?

- Aaron (from the vignette) is adamant about keeping a part-time job, but his mom wants the arguments to stop and his grades to improve. Suppose that you are a family therapist and that they are your clients; what changes would you suggest to them?

Recall answers: (1) specification, (2) social, (3) experience misleading affluence, (4) hold jobs that allow them to use and develop skills

---

9.4 | The Dark Side

LEARNING OBJECTIVES

- Why do teenagers drink and use drugs?

- What leads some adolescents to become depressed? How can depression be treated?

- What are the causes of juvenile delinquency?

Rod was looking forward to going to the senior prom with Peggy, his long-time girlfriend, and then going to the college with her in the fall. Then, without a hint that anything was wrong in their relationship, Peggy dropped Rod and moved in with the drummer of a local rock band. Rod was stunned and miserable. Without Peggy, life meant so little. Some days Rod wondered whether he should just kill himself to make the pain go away.

Some young people do not adapt well to the new demands and responsibilities of adolescence and respond in ways that are unhealthy. In this last section of this chapter, we look at three problems, often interrelated, that create the "three Ds" of adolescent development: drug use, depression, and delinquency. As we look at these problems, you'll understand why Rod feels so miserable without Peggy.

Adolescents often drink because peers encourage them to.

Drug Use

Teenage Drinking

Teen use of illicit drugs like cocaine and methamphetamine often makes headlines, but in reality most adolescents avoid drugs, with one glaring exception—alcohol. About two thirds of U.S. high-school seniors have drunk alcohol within the past year, and nearly half report that they've been drunk (Johnston et al., 2011).

Teens are more likely to drink (1) when drinking is an important part of parents' social lives—for example, stopping at a bar after work—and (2) when parents are relatively uninvolved in their teenager's life or set arbitrary or unreasonable standards for their teens (Reesman & Hogan, 2005). Also, they're more likely to drink when peers do. Finally, teens who report frequent life stresses—problems with parents, with interpersonal relationships, or at school—more often drink (Chassin et al., 2003).

Because teenage drinking has many causes, no single approach can eliminate alcohol abuse. Adolescents who drink to reduce their tension can profit from therapy designed to teach them more effective means of coping with stress. School-based programs that are interactive—featuring student-led discussion—can be effective in teaching the facts about drinking and strategies for resisting peer pressure to drink (Caria et al., 2011; Longshore et al., 2007). Stopping teens from drinking before it becomes habitual is essential because adolescents who drink are at risk for becoming alcohol dependent, depressed, or anxious as adults (Cable & Sacker, 2008; Trim et al., 2007).

Teenage Smoking

Approximately one third of American teens experiment with cigarette smoking at some point in their teenage years (Johnston et al., 2011). As was true for teenage drinking, parents and peers are influential in determining whether youth smoke. When parents smoke, their teenage children are more likely to smoke too. But the parent–child relationship also contributes: Teens are less likely to smoke when they experience supportive parenting (Foster et al., 2007). Like parents, peer influences can be direct and indirect. Teenagers more often smoke when their friends do and when the school norm approves of smoking (Kumar et al., 2002; Mercken et al., 2007).

Because teenage smoking leads to health problems, several school-based programs have been created to reduce teenage smoking (U.S. Department of Health and Human Services, 2000). In these programs, schools have no-smoking policies for all students, staff, and school visitors. In addition, students learn the health and social consequences of smoking and effective ways to respond to peer pressure to smoke.

Depression

The challenges of adolescence can lead some youth to become depressed (Fried, 2005). *When suffering from* **depression**, *adolescents have pervasive feelings of sadness, are irritable, have low self-esteem, sleep poorly, and are unable to concentrate.* About 5 to 15% of adolescents are depressed; adolescent girls are more often affected than boys, probably because social challenges in adolescence are often greater for girls than for boys (Dekker et al., 2007; Hammen & Rudolph, 2003).

Research reveals that unhappiness, anger, and irritation often dominate the lives of depressed adolescents. They believe that family members, friends, and classmates are not friendly to them (Cole & Jordan, 1995), and they are often extremely lonely (Mahon et al., 2006). Rather than being satisfying and rewarding, life is empty and joyless for depressed adolescents.

Depression is often triggered when adolescents experience a serious loss, disappointment, or failure, such as when a loved one dies or a much-anticipated date turns

depression
a disorder characterized by pervasive feelings of sadness, irritability, and low self-esteem

Adolescents sometimes become depressed when they feel as if they've lost control of their lives.

out to be a fiasco (Schneiders et al., 2006). Think back to Rod, the adolescent in the vignette at the beginning of this section. His girlfriend had been the center of his life. When she left him unexpectedly, he felt helpless to control his destiny.

Many adolescents experience negative events like these, but most don't become depressed. Why? One contributing factor is temperament: Children who are less able to regulate their emotions are, as adolescents, more prone to depression (Karevold et al., 2009). Another factor is a belief system in which adolescents see themselves in an extremely negative light. Depression-prone adolescents are, for example, more likely to blame themselves for failure (Cole et al., 2011). Thus, after the disappointing date, a depression-prone teen is likely to think, "I acted like a fool," instead of placing blame elsewhere by thinking, "Gee. He was a real jerk!"

Parents and families can also put an adolescent at risk for depression. Not surprisingly, adolescents more often become depressed when their parents are emotionally distant and uninvolved and when family life is stressful due to economic disadvantage or marital conflict (Karevold et al., 2009; Yap, Allen, & Ladouceur, 2008). And because African American and Hispanic American adolescents more often live in poverty, they're more often depressed (Brown, Meadows, & Elder, 2007). Finally, when parents rely on punitive discipline—hitting and shouting—adolescents often resort to the negative attributions (e.g., blaming themselves) that can lead to depression (Lau et al., 2007).

Heredity also plays a role, putting some adolescents at greater risk for depression (Haeffel et al., 2008). Neurotransmitters may be the underlying mechanism: Some adolescents may feel depressed because lower levels of neurotransmitters make it difficult for them to experience happiness, joy, and other pleasurable emotions (Kaufman & Charney, 2003).

Treating Depression

To treat depression, some adolescents take antidepressant drugs designed to correct the imbalance in neurotransmitters. However, drug treatment has no lasting effects—it only works while people are taking the drugs—and it has been linked to increased risk of suicide (Vitiello & Swedo, 2004). Consequently, psychotherapy is a better choice for treating depressed adolescents. One common approach emphasizes cognitive and social skills—adolescents learn how to have rewarding social interactions and to interpret them appropriately. These treatments are effective (Weisz, McCarty, & Valeri, 2006), and depressed adolescents do need help; left untreated, depression can interfere with performance in school and social relationships and may lead to recurring depression in adulthood (Nevid et al., 2003; Rudolph, Ladd, & Dinella, 2007).

Preventing Teen Suicides

Roughly 10% of adolescents report having attempted suicide at least once, but only 1 in 10,000 commits suicide. Suicide is most frequent in older adolescent boys, particularly among Native American teenage boys (Anderson & Smith, 2005).

Depression is one frequent precursor of suicide; substance abuse is another (Nrugham, Larsson, & Sund, 2008; Renaud et al., 2008). Few suicides are truly spontaneous; in most cases, there are warning signals (Atwater, 1992), including threats of suicide, preoccupation with death, and loss of interest in activities that were once important. When teens show these symptoms, they should not be ignored. Instead, someone should stay with the teen, who should seek professional help. Therapy is essential to treating the feelings of depression and hopelessness that give rise to thoughts of suicide (Capuzzi & Gross, 2004).

Delinquency

Adolescents are responsible for much of the criminal activity committed in the United States (Federal Bureau of Investigation, 2010). *Some of this activity is relatively mild:* **Adolescent-limited antisocial behavior** *refers to relatively minor criminal acts by adolescents who aren't consistently antisocial.* These youth may become involved in petty crimes, such as shoplifting or using drugs, but may be careful to follow all school rules. As the name implies, their antisocial behavior is short lived, usually vanishing in late adolescence or early adulthood (Moffitt, 1993; Moffitt & Caspi, 2005).

A second form of delinquent behavior is far more serious and, fortunately, much less common. **Life-course persistent antisocial behavior** *refers to antisocial behavior that emerges at an early age and continues throughout life.* These individuals may start with hitting at 3 years of age and progress to shoplifting at age 12 and then to car theft at age 16 (Odgers et al., 2008). Perhaps only 5% of youth fit this pattern of antisocial behavior, but they account for most adolescent criminal activity.

Researchers have identified several forces that contribute to this type of antisocial and delinquent behavior (Vitulano, 2005). Twin studies make it clear that heredity contributes: Identical twins are usually more alike in their levels of physical aggression than are fraternal twins (Brendgen et al., 2006). Some children apparently inherit factors that place them at risk for aggressive or violent behavior, such as temperament: Youngsters who are temperamentally difficult, overly emotional, or inattentive are, for example, more likely to be aggressive (Joussemet et al., 2008; Xu, Farver, & Zhang, 2009).

Cognitive skills also play a role in antisocial behavior. Adolescent boys often respond aggressively because they are not skilled at interpreting other people's intentions. Without a clear interpretation in mind, they respond aggressively by default. That is, aggressive boys far too often think, "I don't know what you're up to, and when in doubt, attack" (Crick & Dodge, 1994; Crozier et al., 2008; Fontaine et al., 2009). Antisocial adolescents are often inclined to act impulsively, and they often are unable or unwilling to postpone pleasure (Fontaine, 2007). Seeing a new iPad or a car, delinquent youth are tempted to steal it simply so that they can have it right now. When others inadvertently get in their way, delinquent adolescents often respond without regard to the nature of the other person's acts or intentions.

Antisocial behavior is often related to inadequate parenting. Adolescents are more likely to become involved in delinquent acts when their parents use harsh discipline or don't monitor effectively (Patterson, 2008; Vieno et al., 2009). Parents may also contribute to delinquent behavior if their marital relationship is marked by constant conflict. When parents constantly argue and fight, their children are more likely to be antisocial (Cummings et al., 2006; Feldman, Masalha, & Derdikman-Eiron, 2010).

Aggressive and antisocial behavior is more common among children living in poverty than among children who are economically advantaged (Williams, Conger, & Blozis, 2007). Living in poverty is extremely stressful for parents and often leads to the very parental behaviors that promote aggression—harsh discipline and lax monitoring (Tolan, Gorman-Smith, & Henry, 2003). In addition, children living in poverty-stricken neighborhoods are more often exposed to violence, and such exposure leads to antisocial behavior (Bingenheimer, Brennan, & Earls, 2005).

Many factors contribute to make some adolescents prone to violent behavior. As you can imagine, when risk factors mount up in children's lives, they are at ever-greater risk for aggressive behavior (Greenberg et al., 1999). Efforts to prevent children from taking a developmental path that leads to antisocial behavior in adolescence begin early. One successful intervention program is Fast Track (Conduct Problems Prevention Research Group, 2011), which is designed to teach academic and social skills to elementary-school children plus life and vocational skills to adolescents. In addition,

© Image Source/Age Fotostock

Aggressive teens see the world as a hostile place and typically respond aggressively by default.

HUMAN DEVELOPMENT in action

Imagine that you are a social worker. Plan a workshop for law-enforcement officials in which you describe the factors that predispose some adolescents to antisocial behavior.

adolescent-limited antisocial behavior
behavior of youth who engage in relatively minor criminal acts but aren't consistently antisocial

life-course persistent antisocial behavior
antisocial behavior that emerges at an early age and continues throughout life

parents are taught skills for effective childrearing and, later, how to stay involved with their children and to monitor their behavior. At 12th grade—2 years after the program had ended—aggressive and destructive behavior among children who were at highest risk in kindergarten was cut in half compared to similar high-risk children assigned to a control condition.

In the Linking Research to Life feature, we show how human development research has been used to decide appropriate punishment for adolescent offenders.

Test Yourself

Recall

1. The main factors that determine whether teenagers drink include parents, peers, and _____.

2. Peers influence teenage smoking indirectly by _____.

3. Depression can be triggered when adolescents experience negative events (e.g., a loss) and they are unable to regulate their emotions or they _____.

4. Treatments for depression include drugs that correct imbalances in neurotransmitters and therapy that emphasizes _____.

5. _____ refers to antisocial behavior that begins at an early age and continues throughout life.

6. The factors that contribute to juvenile delinquency include biology, cognitive processes, _____, and poverty.

Interpret

- Describe potential biological and environmental contributions to delinquency.

- How does depression illustrate the interaction of biological, psychological, and sociocultural forces on development?

Apply

- Imagine you are a school counselor. Prepare a fact sheet that middle schools could use with antisocial adolescents to educate them about ways to resolve conflicts and achieve goals without relying on aggression.

- A letter to the editor of your local paper claims that "juvenile delinquents should be thrown in jail because they're born as 'bad apples' and will always be that way." Write a reply that states the facts as you understand them.

Linking Research to life · PROHIBITING CAPITAL PUNISHMENT FOR ADOLESCENTS

Capital punishment—executing a convicted offender—has been practiced throughout U.S. history—and not just with adults: Eight American children age 12 or younger have been executed for crimes, and as recently as 1944 a 14-year-old boy was electrocuted (Banner, 2005). In the late 1980s, the U.S. Supreme Court banned the use of capital punishment with juveniles who were not yet 16 years old when they committed the capital offense (*Thompson v. Oklahoma*, 487 U.S. 815 (1988)) but upheld its use with juveniles who were at least 16 years old at the time of the crime (*Stanford v. Kentucky*, 492 U.S. 361 (1989)).

This changed with a case heard before the court in 2004. A 17-year-old boy had murdered a woman by tying her up and throwing her into a river to drown. The boy confessed to the crime; a jury found him guilty and recommended the death sentence, which the judge imposed.

The boy appealed the death sentence, and the case eventually ended up with the U.S. Supreme Court. The American Psychological Association filed an amicus curiae ("friend of the court") brief arguing that the death sentence for crimes committed as an adolescent constituted cruel and unusual punishment (American Psychological Association, 2004). The brief argued that due to their immature brain development (described on pages 221–222), adolescents are more impulsive, risk prone, and less able than adults to anticipate the consequences of their actions. It was also argued that adolescents are more vulnerable than adults to peer pressure and less capable than adults of contributing to their own defense. The court cited these arguments in deciding, by a 5-4 vote, that capital punishment of adolescents created cruel and unusual punishment (*Roper v. Simmons*, 543 U.S. 551(2005)).

The court's decision means that states can no longer execute juveniles who are younger than 18 years when they commit a crime. Yet important questions remain. What sentences are appropriate for adolescents? Some adolescents are more mature in their reasoning; might we be able to assess such maturity and decide whether some adolescents should be held accountable for their actions in the same way that an adult is held accountable? What do you think?

Summary

9.1 Identity and Self-Esteem

How do adolescents achieve an identity?

- The task for adolescents is to find an identity, a search that typically involves four statuses: Diffusion and foreclosure are more common in early adolescence; moratorium and achievement are more common in late adolescence and young adulthood. As they seek identity, adolescents often believe that others are always watching them and that no one else has felt as they do.

- Adolescents are more likely to achieve an identity when parents encourage discussion and recognize their autonomy; they are least likely to achieve an identity when parents set rules and enforce them without explanation.

What are the stages and results of acquiring an ethnic identity?

- Adolescents from ethnic groups often progress through three phases in acquiring an ethnic identity: initial disinterest, exploration, and identity achievement. Achieving an ethnic identity usually results in higher self-esteem.

How does self-esteem change in adolescence?

- Social comparisons begin anew when children move from elementary to middle or junior high school; consequently, self-esteem usually declines somewhat during this transition. However, self-esteem begins to rise in middle and late adolescence as teenagers see themselves acquiring more adult skills and responsibilities. Self-esteem is linked to adolescents' competence in domains that matter to them and to how parents and peers view them.

- The parent–child relationship becomes more egalitarian during the adolescent years, reflecting adolescents' growing independence. Contrary to myth, adolescence is not usually a period of storm and stress. Most adolescents love their parents, feel loved by them, rely on them for advice, and adopt their values.

9.2 Romantic Relationships and Sexuality

Why do teenagers date?

- Romantic relationships emerge in midadolescence. For younger adolescents, dating is for both companionship and sexual exploration; for older adolescents, it is a source of trust and support. Adolescents in romantic relationships are more self-confident but also report more emotional upheaval.

Why are some adolescents sexually active? Why do so few use contraceptives?

- By the end of adolescence, most American boys and girls have had sexual intercourse, which boys view as recreational but girls see as romantic. Adolescents are more likely to be sexually active if they believe that their parents and peers approve of sex. Adolescents do not use birth control consistently because they do not understand conception, don't know where to obtain contraceptives, and sometimes find pregnancy appealing. Because they use contraception infrequently, they are at risk for sexually transmitted diseases and becoming pregnant.

What determines an adolescent's sexual orientation?

- A small percentage of adolescents are attracted to members of their own sex. Attraction to same-sex individuals follows a different path in boys and girls. For boys, the first step usually involves feeling different and becoming interested in gender-atypical activities. In contrast, for girls, the first step often involves strong feelings toward one particular female. Gay and lesbian youth face many special challenges and thus often experience mental health problems.

What circumstances make dating violence especially likely?

- Many adolescents experience dating violence, and teenage girls are sometimes forced into sex against their will. Girls are more likely to be victims of sexual violence when they've been drinking and when they hold traditional views of gender. Boys are more likely to perpetrate violence when they drink and when their friends perpetrate sexual violence.

9.3 The World of Work

How do adolescents select an occupation?

- In his theory of vocational choice, Super proposes three phases of vocational development during adolescence and young adulthood: crystallization, in which basic interests are identified; specification, in which jobs associated with interests are identified; and implementation, which marks entry into the workforce.

- Holland proposes six work-related personalities: realistic, investigative, social, conventional, enterprising, and artistic. Each is uniquely suited to certain jobs. People are happier when their personality fits their job and less happy when it does not.

What is the impact of part-time employment on adolescents?

- Most adolescents in the United States have part-time jobs. Adolescents who are employed more than 15 hours per week during the school year typically do poorly in school and often have mental health and behavioral problems. Employed adolescents spend most of their income on clothing, food, and their entertainment, which can yield misleading expectations about how to allocate income.

- Part-time employment can be beneficial if adolescents work relatively few hours, if the work allows them to use existing skills or acquire new ones, and if teens save some of their earnings. Summer employment, which does not conflict with the demands of school, can also be beneficial.

9.4 The Dark Side

Why do teenagers drink and use drugs?

- Many adolescents drink alcohol regularly. The primary factors that influence whether adolescents drink are encouragement from others (parents and peers) and stress. Similarly, teenage smoking is influenced by parents and peers.

What leads some adolescents to become depressed? How can depression be treated?

- Depressed adolescents have little enthusiasm for life, believe that others are unfriendly, and wish to be left alone. Depression can be triggered by a negative event; the adolescents most likely to be affected are those who can't control their emotions and who see themselves in a negative light. Treating depression relies on medications that correct the levels of neurotransmitters and on therapy designed to improve social skills and restructure adolescents' interpretation of life events.

What are the causes of juvenile delinquency?

- Many young people engage in antisocial behavior briefly during adolescence. In contrast, the small percentage of adolescents who engage in life-course persistent antisocial behavior commit serious crimes in adolescence and in adulthood. Life-course persistent antisocial behavior has been linked to biology, cognitive processes, family processes, and poverty. Efforts to reduce adolescent criminal activity must address all of these variables.

Key Terms

adolescent egocentrism (241)
imaginary audience (241)
personal fable (241)
illusion of invulnerability (241)
ethnic identity (242)

crystallization (250)
specification (250)
implementation (250)
personality-type theory (251)
depression (254)

adolescent-limited antisocial
  behavior (256)
life-course persistent antisocial
  behavior (256)

Online Resources

Go to CengageBrain.com to access Psychology CourseMate, where you will find an interactive eBook, flashcards, quizzes, videos, websites, and more.

Mycretoucher/Getty Images

Becoming an Adult

Physical, Cognitive, and Personality Development in Young Adulthood

10

There comes a time in life when we turn away from childhood and aspire to be adults. In this chapter, we explore the transition to adulthood, how young adulthood represents the peak of physical development, and key changes in intellectual abilities and personality.

LEARNING OBJECTIVES

- What role transitions mark entry into adulthood?
- How does going to college reflect the transition to adulthood?

- What behavioral criteria mark the transition to adulthood?
- How does achieving financial independence reflect the transition to adulthood?

This couple from India reflects how the passage to adulthood for many occurs with marriage.

Marcus woke up with the worst headache he could ever remember having. "If this is adulthood, they can keep it," he muttered to himself. Like many young adults in the United States, Marcus spent his 21st birthday celebrating at a bar. But the phone call from his mother that woke him in the first place reminds him that he isn't an adult in every way; she called to see if he needs money.

Think for a minute about the first time you felt like an adult. When was it? What was the context? Who were you with? How did you feel?

Even though becoming an adult is one of our most important life transitions, it is difficult to pin down exactly when this occurs in Western societies. In the United States, for example, the age needed to achieve "adult" status ranges from 12 or so for movie theater tickets to 16 for driving a car (in many states), 18 for voting and joining the military, 21 for consuming alcoholic beverages, and 26 for removal from medical insurance coverage on a parent's policy under the 2010 health care law. Certainly Marcus may feel like an adult because he can purchase alcohol legally, but he may not feel that way in other respects, such as financially.

Some human developmentalists view the period from the late teens to the mid- to late 20s as **emerging adulthood**, *a period when individuals are not adolescents but are not yet fully adults* (Arnett, 2012). Emerging adulthood is a time to explore careers, self-identity, and commitments. It is also when certain biological and physiological developmental trends peak and brain development continues in different ways.

Role Transitions Marking Adulthood

When people become adults in different cultures depends on how we define adulthood and the kind of role transitions that cultures create.

Cross-Cultural Evidence of Role Transitions

Cultures in the developing world tend to be clear about when a person becomes an adult (Nelson, Badger, & Wu, 2004). *Rituals marking initiation into adulthood, often among the most important ones in a culture, are termed* **rites of passage**. Rites of passage may involve highly elaborate steps that take days or weeks, or they may be compressed into a few minutes. Initiates are usually dressed in apparel reserved for the ritual to denote their special position. We still have traces of these rites in Western culture; consider, for example, the ritual attire for graduations or weddings.

emerging adulthood
the period between late teens and mid- to late 20s when individuals are not adolescents but are not yet fully adults

rites of passage
rituals marking initiation into adulthood

FIGURE 10.1

Enrollment rates of 18- to 24-year-olds in degree-granting institutions by race/ethnicity, 1975–2008.

Data from U.S. Census Bureau, Current Population Survey CPS, October 1970–October 2008, unpublished tabulations.

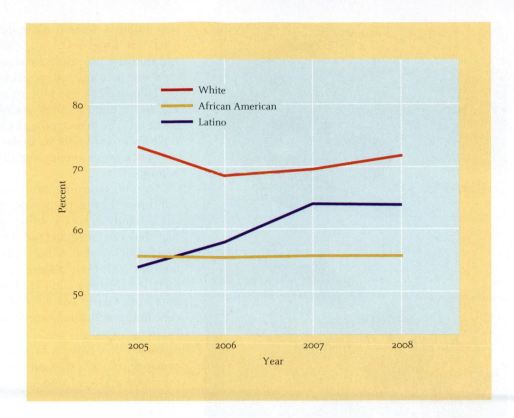

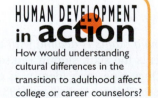

HUMAN DEVELOPMENT in action

How would understanding cultural differences in the transition to adulthood affect college or career counselors?

role transitions

movement into the next stage of development, which is marked by the assumption of new responsibilities and duties

In many cultures, rites of passage to adulthood are connected with religious rituals (Levete, 2010). For example, Christian traditions use a ritual called confirmation to mark the transition from being a child spiritually to being an adult. Judaism celebrates bar and bat mitzvahs. Marriage is the most important rite of passage to adulthood in most cultures because it is a prelude to childbearing, which in turn provides clear evidence of achieving adulthood (Mensch, Singh, & Casterline, 2006).

Role Transitions in Western Cultures

In Western cultures, the most widely used criteria for deciding whether a person has reached adulthood are **role transitions**, *which involve assuming new responsibilities and duties.* Certain role transitions are key markers for attaining adulthood: voting, completing education, beginning full-time employment, leaving home and establishing financial independence, getting married, and becoming a parent. However, many people in their 20s in industrialized countries spread these achievements over several years (Arnett, 2004), and this trend is more common than ever (Burt & Masten, 2010).

The point in the life span when these marker events for role transitions happen has changed a lot over the years. Such changes are examples of cohort effects, described in Chapter 1. For example, in the United States the average age at first marriage has increased by almost 5 years since the 1970s (U.S. Census Bureau, 2010b).

Let's consider a common role transition for many people in industrialized societies, the move from high school to college.

Going to College

For about 69% of all high-school graduates in the United States, a marker of the transition to adulthood is going straight to college—although the rates vary across European Americans, African Americans, and Latino Americans, as shown in Figure 10.1 (National Center for Educational Statistics, 2010). Considerable research has documented

Risky behavior tends to decrease over the course of young adulthood.

how students develop while they are in college (Evans et al., 2010; Kitchener, King, & DeLuca, 2006; Perry, 1970). Students start acting and thinking like adults because of advances in intellectual development and personal and social identity.

Full-time college students tend to be the traditional age (under 25), but a large number are older, with most of them attending part time. For them, going to college isn't the marker of adulthood. *Colleges usually refer to students over age 25 as* **returning adult students**, *which implies that these individuals have already reached adulthood.*

Overall, returning adult students tend to be problem solvers, self-directed, and pragmatic; may have increased stress due to work–family–school conflict; and have relevant life experiences that they can integrate with their course work (Evans et al., 2010; Giancola, Grawitch, & Borchert, 2009). Balancing employment and families with their college courses often causes stress, especially early in returning adult students' academic studies; however, support from family and employers, as well as the positive effects of continuing education, are stress reducers. Many returning adult students, especially middle-aged women, express a sense of self-discovery they had not experienced before (Miles, 2009). The main conclusion here is that going to college affects students of all ages; for traditional-aged students (ages 18 to 25), it helps foster the transition to adulthood.

Behavioral Changes

From a psychological perspective, becoming an adult means behaving in a fundamentally different way. During young adulthood, there is a significant drop in the frequency of risky behaviors, such as driving at high speed, having sex without contraception, engaging in extreme sports, or committing antisocial acts like vandalism (Tanner & Arnett, 2009). *The desire to live life more on the edge through physically and emotionally threatening situations that are on the boundary between life and death is termed* **edgework** (Lois, 2011).

Neuroscience research has raised an intriguing question: Could continuing brain development during adolescence and early adulthood explain shifts in behavior and document a biological marker for adulthood? There is some evidence that the prefrontal cortex, a part of the brain involved in high-level thinking, is not fully developed until a person reaches the mid-20s (Berns, Moore, & Capra, 2009). But Males (2009, 2010) argues that this brain development hypothesis is wrong. He shows that risk-taking behavior does not vary with age between young and middle-aged adults when sociodemographic conditions, such as poverty, are controlled. That is, poverty is a stronger correlate of risky behavior than is brain development.

Establishing Intimacy

According to Erik Erikson, the major task for young adults is dealing with the psychosocial conflict of intimacy versus isolation. This is the sixth step in Erikson's theory of psychosocial development (see Chapter 1). Once a person's identity is established in the stage of Identity vs. Identity Confusion (see Chapter 1), Erikson (1982) believed that he or she is ready to create a shared identity with another—the key ingredient for intimacy. Without a clear sense of identity, Erikson argued, young adults would be

returning adult students
college students over age 25

edgework
the desire to live life more on the edge through physically and emotionally threatening situations that are on the boundary between life and death

afraid of committing to a long-term relationship with another person or might become overly dependent on the partner for their identity.

Research evidence for Erikson's view is conflicting. For example, Montgomery (2005) found that a stronger sense of identity was related to higher levels of intimacy in young adults. However, other research found that identity formation correlated with intimacy in adults age 35 to 45 but that this relationship held even for those people who demonstrated diffusion (the lowest level of identity formation), which Erikson argued should not be the case (Berliner, 2000). After analyzing the results of 21 studies, Årseth et al. (2009) concluded that the conflicting results occurred because men and women resolve identity and intimacy issues differently under certain circumstances.

Gender differences are complex. Identity is related to closeness in same-sex friendships for both men and women and in cross-sex friendships for men; for women, however, identity is unrelated to closeness in cross-sex friendships (Johnson et al., 2007). Why is there a difference in the cross-sex friendship patterns? It turns out that most men and career-oriented women resolve identity issues before intimacy issues (Dyke & Adams, 1990).

Some women resolve intimacy issues before identity issues by marrying and rearing children, and only later do they deal with the question of their identity. Middle-aged women who go to college for the first time are an example of this form of identity development (Miles, 2009).

Still other women deal with both issues simultaneously—for example, by entering into relationships that allow them to develop identities based on caring for others (Dyke & Adams, 1990). For example, a woman could develop a strong identity as a caregiver and a strong intimate relationship with a partner simultaneously.

Thus, Erikson's idea that identity must be resolved before intimacy is most applicable in the cases of men and career-oriented women. Some women show different patterns yet resolve both issues, which indicates that there are likely multiple pathways to achieving identity and intimacy.

HUMAN DEVELOPMENT in action

How might multiple pathways to achieving identity and intimacy influence advice you would give if you were a career coach?

Launching Financial Independence

For many, the key indicator of becoming an adult is establishing financial independence. For the one third of high-school graduates who do not go on to college and for those who do not finish high school, this is likely to occur sooner than it is for college-bound students. Some find their niche through a series of part-time jobs, full-time employment, learning a trade (e.g., carpentry or plumbing), or starting their own business. Others join the military (Kelty, Kleykamp, & Segal, 2010). Military service paves a way to adulthood in several ways, not the least of which is through financial independence.

Eventually, even college-bound students face the need to establish themselves as financially independent. When this happens, though, is changing. It is increasingly common for college graduates to return home to live with their parents prior to establishing financial independence (Henig, 2010).

Regardless of when it occurs, reaching financial independence is a major achievement and serves as a marker of becoming an adult. And where a person lives matters. Research in Western cultures shows clearly that living on one's own accelerates the achievement of adulthood, whereas living with one's parents slows the process of becoming an independent adult (Kins & Beyers, 2010).

The Real People feature presents an example of how financial independence may not be strongly related to age. Read the story of Kristen Jaymes Stewart to see how.

Kristen Jaymes Stewart, born in 1990, achieved international fame for her portrayal of Isabella "Bella" Swan in *The Twilight Saga* films. Her career began in 1999 with a small, uncredited role. Her parents and family have been active in television, in supervising scripts, and in other behind-the-camera activities, so she learned about film and television early on. After acting in several films, she was thrust into major international stardom for being selected to portray Bella, the main female character in the film version of the books by Stephenie Meyer. Kristen's educational career has been different too. After the seventh grade, she completed the rest of her schooling through high school by correspondence.

Clearly, Kristen has not yet experienced many of the transitions we considered in this section that are associated with becoming an adult, such as going to college or marrying and having a child. However, there is also no question that she can be financially independent from her parents. And she certainly lives a public life.

When would you have said that Kristen was an adult? Is it enough to be globally famous and to be extremely wealthy? What effect do these circumstances have on dealing with issues such as Erikson's intimacy versus isolation stage, considering that every person Kristen may want to date will be publicly scrutinized and debated? If you were a counselor, what would you recommend to Kristen?

Kristen Jaymes Stewart

Christopher Polk/Getty Images

Test Yourself

Recall

1. The most widely used criteria for deciding whether a person has reached adulthood are _____.

2. Rituals marking initiation into adulthood are called _____.

3. Students over 25 years of age are referred to as _____.

4. Behaviorally, a major difference between adolescence and adulthood is a significant drop in the frequency of _____.

5. Research indicates that Erikson's idea of resolving identity followed by intimacy best describes men and _____.

Interpret

- Why are formal rites of passage important? What has Western society lost by eliminating them? What has it gained?

- Why is understanding how rites of passage occur in different cultures important?

Apply

- When do you think people become adults? Why?

- How do legal definitions of adulthood matter in professions such as law enforcement and health care?

Recall answers: (1) role transitions, (2) rites of passage, (3) returning adult students, (4) reckless behavior, (5) career-oriented women

LEARNING OBJECTIVES

- In what respects are young adults at their physical peak?
- How healthy are young adults in general?
- How do smoking, drinking alcohol, and nutrition affect young adults' health?

- How does the health of young adults differ as a function of socioeconomic status, gender, and ethnicity?

Juan is a 25-year-old who started smoking cigarettes in high school to be popular. Juan wants to quit, but he knows it will be difficult. He has also heard that it doesn't really matter if he quits or not because his health will never recover. Juan wonders whether it is worthwhile to try.

Juan is at the peak of his physical functioning. Most young adults are in the best physical shape of their lives. Indeed, the early 20s are the best years for strenuous work, trouble-free reproduction, and peak athletic performance. But people's physical functioning is affected by several health-related behaviors, including smoking.

Growth, Strength, and Physical Functioning

Physical functioning generally peaks during young adulthood (Schneider & Davidson, 2003). People are as tall as they will ever be. Physical strength, coordination, and dexterity in both sexes peaks during the late 20s and early 30s, declining slowly throughout the rest of life (Whitbourne, 1996). Because of these trends, few professional athletes remain at the top of their sport in their mid-30s. Indeed, individuals such as Brett Favre, a quarterback who played in the National Football League into his early 40s, and Dara Torres, who set the record for the oldest swimmer to win Olympic medals by winning three in Beijing in 2008 at age 41, are famous partly because they are exceptions.

Sensory acuity is also at its peak in the early 20s (Fozard & Gordon-Salant, 2001). Visual acuity remains high until middle age, when people tend to become farsighted and require glasses for reading. Hearing begins to decline somewhat by the late 20s, especially for high-pitched tones.

Health Status

Because they are so healthy overall, American young adults rarely die from disease (National Center for Health Statistics, 2010a). So what is the leading cause of death among young adults in the United States? Between the ages of 25 and 44, it's accidents.

There are important gender and ethnic differences in death statistics. Young adult men age 25 to 34 are nearly 2.5 times as likely to die in accidents as women of the same age. African American and Latino American young adult males are 2 to 2.5 times as likely to die in accidents as their European American male counterparts, but Asian and Pacific Islander (American) young adult males are likely to die in accidents at only half the rate of their European American male counterparts (National Center for Health Statistics, 2010a).

Lifestyle Factors

To maximize the odds of being healthy, don't smoke, monitor your alcohol consumption, and eat a well-balanced, nutritional diet.

Smoking

Smoking is the single biggest contributor to health problems. In the United States alone, roughly 400,000 people die each year from smoking-related illnesses, and medical treatment of smoking-related ailments costs more than $193 billion annually (Centers for Disease Control and Prevention, 2010c).

The risks of smoking are many. Figure 10.2 shows the various forms of cancer and other chronic diseases that are caused by smoking. And smoking during one's lifetime has a small but measurable negative impact on cognitive functioning in later life (Whalley et al., 2005).

Nonsmokers who breathe secondhand smoke are also at considerably higher risk for smoking-related diseases: Each year, more than 3,400 adult nonsmokers die from lung cancer and 46,000 adult nonsmokers die from cardiovascular disease (American Cancer Society, 2010d). Hundreds of thousands of children have lung problems annually in the United States as a result of environmental smoke. Health problems caused by secondhand smoke cost about $10 billion in health care (Centers for Disease Control and Prevention, 2010c).

Juan, the young man in the vignette, is typical of people who want to stop smoking. Most people begin the process in young adulthood. More than 90% of those who stop do so on their own. But as Juan suspects, quitting is not easy; the American Cancer Society (2010b) estimates that, even with medicinal intervention, between two thirds and three quarters of those who try to quit smoking end up starting again within 6 months. For most people, success is attained only after a long period of stopping and relapsing.

Regardless of how it happens, quitting smoking has enormous health benefits (American Cancer Society, 2010b). For example, in less than a year after quitting, the lungs regain their normal ability to move mucus out. The risks of stroke and coronary heart disease return to normal after a period of roughly 15 years. Even people who do not quit until late life show marked improvements in health (Stop Smoking, 2010). The American Cancer Society offers key information about how to quit and a quiz about whether you need help to quit on its website (2010b, 2010c).

Drinking Alcohol

About two thirds of the people in the United States drink alcohol at least occasionally (National Center for Health Statistics, 2010a). For the majority of people, drinking alcohol poses no serious health problems as long as they do not drink and drive. For example, moderate drinkers (one or two glasses of beer or wine per day for men and one glass per day for women) have a 25% to 40% reduction in risk of cardiovascular disease and stroke than either abstainers or heavy drinkers, even after controlling for hypertension, prior heart attack, and other medical conditions (Harvard School of Public Health, 2010).

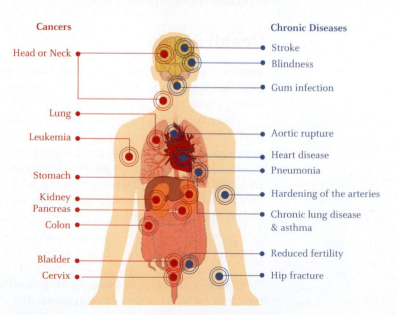

FIGURE 10.2

Smoking can damage every part of the body.

Source: CDC Vital Signs: Tobacco Use-Smoking & Secondhand Smoke, September 2010, pg. 3. Copyright 2010 Centers for Disease Control and Prevention.

FIGURE 10.3

Troublesome behaviors increase with binge drinking. All binge drinkers report more problems than do nonbinge drinkers.

Source: Based on "Trends in college binge drinking during a period of increased prevention efforts," by H. Wechsler, J. E. Lee, M. Kuo, M. Seibrung, T. F. Nelson, & H. Lee, in Journal of American College Health, pp. 203-217. Copyright © American College Health Association 2002.

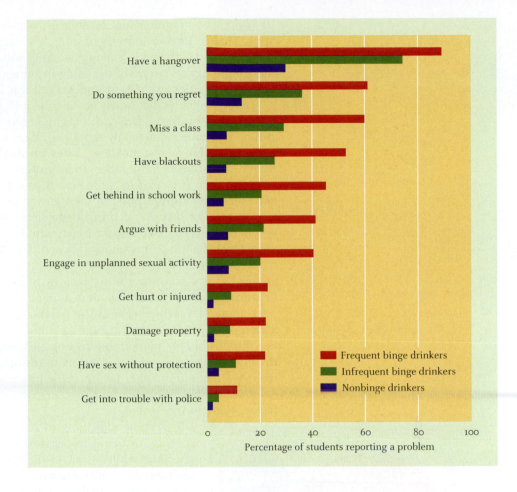

For many students, college parties and drinking alcohol are synonymous. Unfortunately, drinking among college students often goes beyond moderate intake to become binge drinking. **Binge drinking** *is defined for men as consuming five or more drinks in a row and for women as consuming four or more drinks in a row within the past 2 weeks.* Binge drinking has been identified as a major health problem in the United States since the 1990s (National Institute on Alcohol Abuse and Alcoholism, 2007; Wechsler et al., 1994). Surveys of drinking behavior among young adults consistently show that the rate of binge drinking in the general young adult population has declined but that the rate among college students has not (e.g., Grucza, Norberg, & Bierut, 2009).

Students between the ages of 17 and 23 are more likely than older students to binge drink. They are significantly more likely to binge drink if alcohol is readily available (Truong & Sturm, 2009), if they are a member of a fraternity or sorority (McGuckin, 2007), or if they feel really positive about what they are doing (which tends to make some people behave rashly; Cyders et al., 2009). Recent research indicates that average binge drinking among college students is an international problem (Karam, Kypri, & Salamoun, 2007; Kypri et al., 2009), with rates in Europe, South America, Australia, and New Zealand roughly on par with those in the United States.

The notion that binge drinking is just innocent fun is simply wrong. Driving under the influence among binge drinkers, up significantly since the late 1990s to nearly 3 million students per year in the United States, is only one aspect, according to the National Institute on Alcohol Abuse and Alcoholism (NIAAA, 2007). Nearly 100,000 college students annually are victims of alcohol-related date rape, and nearly 700,000 are assaulted by a student who has been drinking (NIAAA, 2007). Researchers estimate that about 1,700 young adult college students age 18 to 24 die every year in the United States from drinking too much (Oster-Aaland et al., 2009). Figure 10.3 shows the rate of a number of drinking-related problems.

binge drinking

a type of drinking defined for men as consuming five or more drinks in a row and for women as consuming four or more drinks in a row within the past 2 weeks

Numerous programs aim to reduce the number of college students who binge drink. These efforts include establishing low tolerance levels for the antisocial behaviors associated with binge drinking; working with athletes, fraternities, and sororities; changing the expectations of incoming freshmen; and increasing the number of non-alcoholic activities available to students (Bishop, 2000; McGuckin, 2007).

In the United States, nearly 8% of adults 18 to 24 years old and 5% of those age 25 to 44 are considered heavy drinkers (Centers for Disease Control and Prevention, 2010c). However, significantly more men than women are alcohol dependent or experience alcohol-related problems. Rates are also higher for European Americans and Native Americans than for other ethnic groups (Grant et al., 2006).

Alcoholism is viewed by most experts as a form of **addiction**, *which means that alcoholics demonstrate physical dependence on alcohol and experience withdrawal symptoms when they do not drink.* Dependence occurs when a drug, such as alcohol, becomes so incorporated into the functioning of the body's cells that the drug becomes necessary for normal functioning (Mayo Clinic, 2010b).

Neuroscience research has discovered that alcohol does a number on the brain, especially in disrupting the balance in neurotransmitters (NIAAA, 2010). These neurotransmitters include gamma-aminobutyric acid, which inhibits impulsiveness; glutamate, which excites the nervous system; norepinephrine, which is released in response to stress; and dopamine, serotonin, and opioid peptides, which are responsible for pleasurable feelings. Excessive, long-term drinking can cause the body to crave alcohol as a means to restore good feelings or to avoid negative feelings. In addition, other factors come into play: genetics; high stress, anxiety, or emotional pain; close friends or partners who drink excessively; and sociocultural factors that glorify alcohol.

Treating addictions such as alcoholism is difficult. Most people seeking treatment for alcohol abuse or dependence for the first time are young adults (Grant et al., 2006). The most widely known treatment option is Alcoholics Anonymous. Other treatment approaches include inpatient and outpatient programs at treatment centers, certain medications, and various forms of counseling (Mayo Clinic, 2010b). Typically, the goal of these approaches is abstinence. Unfortunately, we know little about the long-term success of the various programs.

Nutrition

How many times were you told as a child to eat your vegetables? Most people have disagreements with parents about food while growing up, but as adults they realize that those despised foods are healthful—and don't taste as bad as they once thought.

Experts agree that nutrition directly affects mental, emotional, and physical functioning (Mayo Clinic, 2009). Diet has been linked to cancer, cardiovascular disease, diabetes, anemia, and digestive disorders. As people mature, their nutritional requirements and eating habits change. *This change is due mainly to differences in* **metabolism**, *or how much energy the body needs.* Body metabolism and the digestive process slow with age (Whitney & Ajmera, 2010).

The U.S. Department of Agriculture (USDA) publishes guidelines to help people create healthy diets. In 2011, the USDA launched the Choose MyPlate campaign, which provides a visual guide to healthy eating by showing the relative proportions of various types of food people should eat daily (see Figure 10.4). The guidelines emphasize eating less, making half of the food on a plate fruits and vegetables, ensuring half of the grains eaten are whole grains, switching to fat-free or low-fat (1%) milk, choosing prepared foods with lower sodium, and drinking water instead of sugary drinks (USDA, 2011). The USDA has launched a website supporting the Choose MyPlate program that encourages healthy eating and includes link to the detailed *Dietary Guidelines for Americans, 2010.*

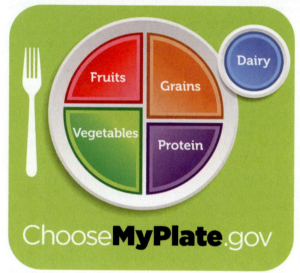

FIGURE 10.4

The USDA depicts a healthy diet by showing the relative portions of various types of food that should be eaten.
Source: © USDA

addiction
physical dependence on a substance (e.g., alcohol) such that withdrawal symptoms are experienced when deprived of that substance

metabolism
how much energy the body needs

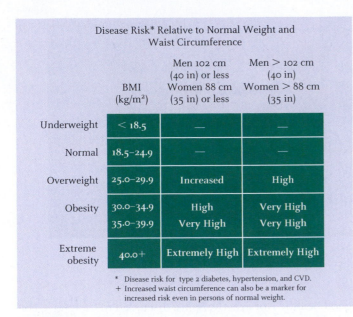

BMI (kg/m²)	Disease Risk* Relative to Normal Weight and Waist Circumference	
	Men 102 cm (40 in) or less Women 88 cm (35 in) or less	Men > 102 cm (40 in) Women > 88 cm (35 in)
Underweight < 18.5	—	—
Normal 18.5–24.9	—	—
Overweight 25.0–29.9	Increased	High
Obesity 30.0–34.9 35.0–39.9	High Very High	Very High Very High
Extreme obesity 40.0+	Extremely High	Extremely High

   * Disease risk for type 2 diabetes, hypertension, and CVD.
   + Increased waist circumference can also be a marker for increased risk even in persons of normal weight.

FIGURE 10.5

Classification of overweight and obesity by BMI, waist circumference, and associated disease risks.

Source: From Classification of Overweight and Obesity by BMI, Waist Circumference, and Associated Disease Risks, by National Heart, Lung, and Blood Institute. Copyright © U.S. Department of Health and Human Services, National Institutes of Health 2012.

The American Heart Association (2010) makes it clear that foods high in saturated fat (e.g., ice cream) should be replaced with foods low in fat (e.g., fat-free frozen yogurt). It also provides a website with recipes and alternatives for a heart-healthy diet (American Heart Association, 2012).

The main goal of these recommendations is to lower cholesterol levels (based on two types of lipoproteins) because high cholesterol is one risk factor for cardiovascular disease. Lipoproteins are fatty chemicals attached to proteins carried in the blood. **Low-density lipoproteins (LDLs)** *cause fatty deposits to accumulate in arteries, impeding blood flow, whereas* **high-density lipoproteins (HDLs)** *help keep arteries clear and break down LDLs.* It is the ratio of LDLs to HDLs that matters most in cholesterol screening. High levels of LDLs are a risk factor in cardiovascular disease, and high levels of HDLs are considered a protective factor (American Heart Association, 2010). LDL levels can be lowered and HDL levels can be raised through various interventions, such as exercise and a high-fiber diet. Weight control is also an important component.

The most popular medications to control cholesterol are called statins (e.g., Lipitor and Zocor). These medications lower LDL and moderately increase HDL. Because of potential side effects on liver functioning, patients taking cholesterol-lowering medications should be monitored regularly.

Obesity is a growing health problem related in part to diet. One good way to assess your status is to compute your body mass index (BMI), a ratio of body weight and height and is related to total body fat. You can compute BMI as follows:

$$BMI = w/h^2,$$

where *w* is weight in kilograms (or weight in pounds divided by 2.2) and *h* is height in meters (or height in inches divided by 39.37). The National Institutes of Health and the American Heart Association define healthy weight as having a BMI of less than 25; the American Heart Association provides a convenient BMI calculator on its website (American Heart Association, 2011).

Figure 10.5 shows the increased risk for several diseases and mortality associated with increased BMI. Based on these estimates, you may want to lower your BMI if it's above 25. But be careful—lowering your BMI too much may not be healthy either. Extremely low BMIs may indicate malnutrition, which is also related to increased mortality.

Social, Gender, and Ethnic Issues in Health

The two most important social influences on health are socioeconomic status (which is a strong predictor of whether a person has access to insurance and good health care) and education (a good predictor of living a healthy lifestyle and avoiding certain diseases). In the United States, the worst health conditions exist in poor, inner-city neighborhoods. For example, African American men in large urban areas have a lower life expectancy than men in some developing countries (U.S. Census Bureau, 2010a).

Even when poor minorities in the United States have access to health care, they are less likely than European Americans to receive treatment for chronic disease (National Center for Health Statistics, 2010a).

Educational level also matters. In one of the largest studies examining this issue that has ever been conducted, results show that—in a representative sample of 5,652 working adults between the ages of 18 and 64—educational level was associated with good health even when the effects of age, gender, ethnicity, and smoking were accounted for (Pincus, Callahan, & Burkhauser, 1987). This is also true when looking at specific conditions such as rheumatoid arthritis (McCollum & Pincus, 2009).

low-density lipoproteins (LDLs)
chemicals that cause fatty deposits to accumulate in arteries, impeding blood flow

high-density lipoproteins (HDLs)
chemicals that help keep arteries clear and break down LDLs

Many inner-city residents must rely on over-crowded clinics for their primary care.

© Tom Carter / PhotoEdit

Does education cause good health? Not exactly. As we discussed in Chapter 1, correlation research does not address cause and effect. In this case, higher educational level is also associated with higher income and with more awareness of dietary and lifestyle influences on health. Thus, more highly educated people are in a better position to afford health care and to know about the kinds of foods and lifestyle that affect health.

Internationally, gender differences matter. As the World Health Organization (2010) points out, in some parts of the world, women cannot receive the health care they need because cultural norms prohibit women from traveling alone to a clinic, or men have much higher rates of lung cancer because smoking is considered a marker of masculinity.

Test Yourself

Recall

1. In young adulthood, most people reach their maximum _____.

2. Sensory acuity peaks during the _____.

3. During the early 20s, death from disease is _____.

4. Young adult _____ are the most likely to die in accidents.

5. _____ is the biggest contributor to health problems.

6. Alcoholism is viewed by most experts as a form of _____.

7. The two most important social influences on health are education and _____.

8. In the United States, the poorest health conditions exist for people living in _____.

Interpret

- How could you design a health care system that provides strong incentives for healthy lifestyles during young adulthood?

- How would you expect that smoking-related health problems are related to socioeconomic status?

Apply

- Imagine that you are a nutritionist. In your job, you have been asked to design a comprehensive educational campaign to promote healthy lifestyles. What information would you be certain to include?

- If you were a nurse, what information besides basic health status would you want to know from a new patient?

Recall answers: (1) height, (2) 20s, (3) rare, (4) men, (5) Smoking, (6) addiction, (7) socioeconomic status, (8) poor, inner-city neighborhoods

LEARNING OBJECTIVES
- What is intelligence in adulthood?
- What are primary and secondary mental abilities? How do they change?
- What are fluid and crystallized intelligence? How do they change?
- How has neuroscience research furthered our understanding of intelligence in adulthood?
- What is postformal thought? How does it differ from formal operations?
- How do emotion and logic become integrated in adulthood?

Susan, a 33-year-old woman recently laid off from her job as a secretary, slides into her seat on her first day of classes at the community college. She is clearly nervous. "I'm worried that I won't be able to compete with these younger students, that I may not be smart enough," she says with a sigh. "Guess we'll find out soon enough, though, huh?"

Many returning adult students like Susan worry that they may not be "smart enough" to keep up with 18- or 19-year-olds. Are these fears realistic? We'll see how the answer to this question depends on the types of intellectual skills being used.

How Should We View Intelligence in Adults?

Take a sheet of paper and write down all the abilities that you think reflect intelligence in adults. It's a safe bet that you listed more than one ability. You are not alone. *Most theories of intelligence are* **multidimensional**—*that is, they identify several types of intellectual abilities.*

Sternberg (1985, 2003; Sternberg, Jarvin, & Grigorenko, 2009) emphasized multidimensionality in his theory of successful intelligence (discussed in Chapter 6). Based on the life-span perspective (described in Chapter 1), Baltes, Lindenberger, and Staudinger (2006) introduced three other concepts as vital to intellectual development in adults: multidirectionality, interindividual variability, and plasticity.

Over time, the various abilities underlying adults' intelligence show **multidirectionality**: *Some aspects of intelligence improve and other aspects decline during adulthood. Closely related to this is* **interindividual variability**: *These patterns of change also vary from one person to another. Finally, people's abilities reflect* **plasticity**: *They are not fixed but can be modified under the right conditions at just about any point in adulthood.* In general, Baltes, Lindenberger, and Staudinger emphasize that intelligence has many components and that these components show varying development in different abilities and different people.

Primary and Secondary Mental Abilities

Since the 1930s, researchers have agreed that intellectual abilities can be studied as groups of related skills (e.g., memory or spatial ability) organized into hypothetical constructs called **primary mental abilities**. *In turn, related groups of primary mental abilities can be clustered into a half dozen or so broader skills, termed* **secondary mental abilities**.

Roughly 25 primary mental abilities have been identified (Horn, 1982). Because it is difficult to study all of them, researchers have focused on five representative ones:

- *Number.* The basic skills underlying our mathematical reasoning.
- *Word fluency.* How easily we produce verbal descriptions of things.

multidimensional
a characteristic of theories of intelligence that identify several types of intellectual abilities

multidirectionality
a developmental pattern in which some aspects of intelligence improve and other aspects decline during adulthood

interindividual variability
patterns of change that vary from one person to another

plasticity
the concept that intellectual abilities are not fixed but can be modified under the right conditions at just about any point in adulthood

primary mental abilities
groups of related intellectual skills (e.g., memory or spatial ability)

secondary mental abilities
broad intellectual skills that subsume and organize primary mental abilities

- *Verbal meaning.* Our vocabulary ability.

- *Inductive reasoning.* Our ability to extrapolate from particular facts to general concepts.

- *Spatial orientation.* Our ability to reason in the three-dimensional world.

The Spotlight on Research feature describes the definitive developmental study of primary mental abilities.

Spotlight on research

The Seattle Longitudinal Study

Who was the investigator, and what was the aim of the study?
To provide a thorough picture of intellectual change, K. Warner Schaie began the Seattle Longitudinal Study in 1956.

How did the investigator measure the topic of interest?
Schaie used standardized tests of primary mental abilities to assess a range of abilities, such as logical reasoning and spatial ability.

Who were the participants in the study?
Over the course of the study, more than 5,000 individuals were tested at eight points in time (1956, 1963, 1970, 1977, 1984, 1991, 1998, and 2005). The participants were representative of the upper 75% of the socioeconomic spectrum and were recruited through a large health maintenance organization in Seattle.

What was the design of the study?
Schaie had invented a new type of research design—the sequential design (see Chapter 1). Participants were tested every 7 years.

Were there ethical concerns with the study?
Because people's names must be retained for future contact, Schaie was careful about keeping personal information secure.

What were the results?
Among the many important findings from the study were differential changes in abilities over time and cohort effects. As you can see in Figure 10.6, scores on tests of primary mental abilities improved gradually until the participants' late 30s or early 40s. Small declines began in their 50s, increased as people aged into their 60s, and became increasingly large in their 70s (Schaie & Zanjani, 2006).

Cohort differences were also found. Figure 10.7 shows that on some skills (e.g., inductive reasoning ability), more recently born younger and middle-aged cohorts performed better than cohorts born earlier. These cohort effects probably reflect differences in educational experiences.

Schaie uncovered many individual differences as well; some people showed developmental patterns closely approximating the overall trends, but others showed unusual patterns. For example, some individuals showed steady declines in most abilities beginning in their 40s and 50s, others showed declines in some abilities but not others, and some people showed little change in most abilities over a 14-year period.

FIGURE 10.6

Longitudinal estimates of age changes on observed measures of five primary mental abilities. T-scores are standardized scores on each dimension for each type. A score of 50 represents the mean. A difference of 10 from the mean indicates a difference of one standard deviation.

Source: From "Intellectual Development Across Adulthood" by K. Warner Schaie and Faika A. K. Zanjani, in Handbook of Adult Development and Learning, ed. by C. Hoare, p. 102. Copyright © 2006 by Oxford University Press. Reprinted by permission of Oxford University Press.

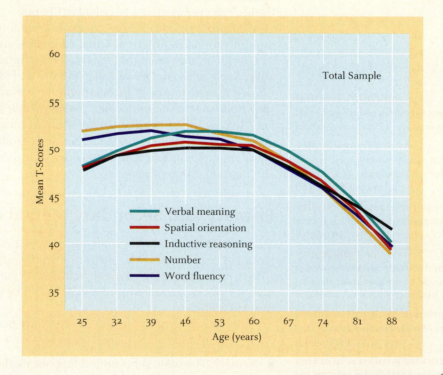

Continued

Continued

FIGURE 10.7

Cohort gradients showing cumulative cohort differences on five primary mental abilities for cohorts born from 1889 to 1973.

From "Intellectual Development Across Adulthood" by K. Warner Schaie and Faika A. K. Zanjani, in Handbook of Adult Development and Learning, ed. by C. Hoare, p. 106. Copyright © 2006 by Oxford University Press. Reprinted by permission of Oxford University Press.

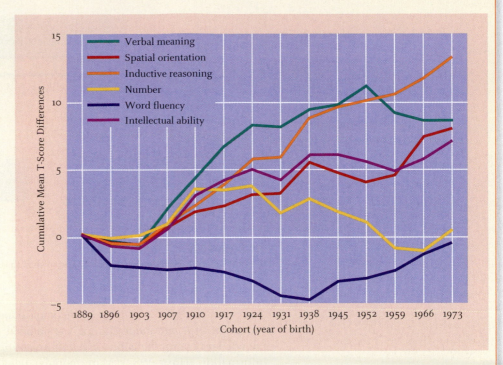

What did the investigator conclude?

Three points are clear. First, intellectual development during adulthood is marked by a gradual leveling off of gains between young adulthood and middle age, followed by a period of relative stability and then a time of gradual decline in most abilities. Second, these trends vary from one cohort to another. Third, individual patterns of change vary considerably from person to person.

What converging evidence would strengthen these conclusions?

Although Schaie's study is one of the most comprehensive ever conducted, it is limited. Studying people who live in different locations around the world would provide evidence as to whether the results are limited geographically. Additional cross-cultural evidence comparing people with different economic backgrounds and differing access to health care would also provide insight into the effects of these variables on intellectual development.

 Go to Psychology CourseMate at **www.cengagebrain.com** to enhance your understanding of this research.

Even with a relatively small number of primary mental abilities, it is hard to discuss intelligence by focusing on separate abilities. As a result, theories of intelligence emphasize clusters of related primary mental abilities as a framework for describing the structure of intelligence. Because they are one step removed from primary mental abilities, however, secondary mental abilities are not measured directly. This can be seen in Figure 10.8 for one of the secondary mental abilities that we consider in the next section: crystallized intelligence.

Fluid and Crystallized Intelligence

Two secondary mental abilities have received a great deal of attention in adult developmental research: fluid intelligence and crystallized intelligence (Horn, 1982).

Fluid intelligence *consists of the abilities that make you a flexible and adaptive thinker, that allow you to make inferences, and that enable you to understand the relations among concepts.* It includes the abilities you need to understand and respond to any situation, but especially new ones: inductive reasoning, integration, abstract thinking, and the like (Horn, 1982). An example of a question that taps fluid abilities is the following: What letter comes next in the series *d f i m r x e*?*

fluid intelligence
the abilities that make people flexible and adaptive thinkers, allow them to make inferences, and enable them to understand the relations among concepts

*The next letter is *m*. The rule is to increase the difference between adjacent letters in the series by one each time and use a continuous circle of the alphabet for counting. Thus, *f* is two letters from *d*, *i* is three letters from *f*, and *e* is seven letters from *x*.

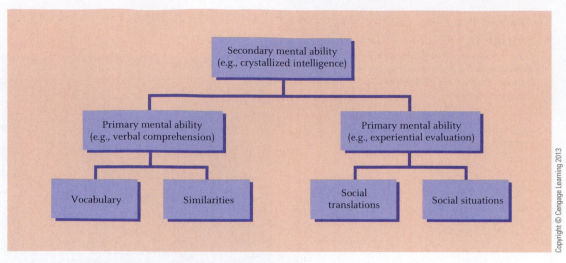

Copyright © Cengage Learning 2013

FIGURE 10.8
Secondary mental abilities reflect several primary mental abilities and their respective measurements.

Crystallized intelligence *is the knowledge acquired through life experience and education in a particular culture.* Crystallized intelligence includes your breadth of knowledge, comprehension of communication, judgment, and sophistication with information (Horn, 1982). Many popular television game shows (e.g., *Jeopardy* and *Wheel of Fortune*) are based on contestants' accumulated crystallized intelligence.

Developmentally, fluid and crystallized intelligence follow different paths, as you can see in Figure 10.9. Fluid intelligence declines throughout adulthood, whereas crystallized intelligence improves. Although we do not yet fully understand why fluid intelligence declines, it may be related to underlying changes in the brain (Horn & Hofer, 1992). In contrast, the increase in crystallized intelligence (at least until late life) indicates that people continue adding knowledge every day.

What do these different developmental trends imply? First, they indicate that—although it continues through adulthood—learning becomes more difficult with age. Second, intellectual development varies a great deal from one set of skills to another.

crystallized intelligence
the knowledge acquired through life experience and education in a particular culture

FIGURE 10.9

Note the opposite developmental patterns for fluid and crystallized intelligence.

From "Organization of data on life-span development of human abilities" by J. L. Horn, in Life-Span Developmental Psychology: Research and Theory, edited by L. R. Goulet and P. B. Bates, p. 463. Copyright © Academic Press 1970. Reprinted with permission of Elsevier.

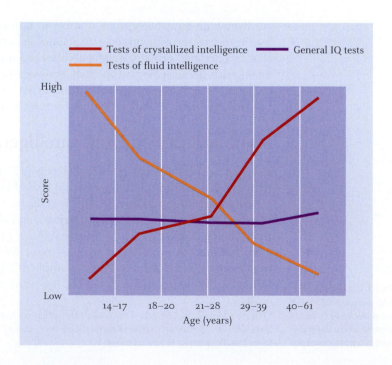

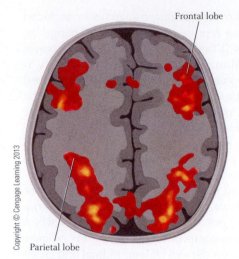

Frontal lobe

Parietal lobe

Copyright © Cengage Learning 2013

FIGURE 10.10
Brain imaging research indicates that active connections between the parietal and the frontal lobes, shown in the colored areas here, are key to understanding intelligence.

Whereas individual differences in fluid intelligence remain relatively uniform over time, individual differences in crystallized intelligence increase with age, largely because maintaining crystallized intelligence depends on being in situations that require its use (Horn, 1982; Horn & Hofer, 1992). For example, few adults get much practice in solving complex letter series tasks like the one on page 277. But because people can improve their vocabulary skills by reading and because people differ considerably in how much they read, differences are likely to emerge.

Neuroscience Research and Intelligence in Young and Middle Adulthood

Intellectual abilities have long been known to correlate with mortality in late life, but increasingly evidence shows this relation holds in middle age, based on research in Sweden (Batty et al., 2009) and Britain (Sabia et al., 2010).

This research shows that specific areas in the brain are associated with intellectual abilities and that developmental changes in these areas are related to changes in performance. On the basis of 37 studies using various brain imaging techniques, Jung and Haier (2007) proposed the parietofrontal integration theory. **Parietofrontal integration theory (P-FIT)** *proposes that intelligence comes from a distributed and integrated network of neurons in the parietal and frontal lobes of the brain.* (The parietal lobe is at the top of the head; the frontal lobe is behind the forehead. Figure 10.10 shows these key brain areas.) In general, P-FIT accounts for individual differences in intelligence as having their origins in individual differences in brain structure and function.

The P-FIT model has been tested in several studies. Results indicate support for the theory when measures of fluid, crystallized, and spatial intelligence are related to brain structures assessed in young adults through magnetic resonance imaging (Shih & Jung, 2009). It is also clear that performance on measures of specific abilities is likely related to specific combinations of brain structures (Haier et al., 2010).

Neuroscience and related research on intelligence will continue to provide many insights into the bases for both development of fluid and crystallized intelligence and understanding of individual differences in them (Nisbett et al., 2012).

Going Beyond Formal Operations: Thinking in Adulthood

Suppose you are faced with the following dilemma:

> You are a member of your college's or university's student judicial board and are currently hearing a case involving plagiarism. The student handbook states that plagiarism is a serious offense that results in expulsion. The student accused of plagiarizing a paper admits copying from Wikipedia but says that she has never been told that she needed to use a formal citation and quotation marks.

Do you vote to expel the student?

When this and similar problems are presented to older adolescents and young adults, interesting differences emerge. Adolescents tend to approach the problem in formal operational terms and point out that the student handbook is clear and the student ignored it, concluding that the student should be expelled. Formal operational thinkers are certain that such solutions are right because they are based on their experiences and are logically driven.

But many adults are reluctant to draw conclusions based on the limited information in the problem, especially when the problem can be interpreted in different ways (Sinnott, 1998). They point out that there is much about the student we don't know: Has she ever been taught the proper procedure for using sources? Was the faculty member clear about what plagiarism is? For adults, the problem is more ambiguous. Adults may eventually decide that the student should (or should not) be expelled, but they do so only after considering aspects of the situation that go well beyond the information given in the problem.

parietofrontal integration theory (P-FIT)
the proposal that intelligence comes from a distributed and integrated network of neurons in the parietal and frontal lobes of the brain

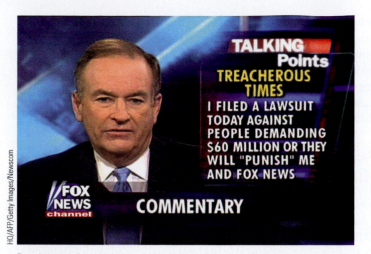

People using the initial stages of reflective judgment believe that what commentators such as Bill O'Reilly say must be true because they are perceived as authority figures.

Based on numerous investigations, researchers concluded that this type of thinking represents a qualitative change beyond formal operations (King & Kitchener, 2004; Kitchener, King, & DeLuca, 2006; Sinnott, 2009). **Postformal thought** *is characterized by a recognition that truth (the correct answer) may vary from situation to situation, that solutions must be realistic to be reasonable, that ambiguity and contradiction are the rule rather than the exception, and that emotion and subjective factors usually play roles in thinking.* In general, research evidence indicates that postformal thinking has its origins in young adulthood (Kitchener et al., 2006; Sinnott, 2009).

Several research-based descriptions of the development of thinking in adulthood have been offered. *One is the description of the development of* **reflective judgment**, *a way in which adults reason through dilemmas involving current affairs, religion, science, personal relationships, and the like.* Based on decades of longitudinal and cross-sectional research, Kitchener and King (1989; Kitchener et al., 2006) refined descriptions and identified a systematic progression of reflective judgment in young adulthood.

The first three stages in the model represent prereflective thought. People in these stages typically do not acknowledge and may not even perceive that knowledge is uncertain. Consequently, they do not understand that some problems exist for which there is not a clear and absolutely correct answer. A student pressuring her instructor for the "right" theory to explain human development reflects this stage. She is also likely to hold firm positions on controversial issues and does so without acknowledging other people's ability to reach a different (but nevertheless equally logical) position.

About halfway through the developmental progression, students think differently. In stages 4 and 5, students are likely to say that nothing can be known for certain and to change their conclusions based on the situation and the evidence. At this point, students argue that knowledge is quite subjective. They are also less persuasive with their positions on controversial issues: "Each person is entitled to his or her own view; I cannot force my opinions on anyone else." Kitchener and King refer to thinking in these stages as quasi-reflective thinking.

As students continue their development into stages 6 and 7, they begin to show true reflective judgment, understanding that people construct knowledge using evidence and argument after careful analysis of the problem or situation. They again hold firm convictions but reach them only after careful consideration of several points of view. They also realize that they must continually reevaluate their beliefs in view of new evidence.

Even though people are able to think at complex levels, do they? Not usually (King & Kitchener, 2004). Why? Mostly, it is because environment does not provide the supports necessary for using their highest-level thinking, especially for issues concerning knowledge and experience they already have. For example, people may not always purchase the product that has the least impact on the environment, such as a fully electric car, even though philosophically they are strong environmentalists, because recharging stations are currently not widely available. However, if pushed and if given the necessary supports (e.g., easily available charging stations), people demonstrate a level of thinking and performance far higher than they typically show each day.

HUMAN DEVELOPMENT in action

If you were a director of training for a company, how would you incorporate reflective judgment into your training program?

postformal thought
thinking characterized by recognizing that the correct answer varies from one situation to another, that solutions should be realistic, that ambiguity and contradiction are typical, and that subjective factors play roles in thinking

reflective judgment
the way in which adults reason through real-life dilemmas

Integrating Emotion and Logic in Life Problems

In addition to an increased understanding that there is more than one "right" answer, adult thinking is characterized by the integration of emotion with logic (Jain & Labouvie-Vief, 2010; Labouvie-Vief, 2006; Labouvie-Vief, Grühn, & Studer, 2010). As they mature, adults tend to make decisions and analyze problems not so much on logical grounds as on pragmatic and emotional grounds. Rules and norms are viewed as relative, not absolute. Mature thinkers realize that thinking is an inherently social enterprise that

demands making compromises with other people and tolerating contradiction and ambiguity. Such shifts mean that their sense of self also undergoes a fundamental change.

A good example of this developmental shift would be the differences in how late adolescents or young adults view an emotionally charged issue—such as unethical behavior at work—compared to the views of middle-aged adults. Younger people may view such behavior as inexcusable, with firing of the employee an inescapable outcome. Middle-aged adults may take contextual factors into account and consider what factors may have forced the person to engage in the behavior. Some might argue that this is because the topic is too emotionally charged for adolescents to deal with intellectually, whereas middle-aged adults are better able to incorporate emotion into their thinking.

The integration of emotion with logic that happens in adulthood provides the basis for decision making in the personal and sometimes difficult arenas of love and work, which we examine in detail in Chapters 11 and 12, respectively. In the present context, it sets the stage for envisioning a future life, a topic we take up later in this chapter.

The developmental integration of thought and emotion during young adulthood and middle age turns out to be influenced by life-cycle forces and cohort effects (see Chapter 1). How strongly people hold beliefs may vary as a function of how particular generations were socialized.

Social cognition researchers argue that individual differences in the strength of social representations of rules, beliefs, and attitudes are linked to specific situations (Blanchard-Fields, 2009; Labouvie-Vief et al., 2010). Such representations can be both cognitive (how we think about the situation) and emotional (how we react to the situation). When we encounter a specific situation, our cognitive belief system triggers an emotional reaction and related goals tied to the content of that situation, which demands integration of cognition and emotion. This, in turn, drives social judgments.

Research exploring social beliefs finds age differences in the types of social rules and evaluations evoked in different types of situations (Blanchard-Fields, 2009). For example, when participants considered a husband who chooses to work long hours instead of spending more time with his wife and children, different evaluations about the husband and the marriage emerged. The belief that "marriage is more important than a career" tended to increase in importance with age. As can be seen in Figure 10.11, this was particularly evident from age 24 to age 65. The social evaluation "the marriage was already in trouble" was also evident and yielded an inverted U-shaped graph; adults between 30 and 55 years of age were most likely to give this evaluation.

HUMAN DEVELOPMENT in action

Suppose you are a manager of a fast-food restaurant. How might types of thinking in adulthood be reflected in your employees?

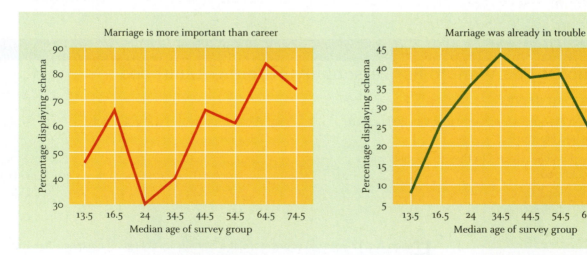

FIGURE 10.11

There are age differences in social rules and relationships evoked in different situations. As people grow older, there is an increase in the belief that marriage is more important than achievement in a career; also, older and younger couples may have explanations different from those of middle-aged adults as to why marriages fail.

Source: Blanchard-Fields, F. (1999). Social schematicity and causal attributions. In T.M. Hess, & F. Blanchard-Fields, F. (Eds.). Social Cognition and Aging. San Diego: Academic Press. Reprinted by permission of Elsevier.

One possible explanation for these findings is that cohort effects or generational differences (as discussed in Chapter 1) influenced whether strong family social rules would be activated (i.e., how cognition and emotion interact). Alternatively, the results could reflect issues concerning different life stages of the respondents; for example, the pressures of providing for children may influence how someone responds in midlife more so than in early or later adulthood. In any case, social beliefs, as expressed through social rules and evaluations, are powerful influences on how we behave in everyday life. Either way, the developmental shift in the integration of cognition and emotion is an important determinant of age differences in social problem solving.

Test Yourself

Recall

1. Most modern theories of intelligence are _____ in that they identify many domains of intellectual abilities.

2. Number, verbal fluency, and spatial orientation are some of the _____ mental abilities.

3. _____ reflects knowledge that acquired through life experience and education in a particular culture.

4. One kind of postformal thinking is called _____.

5. Life problems provide a context for understanding the integration of _____.

Interpret

- Many young adults seemingly get more confused about what field they want to major in and less certain about what they know as they progress through college. From a cognitive-developmental approach, why does this happen?
- Political movements often are led by a combination of late adolescents or young adults and older adults. According

to cognitive-developmental theory, why would this tend to be the case?

Apply

- Two of LuSharon's friends explained their decision to support President Barack Obama during the 2012 U.S. presidential campaign. One friend said that she had an intuition that President Obama's campaign statements were based on facts; the other friend said that the candidate's statements always had to be put into a specific context to be analyzed. Based on the reflective judgment model, what levels of thinking do LuSharon's friends demonstrate?
- How does experience on the job relate to the stages of reflective judgment?

Recall answers: (1) multidimensional, (2) primary, (3) Crystallized intelligence, (4) reflective judgment, (5) emotion and logic

---

10.4 Who Do You Want to Be? Personality in Young Adulthood

LEARNING OBJECTIVES

- What is the life-span construct? How do adults create scenarios and life stories?
- What are possible selves? Do they show differences during adulthood?
- What are personal control beliefs?

Felicia is a 19-year-old sophomore at a community college. She expects her study of early childhood education to be difficult but rewarding. She figures that, along the way, she will meet a great guy whom she will marry soon after graduation. They will have two children before she turns 30. Felicia sees herself getting a good job teaching preschool children and someday owning her own day-care center.

Blogging or posting Tweets has become a modern way of writing an autobiography.

In Chapter 9, we saw how children and adolescents deal with the question "What do you want to be when you grow up?" As a young adult, Felicia has arrived at the "grown up" part and is experimenting with some idealistic answers to the question. Are Felicia's answers typical of most young adults?

Creating Scenarios and Life Stories

Figuring out what (and who) you want to be as an adult takes lots of thought, hard work, and time. *Based on personal experience and input from other people, young adults create a* **life-span construct** *that represents a unified sense of the past, present, and future.* The life-span construct represents a link between Erikson's notion of identity, which is a major focus during adolescence, and our adult view of ourselves.

The first way in which the life-span construct is manifested is through the **scenario***, which consists of expectations about the future.* The scenario takes aspects of a person's identity that are particularly important now and projects them into a plan for the future. In short, a scenario is a game plan for how that person's life will play out.

Felicia, the sophomore college student in the opening vignette, has a fairly typical scenario. She plans on completing a degree in early childhood education, marrying after graduation, and having two children by age 30. *Tagging future events with a particular time or age by which they are to be completed creates a* **social clock**. This personal timetable gives people a way to track progress through adulthood (Hagestad & Neugarten, 1985).

Daniel McAdams argues that a person's sense of identity cannot be understood based on traits or personal concerns (2009; McAdams & Olson, 2010). To him, identity is not just a collection of traits, nor is it a collection of plans, strategies, or goals. Instead, it is based on the story of how each person came into being, where she has been, where she is going, and who she will become. *A* **life story** *is a personal narrative that organizes past events into a coherent sequence.*

Every life story contains episodes that provide insight into perceived change and continuity in life. People prove to themselves and to others that they have either changed or remained the same by pointing to specific events that support the appropriate claim. The main characters in people's lives represent idealizations of the self, such as "the dutiful mother" or "the reliable worker." Integrating these various aspects of the self is a major challenge of midlife and later adulthood. Finally, all life stories need an ending through which the self is able to leave a legacy that creates new beginnings. Life stories in middle-aged and older adults have a clear quality of "giving birth to" a new generation, a notion we will see in Chapters 12 and 13 is essentially identical to Erikson's (1982) idea of generativity.

Overall, McAdams (2008; McAdams & Olson, 2010) believes identity change over time is a process of fashioning and refashioning one's life story. This process appears to be strongly influenced by culture. At times, the reformulation may be at a conscious level, such as when people make explicit decisions about changing careers. At other times, the revision process is unconscious and implicit, growing out of everyday activities. The goal is to create a life story that is coherent, credible, open to new possibilities, richly differentiated, able to reconcile opposing aspects of oneself, and integrated within the sociocultural context.

Possible Selves

When we are asked questions like, "What do you think you'll be like a few years from now?" it requires us to imagine ourselves in the future. When we speculate like this, we create a possible self (Markus & Nurius, 1986). **Possible selves** *represent what we could become, what we would like to become, and what we are afraid of becoming.*

life-span construct
a unified sense of the past, present, and future based on personal experience and input from other people

scenario
a manifestation of the life-span construct through expectations about the future

social clock
tagging future events with a particular time or age by which they are to be completed

life story
a personal narrative that organizes past events into a coherent sequence

possible selves
representations of what we could become, what we would like to become, and what we are afraid of becoming

AP Images / Jae C. Hong

Chad Hurley, co-founder and former chief executive officer of YouTube, is likely to have a high sense of personal control.

HUMAN DEVELOPMENT in action

If you were a career counselor, how would you incorporate people's possible selves in your approach to counseling them?

personal control beliefs
the degree to which you believe your performance in a situation depends on something you do

What we could or would like to become often reflects personal goals; we may see ourselves as leaders, as rich and famous, or as in shape. What we are afraid of becoming may show up in our fear of being alone, overweight, or unsuccessful. Our possible selves are powerful motivators; indeed, how we behave is largely an effort to achieve or avoid these various possible selves and to protect the current view of self (Baumeister, 2010).

Researchers have examined age differences in the construction of possible selves (Bardach et al., 2010; Cotter & Gonzalez, 2009). In a rare set of similar studies conducted across time and research teams by Cross and Markus (1991) and Hooker and colleagues (Frazier et al., 2000, 2002; Hooker, 1999; Hooker et al., 1996; Morfei et al., 2001), people across the adult life span were asked to describe their hoped-for and feared possible selves. The responses were grouped into categories (e.g., family, personal, material, relationships, and occupation).

Several interesting age differences emerged. In terms of hoped-for selves, young adults listed family concerns—for instance, marrying the right person—as most important. In contrast, adults in their 30s listed family concerns last; their main issues involved personal concerns, such as being a more loving and caring person. By ages 40 to 59, family issues again became most common—for example, being a parent who can "let go" of the children. Reaching and maintaining satisfactory performance in one's occupational career, as well as accepting and adjusting to the physiological changes of middle age, were important to this age group.

For adults over 60, researchers found that personal issues were again most prominent—for example, being active and healthy for at least another decade The greatest amount of change occurred in the health domain, which predominated the hoped-for and feared selves. The health domain is the most sensitive and central to the self in the context of aging, and people's possible self related to health is quite resilient in the face of health challenges in later life.

Overall, young adults have multiple possible selves and believe that they can become the hoped-for self and successfully avoid the feared self. Their outlook tends to be quite positive (Remedios, Chasteen, & Packer, 2010). Life experience may dampen this outlook. By old age, both the number of possible selves and the strength of belief have decreased. Older adults are more likely to believe that neither the hoped-for nor the feared self is under their personal control. These findings may reflect differences with age in personal motivation, beliefs in personal control, and the need to explore new options.

The emergence of online social media has created new opportunities for young adults to create possible selves (Lefkowitz, Vukman, & Loken, 2012). Such media present different ways for them to speculate about themselves to others.

Personal Control Beliefs

Do you feel you have control over your life? **Personal control beliefs** *reflect the degree to which you believe your performance in a situation depends on something you do.* For example, suppose you are not offered a job when you think you should have been. Was it your fault? Or was it because the company was too shortsighted to recognize your true talent? Which option you select provides insight into a general tendency. Do you generally believe that outcomes depend on the things you do? Or are they due to factors outside of yourself, such as luck or the power of others?

A high sense of personal control implies a belief that performance is up to you, whereas a low sense of personal control implies that your performance is under the

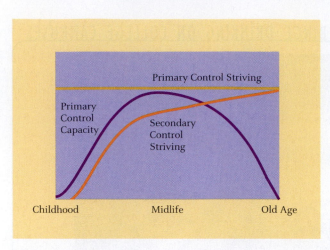

FIGURE 10.12

The use of primary control peaks in midlife, whereas secondary control increases across the adult life span.

Adapted from "A lifespan model of successful aging," by R. Schulz and J. Heckhausen in American Psychologist, *Vol. 51, pp. 702–714. Copyright © American Psychological Association 1996.*

primary control
behavior aimed at affecting the individual's external world

secondary control
behavior or cognition aimed at affecting the individual's internal world

influence of forces other than your own. Personal control is an extremely important idea in a variety of settings and cultures because of the way it guides behavior (Brandtstädter, 1999; Fung & Siu, 2010). Successful people like Stefani Joanne Angelina Germanotta (better known as Lady Gaga) need to exude a high sense of personal control to demonstrate that they are in charge.

Personal control is an important concept that can be applied broadly to several domains, including social networks, health, and careers (Fung & Siu, 2010). The developmental course of personal control beliefs depends on the context of the situation (Vazire & Doris, 2009). These beliefs vary depending on which domain, such as intelligence or health, is being assessed. Heckhausen, Wrosch, and Schulz (2010) pulled together the various perspectives on control beliefs and proposed a motivational theory of life-span development to describe how people optimize primary and secondary control. **Primary control** *is behavior aimed at affecting the individual's external world; working a second job to increase earnings is an example.* Our ability to influence our environment is heavily influenced by biological factors (e.g., stamina to work two jobs), so it changes over time—from very low influence during early childhood to high influence during middle age and then to very low again in late life. **Secondary control** *is behavior or cognition aimed at affecting the individual's internal world; an example is believing that one is capable of success even when faced with challenges.*

The developmental patterns of both types of control are shown in Figure 10.12. The figure also shows that people of all ages strive to control their environment, but how they do this changes over time. For the first half of life, primary control capacity and secondary control striving operate in parallel. During midlife, primary control capacity begins to decline but secondary control striving does not. Thus, the desire for control does not change; what differs with age is whether we can affect our environment or whether we need to think about things differently.

Test Yourself

Recall

1. A _____ is a unified sense of a person's past, present, and future.

2. A personal narrative that organizes past events into a coherent sequence is a _____ .

3. Representations of what we could become, what we would like to be, and what we are afraid of becoming are our _____ .

4. _____ reflect the degree to which a person's performance in a situation is believed to be under his or her control.

Interpret

- How might people's scenarios, life stories, and other aspects of personality vary as a function of cognitive-developmental level and self-definition as an adult?

- How do possible selves reflect people's life experiences?

Apply

- In the context of a bad economy, how could you determine whether your performance on job interviews is under your control?

- How has your view of your possible selves influenced your choice of career?

Recall answers: (1) life-span construct, (2) life story, (3) possible selves, (4) Personal control beliefs

Research reviewed earlier in the chapter showed that binge drinking on college campuses is a major problem. This research also provides ideas about how binge drinking could be reduced.

The NIAAA (2002, 2007) has offered four types or tiers of strategies. The most effective strategy (tier 1) provides one-on-one interventions for at-risk students and programs directly challenging students' expectations regarding alcohol use. Tier 2 strategies are also effective but are not directly implemented on campus, such as working with local officials to make alcohol more difficult to obtain illegally (e.g., by increasing identification checks at restaurants and stores). Tier 3 strategies show promise but are not yet shown to be definitively effective; these include social norms programs, enforcement of campus alcohol policies, and designated driver programs. Tier 4 strategies are ineffective; some of the most typical strategies used by colleges are included here, such as alcohol education programs. NIAAA urges colleges to attack binge drinking in a three-in-one approach, focusing on the individual student, the student body as a whole, and the surrounding community.

Although NIAAA initially listed social norms programs as a tier 3 strategy (a promising strategy not yet proven to be effective), evidence is growing that such programs are effective in the United States (Perkins et al., 2010) and around the world (McAlaney, Bewick, & Hughes, 2011). The social norms approach focuses on changing the culture of drinking in college from one that strongly supports binge drinking to one in which binge drinking is something that popular people do not do. This approach is based on the idea that many college students think their peers' attitudes toward drinking are more permissive than they really are (NIAAA, 2007).

The belief that "everyone is drinking" and that drinking is entirely acceptable is a major correlate of actual binge drinking behavior. The goal of social norms intervention programs is to publicize the true rate of drinking on campus. Equally important for social norms, but often overlooked, are secondhand drinking effects: negative drinking-related consequences that are experienced by others. For example, a nondrinker may be insulted, assaulted, or have to care for an ill binge drinker, which may in turn have important academic consequences for the nondrinking student.

© David Young-Wolff / PhotoEdit

Binge drinking is viewed by many as a rite of passage in college, but it is an especially troublesome behavior for young adults that can cause academic problems.

Clearly, the data indicate that binge drinking among young adults is not inevitable (remember that the rate of binge drinking among young adults not in college has been declining for decades). So it's something about the college experience and culture that's behind it. The social norms approach, with other effective strategies, may offer one way of changing the culture.

Summary

10.1 Emerging Adulthood

What role transitions mark entry into adulthood?

- Some societies use rituals, called rites of passage, to mark this transition clearly. However, such rituals are largely absent in Western culture.

- The most widely used criteria for deciding whether a person has reached adulthood are role transitions, which involve assuming new responsibilities and duties.

How does going to college reflect the transition to adulthood?

- The many college students known as returning adult students are over age 25. These students tend to be more motivated than those who entered college directly from high school, and they have many other positive characteristics.

What behavioral criteria mark the transition to adulthood?

- A major difference between adolescence and adulthood is a drop in the rate of participation in reckless behavior.

- Young adults grapple with issues relating to intimacy, although whether this occurs only after the issue of identity is resolved differs across gender.

How does achieving financial independence reflect the transition to adulthood?

- Launching oneself as financially independent is a major marker of achieving adulthood in Western society.

- Financial independence can be achieved in many ways, such as a series of part-time jobs, joining the military, or going to college and then entering the workforce.

10.2 Physical Development and Health

In what respects are young adults at their physical peak?

- Young adulthood is the time when certain physical abilities peak: strength, muscle development, coordination, dexterity, and sensory acuity. Most of these abilities begin to decline in middle age.

How healthy are young adults in general?

- Young adults are at the peak of health. Death from disease is relatively rare, especially during the 20s. Rather, accidents are the leading cause of death. However, poverty is a major barrier to good health.

How do smoking, drinking alcohol, and nutrition affect young adults' health?

- Smoking is the single biggest contributor to health problems. A person is never too old to quit smoking.

- Smoking is related to many cancers and is a primary cause of respiratory and cardiovascular disease. Although it is difficult, quitting smoking has many health benefits.

- For most people, drinking alcohol in moderation poses few health risks. Several treatment approaches are available for alcoholics.

- Nutritional needs change somewhat during adulthood, mostly due to changes in metabolism. The ratio of low-density to high-density lipoprotein cholesterol, which can be controlled through diet or medication in most people, is an important risk factor in cardiovascular disease.

How does the health of young adults differ as a function of socioeconomic status, gender, and ethnicity?

- The two most important social factors in health are socioeconomic status and education. The poorest health conditions exist for Americans living in poor, inner-city neighborhoods. Ethnic groups with limited access to health care also suffer.

- Higher education is associated with better health via better access to health care and more knowledge about proper diet and lifestyle.

10.3 Cognitive Development

What is intelligence in adulthood?

- Most modern theories of intelligence are multidimensional. For instance, research shows that development in adults varies among individuals and across categories of abilities.

What are primary and secondary mental abilities? How do they change?

- Intellectual abilities can be studied as groups of related skills known as primary mental abilities.

- Clusters of related primary abilities are called secondary mental abilities. Secondary mental abilities are not measured directly.

- Intellectual abilities develop differently and change in succeeding cohorts. More recent cohorts perform better on some skills, such as inductive reasoning, but older cohorts perform better on other skills.

What are fluid and crystallized intelligence? How do they change?

- Fluid intelligence consists of abilities that make people flexible and adaptive thinkers. Fluid abilities generally decline during adulthood.

- Crystallized intelligence reflects knowledge that people acquire through life experience and education in a particular culture. Crystallized abilities improve until late life.

How has neuroscience research furthered our understanding of intelligence in adulthood?

- Neuroscience research has begun mapping specific areas in the brain that relate to intelligence. One prominent theory based on this work is the parietofrontal integration theory.

What is postformal thought? How does it differ from formal operations?

- Postformal thought is characterized by recognition that truth may vary from one situation to another, that solutions must be realistic, that ambiguity and contradiction are the rule, and that emotion and subjectivity play roles in thinking. One example of postformal thought is reflective judgment.

How do emotion and logic become integrated in adulthood?

- Cognition (logic) and emotion become integrated during young adulthood and middle age. This means that the way people approach and solve practical problems in life differs from adolescence through middle age.

10.4 Who Do You Want to Be? Personality in Young Adulthood

What is the life-span construct? How do adults create scenarios and life stories?

- Young adults create a life-span construct that represents a unified sense of the past, present, and future. This is

manifested in two ways: through a scenario that maps the future based on a social clock and in the life story, which creates an autobiography.

What are possible selves? Do they show differences during adulthood?

- People create possible selves by projecting themselves into the future and thinking about what they would like to become, what they could become, and what they are afraid of becoming.

- Age differences in these projections depend on the dimension examined. In hoped-for selves, young and middle-aged adults report family issues as most important, whereas those in their 30s and older adults consider personal issues to be most important. However, all groups include health aspects as part of their most hoped-for and feared selves.

What are personal control beliefs?

- Personal control is an important concept with broad applicability. However, the developmental trends are complex because personal control beliefs vary considerably from one domain to another.

Key Terms

emerging adulthood (264)
rites of passage (264)
role transitions (265)
returning adult students (266)
edgework (266)
binge drinking (271)
addiction (272)
metabolism (272)
low-density lipoproteins (LDLs) (273)
high-density lipoproteins (HDLs) (273)

multidimensional (275)
multidirectionality (275)
interindividual variability (275)
plasticity (275)
primary mental abilities (275)
secondary mental abilities (275)
fluid intelligence (277)
crystallized intelligence (278)
Parietofrontal integration theory (P-FIT) (279)

postformal thought (280)
reflective judgment (280)
life-span construct (283)
scenario (283)
social clock (283)
life story (283)
possible selves (283)
personal control beliefs (284)
primary control (285)
secondary control (285)

Online Resources

Go to CengageBrain.com to access Psychology CourseMate, where you will find an interactive eBook, flashcards, quizzes, videos, websites, and more.

Being With Others

Forming Relationships in Young and Middle Adulthood

11

Imagine yourself years from now. In honor of your 80th birthday, your family and friends' present to you is a video representing the decades of your life. As you watch, you realize how lucky you've been to have so many wonderful people in your life. As you watch, you wonder what it must be like to go through life alone—no family, no friends (even on Facebook), no followers of your Twitter postings. That is what we explore in this chapter—the ways in which we share our lives with others.

LEARNING OBJECTIVES

- What types of friendships do adults have? How do adult friendships develop?

- What is love? How does it develop through adulthood?

- What is the nature of abuse in some relationships?

Jamal and Deb, both 25 years old, have been madly in love since they met at a party about a month ago. They spend as much time together as possible and pledge that they will stay together forever. Deb finds herself daydreaming about Jamal at work and can't wait to go over to his apartment. She wants to move in, but her co-workers tell her to slow down.

You know what Jamal and Deb are going through. Each of us wants to be wanted by someone else. We need people. Without friends and lovers, life would be pretty lonely.

Friendships

Researchers define friendship as a mutual relationship in which those involved influence each other's behaviors and beliefs, and they define friendship quality as the satisfaction derived from the relationship (Flynn, 2007).

The role and influence of friends is of major importance from the late teens to the mid-20s (Arnett, 2007) and continues throughout adulthood. Friendships are predominantly based on feelings, are grounded in reciprocity and choice, and are less emotionally intense and involve less sexual energy or contact than love relationships (Rose & Zand, 2000). Having good friendships helps boost self-esteem (Bagwell et al., 2005).

Friendship in Adulthood

From a developmental perspective, adult friendships have identifiable stages (Levinger, 1980, 1983): acquaintanceship, buildup, continuation, deterioration, and ending. This ABCDE model describes not only the stages of friendships but also the processes by which they change.

Longitudinal research shows how friendships change from adolescence through young adulthood, sometimes in ways that are predictable and sometimes not. Life transitions (e.g., going away to college or getting married) usually result in fewer friends and less contact with the friends you keep (Flynn, 2007). People tend to have more friends and acquaintances during young adulthood than at any subsequent period (Sherman, de Vries, & Lansford, 2000). College students who have strong friendship networks adjust better to stressful life events (Brissette, Scheier, & Carver, 2002) and have better self-esteem (Bagwell et al., 2005). People who have friendships that cross ethnic groups have more positive attitudes toward people with different backgrounds (Aberson, Shoemaker, & Tomolillo, 2004).

The development of online social networks such as Facebook raised concerns that adults' social friendship networks would decline in quality because in-depth interactions would be replaced with quick e-mails or postings. Research shows that this is not true. Wang and Wellman (2010) documented that the quality of the friendship networks in adults age 25 to 74 was good overall and actually improving. This improvement

Despite concerns, social networking websites such as Facebook have not reduced the quality of friendships.

© age fotostock/SuperStock

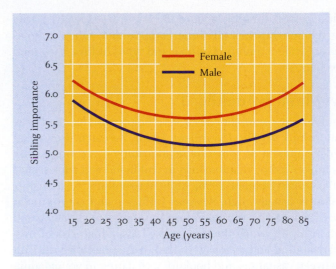

FIGURE 11.1

The importance that men and women place on sibling relationships varies across adulthood and is weakest during middle age.

Source: "When being a brother or sister is important to one's identity: Life stage and gender differences," M. Schmeeckle, M., R. Giarusso, and O. Wang. Paper presented at the annual meeting of the Gerontological Society, Philadelphia (November 1998).

was documented whether people were nonusers of the Internet or heavily virtual. The researchers found that heavy Internet users had the most friends, both online and offline.

In the case of online friendships, trust is an important factor because visual cues may not be present to verify the information being presented. Online environments are more conducive to people who are shy, allowing opportunities to meet others in an initially more anonymous setting in which social interaction and intimacy levels can be carefully controlled (Morahan-Martin & Schumacher, 2003). Online connections can facilitate strong commitment between friends; research shows that most adults who have online, committed friendships report that those friendships can get stronger and that such friendships go through the same cycles as traditional, face-to-face ones (Johnson et al., 2009). However, some argue that online friendships are not true friendships (Fröding & Peterson, 2012).

A special type of friendship exists with siblings (Schulte, 2006), and the importance of these relationships varies with age. As you can see in Figure 11.1, women place more importance on sibling ties across adulthood than do men; however, for both genders, the strength of such ties is greatest in adolescence and late life (Schmeeckle, Giarusso, & Wang, 1998). In young adulthood, siblings report that geographic distance does not affect the quality of the relationship and that expressions of intimacy about the importance of the relationship matter (Corti, 2009).

Men's, Women's, and Cross-Sex Friendships

Men's and women's friendships tend to differ, reflecting continuity in the learned behaviors from childhood (Mehta & Strough, 2009). Women tend to base their friendships on more intimate and emotional sharing and use friendship as a means to confide in others. In contrast, men tend to base friendships on shared activities or interests and are often less intimate (Greif, 2009). Men tend to have a small number of friends with whom they have a close, personal relationship.

Women tend to have more close relationships than do men. But this isn't always an advantage. Sometimes friends can get on people's nerves or make demands. When these things happen, women tend to be less happy even when they have lots of friends (Antonucci, Akiyama, & Lansford, 1998).

What about cross-sex friendships? These have a beneficial effect, especially for men (Piquet, 2007). Cross-sex friendships tend to help men have a lower level of dating anxiety and higher capacity for intimacy; however, such benefits are not evident for women. These patterns hold across ethnic groups. But cross-sex friendships can also prove troublesome as a result of misperceptions and pressures against them from third parties (e.g., spouses or partners) and organizations (e.g., companies that may discourage such friendships) (Mehta & Strough, 2009). Some research shows that men tend to overperceive and women tend to underperceive their friends' sexual interest in them (Koenig, Kirkpatrick, & Ketelaar, 2007). Maintaining cross-sex friendships once individuals enter into exclusive dating relationships, marriage, or committed relationships is difficult, and it often results in one partner feeling jealous (Williams, 2005).

Love Relationships

Love is one of those things everybody feels but nobody can define completely. One way researchers have tried to understand love is to think about what components are essential. Sternberg (2006) found that love has three basic components: (1) passion, an intense physiological desire for someone; (2) intimacy, the feeling that one can share all thoughts and actions with another; and (3) commitment, the willingness to stay

Physical attraction tends to be high early in a relationship.

with a person through good and bad times. Ideally, a true love relationship has all three components; when couples have equivalent amounts of love and types of love, they tend to be happier.

Love Through Adulthood

The different combinations of love help us understand how relationships develop (Sternberg, 2006). Research shows that the development of romantic relationships is a complex process influenced by relationships in childhood and adolescence (Collins & van Dulmen, 2006). Early in a romantic relationship, passion is usually high, whereas intimacy and commitment tend to be low. This is infatuation: an intense, physically based relationship in which the two people have a high risk of misunderstanding and jealousy. Indeed, it is sometimes difficult to establish the boundaries between casual sex and hookups and dating in young adulthood (Giordano et al., 2012).

But infatuation is short lived. As passion fades, either a relationship acquires emotional intimacy or it is likely to end. Trust, honesty, openness, and acceptance must be a part of any strong relationship; when they are present, romantic love develops.

This pattern is a good thing. Research shows that people who select a partner for a more permanent relationship (e.g., marriage) during the height of infatuation are more likely to divorce (Hansen, 2006). But if the couple gives it more time and works at their relationship, they may become committed to each other.

Lemieux and Hale (2002) demonstrated that these developmental trends hold in romantically involved couples between 17 and 75 years of age. As the length of the relationship increases, intimacy and passion decrease but commitment increases.

Falling in Love

In his book *The Prophet,* Kahlil Gibran points out that love is two sided: Just as it can give you great ecstasy, so can it cause you great pain. Yet most of us are willing to take the risk. As you may have experienced, taking the risk is fun (at times) and difficult (at other times).

The best explanation of the process is the theory of **assortative mating**, *which states that people find partners based on their similarity to each other.* Assortative mating occurs along many dimensions, including education, religious beliefs, physical traits, age, socioeconomic status, intelligence, and political ideology (Blossfeld, 2009). Such nonrandom mating occurs most often in Western societies, which allow people to have more control over their dating and pairing behaviors than in other cultures. Common activities are one basis for identifying potential mates—except in speed dating situations. In that case, it comes down to physical attractiveness (Luo & Zhang, 2009).

People meet people in all sorts of places. Does where people meet influence the likelihood that they will "click" on particular dimensions and will form a couple? Kalmijn and Flap (2001) found that it does. Using data from more than 1,500 couples, they found that meeting at school was most likely to result in the most forms of homogamy—the degree to which people are similar. Not surprisingly, the pool of available people to meet is strongly shaped by the opportunities available, which in turn constrain the type of people someone is likely to meet.

Speed dating provides a way to meet several people in a short period. Speed dating is practiced most by young adults (Whitty & Buchanan, 2009). The rules governing partner selection during a speed dating session seem quite similar to traditional dating: physically attractive people, outgoing and self-assured people, and moderately self-focused people are selected more often, and their dates are rated as smoother (Eastwick, Saigal, & Finkel, 2010).

The popularity of online dating means an increasing number of people meet this way (Stevens & Morris, 2007; Whitty & Buchanan, 2009). Surveys indicate that nearly

assortative mating
a theory stating that people find partners based on their similarity to each other

1 in every 5 couples in the United States meet online (compared with 1 in 10 in Australia and 1 in 20 in Spain and the United Kingdom; Dutton et al., 2009). Emerging research indicates that virtual dating sites offer both problems and possibilities, especially in terms of the accuracy of personal descriptions. As in the offline world, physical attractiveness strongly influences initial selections online (Sritharan et al., 2010). Still, many couples who have met via online sites have formed committed relationships (Mazzarella, 2007).

We've seen that physical attractiveness matters in speed dating and online dating, as it does in traditional dating. How does physical attraction operate? Research shows that women tend to choose a more masculine-looking man as a person with whom to have an exciting short-term relationship but tend to select a more feminine-looking man for their husband or as the type of man their parents would want them to date (Kruger, 2006). These findings support a study of nearly 2,000 Spanish respondents (Sangrador & Yela, 2000).

How do these couple-forming behaviors compare cross-culturally? As described in the Spotlight on Research feature, Schmitt et al. (2004) studied 62 cultural regions. They showed that secure romantic attachment was the norm in nearly 80% of cultures and that "preoccupied" romantic attachment was particularly common in East Asian cultures. In general, multicultural studies show that there are global patterns in mate selection and romantic relationships. The romantic attachment profiles of individual nations were correlated with sociocultural indicators in ways that supported evolutionary theories of romantic attachment and basic human mating strategies.

Spotlight on research — Patterns and Universals of Romantic Attachment

Who were the investigators, and what was the aim of the study?
David Schmitt and his colleagues (2004) assembled a large international team of researchers to learn how attachment style influences how someone forms romantic relationships.

How did the investigators measure the topic of interest?
Great care was taken to ensure equivalent translation of the survey across 62 cultural regions. The survey was a measure of adult romantic attachment (the Relationship Questionnaire) that measured models of self and others relative to each other: "secure" romantic attachment (high scores indicate positive models of self and others), "dismissing" romantic attachment (high scores indicate a positive model of self and a negative model of others), "preoccupied" romantic attachment (high scores indicate a negative model of self and a positive model of others), and "fearful" romantic attachment (high scores indicate negative models of self and others).

In addition, there were measures of self-esteem, personality traits, and sociocultural correlates of romantic attachment (e.g., fertility rate and national profiles of individualism [an emphasis that each individual is separate] versus collectivism [an emphasis that each individual is interconnected]).

Who were the participants in the study?
A total of 17,804 people (7,432 men and 10,372 women) from 62 cultural regions around the world took part in the study. Such large and diverse samples are unusual in developmental research.

What was the design of the study?
This was a cross-sectional, nonexperimental study because different age groups were measured once and no independent variable was manipulated.

Were there ethical concerns with the study?
Because the study involved volunteers, there were no ethical concerns.

What were the results?
The researchers first demonstrated that the measures used for model of self and model of others were valid across cultural regions. Specific analyses showed that 79% of the cultural groups studied demonstrated secure romantic attachments but that North American cultures tended to be high on dismissive and East Asian cultures high on preoccupied romantic attachment. These patterns are shown in Figure 11.2. All cultural regions except East Asia showed a pattern in which model of self scores are higher than model of others scores.

What did the investigators conclude?
Overall, Schmitt and his colleagues concluded that although the same attachment pattern holds across most cultures, no one pattern holds across all cultures. East Asian cultures in particular tend to fit a pattern in which people report that others do not get as emotionally close as the respondent would like and that respondents find it difficult to trust others or to depend on them.

What converging evidence would strengthen these conclusions?
Representative samples from the countries under study would provide more accurate insights into people's romantic attachment patterns.

Continued

Continued

FIGURE 11.2

In these model of self and model of others levels across 10 world regions, only in East Asian cultures were model of others scores significantly higher than model of self scores.

Data from "Patterns and universals of adult romantic attachment across 62 cultural regions: Are models of self and of other pancultural constructs?" by D. P. Schmitt, L. Alcalay, M. Allensworth, J. Allik, L. Ault, I. Austers, et al., in Journal of Cross-Cultural Psychology, Vol. 35. Copyright © 2004.

 Go to Psychology CourseMate at **www.cengagebrain.com** to enhance your understanding of this research.

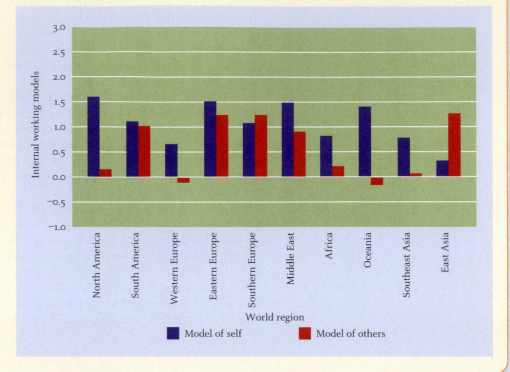

These Egyptian women, performing traditional cultural tasks, are likely to be desired as mates within their society.

Courtesy of John C. Cavanaugh

HUMAN DEVELOPMENT in action

Suppose you were the head of an online company called FindAMate.com. How will Skype and ooVoo continue to affect your company?

abusive relationship
a relationship in which one person becomes aggressive toward the partner

Culture is a powerful force in shaping mate selection choices. For example, despite decades of sociopolitical change in China, research indicates that the same status hierarchy norms from earlier times govern mating patterns in urban China (Xu, Ji, & Tung, 2000). Emotional investment in a romantic relationship also varies by culture (Schmitt et al., 2009). Specifically, across 48 cultures globally, people from cultures that have good health care, education, and resources and that permit young adults to choose their own mates tend to develop more secure romantic attachments than do people from cultures that do not have these characteristics.

Clearly, cultural norms are sometimes highly resistant to change. For example, loyalty of the individual to the family is an important value in India, so despite many changes in mate selection, about 95% of marriages in India are carefully arranged to ensure that an appropriate mate is selected (Dommaraju, 2010). Similarly, Islamic societies use matchmaking as a way to preserve family consistency and continuity and to ensure that couples follow the prohibition on premarital relationships between men and women (Adler, 2001). Matchmaking in these societies occurs both through family connections and personal advertisements in newspapers. To keep up with the Internet age, Muslim matchmaking has gone online too (Lo & Aziz, 2009).

The Dark Side of Relationships: Abuse

Sometimes relationships become violent; one person becomes aggressive toward the partner, creating an **abusive relationship**. Such relationships have received increasing attention since the early 1980s, when the U.S. criminal justice system ruled that, under some circumstances, abusive relationships can be used as an explanation for

Causes of Abuse in Relationships

Type of Abuse	Causes
Verbal abuse	Need to control
	Misuse of power
	Jealousy
	Marital discord
Physical abuse	Acceptance of violence as means of control
	Physically aggressive models
	Abuse as a child
	Aggressive personality style
	Alcohol abuse
Severe physical abuse	Personality disorders
	Emotional swings
	Poor self-esteem

Note: Unemployment and job stressors contribute to all types of abuse.

Source: Based on O'Leary, K.D. (1993). Through a psychological lens: Personality traits, personality disorders, and levels of violence. In Gelles & Loseke (Eds.) Current controversies on family violence. Newbury Park, CA: Sage.

behavior (Walker, 1984). *For example,* **battered woman syndrome** *occurs when a woman believes that she cannot leave an abusive situation and may even go so far as to kill her abuser.*

Being female, being Latina American or African American, having an atypical family structure (something other than two biological parents), having more romantic partners, undergoing early onset of sexual activity, and being a victim of child abuse predict victimization. Although overall national rates of sexual assault have declined more than 60% since the early 1990s, acquaintance rape or date rape is still a major problem; college women are four times more likely to be the victim of sexual assault than are women in other age groups (Rape, Abuse, and Incest National Network, 2010), with 40% experiencing abuse in a dating relationship (Halpern et al., 2009).

What range of aggressive behaviors occurs in abusive relationships? What causes such abuse? Based on considerable research on abusive partners, O'Leary (1993) argues that there is a continuum of aggressive behaviors toward a partner, which progresses as follows: verbally aggressive behaviors, physically aggressive behaviors, severe physically aggressive behaviors (see Table 11.1). The causes of the abuse also vary with the type of abusive behavior being expressed.

Two points about the continuum should be noted. First, there may be fundamental differences in the types of aggression independent of the level of severity. Overall, each year about 4.8 million women and 2.9 million men experience partner-related physical assaults and rape in the United States (Centers for Disease Control and Prevention, 2009); worldwide, between 10% and 69% of women report being physically assaulted or raped (World Health Organization, 2002).

The second point, depicted in the table, is that the suspected underlying causes of aggressive behaviors differ as the type of aggressive behaviors change (O'Leary, 1993). Although anger and hostility in the perpetrator are associated with various forms of physical abuse, the exact nature of this relationship remains elusive (Norlander & Eckhardt, 2005).

In the United States, men are also the victims of violence from intimate partners, though at a rate about one third that of women (Conradi & Geffner, 2009). Studies in New Zealand and the United States revealed that men and women showed similar patterns of holding traditional gendered beliefs and lacking communication and anger management skills; however, intervention programs tend to focus on male perpetrators (Hines & Douglas, 2009; Robertson & Murachver, 2007). Research on violence in gay and lesbian relationships reveals similar findings, and reasons for abuse in such relationships include dissatisfaction with the relationship and alcohol abuse (Fisher-Borne, 2007; Roberts, 2007).

battered woman syndrome
a situation occurring when a woman believes that she cannot leave an abusive situation and may even go so far as to kill her abuser

Culture is also an important contextual factor in understanding partner abuse. In particular, violence against women worldwide reflects cultural traditions, beliefs, and values of patriarchal societies; this can be seen in the commonplace violent practices against women in some countries, which include sexual slavery, female genital cutting, intimate partner violence, and honor killing (Parrot & Cummings, 2006).

In addition, international data indicate that rates of abuse are higher in cultures that emphasize female purity, male status, and family honor. For example, a common cause of women's murders in Arab countries is brothers or other male relatives killing the victim because she violated the family's honor (Kulwicki, 2002). Intimate partner violence is prevalent in China (43% lifetime risk in one study) and has strong associations with patriarchal values and conflict resolutions (Xu et al., 2005).

Alarmed by the seriousness of abuse, many communities have established shelters for battered women and their children, as well as programs that treat abusive men. However, the legal system in many localities is still not set up to deal with domestic violence; women in some locations cannot sue their husbands for assault, and restraining orders all too often offer little real protection from additional violence. Much remains to be done to protect women and their children from the fear and the reality of continued abuse.

Test Yourself

Recall

1. Friendships based on intimacy and emotional sharing are more characteristic of _____.

2. Shared activities is a major part of most friendships among _____.

3. Love relationships in which passion is present but intimacy and commitment are not are termed _____.

4. Aggressive behavior that is based on abuse of power, jealousy, or the need to control is more likely to be displayed as _____.

Interpret

- Why are cultural norms about love relationships so hard to change?

- What do the factors underlying abuse in relationships tell us about the nature of non-abusive relationships?

Apply

- What aspects of cultural differences in mate selection would be important to social workers?

- How would you incorporate information about cultural differences in relationships into international student exchange programs?

Recall answers: (1) women, (2) men, (3) infatuation, (4) verbal abuse

---

11.2 Lifestyles

LEARNING OBJECTIVES

- What's it like to be single?
- What are the characteristics of cohabiting people?
- What are gay and lesbian relationships like?
- What is marriage like through the course of adulthood?

Kevin and Beth are on cloud nine. They got married one month ago and have recently returned from their honeymoon. Everyone who sees them can tell that they love each other a lot. They are highly compatible and have much in common, sharing most of their leisure activities. Kevin and Beth wonder what lies ahead in their marriage.

Developing relationships is only part of the picture in understanding how adults live their lives with other people. Putting relationships like Kevin and Beth's in context is important for us to understand how relationships come into existence and how they change over time.

Single women often face social stereotypes that make life difficult, including lower salaries at work.

Singlehood

Estimates are that approximately 80% of men and 70% of women between ages 20 and 24 are single, with increasing numbers deciding to stay that way (U.S. Census Bureau, 2010a).

What's it like to be single in the United States? It's tougher than you might think. DePaulo (2006) points out numerous stereotypes and biases against single people. Her research found that young adults characterized married people as caring, kind, and giving about 50% of the time compared with only 2% for single people. DePaulo and her colleagues also found that rental agents preferred married couples 60% of the time (Morris, Sinclair, & DePaulo, 2007).

Many women and men remain single as young adults to focus on establishing their careers rather than on marriage or love relationships, which most do later. Others report that they simply did not meet "the right person" or prefer singlehood (Ibrahim & Hassan, 2009; Lamanna & Riedmann, 2003). However, the pressure to marry is especially strong for women.

Men tend to remain single longer in young adulthood because they tend to marry at a later age than women (U.S. Census Bureau, 2010b). Fewer men than women remain unmarried throughout adulthood, though, mainly because men find partners more easily because they select from a larger age range of unmarried women.

Ethnic differences in singlehood reflect differences in age at marriage, as well as social factors. For example, nearly twice as many African Americans are single during young adulthood as European Americans, and more are choosing to remain so (U.S. Census Bureau, 2010a). Singlehood is also increasing among Latino Americans, in part because the average age of Latinos in the United States is lower than that of other ethnic groups and in part because of poor economic opportunities for many Latino Americans (Lamanna & Riedmann, 2003).

Globally, the meanings and implications of remaining single are often tied to strongly held cultural and religious beliefs. For example, Muslim women who remain single in Malaysia speak in terms of *jodoh* (the soul mate found through fate at a time appointed by God) as a reason; they believe that God simply has not decided to have them meet their mate at this time (Ibrahim & Hassan, 2009). But because the role of Malaysian women is to marry, they also understand their marginalized position in society through their singlehood. In Southeast Asia, the number of single adults has increased steadily as education levels have risen over the past several decades (Hull, 2009). This change has challenged traditional definitions of family systems in these cultures (Jones, 2010).

An important distinction is between adults who are temporarily single (i.e., those who are single only until they find a suitable marriage partner) and those who choose to remain single. For most singles, the decision to never marry is a gradual one. This transition is represented by a change in self-attributed status that occurs over time and is associated with a cultural timetable for marriage. It marks the experience of "becoming single" that occurs when an individual identifies more with singlehood than with marriage (Davies, 2003).

Cohabitation

Being unmarried does not necessarily mean living alone. *People in committed, intimate, sexual relationships but who are not married may decide that living together, or* **cohabitation***, provides a way to share daily life.* Cohabitation is becoming an increasingly popular lifestyle choice in the United States, as well as in Canada, Europe, Australia, and elsewhere. Cohabitation in the United States has increased 10-fold over the past three decades: from 523,000 couples in 1970 to 5.5 million couples in 2002, the most recent year in which extensive data were collected (Goodwin, Mosher, & Chandra, 2010). People with lower educational levels cohabit more, and do so in more relationships, than individuals with higher educational

cohabitation

people in committed, intimate, sexual relationships live together but are not married levels. European American, African American, and Latino American men and women cohabit at about the same rates, other factors being equal.

Couples cohabit for three main reasons, most often in connection with testing their relationship in the context of potential marriage but also for convenience and as an alternative to marriage (Rhoades, Stanley, & Markman, 2009).

The global picture differs by culture (Popenoe, 2009; Therborn, 2010). For example, in most European, South American, and Caribbean countries, cohabitation is a common alternative to marriage for young adults. Cohabitation is extremely common in the Netherlands, Norway, and Sweden, where this lifestyle is part of the culture; 99% of married couples in Sweden lived together before they married, and nearly one in four couples are not legally married. Decisions to marry in these countries are typically made to legalize the relationship after children are born—in contrast to Americans, who marry to confirm their love and commitment to each other.

Interestingly, having cohabitated does not seem to make marriages any better; in fact, it may do more harm than good, resulting in lower-quality marriages (Tach & Halpern-Meekin, 2009). These findings reflect two underlying issues: U.S. couples who have children while cohabiting (especially European American women, as compared with African American and Latina American women; Tach & Halpern-Meekin, 2009) and couples who are using cohabitation to test their relationship (Rhoades, Stanley, & Markman, 2009) are most likely to report subsequent problems.

Longitudinal studies find few differences in couples' behavior after living together for many years regardless of whether they married without cohabiting, cohabited and then married, or simply cohabited (Stafford, Kline, & Rankin, 2004). In addition, many countries extend the same rights and benefits to cohabiting couples as they do to married couples and have done so for many years. For instance, Argentina provides pension rights to cohabiting partners, Canada extends insurance benefits, and Australia has laws governing the disposition of property when cohabiting couples sever their relationship (Neft & Levine, 1997).

HUMAN DEVELOPMENT in action

How might different rates of cohabitation affect job benefits in the workplace?

Gay and Lesbian Couples

Less is known about the developmental course of gay and lesbian relationships than that of heterosexual relationships (Rothblum, 2009). What is it like to be gay or lesbian? One woman shares her experience in the Real People feature.

real People APPLYING HUMAN DEVELOPMENT
MAGGIE O'CARROLL'S STORY

I am a 35-year-old woman who believes that each person is here with a purpose to fulfill in his or her lifetime. "Add your light to the sum of light" are words I live by in my teaching career, my personal life with friends and family, and living in general. At times I am very discouraged by the level of hatred that is evident in the world against many groups and against homosexuals in particular.

For me, being a lesbian is the most natural state of being. I do not think of it as a mishap of genetics, a result of an unhappy or traumatic childhood, or an unnatural tendency. However, I am aware of the homophobia that is present at all levels of my own life and in the community. That is where my sense of self and living in the world collide.

Society does not value diversity. We, as a people, do not look to people who are different and acknowledge the strength it takes to live in this society. Being gay in a homophobic, heterosexist society is a burden that manifests itself in many forms, such as through alcohol and drug abuse rates that are much higher than in the heterosexual community. The lack of acknowledgment of gay people's partners by family members, co-workers, and society at large is a stamp of nonexistence and invisibility. How can we build a life with a partner and then not share that person with society?

I consider myself a fortunate gay person in that I have a supportive family. Of the five children in my family, two of us are gay. My parents are supportive and love our partners. My

siblings vary in their attitudes. One sister invited me and my partner to her wedding. Nine years later, my other sister refused to do that. It was very hurtful and hard to forgive.

In the larger community, I have been surprised by the blatant hatred I have experienced. I have demeaning comments aimed at me. The home I live in has been defaced with obscenities. But on a more positive note, I have never been more strongly certain of who I am. I am indebted to those who have supported me over the years with love and enlightenment, knowing that who I am is not a mistake. As I age, it becomes clearer to me that I am meant to share the message that our differences are to be appreciated and respected.

Gay and lesbian couples experience stresses in relationships similar to those of heterosexual couples.

For the most part, the relationships of gay and lesbian couples have many similarities to those of heterosexual couples (Kurdek, 2004). Most gay and lesbian couples are in dual-earner relationships, much like the majority of married heterosexual couples, and are likely to share household chores. However, gay and lesbian couples differ from heterosexual couples in the degree to which both partners are similar on demographic characteristics, such as race, age, and education; gay and lesbian couples tend to be more dissimilar (Schwartz & Graf, 2009).

Gay men, like heterosexual men, tend to separate love and sex and have more short-term relationships (Missildine et al., 2005); both lesbian and heterosexual women are more likely to connect sex and emotional intimacy in fewer, longer-lasting relationships. Lesbians tend to make a commitment and cohabit faster than heterosexual couples (Ganiron, 2007).

Gay and lesbian couples report receiving less support from family members than do either married or cohabiting heterosexual couples (Rothblum, 2009). At a societal level, marriage or civil unions between same-sex couples remain highly controversial in America, with more than half of all states passing constitutional amendments or statutes defining marriage as between a man and a woman. The lack of legal recognition for gay and lesbian relationships in the United States also means that certain rights and privileges, such as certain insurance benefits and hospital visitation rights, are not always granted. Although the legal status of gay and lesbian couples is changing in more countries (most notably in Scandinavia) and a few U.S. states (including New York), most countries and U.S. states do not provide them with the same legal rights as married couples.

Marriage

Most adults want their love relationships to result in marriage. However, over time, U.S. residents have been in less of a hurry to achieve this goal; the median age at first marriage for adults in the United States has been rising for several decades. As shown in Figure 11.3, between 1970 and 2009, the median age for first marriage rose by about 5 years for both men and women (U.S. Census Bureau, 2010b). This trend has some benefits in that, for women, marrying at a later age lessens the likelihood of divorce (U.S. Census Bureau, 2010a).

marital success
an umbrella term referring to any marital outcome

marital quality
a subjective evaluation of the couple's relationship on a number of dimensions

What Is a Successful Marriage, and What Predicts It?

You undoubtedly know couples who appear to have a successful marriage. But what does that mean? *Minnotte (2010) differentiates* **marital success**, *an umbrella term referring to any marital outcome (e.g., divorce rate);* **marital quality**, *a subjective evaluation*

FIGURE 11.3

Median age at first marriage in the United States has increased slightly more for women than for men since 1970.

From Current Population Survey, March and Annual Social and Economic Supplements, *by U.S. Census Bureau, 2010 and earlier.*

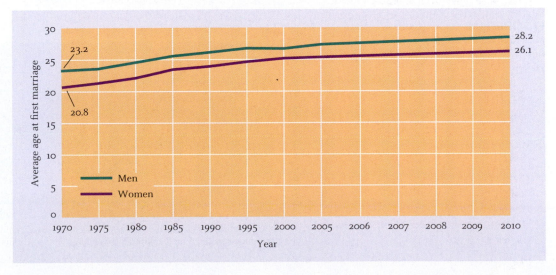

of the couple's relationship on a number of dimensions; **marital adjustment**, *the degree to which a husband and a wife accommodate each other over a certain period; and* **marital satisfaction**, *a global assessment of one's marriage.* Each of these provides a unique insight into the workings of a marriage.

Marriages, like other relationships, differ from one another, but some important predictors of future success can be identified. One key factor is age. In general, the younger the partners are, the lower the odds that the marriage will last—especially when the people are in their teens or early 20s (U.S. Census Bureau, 2010a). Other reasons that increase or decrease the likelihood that a marriage will last include financial security (increase the likelihood) and pregnancy at the time of the marriage (decrease the likelihood).

A second important predictor of successful marriage is **homogamy**, *or the similarity of values and interests a couple shares.* As we saw in relation to choosing a mate, the extent that the partners share similar age, values, goals, attitudes (especially the desire for children), socioeconomic status, certain behaviors (e.g., drinking alcohol), and ethnic background increases the likelihood that their relationship will succeed (Kippen, Chapman, & Yu, 2009).

A third factor in predicting marital success is a feeling that the relationship is equal. *According to* **exchange theory**, *marriage is based on each partner contributing something to the relationship that the other would be hard pressed to provide.* Satisfying and happy marriages result when both partners perceive that there is a fair exchange, or equity, in all dimensions of the relationship. Problems achieving such equity can arise because of the competing demands of work and family, an issue we take up again in Chapter 12.

Cross-cultural research supports these factors. Couples in the United States and Iran (Asoodeh et al., 2010; Hall, 2006; McKenzie, 2003) say that trust, consulting each other, honesty, making joint decisions, and commitment make the difference between a successful marriage and an unsuccessful marriage. Couples for whom religion is important also point to commonly held faith.

Do Married Couples Stay Happy?

Few sights are happier than a couple on their wedding day. Newlyweds, like Kevin and Beth in the vignette, are at the peak of marital bliss. The beliefs people bring into a marriage influence how satisfied they will be as the marriage develops. But as you may have experienced, feelings change over time, sometimes getting better and stronger, sometimes not.

Research shows that, for most couples, overall marital satisfaction is highest at the beginning of the marriage, falls until the children begin leaving home, and rises again in later life; this pattern holds for both married and never-married cohabiting couples with children (see Figure 11.4; Hansen, Moum, & Shapiro, 2007). However, for some couples, satisfaction never rebounds and instead remains low; in essence, they have become emotionally divorced.

marital adjustment
the degree to which a husband and a wife accommodate each other over a certain period

marital satisfaction
a global assessment of one's marriage

homogamy
the similarity of values and interests

exchange theory
the theory that a relationship, such as marriage, is based on each partner contributing something to the relationship that the other would be hard pressed to provide

FIGURE 11.4
Marital satisfaction is highest early on and in later life, dropping off during the childrearing years.

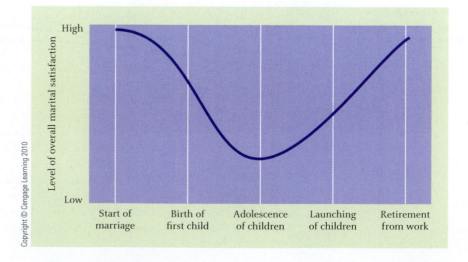

FIGURE 11.5

The vulnerability–stress–adaptation model shows how adapting to vulnerabilities and stress can result in either adaptation or dissolution of the marriage.

From "Keeping marriages healthy, and why it's so difficult," by B. R. Karney. Copyright © American Psychological Association 2010.

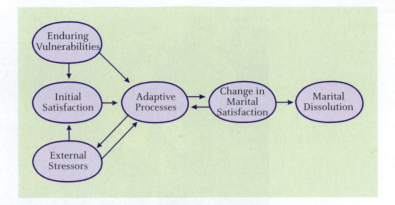

The pattern of a particular marriage over the years is determined by the nature of the dependence of each spouse on the other. When dependence is mutual and about equal, and both people hold similar values that form the basis for their commitment to each other, the marriage is strong and close (Givertz, Segrin, & Hanzal, 2009). When the dependence of one partner is much higher than that of the other, however, the marriage is likely to be characterized by stress and conflict. Learning how to deal with these changes is the secret to long and happy marriages.

Marital satisfaction has a general downward trend but varies widely across couples, which led Karney and Bradbury (1995) to propose a vulnerability–stress–adaptation model of marriage, depicted in Figure 11.5. *The **vulnerability–stress–adaptation model** sees marital quality as a dynamic process resulting from the couple's ability to handle stressful events in the context of their particular vulnerabilities and resources.* For example, as a couple's ability to adapt to stressful situations gets better over time, the quality of the marriage probably will improve. How well couples adapt to various stresses on the relationship determines whether the marriage continues or they get divorced. Let's see how this works over time.

Setting the Stage: The Early Years of Marriage

Marriages are most intense in their early days. Discussing financial matters honestly is key, because many newly married couples experience their first serious marital stresses around money issues (Parkman, 2007). How tough issues early in the marriage are handled sets the stage for the years ahead.

Early in a marriage, the couple must learn to adjust to the different perceptions and expectations each person has for the other. Research indicates that men and women both recognize and admit when problems occur in their marriage (Moynehan & Adams, 2007). The couple must also learn to handle confrontation and resolve conflicts.

Early in a marriage, couples tend to have global adoration for their spouse regarding the spouse's qualities (Karney, 2010; Neff & Karney, 2005). For wives, but not for husbands, more accurate, specific perceptions of what their spouses are like were associated with more supportive behaviors, feelings of control in the marriage, and a decreased risk of divorce. Couples who are happiest in the early stage of their marriage tend to focus on the good aspects, not the annoyances; nit-picking and nagging do not bode well for long-term wedded bliss (Karney, 2010).

As time goes on, and stresses increase, marital satisfaction tends to decline (Lamanna & Riedmann, 2003). For most couples, the primary reason for this drop is having children (Jokela et al., 2009). But it's not just a matter of having a child. The temperament of the child matters, with fussier babies creating more marital problems (Greving, 2007; Meijer & van den Wittenboer, 2007). Parenthood also means having substantially less time to devote to the marriage. Both African American and European American couples report an increase in conflict after the birth of their first child (Crohan, 1996).

vulnerability–stress–adaptation model

a model that proposes that marital quality is a dynamic process resulting from the couple's ability to handle stressful events in the context of their particular vulnerabilities and resources

Young married military couples face special types of stress on their relationship.

Sandy Huffaker/Getty Images

However, using the birth of a child as the explanation for the drop in marital satisfaction is much too simplistic, because child-free couples also experience a decline in marital satisfaction (Hansen, Moum, & Shapiro, 2007). Longitudinal research indicates that disillusionment—as indicated by a decline in feeling in love, in demonstrations of affection, and in the feeling that the spouse is responsive, as well as by an increase in feelings of ambivalence—is a key predictor of marital dissatisfaction (Huston et al., 2001).

During the early years of their marriage, many couples may spend significant amounts of time apart, especially if one spouse is in the military (Fincham & Beach, 2010). Spouses who serve in combat areas on active duty assignment and have post-traumatic stress disorder are particularly vulnerable, because they are at greater risk for other spouse-directed aggression.

What the nondeployed spouse believes turns out to be important. If the nondeployed spouse believes that the deployment will have negative effects on the marriage, then problems are more likely. In contrast, if the nondeployed spouse believes that such challenges make the relationship stronger, then they typically can do so (Renshaw, Rodrigues, & Jones, 2008). Research indicates that the effects of deployment may be greater on wives than husbands; divorce rates for women service members who are deployed are higher than those for their male counterparts (Karney & Crown, 2007).

Keeping Marriages Happy

Couples who have been happily married for many years show an ability to roll with the punches and to adapt to changing circumstances in the relationship. For example, a serious problem of one spouse may not be detrimental to the relationship and may even make the bond stronger if the couple uses good stress- and conflict-reduction strategies. Successful couples also find a way to keep the romance in the relationship, an important determinant of marital satisfaction over the long run (Acevedo & Aron, 2009).

Sharing religious beliefs and spirituality with one's spouse is another good way to help ensure a higher-quality marriage, and that's especially the case among couples in lower socioeconomic groups (Lichter & Carmalt, 2009). But when you get down to basics, it's how well couples communicate their thoughts, actions, and feelings to each other and show intimacy and support each other that largely determines the level of conflict couples experience and, by extension, how happy they are likely to be over the long term (Patrick et al., 2007). This is especially important regarding high-stress areas such as children and work.

HUMAN DEVELOPMENT in action

If you were a marriage counselor, how would research on marriage influence your interventions in troubled marriages?

Test Yourself

Recall

1. A difficulty for many single people is that other people may expect them to _____.

2. Young adults often view cohabitation as a _____ marriage.

3. Gay and lesbian relationships are similar to _____.

4. According to _____, marriage is based on each partner contributing something to the relationship that the other would be hard pressed to provide.

5. For most couples, marital satisfaction _____ after the birth of the first child.

Interpret

- What sociocultural forces affect decisions to marry rather than to cohabit indefinitely?

- Why does education affect rates of cohabitation and marital happiness?

Apply

- Ricardo and Maria are engaged to be married. Ricardo works long hours as a store manager at a local coffee shop, while Maria works regular hours as an administrative assistant for a large communications company. Based on your understanding of the factors that affect marital success, what other characteristics would you, as their marriage counselor, want to know about Ricardo and Maria before evaluating the likely success of their marriage?

- What changes, if any, would you make to your company's job benefits plan regarding support for single, cohabiting, and married employees?

Recall answers: (1) marry, (2) step toward, (3) heterosexual marriages, (4) exchange theory, (5) decreases.

11.3 The Family Life Cycle

LEARNING OBJECTIVES

- What are the common forms of families?
- Why do people have children?
- What is it like to be a parent? What differences are there in types of parenting?

Bob, 32, and Denise, 33, just had their first child, Matthew, after several years of trying. They've heard that having children while in their 30s can have advantages, but Bob and Denise wonder whether people are just saying that to be nice to them. They are also concerned about the financial obligations they are likely to face.

"When are you going to start a family?" is a question that young couples like Bob and Denise are asked frequently. Most couples want children because they believe they will bring great joy, which they often do. But once the child is born, adults may feel inadequate because children don't come with instructions.

The birth of a child transforms a couple (or a single parent) into a family. *The most common form of family in Western societies is the* **nuclear family**, *consisting only of parent(s) and child(ren). The most common family form around the world is the* **extended family**, *in which grandparents and other relatives live with parents and children.* Because we discussed families from the child's perspective in earlier chapters, here we focus on families from the parents' point of view.

Deciding Whether to Have Children

nuclear family
the most common form of family in Western societies, consisting only of parent(s) and child(ren)

extended family
the most common form of family around the world, one in which grandparents and other relatives live with parents and children

One of the biggest decisions couples have to make is whether to have children. This decision appears complicated. You would think that potential parents weigh the many benefits of childrearing against the many drawbacks. But apparently, this is not what most people do.

Rijken (2009) reports that potential parents don't think deliberately or deeply about when to have a child and that those who are career oriented or like their freedom do not often deliberately postpone parenthood because of those factors. Rather, thoughts about having children do not seem to cross their minds until they are ready to start attempting to have children.

Whether the pregnancy is planned or not (and more than half of all U.S. pregnancies are unplanned), a couple's first pregnancy is a milestone event in a relationship, with both benefits and costs (Greving, 2007; Meijer & van den Wittenboer, 2007). Parents largely agree that children add affection, improve family ties, and give parents a feeling of immortality and a sense of accomplishment. Most parents willingly sacrifice a great deal for their children and hope that they grow up to be happy and successful. In this way, children bring happiness to their parents (Angeles, 2010).

Nevertheless, finances are of great concern to most parents because children are expensive. How expensive? According to the U.S. Department of Agriculture (2010), a family in the middle income bracket who had a child in 2009 would spend $286,000 for food, shelter, and other necessities by the time the child turned 17. College expenses would be an additional expense. These costs do not differ significantly between two-parent and single-parent households, but clearly they are a bigger financial burden for single parents.

For many reasons that include personal choice, financial instability, and infertility, an increasing number of couples are child-free. Social attitudes in many countries (e.g., Austria, Germany, Great Britain, Ireland, Netherlands, and United States) are improving toward child-free couples (Gubernskaya, 2010). Couples without children also have some advantages: higher marital satisfaction, more freedom, and higher standards of living.

The Parental Role

Today, couples in the United States typically have fewer children and have their first child later than in the past. The average age at the time of the birth of a woman's first child is about 26. This average age has been increasing steadily since 1970 as a result of two major trends (U.S. Census Bureau, 2010a). First, many women postpone children because they are marrying later, they want to establish careers, or they make a choice to delay childbearing. In addition, the teen birthrate dropped dramatically between the early 1990s and 2005 (but has increased since 2006).

Being older at the birth of the first child is advantageous. Older mothers, like Denise in the vignette, are more at ease being parents, spend more time with their babies, and are more affectionate, sensitive, and supportive to them (Berlin, Brady-Smith, & Brooks-Gunn, 2002). The age of the father also makes a difference in how he interacts with children (Palkovitz & Palm, 2009). Remember Bob, the 32-year-old first-time father in the vignette? Compared to men who become fathers in their 20s, men (like Bob) who become fathers in their 30s are generally more invested in their paternal role and spend up to three times as much time caring for their preschool children as younger fathers do. Father involvement has increased significantly due in part to social attitudes that support it (Fogarty & Evans, 2010).

Parenting skills do not come naturally; they must be acquired. Having a child changes all aspects of couples' lives. Children place a great deal of stress on a relationship. Having a child may create disagreements over division of labor, especially if both parents are employed outside the home. Even when mothers are employed outside the home (and more than 70% of women with children under age 18 are), they still perform most of the childrearing tasks (Seward et al., 2006).

HUMAN DEVELOPMENT in **action**

Should employers modify work assignments for new parents?

Ethnic Diversity and Parenting

Ethnic background matters a great deal in terms of family structure and the parent–child relationship. African American husbands are more likely than their European American counterparts to help with household chores, regardless of their wives' employment status (Dixon, 2009). Overall, most African American parents provide a cohesive, loving environment that often exists within a context of strong religious beliefs (Anderson, 2007; Dixon, 2009), pride in cultural heritage, self-respect, and cooperation with the family (Brissett-Chapman & Issacs-Shockley, 1997).

Family ties among Native Americans tend to be strong.

© Marilyn Angel Wynn/Nativestock Pictures/Corbis

As a result of several generations of oppression, many Native American parents have lost traditional cultural parenting skills: children were valued, women were considered sacred and honored, and men cared for and provided for their families (Witko, 2006). Retaining a strong sense of tribalism is important for Native American families to promote strong ties to parents, siblings, and grandparents (Garrod & Larimore, 1997). Tribal members spend great amounts of time with children imparting the cultural values—such as cooperation, sharing, personal integrity, generosity, harmony with nature, and spirituality—that differ from European American values, which emphasize competitiveness and individuality (Stauss, 1995).

Nearly 25% of all children under 18 in the United States are Latino, and most are at least second generation (Fry, 2009). Among two-parent families, Mexican American mothers and fathers both tend to adopt similar authoritative behaviors toward their preschool children (Gamble, Ramakumar, & Diaz, 2007).

Latino families demonstrate two key values: familism and the extended family. **Familism** *refers to the idea that the well-being of the family takes precedence over the concerns of individual family members.* This value is a defining characteristic of Latino families; for example, Brazilian and Mexican families consider familism a cultural strength (Carlo et al., 2007; Lucero-Liu, 2007). Indeed, familism helps account for the significantly higher trend for Latino American college students to live at home (Desmond & López Turley, 2009). The extended family is also strong among Latino families and serves as the venue for a range of exchanges of goods and services, such as child care and financial support (Almeida et al., 2009).

Asian Americans also value familism (Meyer, 2007) and place an even higher value on extended family. Other key values include obtaining good grades in school, maintaining discipline, being concerned about what others think, and conformity. Asian American adolescents report very high feelings of obligation to their families compared with European American adolescents (Kiang & Fuligni, 2009). In general, males enjoy higher status in traditional Asian families (Tsuno & Homma, 2009).

Raising multiethnic children presents challenges not experienced by parents of same-race children. For example, parents of biracial children report feeling discrimination and targeted for prejudicial behavior from others (Hubbard, 2010; Kilson & Ladd, 2009). These parents also worry that their children may be rejected by members of both racial communities.

Mothers are key in multiethnic families. A study of children of European mothers and Maori fathers in New Zealand showed that the mothers played a major role in establishing the child's Maori identity (Kukutai, 2007). Similarly, European American mothers of biracial children whose fathers were African American tended to raise them as African American in terms of public ethnic identity (O'Donoghue, 2005), and as adults, they were more likely to describe themselves as African American (Khanna, 2010).

familism
the idea that the family's well-being takes precedence over the concerns of individual family members

Research indicates that children raised by gay or lesbian parents may have some advantages in terms of exposure to egalitarian attitudes.

Single Parents

The proportion of births to unwed mothers in the United States is at an all-time high, now more than 40% (Livingston & Cohn, 2010). Rates vary by ethnic group. More than 70% of births to African American mothers, more than 50% of births to Latina American mothers, and nearly 30% of births to European American mothers are to unmarried women (Livingston & Cohn, 2010). Being a single parent raises important questions: How are children affected when only one adult is responsible for child care? And how do single parents meet their own needs for emotional support and intimacy?

Many divorced single parents report complex feelings such as frustration, failure, guilt, and a need to be overindulgent (Lamanna & Riedmann, 2003). Loneliness can be especially difficult to deal with (Anderson et al., 2004). Separation anxiety is a common and strong feeling among military parents who are about to be deployed (Roper, 2007).

Single parents, regardless of gender, face considerable obstacles. Financially, they are usually much less well off than their married counterparts. Integrating the roles of work and parenthood are more difficult. Single mothers are hardest hit, mainly because women typically are paid less than men.

One particular concern for many divorced single parents is dating. Single parents often feel insecure about sexuality and how they should behave around their children in terms of having partners stay overnight (Lampkin-Hunter, 2010). When single parenting happens through divorce, dating often begins fairly quickly; we consider those situations later in this chapter.

Alternative Forms of Parenting

Roughly one third of North American couples become stepparents or foster or adoptive parents at some time during their lives. In general, there are few differences among parents who have biological children and those who become parents in some other way, but there are some unique challenges for the latter (McKay & Ross, 2010).

A big issue for foster parents, adoptive parents, and stepparents is how strongly the child will bond with them. Although infants younger than 1 year will probably bond well, children who are old enough to have formed attachments with their biological parents may have competing loyalties. As a result, the dynamics in blended families can best be understood as a complex system (Dupuis, 2010). These problems are a major reason that second marriages are at high risk for dissolution, as discussed later in this chapter. They are also a major reason behavioral and emotional problems are more common among stepchildren (Crohn, 2006).

Still, many stepparents and stepchildren ultimately develop good relationships with each other. Allowing stepchildren to develop a relationship with the stepparent at their own pace helps. What style of stepparenting ultimately develops is influenced by the expectations of the stepparent, stepchild, spouse, and nonresidential parent (Crohn, 2006).

Adoptive parents also contend with attachment to birth parents, but in different ways. Adopted children may wish to locate and meet their birth parents. Such searches can strain the relationships between these children and their adoptive parents, who may interpret these actions as a form of rejection (Curtis & Pearson, 2010).

Families with children adopted from another culture pose challenges of how to establish and maintain connection with the child's culture of origin (Yngvesson, 2010). For mothers of transracially adopted Chinese and Korean children, becoming connected to the appropriate Asian American community is a way to accomplish this (Johnston et al., 2007). Research in the Netherlands found that children adopted from Columbia, Sri Lanka, and Korea into Dutch homes struggled with looking different, and many expressed desires to be white (Juffer, 2006).

Foster parents tend to have the most tenuous relationship with their children because the bond can be broken for any of a number of reasons having nothing to do with the quality of the care being provided. Dealing with attachment is difficult; foster parents want to provide secure homes, but they may not have the children long enough to establish continuity. Furthermore, because many children in foster care have been unable to form attachments, they are less likely to form ones that will inevitably be broken. Despite the challenges, placement in good foster care results in the development of attachment between foster parents and children who were placed out of institutional settings (Smyke et al., 2010).

Finally, many gay men and lesbian women also want to be parents. Some have biological children, whereas others choose adoption or foster parenting (Braun, 2007; Goldberg, 2009). Although gay men and lesbian women make good parents, they often experience resistance to their having children (Clifford, Hertz, & Doskow, 2010); for example, some states in the United States have laws preventing gay and lesbian couples from adopting. However, research indicates that children reared by gay or lesbian parents do not experience any more problems than children reared by heterosexual parents and are as psychologically healthy as children of heterosexual parents (Biblarz & Savci, 2010). Evidence shows that gay male parents have more egalitarian sharing of childrearing than do fathers in heterosexual households (Biblarz & Savci, 2010).

Test Yourself

Recall

1. the most common form of family in Western society is

   _____.

2. Personal choice, financial instability, and _____ are reasons that couples remain child free.

3. A new father who is invested in his parental role and may feel ambivalent about time lost to his career is probably over age _____.

4. A major issue for foster parents, adoptive parents, and stepparents is _____.

Interpret

- What difference do you think it would make to view children as a financial asset (i.e., a source of income) as opposed to a financial burden (i.e., mainly an expense)?

- From Erikson's perspective, what effects might there be from having difficulty establishing attachment?

Apply

- As a social worker, what factors would you need to keep in mind before placing a child in an adoptive family?

- As a teacher, what would you do if some children in your class made fun of adopted children or children of gay or lesbian parents?

Recall answers: (1) nuclear, (2) infertility, (3) 30, (4) how strongly the child will bond with them

---

11.4 Divorce and Remarriage

LEARNING OBJECTIVES

- Who gets divorced? How does divorce affect parental relationships with children?

- What are remarriages like? How are they similar to and different from first marriages?

Frank and Marilyn, both in their late 40s, thought their marriage would last forever. However, they weren't so lucky and have just divorced. Although two of their children are married, their youngest daughter is still in college. The financial pressures Marilyn feels now that she's on her own are beginning to take their toll. She wonders whether her financial situation is similar to that of other recently divorced women.

Despite what Frank and Marilyn pledged on their wedding day, their marriage did not last until death parted them. Even though marriage can be stressful and difficult, thousands of divorced people each year choose to try marriage again.

Divorce

Most couples enter marriage with the idea that their relationship will be permanent. But rather than growing together, many couples grow apart.

Who Gets Divorced, and Why?

Divorce in the United States is common—couples who marry in the United States today have about a 50–50 chance of divorce; for couples between 20 and 24 at the time of marriage, the odds are 60% (National Center for Health Statistics, 2010c).

How about other countries? As you can see in Figure 11.6, which shows the developed countries with the highest rates of divorce, the divorce rate in nearly every other country is lower than that in the United States. However, divorce rates have increased in many developed countries over the past few decades (National Center for Health Statistics, 2010c; United Nations, 2005, 2010a).

The reasons couples split are complex (Kayser, 2010). Gottman and Levenson (2000) proposed a bold framework for understanding divorce. They developed two models that predict divorce early (within the first 7 years of marriage) and later (when the first child reaches age 14) with 93% accuracy over the 14-year period of their study. Negative emotions displayed during conflict between spouses predict early divorce but not later divorce. Longitudinal research with European and African American couples over a 16-year period demonstrates that how couples deal with conflict changes over time (Birditt et al., 2010). In general, European American wives and African American couples use more accommodating and fewer destructive and quiet withdrawal behaviors over time, indicating that they are looking for ways to defuse conflict and are working through difficult issues more effectively. European American husbands tend to remain

FIGURE 11.6

The United States has one of the highest divorce rates in the world.

From "Marriage and divorce," by National Center for Health Statistics, 2010, and from "Divorces and crude divorce rates by urban/rural residence: 2004–2008," by United Nations, 2010.

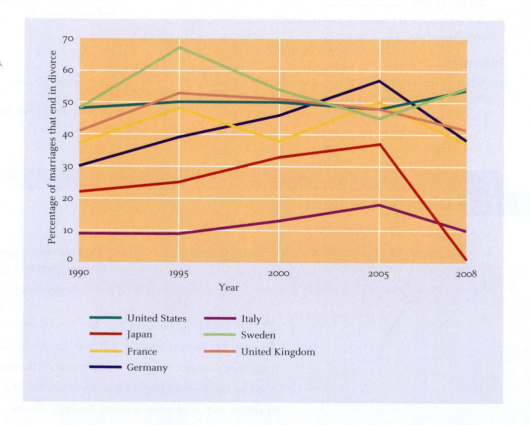

consistent in their behaviors, perhaps because they use less withdrawal early in the marriage. These findings explain why the odds for divorce are higher earlier in marriage: Couples married for shorter times are less able to deal effectively with conflict. It's the absence of positive emotions that eventually takes its toll and results in later divorce. For a marriage to last, people need to be told that they are loved and that what they do and feel matters to their partner.

The high divorce rate in the United States and the reasons typically cited for getting divorced have sparked new approaches, some of them controversial, designed to help keep couples together. **Covenant marriage** *expands the marriage contract to a lifelong commitment between the partners within a supportive community.* This approach is based on the idea that if getting married and getting divorced were grounded in religious and cultural values, and divorce was made more difficult, couples would be more likely to stay together. The couple agrees to participate in mandatory premarital counseling, and that, should problems arise later, the grounds for divorce will be limited (White, 2010). The Linking Research to Life feature at the end of the chapter explores attempts to lower divorce rates in more detail.

Effects of Divorce on the Couple

Although changes in attitudes toward divorce have eased the social trauma associated with it, divorce still takes a high toll on the couple. Studies in the United States and Spain show great similarity in how both partners in a failed marriage feel: deeply disappointed, misunderstood, and rejected (Doohan, Carrère, & Riggs, 2010; Yárnoz-Yaben, 2010). Unlike when a spouse dies, divorce often means the ex-spouse is present to provide a reminder of the unpleasant aspects of the relationship and, in some cases, feelings of personal failure (Doohan, Carrère, & Riggs, 2010).

Divorced people sometimes find the transition difficult; researchers refer to these problems as "divorce hangover" (Walther, 1991). Divorce hangover reflects divorced partners' inability to let go, develop new friendships, or reorient themselves as single people or parents. Forgiving the ex-spouse is also important for eventual adjustment after divorce (Rye et al., 2004).

Divorce in middle age or late life has some special characteristics. If women initiate the divorce, they report self-focused growth and optimism; if they did not initiate the divorce, they tend to ruminate and feel vulnerable (Sakraida, 2005). However, in both cases they report changes in their social networks. Middle-aged and elderly women are at a significant disadvantage for remarriage—an especially traumatic situation for women who obtained much of their identity from their roles as wife and mother.

We must not overlook the financial problems faced by many divorced women (Malone et al., 2010). These problems are especially keen for the middle-aged divorcee who may have spent years as a homemaker and has few marketable job skills. For her, divorce presents an especially difficult financial hardship, which is intensified if she has children in college and if the father provides little support (Lamanna & Riedmann, 2003).

Relationships With Children

When it involves young children, divorce becomes a complicated matter (Clarke-Stewart & Brentano, 2006). In most countries, mothers tend to obtain custody but often do not obtain sufficient financial resources to support the children.

In contrast, divorced fathers pay a psychological price. Although many would like to remain active in their children's lives, few do. Child-support laws in some states also may limit fathers' contact with their children (Wadlington, 2005).

One hopeful direction that addresses the usually difficult custody situations following divorce is the Collaborative Divorce Project, based on collaborative law (Mosten, 2009; Pruett, Insabella, & Gustafson, 2005). **Collaborative divorce** *is a voluntary, contractually based alternative dispute resolution process for couples who want*

covenant marriage
expanding the marriage contract to a lifelong commitment between the partners within a supportive community

collaborative divorce
a voluntary, contractually-based alternative dispute resolution process for couples who want to negotiate a resolution of their situation rather than having a ruling imposed upon them by a court or arbitrator

Single mothers often face difficult challenges financially, as well as the stress of raising their children.

HUMAN DEVELOPMENT in action

What support services would you consider adding to help young adults through their parents' divorce if you ran a college counseling center?

Although remarriage is common, adjusting to it can be difficult.

to negotiate a resolution of their situation rather than having a ruling imposed upon them by a court or arbitrator (DiFonzo, 2010; Mosten, 2009).

Early results from this approach are positive (DeLucia-Waack, 2010). Couples benefited in terms of less conflict, greater father involvement, and better outcomes for children than the control group. Fathers tend to remain more involved after a collaborative divorce (Pruett et al., 2012).

Young adults whose parents divorce experience a great deal of emotional vulnerability and stress (Cooney & Uhlenberg, 1990). One young man put it this way:

> The difficult thing was that it [my parents' divorce] was a time where, you know [you're] making the transition from high school to college. Your high school friends are dispersed. They're all over the place. It's normally a very difficult transition [college]: new atmosphere, new work load, meeting new people. You've got to start deciding what you want to do, you've got to sort of start getting more independent, and so forth. And then, at the same time you find out about a divorce. You know, it's just that much more adjustment you have to make (Cooney et al., 1986).

The effects of experiencing the divorce of one's parents can be long lasting. College-aged students report poorer relations with their parents if their parents are divorced (Yu et al., 2010). Parental divorce may also result in young adults' having negative views on intimate relationships and marriage (Ottaway, 2010). Wallerstein and Lewis (2004) report the findings from a 25-year follow-up study of individuals whose parents divorced when they were between 3 and 18 years old. Results show the difficulties that children of divorce encounter in achieving love, sexual intimacy, and commitment to marriage and parenthood. Clearly, experiencing divorce at any age alters lives.

Remarriage

The trauma of divorce does not deter people from beginning new relationships, which often lead to another marriage. In the United States, about 25% of the adult population has been married more than once (Elliott & Lewis, 2010). Typically, men and women both wait about 3½ years before they remarry (U.S. Census Bureau, 2010a).

An interesting emerging trend reflects an important cohort difference. Compared to older generations, younger generations tend to remarry at a lower rate (Elliott & Lewis, 2010). This may be a reflection of greater social acceptability of cohabitation in the United States, as well as reluctance among younger people to jump back into a marriage.

In contrast to first marriage, remarriage has few norms or guidelines for couples, especially in how to deal with stepchildren and extended families (Elliott & Lewis, 2010). The lack of clear role definitions may be a major reason the divorce rate for remarriages is significantly higher (about 25%, and even higher if stepchildren are involved) than for first marriages.

Although women are more likely to initiate a divorce, they are less likely to remarry (Birditt et al., 2010; Fincham & Beach, 2010; Kayser, 2010) unless they are poor (Elliott & Lewis, 2010). However, women in general benefit more from remarriage than do men, particularly if they have children (Ozawa & Yoon, 2002). Although many people believe that divorced individuals should wait before remarrying to avoid the so-called rebound effect, there is no evidence that those who remarry sooner have less success in remarriage than those who wait longer (Wolfinger, 2007).

Adapting to new relationships in remarriage is stressful. For example, partners may have unresolved issues from the previous marriage that may interfere with satisfaction with the new marriage (Faber, 2004). The effects of remarriage on children are positive, at least for young adult children, who report their own positive intimate relationships when their parent or parents remarry happily (Yu & Adler-Baeder, 2007).

Test Yourself

Recall

1. Following divorce, most women suffer disproportionately in the _____ domain compared with most men.
2. Divorce rates for couples in their early 20s are _____ than for couples in general.
3. Compared to older generations, younger generations tend to remarry at a _____ rate.

Interpret

- Why are divorce rates for second marriages not lower than for first marriages?
- What are the advantages and disadvantages for remarrying?

Apply

- Ricardo and Maria are engaged to be married. Ricardo works long hours as the manager of a local coffee shop, while Maria works regular hours as an administrative assistant at a large communications company. Based on what you know about why couples get divorced, what would you do as a social worker to help them avoid that outcome?
- What would you include in a marriage education program?

Recall answers: (1) financial, (2) higher, (3) lower

Linking Research to life • DOES MARRIAGE EDUCATION WORK?

As a way to combat high divorce rates, the U.S. government created the Healthy Marriage Initiative as part of the Deficit Reduction Act of 2005 and provided $150 million per year through the 2011 fiscal year for promotion of healthy marriages and fatherhood. These in turn resulted in the National Healthy Marriage Center and the National Center for Marriage Research. Research related to these initiatives has focused on the positive aspects of marriage and on the need to do a better job with marriage education (Fincham & Beach, 2010).

The Healthy Marriage Initiative is an example of **marriage education**, *an approach based on the idea that the more couples are prepared for marriage, the better the chances that the relationship will survive over the long run.* More than 40 states have initiated some type of education program. Do they work?

Most marriage education programs focus on communication between spouses. In addition to government or other publicly sponsored programs, several religious denominations have marriage education programs; the Catholic Church's Pre-Cana program is one example.

There are numerous challenges to more extensive community-based marriage education programs. For example, in some cases, the education programs were originally developed to address poverty (Administration for Children and Families, 2010a). In addition, many couples cohabit and are less likely to attend marriage education programs, even though there is little evidence that cohabitation improves communication skills between partners (Fincham & Beach, 2010). As a result, versions of marriage education programs are being adapted for these situations. Programs timed at key transition points (e.g., engagement) have also been developed (Halford, Markman, & Stanley, 2008).

Research to date shows that these skills-based education programs have modest but consistently positive effects on marital quality and communication (Cowan, Cowan, & Knox, 2010; Fincham & Beach, 2010). Perhaps not surprisingly, couples who report more problems at the beginning of the program appear to benefit most.

These positive outcomes are resulting in a broadening of the approaches used by marriage educators to topics beyond communication. How these programs develop, and whether more couples will participate, remains to be seen. What does appear to be the case is that if couples agree to participate in a marriage education program, they may well lower their risk for problems later.

marriage education
the idea that the more couples are prepared for marriage, the better the chances that the relationship will survive over the long run

Summary

11.1 Relationships

What types of friendships do adults have? How do adult friendships develop?

- People tend to have more friendships during young adulthood than during any other period. Friendships are especially important for maintaining life satisfaction throughout adulthood.

- Men tend to have fewer close friendships and to base them on shared activities. Women tend to have more close friendships and to base them on intimate and emotional sharing. Gender differences in same-gender friendship patterns may explain the difficulties men and women have in forming cross-gender friendships.

What is love? How does it develop through adulthood?

- Passion, intimacy, and commitment are the key components of love.

- Selecting a mate works best when there are shared values, goals, and interests. There are cross-cultural differences with regard to the specific aspects of these that are considered most important.

What is the nature of abuse in some relationships?

- Levels of aggressive behavior range from verbal aggression, to physical aggression, to killing one's partner. The causes of aggressive behaviors become more complex as the level of aggression increases. People remain in abusive relationships for many reasons, including low self-esteem and the belief that they cannot leave.

11.2 Lifestyles

What's it like to be single?

- Most young adults in the United States are single. Globally, how long one remains single is rooted in cultural norms.

What are the characteristics of cohabiting people?

- Young adults may cohabit as a step toward marriage, and adults of all ages may cohabit for convenience. Cohabitation is increasingly seen as an alternative to marriage in the United States. Overall, more similarities than differences exist between cohabiting and married couples.

What are gay and lesbian relationships like?

- Gay and lesbian relationships are similar to heterosexual marriages. Some countries and some states in the United States now permit same-sex marriages. Lesbian couples are more likely to remain together than gay male couples.

What is marriage like through the course of adulthood?

- The most important factors in creating marriages that endure are age, similarity of values and interests, and the contribution of unique skills by each partner, as well as effective communication.

- For couples with children, marital satisfaction tends to decline until the children leave home, although individual differences are apparent, especially in long-term marriages.

11.3 The Family Life Cycle

What are the common forms of families?

- Although the nuclear family is the most common form of family in Western societies, the most common form around the world is the extended family.

Why do people have children?

- Although having children is stressful and expensive, most people do it anyway because of the many emotional rewards they bring. However, the number of child-free couples is increasing.

What is it like to be a parent? What differences are there in types of parenting?

- Single parents are faced with many problems, especially if they are women or are divorced. The main problem is significantly reduced financial resources.

- A major issue for adoptive parents, foster parents, and stepparents is how strongly the child will bond with them. Each of these relationships has some special characteristics.

- Gay and lesbian parents face numerous obstacles, but they usually prove to be good parents.

11.4 Divorce and Remarriage

Who gets divorced? How does divorce affect parental relationships with children?

- Currently, odds are about 50–50 that a new marriage will end in divorce. Conflict styles can predict who divorces. Recovery from divorce is different for men and women. Men tend to have a tougher time in the short run, but women clearly have a harder time in the long run, often for financial reasons.

- Difficulties between divorced partners usually involve visitation and child support. Disruptions also occur in divorced parents' relationships with their children, whether the children are young or are adults themselves.

What are remarriages like? How are they similar to and different from first marriages?

- Most divorced couples remarry. Second marriages are especially vulnerable to stress if spouses must adjust to having stepchildren. Remarriage in middle age and beyond tends to be happy, although divorce rates for remarriages remain higher than those for first marriages.

Key Terms

assortative mating (294)
abusive relationship (296)
battered woman syndrome (297)
cohabitation (299)
marital success (301)
marital quality (301)

marital adjustment (302)
marital satisfaction (302)
homogamy (302)
exchange theory (302)
vulnerability–stress–adaptation
    model (303)

nuclear family (305)
extended family (305)
familism (307)
covenant marriage (311)
collaborative divorce (311)
marriage education (313)

Online Resources

Go to CengageBrain.com to access Psychology CourseMate, where you will find an interactive eBook, flashcards, quizzes, videos, websites, and more.

Work

Occupational and Lifestyle Issues in Young and Middle Adulthood

12

From the time we are small children, we think and plan what we will "be" when we grow up. When we are "grown up," we simply change the question "What will I be?" to "And what do you do?" We are socialized, throughout the life span, to consider work a central aspect of life. For some, work is life; for all, it is at least a source of identity.

As in Chapter 11, our focus in this chapter is on issues faced by both young and middle-aged adults. No longer is it only young adults who must deal with occupational selection issues: It is increasingly common for middle-aged people to confront the issues of occupational selection all over again as their industry changes or their company downsizes.

LEARNING OBJECTIVES

- How do people view work?
- How do people choose their occupations?
- What factors influence occupational development?
- What is the relationship between job satisfaction and age?

Monique, a 28-year-old senior communications major, wonders about careers. Should she enter the broadcasting field as a behind-the-scenes producer, or would she be better suited as a public relations spokesperson? She thinks her outgoing personality is a factor that she should consider in making this decision.

Choosing work is serious business. Like Monique, we try to select a field in which we are trained and that is appealing. Work colors much of what we do in life. You may be taking this course as part of your preparation for work. Work is a source for friends. People arrange personal activities around work schedules. Parents often choose child-care centers on the basis of proximity to where they work.

The hassle of commuting makes us think about why we work.

The Meaning of Work

Terkel (1974) wrote in his classic book *Working* that work is "a search for daily meaning as well as daily bread, for recognition as well as cash, for astonishment rather than torpor; in short, for a sort of life rather than a Monday through Friday sort of dying" (p. xiii). Gibran (1923) wrote in his mystical book *The Prophet* (1923), that "Work is love made visible" (p. 28).

The meaning most of us derive from working includes both the money that can be exchanged for life's necessities (and perhaps a few luxuries) and the possibility of personal growth (Rosso, Dekas, & Wrzesniewski, 2010).

The specific occupation a person holds appears to have no effect on his or her need to derive meaning from work. Finding meaning in work can mean the difference between feeling that work is a source of life problems and feeling that it is a source of fulfillment and contentment (Grawitch, Barber, & Justice, 2010).

Lips-Wiersma (2003) found four common meanings: developing self, union with others, expressing self, and serving others. To the extent that these meanings can all be achieved, people experience the workplace as an area of personal fulfillment. This provides a framework for understanding occupational transitions as a means to find better balance among the four meanings.

Contemporary business theory also supports the idea that meaning matters. *Using a concept called* **meaning–mission fit**, *French (2007) showed that corporate executives with better alignment between their personal intentions and their company's mission cared more about their employees' happiness, job satisfaction, and emotional well-being.*

Because work plays such a key role in providing meaning for people, an important question is how people select an occupation. Let's turn our attention to two theories explaining how and why people choose the occupations they do.

Occupational Choice Revisited

meaning–mission fit
the alignment between an executive's personal intentions and the company's mission

In Chapter 9, we saw that early decisions about what people want to do in the world of work are related to their personalities. For adults, two theories have influenced research. First, John Holland's (1997) personality-type theory proposes that people

choose occupations to optimize the fit between their individual traits (e.g., personality, intelligence, skills, and abilities) and their occupational interests. *Second,* **social cognitive career theory (SCCT)** *proposes that career choice is a result of the application of Albert Bandura's social cognitive theory, especially the concept of self-efficacy (see Chapter 1).*

Recall that Holland categorizes occupations by the interpersonal settings in which people must function and by their associated lifestyles. He identifies six personality types that combine these factors: investigative, social, realistic, artistic, conventional, and enterprising, which he believes are optimally related to occupations.

How does Holland's theory help us understand the continued development of occupational interests in adulthood? Monique, the college senior in the vignette, found a good match between her outgoing nature and her major, communications. Indeed, college students of all ages tend to like best the courses and majors that fit well with their personalities.

Complementarily, SCCT proposes that people's career choices are heavily influenced by their interests (Sheu et al., 2010). As depicted in Figure 12.1, SCCT has two versions. The simplest includes four main factors: self-efficacy (your belief in your ability), outcome expectations (what you think will happen in a specific situation), interests (what you like), and choice goals (what you want to achieve). The more complex version also includes supports (environmental things that help you) and barriers (environmental things that block or frustrate you). Several studies show support for the six-variable version of the model (Sheu et al., 2010).

How well do these theories work in practice? Certainly, the relationships among occupation, personality, and demographic variables are complex (Clark, 2007). Although people may have underlying tendencies that relate to certain types of occupations, unless they believe they could be successful in those occupations and careers, they are unlikely to choose them. These beliefs can be influenced by external factors. For example, occupational prestige and gender-related factors need to be taken into account (Deng, Armstrong, & Rounds, 2007).

HUMAN DEVELOPMENT in action

How do your interests relate to your preferred choice of occupation?

social cognitive career theory (SCCT)

a theory that proposes career choice is a result of the application of Bandura's social cognitive theory, especially the concept of self-efficacy

Occupational Development

How a person advances in a career depends on the socialization that occurs when people learn the unwritten rules of an organization.

FIGURE 12.1
The four-variable (paths 1–6) and six-variable (paths 1–13) versions of the SCCT interest and choice models.

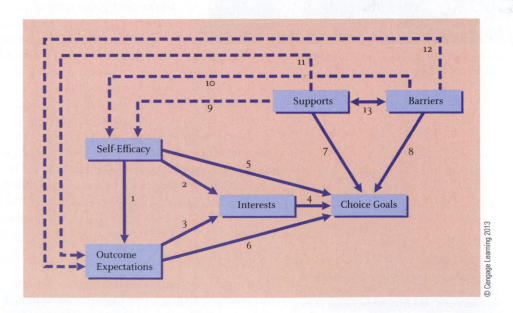

© Cengage Learning 2013

Occupational Expectations

Adolescents form opinions about what work in a particular occupation will be like based on what they learn in school and from their parents, peers, other adults, and the media. These expectations influence what they want to become and when they hope to get there.

In adulthood, personal experiences affect people as they refine and update their occupational expectations and development (Fouad, 2007). This usually involves trying to achieve their occupational goal, monitoring progress toward it, and changing or even abandoning it as necessary. Modifying the goal happens for many reasons, such as realizing that interests have changed, the occupation was not a good fit for them, they never got the chance to pursue the level of education necessary to achieve the goal, or they lack certain essential skills and cannot acquire them. Still other people modify their goals because of age, race, or sex discrimination, a point we consider later in this chapter.

Research shows that most people who know they have both the talent and the opportunity to achieve their occupational and career goals often attain them. When high school students who were identified as academically talented were asked about their career expectations and outcomes, it turned out that 10 and even 20 years later they had been surprisingly accurate (Perrone et al., 2010). What is also clear from research is that the biggest change has been in women's occupational and career expectations (Jacob & Wilder, 2010).

In general, research shows that young adults modify their expectations at least once, usually on the basis of new information and especially about their academic ability. The connection between adolescent expectations and adult reality reinforces the developmental aspects of occupations and careers.

Many writers believe that occupational expectations also vary by generation. Nowhere has this belief been stronger than in the supposed differences between the baby boom generation (born between 1946 and 1964) and the current millennial generation (born since 1983). What people in these generations, on average, expect in occupations appears to be very different (Hershatter & Epstein, 2010). Millennials are more likely to change jobs more often than the older generation did and are likely to view traditional organizations with more distrust and cynicism. But contrary to most stereotypes, millennials are no more egotistical and are just as happy and satisfied as were young adults in every generation since the 1970s (Trzesniewski & Donnellan, 2010). So in many ways, as tech savvy as they may be, the current generation of young adults is, psychologically speaking, quite similar to their parents' generation.

The importance of occupational expectations can be seen clearly in the transition from school to workplace (Moen & Roehling, 2005). The 21st-century workplace is not one in which hard work and long hours necessarily lead to a stable career. *It can also be a place in which you experience* **reality shock**, *a situation in which what you learn in the classroom does not always transfer directly into the "real world" and does not represent all that you need to know.* When reality shock sets in, things never seem to happen the way you expect. Reality shock befalls everyone; for example, you can imagine how a new teacher feels when her long hours preparing a lesson result in students who act bored and unappreciative of her efforts.

Many professions, such as nursing and teaching, have gone to great lengths to alleviate reality shock (Alhija & Fresko, 2010; Hinton & Chirgwin, 2010). This problem is one that is best addressed through internship and practicum experiences for students under the careful guidance of experienced people in the field.

HUMAN DEVELOPMENT in action

What biological, psychological, sociocultural, and life-cycle forces influence the progression of a career?

Reality shock typically hits younger workers soon after they begin an occupation.

reality shock
a situation in which what is learned in the classroom does not always transfer directly into the "real world" and does not represent all that a person needs to know

The Role of Mentors and Coaches

Entering an occupation involves more than the relatively short formal training a person receives. Instead, most people are oriented by a more experienced person who makes a specific effort to do this, taking on the role of a mentor or coach.

Bloom Productions/Getty Images

Women employees typically prefer and may achieve more from a female mentor.

A **mentor or developmental coach** *is part teacher, part sponsor, part model, and part counselor who facilitates on-the-job learning to help the new hire do the work required in his or her present role and to prepare for future roles* (Hunt & Weintraub, 2006). The mentor helps a young worker avoid trouble and provides invaluable information about the unwritten rules that govern day-to-day activities in the workplace, with mentors being sensitive to the employment situation (Smith, Howard, & Harrington, 2005). As part of the relationship, a mentor makes sure that the protégé is noticed and receives credit from supervisors for good work. Thus, occupational success often depends on the quality of the mentor–protégé relationship and the protégé's perceptions of its importance (Eddleston, Baldridge, & Veiga, 2004). In times of economic downturns, mentors can also provide invaluable advice on finding another job (Froman, 2010).

What do mentors get from the relationship? Helping a younger employee learn the job is one way to fulfill aspects of Erikson's phase of generativity. As we see in more detail in Chapter 13, generativity reflects middle-aged adults' need to ensure the continuity of society through activities such as socialization or having children. In addition, leaders may need to serve as mentors to activate transformational leadership (leadership that changes the direction of an organization) and promote positive work attitudes and career expectations of followers, enabling the mentor to rise to a higher level in his or her own career (Scandura & Williams, 2004).

Women and minorities have an especially important need for mentors (Pratt, 2010). When paired with mentors, women benefit by having higher expectations; mentored women also have better perceived career development (Enslin, 2007). For example, Latina nurses in the U.S. Army benefitted from mentors in terms of staying in the military and getting better assignments (Aponte, 2007). It is also critical to adopt a culturally conscious model of mentoring to enhance the advantages of mentoring for minority mentees (Campinha-Bacote, 2010). Culturally conscious mentoring involves understanding how an organization's culture, for example, affects employees and building those assumptions and behaviors into the mentoring situation. It can also involve addressing the cultural background of an employee and incorporating that into the mentoring relationship.

Despite the evidence that having a mentor can have many positive effects on occupational development, there is an important caveat: Having a poor mentor is worse than having no mentor (Ragins, Cotton, & Miller, 2000). Consequently, prospective protégés must be carefully matched with a mentor, and mentorship programs need to select motivated and skilled individuals who are provided with extensive training. How can prospective mentors and protégés meet more effectively? Some organizations have taken a page from dating and created speed mentoring as a way to help create better matches (Berk, 2010; Cook, Bahn, & Menaker, 2010).

Job Satisfaction

What does it mean to be satisfied with a job or occupation? **Job satisfaction** *is the positive feeling that results from an appraisal of one's work.* Research indicates that job satisfaction is a multifaceted concept but that certain characteristics—including hope, resilience, optimism, and self-efficacy—predict both job performance and job satisfaction (Luthans et al., 2007).

Satisfaction with some aspects of one's job tends to increase gradually with age, and successful aging includes a workplace component (Robson et al., 2006). Why is this so?

The factors that predict job satisfaction differ somewhat across cultures (Klassen, Usher, & Bong, 2010). This is explored in more detail in the Spotlight on Research feature.

mentor or developmental coach
a person who is part teacher, part sponsor, part model, and part counselor who facilitates on-the-job learning to help the new hire do the work required in his or her present role and to prepare for future roles

job satisfaction
the positive feeling that results from an appraisal of one's work

Cross-Cultural Aspects of Teachers' Job Satisfaction

Who were the investigators, and what was the aim of the study?

Robert Klassen, Ellen Usher, and Mimi Bong wondered about the similarities and differences in teachers' job satisfaction, self-efficacy, and job stress. To find out more, they studied teachers in the United States, Korea, and Canada. Their main question was whether teachers' cultural values, self-efficacy, and job stress would predict job satisfaction across the three countries.

How did the investigators measure the topic of interest?

The researchers measured self-efficacy by assessing teachers' individual perceptions about their school's collective capabilities to influence student achievement. Job satisfaction was measured through four responses: (1) "I am satisfied with my job," (2) "I am happy with the way my colleagues and superiors treat me," (3) "I am satisfied with what I achieve at work," and (4) "I feel good at work." Job stress was measured using a single response ("I find teaching to be very stressful"). Collectivism, a cultural value, was measured with a six-item scale in which the first part of the question was, "In your opinion, how important is it that you and your family ...," with the conclusion for each item as follows: (1) "take responsibility for caring for older family members?" (2) "turn to each other in times of trouble?" (3) "raise each other's children whenever there is a need?" (4) "do everything you can to help each other move ahead in life?" (5) "take responsibility for caring for older family members?" and (6) "call, write, or see each other often?" The Korean version of the scales was created using a translation–back-translation process to ensure that the meaning of the items was preserved.

Who were the participants in the study?

A total of 500 elementary- and middle-school teachers from the United States ($n = 137$), Canada ($n = 210$), and Korea ($n = 153$) participated. The sample from the United States was included to connect this study to other research on teachers' job satisfaction. Canadian teachers were included to determine the degree to which findings from the United States could be generalized to a country holding similar (but not identical) cultural values. The Korean teachers represented a group with a different geographic and demographic profile (East Asian, Confucian, and collectivist). Careful analyses showed no significant differences in age, teaching experience, job satisfaction, collective efficacy, job stress, or cultural values across the three countries.

What was the design of the study?

The study used a cross-sectional design because participants of different backgrounds were only tested once.

Were there ethical concerns with the study?

Because the study involved voluntary completion of a survey, there were no ethical concerns.

What were the results?

The analyses revealed that North American teachers scored higher on all variables than did Korean teachers. However, there were no differences across countries regarding the efficacy of the teachers and either the strength or the direction of its relationship to job satisfaction. In contrast, analyses revealed that job stress had a bigger impact for North American teachers, whereas the cultural value of collectivism was more important for Korean teachers.

What did the investigators conclude?

The most important finding from the study was the similarity across countries in the connection between the efficacy teachers believe they have and their job satisfaction—the less efficacy, the lower a teacher's satisfaction is likely to be. Second, the higher importance of the cultural value of collectivism for Korean teachers probably reflects a cultural norm of avoiding conflict and working for the betterment of the group. Finally, the finding that job stress was a negative predictor of job satisfaction for North American teachers (the higher the stress, the lower the satisfaction) but a positive predictor for Korean teachers (higher job stress predicted higher satisfaction) indicates that job stress may have different components as a function of culture. For Korean teachers, feeling stressed by the presence of more competent teachers may create an urge to improve, rather than a feeling of defeat. In sum, some predictors of job satisfaction transcend countries; others do not.

What converging evidence would strengthen these conclusions?

Klassen and his colleagues examined only a few countries and cultures, so their study needs to be repeated with others. Also, additional types of teachers (high school and college or university) need to be included.

 Go to Psychology CourseMate at **www.cengagebrain.com** to enhance your understanding of this research.

How does job satisfaction evolve over young and middle adulthood? You may be pleased to learn research shows that, given sufficient time, most people find a job with which they are reasonably happy (Hom & Kinicki, 2001). Optimistically, this indicates that there is a job out there, somewhere, in which you will be happy. That's good, because research grounded in positive psychology theory indicates that happiness fuels success (Achor, 2010).

It's also true that job satisfaction does not increase in all areas and job types with age. White-collar professionals show an increase in job satisfaction with age, whereas those in blue-collar positions generally do not, and these findings hold with both men and women (Aasland, Rosta, & Nylenna, 2010). This is also true across cultures. A study of Filipino and Taiwanese workers in the long-term health care industry in Taiwan showed that workers with 4 or 5 years' experience had lower job satisfaction than did workers with less experience; however, in another study, job satisfaction

among older physicians in Norway was found to increase over time (Aasland, Rosta, & Nylenna, 2010; Tu, 2007).

As you might suspect, the type of job and the kinds of family responsibilities someone has at different career stages—as well as the flexibility of work options, such as telecommuting and family leave benefits to accommodate those responsibilities—influence the relationship between age and job satisfaction (Marsh & Musson, 2008). This suggests that accumulation of experience, changing context, and the stage of career development may contribute to the increase in job satisfaction over time.

Alienation and Burnout

All jobs create a certain level of stress. For most workers, such negatives are merely annoyances. But for others, extremely stressful situations on the job may result in alienation and burnout.

When workers feel that what they are doing is meaningless and that their efforts are devalued, or when they do not see the connection between what they do and the final product, a sense of **alienation** *is likely to result.* Terkel (1974) reported that employees are most likely to feel alienated when they perform routine, repetitive actions. But other workers can become alienated. The financial crisis that began in 2008 and resulted in record levels of job loss is only the most recent example of even high-level managerial employees feeling abandoned by their employers.

It is essential for companies to provide positive work environments to ensure that the workforce remains stable and committed (Griffin et al., 2010). How can employers avoid alienating workers and improve organizational commitment? Research indicates that trust is key (Chen, Aryee, & Lee, 2005), as is a perception among employees that the employer deals with people fairly and impartially (Howard & Cordes, 2010). It is also helpful to involve employees in the decision-making process, create flexible work schedules, and institute employee development and enhancement programs.

Sometimes the pace and pressure of the occupation becomes more than a person can bear, resulting in **burnout**, *the depletion of a person's energy and motivation, the loss of occupational idealism, and the feeling of being exploited.* Burnout is a state of physical, emotional, and mental exhaustion as a result of job stress (Malach-Pines, 2005). Burnout is most common among people in the helping professions—such as teaching, social work, health care (Bozikas et al., 2000), and occupational therapy (Bird, 2001)—and for those in the military (Harrington et al., 2001).

People in these professions must constantly deal with other people's complex problems, usually under difficult time constraints. Dealing with these pressures every day, along with bureaucratic paperwork, may become too much for the worker to bear. Frustration builds, and disillusionment and exhaustion set in—burnout. And burnout can negatively affect the people who are supposed to receive services from the burned-out employee (Rowe & Sherlock, 2005).

But we know that burnout does not affect everyone is a particular profession. Why? R. J. Vallerand (2008), proposes that the difference relates to people feeling different types of passion (obsessive and harmonious) toward their jobs . *A* **passion** *is a strong inclination toward an activity that individuals like (or even love), that they value (and thus find important), and in which they invest time and energy* (Vallerand et al., 2010). Vallerand's (2008) passion model proposes that people develop a passion toward enjoyable activities that are incorporated into identity.

Vallerand's model differentiates between two kinds of passion: obsessive and harmonious. A critical aspect of obsessive passion is that the internal urge to engage in the passionate activity makes it difficult for the person to fully disengage from thoughts

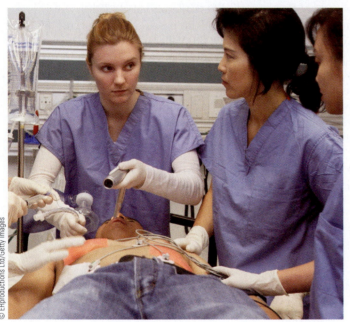

© ERproductions Ltd/Getty Images

High-stress jobs such as intensive care nursing often result in burnout.

alienation

a feeling among workers when their work seems meaningless and their efforts devalued or when they see no connection between their work and the final product

burnout

a depletion of a person's energy and motivation, the loss of occupational idealism, and the feeling of being exploited

passion

a strong inclination toward an activity that individuals like (or even love), that they value (and thus find important), and in which they invest time and energy

FIGURE 12.2

Model of the relationships among passion, satisfaction at work, conflict, and burnout. Harmonious passion predicts higher levels of satisfaction at work, which predict lower levels of burnout. In contrast, obsessive passion predicts higher levels of conflict, which in turn predict higher levels of burnout. ***$p < .001$.

From "On the role of passion for work in burnout: A process model," by R. J. Vallerand, Y. Paquet, F. L. Philippe, and J. Charest, in Journal of Personality, Vol. 78, Figure 1, p. 300. Copyright © Wiley-Blackwell 2010.

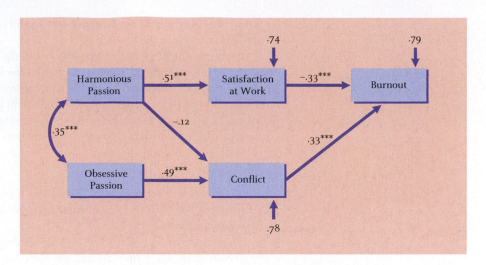

about the activity, leading to conflict with other activities in the person's life (Vallerand et al., 2010). In contrast, harmonious passion results when individuals do not feel compelled to engage in the enjoyable activity; rather, they freely choose to do so, and it is in harmony with other aspects of the person's life (Vallerand et al., 2010).

Research in France and Canada indicates that the passion model accurately predicts employees' feelings of burnout (Vallerand, 2008; Vallerand et al., 2010). As shown in Figure 12.2, obsessive passion predicts higher levels of conflict, which in turn predict higher levels of burnout. In contrast, harmonious passion predicts higher levels of satisfaction at work, which in turn predict lower levels of burnout.

The best ways to lower burnout are intervention programs that focus on both the organization and the employee (Awa, Plaumann, & Walter, 2010). At the organizational level, job restructuring and employee-provided programs are important. For employees, stress-reduction techniques, lowering other people's expectations, cognitive restructuring of the work situation, and finding alternative ways to enhance personal growth and identity are most effective (van Dierendonck, Garssen, & Visser, 2005).

Test Yourself

Recall

1. For most people, the main reason to work is _____.

2. Holland's theory deals with the relationship between occupation and _____.

3. _____ says that occupational selection is based in part on a person's self-efficacy regarding that occupation.

4. The role of a mentor is part teacher, part sponsor, part model, and part _____.

5. For many workers, job satisfaction tends to _____ in midlife.

6. Two salient aspects of job dissatisfaction are alienation and _____.

Interpret

- What is the relationship between occupational development and job satisfaction? Would these relationships

be different in the case of a person with a good match between personality and occupation versus one with a poor match?

- How could interventions to help people avoid alienation be made culturally sensitive?

Apply

- If you were the director of the campus career services office, what would you do to provide students with realistic and accurate information about potential careers?

- If you were the director of human resources at a company, how would you design a new employee orientation program?

Recall answers: (1) to earn a living, (2) personality, (3) Social cognitive career theory, (4) counselor, (5) increase, (6) burnout

Gender, Ethnicity, and Discrimination Issues

LEARNING OBJECTIVES

■ How are people viewed when they enter occupations that are not traditional for their gender?

■ What factors are related to women's occupational development?

■ What factors affect ethnic minority workers' occupational experiences and occupational development?

■ What types of bias and discrimination hinder the occupational development of women and ethnic minority workers?

Janice, a 35-year-old African American manager at a business consulting firm, is concerned because her career is not progressing as rapidly as she had hoped. Janice works hard and has received excellent performance ratings every year. But she has noticed that there are few women in upper management positions in her company. Janice wonders whether she will ever be promoted.

Occupational choice and development are not equally available to all, as Janice is experiencing. Gender, ethnicity, and age may create barriers to achieving occupational goals. Men and women in similar occupations may nonetheless have different life experiences and probably received different socialization as children and adolescents that made it easier or harder for them to set their sights on a career. Bias and discrimination also create barriers to occupational success.

Gender Differences in Occupational Selection

About 60% of all women over age 16 in the United States are working, and they represent roughly 47% of the total workforce (U.S. Bureau of Labor Statistics, 2010c). Across ethnic groups, African American women participate the most (about 62%) and Latina American women are the least likely to work (about 56%). Compared to women in many other countries, women in the United States tend to be employed at a higher rate (see Figure 12.3). However, major structural barriers to women's occupational selection remain (Maume, 2004; Probert, 2005). Let's look at both traditional and nontraditional occupations for women.

Structural Barriers for Women: Traditional and Nontraditional Occupations

In the past, women employed outside the home tended to enter traditional, female-dominated occupations such as secretarial, teaching, and social work jobs. This was due mainly to their socialization into these occupational tracks. However, as more women enter the workforce and as new opportunities are opened for women, a growing number have begun to work in occupations that have been traditionally male dominated, such as construction and engineering. The U.S. Department of Labor (2010a) categorizes women's nontraditional occupations as those in which women constitute 25% or less of the total number of people employed; the skilled trades (electricians, plumbers, and carpenters) still have among the lowest participation rates of women. Trends can be seen in Figure 12.4.

Despite the efforts to counteract gender stereotyping of occupations, women who choose nontraditional occupations and are successful in them tend to be viewed negatively compared with similarly successful men.

In a study conducted in India, both women and men gave higher "respectability" ratings to males than to females in the same occupation (Kanekar, Kolsawalla, & Nazareth, 1989). In the United States, research shows that men still prefer to date women who are in traditional careers (Kapoor et al., 2010).

HUMAN DEVELOPMENT in action
What changes in children's school and other socialization experiences will enable girls to acquire different occupational skills?

FIGURE 12.3

Women's labor force participation rates in
selected countries, 1970–2009.

From "Women at work," by U.S. Bureau of Labor Statistics, p. 13, 2011.

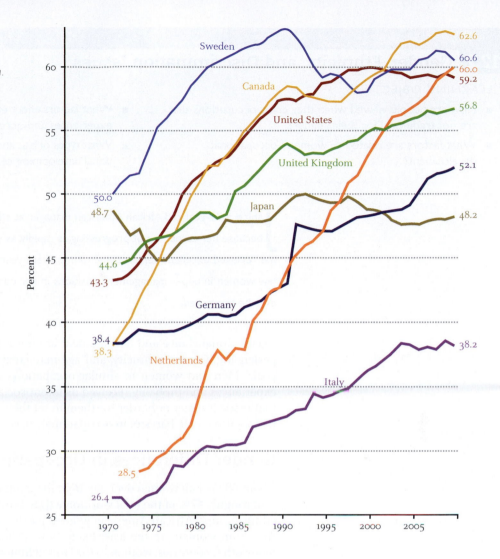

Women and Occupational Development

The characteristics and aspirations of women who entered the workforce in the 1950s, baby boomer women (born between 1946 and 1964), generation X women (born between 1965 and 1982), and millennial women (born since 1983) are significantly different (Howe & Strauss, 1992; Piscione, 2004; Strauss & Howe, 2007). Women in previous generations had fewer opportunities for employment choice and had to overcome more barriers.

In the 21st century, women entrepreneurs are starting small businesses at a faster rate than men and are finding that a home-based business can solve many of the challenges they face in balancing employment and a home life. For those seeking work outside the home, women today negotiate beyond the first offer of a job, salary, and benefits package to make deals with prospective employers that will result in a work environment that is best for their career interests and the needs of their family.

As the millennial generation becomes predominant in the workforce, it will be interesting to see whether their high degree of technological sophistication provides still more occupational and career options. Technologically mediated workplaces may provide solutions to many traditional issues, such as work–family conflict. But when millennial-generation women choose nontraditional occupations, their attitudes toward them are more similar to, rather than different from, previous generations' attitudes (Real, Mitnick, & Maloney, 2010).

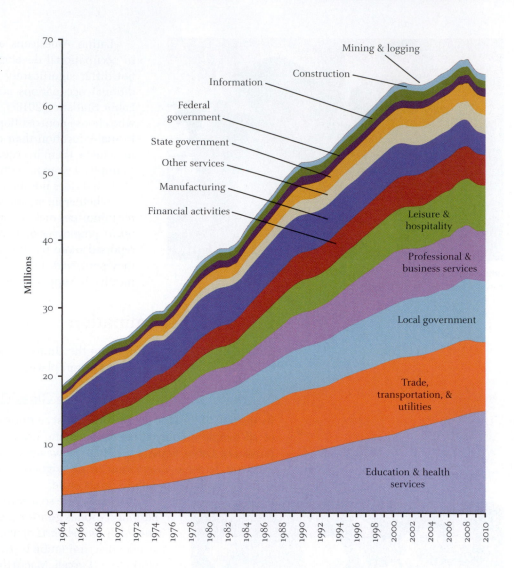

FIGURE 12.4

Employment of women by industry, 1964–2010.

From "Women at work," by U.S. Bureau of Labor Statistics, p. 11, 2011.

Women who graduate from college now have more opportunities in the workplace than their grandmothers did.

In the corporate world, unsupportive or insensitive work environments, organizational politics, and the lack of occupational development opportunities are most important for women working full time (Yamini-Benjamin, 2007). Female professionals leave their jobs for two main reasons, in addition to family obligations. First, the organizations in which women work are felt to idealize and reward masculine values of working—individuality, self-sufficiency, and individual contributions—while emphasizing tangible outputs, competitiveness, and rationality. Most women prefer organizations that more highly value relationships, interdependence, and collaboration.

Second, women may feel disconnected from the workplace. By midcareer, women may conclude that they must leave these unsupportive organizations to achieve satisfaction, growth, and development at work and to be rewarded for the relational skills they consider essential for success.

Ethnicity and Occupational Development

Unfortunately, little research has been conducted from a developmental perspective related to occupational selection and development for people from ethnic minorities. Rather, most researchers have focused on the limited opportunities that ethnic minorities have and on the structural barriers, such as discrimination, that they face.

© Jeff Greenberg/Alamy

Ethnic minority workers face more significant barriers to career development.

Latino Americans are similar to European Americans in occupational development and work values. Women do not differ significantly in terms of participation in nontraditional occupations across ethnic groups (U.S. Bureau of Labor Statistics, 2010c). However, African American women who choose nontraditional occupations tend to plan for more formal education than necessary to achieve their goal. This may make them overqualified for the jobs they then get; for example, a woman with a college degree may be working in a job that does not require that level of education.

Whether an organization is responsive to the needs of ethnic minorities makes a big difference for employees. Ethnic minority employees of a diverse organization in the Netherlands reported more positive feelings about their workplace when they perceived their organization as responsive and communicative in supportive ways (Dinsbach, Fiej, & de Vries, 2007).

Bias and Discrimination

Since the 1960s, organizations in the United States have been sensitized to the issues of bias and discrimination in the workplace.

Gender Discrimination and the Glass Ceiling

By the end of the first decade of the 21st century, women accounted for more than half of all people employed in management, professional, and related occupations (U.S. Bureau of Labor Statistics, 2010c). However, women are still underrepresented at the very top. Janice's observation in the vignette, that few women serve in the highest ranks of major corporations, is accurate.

© ITAR-TASS Photo Agency/Alamy

Women like Hillary Clinton who make it to the highest ranks of their profession have had to contend with both the glass ceiling and the glass cliff.

Why are there so few women in such positions? *The most important reason is* **gender discrimination***: denying a job to someone solely on the basis of whether the person is a man or a woman.* Gender discrimination is still pervasive in too many aspects of the workplace (Purcell, MacArthur, & Samblanet, 2010).

In addition, research in the United States and Britain confirms that women are forced to work harder than men (Gorman & Kmec, 2007). Neither differences in job characteristics nor family obligations account for this difference; the results clearly point to stricter job performance standards being applied to women.

Women themselves refer to a **glass ceiling***, the level to which they may rise in an organization but beyond which they may not go.* The glass ceiling is a major barrier for women (Maume, 2004; Purcell, MacArthur, & Samblanet, 2010), and the greatest barrier facing them is at the boundary between lower-tier and upper-tier jobs. Men are largely blind to the existence of the glass ceiling (Heppner, 2007).

The glass ceiling is pervasive across higher management and professional workplace settings (Heppner, 2007). The glass ceiling has also been used to account for why African Americans and Asian Americans do not advance as much in their careers as do European American men (Hwang, 2007; Johnson, 2000; Phelps & Constantine, 2001). It also provides a framework for understanding limitations to women's careers in many countries around the world (Mugadza, 2005; Zafarullah, 2000).

Interestingly, a different trend emerges if we examine who is appointed to critical positions in organizations in times of crisis. Research shows that at such times women are more likely to be put into leadership positions. *Consequently, women often confront a* **glass cliff** *in which their leadership position is precarious.* For example,

gender discrimination
denying a job to someone solely on the basis of whether the person is a man or a woman

glass ceiling
the level to which women may rise in an organization but beyond which they may not go

glass cliff
a situation that women confront in which their leadership position is precarious

evidence shows that companies are more likely to appoint a woman to their board of directors if their financial performance had been poor in the recent past, and women are more likely to be political candidates if the seat is a highly contested one (Ryan, Haslam, & Kulich, 2010).

What can be done to eliminate the glass ceiling and the glass cliff? Kolb, Williams, and Frohlinger (2010) argue that women can and must be assertive in getting their rightful place at the table by focusing on five key things: drilling deep into the organization so that they can make informed decisions, getting critical support, acquiring the necessary resources, getting buy-in, and making a difference.

Equal Pay for Equal Work

In addition to discrimination in hiring and promotion, women are subject to pay discrimination. According to the U.S. Bureau of Labor Statistics (2010d), women are paid about 80% of what men are paid on an average annual basis. As you can see in Figure 12.5, the wage gap depends on age and has been narrowing since the late 1970s. When the first equal-pay legislation passed in the United States in 1963, women were paid only 59 cents for every dollar men were paid.

What can be done to eliminate the pay inequity problem permanently? In their comprehensive look at pay inequity, Dey and Hill (2007) suggested several actions: encouraging women to negotiate salary more effectively, rethinking the use of hours worked as the primary measure of productivity, creating more work options for working mothers, and ending gender discrimination in the workplace. The Linking Research to Life feature at the end of the chapter explores this issue in more detail.

Sexual Harassment

Suppose you have been working hard on a paper for a course and think you've done a good job. When you receive an A for the paper, you are elated. When you discuss your paper (and your excitement) with your instructor, you receive a big hug. How do you feel? What if this situation involved a major project at work and the hug came from your boss? Your co-worker? What if it were a kiss on your lips instead of a hug?

Whether such behavior is acceptable, or whether it constitutes sexual harassment, depends on many situational factors, including the setting and the people involved and the relationship between them.

How many people have been sexually harassed? That's a hard question to answer for several reasons: there is no universal definition of it, men and women

FIGURE 12.5

Women's earnings as a percentage of men's, showing median usual weekly earnings of full-time wage and salary workers by age, 1979–2009.

Source: From Women's-to-men's Earnings Ratio by Age, 2009. U.S. Bureau of Labor Statistics.

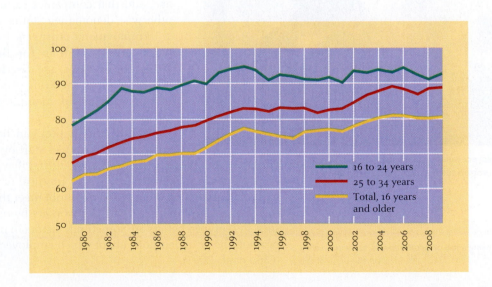

have different perceptions, and many victims do not report it (Advocates for Human Rights, 2010). Even given these difficulties, evidence indicates that at least 28% of women report having been sexually harassed in the workplace (Ilies et al., 2003), and harassment of men is increasing. Victims are most often single or divorced young adult women (Zippel, 2006), but about 16% of workplace cases that result in formal legal charges involve male victims (Equal Employment Opportunity Commission, 2010). In 1998, the U.S. Supreme Court (in *Oncale v. Sundowner Offshore Services*) ruled that the relevant laws also protect men. Thus, the standard by which sexual harassment is judged could now be said to be a "reasonable person" standard.

What are the effects of being sexually harassed? As you might expect, research evidence clearly shows negative job-related, psychological, and physical health outcomes (Lim & Cortina, 2005). Cultural differences in labeling behaviors as sexually harassing, and how this harassment is addressed, are also important. Research comparing countries in the European Union reveals differences across these countries in terms of definitions and corrective action (Zippel, 2006). Compared to women who work in traditional occupations, women who work in nontraditional occupations are less likely to believe that they are being sexually harassed when confronted with the same behavior (Bouldin & Grayson, 2010; Maeder, Wiener, & Winter, 2007).

Unfortunately, little research has been done to identify what aspects of organizations foster harassment or to determine the impact of educational programs aimed at addressing the problem.

What can be done to provide people with safe work and learning environments, free from sexual harassment? Training in gender awareness is a common approach that often works (Tang & McCollum, 1996), especially given that gender differences exist in perceptions of behavior (Lindgren, 2007).

HUMAN DEVELOPMENT in action

What are the key biological, psychological, sociocultural, and life-cycle factors that should inform training programs concerning sexual harassment in the workplace?

Age Discrimination

Another structural barrier to occupational development is **age discrimination***, which involves denying a job or promotion to someone solely on the basis of age.* The U.S. Age Discrimination in Employment Act of 1986 protects workers over age 40. A similar law, the Employment Equality (Age) Regulations, went into effect in the United Kingdom in 2006, and more European countries are protecting middle-aged and older workers (Lahey, 2010). These laws stipulate that people must be hired based on their ability, not their age, and that companies cannot segregate or classify workers or otherwise denote their status on the basis of age.

Employment prospects for middle-aged people around the world are lower than for their younger counterparts (Lahey, 2010). For example, age discrimination toward those over age 45 is common in Hong Kong (Cheung, Kam, & Ngan, 2011), resulting in longer periods of unemployment, early retirement, or negative attitudes.

Age discrimination can happen prior to or after interaction with human resources staff by other employees making the hiring decisions, and it can be covert (Lahey, 2010; Pillay, Kelly, & Tones, 2006). For example, employers can make certain types of physical or mental performance a job requirement and argue that older workers cannot meet the standard prior to an interview. Or they can attempt to get rid of older workers by using retirement incentives. Supervisors' stereotyped beliefs are sometimes factors in performance evaluations for raises or promotions or in decisions about which employees are eligible for additional training (Chiu et al., 2001).

Dennis Wise/Getty Images

Employers cannot make a decision not to hire this woman solely on the basis of her age.

age discrimination

denying a job or promotion to someone solely on the basis of age

Test Yourself

Recall

1. Women who choose nontraditional occupations are often viewed _____ by their peers.

2. Research shows that men tend to prefer to date women who are in _____ occupations.

3. Ethnic minority workers are more satisfied with and committed to organizations that are responsive and _____.

4. Three barriers to women's occupational development are sex discrimination, the glass ceiling, and _____.

Interpret

- What steps need to be taken to eliminate gender, ethnic, and age bias in the workplace?

- How could you help foster a culture of support in your workplace?

Apply

- Suppose that you are the CEO of a large organization and that you need to make personnel reductions through layoffs. Many of your most expensive employees are over age 40. How could you accomplish this without being accused of age discrimination?

- How would you develop a sexual harassment prevention program?

Recall answers: (1) traditional, (2) family obligations, (3) communicative in supportive ways, (4) pay discrimination

---

12.3 Occupational Transitions

LEARNING OBJECTIVES

- Why do people change occupations?
- Is worrying about potential job loss a major source of stress?
- How does job loss affect the amount of stress experienced?

Fred has 32 years of service for an automobile manufacturer. Over the years, increasing numbers of assembly-line jobs have been eliminated by new technology (including robots) and by the export of manufacturing jobs to other countries. Although Fred has been assured that his job is safe, he isn't so sure. He worries that he could be laid off at any time.

In the past, people like Fred commonly chose an occupation during young adulthood and stayed in it throughout their working years. Today, however, not many people have that option. Corporations have restructured so often that employees now assume occupational changes are part of the career process. Such corporate actions mean that people's conceptions of work and career are in flux and that losing a job no longer has only negative meanings (Haworth & Lewis, 2005).

Several factors have been identified as important in determining who will remain in an occupation and who will change. Some factors—such as whether the person likes the occupation—lead to self-initiated occupation changes. However, other factors—such as obsolete skills and economic trends—may cause forced occupational changes. For example, continued improvement of robots has caused some auto industry workers to lose their jobs; corporations send jobs overseas to increase profits; and economic recessions usually result in large-scale layoffs and high levels of unemployment.

Retraining Workers

When you are hired into a specific job, you are selected because your employer believes you offer the best fit between the abilities you already have and those needed to perform the job. As most people can attest, though, the skills needed to perform a

Seminars such as this are taken by thousands of workers around the world each year as part of worker training and retraining programs.

job usually change over time. Such changes may be due to the introduction of new technology, additional responsibilities, or reorganization.

Unless a person's skills are kept up to date, the outcome is likely to be either job loss or career plateau (McCleese & Eby, 2006; Rose & Gordon, 2010). **Career plateauing** *occurs when there is a lack of challenge in the job or promotional opportunity in the organization or when a person decides not to seek advancement.* Research in Canada (Lemire, Saba, & Gagnon, 1999), Asia (Lee, 2003), and Australia (Rose & Gordon, 2010) shows that feeling one's career has plateaued usually results in less organizational commitment, lower job satisfaction, and a greater tendency to leave. But attitudes can remain positive if it is only the lack of challenge and not a lack of promotion opportunity that is responsible for the plateauing (McCleese & Eby, 2006).

In cases of job loss or career plateau, retraining may be an appropriate response. Around the world, large numbers of employees participate each year in programs and courses that are offered by their employer or by a college or university and are aimed at improving existing skills or adding new job skills. For midcareer employees, retraining might focus on how to advance in occupation or on how to find new career opportunities—for example, through resumé preparation and career counseling. Increasingly, such programs are offered online to make them easier and more convenient for people to access (Githens & Sauer, 2010).

Many corporations, as well as community and technical colleges, offer retraining programs in a variety of fields. Organizations that promote employee development typically promote in-house courses to improve employee skills. They may also offer tuition reimbursement programs for individuals who successfully complete courses at colleges or universities.

The retraining of midcareer and older workers highlights the need for lifelong learning (Armstrong-Stassen & Templer, 2005; Sinnott, 1994). If corporations are to meet the challenges of a global economy, it is imperative that they include retraining in their employee development programs. Such programs will help improve people's chances of advancement in their chosen occupations and can assist people in making successful transitions from one occupation to another.

Occupational Insecurity

Over the past few decades, changing U.S. economic conditions (e.g., the move toward a global economy), changing demographics, and a global recession have forced many people out of their jobs. Heavy manufacturing and support businesses (e.g., the steel, oil, and automotive industries) and farming were the hardest-hit sectors during the 1970s and 1980s. But no one is immune. The Great Recession that began in 2008 put many middle- and upper-level corporate executives out of work worldwide.

As a result, many people today feel insecure about their jobs. Economic downturns create significant levels of stress, especially when such downturns create massive job loss (Sinclair et al., 2010). Like Fred, the autoworker in the vignette, many worried workers have numerous years of dedicated service to a company. Unfortunately, people who worry about their jobs tend to have poorer physical and psychological well-being (McKee-Ryan et al., 2005). For example, people's anxiety about their job may result in negative attitudes about their employer or even about work in general, which in turn may result in diminished desire to be successful. Whether there is any basis for people's feelings of job insecurity may not matter; sometimes what people think is true about their work situation is more important than what is actually the case. Just the possibility of losing one's job can negatively affect physical and psychological health.

career plateauing
when promotional advancement is either not possible or not desired by the worker

When Jo Ann graduated from college, she thought she had hit the jackpot by getting a great job with a major technology company. She was a rising star for her first 16 years with the company, being named to all-company lists of the best systems marketing employees, exceeding her sales goals every year, and being promoted quickly up the ranks. So when the rumors of lay-offs began circulating through the company, she thought she had little to worry about.

She was wrong.

To Jo Ann's great shock, she was laid off. The entire division of the company was eliminated or outsourced. She was devastated. The severance package the company provided was no consolation. Unemployment benefits did not pay the mortgage. Her savings would soon be gone. She felt as if someone had punched her, hard, right in the gut. She had lost much of her identity. She felt ashamed. She felt at fault.

Jo Ann became seriously depressed. She realized it was going to be a difficult process finding a new job with so many others like herself out of work.

Jo Ann finally got a job, at far less pay than she had made in the tech company. She still feels angry and hurt, years later.

So how does the possibility of losing their job affect employees? Mantler et al. (2005) examined coping strategies for comparable samples of laid-off and employed high-technology workers. They found that although unemployed participants reported higher levels of stress compared with employed participants, employment uncertainty mediated the association between employment status and perceived stress. That is, people who believe that their job is in jeopardy—even if it is not—show levels of stress similar to unemployed participants. This result is due to differences in coping strategies. There are several ways that people deal with stress, and two of the more common are emotion-focused coping and problem-focused coping. Some people focus on how the stressful situation makes them feel, so they cope by making themselves feel better about it. Others focus on the problem itself and do something to solve it. People who avoided addressing stressful situations reported higher levels of stress, particularly when they were fairly certain of the outcome. Thus, even people whose jobs aren't really in jeopardy can report high levels of stress if they tend to use emotion-focused coping strategies.

Coping With Unemployment

What does it feel like to lose one's job after many years of dedicated service? Read the Real People feature to get a sense of this experience.

As Jo Ann's case so poignantly reflects, losing one's job can have enormous personal impact that can last a long time (Lin & Leung, 2010; McKee-Ryan et al., 2005). When U.S. unemployment rates hit 10.6% in January 2010, millions of people could relate to these feelings. When unemployment lasts and reemployment does not occur soon, unemployed people commonly experience a variety of negative effects (Lin & Leung, 2010) that range from a decline in immune system functioning (Cohen et al., 2007) to decreases in well-being (McKee-Ryan et al., 2005).

In a comprehensive study of the effects of unemployment, McKee-Ryan et al. (2005) found several specific results from losing one's job. Unemployed workers had significantly lower mental health, life satisfaction, marital or family satisfaction, and subjective physical health (how they perceive their health to be) than their employed counterparts. With reemployment, these negative effects disappear. Figure 12.6 shows that physical health and psychological health following job displacement are influenced by several factors (McKee-Ryan et al., 2005).

The effects of job loss vary with age and gender. In the United States, middle-aged men are more vulnerable to negative effects than older or younger men—largely because they have greater financial responsibilities than the other two groups—but older women report more negative effects over time than younger women (Bambra, 2010). Research in Spain indicates that gender differences in responding to job loss are complexly related to family responsibilities and social class

FIGURE 12.6

Psychological and physical well-being after losing one's job are affected by many variables.

From "Psychological and physical well-being during unemployment: A meta-analytic study," by F. McKee-Ryan, Z. Song, C. R. Wanberg, and A. J. Kinicki, in Journal of Applied Psychology, Vol. 90, p. 56, 2005.

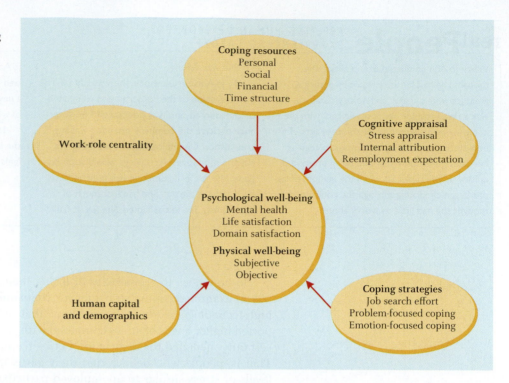

HUMAN DEVELOPMENT in action

What are some of the broader effects of unemployment on you or people you know?

(Artazcoz et al., 2004). Specifically, to the extent that work is viewed as the expected contribution to the family, losing one's job has a more substantial negative effect. Because this tends to be more the case for men than for women, it helps explain the gender differences.

Because unemployment rates for many ethnic minority groups are substantially higher than those for European Americans (U.S. Bureau of Labor Statistics, 2010b), the effects of unemployment are experienced by a greater proportion of people in these groups. Cultural differences need to be considered in understanding the effects of unemployment (Grosso & Smith, 2012). Compared to European Americans, however, it usually takes minority workers longer to find another job.

How long you are unemployed also affects how people react. People who are unemployed for at least a year perceive their mental health significantly more negatively than either employed people or those who have removed themselves from the labor force (e.g., have stopped looking for work) (Pharr, Moonie, & Bungum, 2012). Those who lost their jobs involuntarily feel a loss of control over their work environment and feel less demand placed on them. Importantly, a reasonable amount of demand is critical to maintaining good health, whereas too little demand lowers health.

Research also offers some advice for adults who are trying to manage occupational transitions (Ebberwein, 2001):

- Approach job loss with a healthy sense of urgency.

- Consider your next career move and what you must do to achieve it, even if there are no prospects for it in sight.

- Acknowledge and react to change as soon as it is evident.

- Be cautious of stopgap employment.

- Identify a realistic goal and then list the steps you must take to achieve it.

In addition, the U.S. Department of Labor (2012) offers tips for job seekers, as do online services such as LinkedIn, which also provides networking groups. These steps may not guarantee that you will find a new job quickly, but they help create a better sense that you are in control.

Test Yourself

Recall

1. One response to the pressures of a global economy and an aging workforce is to provide _____.

2. Two factors that could cause involuntary occupational change are economic trends and _____.

3. Fear of job loss is often a more important determinant of stress than _____.

4. The group that is most at risk for negative effects of job loss is _____.

Interpret

- A trend toward multiple careers has become the norm. What implications does this have for theories of career development?

- Analyze the effects of being laid off from a biological, psychological, sociocultural, and life-cycle perspective.

Apply

- You have been asked to design a program to help employees cope with losing their job. What key components would you include in this program?

- How might education affect the outcome of being laid off?

12.4 Work and Family

LEARNING OBJECTIVES

- What are the issues faced by employed people who care for dependents?

- How do partners typically view the division of household chores? What is work–family conflict? How does it affect couples' lives?

Jennifer, a 38-year-old sales clerk at a department store, feels that her husband, Bill, doesn't do his share of the housework or child care. Bill says that real men don't do housework and that he's really tired when he comes home from work. Jennifer thinks that this isn't fair, especially because she works as many hours as her husband.

One of the most difficult challenges facing adults like Jennifer is trying to balance the demands of occupation with the demands of family. Over the past few decades, the rapid increase in the number of families in which both parents are employed has fundamentally changed how we view the relationship between work and family. This can even mean taking a young child to work as a way to deal with the pushes and pulls of being an employed parent. In roughly 60% of two-parent households today, both adults work outside the home, a rate slightly lower than previous years due to the economic recession (U.S. Bureau of Labor Statistics, 2010a). The main reason? Families need the dual income to pay their bills and maintain a moderate standard of living.

We will see that dual-earner couples with children experience both benefits and disadvantages. The stresses of living in this arrangement are substantial, and gender differences are clear—especially in the division of household chores.

The Dependent Care Dilemma

Many employed adults must also provide care for dependent children or parents. As we will see, the issues they face are complex.

Employed Caregivers

Many mothers have no option but to return to work after the birth of a child. About 55% of married and unmarried mothers with children under the age of 3 years work for pay, with another 9% officially considered unemployed but looking for employment (U.S. Department of Labor, 2010b).

Some women, though, grapple with the decision of whether they want to return to work. Surveys of mothers with preschool children reveal that the motivation for returning to work tends to be related to financial need and how attached mothers are to their work. The amount of leave time a woman has matters; the passage of the Family and Medical Leave Act in 1993 entitled workers to take unpaid time off to care for their dependents with the right to return to their jobs. This act resulted in an increase in the number of women who returned to work at least part time (Schott, 2010). Although part-time work may seem appealing, what matters more is whether mothers are working hours that are close to what they consider ideal and are accommodating to their family's needs (Kim, 2000). Perceptions of ideal working hours differ as a function of gender and life-cycle stage regarding children.

A concern for many women is whether stepping out of their occupations following childbirth will negatively affect their career paths. Evidence clearly indicates that it does (Aisenbrey, Evertsson, & Grunow, 2009). Women in the United States are punished, even for short leaves. But even in women-friendly countries such as Sweden, long leaves typically result in a negative effect on upward career movement.

Often overlooked is the increasing number of workers who must also care for a parent or partner. Of women caring for parents or parents-in-law, more than 80% provide an average of 23 hours per week of care and 70% contribute money (Pierret, 2006). We consider their situation in more detail in Chapter 13.

Whether assistance is needed for a person's children or parents, key factors in selecting an appropriate care site are quality of care, price, and hours of availability (Helpguide.org, 2005; Mitchell & Messner, 2003–2004). Depending on the individual's economic situation, it may not be possible to find affordable and quality care that is available when needed. In such cases, there may be no option but to drop out of the workforce or enlist the help of friends and family.

Dependent Care and Effects on Workers

Being responsible for dependent care has significant negative effects on caregivers. For example, whether responsible for the care of an older parent or a child, women and men report negative effects on their work, higher levels of stress, and problems with coping (Neal & Hammer, 2006). Because women serve as caregivers more often than men, the related problems are greater for women; for example, women experience far more negative consequences on their career advancement if they both are employed full time and serve as a primary caregiver (Roxburgh, 2002).

How can these negative effects be lessened? When women's partners provide good support and women have average or high control over their jobs, employed mothers are significantly less distressed than employed nonmothers (Roxburgh, 2002) or mothers without support (Rwampororo, 2001). Research focusing on single working mothers also shows that those who have support from their families manage to figure out a balance between work and family obligations (Son & Bauer, 2010).

Dependent Care and Employer Responses

Employed parents with small children or dependent spouses, partners, or parents are confronted with the difficult prospect of leaving them in the care of others. This is especially problematic when the usual care arrangement is unavailable. *A growing need in the workplace is for*

Balancing work and family obligations is especially difficult for women.

Keith Brofsky/Getty Images

backup care, *which provides emergency care for dependent children or adults so that the employee does not need to lose a day of work.*

Does providing a workplace care center or backup care make a difference in terms of an employee's feelings about work, absenteeism, and productivity? There is no simple answer. For example, just making a child-care center available to employees does not necessarily reduce parents' work–family conflict or their absenteeism, particularly among younger employees (Connelly, Degraff, & Willis, 2004). A "family-friendly" company must also pay attention to the attitudes of their employees and make sure that the company provides broad-based support (Allen, 2001; Grandey, 2001). The keys are how supervisors act and the number and type of benefits the company provides. The most important single thing a company can do is allow the employee to leave work without penalty to tend to family needs (Lawton & Tulkin, 2010).

Research also indicates that there may not be differences for either mothers or their infants between work-based and non-work-based child-care centers in terms of the mothers' ease in transitioning back to work or the infants' ability to settle into day care (Skouteris, McNaught, & Dissanayake, 2007).

It will be interesting to watch how these issues—especially flexible schedules—play out in the United States, where such practices are not yet common. A global study of parental leave, such as that granted under the U.S. Family and Medical Leave Act, showed that the more generous parental leave policies are, the lower the infant mortality rates, clearly indicating that parental leave policies are a good thing (Ferrarini & Norström, 2010).

HUMAN DEVELOPMENT in action

How could your workplace or the college or university you are attending provide a more supportive environment for dependent care?

Juggling Multiple Roles

When both members of a heterosexual couple with dependents are employed, who cleans the house, cooks the meals, and takes care of the children when they are ill? This question goes to the heart of the core dilemma of modern, dual-earner couples: How are household chores divided? How are work and family role conflicts handled?

Dividing Household Chores

Despite much media attention and claims of increased sharing in the duties, women still perform the lion's share of housework, regardless of employment status. As shown in Figure 12.7, this is true globally (Ruppanner, 2010). This unequal division of labor causes the most arguments and the most unhappiness for dual-earner couples. This is the case with Jennifer and Bill, the couple in the vignette; Jennifer does most of the housework.

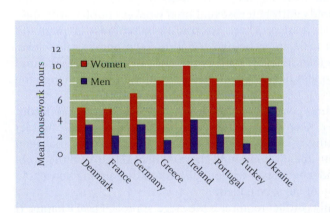

FIGURE 12.7

Women spend much more time on household chores than men,

Data from "Cross-national reports of housework: An investigation of the gender empowerment measure," by L. E. Ruppanner, in Social Science Research, Vol. 19, Table 1, p. 968. Copyright © Elsevier 2010.

Although women still do most of the household chores, things are getting a bit better. Women have reduced the amount of time they spend on housework (especially when they are employed), and men have increased the amount of time they spend on such tasks (Saginak & Saginak, 2005). The increased participation of men in these tasks is not all that it seems, however. Most of the increase is on weekends, involves specific tasks that they agree to perform, and is largely unrelated to women's employment status. In short, the increase in men's participation has not done much to lower women's burdens around the house.

Men and women view the division of labor differently. Men are often most satisfied with an equitable division of labor based on the number of hours spent, especially if the amount of time needed to perform household tasks is relatively small. Women are often most satisfied when men are willing to perform women's traditional chores (Saginak & Saginak, 2005). When different ethnic groups are studied, similarities concerning satisfaction among men and women across groups are found.

Ethnic differences in the division of household labor are also apparent. In Mexican American families with husbands born in Mexico, men help more when family

backup care

emergency care for dependent children or adults so that the employee does not need to lose a day of work

Dual-earner couples must learn how to grapple with work–family conflict in balancing job and family demands.

income is lower and their wives contribute a proportionately higher share of the household income (Pinto & Coltrane, 2009). Comparisons of Latino American, African American, and European American men consistently show that European American men help with chores less than Latino American or African American men (Omori & Smith, 2009).

Work–Family Conflict

When people have both occupations and children, they must figure out how to balance the demands of each. *These competing demands cause* **work–family conflict**, *which is the feeling of being pulled in multiple directions by incompatible demands from job and family.*

Dual-earner couples must find a balance between their occupational and family roles. Because nearly 60% of married couples with children consist of dual-earner households (U.S. Bureau of Labor Statistics, 2010a), how to divide the household chores and how to care for the children have become increasingly important questions.

Many people believe that, in such cases, work and family roles influence each other: When things go badly at work, the family suffers, and when there are troubles at home, work suffers. That's true, but the influence is not the same in each direction (Andreassi, 2007). Whether work influences family, or vice versa, is a complex function of support resources, type of job, and a host of other issues (Saginak & Saginak, 2005). One key but often overlooked factor is whether the work schedules of both partners allow them to coordinate activities such as child care (Jacobs & Gerson, 2001).

It is important that the partners negotiate agreeable arrangements of household and child-care tasks, but truly equitable divisions of labor are clearly the exception. Most U.S. households with heterosexual dual-worker couples still operate under a gender-segregated system: There are traditional chores for men and for women. These important tasks must be performed to keep homes safe, clean, and sanitary, and these tasks take time. Men may mow the lawn, wash the car, and even cook, but they are much less likely to vacuum, scrub the toilet, or change the baby's diaper.

So how and when will things change? An important step would be to talk about these issues with your partner. Keep communication lines open all the time, and let your partner know if something is bothering you. Teaching your children that men and women are equally responsible for household chores will also help end the problem. Only by creating true gender equality—without differentiating among household tasks—will this unfair division of labor be ended.

Understanding work–family conflict requires a life-stage approach (see Chapter 1) to the issue (Blanchard-Fields, Baldi, & Constantin, 2004). For example, several studies have found that the highest conflict between the competing demands of work and family occurs during the peak parenting years, when there are at least two preschool children in the home. Inter-role conflict diminishes in later life stages, especially when the quality of the marriage is high.

Dual-earner couples often have difficulty finding time for each other, especially if both work long hours. The amount of time together is not necessarily the most important issue; as long as the time is spent in shared activities such as eating, playing, and conversing, couples tend to be happy (Jacobs & Gerson, 2001). Especially when both partners are employed, getting all of the schedules to work together smoothly can be a major challenge. Unfortunately, many couples find themselves in the same position as Hi and Lois; by the time they have an opportunity to be alone together, they are too tired to make the most of it.

work–family conflict
the feeling of being pulled in multiple directions by incompatible demands from job and family

Hi and Lois. Reprinted with permission of King Features Syndicate.

Some effects are global: For example, burnout from the dual demands of work and parenting is more likely to affect women (Spector et al., 2005). Japanese career women's job satisfaction declines, and turnover becomes more likely, to the extent they have high work–family conflict (Honda-Howard & Homma, 2001). Research comparing sources of work–family conflict in the United States and China reveals that when work demands do not differ, work pressure is a significant source of work–family conflict in both countries (Yang et al., 2000).

So exactly what effects do family matters have on work performance, and vice versa? Evidence suggests that work–family conflict is a major source of stress in couples' lives. In general, women feel the work-to-family spillover to a greater extent than men, but both men and women feel the pressure (Saginak & Saginak, 2005).

Test Yourself

Recall

1. Parents report lower work–family conflict and have lower absenteeism when supervisors are sympathetic and supportive regarding _____.

2. Men are satisfied with an equitable division of labor based on _____, whereas women are satisfied _____.

Interpret

- What can organizations do to help ease work–family conflict?

- What changes in childrearing are needed to change the imbalance between partners when it comes to sharing household chores?

Apply

- Suppose you are the vice president for human resources and you are thinking about creating a way to help employees who face dependent care issues. What factors do you need to consider before implanting a plan?

- What programs would you create to rebalance the division of labor?

Recall answers: (1) family issues and child care, (2) number of hours spent; when men perform traditionally female chores

Linking **Research to life** • UNEQUAL PAY FOR EQUAL WORK

Despite the progress that women have made in American society over many decades, there remains one area where gender differences are so entrenched they almost seem normal: pay equity. In the United States, the first law regarding pay equity was passed by Congress in 1963. Forty-six years later, in 2009, President Obama signed the Lilly Ledbetter Fair Pay Act, showing clearly that the problem of pay inequity still exists. In their comprehensive and insightful analysis of the continuing gap between men's and women's paychecks for the same work, Dey and Hill (2007) make a clear case that much needs to be done, and now.

Why? Consider this: On average, a woman earns on average about $0.80 for every $1.00 a male earns. This is even after controlling for such important variables as occupation, hours worked, parenthood, and other factors associated with pay.

What if women choose a college major that is associated with high-paying jobs, such as those in science, technology, engineering, and mathematics? Will that help reduce the pay differential? No. Choosing a traditionally "male-dominated" major will not solve the problem alone. For example, women in mathematics occupations earn only about $0.76 for every $1.00 a male mathematics graduate earns.

A woman is also significantly disadvantaged when it comes to the division of labor at home if she is married or living with a man. Despite decades of effort in getting men to do more of the housework and child-care tasks, little has changed in terms of the amount of time men spend on these tasks. In effect, this means that women have two careers, one in the workplace and the other at home. And if a college-educated woman stays at home to care for a child or parent, then her

Saul Loeb/AFP/Getty Images

The Fair Pay Act of 2009 was named for Lilly Ledbetter (standing behind President Obama), who refused to accept being paid $500 to $1,000 less a month than men doing the same job.

return to the workforce will be at a lower salary than it would have been otherwise.

So what can be done about pay inequity? First, we must recognize that it exists; only then can other steps be taken. Women and men deserve to be treated fairly and paid the same for the same work. But that's not enough—laws against it have been on the books for years. Workplaces must change by making accommodations for people who take care of a child or parent and carefully analyzing salary policies. Making this a reality will take a cooperative effort by everyone.

Summary

12.1 Occupational Selection and Development

How do people view work?

■ Most people work for money and ideally for one of four meanings they find in work: developing self, union with others, expressing self, and serving others.

How do people choose their occupations?

■ Holland's theory is based on the idea that people choose occupations to optimize the fit between their individual traits and their occupational interests. Six personality types, representing different combinations of these, have been identified. Support for these types has been found in several studies.

■ Social cognitive career theory emphasizes that how people choose careers is influenced by what they think they can do and how well they can do it, as well as how motivated they are to pursue a career.

What factors influence occupational development?

■ Reality shock is the realization that expectations about an occupation are different from what is experienced. Reality shock is common among young workers.

■ Few differences exist across generations in terms of occupational expectations.

■ A mentor or developmental coach is a co-worker who teaches a new employee the unwritten rules and fosters occupational development. Mentor–protégé relationships, like other relationships, develop through stages over time.

What is the relationship between job satisfaction and age?

■ Older workers report higher job satisfaction than younger workers, mainly because they eventually find a job in which they are happy.

- Alienation and burnout are important considerations in understanding job satisfaction. Both involve significant stress for workers.

- Vallerand's passion model proposes that people develop a passion toward enjoyable activities that are incorporated into identity. Obsessive passion happens when people experience an uncontrollable urge to engage in the activity; harmonious passion results when individuals have freely accepted the activity as important for them without contingencies attached to it.

12.2 Gender, Ethnicity, and Discrimination Issues

How are people viewed when they enter occupations that are not traditional for their gender?

- Boys and girls are socialized differently for work, and their occupational choices are affected as a result. Women in nontraditional occupations today are still viewed more negatively than men in the same occupations.

What factors are related to women's occupational development?

- Women leave well-paid occupations for many reasons, including family obligations and workplace environment. Women who continue to work full-time look for ways to further their occupational development.

What factors affect ethnic minority workers' occupational experiences and occupational development?

- Whether an organization is sensitive to ethnicity issues is a strong predictor of satisfaction among ethnic minority employees.

What types of bias and discrimination hinder the occupational development of women and ethnic minority workers?

- The glass ceiling, which limits women's occupational attainment, and the glass cliff, which puts women leaders in a precarious position, affect how often women achieve top executive positions and how successful women leaders are.

- Gender discrimination remains the chief barrier to women's occupational development. In many cases, this operates as a glass ceiling. Pay inequity is also a problem; women are often paid less than what men earn in similar jobs.

- Sexual harassment is a problem in the workplace. Current criteria for judging harassment are based on the "reasonable person" standard. Denying employment to any American over 40 because of age is age discrimination.

12.3 Occupational Transitions

Why do people change occupations?

- Important reasons people change occupations include personality, obsolescence, and economic trends.

- To adapt to the effects of a global economy and an aging workforce, many corporations are providing retraining opportunities for workers. Retraining is especially important in cases of outdated skills and career plateauing.

Is worrying about potential job loss a major source of stress?

- Occupational insecurity is a growing problem. Fear of losing a job is a better predictor of anxiety than the actual likelihood of job loss.

How does job loss affect the amount of stress experienced?

- Job loss is a traumatic event that can affect every aspect of a person's life. Degree of financial distress is a predictor of distress.

12.4 Work and Family

What are the issues faced by employed people who care for dependents?

- Caring for children or aging parents creates dilemmas for workers. Whether a woman returns to work after having a child depends largely on how attached she is to her work. Simply providing child care on site does not always result in higher job satisfaction. A more important factor is the degree to which supervisors are sympathetic.

How do partners typically view the division of household chores? What is work–family conflict? How does it affect couples' lives?

- Although women have reduced the amount of time they spend on household tasks, they still do most of the work. European American men are less likely than either African American or Latino American men to help with traditionally female household tasks.

- Flexible work schedules and number of children are important factors in role conflict. Recent evidence shows that work stress can affect family life and family stress can affect work performance. Some women pay a high personal price for having careers.

Key Terms

meaning–mission fit (318)
social cognitive career theory
  (SCCT) (319)
reality shock (320)
mentor or developmental coach (321)
job satisfaction (321)

alienation (323)
burnout (323)
passion (323)
gender discrimination (328)
glass ceiling (328)

glass cliff (328)
age discrimination (330)
career plateauing (332)
backup care (337)
work–family conflict (338)

Online Resources

Go to CengageBrain.com to access Psychology CourseMate, where you will find an interactive eBook, flashcards, quizzes, videos, websites, and more.

Making It in Midlife

The Biopsychosocial Challenges of Middle Adulthood

13

There's an old saying that life begins at 40. That's good news for middle-aged adults. As we will see, they face many stressful events, but they also leave many of the pressures of young adulthood behind. In some respects, middle age is the prime of life: People's health is generally good, and their earnings are at their peak. But in other ways, things change. Let's see what happens in more detail.

- How does appearance change in middle age?
- What changes occur in bones and joints?
- What reproductive changes occur in men and women in middle age?

- What is stress? How does it affect physical and psychological health?
- What benefits are there to exercise?

By all accounts, Dean is extremely successful. Among other things, he became the head of a moderate-sized manufacturing firm by the time he was 43 years old. Dean has always considered himself to be a rising young star in the company. Then one day he found more than the usual number of hairs in his brush. "Oh no!" he exclaimed. "I can't be going bald! What will people say?" What does Dean think about these changes?

One morning, when you least expect it, you see *it.* One solitary gray hair or one tiny wrinkle at the corner of your eye—or, like Dean, some excess hairs falling out—and you worry that your youth is gone, your life is over, and you will soon be acting the way your parents did when they embarrassed you in your younger days.

Crossing the boundary to middle age in the United States is typically associated with turning 40. As people move into middle age, they begin experiencing some physical changes associated with aging. In this section, we focus on the changes most obvious in middle-aged adults: appearance, reproductive capacity, and stress and coping.

Changes in Appearance

On that fateful day when the hard truth stares at you in the bathroom mirror, it probably doesn't matter to you that getting wrinkles and gray hair is universal and inevitable. Wrinkles are caused by changes in the structure of the skin and its connective and supporting tissues, as well as by the cumulative effects of damage from exposure to sunlight and smoking cigarettes (Aldwin & Gilmer, 2004). It may not make you feel better to know that gray hair is natural and caused by a normal cessation of pigment production in hair follicles. Male pattern baldness, a genetic trait in which hair is lost progressively beginning with the top of the head, often begins to appear in middle age. Most people gain weight between their early 30s and mid-50s, producing the infamous "middle-aged bulge" as metabolism slows (Aldwin & Gilmer, 2004).

People's reactions to these changes in appearance vary. As the cartoon depicts, certain changes to men in Western society are viewed as positive, but the same changes to women are not.

Changes in Bones and Joints

The bones and the joints change with age, sometimes in potentially preventable ways and sometimes because of genetic predisposition or disease.

Osteoporosis

Bone mass stays about the same until women experience menopause and men reach late life. For women, there is a rapid loss of bone mass in the first few years after menopause, which greatly increases the risk of problems with disease and broken bones (National Institute of Arthritis and Musculoskeletal and Skin Diseases, 2009).

Loss of bone mass makes bones weaker and more brittle, thereby making them easier to break. *Severe loss of bone mass results in* **osteoporosis**, *a disease in which bones become porous and extremely easy to break* (see Figure 13.1). In severe cases, osteoporosis can cause spinal vertebrae to collapse, causing the person to stoop and to become shorter (National Institutes of Health, 2000a; see Figure 13.2). About 40 million Americans either have osteoporosis or are at high risk due to low bone density (National Institute of Arthritis and Musculoskeletal and Skin Diseases, 2010c).

Osteoporosis is caused in part by having low bone mass at skeletal maturity (the point at which your bones reach peak development), deficiencies of calcium and vitamin D, estrogen depletion, and lack of weight-bearing exercise that builds up bone mass (National Institute of Arthritis and Musculoskeletal and Skin Diseases, 2010c).

The National Institute of Arthritis and Musculoskeletal and Skin Diseases (2010c) recommends getting enough dietary calcium and vitamin D as ways to prevent osteoporosis. There is evidence that calcium and vitamin D supplements after menopause may slow the rate of bone loss and delay the onset of osteoporosis. People should consume foods (e.g., milk and broccoli) that are high in calcium and vitamin D. Recommended calcium and vitamin D intakes for men and women of various ages as determined by the Institute of Medicine (2010) are shown in Table 13.1.

To reduce the risk of osteoporosis, the National Institutes of Health recommends dietary, medication, and activity approaches. There is also some evidence that regular exercise is beneficial, but results vary depending on the type and intensity of the regimen. The best results come from a regular regimen of moderate weight- or load-bearing exercise, such as weight lifting, jogging, or other exercises that require you to work against gravity.

Arthritis

Many middle-aged adults complain of aching joints. They have good reason. Beginning in the 20s, the protective cartilage in joints shows signs of deterioration, such as thinning and becoming cracked and frayed. *Over time the bones underneath the cartilage*

osteoporosis
a disease in which bones become porous and extremely easy to break

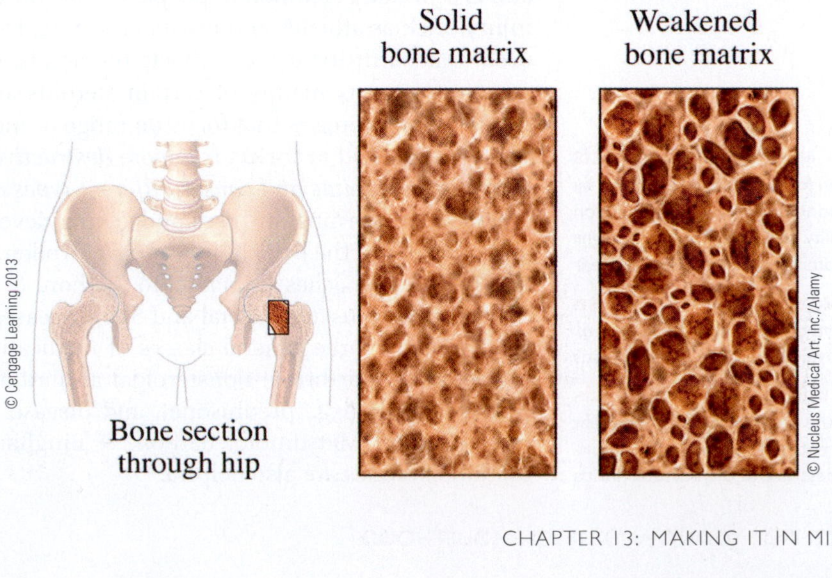

FIGURE 13.1
The difference between normal bone (on the left) and osteoporosis (on the right) is easy to see in these sections of bone tissue from a hip.

Solid bone matrix   Weakened bone matrix

Bone section through hip

© Cengage Learning 2013

© Nucleus Medical Art, Inc./Alamy

FIGURE 13.2
Osteoporosis eventually causes a person to
stoop and to lose height because of compres-
sion of the vertebrae.
*Source: Reprinted from Ebersole, P., & Hess, P. (1998). Toward healthy
aging (5th ed., p. 395), with permission from Elsevier Science.*

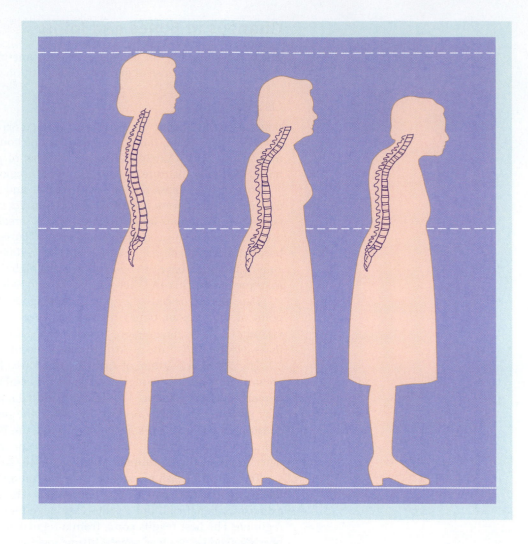

become damaged, which can result in **osteoarthritis***, a disease marked by gradual
onset of bone damage with progression of pain and disability, together with minor signs
of inflammation.*

Osteoarthritis is an example of a **wear-and-tear disease***, a degenerative disease
caused by injury or overuse* (National Arthritis Foundation, 2010). This most common
form of arthritis usually occurs in late middle age or early old age, progresses slowly,
and is especially common in people whose joints are subjected to routine overuse and
injury, such as athletes and manual laborers. Pain typically is worse when the joint is
used. Osteoarthritis usually affects the hands, spine, hips, and knees. Effective management consists mainly of certain steroids and anti-inflammatory drugs, rest and
nonstressful exercises that focus on range of motion, and dietary modifications.

Rheumatoid arthritis *is a more destructive disease of the joints that typically affects different joints and causes different types of pain than osteoarthritis.* Most often,
a pattern of morning stiffness and aching develops in the fingers, wrists, and ankles
on both sides of the body. Joints appear swollen. There is no cure, but there are several
treatment approaches (Matsumoto, Bathon, & Bingham, 2010; National Institute of
Arthritis and Musculoskeletal and Skin Diseases, 2010a).

There are three general classes of medications commonly used in the treatment
of rheumatoid arthritis: nonsteroidal anti-inflammatory drugs (e.g., Advil or Aleve),
corticosteroids (e.g., prednisone), and disease modifying antirheumatic drugs (e.g.,
methotrexate; Matsumoto, Bathon, & Bingham, 2010). Rest and passive range-of-
motion exercises are also helpful.

osteoarthritis
the most common form of arthritis, marked by
gradual onset of bone damage with progression
of pain and disability, together with minor signs
of inflammation from wear and tear

wear-and-tear disease
a degenerative disease caused by injury or
overuse, such as osteoarthritis

rheumatoid arthritis
a disease of the joints that affects different
joints, causes different types of pain, and is more
destructive than osteoarthritis

Recommended Calcium and Vitamin D Intakes

Age	Calcium (milligrams)	Vitamin D (international units)
Infants		
Birth to 6 months	200	400
6 months to 1 year	260	400
Children and Young Adults		
1 to 3 years	700	600
4 to 8 years	1,000	600
9 to 13 years	1,300	600
14 to 18 years	1,300	600
Adult Women and Men		
19 to 30 years	1,000	600
31 to 50 years	1,000	600
51- to 70-year-old males	1,000	600
51- to 70-year-old females	1,200	600
Over 70 years	1,200	800

SOURCE: National Institute of Arthritis and Musculoskeletal and Skin Diseases, 2010d.

Telling the differences among osteoporosis, osteoarthritis, and rheumatoid arthritis can be tricky. A comparison of the risk factors and effects of each is shown in Table 13.2.

Reproductive Changes

Besides changes in the way we look, middle age brings transitions in our reproductive systems. These changes differ dramatically for women and men. Yet even in the context of these changes, a major national survey by AARP (Fisher, 2010) found that middle-aged adults continue to enjoy active sex lives.

The Climacteric and Menopause

As women enter midlife, they experience a major biological process, called the **climacteric**, *during which they pass from their reproductive to nonreproductive years.* **Menopause** *is the point at which menstruation stops.* It is complete when periods have stopped for one year. Men do not endure such sweeping biological changes but experience several gradual changes.

The major reproductive change in women during adulthood is the loss of the ability to bear children. This change begins in the 40s as menstrual cycles become irregular, and by age 50 to 55 it is usually complete (Robertson, 2006). *This time of transition from regular menstruation to menopause is called* **perimenopause**, *and how long it lasts varies considerably* (Mayo Clinic, 2010f). The gradual loss and eventual end of monthly periods is accompanied by decreases in estrogen and progesterone levels, changes in the reproductive organs, and changes in sexual functioning (Aldwin & Gilmer, 2004).

A variety of physical and psychological symptoms may accompany perimenopause and menopause as a result of decreases in hormonal levels (Mayo Clinic, 2010f; Robertson, 2006): hot flashes, night sweats, headaches, mood changes, difficulty concentrating, vaginal dryness, changing cholesterol levels, and a variety of aches and pains. Negative effects on sexuality, such as low libido, are common (Myskow, 2002). Many women report no symptoms, but most women experience at least some, and

climacteric
the biological process during which women pass from their reproductive to nonreproductive years

menopause
the point at which menstruation stops

perimenopause
the individually varying time of transition from regular menstruation to menopause

TABLE 13.2

Similarities and Differences Among Osteoporosis, Osteoarthritis, and Rheumatoid Arthritis

	Osteoporosis	Osteoarthritis	Rheumatoid Arthritis
Risk Factors	×	×	
Age-related	×	×	
Menopause	×		
Family history	×	×	×
Use of certain medications (e.g., glucocorticoids or seizure medications)	×		
Calcium deficiency or inadequate vitamin D	×		
Inactivity	×		
Overuse of joints		×	
Smoking	×		
Excessive alcohol	×		
Anorexia nervosa	×		
Excessive weight		×	
Physical Effects			
Affects entire skeleton	×		
Affects joints		×	×
Is an autoimmune disease			×
Causes bony spurs		×	×
Enlarges or malforms joints	×	×	
Leads to height loss	×		

SOURCE: *National Institute of Arthritis and Musculoskeletal and Skin Diseases, 2010b.*

there are large ethnic and cultural group differences in how they are expressed (Banger, 2003). For example, Chinese women reported increased sleep disturbances and fatigue (Chang et al., 2010).

Women's genital organs undergo progressive change after menopause (Aldwin & Gilmer, 2004). The vaginal walls shrink and become thinner, the size of the vagina decreases, vaginal lubrication is reduced and delayed, and some shrinkage of the external genitalia occurs. These changes have important effects on sexual activity, such as an increased possibility of painful intercourse and a longer time and more stimulation needed to reach orgasm. Failure to achieve orgasm is more common than in a woman's younger years. However, maintaining an active sex life throughout adulthood lowers the degree to which problems are encountered.

Despite the physical changes, there is no physiological reason most women cannot continue sexual activity and enjoy it well into old age. The primary reason for the decline in women's sexual activity with age is the lack of a willing or appropriate partner, not a lack of physical ability or desire (AARP, 1999; Fisher, 2010; Jacoby, 2005).

Reproductive technology such as fertility drugs and in vitro fertilization (see Chapter 2) has made it possible for postmenopausal women to have children. Indeed, in 2008 Rajo Devi Lohan of India gave birth at age 70 through in vitro fertilization, making her the world's oldest woman to become pregnant and deliver.

Some adults do not achieve generativity. Instead, they become bored, self-indulgent, and unable to contribute to the continuation of society. *Erikson referred to this state as* **stagnation**, *in which people are unable to deal with the needs of their children or to provide mentoring to younger adults.*

What Are Generative People Like?

Research shows that generativity is different from traits; for example, generativity is more related to societal engagement than are traits (Cox et al., 2010).

One of the best approaches to generativity is McAdams's model (McAdams, 2001, 2008; McAdams & Olson, 2010), shown in Figure 13.7. This multidimensional model shows how generativity results from the complex interconnections among societal and inner forces, which create a concern for the next generation and a belief in the goodness of the human enterprise; this leads to generative commitment, which produces generative actions. *A person derives personal meaning from being generative by constructing a life story or* **narrative**, *which helps create the person's identity* (see Chapter 10).

The components of McAdams's model constitute an approach that differs from personality traits (McAdams, 2008; McAdams & Olson, 2010). In McAdams's model, generative concern (a trait) relates to life satisfaction and overall happiness, whereas generative action does not (de St. Aubin & McAdams, 1995). For instance, new grandparents may derive much satisfaction from their grandchildren and are greatly concerned with their well-being (concern), but they have little desire to engage in the daily hassles of caring for them regularly (action).

How well do these ideas generalize across ethnic groups and cultures? In one of the few studies to examine generativity across cultures, Hofer et al. (2008) examined it in Cameroon, Costa Rica, and Germany. They found that McAdams's model could be successfully applied across the three cultures.

The growing evidence on generativity indicates that the personal concerns and priorities of middle-aged adults are different from those of younger adults. But is this view consistent with other aspects of personality? Let's consider the evidence.

Life Transition Theories and the Midlife Crisis

We have seen that theorists such as Erikson believe that adults face several important challenges and that, by struggling with these issues, people develop new aspects of themselves. Carl Jung (1875–1961), one of the founders of psychoanalytic theory, believed that

stagnation

in Erikson's theory, the state in which people are unable to deal with the needs of their children or to provide mentoring to younger adults

narrative

a way in which a person derives personal meaning from being generative and by constructing a life story, which helps create the person's identity

FIGURE 13.7

McAdam's model of generativity. How someone shows generativity (action) is influenced by several factors.

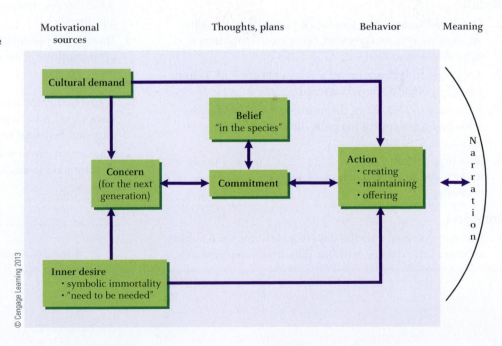

© Cengage Learning 2013

adults may experience a midlife crisis. This belief led to the development of several theories suggesting that adulthood consists of alternating periods of stability and transition that people experience in a fixed sequence.

These theoretical approaches led to a popularization of the midlife crisis so that many considered people like Jim, the recently divorced guy with the red sports car in the vignette, to be typical. Is there such a thing as a midlife crisis? Not really. The evidence indicates that, for most people, midlife is no more or no less traumatic than any other period. Thus, Jim's behavior may have an explanation, but it's not because he's going through a universal midlife crisis. Perhaps it is better to view midlife as a time that presents unique challenges and issues that must be negotiated (Bumpass & Aquilino, 1995).

If midlife is not characterized by a crisis but does present unique challenges and issues, then how do people negotiate it successfully? *The secret seems to be* **ego resilience**, *a powerful personality resource that enables people to handle midlife changes.* Longitudinal data from two samples indicate that people who enter middle age with high ego resilience are more likely to experience it as an opportunity for change and growth, whereas people with low ego resilience are more likely to experience it as a time of stagnation or decline (Klohnen, Vandewater, & Young, 1996).

In sum, perhaps the best way to view the life transitions associated with middle age is through the words of a 52-year-old woman:

> Middle age. The time when you realize you've moved to the caretaker, senior responsibility role. A time of discomfort because you watch the generation before you, whom you have loved and respected and counted on for emotional back-up, for advice, become more dependent on you and then die. Your children grow up, move out, try their wings; indeed, they attempt to teach you the "truths" they've discovered about life. It's time to make some new choices—groups, friends, activities need not be so child-related anymore. (Klohnen, Vandewater, & Young, 1996, p. 431)

ego resilience
a powerful personality resource that enables people to handle midlife changes

Test Yourself

Recall

1. The dimensions in the five-factor theory of personality are neuroticism, extraversion, openness to experience, agreeableness, and _____.

2. According to Erikson, an increasing concern with helping younger people achieve is termed _____.

3. According to McAdams, the meaning someone derives from being generative happens through the process of _____.

4. Research indicates that _____ is a key personality factor in predicting who will negotiate midlife successfully.

Interpret

- How can you reconcile the data from trait research, which indicates little change, with the data from other research, which shows substantial change, in personality during adulthood?

- How might personality development in adulthood influence cognitive development (e.g., reflective judgment)?

Apply

- If psychotherapy assumes that a person can change behavior over time, what is the relationship between personality and behavior from this perspective?

- How might career coaches use the research on personality in adulthood to advise their clients?

LEARNING OBJECTIVES

- Who are the kinkeepers in families?
- How does the relationship between middle-aged parents and their young adult children change?
- How do middle-aged adults deal with their aging parents?

- What styles of grandparenthood do middle-aged adults experience? How do grandchildren and grandparents interact?

Esther is facing a major milestone: Her youngest child, Megan, is about to head off to college. But instead of feeling depressed, as she thought she would, Esther feels almost elated at the prospect. She and Bill are finally free of the day-to-day parenting duties of the past 30 years. Esther is looking forward to getting to know her husband again. She wonders whether there is something wrong with her for being excited that her daughter is moving away.

© Blend Images/Alamy

Adult children's relationships with their parents often include a friendship dimension.

People like Esther connect generations. Members of the middle-aged generation, like Esther, serve as the links between their aging parents and their maturing children (Hareven, 2001). *Middle-aged mothers (more than fathers) tend to take on this role of* **kinkeeper**, *the person who gathers family members together for celebrations and keeps them in touch with one another.*

Think about the major issues confronting a typical middle-aged couple: maintaining a good marriage, parenting responsibilities, dealing with children who are becoming adults themselves, handling job pressures, and worrying about aging parents, just to name a few. Middle-aged adults truly have quite a lot to deal with every day in balancing their responsibilities to their children and their aging parents (Riley & Bowen, 2005). *Indeed, middle-aged adults are sometimes referred to as the* **sandwich generation** *because they are caught between the competing demands of two generations: their parents and their children.*

Letting Go: Middle-Aged Adults and Their Children

For most parents, the major child-related event in middle age is their leaving (and sometimes returning).

Becoming Friends and the Empty Nest

Sometime during middle age, most parents experience two positive developments with regard to their children (Buhl, 2008): Suddenly their children see them in a new light, and the children leave home.

The extent to which parents foster and approve of their children's attempts at being independent matters. Most parents manage the transition successfully (Owen, 2005). That's not to say that parents are heartless. As depicted in the cartoon, when children leave home, emotional bonds are disrupted. Mothers in all ethnic groups report feeling sad at the time that children leave but having many more positive feelings about the potential for growth in their relationships with their children (Feldman, 2010).

Still, parents provide considerable emotional support (by staying in touch) and financial help (e.g., paying college tuition and providing a free place to live until the child finds employment) when possible (Mitchell, 2006; Warner, Henderson-Wilson, & Andrew, 2010).

kinkeeper

the person, usually a middle-aged mother, who gathers family members together for celebrations and keeps them in touch with one another

sandwich generation

middle-aged adults who are caught between the competing demands of two generations: their parents and their children

A positive experience with launching children is strongly influenced by the extent to which parents perceive a job well done and that their children have turned out well (Mitchell, 2010). Children are regarded as successes when they meet parents' culturally based developmental expectations, and they are seen as "good kids" when there is agreement between parents and children in basic values.

When Children Come Back

Parents' satisfaction with the empty nest is sometimes short lived. Roughly half of young adults in the United States return to their parents' home at least once after moving out (Osgood et al., 2005). There is evidence that these young adults, called "boomerang kids" (Mitchell, 2006), reflect a less permanent, more mobile contemporary society.

Why do children move back? A major impetus is the increased costs of living on one's own when saddled with college debt, especially if the societal economic situation is bad and jobs are not available.

This trend reflects the changing definition of adulthood we considered in Chapter 10. As the ages at which young people take on the roles of adulthood increase, we are likely to see more children living at home longer or returning to their parents' home after graduating from college.

Giving Back: Middle-Aged Adults and Their Aging Parents

How do middle-aged adults relate to their parents? What happens when their parents become frail? How do middle-aged adults deal with the need to care for their parents?

Caring for Aging Parents

Most middle-aged adults have parents who are in reasonably good health. For a growing number of people, however, being a middle-aged child of aging parents involves providing some level of care. The job of caring for older parents usually falls to a daughter or a daughter-in-law (Stephens & Franks, 1999), and daughters tend to coordinate care provided by multiple siblings (Friedman & Seltzer, 2010). The cartoon depicts a common situation: a daughter worrying about her aging parents and wondering whether she should be doing more. In Japan, even though the oldest son is responsible for parental care, it is his wife who does the day-to-day caregiving for her parents and her in-laws (Lee, 2010).

As described in the Real People feature, caring for one's parent presents a dilemma, especially for women (Baek, 2005; Lai, 2010; Lee, 2010; Stephens et al., 2001). *Most adult children feel a sense of responsibility, termed* **filial obligation**, *to care for their parents if necessary.* For example, family caregivers sometimes express the feeling that they "owe it to Mom or Dad" to care for them; after all, their parents provided for

filial obligation
a sense of obligation to care for one's parents if necessary

them for many years, and now the shoe is on the other foot (Gans, 2007). Adult children often provide the majority of care when needed to their parents in all Western and non-Western cultures studied but especially in Asian cultures (Hareven & Adams, 1996; Lai, 2010).

Joan's experience embodies the notion of the sandwich generation noted earlier. Joan's need to balance caring for her daughter and caring for her mother can create conflict, both within herself and among the individuals involved (Neal & Hammer, 2006).

Roughly 50 million Americans provide unpaid care for older parents, in-laws, grandparents, and other older loved ones (National Alliance for Caregiving & AARP, 2010). The typical family caregiver is a 48-year-old woman who is employed outside the home and who provides more than 20 hours per week of unpaid caregiving. These family caregivers spend as much as $7,000 per year, on average, in support of their loved one (National Endowment for Financial Education, 2010).

Caregiving Stresses and Rewards

Caregiving is a major source of both stresses and rewards. On the stress side, adult children and other family caregivers are especially vulnerable from two main sources (Pearlin et al., 1990):

- Adult children may have trouble coping with declines in their parents' functioning, especially those involving cognitive abilities and problematic behavior, and with work overload, burnout, and loss of the previous relationship with a parent.

real People APPLYING HUMAN DEVELOPMENT
TAKING CARE OF MOM

Everything seemed to be going well for Joan. Her career was really taking off, her youngest daughter Kelly had just entered high school, and her marriage to Bill was better than ever. So when her phone rang one June afternoon, she was taken by surprise.

The voice on the other end was matter of fact. Joan's mother had experienced a major stroke and would need someone to care for her. Because her mother did not have sufficient medical and long-term care insurance to afford a nursing home, Joan made the only decision she could—her mom would move in with her, Bill,

and Kelly. Joan firmly believed that, because her mom had provided for her, Joan owed it to her mom to do the same now that she was in need.

What Joan didn't count on was that taking care of her mom was the most difficult yet the most rewarding thing she had ever done. Joan quickly realized that her days of lengthy business trips and seminars were over, as was her quick rise up the company leadership ladder. Other employees were now the ones who brought back the great new ideas and could respond to out-of-town crises quickly. Hard as it was, Joan knew that her career trajectory

had taken a different turn. And she and Bill had more disagreements than she could ever remember, usually about the decreased amount of time they had to spend with each other. Kelly's demands to be driven here and there added to Joan's stress.

But Joan and her mom were able to develop the kind of relationship that they could not have otherwise and to talk about issues that they had long suppressed. Although caring for a physically disabled mother was extremely taxing, Joan and her mother's ability to connect on a different level made it worthwhile.

Caring for an older parent creates both stresses and rewards.

HUMAN DEVELOPMENT in action

How does parental caregiving affect employees?

- If the caregiving situation is perceived as confining or seriously infringes on the adult son's or daughter's other responsibilities (spouse, parent, employee, etc.), then the situation is likely to be perceived negatively, which may lead to family or job conflicts, economic problems, loss of self-identity, and decreased competence.

When caring for an aging parent, even the most devoted family caregiver will at times feel depressed, resentful, angry, or guilty (Cavanaugh, 1999; Stephens et al., 2001). Many middle-aged caregivers are hard pressed financially: they may still be paying child-care or college tuition expenses, perhaps trying to save adequately for their own retirement, and having to work more than one job to do it. Financial pressures are especially serious for those caring for parents with chronic conditions, such as Alzheimer's disease, that require services, such as adult day care, not adequately covered by medical insurance even if the older parent has supplemental coverage. In some cases, adult children may even need to quit their jobs to provide care if adequate alternatives, such as adult day care, are unavailable or unaffordable.

The stresses of caring for a parent mean that the caregiver needs to carefully monitor his or her own health. Indeed, many professionals point out that "caregiving for the caregiver" is an important consideration to avoid caregiver burnout (Tamayo et al., 2010).

On the plus side, caring for an aging parent has rewards. Caring for aging parents can bring parents and their adult children closer together and can provide a way for adult children to feel that they are giving back to their parents (Miller et al., 2008). Cross-cultural research examining Taiwanese (Lee, 2007) and Chinese (Zhan, 2006) participants confirms that adults caring for aging parents can find the experience rewarding.

Cultural values enter into the caregiving relationship in an indirect way (Knight & Sayegh, 2010). Caregivers in all cultures studied to date show a common set of outcomes: caregiver stressors are appraised as burdensome, which creates negative health consequences for the caregiver. However, cultural values influence the kinds of social support that are available to the caregiver.

Things aren't always rosy from the parents' perspective, either. Independence and autonomy are important traditional values in some ethnic groups, and their loss is not taken lightly. Older adults in these groups are more likely to express the desire to pay a professional for assistance rather than ask a family member for help; they may find it demeaning to live with their children and express strong feelings about "not wanting to burden them" (Cahill et al., 2009). Most move in only as a last resort. As many as two thirds of older adults who receive help with daily activities feel negatively about the help they receive (Newsom, 1999).

Determining whether older parents are satisfied with the help their children provide is a complex issue (Cahill et al., 2009; Newsom, 1999). Based on a critical review of the research, Newsom (1999) proposes a model of how certain aspects of care can produce negative perceptions of care directly or by affecting the interactions between caregiver and care recipient (see Figure 13.8). The important thing to conclude from the model is that, even under the best circumstances, there is no guarantee that the help adult children provide their parents will be well received. Misunderstandings can occur, and the frustration that caregivers feel may be translated directly into negative interactions.

In sum, taking care of one's aging parents is a difficult task. Despite the numerous challenges and risks of negative psychological and financial outcomes, many caregivers nevertheless experience positive outcomes.

FIGURE 13.8

Whether a care recipient perceives care to be good depends on interactions with the caregiver and whether those interactions are perceived negatively.

Source: From Newsom, J.T., 1999, "Another side to caregiving: Negative reactions to being helped," Current Directions in Psychological Science, 8, 185. Reprinted by permission of Sage Publications.

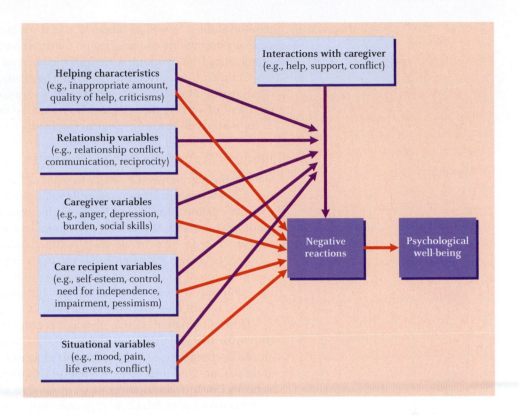

Grandparenthood

Becoming a grandparent takes some help. Being a parent yourself is a prerequisite. But it is your children's decisions and actions that determine whether you will experience the transition to grandparenthood, making this role different from most others we experience throughout life. Most people become grandparents in their 40s and 50s, though some are older or perhaps as young as their late 20s or early 30s. For many middle-aged adults, becoming a grandparent is a peak experience (Hoffman, Kaneshiro, & Compton, 2012).

Grandparents can forge strong relationships with their grandchildren and get great enjoyment from them.

How Do Grandparents Interact With Grandchildren?

Grandparents have many ways of interacting with their grandchildren. Categorizing these styles has been attempted over many decades (e.g., Neugarten & Weinstein, 1964), but none of these attempts have been particularly successful because grandparents use different styles with different grandchildren and styles change as grandparents and grandchildren age (Stephens & Clark, 1996).

An alternative approach involves considering the many functions grandparents serve and the changing nature of families (Hills, 2010). The social dimension includes societal needs and expectations of what grandparents are to do, such as passing on family history to grandchildren. The personal dimension includes the personal satisfaction and individual needs that are fulfilled by being a grandparent. Many grandparents pass on skills—as well as religious, social, and vocational values (social dimension)—through storytelling and advice, and they may feel great pride and satisfaction (personal dimension) from working with grandchildren on joint projects.

Grandchildren give grandparents a great deal in return. For example, grandchildren keep grandparents in touch with youth and the latest trends. Sharing the excitement of surfing the web in school may be one way in which grandchildren keep grandparents on the technological forefront.

Being a Grandparent Is Meaningful

Does being a grandparent matter to people? You bet it does, at least to the vast majority of grandparents. In her groundbreaking research, Kivnick (1982, 1985) identified five dimensions of meaning that grandparents often assign to their roles. However, additional research shows that grandparents can derive multiple meanings and that they are linked with generativity (Hayslip, Henderson, & Shore, 2003; Thiele & Whelan, 2010). For some, grandparenting is the most important thing in their lives. For others, meaning comes from being seen as wise, from spoiling grandchildren, from recalling the relationship they had with their own grandparents, or from taking pride in being followed by not one but two generations.

Most grandparents derive several meanings, regardless of the style of their relationship with the grandchildren (Alley, 2004). Similar findings are reported when overall satisfaction with being a grandparent is examined; no matter what their style is, grandparents find their role meaningful (Hayslip, Henderson, & Shore, 2003; Thiele & Whelan, 2010). These findings have resulted in viewing grandparenthood as an aspect of generativity from which most grandparents derive a great deal of satisfaction (Thiele & Whelan, 2010).

Grandchildren also highly value their relationships with grandparents, even when they are young adults (Alley, 2004). Grandparents are valued as role models, as well as for their personalities, the activities they share, and the attention they show to grandchildren. Grandchildren also note that, when their grandparents are frail, helping their grandparents is a way for them to act on their altruistic beliefs (Kennedy, 1991). Young adult grandchildren (ages 21 to 29) derive both stress and rewards from caring for grandparents, much the same way that middle-aged adults do when they care for their aging parents (Fruhauf, 2007).

Ethnic Differences

How grandparents and grandchildren interact varies among ethnic groups. Intergenerational relationships are especially important and have historically been a source of strength in African American families (Waites, 2009) and Latino American families (Gladding, 2002). African American grandparents play an important role in many aspects of their grandchildren's lives, such as religious education (King et al., 2006). African American grandfathers, in particular, tend to perceive grandparenthood as a central role to a greater degree than do European American grandfathers (Kivett, 1991). And Latino American grandparents are more likely to participate in childrearing because of a cultural core value of family (Burnette, 1999).

Native American grandparents appear to have some interactive styles that differ from those of other groups (Weibel-Orlando, 1990). Fictive grandparenting is a style that allows adults to fill in for missing or deceased biological grandparents, functionally creating the role of surrogate grandparent. These adults provide a connection to the older generation that would otherwise be absent for these children. In the cultural conservator style, grandparents request that their grandchildren be allowed to live with them to ensure that the grandchildren learn the native ways. These grandparents provide grandchildren with a way to connect with their cultural heritage, and they are likely to provide a great deal of care for their grandchildren (Mutchler, Baker, & Lee, 2007). In general, Native American grandmothers take a more active role in

How grandparents and grandchildren interact varies across ethnic groups.

these styles than do grandfathers and are more likely to pass on traditional rituals (Woodbridge, 2008).

Asian American grandparents, particularly if they are immigrants, serve as a primary source of traditional culture for their grandchildren (Yoon, 2005). When these grandparents become heavily involved in caring for their grandchildren, they especially want and need services that are culturally and linguistically appropriate. Grandparents caring for grandchildren is a topic to which we now turn.

When Grandparents Care for Grandchildren

Grandparenthood today is tougher than it used to be. Families are more mobile, which means that grandparents are more often separated from their grandchildren by geographical distance. Grandparents are more likely to have independent lives apart from their children and grandchildren. What being a grandparent entails in the 21st century is more ambiguous than it once was (Fuller-Thompson, Hayslip, & Patrick, 2005).

Perhaps the biggest change worldwide for grandparents is the increasing number who serve as custodial parents or primary caregivers for their grandchildren (Moorman & Greenfield, 2010). Estimates are that about 6.4 million U.S. grandparents have grandchildren living with them, and 2.6 million of these grandparents provide basic needs (food, shelter, and clothing) for one or more of their grandchildren (U.S. Census Bureau, 2010c). These situations result most often when both parents are employed outside the home (Uhlenberg & Cheuk, 2010); when the parents are deceased, addicted, incarcerated, or unable to raise their children for some other reason (Backhouse, 2006; Moorman & Greenfield, 2010); or when discipline or behavior problems have been exhibited by the grandchild (Giarusso et al., 2000). Lack of legal recognition stemming from the grandparents' lack of legal guardianship also poses problems and challenges—for example, in dealing with schools and obtaining records. Typically, social service workers must assist grandparents in navigating the many unresponsive policies and systems they encounter when trying to provide the best possible assistance to their grandchildren (Cox, 2007). Clearly, public policy changes are needed to address these issues, especially regarding grandparents' rights regarding schools and health care for their grandchildren (Ellis, 2010).

Raising grandchildren is not easy. Financial stress, cramped living space, and social isolation are only some of the issues facing custodial grandparents (Bullock, 2004). Rates of problem behavior, hyperactivity, and learning problems in grandchildren are high and may negatively affect the grandparent–grandchild relationship (Hayslip et al., 1998). The grandchildren's routines, activities, and school-related issues also cause stress (Musil & Standing, 2005). All of these stresses are also reported cross-culturally; for example, full-time custodial grandmothers in Kenya reported higher levels of stress than do part-time caregivers (Oburu & Palmérus, 2005).

Even custodial grandparents raising grandchildren without these problems report more stress and role disruption than noncustodial grandparents (Emick & Hayslip, 1999). Custodial grandmothers who are employed report that they arrive late, miss work, must leave work suddenly, or leave early to tend to the grandchild's needs (Pruchno, 1999). But most custodial grandparents consider their situation better for their grandchild than any other alternative and report surprisingly few negative effects on their marriages.

HUMAN DEVELOPMENT in action

Suppose you are a school principal. What changes would you need to make to include custodial grandparents in school-related decisions?

Test Yourself

Recall

1. The term _____ refers to middle-aged adults who have both living parents and children.
2. The people who gather the family together for celebrations and keep family members in touch are called _____.
3. Most caregiving for aging parents is provided by _____.
4. The sense of personal responsibility to care for one's parents is called _____.
5. _____ grandparents have a grandparenting style called cultural conservator.

Interpret

- If you were to create a guide to families for middle-aged adults, what would your most important pieces of advice be? Why did you select these?

- How does practical intelligence factor into good parenting and grandparenting?

Apply

- What are the connections between the first part of this chapter, on health, and this section, on caregiving?
- What employment policies would be most beneficial for middle-aged employees?

Linking Research to life • MENOPAUSAL HORMONE THERAPY

For many years, women have had the choice of taking medications to replace the female hormones that are not produced naturally by the body after menopause. Hormone therapy may involve taking estrogen alone or in combination with progesterone (called progestin in its synthetic form). Research on the effects of MHT has helped clarify the appropriate use of such medications.

Until about 2003, it was thought that MHT was beneficial for most women, and results from several studies were positive. But results from the Women's Health Initiative (WHI) in the United States and from the Million Women Study in the United Kingdom indicated that, for some types of MHT, there were several potentially serious side effects. As a result, physicians are now far more cautious in recommending MHT.

The WHI, begun in 1991, was a very large study (National Heart, Lung, and Blood Institute, 2003). The estrogen-plus-progestin trial used 0.625 milligram of estrogens taken daily plus 2.5 milligrams of medroxyprogesterone acetate (Prempro) taken daily. This combination was chosen because it is the mostly commonly prescribed form of the combined hormone therapy in the United States and, in several observational studies, had appeared to benefit women's health. The women in the WHI estrogen-plus-progestin study were age 50 to 79 when they enrolled in the study between 1993 and 1998. The health of study participants was carefully monitored by an independent panel called the Data and Safety Monitoring Board. The study was stopped in July 2002 because investigators discovered a significant increased risk for breast cancer and that overall the risks outnumbered the benefits. However, in addition to the increased risk of breast cancer—as well as heart attack, stroke, and blood clots—MHT resulted in fewer hip fractures and lower rates of colorectal cancer.

The Million Women Study began in 1996 and includes one in four women over age 50, the largest study of its kind ever conducted. Like the WHI, the study examines how MHT (both estrogen–progestin combinations and estrogen alone) affects breast cancer, cardiovascular disease, and other aspects of women's health. Results from this study confirm the WHI outcome of increased risk for breast cancer associated with MHT.

The combined results from the WHI and the Million Women Study led physicians to recommend that women over age 60 should not begin MHT to relieve menopausal symptoms or protect their health. Women over age 60 who begin MHT are at increased risk for certain cancers.

In sum, women face difficult choices when deciding whether to use MHT as a means of combating certain menopausal symptoms and protecting themselves against other diseases. For example, MHT can help reduce hot flashes and night sweats, help reduce vaginal dryness and discomfort during sexual intercourse, slow bone loss, and perhaps ease mood swings. On the other hand, MHT can increase a woman's risk of blood clots, heart attack, stroke, breast cancer, and gallbladder disease.

The best course of action is to consult closely with a physician to weigh the benefits and risks. It's also a good idea to keep in mind several key points (Womenshealth.gov, 2010):

- Once a woman reaches menopause, MHT is recommended only as a short-term treatment.
- Doctors rarely recommend MHT to prevent certain chronic diseases like osteoporosis.
- Women who have gone through menopause should not take MHT to prevent heart disease.
- MHT should not be used to prevent memory loss, dementia, or Alzheimer's disease.

Summary

13.1 Physical Changes and Health

How does appearance change in middle age?

■ Some signs of aging appearing in middle age include wrinkles, gray hair, and weight gain.

What changes occur in bones and joints?

■ An important change—especially in women—is loss of bone mass, which in severe form may result in the disease osteoporosis.

■ Osteoarthritis generally becomes noticeable in late middle or early old age. Rheumatoid arthritis is a more destructive disease affecting fingers, wrists, and ankles.

What reproductive changes occur in men and women in middle age?

■ The climacteric (loss of the ability to bear children by natural means) and menopause (cessation of menstruation) occur in the 40s and 50s and constitute a major change in reproductive ability in women.

■ Menopausal hormone therapy is a controversial approach to treatment of menopausal symptoms.

■ Reproductive changes in men are much less dramatic than in women; even older men are usually still fertile. Still, physical changes affect sexual response.

What is stress? How does it affect physical and psychological health?

■ In the stress and coping paradigm, stress results from a person's appraisal of an event as taxing his or her resources. Daily hassles are viewed as the primary source of stress.

■ The Type A behavior pattern is characterized by intense competitiveness, anger, hostility, restlessness, aggression, and impatience. It is linked with cardiovascular disease. The Type B behavior pattern is the opposite of the Type A one.

What benefits are there to exercise?

■ Aerobic exercise has numerous benefits, especially to cardiovascular health and fitness. The best results are obtained with a moderate exercise program maintained throughout adulthood.

13.2 Cognitive Development

How does practical intelligence develop in adulthood?

■ Research on practical intelligence reveals differences between it and general cognitive ability. Practical intelligence appears not to decline appreciably until late life.

How does a person become an expert?

■ People tend to become experts in some areas and not in others. Experts tend to think in more flexible ways than novices and are able to skip steps in solving problems. Expert performance tends to peak in middle age.

What differences are there between adults and young people in how they learn?

■ Adults learn differently from children and youth. Older students need practical connections and a rationale for learning, and they are more motivated by internal factors.

13.3 Personality

What is the five-factor model? What evidence is there for stability in personality traits?

■ The five-factor model postulates five dimensions of personality: neuroticism, extraversion, openness to experience, agreeableness, and conscientiousness. Several longitudinal studies indicate that personality traits show long-term stability, but increasing evidence shows that traits change across adulthood.

What changes occur in people's priorities and personal concerns? How does a person achieve generativity? How is midlife best described?

■ Erikson believed that middle-aged adults become more concerned with helping others and passing social values and skills to the next generation—a set of behaviors and beliefs he labeled generativity. Those who do not achieve generativity are thought to experience stagnation.

■ For the most part, there is little support for theories based on the premise that adults go through a midlife crisis during a specific period. Rather, midlife is a period of challenges and issues that varies from person to person.

13.4 Family Dynamics and Middle Age

Who are the kinkeepers in families?

■ Middle-aged mothers tend to adopt the role of kinkeepers to keep family traditions alive and as a way of linking generations.

■ Middle age is sometimes referred to as the sandwich generation.

How does the relationship between middle-aged parents and their young adult children change?

■ Parent–child relations improve dramatically when children grow out of adolescence. Most parents look forward to having an empty nest. Difficulties emerge to the extent that raising children has been a primary source of personal identity for parents. However, once children have left home, parents still provide considerable support.

■ Children move back home primarily for financial reasons.

How do middle-aged adults deal with their aging parents?

■ Caring for aging parents usually falls to a daughter or daughter-in-law. Caregiving creates a stressful situation due to conflicting feelings and roles. The potential for conflict is high, as is financial pressure.

■ Older parents are often dissatisfied with the situation as well.

What styles of grandparenthood do middle-aged adults experience? How do grandchildren and grandparents interact?

■ Becoming a grandparent means assuming new roles. Styles of interaction vary across grandchildren and with the age of the grandchild. Also relevant are the social and personal dimensions of grandparenting.

■ Grandparents derive several types of meaning regardless of style. Most children and young adults report positive relationships with grandparents, and young adults feel a responsibility to care for them if necessary.

■ Ethnic differences are found in the extent to which grandparents take an active role in their grandchildren's lives.

■ In an increasingly mobile society, grandparents are more frequently assuming a distant relationship with their grandchildren. An increasing number of grandparents serve as the custodial parent. These arrangements are typically stressful.

Key Terms

osteoporosis (347)	Type A behavior pattern (353)	openness to experience (360)
osteoarthritis (348)	Type B behavior pattern (353)	agreeableness (360)
wear-and-tear disease (348)	post-traumatic stress disorder (PTSD) (353)	conscientiousness (360)
rheumatoid arthritis (348)		generativity (361)
climacteric (349)	aerobic exercise (353)	stagnation (363)
menopause (349)	practical intelligence (356)	narrative (363)
perimenopause (349)	mechanics of intelligence (356)	ego resilience (364)
menopausal hormone therapy (MHT) (351)	pragmatics of intelligence (356)	kinkeeper (365)
stress and coping paradigm (352)	neuroticism (360)	sandwich generation (365)
coping (352)	extraversion (360)	filial obligation (366)

Online Resources

Go to CengageBrain.com to access Psychology CourseMate, where you will find an interactive eBook, flashcards, quizzes, videos, websites, and more.

© Stock4B/Corbis

The Personal Context of Later Life

Physical, Cognitive, and Mental Health Issues

14

Stop! Before you read this chapter, write down all the words or phrases you can think of to describe aging and older adults and all the "facts" about them you know. Look over your list carefully. As we go through the next two chapters, keep track of whether your descriptions are correct.

LEARNING OBJECTIVES

- What are the characteristics of older adults in the population?

- How long will most people live? What factors influence this?

Sarah is an 87-year-old African American woman who comes from a family of long-lived individuals. She has never been to a physician in her life, and she has never really been seriously ill. Sarah figures it's just as well that she has never needed a physician, because for most of her life she had no health insurance. Because she feels healthy and has more living that she wants to do, Sarah believes that she'll live for several more years.

What is it like to be old? Do you want your late life to be described by the words and phrases you wrote at the beginning of the chapter? Most of us probably want to be like Sarah and enjoy a long, healthy life.

The Demographics of Aging

There have never been as many older adults alive as there are now, so you see many more older people than your great-grandparents (or even your parents) did. The proportion of older adults in the population of industrialized countries has increased tremendously, mainly due to better health care and to lowering women's mortality rate during childbirth.

People who study population trends, called **demographers**, *use a graphic technique called a* **population pyramid** *to illustrate these changes.* Figure 14.1 shows population pyramids for both developed and developing countries around the world. Let's consider developed countries first (they're designated by the darker color in the figure). Notice the shape of the population pyramid in 1950, shown in the top panel of the figure. In the middle of the 20th century, there were fewer people over age 60 than under age 60, so the figure tapers toward the top. By 2011, the shape had begun to change as more older adults were still alive. Compare this to projections for 2050, and you can see that a dramatic change will occur in the number of people over 65.

These changes also occur in developing countries, shown in the lighter color. The figures for both 1950 and 2011 look more like pyramids because there are substantially fewer older adults than younger people. But by 2050, the number of older adults in developing countries will also have increased dramatically, changing the shape of the figure.

In the United States, the sheer number of older adults will place enormous pressure on pension systems (especially Social Security), health care (especially Medicare, Medicaid, and long-term care), and other human services. The costs will be borne by smaller cohorts of taxpaying workers behind them.

The growing strain on social service systems will intensify because the most rapidly growing segment of the U.S. population is the group of people over age 85 (U.S. Census Bureau, 2010a). Individuals over age 85 generally need more assistance with daily living than do people under 85, straining the health care system.

The Diversity of Older Adults

Older women outnumber older men in all ethnic groups in the United States. The number of older adults among ethnic minority groups is increasing faster than the number among European Americans (U.S. Census Bureau, 2010a). Projections for the future diversity of the U.S. population are shown in Figure 14.2. You can see very large

HUMAN DEVELOPMENT in action

How will demographic changes affect your job opportunities?

demographers
people who study population trends

population pyramid
a graphic technique for illustrating population trends

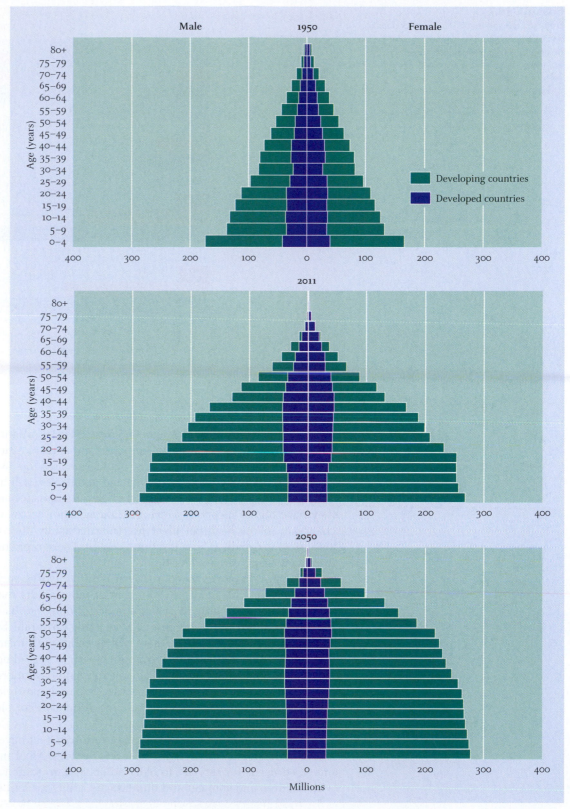

FIGURE 14.1

Changing shapes of distributions in terms of the proportion of the population that is young versus old over time and as a function of whether countries are considered developed or developing.

From International programs: International data base, by U.S. Census Bureau. Copyright © U.S. Census Bureau 2010. Retrieved from www.census.gov/ipc/www/idb

FIGURE 14.2

Projected changes in the U.S. minority population of older adults. The number of older Latino Americans will increase the fastest.

Data from The 2008 statistical abstract: 2008 edition, *by U.S. Census Bureau. Copyright © U.S. Census Bureau 2008.*

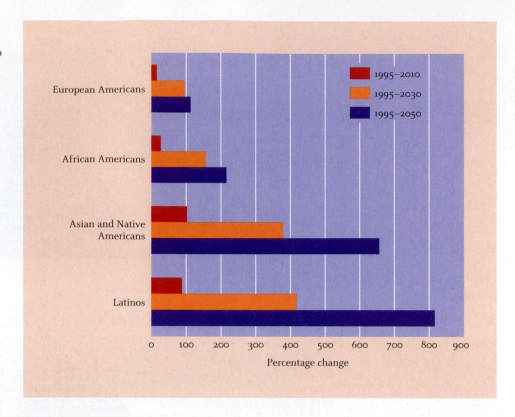

increases in the number of Asian American, Native American, and Latino American older adults relative to European American and African American older adults.

Older adults in the future will be better educated too. By 2030, it is estimated that 85% will have a high-school diploma and about 75% will have a college degree (U.S. Census Bureau, 2010a). Better-educated people tend to live longer—mostly because they have higher incomes, which give them better access to good health care and a chance to follow healthier lifestyles. Internationally, the number of older adults is also growing rapidly (United Nations, 2010b). These rapid increases are due mostly to improved health care in developing countries.

Economically powerful countries around the world, such as Japan and China, are trying to cope with increased numbers of older adults that strain the country's resources. The rate of growth of the number of older adults in Japan is the highest in the industrialized world; because of a declining birth rate, by 2025 there will be twice as many adults over age 65 as there will be children (Ministry of Internal Affairs and Communication, 2010). China is grappling with increased needs for health care for its older adult population. By 2040, China expects to have more than 300 million people over age 60. So the country is already addressing issues related to providing services for many more older adults, especially regarding care for older adults with dementia, such as Alzheimer's disease (Barboza, 2011).

As you can see in Figure 14.3, many countries will have substantially more older adults in the population over the next few decades. All of them will need to deal with increased needs for services to older adults and, in some cases, competing demands with children and younger and middle-aged adults for limited resources.

Longevity

longevity
the number of years a person can expect to live

average life expectancy
the age at which half of the people born in a particular year will have died

The number of years a person can expect to live, termed **longevity**, *is jointly determined by genetic and environmental factors.* Researchers distinguish among three types of longevity: average life expectancy, useful life expectancy, and maximum life expectancy. **Average life expectancy** *(or median life expectancy) is the age at which half of the*

380 | PART FOUR: LATE ADULTHOOD

FIGURE 14.3

The proportion of older adults (65 years and older) is increasing in many countries and will continue to do so in the coming decades.

From United Nations, Statistics Bureau, Ministry of Public Management, Home Affairs, Post, and Telecommunications, Ministry of Health, Labour and Welfare.

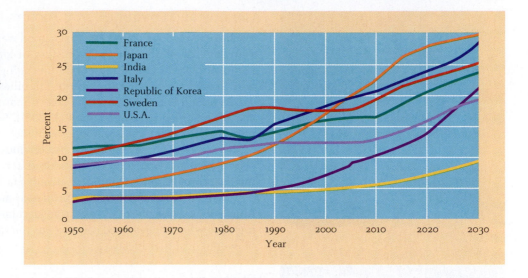

people born in a particular year will have died. As you can see in Figure 14.4, average life expectancy at birth for people in the United States has increased, mainly due to significant declines in infant mortality and in the number of women dying during childbirth, elimination of major diseases, and improvements in medical technology. Currently, average life expectancy at birth for American women is 80.4 years; for men, it's 75.4 years (National Center for Health Statistics, 2010b).

Useful life expectancy *is the number of years that a person is free from debilitating chronic disease and impairment.* Ideally, useful life expectancy matches the length of a person's life. However, medical technology sometimes enables people to live on for years even though they may no longer be able to perform routine daily tasks. Accordingly, when making medical treatment decisions, people are now placing greater emphasis on useful life expectancy and less emphasis on the sheer number of years they may live.

Maximum life expectancy *is the oldest age to which any person lives.* Currently, scientists estimate that the maximum limit for humans is around 120 years, mostly because the heart and other key organ systems are limited in how long they can last without replacement (Hayflick, 1998).

useful life expectancy
the number of years that a person is free from debilitating chronic disease and impairment

maximum life expectancy
the oldest age to which any person lives

FIGURE 14.4

Life expectancy at birth and at 65 years of age in the United States, 1900–2007.

Data from Health, United States, 2010: With special feature on medical technology, by National Center for Health Statistics. Copyright © Centers for Disease Control and Prevention, National Center for Health Statistics, National Vital Statistics System 2011. (2010). Retrieved from http://www.cdc.gov/nchs/data/hus/hus10.pdf#022

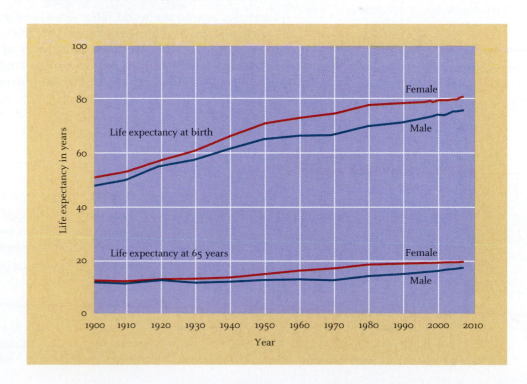

Genetic and Environmental Factors in Longevity

We have known for some time that a good way to increase the chance of a long life is to come from a family with a history of long-lived individuals (Hayflick, 1998). For example, genomic studies of human aging are advancing our understanding of why longevity tends to run in certain families (Slagboom et al., 2011).

Although heredity is a major determinant of longevity, environmental factors also affect life span (Slagboom et al., 2011). Some environmental factors are obvious; diseases, toxins, lifestyle, and social class are among the most important. Some of the causes of these factors are also obvious; as an example, the impact of social class on longevity results from reduced access to goods and services, especially medical care (National Center for Health Statistics, 2007).

How environmental factors influence average life expectancy changes over time. For example, the effect of cardiovascular diseases on life expectancy is lessening somewhat in developed countries as the rates of those diseases decline because of overall healthier lifestyles.

Ethnic and Gender Differences in Longevity

Ethnic differences in average life expectancy are clear (National Center for Health Statistics, 2010b). Although African Americans start life with lower average longevity than European Americans, by age 85 they typically outlive them. Latino Americans expect to live longer than European Americans at every age.

Women's average longevity is about 5 years longer than men's at birth, narrowing to roughly 1 year by age 85 (National Center for Health Statistics, 2010d). These differences are fairly typical of most developed countries but not of developing countries. Why? Death in childbirth partially explains the lack of a female advantage in developing countries; however, part of the difference in some countries also results from infanticide of baby girls.

What accounts for women's longevity advantage, especially in developed countries? Overall, men's rates of dying from 12 of the top 15 causes of death are significantly higher than women's at nearly every age, and men are more susceptible to infectious diseases (Pinkhasov et al., 2010).

International Differences in Longevity

Countries around the world differ dramatically in how long their populations live on average. As you can see in Figure 14.5, the current range extends from 38 years in Sierra Leone, Africa, to more than 82 years in Japan. Such wide divergence in life expectancy reflects vast discrepancies in genetics, sociocultural and economic conditions, health care, disease, and the like across developed and developing nations.

Being able to continue doing enjoyable things is one hallmark of useful life expectancy.

HUMAN DEVELOPMENT in action

How do ethnic and gender differences influence the need for professionals in health care?

Test Yourself

Recall

1. The fastest growing segment of the population in the United States is people over age _____.
2. The age at which half of the people born in a particular year will have died is called _____.

Interpret

- Think back to the lifestyle influences on health discussed in Chapter 12. If most people exhibited a healthy lifestyle, what do you think would happen to average life expectancy?
- How could men's average longevity be increased?

Apply

- If you were to design an intervention program to maximize the odds that people will live to maximum longevity, what would you emphasize?
- What are the social impacts of increased longevity?

Recall answers: (1) 85, (2) average life expectancy

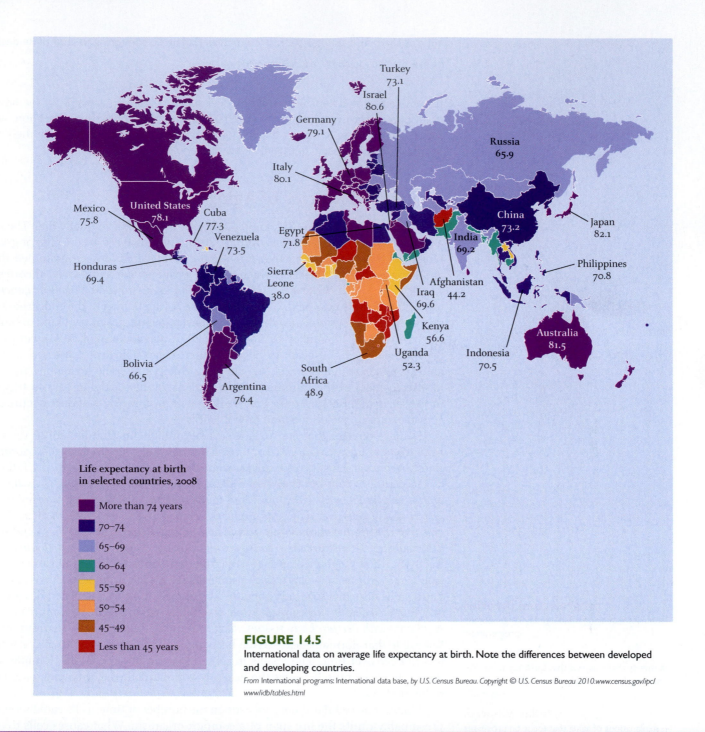

FIGURE 14.5

International data on average life expectancy at birth. Note the differences between developed and developing countries.

From International programs: International data base, by U.S. Census Bureau. Copyright © U.S. Census Bureau 2010.www.census.gov/ipc/ www.idb/tables.html

Life expectancy at birth in selected countries, 2008

- More than 74 years
- 70–74
- 65–69
- 60–64
- 55–59
- 50–54
- 45–49
- Less than 45 years

14.2 Physical Changes and Health

LEARNING OBJECTIVES

- What are the major biological theories of aging?
- What physiological changes normally occur in later life?
- What are the principal health issues for older adults?

Frank is an 80-year-old man who has been physically active his whole life. He still enjoys sailing, long-distance biking, and cross-country skiing. Although he considers himself to be in excellent shape, he has noticed that his endurance has decreased and that his hearing isn't

quite as sharp as it used to be. Frank wonders: Can he do something to stop these declines, or are they an inevitable part of growing older?

If your family has kept photographs over many years, you are able to see how your grandparents or great-grandparents changed over their lives. In this section, we consider some of these changes, as well as things adults can do to improve their health. But first, we ask a basic question: Why do people grow old?

Biological Theories of Aging

Why does everyone who lives long enough grow old and eventually die? There is no adequate theory or explanation (Kunlin, 2010). Instead, there are two major groups of biological theories of aging that provide partial explanations: programmed theories and damage or error theories, which include wear-and-tear and cellular theories.

Programmed theories *suggest that aging is due to a biological or genetic program.* Researchers now believe that the decline in functioning in the endocrine system, and the immune system, may be part of a master genetic program, a kind of biological clock (Kunlin, 2010; Pankow & Solotoroff, 2007; Slagboom et al., 2011). For example, programmed aging appears to be a function of physiological processes, the innate ability of cells to self-destruct, the clocklike changes in some hormones, the decline in effectiveness of the immune system, and the ability of dying cells to trigger key processes in other cells. At present, we do not know how this self-destruct program is activated, nor do we understand how it works.

Damage or error theories include several components (Kunlin, 2010). **Wear-and-tear theory** *suggests that the body, much like any machine, gradually deteriorates and finally wears out.* This theory explains some diseases, such as osteoarthritis, rather well.

In contrast, **cellular theories** *explain aging by focusing on processes that occur within individual cells, which may lead to the buildup of harmful substances or the deterioration of cells over a lifetime.* Some researchers believe that **free radicals**—*chemicals that are produced randomly during normal cell metabolism and that bond easily to other substances inside cells*—*cause cellular damage that impairs functioning.* According to this theory, aging is caused by the cumulative effects of free radicals over the life span. Free radicals may play a role in some diseases, such as atherosclerosis and cancer. Eating a healthy diet may postpone the occurrence of some age-related diseases.

Another cellular theory focuses on **cross-linking,** *in which some proteins interact randomly with certain body tissues, such as muscles and arteries.* The result of cross-linking is that normal, elastic tissue becomes stiffer so that muscles and arteries are less flexible over time. The results in some cases can be serious; for example, stiffening in the heart muscle forces the heart to work harder, which may increase the risk of heart attacks.

Finally, one cellular theory focuses on the number of times cells can divide, which presumably limits the life span of a complex organism. What causes cells to restrict their number of divisions? *Evidence suggests that the tips of the chromosomes, called* **telomeres,** *play a major role* (Sahin & DePinho, 2010). An enzyme called telomerase is needed in DNA replication to fully replicate the telomeres. But telomerase is not normally present in cells, so with each replication, the telomeres become shorter. Eventually, the chromosomes become unstable and cannot replicate because the telomeres become too short with age (Lung et al., 2005); they are also susceptible to prolonged stress (Epel, Burke, & Wolkowitz, 2007). Some researchers believe that cancer cells proliferate so quickly in some cases because they can activate telomerase. Current thinking is that cancer cells may thus become functionally immortal and that effective cancer therapy may involve targeting telomerase (Artandi & DePinho, 2010; Harley, 2008). Some good news comes from research indicating that aerobic exercise may help maintain telomere length, which may help slow the aging process (LaRocca, Seals, & Pierce, 2010).

programmed theories
theories that aging is biologically or genetically programmed

wear-and-tear theory
a theory that suggests that the body, much like any machine, gradually deteriorates and finally wears out

cellular theories
explanations of aging that focus on processes that occur within individual cells, which may lead to the buildup of harmful substances or the deterioration of cells over a lifetime

free radicals
chemicals that are produced randomly during normal cell metabolism and that bond easily to other substances inside cells

cross-linking
the random interaction of some proteins with certain body tissues, such as muscles and arteries

telomeres
tips of the chromosomes that shorten and break with increasing age

Eating a healthy diet can delay the appearance of age-related diseases.

R. Ian Lloyd/Masterfile

Physiological Changes

Growing older brings with it several inevitable physiological changes—like Frank, whom we met in the vignette, discovered.

Neural Changes

Neuroscience research indicates that the most important normative changes with age involve changes in the structure of neurons and in how they communicate (Bishop, Lu, & Yankner, 2010; Deary, Penke, & Johnson, 2010; Reuter-Lorenz & Park, 2010). Recall the basic structures of the neuron we encountered in Chapter 3, shown again in Figure 14.6. Each of the changes we consider in this section impairs the neurons' ability to transmit information, which ultimately affects how well a person functions (Bishop, Lu, & Yankner, 2010).

For reasons that are not understood, fibers that compose the axon sometimes become twisted together to form spiral-shaped masses called **neurofibrillary tangles**. These tangles interfere with the neuron's ability to transmit information down the axon. Some degree of tangling occurs normally with age, but large numbers of neurofibrillary tangles are associated with Alzheimer's disease and other forms of dementia (Ribe et al., 2011; Risacher & Saykin, 2011).

Changes in the dendrites are more complicated. Some dendrites shrivel up and die, making it more difficult for neurons to communicate with one another and transmit information (von Bohlen und Halbach, 2010). However, research indicates that dendrites continue to grow in some areas of the brain, and embryonic stem cell research indicates that inducing growth may be a future way to treat brain disease and injury (West, 2010). This may help explain why older adults continue to improve in some areas, as we discover later. Why some dendrites degenerate and others do not is poorly understood; it may reflect the existence of two families of neurons.

Damaged and dying neurons sometimes collect around a core of protein and produce **neuritic plaques**. It is likely that plaques interfere with normal functioning of healthy neurons. Although large numbers of plaques are considered a defining criterion of dementia, researchers have not established an "allowable number" of plaques that indicate a healthy aging brain (Takata, Kitamura, & Taniguchi, 2011).

neurofibrillary tangles
spiral-shaped masses formed when fibers that compose the axon become twisted together

neuritic plaques
structural changes in the brain produced when damaged and dying neurons collect around a core of protein

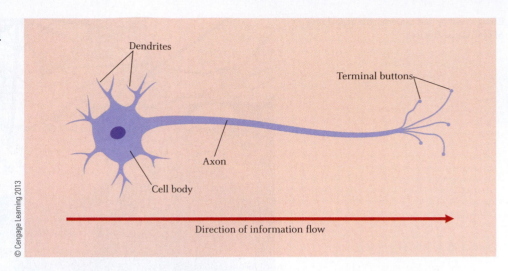

FIGURE 14.6
Basic structure of the neuron.

Dendrites

Terminal buttons

Axon

Cell body

Direction of information flow

© Cengage Learning 2013

Because neurons do not physically touch one another, they must communicate via chemicals called neurotransmitters. With age, the levels of these neurotransmitters decline (Björklund & Dunnett, 2007). These declines are believed to be responsible for numerous age-related behavioral changes, including those in memory and sleep, and perhaps for diseases such as Parkinson's disease (Björklund & Dunnett, 2007).

We are learning a great deal about the relationships between changes in the brain and changes in behavior through technological advances in noninvasive imaging and in assessing psychological functioning (Blanchard-Fields, 2010; Reuter-Lorenz & Park, 2010). Neuroimaging is an important tool for understanding both normal and abnormal cognitive aging. Two neuroimaging techniques are used:

- *Structural neuroimaging* provides highly detailed images of anatomical features in the brain. The most commonly used are X-rays, computerized tomography (CT) scans, and magnetic resonance imaging (MRI).

- *Functional neuroimaging* provides an indication of brain activity but not high anatomical detail. The most commonly used are single photon emission computerized tomography, positron emission tomography, functional magnetic resonance imaging (fMRI), magnetoencephalograpy (or multichannel encephalography), and near-infrared spectroscopic imaging. In general, fMRI is the most commonly used technique in cognitive neuroscience research (Reuter-Lorenz & Park, 2010).

These techniques, coupled with tests of cognitive processing, have shown quite convincingly that age-related brain changes are responsible for age-related declines (Blanchard-Fields, 2010; Reuter-Lorenz & Park, 2010).

Cardiovascular and Respiratory Systems

The incidence of cardiovascular diseases increases dramatically with age and is higher among African Americans (Keenan & Shaw, 2011). However, the overall death rates from these diseases have been declining over recent decades, although the death rate for some ethnic groups remains much higher because of poorer preventive health care and lack of financial resources (Keenan & Shaw, 2011).

As people grow older, their chances of having a stroke increase. *A* **stroke or cerebral vascular accident (CVA)** *is caused by an interruption of blood flow in the brain due to blockage or hemorrhage in a cerebral artery.* Blockages of an artery may be caused by clots or by deposits of fatty substances due to the disease atherosclerosis. Hemorrhages are caused by ruptures of the artery. CVAs are the leading cause of disability (and the third-leading cause of death) in the United States.

stroke or cerebral vascular accident (CVA)
an interruption of blood flow in the brain due to blockage or hemorrhage in a cerebral artery

Research indicates that quick intervention and aggressive rehabilitation result in better recovery (DeAngelis, 2010).

Older adults often experience **transient ischemic attacks (TIAs)**, *which involve interruptions of blood flow to the brain and are often early warning signs of stroke.* A single, large CVA may produce serious cognitive impairment, such as the loss of the ability to speak, or physical problems, such as the inability to move an arm. Recovery from a single stroke depends on many factors, including the extent and type of the loss.

Numerous small CVAs can result in a disease termed **vascular dementia**. Unlike Alzheimer's disease (discussed later), vascular dementia can have a sudden onset and may progress slowly (Oh et al., 2011). Single CVAs and vascular dementia are diagnosed by structural imaging (e.g., CT scan or MRI), and by neuropsychological tests. Known risk factors for both conditions include hypertension and a family history of the disorders. Typical symptoms of vascular dementia include specific and extensive alterations on an MRI and differential impairment on neuropsychological tests. Individuals' specific symptom patterns and the course of the disease may vary a great deal.

When it comes to the respiratory system, the decline in maximum lung capacity is the main cause of shortness of breath in later life. *The most common form of incapacitating respiratory disease among older adults is* **chronic obstructive pulmonary disease (COPD)**. COPD can be an extremely debilitating condition and may result in depression, anxiety, and the need to be continually connected to oxygen (Borson, 2011; Vestbo, 2011). Emphysema is the most common form of COPD; although most cases of emphysema are due to smoking, some forms are genetic.

Parkinson's Disease

Parkinson's disease *is known primarily for its characteristic motor symptoms: very slow walking, difficulty getting into and out of chairs, and a slow hand tremor.* These problems are caused by a deterioration of neurons in the midbrain that produce the neurotransmitter dopamine. More than 1 million people in the United States (and more than 4 million globally) have Parkinson's disease (National Parkinson's Foundation, 2011b).

Symptoms of Parkinson's disease are managed effectively with two primary approaches: medication and surgery (Bhidayasiri & Brenden, 2011; National Parkinson's Foundation, 2011a). The most common medication is levodopa, which raises the functional level of dopamine in the brain. Surgical intervention involves using a device called a neurostimulator, which acts like a brain pacemaker, regulating brain activity when implanted deep inside the brain (National Institute of Neurological Disorders and Stroke, 2010).

Sensory Changes

VISION. Two major kinds of age-related structural changes occur in the eye as we reach old age. One is a decrease in the amount of light that passes through the eye, resulting in the need for more light to do tasks such as reading. One possible logical response to the need for more light would be to increase illumination levels in general. However, this solution does not work in all situations, because we also become increasingly sensitive to glare (Lighthouse International, 2011). The second major change is that our ability to adjust to changes in illumination, called adaptation, declines. These changes are especially important for older drivers, who have more difficulty seeing after being confronted with the headlights of an oncoming car.

As we grow older, the eye's lens becomes more yellow, causing poorer color discrimination in the green–blue–violet end of the color spectrum, and the ability of the lens to adjust and focus declines as the muscles around it stiffen (Fozard & Gordon-Salant, 2001). *This is what causes* **presbyopia**, *difficulty in seeing close objects clearly,*

transient ischemic attacks (TIAs)
interruptions of blood flow to the brain that are often early warning signs of stroke

vascular dementia
a disease caused by numerous small CVAs

chronic obstructive pulmonary disease (COPD)
the most common form of incapacitating respiratory disease among older adults

Parkinson's disease
a brain disease known primarily for its characteristic motor symptoms: very slow walking, difficulty getting into and out of chairs, and a slow hand tremor

presbyopia
difficulty in seeing close objects clearly

necessitating either longer arms or corrective lenses. To complicate matters further, the time our eyes need to change focus from near to far, and vice versa, increases (Fozard & Gordon-Salant, 2001). This also poses a major problem in driving.

Some people experience diseases caused by abnormal structural changes. First, opaque spots called cataracts may develop on the lens, which limit the amount of light transmitted. Cataracts often are treated by surgical removal and use of corrective lenses. Second, the fluid in the eye may not drain properly, causing very high pressure; this condition, called glaucoma, can cause internal damage and loss of vision. Glaucoma is usually treated with eyedrops.

The second major family of changes in vision results from changes in the retina. Macular degeneration involves the progressive and irreversible destruction of receptors in the retina from any number of causes. This disease results in loss of the ability to see details; for example, reading becomes extremely difficult, and television is often reduced to a blur. It is the leading cause of functional blindness in older adults.

Diabetic retinopathy, which can cause blindness, can involve fluid retention in the macula, detachment of the retina, hemorrhage, and aneurysms (Fozard & Gordon-Salant, 2001). Because it takes many years to develop, diabetic retinopathy is more common among people who developed diabetes early in life.

HEARING. Age-related changes in hearing can interfere with people's ability to communicate with others. Hearing loss is one of the well-known normative changes associated with aging (National Institute on Aging, 2010).

Loud noise is the enemy of hearing at any age. You probably have seen people who work in noisy environments (e.g., factories and airports) wearing protective gear on their ears so that they are not exposed to loud noise over extended periods. But you don't need to be in a loud environment to damage your hearing. Using headphones or earbuds, especially at high volume, can cause the same serious damage and should be avoided. It is especially easy to cause hearing loss with headphones or earbuds if you wear them while exercising; the increased blood flow to the ear during exercise makes hearing receptors more vulnerable to damage.

The cumulative effects of noise and normative age-related changes create the most common age-related hearing problem: reduced sensitivity to high-pitched tones, or **presbycusis**, *which occurs earlier and more severely than loss of sensitivity to low-pitched tones.* Research indicates that, by their late 70s, roughly half of older adults

presbycusis
reduced sensitivity to high-pitched tones

Exercising while wearing headphones or earbuds and listening to loud music when you are young can result in serious hearing loss in later life.

iStockphoto.com/webphotographeer

have presbycusis. Hearing loss usually is gradual at first but accelerates during the 40s, a pattern seen clearly in Figure 14.7.

Loss of hearing in later life may cause numerous adverse emotional reactions, such as loss of independence, social isolation, irritation, paranoia, and depression. Much research indicates that hearing loss per se does not cause social maladjustment or emotional disturbance. However, friends and relatives of an older person with hearing loss often attribute emotional changes to hearing loss, which strains the quality of interpersonal relationships, and the older person's emotional well-being can be negatively affected (Sprinzl & Riechelmann, 2010). Thus, while hearing loss may not directly affect older adults' self-concept or emotions, it may negatively affect how they feel about interpersonal communication. By understanding hearing-loss problems and ways to overcome them, those without hearing loss can play a large part in minimizing the effects of hearing loss on the older people in their lives.

FALLS. Changes in eyesight and hearing, as well as in muscle tone, reflexes, and balance, make older people increasingly likely to fall. The fear of falling and becoming injured is a real concern for many older adults and can affect their willingness to

FIGURE 14.7

Hearing loss occurs in all adults but is greatest for high-pitched tones and greater for men than for women. As a reference, the highest note on a piano is 4,186 Hz; normal human hearing ranges from 27 Hz to 20,000 Hz.

Based on "Age differences in the functional and structural organization of the auditory system in man," by J. M. Ordy, K. R. Brizzee, T. Beavers, and P. Medart, in Sensory Systems and Communication in the Elderly, edited by J. M. Ordy and K. R. Brizzee. Copyright © Raven Press 1979.

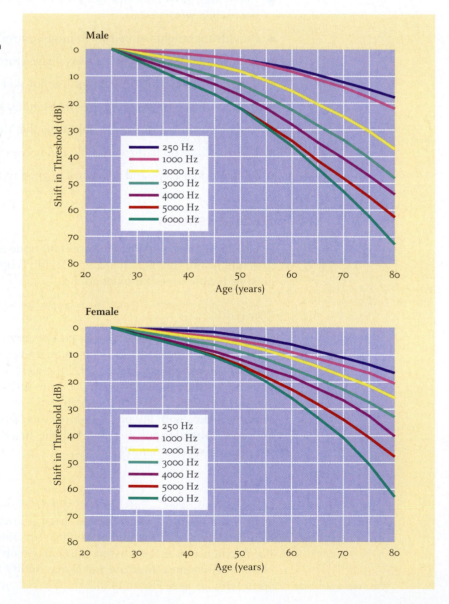

HUMAN DEVELOPMENT in **action**

What physical changes in the workplace would provide support and reduce the impact of sensory ability changes with age?

engage in certain types of activities (Li et al., 2005). Staying active and fit, along with taking precautions, such as ensuring that there is sufficient light and no loose carpets, can also help reduce falls.

EFFECTS ON EVERYDAY LIFE. The sensory changes that people experience as they age have important implications for their everyday lives (Schneider, Pichora-Fuller, & Daneman, 2010; Whitbourne, 1996). Some (e.g., difficulty reading things close up) are minor annoyances that are easily corrected (e.g., by wearing reading glasses). Others are more serious and less easily addressed. For example, the ability to drive a car is affected by changes in vision and in hearing.

Because sensory changes may also lead to accidents around the home, it is important to design a safer environment that takes these changes into account. Many accidents can be prevented by maintaining health through prevention and conditioning. But making some relatively simple environmental changes also helps. For example, falls are the most common cause of accidental serious injury and death among older adults. Here are some steps that can help reduce the potential for falls:

- Illuminate stairways and provide light switches at both the top and the bottom of the stairs.

- Avoid high-gloss floor finishes because of their glare and their tendency to be slippery when wet.

- Provide nightlights or bedside remote-control light switches.

- Be sure that both sides of stairways have sturdy handrails.

- Tack down carpeting on stairs or use nonskid treads.

- Remove throw rugs or area rugs that tend to slide on the floor.

- Arrange furniture and other objects so that they are not obstacles.

- Use grab bars on bathroom walls and nonskid mats or strips in bathtubs.

- Keep outdoor steps and walkways in good repair.

Health Issues

Health promotion remains an important issue as people age. Integrating lifestyle issues into health care is a challenge (HealthyPeople.gov, 2011). Let's focus on some key lifestyle health issues for older adults.

Sleep

Compared to younger adults, older adults report that it takes roughly twice as long to fall asleep, that they get less sleep on an average night, and that they feel more negative effects following a night with little sleep (Ancoli-Israel & Alessi, 2005). Several physical and mental health problems can disrupt sleep. *Sleep problems can disrupt a person's* **circadian rhythm**, *or sleep–wake cycle.* Circadian rhythm disruptions can cause problems with attention and memory. Research shows that interventions, such as properly timed exposure to bright light, are effective in correcting circadian rhythm sleep disorders (Terman, 1994).

Nutrition

Most healthy older adults do not require vitamin or mineral supplements as long as they are eating a well-balanced diet (Ahluwalia, 2004). A good nutritional guide for older adults is the modified MyPlate for Older Adults developed by Tufts University (Lichtenstein & Rasmussen, 2011). Based on the U.S. Department of Agriculture's MyPlate guidelines, MyPlate for Older Adults takes into account the changes that occur with age (see Figure 14.8).

circadian rhythm
the sleep–wake cycle

FIGURE 14.8

Dietary guidelines for older adults.

Source: Copyright 2011 Tufts University. For details about the My Plate for Older Adults, please see http://nutrition.tufts.edu/research/ myplate-older-adults

MyPlate for Older Adults

2011© TUFTS UNIVERSITY

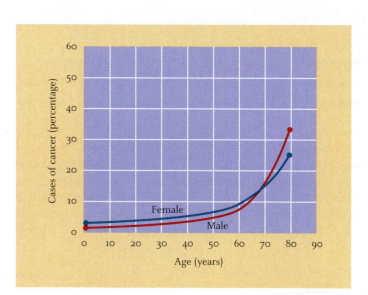

FIGURE 14.9

The risk of cancer increases greatly with age.

Adapted from data from Lifetime risk of developing or dying from cancer, by American Cancer Society. Copyright © American Cancer Society 2010) www.cancer.org/Cancer/CancerBasics/lifetime-probability-of-developing-or-dyingfrom-cancer.

Cancer

As shown in Figure 14.9, the risk of getting cancer increases markedly with age. Unhealthy lifestyles (smoking and poor diet), genetics, and exposure to cancer-causing chemicals certainly are important, but they do not fully explain the age-related increase in risk. Early detection of cancer—even in older adults—is essential to maximize the odds of surviving most cancers, and survival rates for most cancers are improving (American Cancer Society, 2010a).

Immigrant Status

Whether an older adult was born in the United States or emigrated from another country affects health. Whereas immigrants in the United States face numerous barriers in obtaining adequate health care (Glick, 2010), immigrants to Canada largely do not (Prus, Tfaily, & Lin, 2010).

Language and cultural differences need to be considered in performing examinations with immigrants. Cultures vary regarding how comfortable people are about allowing strangers (i.e., physicians) to examine them (Bylsma, Ostendorf, & Hofer, 2002), and cultural differences can result in mislabeling or misdiagnosing problems (McConatha, Stoller, & Oboudiat, 2001).

Research comparing the health status of immigrants and U.S.-born older adults shows that even when socioeconomic status is controlled, immigrants show poorer health than U.S.-born people with the same ethnic background (e.g., Angel, Buckley, & Sakamoto, 2001; Berdes & Zych, 2000). One mitigating factor is when immigrants have an excellent relationship with their child; in these cases, older immigrants have fewer chronic illnesses (Ajrouch, 2007).

Test Yourself

Recall

1. Two major groups of biological theories of aging are _____ theories and damage or error theories.

2. Damaged and dying neurons that collect around a core of protein produce _____.

3. The risk of getting cancer _____ markedly with age.

Interpret

- In this section we concentrated on the biological forces in development. Think about other forces (psychological, social, and life cycle), and list some reasons as to why scientists have yet to propose a purely biological theory that accounts for all aspects of aging.

- How might changes in sensory abilities result in behavior that appears to reflect cognitive changes?

Apply

- How do the sensory changes that occur with age affect an older adult's everyday life?

- What policies and procedures should employers have to be sensitive to sensory and physical changes with age?

14.3 Cognitive Processes

LEARNING OBJECTIVES

- What changes occur in information processing as people age? How do these changes relate to everyday life?

- What changes occur in memory with age? What can be done to remediate these changes?

- What are creativity and wisdom? How do they relate to age?

Rocio is a 75-year-old widow who feels that she does not remember recent events—such as whether she took her medicine—as well as she used to, but she has no trouble remembering things that happened in her 20s. Rocio wonders whether this is normal or she should be worried.

Rocio, like many older people, takes medications for arthritis, allergies, and high blood pressure. However, each drug has its own pattern; some are taken only with meals, others are taken every 8 hours, and still others are taken twice daily. Keeping these regimens straight is important to avoid potentially dangerous interactions and side effects, and older people face the problem of remembering to take each medication at the proper time.

Information Processing

Innovations and discoveries in neuroscience have resulted in major advances in our understanding of how people process information across their life span (Blanchard-Fields, 2010; Reuter-Lorenz & Park, 2010). The most common approach involves using a task-related neuroimaging technique, such as fMRI, to measure brain activity while the person is performing the cognitive task.

Psychomotor Speed

You are driving home from a friend's house when all of a sudden a car pulls out of a driveway right into your path. You must hit the brakes as fast as possible, or you will have an accident. How quickly can you move your foot from the accelerator to the brake?

This real-life situation is an example of **psychomotor speed or reaction time**, *the speed with which a person can make a specific response.* Hundreds of studies of psychomotor speed all point to the same conclusion: People slow down as they get older. The slowing-with-age finding is so well documented that many researchers accept it as the only universal behavioral change in aging discovered so far (Salthouse, 2000, 2006, 2010a, 2010b).

The most important reason reaction times slow down is that older adults take longer to decide that they need to respond, especially when the situation involves ambiguous information (Salthouse, 2010a, 2010b). Although response slowing is inevitable, the amount of the decline can be reduced if older adults are allowed to practice making quick responses or if they are experienced in the task. Because psychomotor slowing is a universal phenomenon, researchers have argued that it may explain a great deal of the age differences in cognition (e.g., Salthouse, 2010a, 2010b). Psychomotor slowing is a good predictor of cognitive performance, but there's a catch: The prediction is best when the task requires little effort (Park et al., 1996). If the task requires more effort and is more difficult, then working memory (which we consider later) is a better predictor of performance (Park et al., 1996). Also, exercise can mediate the effects of normative aging on cognitive slowing (Spirduso, Poon, & Chodzko-Zajko, 2008).

Psychomotor slowing with age has also sparked considerable controversy concerning whether older adults should be allowed to drive. As we have seen, age-related changes in vision, hearing, attention, and reaction time affect people's competence as drivers.

As you can see in Figure 14.10, statistics compiled by the Insurance Institute for Highway Safety (Cheung & McCartt, 2010) show that although the fatality rate for drivers over age 75 has declined, it is higher than that for middle-aged adults. Research shows that the higher fatality rate is due to older drivers' age-related decline in key sensory, attentional, and psychomotor abilities (Horswill et al., 2010; Krishnasamy & Unsworth, 2011).

Experts agree that decisions about whether "at risk" drivers should be allowed to continue driving must be based on performance measures rather than age or medical diagnosis alone (Carr & Ott, 2010). *Ball and Owsley (1993) developed the* **useful field of view (UFOV)** *measure, an area from which someone can extract visual information in a single glance without turning the head or moving the eyes.* This measure can easily be assessed via a personal desktop computer (Edwards et al., 2005). A prototype assessment

psychomotor speed or reaction time

the speed with which a person can make a specific response

useful field of view (UFOV)

an area from which someone can extract visual information in a single glance without turning the head or moving the eyes

FIGURE 14.10

National fatal passenger vehicle driver crash involvements per 100,000 licensed drivers by driver age group, 1997–2008.

Source: From "Declines in Fatal Crashes of Older Drivers: Changes in Crash Risk and Survivability, by Ivan Sheung, Anne T. McCartt, June 2010. Insurance Institute for Highway Safety.www.iihs.org. Reprinted by permission.

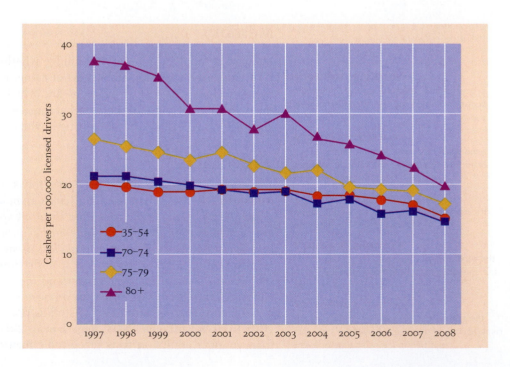

that can be used during normal driving has also been developed (Danno et al., 2010). The size of the UFOV is important; it may mean the difference between "seeing" a car running a stop sign, or a child running out from between two parked cars, and "not seeing" such information. Performance on the UFOV measure predicts driving performance (e.g., Danno et al., 2010; Hoffman et al., 2005).

To assist states in adopting more uniform standards, the American Automobile Association (2005) created the *AAA Roadwise Review Online: A Tool to Help Seniors Drive Safely Longer.* Designed to be administered online, the review assesses eight key functional areas: leg strength and general mobility, head and neck flexibility, high-contrast visual acuity, low visual acuity, working memory, visualization of missing information, visual search, and visual information-processing speed. Drivers with a significant loss in the functional capabilities tested by the *AAA Roadwise Review* are two to five times more likely to cause a motor vehicle crash (American Automobile Association, 2005). You can find out more about *AAA Roadwise Review* and download the test from SeniorDriving.AAA.com.

Working Memory

One evening, you remember that your significant other's birthday is a week from tomorrow. So you go online, find a restaurant that is perfect for a romantic dinner, see that you must call to make reservations, look at the phone number, and start to dial. Remembering the number long enough to dial it successfully requires good working memory. **Working memory** *consists of the processes and structures involved in holding information in mind and simultaneously using it to solve a problem, make a decision, perform some function, or learn new information.*

Working memory generally declines with age (Braver & West, 2008). Taken together, working memory and psychomotor speed provide a powerful set of explanatory constructs for predicting cognitive performance (Salthouse, 2010a, 2010b).

Neuroimaging studies reveal why these age differences occur. Both younger and older adults activate the prefrontal area of their brains (an area behind the forehead) during working memory tasks. But older adults activate more of it on easier tasks, and they exhaust their resources sooner (Cappell, Gmeindl, & Reuter-Lorenz, 2010; Reuter-Lorenz & Park, 2010). In a sense, older adults have to devote more "brain power" to working memory than younger adults, so older adults run out of resources sooner, resulting in poorer performance.

Memory

Many older adults use memory to judge whether their mind is intact. Poor memory is often viewed as an inevitable part of aging. But is it? And if it is, which aspects of memory change happen to everyone and which ones don't? Many people, like Rocio, the woman in the vignette, believe that forgetting a loaf of bread at the store when age 25 is not a big deal but that forgetting it when age 65 is cause for alarm. Is this true?

What Changes?

The study of memory aging generally focuses on two types of memory: **explicit memory***, the deliberate and conscious remembering of information learned and remembered at a specific time, and* **implicit memory***, the unconscious remembering of information learned at some earlier time. Explicit memory is further divided into* **episodic memory***, the general class of memory having to do with the conscious recollection of information from a specific time or event, and* **semantic memory***, the general class of memory concerning the remembering of meanings of words or concepts not tied to a specific time or event.*

The results from hundreds of studies point to several conclusions (Berry et al., 2010; Craik & Salthouse, 2008; Negash et al., 2011). Older adults tend to perform worse than younger adults on tests of episodic memory recall (such as remembering the

working memory
the processes and structures involved in holding information in mind and simultaneously using it for other functions

explicit memory
the deliberate and conscious remembering of information learned and remembered at a specific time

implicit memory
the unconscious remembering of information learned at some earlier time

episodic memory
the general class of memory having to do with the conscious recollection of information from a specific time or event

semantic memory
the general class of memory concerning the remembering of meanings of words or concepts not tied to a specific time or event

Older adults perform as well as younger adults at semantic memory tasks, like the TV show *Jeopardy*, shown here, that involve remembering facts or words.

Amanda Edwards/Getty Images

specific items on a list). On recognition tests (such as picking out the specific face you saw earlier from a group of faces), age differences are smaller but still present (Zacks, Hasher, & Li, 2000). Older adults also tend to be less efficient at spontaneously using memory strategies to help themselves remember (Hertzog & Dunlosky, 2004) but can learn to use such strategies effectively (Berry et al., 2010).

In contrast, age differences on semantic memory tasks are typically absent in normative aging but are found in people with dementia, making this difference one way to diagnose probable cases of abnormal cognitive aging (Paraita, Díaz, & Anllo-Vento, 2008). Similarly, age differences are typically absent on tests of implicit memory. However, one area in which older adults have difficulty is in word finding, such as experiencing delays in coming up with the right word based on a definition and having more tip-of-the-tongue experiences.

In general, neuroscience research provides evidence that structural changes in the brain underlie changes in memory. Neuroimaging results show that the areas of the brain involved in encoding memories (e.g., the hippocampus and the medial temporal lobe) shrink in older adults, making it harder for them to get information stored properly (Mitchell & Johnson, 2009). Older adults tend to activate their prefrontal cortex as a way to try to compensate, but their resources there are limited (Reuter-Lorenz & Park, 2010).

In sum, contrary to social stereotypes of a broad-based decline in memory ability with age, research shows that the facts are more complex and related to underlying changes in the brain. Whether memory declines with age depends on the type of memory.

When Is Memory Change Abnormal?

The older man in the *For Better or For Worse* cartoon voices a concern that many older adults have: that their forgetfulness is indicative of something worse. Differentiating normal and abnormal memory changes is usually accomplished through an array of tests grounded in the research findings that document the various developmental patterns discussed previously (American Psychological Association, 2004). Such testing focuses on measuring performance and identifying declines in aspects of memory that typically do not change, such as tertiary memory (which is essentially long-term memory) (Stoner, O'Riley, & Edelstein, 2010).

A first step in diagnosing memory-related problems is to find out whether the memory problem is interfering with everyday functioning. When the memory problem does

interfere with functioning, such as not remembering your spouse's name or how to get home, it is appropriate to suspect a serious, abnormal underlying reason.

Once a serious problem is suspected, the next step is to obtain a thorough examination (Stoner, O'Riley, & Edelstein, 2010). This should include a complete physical and neurological examination and a complete battery of neuropsychological tests.

Many memory-impairing diseases progress slowly, and poor memory performance may only be noticed gradually over an extended period. Only with complete and thorough testing can concerns about memory be checked appropriately.

Remediating Memory Problems

Support programs can be designed for people to help them remember. Sometimes, people like Rocio who are experiencing normal age-related memory changes need extra help because of the high memory demands they face. At other times, people need help because the memory changes they are experiencing are greater than normal.

Camp et al. (1993; Camp, 2001; Malone & Camp, 2007) developed the E-I-E-I-O framework to handle both situations. The E-I-E-I-O framework combines the two primary types of memory: explicit and implicit, the first E-I pair. The framework also includes two types of memory aids that form the second E-I pair. **External aids** *are memory aids that rely on environmental resources, such as notebooks or calendars.* **Internal aids** *are memory aids that rely on mental processes, such as imagery.* The "aha" experience that comes with suddenly remembering something (i.e., "Oh, now I remember!") is the O that follows these Es and Is. As you can see in Figure 14.11, the E-I-E-I-O framework allows different types of memory to be combined with different types of memory aids to provide a range of intervention options that help people remember.

In general, explicit–external interventions are most frequently used to remediate the kinds of memory problems that older adults face, probably because such methods are easy to use and widely available (Berry et al., 2010). For example, virtually everyone owns either a smart phone or an address book in which they store addresses and phone numbers, and a pillbox divided into compartments corresponding to days of the week and times of the day is an effective way to help people remember to take medications (Park, Morrell, & Shifren, 1999). Memory interventions like this can help older adults maintain their independence. Nursing homes also use explicit–external interventions, such as bulletin boards with the date and weather conditions or activities charts, to help residents keep in touch with current events.

Type of memory	Type of memory aid	
	External	Internal
Explicit	Appointment book	Mental imagery
	Grocery list	Rote rehearsal
Implicit	Color-coded maps	Spaced retrieval
	Sandpaper letters	Conditioning

FIGURE 14.11

The E-I-E-I-O model of memory helps categorize different types of memory and their aids.

external aids

memory aids that rely on environmental resources, such as notebooks or calendars

internal aids

memory aids that rely on mental processes, such as imagery

Creativity and Wisdom

Two additional aspects of cognition that have been examined for age-related differences are creativity and wisdom. Each has been the focus of stereotypes: creativity is assumed to be a function of young people, whereas wisdom is assumed to be the province of older adults. Let's see whether these views are accurate.

Creativity

What makes a person creative? Is it exceptional productivity? Does creativity mean having a career marked by precocity and longevity?

Researchers define creativity in adults as the ability to produce work that is novel, high in demand, and task appropriate (Sternberg & Lubart, 2001). Creative output, in terms of the number of creative ideas a person has or the major contributions a person makes, varies across the adult life span and across disciplines (Jones, 2010; Kozbelt & Durmysheva, 2007; Simonton, 1997, 2007). When considered as a function of age, the overall number of creative contributions a person has tends to increase through the 30s, peak in the early 40s, and decline thereafter. The age-related decline does not mean that people stop being creative, just that they produce fewer creative ideas than when they were younger (Dixon & Hultsch, 1999). Still, the age at which people made major creative contributions, such as research that resulted in winning the Nobel Prize, increased throughout the 20th century (Jones, 2010). In short, creativity never stops, as illustrated in the Real People feature.

Exciting new neuroimaging research is supporting previous research that a person's most innovative contribution tends to happen most often during the 30s or 40s, as well as showing that a creative person's brain is different. This new research shows that white matter brain structures that connect distant brain regions, and coordinate the cognitive control of information among them, are related to creativity and are more apparent in a creative person (Jung et al., 2010; Takeuchi et al., 2010). This research supports the belief that creativity involves connecting disparate ideas in new ways, as different areas of the brain are responsible for processing different kinds of information. Because white matter tends to change with age, this finding also suggests that there are underlying brain maturation reasons for which innovative thinking tends to occur most often during late young adulthood and early middle age.

Wisdom

For thousands of years, cultures around the world have greatly admired people who were wise. Based on years of research using in-depth think-aloud interviews with young, middle-aged, and older adults about normal and unusual problems that

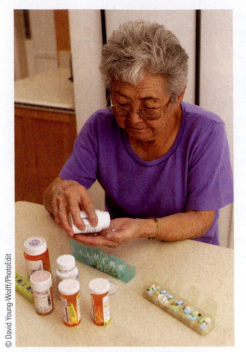

External memory aids such as pill organizers help people remember when certain medications need to be taken.

© David Young-Wolff/PhotoEdit

---

real People   APPLYING HUMAN DEVELOPMENT
CREATIVITY NEVER STOPS

Susan Perlstein has never believed that creativity stopped at a certain age. Rather, she believes that no matter how old you are, you need to be striving to reach your potential. For her, being creative is one of those potentials.

To help older adults reach their creative potential, Susan founded the National Center for Creative Aging (NCCA). The NCCA showcases the creative work of older adults through its blog, which includes works by older artists and photographers, among others,

and personal stories of ways in which older adults are creative.

Examples of people who found their creative expression through Susan's efforts abound. Among them are numerous older military veterans who started painting in later life. The NCCA also showcases active, creative people, such as women who returned to complete their education. In one case, a woman returned at age 52 as a young widow to complete her degree and worked to educate the

military about human sexuality through the 1990s. She was reelected to her city council at age 78 (for a fifth term), works out with her Wii, and enjoys living with her daughter, son-in-law, and grandchildren.

Susan's efforts to promote creative aging remind us that although the quantity of creative output may decrease, the fact of creative output never ends. So no matter how old you are, you can, and should, be creative in some way.

people face, Baltes and colleagues (Ardelt, 2010; Baltes & Staudinger, 2000; Scheibe, Kunzmann, & Baltes, 2007) describe four characteristics of wisdom:

- Wisdom deals with important or difficult matters of life and the human condition.
- Wisdom is truly "superior" knowledge, judgment, and advice.
- Wisdom is knowledge with extraordinary scope, depth, and balance that is applicable to specific situations.
- Wisdom, when used, is well intended and combines mind and virtue (character).

Researchers have used this framework to discover that people who are wise are experts in the basic issues in life (Ardelt, 2010; Baltes & Staudinger, 2000). Wise people know a great deal about how to conduct life, how to interpret life events, and what life means. Kunz (2007) refers to this as the strengths, knowledge, and understanding learned only by living through the earlier stages of life.

Research studies indicate that, contrary to what many people expect, there is no association between age and wisdom (Ardelt, 2010; Baltes & Staudinger, 2000; De Andrade, 2000; Hartman, 2001). As envisioned by Baltes and colleagues, whether a person is wise depends on whether he or she has extensive life experience with the type of problem given and has the requisite cognitive abilities and personality. Thus, wisdom could be related to crystallized intelligence, knowledge that builds over time and through experience (Ardelt, 2010).

So what specific factors help someone become wise? Baltes (1993) identified three factors: (1) general personal conditions, such as mental ability; (2) specific expertise conditions, such as mentoring or practice; and (3) facilitative life contexts, such as education or leadership experience. Personal growth during adulthood, reflecting Erik Erikson's concepts of generativity and integrity, also helps foster the process, as do facing and dealing with life crises (Ardelt, 2010). All of these factors take time. Thus, although growing old is no guarantee of wisdom, it does provide the time that, if used well, creates a supportive context for developing wisdom.

Test Yourself

Recall

1. One universal factor regarding information processing and aging is the slowing of _____.
2. The two types of explicit memory are _____.
3. Three factors that help a person become wise are general personal conditions, special expertise conditions, and _____.

Interpret

- How would the view that wisdom involves life experience fit into the discussion of expertise in Chapter 13?
- How might normative changes in memory affect sense of self?

Apply

- If you were to design a training program for older drivers, what elements would you include?
- If you were an attorney, what would concern you about normative changes in memory?

Recall answers: (1) psychomotor speed, (2) episodic and semantic, (3) facilitative life contexts

LEARNING OBJECTIVES

- How does depression in older adults differ from depression in younger adults? How is it diagnosed and treated?

- What is Alzheimer's disease? How is it diagnosed and managed? What causes it?

Mary lived by herself for 30 years after her husband died. For all but the last 5 years or so, she managed well. Little by little, family members and friends began noticing that Mary wasn't behaving quite right. For example, her memory slipped, she sounded confused sometimes, and her moods changed without warning. Her appearance deteriorated. Some of her friends attribute these changes to the fact that Mary is in her 80s. But others wonder whether this is something more than normal aging.

Suppose Mary is a relative of yours. How would you deal with the situation? How would you decide whether her behavior is normal? What would you do to try to improve Mary's life?

Every day, families turn to mental health professionals for help in dealing with the psychological problems of their aging relatives. Unfortunately, myths interfere with appropriate mental health diagnoses and interventions for older adults. For example, many people mistakenly believe that nearly all older adults are depressed, demented, or both. When they observe older adults behaving in these ways, they take no action because they believe that nothing can be done.

In this section, we see that such beliefs are wrong. Only a minority of older adults have mental health problems, and most such problems respond to therapy.

Depression

Most people feel down or sad from time to time, perhaps in reaction to a problem at work or in a relationship. But does this mean that most people are depressed? How is depression diagnosed? Are there age-related differences in the symptoms examined in diagnosis? How is depression treated?

First, let's dispense with a myth: Contrary to the popular belief that most older adults are depressed, for healthy people the rate of severe depression *declines* from young adulthood to old age. The average age of onset is the early 30s (National Institute of Mental Health, 2010a), a fact that also holds cross-culturally (Chou & Chi, 2005).

How Is Depression Diagnosed in Older Adults?

Depression in later life is usually diagnosed on the basis of two clusters of symptoms that must be present for at least 2 weeks: feelings and physical changes. *As with younger people, the most prominent symptom of depression in older adults is feeling sad or down, termed* **dysphoria**. But whereas younger people are likely to label these feelings directly as "feeling depressed," older adults may refer to them as "feeling helpless" or in terms of physical health, such as "feeling tired" (Stoner, O'Riley, & Edelstein, 2010). Older adults are also more likely than younger people to appear apathetic and expressionless, to confine themselves to bed, to neglect themselves, and to make derogatory statements about themselves.

The second cluster of symptoms includes physical changes, such as loss of appetite, insomnia, and trouble breathing (Stoner, O'Riley, & Edelstein, 2010). In young people, these symptoms usually indicate an underlying psychological problem, but in older adults they may simply reflect normal, age-related changes. Thus, older adults'

dysphoria
feeling sad or down

physical symptoms of depression must be evaluated carefully (Whitbourne & Spiro, 2010). Memory problems are also a common long-term feature of depression in older adults (González, Bowen, & Fisher, 2008).

An important step in diagnosis is ruling out other possible causes of the symptoms, such as neurological disorders, medication side effects, metabolic conditions, and substance abuse (Stoner, O'Riley, & Edelstein, 2010; Whitbourne & Spiro, 2010). For many minorities, immigration status and degree of acculturation and assimilation matter (Jimenez et al., 2010). Finally, true clinical depression significantly impairs daily living (Stoner, O'Riley, & Edelstein, 2010).

Although rates of serious depression decline with age, depression remains a significant problem for many older adults.

What Causes Depression?

There are two main ideas about the causes of depression. One focuses on biological and physiological processes, particularly on imbalances of specific neurotransmitters. Because most neurotransmitter levels decline with age, some researchers believe that depression in later life is likely to be a biochemical problem (Ciraulo et al., 2011; Way, 2011). The general view that depression has a biochemical basis underlies current approaches to drug therapies, discussed later.

The second view focuses on psychosocial factors, such as loss and internal belief systems. It is how a person interprets a loss, rather than the event itself, that causes depression (Gaylord & Zung, 1987). *In this approach,* **internal belief systems**, *or what one tells oneself about why certain things are happening, are emphasized as the cause of depression.* For example, experiencing an unpredictable and uncontrollable event, such as the death of a spouse, may cause depression if you believe it happened because you are a bad person (Beck, 1967). People who are depressed tend to believe that they are personally responsible for all the bad things that happen to them, that things are unlikely to get better, and that their whole life is a shambles.

How Is Depression Treated in Older Adults?

Regardless of how severe depression is, people benefit from treatment, often through a combination of medication and psychotherapy (Ciraulo et al., 2011; Qualls & Layton, 2010). Medications work by altering the balance of specific neurotransmitters in the brain. *For severe cases of depression, medications such as* **selective serotonin reuptake inhibitors (SSRIs), heterocyclic antidepressants (HCAs), and monoamine oxidase (MAO) inhibitors** *can be administered.* SSRIs are the medication of first choice because they have the lowest overall side effects of any antidepressant. SSRIs work by boosting the level of serotonin, which is a neurotransmitter involved in regulating moods.

If SSRIs are not effective, the next family of medications is the HCAs. However, HCAs cannot be used if the person is also taking medications to control hypertension or has certain metabolic conditions. As a last resort, MAO inhibitors may be used. But MAO inhibitors cause dangerous, potentially fatal interactions with certain foods—such as cheddar cheese, wine, and chicken liver—containing tyramine or dopamine.

Either as an alternative to medication or in conjunction with it, psychotherapy is a popular approach to treating depression. Two forms of psychotherapy have been shown to be effective with older adults. *The basic idea in* **behavior therapy** *is that depressed people experience too few rewards or reinforcements from their environment.* Thus, the goal of behavior therapy is to increase the good things that happen and minimize the negative things (Lewinsohn, 1975). This is often accomplished by having people increase their activities; simply by doing more, the likelihood that something nice will happen is increased.

A second effective approach is **cognitive therapy**, *which is based on the idea that maladaptive beliefs or cognitions about oneself are responsible for depression.* From this

internal belief systems
what one tells oneself about why certain things are happening

selective serotonin reuptake inhibitors (SSRIs), heterocyclic antidepressants (HCAs), or monoamine oxidase (MAO) inhibitors
medications for severe depression

behavior therapy
a type of therapy based on the notion that depressed people experience too few rewards or reinforcements from their environment

cognitive therapy
a type of therapy based on the idea that maladaptive beliefs or cognitions about oneself are responsible for depression

© Tim Pannell/Corbis

perspective, those who are depressed view themselves as unworthy and inadequate, the world as insensitive and ungratifying, and the future as bleak and unpromising (Beck et al., 1979). In a cognitive therapy session, a person is taught how to recognize these thoughts and to reevaluate the self, the world, and the future more positively, resulting in a change in the underlying beliefs. Cognitive therapy is the psychotherapy approach of choice for older adults (Laidlaw, 2007).

The most important fact to keep in mind about depression is that it *is* treatable. Thus, if an older person behaves in ways that indicate depression, it is a good idea to have him or her examined by a mental health professional. A major health care problem in the United States is that less than 40% of adults of all ages receive minimally adequate treatment for depression (National Institute of Mental Health, 2010a).

Dementia: Alzheimer's Disease

Arguably the most serious age-related condition is **dementia**, *a family of diseases involving serious impairment of behavioral and cognitive functioning.* Of these disorders, Alzheimer's disease is the most common.

Alzheimer's disease can cause people to change from thinking, communicative humans to confused, bedridden people unable to recognize their family members and close friends. Because these symptoms can be so life-changing, the *fear* of Alzheimer's disease among healthy older adults—especially those who are married to or related to a person with Alzheimer's disease—is often a significant concern (Kaiser & Panegyres, 2007).

Millions of people have Alzheimer's disease, including such notable individuals as former U.S. President Ronald Reagan, who died from it in 2004, and Margaret Thatcher, former prime minister of the United Kingdom. About 5.3 million Americans have Alzheimer's disease, which cuts across ethnic, racial, and socioeconomic groups (Alzheimer's Association, 2010). The prevalence increases with age, rising from extremely low rates in the 50s to about half of all people age 85 and older. As the number of older adults increases rapidly over the next several decades, the number of cases is expected to roughly triple.

What Are the Symptoms of Alzheimer's Disease?

The key symptoms of **Alzheimer's disease** *are gradual declines in memory, learning, attention, and judgment; confusion as to time and place; difficulties in communicating and finding the right words; decline in personal hygiene and self-care skills; inappropriate social behavior; and changes in personality.* These classic symptoms may be vague and may occur only occasionally in the beginning with little behavioral impact, but as the disease progresses, the symptoms become more pronounced and are exhibited more regularly (Roberson, 2011). Wandering away from home and not being able to remember how to return increases. Delusions, hallucinations, and related behaviors develop and get worse over time. Spouses become strangers. Patients may not even recognize themselves in a mirror; they wonder who is looking back at them. *In its advanced stages, Alzheimer's disease often causes* **incontinence**, *loss of control of the bladder or bowels.* It may also result in a total loss of mobility. People with the disease eventually become completely dependent on others for care. At this point, many caregivers seek facilities, such as adult day-care centers, and other sources of help, such as family and friends, to provide a safe environment for the Alzheimer's patient while the primary caregiver is at work or needs to run basic errands.

The rate of deterioration in Alzheimer's disease varies widely from one patient to another but averages around 12 years from onset of symptoms, although progression usually is faster when onset occurs earlier in adulthood (Roberson, 2011). It is difficult to predict how long a specific patient will survive, which only adds to the stress experienced by the caregiver (Cavanaugh & Nocera, 1994).

dementia
a family of diseases involving serious impairment of behavioral and cognitive functioning

Alzheimer's disease
a disease marked by gradual declines in memory, attention, and judgment; confusion as to time and place; difficulties in communicating; decline in self-care skills; inappropriate behavior; and personality changes

incontinence
loss of bladder or bowel control

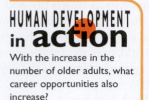

HUMAN DEVELOPMENT
in action

With the increase in the number of older adults, what career opportunities also increase?

How Is Alzheimer's Disease Diagnosed?

Despite intensive research to find specific indicators, certainty that a person has Alzheimer's disease cannot be achieved while the individual is alive (Roberson, 2011). Definitive diagnosis must be based on an autopsy of the brain after death, because the defining criteria for diagnosing Alzheimer's disease involve documenting large numbers of amyloid plaques and neurofibrillary tangles, structural changes in neurons that occur normally with age but occur in very large numbers and much earlier in Alzheimer's disease.

We are still left with the issue of figuring out whether a person probably has Alzheimer's disease while he or she is still alive. Although not definitive, the number and severity of behavioral changes lead clinicians to make fairly accurate diagnoses of probable Alzheimer's disease (Roberson, 2011). Several brief screening measures have been developed, with some, such as the 7-Minute Screen (Ijuin et al., 2008), showing about 90% accuracy. Greater accuracy depends on a broad-based and thorough series of medical and psychological tests, including complete blood tests, metabolic and neurological tests, and neuropsychological tests (Roberson, 2011). A great deal of diagnostic work goes into ruling out virtually all other possible causes of the observed symptoms. This effort is essential. Because Alzheimer's disease is an incurable, fatal disease, every treatable cause of the symptoms must be explored first. In essence, Alzheimer's disease is diagnosed by excluding all other possible explanations. A model plan for making sure the diagnosis is correct is shown in Figure 14.12.

In an attempt to be as thorough as possible, clinicians usually interview family members about their perceptions of the observed behavioral symptoms. Most clinicians view this information as critical to understanding the history of the difficulties the person is experiencing. However, research indicates that spouses are often inaccurate in their assessments of the level of their partner's impairment (McGuire & Cavanaugh, 1992). In part, this inaccuracy is due to lack of knowledge about the disease; if people do not understand or know what to look for, they are less accurate in reporting changes in their spouse's behavior. Also, spouses may wish to portray themselves as being in control, either by denying that the symptoms are severe or by exaggerating the severity to give the appearance that they are coping well in a difficult situation. Some spouses describe their partner's symptoms accurately, but family reports should not be the only source of information about the person's ability to function.

A great deal of attention has been given to the development of more definitive tests for Alzheimer's disease while the person is still alive. *Much of this work has focused on* **amyloid***, a protein that is produced in abnormally high levels in Alzheimer's patients, perhaps causing the neurofibrillary tangles and neuritic plaques described earlier.* Research is progressing toward developing a way to measure amyloid concentrations in cerebrospinal fluid and blood, but there is no definitive test as yet, especially in predicting later onset cases.

In 2011, a draft of revised diagnostic criteria was released for comment by professionals (Albert et al., 2011; Jack et al., 2011; McKhann et al., 2011; Sperling et al., 2011). The controversies around these revisions, along with recent research discoveries, are discussed in the Linking Research to Life feature at the end of the chapter.

What Causes Alzheimer's Disease?

We do not know for sure what causes Alzheimer's disease (Roberson, 2011). Currently, most research concentrates on identifying genetic links (Bekris et al., 2011) and the role of certain proteins, such as amyloid (Liu et al., 2012; Okonkwo et al., 2011; Roe et al., 2011). To understand the evidence better, we need to think about two general types of Alzheimer's disease: early onset (before age 60) and later onset (after age 60).

The early onset version tends to run in families. *It has an* **autosomal dominant inheritance** *in that the presence of certain genes means that there is a 100% chance of the person eventually getting the disease.* Familial Alzheimer's disease is linked to three causative genes: *APP, PSEN1,* and *PSEN2.* If you have one of these genes, symptoms always appear before age 60 and sometimes as early as the 30s or 40s.

amyloid
a protein that is produced in abnormally high levels in Alzheimer's patients

autosomal dominant inheritance
the presence of certain genes that means there is a 100% chance of the person eventually getting a disease such as Alzheimer's

FIGURE 14.12

Diagnosing Alzheimer's disease requires a thorough process of ruling out other possibilities.

Alzheimer's Association online document, developed and endorsed by the TriAD Advisory Board. Copyright 1996 Pfizer Inc. and Esai Inc. with special thanks to J. L. Cummings. Algorithm reprinted from TriAD, Three for the Management of Alzheimer's Disease.

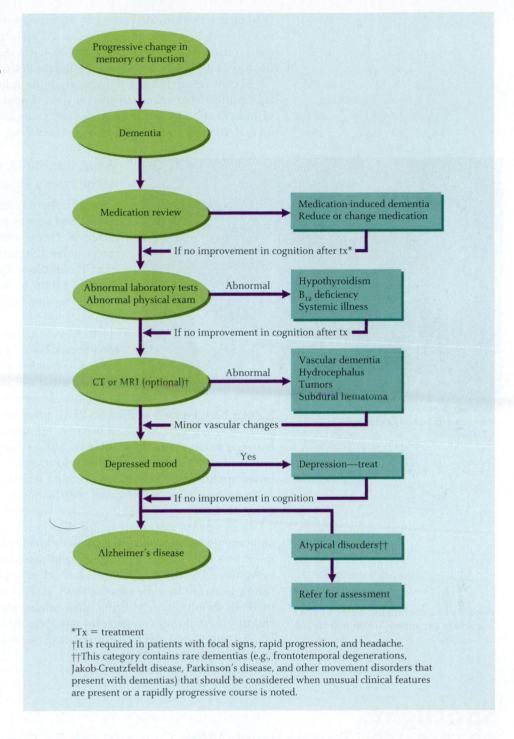

Progressive change in memory or function

Dementia

Medication review → Medication-induced dementia Reduce or change medication

If no improvement in cognition after tx*

Abnormal laboratory tests Abnormal physical exam — Abnormal → Hypothyroidism B$_{12}$ deficiency Systemic illness

If no improvement in cognition after tx

CT or MRI (optional)† — Abnormal → Vascular dementia Hydrocephalus Tumors Subdural hematoma

Minor vascular changes

Depressed mood — Yes → Depression—treat

If no improvement in cognition

Alzheimer's disease   Atypical disorders††

Refer for assessment

*Tx = treatment
†It is required in patients with focal signs, rapid progression, and headache.
††This category contains rare dementias (e.g., frontotemporal degenerations, Jakob-Creutzfeldt disease, Parkinson's disease, and other movement disorders that present with dementias) that should be considered when unusual clinical features are present or a rapidly progressive course is noted.

Later onset Alzheimer's disease may be linked to **risk genes**, *that is, genes that increase risk of getting the disease.* The most common later onset risk gene is the *APOE-e4* gene, which appears to be related to the formation of amyloid plaques (Kester, 2011). *APOE-e4* is one of three common forms of the *APOE* gene; the others are *APOE-e2* and *APOE-e3*. Everyone inherits a copy of some form of *APOE* from each parent. If you inherit *APOE-e4* from one parent, you have an increased risk of Alzheimer's disease. If you inherit *APOE-e4* from both parents, you have an even higher risk, but still it is not a certainty that you will get the disease. No one knows for sure yet how *APOE-e4* works.

Neuroimaging studies of people with Alzheimer's disease are providing supportive evidence of the structural changes caused by the genes identified so far

risk genes
genes that increase the risk of getting a disease such as Alzheimer's

(Risacher & Saykin, 2011). An important opportunity in this regard is the Alzheimer's Disease Neuroimaging Initiative (ADNI) that is following 800 people (200 with early onset Alzheimer's disease, 400 with mild cognitive impairment, and 200 healthy individuals as controls). All data discovered in the ADNI are made public.

Recent research has also focused on the role of tau protein, which appears to be transmitted from neuron to neuron and is found in high concentration in the neurons of individuals who die from Alzheimer's disease (Liu et al., 2012). This transmission across synapses could be the basis for new drug research.

Alzheimer's disease involves memory loss to an extent that may include forgetting the names of family members.

What Can Be Done for People With Alzheimer's Disease?

Currently, there is no effective treatment for Alzheimer's disease and no way to prevent it. The best we can do today is alleviate some symptoms. Most research is focused on drugs aimed at improving cognitive functioning. However, most medications approved by the U.S. Food and Drug Administration to date provide little relief over the long run, and few medications in development show promising results.

However, numerous behavioral and educational interventions have been developed. *One behavioral intervention, grounded in the E-I-E-I-O model discussed earlier, involves using the implicit–internal memory intervention called* **spaced retrieval**. Adapted by Camp and colleagues (Camp, 2001; Camp & McKitrick, 1991), spaced retrieval involves teaching people with Alzheimer's disease to remember new information by gradually increasing the time between retrieval attempts. This easy, almost magical technique has been used to teach names of staff members and other information, and it holds considerable potential for broad application. It is superior to other techniques (Haslam, Hodder, & Yates, 2011), and combining spaced retrieval with additional memory-encoding aids helps even more (Kinsella et al., 2007).

In designing interventions for those with Alzheimer's disease, the guiding principle should be optimizing the person's functioning. Regardless of the level of impairment, attempts should be made to help the person cope as well as possible with the symptoms. The key is helping all individuals maintain their dignity as humans. This can be achieved in some creative ways, such as adapting the principles of Montessori methods of education to bring older adults with dementia together with preschool children so that they can perform tasks together (Camp et al., 1997; Malone & Camp, 2007). One example of this approach is discussed in the Spotlight on Research feature.

spaced retrieval
a memory intervention based on the E-I-E-I-O approach that involves implicit memory and internal aids

---

Spotlight on research Training People With Dementia to Be Group Activity Leaders

Who were the investigators, and what was the aim of the study?
Dementia is marked by progressive and severe cognitive decline. But despite these losses, can people with dementia be trained to be group leaders? Most people might think the answer is "no," but Cameron Camp and Michael Skrajner (2005) decided to find out by using a training technique based on the Montessori method.

How did the investigators measure the topic of interest?
The Montessori method is based on self-paced learning and developmentally appropriate activities. As Camp and Skrajner point out, many techniques used in rehabilitation (e.g., task breakdown, guided repetition, and moving from simple to complex and concrete to abstract) and in intervention programs for people with dementia (e.g., use of external cues and implicit memory) are consistent with the Montessori method.

Continued

For this study, a program was developed to train group leaders for memory bingo (see Camp, 1999a, 1999b, for details about this game). Group leaders had to learn which cards to pick for the game, where the answers were located on the card, where to "discard" the used (but not the winning) cards, and where to put the winning cards. Success in the program was measured by research staff raters, who made ratings of the type and quality of engagement in the task shown by the group leader.

Who were the participants in the study?
Camp and Skrajner tested four people who had been diagnosed as probably having dementia who were also residents of a special care unit of a nursing home.

What was the design of the study?
The study used a longitudinal design so that Camp and Skrajner could track participants' performance over several weeks.

Were there ethical concerns with the study?
Having people with dementia as research participants raises important issues regarding informed consent. Because of their serious cognitive impairments, these individuals may not fully understand the procedures. Thus, family members such as a spouse or adult child caregiver are also asked to give informed consent. In addition, researchers must pay careful attention to participants' emotions; if participants become agitated or frustrated, the training or testing session must be stopped. Camp and Skrajner took all these precautions.

What were the results?
Results showed that at least partial adherence to the established game protocols was achieved at a very high rate. Staff assistance was not required for most game sessions for any leader. All leaders said that they enjoyed their role, and one recruited another resident to become a leader in the next phase of the project.

What did the investigators conclude?
It appears that people with dementia can be taught to be group activity leaders through a procedure based on the Montessori method. This is important because it provides a way for such individuals to become more engaged in an activity and to be more productive. Although more work is needed to continue refining the technique, applications of the Montessori method offer a promising intervention approach for people with cognitive impairments.

What converging evidence would strengthen these conclusions?
Camp and Skrajner studied only four residents; more evidence that the approach works with different types of people would bolster their conclusions. Although the Montessori method is effective for training people with dementia, the approach has not yet been demonstrated to be effective with other diseases that cause serious memory loss.

 Go to Psychology CourseMate at **www.cengagebrain.com** to enhance your understanding of this research.

One of the best ways to find out about the latest medical and behavioral research, and about the educational and support programs available in your area, is to contact your local chapter of the Alzheimer's Association. The chapter in your area will be happy to supply a range of educational material and information about local programs.

Test Yourself

Recall

1. Compared to younger adults, older adults are less likely to label their feelings of sadness as _____.
2. A form of psychotherapy that focuses on people's beliefs about the self, the world, and the future is called _____.
3. The only way to definitively diagnose Alzheimer's disease is through a _____.
4. Twisted fibers called _____ occur in the axon of neurons in people with Alzheimer's disease.

Interpret

- After reading about the symptoms of Alzheimer's disease, what do you think would be the most stressful aspects of caring for a parent who has the disease?

(You may want to refer to the section on caring for aging parents in Chapter 13.)

- Why is it important to differentially diagnose depression and Alzheimer's disease?

Apply

- If a friend asked you the difference between dementia and normative increases in forgetting that occur with age, what would you say?
- What programs should employers offer with regard to Alzheimer's disease?

Recall answers: (1) depression, (2) cognitive therapy, (3) brain autopsy, (4) neurofibrillary tangles

The diagnostic criteria for Alzheimer's disease currently in use were developed in 1984. Because a great deal of research has been done, resulting in considerably more knowledge about Alzheimer's disease, researchers and clinicians alike believe that the criteria are overdue for revision. In 2011, a draft of new criteria was released that took the roughly 30 years of research into consideration.

The draft criteria created considerable controversy. Research has indicated that Alzheimer's disease progresses through a series of stages, from a "preclinical" phase in which no symptoms can be detected, through mild cognitive impairment, to clinical Alzheimer's disease (Albert et al., 2011; Jack et al., 2011; McKhann et al., 2011; Sperling et al., 2011). In addition, the draft included a call

for biomarkers to be linked with the various categories. The main controversy concerned whether people should be diagnosed with a "preclinical" form of Alzheimer's disease, especially when there is no treatment and many people never go on to develop clinical Alzheimer's disease (Brickman, 2011).

Research has also clearly shown that abnormal levels of amyloid protein is associated with mild cognitive impairment (Rodrigue, Kennedy, & Park, 2009), but again, whether everyone with high levels of amyloid should have a diagnosis is controversial (Brickman, 2011). However, the recent research linking tau protein transmission across neurons offers hope that a drug or other effective therapy could be invented to prevent such transmission (Liu et al., 2012).

Summary

14.1 What Are Older Adults Like?

What are the characteristics of older adults in the population?

- The number of older adults is growing rapidly, especially the number of people over age 85. In the future, older adults will be more ethnically diverse and better educated than they are now.

How long will most people live? What factors influence this?

- Average life expectancy has increased dramatically in this century, mainly due to improvements in health care. Useful life expectancy refers to the number of years that a person is free from debilitating disease. Maximum life expectancy is the longest time any human can live.

- Genetic factors that can influence longevity include familial longevity and a family history of certain diseases. Environmental factors include acquired diseases, toxins, pollutants, and lifestyle.

- Women have a longer average life expectancy at birth than do men. Ethnic group differences are complex; depending on how old people are, the patterns of differences change.

14.2 Physical Changes and Health

What are the major biological theories of aging?

- There are two main groups of theories of biological aging. Programmed theories argue that aging is the result of a biological or genetic program. The damage or error theories include wear-and-tear theory, which postulates aging is caused by body systems simply wearing out, and cellular theories, which focus on reactions within cells that involve free radicals, cross-linking, and telomeres. No single theory is sufficient to explain aging.

What physiological changes normally occur in later life?

- Three important structural changes in the neurons are neurofibrillary tangles, dendritic changes, and neuritic plaques. These have important consequences for functioning because they reduce the effectiveness with which neurons transmit information.

- The risk of cardiovascular disease increases with age. Stroke and vascular dementia cause significant cognitive impairment, depending on the location of the brain damage.

- Older adults may suffer shortness of breath and face an increased risk of chronic obstructive pulmonary disease.

- Parkinson's disease is caused by insufficient levels of dopamine but can be effectively managed with levodopa.

- Age-related declines in vision and hearing are well documented. The main changes in vision concern the structure of the eye and the retina. Changes in hearing mainly involve presbycusis, reduced sensitivity to high-pitched tones.

What are the principal health issues for older adults?

- Older adults have more sleep disturbances than younger adults. Nutritionally, most older adults do not need vitamin or mineral supplements. Cancer risk increases sharply with age. The poorer health status of aging immigrants is largely due to communication problems and barriers to care.

14.3 Cognitive Processes

What changes occur in information processing as people age? How do these changes relate to everyday life?

- Older adults' psychomotor speed is slower than younger adults'. However, the amount of slowing is lessened if older adults have practice or expertise in the task.

- Sensory and information-processing changes create problems for older drivers. Working memory is another powerful explanatory concept for changes in information processing with age.

What changes occur in memory with age? What can be done to remediate these changes?

- Older adults typically do worse on tests of episodic recall; age differences are less on recognition tasks. The semantic and implicit memory classes are both largely unaffected by aging.

- Distinguishing memory changes associated with aging from memory changes due to disease should be accomplished through comprehensive evaluations.

- Memory training can be achieved in many ways. A useful framework is to combine explicit–implicit memory distinctions with external–internal types of memory aids.

What are creativity and wisdom? How do they relate to age?

- Research indicates that creative output peaks in late young adulthood or early middle age and declines thereafter, but the point of peak activity varies across disciplines and occupations.

- Wisdom has more to do with being an expert in living than with age per se. Three factors that help people become wise are personal attributes, specific expertise, and facilitative life contexts.

14.4 Mental Health and Intervention

How does depression in older adults differ from depression in younger adults? How is it diagnosed and treated?

- The key symptom of depression is persistent sadness. Other psychological and physical symptoms also occur,

but the importance of these depends on the age of the person reporting them.

- Major causes of depression include imbalances in neurotransmitters and psychosocial forces, such as loss and internal belief systems.

- Depression can be treated with medications (e.g., selective serotonin reuptake inhibitors, heterocyclic antidepressants, or monoamine oxidase inhibitors) and through psychotherapy, such as behavioral or cognitive therapy.

What is Alzheimer's disease? How is it diagnosed and managed? What causes it?

- Dementia is a family of diseases that cause severe cognitive impairment. Alzheimer's disease is the most common form of dementia.

- Symptoms of Alzheimer's disease include memory impairment, personality changes, and behavioral changes. These symptoms usually worsen gradually, with rates varying considerably among individuals.

- Definitive diagnosis of Alzheimer's disease can only be made following a brain autopsy. Diagnosis of probable Alzheimer's disease in a living person involves a thorough process by which other potential causes are eliminated.

- Most researchers are focusing on a probable genetic cause of Alzheimer's disease.

- Although Alzheimer's disease is incurable, various therapeutic interventions may improve the quality of the patient's life.

Key Terms

demographers (378)
population pyramid (378)
longevity (380)
average life expectancy (380)
useful life expectancy (381)
maximum life expectancy (381)
programmed theories (384)
wear-and-tear theory (384)
cellular theories (384)
free radicals (384)
cross-linking (384)
telomeres (384)
neurofibrillary tangles (385)
neuritic plaques (385)
stroke or cerebral vascular accident (CVA) (386)

transient ischemic attacks (TIAs) (387)
vascular dementia (387)
chronic obstructive pulmonary disease (COPD) (387)
Parkinson's disease (387)
presbyopia (387)
presbycusis (388)
circadian rhythm (390)
psychomotor speed or reaction time (393)
useful field of view (UFOV) (393)
working memory (394)
explicit memory (394)
implicit memory (394)
episodic memory (394)
semantic memory (394)
external aids (396)

internal aids (396)
dysphoria (399)
internal belief systems (400)
selective serotonin reuptake inhibitors (SSRIs), heterocyclic antidepressants (HCAs), and monoamine oxidase (MAO) inhibitors (400)
behavior therapy (400)
cognitive therapy (400)
dementia (401)
Alzheimer's disease (401)
incontinence (401)
amyloid (402)
autosomal dominant inheritance (402)
risk genes (403)
spaced retrieval (404)

Online Resources

Go to CengageBrain.com to access Psychology CourseMate, where you will find an interactive eBook, flashcards, quizzes, videos, websites, and more.

Social Aspects of Later Life

Psychosocial, Retirement, Relationship, and Societal Issues

15

What is it like to be an older adult? As we saw in Chapter 14, aging brings with it both physical limits and psychological gains. Old age also brings social challenges. Older adults are sometimes stereotyped as being marginal and powerless in society.

LEARNING OBJECTIVES
- What is continuity theory?
- What is the competence–environmental press model?

Since Sandy retired from her job as secretary at the local African Methodist Episcopal Church, she has hardly slowed down. She sings in the gospel choir, is involved in the Black Women's Community Action Committee, and volunteers one day a week at a local Head Start school. Sandy's friends say that she has to stay involved, because that's the only way she's ever known. They claim you'd never know that Sandy is 71 years old.

Understanding how people grow old is not as simple as asking someone how old he or she is, as Sandy shows. As Dennis the Menace notes, older adults are often marginalized in society. Psychosocial approaches to aging recognize these issues. And Sandy's life reflects several key points. Her level of activity has remained constant across her adult life. This consistency fits well in continuity theory, the first framework considered in this section. Her ability to maintain this level of commitment indicates that the match between her abilities and her environment is just about right, as discussed in competence–environmental press theory later in this section.

Dennis the Menace. © North America Syndicate. Reprinted with permission of Hank Ketcham Enterprises.

"WE HAVE A LOT IN COMMON, DON'T WE? I'M TOO YOUNG TO DO MOST EVERYTHING AND YOU'RE TOO OLD TO DO MOST EVERYTHING."

Continuity Theory

People tend to keep doing whatever works for them (Atchley, 1989). *According to* **continuity theory**, *people tend to cope with daily life in later adulthood by applying familiar strategies based on past experience to maintain and preserve both internal and external structures.* By building on and linking to their past life, change becomes part of continuity. Thus, Sandy's new activities represent both change (because they are new) and continuity (because she has always been engaged in her community). In this sense, continuity represents an evolution, not a complete break with the past.

Continuity can be either internal or external (Atchley, 1989). Internal continuity refers to a remembered inner past, such as temperament, experiences, emotions, and skills; in brief, it is personal identity. Internal continuity enables you to see that how you are now is connected with your past, even if your current behavior looks different. One of the most destructive aspects of Alzheimer's disease is that it destroys internal continuity as it strips away a person's identity.

External continuity concerns remembered physical and social environments, role relationships, and activities. For example, continuity theory provides a framework for understanding how social participation and volunteer activity in recently widowed older adults helps them maintain connections with people, sometimes over many years (Donnelly & Hinterlong, 2010).

There is considerable evidence that people in late life typically continue to engage in activities they did earlier in adulthood (Agahi, Ahacic, & Parker, 2006; Donnelly & Hinterlong, 2010). And within a broad continuity of activities, people strike out in some new directions; this is due in part to increased flexibility in their time and in part to emerging personal interests (Agahi, Ahacic, & Parker, 2006; Nimrod & Kleiber, 2007). This aspect of exploration has been called an innovation theory of successful aging (Nimrod & Kleiber, 2007). Innovation in such things as leisure activities helps preserve a sense of continuity (Nimrod & Hutchinson, 2010).

HUMAN DEVELOPMENT in action

If you were an activity therapist in a long-term care facility, how would you incorporate continuity theory into your activities for the residents?

continuity theory
a theory based on idea that people tend to cope with daily life in later adulthood by applying familiar strategies based on past experience to maintain and preserve both internal and external structures

Competence and Environmental Press

Understanding psychosocial aging requires a focus on the relation between person and environment (Wahl & Oswald, 2010). As discussed in Chapter 1, the competence–environmental press approach is a good example of a theory that incorporates elements of the biopsychosocial model into the person–environment relationship (Lawton & Nahemow, 1973; Nahemow, 2000; Wahl & Oswald, 2010).

Competence is defined as the upper limit of a person's ability to function in five domains: physical health, sensory–perceptual skills, motor skills, cognitive skills, and ego strength. These domains are viewed as underlying all other abilities and reflect biological and psychological forces. Environmental press refers to the physical, interpersonal, or social demands that environments put on people. Physical demands might include having to walk up three flights of stairs to your apartment. Interpersonal demands include having to adjust your behavior patterns to different types of people. Social demands include dealing with laws or customs that place certain expectations on people. These aspects of the theory reflect biological, psychological, and social forces. Both competence and environmental press change as people move through the life span; what you are capable of doing as a 5-year-old differs from what you are capable of doing as a 25-, 45-, 65-, or 85-year-old. Similarly, the demands put on you by your environment change as you age. Thus, the competence–environmental press framework reflects life-cycle factors as well.

The competence–environmental press model, depicted in Figure 15.1, shows how the two components are related. Low to high competence is represented on the vertical axis, and weak to strong environmental press is represented on the horizontal axis. Sections of the figure represent various combinations of the two. Most important, the shaded areas show that adaptive behavior and positive affect (emotion) can result from many combinations of competence and environmental press levels. **Adaptation level** *is the area where the press level is average for a particular level of competence; this is*

adaptation level
when the press level is average for a particular level of competence

FIGURE 15.1

The competence–environmental press model.

From "Ecology of the Aging Process," by M. P. Lawton and L. Nahemow. In The psychology of adult development and aging, *edited by C. Eisdorfer and M. P. Lawton. Copyright © American Psychological Association 1973.*

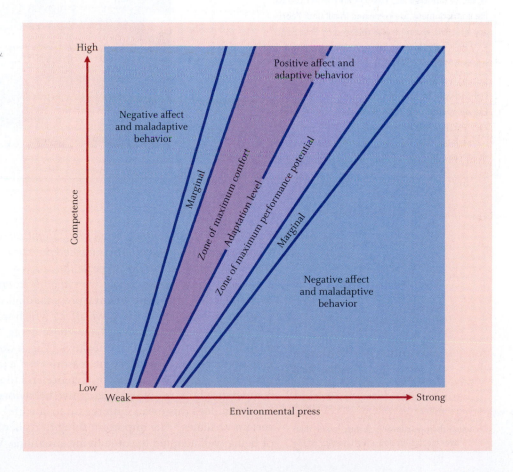

Few people have had the impact on their native country that Nelson Mandela has. Born July 18, 1918, Mandela was the first member of his family to attend a school, eventually earning his bachelor's degree at the University of South Africa. In 1948, he began his political career by opposing the Afrikaner-dominated National Party, which supported the apartheid policy of racial segregation. It was a decision that changed his life.

Mandela was initially dedicated to nonviolent opposition and was influenced by Mahatma Gandhi, who had begun his efforts at social activism in South Africa years earlier. However, after Mandela's arrest for treason in 1956, and his subsequent 5-year trial (he was acquitted), he changed his view about nonviolent opposition. The Sharpeville Massacre in 1960, in which 69 peaceful protesters were killed by South African police, convinced him that armed struggle was now necessary to overthrow the apartheid government. So in 1961 he formed the armed wing of the African National Congress and began a guerrilla campaign of sabotage against military and government targets.

Mandela was arrested again in 1962, convicted of sabotage and treason, and sentenced to life imprisonment. He remained in jail until February 11, 1990, when he was released by President F. W. de Klerk. During a speech right after his release, Mandela said his main focus was to bring peace to the black majority and give them the right to vote in both national and local elections. Between 1990 and 1994, he negotiated the first multiracial elections in South Africa's history.

Mandela was elected president and served from 1994 to 1999. He helped the country move from white minority apartheid rule to a multiracial model of government built on reconciliation. His support of the Springboks rugby team that won the 1996 world title was especially important and was the subject of the 2009 film *Invictus*.

Since his retirement in 1999, Mandela has remained politically active. He became an advocate for human rights organizations and has been active in the fight against AIDS. He has founded three organizations: the Nelson Mandela Foundation, the Nelson Mandela Children's Fund, and the Mandela Rhodes Foundation.

Mandela is a true world leader, a person who reshaped the history of his country. He shows continuity in his life through his political activity, as well as showing the match between competence and environmental press through his changing approach to situations across his life.

Nelson Mandela

© Gallo Images/Alamy

where behavior and affect are normal. Slight increases in press tend to improve performance; this area on the figure is labeled the **zone of maximum performance potential**. Slight decreases in press create the **zone of maximum comfort**, in which people are able to live happily without worrying about environmental demands. Combinations of competence and environmental press that fall within either of these two zones result in adaptive behavior and positive affect, which translate into a high quality of life.

As a person moves away from these areas, behavior becomes increasingly maladaptive and affect becomes negative. These outcomes also can result from several combinations and for different reasons. For example, too many environmental demands on a person with low competence and too few demands on a person with high competence both result in maladaptive behaviors and negative affect.

What does this mean with regard to late life? Is aging merely an equation relating certain variables? The important thing to realize is that each person has the potential of being well adapted to some living situations. Whether people are functioning well

zone of maximum performance potential
when the press level is slightly higher than average, tending to improve performance

zone of maximum comfort
when the press level is slightly lower than average, facilitating a high quality of life

depends on whether their abilities fit the demands of their environment. When their abilities match these demands, people adapt; when there is a mismatch, they don't.

Understanding how people age usually entails taking a broader perspective than any single theory can offer. The Real People feature about Nelson Mandela, a Nobel Peace Prize winner and world leader from South Africa, shows that both continuity theory and competence–environmental press theory are important.

Test Yourself

Recall

1. A central premise of _____ theory is that people make adaptive choices to maintain and preserve existing internal and external structures.

2. A person's ability to function in several key domains is termed _____, whereas demands put on a person from external sources are termed _____.

Interpret

- How does continuity theory incorporate aspects of the biopsychosocial model?

- How might competence and environmental press be used to understand an older adult's feelings of safety or insecurity?

Apply

- How would a new state law requiring older adults to pass a vision test before renewing their driver's license be an example of changes in environmental press?

- How might a nurse increase an older adult's feelings of competence?

Recall answers: (1) continuity, (2) competence, environmental press

---

Personality, Social Cognition, and Spirituality

LEARNING OBJECTIVES

- What is integrity in late life? How can people achieve it?

- How is well-being defined in adulthood? How do people view themselves differently as they age?

- What role does spirituality play in late life?

Olive is a spry 88-year-old who spends more time thinking and reflecting about her past than she used to. She also tends to be less critical now of decisions made years ago than she was at the time. Olive remembers her visions of the woman she wanted to become and concludes that she's come pretty close. She wonders whether this process of reflection is something that most older adults go through.

Think for a minute about the older adults you know. Do they see themselves as the same or different from the way they were in the past? In this section, we explore how people like Olive assemble the final pieces in the personality puzzle and see how important aspects of personality continue to evolve in later life.

Integrity Versus Despair

integrity versus despair
according to Erikson, the process in late life by which people try to make sense of their lives

As people enter late life, they begin the struggle of **integrity versus despair**, which involves the process by which people try to make sense of their lives. According to Erik Erikson

(1982), this struggle comes about as older adults like Olive try to understand their lives in terms of the future of their family and community. Thoughts of their own death are balanced by the realization that they will "live" on through children, grandchildren, great-grandchildren, and the community. This realization produces what Erikson calls a life-affirming involvement in the present.

The struggle of integrity versus despair requires people to engage in a **life review**, *the process by which they reflect on the events and experiences of their lifetimes.* To achieve integrity, a person must come to terms with the choices and events that have made his or her life unique. There must also be acceptance that life is drawing to a close. Research shows a connection between engaging in a life review and achieving integrity, so life review forms the basis for effective mental health interventions (Westerhof, Bohlmeijer, & Webster, 2010).

Who reaches integrity? Erikson (1982) emphasizes that people who demonstrate integrity have made many choices and follow many lifestyles; the point is that everyone has this opportunity to achieve integrity if they strive for it. Those who reach integrity become self-affirming and self-accepting; they judge their lives to have been worthwhile and good. They are glad to have lived the lives they did.

Well-Being and Emotion

How is your life going? Are you reasonably content, or do you think you could be doing better? *Answers to these questions provide insight into your* **subjective well-being**, *an evaluation of one's life that is associated with positive feelings.* Subjective well-being is usually assessed by measures of life satisfaction, happiness, and self-esteem (Oswald & Wu, 2010).

Overall, young-older adults are characterized by improved subjective well-being compared to earlier in adulthood (Charles & Carstensen, 2010). The differences in people's typical level of happiness across adulthood are illustrated in results from the United Kingdom, shown in Figure 15.2. These happiness-related factors hold across cultures as well; for example, a study of Taiwanese and Tanzanian older adults showed similar predictors of successful aging (Hsu, 2005; Mwanyangala et al., 2010).

Emotion-focused research in neuroscience is providing answers to the question of why subjective well-being tends to increase with age (Cacioppo et al., 2011). A brain structure called the amygdala, an almond-shaped set of nuclei deep in the brain, helps regulate emotion. Evidence is growing that age-related changes in how the amygdala functions may play a key role in understanding emotional regulation in older adults. Here's how: In young adults, arousal of the amygdala is associated with negative emotional arousal. When negative emotional arousal occurs, for example, memory for events associated with the emotion is stronger. But the situation is different for older adults—both amygdala activation and emotional arousal are lower. That may be one

life review
the process by which people reflect on the events and experiences of their lifetimes

subjective well-being
an evaluation of one's life that is associated with positive feelings

FIGURE 15.2
The pattern of a typical person's happiness through life.
From Happiness, health, and economics, by A. Oswald. Copyright © Warwick University. http://limechanica.org/files/andrew_oswald_presentation_071129.pdf.

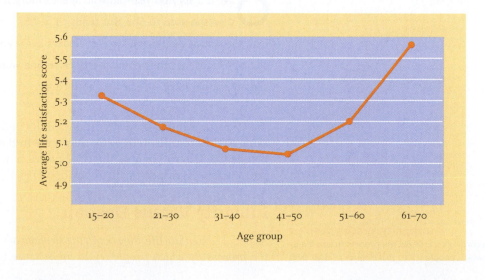

The Aging Emotional Brain

Who were the investigators, and what was the aim of the study?
Little research has examined the specific underlying neural mechanisms of emotion. Amy Winecoff and her colleagues (2011) decided to examine these mechanisms and discover whether they differed with age.

How did the investigators measure the topic of interest?
Winecoff and her colleagues used a battery of tests to measure cognitive performance and emotional behavior. They tested participants' immediate recall, delayed recall, and recognition. They also administered a response-time test to measure psychomotor speed and a digit-span test to measure working memory. The researchers also had participants complete three questionnaires to measure various types of emotions.

After these measures were obtained, participants were given the cognitive reappraisal task depicted in Figure 15.3. In brief, participants learned a reappraisal strategy that involved thinking of themselves as an emotionally detached and objective third party. During the training session, they told the experimenter how they were thinking about the image to ensure task compliance, but they were instructed not to speak during the scanning session. During the functional magnetic resonance imaging (fMRI) session, participants completed 60 positive image trials (30 "experience" and 30 "reappraise"), 60 negative image trials (30 "experience" and 30 "reappraise") trials, and 30 neutral image trials (all "experience"). Within each condition, half of the images contained people, and the other half did not. The fMRI session provided images of ongoing brain activity.

Who were the participants in the study?
The sample consisted of 22 younger adults (average age = 23 years, range = 19 to 33 years) and 20 older adults (average age = 69 years; range = 59 to 73 years). Participants were matched on demographic variables, including education. Participants received the cognitive, memory, and emotion tests on one day and the reappraisal task in the fMRI session on a second day. Participants were paid $55.

What was the design of the study?
The study used a cross-sectional design, with testing of two age groups over two sessions.

Were there ethical concerns with the study?
All participants provided written consent under a protocol approved by the Institutional Review Board of Duke University Medical Center.

What were the results?
Younger and older adults performed the reappraisal tasks similarly; that is, in the reappraisal condition, positive images were reported as less positive and negative images were reported as less negative. However, older adults' reports of negative emotion were higher than those of younger adults in the negative reappraisal situation.

Examination of the fMRI results showed that reappraisals involved significant activation of specific areas in the prefrontal cortex for both positive and negative emotions. For both age groups, activity in the

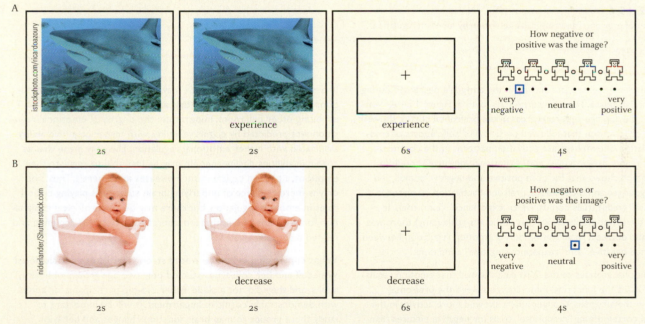

FIGURE 15.3

Cognitive reappraisal task. Participants were trained in the use of a reappraisal strategy for emotion regulation. (A) On "experience" trials, participants viewed an image and then received an instruction to experience naturally the emotions evoked by that image. The image then disappeared, but participants continued to experience their emotions throughout a 6-second delay period. At the end of the trial, the participants rated the perceived emotional valence of that image using an eight-item rating scale. (B) "Reappraise" trials had similar timing, except that the cue instructed participants to decrease their emotional response to the image by reappraising the image (e.g., distancing themselves from the scene). Shown are examples of images similar to those of the negative (A) and positive (B) images used in the study.

Source: Winecoff, A., LaBar, K. S. Madden, D. J., Cabeza, R., & Huettel, S. A. (in press). Cognitive and neural contributions to emotion regulation in aging. Social Cognitive and Affective Neuroscience, 6. By permission of Oxford University Press.

Continued

Continued

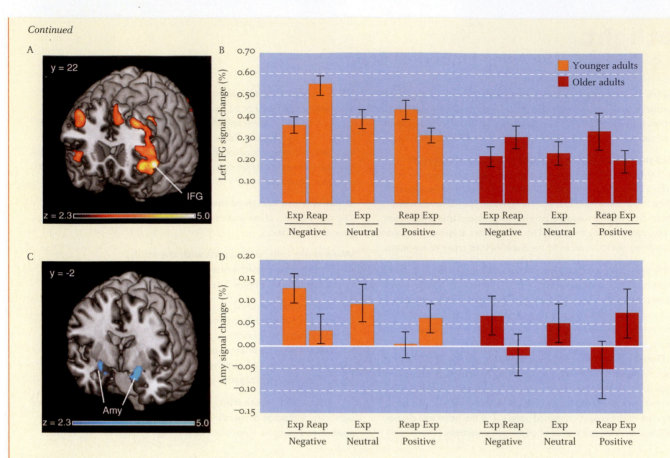

FIGURE 15.4

Modulation of prefrontal and amygdalar activation by emotion regulation.

Source: Winecoff, A., LaBar, K. S. Madden, D. J., Cabeza, R., & Huettel, S. A. (in press). Cognitive and neural contributions to emotion regulation in aging.
Social Cognitive and Affective Neuroscience, 6. By permission of Oxford University Press.

prefrontal area increased and activity in the amygdala decreased during the reappraisal phase. These patterns are shown in Figure 15.4. As you can see in the top figure, certain areas in the prefrontal cortex showed a pattern of activation that followed participants' self-reports of emotion regulation. Shown here are activation patterns in the contrast between "reappraise-negative" and "experience-negative" conditions. The top graph shows that for both positive and negative stimuli, and for both younger and older adults, prefrontal activation increased in "reappraise" (reap) trials compared to "experience" (exp) trials. In contrast, the lower graph shows that in the amygdala (amy) there was a systematic decrease in activation during emotion regulation between "experience-negative" and "reappraise-negative" conditions.

Additional analyses of the fMRI data showed that emotion regulation modulates the functional interaction between the prefrontal cortex and the amygdala. Younger adults showed more activity in the prefrontal cortex during "reappraise" trials for negative pictures than older adults did. Cognitive abilities were related to the degree of decrease in amygdala activation, independent of age.

What did the investigators conclude?

Winecoff and her colleagues concluded that the prefrontal cortex plays a major role in emotional regulation, especially for older adults.

In essence, the prefrontal cortex may help suppress (regulate) emotions in the same way in which that area of the brain is involved in inhibiting other behaviors. Importantly, the degree of emotional regulation was predicted by cognitive ability, with higher cognitive ability associated with higher emotional regulation. This may mean that as cognitive abilities decline, people may be less able to regulate their emotions, a pattern typical in such diseases as dementia. Thus, not only is there evidence of underlying brain structures playing critical roles in emotion regulation, but there may be a neurological explanation for the kinds of emotional outbursts that occur in dementia and related disorders.

What converging evidence would strengthen these conclusions?

Winecoff and her colleagues studied only two age groups of healthy adults, and they did not include either old-old participants or adults with demonstrable cognitive impairment. It will be important to study these groups to map brain function changes and behavior more completely.

 Go to Psychology CourseMate at **www.cengagebrain.com** to enhance your understanding of this research.

reason older adults experience less negative emotion, lower rates of depression, and better well-being (Cacioppo et al., 2011; Winecoff et al., 2011). But that's not the whole story. Neuroimaging research shows that changes in cognitive processing in the prefrontal cortex are also associated with changes in emotional regulation in older adults, as described in the Spotlight on Research feature.

Spirituality in Later Life

When faced with the daily problems of living, how do many older adults cope? Older adults in many countries use their religious faith and spirituality, often more than they use family or friends (Ai, Wink, & Ardelt, 2010). For some older adults, especially African Americans, a strong attachment to God is what they believe helps them deal with the challenges of life (Dilworth-Anderson, Boswell, & Cohen, 2007).

There is considerable evidence linking spirituality and health (Krause, 2006; Park, 2007). In general, older adults who are more involved with and committed to their faith have better physical and mental health than older adults who are not religious (Ai, Wink, & Ardelt, 2010). For example, older Mexican Americans who pray to the saints and the Virgin Mary regularly tend to have greater optimism and better health (Krause & Bastida, 2011).

When asked to describe ways of dealing with problems in life that affect physical and mental health, many people list coping strategies associated with spirituality (Ai, Wink, & Ardelt, 2010; White, Peters, & Shim, 2011). Of these, the most frequently used were placing trust in God, praying, and getting strength and help from God.

Researchers have increasingly focused on **spiritual support**—*which includes seeking pastoral care, participating in organized and nonorganized religious activities, and expressing faith in a God who cares for people*—*as a key factor in understanding how older adults cope.* Even when under high levels of stress, people who rely on spiritual support report greater personal well-being (Ai, Wink, & Ardelt, 2010; White, Peters, & Shim, 2011). Krause (2006) reports that feelings of self-worth are lowest in older adults who have little religious commitment, a finding supported by cross-cultural research with Muslims, Hindus, and Sikhs (Mehta, 1997).

These Buddhist monks' spirituality can serve as an important coping strategy.

When people rely on spirituality to cope, how do they do it? Older adults reported that turning problems over to God was a three-step process: (1) differentiating between things that can and those that cannot be changed, (2) focusing personal efforts on the parts of the problem that can be changed, and (3) emotionally disconnecting from those aspects of the problem that cannot be changed by focusing on the belief that God will provide the best outcome possible for those aspects (Krause et al., 2000). These findings show that reliance on spiritual beliefs helps people focus their attention on parts of a problem that may be under their control.

Reliance on religion in times of stress appears to be especially important for many African Americans, who as a group are more intensely involved in religious activities than are European Americans (Taylor, Chatters, & Levin, 2004; Troutman et al., 2011). They also are more likely to rely on God for support (Lee & Sharpe, 2007). Churches have historically offered considerable social support for the African American community and have served an important function in advocating social justice, and ministers play a major role in providing support in times of personal need (Chatters et al., 2011).

Similar effects of spirituality are observed in Asian and Asian American groups. For example, the risk of dying in a given year among the old-old in China was found to be 21% lower among frequent religious participants compared to nonparticipants, after their initial health condition was equated (Zeng, Gu, & George, 2011). Asian care-

HUMAN DEVELOPMENT in action

If you were part of a multidisciplinary support team, how would you include spirituality as part of an overall plan to help your clients cope with life issues?

spiritual support
a type of coping strategy that includes seeking pastoral care, participating in organized and nonorganized religious activities, and expressing faith in a God who cares for people

givers of dementia patients who are more religious report being able to handle the stresses and burden of caregiving better than nonreligious caregivers can (Chan, 2010).

Neuroscience research has shown a connection between certain practices and brain activity. For example, there is evidence that people who have practiced meditation show more organized attention systems and less activity in areas of the brain that focus on the self (Davidson, 2010; Lutz et al., 2009). Thus, neurological evidence indicates there may be changes in brain activity associated with spiritual practices that help people cope.

Health care and social service providers would be well advised to keep in mind the self-reported importance of spirituality in the lives of many older adults when designing interventions to help them adapt to life stressors. For example, older adults may be more willing to talk with their minister or rabbi about a personal problem than they would be to talk with a psychotherapist. Overall, many churches offer a wide range of programs to assist poor or homebound older adults in the community. Such programs may be more palatable to the people served than programs based in social service agencies. To be successful, service providers should try to view life as their clients see it.

Test Yourself

Recall

1. The Eriksonian struggle that older adults face is termed _____.

2. An evaluation of one's life that is associated with positive feelings is termed _____.

3. One of the most commonly reported methods for coping with life stress among older adults is _____.

Interpret

- How might different spiritual traditions influence personal well-being?

- How are normative changes in cognitive ability related to life review?

Apply

- If you were the activities director at a senior center, how would you incorporate Erikson's notion of life review?

- If you ran a health promotion program, how would you build a spirituality component into your programs?

Recall answers: (1) integrity versus despair, (2) subjective well-being, (3) religion or spiritual support

---

I Used to Work at . . . : Living in Retirement

LEARNING OBJECTIVES

- What does being retired mean?
- Why do people retire?

- How satisfied are retired people?
- How do retirees keep busy?

Marcus is a 77-year-old retired construction worker who labored hard all his life. He managed to save a little money, but he and his wife live primarily off of his monthly Social Security checks. Though not rich, they have enough to pay the bills. Marcus is largely happy with retirement, and he stays in touch with his friends. He thinks maybe he's a little strange, though, since he has heard that retirees are supposed to be isolated and lonely.

Did you know that until 1934, when a railroad union sponsored a bill promoting mandatory retirement, and 1935, when Social Security was inaugurated, retirement was not even considered a possibility by most Americans like Marcus (McClinton, 2010)? Only

Retirement provides many people with the opportunity to do things they want to do rather than things they must do.

since World War II has there been a substantial number of retired people in the United States (McClinton, 2010). Although we take retirement for granted, economic downturns have a major disruptive effect on people's retirement decisions and plans—after declining for decades, the number of people over age 65 still in the workforce has increased significantly (Sterns & Chang, 2010). As more people retire and take advantage of longer lives, a significant social challenge is created regarding how to fund retiree benefits and how to view older adults who are still very active (Bengtsson & Scott, 2011; McClinton, 2010; Tsao, 2004).

What Does Being Retired Mean?

Retirement means different things to people in different ethnic groups (Luborsky & LeBlanc, 2003; McClinton, 2010). Part of the reason it is difficult to define retirement precisely is that the decision to retire involves the loss of occupational identity (see Chapter 12), not what people may add to their lives. What people do for a living is a major part of their identity; we introduce ourselves as postal workers, teachers, builders, or nurses as a way to tell people something about ourselves. Not doing those jobs any more means that we either put that aspect of our lives in the past tense—"I used to work as a manager at the Hilton"—or say nothing. Loss of this aspect of ourselves can be difficult to face, so some look for a label other than "retired" to describe themselves.

That's why researchers view retirement as one of the many transitions people experience in life (Schlossberg, 2004; Sterns & Chang, 2010). This view makes retirement a complex process by which people withdraw from full-time participation in an occupation (Beehr & Bennett, 2007; Henretta, 2001), recognizing that there are many pathways to this end (Everingham, Warner-Smith, & Byles, 2007).

Why Do People Retire?

Provided that they have good health, more workers retire by choice than for any other reason (Ekerdt, 2010; McClinton, 2010; Sterns & Chang, 2010). Individuals usually retire when they feel financially secure after considering projected income from Social Security, pensions and other structured retirement programs, and personal savings. Some people are forced to retire because of health problems or because they lose their jobs. As corporations downsize during economic downturns or after corporate mergers, some older workers accept buyout packages involving supplemental payments if they retire. Others are permanently furloughed, laid off, or dismissed.

The decision to retire is influenced by occupational history and goal expectations (Brougham & Walsh, 2005; Ekerdt, 2010; McClinton, 2010). Whether people perceive that they will achieve their personal goals through work or retirement influences the decision to retire and its connection with health and disability.

Gender and Ethnic Differences

Women's experience of retiring can be quite different from men's (Everingham, Warner-Smith, & Byles, 2007; Frye, 2008). For example, women may enter the workforce after they have stayed home and raised children and in general have more discontinuous work histories; also, having fewer financial resources may affect women's decisions to retire. Women also tend to spend less time planning their retirement (Jacobs-Lawson, Hershey, & Neukam, 2004).

For women who were never employed outside the home, the process of retirement is especially unclear (Gardiner et al., 2007). Because they most likely were not paid for all of their work raising children and caring for the home, it is rare for them to have pensions or other sources of income in retirement. In addition, the work they have always done in caring for the home continues, often nearly uninterrupted.

HUMAN DEVELOPMENT in action

In the absence of mandatory retirement, what does the term "early retirement" mean to a human resources professional?

There has not been much research examining the process of retirement as a function of ethnicity. African American older adults are likely to continue working beyond age 65 (Troutman et al., 2011). However, there are no ethnic-based differences in health outcomes between African American women and men following retirement (Curl, 2007).

Adjustment to Retirement

How do people who go through the process of retirement adjust to it? Researchers agree on one point: New patterns of personal involvement must be developed in the context of changing roles and lifestyles in retirement (McClinton, 2010; Schlossberg, 2004). People's adjustment to retirement evolves over time as a result of complex interrelations involving physical health, financial status, the degree to which their retirement was voluntary, and feelings of personal control (Ekerdt, 2010; McClinton, 2010).

How do most people fare? As long as people have financial security, health, a supportive network of relatives and friends, and an internally driven sense of motivation, they report feeling good about being retired (Ekerdt, 2010; Stephan, Fouquereau, & Fernandez, 2007).

One widely held view is that being retired has negative effects on health. Research findings show that the relationship between health and retirement is complex. There is no evidence that voluntary retirement has any immediate negative effects on health (Weymouth, 2005). In contrast, there is ample evidence that being forced to retire likely leads to significant declines in physical and mental health (Donahue, 2007). Health issues are also a major predictor of when a person retires, as a longitudinal study in England showed (Rice et al., 2010).

Some retired adults take up hobbies to develop their creative side.

Keeping Busy in Retirement

Retirement is an important life transition, one that is best understood through a life-course perspective (see Chapter 1; McClinton, 2010; Schlossberg, 2004). This life change means that retirees must look for ways to maintain social integration and to be active in various ways.

For some people, being active means being employed, either part or full time. Employment may be a financial necessity for people without sufficient means to make ends meet, especially for those whose entire income would consist only of Social Security benefits. For others, the need to stay employed at least part time represents a way to stay connected with their former lives and careers.

The past few decades have witnessed a rapid growth of organizations devoted to offering such opportunities to retirees. Groups at the local community level, including senior centers and clubs, promote the notion of lifelong learning and help keep older adults cognitively active. Many also offer travel opportunities specifically designed for active older adults.

Healthy, active retired adults also maintain community ties by volunteering (Moen et al., 2000a, 2000b). Older adults report they volunteer for many reasons that benefit their well-being (Greenfield & Marks, 2005): to provide service to others, to maintain social interactions and improve their communities, and to keep active.

Why do so many people volunteer? Several factors are responsible (Tang, Morrow-Howell, & Choi, 2010): developing a new aspect of the self, finding a personal sense of purpose, desiring to share skills and expertise, redefining the nature and merits of volunteer work, creating a more highly educated and healthy population of older adults, and greatly expanding opportunities for people to become involved in volunteer work that they enjoy. Brown et al. (2011) argue that volunteerism offers a way for society to tap into the vast resources that older adults offer.

HUMAN DEVELOPMENT in action

What might the opportunity for more older adults to volunteer for organizations mean politically? Check your answer with the research data cited later in the chapter.

Some retired adults do volunteer work as a way to stay active.

© Mike Greenlar/The Image Works

Test Yourself

Recall

1. One useful way to view retirement is as a _____.
2. The most common reason people retire is _____.
3. Overall, most retirees are _____ with retirement.
4. Many retirees keep contacts in their communities by _____.

Interpret

- Why does forced retirement have a negative effect on health?
- How are cognitive development and retirement related?

Apply

- Using the information from Chapter 12 on occupational development, create a developmental description of occupations that incorporates retirement.
- How might you, a social worker, use a person's work history to provide therapy in long-term care settings?

Recall answers: (1) complex process by which people gradually withdraw from employment, (2) by choice, (3) satisfied, (4) volunteering

---

15.4 Friends and Family in Late Life

LEARNING OBJECTIVES

- What role do friends and family play in late life?
- What are older adults' marriages and same-sex partnerships like?

- What is it like to provide basic care for a partner?
- How do people cope with widowhood? How do men and women differ?

Alma was married to Charles for 46 years. Even though he died 20 years ago, Alma still speaks about him as if he had only recently passed away. Alma still gets sad on special dates—their anniversary, Charles's birthday, and the date on which he died. Alma tells everyone that she and Chuck, as she called him, had a wonderful marriage and that she misses him terribly even after all these years.

To older adults like Alma, the most important thing in life is relationships. In this section, we consider many of the relationships older adults have. Whether it is friendship or family ties, having relationships with others is what keeps us connected.

We have seen throughout this text how our lives are shaped and shared by the company of others. *The term* **social convoy** *is used to suggest how a group of people journeys with us throughout our lives, providing support in good and bad times.* People form the convoy, and under ideal conditions that convoy provides a protective, secure cushion that affirms people and permits them to explore and learn about the world (Antonucci, 2001; Luong, Charles, & Fingerman, 2011).

The size of an individual's social convoy and the amount of support it provides do not differ across generations. This strongly supports the conclusion that friends and family are essential aspects of all adults' lives. Social support is especially important in the African American and Mexican American immigrant communities, because these networks provide informal assistance for health-related and other issues (Miller-Martinez & Wallace, 2007; Warren-Findlow & Issel, 2010).

Siblings play an important role in the lives of older adults.

Friends and Siblings

By late life, some members of a person's social network have been friends for several decades. Research consistently finds that older adults have the same need for friends as do people in younger generations.

Friendships

The quality of late-life friendships is particularly important (Moorman & Greenfield, 2010; Rawlins, 2004). Having at least one close friend or confidant provides a buffer against the losses of roles and status that accompany old age, such as retirement or the death of a loved one, and can increase people's happiness and self-esteem (Moorman & Greenfield, 2010; Rawlins, 2004). Patterns of friendship among older adults tend to mirror those in young adulthood described in Chapter 11 (Rawlins, 2004). One major difference is that cross-sex friendships in late life are more important, especially for men whose male friendship network may have been depleted through death (Adams & Ueno, 2006; Moorman & Greenfield, 2010).

In general, older adults have fewer relationships and develop fewer new relationships than younger or middle-aged adults, and they do not replace friends lost through death or other reasons with people in younger generations (Moorman & Greenfield, 2010). This decline in numbers does not just reflect the loss of relationships; instead, the changes reflect a more complicated process (Carstensen, 1993, 1995). *This process, termed* **socioemotional selectivity**, *implies that social contact is motivated by many goals, including information seeking, self-concept, and emotional regulation.* Each of these goals is differentially relevant at different times and results in different social behaviors.

With time, older adults begin to lose members of their friendship network, usually through death. Loneliness matters a great deal in explaining the relationship between social network and life satisfaction for older adults (Gow et al., 2007). But newer cohorts of older adults have both more friends and more long-term friends on average than previous cohorts (Stevens & Van Tilburg, 2011).

Online friendship opportunities have been embraced by older adults. For example, Ledbetter and Kuznekoff (2012) found that some online gamers were young-older adults (about 25% of online gamers are over age 50). Regardless of age, heavy Internet users tend to have more friends online and offline than light users or nonusers of the Internet (Wang & Wellman, 2010). In addition, older adults use online services for finding friends that could lead to dating relationships (McIntosh et al., 2011).

social convoy
a group of people that journeys with us throughout our lives, providing support in good times and bad

socioemotional selectivity
the process by which social contact is motivated by many goals, including information seeking, self-concept, and emotional regulation

Sibling Relationships

Siblings constitute the longest-lasting relationships in most people's lives (Moorman & Greenfield, 2010). The importance of sibling relationships varies a lot within and across families, but such relationships are typically more important in late life than they were earlier in adulthood.

As social emotional selectivity theory would predict, sibling relationships provide a way for older adults to have close, emotionally based relationships because siblings have a long, shared past. Even though there are many grounds for good relationships among older siblings, closeness does not always occur. Sometimes siblings become rivals, even to the point of having hostile relationships. Older adult siblings whose lives took very different paths are the least likely to be close (Moorman & Greenfield, 2010).

Marriage and Same-Sex Partnerships

Older married couples show several specific characteristics (Moorman & Greenfield, 2010; O'Rourke & Cappeliez, 2005). Many older couples exhibit selective memory regarding the occurrence of negative events and perceptions of their partner. Like the older couple in the *For Better or Worse* cartoon, older couples typically have a reduced potential for marital conflict and greater potential for pleasure, are more likely to be similar in terms of mental and physical health than are younger couples, and show fewer gender differences in sources of pleasure. In short, most older married couples have developed adaptive ways to avoid conflict.

Being married in late life has several benefits. A study of 9,333 European Americans, African Americans, and Latino Americans showed that marriage helps people deal better with chronic illness, functional problems, and disabilities (Pienta, Hayward, & Jenkins, 2000). The division of household chores becomes more egalitarian after the

husband retires than it was when the husband was employed, irrespective of whether the wife was working outside the home (Kulik, 2001a, 2001b).

Little research has been conducted on long-term gay and lesbian partnerships (Moorman & Greenfield, 2010). Based on the available data, it appears that such relationships do not differ in quality from long-term heterosexual marriages (Connidis, 2001; O'Brien & Goldberg, 2000). Research on lesbians indicates they are flexible and adapt to the challenges they face, including social marginalization and discrimination (Averett & Jenkins, 2012).

Caring for a Partner

Francine and Ron are a couple who have tested the "in sickness and in health" part of their vows. After 42 years of mainly good times together, Ron was diagnosed as having Alzheimer's disease. When first contacted by researchers, Francine had been caring for Ron for 6 years. "At times it's very hard, especially when he looks at me and doesn't have any idea who I am. Imagine, after all these years, not to recognize me. But I love him, and I know that he would do the same for me. But, to be perfectly honest, we're not the same couple we once were. We're just not as close; I guess we really can't be."

Caring for a spouse can be both extremely stressful and highly rewarding.

Caring for a chronically ill partner presents challenges different from those of caring for a chronically ill parent. The partner caregiver is assuming a new role. Such change inevitably puts stress on the relationship (Cavanaugh & Kinney, 1994). Studies of spousal caregivers of people with Alzheimer's disease show that marital satisfaction is much lower than for healthy couples (Bouldin & Andresen, 2010; Dow & Meyer, 2010). Spousal caregivers report a loss of companionship and intimacy over the course of caregiving but also more rewards than do adult child caregivers (Raschick & Ingersoll-Dayton, 2004). Marital satisfaction is also an important predictor of spousal caregivers' reports of depressive symptoms: The better the perceived quality of the marriage, the fewer symptoms caregivers report (Dow & Meyer, 2010). Providing full-time care for a partner is both stressful and rewarding in terms of the marital relationship (Baek, 2005; Carbonneau, Caron, & Desrosiers, 2010). For example, coping with a wife who may not remember her husband's name, who may act strangely, and who has a chronic and fatal disease presents serious challenges even to the happiest of couples, as depicted in the *Doonesbury* cartoon. Yet even in that situation, the caregiving husband may experience no change in marital happiness, despite the changes in his wife due to the disease.

Widowhood

Like Alma and Chuck, virtually all older married couples will see their marriages end because one partner dies. For most people, the death of a partner is one of the most traumatic events they will ever experience, causing an increased risk of death among older European Americans (but not African Americans), an effect that lasts several years (Moorman & Greenfield, 2010). For example, an extensive study of widowed adults in Scotland showed that the increased likelihood of dying lasted at least 10 years (Boyle, Feng, & Raab, 2011). Despite the stress of losing one's partner, though, most widowed older adults cope reasonably well (Moorman & Greenfield, 2010).

Women are more likely to be widowed than are men. More than half of all women over age 65 are widows, but only 15% of men the same age are widowers. Women have longer life expectancies and typically marry men older than themselves. Consequently, the average married woman can expect to live at least 10 years as a widow.

The impact of widowhood goes well beyond the ending of a long-term partnership (Boyle et al., 2011; Guiaux, 2010). Loneliness is a major problem. Widowed people may be left alone by family and friends who do not know how to deal with a bereaved person. As a result, widows and widowers may lose not only a partner but also those friends and family who feel uncomfortable with including a single person rather than a couple in social functions (Guiaux, 2010). Feelings of loss do not dissipate quickly, as the case of Alma shows clearly.

Men and women react differently to widowhood. In general, those who were most dependent on their partners during the marriage report the highest increase in self-esteem in widowhood because they have learned to do the tasks formerly done by their partners (Carr, 2004). Widowers may recover more slowly unless they have strong social support systems (Bennett, 2010). Widows often suffer more financially because survivor's benefits are usually only half of their husband's pensions (Weaver, 2010). For many women, widowhood results in difficult financial circumstances, particularly regarding medical expenses (McGarry & Schoeni, 2005).

For many reasons, including the need for companionship and financial security, some widowed people cohabit or remarry. A newer variation on repartnering is "living alone together," an arrangement in which two older adults form a romantic relationship but maintain separate living arrangements (Moorman & Greenfield, 2010). Repartnering in widowhood can be difficult due to family objections (e.g., resistance from children), objective limitations (decreased mobility, poorer health, or poorer finances), absence of incentives common to younger ages (desire for children), and social pressures to protect one's estate.

Widowers are less likely than widows to form new friendships, continuing a trend throughout adulthood that men have fewer close friendships than women have.

Test Yourself

Recall

1. The longest relationship most people have is with their _____.

2. In general, older couples have reduced likelihood of _____.

3. Compared to noncaregiver spouses, marital satisfaction in spousal caregivers is _____.

4. _____ are at special risk of experiencing a drop in financial status following the death of their spouse.

Interpret

• Why would widows and widowers want to establish a new cohabitation relationship?

• How does the meaning of friendship change across the life span?

Apply

• If you were a marriage counselor, how would you incorporate the data on marital satisfaction among older couples in your work?

• If you were a nurse, how would you use a spousal caregiver in caring for a patient?

Recall answers: (1) siblings, (2) marital conflict, (3) lower, (4) Widows

LEARNING OBJECTIVES

- Who are frail older adults? How common is frailty?
- What housing options are there for older adults?
- How do you know whether an older adult is abused or neglected? Which people are most likely to be abused and to be abusers?

- What are the key social policy issues affecting older adults?

Older adults over age 85 are more likely to be frail and to need help with basic daily tasks.

© John Birdsall/The Image Works

frail older adults
adults who have physical disabilities, are very ill, and may have cognitive or psychological disorders

activities of daily living (ADLs)
basic self-care tasks such as eating, bathing, toileting, walking, and dressing

instrumental activities of daily living (IADLs)
actions that require some intellectual competence and planning

Rosa is an 82-year-old woman who still lives in the neighborhood in which she grew up. She has been in relatively good health for most of her life, but in the last year she has needed help with tasks, such as preparing meals and shopping for personal items. Rosa wants to continue living in her home. She dreads being placed in a nursing home, but her family wonders whether that might be the best option.

Our consideration of late life thus far has focused on the experiences of the typical older adult. In this final section, we consider people like Rosa, who need daily assistance. We also consider those who are abused or neglected. Finally, we conclude with an overview of the most important emerging social policy issues for older adults.

Frail Older Adults

Some older adults experience difficulties as they age. *They are the* **frail older adults** *who have physical disabilities, are very ill, and may have cognitive or psychological disorders.* These frail older adults constitute a minority of the population over age 65, but it is a proportion that increases with age.

Frail older adults are people whose competence (in terms of the competence–environmental press model presented earlier) is declining. They do not have one specific problem that differentiates them from their active, healthy counterparts; instead, they tend to have multiple problems (Crews, 2011). Given the rise in the population of older adults, the number of people who could be considered frail is increasing.

Assessing everyday competence consists of examining how well people can complete activities of daily living and instrumental activities of daily living (Crews, 2011). **Activities of daily living (ADLs)** *are basic self-care tasks such as eating, bathing, toileting, walking, or dressing.* A person could be considered frail if he or she needs help with one of these tasks. Other tasks are also deemed important for living independently. *These* **instrumental activities of daily living (IADLs)** *are actions that require some intellectual competence and planning.* Which actions constitute IADLs vary considerably from one culture to another and factor into cross-cultural differences in conceptions of competence (Sternberg & Grigorenko, 2004). For example, for most older adults in Western cultures, IADLs would include shopping for personal items, paying bills, making telephone calls, taking medications appropriately, and keeping appointments. In other cultures, IADLs might include caring for animal herds, making bread, threshing grain, and tending crops.

Prevalence of Frailty

As you can see in Figure 15.5, if you add together all people over age 65 who have some level of limitation, about 40% of people over age 65 report a functional limitation of some kind (Federal Interagency Forum on Aging-Related Statistics, 2010). As you can see in Figure 15.6, the percentage of people needing assistance increases with age, from 7.6% of people age 65 to 69 to 29.2% of those over age 80 (Brault, 2008).

FIGURE 15.5

Limitations in activities of daily living and instrumental activities of daily living, 2003–2007.

Source: Based on Limitations in Activities of Daily Living and Instrumental Activities of Daily Living, 2003-2007. Centers for Disease Control and Prevention.

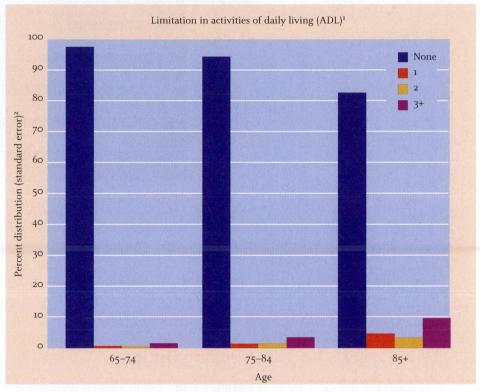

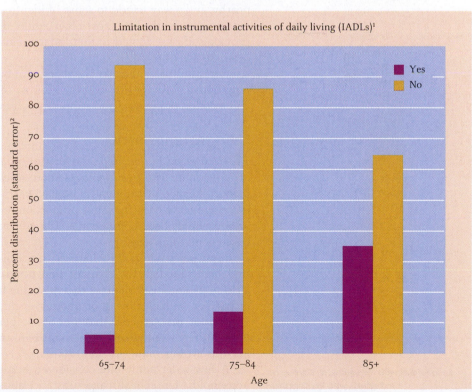

FIGURE 15.6

Prevalence of disability and the need for assistance by age, 2005.

From U.S. Census Bureau, Survey of Income and Program Participation, June–September 2005.

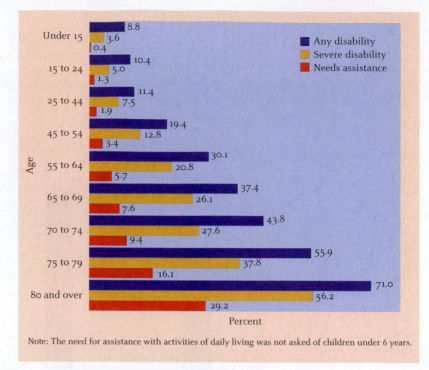

Note: The need for assistance with activities of daily living was not asked of children under 6 years.

In addition to basic assistance with ADLs and IADLs, frail older adults are also prone to higher rates of anxiety disorders and depression, especially if they are living in a long-term care facility (Qualls & Layton, 2010).

Housing Options

Having a stable home offers a place where things are familiar, a place with services nearby, and a way to add to sense of identity (Pynoos, Caraviello, & Cicero, 2010). Living independently, like most older adults do, provides a measure of their ability to provide self-care, rooted in their attachment to their home, and a way to fulfill their desire to age in place.

Communities must take the rising number of older adults into account when planning housing. As we just saw, the number of frail older adults is rising, so the design and location of housing and support services is a major issue.

Living Arrangements

The U.S. Census Bureau defines a **household** *as an individual who lives alone or a group of individuals who live together.* About one in every five households in the United States is headed by someone at least 65 years old (U.S. Census Bureau, 2011). Including those age 60 to 64 brings that proportion to one in every three. By 2015, the number of households headed by people 60 to 69 years old is expected to double as the baby boom generation ages.

Most older adults do whatever they can to adapt their homes and activities and thus accommodate the changes that occur with age (Pynoos, Caraviello, & Cicero, 2010). Despite the challenges that arise due to physical changes, the death of a spouse or partner, sudden illness, or another event, nearly all older adults report that their very strong preference is that they age in place. About half of adults over age 55 who thought they would likely need to move in with family or friends said they would not like this arrangement (Keenan, 2009).

A few older adults are considered homeless in that they are not members of a household. Mental health and substance abuse problems are much higher in homeless

household
an individual who lives alone or a group of individuals who live together

One way older adults can age in their own home is to renovate it to accommodate wheelchairs.

individuals, and the lack of adequate services, coupled with the increased number of people age 65 and older, is raising concerns that there may be a significant increase in the number of homeless older adults (Deutsch, 2010).

In general, older adults live in their own home or apartment, in an assisted living situation (a formal assisted living facility or a shared single-family home with family or friend), or in long-term care facilities. Which of these arrangements provides the optimal setting for a particular person depends on the person's functional health. **Functional health** *refers to the ability to perform the ADLs and IADLs discussed earlier in this section.* As a person's functional health diminishes, the level of supports needed from his or her environment increases, and the optimal housing situation changes. Let's take a closer look at each of the major types of housing to see how this works.

Independent Living Situations

Where one lives usually takes on special meaning. *A* **sense of place** *refers to the cognitive and emotional attachments that a person puts on their place of residence, by which a "house" is made into a "home."* Scheidt and Schwarz (2010) point out that a sense of place comprises an important part of people's identity. As a result, aging in their own home carries enormous psychological meaning for older adults.

Because aging in place is so important, there are many approaches to ensuring that this is at least a possibility. One common way of achieving this is through home modification, which can range from minor changes, such as replacing knobs on cabinets with pull handles that are more easily grasped, to extensive renovation, such as widening doorways and bathrooms to provide access for wheelchairs.

Assisted Living

Assisted living facilities *provide a supportive living arrangement for people who need assistance with ADLs or IADLs but who are not so impaired physically or cognitively that they need 24-hour care.* Estimates are that nearly two thirds of residents of assisted living facilities over age 65 have an ADL or IADL limitation (Federal Interagency Forum on Aging-Related Statistics, 2010) and about half have some degree of memory impairment (Pynoos, Caraviello, & Cicero, 2010). Assisted living facilities usually provide support for ADLs (e.g., assistance with bathing), as well as meals and other services. There are health care personnel to assist with medications and certain other procedures.

Assisted living facilities provide a range of services and care but are not designed to provide intensive, around-the-clock medical care. As residents become frailer, their needs may go beyond those the facility can provide. Policies governing discharge for this reason, usually to a long-term care facility, may result in competing interests between providing for the residents increasing medical needs and providing a familiar environment.

Long-Term Care Facilities

Long-term care facilities provide medical care 24 hours a day, 7 days a week by a team of health care professionals that includes physicians (who must be on call at all times), nurses, therapists (e.g., physical and occupational), and others. Misconceptions about long-term care facilities are common. Contrary to what some people believe, only about 5% of older adults in the United States live in a long-term care facility such as a nursing home. As you can see in Figure 15.7, the percentage of older adults who live in a long-term care facility at any given point in time increases from around 1% in those age 65 to 74 to about 15% of adults over age 85; however, over their lifetime,

functional health
the ability to perform ADLs and IADLs

sense of place
the cognitive and emotional attachments that a person puts on their place of residence, by which a "house" is made into a "home"

assisted living facilities
a supportive living arrangement for people who need assistance with ADLs or IADLs but who are not so impaired physically or cognitively that they need 24-hour care

FIGURE 15.7

Percentage of Medicare enrollees age 65 and older residing in selected residential settings by age group, 2007.

Data from Older Americans 2010: Key indicators of well-being, by Federal Interagency Forum on Aging-Related Statistics, p. 131. 2010.

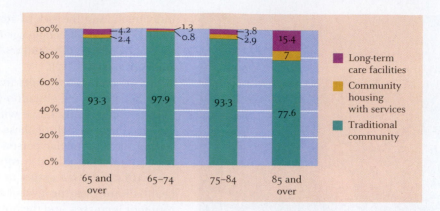

adults over age 65 have about a 50% chance of spending at least some time in a long-term care facility (Centers for Disease Control and Prevention, 2010a).

Who is the typical resident? She is very old, European American, financially disadvantaged (and eligible for Medicaid), probably widowed or divorced, and possibly without living children, and she has lived in the nursing home for more than a year (Centers for Disease Control and Prevention, 2010a).

The decision to place a family member in a long-term care facility is a difficult one (Caron, Ducharme, & Griffith, 2006) and often is made quickly in reaction to a crisis, such as a person's impending discharge from a hospital or other health emergency. The decision tends to be made by partners or adult children, a finding that generalizes across ethnic groups—especially when there is evidence of cognitive impairment (Almendarez, 2008; Caron, Ducharme, & Griffith, 2006).

Selecting a long-term care facility such as a nursing home should be done carefully. The Centers for Medicare and Medicaid Services of the U.S. Department of Health and Human Services provides a detailed *Nursing Home Quality Initiatives* website (U.S. Department of Health and Human Services, 2012). Among the most important things to consider are quality of life for residents (e.g., whether residents are well groomed, the food is tasty, and the rooms contain comfortable furniture), quality of care (e.g., whether staff members respond quickly to calls and whether staff and family members are involved in care decisions), safety (e.g., whether there are enough staff members and whether hallways are free of clutter), and other issues (e.g., whether there are outdoor areas for residents to use). These aspects of nursing homes reflect those dimensions considered by states in their inspections and licensing process.

The Eden Alternative, Green House Project, and Cohousing Initiatives

In response to the need to provide support for older adults who require assistance with ADLs and IADLs and to their desire to age in place, new approaches to housing options have emerged that provide both. These movements include programs that infuse a different culture into nursing homes, as well as those that create small-scale living (usually 6 to 10 residents) in a community-based setting with an emphasis on living well rather than on receiving care (Pynoos, Caraviello, & Cicero, 2010).

The Eden Alternative seeks to eliminate loneliness, helplessness, and boredom from the lives of those living in long-term care facilities and to create a community in which life is worth living. This can be achieved by rethinking how care is provided in the older person's own home or in long-term care facilities through training.

The Green House Project creates small neighborhood-integrated homes for 6 to 10 residents in which older adults receive a high level of personal and professional care. The Green House Project takes the principles of the Eden Alternative and creates a different culture of care in the community.

Various cohousing options provide another alternative approach. Cohousing is a planned community that is modest in size and built around an open, walkable space designed to foster social interaction among neighbors (Pynoos, Caraviello, & Cicero, 2010). Neighbors provide care for one another when it is needed. Personal autonomy is a core value for the people who create cohousing developments (Nusbaum, 2010).

These alternatives to traditional housing options for older adults indicate that the choices for how to spend late life and that assurance that appropriate support systems are in place are becoming more varied.

Elder Abuse and Neglect

Unfortunately, some older adults who need quality caregiving by family members or in other settings do not receive it. In some cases, older adults are treated inappropriately and experience elder abuse and neglect.

Defining Elder Abuse and Neglect

Like child abuse (see Chapter 7) and partner abuse (see Chapter 11), elder abuse has been extremely difficult to define precisely (Nerenberg, 2010). In general, researchers and public policy advocates describe seven categories of elder abuse (National Center on Elder Abuse, 2010b; Nerenberg, 2010):

- *Physical abuse.* The use of physical force that may result in bodily injury, physical pain, or impairment.

- *Sexual abuse.* Nonconsensual sexual contact of any kind.

- *Emotional or psychological abuse.* Infliction of anguish, pain, or distress.

- *Financial or material exploitation.* Illegal or improper use of an older adult's funds, property, or assets.

- *Abandonment.* Desertion of an older adult by an individual who had physical custody or otherwise had assumed responsibility for providing care for the older adult.

- *Neglect.* Refusal or failure to fulfill any part of a person's obligation or duties to an older adult.

- *Self-neglect.* Behaviors of an older person that threaten his or her own health or safety, excluding those conscious and voluntary decisions by a mentally competent and healthy adult.

Part of the problem in agreeing on definitions of elder abuse and neglect is that perceptions of what constitutes elder abuse differ among ethnic groups. Cultural values, such as multiple families sharing an older adult's pension, a group's history of oppression, or an unwillingness to report problems to strangers also create difficulties in understanding and preventing elder abuse across ethnic groups (Horsford et al., 2011; Nerenberg, 2010).

Prevalence

As many as 5 million older adults in the United States may be victims of elder abuse (National Center on Elder Abuse, 2010a), but only about one in every six cases comes to the attention of authorities. The most common forms are neglect (roughly 60%), physical abuse (16%), and financial or material exploitation (12%). Identification by professionals, such as physicians, of abuse or neglect is essential for understanding prevalence and getting victims help (Schulman & Hohler, 2012).

HUMAN DEVELOPMENT in action

If you were a social worker, what signs would you look for to detect elder abuse or neglect?

Risk Factors

Who is likely to be at risk for elder abuse? It's hard to say precisely; studies of risk factors in elder abuse have produced conflicting results. For example, there is evidence both that people living with others and that people living alone are at greater risk, depending on the nature of the living situation (National Center on Elder Abuse, 2010c; Nerenberg, 2010).

In roughly two thirds of elder abuse and neglect incidents, the abuser is a family member—typically the victim's partner or an adult child (National Center on Elder Abuse, 2010c). People who provide care (e.g., nursing home employees) or are in positions of trust (e.g., bankers, accountants, and attorneys) are also in a position to take advantage of an older adult (National Center on Elder Abuse, 2010c; Nerenberg, 2010). Telemarketing and Internet fraud against older adults is a growing problem (Barnard, 2010; Grimes et al., 2010). Why elder abuse occurs is a matter of debate and often conflicting data (National Center on Elder Abuse, 2010c). Nerenberg (2010) summarizes decades of research by pointing to several possible causes, all of which have some research support: external stresses (e.g., poverty and family problems), social isolation, dependency on the victim (usually financial dependency), retribution for spousal abuse, caregiver stress, potential financial gain, and feeling a sense of power or control.

Social Security and Medicare

The 20th century saw a dramatic improvement in the everyday lives of older adults in industrialized countries. Perhaps the most important gain was the creation of government-funded retirement programs such as Social Security (Polivka, 2010). Such programs have helped reduce the number of older adults below the poverty line; for example, in the 1950s, roughly 35% of older adults were below the federal poverty line compared to only about 10% today (Johnson & Wilson, 2010).

The aging of the baby boomers presents difficult and expensive problems (Office of Management and Budget, 2010). In fiscal year 2011, federal spending on Social Security and Medicare alone topped $1.2 trillion. As you can see in Figure 15.8, if spending patterns do not change, then by 2039 the expenditures for Social Security and Medicare alone are projected to consume roughly 12% of the U.S. gross domestic product, a 50% increase over rates in 2010. Without major reforms in these programs, such growth will force extremely difficult choices in how to pay for them.

Clearly, the political and social issues concerning benefits to older adults are quite complex. The first of the baby boomers became eligible for Medicare benefits in 2011 and full Social Security benefits in 2012, so action to ensure that these programs remain solvent is increasingly urgent. Let's look more closely at the Social Security and Medicare issues.

FIGURE 15.8

Cost of Social Security (blue line) and Medicare (purple line) as percentage of U.S. gross domestic product.

Adapted from 2012 annual report of the Boards of Trustees of the Federal Hospital Insurance and Federal Supplementary Medical Insurance Trust Funds. https://www.cms.gov/Research-Statistics-Data-and-Systems/Statistics-Trends-and-Reports/ReportsTrustFunds/downloads/tr2012.pdf, p. 22, and OASDI and HI annual income, cost, and balance as a percentage of GDP, http://www.ssa.gov/oact/tr/2012/lr6f4.html.

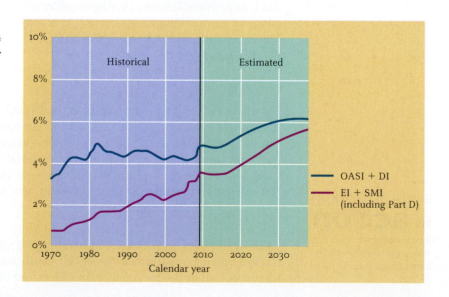

Social Security

Social Security began in 1935 as an initiative by President Franklin D. Roosevelt to "frame a law which will give some measure of protection to the average citizen and to his family against the loss of a job and against poverty-ridden old age" (Roosevelt, 1935). Thus, Social Security was originally intended to provide a supplement to savings and other means of financial support.

Over the years, revisions to the original law have changed Social Security to the point that now it represents the primary source of financial support after retirement for most U.S. citizens and the only source for many (Polivka, 2010). Since the 1970s, however, increasing numbers of workers have been included in employer-sponsored pension plans such as 401(k), 403(b), and 457 plans, as well as mutual funds and various types of individual retirement accounts (McGill et al., 2010; Polivka, 2010). These various retirement plans, especially savings options, plus financial pressure to reform Social Security, may force future retirees to use Social Security as the supplemental financial source for which it was intended, thereby shifting responsibility for retirement financial planning to the individual (Polivka, 2010).

The primary challenge facing Social Security is the aging of the baby boomers and the much smaller generation that follows. Because Social Security is not a savings account but is funded by current workers' payroll taxes, the amount of money each worker must pay depends on the ratio of the number of people paying Social Security taxes to the number of people collecting benefits. By 2030 this ratio will have been reduced by nearly half of what it was in 2010; that is, there will be nearly twice as many people collecting Social Security per worker paying into the system (Social Security Administration, 2011). Congress has not yet taken the actions necessary to ensure the long-term financial stability of the system. As discussed in the Linking Research to Life feature at the end of the chapter, the suggestions for doing this present difficult choices.

Medicare

Roughly 40 million U.S. citizens depend on Medicare for their medical insurance (Kaiser Family Foundation, 2010). To be eligible, a person must meet one of the following criteria: be over age 65, be disabled, or have permanent kidney failure. Medicare consists of four parts (Medicare.gov, 2011). Part A covers inpatient hospital services, skilled nursing facilities, home health services, and hospice care. Part B covers the cost of physician services, outpatient hospital services, medical equipment and supplies, and other health services and supplies, and part D provides some coverage for prescription medications. Part C, also called Medicare Advantage, is offered by private companies approved by Medicare, and includes all benefits of parts A and B, plus additional coverage (e.g., vision and dental) and usually part D.

Expenses relating to most long-term care needs are funded by Medicaid, another major health care program funded by the U.S. government and targeted to people who are poor. Out-of-pocket expenses associated with copayments and other charges are often paid by supplemental insurance policies, sometimes referred to as "Medigap" policies (Medicare.gov, 2011).

Like Social Security, Medicare is funded by a payroll tax. Hence, the funding problems facing Medicare are similar to those facing Social Security. Medicare costs have increased dramatically as a result of the rapidly increasing costs of health care.

Because Medicare is a government-run health care program, it continues to be controversial among those who oppose such approaches. But unlike Social Security, Medicare has already been subjected to significant cuts in expenditures, typically through reduced payouts to health care providers. Whether this practice will continue is unclear.

Taken together, the challenges facing society concerning older adults' financial security and health will continue to be major political issues throughout the first few decades of the 21st century. There are no easy answers, but open discussion of the various arguments will be essential for creating the optimal solution.

Test Yourself

Recall

1. ADLs include functioning in the areas of bathing, toileting, walking, dressing, and _____.

2. Most people who live in long-term care facilities are _____.

3. The people who most often abuse older adults are _____.

4. The two most important public policy issues in the United States that are being affected by the aging baby boom generation are Social Security and _____.

Interpret

- How might the large generation that graduated from high school in the early 2000s affect Social Security in the future?

- What mental health needs are most likely to be found in long-term care facilities?

Apply

- How would you design the various types of housing and nursing homes discussed in this section?

- If you were in Congress, how would you address the problems facing Social Security and Medicare?

Linking **Research to life** • SAVING SOCIAL SECURITY

Few political issues have been around as long and are as politically sensitive as those that concern making Social Security fiscally sound for the long term. The basic issues have been well known for decades: The present method for raising and distributing revenues in Social Security is not sustainable (Office of Management and Budget, 2010; Social Security Administration, 2011).

Because Social Security is based on current workers paying a tax to support current retirees, the looming funding problems depend critically on the worker-to-retiree ratio. As Figure 15.9 shows, this ratio has declined precipitously since Social Security began and will continue to decline until about 2030, when there will only be about two workers paying to support every beneficiary. This declining ratio places an increasing financial burden on workers to provide the level of benefits to retirees that people have come to expect. Because of this declining ratio, unless major structural changes are made, major reductions in

benefits would be required (Social Security Administration, 2011). So it's no wonder that young adults have little faith that Social Security will be there for them.

What steps can be taken to keep Social Security sound in the long term? For decades, U.S. presidents, Congress, and others have proposed numerous strategies (Polivka, 2010). Among the changes proposed over the years are the following.

- *Privatize the system.* Various proposals have been made for allowing or requiring workers to invest at least part of their money in personal retirement accounts managed either by the federal government or by private investment companies. A variation would take trust funds and invest them in private-sector equity markets. Another option would allow individuals to create personal accounts with a portion of the funds paid in payroll taxes.

FIGURE 15.9

Ratio of covered workers to Social Security beneficiaries, 2009 data.

From Ratio of covered workers to beneficiaries. http://www.ssa.gov/history/ratios.html.

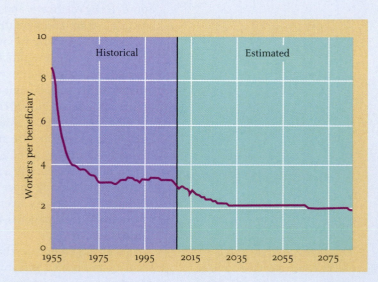

Continued

- *Institute means-test benefits.* This proposal would reduce or eliminate benefits to people with high incomes.
- *Increase the number of years used to compute benefits.* Currently, benefits are based on a person's history of contributions over a 35-year period. This proposal would increase that period to 38 or 40 years.
- *Increase the retirement age.* The age of eligibility for full Social Security benefits is increasing slowly from age 65 in 2000 to age 67 in 2027. Various proposals have been made to speed up the increase, to increase the age to 70, or to connect age at which a person becomes fully eligible to average longevity statistics.
- *Adjust cost-of-living increases downward.* Some proposals have been made to lower those increases given to beneficiaries that result from increases in the cost of living.
- *Increase the payroll tax rate.* One direct way to address the coming funding shortfall is to increase revenues through a higher tax rate.
- *Increase the earnings cap for payroll tax purposes.* This proposal would either raise or remove the cap on income subject to the Social Security payroll tax (the maximum taxable earnings for Social Security was $106,800 in 2011).
- *Make across-the-board reductions in Social Security pension benefits.* A reduction in benefits of 3 to 5% would resolve most of the funding problem.

None of these proposals has universal support. Many proposed solutions would significantly disadvantage certain people—especially minorities and older widows—who depend almost entirely on Social Security for their retirement income (Polivka, 2010). Given the political difficulties inherent in tackling the issue and the lack of perfect solutions, it is likely that Social Security will remain a major controversy.

Solving the funding problems facing Social Security will become increasingly important in the next few years. What do you think should be done to stabilize the system?

Summary

15.1 Theories of Psychosocial Aging

What is continuity theory?

- Continuity theory is based on the view that people tend to cope with daily life in later adulthood by applying familiar strategies based on past experience to maintain and preserve both internal and external structures.

What is the competence–environmental press model?

- According to competence–environmental press theory, people's optimal adaptation occurs when there is balance between their ability to cope and the level of environmental demands placed on them. When balance is not achieved, behavior becomes maladaptive.

15.2 Personality, Social Cognition, and Spirituality

What is integrity in late life? How can people achieve it?

- Older adults face the Eriksonian struggle of integrity versus despair primarily through a life review. Integrity involves accepting one's life for what it is; despair involves bitterness about one's past. People who reach integrity become self-affirming and self-accepting, and they judge their lives to have been worthwhile and good.

How is well-being defined in adulthood? How do people view themselves differently as they age?

- Subjective well-being is an evaluation of one's life that is associated with positive feelings. In life-span developmental psychology, subjective well-being is usually assessed by measures of life satisfaction, happiness, and self-esteem.
- Neuroscience research shows a developmental connection with brain activity in the prefrontal cortex and the amygdala.

What role does spirituality play in late life?

- Older adults typically use religion and spiritual support more often than they use friends or family to help them cope with problems of life. This is especially true for African Americans, but all ethnic groups use spiritual-based coping to some degree.

15.3 I Used to Work at . . . : Living in Retirement

What does being retired mean?

- Retirement is a complex process by which people withdraw from full-time employment. No single definition is adequate for all ethnic groups. An individual's decision to retire involves several factors, including eligibility for certain social programs.

Why do people retire?

- People generally retire because they choose to, although some people are forced to retire because of job loss or serious health problems, such as cardiovascular disease or cancer.

How satisfied are retired people?

■ Retirement is an important life transition. Most people are satisfied with retirement. Many retired people maintain their health, friendship networks, and activity levels.

How do retirees keep busy?

■ Most retired people stay busy in activities such as volunteer work and helping others. From a life-course perspective, it is important to maintain social integration in retirement. Participation in community organizations and volunteering are primary ways of achieving this.

15.4 Friends and Family in Late Life

What role do friends and family play in late life?

■ A person's social convoy is an important source of satisfaction in late life. Patterns of friendships among older adults are similar to those among young adults, but older adults are more selective. Sibling relationships are especially important in old age.

What are older adults' marriages and same-sex partnerships like?

■ Long-term marriages tend to be happy until one partner develops serious health problems. Older married couples show a lower potential for marital conflict and greater potential for pleasure. Long-term gay and lesbian relationships tend to be similar in characteristics to long-term heterosexual marriages.

What is it like to provide basic care for a partner?

■ Caring for a partner puts considerable strain on the spousal relationship. The degree of marital satisfaction strongly affects how spousal caregivers perceive stress.

How do people cope with widowhood? How do men and women differ?

■ Widowhood is a difficult transition for most people. Feelings of loneliness are hard to cope with, especially during the first few months following bereavement. Women tend to have more severe financial problems. Some widowed people remarry, partly to solve loneliness and financial problems.

15.5 Social Issues and Aging

Who are frail older adults? How common is frailty?

■ The number of frail older adults is growing. Frailty is defined in terms of impairment in activities of daily living (basic self-care skills) and instrumental activities of daily living (actions that require intellectual competence or planning). Many of those over age 85 may need assistance with such activities.

What housing options are there for older adults?

■ Most older adults prefer to stay in their community; home modification offers one option to achieve that. Assisted living facilities offer support for ADLs and IADLs while providing a significant degree of independence. Long-term care facilities such as nursing homes provide 24-7 medical care for those who need continual assistance. Newer alternatives include the Eden Alternative, the Green House Project, and cohousing options that focus on providing greater support for people to remain in their community.

How do you know whether an older adult is abused or neglected? Which people are most likely to be abused and to be abusers?

■ Abuse and neglect of older adults is an increasing problem. However, abuse and neglect are difficult to define precisely. Several categories are used, generally physical abuse, sexual abuse, emotional or psychological abuse, financial or material exploitation, abandonment, neglect, and self-neglect. Most perpetrators are family members, usually partners or adult children of the victims. Research indicates that abuse results from a complex interaction of characteristics of the caregiver and care recipient.

What are the key social policy issues affecting older adults?

■ Although initially designed as an income supplement, Social Security has become the primary source of retirement income for most U.S. citizens. The aging of the baby boom generation will place considerable stress on the system's financing.

■ Medicare is the principal health insurance program for adults in the United States over age 65. Cost containment is a major concern, and there are no easy answers for ensuring the system's future viability.

Key Terms

continuity theory (410)
adaptation level (411)
zone of maximum performance
potential (412)
zone of maximum comfort (412)
integrity versus despair (413)
life review (414)

subjective well-being (414)
spiritual support (417)
social convoy (422)
socioemotional selectivity (422)
frail older adults (426)
activities of daily living (ADLs) (426)

instrumental activities of daily living
(IADLs) (426)
household (428)
functional health (429)
sense of place (429)
assisted living facilities (429)

Online Resources

Go to CengageBrain.com to access Psychology CourseMate, where you will find an interactive eBook, flashcards, quizzes, videos, websites, and more.

The Final Passage

Dying and Bereavement

We have a paradoxical relationship with death. As French writer and reformer Duc François de La Rochefoucauld (1613–1680) wrote more than 300 years ago, looking into the sun is easier than contemplating our death. When death is personal, we become uneasy. And looking at the sun is hard indeed.

In this chapter, we delve into thanatology. **Thanatology** *is the study of death, dying, grief, bereavement, and social attitudes toward these issues.* We consider societal and personal perspectives of dying and bereavement.

LEARNING OBJECTIVES

- How is death defined?
- What legal and medical criteria are used to determine when death occurs?

- What are the ethical dilemmas surrounding euthanasia?

Greta, a college sophomore, was upset when she learned that her roommate's mother had died suddenly. Her roommate is Jewish, and Greta had no idea what customs would be followed during the funeral. When Greta arrived at her roommate's house, she was surprised to find all mirrors in the house covered. Greta realized for the first time that death rituals vary in different religious traditions.

Max Milligan/John Warburton-Lee Photography/Photolibrary/Getty Images

The symbols we use when people die, such as these caskets from Ghana, provide insights into how cultures think about death.

thanatology
the study of death, dying, grief, bereavement, and social attitudes toward these issues

Death seems a simple concept to define: It is the point at which a person is no longer alive. Similarly, dying is simply the process of making the transition from being alive to being dead. But death and dying are far more complicated concepts. As we see, Greta's experience reflects the many cultural and religious differences in the definition of death and the customs surrounding it.

Sociocultural Definitions of Death

What comes to mind when you hear the word *death?* A transition to an eternal reward? Flags at half-staff? A cemetery? Each of these represents a way that death can be considered in Western culture (Bustos, 2007; Penson, 2004). All cultures have their own views. Among Melanesians, the term *mate* includes the very sick, the very old, and the dead; the term *toa* refers to all other living people (Counts & Counts, 1985). In Ghana, people are said to have a "peaceful" or "good" death if the dying person finished all business and made peace with others before death (van der Geest, 2004).

Mourning rituals and states of bereavement also vary in different cultures (Lee, 2010; Rosenblatt, 2001). Some cultures have formalized periods during which certain prayers or rituals are performed. For example, after the death of a close relative, Orthodox Jews recite ritual prayers and cover all mirrors in the house. The men slash their ties as a symbol of loss. (These are the customs that Greta, the college student in the vignette, experienced.) In Papua New Guinea, there are accepted time periods for phases of grief (Herner, 2010). In the United States, the Muscogee Creek tribe's rituals include digging the grave by hand and giving a "farewell handshake" by throwing a handful of dirt into the grave before covering it (Walker & Balk, 2007). Ancestor worship, a deep, respectful feeling toward individuals from whom a family is descended or who are important to them, is an important part of customs of death in many Asian cultures (Roszko, 2010). We must keep in mind that the experiences of our culture or particular group may not generalize to other cultures or groups.

The many ways of viewing death can be seen in various customs involving funerals. You may have experienced a range of types of funerals, from small, private services to elaborate rituals. Variations in the customs surrounding death are reflected in some of the most iconic structures on earth, such as the pyramids in Egypt and the Taj Mahal in India.

Legal and Medical Definitions

Sociocultural approaches do not address a fundamental question: How do we determine that someone has died? The medical and legal communities have grappled with this question for centuries and continue to do so today.

Determining when death occurs has always been subjective. *For hundreds of years, people accepted and applied the criteria that now define* **clinical death***: lack of heartbeat and respiration. Today, however, the most widely accepted criteria are those that characterize* **whole-brain death***.* These criteria are as follows:

- No spontaneous movement in response to any stimuli
- No spontaneous respirations for at least 1 hour
- Total lack of responsiveness to even the most painful stimuli
- No eye movements, blinking, or pupil responses
- No postural activity, swallowing, yawning, or vocalizing
- No motor reflexes
- A flat electroencephalogram (EEG) for at least 10 minutes
- No change in any of these criteria when they are tested again 24 hours later

For a person to be declared dead, all eight criteria must be met. Moreover, other conditions that might mimic death—such as deep coma, hypothermia, or drug overdose—must be ruled out. Finally, according to most hospitals, the lack of brain activity must occur both in the brainstem, which involves vegetative functions such as heartbeat and respiration, and in the cortex, which involves higher processes such as thinking. In the United States, all 50 states and the District of Columbia use the whole-brain standard to define death.

A major problem facing the medical profession is to determine brain death in practice (Sung & Greer, 2011). This is partly because of variable intervals taken to make the second assessment that is required as the final item in the criteria listed previously (Lustbader et al., 2011). Because patients declared brain dead on first examination do not spontaneously recover brainstem function, and because long delays in second assessments lower the rate at which patients' families agree to organ donation, some medical professionals are calling for a single assessment or at least a simpler, more direct process (Sung & Greer, 2011).

Brain death is also controversial from some religious perspectives. For example, some Islamic scholars argue that brain death is not complete death; complete death must include the cessation of respiration (Bedir & Aksoy, 2011). Specifically, the Resolution of the Pan-Islamic Council Jurisprudence on Resuscitation Apparatus (1986) adopted a definition of death that is similar to the one currently used in the United States (Ebrahim, 1998). Based on this Resolution the legal definition of death in Islam was changed to:

> A person is pronounced legally dead and consequently, all dispositions of the Islamic law in case of death apply if one of the two following conditions has been established: (1) there is total cessation of cardiac and respiratory functions, and doctors have ruled that such cessation is irreversible; (2) there is total cessation of all cerebral functions and experienced specialized doctors have ruled that such cessation is irreversible and the brain has started to disintegrate. In this case, it is permissible to take the person off the resuscitation apparatus, even if the function of some organs e.g., heart, are still artificially maintained.

Roman Catholics focus on what they term "natural death" (Verheijde, 2010). That means that Catholics are encouraged to stipulate that if due to illness or injury death will occur with or without medical intervention, then no medical intervention should be used at all.

It is possible for a person's cortical functioning to cease while brainstem activity continues; this is a **persistent vegetative state***, from which the person does not recover.*

clinical death
the lack of heartbeat and respiration

whole-brain death
declared only when the deceased meets eight criteria related to movement, respiration, and responsiveness upon an initial test and again 24 hours later

persistent vegetative state
a situation in which a person's cortical functioning ceases while brainstem activity continues

This condition can occur following a disruption of blood flow to the brain, a severe head injury, or a drug overdose. A persistent vegetative state allows for spontaneous heartbeat and respiration but not for consciousness. The whole-brain standard does not permit a declaration of death for someone who is in a persistent vegetative state. Because of conditions like persistent vegetative state, family members sometimes face difficult ethical decisions concerning care for the individual.

Ethical Issues

An ambulance screeches to a halt, and emergency personnel rush a woman into the emergency room. As a result of an accident, she has no pulse and no respiration. The trauma team reestablishes a heartbeat, and a respirator is connected. An EEG and other tests reveal that she is in a persistent vegetative state. What should be done now?

This is an example of the kinds of problems faced in the field of **bioethics**, *the study of the interface between human values and technological advances in health and life sciences.* Bioethics grew from two bases: a respect for individual freedom and the impossibility of establishing any single version of morality by rational argument or common sense. Both of these factors are increasingly based on empirical evidence and cultural contexts (Holloway, 2011; Sherwin, 2011). In practice, bioethics emphasizes the importance of individual choice and the minimization of harm over the maximization of good. That is, bioethics requires people to weigh how much the patient will benefit from a treatment relative to the amount of suffering he or she will endure as a result of the treatment. Examples of the tough choices required are those facing cancer patients about aggressive treatment for cancer that is quite likely to be fatal in any case and those facing family members about whether to turn off a life-support machine that is attached to their loved one.

In the arena of death and dying, the most important bioethical issue is **euthanasia**— *the practice of ending life for reasons of mercy.* The moral dilemma posed by euthanasia becomes apparent when we try to decide the circumstances under which a person's life should be ended, which forces one person to place a value on another's life (Bedir & Aksoy, 2011; Elliott & Oliver, 2008; Verheijde, 2010). It also makes us think about the difference between "killing" and "letting die" at the end of life (Dickens, Boyle, & Ganzini, 2008). In Western society, this dilemma occurs most often when a person is being kept alive by machines or when someone has a terminal illness.

Euthanasia

Euthanasia can be carried out in two ways: actively and passively (Moeller, Lewis, & Werth, 2010). **Active euthanasia** *involves the deliberate ending of someone's life, which may be based on a clear statement of the person's wishes or be a decision made by someone else who has the legal authority to do so.* Usually, this involves situations in which people are in a persistent vegetative state or the end stages of a terminal disease. Examples of active euthanasia would be administering a drug overdose or ending a person's life through so-called mercy killing.

A second form of euthanasia, **passive euthanasia**, *involves allowing a person to die by withholding available treatment.* For example, a ventilator might be disconnected, chemotherapy might be withheld from a patient with terminal cancer, a surgical procedure might not be performed, or food could be withdrawn.

Some ethicists and medical professionals do not differentiate active and passive euthanasia. For example, the European Association of Palliative Care (2011) established an ethics task force opposing euthanasia, and the group claims that the expression "passive euthanasia" is a contradiction in terms because any ending of a life is by definition active. Despite these concerns, Garrard and Wilkinson (2005) conclude that there is no reason to abandon the category provided that it is properly and narrowly understood and provided that "euthanasia reasons" for withdrawing or withholding life-prolonging treatment are carefully distinguished from other reasons, such as family members not wanting to wait to divide the patient's estate. Still, whether there is a difference between active and passive euthanasia remains controversial (Busch & Rodogno, 2011).

bioethics
the study of the interface between human values and technological advances in health and life sciences

euthanasia
the practice of ending life for reasons of mercy

active euthanasia
the deliberate ending of someone's life

passive euthanasia
allowing a person to die by withholding available treatment

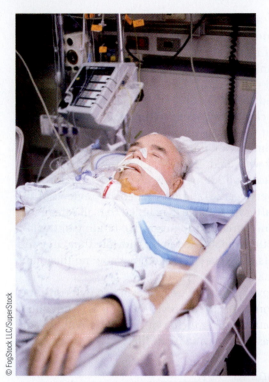

© FogStock LLC/SuperStock

Disconnecting life-support systems is a difficult bioethical issue.

HUMAN DEVELOPMENT in action

If you were a hospital counselor, how would you include cultural issues in your work with families grappling with ending the life of a loved one who is on life support?

Most Americans favor such actions as disconnecting life support in situations involving patients in a persistent vegetative state, withholding treatment if the person agrees or is already in the later stages of a terminal illness, and even the concept of assisted death. But feelings also run strongly against such actions for religious or other reasons (Bedir & Aksoy, 2011; Dickens, Boyle, & Ganzini, 2008; Verheijde, 2010).

Globally, opinions about euthanasia vary (Bosshard & Materstvedt, 2011). Opinions are often related to religious or political beliefs (Swinton & Payne, 2009). For example, Western Europeans tend to view active euthanasia more positively than residents of Eastern European and Islamic countries, who tend to be more influenced by religious beliefs that argue against such practices (Baumann et al., 2011; Góra & Mach, 2010; Nayernouri, 2011).

Disconnecting a life-support system is one thing; withholding nourishment from a terminally ill person is quite another for many people. Such cases often end up in court. The most widely publicized and politicized case of euthanasia in the United States involved Terri Schiavo, who died in Florida in 2005. This extremely controversial case involving the withdrawal of forced feeding had its origins in a disagreement between Terri's husband Michael, who said that Terri would have wanted to die with dignity and therefore the feeding tube should be removed, and her parents, who argued the opposite. The debate resulted in the involvement of government officials, state and federal legislators, and the courts. As discussed in the Linking Research to Life feature at the end of the chapter, such cases reveal the difficult legal, medical, and ethical issues, as well as the high degree of emotion, surrounding the topic of death with dignity.

Physician-Assisted Suicide

Taking one's own life has never been popular in the United States because of religious and other prohibitions. In other cultures, such as Japan, suicide is viewed as an honorable way to die under certain circumstances (Joiner, 2010).

But attitudes regarding suicide in certain situations are changing. *Much of this change concerns the topic of* **physician-assisted suicide**, *in which physicians provide dying patients with a fatal dose of medication that the patient self-administers.* A Harris Poll released in 2011 indicated that 70% of all adult respondents (and 62% of those over age 65) agreed that people who are terminally ill, in great pain, and have no chance of recovery should have the right to choose to end their lives. Only 17% of the respondents disagreed. By a margin of 58% to 20%, respondents supported physician-assisted suicide for such patients (Harris Interactive, 2011).

Several countries—including Switzerland, Belgium, and Colombia—tolerate physician-assisted suicide. In 1984, the Dutch Supreme Court eliminated prosecution of physicians who assist in suicide if five criteria are met:

- The patient's condition is intolerable with no hope for improvement.

- No relief is available.

- The patient is competent.

- The patient makes a request repeatedly over time.

- Two physicians have reviewed the case and agree with the patient's request.

The Dutch Parliament approved the policy in April 2001, making the Netherlands the first country to have an official policy legalizing physician-assisted suicide (Deutsch, 2001).

Voters in Oregon passed the Death With Dignity Act in 1994, the first physician-assisted suicide law in the United States, and I-1000 passed in Washington state in 2008, modeled after the Oregon law. These laws make it legal for people to request a lethal dose of medication if they have a terminal disease and make the request voluntarily. Although the U.S. Supreme Court ruled in two cases in 1997 (*Vacco v. Quill* and *Washington v. Glucksberg*) that there is no right to assisted suicide, the court decided in 1998 not to overturn the Oregon law.

physician-assisted suicide
the process in which physicians provide dying patients with a fatal dose of medication that the patient self-administers

The Oregon and Washington laws are more restrictive than the law in the Netherlands (Deutsch, 2001). Both laws provide for people to obtain and use prescriptions for self-administered lethal doses of medication. The law requires the physician to inform the person that he or she is terminally ill and to describe alternative options (e.g., hospice care and pain control), and the terminally ill person must be mentally competent and make two oral requests and a written one, with at least 15 days between each oral request. Such provisions are included to ensure that people making the request fully understand the issues and that the request is not made hastily.

Several studies have examined the impact of the Oregon law. The numbers of patients who received prescriptions and who died between 1998 and early 2011 are shown in Figure 16.1. Over the period, a total of 525 patients died under the terms of the law (Oregon Department of Human Services, 2012). Comprehensive reviews of the implementation of the Oregon law soon after its passage concluded that all safeguards worked and that such things as depression, coercion, and misunderstanding of the law were carefully screened (Orentlicher, 2000). Available data also indicate that Oregon's law has psychological benefits for patients, who are comforted by knowing they have this option (Cerminara & Perez, 2000).

There is no question that the debate over physician-assisted suicide will continue. As the technology to keep people alive continues to improve, the ethical issues about active euthanasia in general and physician-assisted suicide in particular will become more complex and will likely focus increasingly on quality of life.

Making Your End-of-Life Intentions Known

As has been clearly shown, euthanasia raises complex legal, political, and ethical issues. In most jurisdictions, euthanasia is legal only when a person has made known his or her wishes concerning medical intervention. Unfortunately, many people fail to take this step, perhaps because it is difficult to think about such situations or because they do not know the options available to them. But without clear directions, medical personnel may be unable to take a patient's preferences into account.

There are two ways to make intentions known. *In a* **living will**, *a person simply states his or her wishes about life support and other treatments. In a* **durable power of attorney for health care**, *an individual appoints someone to act as his or her agent for health care decisions.* A major purpose of both is to make wishes known about the use of life-support interventions in the event that the person is incapable of expressing them, along with other related end-of-life issues such as organ transplantation

living will
a document in which a person states his or her wishes about life support and other treatments

durable power of attorney for health care
a document in which an individual appoints someone to act as his or her agent for health care decisions

FIGURE 16.1
Number of Oregon Death With Dignity Act prescription (Rx) recipients and deaths, 1998–2011.

From Oregon's Death With Dignity Act—2011, by Oregon Department of Human Services, p. 1. Copyright © Oregon Public Health Division 2012.

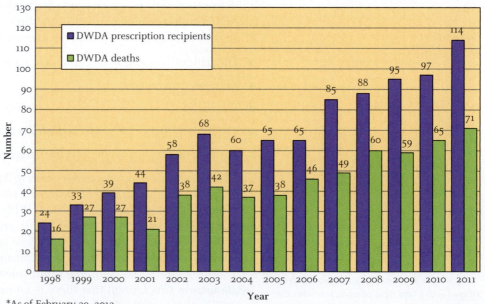

*As of February 29, 2012

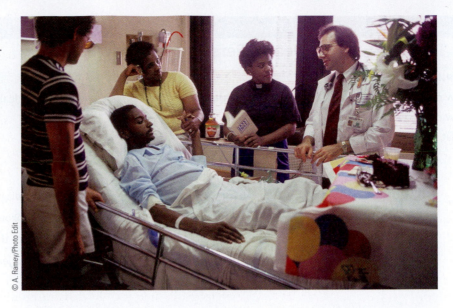

Frank discussions of end-of-life issues with patients and their families by health care workers provide a better context for handling these issues.

© A. Ramey/Photo Edit

(Baumann et al., 2011; Castillo et al., 2011). A durable power of attorney for health care has an additional advantage: It names an individual who has the legal authority to speak for the person if necessary.

Although there is considerable support for both mechanisms, there are several problems as well (Castillo et al., 2011). States vary in their laws relating to such advance directives. Many people fail to inform their relatives and physicians about their health care decisions. Others do not tell the person named in a durable power of attorney where the document is kept. This puts relatives at a serious disadvantage if decisions concerning the use of life-support systems need to be made.

A living will or a durable power of attorney for health care can be the basis for a "do not resuscitate" medical order. *A* **do not resuscitate (DNR) order** *means that cardiopulmonary resuscitation (CPR) is not started should the heart and breathing stop.* In the normal course of events, a medical team will immediately try to restore normal heartbeat and respiration. With a DNR order, this treatment is not done. As with living wills and durable powers of attorney, it is extremely important to let all appropriate medical personnel know that a DNR order is in effect.

do not resuscitate (DNR) order
a medical order that means CPR is not started should the heart and breathing stop

Test Yourself

Recall

1. Different funeral rituals are an example of the _____ definition of death.

2. The difference between brain death and a persistent vegetative state is _____.

3. Withholding an antibiotic from a person who dies as a result is an example of _____.

Interpret

- What is the difference between Oregon's Death With Dignity Act and active euthanasia?

- How is cognitive competence related to the validity of a living will or durable power of attorney for health care?

Apply

- If you were a bioethicist, how would you advise a hospital to handle patients who are in a persistent vegetative state?

- If you were an elected official, what input would you seek regarding a bill modeled after Oregon's Death With Dignity Act?

Recall answers: (1) sociocultural, (2) the brainstem still functions in a persistent vegetative state, (3) passive euthanasia

LEARNING OBJECTIVES

- How do feelings about death change over adulthood?
- How do people deal with their own death?
- What is death anxiety? How do people show it?
- How do people deal with end-of-life issues and create a final scenario?
- What is hospice?

Jean is a 72-year-old woman who was recently diagnosed with advanced colon cancer. She has vivid memories of her father dying a long, protracted death in great pain. Jean is afraid that she will have the same fate. She has heard that the hospice in town emphasizes pain management and provides a lot of support for families. Jean wonders whether this is something she should explore in the time she has left.

Like Jean, most people are uncomfortable thinking about their own death, especially if they think it will be unpleasant. In this section, we focus on two questions: (1) How do people's feelings about death differ with age? (2) What is it about death that we fear or that makes us anxious?

Before proceeding, however, take a few minutes to complete the following self-reflective exercise on death:

- In 200 words or less, write your own obituary. Be sure to include your age and cause of death. List your lifetime accomplishments. Don't forget to list your survivors.

- Think about all the things you will have done that are not listed in your obituary. List some of them.

- Think of all the friends you will have made and how you will have affected them.

- Would you make any changes in your obituary now?

A Life-Course Approach to Dying

It probably doesn't surprise you to learn that feelings about dying vary across adulthood. For example, adults of various ages who live with a person who has a life-threatening illness come to terms with death in an individual and a family-based way (Carlander, 2011).

Midlife is when most people in developed countries confront the death of their parents. Until that point, people tend not to think much about their own death. Once their parents have died, people realize that they are now the oldest generation of their family—the next in line to die. Probably as a result of this growing realization of their own mortality, middle-aged adults' sense of time changes from an emphasis on how long they have already lived to how long they have left to live, a shift that increases into late life (Cicirelli, 2006; Neugarten, 1969). This may lead to occupational change or other redirection, such as improving relationships that had deteriorated over the years.

Older adults are generally less anxious about death and more accepting of it than any other age group. In part, the greater overall acceptance of death results from the achievement of integrity, as described in Chapter 15.

Dealing With One's Own Death

Thinking about one's own death, like Jean is doing in the vignette, is often hard. Many authors have tried to describe the dying process, often using the metaphor of

Dealing with the death of friends is often especially difficult for young adults.

© DreamPictures/Blend/Glow Images

a trajectory that captures the period between onset of dying (e.g., from the diagnosis of a fatal disease) and death (Field & Cassel, 2010; Wilkinson & Lynn, 2001). These dying trajectories vary a great deal across diseases, as illustrated in Figure 16.2. Some diseases, such as some cancers (represented by the green line), have a clear and rapid period of decline. Other diseases, such as a series of cerebral vascular accidents (represented by the red line), have some periods of rapid decline followed by some recovery but result in gradual overall decline over time. A third situation, represented by the gold line, involves a long-term chronic condition that ends in death.

Kübler-Ross's Theory

Elisabeth Kübler-Ross (1926-2004) changed the way we approach dying. She described five reactions that represented the ways in which people dealt with death: denial, anger, bargaining, depression, and acceptance (Kübler-Ross, 1969). Although she believed that these five stages represent the typical range of emotional development in the dying process, Kübler-Ross (1974) cautioned that not everyone experiences all of them or progresses through them at the same rate or in the same order. Research supports the view that her "stages" should not be viewed as a sequence (Charlton & Verghese, 2010; Neimeyer, 1997).

FIGURE 16.2

The three main trajectories of decline at the end of life.

Source: Reproduced from Murray, SA. and Sheikh, A. (2008). Care for all at the end of life. Figure 1, the three main trajectories of decline at the end of life. British Medical Journal, 336;958-959. Reprinted with permission from BMJ Publishing Group Ltd.

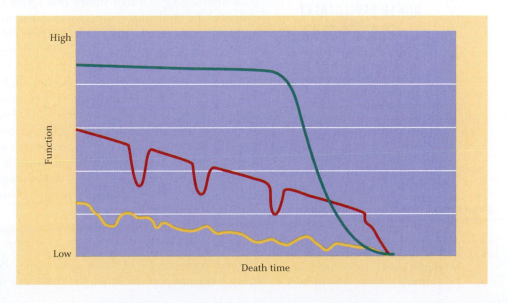

Bob Strong/Reuters/Landov

Facing death regularly often forces people to confront their death anxiety.

A Contextual Theory of Dying

There is no one right way to die, although there may be better or worse ways of coping (Corr, 1991–1992, 2010; Corr, Corr, & Nabe, 2008). A perspective that recognizes this approaches the issue from the mind-set of the dying person and the issues or tasks that he or she must face. Corr identified four dimensions of such tasks: bodily needs, psychological security, interpersonal attachments, and spiritual energy and hope. This holistic approach acknowledges individual differences and rejects broad generalizations. Corr's task approach also recognizes the importance of the coping efforts of family members, friends, and caregivers, as well as those of the dying person.

Kastenbaum and Thuell (1995) argue that the socioenvironmental context within which dying occurs, which often changes over time, must be recognized. For example, a person may begin the dying process living independently but end up in a long-term care facility. Such moves may have profound implications for how the person copes with dying. A contextual approach would provide guidance for health care professionals and families for discussing how to protect the quality of life, provide better care, and prepare caregivers for dealing with the end of life.

Death Anxiety

We have seen that how people view death varies with age. In the process, we encountered the notion of feeling anxious about death. **Death anxiety** *refers to people's anxiety or even fear of death and dying.* Death anxiety is tough to pin down; we cannot say what specifically about death is causing us to feel uneasy.

For nearly three decades, researchers have applied terror management theory as a framework to study death anxiety (Burke, Martens, & Faucher, 2010). **Terror management theory** *addresses the issue of why people engage in certain behaviors to achieve particular psychological states based on their deeply rooted concerns about mortality* (Arndt & Vess, 2008). The theory proposes that ensuring the continuation of one's life is the primary motive underlying behavior. Thus, death anxiety is a reflection of concern over dying, an outcome that would violate the prime motive.

Neuroimaging research shows that terror management theory provides a useful framework for studying brain activity related to death anxiety. Quirin et al. (2012) found that brain activity in the right amygdala, left rostral anterior cingulate cortex, and right caudate nucleus was greater when male participants were answering questions about fear of death and dying than when they were answering questions about dental pain.

Research on American and Canadian adults indicates that components of death anxiety included pain, body malfunction, humiliation, rejection, nonbeing, punishment, interruption of goals, being destroyed, and negative impact on survivors (Fortner & Neimeyer, 1999; Power & Smith, 2008). To complicate matters further, each of these components can be assessed at any of three levels: public, private, and nonconscious. That is, what we admit feeling about death in public may differ greatly from what we feel when we are alone with our own thoughts or what we feel subconsciously. In short, the measurement of death anxiety is complex, and researchers need to specify which aspects they are assessing.

Learning to Deal With Death Anxiety

Although some degree of death anxiety may be appropriate, we must guard against letting it become powerful enough to interfere with our normal daily routines. Perhaps

HUMAN DEVELOPMENT in action

If you were a health professional, how would understanding the components of death anxiety help you provide better care for dying patients?

death anxiety
people's anxiety or even fear of death and dying

terror management theory
a theory that addresses the issue of why people engage in certain behaviors to achieve particular psychological states based on their deeply rooted concerns about mortality

the one most often used ways to deal with death anxiety is to live life to the fullest. Adolescents are particularly likely to do this; research shows that teenagers, especially males, engage in risky behavior that is correlated with low death anxiety (Cotter, 2001).

Koestenbaum (1976) proposed several exercises and questions to increase death awareness. Some of these are to write your own obituary (like you did earlier in this chapter) and to plan your own death and funeral services.

These actions serve as a basis for an increasingly popular way to reduce anxiety: death education. Most death education programs combine factual information about death with issues aimed at reducing anxiety and fear. It is important to make education programs reflect the diverse backgrounds of the participants (Fowler, 2008). Research shows that participating in experiential workshops about death significantly lowers death anxiety in younger, middle-aged, and older adults and raises awareness about the importance of advance directives (Moeller, Lewis, & Werth, 2010).

Creating a Final Scenario

When given the chance, many adults like to discuss **end-of-life issues***: management of the final phase of life, after-death disposition of their body and memorial services, and distribution of assets* (Green, 2008; Kleespies, 2004). People want to manage the final part of their lives by thinking through the choices between traditional care (e.g., that provided by hospitals and nursing homes) and alternatives (e.g., hospices, which we discuss in the next section), completing advance directives (e.g., durable power of attorney for health care or living will), resolving key personal relationships, and perhaps choosing the alternative of ending life prematurely through euthanasia.

What happens to one's body and how one is memorialized is important to most people. Making a will is especially important in ensuring that wishes are carried out. Whether people choose to address these issues formally or informally, it is important that they be given the opportunity to do so. In many cases, family members are reluctant to discuss these matters with the dying relative because of their own anxiety about death. *People making known such choices about how they do and do not want their life to end constitutes a* **final scenario**.

One of the most difficult and important parts of a final scenario for most people is the process of separation from family and friends (Corr et al., 2008; Wanzer & Glenmullen, 2007). The final days, weeks, and months of life provide opportunities to

end-of-life issues
issues pertaining to the management of the final phase of life, after-death disposition of the body and memorial services, and distribution of assets

final scenario
people making their choices known about how they do and do not want their life to end

Deciding whether to have a traditional funeral is part of the creation of one's final scenario.

affirm love, resolve conflicts, and provide peace to dying people. The failure to complete this process often leaves survivors feeling that they did not achieve closure in the relationship, which can result in bitterness toward the deceased.

Health care workers realize the importance of giving dying patients the chance to create a final scenario and recognize the uniqueness of each person's final passage. A key part of their role is to ease this process (Wanzer & Glenmullen, 2007). Primary attention is paid to how people's total life experiences have prepared them to face end-of-life issues (Moeller, Lewis, & Werth, 2010).

A final scenario helps family and friends interpret one's death, especially when the scenario is constructed jointly, such as between spouses, and when communication is open and honest (Green, 2008). The perspectives of everyone involved are unlikely to converge without clear communication and discussion. Respecting each person's perspective is key and greatly helps in creating a good final scenario.

The Hospice Option

Most people would like to die at home among family and friends. An important barrier to this choice is the availability of support systems when the person has a terminal disease. Most people believe that they have no choice but to go to a hospital or nursing home. However, another alternative exists. **Hospice** *is an approach to assisting dying people that emphasizes pain management and death with dignity* (Knee, 2010; Russo, 2008). The emphasis in a hospice is on the dying person's quality of life. This approach grows out of an important distinction between the prolongation of life and the prolongation of death, a distinction that is important to Jean, the woman we met in the vignette. In a hospice, the concern is to make the person as peaceful and comfortable as possible, not to delay an inevitable death. Although medical care is available at a hospice, it is aimed primarily at controlling pain and restoring normal functioning. *The approach to care in hospice is called* **palliative care** *and is focused on providing relief from pain and other symptoms of disease at any point during the disease process* (Reville, 2011).

Hospice services are requested only after the person or physician believes that no treatment or cure is possible, making the hospice program markedly different from hospital or home care. The differences are evident in the principles that underlie hospice care: Clients and their families are viewed as a unit, clients should be kept free of pain, emotional and social impoverishment must be minimal, clients must be encouraged to maintain competencies, conflict resolution and fulfillment of realistic desires must be assisted, clients must be free to begin or end relationships, an interdisciplinary team approach is used, and staff members must seek to alleviate pain and fear (Knee, 2010).

The Real People feature provides some insight into one family's experience with a hospice.

hospice

an approach to assisting dying people that emphasizes pain management, or palliative care, and death with dignity

palliative care

care that is focused on providing relief from pain and other symptoms of disease at any point during the disease process

realPeople APPLYING HUMAN DEVELOPMENT
ONE FAMILY'S EXPERIENCE WITH DYING

The news from Roseanne's oncologist had been expected, but it still came as a shock to her, her husband Harry, and their two daughters: Her cancer had spread, and she had only about 3 months to live. At first, the family didn't know what to do. But her oncologist made a suggestion that turned out to be extremely helpful: Roseanne and her family should contact the local hospice for help.

The hospice in Roseanne's city was typical. The nurse and full backup team who visited the family's house were the most caring people the family had ever met. Far from being in a rush to complete the workup, the nurse spent a great deal of time asking Roseanne about her pain and how she wanted to manage it, her wishes and desires about her process of dying, and many other personal

topics. This approach made Roseanne and her family members feel more at ease. They knew that their feelings mattered and that Roseanne would be well cared for.

As Roseanne's condition deteriorated, the home hospice nurse made sure that her pain medication was adequate to provide physical comfort. Counselors worked with the family to help them discuss their feelings about

Continued

Roseanne's pending death and with Roseanne to help her prepare to die. They also explained to the family that they should call the hospice first if Roseanne died when no one from the hospice was present. This would ensure that Roseanne's wishes concerning life support and resuscitation were honored.

Two and a half months after contacting the hospice, Roseanne died at home—surrounded by her family and the hospice nurse, just as she wanted. Because her pain was well managed, she was comfortable even at the end. The grief of Harry and Roseanne's daughters was made easier through the constant support and counseling they received.

The hospice staff members who worked with Roseanne and her family had Roseanne's physical comfort as their primary goal, followed by supporting the family. The way they helped Roseanne die, and Harry and their daughters to grieve with support, made a difficult process a bit easier.

Although the hospice is a valuable alternative for many people, it may not be appropriate for everyone. Those who trust their physician regarding medical care options are more likely to select hospice than those who do not trust their physician, especially among African Americans (Ludke & Smucker, 2007). Most people who select hospice have cancer, AIDS, cardiovascular disease, pulmonary disease, or a progressive neurological condition; two thirds are over age 65; and most are in the last 6 months of life (Hospice Foundation of America, 2011b).

How do people decide to explore the hospice option? Families need to consider several things (Hospice Foundation of America, 2011a; Kastenbaum, 1999):

- *Is the person completely informed about the nature and prognosis of his or her condition?* Full knowledge and the ability to communicate with health care personnel are essential to understanding what hospice has to offer.

- *What options are available at this point in the progress of the person's disease?* Knowing about all available treatment options is critical. Exploring treatment options also requires health care professionals to be aware of the latest approaches and be willing to disclose them.

- *What are the person's expectations, fears, and hopes?* Some older adults, like Jean, remember or have heard stories about people who suffered greatly at the end of their lives. This can produce anxiety about their own death. Similarly, fears of becoming dependent play an important role in a person's decision making. Discovering and discussing these anxieties helps clarify options.

- *How well do people in the person's social network communicate with one another?* Talking about death is taboo in many families (Book, 1996). In others, intergenerational communication is difficult or impossible. Even in families with good communication, the pending death of a loved relative is difficult. As a result, the dying person may have difficulty expressing his or her wishes. The decision to explore the hospice option is best made when it is discussed openly.

- *Are family members available to participate actively in terminal care?* Hospice relies on family members to provide much of the care, which is supplemented by professionals and volunteers. We saw in Chapter 13 that being a primary caregiver can be highly stressful. Having a family member who is willing to accept this responsibility is essential for the hospice option to work.

- *Is a high-quality hospice care program available?* Hospice programs are not uniformly good. As with any health care provider, patients and family members must investigate the quality of local hospice programs before making a choice. The Hospice Foundation of America provides excellent material for evaluating a hospice.

- *Is hospice covered by insurance?* Hospice services are reimbursable under Medicare in most cases, but any additional expenses may or may not be covered under other forms of insurance (Knee, 2010).

Hospice outpatient health care workers provide help for people with terminal diseases who choose to die at home.

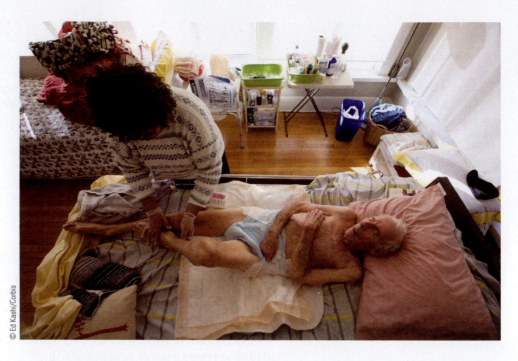

© Ed Kashi/Corbis

Hospice provides an important end-of-life option for many terminally ill people and their families. Moreover, the supportive follow-up services they provide are often used by surviving family and friends. Most important, the success of the hospice option has had influences on traditional health care. For example, the American Academy of Pain Medicine (2009) published an official position paper advocating the use of medical and behavioral interventions to provide pain management.

Despite the importance of the hospice option for end-of-life decisions, terminally ill people may face barriers of family reluctance to face the reality of terminal illness and participate in the decision-making process and health care providers hindering access to hospice care (Knee, 2010; Melhado & Byers, 2011; Reville, 2011). Irrespective of the choice of traditional health care or hospice, the wishes of the dying person should be honored, and family members must participate.

Test Yourself

Recall

1. _____ are most likely to face the death of their parents.

2. A _____ approach to dying acknowledges individual differences and rejects broad generalizations.

3. The primary framework for studying death anxiety is _____.

4. People making their choices known about how they do and do not want their lives to end constitutes a _____.

5. _____ is an approach to assisting dying people that emphasizes pain management, or palliative care, and death with dignity.

Interpret

- Why is there a difference in treatment approach between hospitals and hospices?

- How might ego integrity be related to the choice of using hospice?

Apply

- If you were an educator, what would you include in a death education program?

- Is hospice care included in employers' health care benefits package?

Recall answers: (1) Middle-aged adults, (2) holistic, (3) terror management theory, (4) final scenario, (5) Hospice

LEARNING OBJECTIVES

- How do people experience the grief process?
- What feelings do grieving people have?
- What is the difference between typical and prolonged grief?

After 67 years of marriage, Bertha recently lost her husband. At 90, Bertha knew that neither she nor her husband was likely to live much longer, but the death was a shock just the same. Bertha thinks about him much of the time and often finds herself making decisions on the basis of "what John would have done" in the same situation.

Each of us experiences many losses over a lifetime. Whenever we lose someone close to us through death or other separation, like Bertha we experience bereavement, grief, and mourning. **Bereavement** *is the state or condition caused by loss through death.* **Grief** *is the sorrow, hurt, anger, guilt, confusion, and other feelings that arise after experiencing a loss.* **Mourning** *concerns the ways in which we express our grief.* For example, you can tell that people in some cultures are bereaved and in mourning because of the clothing they wear. Mourning is highly influenced by culture. For some, mourning may involve wearing black, attending funerals, and observing an official period of grieving; for others, it means drinking, wearing white, and marrying the deceased spouse's sibling. Grief corresponds to the emotional reactions following loss, whereas mourning is the culturally approved behavioral manifestations of those feelings. Even though mourning rituals may be fairly standard within a culture, how people grieve varies, as we see next. We also see how Bertha's reactions are fairly typical of most people.

The Grief Process

How do people grieve? What do they experience? Just as there is no right way to die, there is no right way to grieve.

Like the process of dying, grieving does not have clearly demarcated stages through which we pass in a neat sequence, although there are certain issues people must face that are similar to those faced by dying people. When someone close to us dies, we must reorganize our lives, establish new patterns of behavior, and redefine relationships with family and friends. Attig (1996) provided one of the best descriptions of grief when he wrote that grief is the process by which we relearn the world.

Unlike bereavement, over which we have no control, grief is a process that involves choices in coping (Ivancovich & Wong, 2008). Grief is an active process in which a person must do the following (Worden, 1991):

- Acknowledge the reality of the loss.
- Work through the emotional turmoil.
- Adjust to an environment from which the deceased is absent.
- Loosen ties to the deceased.

Grief is an active coping process in which survivors must come to terms with the physical world, as well as the spiritual world; the interpersonal world of interactions with family and friends, the dead, and in some cases, God; and aspects of their inner

bereavement
the state or condition caused by loss through death

grief
the sorrow, hurt, anger, guilt, confusion, and other feelings that arise after experiencing a loss

mourning
the ways in which we express our grief

Going through the personal effects of a deceased loved one can be a difficult process for survivors.

selves and their personal experiences (Ivancovich & Wong, 2008; Papa & Litz, 2011). Bertha, the woman in the vignette, is in the middle of this process. Even the matter of deciding what to do with the deceased's personal effects can be part of this active coping process (Attig, 1996).

Grieving is a highly individual experience (Mallon, 2008; Papa & Litz, 2011). People need time to grieve. To a casual observer, it may appear that a survivor is "back to normal" after a few weeks. Actually, it takes much longer to resolve the complex emotional issues that are faced during bereavement (Mallon, 2008; Papa & Litz, 2011). Researchers and therapists alike agree that a person needs at least a year following the loss to begin recovery, and 2 years is not uncommon. Finally, it is probably more accurate to say that we learn to live with our loss rather than that we recover from it (Attig, 1996). Still, most people reach a point of moving on with their lives in a reasonable time frame (Bonanno, 2009; Mancini & Bonnano, 2010).

Recognizing these aspects of grief makes it easier to know what to say and do for bereaved people. Among the most useful things are to simply let the person know that you are sorry for his or her loss, that you are there for support, and that you mean what you say.

Typical Grief Reactions

The feelings experienced during grieving are intense, which not only makes it difficult to cope but can also make a person question her or his reactions. The feelings involved usually include sadness, denial, anger, loneliness, and guilt.

Many authors refer to the psychological side of coming to terms with bereavement as **grief work**. Whether the loss is ambiguous and lacking closure (e.g., waiting to learn the fate of a missing loved one) or certain (e.g., verification of death through a dead body), people need space and time in which to grieve (Boss, 2006; Papa & Litz, 2011). Even without the personal experience of the death of close family members, people recognize the need to give survivors time to deal with their many feelings.

Muller and Thompson (2003) examined people's experience of grief in a detailed interview study and found five themes. *Coping* concerns what people do to deal with their loss in terms of what helps them. *Affect* refers to people's emotional reactions to the death of their loved one. *Change* involves the ways in which survivors' lives change as a result of the loss; personal growth (e.g., "I didn't think I could deal with something that painful, but I did") is a common experience. *Narrative* relates to the stories survivors tell about their deceased loved one, which sometimes include details about the process of the death. Finally, *relationship* reflects who the deceased person was and the nature of the ties between that person and the survivor. Collectively, these themes indicate that the experience of grief is complex and involves dealing with one's feelings as a survivor as well as memories of the deceased person.

In addition to psychological grief reactions, there are physiological ones. Widows report sleep disturbances, as well as neurological and circulatory problems (Kowalski & Bondmass, 2008). Physical health may decline, illness may result, and use of health care services may increase (Stroebe, Schut, & Stroebe, 2007).

In the time following the death of a loved one, dates that have personal significance may reintroduce feelings of grief. The anniversary of the death can be especially troublesome. *The term* **anniversary reaction** *refers to changes in behavior related to feelings of sadness on this date.* Personal experience and research show that recurring feelings of sadness or other examples of the anniversary reaction are common in normal grief (Holland & Neimeyer, 2010).

Grief can last a long time. Some widows show no sign of lessening of grief after 5 years (Kowalski & Bondmass, 2008). Rosenblatt (1996) reported that people still felt

grief work
the psychological side of coming to terms with bereavement

anniversary reaction
changes in behavior related to feelings of sadness on the anniversary date of a loss

the effects of the deaths of family members 50 years after the event. The depth of the emotions over the loss of loved ones never totally went away, because people still cried and felt sad when discussing the loss despite the length of time that had passed. In general, though, people move on with their lives within a relatively short period and deal with their feelings reasonably well (Bonanno, 2009).

Coping With Grief

Two integrative approaches have been proposed that are specific to the grief process: the four-component model and the dual-process model of coping with bereavement.

The Four-Component Model

The **four-component model** *proposes that understanding grief is based on four things: (1) the context of the loss, referring to risk factors such as whether the death was expected; (2) the continuation of subjective meaning associated with the loss, ranging from evaluations of everyday concerns to major questions about the meaning of life; (3) changing representations of the lost relationship over time; and (4) the role of coping and emotion regulation processes that cover all coping strategies used to deal with grief* (Bonanno, 2009; Bonanno & Kaltman, 1999). The four-component model relies heavily on emotion theory, has much in common with the transactional model of stress, and has empirical support. According to the four-component model, dealing with grief is a complicated process that can only be understood as a complex outcome that unfolds over time.

One of the most important implications of this model is that helping grieving people involves helping them make meaning from the loss (Bratkovich, 2010; Wong, 2008). Second, this model implies that encouraging people to express their grief may not be helpful. *An alternative view, called the* **grief-work-as-rumination hypothesis**, *does not merely reject the necessity of grief processing for recovery from loss but views extensive grief processing as a form of rumination that may increase distress* (Bonanno, Papa, & O'Neill, 2001). Although it may seem that people who think obsessively about their loss or who ruminate about it are confronting the loss, rumination is considered a form of avoidance, because the people not dealing with their real feelings and moving on (Stroebe et al., 2007).

The grief-work-as-rumination hypothesis views grief avoidance as an independent but maladaptive form of coping with loss (Stroebe et al., 2007). In contrast to the traditional perspective, which equates the absence of grief processing with grief avoidance, the grief-work-as-rumination framework assumes that resilient individuals are able to minimize processing of a loss through relatively automated processes, such as distraction or shifting attention toward more positive emotional experiences (Bonanno, 2009). This framework argues that the deliberate avoidance or suppression of grief represents a less effective form of coping (Wegner & Gold, 1995) that tends to exacerbate rather than minimize the experience of grief (Bonanno, 2009).

The Spotlight on Research feature explores grief work regarding the loss of a spouse and the loss of a child in two cultures, the United States and China. As you read it, pay special attention to the question of whether encouraging people to express and deal with their grief is necessarily a good idea.

The Dual Process Model

The **dual process model (DPM)** *of coping with bereavement integrates existing ideas regarding stressors* (Stroebe & Schut, 2001; Stroebe, Schut, & Boerner, 2010). As shown in Figure 16.4, the DPM defines two broad types of stressors. Loss-oriented stressors concern the loss itself, such as the grief work that needs to be done. Restoration-oriented stressors are those that involve adapting to the survivor's new

four-component model
a model for understanding grief that is based on (1) the context of the loss, (2) the continuation of subjective meaning associated with the loss, (3) changing representations of the lost relationship over time, and (4) the role of coping and emotion regulation processes

grief-work-as-rumination hypothesis
an approach that does not merely reject the necessity of grief processing for recovery from loss but views extensive grief processing as a form of rumination that may increase distress

dual process model (DPM)
the view of coping with bereavement that integrates loss-oriented stressors, concerning the loss itself, and restoration-oriented stressors, related to moving on with life

Spotlight on research

Grief Processing and Avoidance in the United States and China

Who were the investigators, and what was the aim of the study?
George Bonanno and his colleagues (2005) noted that grief following the loss of a loved one often tends to be denied. However, research evidence related to positive benefits of resolving grief is largely lacking. Thus, whether unresolved grief is "bad" remains an open issue. Likewise, cross-cultural evidence is also lacking.

How did the investigators measure the topic of interest?
Collaborative meetings between U.S. and Chinese researchers resulted in a 13-item grief processing scale and a 7-item grief avoidance scale, with both English and Mandarin Chinese versions. Self-reported psychological symptoms and physical health were also collected.

Who were the participants in the study?
Adults under age 66 who had experienced the loss of either a spouse or a child approximately 4 months prior to the start of data collection were asked to participate through solicitation letters. Participants were from either the metropolitan areas of Washington, D.C., or the Nanjing, Jiangsu, province in China.

What was the design of the study?
The study used a longitudinal design. Two sets of measures were collected at approximately 4 months and 18 months after the loss.

Were there ethical concerns with the study?
Because participation was voluntary, there were no ethical concerns.

What were the results?
Consistent with the grief-work-as-rumination view, scores on the two grief measures were uncorrelated. Overall, women tended to show more grief processing than men, and grief processing decreased over time. As you can see in Figure 16.3, Chinese participants reported more grief processing and grief avoidance than U.S. participants at the first time of measurement, but differences disappeared by the second measurement for grief processing.

What did the investigators conclude?
Based on converging results from the United States and China, the researchers concluded that the data supported the grief-work-as-rumination view. The results support the notion that excessive processing of grief may increase a bereaved person's stress and feelings of discomfort rather than being helpful. These findings contradict the idea that people should be encouraged to work through their grief and that doing so will always be helpful.

What converging evidence would strengthen these conclusions?
Although the data were collected in two cities in two countries, additional areas (e.g., rural and urban) and more cross-cultural data would be helpful. Also, the sample was limited to people under age 66 and to those who had recently experienced the loss of either a spouse or a child. Older adults and people experiencing different types of loss (parent, partner, sibling, or friend) would provide a richer data set.

 Go to Psychology CourseMate at **www.cengagebrain.com** to enhance your understanding of this research.

FIGURE 16.3

Grief processing and deliberate grief avoidance across time in China and the United States.

From "Grief processing and deliberate grief avoidance: A prospective comparison of bereaved spouses and parents in the United States and the People's Republic of China," by G.A. Bonanno, A. Papa, K. Lalande, N. Zhang, and , J. G. Noll, in Journal of Consulting and Clinical Psychology, Vol. 73, pp. 86–98. Copyright © American Psychological Association 2005. P. 92

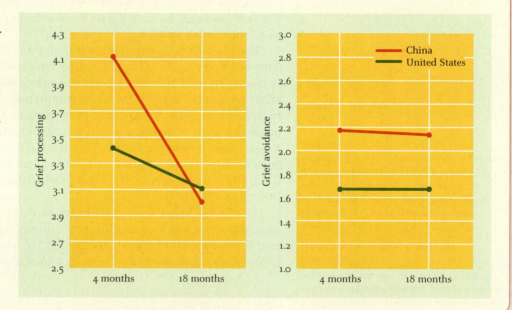

FIGURE 16.4
The DPM of coping with bereavement shows the relationship between dealing with the stresses of the loss itself (loss oriented) and moving on with life (restoration oriented).

From "Models of coping with bereavement: A review," by M. S. Stroebe, and H. Schut, in Handbook of bereavement research: Consequences, coping, and care, *edited by M. S. Stroebe, R. O., Hansson, W. Stroeve, and H. Schut , pp. 375–403). Copyright © American Psychological Association 2001.*

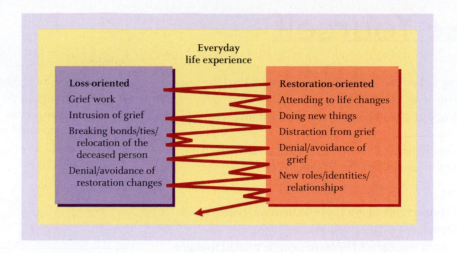

life situation, such as building new relationships and finding new activities. The DPM proposes that dealing with these stressors is a dynamic process, as indicated by the lines connecting them in the figure. This is a distinguishing feature of DPM. It shows how bereaved people cycle back and forth between dealing mostly with grief and trying to move on with life. At times the emphasis will be on grief; at other times it's on moving forward.

The DPM captures well the process that bereaved people report—at times they are nearly overcome with grief, while at other times they handle life well. The DPM also helps us understand how, over time, people come to a balance between the long-term effects of bereavement and the need to live life. Understanding how people handle grief requires understanding of the various contexts in which people live and interact with others (Sandler, Wolchik, & Ayers, 2008).

Complicated or Prolonged Grief Disorder

Not everyone is able to cope with grief well and begin rebuilding a life. Sometimes the feelings of hurt, loneliness, and guilt are so overwhelming that they become the focus of the survivor's life to such an extent that there is never any closure and the grief continues to interfere indefinitely with the person's ability to function. *When this occurs, the individual is viewed as having* **complicated or prolonged grief disorder**, *which is distinguished from depression and from normal grief in terms of separation distress and traumatic distress* (Boelen & Prigerson, 2007; Kersting et al., 2011; Shear et al., 2011). *Symptoms of* **separation distress** *include preoccupation with the deceased to the point that it interferes with everyday functioning, upsetting memories of the deceased, longing and searching for the deceased, and isolation following the loss. Symptoms of* **traumatic distress** *include disbelief about the death; mistrust, anger, and detachment from others as a result of the death; feeling shocked by the death; and experiencing the physical presence of the deceased.*

Complicated grief forms a separate set of symptoms from depression (Bonanno, 2009; Kersting et al., 2011; Papa & Litz, 2011; Shear et al., 2011). Individuals experiencing complicated grief report high levels of separation distress (e.g., yearning, pining, or longing for the deceased person), along with specific cognitive, emotional, or behavioral indicators (e.g., avoiding reminders of the deceased, diminished sense of self, difficulty in accepting the loss, feeling bitter or angry), as well as increased morbidity, increased smoking and substance abuse, and difficulties with family and other social relationships. Similar distinctions have been made between complicated or prolonged grief disorder and anxiety disorders.

complicated or prolonged grief disorder
an expression of grief that is distinguished from depression and from normal grief in terms of separation distress and traumatic distress

separation distress
the expression of complicated or prolonged grief disorder that includes preoccupation with the deceased to the point that it interferes with everyday functioning, upsetting memories of the deceased, longing and searching for the deceased, and isolation following the loss

traumatic distress
the expression of complicated or prolonged grief disorder that includes disbelief about the death; mistrust, anger, and detachment from others as a result of the death; feeling shocked by the death; and experiencing the physical presence of the deceased

Test Yourself

Recall

1. Feeling sad on the date your grandmother died the previous year is an example of an _____ .

2. Dealing with the psychological effects of loss is called _____ .

3. Separation distress and _____ are two characteristics of complicated or prolonged grief disorder.

Interpret

- What connections might there be between bereavement and stress?
- How might reactions to bereavement be related to cognitive development?

Apply

- If you were to create a brochure listing the five most important things to do and not to do in reacting to someone who just lost a close family member or friend through death, what would you include? Why?
- What would an effective employee bereavement leave policy look like?

16.4 Dying and Bereavement Experiences Across the Life Span

LEARNING OBJECTIVES

- What do children understand about death? How should adults help them deal with it?
- How do adolescents deal with death?
- How do adults deal with death? What are the special issues they face concerning the death of a child or parent?
- How do older adults face their own death or the loss of a child, grandchild, or partner?

Donna and Carl have a 6-year-old daughter, Jennie, whose grandmother just died. Jennie and her grandmother were close; the two saw each other almost every day. Other adults have told her parents not to take Jennie to the funeral. Donna and Carl aren't sure what to do. They wonder whether Jennie will understand what happened to her grandmother, and they worry about how she will react.

Coming to grips with the reality of death is probably one of the hardest things we have to do in life. American society does not help much either, because it tends to distance itself from death through euphemisms, such as "passed away," and by eliminating many rituals.

These trends make it difficult for people like Donna, Carl, and Jennie to learn about death in its natural context. Dying has been moved from the home to hospitals and other institutions. The closest most people get to death is a quick glance inside a nicely lined casket at a corpse that has been made to look as if the person were still alive.

Childhood

Many adults, like Donna and Carl in the vignette, wonder whether young children really know what death means. Children's understanding of death changes with their development (Webb, 2010b). Preschoolers tend to believe that death is temporary and magical, something dramatic that comes to get you in the middle of the night like a burglar or a ghost. Not until children are 5 to 7 years of age do they realize that death is permanent, that it eventually happens to everyone, and that dead people no longer have any biological functions.

Why does this shift occur? There are three major areas of developmental change in children that affect their understanding of death and grief (Oltjenbruns, 2001; Webb, 2010b): cognitive-language ability, psychosocial development, and coping skills.

Research shows that bereavement per se during childhood typically does not have long-lasting effects, such as depression (Oltjenbruns & Balk, 2007; Webb, 2010a). Problems are more likely to occur if the child does not receive adequate care and attention following the death.

Understanding death can be particularly difficult for children when adults are not open and honest with them, especially about the meaning of death (Buchsbaum, 1996). The use of euphemisms, such as "Grandma has gone away" or "Mommy is only sleeping," is unwise. Young children do not understand the deeper level of meaning in such statements and are likely to take them literally (Attig, 1996; Silverman & Nickman, 1996).

When explaining death to children, it is best to deal with them on their terms. Keep explanations simple, at a level they can understand. Try to allay their fears and reassure them that whatever reaction they have is okay. Providing loving support for the child maximizes the potential for a successful (albeit painful) introduction to one of life's realities.

It is important for children to know that it is okay for them to feel sad, to cry, or to show their feelings in whatever way they want. Reassuring children that it's okay to feel this way helps them deal with their confusion at some adults' explanations of death. Researchers believe it is important for children to attend the funeral of a relative or to have a private viewing (Webb, 2010a).

Adolescence

Adolescents are more experienced with death and grief than many people realize. Surveys of college students who are late adolescents or in their very early twenties indicate that between 40% and 70% of traditional-age college students will experience the death of someone close to them during their college years (Knox, 2007). Still, when teenagers experience the death of someone close to them, they may have considerable trouble making sense of the event, especially if this is their first experience (Oltjenbruns & Balk, 2007). The effects of bereavement in adolescence can be quite severe, especially when the death was unexpected, and can be expressed in many ways, such as chronic illness, enduring guilt, low self-esteem, poorer performance in school and on the job, substance abuse, problems in interpersonal relationships, and suicidal thinking (Malone, 2010; Morgan & Roberts, 2010). Despite these immediate effects, bereaved adolescent siblings experience continued personal growth following the death of a loved one in much the same way as adolescents who did not experience such a loss (Morgan & Roberts, 2010).

Adulthood

HUMAN DEVELOPMENT in action

How might a high-school teacher help a bereaved student?

When asked how they feel about death, young adults report a strong sense that those who die at this point in their lives would be cheated out of their future (Attig, 1996). Wrenn (1999) relates that one of the challenges faced by bereaved college students is learning "how to respond to people who ignore their grief, or who tell them that they need to get on with life, that it's not good for them to continue to grieve" (p. 134). College students have a need to express their grief like other bereaved people do, so providing them the opportunity to do so is crucial (Servaty-Seib & Taub, 2010).

Experiencing the loss of one's partner in young adulthood can be traumatic, not only because of the loss itself but also because such loss is typically unexpected. As Trish Straine, a 32-year-old widow whose husband was killed in the World Trade Center attack, put it: "I suddenly thought, 'I'm a widow.' Then I said to myself, 'A widow? That's an older woman, who's dressed in black. It's certainly not a 32-year-old like me'" (Lieber, 2001). A study on young Canadian widows reported intense feelings and a desire to stay connected through memories (Lowe & McClement, 2010–2011).

Becoming a widow as a young adult can be especially traumatic.

Losing one's spouse in midlife often results in the survivor challenging basic assumptions about self, relationships, and life options, especially if the survivor is a parent of a child still at home (Glazer et al., 2010). By the first-year anniversary of the loss, the surviving spouse has usually begun transforming his or her perspectives on these issues. The important part of this process is to make meaning of the death and to continue working on and revising it over time (Gillies & Neimeyer, 2006).

Death of One's Child in Young and Middle Adulthood

Many people believe that the death of one's child is the worst type of loss (Woodgate, 2006). Mourning is always intense, and some parents never recover or reconcile themselves to the death of their child and may terminate their relationship with each other (Rosenbaum, Smith, & Zollfrank, 2011). The intensity of feelings is due to the strong parent–child bond that begins before birth and lasts a lifetime (Maple et al., 2010; Rosenbaum et al., 2011).

Young parents who lose a child due to sudden infant death syndrome report high anxiety, a more negative view of the world, and much guilt, which results in a devastating experience (Seyda & Fitzsimons, 2010). The most overlooked losses of a child are those that happen through stillbirth, miscarriage, abortion, or neonatal death (Rosenbaum et al., 2011). The loss of a young adult child for a middle-aged parent is experienced differently but is equally devastating (Maple et al., 2010; Rubin & Malkinson, 2001). For example, parents who lost sons in wars (Rubin, 1996) and in traffic accidents (Shalev, 1999) still report strong feelings of anxiety, problems in functioning, and difficulties in relationships with both the surviving siblings and the deceased as long as 13 years after the loss.

Death of One's Parent

Losing a parent in adulthood is a rite of passage as a person is transformed from being a "son" or "daughter" to being "without parents" (Edwards, 2006). The death of a parent often leads the surviving children to redefine the meaning of their relationships with their siblings, children, and other family members (Moss, Moss, & Hansson, 2001).

The loss of a parent is perceived as a significant one no matter how old we are. For young adult women transitioning to motherhood, having lost their mother during adolescence raises many feelings, such as deep loss at not being able to share their pregnancies with their mothers and fear of dying young themselves (Franceschi, 2005). Middle-aged women who lose a parent report feeling a complex set of emotions (Westbrook, 2002): They have intense emotional feelings of both loss and freedom, they remember both positive and negative aspects of their parent, and they experience shifts in their sense of self.

Regardless of one's age, the loss of a parent is typically a difficult experience.

The feelings accompanying the loss of an older parent reflect a sense of letting go, the loss of a buffer against death, better acceptance of one's eventual death, and a sense of relief that the parent's suffering is over (Moss, Moss, & Hansson, 2001). Yet, if the parent died from a cause, such as Alzheimer's disease, that involves the loss of the parent–child relationship along the way, then bodily death can feel like the second time the parent died (Shaw, 2007).

Late Adulthood

Although anxiety about their own death is less of an issue as adults age, the deaths of those close to them can still be traumatic. They may feel that their most important life tasks have been completed (Kastenbaum, 1999). However, they, like young adults, feel that people from later generations have had their lives cut short if they die young.

Death of One's Child or Grandchild in Late Life

The loss of a child can happen at any point over the adult life span. Older bereaved parents tend to reevaluate their grief as experienced shortly after the loss and years and decades later. Even more than 30 years after the death of a child, older adults still feel a keen sense of loss and have continued difficulty coming to terms with it (Malkinson & Bar-Tur, 2004–2005). The long-lasting effects of the loss of a child are often accompanied by a sense of guilt that the pain affected the parents' relationships with the surviving children.

The loss of a grandchild results in similar feelings: intense emotional upset, survivor guilt, regrets about the relationship with the deceased grandchild, and a need to restructure relationships with the surviving family. However, bereaved grandparents tend to control and hide their grief behavior in an attempt to shield their child (the bereaved parent) from the level of pain being felt. In cases in which older adults were the primary caregivers for grandchildren, feelings can be especially difficult (Boon et al., 2010).

Death of One's Partner

Experiencing the loss of one's partner is the type of loss in late life we know most about. The death of a partner differs from other losses. It clearly represents a deep personal loss, especially when the couple has had a long and close relationship (Moss, Moss, & Hansson, 2001). In a real way, when someone's partner dies, a part of the surviving person dies too.

Older bereaved spouses may grieve a great deal for a long time (Hansson & Stroebe, 2007); results from one study showed that such grief can last at least 30 months (Thompson et al., 1991). Survivors who have close confidants are better off than survivors who have many acquaintances (Hansson & Stroebe, 2007).

When someone's partner dies, how that person felt about the relationship could play a role in coping with bereavement. One study of spousal bereavement measured how the surviving spouse rated the marriage. Bereaved older widows and widowers rated their relationships at 2, 12, and 30 months after the death of their spouse; nonbereaved older adults served as a comparison group. The results are summarized in Figure 16.5. Overall, bereaved widows and widowers gave their marriages more positive ratings than nonbereaved older adults. A marriage lost through death left a positive bias

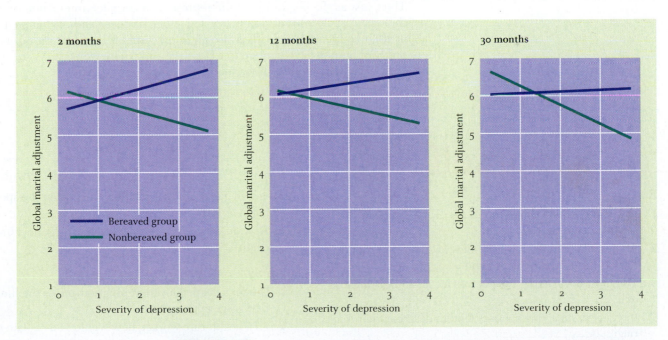

FIGURE 16.5

In general, bereaved spouses rate their marriages more positively than nonbereaved spouses, and they tend to be more positive the more depressed they are after the loss.

From "Retrospective assessment of marital adjustment and depression during the first two years of spousal bereavement," by A. Futterman, D. Gallagher, L. W. Thompson, S. Lovett, and M. Gilewski, in Psychology and Aging, 5, 277–283. Copyright © American Psychological Association 1990.

in memory. However, bereaved spouses' ratings were related to depression in an interesting way. The more depressed the bereaved spouse, the more positive the marriage's rating. In contrast, depressed nonbereaved spouses gave their marriages negative ratings. This result suggests that depression following bereavement signifies positive aspects of a relationship, whereas depression not connected with bereavement indicates a troubled relationship (Futterman et al., 1990).

Several studies of widows document a tendency for some older women to sanctify their husbands (Lopata, 1996). Sanctification involves describing deceased husbands in idealized terms, and it serves several functions, validating that the widow had a strong marriage, is a good and worthy person, and is capable of rebuilding her life. European American women who view being a wife as above all other roles a woman can perform are somewhat more likely to sanctify their husbands. The higher the quality of the relationship, the more bereaved spouses yearn for their lost spouse (Stroebe, Abakoumkin, & Stroebe, 2010).

Gay and lesbian couples may experience other feelings and reactions, in addition to typical feelings of grief (V. Clarke et al., 2010). For example, family members of the deceased may not make the partner feel welcome at the funeral, making it hard for the partner to bring closure to the relationship. For gay partners who were also caregivers, the loss affects their sense of identity in much the same way as the death of a spouse, and making sense of the death becomes the primary issue (Cadell & Marshall, 2007). Lesbian widows report similar feelings (Bent & Magilvy, 2006).

Conclusion

Death is the last life-cycle force we encounter, the ultimate triumph of biological forces that limit the length of life. Yet the same psychological and social forces that are so influential throughout life help us deal with death, either our own or someone else's. As we come to the end of our life journey, we understand death through an interaction of psychological forces—such as coping skills and intellectual and emotional understanding of death—and sociocultural forces expressed in a particular society's traditions and rituals. When death happens in the course of the life span also matters.

Thus, just as the beginning of life represents a complex interaction of biological, psychological, sociocultural, and life-cycle factors, so does death. What people believe about what happens after death is also an interaction of these factors. So, as we bring our study of human development to a close, we end where we began: What we experience in our lives cannot be understood from a single perspective.

Test Yourself

Recall

1. In general, adults should be _____ when discussing death with children.

2. Adolescents usually have trouble _____ of the death of someone close to them.

3. The most devastating type of loss for an adult is the loss of a _____.

4. In general, surviving spouses tend to describe their marriages as _____.

Interpret

• What similarities and differences would you expect to find between the survivors in heterosexual marriages and in gay or lesbian relationships when the spouse or partner dies?

• How does cognitive development affect understanding of death?

Apply

• Design a death education program across the life span that is age appropriate.

• As a health care worker, how would you explain death to a young child?

Recall answers: (1) honest, (2) making sense, (3) child, (4) more positively

On February 25, 1990, 26-year-old Terri Schiavo collapsed in her home from a possible potassium imbalance caused by an eating disorder, temporarily stopping her heart and cutting off oxygen to her brain. On March 31, 2005, Terri Schiavo died after her feeding tube had been removed 13 days earlier. On these two points everyone connected with Terri's case agreed. But on all other essential aspects of it, Terri's husband Michael and Terri's parents deeply disagreed.

The central point of disagreement was Terri's medical condition. Terri's husband and numerous physicians argued that she was in a persistent vegetative state. Based on this diagnosis, Michael Schiavo requested that Terri's feeding tube be withdrawn and that she be allowed to die with dignity in the way he asserted she would have wanted to.

Terri's parents and some other physicians said she was not in a persistent vegetative state and that she was capable of recognizing them and others. Based on this diagnosis, their belief that Terri would not want the intervention stopped, and their contention that passive euthanasia is morally wrong, they fought Michael's attempts to remove the feeding tube.

What made this case especially difficult was that Terri had left no written instructions that clearly stated her thoughts and intentions on the issue. So the ensuing legal and political debates became based on what various people thought Terri would have wanted and reflected various aspects of people's positions on personal rights regarding life and death.

The legal and political battles began in 1993, when Terri's parents tried unsuccessfully to have Michael removed as Terri's guardian. But the most heated aspects of the case began in 2000, when a circuit court judge ruled that Terri's feeding tube could be removed based on his belief that she had told Michael that she would not have wanted it. In April 2001, the feeding tube was removed after state courts and the U.S. Supreme Court refused to hear the case. However, the tube was reinserted 2 days later upon another judge's order. In November 2002, the original circuit court judge ruled that Terri had no hope of recovery and again ordered the tube removed, an order eventually carried out in October 2003. Within a week, however, Florida Governor Jeb Bush signed a bill passed by the Florida legislature requiring that the tube be reinserted. This law was ruled unconstitutional by the Florida Supreme Court in September 2004. In February 2005, the original circuit court judge again ordered the tube removed. Between March 16 and 27, the Florida House introduced and passed a bill that would have required the tube to be reinserted, but the Florida Senate defeated a somewhat different version of the bill. From March 19 to 21, bills that would have allowed a federal court to review the case passed in the U.S. House of Representatives and the U.S. Senate, but the two versions could not be reconciled. Over the next 10 days, the Florida Supreme Court, the U.S. district court, and a U.S. circuit court refused to hear the case, as did the U.S. Supreme Court. The original circuit court judge rejected a final attempt by Terri's parents to have the feeding tube reinserted.

The public debate on the case was as long and complex as the legal and political arguments. The debate had several positive outcomes. The legal and political complexities dramatically illustrated the need for people to reflect on end-of-life issues and to make their wishes known to family members and others (e.g., health care providers) in writing. The case also brought to light the high cost of long-term care, the difficulties in determining whether someone is in a persistent vegetative state (and, in turn, what that implies about life), the tough moral and ethical issues surrounding the withdrawal of nutrition, and the individual's personal feelings about death. The legal and medical communities have proposed reforms concerning how these types of cases are heard in the courts and the processes used to resolve them (Dickinson, 2011; Moran, 2008).

Summary

16.1 Definitions and Ethical Issues

How is death defined?

- Death is a difficult concept to define precisely. Different cultures have different meanings for death that are reflected, for example, in funeral rituals.

What legal and medical criteria are used to determine when death occurs?

- For centuries, a clinical definition of death was used: the absence of a heartbeat and respiration. Currently, whole-brain death is the most widely used definition. It is based on several highly specific criteria, including brain activity and responses to specific stimuli.

What are the ethical dilemmas surrounding euthanasia?

- Two types of euthanasia are distinguished. Active euthanasia consists of deliberately ending someone's life, such as turning off a life-support system. Physician-assisted suicide is a controversial issue and a form of active euthanasia. Passive euthanasia is ending someone's life by withholding some type of intervention or treatment (e.g., by stopping nutrition). It is essential that people make their wishes known through either a durable power of attorney for health care or a living will.

16.2 Thinking About Death: Personal Aspects

How do feelings about death change over adulthood?

- Middle-aged adults begin to confront their own mortality and undergo a change in their sense of time lived and time until death. Older adults are more accepting of death.

How do people deal with their own death?

- Kübler-Ross's theory consists of five stages: denial, anger, bargaining, depression, and acceptance. Some people do not progress through all these stages, and some people move through them at different rates. People may be in more than one stage at a time and do not necessarily go through them in order.

■ A contextual theory of dying emphasizes the tasks a dying person must face. Four dimensions of these tasks have been identified: bodily needs, psychological security, interpersonal attachments, and spiritual energy and hope. A contextual theory incorporates differences in the reasons people die and the places people die.

What is death anxiety? How do people show it?

■ Most people exhibit some degree of anxiety about death, though it is difficult to define and measure. Several ways to deal with anxiety exist: living life to the fullest, personal reflection, and education. Death education has been shown to be extremely effective.

How do people deal with end-of-life issues and create a final scenario?

■ Managing the final aspects of life, after-death disposition of the body and memorial services, and distribution of assets are important end-of-life issues. Making choices about what people do and do not want done constitutes a final scenario.

What is hospice?

■ The goals of a hospice are to maintain the quality of life and to manage the pain of terminally ill patients.

16.3 Surviving the Loss

How do people experience the grief process?

■ Grief is an active process of coping with loss. Four aspects of grieving must be confronted: the reality of the loss, the emotional turmoil, the environmental adjustment, and the loosening of ties with the deceased.

What feelings do grieving people have?

■ Dealing with grief, called grief work, usually takes 1 to 2 years and sometimes 5 or more years. Typical grief reactions include sadness, denial, disbelief, guilt, and anniversary reactions.

What is the difference between typical and prolonged grief?

■ The four-component model proposes that the grief process is described by the context of the loss, the continuation of subjective meaning associated with the loss, changing representations of the lost relationship over time, and the role of coping and emotion regulation processes.

■ The dual-process model of coping with bereavement focuses on loss-oriented and restoration-oriented stressors.

■ Prolonged grief involves symptoms of separation distress and symptoms of traumatic distress.

16.4 Dying and Bereavement Experiences Across the Life Span

What do children understand about death? How should adults help them deal with it?

■ The cognitive and psychosocial developmental levels of children determine their understanding of and ability to cope with death.

■ Research indicates that there are few long-lasting effects of bereavement in childhood.

How do adolescents deal with death?

■ Adolescents may have difficulty making sense of death and are often severely affected by bereavement.

How do adults deal with death? What are the special issues they face concerning the death of a child or parent?

■ Young and middle-aged adults usually have intense feelings about death.

■ The death of one's child is especially difficult to cope with.

■ Midlife is when people usually deal with the death of their parents and confront their own mortality. The death of one's parent deprives an adult of many important things, and the feelings accompanying it are often complex.

How do older adults face their own death or the loss of a child, grandchild, or partner?

■ Older adults are usually less anxious about their own death and deal with it better than does any other age group.

■ The death of a child or grandchild can be traumatic for older adults, and the feelings of loss may never go away.

■ The death of one's partner represents a deep personal loss, especially when the couple had a long and close relationship.

Key Terms

thanatology (440)
clinical death (441)
whole-brain death (441)
persistent vegetative state (441)
bioethics (442)
euthanasia (442)
active euthanasia (442)
passive euthanasia (442)
physician-assisted suicide (443)
living will (444)
durable power of attorney for health care (444)

do not resuscitate (DNR) order (445)
death anxiety (448)
terror management theory (448)
end-of-life issues (449)
final scenario (449)
hospice (450)
palliative care (450)
bereavement (453)
grief (453)
mourning (453)
grief work (454)
anniversary reaction (454)

four-component model (455)
grief-work-as-rumination hypothesis (455)
dual process model (DPM) (455)
complicated or prolonged grief disorder (457)
separation distress (457)
traumatic distress (457)

Online Resources

Go to CengageBrain.com to access Psychology CourseMate, where you will find an interactive eBook, flashcards, quizzes, videos, websites, and more.

Glossary

abusive relationship a relationship in which one person becomes aggressive toward the partner

accommodation according to Piaget, changing existing knowledge based on new knowledge

active euthanasia the deliberate ending of someone's life

activities of daily living (ADLs) basic self-care tasks such as eating, bathing, toileting, walking, and dressing

adaptation level when the press level is average for a particular level of competence

addiction physical dependence on a substance (e.g., alcohol) such that withdrawal symptoms are experienced when deprived of that substance

adolescent egocentrism self-absorption that is characteristic of teenagers as they search for identity

adolescent-limited antisocial behavior behavior of youth who engage in relatively minor criminal acts but aren't consistently antisocial

aerobic exercise exercise that places moderate stress on the heart by maintaining a pulse rate between 60 and 90% of the person's maximum heart rate

age discrimination denying a job or promotion to someone solely on the basis of age

age of viability the age, typically 22–28 weeks after conception, at which a fetus can survive if born because most of its bodily systems function adequately

agreeableness a personality dimension associated with being accepting, willing to work with others, and caring

alert inactivity the state in which a baby is calm, with eyes open and attentive, and seems to be deliberately inspecting its environment

alienation a feeling among workers when their work seems meaningless and their efforts devalued or when they see no connection between their work and the final product

alleles variations of genes

altruism prosocial behavior such as helping and sharing in which the individual does not benefit directly from the behavior

Alzheimer's disease a disease marked by gradual declines in memory, attention, and judgment; confusion as to time and place; difficulties in communicating; decline in self-care skills; inappropriate behavior; and personality changes

amniocentesis a prenatal diagnostic technique that uses a syringe to withdraw a sample of amniotic fluid through the pregnant woman's abdomen

amnion the inner sac in which the developing child rests

amniotic fluid the fluid that surrounds the fetus

amyloid a protein that is produced in abnormally high levels in Alzheimer's patients

analytic ability in Sternberg's theory of successful intelligence, the ability to analyze problems and generate different solutions

anniversary reaction changes in behavior related to feelings of sadness on the anniversary date of a loss

anorexia nervosa a persistent refusal to eat accompanied by an irrational fear of being overweight

assimilation according to Piaget, taking in information that is compatible with what is already known

assisted living facilities a supportive living arrangement for people who need assistance with ADLs or IADLs but who are not so impaired physically or cognitively that they need 24-hour care

assortative mating a theory stating that people find partners based on their similarity to each other

attachment enduring socioemotional relationships between infants and their caregivers

attention processes that determine which information is processed further by an individual

authoritarian parenting a style of parenting in which parents show high levels of control and low levels of warmth toward their children

authoritative parenting a style of parenting in which parents use a moderate amount of control and are warm and responsive to their children

autobiographical memory memories of the significant events and experiences of someone's own life

autosomal dominant inheritance the presence of certain genes that means there is a 100% chance of the person eventually getting a disease such as Alzheimer's

autosomes the first 22 pairs of chromosomes

average children as applied to children's popularity, children who are liked and disliked by different classmates, but with relatively little intensity

average life expectancy the age at which half of the people born in a particular year will have died

avoidant attachment a relationship in which infants turn from their mothers when they are reunited following a brief separation

axon a tubelike structure that emerges from the cell body and transmits information to other neurons

babbling speechlike sounds that consist of vowel–consonant combinations and are common at about 6 months

backup care emergency care for dependent children or adults so that the employee does not need to lose a day of work

basal metabolic rate the speed at which the body consumes calories

basic cry a cry that starts softly, gradually becomes more intense, and is often heard when babies are hungry or tired

basic emotions emotions experienced by humankind and that consist of three elements: a subjective feeling, a physiological change, and an overt behavior

battered woman syndrome a situation occurring when a woman believes that she cannot leave an abusive situation and may even go so far as to kill her abuser

behavior therapy a type of therapy based on the notion that depressed people experience too few rewards or reinforcements from their environment

bereavement the state or condition caused by loss through death

binge drinking a type of drinking defined for men as consuming five or more drinks in a row and for women as consuming four or more drinks in a row within the past 2 weeks

bioethics the study of the interface between human values and technological advances in health and life sciences

biopsychosocial framework a useful way to organize the biological, psychological, and sociocultural forces on human development

blended family a family consisting of a biological parent, a stepparent, and children

body mass index (BMI) an adjusted ratio of weight to height that is used to define *overweight*

bulimia nervosa a disease in which people alternate between binge eating—periods when they eat uncontrollably—and purging through use of laxatives or self-induced vomiting

burnout a depletion of a person's energy and motivation, the loss of occupational idealism, and the feeling of being exploited

cardinality principle a counting principle in which the last number name denotes the number of objects being counted

career plateauing when promotional advancement is either not possible or not desired by the worker

cell body the center of a neuron that keeps the neuron alive

cellular theories explanations of aging that focus on processes that occur within individual cells, which may lead to the buildup of harmful substances or the deterioration of cells over a lifetime

centration according to Piaget, a narrowly focused type of thought characteristic of preoperational children

cerebral cortex the wrinkled surface of the brain that regulates many functions that are distinctly human

chorionic villus sampling (CVS) a prenatal diagnostic technique that involves taking a sample of tissue from the chorion

chromosomes threadlike structures in the nuclei of cells that contain genetic material

chronic obstructive pulmonary disease (COPD) the most common form of incapacitating respiratory disease among older adults

circadian rhythm the sleep–wake cycle

classical conditioning a form of learning that involves pairing a neutral stimulus and a response originally produced by another stimulus

climacteric the biological process during which women pass from their reproductive to nonreproductive years

clinical death the lack of heartbeat and respiration

clique a small group of friends who are similar in age, sex, race, and attitudes

cognitive therapy a type of therapy based on the idea that maladaptive beliefs or cognitions about oneself are responsible for depression

cohabitation people in committed, intimate, sexual relationships who live together but are not married

cohort effects problems with cross-sectional designs in which differences between age groups (cohorts) may result as easily from environmental events as from developmental processes

collaborative divorce a voluntary, contractually based alternative dispute resolution process for couples who want to negotiate a resolution of their situation rather than having a ruling imposed upon them by a court or arbitrator

competence a person's abilities

complicated or prolonged grief disorder an expression of grief that is distinguished from depression and from normal grief in terms of separation distress and traumatic distress

conscientiousness a personality dimension in which people tend to be hardworking, ambitious, energetic, scrupulous, and persevering

constricting actions interactions in which one partner tries to emerge as the victor by threatening or contradicting the other

continuity theory a theory based on idea that people tend to cope with daily life in later adulthood by applying familiar strategies based on past experience to maintain and preserve both internal and external structures

continuity–discontinuity issue whether a particular developmental phenomenon represents a smooth progression throughout the life span (continuity) or a series of abrupt shifts (discontinuity)

controversial children as applied to children's popularity, children who are both liked and disliked intensely by classmates

conventional level the second level in Kohlberg's theory, in which moral reasoning is based on society's norms

convergent thinking using information to arrive at one standard and correct answer

cooing early vowel-like sounds that babies produce

cooperative play play that is organized around a theme, with each child taking on a different role, and that begins at about 2 years of age

coping any attempt to deal with stress

core knowledge hypothesis the theory that infants are born with rudimentary knowledge of the world, which is elaborated based on experiences

corpus callosum a thick bundle of neurons that connects the brain's two hemispheres

correlation coefficient an expression of the strength and direction of a relation between two variables

correlational study an investigation that looks at relations between variables as they exist naturally in the world

co-rumination conversations about personal problems, common among adolescent girls

covenant marriage expanding the marriage contract to a lifelong commitment between the partners within a supportive community

creative ability in Sternberg's theory of successful intelligence, the ability to deal adaptively with novel situations and problems

cross-linking the random interaction of some proteins with certain body tissues, such as muscles and arteries

cross-sectional study a study in which developmental differences are identified by testing people of different ages

crowd a large group including many cliques that have similar attitudes and values

crying the state in which a baby cries vigorously, usually accompanied by agitated but uncoordinated movement

crystallization the first phase in Super's theory of career development, in which adolescents use their emerging identities to form ideas about careers

crystallized intelligence the knowledge acquired through life experience and education in a particular culture

death anxiety people's anxiety or even fear of death and dying

deductive reasoning a characteristic of formal-operational thought that involves drawing conclusions from facts

dementia a family of diseases involving serious impairment of behavioral and cognitive functioning

demographers people who study population trends

dendrite the end of the neuron that receives information, which looks like a tree with many branches

deoxyribonucleic acid (DNA) the molecule that composes one chromosome, making it the biochemical basis of heredity

dependent variable the behavior being observed

depression a disorder characterized by pervasive feelings of sadness, irritability, and low self-esteem

differentiation distinguishing and mastering individual motions

direct instruction telling a child what to do, when, and why

disorganized (disoriented) attachment a relationship in which infants don't seem to understand what's happening when they are separated and later reunited with their mothers

divergent thinking thinking in novel and unusual directions

dizygotic twins the result of two separate eggs fertilized by two sperm; also called fraternal twins

do not resuscitate (DNR) order a medical order that means CPR is not started should the heart and breathing stop

dominance hierarchy the ordering of individuals within a group in which group members with lower status defer to those with greater status

dominant the allele whose chemical instructions are followed

dual process model (DPM) the view of coping with bereavement that integrates loss-oriented stressors, concerning the loss itself, and restoration-oriented stressors, related to moving on with life

durable power of attorney for health care a document in which an individual appoints someone to act as his or her agent for health care decisions

dynamic systems theory the theory that views motor development as involving many distinct skills that are organized and reorganized over time to meet specific needs

dysphoria feeling sad or down

ecological theory a theory based on the idea that human development is inseparable from the environmental contexts in which a person develops

edgework the desire to live life more on the edge through physically and emotionally threatening situations that are on the boundary between life and death

ego resilience a powerful personality resource that enables people to handle midlife changes

egocentrism having difficulty in seeing the world from another's point of view, a characteristic typical of children in the preoperational period

elaboration a memory strategy in which information is embellished to make it more memorable

embryo the term given to the zygote after it is completely implanted in the uterine wall

emerging adulthood the period between late teens and mid- to late 20s when individuals are not adolescents but are not yet fully adults

emotional intelligence the ability to use one's own and others' emotions effectively for solving problems and living happily

empathy experiencing another person's feelings

enabling actions individuals' actions and remarks that tend to support others and sustain the interaction

end-of-life issues issues pertaining to the management of the final phase of life, after-death disposition of the body and memorial services, and distribution of assets

environmental press the demands put on an individual by the environment

epigenetic principle in Erikson's theory, the idea that each psychosocial strength has its own period of particular importance

episodic memory the general class of memory having to do with the conscious recollection of information from a specific time or event

equilibration according to Piaget, a process by which when disequilibrium occurs, children reorganize their schemes to return to a state of equilibrium

ethnic identity the feeling of belonging to a specific ethnic group

eugenics the effort to improve the human species by letting only people whose characteristics are valued by a society mate and pass along their genes

euthanasia the practice of ending life for reasons of mercy

exchange theory the theory that a relationship, such as marriage, is based on each partner contributing something to the relationship that the other would be hard pressed to provide

exosystem the social settings that a person may not experience firsthand but that still influence development

experience-expectant growth the process by which the wiring of the brain is organized by experiences that are common to most humans

experiment a systematic way of manipulating the key factor or factors that the investigator thinks causes a particular behavior

explicit memory the deliberate and conscious remembering of information learned and remembered at a specific time

expressive style a language-learning style of children whose vocabularies include many social phrases that are used like one word

extended family the most common form of family around the world, one in which grandparents and other relatives live with parents and children

external aids memory aids that rely on environmental resources, such as notebooks or calendars

extraversion a personality dimension associated with the tendencies to thrive on social interaction, enjoy talking, take charge easily, readily express opinions and feelings, like keeping busy, have boundless energy, and prefer stimulating and challenging environments

extremely low birth weight newborns who weigh less than 1,000 grams (2.2 pounds)

familism the idea that the family's well-being takes precedence over the concerns of individual family members

fast mapping a child's connections between words and referents that are made so quickly that he or she cannot consider all possible meanings of the word

fetal alcohol spectrum disorder a disorder affecting babies whose mothers consumed large amounts of alcohol while they were pregnant

fetal medicine a field of medicine concerned with treating prenatal problems before birth

filial obligation a sense of obligation to care for one's parents if necessary

final scenario people making their choices known about how they do and do not want their life to end

fine motor skills body movements associated with grasping, holding, and manipulating objects

fluid intelligence the abilities that make people flexible and adaptive thinkers, allow them to make inferences, and enable them to understand the relations among concepts

four-component model a model for understanding grief that is based on (1) the context of the loss, (2) the continuation of subjective meaning associated with the loss, (3) changing representations of the lost relationship over time, and (4) the role of coping and emotion regulation processes

frail older adults adults who have physical disabilities, are very ill, and may have cognitive or psychological disorders

free radicals chemicals that are produced randomly during normal cell metabolism and that bond easily to other substances inside cells

friendship a voluntary relationship between two people involving mutual liking

frontal cortex the brain region that regulates personality and goal-directed behavior

functional health the ability to perform ADLs and IADLs

gender constancy the understanding that maleness and femaleness do not change over situations or personal wishes

gender discrimination denying a job to someone solely on the basis of whether the person is a man or a woman

gender identity a sense of oneself as male or female

gender labeling young children's understanding that they are either boys or girls and naming of themselves accordingly

gender stability the understanding in preschool children that boys become men and girls become women

gender stereotypes beliefs and images about males and females that are not necessarily true

gender-schema theory a theory that states that children want to learn more about an activity only after first deciding whether it is masculine or feminine

gene a group of compounds that provides a specific set of biochemical instructions

generativity in Erikson's theory, being productive by helping others to ensure the continuation of society by guiding the next generation

genotype the complete set of genes that makes up a person's hereditary

germ disc small cluster of cells near the center of the zygote that will eventually develop into a baby

glass ceiling the level to which women may rise in an organization but beyond which they may not go

glass cliff a situation that women confront in which their leadership position is precarious

grammatical morphemes words or endings of words that make a sentence grammatical

grief the sorrow, hurt, anger, guilt, confusion, and other feelings that arise after experiencing a loss

grief work the psychological side of coming to terms with bereavement

grief-work-as-rumination hypothesis an approach that does not merely reject the necessity of grief processing for recovery from loss but views extensive grief processing as a form of rumination that may increase distress

habituation becoming unresponsive to a stimulus that is presented repeatedly

hemispheres right and left halves of the cortex

heterozygous alleles in a pair of chromosomes that differ from each other

high-density lipoproteins (HDLs) chemicals that help keep arteries clear and break down LDLs

homogamy the similarity of values and interests

homozygous alleles in a pair of chromosomes that are the same

hope according to Erikson, openness to new experience tempered by wariness that occurs when trust and mistrust are in balance

hospice an approach to assisting dying people that emphasizes pain management, or palliative care, and death with dignity

hostile aggression unprovoked aggression that seems to have the sole goal of intimidating, harassing, or humiliating another child

household an individual who lives alone or a group of individuals who live together

human development the multidisciplinary study of how people change and how they remain the same over time

hypoxia a birth complication in which umbilical blood flow is disrupted and the infant does not receive adequate oxygen

illusion of invulnerability adolescents' belief that misfortunes cannot happen to them

imaginary audience adolescents' feeling that their behavior is constantly being watched by their peers

imitation or observational learning learning that occurs by simply watching how others behave

implantation the zygote burrows into the uterine wall and establishes connections with a woman's blood vessels

implementation the third phase in Super's theory of career development, in which individuals enter the workforce

implicit memory the unconscious remembering of information learned at some earlier time

in vitro fertilization the process by which sperm and an egg are mixed in a petri dish to create a zygote, which is then placed in a woman's uterus

incontinence loss of bladder or bowel control

independent variable the factor being manipulated

infant mortality rate the percentage of infants who die before their first birthday

infant-directed speech speech that adults use with infants that is slow, has exaggerated changes in pitch and volume, and is thought to aid language acquisition

information-processing theory a theory proposing that human cognition consists of mental hardware and mental software

instrumental activities of daily living (IADLs) actions that require some intellectual competence and planning

instrumental aggression aggression used to achieve an explicit goal

instrumental orientation a characteristic of Kohlberg's stage 2, in which moral reasoning is based on the aim of looking out for one's needs

integration linking individual motions into a coherent, coordinated whole

integrity versus despair according to Erikson, the process in late life by which people try to make sense of their lives

intellectual disability substantially below-average intelligence and problems adapting to an environment that emerge before the age of 18

intelligence quotient (IQ) a mathematical representation of how a person scores on an intelligence test in relation to how other people of the same age score

interindividual variability patterns of change that vary from one person to another

internal aids memory aids that rely on mental processes, such as imagery

internal belief systems what one tells oneself about why certain things are happening

internal working model an infant's understanding of how responsive and dependable the mother is, which is thought to influence close relationships throughout the child's life

interpersonal norms a characteristic of Kohlberg's stage 3, in which moral reasoning is based on winning the approval of others

intersensory redundancy being attuned to information presented simultaneously to different sensory modes

intimacy versus isolation the sixth stage in Erikson's theory and the major psychosocial task for young adults

irregular or rapid-eye-movement (REM) sleep sleep in which an infant's eyes dart rapidly beneath the eyelids while the body is quite active

job satisfaction the positive feeling that results from an appraisal of one's work

joint custody when both parents retain legal custody of their children following divorce

kinetic cues cues to depth perception in which motion is used to estimate depth

kinkeeper the person, usually a middle-aged mother, who gathers family members together for celebrations and keeps them in touch with one another

knowledge-telling strategy writing down information as it is retrieved from memory, a common practice for young writers

knowledge-transforming strategy deciding what information to include and how best to organize it to convey a point

learning disability difficulty mastering at least one academic subject when a child has normal intelligence yet does not suffer other conditions that explain the poor performance

life-course persistent antisocial behavior antisocial behavior that emerges at an early age and continues throughout life

life-course perspective the ways in which various generations experience the biological, psychological, and sociocultural forces of development in their respective historical contexts

life review the process by which people reflect on the events and experiences of their lifetimes

life-span construct a unified sense of the past, present, and future based on personal experience and input from other people

life-span perspective the view that human development is multiply determined and cannot be understood within the scope of a single framework

life story a personal narrative that organizes past events into a coherent sequence

linear perspective a cue to depth perception based on parallel lines coming together at a single point in the distance

living will a document in which a person states his or her wishes about life support and other treatments

locomote the ability to move around in the world

longevity the number of years a person can expect to live

longitudinal study a research design in which the same individuals are observed or tested repeatedly at different points in their lives

low birth weight newborns who weigh less than 2,500 grams (5.5 pounds)

low-density lipoproteins (LDLs) chemicals that cause fatty deposits to accumulate in arteries, impeding blood flow

macrosystem the cultures and subcultures in which the microsystem, mesosystem, and exosystem are embedded

mad cry a more intense version of a basic cry

malnourished being small for age because of inadequate nutrition

marital adjustment the degree to which a husband and a wife accommodate each other over a certain period

marital quality a subjective evaluation of the couple's relationship on a number of dimensions

marital satisfaction a global assessment of one's marriage

marital success an umbrella term referring to any marital outcome

marriage education the idea that the more couples are prepared for marriage, the better the chances that the relationship will survive over the long run

maximum life expectancy the oldest age to which any person lives

meaning–mission fit the alignment between an executive's personal intentions and the company's mission

mechanics of intelligence those aspects of intelligence comprising fluid intelligence

menarche the onset of menstruation

menopausal hormone therapy (MHT) medication therapy in which women take low doses of estrogen, which is often combined with progestin (a synthetic form of progesterone) to counter symptoms associated with menopause

menopause the point at which menstruation stops

mental age (MA) in intelligence testing, a measure of children's performance corresponding to the chronological age of those whose performance equals the child's

mental hardware mental and neural structures that are built in and that allow the mind to operate

mental operations cognitive actions that can be performed on objects or ideas

mental software mental "programs" that are the basis for performing particular tasks

mentor or developmental coach a person who is part teacher, part sponsor, part model, and part counselor who facilitates on-the-job learning to help the new hire do the work required in his or her present role and to prepare for future roles

mesosystem provides connections across microsystems

metabolism how much energy the body needs

metacognitive knowledge a person's knowledge and awareness of cognitive processes

metamemory a person's informal understanding of memory, including the ability to diagnose memory problems accurately and to monitor the effectiveness of memory strategies

microsystem the people and objects in an individual's immediate environment

monozygotic twins the result of a single fertilized egg splitting to form two new individuals; also called identical twins

motion parallax a kinetic cue to depth perception based nearby objects moving across our visual field faster than distant moving objects

motor skills coordinated movements of the muscles and limbs

mourning the ways in which we express our grief

multidimensional a characteristic of theories of intelligence that identify several types of intellectual abilities

multidirectionality a developmental pattern in which some aspects of intelligence improve and other aspects decline during adulthood

myelin a fatty sheath that wraps around neurons and enables them to transmit information more rapidly

narrative a way in which a person derives personal meaning from being generative and by constructing a life story, which helps create the person's identity

naturalistic observation a technique in which people are observed as they behave spontaneously in some real-life situation

nature–nurture issue the degree to which genetic or hereditary influences (nature) and experiential or environmental influences (nurture) determine the kind of person you are

negative reinforcement trap unwittingly reinforcing a behavior you want to discourage

neglected children as applied to children's popularity, children who are ignored—neither liked nor disliked—by their classmates

neural plate a flat group of cells present in prenatal development that becomes the brain and spinal cord

neuritic plaques structural changes in the brain produced when damaged and dying neurons collect around a core of protein

neurofibrillary tangles spiral-shaped masses formed when fibers that compose the axon become twisted together

neuron a basic cellular unit of the brain and nervous system that specializes in receiving and transmitting information

neuroscience the study of the brain and nervous system, especially in terms of brain–behavior relationships

neuroticism a personality dimension that reflects the tendencies to be anxious, hostile, self-conscious, depressed, impulsive, and vulnerable

neurotransmitters chemicals released by terminal buttons that allow neurons to communicate with one another

niche-picking the process of deliberately seeking environments that are compatible with one's genetic makeup

nonshared environmental influences forces within a family that make siblings different from one another

nuclear family the most common form of family in Western societies, consisting only of parent(s) and child(ren)

obedience orientation a characteristic of Kohlberg's stage 1, in which moral reasoning is based on the belief that adults know what is right and wrong

object permanence the understanding, acquired in infancy, that objects exist independently

one-to-one principle a counting principle that states that there must be one and only one number name for each object counted

openness to experience a personality dimension that reflects the tendencies to have a vivid imagination and dream life, an appreciation of art, and a strong desire to try anything once

operant conditioning a form of learning related to the relation between the consequences of behavior and the likelihood that the behavior will recur

organization as applied to children's memory, a strategy in which information to be remembered is structured so that related information is placed together

orienting response an individual views a strong or unfamiliar stimulus, and changes in heart rate and brain-wave activity occur

osteoarthritis the most common form of arthritis, marked by gradual onset of bone damage with progression of pain and disability, together with minor signs of inflammation from wear and tear

osteoporosis a disease in which bones become porous and extremely easy to break

overextension when children define words more broadly than adults do

overregularizations grammatical usage that results from applying rules to words that are exceptions to the rule

pain cry a cry that begins with a sudden long burst, followed by a long pause and gasping

palliative care care that is focused on providing relief from pain and other symptoms of disease at any point during the disease process

parallel play when children play alone but are aware of and interested in what another child is doing

parietofrontal integration theory (P-FIT) the proposal that intelligence comes from a distributed and integrated network of neurons in the parietal and frontal lobes of the brain

Parkinson's disease a brain disease known primarily for its characteristic motor symptoms: very slow walking, difficulty getting into and out of chairs, and a slow hand tremor

passion a strong inclination toward an activity that individuals like (or even love), that they value (and thus find important), and in which they invest time and energy

passive euthanasia allowing a person to die by withholding available treatment

perception processes by which the brain receives, selects, modifies, and organizes incoming nerve impulses that are the result of physical stimulation

perimenopause the individually varying time of transition from regular menstruation to menopause

period of the fetus the longest period of prenatal development, extending from the 9th until the 38th week after conception

permissive parenting a style of parenting that offers warmth and caring but little parental control over children

persistent vegetative state a situation in which a person's cortical functioning ceases while brainstem activity continues

personal control beliefs the degree to which you believe your performance in a situation depends on something you do

personal fable the attitude of many adolescents that their feelings and experiences are unique and have never before been experienced by anyone

personality-type theory the view proposed by Holland that people find their work fulfilling when the important features of a job or profession fit the worker's personality

phenotype physical, behavioral, and psychological features that result from the interaction between an individual's genes and environment

phonemes unique sounds used to create words, making them the basic building blocks of language

phonological awareness the ability to hear the distinctive sounds of letters

physician-assisted suicide the process in which physicians provide dying patients with a fatal dose of medication that the patient self-administers

pictorial cues cues to depth perception that are used to convey depth in drawings and paintings

placenta a structure through which nutrients and wastes are exchanged between the pregnant woman and the developing child

plasticity the concept that intellectual abilities are not fixed but can be modified under the right conditions at just about any point in adulthood

polygenic inheritance phenotypes that are the result of the combined activity of many separate genes

popular children children who are liked by many classmates

population pyramid a graphic technique for illustrating population trends

populations broad groups of people that are of interest to researchers

possible selves representations of what we could become, what we would like to become, and what we are afraid of becoming

postconventional level the third level in Kohlberg's theory, in which moral reasoning is based on a personal moral code

postformal thought thinking characterized by recognizing that the correct answer varies from one situation to another, that solutions should be realistic, that ambiguity and contradiction are typical, and that subjective factors play roles in thinking

post-traumatic stress disorder (PTSD) an anxiety disorder that can develop after exposure to a terrifying event or ordeal in which grave physical harm occurred or was threatened

practical ability in Sternberg's theory of successful intelligence, the ability to know which solutions to a problem are likely to work

practical intelligence the range of skills related to how individuals shape, select, or adapt to their physical and social environments

pragmatics of intelligence those aspects of intelligence reflecting crystallized intelligence

preconventional level the first level in Kohlberg's theory, in which moral reasoning is based on external forces

prejudice a view of other people, usually negative, that is based on their membership in a specific group

prenatal development the many changes that turn a fertilized egg into a newborn human

presbycusis reduced sensitivity to high-pitched tones

presbyopia difficulty in seeing close objects clearly

preterm (premature) babies born before the 36th week after conception

primary control behavior aimed at affecting the individual's external world

primary mental abilities groups of related intellectual skills (e.g., memory or spatial ability)

primary sex characteristics physical signs of maturity that are directly linked to the reproductive organs

private speech a child's comments that are not intended for others but are designed instead to help regulate the child's behavior

programmed theories theories that aging is biologically or genetically programmed

prosocial behavior any behavior that benefits another person

psychodynamic theories theories proposing that development is largely determined by how well people resolve conflicts they face at different ages

psychomotor speed or reaction time the speed with which a person can make a specific response

psychosocial theory Erikson's proposal that personality development is determined by the interaction of an internal maturational plan and external societal demands

puberty a collection of physical changes that mark the onset of adolescence, including a growth spurt and the growth of breasts or testes

punishment a consequence that decreases the future likelihood of the behavior that it follows

purpose according to Erikson, a balance between individual initiative and willingness to cooperate with others

qualitative research a method that involves gaining in-depth understanding of human behavior and what governs it

reality shock a situation in which what is learned in the classroom does not always transfer directly into the "real world" and does not represent all that a person needs to know

recessive the allele whose instructions are ignored in the presence of a dominant allele

referential style a language-learning style of children whose vocabularies are dominated by names of objects, people, or actions

reflective judgment the way in which adults reason through real-life dilemmas

reflexes unlearned responses triggered by specific stimulation

regular (non-REM) sleep sleep in which heart rate, breathing, and brain activity are steady

reinforcement a consequence that increases the future likelihood of the behavior that it follows

rejected children as applied to children's popularity, children who are disliked by many classmates

relational aggression aggression used to hurt others by undermining their social relationships

reliability the extent to which a measure provides a consistent index of a characteristic

resistant attachment a relationship in which, after a brief separation, infants want to be held but are difficult to console

retinal disparity a way of inferring depth based on differences in the retinal images in the left and right eyes

returning adult students college students over age 25

rheumatoid arthritis a disease of the joints that affects different joints, causes different types of pain, and is more destructive than osteoarthritis

risk genes genes that increase the risk of getting a disease such as Alzheimer's

rites of passage rituals marking initiation into adulthood

role transitions movement into the next stage of development, which is marked by the assumption of new responsibilities and duties

sample a subset of the population

sandwich generation middle-aged adults who are caught between the competing demands of two generations: their parents and their children

scaffolding a style in which teachers gauge the amount of assistance they offer to match the learner's needs

scenario a manifestation of the life-span construct through expectations about the future

schemes according to Piaget, mental structures that organize information and regulate behavior

secondary control behavior or cognition aimed at affecting the individual's internal world

secondary mental abilities broad intellectual skills that subsume and organize primary mental abilities

secondary sex characteristics physical signs of maturity that are not directly linked to reproductive organs

secure attachment a relationship in which infants have come to trust and depend on their mothers

selective optimization with compensation model the model in which three processes (selection, optimization, and compensation) form a system of behavioral action that generates and regulates development and aging

selective serotonin reuptake inhibitors (SSRIs), heterocyclic antidepressants (HCAs), or monoamine oxidase (MAO) inhibitors medications for severe depression

self-efficacy people's beliefs about their own abilities and talents

self-reports people's answers to questions about the topic of interest

semantic memory the general class of memory concerning the remembering of meanings of words or concepts not tied to a specific time or event

sense of place the cognitive and emotional attachments that a person puts on their place of residence, by which a "house" is made into a "home"

sensorimotor period the first of Piaget's four stages of cognitive development, which lasts from birth to approximately 2 years

separation distress the expression of complicated or prolonged grief disorder that includes preoccupation with the deceased to the point that it interferes with everyday functioning, upsetting memories of the deceased, longing and searching for the deceased, and isolation following the loss

sequential design a developmental research design based on cross-sectional and longitudinal designs

sex chromosomes the 23rd pair of chromosomes, which determines the sex of the child

simple social play play that begins at about 15 to 18 months and continues into toddlerhood, when talking and smiling at each other also occur

sleeping the state in which a baby alternates from being still and breathing regularly to moving gently and breathing irregularly, with the eyes closed throughout

social clock tagging future events with a particular time or age by which they are to be completed

social cognitive career theory (SCCT) a theory that proposes career choice is a result of the application of Bandura's social cognitive theory, especially the concept of self-efficacy

social contract a characteristic of Kohlberg's stage 5, in which moral reasoning is based on the belief that laws are for the good of all members of society

social convoy a group of people that journeys with us throughout our lives, providing support in good times and bad

social referencing behavior in which infants in unfamiliar or ambiguous environments look at an adult for cues to help them interpret the situation

social role a set of cultural guidelines about how one should behave, especially with other people

social smiles smiles that infants produce when they see a human face

social system morality a characteristic of Kohlberg's stage 4, in which moral reasoning is based on maintenance of order in society

socialization teaching children the values, roles, and behaviors of their culture

socioemotional selectivity the process by which social contact is motivated by many goals, including information seeking, self-concept, and emotional regulation

spaced retrieval a memory intervention based on the E-I-E-I-O approach that involves implicit memory and internal aids

specification the second phase in Super's theory of career development, in which adolescents learn more about specific lines of work and begin training

spermarche the first spontaneous ejaculation of sperm

spiritual support a type of coping strategy that includes seeking pastoral care, participating in organized and nonorganized religious activities, and expressing faith in a God who cares for people

stable-order principle a counting principle that states that number names must always be counted in the same order

stagnation in Erikson's theory, the state in which people are unable to deal with the needs of their children or to provide mentoring to younger adults

stem cells unspecialized human or animal cells that can produce mature specialized body cells and can replicate themselves

stranger wariness the first distinct signs of fear that emerge around 6 months of age when infants become wary in the presence of unfamiliar adults

stress and coping paradigm the dominant framework used to study stress, which emphasizes the transactions between a person and his or her environment

stroke or cerebral vascular accident (CVA) an interruption of blood flow in the brain due to blockage or hemorrhage in a cerebral artery

structured observations the researcher creates a setting that is likely to elicit the behavior of interest

subjective well-being an evaluation of one's life that is associated with positive feelings

sudden infant death syndrome (SIDS) when a healthy baby dies suddenly for no apparent reason

synaptic pruning a gradual reduction in the number of synapses, beginning in infancy and continuing until early adolescence

systematic observation watching people and carefully recording what they do or say

telegraphic speech speech used by young children that contains only words necessary to convey a message

telomeres tips of the chromosomes that shorten and break with increasing age

temperament a consistent style or pattern of behavior

teratogen an agent that causes abnormal prenatal development

terminal buttons small knobs at the end of the axon that release neurotransmitters

terror management theory a theory that addresses the issue of why people engage in certain behaviors to achieve particular psychological states based on their deeply rooted concerns about mortality

texture gradient a perceptual cue to depth based on the texture of objects changing from coarse and distinct for nearby objects to finer and less distinct for distant objects

thanatology the study of death, dying, grief, bereavement, and social attitudes toward these issues

theory an organized set of ideas that is designed to explain development

theory of mind ideas about connections among thoughts, beliefs, intentions, and behavior that create an intuitive understanding of the link between mind and behavior

time-out a punishment that involves removing children who are misbehaving from a situation to a quiet, unstimulating environment

transient ischemic attacks (TIAs) interruptions of blood flow to the brain that are often early warning signs of stroke

traumatic distress the expression of complicated or prolonged grief disorder that includes disbelief about the death; mistrust, anger, and detachment from others as a result of the death; feeling shocked by the death; and experiencing the physical presence of the deceased

Type A behavior pattern a behavior pattern in which people tend to be intensely competitive, angry, hostile, restless, aggressive, and impatient

Type B behavior pattern a behavior pattern that is the opposite of Type A

ultrasound a prenatal diagnostic technique that uses sound waves to generate an image of the fetus

umbilical cord the structure containing veins and arteries that connects the developing child to the placenta

underextension when children define words more narrowly than adults do

uninvolved parenting a style of parenting that provides neither warmth nor control and that minimizes the amount of time parents spend with children

universal versus context-specific development issue whether there is just one path of development or several paths

useful field of view (UFOV) an area from which someone can extract visual information in a single glance without turning the head or moving the eyes

useful life expectancy the number of years that a person is free from debilitating chronic disease and impairment

validity the extent to which a measure actually assesses what researchers think it assesses

vascular dementia a disease caused by numerous small CVAs

very low birth weight newborns who weigh less than 1,500 grams (3.3 pounds)

visual cliff a glass-covered platform that appears to have a "shallow" side and a "deep" side and is used to study infants' depth perception

visual expansion a kinetic cue to depth perception that is based an object filling an ever-greater proportion of the retina as it moves closer

vulnerability–stress–adaptation model a model that proposes that marital quality is a dynamic process resulting from the couple's ability to handle stressful events in the context of their particular vulnerabilities and resources

waking activity the state in which a baby's eyes are open but seem unfocused while the arms or legs move in bursts of uncoordinated motion

wear-and-tear disease a degenerative disease caused by injury or overuse, such as osteoarthritis

wear-and-tear theory a theory that suggests that the body, much like any machine, gradually deteriorates and finally wears out

whole-brain death declared only when the deceased meets eight criteria related to movement, respiration, and responsiveness upon an initial test and again 24 hours later

will according to Erikson, a young child's understanding that he or she can act on the world intentionally, which occurs when autonomy, shame, and doubt are in balance

work–family conflict the feeling of being pulled in multiple directions by incompatible demands from job and family

working memory the processes and structures involved in holding information in mind and simultaneously using it for other functions

zone of maximum comfort when the press level is slightly lower than average, facilitating a high quality of life

zone of maximum performance potential when the press level is slightly higher than average, tending to improve performance

zone of proximal development the difference between what children can do with assistance and what they can do alone

zygote the fertilized egg

References

AARP. (1999). *AARP/Modern Maturity sexuality survey: Summary of findings.* Retrieved from http://assets.aarp.org/rgcenter/health/mmsexsurvey.pdf

Aasland, O. G., Rosta, J., & Nylenna, M. (2010). Healthcare reforms and job satisfaction among doctors in Norway. *Scandinavian Journal of Public Health, 38,* 253–258.

Aberson, C. L., Shoemaker, C., & Tomolillo, C. (2004). The role of interethnic friendships. *Journal of Social Psychology, 144,* 335–347.

Aboud, F. E. (1993). The developmental psychology of racial prejudice. *Transcultural Psychiatric Research Review, 30,* 229–242.

Aboud, F. E. (2003). The formation of in-group favoritism and out-group prejudice in young children: Are they distinct attitudes? *Developmental Psychology, 39,* 48–60.

Acevedo, B. P., & Aron, A. (2009). Does a long-term relationship kill romantic love? *Review of General Psychology, 13,* 59–65.

Achor, S. (2010). *The happiness advantage: The seven principles of positive psychology that fuel success and performance at work.* New York: Random House.

Ackerman, B. P. (1993). Children's understanding of the speaker's meaning in referential communication. *Journal of Experimental Child Psychology, 55,* 56–86.

Adams, J. (1999). On neurodevelopmental disorders: Perspectives from neurobehavioral teratology. In H. Tager-Flusberg (Ed.), *Neurodevelopmental disorders* (pp. 451–468). Cambridge, MA: MIT Press.

Adams, M. J., Treiman, R., & Pressley, M. (1998). Reading, writing, and literacy. In W. Damon (Ed.), *Handbook of child psychology* (5th ed., Vol. 4, pp. 275–356). New York: Wiley.

Adams, R. G., & Ueno, K. (2006). Middle-aged and older adult men's friendships. In V. H. Bedford & B. Formaniak Turner (Eds.), *Men in relationships: A new look from a life course perspective* (pp. 103–124). New York: Springer.

Adler, L. L. (2001). Women and gender roles. In L. L. Adler & U. P. Gielen (Eds.), *Cross-cultural topics on psychology* (2nd ed., pp. 103–114). Westport, CT: Praeger/Greenwood Press.

Administration for Children and Families. (2010a). *Administration for Children and Families healthy marriage initiative, 2002–2009.* Retrieved from http://www.healthymarriageinfo.org/docs/ACFGuideto09.pdf

Administration for Children and Families. (2010b). *Head Start facts.* Author.

Adolph, K. E. (2000). Specificity of learning: Why infants fall over a veritable cliff. *Psychological Science, 11,* 290–295.

Adolph, K. E. (2002). Learning to keep balance. In R. V. Kail (Ed.), *Advances in child development and behavior* (Vol. 30, pp. 1–40). Orlando, FL: Academic Press.

Adzick, N. S. (2010). Fetal myelomeningocele: Natural history, pathophysiology, and in-utero intervention. *Seminars in Fetal and Neonatal Medicine, 15,* 9–14.

Agahi, N., Ahacic, K., & Parker, M. G. (2006). Continuity of leisure participation from middle age to old age. *Journals of Gerontology: Psychological Sciences and Social Sciences, 61B,* S340–S346.

Ahluwalia, N. (2004). Aging, nutrition and immune function. *Journal of Nutrition, Health & Aging, 8,* 2–6.

Ai, A. L., Wink, P., & Ardelt, M. (2010). Spirituality and aging: A journey for meaning through deep interconnection in humanity. In J. C. Cavanaugh & C. K. Cavanaugh (Eds.), *Aging in America* (Vol. 3, pp. 222–246). Santa Barbara, CA: Praeger Perspectives.

Ainsworth, M. S. (1978). The development of infant–mother attachment. In B. M. Caldwell & H. N. Ricciuti (Eds.), *Review of child development research* (Vol. 3, pp. 1–94). Chicago: University of Chicago Press.

Ainsworth, M. S. (1993). Attachment as related to mother–infant interaction. *Advances in Infancy Research, 8,* 1–50.

Aisenbrey, S., Evertsson, M., & Grunow, D. (2009). Is there a career penalty for mothers' time out? A comparison of Germany, Sweden, and the United States. *Social Forces, 88,* 573–605.

Ajrouch, K. J. (2007). Health disparities and Arab-American elders: Does intergenerational support buffer the inequality-health link? *Journal of Social Issues, 63,* 745–758.

Albert, M. S., DeKosky, S. T., Dickson, D., Dubois, B., Feldman, H. A., Fox, N. C., et al. (2011). The diagnosis of mild cognitive impairment due to Alzheimer's disease: Recommendations from the National Institute on Aging–Alzheimer's Association workgroups on diagnostic guidelines for Alzheimer's disease. *Alzheimer's & Dementia: Journal of the Alzheimer's Association, 7,* 270–279.

Alberts, A. E. (2005). Neonatal behavioral assessment scale. In C. B. Fisher & R. M. Lerner (Eds.), *Encyclopedia of applied developmental science* (Vol. 1, pp. 111–115). Thousand Oaks, CA: Sage.

Aldridge, V., Dovey, T. M., & Halford, J. C. G. (2009). The role of familiarity in dietary development. *Developmental Review, 29,* 32–44.

Aldwin, C. M., & Gilmer, D. F. (2004). *Health, illness, and optimal aging: Biological and psychosocial perspectives.* Thousand Oaks, CA: Sage.

Alhija, F. N.-A., & Fresko, B. (2010). Socialization of new teachers: Does induction matter? *Teaching and Teacher Education, 26,* 1592–1597.

Allaire, J. C., & Marsiske, M. (1999). Everyday cognition: Age and intellectual ability correlates. *Psychology and Aging, 14,* 627–644.

Allen, T. D. (2001). Family-supportive work environments: The role of organizational perceptions. *Journal of Vocational Behavior, 58,* 414–435.

Alley, J. L. (2004). The potential meaning of the grandparent–grandchild relationship as perceived by young adults: An exploratory study. *Dissertation Abstracts International. Section B. Sciences and Engineering, 65*(3-B), 1536.

Almeida, J., Molnar, B. E., Kawachi, I., & Subramanian, S. V. (2009). Ethnicity and nativity status as determinants of perceived social support: Testing the concept of familism. *Social Science and Medicine, 68,* 1852–1858.

Almendarez, B. L. (2008). Mexican American elders and nursing home transition. *Dissertation Abstracts International. Section B. Sciences and Engineering, 68*(7-B), 4384.

Altschul, I., Oyserman, D., & Bybee, D. (2006). Racial–ethnic identity in mid-adolescence: Content and change as predictors of academic achievement. *Child Development, 77,* 1155–1169.

Alzheimer's Association. (2010). *2010 Alzheimer's disease facts and figures.* Retrieved from http://www.alz.org/documents_custom/report_alzfactsfigures2010.pdf

Amato, P. R. (2001). Children of divorce in the 1990s: An update of the Amato and Keith (1991) meta-analysis. *Journal of Family Psychology, 15,* 355–370.

Amato, P. R., & Fowler, F. (2002). Parenting practices, child adjustment, and family diversity. *Journal of Marriage and Family, 64,* 703–716.

American Academy of Pain Medicine. (2009). Pain medicine position paper. *Pain Medicine, 10,* 972–1000. doi:10.1111/j.1526-4637.2009.00696.x

American Academy of Pediatrics. (2005). Policy statement: Use of performance-enhancing substances. *Pediatrics, 115,* 1103–1106.

American Association on Intellectual and Developmental Disabilities Ad Hoc Committee on Terminology and Classification. (2010). *Intellectual disability* (11th ed.). Washington, DC: Author.

American Automobile Association. (2005). *AAA roadwise review—A tool to help seniors drive safely, longer: Overview.* Retrieved from http://seniordriving.aaa.com/evaluate-your-driving-ability/interactive-driving-evaluation

American Cancer Society. (2010a). *Cancer facts and figures 2010.* Retrieved from http://www.cancer.org/acs/groups/content/@nho/documents/document/acspc-024113.pdf

American Cancer Society. (2010b). *Guide to quitting smoking.* Retrieved from http://www.cancer.org/Healthy/StayAwayfromTobacco/GuidetoQuittingSmoking/index

American Cancer Society. (2010c). *Quiz: Do you need help to quit? Take the stop smoking quiz.* Retrieved from http://www.cancer.org/Healthy/ToolsandCalculators/Quizzes/app/smoking-habits-quiz

American Cancer Society. (2010d). *Secondhand smoke.* Retrieved from http://www.cancer.org/Cancer/CancerCauses/TobaccoCancer/secondhand-smoke

American Heart Association. (2010). *Cholesterol.* Retrieved from http://www.heart.org/HEARTORG/Conditions/Cholesterol/CholestrolATH_UCM_001089_SubHomePage.jsp

American Heart Association. (2011). *Body mass index (BMI calculator).* Retrieved from http://www.heart.org/HEARTORG/GettingHealthy/WeightManagement/BodyMassIndex/Body-Mass-Index-BMI-Calculator_UCM_307849_Article.jsp

American Heart Association. (2012). *Delicious decisions.* Retrieved from http://www.heart.org/HEARTORG/GettingHealthy/NutritionCenter/Recipes/Welcome-to-Delicious-Decisions_UCM_301068_SubHomePage.jsp

American Psychiatric Association. (1994). *Diagnostic and statistical manual of mental disorders* (4th ed.). Washington, DC: Author.

American Psychological Association. (2004). Guidelines for psychological practice with older adults. *American Psychologist, 59,* 236–260.

Amso, D., & Johnson, S. P. (2006). Learning by selection: Visual search and object perception in young infants. *Developmental Psychology, 42,* 1236–1245.

Ancoli-Israel, S., & Alessi, C. (2005). Sleep and aging. *American Journal of Geriatric Psychiatry, 13,* 341–343.

Anderson, C. A., Shibuya, A., Ihori, N., Swing, E. L., Bushman, B. J., Sakamoto, A., et al. (2010). Violent video game effects on aggression, empathy, and prosocial behavior in Eastern and Western countries: A meta-analytic review. *Psychological Bulletin, 136,* 151–173.

Anderson, D. R., Huston, A. C., Schmitt, K. L., Linebarger, D. L., & Wright, J. C. (2001). Early childhood television viewing and adolescent behavior. *Monographs of the Society for Research in Child Development, 66* (Serial No. 264).

Anderson, E. R., Greene, S. M., Walker, L., Malerba, C., Forgatch, M. S., & DeGarmo, D. S. (2004). Ready to take a chance again: Transitions into dating among divorced parents. *Journal of Divorce & Remarriage, 40,* 61–75.

Anderson, K. G., Tomlinson, K., Robinson, J. M., & Brown, S. A. (2011). Friends or foes: Social anxiety, peer affiliation, and drinking in middle school. *Journal of Studies on Alcohol and Drugs, 72,* 61–69.

Anderson, R. N., & Smith, B. L. (2005). Deaths: Leading causes for 2002. *National Vital Statistics Reports, 53*(17).

Anderson, S. W., Damasio, H., Tranel, D., & Damasio, A. R. (2001). Long-term sequelae of prefrontal cortex damage acquired in early childhood. *Developmental Neuropsychology, 18,* 281–296.

Anderson, V. D. (2007). Religiosity as it shapes parenting processes in preadolescence: A contextualized process model. *Dissertation Abstracts International. Section B. Sciences and Engineering, 67*(9-B), 5439.

Andreassi, J. K. (2007). The role of personality and coping in work–family conflict: New directions. *Dissertation Abstracts International. Section A. Humanities and Social Sciences, 67*(8-A), 3053.

Angel, J. L., Buckley, C. J., & Sakamoto, A. (2001). Duration or disadvantage? Exploring nativity, ethnicity, and health in midlife. *Journal of Gerontology: Social Sciences, 56B,* S275–S284.

Angeles, L. (2010). Children and life satisfaction. *Journal of Happiness Studies, 11,* 523–538.

Anisfeld, M. (1991). Neonatal imitation. *Developmental Review, 11,* 60–97.

Anisfeld, M. (1996). Only tongue protrusion modeling is matched by neonates. *Developmental Review, 16,* 149–161.

Annett, M. (2008). Test of the right shift genetic model for two new samples of family handedness and for the data of McKeever (2000). *Laterality, 13,* 105–123.

Antonucci, T. (2001). Social relations: An examination of social networks, social support, and sense of control. In J. E. Birren & K. W. Schaie (Eds.), *Handbook of the psychology of aging* (5th ed., pp. 427–453). San Diego, CA: Academic Press.

Antonucci, T. C., Akiyama, H., & Lansford, J. E. (1998). Negative effects of close social relations. *Family Relations, 47,* 379–384.

Apfelbaum, E. P., Pauker, K., Ambady, N., Sommers, S. R., & Norton, M. I. (2008). Learning (not) to talk about race: When older children underperform in social categorization. *Developmental Psychology, 44,* 1513–1518.

Apgar, V. (1953). A proposal for a new method of evaluation of the newborn infant. *Current Researches in Anesthesia and Analgesia, 32,* 260–267.

Aponte, M. (2007). Mentoring: Career advancement of Hispanic army nurses. *Dissertation Abstracts International. Section A. Humanities and Social Sciences, 68*(4-A), 1609.

Appleyard, K., Yang, C. M., & Runyan, D. K. (2010). Delineating the maladaptive pathways of child maltreatment: A mediated moderation analysis of the roles of self-perception and social support. *Development and Psychopathology, 22,* 337–352.

Archer, N., & Bryant, P. (2001). Investigating the role of context in learning to read: A direct test of Goodman's model. *British Journal of Psychology, 92,* 579–591.

Ardelt, M. (2010). Age, experience, and the beginning of wisdom. In D. Dannefer & C. Phillipson (Eds.), *The Sage handbook of social gerontology* (pp. 306–316). Thousand Oaks, CA: Sage.

Armstrong-Stassen, M., & Templer, A. (2005). Adapting training for older employees: The Canadian response to an aging workforce. *Journal of Management Development, 24,* 57–67.

Arndt, J., & Vess, M. (2008). Tales from existential oceans: Terror management theory and how the awareness of our mortality affects us all. *Social and Personality Psychology Compass, 2,* 909–928.

Arnett, J. J. (2004). *Emerging adulthood: The winding road from the late teens through the twenties.* New York: Oxford University Press.

Arnett, J. J. (2007). Socialization in emerging adulthood: From the family to the wider world, from socialization to self-socialization. In J. E. Grusec & P. D. Hastings (Eds.), *Handbook of socialization: Theory and research* (pp. 208–231). New York: Guilford.

Arnett, J. J. (2012). New horizons in research on emerging and young adult-hood. In A. Booth, S. L. Brown, N. S. Landale, W. D. Manning, & S. M. McHale (Eds.), *Early adulthood in family context* (Vol. 2, Pt. 5, pp. 231–244). New York: Springer.

Arseneault, L., Tremblay, R. E., Boulerice, B., & Saucier, J. F. (2002). Obstetrical complications and violent delinquency: Testing two developmental pathways. *Child Development, 73,* 496–508.

Årseth, A. K., Kroger, J., Martinussen, M., & Marcia, J. E. (2009). Meta-analytic studies of identity status and the relational issues of attachment and intimacy. *Identity, 9,* 1–32.

Artandi, S. E., & DePinho, R. A. (2010). Telomeres and telomerase in cancer. *Carcinogenesis, 31,* 9–18.

Artazcoz, L., Benach, J., Borrell, C., & Cortès, I. (2004). Unemployment and mental health: Understanding the interactions among gender, family roles, and social class. *American Journal of Public Health, 94,* 82–88.

Asbury, K., Dunn, J. F., Pike, A., & Plomin, R. (2003). Nonshared environmental influences on individual differences in early behavioral development: A monozygotic twin differences study. *Child Development, 74,* 933–943.

Asendorpf, J. B., Denissen, J. J. A., & van Aken, M. A. G. (2008). Inhibited and aggressive preschool children at 23 years of age: Personality and social transitions into adulthood. *Developmental Psychology, 44,* 997–1011.

Ashcraft, M. H. (1982). The development of mental arithmetic: A chronometric approach. *Developmental Review, 2,* 212–236.

Asher, S. R., & Paquette, J. A. (2003). Loneliness and peer relations in childhood. *Current Directions in Psychological Science, 12,* 75–78.

Aslin, R. N., Jusczyk, P. W., & Pisoni, D. B. (1998). Speech and auditory processing during infancy: Constraints on and precursors to language. In W. Damon (Ed.), *Handbook of child psychology* (5th ed., Vol. 2, pp. 147–198). New York: Wiley.

Aslin, R. N., Saffran, J. R., & Newport, W. L. (1998). Computation of conditional probability statistics by 8-month-old infants. *Psychological Science, 9,* 321–324.

Asoodeh, M. H., Khalili, S., Daneshpour, N., & Lavasani, M. G. (2010). Factors of successful marriage: Accounts from self described happy couples. *Procedia Social and Behavioral Sciences, 5,* 2042–2046.

Aspenlieder, L., Buchanan, C. M., McDougall, P., & Sippola, L. K. (2009). Gender nonconformity and peer victimization in pre- and early adolescence. *European Journal of Developmental Science, 3,* 3–16.

Atchley, R. C. (1989). A continuity theory of normal aging. *The Gerontologist, 29,* 183–190.

Attig, T. (1996). *How we grieve: Relearning the world.* New York: Oxford University Press.

Atwater, E. (1992). *Adolescence.* Englewood Cliffs, NJ: Prentice Hall.

Au, T. K., & Glusman, M. (1990). The principle of mutual exclusivity in word learning: To honor or not to honor? *Child Development, 61,* 1474–1490.

Aunola, K., Stattin, H., & Nurmi, J.-E. (2000). Parenting styles and adolescents' achievement strategies. *Journal of Adolescence, 23,* 205–222.

Averett, P., & Jenkins, C. (2012). Review of the literature on older lesbians: Implications for education, practice, and research. *Journal of Applied Gerontology, 31,* 537–561.

Awa, W. L., Plaumann, M., & Walter, U. (2010). Burnout prevention: A review of intervention programs. *Patient Education and Counseling, 78,* 184–190.

Bach, P. B. (2010). Postmenopausal hormone therapy and breast cancer: An uncertain trade-off. *JAMA, 304,* 1719–1720.

Bachman, J. G., Staff, J. G., O'Malley, P. M., Schulenberg, J. E., & Freedman-Doan, P. (2011). Twelfth-grade student work intensity linked to later educational attainment and substance use: New longitudinal evidence. *Developmental Psychology, 47,* 344–363.

Backhouse, J. (2006, October). *Grandparents-as-parents: Social change and its impact on grandparents who are raising their grandchildren.* Paper presented at the Social Change in the 21st Century Conference, Carseldine Queensland University of Technology, Brisbane, Australia. Retrieved from http://eprints.qut.edu.au/6072/1/6072.pdf

Backscheider, A. G., Shatz, M., & Gelman, S. A. (1993). Preschoolers' ability to distinguish living kinds as a function of regrowth. *Child Development, 64,* 1242–1257.

Baek, J. (2005). Individual variations in family caregiving over the caregiving career. *Dissertation Abstracts International. Section B. Sciences and Engineering, 65*(X-B), 3769.

Bagwell, C. L. (2004). Friendships, peer networks and antisocial behavior. In J. B. Kupersmidt & K. A. Dodge (Eds.), *Children's peer relations* (pp. 37–57). Washington, DC: American Psychological Association.

Bagwell, C. L., Bender, S. E., Andreassi, C. L., Kinoshita, T. L., Montarello, S. A., & Muller, J. G. (2005). Friendship quality and perceived relationship changes predict psychosocial adjustment in early adulthood. *Journal of Social & Personal Relationships, 22,* 235–254.

Bagwell, C. L., Newcomb, A. F., & Bukowski, W. M. (1998). Preadolescent friendship and peer rejection as predictors of adult adjustment. *Child Development, 69,* 140–153.

Bahrick, L. E., & Lickliter, R. (2002). Intersensory redundancy guides early perceptual and cognitive development. In R. V. Kail (Ed.), *Advances in child development and behavior* (Vol. 30, pp. 153–187). Orlando, FL: Academic Press.

Bahrick, L. E., Lickliter, R., & Flom, R. (2004). Intersensory redundancy guides the development of selective attention, perception, and cognition in infancy. *Current Directions in Psychological Science, 13,* 99–102.

Bailey, D. A., & Rasmussen, R. L. (1996). Sport and the child: Physiological and skeletal issues. In F. L. Smoll & R. E. Smith (Eds.), *Children and youth in sport: A biopsychological perspective* (pp. 187–199). Dubuque, IA: Brown & Benchmark.

Bailey, J. A., Hill, K. G., Oesterle, S., & Hawkins, J. D. (2009). Parenting practices and problem behavior across three generations: Monitoring, harsh discipline, and drug use in the intergenerational transmission of externalizing behavior. *Developmental Psychology, 45,* 1214–1226.

Baillargeon, R. (1987). Object permanence in 3½- and 4½-month-old infants. *Developmental Psychology, 23,* 655–664.

Baillargeon, R. (1994). How do infants learn about the physical world? *Current Directions in Psychological Science, 3,* 133–140.

Baillargeon, R. H., Zoccolillo, M., Keenan, K., Côté, S., Pérusse, D., Wu, H., et al. (2007). Gender differences in physical aggression: A prospective population-based survey of children before and after 2 years of age. *Developmental Psychology, 43,* 13–26.

Baker, L. (1994). Fostering metacognitive development. In H. W. Reese (Ed.), *Advances in child development and behavior* (Vol. 25, pp. 201–239). San Diego, CA: Academic Press.

Bakermans-Kranenburg, M., van IJzendoorn, M. H., & Juffer, F. (2003). Less is more: Meta-analyses of sensitivity and attachment interventions in early childhood. *Psychological Bulletin, 129,* 195–215.

Ball, K., & Owsley, C. (1993). The useful field of view test: A new technique for evaluating age-related declines in visual function. *Journal of the American Optometric Association, 64,* 71–79.

Baltes, P. B. (1993). The aging mind: Potential and limits. *The Gerontologist, 33,* 580–594.

Baltes, P. B. (1997). On the incomplete architecture of human ontogeny: Selection, optimization, and compensation as foundation of developmental theory. *American Psychologist, 52,* 366–380.

Baltes, P. B., Lindenberger, U., & Staudinger, U. M. (2006). Life span theory in developmental psychology. In R. M. Lerner & W. Damon (Eds.), *Handbook of child psychology* (6th ed., Vol. 1, pp. 569–664). Hoboken, NJ: Wiley.

Baltes, P. B., & Smith, J. (2003). New frontiers in the future of aging: From successful aging of the young old to the dilemmas of the fourth age. *Gerontology, 49,* 123–135.

Baltes, P. B., & Staudinger, U. M. (2000). Wisdom: A metaheuristic (pragmatic) to orchestrate mind and virtue toward excellence. *American Psychologist, 55,* 122–136.

Bambra, C. (2010). Yesterday once more? Unemployment and health in the 21st century. *Journal of Epidemiology and Community Health, 64,* 213–215.

Bandura, A., & Bussey, K. (2004). On broadening the cognitive, motivational, and sociostructural scope of theorizing about gender development and functioning: Comment on Martin, Ruble, and Szkrybalo (2002). *Psychological Bulletin, 130,* 691–701.

Banger, M. (2003). Affective syndrome during perimenopause. *Maturitas, 41*(Suppl. I), S13–S18.

Bannard, C., & Mathews, D. (2008). Stored word sequences in language learning: The effect of familiarity on children's repetition of four-word combinations. *Psychological Science, 19,* 241–248.

Banner, S. (2005, March 5). When killing a juvenile was routine. *New York Times,* p. 6.

Barber, B. K., & Olsen, J. A. (1997). Socialization in context: Connection, regulation, and autonomy in the family, school, and neighborhood, and with peers. *Journal of Adolescent Research, 12,* 287–315.

Barboza, D. (2011, January 12). *China, in a shift, takes on its Alzheimer's problem.* Retrieved from http://www.nytimes.com/2011/01/13/world/asia/13shanghai.html?_r51&scp51&sq5china%20alzheimer%27s&st5cse

Bardach, S. H., Gayer, C. C., Clinkinbeard, T., Zanjani, F., & Watkins, J. F. (2010). The malleability of possible selves and expectations regarding aging. *Educational Gerontology, 36,* 407–424.

Barenboim, C. (1981). The development of person perception in childhood and adolescence: From behavioral comparisons to psychological constructs to psychological comparisons. *Child Development, 52,* 129–144.

Barkley, R. A. (2003). Attention-deficit/hyperactivity disorder. In E. J. Mash & R. A. Barkley (Eds.), *Child psychopathology* (2nd ed., pp. 63–112). New York: Guilford.

Barkley, R. A. (2004). Adolescents with attention deficit/hyperactivity disorder: An overview of empirically based treatments. *Journal of Psychiatric Review, 10,* 39–56.

Barnard, J. W. (2010). Deception, decisions, and investor education. *Elder Law Journal, 17,* 201.

Baron-Cohen, S. (1995). *Mindblindness: An essay on autism and theory of mind.* Cambridge, MA: MIT Press/Bradford Books.

Barr, R., & Hayne, H. (1999). Developmental changes in imitation from television during infancy. *Child Development, 70,* 1067–1081.

Barton, M. E., & Tomasello, M. (1991). Joint attention and conversation in mother–infant–sibling triads. *Child Development, 62,* 517–529.

Bartsch, K., & Wellman, H. M. (1995). *Children talk about the mind.* New York: Oxford University Press.

Baskett, L. M. (1985). Sibling status effects: Adult expectations. *Developmental Psychology, 21,* 441–445.

Bates, E., Bretherton, I., & Snyder, L. (1988). *From first words to grammar: Individual differences and dissociable mechanisms.* New York: Cambridge University Press.

Bates, J. S. (2009). *Generative grandfathering, commitment, and contact: How grandfathers nurture relationships with grandchildren and the relational and mental health benefits for aging men* (Unpublished doctoral dissertation). Syracuse University, Syracuse, NY.

Batty, G. D., Wennerstad, K. M., Smith, G. D., Gunnell, D., Deary, I. J., Tynelius, P., & Rasmussen, F. (2009). IQ in early adulthood and morality in middle age: Cohort study of 1 million Swedish men. *Epidemiology, 20,* 100–109.

Bauer, P. J. (2006). Event memory. In W. Damon & R. M. Lerner (Eds.), *Handbook of child psychology* (6th ed., Vol. 2, pp. 373–425). Hoboken, NJ: Wiley.

Bauer, P. J. (2007). *Remembering the times of our lives: Memory in infancy and beyond.* Mahwah, NJ: Erlbaum.

Bauer, P. J., & Lukowski, A. F. (2010). The memory is in the details: Relations between memory for the specific features of events and long-term recall during infancy. *Journal of Experimental Child Psychology, 107,* 1–14.

Baumann, A., Claudot, F., Audibert, G., Mertes, P.-M., & Puybasset, M. (2011). The ethical and legal aspects of palliative sedation in severely brain-injured patients:

a French perspective. *Philosophy, Ethics, and Humanities in Medicine, 6*. Retrieved from http://preview.peh-med.com/content/pdf/1747-5341-6-4.pdf

Baumeister, R. F. (2010). The self. In R. F. Baumeister & E. J. Finkel (Eds.), *Advanced social psychology: The state of the science* (pp. 139–175). New York: Oxford University Press.

Baumrind, D. (1975). *Early socialization and the discipline controversy*. Morristown, NJ: General Learning Press.

Baumrind, D. (1991). Parenting styles and adolescent development. In R. M. Lerner, A. C. Petersen, & J. Brooks-Gunn (Eds.), *Encyclopedia of adolescence* (pp. 746–758). New York: Garland.

Bauserman, R. (2002). Child adjustment in joint-custody versus sole-custody arrangements: A meta-analytic review. *Journal of Family Psychology, 16*, 91–102.

Bava, S., & Tapert, S. F. (2010). Adolescent brain development and the risk for alcohol and other drug problems. *Neuropsychology Review, 20*, 398–413.

Beal, C. R., & Belgrad, S. L. (1990). The development of message evaluation skills in young children. *Child Development, 61*, 705–712.

Beck, A. T. (1967). *Depression: Clinical, experimental, and theoretical aspects*. New York: Harper & Row.

Beck, A. T., Rush, J., Shaw, B., & Emery, G. (1979). *Cognitive therapy of depression*. New York: Guilford.

Beck, E., Burnet, K. L., & Vosper, J. (2006). Birth-order effects on facets of extraversion. *Personality and Individual Differences, 40*, 953–959.

Becker, B. J. (1986). Influence again: An examination of reviews and studies of gender differences in social influence. In J. S. Hyde & M. C. Linn (Eds.), *The psychology of gender differences: Advances through meta-analysis* (pp. 178–209). Baltimore: Johns Hopkins University Press.

Bedir, A., & Aksoy, Ş. (2011). Brain death revisited: It is not "complete death" according to Islamic sources. *Journal of Medical Ethics, 37*, 290–294.

Beehr, T. A., & Bennett, M. M. (2007). Examining retirement from a multi-level perspective. In K. S. Shultz & G. A. Adams (Eds.), *Aging and work in the 21st century* (pp. 277–302). Mahwah, NJ: Erlbaum.

Behnke, M., & Eyler, F. D. (1993). The consequences of prenatal substance use for the developing fetus, newborn, and young child. *International Journal of the Addictions, 28*, 1341–1391.

Bekris, L. M., Yu, C.-E., Bird, T. D., & Tsuang, D. (2011). The genetics of Alzheimer's disease and Parkinson's disease. In J. P. Blass (Ed.), *Neurochemical mechanisms in disease* (pp. 695–756). New York: Springer.

Belsky, J., Houts, R. M., & Fearon, R. M. P. (2010). Infant attachment security and the timing of puberty: Testing an evolutionary hypothesis. *Psychological Science, 21*, 1195–1201.

Belsky, J., Steinberg, L., & Draper, P. (1991). Childhood experience, interpersonal development, and reproductive strategy: An evolutionary theory of socialization. *Child Development, 62*, 647–670.

Belsky, J., Steinberg, L. D., Houts, R. M., Friedman, S. L., DeHart, G., Cauffman, E., et al. (2007). Family rearing antecedents of pubertal timing. *Child Development, 78*, 1302–1321.

Belsky, J., Steinberg, L., Houts, R. M., Halpern-Felsher, B., & the National Institute of Child Health and Human Development Early Child Care Research Network. (2010). The development of reproductive strategy in females: Early maternal harshness → earlier menarche → increased sexual risk taking. *Developmental Psychology, 46*, 120–128.

Ben Bashat, D., Ben Sira, L., Graif, M., Pianka, P., Hendler, T., Cohen, Y., et al. (2005). Normal white matter development from infancy to adulthood: Comparing diffusion tensor and high b value diffusion weighted MR images. *Journal of Magnetic Resonance Imaging, 21*, 503–511.

Benenson, J. F., & Christakos, A. (2003). The greater fragility of females' versus males' closest same-sex friendships. *Child Development, 74*, 1123–1129.

Bengtsson, T., & Scott, K. (2011). Population aging and the future of the welfare state: The example of Sweden. *Population and Review, 37*(Suppl. S1), 158–170.

Bennett, D. S., Bendersky, M., & Lewis, M. (2008). Children's cognitive ability from 4 to 9 years old as a function of prenatal cocaine exposure, environmental risk, and maternal verbal intelligence. *Developmental Psychology, 44*, 919–928.

Bennett, K. M. (2010). How to achieve resilience as an older widower: Turning points or gradual change? *Ageing and Society, 30*, 369–382.

Bent, K. N., & Magilvy, J. K. (2006). When a partner dies: Lesbian widows. *Issues in Mental Health Nursing, 27*, 447–459.

Benton, S. L., Corkill, A. J., Sharp, J. M., Downey, R. G., & Khramtsova, I. (1995). Knowledge, interest, and narrative writing. *Journal of Educational Psychology, 87*, 66–79.

Berch, D. B. (2005). Making sense of number sense: Implications for children with mathematical disabilities. *Journal of Learning Disabilities, 38*, 333–339.

Berdes, C., & Zych, A. A. (2000). Subjective quality of life of Polish, Polish-immigrant, and Polish-American elderly. *International Journal of Aging and Human Development, 50*, 385–395.

Bereiter, C., & Scardamalia, M. (1987). *The psychology of written composition*. Hillsdale, NJ: Erlbaum.

Bergen, D., & Mauer, D. (2000). Symbolic play, phonological awareness, and literacy skills at three age levels. In K. A. Roskos & J. F. Christie (Eds.), *Play and literacy in early childhood: Research from multiple perspectives* (pp. 45–62). Mahwah, NJ: Erlbaum.

Berger, S. E., Adolph, K. E., & Lobo, S. A. (2005). Out of the toolbox: Toddlers differentiate wobbly and wooden handrails. *Child Development, 76*, 1294–1307.

Berk, R. A. (2010). Where's the chemistry in mentor–mentee academic relationships? Try spend mentoring. *International Journal of Mentoring and Coaching, 8*, 85–92. Retrieved from http://www.ronberk.com/articles/2010_mentor.pdf

Berko, J. (1958). The child's learning of English morphology. *Word, 14*, 150–177.

Berkowitz, M. W., Sherblom, S., Bier, M., & Battistich, V. (2006). Educating for positive youth development. In M. Killen & J. G. Smetana (Eds.), *Handbook of moral development* (pp. 683–702). Mahwah, NJ: Erlbaum.

Berlin, L. J., Appleyard, K., & Dodge, K. A. (2011). Intergenerational continuity in child maltreatment: Mediating mechanisms and implications for prevention. *Child Development, 82*, 162–176.

Berlin, L. J., Brady-Smith, C., & Brooks-Gunn, J. (2002). Links between childbearing age and observed maternal behaviors with 14-month-olds in the Early Head Start Research and Evaluation Project. *Infant Mental Health Journal, 23*, 104–129.

Berliner, A. J. (2000). Re-visiting Erikson's developmental model: The impact of identity crisis resolution on intimacy motive, generativity formation, and psychological adaptation in never-married, middle-aged adults. *Dissertation Abstracts International. Section B. Sciences and Engineering, 61*(X-B), 560.

Berndt, T. J., & Keefe, K. (1995). Friends' influence on adolescents' adjustment to school. *Child Development, 66*, 1312–1329.

Berndt, T. J., & Murphy, L. M. (2002). Influences of friends and friendships: Myths, truths, and research recommendations. *Advances in Child Development and Behavior, 30*, 275–310.

Berns, G. S., Moore, S., & Capra, C. M. (2009). *Adolescent engagement in dangerous behaviors is associated with increased white matter maturity of frontal cortex*. Retrieved from http://www.ncbi.nlm.nih.gov/pmc/articles/PMC2728774/

Berry, J. M., Hastings, E., West, R. L., Lee, C., & Cavanaugh, J. C. (2010). Memory aging: Deficits, beliefs, and interventions. In J. C. Cavanaugh & C. K. Cavanaugh (Eds.), *Aging in America* (Vol. 1, pp. 255–299). Santa Barbara, CA: Praeger Perspectives.

Bertenthal, B. H., & Clifton, R. K. (1998). Perception and action. In W. Damon (Ed.), *Handbook of child psychology* (5 ed., Vol. 2, pp. 51–102). New York: Wiley.

Besharov, D. J., & Gardiner, K. N. (1997). Trends in teen sexual behavior. *Children and Youth Services Review, 19*, 341–367.

Best, C. T. (1995). Learning to perceive the sound pattern of English. In C. Rovee-Collier (Ed.), *Advances in infancy research*. Norwood, NJ: Ablex.

Best, J. R. (2010). Effects of physical activity on children's executive function: Contributions of experimental research on aerobic exercise. *Developmental Review, 30*, 331–351.

Bhatt, R. S., Bertin, E., Hayden, A., & Reed, A. (2005). Face processing in infancy: Developmental changes in the use of different kinds of relational information. *Child Development, 76*, 169–181.

Bhidayasiri, R., & Brenden, N. (2011). 10 commonly asked questions about Parkinson's disease. *The Neurologist, 17*, 57–62.

Bialystok, E. (1988). Levels of bilingualism and levels of linguistic awareness. *Developmental Psychology, 24*, 560–567.

Bialystok, E. (2010). Global–local and trail-making tasks by monolingual and bilingual children: Beyond inhibition. *Developmental Psychology, 46*, 93–105.

Biblarz, T. J., & Savci, E. (2010). Lesbian, gay, bisexual, and transgender families. *Journal of Marriage and Family, 72*, 480–497.

Biddle, S. J. H., & Asare, M. (2011). Physical activity and mental health in children and adolescents: a review of reviews. *British Journal of Sports Medicine, 45*, 886–895.

Biederman, J., Petty, C. R., Evans, M., Small, J., & Faraone, S. V. (2010). How persistent is ADHD? A controlled 10-year follow-up study of boys with ADHD. *Psychiatry Research, 177,* 299–304.

Bigler, R. S., Jones, L. C., & Lobliner, D. B. (1997). Social categorization and the formation of intergroup attitudes in children. *Child Development, 68,* 530–543.

Bigler, R. S., & Liben, L. S. (2007). Developmental intergroup theory: Explaining and reducing children's social stereotyping and prejudice. *Current Directions in Psychological Science, 16,* 162–166.

Bingenheimer, J. B., Brennan, R. T., & Earls, F. J. (2005). Firearm violence exposure and serious violent behavior. *Science, 308,* 1323–1326.

Bird, D. J. (2001). The influences and impact of burnout on occupational therapists. *Dissertation Abstracts International. Section B. Sciences and Engineering, 62*(1-B), 204.

Birditt, K. S., Brown, E., Orbuch, T. L., & McIlvane, J. M. (2010). Marital conflict behaviors and implications for divorce over 16 years. *Journal of Marriage and Family, 72,* 1188–1204.

Biro, S., & Leslie, A. M. (2007). Infants' perception of goal-directed actions: Development through cue-based bootstrapping. *Developmental Science, 8,* 36–43.

Bishop, J. B. (2000). An environmental approach to combat binge drinking on college campuses. *Journal of College Student Psychotherapy, 15,* 15–30.

Bishop, N. A., Lu, T., & Yankner, B. A. (2010). Neural mechanisms of ageing and cognitive decline. *Nature, 464,* 529–535.

Bjerkedal, T., Kristensen, P., Skjeret, G. A., & Brevik, J. I. (2007). Intelligence test scores and birth order among young Norwegian men (conscripts) analyzed within and between families. *Intelligence, 35,* 503–514.

Björklund, A., & Dunnett, S. B. (2007). Dopamine neuron systems in the brain: An update. *Trends in Neurosciences, 30,* 194–202.

Bjorklund, D. F. (2005). *Children's thinking: Cognitive development and individual differences* (4th ed.). Belmont, CA: Wadsworth.

Black, J. E. (2003). Environment and development of the nervous system. In I. B. Weiner, M. Gallagher, & R. J. Nelson (Eds.), *Handbook of psychology* (Vol. 3, pp. 655–668). Hoboken, NJ: Wiley.

Black-Gutman, D., & Hickson, F. (1996). The relationship between racial attitudes and social-cognitive development in children: An Australian study. *Developmental Psychology, 32,* 448–456.

Blanchard-Fields, F. (2007). Everyday problem solving and emotion: An adult developmental perspective. *Current Directions in Psychological Science, 16,* 26–31.

Blanchard-Fields, F. (2009). Flexible and adaptive socio-emotional problem solving in adult development and aging. *Restorative Neurology and Neuroscience, 27,* 539–550.

Blanchard-Fields, F. (2010). Neuroscience and aging. In J. C. Cavanaugh & C. K. Cavanaugh (Eds.), *Aging in America* (Vol. 1, pp. 1–25). Santa Barbara, CA: Praeger Perspectives.

Blanchard-Fields, F., Baldi, R. A., & Constantin, L. P. (2004). *Interrole conflict across the adult lifespan: The role of parenting stage, career stages and quality of experiences.* Unpublished manuscript, School of Psychology, Georgia Institute of Technology, Atlanta, GA.

Blanchard-Fields, F., Janke, H. C., & Camp, C. J. (1995). Age differences in problem-solving style: The role of emotional salience. *Psychology and Aging, 10,* 173–180.

Bloom, L. (1998). Language acquisition in its developmental context. In W. Damon (Ed.), *Handbook of child psychology* (5th ed., Vol. 2, pp. 309–370). New York: Wiley.

Bloom, L., Margulis, C., Tinker, E., & Fujita, N. (1996). Early conversations and word learning: Contributions from child and adult. *Child Development, 67,* 3154–3175.

Bloom, L., & Tinker, E. (2001). The intentionality model and language acquisition. *Monographs of the Society for Research in Child Development, 66* (Serial No. 267).

Blossfeld, H.-P. (2009). Educational assortative marriage in comparative perspective. *Annual Review of Sociology, 35,* 513–530.

Boelen, P. A., & Prigerson, H. G. (2007). The influence of symptoms of prolonged grief disorder, depression, and anxiety on quality of life among bereaved adults: A prospective study. *European Archives of Psychiatry and Clinical Neuroscience, 257,* 444–452.

Boivin, M., Vitaro, F., & Gagnon, C. (1992). A reassessment of the self-perception profile for children: Factor structure, reliability, and convergent validity of a French version among second through sixth grade children. *International Journal of Behavioral Development, 15,* 275–290.

Bonanno, G. A. (2009). *The other side of sadness: What the new science of bereavement tells us about life after loss.* New York: Basic Books.

Bonanno, G. A., & Kaltman, S. (1999). Toward an integrative perspective on bereavement. *Psychological Bulletin, 125,* 760–776.

Bonanno, G. A., Papa, A., Lalande, K., Zhang, N., & Noll, J. G. (2005). Grief processing and deliberate grief avoidance: A prospective comparison of bereaved spouses and parents in the United States and the People's Republic of China. *Journal of Consulting and Clinical Psychology, 73,* 86–98.

Bonanno, G. A., Papa, A., & O'Neill, K. (2001). Loss and human resilience. *Applied and Preventive Psychology, 10,* 193–206.

Book, P. L. (1996). How does the family narrative influence the individual's ability to communicate about death? *Omega: Journal of Death and Dying, 33,* 323–342.

Boon, H., Ruiter, R. U. C., James, S., van den Borne, B., Williams, E., & Reddy, P. (2010). Correlates of grief among older adults caring for children and grandchildren as a consequence of HIV and AIDS in South Africa. *Journal of Aging and Health, 22,* 48–67.

Bornstein, M. H., & Arterberry, M. E. (2003). Recognition, discrimination, and categorization of smiling by 5-month-old infants. *Developmental Science, 6,* 585–599.

Bornstein, M. H., Putnick, D. L., Suwalsky, J. T., & Gini, M. (2006). Maternal chronological age, prenatal and perinatal history, social support, and parenting of infants. *Child Development, 77,* 875–892.

Borson, S. (2011). Depression and anxiety in COPD: Diagnosis and management issues. In N. A. Hanania & A. Sharafkhaneh (Eds.), *COPD: A guide to diagnosis and clinical management* (pp. 271–281). New York: Springer.

Boseovski, J. J. (2010). Evidence for "rose-colored glasses": An examination of the positivity bias in young children's personality judgments. *Child Development Perspectives, 4,* 212–218.

Boseovski, J. J. (2012). Trust in testimony about strangers: Young children prefer reliable informants who make positive attributions. *Journal of Experimental Child Psychology, 111,* 543–551.

Bosma, H. A., & Kunnen, E. S. (2001). Determinants and mechanisms in ego identity development: A review and synthesis. *Developmental Review, 21,* 39–66.

Boss, P. (2006). *Loss, trauma, and resilience: Therapeutic work with ambiguous loss.* New York: Norton.

Bosshard, G., & Materstvedt, L. J. (2011). Medical and societal issues in euthanasia and assisted suicide. In R. Chadwick, H. ten Have, & E. M. Meslin (Eds.), *The Sage handbook of health care ethics* (pp. 202–218). Thousand Oaks, CA: Sage.

Bot, S. M., Engels, R. C. M. E., Knibbe, R. A., & Meeus, W. H. J. (2005). Friends' drinking behavior and adolescent alcohol consumption: The moderating role of friendship characteristics. *Addictive Behaviors, 30,* 929–947.

Bouchard, T. J. (2009). Genetic influence on human intelligence (Spearman's *g*): How much? *Annals of Human Biology, 36,* 527–544.

Bouldin, E. D., & Andresen, E. (2010). Caregiving and health. Personal relationships in later life. In J. C. Cavanaugh & C. K. Cavanaugh (Eds.), *Aging in America* (Vol. 2, pp. 81–99). Santa Barbara, CA: Praeger Perspectives.

Bouldin, P. L., & Grayson, A. M. (2010). *Perceptions of sexual harassment and sexual assault: A study of gender differences among U.S. Navy officers* (Master's thesis, Naval Postgraduate School, Monterey, CA). Retrieved from http://edocs.nps.edu/npspubs/scholarly/theses/2010/Mar/10Mar_Bouldin.pdf

Bowker, A. (2006). The relationship between sports participation and self-esteem during early adolescence. *Canadian Journal of Behavioral Science, 38,* 214–229.

Bowlby, J. (1969). *Attachment and loss* (Vol. 1). New York: Basic Books.

Bowlby, J. (1991). Ethological light on psychoanalytical problems. In P. Bateson (Ed.), *The development and integration of behaviour: Essays in honour of Robert Hinde* (pp. 301–313). New York: Cambridge University Press.

Boyle, P. J., Feng, Z., & Raab, G. M. (2011). Does widowhood increase mortality risk? Testing for selection effects by comparing causes of spousal death. *Epidemiology, 22,* 1–5.

Bozikas, V., Kioseoglou, V., Palialia, M., Nimatoudis, I., Iakovides, A., Karavatos, A., & Kaprinis, G. (2000). Burnout among hospital workers and community-based mental health staff. *Psychiatriki, 11,* 204–211.

Bradley, R. H., Corwyn, R. F., Burchinal, M., McAdoo, H. P., & Coll, C. G. (2001). The home environment of children in the United States: Part II. Relations with behavioral development through age thirteen. *Child Development, 72,* 1868–1886.

Braine, M. D. S. (1976). Children's first word combinations. *Monographs of the Society for Research in Child Development, 41* (Serial No. 164).

Braine, M. D. S. (1992). What sort of innate structure is needed to "bootstrap" into syntax? *Cognition, 45,* 77–100.

Brandone, A. C., & Wellman, H. M. (2009). You can't always get what you want: Infants understand failed goal-directed actions. *Psychological Science, 20,* 85–91.

Brandtstädter, J. (1999). Sources of resilience in the aging self. In T. M. Hess & F. Blanchard-Fields (Eds.), *Social cognition and aging* (pp. 123–141). San Diego, CA: Academic Press.

Bratkovich, K. L. (2010). *The relationship of attachment and spirituality with post-traumatic growth following a death for college students.* (Unpublished doctoral dissertation). Oklahoma State University, Stillwater, OK.

Brault, M. W. (2008). *Americans with disabilities: 2005.* Retrieved from http://www.census.gov/prod/2008pubs/p70-117.pdf

Braun, S. D. (2007). Gay fathers with children adopted from foster care: Understanding their experiences and predicting adoption outcomes. *Dissertation Abstracts International. Section B. Sciences and Engineering, 68*(2-B), 1296.

Braungart, J. M., Plomin, R., DeFries, J. C., & Fulker, D. W. (1992). Genetic influence on tester-rated infant temperament as assessed by Bayley's Infant Behavior Record: Nonadoptive and adoptive siblings and twins. *Developmental Psychology, 28,* 40–47.

Braungart-Rieker, J. M., Hill-Soderlund, A. L., & Karrass, J. (2010). Fear and anger reactivity trajectories from 4 to 16 months: The roles of temperament, regulation, and maternal sensitivity. *Developmental Psychology, 46,* 791–804.

Braver, T. S., & West, R. F. (2008). Working memory, executive control, and aging. In F. I. M. Craik & T. A. Salthouse (Eds.). *Handbook of aging and cognition* (3rd ed., pp. 311–372). New York: Psychology Press.

Brazelton, T. B., & Nugent, J. K. (1995). *Neonatal behavioral assessment scale* (3rd ed.). London: Mac Keith.

Brazelton, T. B., Nugent, J. K., & Lester, B. M. (1987). Neonatal behavioral assessment scale. In J. D. Osofsky (Ed.), *Handbook of infant development* (2nd ed.). New York: Wiley.

Brechwald, W. A., & Prinstein, M. J. (2011). Beyond homophily: A decade of advances in understanding peer influence processes. *Journal of Research on Adolescence, 21,* 166–179.

Bremner, J. G. (2011). Four themes from 20 years of research on infant perception and cognition. *Infant and Child Development, 20,* 137–147.

Brendgen, M., Lamarche, V., Wanner, B., & Vitaro, F. (2010). Links between friendship relations and early adolescents' trajectories of depressed mood. *Developmental Psychology, 46,* 491–501.

Brendgen, M., Vitaro, F., Boivin, M., Dionea, G., & Pérusse, D. (2006). Examining genetic and environmental effects on reactive versus proactive aggression. *Developmental Psychology, 42,* 1299–1312.

Brennan, P. A., Grekin, E. R., Mortensen, E. L., & Mednick, S. A. (2002). Relationship of maternal smoking during pregnancy with criminal arrest and hospitalization for substance abuse in male and female adult offspring. *American Journal of Psychiatry, 159,* 48–54.

Brickman, A. D. (2011, August). *Loosely formed semi-related thoughts about the diagnosis of AD (and related disorders) from a neuropsychologist.* Paper presented at the annual meeting of the American Psychological Association, Washington, DC.

Bribiescas, R. G. (2010). An evolutionary and life history perspective on human male reproductive senescence. *Annals of the New York Academy of Sciences, 1204,* 54–64.

Brissett-Chapman, S., & Isaacs-Shockley, M. (1997). *Children in social peril: A community vision for preserving family care of African American children and youth.* Washington, DC: Child Welfare League of America.

Brissette, I., Scheier, M. F., & Carver, C. S. (2002). The role of optimism in social network development, coping, and psychological adjustment during a life transition. *Journal of Personality and Social Psychology, 82,* 102–111.

Brockington, I. (1996). *Motherhood and mental health.* Oxford, England: Oxford University Press.

Brody, G. H., & Ge, X. (2001). Linking parenting processes and self-regulation to psychological functioning and alcohol use during early adolescence. *Journal of Family Psychology, 15,* 82–94.

Brody, G. H., Kim, S., Murry, V. M., & Brown, A. C. (2003). Longitudinal direct and indirect pathways linking older sibling competence to the development of younger sibling competence. *Developmental Psychology, 39,* 618–628.

Brody, G. H., Stoneman, A., & McCoy, J. K. (1994). Forecasting sibling relationships in early adolescence from child temperament and family processes in middle childhood. *Child Development, 65,* 771–784.

Brody, N. (1992). *Intelligence* (2nd ed.). San Diego, CA: Academic Press.

Bronfenbrenner, U. (1979). Contexts of child rearing: Problems and prospects. *American Psychologist, 34,* 844–850.

Bronfenbrenner, U. (1989). Ecological systems theory. In R. Vasta (Ed.), *Annals of child development* (Vol. 6, pp. 187–249). Greenwich, CT: JAI Press.

Bronfenbrenner, U. (1995). Developmental ecology through space and time: A future perspective. In P. Moen, G. H. Elder, Jr., & K. Luscher (Eds.), *Examining lives in context: Perspectives on the ecology of human development* (pp. 619–647). Washington, DC: American Psychological Association.

Bronfenbrenner, U., & Morris, P. (2006). The ecology of developmental processes. In R. M. Lerner & W. Damon (Eds.), *Handbook of child psychology* (6th ed., Vol. 1, pp. 793–828). Hoboken, NJ: Wiley.

Brooks-Gunn, J., & Paikoff, R. (1993). "Sex is a gamble, kissing is a game": Adolescent sexuality, contraception, and sexuality. In S. P. Millstein, A. C. Petersen, & E. O. Nightingale (Eds.), *Promoting the health behavior of adolescents* (pp. 180–208). New York: Oxford University Press.

Brougham, R. R., & Walsh, D. A. (2005). Goal expectations as predictors of retirement intentions. *International Journal of Aging and Human Development, 61,* 141–160.

Brown, B. B., & Klute, C. (2003). Friendships, cliques, and crowds. In G. R. Adams & M. D. Berzonsky (Eds.), *Blackwell handbook of adolescence* (pp. 330–348). Malden, MA: Blackwell.

Brown, B. B., Lohr, M. J., & McClenahan, E. L. (1986). Early adolescents' perceptions of peer pressure. *Journal of Early Adolescence, 6,* 139–154.

Brown, B. B., Mounts, N., Lamborn, S. D., & Steinberg, L. (1993). Parenting practices and peer group affiliation in adolescence. *Developmental Psychology, 64,* 467–482.

Brown, J. R., & Dunn, J. (1996). Continuities in emotion understanding from three to six years. *Child Development, 67,* 789–802.

Brown, J. V., Bakeman, R., Coles, C. D., Platzman, K. A., & Lynch, M. E. (2004). Prenatal cocaine exposure: A comparison of 2-year-old children in parental and nonparental care. *Child Development, 75,* 1282–1295.

Brown, J. W., Chen, S.-L., Mefford, L., Brown, A., Callen, B., & McArthur, P. (2011). Becoming an older volunteer: A grounded theory study. *Nursing Research and Practice.* doi:10.1155/2011/361250

Brown, J., Meadows, S. O., & Elder, G. H., Jr. (2007). Race–ethnic inequality and psychological distress: Depressive symptoms from adolescence to young adulthood. *Developmental Psychology, 43,* 1295–1311.

Brown, R., Pressley, M., Van Meter, P., & Schuder, T. (1996). A quasi-experimental validation of transactional strategies instruction with low-achieving second-grade readers. *Journal of Educational Psychology, 88,* 18–37.

Browne, K. D., & Hamilton-Giachritsis, C. (2005). The influence of violent media on children and adolescents: A public-health approach. *Lancet, 365,* 702–710.

Bruno, J. L., Manis, F. R., Keating, P., Sperling, A. J., Nakamoto, J., & Seidenberg, M. S. (2007). Auditory word identification in dyslexic and normally achieving readers. *Journal of Experimental Child Psychology, 97,* 183–204.

Buchanan, C. M., & Heiges, K. L. (2001). When conflict continues after the marriage ends: Effects of postdivorce conflict on children. In J. Grych & F. D. Fincham (Eds.), *Interparental conflict and child development* (pp. 337–362). New York: Cambridge University Press.

Buchsbaum, B. C. (1996). Remembering a parent who has died: A developmental perspective. In D. Klass, P. R. Silverman, & S. L. Nickman (Eds.), *Continuing bonds: New understandings of grief* (pp. 113–124). Washington, DC: Taylor & Francis.

Bugental, D. B., & Happaney, K. (2004). Predicting infant maltreatment in low-income families: The interactive effects of maternal attributions and child status at birth. *Developmental Psychology, 40,* 234–243.

Bugental, D. B., & Schwartz, A. (2009). A cognitive approach to child maltreatment prevention among medically at-risk infants. *Developmental Psychology, 45,* 284–288.

Buhl, H. (2008). Development of a model describing individuated adult child–parent relationships. *International Journal of Behavioral Development, 32,* 381–389.

Buhrmester, D., & Furman, W. (1990). Perceptions of sibling relationships during middle childhood and adolescence. *Child Development, 61,* 1387–1398.

Bullard, L., Wachlarowicz, M., DeLeeuw, J., Snyder, J., Low, S., Forgatch, M., et al. (2010). Effects of the Oregon model of parent management training (PMTO) on marital adjustment in new stepfamilies: A randomized trial. *Journal of Family Psychology, 24,* 485–496.

Bullock, K. (2004). Family social support. In P. J. Bomar (Ed.), *Promoting health in families: Applying family research and theory to nursing practice* (3rd ed., pp. 142–161). Philadelphia: W. B. Saunders.

Bullock, M., & Lütkenhaus, P. (1990). Who am I? The development of self-understanding in toddlers. *Merrill-Palmer Quarterly, 36,* 217–238.

Bumpass, L. L., & Aquilino, W. S. (1995). *A social map of midlife: Family and work over the middle years.* Madison, WI: University of Wisconsin, Center for Demography and Ecology.

Burack, J. A., Flanagan, T., Peled, T., Sutton, H. M., Zygmuntowicz, C., & Manly, J. T. (2006). Social perspective-taking skills in maltreated children and adolescents. *Developmental Psychology, 42,* 207–217.

Burchinal, M. R., Roberts, J. E., Riggins, R., Zeisel, S. A., Neebe, E., & Bryant, D. (2000). Relating quality of center-based child care to early cognitive and language development longitudinally. *Child Development, 71,* 338–357.

Burk, W. J., & Laursen, B. (2005). Adolescent perceptions of friendship and their associations with individual adjustment. *International Journal of Behavioral Development, 29,* 156–164.

Burke, B. L., Martens, A., & Faucher, E. H. (2010). Two decades of terror management theory: a meta-analysis of mortality salience research. *Personality and Social Psychology Review, 14,* 155–195.

Burnette, D. (1999). Social relationships of Latino grandparent caregivers: A role theory perspective. *The Gerontologist, 39,* 49–58.

Burt, K. B., & Masten, A. S. (2010). Development in the transition to adulthood: Vulnerabilities and opportunities. In J. E. Grant & M. N. Potenza (Eds.), *Young adult mental health* (pp. 5–18). Oxford, England: Oxford University Press.

Busch, J., & Rodogno, R. (2011). Life support and euthanasia, a perspective on Shaw's new perspective. *Journal of Medical Ethics, 37,* 81–83.

Buss, K. A., & Goldsmith, H. H. (1998). Fear and anger regulation in infancy: Effects on the temporal dynamics of affective expression. *Child Development, 69,* 359–374.

Buss, K. A., & Kiel, E. J. (2004). Comparison of sadness, anger, and fear facial expressions when toddlers look at their mothers. *Child Development, 75,* 1761–1773.

Bustos, M. L. C. (2007). La muerte en la cultura occidental: Antropología de la muerte [Death in Western culture: Anthropology of death]. *Revista Colombiana de Psiquiatría, 36,* 332–339.

Bylsma, F. W., Ostendorf, C. A., & Hofer, P. J. (2002). Challenges in providing neuropsychological and psychological services in Guam and the Commonwealth of the Northern Marianas Islands (CNMI). In F. R. Ferraro (Ed.), *Minority and cross-cultural aspects of neuropsychological assessment: Studies on neuropsychology, development, and cognition* (pp. 145–157). Bristol, PA: Swets & Zeitlinger.

Cable, N., & Sacker, A. (2008). Typologies of alcohol consumption in adolescence: Predictors and adult outcomes. *Alcohol and Alcoholism, 43,* 81–90.

Cacioppo, J. T., Berntson, G. G., Bechara, A., Tranel, D., & Hawkley, H. C. (2011). Could an aging brain contribute to subjective well-being? The value added by a social neuroscience perspective. In A. Todorov, S. Fiske, & D. Prentice (Eds.), *Social neuroscience: Toward understanding the underpinnings of the social mind* (pp. 249–262). New York: Oxford University Press.

Cadell, S., & Marshall, S. (2007). The (re)construction of self after the death of a partner to HIV/AIDS. *Death Studies, 31,* 537–548.

Cahill, E., Lewis, L. M., Barg, F. K., & Bogner, H. R. (2009). "You don't want to burden them": Older adults' views on family involvement in care. *Journal of Family Nursing, 27,* 295–317.

Cain, K. (1999). Ways of reading: How knowledge and use of strategies are related to reading comprehension. *British Journal of Developmental Psychology, 17,* 293–312.

Callaghan, R., Rochat, P., Lillard, A., Claux, M. L., Odden, H., Itakura, S., et al. (2005). Synchrony in the onset of mental-state reasoning: Evidence from five cultures. *Psychological Science, 16,* 378–384.

Callahan, C. M. (2000). Intelligence and giftedness. In R. J. Sternberg (Ed.), *Handbook of intelligence* (pp. 159–175). Cambridge, England: Cambridge University Press.

Cameron, L., Rutland, A., Brown, R., & Douch, R. (2006). Changing children's intergroup attitudes toward refugees: Testing different models of extended contact. *Child Development, 77,* 1208–1219.

Camp, C. J. (1999a). Memory interventions for normal and pathological older adults. In R. Schulz, M. P. Lawton, & G. Maddox (Eds.), *Annual review of gerontology and geriatrics* (Vol. 18, pp. 155–189). New York: Springer.

Camp, C. J. (2001). From efficacy to effectiveness to diffusion: Making the transitions in dementia intervention research. *Neuropsychological Rehabilitation, 11,* 495–517.

Camp, C. J. (Ed.). (1999b). *Montessori-based activities for persons with dementia* (Vol. 1). Beachwood, OH: Menorah Park Press.

Camp, C. J., Foss, J. W., Stevens, A. B., Reichard, C. C., McKitrick, L. A., & O'Hanlon, A. M. (1993). Memory training in normal and demented elderly populations: The E-I-E-I-O model. *Experimental Aging Research, 19,* 277–290.

Camp, C. J., Judge, K. S., Bye, C. A., Fox, K. M., Bowden, J., Bell, M., et al. (1997). An intergenerational program for persons with dementia using Montessori methods. *The Gerontologist, 37,* 688–692.

Camp, C. J., & McKitrick, L. A. (1991). Memory interventions in Alzheimer-type dementia populations: Methodological and theoretical issues. In R. L. West & J. D. Sinnott (Eds.), *Everyday memory and aging: Current research and methodology* (pp. 155–172). New York: Springer.

Camp, C. J., & Skrajner, M. J. (2005). Resident-assisted Montessori programming (RAMP): Training persons with dementia to serve as group activity leaders. *The Gerontologist, 44,* 426–431.

Campbell, F. A., Pungello, E. P., Miller-Johnson, S., Burchinal, M., & Ramey, C. T. (2001). The development of cognitive and academic abilities: Growth curves from an early childhood educational experiment. *Developmental Psychology, 37,* 231–242.

Campbell, R., & Sais, E. (1995). Accelerated metalinguistic (phonological) awareness in bilingual children. *British Journal of Developmental Psychology, 13,* 61–68.

Campinha-Bacote, J. (2010). A culturally conscious model of mentoring. *Nurse Educator, 35,* 130–135.

Camras, L. A., Chen, Y., Bakeman, R., Norris, K., & Cain, R. T. (2006). Culture, ethnicity, and children's facial expressions: A study of European American, mainland Chinese, Chinese American, and adopted Chinese girls. *Emotion, 6,* 103–114.

Cannon, T. D., Rosso, I. M., Hollister, J. M., Bearden, C. E., Sanchez, L. E., & Hadley, T. (2000). A prospective cohort study of genetic and perinatal influences in the etiology of schizophrenia. *Schizophrenia Bulletin, 26,* 351–366.

Cappell, K. A., Gmeindl, L., & Reuter-Lorenz, P. A. (2010). Age differences in prefrontal recruitment during verbal working memory maintenance depend on memory load. *Cortex, 46,* 462–473.

Capuzzi, D., & Gross, D. R. (2004). Counseling suicidal adolescents. In D. Capuzzi (Ed.), *Suicide across the lifespan: Implications for counselors* (pp. 235–270). Alexandria, VA: American Counseling Association.

Carbonneau, H., Caron, C., & Desrosiers, J. (2010). Development of a conceptual framework of positive aspects of caregiving in dementia. *Dementia, 9,* 327–353.

Card, N. A., Stucky, B. D., Sawalani, G. M., & Little, T. D. (2008). Direct and indirect aggression during childhood and adolescence: A meta-analytic review of gender differences, intercorrelations, and relations to maladjustment. *Child Development, 79,* 1185–1229.

Caria, M. P., Faggiano, F., Bellocco, R., & Galanti, M. R. (2011). Effects of a school-based prevention program on European adolescents' patterns of alcohol use. *Journal of Adolescent Health, 48,* 182–188.

Carlander, I., Ternestedt, B.-M., Sahlberg-Blom, E., Hellström, I., & Sandberg, J. (2011). Being me and being us in a family living close to death at home. *Qualitative Health Research, 5,* 683–695.

Carlo, G., Koller, S., Raffaelli, M., & de Guzman, M. R. T. (2007). Culture-related strengths among Latin American families: A case study of Brazil. *Marriage & Family Review, 41,* 335–360.

Carlson Jones, D. (2004). Body image among adolescent girls and boys: A longitudinal study. *Developmental Psychology, 40,* 823–835.

Carlson, S. M., & Meltzoff, A. N. (2008). Bilingual experience and executive functioning in young children. *Developmental Science, 11,* 282–298.

Caron, C. D., Ducharme, F., & Griffith, J. (2006). Deciding on institutionalization for a relative with dementia: The most difficult decision for caregivers. *Canadian Journal on Aging, 25,* 193–205.

Carpenter, P. A., & Daneman, M. (1981). Lexical retrieval and error recovery in reading: A model based on eye fixations. *Journal of Verbal Learning and Verbal Behavior, 20,* 137–160.

Carr, D. (2004). Gender, preloss marital dependence, and older adults' adjustment to widowhood. *Journal of Marriage and Family, 66,* 220–235.

Carr, D. B., & Ott, B. R. (2010). The older adult driver with cognitive impairment: "It's a very frustrating life." *JAMA, 303,* 1632–1641.

Carrere, S., & Gottman, J. M. (1999). Predicting the future of marriages. In E. M. Hetherington (Ed.), *Coping with divorce, single parenting, and remarriage: A risk and resiliency perspective* (pp. 3–22). Mahwah, NJ: Erlbaum.

Carroll, J. B. (1993). *Human cognitive abilities: A survey of factor-analytic studies.* New York: Cambridge University Press.

Carroll, J. B. (1996). A three-stratum theory of intelligence: Spearman's contribution. In I. Dennis & P. Tapsfield (Eds.), *Human abilities: Their nature and measurement* (pp. 1–18). Mahwah, NJ: Erlbaum.

Carroll, J. L., & Loughlin, G. M. (1994). Sudden infant death syndrome. In F. A. Oski, C. D. DeAngelis, R. D. Feigin, J. A. McMillan, & J. B. Warshaw (Eds.), *Principles and practice of pediatrics.* Philadelphia: Lippincott.

Carstensen, L. L. (1993). Motivation for social contact across the life span: A theory of socioemotional selectivity. *Nebraska Symposium on Motivation, 40,* 209–254.

Carstensen, L. L. (1995). Evidence for a life-span theory of socioemotional selectivity. *Current Directions in Psychological Science, 4,* 151–156.

Carver, K., Joyner, K., & Udry, J. R. (2003). National estimates of adolescent romantic relationships. In P. Florsheim (Ed.), *Adolescent romantic relations and sexual behavior: Theory, research, and practical implications* (pp. 23–56). Mahwah, NJ: Erlbaum.

Carver, P. R., Egan, S. K., & Perry, D. G. (2004). Children who question their hetero-sexuality. *Developmental Psychology, 40,* 43–53.

Casaer, P. (1993). Old and new facts about perinatal brain development. *Journal of Child Psychology and Psychiatry, 34,* 101–109.

Casey, B. J., Jones, R. M., & Somerville, L. H. (2011). Braking and accelerating of the adolescent brain. *Journal of Research on Adolescence, 21,* 21–33.

Casey, M. B. (1996). Understanding individual differences in spatial ability within females: A nature/nurture interactionist framework. *Developmental Review, 16,* 241–260.

Caspi, A., Roberts, B. W., & Shiner, R. L. (2005). Personality development: Stability and change. *Annual Review of Psychology, 56,* 453–484.

Castelli, L., Zogmaister, C., & Tomelleri, S. (2009). The transmission of racial attitudes within the family. *Developmental Psychology, 45,* 586–591.

Castillo, L. S., Williams, B. A., Hooper, S. M., Sabatino, C. P., Weithorn, L. A., & Sudore, R. L. (2011). Lost in translation: The unintended consequences of advance directive law on clinical care. *Annals of Internal Medicine, 154,* 121–128.

Cavanagh, S. E. (2004). The sexual debut of girls in early adolescence: The intersection of race, pubertal timing, and friendship group characteristics. *Journal of Research on Adolescence, 14,* 285–312.

Cavanaugh, J. C. (1999). Caregiving to adults: A life event challenge. In I. H. Nordhus, G. R. VandenBos, S. Berg, & P. Fromholt (Eds.), *Clinical geropsychology* (pp. 131–135). Washington, DC: American Psychological Association.

Cavanaugh, J. C., & Kinney, J. M. (1994, July). *Marital satisfaction as an important contextual factor in spousal caregiving.* Paper presented at the 7th International Conference on Personal Relationships, Groningen, the Netherlands.

Cavanaugh, J. C., & Nocera, R. (1994). Cognitive aspects and interventions in Alzheimer's disease. In J. D. Sinnott (Ed.), *Interdisciplinary handbook of adult lifespan learning* (pp. 389–407). New York: Greenwood Press.

Centers for Disease Control and Prevention. (2007a). *2005 assisted reproductive technology success rates.* Atlanta, GA: Author.

Centers for Disease Control and Prevention. (2007b). *Sexually transmitted disease surveillance, 2006.* Atlanta, GA: Author.

Centers for Disease Control and Prevention. (2008). *Understanding teen dating violence fact sheet.* Atlanta, GA: Author.

Centers for Disease Control and Prevention. (2009). *Understanding intimate partner violence.* Retrieved from http://www.cdc.gov/violenceprevention/pdf/IPV_fact-sheet-a.pdf

Centers for Disease Control and Prevention. (2010a). *Nursing home care.* Retrieved from http://www.cdc.gov/nchs/fastats/nursingh.htm

Centers for Disease Control and Prevention. (2010b). *Sexually transmitted disease surveillance 2009.* Atlanta, GA: Author.

Centers for Disease Control and Prevention. (2010c). *Smoking and tobacco use: Fast facts.* Retrieved from http://www.cdc.gov/tobacco/data_statistics/fact_sheets/fast_facts/index.htm

Cerminara, K. L., & Perez, A. (2000). Therapeutic death: A look at Oregon's law. *Psychology, Public Policy, and Law, 6,* 503–525.

Cervantes, C. A., & Callanan, M. A. (1998). Labels and explanations in mother–child emotion talk: Age and gender differentiation. *Developmental Psychology, 34,* 88–98.

Chan, S. W.-C. (2010). Family caregiving in dementia: The Asian perspective of a global problem. *Dementia and Geriatric Cognitive Disorders, 30,* 469–478.

Chang, J. W., Sy, T., & Choi, J. N. (2012). Team emotional intelligence and performance: Interactive dynamics between leaders and members. *Small Group Research, 43,* 75–104.

Chang, Y.-C., Jou, H.-J., Hsiao, H.-C., & Tsao, L.-I. (2010). Sleep quality, fatigue, and related factors among perimenopausal women in Taipei city. *Journal of Nursing Research, 18,* 275–282.

Charles, S. T., & Carstensen, L. L. (2010). Social and emotional aging. *Annual Review of Psychology, 61,* 383–409.

Charlton, B., & Verghese, A. (2010). Caring for Ivan Ilyich. *Journal of General Internal Medicine, 25,* 93–95.

Charness, N., & Bosman, E. A. (1990). Expertise and aging: Life in the lab. In T. M. Hess (Ed.), *Aging and cognition: Knowledge organization and utilization* (pp. 343–385). Amsterdam: North-Holland.

Chassin, L., Ritter, J., Trim, R. S., & King, K. M. (2003). Adolescent substance use disorders. In E. J. Mash & R. A. Barkely (Eds.), *Child psychopathology* (2nd ed., pp. 199–230). New York: Guilford.

Chatters, L. M., Mattis, J. S., Woodward, A. T., Taylor, R. J., Neighbors, H. J., & Grayman, N. A. (2011). Use of ministers for a serious personal problem among African Americans: Findings from the National Survey of American Life. *American Journal of Orthopsychiatry, 81,* 118–127.

Chavous, T. M., Bernat, D. H., Schmeelk-Cone, K., Caldwell, C. H., Kohn-Wood, L., & Zimmerman, M. A. (2003). Racial identity and academic attainment among African American adolescents. *Child Development, 74,* 1076–1090.

Chen, J., & Gardner, H. (2005). Assessment based on multiple intelligences theory. In D. P. Flanagan & P. L. Harrison (Eds.), *Contemporary intellectual assessment: Theories, tests, and issues* (pp. 77–102). New York: Guilford.

Chen, Z. X., Aryee, S., & Lee, C. (2005). Test of a mediation model of perceived organizational support. *Journal of Vocational Behavior, 66,* 457–470.

Cheung, C.-K., Kam, P. K., & Ngan, R. M.-H. (2011). Age discrimination in the labour market from the perspectives of employers and older workers. *International Social Work, 54,* 118–136.

Cheung, I. and McCartt, A.T. (2011). Declines in fatal crashes of older drivers: changes in crash risk and survivability. *Accident Analysis and Prevention, 43,* 666-674.

Chi, M. T. H. (2006). Laboratory methods for assessing experts' and novices' knowledge. In K. A. Ericsson, N. Charness, P. J. Feltovich, & R. R. Hoffman (Eds.), *The Cambridge handbook of expertise and expert performance* (pp. 167–184). New York: Cambridge University Press.

Chilman, C. S. (1983). *Adolescent sexuality in a changing American society* (2nd ed.). New York: Wiley.

Chiu, W. C. K., Chan, A. W., Snape, E., & Redman, T. (2001). Age stereotypes and discriminatory attitudes towards older workers: An East–West comparison. *Human Relations, 54,* 629–661.

Choi, J., Johnson, D. W., & Johnson, R. (2011). Relationships among cooperative learning experiences, social interdependence, children's aggression, victimization, and prosocial behaviors. *Journal of Applied Social Psychology, 41,* 976–1003.

Chomitz, V. R., Cheung, L. W. Y., & Lieberman, E. (1995). The role of lifestyle in preventing low birth weight. *The Future of Children, 5,* 121–138.

Chomsky, N. (1957). *Syntactic structures.* The Hague: Mouton.

Chomsky, N. (1995). *The minimalist program.* Cambridge, MA: MIT Press.

Chorpita, B. F., & Barlow, D. H. (1998). The development of anxiety: The role of control in the early environment. *Psychological Bulletin, 124,* 3–21.

Chou, K.-L., & Chi, I. (2005). Prevalence and correlates of depression in Chinese oldest-old. *International Journal of Geriatric Psychiatry, 20,* 41–50.

Chow, B. W., McBride-Chang, C., Cheung, H., & Chow, C. S. (2008). Dialogic reading and morphology training in Chinese children: Effects on language and literacy. *Developmental Psychology, 44,* 233–244.

Cicchetti, D., & Toth, S. L. (2006). Developmental psychopathology and preventive intervention. In W. Damon & R. M. Lerner (Eds.), *Handbook of child psychology* (6th ed., Vol. 4, pp. 497–547). Hoboken, NJ: Wiley.

Cicirelli, V. G. (2006). Fear of death in mid-old age. *Journals of Gerontology: Psychological Sciences, 61B,* P75–P81.

Cillessen, A. H. N., & Rose, A. (2005). Understanding popularity in the peer system. *Current Directions in Psychological Science, 14,* 102–105.

Ciraulo, D. A., Evans, J. A., Qiu, W. Q., Shader, R. I., & Salzman, C. (2011). Antidepressant treatment of geriatric depression. In D. A. Ciraulo & R. I. Shader (Eds.), *Pharmacotherapy of depression* (2nd ed., pp. 125–183). New York: Humana Press.

Clark, L. A. (2007). Relationships between the big five personality dimensions and attitudes toward telecommuting. *Dissertation Abstracts International. Section A. Humanities and Social Sciences, 68*(5-A), 2041.

Clarke, P. J., Snowling, M. J., Truelove, E., & Hulme, C. (2010). Ameliorating children's reading-comprehension difficulties: A randomized controlled trial. *Psychological Science, 21,* 1106–1116.

Clarke, V., Ellis, S. J., Peel, E., & Riggs, D. W. (2010). *Lesbian, gay, bisexual, trans and queer psychology: An introduction.* Cambridge, England: Cambridge University Press.

Clarke-Stewart, K. A., & Brentano, C. (2005). *Till divorce do us part.* New Haven, CT: Yale University Press.

Clarke-Stewart, K. A., & Brentano, C. (2006). *Divorce: Causes and consequences.* New Haven, CT: Yale University Press.

Clifford, D., Hertz, F., & Doskow, E. (2010). *A legal guide for lesbian and gay couples* (15th ed.). Berkeley, CA: Nolo.

Cnattingius, S. (2004). The epidemiology of smoking during pregnancy: Smoking prevalence, maternal characteristics, and pregnancy outcomes. *Nicotine & Tobacco Research, 6,* S125–S140.

Coatsworth, J. D., & Conroy, D. E. (2009). The effects of autonomy-supporting coaching, need satisfaction, and self-perceptions on initiative and identity in youth swimmers. *Developmental Psychology, 45,* 320–328.

Coelho, J. S., Jansen, A., Roefs, A., & Nederkoorn, C. (2009). Eating behavior in response to food-cue exposure: Examining the cue-reactivity and counteractive-control models. *Psychology of Addictive Behaviors, 23,* 131–139.

Cohen, F., Kemeny, M. E., Zegans, L., Johnson, P., Kearney, K. A., & Sites, D. P. (2007). Immune function declines with unemployment and recovers after stressor termination. *Psychosomatic Medicine, 69,* 225–234.

Cohen, R. W., Martinez, M. E., & Ward, B. W. (2010). *Health insurance coverage: Early release of estimates from the National Health Interview Survey, 2009.* Hyattsville, MD: National Center for Health Statistics.

Cohen, S., & Williamson, G. M. (1991). Stress and infectious disease in humans. *Psychological Bulletin, 109,* 5–24.

Coie, J. D., Dodge, K. A., Terry, R., & Wright, V. (1991). The role of aggression in peer relations: An analysis of aggression episodes in boys' play groups. *Child Development, 62,* 812–826.

Colby, A., Kohlberg, L., Gibbs, J. C., & Lieberman, M. (1983). A longitudinal study of moral development. *Monographs of the Society for Research in Child Development, 48* (Serial No. 200).

Cole, D. A., Jacquez, F. M., LaGrange, B., Pineda, A. Q., Truss, A. E., Weitlauf, A. S., et al. (2011). A longitudinal study of cognitive risks for depressive symptoms in children and young adolescents. *Journal of Early Adolescence, 31,* 782–816.

Cole, D. A., & Jordan, A. E. (1995). Competence and memory: Integrating psychosocial and cognitive correlates of child depression. *Child Development, 66,* 459–473.

Cole, M. (2006). Culture and cognitive development in phylogenetic, historical and ontogenetic perspective. In W. Damon & R. M. Lerner (Eds.), *Handbook of child psychology* (6th ed., Vol. 2, pp. 636–683). Hoboken, NJ: Wiley.

Collins, W. A. (2003). More than myth: The developmental significance of romantic relationships during adolescence. *Journal of Research on Adolescence, 13,* 1–24.

Collins, W. A., & van Dulmen, M. (2006). "The course of true love(s)": Origins and pathways in the development of romantic relationships. In A. C. Crouter & A. Booth (Eds.), *Romance and sex in adolescence and emerging adulthood: Risks and opportunities* (pp. 63–86). Mahwah, NJ: Erlbaum.

Collins, W. A., Welsh, D. P., & Furman, W. (2009). Adolescent romantic relationships. *Annual Review of Psychology, 60,* 631–652.

Conduct Problems Prevention Research Group. (2011). The effects of the Fast Track preventive intervention on the development of conduct disorder across childhood. *Child Development, 82,* 331–345.

Connelly, R., Degraff, D. S., & Willis, R. A. (2004). The value of employer-sponsored child care to employees. *Industrial Relations: A Journal of Economy & Society, 43,* 759–792.

Connidis, I. A. (2001). *Family ties and aging.* Thousand Oaks, CA: Sage.

Conradi, L., & Geffner, R. (2009). Introduction to part I of the special issue on female offenders of intimate partner violence. *Journal of Aggression, Maltreatment and Trauma, 18,* 547–551.

Cook, D. A., Bahn, R. S., & Menaker, R. (2010). Speed mentoring: An innovative method to facilitate mentoring relationships. *Medical Teacher, 32,* 692–694.

Cooney, T. M., & Uhlenberg, P. (1990). The role of divorce in men's relations with their adult children after mid-life. *Journal of Marriage and the Family, 52,* 677–688.

Cooney, T. M., Smyer, M. A., Hagestad, G. O., & Klock, R. (1986). Parental divorce in young adulthood: Some preliminary findings. *American Journal of Orthopsychiatry, 56,* 470–477.

Coplan, R. J., & Armer, M. (2007). A "multitude" of solitude: A closer look at social withdrawal and nonsocial play in early childhood. *Child Development Perspectives, 1,* 26–32.

Coplan, R. J., Gavinski-Molina, M. H., Lagace-Seguin, D. G., & Wichman, C. (2001). When girls versus boys play alone: Nonsocial play and adjustment in kindergarten. *Developmental Psychology, 37,* 464–474.

Copper, R. L., Goldenberg, R. L., Das, A., Elder, N., Swain, M., Norman, G., et al. (1996). The preterm prediction study: Maternal stress is associated with spontaneous preterm birth at less than thirty-five weeks' gestation. *American Journal of Obstetrics and Gynecology, 175,* 1286–1292.

Cordes, S., & Brannon, E. M. (2009). The relative salience of discrete and continuous quantity in young infants. *Developmental Science, 12,* 453–463.

Corr, C. A. (1991–1992). A task-based approach to coping with dying. *Omega: Journal of Death and Dying, 24,* 81–94.

Corr, C. A. (2010). Children's emerging awareness and understandings of loss and death. In C. A. Corr & D. E. Balk (Eds.), *Children's encounters with death, bereavement, and coping* (pp. 21–37). New York: Springer.

Corr, C. A., Corr, D. M., & Nabe, C. M. (2008). *Death and dying: Life and living.* Belmont, CA: Wadsworth.

Corti, J. K. (2009). *Sibling relationships during the young adult years: An analysis of closeness, relational satisfaction, everyday talk, and turning points.* Retrieved from https://adr.coalliance.org/codu/fez/eserv/codu:55639/Corti_denver_0061D_10200.pdf

Costa, P. T., Jr., & McCrae, R. R. (1988). Personality in adulthood: A six-year longitudinal study of self-reports and spouse ratings on the NEO Personality Inventory. *Journal of Personality and Social Psychology, 54,* 853–863.

Costa, P. T., Jr., & McCrae, R. R. (1997). Longitudinal stability of adult personality. In R. Hogan, J. Johnson, & S. Briggs (Eds.), *Handbook of personality psychology* (pp. 269–292). San Diego, CA: Academic Press.

Costin, S. E., & Jones, D. C. (1992). Friendship as a facilitator of emotional responsiveness and prosocial interventions among young children. *Developmental Psychology, 28,* 941–947.

Cotter, R. P. (2001). High-risk behaviors in adolescence and their relationship to death anxiety and death personification. *Dissertation Abstracts International. Section B. Sciences and Engineering, 61*(8-B), 4446.

Cotter, V. T., & Gonzalez, E. W. (2009). Self-concept in older adults: An integrative review of empirical literature. *Holistic Nursing Practice, 23,* 335–348.

Coulton, C. J., Crampton, D. S., Irwin, M., Spilsbury, J. C., & Korbin, J. E. (2007). How neighborhoods influence child maltreatment: A review of the literature and alternative pathways. *Child Abuse and Neglect, 31,* 1117–1142.

Counts, D., & Counts, D. (Eds.). (1985). *Aging and its transformations: Moving toward death in Pacific societies.* Lanham, MD: University Press of America.

Coutelle, C., Themis, M., Waddington, S. N., Buckley, S. M., Gregory, L. G., Nivsarkar, M. S., et al. (2005). Gene therapy progress and prospects: Fetal gene therapy—first proofs of concept—some adverse effects. *Gene Therapy, 12,* 1601–1607.

Cowan, P. A., Cowan, C. P., & Knox, V. (2010). Marriage and fatherhood programs. *Fragile Families, 20.* Retrieved from http://www.futureofchildren.org/futureof-children/publications/journals/article/index.xml?journalid=73&articleid=537

Cox, C. B. (2007). Grandparent-headed families: Needs and implications for social work interventions and advocacy. *Families in Society, 88,* 561–566.

Cox, K. S., Wilt, J., Olson, B. D., & McAdams, D. P. (2010). Generativity, the Big Five, and psychosocial adaptation in midlife adults. *Journal of Personality, 78,* 1185–1208.

Cox, M. J., Paley, B., & Harter, K. (2001). Interparental conflict and parent–child relationships. In J. H. Grych & F. D. Fincham (Eds.), *Interparental conflict and child development* (pp. 249–272). New York: Cambridge University Press.

Cox, T., & Griffiths, A. (2010). Work-related stress: A theoretical perspective. In S. Leka & J. Houdmont (Eds.), *Occupational health psychology* (pp. 31–56). Chichester, England: Blackwell.

Craig, K. D., Whitfield, M. F., Grunau, R. V. E., Linton, J., & Hadjistavropoulos, H. D. (1993). Pain in the preterm neonate: Behavioural and physiological indices. *Pain, 52,* 238–299.

Craik, F. I. M., & Salthouse, T. A. (Eds.). (2008). *Handbook of aging and cognition* (3rd ed.). New York: Psychology Press.

Crews, J. (2011). Aging, disability, and public health. In D. L. Lollar & E. M. Andresen (Eds.), *Public health perspectives on disability: Epidemiology to ethics and beyond* (pp. 163–183). New York: Springer.

Crick, N. R., & Dodge, K. A. (1994). A review and reformulation of social-information processing mechanisms in children's social adjustment. *Psychological Bulletin, 115*, 74–101.

Crick, N. R., Ostrov, J. M., Appleyard, K., Jansen, E. A., & Casas, J. F. (2004). Relational aggression in early childhood: "You can't come to my birthday party unless." In M. Puttalaz & K. L. Bierman (Eds.), *Aggression, antisocial behavior, and violence among girls* (pp. 71–89). New York: Guilford.

Cristia, A. (2010). Phonetic enhancement of sibilants in infant-directed speech. *Journal of the Acoustical Society of America, 128*, 424–434.

Crocetti, E., Rubini, M., Luyckx, K., & Meeus, W. (2008). Identity formation in early and middle adolescents from various ethnic groups: From three dimensions to five statuses. *Journal of Youth and Adolescence, 37*, 983–996.

Crohan, S. E. (1996). Marital quality and conflict across the transition to parenthood in African American and white couples. *Journal of Marriage and Family, 58*, 933–944.

Crohn, H. M. (2006). Five styles of positive stepmothering from the perspective of young adult stepdaughters. *Journal of Divorce & Remarriage, 46*, 119–134.

Cross, S., & Markus, H. (1991). Possible selves across the lifespan. *Human Development, 34*, 230–255.

Crouter, A. C., & Bumpus, M. F. (2001). Linking parents' work stress to children's and adolescents' psychological adjustment. *Current Directions in Psychological Science, 10*, 156–159.

Crouter, A. C., Whiteman, S. D., McHale, S. M., & Osgood, D. (2007). Development of gender attitude traditionality across middle childhood and adolescence. *Child Development, 78*, 911–926.

Crozier, J. C., Dodge, K. A., Fontaine, R. G., Lansford, J. E., Bates, J. E., Pettit, G. S., et al. (2008). Social information processing and cardiac predictors of adolescent antisocial behavior. *Journal of Abnormal Psychology, 117*, 253–267.

Csikszentmihalyi, M., & Larson, R. (1984). *Being adolescent: Conflict and growth in the teenage years.* New York: Basic Books.

Cullerton-Sen, C., Cassidy, A. R., Murray-Close, D., Cicchetti, D., Crick, N. R., & Rogosch, F. A. (2008). Child maltreatment and the development of relational and physical aggression: The importance of a gender-informed approach. *Child Development, 79*, 1736–1751.

Cummings, E., Schermerhorn, A. C., Davies, P. T., Goeke-Morey, M. C., & Cummings, J. S. (2006). Interparental discord and child adjustment: Prospective investigations of emotional security as an explanatory mechanism. *Child Development, 77*, 132–152.

Cunningham, A. E., Perry, K. E., Stanovich, K. E., & Share, D. L. (2002). Orthographic learning during reading: Examining the role of self-teaching. *Journal of Experimental Child Psychology, 82*, 185–199.

Curl, A. L. (2007). The impact of retirement on trajectories of physical health of married couples. *Dissertation Abstracts International. Section A. Humanities and Social Sciences, 68*(4-A), 1606.

Curtis, R., & Pearson, F. (2010). Contact with birth parents: Differential psychological adjustment for adults adopted as infants. *Journal of Social Work, 10*, 347–367.

Cyders, M. A., Flory, K., Rainer, S., & Smith, G. T. (2009). The role of personality dispositions to risky behavior in predicting first-year college drinking. *Addiction, 104*, 193–202.

D'Onofrio, B. M., Goodnight, J. A., Van Hulle, C. A., Rodgers, J. L., Rathouz, P. J., Waldman, I. D., & Lahey, B. B. (2009). Maternal age at childbirth and offspring disruptive behaviors: Testing the causal hypothesis. *Journal of Child Psychology and Psychiatry, 50*, 1018–1028.

D'Onofrio, B. M., Singh, A. L., Iliadou, A., Lambe, M., Hultman, C. M., Neiderhiser, J. M., Långström, N., & Lichtenstein, P. (2010). A quasi-experimental study of maternal smoking during pregnancy and offspring academic achievement. *Child Development, 81*, 80–100.

Daley, T. C., Whaley, S. E., Sigman, M. D., Espinosa, M. P., & Neumann, C. (2003). IQ on the rise: The Flynn effect in rural Kenyan children. *Psychological Science, 14*, 215–219.

Daly, M., & Wilson, M. (1996). Violence against stepchildren. *Current Directions in Psychological Science, 5*, 77–81.

Dannefer, D., & Miklowski, C. (2006). Developments in the life course. In J. A. Vincent, C. R. Phillipson, & M. Downs (Eds.), *The futures of old age* (pp. 30–39). Thousand Oaks, CA: Sage.

Dannemiller, J. L. (1998). Color constancy and color vision during infancy: Methodological and empirical issues. In V. Walsh & J. Kulikowski (Eds.), *Perceptual constancy: Why things look as they do.* New York: Cambridge University Press.

Danno, M., Miyaji, M., Kortelainen, J. M., & Kutila, M. (2010, September). *Detection of a driver's visual attention using the online UFOV method.* Paper presented at the 13th International Conference on Intelligent Transportation Systems, Funchal, Portugal.

Darling, H., Reeder, A. I., McGee, T., & Williams, S. (2006). Brief report: Disposable income, and spending on fast food, alcohol, cigarettes, and gambling by New Zealand secondary school students. *Journal of Adolescence, 29*, 837–843.

David, A., & Rodeck, C. H. (2009). Fetal gene therapy. In C. H. Rodeck & M. J. Whittle (Eds.), *Fetal medicine: Basic science and clinical practice.* London: Churchill Livingstone.

Davidson, F. H., & Davidson, M. M. (1994). *Changing childhood prejudice: The caring work of the schools.* Westport, CT: Bergin & Garvey/Greenwood Press.

Davidson, R. J. (2010). Empirical explorations of mindfulness: Conceptual and methodological conundrums. *Emotion, 10*, 8–11.

Davies, L. (2003). Singlehood: Transitions within a gendered world. *Canadian Journal on Aging, 22*, 343–352.

De Andrade, C. E. (2000). Becoming the wise woman: A study of women's journeys through midlife transformation. *Dissertation Abstracts International. Section B. Sciences and Engineering, 61*(2-B), 1109.

de Haan, M., Wyatt, J. S., Roth, S., Vargha-Khadem, F., Gadian, D., & Mishkin, M. (2006). Brain and cognitive-behavioral development after asphyxia at term birth. *Developmental Science, 9*, 441–442.

De Neys, W., & Everaerts, D. (2008). Developmental trends in everyday conditional reasoning: The retrieval and inhibition interplay. *Journal of Experimental Child Psychology, 100*, 252–263.

de St. Aubin, E., & McAdams, D. P. (1995). The relations of generative concern and generative action to personality traits, satisfaction/happiness with life, and ego development. *Journal of Adult Development, 2*, 99–112.

De Wolff, M. S., & van IJzendoorn, M. H. (1997). Sensitivity and attachment: A meta-analysis on parental antecedents of infant attachment. *Child Development, 68*, 571–591.

DeAngelis, T. (2010). New help for stroke survivors. *Monitor on Psychology, 41*(3), 52–55.

Deary, I. J., Batty, G. D., & Gale, C. R. (2008). Bright children become enlightened adults. *Psychological Science, 19*, 1–6.

Deary, I. J., Penke, L., & Johnson, W. (2010). The neuroscience of human intelligence differences. *Nature Reviews Neuroscience, 11*, 201–211.

Dekker, M. C. Ferdinand, R. F., van Lang, D. J., Bongers, I. L. van der Ende, J., & Verhulst, F. C. (2007). Developmental trajectories of depressive symptoms from early childhood to late adolescence: gender differences and adult outcome. *Journal of Child Psychology and Psychiatry, 48*, 657–666.

Dekovic, M., & Janssens, J. M. (1992). Parents' child-rearing style and child's sociometric status. *Developmental Psychology, 28*, 925–932.

del Valle, J. F., Bravo, A., & Lopez, M. (2010). Parents and peers as providers of support in adolescents' social network: A developmental perspective. *Journal of Community Psychology, 38*, 16–27.

Delaney, C. (2000). Making babies in a Turkish village. In J. S. DeLoache & A. Gottlieb (Eds.), *A world of babies: Imagined childcare guides for seven societies.* New York: Cambridge University Press.

DeLoache, J. S. (1995). Early understanding and use of models: The model model. *Current Directions in Psychological Science, 4*, 109–113.

DeLoache, J. S., Chiong, C., Sherman, K., Islam, N., Vanderborght, M., Troseth, G. L., et al. (2010). Do babies learn from baby media? *Psychological Science, 21*, 1570–1574.

DeLucia-Waack, J. L. (2010). Children of divorce groups. In G. L. Greif & P. H. Ephross (Eds.), *Group work with populations at risk* (3rd ed., pp. 93–114). New York: Oxford University Press.

Demir, A., Levine, S. C., & Goldin-Meadow, S. (2010). Narrative skill in children with unilateral brain injury: A possible limit to functional plasticity. *Developmental Science, 13*, 636–647.

Deng, C.-P., Armstrong, P. I., & Rounds, J. (2007). The fit of Holland's RIASEC model to U.S. occupations. *Journal of Vocational Behavior, 71*, 1–22.

Denissen, J. J., Zarrett, N. R., & Eccles, J. S. (2007). I like to do it, I'm able, and I know I am: Longitudinal couplings between domain-specific achievement, self-concept, and interest. *Child Development, 78,* 430–447.

Denney, N. W. (1989). Everyday problem solving: Methodological issues, research findings, and a model. In L. W. Poon, D. C. Rubin, & B. A. Wilson (Eds.), *Everyday cognition in adulthood and late life* (pp. 330–351). Cambridge, England: Cambridge University Press.

Denney, N. W. (1990). Adult age differences in traditional and practical problem solving. In E. A. Lovelace (Ed.), *Aging and cognition: Mental processes, self-awareness, and interventions* (pp. 329–349). Amsterdam: North-Holland.

Denney, N. W., Pearce, K. A., & Palmer, A. M. (1982). A developmental study of adults' performance on traditional and practical problem-solving tasks. *Experimental Aging Research, 8,* 115–118.

Dennis, T., Bendersky, M., Ramsay, D., & Lewis, M. (2006). Reactivity and regulation in children prenatally exposed to cocaine. *Developmental Psychology, 42,* 84–97.

DePaulo, B. M. (2006). *Singled out: How singles are stereotyped, stigmatized, and ignored, and still live happily ever after.* New York: St. Martin's Press.

Desmond, N., & López Turley, R. N. (2009). The role of familism in explaining the Hispanic–white college application gap. *Social Problems, 56,* 311–334.

Deutsch, A. (2001, April 11). Dutch parliament OKs strict euthanasia bill. *Wilmington (NC) Morning Star,* p. 2A.

Deutsch, D. (2010). *Increased mental health services for the homeless* (Master's thesis, California State University at Humboldt, Arcata, CA). Retrieved from http://gradworks.umi.com/1486303.pdf

Dewey, K. G. (2001). Nutrition, growth, and complementary feeding of the breastfed infant. *Pediatric Clinics of North America, 48,* 87–104.

Dey, J. G., & Hill, C. (2007). *Behind the pay gap.* Washington, DC: American Association of University Women Educational Foundation.

Diamond, A. (2007). Interrelated and interdependent. *Developmental Science, 10,* 152–158.

Dickens, B. M., Boyle, J. M., Jr., & Ganzini, L. (2008). Euthanasia and assisted suicide. In P. A. Singer & A. M. Viens (Eds.), *The Cambridge textbook of bioethics* (pp. 72–77). New York: Cambridge University Press.

Dickens, W. T., & Flynn, J. R. (2001). Heritability estimates versus large environmental effects: The IQ paradox resolved. *Psychological Review, 108,* 346–369.

Dickinson, G. E. (2011). Thirty-five years of end-of-life issues in U.S. medical schools. *American Journal of Hospice and Palliative Medicine, 28,* 412–417.

Dick-Read, G. (1959). *Childbirth without fear.* New York: Harper.

Diehl, M. (1998). Everyday competence in later life: Current status and future directions. *The Gerontologist, 4,* 422–433.

Diehl, M., Marsiske, M., Horgas, A. L., Rosenberg, A., Saczynski, J. S., & Willis, S. L. (2005). The revised observed tasks of daily living: A performance-based assessment of everyday problem solving in older adults. *Journal of Applied Gerontology, 24,* 211–230.

DiFonzo, J. H. (2010). A vision for collaborative practice: The final report of the Hofstra Collaborative Law Conference. *Hofstra Law Review, 39,* 101.

Dilworth-Anderson, P., Boswell, G., & Cohen, M. D. (2007). Spiritual and religious coping values and beliefs among African American caregivers: A qualitative study. *Journal of Applied Gerontology, 26,* 355–369.

Dinsbach, A. A., Fiej, J. A., & de Vries, R. E. (2007). The role of communication content in an ethnically diverse organization. *International Journal of Intercultural Relations, 31,* 725–745.

DiPietro, J. A., Caulfield, L., Costigan, K. A., Merialdi, M., Nguyen, R. H. N., Zavaleta, N., & Gurewitsch, E. D. (2004). Fetal neurobehavioral development: A tale of two cities. *Developmental Psychology, 40,* 445–456.

Dishion, T. J., Poulin, F., & Burraston, B. (2001). Peer group dynamics associated with iatrogenic effects in group interventions with high-risk young adolescents. In D. W. Nangle & C. A. Erdley (Eds.), *The role of friendship in psychological adjustment* (pp. 79–92). San Francisco: Jossey-Bass.

Dixon, P. (2009). Marriage among African Americans: What does the research reveal? *Journal of African American Studies, 13,* 29–46.

Dixon, R. A., & Hultsch, D. F. (1999). Intelligence and cognitive potential in late life. In J. C. Cavanaugh & S. K. Whitbourne (Eds.), *Gerontology: An interdisciplinary perspective.* New York: Oxford University Press.

Dockstader, C., Gaetz, W., Rockel. C., & Mabbot, D. J. (2012). White matter maturation in visual and motor areas predicts the latency of visual activation in children. *Human Brain Mapping, 33,* 179–191.

Dodge, K. A., Coie, J. D., & Lynam, D. (2006). Aggression and antisocial behavior in youth. In N. Eisenberg, W. Damon, & R. M. Lerner (Eds.), *Handbook of child psychology* (6th ed., Vol. 3, pp. 719–788). Hoboken, NJ: Wiley.

Dohnt, H., & Tiggemann, M. (2006). The contribution of peer and media influences to the development of body satisfaction and self-esteem in young girls: A prospective study. *Developmental Psychology, 42,* 929–936.

Dommaraju, P. (2010). *The changing demography of marriage in India.* Audio available at http://itunes.apple.com/us/itunes-u/changing-family-asia-research/id387325084

Donahue, P. J. D. (2007). Retirement reconceptualized: Forced retirement and its relationship to health. *Dissertation Abstracts International. Section A. Humanities and Social Sciences, 67*(7-A), 2750.

Donaldson, S. J., & Ronan, K. R. (2006). The effects of sports participation on young adolescents' emotional well-being. *Adolescence, 41,* 369–389.

Donnelly, E. A., & Hinterlong, J. E. (2010). Changes in social participation and volunteer activity among recently widowed older adults. *The Gerontologist, 50,* 158–169.

Doohan, E.-A. M., Carrère, S., & Riggs, M. L. (2010). Using relational stories to predict the trajectory toward marital dissolution: The oral history interview and spousal feelings of flooding, loneliness, and depression. *Journal of Family Communication, 10,* 57–77.

Dow, B., & Meyer, C. (2010). Caring and retirement: Crossroads and consequences. *International Journal of Health Services, 40,* 645–665.

Draghi-Lorenz, R., Reddy, V., & Costall, A. (2001). Rethinking the development of "nonbasic" emotions: A critical review of existing theories. *Developmental Review, 21,* 263–304.

Driscoll, A. K., Russell, S. T., & Crockett, L. J. (2008). Parenting styles and youth well-being across immigrant generations. *Journal of Family Issues, 29,* 185–209.

Duckworth, A. L., & Seligman, M. E. (2005). Self-discipline outdoes IQ in predicting academic performance of adolescents. *Psychological Science, 16,* 939–944.

Duff, L. J., Ericsson, K. A., & Baluch, B. (2007). In search of the loci for sex differences in throwing: The effects of physical size and differential recruitment rates on high levels of dart performance. *Research Quarterly for Exercise and Sport, 78,* 71–78.

Dumas, J. A., McDonald, B. C., Saykin, A. J., McAllister, T. W., Hynes, M. L., West, J. D., et al. (2010). Cholinergic modulation of hippocampal activity during episodic memory encoding in postmenopausal women: A pilot study. *Menopause, 17,* 852–859.

Duncan, G. J., & Brooks-Gunn, J. (2000). Family poverty, welfare reform, and child development. *Child Development, 71,* 188–196.

Dunham, P. J., Dunham, F., & Curwin, A. (1993). Joint attentional states and lexical acquisition at 18 months. *Developmental Psychology, 29,* 827–831.

Dunn, J., & Brophy, M. (2005). Communication, relationships, and individual differences in children's understanding of mind. In J. W. Astington & J. A. Baird (Eds.), *Why language matters for theory of mind* (pp. 50–69). New York: Oxford University Press.

Dunn, J., & Davies, L. (2001). Sibling relationships and interpersonal conflict. In J. Grych & F. D. Fincham (Eds.), *Interparental conflict and child development* (pp. 273–290). New York: Cambridge University Press.

Dunn, J., & Kendrick, C. (1981). Social behavior of young siblings in the family context: Differences between same-sex and different-sex dyads. *Child Development, 52,* 1265–1273.

Dunn, J., O'Connor, T. G., & Cheng, H. (2005). Children's responses to conflict between their different parents: Mothers, stepfathers, nonresident fathers, and nonresident stepmothers. *Journal of Clinical Child and Adolescent Psychology, 34,* 223–234.

Dunn, M., & White, V. (2011). The epidemiology of anabolic–androgenic steroid use among Australian secondary school students. *Journal of Science and Medicine in Sport, 14,* 10–14.

Dunson, D. B., Colombo, B., & Baird, D. D. (2002). Changes in age in the level and duration of fertility in the menstrual cycle. *Human Reproduction, 17,* 1399–1403.

Dupuis, S. (2010). Examining the blended family: The application of systems theory toward an understanding of the blended family system. *Journal of Couple and Relationship Therapy, 9,* 239–251.

Durston, S., Davidson, M. C., Tottenham, N., Galvan, A., Spicer, J., Fossella, J. A., et al. (2006). A shift from diffuse to focal cortical activity with development. *Developmental Science, 9,* 1–8.

Dutton, W. H., Helsper, E. J., Whitty, M. T., Li, N., Buckwalter, J. G., & Lee, E. (2009). The role of the Internet in reconfiguring marriages: A cross-national study. *Interpersona: An International Journal on Personal Relationships, 3*(Suppl. 2). Retrieved from http://abpri.files.wordpress.com/2010/12/interpersona-3-suppl-2_1.pdf

Dwyer, T., & Ponsonby, A. L. (2009). Sudden infant death syndrome and prone sleeping position. *Annals of Epidemiology, 19,* 245–249.

Dyke, P. H., & Adams, G. R. (1990). Identity and intimacy: An initial investigation of three theoretical models using cross-lag panel correlations. *Journal of Youth and Adolescence, 19,* 91–110.

Eagly, A. H., Karau, S. J., & Makhijani, M. G. (1995). Gender and the effectiveness of leaders: A meta-analysis. *Psychological Bulletin, 117,* 125–145.

Eastwick, P. W., Saigal, S. D., & Finkel, E. J. (2010). *Smooth operating: A structural analysis of social behavior (SASB) perspective on initial romantic encounters.* Social Psychological and Personality Science, 1, DOI: 10.1177/1948550610373402. http://faculty.wcas.northwestern.edu/eli-finkel/documents/2010_EastwickSaigalFinkel_SPPS.pdf

Eaton, D. K., Kann, L., Kinchen, S., Shanklin, S., Ross, J., Hawkins, J., et al. (2008). Youth risk behavior surveillance—United States, 2007. *Morbidity and Mortality Weekly Report, 57,* 1–131.

Eaton, J., & Salari, S. (2005). Environments for lifelong learning in senior centers. *Educational Gerontology, 31,* 461–480.

Ebberwein, C. A. (2001). Adaptability and the characteristics necessary for managing adult career transition: A qualitative investigation. *Dissertation Abstracts International. Section B. Sciences and Engineering, 62*(1-B), 545.

Ebrahim, A. F. (1998). Islamic jurisprudence and the end of human life. *Medications Law, 17*(189), 1998.

Eddleston, K. A., Baldridge, D. C., & Veiga, J. F. (2004). Toward modeling the predictors of managerial career success: Does gender matter? *Journal of Managerial Psychology, 19,* 360–385.

Edwards, C. A. (1994). Leadership in groups of school-age girls. *Developmental Psychology, 30,* 920–927.

Edwards, J. D., Vance, D. E., Wadley, V. G., Cissell, G. M., Roenker, D. L., & Ball, K. K. (2005). Reliability and validity of useful field of view test scores as administered by personal computer. *Journal of Clinical & Experimental Neuropsychology, 27,* 529–543.

Edwards, M. B. (2006). The relationship between the internal working model of attachment and patterns of grief experienced by college students after the death of a parent. *Dissertation Abstracts International. Section A. Humanities and Social Sciences, 66*(11-A), 4197.

Egan, S. K., Monson, T. C., & Perry, D. G. (1998). Social-cognitive influences on change in aggression over time. *Developmental Psychology, 34,* 996–1006.

Eisenberg, N. (2000). Emotion, regulation, and moral development. *Annual Review of Psychology, 51,* 665–697.

Eisenberg, N., Cumberland, A., Spinrad, T. L., Fabes, R. A., Shepard, S. A., Reiser, M., et al. (2001). The relations of regulation and emotionality to children's externalizing and internalizing problem behavior. *Child Development, 72,* 1112–1134.

Eisenberg, N., & Fabes, R. A. (1998). Prosocial development. In W. Damon (Ed.), *Handbook of child psychology* (5th ed., Vol. 3, pp. 701–778). New York: Wiley.

Eisenberg, N., Fabes, R. A., & Spinrad, T. (2006). Prosocial development. In W. Damon & R. M. Lerner (Eds.), *Handbook of child psychology* (6th ed., Vol. 3, pp. 646–718). Hoboken, NJ: Wiley.

Eisenberg, N., Hofer, C., Spinrad, T., Gershoff, E., Valiente, C., Losoya, S. L., et al. (2008). Understanding parent–adolescent conflict discussions: Concurrent and across-time prediction from youths' dispositions and parenting. *Monographs of the Society for Research in Child Development, 73* (Serial No. 290).

Eisenberg, N., Michalik, N., Spinrad, T. L., Hofer, C., Kupfer, A., Valiente, C., et al. (2007). The relations of effortful control and impulsivity to children's symptoms: A longitudinal study. *Cognitive Development, 22,* 544–567.

Eisenberg, N., & Morris, A. S. (2002). Children's emotion-related regulation. *Advances in Child Development and Behavior, 30,* 189–229.

Eisenberg, N., Sadovsky, A., Spinrad, T. L., Fabes, R. A., Losoya, S. H., Valienta, C., et al. (2005). The relations of problem behavior status to children's negative emotionality, effortful control, and impulsivity: Concurrent relations and predictions of change. *Developmental Psychology, 41,* 193–211.

Eisenberg, N., & Shell, R. (1986). Prosocial moral judgment and behavior in children: The mediating role of cost. *Personality and Social Psychology Bulletin, 12,* 426–433.

Eizenman, D. R., & Bertenthal, B. I. (1998). Infants' perception of object unity in translating and rotating displays. *Developmental Psychology, 34,* 426–434.

Ekerdt, D. J. (2010). Frontiers of research on work and retirement. *Journal of Gerontology: Social Sciences, 65*(B), S69–S80.

El Nokali, N. E., Bachman, H. J., & Votruba-Drzal, E. (2010). Parent involvement and children's academic and social development in elementary school. *Child Development, 81,* 988–1005.

Elkind, D. (1978). *The child's reality: Three developmental themes.* Hillsdale, NJ: Erlbaum.

Elkind, D., & Bowen, R. (1979). Imaginary audience behavior in children and adolescents. *Developmental Psychology, 15,* 38–44.

Elliott, D. B., & Lewis, J. M. (2010). *Embracing the institution of marriage: The characteristics of remarried Americans.* Retrieved from http://www.census.gov/hhes/socdemo/marriage/data/acs/Remarriage.pdf

Elliott, J., & Oliver, I. (2008). Choosing between life and death: Patient and family perceptions of the decision not to resuscitate the terminally ill cancer patient. *Bioethics, 22,* 179–189.

Ellis, B. J. (2004). Timing of pubertal maturation in girls: An integrated life history approach. *Psychological Bulletin, 130,* 920–958.

Ellis, J. W. (2010). Comment: Yours, mine, ours? Why the Texas legislature should simplify caretaker consent capabilities for minor children and the implications of the addition of Chapter 34 to the Texas Family Code. *Texas Tech Law Review, 42,* 987.

Else-Quest, N. M., Hyde, J. S., Goldsmith, H., & Van Hulle, C. A. (2006). Gender differences in temperament: A meta-analysis. *Psychological Bulletin, 132,* 33–72.

Else-Quest, N. M., Hyde, J. S., & Linn, M. C. (2010). Cross-national patterns of gender differences in mathematics: A meta-analysis. *Psychological Bulletin, 136,* 103–127.

Emick, M. A., & Hayslip, B., Jr. (1999). Custodial grandparenting: Stresses, coping skills, and relationships with grandchildren. *International Journal of Aging and Human Development, 48,* 35–61.

Engel, S. M., Berkowitz, G. S., Wolff, M. S., & Yehuda, R. (2005). Psychological trauma associated with the World Trade Center attacks and its effect on pregnancy outcome. *Paediatric and Perinatal Epidemiology, 19,* 334–341.

Engle, P., & Huffman, S. L. (2010). Growing children's bodies and minds: Maximizing child nutrition and development. *Food and Nutrition Bulletin, 31,* S186–S197.

Enslin, C. (2007). Women in organizations: A phenomenological study of female executives mentoring junior women in organizations. *Dissertation Abstracts International. Section A. Humanities and Social Sciences, 68*(4-A), 1692.

Epel, E. S., Burke, H. M., & Wolkowitz, O. M. (2007). The psychoneuroendocrinology of aging: Anabolic and catabolic hormones. In C. M. Aldwin, C. L. Park, & A. Spiro III (Eds.), *Handbook of health psychology and aging* (pp. 119–141). New York: Guilford.

Epstein, L. H., & Cluss, P. A. (1986). Behavioral genetics of childhood obesity. *Behavior Therapy, 17,* 324–334.

Epstein, L. H., Leddy, J. J., Temple, J. L., & Faith, M. S. (2007). Food reinforcement and eating: A multilevel analysis. *Psychological Bulletin, 133,* 884–906.

Equal Employment Opportunity Commission. (2010). *Sexual harassment charges: EEOC and FEPAs combined: FY1997-FY2009.* Retrieved from http://www.eeoc.gov/eeoc/statistics/enforcement/sexual_harassment.cfm

Erel, O., Margolin, G., & John, R. S. (1998). Observed sibling interaction: Links with the marital and the mother–child relationship. *Developmental Psychology, 34,* 288–298.

Ericsson, K. A., & Towne, T. J. (2010). Expertise. *Wiley Interdisciplinary Reviews: Cognitive Science, 1,* 404–416.

Erikson, E. H. (1968). *Identity: Youth and crisis.* New York: Norton.

Erikson, E. H. (1982). *The life cycle completed: Review.* New York: Norton.

Ernst, M., Moolchan, E. T., & Robinson, M. L. (2001). Behavioral and neural consequences of prenatal exposure to nicotine. *Journal of the American Academy of Child & Adolescent Psychiatry, 40,* 630–641.

Eskritt, M., & McLeod, K. (2008). Children's note taking as a mnemonic tool. *Journal of Experimental Child Psychology, 101,* 52–74.

European Association for Palliative Care. (2011). *The EAPC ethics task force on palliative care and euthanasia.* Retrieved from http://www.eapcnet.eu/Themes/Ethics/PCeuthanasiataskforce.aspx

Evans, N. J., Forney, D. S., Guido, F. M., Patton, L. D., & Renn, K. A. (2010). *Student development in college: Theory, research, and practice* (2nd ed.). San Francisco: Jossey-Bass.

Everingham, C., Warner-Smith, P., & Byles, J. (2007). Transforming retirement: Re-thinking models of retirement to accommodate the experiences of women. *Women's Studies International Forum, 30,* 512–522.

Faber, A. J. (2004). Examining remarried couples through a Bowenian family systems lens. *Journal of Divorce & Remarriage, 40,* 121–133.

Fabricius, W. V., & Luecken, L. J. (2007). Postdivorce living arrangements, parent conflict, and long-term physical health correlates for children of divorce. *Journal of Family Psychology, 21,* 195–205.

Fagot, B. I. (1985). Changes in thinking about early sex role development. *Developmental Review, 5,* 83–98.

Falbo, T., & Polit, E. F. (1986). Quantitative review of the only child literature: Research evidence and theory development. *Psychological Bulletin, 100,* 176–186.

Farrant, B. M., Maybery, M. T., & Fletcher, J. (2012). Language, cognitive flexibility, and explicit false belief understanding: Longitudinal analysis in typical development and specific language impairment. *Child Development, 83,* 225–235.

Fearon, R. P., Bakermans-Kranenburg, M. J., van IJzendoorn, M. H., Lapsley, A., & Roisman, G. I. (2010). The significance of insecure attachment and disorganization in the development of children's externalizing behavior: A meta-analytic study. *Child Development, 81,* 435–456.

Feddes, A. R., Noack, P., & Rutland, A. (2009). Direct and extended friendship effects on minority and majority children's interethnic attitudes: A longitudinal study. *Child Development, 80,* 377–390.

Federal Bureau of Investigation. (2010). *Crime in the United States, 2009.* Retrieved from http://www.fbi.gov/ucr/09cius.htm

Federal Interagency Forum on Aging-Related Statistics. (2010). *Older Americans 2010: Key indicators of well-being.* Retrieved from http://www.agingstats.gov/agingstatsdotnet/Main_Site/Data/2010_Documents/Docs/OA_2010.pdf

Federal Interagency Forum on Child and Family Statistics. (2005). *America's children: Key national indicators of well-being, 2005.* Washington, DC: U.S. Government Printing Office.

Feldhusen, J. F. (1996). Motivating academically able youth with enriched and accelerated learning experiences. In C. P. Benbow & D. J. Lubinski (Eds.), *Intellectual talent: Psychometric and social issues.* Baltimore: Johns Hopkins University Press.

Feldman, K. (2010). *Post parenthood redefined: Race, class, and family structure differences in the experience of launching children* (Doctoral dissertation, Case Western Reserve University). Retrieved from http://etd.ohiolink.edu/send-pdf.cgi/Feldman%20Karie%20Ellen.pdf?case1267730564

Feldman, R., Masalha, S., & Derdikman-Eiron, R. (2010). Conflict resolution in the parent–child, marital, and peer context and children's aggression in the peer group: A process-oriented cultural perspective. *Developmental Psychology, 46,* 310–325.

Fennell, C. T., Byers-Heinlein, K., & Werker, J. F. (2007). Using speech sounds to guide word learning: The case of bilingual infants. *Child Development, 78,* 1510–1525.

Fenson, L., Dale, P. S., Reznick, J. S., Bates, E., Thal, D. J., & Pethick, S. J. (1994). Variability in early communicative development. *Monographs of the Society for Research in Child Development, 59*(5, Serial No. 242).

Fergusson, D. M., & Woodward, L. J. (2000). Teenage pregnancy and female educational underachievement: A prospective study of a New Zealand birth cohort. *Journal of Marriage and Family, 62,* 147–161.

Fernyhough, C. (2010). Inner speech. In H. Pashler (Ed.), *Encyclopedia of the mind.* Thousand Oaks, CA: Sage.

Ferrarini, T., & Norström, T. (2010). Family policy, economic development, and infant mortality: A longitudinal comparative analysis. *International Journal of Social Welfare, 19,* S89–S102.

Ferreol-Barbey, M., Piolat, A., & Roussey, J. (2000). Text recomposition by eleven-year-old children: Effects of text length, level of reading comprehension, and mastery of prototypical schema. *Archives de Psychologie, 68,* 213–232.

Field, M. J., & Cassel, C. K. (2010). Approaching death: Improving care at the end of life. In D. Meier, S. L. Isaacs, & R. G. Hughes (Eds.), *Palliative care: Transforming the care of serious illness* (pp. 79–91). San Francisco: Jossey-Bass.

Field, T. (2010). Postpartum depression effects on early interactions, parenting, and safety practices: A review. *Infant Behavior and Development, 33,* 1–6.

Field, T., & Diego, M. (2010). Preterm infant massage therapy research: A review. *Infant Behavior and Development, 33,* 115–124.

Field, T. M. (1990). *Infancy.* Cambridge, MA: Harvard University Press.

Field, T. M., & Widmayer, S. M. (1982). Motherhood. In B. B. Wolman (Ed.), *Handbook of developmental psychology* (pp. 681–701). Englewood Cliffs, NJ: Prentice Hall.

Fincham, F. D., & Beach, S. R. H. (2010). Marriage in the new millennium: A decade in review. *Journal of Marriage and Family, 72,* 630–649.

Fisher, C. (1996). Structural limits on verb mapping: The role of analogy in children's interpretations of sentences. *Cognitive Psychology, 31,* 41–81.

Fisher, L. L. (2010). Sex, romance, and relationships: AARP survey of midlife and older adults. Retrieved from http://assets.aarp.org/rgcenter/general/srr_09.pdf

Fisher-Borne, M. (2007). Making the link: Domestic violence in the GLBT community. In L. Messinger & D. F. Morrow (Eds.), *Case studies on sexual orientation and gender expression in social work practice* (pp. 96–98). New York: Columbia University Press.

FitzGerald, D. P., & White, K. J. (2003). Linking children's social worlds: Perspective-taking in parent–child and peer contexts. *Social Behavior and Personality, 31,* 509–522.

Fivush, R. (2011). The development of autobiographical memory. *Annual Review of Psychology, 62,* 559–582.

Fivush, R., Reese, E., & Haden, C. A. (2006). Elaborating on elaborations: Role of maternal reminiscing style in cognitive and socioemotional development. *Child Development, 77,* 1568–1588.

Flavell, J. H. (1985). *Cognitive development* (2nd ed.). Englewood Cliffs, NJ: Prentice Hall.

Flavell, J. H. (1996). Piaget's legacy. *Psychological Science, 7,* 200–203.

Flavell, J. H. (2000). Development of children's knowledge about the mental world. *International Journal of Behavioral Development, 24,* 15–23.

Flom, R., & Bahrick, L. E. (2007). The development of infant discrimination of affect in multimodal and unimodal stimulation: The role of intersensory redundancy. *Developmental Psychology, 43,* 238–252.

Flynn, H. K. (2007). Friendship: A longitudinal study of friendship characteristics, life transitions, and social factors that influence friendship quality. *Dissertation Abstracts International. Section A. Humanities and Social Sciences, 67*(9-A), 3608.

Flynn, J. R. (1999). Searching for justice: The discovery of IQ gains over time. *American Psychologist, 54,* 5–20.

Fogarty, K., & Evans, G. D. (2010). Being an involved father: What does it mean? Retrieved from http://edis.ifas.ufl.edu/he141

Folkman, S. (2008). The case for positive emotions in the stress process. *Anxiety, Stress & Coping, 21,* 3–14.

Fontaine, R. G. (2007). On-line social decision making and antisocial behavior: Some essential but neglected issues. *Clinical Psychology Review, 28,* 17–35.

Fontaine, R. G., Yang, C., Dodge, K. A., Pettit, G. S., & Bates, J. E. (2009). Development of response evaluation and decision (RED) and antisocial behavior in childhood and adolescence. *Developmental Psychology, 45,* 447–459.

Fonzi, A., Schneider, B. H., Tani, F., & Tomada, G. (1997). Predicting children's friendship status from their dynamic interaction in structured situations of potential conflict. *Child Development, 68,* 496–506.

Foreyt, J. P., & Goodrick, G. K. (1995). Obesity. In R. T. Ammerman & M. Hersen (Eds.), *Handbook of child behavior therapy in the psychiatric setting* (pp. 409–426). New York: Wiley.

Fortner, B. V., & Neimeyer, R. A. (1999). Death anxiety in older adults: A quantitative review. *Death Studies, 23,* 387–411.

Foshee, V. A., & Langwick, S. (2004). *Safe dates: An adolescent dating abuse prevention curriculum.* Center City, MN: Hazelden Publishing and Educational Services.

Foshee, V. A., Benefield, T. S., Ennett, S. T., Bauman, K. E., & Suchindran, S. (2004). Longitudinal predictors of serious physical and sexual dating violence victimization during adolescence. *Preventive Medicine, 39,* 1007–1016.

Foshee, V. A., Linder, F., MacDougall, J. E., & Bangdiwala, S. (2001). Gender differences in the longitudinal predictors of adolescent dating violence. *Preventive Medicine, 32,* 128–141.

Foster, E. M., & Watkins, S. (2010). The value of reanalysis: TV viewing and attention problems. *Child Development, 81,* 368–375.

Foster, S. E., Jones, D. J., Olson, A. L., Forehand, R., Gaffney, C. A., Zens, M. S., et al. (2007). Family socialization of adolescents' self-reported cigarette use: The role of parents' history of regular smoking and parenting style. *Journal of Pediatric Psychology, 32,* 481–493.

Fouad, N. A. (2007). Work and vocational psychology: Theory, research, and applications. *Annual Review of Psychology, 58,* 543–564.

Fowler, K. L. (2008). "The wholeness of things": Infusing diversity and social justice into death education. *Omega: Journal of Death and Dying, 57,* 53–91.

Fox, S. E., Levitt, P., & Nelson, C. A. (2010). How the timing and quality of early experiences influence the development of brain architecture. *Child Development, 81,* 28–40.

Fozard, J. L., & Gordon-Salant, S. (2001). Changes in vision and hearing with aging. In J. E. Birren & K. W. Schaie (Eds.), *Handbook of the psychology of aging* (5th ed., pp. 241–266). San Diego, CA: Academic Press.

Franceschi, K. A. (2005). The experience of the transition to motherhood in women who have suffered maternal loss in adolescence. *Dissertation Abstracts International. Section B. Sciences and Engineering, 65*(8-B), 4282.

Frank, D. A., Augustyn, M., Knight, W. G., Pell, T., & Zuckerman, B. (2001). Growth, development, and behavior in early childhood following prenatal cocaine exposure: A systematic review. *JAMA, 285,* 1613–1625.

Frazier, L. D., Hooker, K., Johnson, P. M., & Kaus, C. R. (2000). Continuity and change in possible selves in later life: A 5-year longitudinal study. *Basic and Applied Social Psychology, 22,* 237–243.

Frazier, L. D., Johnson, P. M., Gonzalez, G. K., & Kafka, C. L. (2002). Psychosocial influences on possible selves: A comparison of three cohorts of older adults. *International Journal of Behavioral Development, 26,* 308–317.

Fredricks, J. A., & Eccles, J. S. (2005). Family socialization, gender, and sport motivation and involvement. *Journal of Sport & Exercise Psychology, 27,* 3–31.

French, M. L. (2007). The alignment between personal meaning and organizational mission among music executives: A study of happiness, job satisfaction, and responsibility toward employees. *Dissertation Abstracts International. Section A. Humanities and Social Sciences, 67*(11-A), 4247.

Fretz, B. R. (2001). Coping with licensing, credentialing, and lifelong learning. In S. Walfish & A. K. Hess (Eds.), *Succeeding in graduate school: The career guide for psychology students* (pp. 353–367). Mahwah, NJ: Erlbaum.

Fried, A. (2005). Depression in adolescence. In C. B. Fisher & R. M. Lerner (Eds.), *Encyclopedia of applied developmental science* (Vol. 1, pp. 332–334). Thousand Oaks, CA: Sage.

Friedman, E. M., & Seltzer, J. A. (2010). *Providing for older parents: Is it a family affair?* California Center for Population (Research Paper No. PWP-CCPR-2010-12). Retrieved from http://www.n4a.org/pdf/PWP-CCPR-2010-012.pdf

Friedman, J. M., & Polifka, J. E. (1996). *The effects of drugs on the fetus and nursing infant: A handbook for health care professionals.* Baltimore: Johns Hopkins University Press.

Friedman, M., & Rosenman, R. H. (1974). *Type A behavior and your heart.* New York: Random House.

Fröding, B., & Peterson, M. (2012). Why virtual friendship is not genuine friendship. Ethics and Information Technology. Retrieved from http://www.springerlink.com/content/l14160v427w87wh2/fulltext.html

Froman, L. (2010). Positive psychology in the workplace. *Journal of Adult Development, 17,* 59–69.

Fruhauf, C. A. (2007). Grandchildren's perceptions of caring for grandparents. *Dissertation Abstracts International. Section A. Humanities and Social Sciences, 68*(3-A), 1120.

Fry, R. (2009). *Latino children: A majority are U.S.-born offspring of immigrants.* Retrieved from http://pewhispanic.org/reports/report.php?ReportID5110

Frye, K. L. (2008). Perceptions of retirement and aging as experienced by self-identified lesbians ages 51 through 60. *Dissertation Abstracts International. Section B. Sciences and Engineering, 68*(7-B), 4886.

Fujita, F., & Diener, E. (2005). Life satisfaction set point: Stability and change. *Journal of Personality and Social Psychology, 88,* 158–164.

Fuller-Thompson, E., Hayslip, B., Jr., & Patrick, J. H. (2005). Introduction to the special issue: Diversity among grandparent caregivers. *International Journal of Aging and Human Development, 60,* 269–272.

Fung, H. H., & Siu, T. M. Y. (2010). Time, culture, and life-cycle changes of social goals. In T. W. Miller (Ed.), *Handbook of stressful transitions across the lifespan* (pp. 441–464). New York: Springer.

Futterman, A., Gallagher, D., Thompson, L. W., Lovett, S., & Gilewski, M. (1990). Retrospective assessment of marital adjustment and depression during the first two years of spousal bereavement. *Psychology and Aging, 5,* 277–283.

Gagliardi, A. (2005). Postpartum depression. In C. B. Fisher & R. M. Lerner (Eds.), *Encyclopedia of applied developmental science* (Vol. 2, pp. 867–870). Thousand Oaks, CA: Sage.

Gamble, W. C., Ramakumar, S., & Diaz, A. (2007). Maternal and paternal similarities and differences in parenting: An examination of Mexican-American parents of young children. *Early Childhood Research Quarterly, 22,* 72–88.

Ganiron, E. E. (2007). Mutuality and relationship satisfaction in the formation of lesbian relationships across the life cycle: Unpacking the U-Haul myth. *Dissertation Abstracts International. Section B. Sciences and Engineering, 68*(3-B), 1924.

Gans, D. (2007). Normative obligations and parental care in social context. *Dissertation Abstracts International. Section A. Humanities and Social Sciences, 68*(5-A), 2115.

Garciaguirre, J. S., Adolph, K. E., & Shrout, P. E. (2007). Baby carriage: Infants walking with loads. *Child Development, 78,* 664–680.

Gardiner, J., Stuart, M., Forde, C., Greenwood, I., MacKenzie, R., & Perrett, R. (2007). Work–life balance and older workers: Employees' perspectives on retirement transitions following redundancy. *International Journal of Human Resource Management, 18,* 476–489.

Gardner, H. (1983). *Frames of mind: The theory of multiple intelligences.* New York: Basic Books.

Gardner, H. (1993). *Multiple intelligences: The theory in practice.* New York: Basic Books.

Gardner, H. (1995). Reflections on multiple intelligences: Myths and messages. *Phi Delta Kappan, 77,* 200–203, 206–209.

Gardner, H. (1999). *Intelligence reframed: Multiple intelligences for the 21st century.* New York: Basic Books.

Gardner, H. (2002). *MI millennium: Multiple intelligences for the new millennium* [Video recording]. Los Angeles: Into the Classroom Media.

Gardner, H. (2006). *Multiple intelligences: New horizons.* New York: Basic Books.

Gardner, M., Roth, J., & Brooks-Gunn, J. (2009). Sports participation and juvenile delinquency: The role of the peer context among adolescent boys and girls with varied histories of problem behavior. *Developmental Psychology, 45,* 341–353.

Garrard, E., & Wilkinson, S. (2005). Passive euthanasia. *Journal of Medical Ethics, 31,* 64–68.

Garrod, A., & Larimore, C. (Eds.). (1997). *First person, first peoples: Native American college graduates tell their life stories.* Ithaca, NY: Cornell University Press.

Gartstein, M. A., Bridgett, D. J., Rothbart, M. K., Robertson, C., Iddins, E., & Ramsay, K. & Schlect, S. (2010). A latent growth examination of fear development in infancy: Contributions of maternal depression and the risk for toddler anxiety. *Developmental Psychology, 46,* 651–668.

Gartstein, M. A., Knyazev, G. G., & Slobodskaya, H. R. (2005). Cross-cultural differences in the structure of infant temperament: United States of America and Russia. *Infant Behavior and Development, 28,* 54–61.

Gartstein, M. A., Slobodskaya, H. R., & Kinsht, I. A. (2003). Cross-cultural differences in temperament in the first year of life: United States of America (U.S.) and Russia. *International Journal of Behavioral Development, 27,* 316–328.

Garvey, C., & Berninger, G. (1981). Timing and turn taking in children's conversations. *Discourse Processes, 4,* 27–59.

Gass, K., Jenkins, J., & Dunn, J. (2007). Are sibling relationships protective? A longitudinal study. *Journal of Child Psychology and Psychiatry, 48,* 167–175.

Gavin, L. A., & Furman, W. (1996). Adolescent girls' relationships with mothers and best friends. *Child Development, 67,* 375–386.

Gaylord, S. A., & Zung, W. W. K. (1987). Affective disorders among the aging. In L. L. Carstensen & B. A. Edelstein (Eds.), *Handbook of clinical gerontology* (pp. 76–95). New York: Pergamon Press.

Ge, X., Brody, G. H., Conger, R. D., Simons, R. L., & Murphy, V. M. (2002). Contextual amplification of pubertal transition effects on deviant peer affiliation and externalizing behavior among African American children. *Developmental Psychology, 38,* 45–54.

Ge, X., Conger, R. D., & Elder, G. H. (2001). Pubertal transition, stressful life events, and the emergence of gender differences in adolescent depressive symptoms. *Developmental Psychology, 37,* 404–417.

Geary, D. C. (2002). Sexual selection and human life history. In R. V. Kail (Ed.), *Advances in child development and behavior* (Vol. 30, pp. 41–102). Orlando, FL: Academic Press.

Geary, D. C. (2005). *The origin of mind: Evolution of brain, cognition, and general intelligence.* Washington, DC: American Psychological Association.

Geary, D. C., Hoard, M. K., Byrd-Craven, J., Nugent, L., & Numtee, C. (2007). Cognitive mechanisms underlying achievement deficits in children with mathematical learning disability. *Child Development, 78,* 1343–1359.

Gelman, R., & Meck, E. (1986). The notion of principle: The case of counting. In J. Hiebert (Ed.), *Conceptual and procedural knowledge: The case of mathematics* (pp. 29–57). Hillside, NJ: Erlbaum.

Gelman, S. A., Taylor, M. G., & Nguyen, S. P. (2004). Mother–child conversations about gender. *Monographs of the Society for Research in Child Development, 69* (Serial No. 275).

Gentile, D. (2009). Pathological video-game use among youth ages 8 to 18: A national study. *Psychological Science, 20,* 594–602.

George, J. B. F., & Franko, D. L. (2010). Cultural issues in eating pathology and body image among children and adolescents. *Journal of Pediatric Psychology, 35,* 231–242.

Gerry, D. W., Faux, A. L., & Trainor, L. J. (2010). Effects of Kindermusik training on infants' rhythmic enculturation. *Developmental Science, 13,* 545–551.

Gershkoff-Stowe, L., & Smith, L. B. (2004). Shape and the first hundred nouns. *Child Development, 75,* 1098–1114.

Gershoff, E. T., Grogan-Kaylor, A., Lansford, J. E., Chang, L., Zelli, A., Deater-Deckard, K., et al. (2010). Parent discipline practices in an international sample: Associations with child behavior and moderation by perceived normativeness. *Child Development, 81,* 487–502.

Ghetti, S. (2008). Rejection of false events in childhood: A metamemory account. *Current Directions in Psychological Science, 17,* 16–20.

Giancola, J., Grawitch, M. J., & Borchert, D. (2009). Dealing with the stress of college: A model for adult students. *Adult Education Quarterly, 59,* 246–263.

Giarusso, R., Feng, D., Silverstein, M., & Marenco, A. (2000). Primary and secondary stressors of grandparents raising grandchildren: Evidence from a national survey. *Journal of Mental Health and Aging, 6,* 291–310.

Gibbs, D. A., Martin, S. L., Kupper, L. L., & Johnson, R. E. (2007). Child maltreatment in enlisted soldiers' families during combat-related deployments. *JAMA, 298,* 528–535.

Gibbs, J. C., Clark, P. M., Joseph, J. A., Green, J. L., Goodrick, T. S., & Makowski, D. (1986). Relations between moral judgment, moral courage, and field independence. *Child Development, 57,* 185–193.

Gibran, K. (1923). *The prophet.* New York: Knopf.

Gibson, E. J., & Walk, R. D. (1960). The visual cliff. *Scientific American, 202,* 64–71.

Giles, J. W., & Heyman, G. D. (2005). Reconceptualizing children's suggestibility: Bidirectional and temporal properties. *Child Development, 76,* 40–53.

Gillies, J., & Neimeyer, R. A. (2006). Loss, grief, and the search for significance: Toward a model of meaning reconstruction in bereavement. *Journal of Constructivist Psychology, 19,* 31–65.

Gilligan, C. (1982). *In a different voice: Psychological theory and women's development.* Cambridge, MA: Harvard University Press.

Gilligan, C., & Attanucci, J. (1988). Two moral orientations: Gender differences and similarities. *Merrill-Palmer Quarterly, 34,* 223–237.

Giordano, P. C., Manning, W. D., Longmore, M. A., & Flanigan, C. M. (2012). Developmental shifts in the character of romantic and sexual relationships from adolescence to young adulthood. In A. Booth, S. L. Brown, N. S. Landale, W. D. Manning, & S. M. McHale (Eds.), *Early adulthood in family context* (Vol. 2, Pt. 3, pp. 133–164). New York: Springer.

Githens, R., & Sauer, T. (2010). Going green online: Distance learning prepares students for success in green-collar job markets. *Community College Journal, 80,* 32–35.

Givertz, M., Segrin, C., & Hansal, A. (2009). The association between satisfaction and commitment differs across marital couple types. *Communication Research, 36,* 561–584.

Gladding, S. T. (2002). *Family therapy: History, theory, and practice* (3rd ed.). Upper Saddle River, NJ: Merrill Prentice Hall.

Glazer, H. R., Clark, M. D., Thomas, R., & Haxton, H. (2010). Parenting after the death of a spouse. *Journal of Hospice and Palliative Care, 27,* 532–536.

Gleason, T. R., & Hohmann, L. M. (2006). Concepts of real and imaginary friendships in early childhood. *Social Development, 15,* 128–144.

Glick, J. E. (2010). Connecting complex processes: A decade of research on immigrant families. *Journal of Marriage and Family, 72,* 498–515.

Goeke-Morey, M. C., Cummings, E. M., Harold, G. T., & Shelton, K. H. (2003). Categories and continua of destructive and constructive conflict tactics from the perspective of U.S. and Welsh children. *Journal of Family Psychology, 17,* 327–338.

Goldberg, A. E. (2009). *Lesbian and gay parents and their children: Research on the family life cycle.* Washington, DC: American Psychological Association.

Goldman, L. S., Genel, M., Bezman, R. J., & Slanetz, P. J. (1998). Diagnosis and treatment of attention-deficit/hyperactivity disorder in children and adolescents. *JAMA, 279,* 1100–1107.

Goldsmith, H. H., Pollak, S. D., & Davidson, R. J. (2008). Developmental neuroscience perspectives on emotion regulation. *Child Development Perspectives, 2,* 132–140.

Golinkoff, R. M. (1993). When is communication a "meeting of minds"? *Journal of Child Language, 20,* 199–207.

Golombok, S., Murray, C., Jadva, V., MacCallum, F., & Lycett, E. (2004). Families created through surrogacy arrangements: Parent–child relationships in the first year of life. *Developmental Psychology, 40,* 400–411.

González, H. M., Bowen, M. E., & Fisher, G. G. (2008). Memory decline and depressive symptoms in a nationally representative sample of older adults: The Health and Retirement Study (1998–2004). *Dementia and Geriatric Cognitive Disorders, 25,* 266–271.

Good, T. L., & Brophy, J. E. (1994). *Looking in classrooms* (6th ed.). New York: HarperCollins.

Good, T. L., & Brophy, J. E. (2008). *Looking in classrooms.* Boston: Pearson/Allyn & Bacon.

Goodnow, J. J. (1992). *Parental belief systems: The psychological consequences for children.* Hillsdale, NJ: Erlbaum.

Goodwin, P. Y., Mosher, W. D., & Chandra, A. (2010). *Marriage and cohabitation in the United States: A statistical portrait based on cycle 6 (2002) of the National Survey of Family Growth.* Retrieved from http://www.cdc.gov/nchs/data/series/sr_23/sr23_028.pdf

Goodwyn, S. W., & Acredolo, L. P. (1993). Symbolic gesture versus word: Is there a modality advantage for onset of symbol use? *Child Development, 64,* 688–701.

Góra, M., & Mach, Z. (2010). Between old fears and new challenges: The Polish debate on Europe. In J. Lacroix & K. Nicholaïdis (Eds.), *European stories: Intellectual debates on Europe in national contexts* (pp. 221–240). Oxford: Oxford University Press.

Gordon, C. P. (1996). Adolescent decision making: A broadly based theory and its application to the prevention of early pregnancy. *Adolescence, 31,* 561–584.

Gordon, R. A., Chase-Lansdale, P. L., & Brooks-Gunn, J. (2004). Extended households and the life course of young mothers: Understanding the associations using a sample of mothers with premature, low birth weight babies. *Child Development, 75,* 1013–1038.

Gorman, E. H., & Kmec, J. A. (2007). We (have to) try harder: Gender and required work effort in Britain and the United States. *Gender & Society, 21,* 828–856.

Gottlieb, L. N., & Mendelson, M. J. (1990). Parental support and firstborn girls' adaptation to the birth of a sibling. *Journal of Applied Developmental Psychology, 11,* 29–48.

Gottman, J. M. (1986). The world of coordinated play: Same- and cross-sex friendships in children. In J. M. Gottman & J. G. Parker (Eds.), *Conversations of friends* (pp. 131–191). New York: Cambridge University Press.

Gottman, J. M., & Levenson, R. W. (2000). The timing of divorce: Predicting when a couple will divorce over a 14-year period. *Journal of Marriage and the Family, 62,* 737–745.

Goubet, N., Clifton, R. K., & Shah, B. (2001). Learning about pain in preterm newborns. *Journal of Developmental and Behavioral Pediatrics, 22,* 418–424.

Gow, A. J., Pattie, A., Whiteman, M. C., Whalley, L. J., & Deary, I. J. (2007). Social support and successful aging: Investigating the relationships between lifetime cognitive change and life satisfaction. *Journal of Individual Differences, 28,* 103–115.

Graham, S., & Perin, D. (2007). A meta-analysis of writing instruction for adolescent students. *Journal of Educational Psychology, 99,* 445–476.

Graham, S., Harris, K. R., & Fink, B. (2000). Is handwriting causally related to learning to write? Treatment of handwriting problems in beginning writers. *Journal of Educational Psychology, 92,* 620–633.

Grandey, A. A. (2001). Family friendly policies: Organizational justice perceptions of need-based allocations. In R. Cropanzano (Ed.), *Justice in the workplace: From theory to practice* (pp. 145–173). Mahwah, NJ: Erlbaum.

Grant, B. F., Dawson, D. A., Stinson, F. S., Chou, S. P., Dufour, M. C., & Pickering, R. P. (2006). The 12-month prevalence and trends in DSM-IV alcohol abuse and dependence: United States, 1991–1992 and 2001–2002. *Alcohol Research and Health, 29,* 79–91.

Grawitch, M. J., Barber, L. K., & Justice, L. (2010). Rethinking the work–life interface: It's not about balance, it's about resource allocation. *Applied Psychology: Health and Well-Being, 2,* 127–159.

Graziano, P. A., Keane, S. P., & Calkins, S. D. (2007). Cardiac vagal regulation and early peer status. *Child Development, 78,* 264–278.

Green, J. S. (2008). *Beyond the good death: An anthropology of modern dying.* Baltimore: University of Pennsylvania Press.

Greenberg, M. T., & Crnic, K. A. (1988). Longitudinal predictors of developmental status and social interaction in premature and full-term infants at age two. *Child Development, 59,* 554–570.

Greenberg, M. T., Lengua, L. J., Coie, J. D., Pinderhughes, E. E., & the Conduct Problems Prevention Research Group. (1999). Predicting developmental outcomes at school entry using a multiple-risk model: Four American communities. *Developmental Psychology, 35,* 403–417.

Greenfield, E. A., & Marks, N. F. (2005). Formal volunteering as a protective factor for older adults' psychological well-being. *Journals of Gerontology: Social Sciences, 59,* S258–S264.

Greenough, W. T., & Black, J. E. (1992). Induction of brain structure by experience: Substrates for cognitive development. In M. Gunnar & C. Nelson (Eds.), *Minnesota symposia on child psychology* (Vol. 24, pp. 155–200). Hillsdale, NJ: Erlbaum.

Greif, G. L. (2009). *Buddy system: Understanding male friendships.* New York: Oxford University Press.

Greving, K. A. (2007). Examining parents' marital satisfaction trajectories: Relations with children's temperament and family demographics. *Dissertation Abstracts International. Section A. Humanities and Social Sciences, 68*(4-A), 1676.

Grice, H. P. (1975). Logic and conversation. In P. Cole & J. Morgan (Eds.), *Speech acts: Syntax and semantics* (Vol. 3, pp. 41–58). New York: Academic Press.

Griffin, M. L., Hogan, N. L., Lambert, E. G., Tucker-Gail, K. A., & Baker, D. N. (2010). Job involvement, job stress, job satisfaction, and organizational commitment and the burnout of correctional staff. *Criminal Justice and Behavior, 37,* 239–255.

Grimes, G., Hough, M., Mazur, E., & Signorella, M. (2010). Older adults' knowledge of Internet hazards. *Educational Gerontology, 36*(3), 173–192.

Grosso, J.-L., & Smith, T. L. (2012). Poverty and unemployment: A cultural approach. *Thunderbird International Business Review, 54,* 79–90.

Grucza, R. A., Norberg, K. E., & Bierut, L. J. (2009). Binge drinking among youths and young adults in the United States: 1979–2006. *Child and Adolescent Psychiatry, 48,* 692–702.

Grusec, J. E., Goodnow, J. J., & Cohen, L. (1996). Household work and the development of concern for others. *Developmental Psychology, 32,* 999–1007.

Gubernskaya, Z. (2010). Changing attitudes toward marriage and children in six countries. *Sociological Perspectives, 53,* 179–200.

Gudmundson, J. A., & Leerkes, E. M. (2012). Links between mothers' coping styles, toddler reactivity, and sensitivity to toddlers' negative emotions. *Infant Behavior and Development, 35,* 158–166.

Guerra, N. G., Williams, K. R., & Sadek, S. (2011). Understanding bullying and victimization during childhood and adolescence: A mixed methods study. *Child Development, 82,* 295–310.

Guiaux, M. (2010). *Social adjustment to widowhood: Changes in personal relationships and loneliness before and after partner loss* (Doctoral dissertation, Vrije Universiteit, Amsterdam). Retrieved from http://dspace.ubvu.vu.nl/bitstream/1871/17427/2/2010%20PhD%20Dissertation%20Guiaux.pdf

Güngör, D., & Bornstein, M. H. (2010). Culture-general and -specific associations of attachment avoidance and anxiety with perceived parental warmth and psychological control among Turk and Belgian adolescents. *Journal of Adolescence, 33,* 593–602.

Gupta, S., Tracey, T. J. G., & Gore, P. A. (2008). Structural examination of RIASEC scales in high school students: Variation across ethnicity and method. *Journal of Vocational Behavior, 72,* 1–13.

Haagsma, J. A., Polinder, S., Olff, M., Toet, H., Bonsel, G. J., & van Beeck, E. F. (2012). Posttraumatic stress symptoms and health-related quality of life: A two-year follow-up study of injury treated at the emergency department. *BMC Psychiatry, 12.* doi:10.1186/1471-244X-12-1

Haeffel, G. J., Gibb, B. E., Metalsky, G. I., Alloy, L. B., Abramson, L. Y., Hankin, B. L., et al. (2008). Measuring cognitive vulnerability to depression: Development and validation of the cognitive style questionnaire. *Clinical Psychology Review, 28,* 824–836.

Hagestad, G. O., & Neugarten, B. L. (1985). Age and the life course. In R. H. Binstock & E. Shanas (Eds.), *Handbook of aging and the social sciences* (2nd ed., pp. 35–61). New York: Van Nostrand Reinhold.

Haier, R. J., Schroeder, D. H., Tang, C., Head, K., & Colom, R. (2010). Gray matter correlates of cognitive ability tests used for vocational guidance. *BMC Research Notes, 3.* Retrieved from http://www.biomedcentral.com/content/pdf/1756-0500-3-206.pdf

Halford, W. K., Markman, H. J., & Stanley, S. (2008). Strengthening couples' relationships with education: Social policy and public health perspectives. *Journal of Family Psychology, 22,* 497–505.

Halgunseth, L. C., Ispa, J. M., & Rudy, D. (2006). Parental control in Latino families: An integrated review of the literature. *Child Development, 77,* 1282–1297.

Hall, J. A., & Halberstadt, A. G. (1981). Sex roles and nonverbal communication skills. *Sex Roles, 7,* 273–287.

Hall, S. S. (2006). Marital meaning: Exploring young adult's belief systems about marriage. *Journal of Family Issues, 27,* 1437–1458.

Halpern, C. T., Spriggs, A. L., Martin, S. L., & Kupper, L. L. (2009). Patterns of intimate partner violence victimization from adolescence to young adulthood in a nationally representative sample. *Journal of Adolescent Health, 45,* 508–516.

Halpern, D. F., Benbow, C. P., Geary, D. C., Gur, R. C., Hyde, J. S., & Gernsbacher, M. A. (2007). The science of sex differences in science and mathematics. *Psychological Science in the Public Interest, 8,* 1–51.

Halpern, L. F., MacLean, W. E., & Baumeister, A. A. (1995). Infant sleep–wake characteristics: Relation to neurological status and the prediction of developmental outcome. *Developmental Review, 15,* 255–291.

Halpern-Felsher, B. L., & Cauffman, E. (2001). Costs and benefits of a decision: Decision-making competence in adolescents and adults. *Journal of Applied Developmental Psychology, 22,* 257–273.

Hamilton, B. E., Martin, J. A., & Ventura, S. J. (2010). Births: Preliminary data for 2008. *National Vital Statistics Reports, 58.*

Hamm, J. V. (2000). Do birds of a feather flock together? The variable bases for African American, Asian American, and European American adolescents' selection of similar friends. *Developmental Psychology, 36,* 209–219.

Hammen, C., & Rudolph, K. D. (2003). Childhood mood disorders. In E. J. Mash & R. A. Barkley (Eds.), *Child psychopathology* (2nd ed., pp. 233–278). New York: Guilford.

Hammer, L. B., Neal, M. B., Newsom, J. T., Brockwood, K.-J., & Colton, C. L. (2005). A longitudinal study of the effects of dual-earner couples' utilization of family-friendly workplace supports on work and family outcomes. *Journal of Applied Psychology, 90,* 799–810.

Hane, A. A., & Fox, N. W. (2006). Ordinary variations in maternal caregiving influence human infants' stress reactivity. *Psychological Science, 17,* 550–556.

Hansen, S. R. (2006). Courtship duration as a correlate of marital satisfaction and stability. *Dissertation Abstracts International. Section B. Sciences and Engineering, 67*(4-B), 2279.

Hansen, T., Moum, T., & Shapiro, A. (2007). Relational and individual well-being among cohabitors and married individuals in midlife: Recent trends from Norway. *Journal of Family Issues, 28,* 910–933.

Hansson, R. O., & Stroebe, M. S. (2007). *Bereavement in late life: Coping, adaptation, and developmental influences.* Washington, DC: American Psychological Association.

Harden, K. P., & Mendle, J. (2012). Gene–environment interplay in the association between pubertal timing and delinquency in adolescent girls. *Journal of Abnormal Psychology, 121,* 73–87.

Hareven, T. K. (1995). Introduction: Aging and generational relations over the life course. In T. K. Hareven (Ed.), *Aging and generational relations over the life course: A historical and cross-cultural perspective* (pp. 1–12). Berlin: de Gruyter.

Hareven, T. K. (2001). Historical perspectives on aging and family relations. In R. H. Binstock & L. K. George (Eds.), *Handbook of aging and the social sciences* (5th ed., pp. 141–159). San Diego, CA: Academic Press.

Hareven, T. K., & Adams, K. (1996). The generation in the middle: Cohort comparisons in assistance to aging parents in an American community. In T. K. Hareven (Ed.), *Aging and generational relations: Life course and cross-cultural perspectives* (pp. 3–29). New York: Aldine de Gruyter.

Harley, C. B. (2008). Telomerase and cancer therapeutics. *Nature Reviews: Cancer, 8,* 167–179.

Harre, N. (2007). Community service or activism as an identity project for youth. *Journal of Community Psychology, 35,* 711–724.

Harrington, D., Bean, N., Pintello, D., & Mathews, D. (2001). Job satisfaction and burnout: Predictors of intentions to leave a job in a military setting. *Administration in Social Work, 25,* 1–16.

Harris, K. R., Graham, S., Mason, L., & Friedlander, B. (2008). *Powerful writing strategies for all students.* Baltimore: Brookes.

Harris, P. L., Brown, E., Marriot, C., Whithall, S., & Harmer, S. (1991). Monsters, ghosts, and witches: Testing the limits of the fantasy–reality distinction in young children. *British Journal of Developmental Psychology, 9,* 105–123.

Harris Interactive. (2011). *Large majorities support doctor assisted suicide for terminally ill patients in great pain.* Retrieved from http://www.harrisinteractive.com/NewsRoom/HarrisPolls/tabid/447/mid/1508/articleId/677/ctl/ReadCustom%20Default/Default.aspx

Harrist, A. W., Zaia, A. F., Bates, J. E., Dodge, K. A., & Pettit, G. S. (1997). Subtypes of social withdrawal in early childhood: Sociometric status and social-cognitive differences across four years. *Child Development, 68,* 278–294.

Harter, S. (1994). Developmental changes in self-understanding across the 5 to 7 shift. In A. Sameroff & M. M. Haith (Eds.), *Reason and responsibility: The passage through childhood.* Chicago: University of Chicago Press.

Harter, S. (2006). The self. In N. Eisenberg, W. Damon, & R. M. Lerner (Eds.), *Handbook of child psychology* (6th ed., Vol. 3, pp. 505–570). Hoboken, NJ: Wiley.

Harter, S., Waters, P., & Whitesell, N. R. (1998). Relational self-worth: Differences in perceived worth as a person across interpersonal contexts among adolescents. *Child Development, 69,* 756–766.

Harter, S., Whitesell, N. R., & Kowalski, P. S. (1992). Individual differences in the effects of educational transitions on young adolescents' perceptions of competence and motivational orientation. *American Educational Research Journal, 29,* 777–807.

Hartman, P. S. (2001). Women developing wisdom: Antecedents and correlates in a longitudinal sample. *Dissertation Abstracts International. Section B. Sciences and Engineering, 62*(1-B), 591.

Hartup, W. W., & Stevens, N. (1999). Friendships and adaptation across the life span. *Current Directions in Psychological Science, 8,* 76–79.

Harvard School of Public Health. (2010). *The nutrition source: Alcohol: Balancing risks and benefits.* Retrieved from http://www.hsph.harvard.edu/nutritionsource/what-should-you-eat/alcohol-full-story

Haslam, C., & Lawrence, W. (2004). Health-related behavior and beliefs of pregnant smokers. *Health Psychology, 23,* 486–491.

Haslam, C., Hodder, K. I., & Yates, P. J. (2011). Errorless learning and spaced retrieval: How do these methods fare in healthy and clinical populations? *Journal of Clinical and Experimental Neuropsychology, 33,* 1–16.

Hastings, P. D., & Rubin, K. H. (1999). Predicting mothers' beliefs about preschool-aged children's social behavior: Evidence for maternal attitudes moderating child effects. *Child Development, 70,* 722–741.

Hastings, P. D., Zahn-Waxler, C., & McShane, K. (2006). We are, by nature, moral creatures: Biological bases of concern for others. In M. Killen & J. G. Smetana (Eds.), *Handbook of moral development* (pp. 483–516). Mahwah, NJ: Erlbaum.

Hatania, R., & Smith, L. B. (2010). Selective attention and attention switching: Toward a unified developmental approach. *Developmental Science, 13,* 622–635.

Haviland, J. M., & Lelwica, M. (1987). The induced affect response: 10-week-old infants' responses to three emotion expressions. *Developmental Psychology, 23,* 97–104.

Hawley, P. H. (1999). The ontogenesis of social dominance: A strategy-based evolutionary perspective. *Developmental Review, 19,* 7–132.

Haworth, J., & Lewis, S. (2005). Work, leisure and well-being. *British Journal of Guidance & Counselling, 33,* 67–78.

Hayflick, L. (1998). How and why we age. *Experimental Gerontology, 33,* 639–653.

Hayslip, B., Jr., Henderson, C. E., & Shore, R. J. (2003). The structure of grandparental role meaning. *Journal of Adult Development, 10,* 1–11.

Hayslip, B., Jr., Shore, R. J., Hendereson, C. E., & Lambert, P. L. (1998). Custodial grandparenting and the impact of grandchildren with problems on role satisfaction and role meaning. *Journal of Gerontology: Social Sciences, 53B,* S164–S173.

Hazell, P. L. (2009). 8-year follow-up of the MTA sample. *Journal of the American Academy of Child & Adolescent Psychiatry, 48,* 461–462.

Health and Safety Executive. (2010). *About us.* Retrieved from http://www.hse.gov.uk/aboutus/index.htm

HealthyPeople.gov. (2011). *Healthy People 2020.* Retrieved from http://www.healthypeople.gov/2020/default.aspx

Heatherington, L., & Lavner, J. A. (2008). Coming to terms with coming out: Review and recommendations for family systems–focused research. *Journal of Family Psychology, 22,* 329–343.

Heckhausen, J., Wrosch, C., & Schulz, R. (2010). A motivational theory of life-span development. *Psychological Review, 117,* 32–60.

Heidrich, S. M., & Denney, N. W. (1994). Does social problem solving differ from other types of problem solving during the adult years? *Experimental Aging Research, 20,* 105–126.

Helpguide.org. (2005). *Adult day care centers: A guide to options and selecting the best center for your needs.* Retrieved from http://www.helpguide.org/elder/adult_day_care_centers.htm

Henderson, N. D. (2010). Predicting long-term firefighter performance from cognitive and physical ability measures. *Personnel Psychology, 63,* 999–1039.

Henig, R. M. (2010). *What is it about 20-somethings?* Retrieved from http://www.nytimes.com/2010/08/22/magazine/22Adulthood-t.html?_r51&ref5families_and_family_life

Henretta, J. C. (2001). Work and retirement. In R. H. Binstock & L. K. George (Eds.), *Handbook of aging and the social sciences* (5th ed., pp. 255–271). San Diego, CA: Academic Press.

Henry, D. B., Schoeny, M. E., Deptula, D. P., & Slavick, J. T. (2007). Peer selection and socialization effects on adolescent intercourse without a condom and attitudes about the costs of sex. *Child Development, 78,* 825–838.

Heppner, R. S. (2007). A paradox of diversity: Billions invested, but women still leave. *Dissertation Abstracts International. Section A. Humanities and Social Sciences, 68*(4-A), 1527.

Herner, S. R. (2010). Grief as a social experience: Death and bereavement in Lihir, Papua New Guinea. *Australian Journal of Anthropology, 21,* 281–297.

Hershatter, A., & Epstein, M. (2010). Millennials and the world of work: An organization and management perspective. *Journal of Business and Psychology, 25,* 211–223.

Hertzog, C., & Dunlosky, J. (2004). Aging, metacognition, and cognitive control. In B. H. Ross (Ed.), *The psychology of learning and motivation: Advances in research and theory* (Vol. 45, pp. 215–251). San Diego, CA: Elsevier.

Hespos, S. J., Ferry, A. L., & Rips, L. J. (2009). Five-month-old infants have different expectations for solids and liquids. *Psychological Science, 20,* 603–611.

Hespos, S. J., & vanMarle, K. (2012). Physics for infants: Characterizing the origins of knowledge about objects, substances, and number. *Wiley Interdisciplinary Reviews: Cognitive Science, 3,* 19–27.

Hess, U., & Kirouac, G. (2000). Emotion expression in groups. In M. Lewis & J. Haviland-Jones (Eds.), *Handbook of emotions* (2nd ed., pp. 368–381). New York: Guilford.

Hetherington, E. M., & Kelly, J. (2002). *For better or for worse: Divorce reconsidered.* New York: W. W. Norton.

Heyman, G. D. (2009). Children's reasoning about traits. In P. Bauer (Ed.), *Advances in child development and behavior* (Vol. 37, pp. 105–143). London: Elsevier.

Heyman, G. D., & Legare, C. H. (2004). Children's beliefs about gender differences in the academic and social domains. *Sex Roles, 50,* 227–239.

Hill, J. L., Brooks-Gunn, J., & Waldfogel, J. (2003). Sustained effects of high participation in an early intervention for low-birth-weight premature infants. *Developmental Psychology, 39,* 730–744.

Hill, N. E., & Taylor, L. E. (2004). Parental school involvement and children's academic achievement: Pragmatics and issues. *Current Directions in Psychological Science, 13,* 161–164.

Hillman, C. H., Buck, S. M., Themanson, J. R., Pontifex, M. B., & Castelli, D. M. (2009). Aerobic fitness and cognitive development: Event-related brain potential and task performance indices of executive control in preadolescent children. *Developmental Psychology, 45,* 114–129.

Hills, W. E. (2010). Grandparenting roles in the evolving American family. In D. Wiseman (Ed.), *The American family: Understanding its changing dynamics and place in society* (pp. 65–78.) Springfield, IL: Charles C. Thomas.

Hines, D. A., & Douglas, E. M. (2009). Women's use of intimate partner violence against men: Prevalence, implications, and consequences. *Journal of Aggression, Maltreatment and Trauma, 18,* 572–586.

Hines, M. (2011). Gender development and the human brain. *Annual Review of Neuroscience, 34,* 69–88.

Hinton, A., & Chirgwin, S. (2010). Nursing education: Reducing reality shock for graduate indigenous nurses—It's all about time. *Australian Journal of Advanced Nursing, 28,* 60–66.

Hipwell, A. E., Keenan, K., Loeber, R., & Battista, D. (2010). Early predictors of sexually intimate behaviors in an urban sample of young girls. *Developmental Psychology, 46,* 366–378.

Hirsh-Pasek, K., & Golinkoff, R. M. (2008). King Solomon's take on word learning: An integrative account from the radical middle. In R. V. Kail (Ed.), *Advances in child development and behavior* (Vol. 36, pp. 1–29). San Diego, CA: Elsevier.

Hofer, J., Busch, H., Chasiotis, A., Kärtner, J., & Campos, D. (2008). Concern for generativity and its relation to implicit pro-social power motivation, generative goals, and satisfaction with life: A cross-cultural investigation. *Journal of Personality, 76,* 1–30.

Hofer, M. A. (2006). Psychobiological roots of early attachment. *Current Directions in Psychological Science, 15,* 84–88.

Hoff, E. (2009). *Language development* (4th ed.). Belmont, CA: Wadsworth Cengage Learning.

Hoff, E., & Naigles, L. (2002). How children use input to acquire a lexicon. *Child Development, 73,* 418–433.

Hoff-Ginsberg, E. (1997). *Language development.* Pacific Grove, CA: Brooks/Cole.

Hoff-Ginsberg, E., & Tardif, T. (1995). Socioeconomic status and parenting. In M. H. Bornstein (Ed.), *Handbook of parenting* (Vol. 2, pp. 161–188). Mahwah, NJ: Erlbaum.

Hoffman, E., Kaneshiro, S., & Compton, W. C. (2012). Peak experiences among Americans in midlife. *Journal of Humanistic Psychology, 52.* doi:10.1177/0022167811433851

Hoffman, L., McDowd, J. M., Atchley, P., & Dubinsky, R. (2005). The role of visual attention in predicting driving impairment in older adults. *Psychology and Aging, 20,* 610–622.

Hoffman, M. L. (1988). Moral development. In M. H. Bornstein & M. E. Lamb (Eds.), *Developmental psychology: An advanced textbook* (2nd ed., pp. 497–538). Hillsdale, NJ: Erlbaum.

Hoffman, M. L. (1994). Discipline and internalization. *Developmental Psychology, 30,* 26–28.

Hogan, A. M., de Haan, M., Datta, A., & Kirkham, F. J. (2006). Hypoxia: An acute, intermittent and chronic challenge to cognitive development. *Developmental Science, 9,* 335–337.

Hogge, W. A. (1990). Teratology. In I. R. Merkatz & J. E. Thompson (Eds.), *New perspectives on prenatal care.* New York: Elsevier.

Holden, G. W., & Miller, P. C. (1999). Enduring and different: A meta-analysis of the similarity in parents' child rearing. *Psychological Bulletin, 125,* 223–254.

Holland, J. L. (1985). *Making vocational choices: A theory of vocational personalities and work environments* (2nd ed.). Englewood Cliffs, NJ: Prentice Hall.

Holland, J. L. (1987). Current status of Holland's theory of careers: Another perspective. *Career Development Quarterly, 36,* 24–30.

Holland, J. L. (1996). Exploring careers with a typology: What we have learned and some new directions. *American Psychologist, 51,* 397–406.

Holland, J. L. (1997). *Making vocational choices: A theory of vocational personalities and work environments* (3rd ed.). Baltimore: Johns Hopkins University Press.

Holland, J. M., & Neimeyer, R. A. (2010). An examination of stage theory of grief among individuals bereaved by natural and violent causes: A meaning-oriented contribution. *Omega: Journal of Death and Dying, 61,* 103–120.

Hollich, G. J., Hirsh-Pasek, K., & Golinkoff, R. M. (2000). Breaking the language barrier: An emergentist coalition model for the origins of word learning. *Monographs of the Society for Research in Child Development, 65* (Serial No. 262),.

Holloway, K. F. C. (2011). *Private bodies, public texts: Race, gender, and a cultural bioethics.* Durham, NC: Duke University Press.

Hom, P. W., & Kinicki, A. J. (2001). Toward a greater understanding of how dissatisfaction drives employee turnover. *Academy of Management Journal, 44,* 975–987.

Honda-Howard, M., & Homma, M. (2001). Job satisfaction of Japanese career women and its influence on turnover intention. *Asian Journal of Social Psychology, 4,* 23–38.

Hood, B., Carey, S., & Prasada, S. (2000). Predicting the outcomes of physical events: Two-year-olds fail to reveal knowledge of solidity and support. *Child Development, 71,* 1540–1554.

Hooker, K. (1999). Possible selves in adulthood. In T. M. Hess & F. Blanchard-Fields (Eds.), *Social cognition and aging* (pp. 97–122). San Diego, CA: Academic Press.

Hooker, K., Fiese, B. H., Jenkins, L., Morfei, M. Z., & Schwagler, J. (1996). Possible selves among parents of infants and preschoolers. *Developmental Psychology, 32,* 542–550.

Horn, J. L. (1982). The aging of human abilities. In B. B. Wolman (Ed.), *Handbook of developmental psychology* (pp. 847–870). Englewood Cliffs, NJ: Prentice Hall.

Horn, J. L., & Hofer, S. M. (1992). Major abilities and development in the adult period. In R. J. Sternberg & C. A. Berg (Eds.), *Intellectual development* (pp. 44–99). New York: Cambridge University Press.

Horsford, S. R., Parra-Cardona, J. R., Post, L. A., & Schiamberg, L. (2011). Elder abuse and neglect in African American families: Informing best practice based on ecological and cultural frameworks. *Journal of Elder Abuse and Neglect, 23,* 75–88.

Horswill, M. S., Kemala, C. N., Wetton, M., Scialfa, C. T., & Pachana, N. A. (2010). Improving older drivers' hazard perception ability. *Psychology and Aging, 25,* 464–469.

Hospice Foundation of America. (2011a). *Choosing hospice: Questions to ask.* Retrieved from http://www.hospicefoundation.org/pages/page.asp?page_id571942

Hospice Foundation of America. (2011b). *Hospice patients and staff.* Retrieved from http://www.hospicefoundation.org/pages/page.asp?page_id553123

Houston, D. M., & Jusczyk, P. W. (2003). Infants' long-term memory for the sound patterns of words and voices. *Journal of Experimental Psychology: Human Perception and Performance, 29,* 1143–1154.

Howard, L. W., & Cordes, C. L. (2010). Flight from unfairness: Effects of perceived injustice on emotional exhaustion and employee withdrawal. *Journal of Business and Psychology, 25,* 409–428.

Howe, N., & Ross, H. S. (1990). Socialization, perspective taking and the sibling relationship. *Developmental Psychology, 26,* 160–165.

Howe, N., & Strauss, W. (1992). *Generations: The history of America's future, 1584–2069.* New York: Harper Perennial.

Howell, K. K., Lynch, M. E., Platzman, K. A., Smith, G. H., & Coles, C. D. (2006). Prenatal alcohol exposure and ability, academic achievement, and school functioning in adolescence: A longitudinal follow-up. *Journal of Pediatric Psychology, 31,* 116–126.

Howes, C., & Matheson, C. C. (1992). Sequences in the development of competent play with peers: Social and social pretend play. *Developmental Psychology, 28,* 961–974.

Hsu, H.-C. (2005). Gender disparity of successful aging in Taiwan. *Women & Health, 42,* 1–21.

Hubbard, R. R. (2010). *Afro-German biracial identity development.* Retrieved from http://digarchive.library.vcu.edu/bitstream/10156/2804/1/Afro-German%20HEMBAGI%20%28F3%29.pdf

Huesmann, L. R. (2007). The impact of electronic media violence: Scientific theory and research. *Journal of Adolescent Health Care, 41,* S6–S13.

Hughes, J. M., Bigler, R. S., & Levy, S. R. (2007). Consequences of learning about historical racism among European American and African American children. *Child Development, 78,* 1689–1705.

Huizink, A., Robles de Medina, P., Mulder, E., Visser, G., & Buitelaar, J. (2002). Psychological measures of prenatal stress as predictors of infant temperament. *Journal of the American Academy of Child & Adolescent Psychiatry, 41,* 1078–1085.

Hull, T. H. (2009). *Fertility prospects in south-eastern Asia: Report of the United Nations Expert Group meeting on recent and future trends in fertility.* Retrieved from http://www.un.org/esa/population/meetings/EGM-Fertility2009/P14_Hull.pdf

Hulme, C., & Snowling, M. J. (2009). *Developmental disorders of language learning and cognition.* Chichester, England: Wiley-Blackwell.

Human Genome Project. (2003). *Genomics and its impact on science and society: A 2003 primer.* Washington, DC: U.S. Department of Energy.

Hunt, E., & Carlson, J. (2007). Considerations relating to the study of group differences in intelligence. *Perspectives on Psychological Science, 2,* 194–213.

Hunt, J. M., & Weintraub, J. R. (2006). *The coaching organization: A strategy for developing leaders.* Thousand Oaks, CA: Sage.

Huston, A. C., & Wright, J. C. (1998). Mass media and children's development. In W. Damon (Ed.), *Handbook of child psychology* (5th ed., Vol. 4, pp. 998–1058). New York: Wiley.

Huston, T. L., Caughlin, J. P., Houts, R. M., Smith, S. E., & George, L. J. (2001). The connubial crucible: Newlywed years as a predictor of marital delight, distress, and divorce. *Journal of Personality and Social Psychology, 80,* 237–252.

Hutchinson, D. M., Rapee, R. M., & Taylor, A. (2010). Body dissatisfaction and eating disturbances in early adolescence: A structural modeling investigation examining negative affect and peer factors. *Journal of Early Adolescence, 30,* 489–517.

Huth-Bocks, A. C., Levendosky, A. A., Bogat, G. A., & von Eye, A. (2004). The impact of maternal characteristics and contextual variables on infant–mother attachment. *Child Development, 75,* 480–496.

Huttenlocher, J., Haight, W., Bryk, A., Seltzer, M., & Lyons, T. (1991). Early vocabulary growth: Relation to language input and gender. *Developmental Psychology, 27*, 236–248.

Hwang, M. J. (2007). Asian social workers' perceptions of glass ceiling, organizational fairness and career prospects. *Journal of Social Service Research, 33*, 13–24.

Hyde, J. S. (2007). New directions in the study of gender similarities and differences. *Current Directions in Psychological Science, 16*, 259–263.

Hymel, S., Vaillancourt, T., McDougall, P., & Renshaw, P. D. (2004). Peer acceptance and rejection in childhood. In P. K. Smith & C. H. Hart (Eds.), *Blackwell handbook of childhood social development* (pp. 265–284). Malden, MA: Blackwell.

Ibrahim, R., & Hassan, Z. (2009). Understanding singlehood from the experiences of never-married Malay Muslim women in Malaysia: Some preliminary findings. *European Journal of Social Sciences, 8*, 395–405.

Iervolino, A. C., Hines, M., Golombok, S. E., Rust, J., & Plomin, R. (2005). Genetic and environmental influences on sex-typed behavior during the preschool years. *Child Development, 76*, 826–840.

Ijuin, M., Homma, A., Mimura, M., Kitamura, S., Kawai, Y., Imai, Y., & Gondo, Y. (2008). Validation of the 7-minute screen for the detection of early-stage Alzheimer's disease. *Dementia and Geriatric Cognitive Disorders, 25*, 248–255.

Ilies, R., Hauserman, N., Schwochau, S., & Stibal, J. (2003). Reported incidence rates of work-related sexual harassment in the United States: Using meta-analysis to explain reported rate disparities. *Personnel Psychology, 56*, 607–631.

Inhelder, B., & Piaget, J. (1958). *The growth of logical thinking from childhood to adolescence.* New York: Basic Books.

Institute of Medicine. (2010). *DRIs for calcium and vitamin D.* Retrieved from http://iom.edu/Reports/2010/Dietary-Reference-Intakes-for-Calcium-and-Vitamin-D/~/media/Files/Report%20Files/2010/Dietary-Reference-Intakes-for-Calcium-and-Vitamin-D/calciumvitd_lg.jpg

Ivancovich, D. A., & Wong, T. P. (2008). The role of existential and spiritual coping in anticipatory grief. In A. Tomer, G. T. Eliason, & P. T. P. Wong (Eds.), *Existential and spiritual issues in death attitudes* (pp. 209–233). Mahwah, NJ: Erlbaum.

Izard, C. E. (2007). Basic emotions, natural kinds, emotion schemas, and a new paradigm. *Perspectives on Psychological Science, 2*, 260–280.

Jack, C. R., Jr., Albert, M. A., Knopman, D. S., McKhann, G. M., Sperling, R. A., Carrillo, M. C., et al. (2011). Introduction to the recommendations from the National Institute on Aging–Alzheimer's Association workgroups on diagnostic guidelines for Alzheimer's disease. *Alzheimer's & Dementia: Journal of the Alzheimer's Association, 7*, 257–262.

Jack, F., MacDonald, S., Reese, E., & Hayne, H. (2009). Maternal reminiscing style during early childhood predicts the age of adolescents' earliest memories. *Child Development, 80*, 496–505.

Jacob, B., & Wilder, T. (2010). *Educational expectations and attainment.* National Bureau of Economic Research (Working Paper No. w156983). Retrieved from http://papers.ssrn.com/sol3/papers.cfm?abstract_id51540987

Jacobi, C., Hayward, C., de Zwaan, M., Kraemer, H. C., & Agras, W. S. (2004). Coming to terms with risk factors for eating disorders: Application of risk terminology and suggestions for a general taxonomy. *Psychological Bulletin, 130*, 19–65.

Jacobs, J. A., & Gerson, K. (2001). Overworked individuals or overworked families? Explaining trends in work, leisure, and family time. *Work and Occupations, 28*, 40–63.

Jacobs, J. E., & Eccles, J. S. (1992). The impact of mothers' gender-role stereotypic beliefs on mothers' and children's ability perceptions. *Journal of Personality and Social Psychology, 63*, 932–944.

Jacobs-Lawson, J. M., Hershey, D. A., & Neukam, K. A. (2004). Gender differences in factors that influence time spent planning for retirement. *Journal of Women & Aging, 16*, 55–69.

Jacobson, S. W., & Jacobson, J. L. (2000). Teratogenic insult and neurobehavioral function in infancy and childhood. In C. A. Nelson (Ed.), *The Minnesota symposium on child psychology* (Vol. 31, pp. 61–112). Mahwah, NJ: Erlbaum.

Jacoby, S. (2005). *Sex in America.* AARP report. Retrieved from http://assets.aarp.org/rgcenter/general/2004_sexuality.pdf

Jaffee, S., & Hyde, J. S. (2000). Gender differences in moral orientation: A meta-analysis. *Psychological Bulletin, 126*, 703–726.

Jain, E., & Labouvie-Vief, G. (2010). Compensatory effects of emotional avoidance in adult development. *Biological Psychology, 84*, 497–513.

Jansen, J., de Weerth, C., & Riksen-Walraven, J. M. (2008). Breastfeeding and the mother–infant relationship—A review. *Developmental Review, 28*, 503–521.

Janson, H., & Mathiesen, K. S. (2008). Temperament profiles from infancy to middle childhood: Development and associations with behavioral problems. *Developmental Psychology, 44*, 1314–1328.

Janssen, J., Tattersall, C., Waterink, W., van den Berg, B., van Es, R., Bolman, C., & Koper, R. (2007). Self-organising navigational support in lifelong learning: How predecessors can lead the way. *Computers & Education, 49*, 781–793.

Jiao, Z. (1999, April). *Which students keep old friends and which become new friends across a school transition?* Paper presented at the 1999 meeting of the Society for Research in Child Development, Albuquerque, New Mexico.

Jimenez, D. E., Alegria, M., Chen, C.-N., Chan, D., & Laderman, N. (2010). Prevalence of psychiatric illnesses in older ethnic minority adults. *Journal of the American Geriatrics Society, 58*, 256–264.

Johanson, R. B., Rice, C., Coyle, M., Arthur, J., Anyanwu, L., Ibrahim, J., et al. (1993). A randomized prospective study comparing the new vacuum extractor policy with forceps delivery. *British Journal of Obstetrics and Gynecology, 100*, 524–530.

John, O. P., & Gross, J. J. (2007). Individual differences in emotion regulation. In J. J. Gross (Ed.), *Handbook of emotion regulation* (pp. 351–372). New York: Guilford.

Johnson, A. J., Becker, J. A. H., Craig, E. A., Gilchrist, E. S., & Haigh, M. M. (2009). Changes in friendship commitment: Comparing geographically close and long-distance young-adult friendships. *Communication Quarterly, 57*, 395–415.

Johnson, D. L. (2000). The black corporate experience: Perceptions of the impact of skin color and gender on black professionals' success. *Dissertation Abstracts International. Section B. Sciences and Engineering, 60*(8-B), 4282.

Johnson, H. D., Brady, E., McNair, R., Congdon, D., Niznik, J., & Anderson, S. (2007). Identity as a moderator of gender differences in the emotional closeness of emerging adults' same- and cross-sex friendships. *Adolescence, 42*, 1–23.

Johnson, K., & Wilson, K. (2010). *Current economic status of older adults in the United States: demographic analysis.* Report prepared for the National Council on Aging. Retrieved from http://www.ncoa.org/assets/files/pdf/Economic-Security-Trends-for-Older-Adults-65-and-Older_March-2010.pdf

Johnson, M. H., Grossman, T., & Cohen Kadosh, K. (2009). Mapping functional brain development: Building a social brain through interactive specialization. *Developmental Psychology, 45*, 151–159.

Johnson, M. J., Grossman, T., & Farroni, T. (2008). The social cognitive neuroscience of infancy: Illuminating the early development of social brain functions. In R. V. Kail (Ed.), *Advances in child development and behavior* (Vol. 36, pp. 331–372). San Diego, CA: Elsevier.

Johnson, R. M., Miller, M., Vriniotis, M., Azrael, D., & Hemenway, D. (2006). Are household firearms stored less safely in home with adolescents? Analysis of a national random sample of parents. *Archives of Pediatrics and Adolescent Medicine, 160*, 788–792.

Johnson, S. P. (2001). Visual development in human infants: Binding features, surfaces, and objects. *Visual Cognition, 8*, 565–578.

Johnston, K. E., Swim, J. K., Saltsman, B. M., Deater-Deckard, K., & Petrill, S. A. (2007). Mothers' racial, ethnic, and cultural socialization of transracially adopted Asian children. *Family Relations, 56*, 390–402.

Johnston, L. D., Delva, J., & O'Malley, P. M. (2007). Sports participation and physical education in American secondary schools: Current levels and racial/ethnic and socioeconomic disparities. *American Journal of Preventive Medicine, 33*, S195–S208.

Johnston, L. D., O'Malley, P. M., Bachman, J. G., & Schulenberg, J. E. (2011). *Monitoring the Future national results on adolescent drug use: Overview of key findings, 2010.* Ann Arbor, MI: Institute for Social Research, The University of Michigan.

Joiner, T. (2010). *Myths about suicide.* Cambridge, MA: Harvard University Press.

Jokela, M., Kivimäki, M., Elovainio, M., & Keltikangas-Järvinen, L. (2009). Personality and having children: A two-way relationship. *Journal of Personality and Social Psychology, 96*, 218–230.

Jones, B. F. (2010). Age and great invention. *Review of Economics and Statistics, 92*, 1–14. doi:10.1162/rest.2009.11724

Jones, C. J., & Meredith, W. (1996). Patterns of personality change across the life span. *Psychology and Aging, 11*, 57–65.

Jones, G. W. (2010). *Changing marriage patterns in Asia.* Asia Research Institute (Working Paper Series No. 131). Retrieved from http://www.ari.nus.edu.sg/docs/wps/wps10_131.pdf

Jones, H. E. (2006). Drug addiction during pregnancy: Advances in maternal treatment and understanding child outcomes. *Current Directions in Psychological Science, 15,* 126–130.

Jordan, N. C. (2007). The need for number sense. *Educational Leadership, 65,* 63–66.

Jordan, N. C., Kaplan, D., Ramineni, C., & Locuniak, M. N. (2008). Development of number combination skill in the early school years: When do fingers help? *Developmental Science, 11,* 662–668.

Joseph, D. L., & Newman, D. A. (2010). Emotional intelligence: An integrative meta-analysis and cascading model. *Journal of Applied Psychology, 95,* 54–78.

Joseph, R. (2000). Fetal brain behavior and cognitive development. *Developmental Review, 20,* 81–98.

Joseph, R. M., Keehn, B., Connolly, C., Wolfe, J. M., & Horowitz, T. S. (2009). Why is visual search superior in autism spectrum disorder? *Developmental Science, 12,* 1083–1096.

Joussemet, M., Vitaro, F., Barker, E. D., Côté, S., Zoccolillo, M., Nagin, D. S., et al. (2008). Controlling parenting and physical aggression during elementary school. *Child Development, 79,* 411–425.

Joyner, K., & Udry, J. R. (2000). You don't bring me anything but down: Adolescent romance and depression. *Journal of Health and Social Behavior, 41,* 369–391.

Judge, T. A., Klinger, R. L., & Simon, L. S. (2010). Time is on my side: Time, general mental ability, human capital, and extrinsic career success. *Journal of Applied Psychology, 95,* 92–107.

Juffer, F. (2006). Children's awareness of adoption and their problem behavior in families with 7-year-old internationally adopted children. *Adoption Quarterly, 9,* 1–22.

Jung, R. E., & Haier, R. J. (2007). The parieto-frontal integration theory (P-FIT) of intelligence: Converging neuroimaging evidence. *Behavioral and Brain Sciences, 30,* 135–154.

Jung, R. E., Segall, J. M., Bockholt, H. J., Flores, R. A., Smith, S. M., Chavez, R. S., et al. (2010). Neuroanatomy of creativity. *Human Brain Mapping, 31,* 398–409.

Jusczyk, P. W. (1995). Language acquisition: Speech sounds and phonological development. In J. L. Miller & P. D. Eimas (Eds.), *Handbook of perception and cognition* (Vol. 11, pp. 263–301). Orlando, FL: Academic Press.

Jusczyk, P. W. (2002). How infants adapt speech-processing capacities to native-language structure. *Current Directions in Psychological Science, 11,* 15–18.

Justice, L. M., Pullen, P. C., & Pence, K. (2008). Influence of verbal and nonverbal references to print on preschoolers' visual attention to print during storybook reading. *Developmental Psychology, 44,* 855–866.

Kagan, J., Arcus, D., Snidman, N., Feng, W. Y., Hendler, J., & Greene, S. (1994). Reactivity in infants: A cross-national comparison. *Developmental Psychology, 30,* 342–345.

Kaijura, H., Cowart, B. J., & Beauchamp, G. K. (1992). Early developmental change in bitter taste responses in human infants. *Developmental Psychobiology, 25,* 375–386.

Kail, R. (2004). Cognitive development includes global and domain-specific processes. *Merrill-Palmer Quarterly, 50,* 445–455.

Kail, R., & Bisanz, J. (1992). The information-processing perspective on cognitive development in childhood and adolescence. In R. J. Sternberg & C. A. Berg (Eds.), *Intellectual development* (pp. 229–260). New York: Cambridge University Press.

Kaiser Family Foundation. (2010). *Medicare chartbook* (4th ed.). Retrieved from http://facts.kff.org/chart.aspx?cb558&sctn5162&p51

Kaiser, S., & Panegyres, P. K. (2007). The psychosocial impact of young onset dementia on spouses. *American Journal of Alzheimer's Disease and Other Dementias, 21,* 398–402.

Kalmijn, M., & Flap, H. (2001). Assortative meeting and mating: Unintended consequences of organized settings for partner choices. *Social Forces, 79,* 1289–1312.

Kanayama, G., Hudson, J. I., & Pope, H. G. (2008). Long-term psychiatric and medical consequences of anabolic–androgenic steroid use: A looming public health concern? *Drug and Alcohol Dependence, 98,* 1–12.

Kanekar, S., Kolsawalla, M. B., & Nazareth, T. (1989). Occupational prestige as a function of occupant's gender. *Journal of Applied Social Psychology, 19,* 681–688.

Kann, L., Collins, J. L., Pateman, B. C., Small, M. L., Ross, J.-G., & Kolbe, L. J. (1995). The School Health Policies and Programs Study (SHPPS): Rationale for a nationwide status report on school health programs. *Journal of School Health, 65,* 291–294.

Kapoor, U., Pfost, K. S., House, A. E., & Pierson, E. (2010). Relation of success and nontraditional career choice to selection for dating and friendship. *Psychological Reports, 107,* 177–184.

Karam, E., Kypri, K., & Salamoun, M. (2007). Alcohol use among college students: An international perspective. *Current Opinion in Psychiatry, 20,* 213–221.

Karevold, E., Røysamb, E., Ystrom, E., & Mathiesen, K. S. (2009). Predictors and pathways from infancy to symptoms of anxiety and depression in early adolescence. *Developmental Psychology, 45,* 1051–1060.

Kärnä, A., Voeten, M., Little, T. D., Poskiparta, E., Kaljonen, A., & Salmivalli, C. (2011). A large-scale evaluation of the KiVa antibullying program: Grades 4–6. *Child Development, 82,* 311–330.

Karney, B. R. (2010). *Keeping marriages healthy, and why it's so difficult.* Retrieved from http://www.apa.org/science/about/psa/2010/02/sci-brief.aspx

Karney, B. R., & Bradbury, T. N. (1995). The longitudinal course of marital quality and stability: A review of theory, method, and research. *Psychological Bulletin, 118,* 3–34.

Karney, B. R., & Crown, J. S. (2007). *Families under stress: An assessment of data, theory, and research on marriage and divorce in the military* (Report No. MG-599-OSD). Santa Monica, CA: RAND Corporation.

Karniol, R. (1989). The role of manual manipulative states in the infant's acquisition of perceived control over objects. *Developmental Review, 9,* 205–233.

Kastenbaum, R. (1999). Dying and bereavement. In J. C. Cavanaugh & S. K. Whitbourne (Eds.), *Gerontology: An interdisciplinary perspective.* New York: Oxford University Press.

Kastenbaum, R., & Thuell, S. (1995). Cookies baking, coffee brewing: Toward a contextual theory of dying. *Omega: Journal of Death and Dying, 31,* 175–187.

Katz, L. F., & Woodin, E. M. (2002). Hostility, hostile detachment, and conflict engagement in marriages: Effects on child and family functioning. *Child Development, 73,* 636–652.

Kaufman, J., & Charney, D. (2003). The neurobiology of child and adolescent depression: Current knowledge and future directions. In D. Cicchetti & E. Walker (Eds.), *Neurodevelopmental mechanisms in psychopathology* (pp. 461–490). New York: Cambridge University Press.

Kavsek, M., & Bornstein, M. H. (2010). Visual habituation and dishabituation in preterm infants: A review and meta-analysis. *Research in Developmental Disabilities, 31,* 951–975.

Kawabata, Y., Alink, L. R. A., Tseng, W. L., van IJzendoorn, M. H., & Crick, N. R. (2011). Maternal and paternal parenting styles associated with relational aggression in children and adolescents: A conceptual analysis and meta-analytic review. *Developmental Review, 31,* 240–278.

Kayser, K. (2010). Couples therapy. In J. R. Brandell (Ed.), *Theory and practice in clinical social work* (2nd ed., pp. 259–288). Thousand Oaks, CA: Sage.

Keenan, N. L., & Shaw, K. M. (2011). *Coronary heart disease and stroke deaths—United States 2006.* Retrieved from http://www.cdc.gov/mmwr/preview/mmwrhtml/su6001a13.htm?s_cid5su6001a13_w

Keenan, T. (2009). *Multi-generational housing patterns.* Washington, DC: AARP.

Kellman, P. J., & Arterberry, M. E. (2006). Infant visual perception. In W. Damon & R. M. Lerner (Eds.), *Handbook of child psychology* (6th ed., Vol. 2, pp. 109–160). Hoboken, NJ: Wiley.

Kelly, D. J., Quinn, P. C., Slater, A. M., Lee, K., Ge, L., & Pascalis, O. (2009). Development of the other-race effect during infancy: Evidence toward universality? *Journal of Experimental Child Psychology, 104,* 105–114.

Kelly, P. (2011). Corporal punishment and child maltreatment in New Zealand. *Acta Paediatrica, 100,* 14–20.

Kelty, R., Kleykamp, M., & Segal, D. R. (2010). The military and the transition to adulthood. *The Future of Children, 20,* 181–207.

Kennedy, G. E. (1991). Grandchildren's reasons for closeness with grandparents. *Journal of Social Behavior and Personality, 6,* 697–712.

Kersting, A., Brähler, E., Glaesmer, H., & Wagner, B. (2011). Prevalence of complicated grief in a representative population-based sample. *Journal of Affective Disorders, 131,* 339–343.

Kester, M. I. (2011). *Biomarkers for Alzheimer's pathology: Monitoring, predicting, and understanding the disease.* Retrieved from http://dare.ubvu.vu.nl/bitstream/1871/18384/2/abstract_english.pdf

Khanna, N. (2010). "If you're half black, you're just black": Reflected appraisals and the persistence of the one-drop rule. *Sociological Quarterly, 51,* 96–121.

Kiang, L., & Fuligni, A. J. (2009). Ethnic identity and family processes among adolescents from Latin American, Asian, and European backgrounds. *Journal of Youth and Adolescence, 38,* 228–241.

Kidd, E., & Holler, J. (2009). Children's use of gesture to resolve lexical ambiguity. *Developmental Science, 12,* 903–913.

Killen, M., & McGlothlin, H. (2005). Prejudice in children. In C. B. Fisher & R. M. Lerner (Eds.), *Encyclopedia of applied developmental science* (Vol. 2, pp. 870–872). Thousand Oaks, CA: Sage.

Kilson, M., & Ladd, F. (2009). *Is that your child? Mothers talking about rearing biracial children.* Lanham, MD: Lexington Books.

Kim, J.-Y., McHale, S. M., Crouter, A. C., & Osgood, D. (2007). Longitudinal linkages between sibling relationships and adjustment from middle childhood through adolescence. *Developmental Psychology, 43,* 960–973.

Kim, J.-Y., McHale, S. M., Osgood, D., & Crouter, A. C. (2006). Longitudinal course and family correlates of sibling relationships from childhood through adolescence. *Child Development, 77,* 1746–1761.

Kim, S. S. (2000). Gradual return to work: The antecedents and consequences of switching to part-time work after first childbirth. *Dissertation Abstract International. Section A. Humanities and Social Sciences, 61*(3-A), 1182.

Kim, Y. H., & Goetz, E. T. (1994). Context effects on word recognition and reading comprehension of good and poor readers: A test of the interactive compensatory hypothesis. *Reading Research Quarterly, 29,* 178–188.

Kindermann, T. A. (2007). Effects of naturally existing peer groups on changes in academic engagement in a cohort of sixth graders. *Child Development, 78,* 1186–1203.

King, P. E., & Furrow, J. L. (2004). Religion as a resource for positive youth development: Religion, social capital, and moral outcomes. *Developmental Psychology, 40,* 703–713.

King, P. M., & Kitchener, K. S. (2004). Reflective judgment: Theory and research on the development of epistemic assumptions through adulthood. *Educational Psychologist, 39,* 5–18.

King, S. V., Burgess, E. O., Akinyela, M., Counts-Spriggs, M., & Parker, N. (2006). The religious dimensions of the grandparent role in three-generation African American households. *Journal of Religion, Spirituality & Aging, 19,* 75–96.

King, V., Elder, G. H., & Whitbeck, L. B. (1997). Religious involvement among rural youth: An ecological and life-course perspective. *Journal of Research on Adolescence, 7,* 431–456.

Kinney, J. M., Ishler, K. J., Pargament, K. I., & Cavanaugh, J. C. (2003). Coping with the uncontrollable: The use of general and religious coping by caregivers to spouses with dementia. *Journal of Religious Gerontology, 14,* 171–188.

Kins, E., & Beyers, W. (2010). Failure to launch, failure to achieve criteria for adulthood? *Journal of Adolescent Research, 25,* 743–777.

Kinsella, G. J., Ong, B., Storey, E., Wallace, J., & Hester, R. (2007). Elaborated spaced-retrieval and prospective memory in mild Alzheimer's disease. *Neuropsychological Rehabilitation, 17,* 688–706.

Kippen, R., Chapman, B., & Yu, P. (2009). *What's love got to do with it? Homogamy and dyadic approaches to understanding marital instability.* Retrieved from http://www.datingsitesreviews.com/images/other/Kippen-Rebecca-paper.pdf

Kirby, D. (2001). *Emerging answers: Research findings on programs to reduce teen pregnancy* [Summary]. Washington, DC: National Campaign to Prevent Teen Pregnancy.

Kirby, D., & Laris, B. A. (2009). Effective curriculum-based sex and STD/HIV education programs for adolescents. *Child Development Perspectives, 3,* 21–29.

Kitchener, K. S., & King, P. M. (1989). The reflective judgment model: Ten years of research. In M. L. Commons, C. Armon, L. Kohlberg, F. A. Richards, T. A. Grotzer, & J. D. Sinnott (Eds.), *Adult development* (Vol. 2, pp. 63–78). New York: Praeger.

Kitchener, K. S., King, P. M., & DeLuca, S. (2006). Development of reflective judgment in adulthood. In C. Hoare (Ed.), *Handbook of adult development and learning* (pp. 73–98). New York: Oxford University Press.

Kivett, V. R. (1991). Centrality of the grandfather role among older rural black and white men. *Journal of Gerontology: Social Sciences, 46,* S250–S258.

Kivnick, H. Q. (1982). *The meaning of grandparenthood.* Ann Arbor, MI: UMI Research.

Kivnick, H. Q. (1985). Grandparenthood and mental health: Meaning, behavior, and satisfaction. In V. L. Bengtson & J. F. Robertson (Eds.), *Grandparenthood* (pp. 151–158). Beverly Hills, CA: Sage.

Klaczynski, P. A., & Lavallee, K. L. (2005). Domain-specific identity, epistemic regulation, and intellectual ability as predictors of belief-biased reasoning: A dual-process perspective. *Journal of Experimental Child Psychology, 92,* 1–24.

Klaczynski, P. A., & Narasimham, G. (1998). Development of scientific reasoning biases: Cognitive versus ego-protective explanations. *Developmental Psychology, 34,* 175–187.

Klassen, R. M., Usher, E. L., & Bong, M. (2010). Teachers' collective efficacy, job satisfaction, and job stress in cross-cultural context. *Journal of Experimental Education, 78,* 464–486.

Kleespies, P. M. (2004). *Life and death decisions: Psychological and ethical considerations in end-of-life care.* Washington, DC: American Psychological Association.

Klohnen, E. C., Vandewater, E. A., & Young, A. (1996). Negotiating the middle years: Ego-resiliency and successful midlife adjustment in women. *Psychology and Aging, 11,* 431–442.

Knee, D. O. (2010). Hospice care for the aging population in the United States. In J. C. Cavanaugh & C. K. Cavanaugh (Eds.), *Aging in America* (Vol. 3, pp. 203–221). Santa Barbara, CA: Praeger Perspectives.

Knight, B. G., & Sayegh, P. (2010). Cultural values and caregiving: The updated sociocultural stress and coping model. *Journal of Gerontology: Psychological Sciences and Social Sciences, 65B,* P5-P13.

Knowles, D. R. (2006). *Aging changes in the male reproductive system.* Retrieved from http://www.nlm.nih.gov/medlineplus/ency/article/004017.htm

Knowles, M. S., Swanson, R. A., & Holton, E. F. (2005). *The adult learner: The definitive classic in adult education and human resource development.* New York: Elsevier.

Kochanska, G., Gross, J. N., Lin, M., & Nichols, K. E. (2002). Guilt in young children: Development, determinants, and relations with a broader system of standards. *Child Development, 73,* 461–482.

Koenig, B. L., Kirkpatrick, L. A., & Ketelaar, T. (2007). Misperception of sexual and romantic interests in opposite-sex friendships: Four hypotheses. *Personal Relationships, 14,* 411–429.

Koestenbaum, P. (1976). *Is there an answer to death?* Englewood Cliffs, NJ: Prentice Hall.

Kogan, N. (1983). Stylistic variation in childhood and adolescence: Creativity, metaphor, and cognitive style. In P. H. Mussen (Ed.), *Handbook of child psychology* (Vol. 3, pp. 630–706). New York: Wiley.

Kohlberg, L. (1966). A cognitive-developmental analysis of children's sex-role concepts and attitudes. In E. E. Maccoby (Ed.), *The development of sex differences* (pp. 87–123). Stanford, CA: Stanford University Press.

Kohlberg, L. (1969). Stage and sequence: The cognitive-developmental approach to socialization. In D. Goslin (Ed.), *Handbook of socialization: Theory and research* (pp. 347–480). Chicago: Rand McNally.

Kohlberg, L., & Ullian, D. Z. (1974). Stages in the development of psychosexual concepts and attitudes. In R. C. Friedman, R. M. Richart, & R. L. Van Wiele (Eds.), *Sex differences in behavior* (pp. 209–222). New York: Wiley.

Kokis, J. V., Macpherson, R., Toplak, M. E., West, R. F., & Stanovich, K. E. (2002). Heuristic and analytic processing: Age trends and associations with cognitive ability and cognitive styles. *Journal of Experimental Child Psychology, 83,* 26–52.

Kolb, D. M., Williams, J., & Frohlinger, C. (2010). *Her place at the table: A woman's guide to negotiating five key challenges to leadership success.* San Francisco: Jossey-Bass.

Kolberg, K. J. S. (1999). Environmental influences on prenatal development and health. In T. L. Whitman & T. V. Merluzzi (Eds.), *Life-span perspectives on health and illness* (pp. 87–103). Mahwah, NJ: Erlbaum.

Konijn, E. A., Bijvank, M. N., & Bushman, B. J. (2007). I wish I were a warrior: The role of wishful identification in the effects of violent video games on aggression in adolescent boys. *Developmental Psychology, 43,* 1038–1044.

Kornhaber, M., Fierros, E., & Veenema, S. (2004). *Multiple intelligences: Best ideas from research and practice.* Boston: Allyn & Bacon.

Kowalski, S. D., & Bondmass, M. D. (2008). Physiological and psychological symptoms of grief in widows. *Research in Nursing & Health, 31,* 23–30.

Kozbelt, A., & Durmysheva, Y. (2007). Lifespan creativity in a non-Western artistic tradition: A study of Japanese Ukiyo-e printmakers. *International Journal of Aging and Human Development, 65,* 23–51.

Kramer, L. (2010). The essential ingredients of successful sibling relationships: An emerging framework for advancing theory and practice. *Child Development Perspectives, 4,* 80–86.

Krause, N. (2006). Religion and health in late life. In J. E. Birren & K. W. Schaie (Eds.), *Handbook of the psychology of aging* (6th ed., pp. 499–518). Amsterdam: Elsevier.

Krause, N., & Bastida, E. (2011). Prayer to the saints or the Virgin and health among older Mexican Americans. *Hispanic Journal of Behavioral Sciences, 33,* 71–87.

Krause, N., Morgan, D., Chatters, L., & Meltzer, T. (2000). Using focus groups to explore the nature of prayer in late life. *Journal of Aging Studies, 14,* 191–212.

Krishnasamy, C., & Unsworth, C. A. (2011). Normative data, preliminary inter-rater reliability and predictive validity of the Drive Home Maze Test. *Clinical Rehabilitation, 25,* 88–95.

Kruger, D. J. (2006). Male facial masculinity influences attributions of personality and reproductive strategy. *Personal Relationships, 13,* 451–463.

Kübler-Ross, E. (1969). *On death and dying.* New York: Macmillan.

Kübler-Ross, E. (1974). *Questions and answers on death and dying.* New York: Macmillan.

Kuhl, P. K., Andruski, J. E., Chistovich, I. A., Chistovich, L.-A., Kozhevnikova, E. V., Ryskina, V. L., et al. (1997). Cross-language analysis of phonetic units in language addressed to infants. *Science, 277,* 684–686.

Kuhl, P. K., Stevens, E., Hayashi, A., Deguchi, T., Kiritani, S., & Iverson, P. (2006). Infants show a facilitation effect for native language phonetic perception between 6 and 12 months. *Developmental Science, 9,* F13–F21.

Kukutai, T. H. (2007). White mothers, brown children: Ethnic identification of Maori–European children in New Zealand. *Journal of Marriage and Family, 69,* 1150–1161.

Kulik, L. (2001a). The impact of men's and women's retirement on marital relations: A comparative analysis. *Journal of Women & Aging, 13,* 21–37.

Kulik, L. (2001b). Marital relationships in late adulthood: Synchronous versus asynchronous couples. *International Journal of Aging and Human Development, 52,* 323–339.

Kulwicki, A. D. (2002). The practice of honor crimes: A glimpse of domestic violence in the Arab world. *Issues in Mental Health Nursing, 23,* 77–87.

Kumar, R., O'Malley, P. M., Johnston, L. D., Schulenberg, J.-E., & Bachman, J. G. (2002). Effects of school-level norms on student substance use. *Prevention Science, 3,* 105–124.

Kunlin, J. (2010). Modern biological theories of aging. *Aging and Disease, 1,* 72–74.

Kunz, J. A. (2007). Older adult development. In J. A. Kunz & F. G. Soltys (Eds.), *Transformational reminiscence: Life story work* (pp. 19–39). New York: Springer.

Kurdek, L. A. (2004). Are gay and lesbian cohabiting couples really different from heterosexual married couples? *Journal of Marriage and Family, 66,* 880–900.

Kypri, K., Paschall, M. J., Langley, J., Baxter, J., Cashell-Smith, M., & Bourdeau, B. (2009). Drinking and alcohol-related harm among New Zealand university students: findings from a national web-based survey. *Alcoholism: Clinical and Experimental Research, 33,* 307–314.

Labouvie-Vief, G. (2006). Emerging structures of adult thought. In J. J. Arnett & J. L. Tanner (Eds.), *Emerging adults in America: Coming of age in the 21st century* (pp. 59–84). Washington, DC: American Psychological Association.

Labouvie-Vief, G., Grühn, D., & Studer, J. (2010). Dynamic integration of emotion and cognition: Equilibrium regulation in development and aging. In M. E. Lamb & A. M. Freund (Eds.), *The handbook of life-span development* (Vol. 2, pp. 79–115). Hoboken, NJ: Wiley.

Ladd, G. W. (1998). Peer relationships and social competence during early and middle childhood. *Annual Review of Psychology, 50,* 333–359.

Ladd, G. W. (2003). Probing the adaptive significance of children's behavior and relationships in the school context: A child by environment perspective. In R. V. Kail (Ed.), *Advances in child development and behavior* (Vol. 31, pp. 44–104). San Diego, CA: Academic Press.

Ladd, G. W. (2006). Peer rejection, aggressive or withdrawn behavior, and psychological maladjustment from ages 5 to 12: An examination of four predictive models. *Child Development, 77,* 822–846.

Ladd, G. W., & Ladd, B. K. (1998). Parenting behaviors and parent–child relationships: Correlates of peer victimization in kindergarten? *Developmental Psychology, 34,* 1450–1458.

Ladd, G. W., & Pettit, G. S. (2002). Parents and children's peer relationships. In M. H. Bornstein (Ed.), *Handbook of parenting* (2nd ed., Vol. 4, pp. 377–409). Mahwah, NJ: Erlbaum.

La Greca, A. M. (1993). Social skills training with children: Where do we go from here? *Journal of Clinical Child Psychology, 22,* 288–298.

Lahey, J. N. (2010). International comparison of age discrimination laws. *Research on Aging, 32,* 679–697.

Lai, D. W. L. (2010). Filial piety, caregiving appraisal, and caregiving burden. *Research on Aging, 32,* 200–223.

Laible, D. (2011). Does it matter if preschool children and mothers discuss positive vs. negative events during reminiscing? Links with mother-reported attachment, family emotional climate, and socioemotional development. *Social Development, 20,* 394–411.

Laible, D. J., & Carlo, G. (2004). The differential relations of maternal and paternal support and control to adolescent social competence, self-worth, and sympathy. *Journal of Adolescent Research, 19,* 759–782.

Laidlaw, K. (2007). Cognitive behavior therapy with older adults. In S. H. Qualls & B. G. Knight (Eds.), *Psychotherapy for depression in older adults* (pp. 83–109). Hoboken, NJ: Wiley.

Lako, M., Trounson, A., & Daher, S. (2010). Law, ethics, and clinical translation in the 21st century—A discussion with Stephen Bellamy. *Stem Cells, 28,* 177–180.

Lamanna, M. A., & Riedmann, A. (2003). *Marriages and families: Making choices in a diverse society* (8th ed.). Belmont, CA: Wadsworth.

Lamaze, F. (1958). *Painless childbirth.* London: Burke.

Lamb, M. E. (1999). Nonparental child care. In M. E. Lamb (Ed.), *Parenting and child development in "nontraditional" families* (pp. 39–55). Mahwah, NJ: Erlbaum.

Lamb, M. E., Orbach, Y., Hershkowitz, I., Esplin, P. W., & Horowitz, D. (2007). A structured forensic interview protocol improves the quality and informativeness of investigative interviews with children: A review of research using the NICHD Investigative Interview Protocol. *Child Abuse and Neglect, 31,* 1201–1231.

Lampkin-Hunter, T. (2010). *Single parenting.* Bloomington, IN: Xlibris.

Landerl, K., Fussenegger, B., Moll, K., & Willburger, E. (2009). Dyslexia and dyscalculia: Two learning disorders with different cognitive profiles. *Journal of Experimental Child Psychology, 103,* 309–324.

Lansford, J. E. (2009). Parental divorce and children's adjustment. *Perspectives on Psychological Science, 4,* 140–152.

Laplante, D. P., Barr, R. G., Brunet, A., Du Fort, G. G., Meaney, M. L., Saucier, J., et al. (2004). Stress during pregnancy affects general intellectual and language functioning in human toddlers. *Pediatric Research, 56,* 400–410.

LaRocca, T. J., Seals, D. R., & Pierce, G. L. (2010). Leukocyte telomere length is preserved with aging in endurance exercise-trained adults and related to maximal aerobic capacity. *Mechanisms of Ageing and Development, 131,* 165–167.

Lau, J. Y., Rijsdijk, F., Gregory, A. M., McGuffin, P., & Eley, T. C. (2007). Pathways to childhood depressive symptoms: The role of social, cognitive, and genetic risk factors. *Developmental Psychology, 43,* 1402–1414.

Laursen, B., & Collins, W. A. (1994). Interpersonal conflict during adolescence. *Psychological Bulletin, 115,* 197–209.

Laus, M. F., Vales, L. D. M. F., Costa, T. M. B., & Almeida, S. S. (2011). Early postnatal protein-calorie malnutrition and cognition: A review of human and animal studies. *International Journal of Environmental Research and Public Health, 8,* 590–612.

Lawton, L. E., & Tulkin, D. O. (2010). Work–family balance, family structure and family-friendly employer programs. Paper presented at the annual meeting of the Population Association of America, Dallas, TX. Retrieved from http://paa2010.princeton.edu/download.aspx?submissionId5100573

Lawton, M. P., & Nahemow, L. (1973). Ecology of the aging process. In C. Eisdorfer & M. P. Lawton (Eds.), *The psychology of adult development and aging* (pp. 619–674). Washington, DC: American Psychological Association.

Lazarus, R. S., & Folkman, S. (1984). *Stress, appraisal, and coping.* New York: Springer.

Leaper, C., & Smith, T. E. (2004). A meta-analytic review of gender variations in children's language use: Talkativeness, affiliative speech, and assertive speech. *Developmental Psychology, 40,* 993–1027.

Lecanuet, J. P., Granier-Deferre, C., & Busnel, M. C. (1995). Human fetal auditory perception. In J. P. Lecanuet, W. P. Fifer, N. A. Krasnegor, & W. P. Smotherman (Eds.), *Fetal development: A psychobiological perspective.* Hillsdale, NJ: Erlbaum.

Ledbetter, A. M., & Kuznekoff, J. H. (2012). More than a game: Friendship relational maintenance and attitudes toward Xbox LIVE communication. *Communication Research, 39,* 269–290.

Ledebt, A., van Wieringen, P. C. W., & Saveslsbergh, G. J. P. (2004). Functional significance of foot rotation in early walking. *Infant Behavior and Development, 27,* 163–172.

Lee, E.-K. O., & Sharpe, T. (2007). Understanding religious/spiritual coping and support resources among African American older adults: A mixed-method approach. *Journal of Religion, Spirituality & Aging, 19,* 55–75.

Lee, K. S. (2010). Gender, care work, and the complexity of family membership in Japan. *Gender & Society, 24,* 647–671.

Lee, K. T., Mattson, S. N., & Riley, E. P. (2004). Classifying children with heavy prenatal alcohol exposure using measures of attention. *Journal of the International Neuropsychological Society, 10,* 271–277.

Lee, M.-D. (2007). Correlates of consequences of intergenerational caregiving in Taiwan. *Journal of Advanced Nursing, 59,* 47–56.

Lee, M. H., Ranganathan, R., & Newell, K. M. (2011). Changes in object-oriented arm movements that precede the transition to goal-directed reaching in infancy. *Developmental Psychobiology, 53,* 685–693.

Lee, P. C. B. (2003). Going beyond career plateau: Using professional plateau to account for work outcomes. *Journal of Management Development, 22,* 538–551.

Lefkowitz, E. S., Vukman, S. N., & Loken, E. (2012). Young adults in a wireless world. In A. Booth, S. L. Brown, N. S. Landale, W. D. Manning, & S. M. McHale (Eds.), *Early adulthood in family context* (Vol. 2, Pt. 1, pp. 45–56). New York: Springer.

LeMare, L. J., & Rubin, K. H. (1987). Perspective taking and peer interaction: Structural and developmental analyses. *Child Development, 58,* 306–315.

Lemieux, R., & Hale, J. L. (2002). Cross-sectional analysis of intimacy, passion, and commitment: Testing the assumptions of the triangular theory of love. *Psychological Reports, 90,* 1009–1014.

Lemire, L., Saba, T., & Gagnon, Y. C. (1999). Managing career plateauing in the Quebec public sector. *Public Personnel Management, 28,* 375–391.

Lengua, L. J., Sandler, I. N., West, S. G., Wolchik, S. A., & Curran, P. J. (1999). Emotionality and self-regulation, threat appraisal, and coping in children of divorce. *Development & Psychopathology, 11,* 15–37.

Lervåg, A., Bråten, I., & Hulme, C. (2009). The cognitive and linguistic foundations of early reading development: A Norwegian latent variable longitudinal study. *Developmental Psychology, 45,* 764–781.

Levete, S. (2010). *Coming of age.* New York: Wayland/Rosen.

Levinger, G. (1980). Toward the analysis of close relationships. *Journal of Experimental Social Psychology, 16,* 510–544.

Levinger, G. (1983). Development and change. In H. H. Kelley, E. Berscheid, A. Christensen, J. H. Harvey, T. L. Hutson, G. Levinger, et al. (Eds.), *Close relationships* (pp. 315–359). New York: Freeman.

Levitt, A. G., & Utman, J. A. (1992). From babbling towards the sound systems of English and French: A longitudinal two-case study. *Journal of Child Language, 19,* 19–49.

Levitt, M. J., Guacci-Franco, N., & Levitt, J. L. (1993). Convoys of social support in childhood and early adolescence: Structure and function. *Developmental Psychology, 29,* 811–818.

Levy, B. A., Gong, Z., Hessels, S., Evans, M. A., & Jared, D. (2006). Understanding print: Early reading development and the contributions of home literacy experiences. *Journal of Experimental Child Psychology, 93,* 63–93.

Levy, G. D., Taylor, M. G., & Gelman, S. A. (1995). Traditional and evaluative aspects of flexibility in gender roles, social conventions, moral rules, and physical laws. *Child Development, 66,* 515–531.

Levy, J. (1976). A review of evidence for a genetic component in the determination of handedness. *Behavior Genetics, 6,* 429–453.

Lewinsohn, P. M. (1975). The behavioral study and treatment of depression. In M. Hersen, R. M. Eisler, & P. M. Miller (Eds.), *Progress in behavior modification* (Vol. 1, pp. 19–64). New York: Academic Press.

Lewis, M. (2000). The emergence of human emotions. In M. Lewis & J. Haviland-Jones (Eds.), *Handbook of emotions* (2nd ed., pp. 265–280). New York: Guilford.

Lewis, M. (2011). The origins and uses of self-awareness or the mental representations of me. *Consciousness and Cognition, 20,* 120–129.

Lewis, M., & Brooks-Gunn, J. (1979). *Social cognition and the acquisition of self.* New York: Plenum.

Lewis, M., Takai-Kawakami, K., Kawakami, K., & Sullivan, M. W. (2010). Cultural differences in emotional responses to success and failure. *International Journal of Behavioral Development, 34,* 53–61.

Lewontin, R. (1976). Race and intelligence. In N. J. Block & G. Dworkin (Eds.), *The IQ controversy* (pp. 78–92). New York: Pantheon.

Li, F., Fisher, K. J., Harmer, P., & McAuley, E. (2005). Falls self-efficacy as a mediator of fear of falling in an exercise intervention for older adults. *Journals of Gerontology: Psychological Sciences & Social Sciences, 60B,* P34–P40.

Li, Y., Anderson, R. C., Nguyen-Jahiel, K., Dong, T., Archodidou, A., Kim, I.-H., et al. (2007). Emergent leadership in children's discussion groups. *Cognition and Instruction, 25,* 75–111.

Liang, H., & Eley, T. C. (2005). A monozygotic twin differences study of nonshared environmental influence on adolescent depressive symptoms. *Child Development, 76,* 1247–1260.

Liben, L. S., & Bigler, R. S. (2002). The developmental course of gender differentiation. *Monographs of the Society for Research in Child Development, 67* (Serial No. 269).

Lichtenstein, A. H., & Rasmussen, H. (2011). *MyPlate for older adults.* Retrieved from http://www.nutrition.tufts.edu/research/myplate-older-adults

Lichter, D. T., & Carmalt, J. H. (2009). Religion and marital quality among low-income couples. *Social Science Research, 38,* 168–187.

Liebal, K., Behne, T., Carpenter, M., & Tomasello, M. (2009). Infants use shared experience to interpret pointing gestures. *Developmental Science, 12,* 264–271.

Lieber, J. (2001, October 10). Widows of tower disaster cope, but with quiet fury. *USA Today,* pp. A1–A2.

Lighthouse International. (2011). *Illumination.* Retrieved from http://www.lighthouse.org/for-professionals/practice-management/professional-products/illumination

Lim, S., & Cortina, L. M. (2005). Interpersonal mistreatment in the workplace: The interface and impact of general incivility and sexual harassment. *Journal of Applied Psychology, 90,* 483–496.

Lin, X., & Leung, K. (2010). Differing effects of coping strategies on mental health during prolonged unemployment: A longitudinal analysis. *Human Relations, 63,* 637–665.

Lindberg, S. M., Hyde, J. S., Petersen, J. L., & Linn, M. C. (2010). New trends in gender and mathematics performance: A meta-analysis. *Psychological Bulletin, 136,* 1123–1135.

Lindgren, K. P. (2007). Sexual intent perceptions: Review and integration of findings, investigation of automatic processes, and development and implementation of a dynamic assessment methodology. *Dissertation Abstracts International. Section B. Sciences and Engineering, 67*(9-B), 5469.

Lindsey, E. W., & Colwell, M. J. (2003). Preschoolers' emotional competence: Links to pretend and physical play. *Child Study Journal, 33,* 39–52.

Lindsey, E. W., & Mize, J. (2000). Parent–child physical and pretense play: Links to children's social competence. *Merrill-Palmer Quarterly, 46,* 565–591.

Linebarger, D. L., & Vaala, S. E. (2010). Screen media and language development in infants and toddlers: An ecological perspective. *Developmental Review, 30,* 176–202.

Linver, M. R., Roth, J. L., & Brooks-Gunn, J. (2009). Patterns of adolescents' participation in organized activities: Are sports best when combined with other activities? *Developmental Psychology, 45,* 354–367.

Lipsitt, L. P. (1990). Learning and memory in infants. *Merrill-Palmer Quarterly, 36,* 53–66.

Lipsitt, L. P. (2003). Crib death: A biobehavioral phenomenon. *Psychological Science, 12,* 164–170.

Lips-Wiersma, M. S. (2003). Making conscious choices in doing research on workplace spirituality: Utilizing the "holistic development model" to articulate values, assumptions and dogmas of the knower. *Journal of Organizational Change Management, 16,* 406–425.

Liu, D., Gelman, S. A., & Wellman, H. M. (2007). Components of young children's trait understanding: Behavior-to-trait and trait-to-behavior predictions. *Child Development, 78,* 1543–1558.

Liu, D., Wellman, H. M., Tardif, T., & Sabbagh, M. A. (2008). Theory of mind development in Chinese children: A meta-analysis of false-belief understanding across cultures and languages. *Developmental Psychology, 44,* 523–531.

Liu, H.-M., Tsao, F.-M., & Kuhl, P. K. (2007). Acoustic analysis of lexical tone in Mandarin infant-directed speech. *Developmental Psychology, 43,* 912–917.

Liu, L., Drouet, V., Wu, J. W., Witter, M. P., Small, S. A., Clelland, C., & Duff, K. (2012). Trans-synaptic spread of tau pathology *in vivo. PLoS One, I,* e31302. doi:10.1371/journal.pone.0031302

Liu, R X., Lin, W., & Chen, Z. Y. (2010). School performance, peer association, psychological and behavioral adjustments: A comparison between Chinese adolescents with and without siblings. *Journal of Adolescence, 33,* 411–417.

Livesley, W. J., & Bromley, D. B. (1973). *Person perception in childhood and adolescence.* New York: Wiley.

Livingston, G., & Cohn, D. (2010). *The new demography of American motherhood.* Retrieved from http://pewresearch.org/pubs/1586/changing-demographic-characteristics-american-mothers?src5prc-latest&proj5peoplepress

Lo, M., & Aziz, T. (2009). Muslim marriage goes online: The use of Internet matchmaking by American Muslims. *Journal of Religion and Popular Culture, 21*(3). Retrieved from http://www.usask.ca/relst/jrpc/art21%283%29-Muslim-Marriage.html

Lobelo, F., Dowda, M., Pfeiffer, K. A., & Pate, R. R. (2009). Electronic media exposure and its association with activity-related outcomes in female adolescents: Cross-sectional and longitudinal analyses. *Journal of Physical Activity and Health, 6,* 137–143.

LoBue, V., & DeLoache, J. S. (2010). Superior detection of threat-relevant stimuli in infancy. *Developmental Science, 13,* 221–228.

Lockl, K., & Schneider, W. (2007). Knowledge about the mind: Links between theory of mind and later metamemory. *Child Development, 78,* 148–167.

Lois, J. (2011). Gender and emotion management in the stages of edgework. In J. Z. Spade & C. G. Valentine (Eds.), *The kaleidoscope of gender: Prisms, patterns, and possibilities* (3rd ed., pp. 333–343). Thousand Oaks, CA: Pine Forge Press.

Longshore, D., Ellickson, P. L., McCaffrey, D. F., & St. Clair, P. A. (2007). School-based drug prevention among at-risk adolescents: Effects of ALERT Plus. *Health Education and Behavior, 34,* 651–668.

Lopata, H. Z. (1996). Widowhood and husband sanctification. In D. Klass, P. R. Silverman, & S. L. Nickman (Eds.), *Continuing bonds: New understandings of grief* (pp. 149–162). Washington, DC: Taylor & Francis.

Lord, S. E., Eccles, J. S., & McCarthy, K. A. (1994). Surviving the junior high transition: Family processes and self-perception as protective and risk factors. *Journal of Early Adolescence, 14,* 162–199.

Lowe, M. E., & McClement, S. E. (2010–2011). Spousal bereavement: The lived experience of young Canadian widows. *Omega: Journal of Death and Dying, 62,* 127–148.

Lowry, R., Wechsler, H., Kann, L., & Collins, J. L. (2001). Recent trends in participation in physical education among U.S. high school students. *Journal of School Health, 71,* 145–152.

Luborsky, M. R., & LeBlanc, I. M. (2003). Cross-cultural perspectives on the concept of retirement: An analytic redefinition. *Journal of Cross-Cultural Gerontology, 18,* 251–271.

Lucas, J. L. (2000). Mentoring as a manifestation of generativity among university faculty. *Dissertation Abstracts International. Section A. Humanities and Social Sciences, 61*(3-A), 881.

Lucero-Liu, A. A. (2007). Exploring intersections in the intimate lives of Mexican origin women. *Dissertation Abstracts International. Section A. Humanities and Social Sciences, 68*(3-A), 1175.

Ludke, R. L., & Smucker, D. R. (2007). Racial differences in the willingness to use hospice services. *Journal of Palliative Medicine, 10,* 1329–1337.

Ludwig, J., & Phillips, D. (2007). The benefits and costs of Head Start. *SRCD Social Policy Report, 21,* 3–11, 16–18.

Luecke-Aleksa, D., Anderson, D. R., Collins, P. A., & Schmitt, K. L. (1995). Gender constancy and television viewing. *Developmental Psychology, 31,* 773–780.

Lung, F.-W., Fan, P.-L., Chen, N. C., & Shu, B.-C. (2005). Telomeric length varies with age and polymorphisms of the MAOA gene promoter in peripheral blood cells obtained from a community in Taiwan. *Psychiatric Genetics, 15,* 31–35.

Luo, S., & Zhang, G. (2009). What leads to romantic attraction: Similarity, reciprocity, security, or beauty? Evidence from a speed-dating study. *Journal of Personality, 77,* 933–964.

Luo, Y., Kaufman, L., & Baillargeon, R. (2009). Young infants' reasoning about physical events involving inert and self-propelled objects. *Cognitive Psychology, 58,* 441–486.

Luong, G., Charles, S. T., & Fingerman, K. L. (2011). Better with age: Social relationships across adulthood. *Journal of Social and Personal Relationships, 28,* 9–23.

Lustbader, D., O'Hara, M. S., Wijdicks, E. F. M., MacLean, L., Tajik, W., Ying, A., et al. (2011). Second brain death examination may negatively affect organ donation. *Neurology, 76,* 119–124.

Luthans, F., Avolio, B. J., Avey, J. B., & Norman, S. M. (2007). Positive psychological capital: Measurement and relationship with performance and satisfaction. *Personnel Psychology, 60,* 541–572.

Lutz, A., Slagter, H. A., Rawlings, N. B., Francis, A. D., Greischar, L. L., & Davidson, R. J. (2009). Mental training enhances attentional stability: Neural and behavioral evidence. *Journal of Neuroscience, 29,* 13418–13427.

Lyness, D. (2007). *Stress.* Retrieved from http://kidshealth.org/teen/your_mind/emotions/stress.html

Lytton, H. (2000). Toward a model of family–environmental and child–biological influences on development. *Developmental Review, 20,* 150–179.

Lytton, H., & Romney, D. M. (1991). Parents' differential socialization of boys and girls: A meta-analysis. *Psychological Bulletin, 109,* 267–296.

MacCallum, F., Golombok, S., & Brinsden, P. (2007). Parenting and child development in families with a child conceived through embryo donation. *Journal of Family Psychology, 21,* 278–287.

Maccoby, E. E. (1990). Gender and relationships: A developmental account. *American Psychologist, 45,* 513–520.

Maccoby, E. E. (1998). *The two sexes: Growing up apart, coming together.* Cambridge, MA: Belknap Press.

Maccoby, E. E., & Jacklin, C. N. (1974). *The psychology of sex differences.* Stanford, CA: Stanford University Press.

Mackey, A. P., Hill, S. S., Stone, S. I., & Bunge, S. A. (2011). Differential effects of reasoning and speed training in children. *Developmental Science, 14,* 582–590.

MacWhinney, B. (1998). Models of the emergence of language. *Annual Review of Psychology, 49,* 199–227.

Maeder, E. M., Wiener, R. L., & Winter, R. (2007). Does a truck driver see what a nurse sees? The effects of occupation type on perceptions of sexual harassment. *Sex Roles, 56,* 801–810.

Maggi, S., Ostry, A., Tansey, J., Dunn, J., Hershler, R., Chen, L., & Hertzman, C. (2008). Paternal psychosocial work conditions and mental health outcomes: A case-control study. *BMC Public Health, 8,* 104.

Magnuson, K., & Duncan, G. (2006). The role of family socioeconomic resources in black and white test score gaps among young children. *Developmental Review, 26,* 365–399.

Maguire, A. M., High, K. A., Auricchio, A., Wright, J. F., Pierce, E. A., Testa, F., et al. (2009). Age-dependent effects of RPE65 gene therapy for Leber's congenital amaurosis: A phase 1 dose-escalation trial. *Lancet, 374,* 1597–1605.

Mahon, N. E., Yarcheski, A., Yarcheski, T., Cannella, B. L., & Hanks, M. M. (2006). A meta-analytic study of predictors for loneliness during adolescence. *Nursing Research, 55,* 308–315.

Maiden, R. J., Peterson, S. A., Caya, M., & Hayslip, B. (2003). Personality changes in the old–old: A longitudinal study. *Journal of Adult Development, 10,* 31–39.

Maimburg, R. D., Vaeth, M., Durr, J., Hvidman, L., & Olsen, J. (2010). Randomised trial of structured antenatal training sessions to improve the birth process. *BJOG—An International Journal of Obstetrics and Gynaecology, 117,* 921–927.

Malach-Pines, A. (2005). The burnout measure, short version. *International Journal of Stress Management, 12,* 78–88.

Males, M. (2009). Does the adolescent brain make risk taking inevitable? A skeptical appraisal. *Journal of Adolescent Research, 24,* 3–20.

Males, M. (2010). Is jumping off the roof always a bad idea? A rejoinder on risk taking and the adolescent brain. *Journal of Adolescent Research, 25,* 48–63.

Malkinson, R., & Bar-Tur, L. (2004–2005). Long term bereavement processes of older parents: The three phases of grief. *Omega: Journal of Death and Dying, 50,* 103–129.

Mallon, B. (2008). *Dying, death, and grief: Working with adult bereavement.* Thousand Oaks, CA: Sage.

Malone, K., Stewart, S. D., Wilson, J., & Korsching, P. F. (2010). Perceptions of financial well-being among American women in diverse families. *Journal of Family and Economic Issues, 31,* 63–81.

Malone, M. L., & Camp, C. J. (2007). Montessori-based dementia programming: Providing tools for engagement. *Dementia: The International Journal of Social Research and Practice, 6,* 150–157.

Malone, P. A. (2010). *The impact of peer death on adolescent girls: An efficacy study of the Adolescent Grief and Loss group.* (Unpublished doctoral dissertation). University of Texas at Austin, Austin, TX.

Malti, T., Gummerum, M., Keller, M., & Buchmann, M. (2009). Children's moral motivation, sympathy, and prosocial behavior. *Child Development, 80,* 442–460.

Mancini, A. D., & Bonanno, G. A. (2010). Resilience to potential trauma: Toward a lifespan approach. In J. W. Reich, A. Zautra, & J. S. Hall (Eds.), *Handbook of adult resilience* (pp. 258–280). New York: Guilford.

Mandara, J., Gaylord-Harden, N. K., Richard, M H., & Ragsdale, B. L. (2009). The effects of changes in racial identity and self-esteem on changes in African American adolescents' mental health. *Child Development, 80,* 1660–1675.

Mandel, D. R., Jusczyk, P. W., & Pisoni, D. B. (1995). Infants' recognition of the sound patterns of their own names. *Psychological Science, 6,* 314–317.

Mangelsdorf, S. C. (1992). Developmental changes in infant–stranger interaction. *Infant Behavior and Development, 15,* 191–208.

Mangelsdorf, S. C., Gunnar, M., Kestenbaum, R., Lang, S., & Andreas, D. (1990). Infant proneness-to-distress temperament, maternal personality, and mother–infant attachment: Associations and goodness of fit. *Child Development, 61,* 820–831.

Mangelsdorf, S. C., Shapiro, J. R., & Marzolf, D. (1995). Developmental and temperamental differences in emotional regulation in infancy. *Child Development, 66,* 1817–1828.

Mantler, J., Matejicek, A., Matheson, K., & Anisman, H. (2005). Coping with employment uncertainty: A comparison of employed and unemployed workers. *Journal of Occupational Health Psychology, 10,* 200–209.

Maple, M., Edwards, H., Plummer, D., & Minichiello, V. (2010). Silenced voices: Hearing the stories of parents bereaved through the suicide death of a young adult child. *Health and Social Care in the Community, 18,* 241–248.

Maratsos, M. (1998). The acquisition of grammar. In W. Damon (Ed.), *Handbook of child psychology* (5th ed., Vol. 2, pp. 421–455). New York: Wiley.

Marcia, J. E. (1980). Identity in adolescence. In J. Adelson (Ed.), *Handbook of adolescent psychology* (pp. 159–187). New York: Wiley.

Marcus, G. F., Pinker, S., Ullman, M., Hollander, M., Rosen, T. J., & Xu, F. (1992). Overregularization in language acquisition. *Monographs of the Society for Research in Child Development, 58*(4, Serial No. 228).

Margett, T. E., & Witherington, D. C. (2011). The nature of preschoolers' concept of living and artificial objects. *Child Development, 82,* 2067–2082.

Margrett, J. A., Allaire, J. C., Johnson, T. L., Daugherty, K. E., & Weatherbee, S. R. (2010). Everyday problem solving. In J. C. Cavanaugh & C. K. Cavanaugh (Eds.), *Aging in America* (Vol. 1, pp. 79–101). Santa Barbara, CA: Praeger Perspectives.

Markovits, H., Benenson, J., & Dolenszky, E. (2001). Evidence that children and adolescents have internal models of peer interactions that are gender differentiated. *Child Development, 72,* 879–886.

Markus, H., & Nurius, P. (1986). Possible selves. *American Psychologist, 41,* 954–969.

Marschik, P. B., Einspieler, C., Strohmeier, A., Plienegger, J., Garzarolli, B., & Prechtl, H. F. R. (2008). From the reaching behavior at 5 months of age to hand preference at preschool age. *Developmental Psychobiology, 50,* 511–518.

Marsh, H. W. (1991). Employment during high school: Character building or a subversion of academic goals? *Sociology of Education, 64,* 172–189.

Marsh, K., & Musson, G. (2008). Men at work and at home: Managing emotion in telework. *Gender, Work & Organization, 15,* 31–48.

Marshal, M. P., Friedman, M. S., Stall, R., King, K. M., Miles, J., Gold, M. A., et al. (2008). Sexual orientation and adolescent substance use: A meta-analysis and methodological review. *British Journal of Addiction, 103,* 546–556.

Marsiske, M., & Margrett, J. A. (2006). Everyday problem solving with decision making. In J. E. Birren & K. W. Schaie (Eds.), *Handbook of the psychology of aging* (6th ed., pp. 315–342). Boston: Academic Press.

Martin, C. L., & Fabes, R. A. (2001). The stability and consequences of young children's same-sex peer interactions. *Developmental Psychology, 37,* 431–446.

Martin, C. L., Fabes, R. A., Evans, S. M., & Wyman, H. (1999). Social cognition on the playground: Children's beliefs about playing with girls versus boys and their relationships to sex-segregated play. *Journal of Social and Personal Relationships, 16,* 751–772.

Martin, C. L., & Halverson, C. F. (1987). The roles of cognition in sex role acquisition. In D. B. Carter (Ed.), *Current conceptions of sex roles and sex typing: Theory and research* (pp. 123–137). New York: Praeger.

Martin, C. L., & Ruble, D. (2004). Children's search for gender cues: Cognitive perspectives on gender development. *Current Directions in Psychological Science, 13,* 67–70.

Martin, J. L., & Ross, H. S. (2005). Sibling aggression: Sex differences and parents' reactions. *International Journal of Behavioral Development, 29,* 129–138.

Martin, M., Long, M. V., & Poon, L. W. (2003). Age changes and differences in personality traits and states of the old and very old. *Journal of Gerontology: Psychological Sciences, 57B,* 144–152.

Mascolo, M. F., Fischer, K. W., & Li, J. (2003). Dynamic development of component systems of emotions: Pride, shame, and guilt in China and the United States. In R. J. Davidson, K. R. Scherer, & H. H. Goldsmith (Eds.), *Handbook of affective sciences* (pp. 375–408). Oxford, England: Oxford University Press.

Mash, E. J., & Wolfe, D. A. (2010). *Abnormal child psychology* (4th ed.). Belmont, CA: Cengage.

Masunaga, H., & Horn, J. (2001). Expertise and age-related changes in components of intelligence. *Psychology and Aging, 16,* 293–311.

Masur, E. F. (1995). Infants' early verbal imitation and their later lexical development. *Merrill-Palmer Quarterly, 41,* 286–306.

Matsumoto, A. K., Bathon, J., & Bingham, C. O., III. (2010). *Rheumatoid arthritis treatment.* Retrieved from http://www.hopkins-arthritis.org/arthritis-info/rheumatoid-arthritis/rheum_treat.html

Mattys, S. L., Jusczyk, P. W., Luce, P. A., & Morgan, J. L. (1999). Phonotactic and prosodic effects on word segmentation in infants. *Cognitive Psychology, 38,* 465–494.

Maughan, A., & Cicchetti, D. (2002). Impact of child maltreatment and interadult violence on children's emotion regulation abilities and socioemotional adjustment. *Child Development, 73,* 1525–1542.

Maume, D. J., Jr. (2004). Is the glass ceiling a unique form of inequality? Evidence from a random-effects model of managerial attainment. *Work and Occupations, 31,* 250–274.

Maurer, T. W., & Robinson, D. W. (2008). Effects of attire, alcohol, and gender on perceptions of date rape. *Sex Roles, 58,* 423–434.

Maye, J., Weiss, D. J., & Aslin, R. N. (2008). Statistical phonetic learning in infants: Facilitation and feature generalization. *Developmental Science, 11,* 122–134.

Mayer, H. U. (2009). New directions in life course research. *Annual Review of Sociology, 35,* 413–433.

Mayer, J. D., Salovey, P., & Caruso, D. R. (2008). Emotional intelligence: New ability or eclectic traits. *American Psychologist, 63,* 503–517.

Maynard, A. E. (2002). Cultural teaching: The development of teaching skills in Maya sibling interactions. *Child Development, 73,* 969–982.

Mayo Clinic. (2009). *Nutrition and healthy eating.* Retrieved from http://www.mayoclinic.com/health/nutrition-and-healthy-eating/MY00431

Mayo Clinic. (2010a). *Aerobic exercise: Top 10 reasons to get physical.* Retrieved from http://www.mayoclinic.com/health/aerobic-exercise/EP00002/NSECTIONGROUP52

Mayo Clinic. (2010b). *Alcoholism.* Retrieved from http://www.mayoclinic.com/health/alcoholism/DS00340

Mayo Clinic. (2010c). *Alternative medicine.* Retrieved from http://www.mayoclinic.com/health/menopause/DS00119/DSECTION5alternative-medicine

Mayo Clinic. (2010d). *Hormone therapy: Is it right for you?* Retrieved from http://www.mayoclinic.com/health/hormone-therapy/WO00046

Mayo Clinic. (2010e). *Lifestyle and home remedies.* Retrieved from http://www.mayoclinic.com/health/menopause/DS00119/DSECTION5lifestyle-and-home-remedies

Mayo Clinic. (2010f). *Perimenopause.* Retrieved from http://www.mayoclinic.com/health/perimenopause/DS00554

Mayo Clinic. (2011). *Fitness: Fitness basics.* Retrieved from http://www.mayoclinic.com/health/fitness/MY00396/TAB_indepth

Mazur, E., Wolchik, S. A., Virdin, L., Sandler, I. N., & West, S. G. (1999). Cognitive moderators of children's adjustment to stressful divorce events: The role of negative cognitive errors and positive illusions. *Child Development, 70,* 231–245.

Mazzarella, S. R. (2007). Cyberdating success stories and the mythic narrative of living "happily-ever-after with the one." In M.-L. Galician & D. L. Merskin (Eds.), *Critical thinking about sex, love, and romance in the mass media* (pp. 23–37). Mahwah, NJ: Erlbaum.

McAdams, D. P. (2001). Generativity at midlife. In M. E. Lachman (Ed.), *Handbook of midlife development* (pp. 395–443). New York: Wiley.

McAdams, D. P. (2008). Personal narratives and the life story. In O. P. John, R. W. Robins, & L. A. Pervin (Eds.), *Handbook of personality: Theory and research* (3rd ed., pp. 241–61). New York: Guilford.

McAdams, D. P. (2009). The problem of meaning in personality psychology from the standpoints of dispositional traits, characteristic adaptations, and life stories. *Japanese Journal of Psychology, 18,* 173–186.

McAdams, D. P., & Olson, B. D. (2010). Personality development: Continuity and change over the life course. *Annual Review of Psychology, 61,* 517–542.

McAlaney, J., Bewick, B., & Hughes, C. (2011). The international development of the "social norms" approach to drug education and prevention. *Drugs: Education, Prevention, and Policy, 18,* 81–89.

McCall, R. B. (1979). *Infants.* Cambridge, MA: Harvard University Press.

McCarty, M. E., & Ashmead, D. H. (1999). Visual control of reaching and grasping in infants. *Developmental Psychology, 35,* 620–631.

McCleese, C. S., & Eby, L. T. (2006). Reactions to job content plateaus: Examining role ambiguity and hierarchical plateaus as moderators. *Career Development Quarterly, 55,* 64–76.

McClinton, B. E. (2010). *Preparing for the third age: A retirement planning course outline for lifelong learning programs* (Master's thesis, California State University at Long Beach, Long Beach, CA). Retrieved from http://gradworks.umi.com/1486345.pdf

McClure, E. B. (2000). A meta-analytic review of sex differences in facial expression processing and their development in infants, children, and adolescents. *Psychological Bulletin, 126,* 424–453.

McCollum, L., & Pincus, T. (2009). A biopsychosocial model to complement a biomedical model: Patient questionnaire data and socioeconomic status usually are more significant than laboratory tests and imaging studies in prognosis of rheumatoid arthritis. *Rheumatoid Disease Clinics of North America, 35,* 699–712.

McConatha, J. T., Stoller, P., & Oboudiat, F. (2001). Reflections of older Iranian women: Adapting to life in the United States. *Journal of Aging Studies, 15,* 369–381.

McCormick, C. B. (2003). Metacognition and learning. In I. B. Weiner, W. M. Reynolds, & G. E. Miller (Eds.), *Handbook of psychology* (Vol. 7, pp. 79–102). New York: Wiley.

McCrae, R. R. (2002). The maturation of personality psychology: Adult personality development and psychological well-being. *Journal of Research in Personality, 36,* 307–317.

McCrae, R. R., & Costa, P. T. (1994). The stability of personality: Observation and evaluations. *Current Directions in Psychological Sciences, 3,* 173–175.

McCrae, R. R., & Terracciano, A. (2005). Universal features of personality traits from the observer's perspective: Data from 50 cultures. *Journal of Personality and Social Psychology, 88,* 547–561.

McDonald, K. L., Bowker, J. C., Rubin, K. H., Laursen, B., & Duchene, M. S. (2010). Interactions between rejection sensitivity and supportive relationships in the prediction of adolescents' internalizing difficulties. *Journal of Youth and Adolescence, 39,* 563–574.

McElwain, N. L., Booth-LaForce, C., & Wu, X. (2011). Infant–mother attachment and children's friendship quality: Maternal mental-state talk as an intervening mechanism. *Developmental Psychology, 47,* 1295–1311.

McEwen, B. S., & Gianaros, P. J. (2010). Central role of the brain in stress and adaptation: Links to socioeconomic status, health, and disease. *Annals of the New York Academy of Sciences, 1186,* 190–222.

McGarry, K., & Schoeni, R. F. (2005). Widow(er) poverty and out-of-pocket medical expenditures near the end of life. *Journal of Gerontology: Social Sciences, 60,* S160–S168.

McGill, D., Brown, K., Haley, J., Schieber, S., & Warshawsky, M. (2010). *Fundamentals of private pensions* (9th ed.). New York: Oxford University Press.

McGuckin, T. L. (2007). *Examining the patterns of alcohol use on campus and the perceptions of faculty related to student alcohol use.* (Unpublished doctoral dissertation) University of West Florida, Pensacola, FL.

McGuire, L. C., & Cavanaugh, J. C. (1992, April). *Objective measures versus spouses' perceptions of cognitive status in dementia patients.* Paper presented at the biennial Cognitive Aging Conference, Atlanta, GA.

McGuire, S., & Shanahan, L. (2010). Sibling experiences in diverse family contexts. *Child Development Perspectives, 4,* 72–79.

McHale, J. P., Laurette, A., Talbot, J., & Pourquette, C. (2002). Retrospect and prospect in the psychological study of coparenting and family group process. In J. P. McHale & W. Grolnick (Eds.), *Retrospect and prospect in the psychological study of families* (pp. 127–165). Mahwah, NJ: Erlbaum.

McIntosh, W. D., Locker, L., Briley, K., Ryan, R., & Scott, A. (2011). What do older adults seek in their potential romantic partners? Evidence from online personal ads. *International Journal of Aging and Human Development, 72,* 67–82.

McKay, K., & Ross, L. E. (2010). The transition to adoptive parenthood: A pilot study of parents adopting in Ontario, Canada. *Children and Youth Services Review, 32,* 604–610.

McKee-Ryan, F., Song, Z., Wanberg, C. R., & Kinicki, A. J. (2005). Psychological and physical well-being during unemployment: A meta-analytic study. *Journal of Applied Psychology, 90,* 53–76.

McKenzie, P. T. (2003). *Factors of Successful Marriage: Accounts from Self-Described Happy Couples.* (Unpublished doctoral dissertation). Howard University, Washington, DC.

McKhann, G. M., Knopman, D. S., Chertkow, H., Hyman, B. T., Jack, C. R., Jr., Kawas, C. H., et al. (2011). The diagnosis of dementia due to Alzheimer's disease: Recommendations from the National Institute on Aging–Alzheimer's Association workgroups on diagnostic guidelines for Alzheimer's disease. *Alzheimer's & Dementia: Journal of the Alzheimer's Association, 7,* 263–269.

McKusick, V. A. (1995). *Mendelian inheritance in man: Catalogs of autosomal dominant, autosomal recessive, and X-linked phenotypes* (10th ed.). Baltimore: Johns Hopkins University Press.

McLanahan, S. (1999). Father absence and the welfare of children. In E. M. Hetherington (Ed.), *Coping with divorce, single parenting, and remarriage: A risk and resiliency perspective* (pp. 117–145). Mahwah, NJ: Erlbaum.

McLellan, J. A., & Youniss, J. (2003). Two systems of youth service: Determinants of voluntary and required youth community service. *Journal of Youth and Adolescence, 32,* 47–58.

McMurray, B. (2007). Defusing the childhood vocabulary explosion. *Science, 317,* 631.

Meaney, M. J. (2010). Epigenetics and the biological definition of gene X environment interactions. *Child Development, 81,* 41–79.

Medicare.gov. (2011). *Medicare basics.* Retrieved from http://www.medicare.gov/navigation/medicare-basics/medicare-basics-overview.aspx

Meeus, W., Oosterwegel, A., & Vollebergh, W. (2002). Parental and peer attachment and identity development in adolescence. *Journal of Adolescence, 25,* 93–106.

Meeus, W., van de Schoot, R., Keijsers, L., Schwartz, S. J., & Branje, S. (2010). On the progression and stability of adolescent identity formation: A five-wave longitudinal study in early-to-middle and middle-to-late adolescence. *Child Development, 81,* 1565–1581.

Mehta, C. M., & Strough, J. (2009). Sex segregation in friendships and normative contexts across the life span. *Developmental Review, 29,* 201–220.

Mehta, K. K. (1997). The impact of religious beliefs and practices on aging: A cross-cultural comparison. *Journal of Aging Studies, 11,* 101–114.

Meijer, A. M., & van den Wittenboer, G. L. H. (2007). Contribution of infants' sleep and crying to marital relationship of first-time parent couples in the 1st year after childbirth. *Journal of Family Psychology, 21,* 49–57.

Melby, J. N., Conger, R. D., Fang, S., Wickrama, K. A. S., & Conger, K. J. (2008). Adolescent family experiences and educational attainment during early adulthood. *Developmental Psychology, 44,* 1519–1536.

Melby-Lervag, M., Lyster, S. A. H., & Hulme, C. (2012). Phonological skills and their role in learning to read: A meta-analytic review. *Psychological Bulletin, 138,* 322–352.

Melhado, L. W., & Byers, J. F. (2011). Patients' and surrogates' decision-making characteristics: Withdrawing, withholding, and continuing life-sustaining treatments. *Journal of Hospice and Palliative Nursing, 13,* 16–28.

Meltzoff, A. N., & Moore, M. K. (1989). Imitation in newborn infants: Exploring the range of gestures imitated and the underlying mechanisms. *Developmental Psychology, 25,* 954–962.

Meltzoff, A. N., & Moore, M. K. (1994). Imitation, memory, and the representation of persons. *Infant Behavior and Development, 17,* 83–99.

Mendle, J., Turkheimer, E., & Emery, R. E. (2007). Detrimental psychological outcomes associated with early pubertal timing in adolescent girls. *Developmental Review, 27,* 151–171.

Mennella, J. A., & Beauchamp, G. K. (1997). The ontogeny of human flavor perception. In G. K. Beauchamp & L. Bartoshuk (Eds.), *Tasting and smelling: Handbook of perception and cognition.* San Diego, CA: Academic Press.

Mennella, J. A., Jagnow, C. P., & Beauchamp, G. K. (2001). Prenatal and post-natal flavor learning by human infants. *Pediatrics, 107,* E88.

Mensch, B. S., Singh, S., & Casterline, J. B. (2006). Trends in the timing of first marriage among men and women in the developing world. In C. B. Lloyd, J. R. Behrman, N. P. Stromquist, & B. Cohen (Eds.), *The changing transitions to adulthood in developing countries: Selected studies* (pp. 1180–171). Washington, DC: National Research Council.

Mercken, L., Candel, M., Willems, P., & de Vries, H. (2007). Disentangling social selection and social influence effects on adolescent smoking: The importance of reciprocity in friendships. *British Journal of Addiction, 102,* 1483–1492.

Mervis, C. B., & Johnson, K. E. (1991). Acquisition of the plural morpheme: A case study. *Developmental Psychology, 27,* 222–235.

Meyer, J. F. (2007). Confucian "familism" in America. In D. S. Browning & D. A. Clairmont (Eds.), *American religions and the family: How faith traditions cope with modernization and democracy* (pp. 168–184). New York: Columbia University Press.

Milberger, S., Biederman, J., Faraone, S. V., Guite, J., & Tsuang, M. T. (1997). Pregnancy, delivery and infancy complication, and attention deficit hyperactivity disorder: Issues of gene–environment interaction. *Biological Psychiatry, 41,* 65–75.

Miles, J. (2009). *Autobiographical reflection and perspective transformation in adult learners returning to study: research in progress.* Retrieved from http://www.avetra.org.au/papers-2009/papers/37.00.pdf

Miller, G. E., & Chen, E. (2010). Harsh family climate in early life presages the emergence of proinflammatory phenotype in adolescence. *Psychological Science, 21,* 848–856.

Miller, J. G., & Bersoff, D. M. (1992). Culture and moral judgment: How are conflicts between justice and interpersonal responsibilities resolved? *Journal of Personality and Social Psychology, 62,* 541–554.

Miller, K. I., Shoemaker, M. M., Willyard, J., & Addison, P. (2008). Providing care for elderly parents: A structurational approach to family caregiver identity. *Journal of Family Communication, 8,* 19–43.

Miller, P. M., Danaher, D. L., & Forbes, D. (1986). Sex-related strategies of coping with interpersonal conflict in children aged five to seven. *Developmental Psychology, 22,* 543–548.

Miller-Martinez, D., & Wallace, S. P. (2007). Structural contexts and life-course processes in the social networks of older Mexican immigrants in the United States. In S. Carmel, C. Morse, & F. Torres-Gil (Eds.), *Lessons on aging from three nations* (Vol. 1, pp. 141–154). Amityville, NY: Baywood.

Millstein, S. G., & Halpern-Felsher, B. L. (2002). Judgments about risk and perceived invulnerability in adolescents and young adults. *Journal of Research on Adolescence, 12,* 399–422.

Ministry of Internal Affairs and Communications. (2010). *Statistical handbook of Japan 2010.* Retrieved from http://www.stat.go.jp/english/data/handbook/index.htm

Minnotte, K. L. (2010). *Methodologies of assessing marital success.* Retrieved from http://wfnetwork.bc.edu/encyclopedia_entry.php?id516779&area5All

Mischel, W. (1970). Sex-typing and socialization. In P. H. Mussen (Ed.), *Carmichael's manual of child psychology* (Vol. 2, pp. 3–72). New York: Wiley.

Missildine, W., Feldstein, G., Punzalan, J. C., & Parsons, J. T. (2005). S/he loves me, s/he loves me not: Questioning heterosexist assumptions of gender differences for romantic and sexually motivated behaviors. *Sexual Addiction & Compulsivity, 12,* 65–74.

Missotten, L. C., Luyckx, K., Branje, S., Vanhalst, J., & Goossens, L. (2011). Identity styles and conflict resolution styles: Associations in mother-adolescent dyads. *Journal of Youth and Adolescence, 40,* 972–982.

Mitchell, B. A. (2006). *The boomerang age: Transitions to adulthood in families.* New Brunswick, NJ: AldineTransaction.

Mitchell, B. A. (2010). Happiness in midlife parental roles: A contextual mixed methods analysis. *Family Relations, 59,* 326–339.

Mitchell, K. J., & Johnson, M. K. (2009). Source monitoring 15 years later: What have we learned from fMRI about the neural mechanisms of source memory? *Psychological Bulletin, 135,* 638–677.

Mitchell, L. M., & Messner, L. (2003–2004). Relative child care: Supporting the providers. *Journal of Research in Childhood Education, 18,* 105–113.

Mix, K. S., Huttenlocher, J., & Levine, S. C. (2002). Multiple cues for quantification in infancy: Is number one of them? *Psychological Bulletin, 128,* 278–294.

Mize, J., & Ladd, G. W. (1990). A cognitive social-learning approach to social skill training with low-status preschool children. *Developmental Psychology, 26,* 388–397.

Mize, J., Pettit, G. S., & Brown, E. G. (1995). Mothers' supervision of their children's peer play: Relations with beliefs, perceptions, and knowledge. *Developmental Psychology, 31,* 311–321.

Mizes, J., & Palermo, T. M. (1997). Eating disorders. In M. Hersen & R. T. Ammerman (Eds.), *Handbook of prevention and treatment with children and adolescents: Intervention in the real world context* (pp 572–603). New York: Wiley.

Moeller, J. R., Lewis, M. M., & Werth, J. L., Jr. (2010). End of life issues. In J. C. Cavanaugh & C. K. Cavanaugh (Eds.), *Aging in America* (Vol. 1, pp. 202–231). Santa Barbara, CA: Praeger Perspectives.

Moen, P., Fields, V., Meador, R., & Rosenblatt, H. (2000a). Fostering integration: A case study of the Cornell Retirees Volunteering in Service (CRVIS) program. In K. Pillemer & P. Moen (Eds.), *Social integration in the second half of life* (pp. 247–264). Baltimore: Johns Hopkins University Press.

Moen, P., Fields, V., Quick, H. E., & Hofmeister, H. (2000b). A life course approach to retirement and social integration. In K. Pillemer & P. Moen (Eds.), *Social integration in the second half of life* (pp. 75–107). Baltimore: Johns Hopkins University Press.

Moen, P., & Roehling, P. (2005). *The career mystique: Cracks in the American dream.* Lanham, MD: Rowman & Littlefield.

Moerk, E. L. (2000). *The guided acquisition of first language skills.* Westport, CT: Ablex.

Moffitt, T. E. (1993). Adolescence-limited and life-course-persistent antisocial behavior: A developmental taxonomy. *Psychological Review, 100,* 674–701.

Moffitt, T. E., & Caspi, A. (2005). Life-course persistent and adolescence-limited antisocial males: Longitudinal follow-up to adulthood. In D. M. Stoff & E. J. Susman (Eds.), *Developmental psychobiology of aggression* (pp. 161–186). New York: Cambridge University Press.

Moffitt, T. E., Caspi, A., Belsky, J., & Silva, P. A. (1992). Childhood experience and the onset of menarche: A test of a sociobiological model. *Child Development, 63,* 47–58.

Molfese, D. L., & Burger-Judisch, L. M. (1991). Dynamic temporal–spatial allocation of resources in the human brain: An alternative to the static view of hemisphere differences. In F. L. Ketterle (Ed.), *Cerebral laterality: Theory and research. The Toledo symposium.* Hillsdale, NJ: Erlbaum.

Molina, B. S. G., Hinshaw, S. P., Swanson, J. M., Arnold, L. E., Vitiello, B., Jensen, P. S., et al. (2009). The MTA at 8 years: Prospective follow-up of children treated for combined-type ADHD in a multisite study. *Journal of the American Academy of Child & Adolescent Psychiatry, 48,* 484–500.

Molloy, L. E., Gest, S. D., & Rulison, K. L. (2011). Peer influences on academic motivation: Exploring multiple methods of assessing youths' most "influential" peer relationships. *Journal of Early Adolescence, 31,* 13–40.

Molloy, L. E., Ram, N., & Gest, S. D. (2011). The storm and stress (or calm) of early adolescent self-concepts: Within- and between-subjects variability. *Developmental Psychology, 47,* 1589–1607.

Monahan, K. C., Lee, J. M., & Steinberg, L. (2011). Revisiting the impact of part-time work on adolescent adjustment: Distinguishing between selection and socialization using propensity score matching. *Child Development, 82,* 96–112.

Monk, C., Fifer, W. P., Myers, M. M., Sloan, R. P., Trien, L., & Hurtado, A. (2000). Maternal stress responses and anxiety during pregnancy: Effects on fetal heart rate. *Developmental Psychobiology, 36,* 67–77.

Montague, D. P., & Walker-Andrews, A. S. (2001). Peekaboo: A new look at infants' perception of emotion expressions. *Developmental Psychology, 37,* 826–838.

Montgomery, M. J. (2005). Psychosocial intimacy and identity: From early adolescence to emerging adulthood. *Journal of Adolescent Research, 20,* 346–374.

Moore, C. (2007). Understanding self and others in the second year. In C. A. Brownell & C. B. Kopp (Eds.), *Socioemotional development in the toddler years.* New York: Guilford.

Moore, K. L., & Persaud, T. V. N. (1993). *Before we are born* (4th ed.). Philadelphia: W. B. Saunders.

Moore, M. R., & Brooks-Gunn, J. (2002). Adolescent parenthood. In M. H. Bornstein (Ed.), *Handbook of parenting* (2nd ed., Vol. 3, pp. 173–214). Mahwah, NJ: Erlbaum.

Moorman, S. M., & Greenfield, E. A. (2010). Personal relationships in later life. In J. C. Cavanaugh & C. K. Cavanaugh (Eds.), *Aging in America* (Vol. 3, pp. 20–52). Santa Barbara, CA: Praeger Perspectives.

Morahan-Martin, J., & Schumacher, P. (2003). Loneliness and social uses of the Internet. *Computers in Human Behavior, 19,* 659–671.

Moran, J. D. (2008). Families, courts, and the end of life: Schiavo and its implications for the family justice system. *Family Court Review, 46,* 297–330.

Morfei, M. Z., Hooker, K., Fiese, B. H., & Cordeiro, A. M. (2001). Continuity and change in parenting possible selves: A longitudinal follow-up. *Basic and Applied Social Psychology, 23,* 217–223.

Morgan, B., & Gibson, K. R. (1991). Nutritional and environmental interactions in brain development. In K. R. Gibson & A. C. Peterson (Eds.), *Brain maturation and cognitive development: Comparative and crosscultural perspectives.* New York: de Gruyter.

Morgan, J. P., & Roberts, J. E. (2010). Helping bereaved children and adolescents: Strategies and implications for counselors. *Journal of Mental Health Counseling, 32,* 206–217.

Morgane, P. J., Austin-Lafrance, R., Bronzino, J. D., Tonkiss, J., Diaz-Cintra, S., Cintra, L., et al. (1993). Prenatal malnutrition and development of the brain. *Neuroscience & Biobehavioral Reviews, 17,* 91–128.

Morris, W. L., Sinclair, S., & DePaulo, B. M. (2007). No shelter for singles: The perceived legitimacy of marital status discrimination. *Group Processes & Intergroup Relation, 10,* 457–470.

Morrow, J. R. (2005). Are American children and youth fit? It's time we learned. *Research Quarterly for Exercise and Sport, 76,* 377–388.

Moss, E., Smolla, N., Guerra, I., Mazzarello, T., Chayer, D., & Berthiaume, C. (2006). Attachement et problèmes de comportements intériorisés et extériorisés auto-rapportés á la période scolaire. *Canadian Journal of Behavioural Science, 38,* 142–157.

Moss, M. S., Moss, S. Z., & Hansson, R. O. (2001). Bereavement and old age. In M. S. Stroebe, R. O. Hansson, W. Stroebe, & H. Schut (Eds.), *Handbook of bereavement research: Consequences, coping, and care* (pp. 241–260). Washington, DC: American Psychological Association.

Mosten, F. S. (2009). *Collaborative divorce handbook: Helping families without going to court.* San Francisco: Jossey-Bass.

Moynehan, J., & Adams, J. (2007). What's the problem? A look at men in marital therapy. *American Journal of Family Therapy, 35,* 41–51.

MTA Cooperative Group. (1999). Moderators and mediators of treatment response for children with attention-deficit/hyperactivity disorder. *Archives of General Psychiatry, 56,* 1088–1096.

Mugadza, T. (2005). Discrimination against women in the world of human rights: The case of women in southern Africa. In A. Barnes (Ed.), *The handbook of women, psychology, and the law* (pp. 354–365). New York: Wiley.

Muller, E. D., & Thompson, C. L. (2003). The experience of grief after bereavement: A phenomenological study with implications for mental health counseling. *Journal of Mental Health Counseling, 25,* 183–203.

Mumme, D. L., Fernald, A., & Herrera, C. (1996). Infants' responses to facial and vocal emotional signals in a social referencing paradigm. *Child Development, 67,* 3219–3237.

Murray-Close, D., Hoza, B., Hinshaw, S.P., Arnold, L.E., Swanson, J., Jensen, P.S., et al. (2010). Developmental processes in peer problems of children with attention-deficit/hyperactivity disorder in the Multimodal Treatment Study of Children with ADHD: Developmental cascades and vicious cycles. *Development and Psychopathology, 22,* 785–802.

Musil, C. M., & Standing, T. (2005). Grandmothers' diaries: A glimpse at daily lives. *International Journal of Aging and Human Development, 60,* 317–329.

Mustillo, S. A., Hendrix, K. L., & Schafer, M. H. (2012). Trajectories of body mass and self-concept in black and white girls: The lingering effects of stigma. *Journal of Health and Social Behavior, 53,* 2–16.

Mutchler, J. E., Baker, L. A., & Lee, S. A. (2007). Grandparents responsible for grandchildren in Native-American families. *Social Science Quarterly, 88,* 990–1009.

Mwanyangala, M. A., Mayombana, C., Urassa, H., Charles, J., Mahutanga, C., Abdullah, S., et al. (2010). Health status and quality of life among older adults in rural Tanzania. *Global Health Action, 3.* Retrieved from http://journals.sfu.ca/coaction/index.php/gha/article/viewArticle/2142/6055

Myskow, L. (2002). Perimenopausal issues in sexuality. *Sexual & Relationship Therapy, 17,* 253–260.

Nadig, A. S., & Sedivy, J. C. (2002). Evidence of perspective-taking constraints in children's on-line reference resolution. *Psychological Science, 13,* 329–336.

Nahemow, L. (2000). The ecological theory of aging: Powell Lawton's legacy. In R. L. Rubinstein & M. Moss (Eds.), *The many dimensions of aging* (pp. 22–40). New York: Springer.

Nánez, J., Sr., & Yonas, A. (1994). Effects of luminance and texture motion on infant defensive reactions to optical collision. *Infant Behavior and Development, 17,* 165–174.

National Alliance for Caregiving & AARP. (2010). *Caregiving in the U.S.: Executive Summary.* Retrieved from http://assets.aarp.org/rgcenter/il/caregiving_09_es.pdf

National Arthritis Foundation. (2010). *Osteoarthritis fact sheet.* Retrieved from http://www.arthritis.org/media/newsroom/media-kits/Osteoarthritis_fact_sheet.pdf

National Association for Sport and Physical Education. (2004). *Appropriate practices for high school physical education.* Reston, VA: Author.

National Cancer Institute. (2006). *Diethylstilbestrol (DES) and Cancer.* Retrieved from http://www.cancer.gov/cancertopics/factsheet/Risk/DES

National Center for Educational Statistics. (2010). *The condition of education 2010.* Retrieved from http://nces.ed.gov/pubsearch/pubsinfo.asp?pubid52010028

National Center for Health Statistics. (2007). *The state of aging and health in America.* Retrieved from http://www.cdc.gov/aging/pdf/saha_2007.pdf

National Center for Health Statistics. (2010a). *Health, United States, 2009: With special feature on medical technology.* Retrieved from http://www.cdc.gov/nchs/data/hus/hus09.pdf

National Center for Health Statistics. (2010b). *Life expectancy.* Retrieved from http://www.cdc.gov/nchs/data/hus/hus2009tables/Table024.pdf

National Center for Health Statistics. (2010c). *Marriage and divorce.* Retrieved from http://www.cdc.gov/nchs/fastats/divorce.htm

National Center for Health Statistics. (2010d). *United States life tables by Hispanic origin.* Retrieved from http://www.cdc.gov/nchs/data/series/sr_02/sr02_152.pdf

National Center on Elder Abuse. (2010a). *Frequently asked questions.* Retrieved from http://www.ncea.aoa.gov/NCEAroot/Main_Site/FAQ/Questions.aspx

National Center on Elder Abuse. (2010b). *Major types of elder abuse.* Retrieved from http://www.ncea.aoa.gov/NCEAroot/Main_Site/FAQ/Basics/Types_Of_Abuse.aspx

National Center on Elder Abuse. (2010c). *Who are the abusers?* Retrieved from http://www.ncea.aoa.gov/NCEAroot/Main_Site/FAQ/Basics/Abusers.aspx

National Endowment for Financial Education. (2010). *Costs of caring for an aging parent.* Retrieved from http://www.smartaboutmoney.org/LifeEventsFinancial-Decisions/HealthandFamilySupport/AgingParents/CostsofCaregiving/tabid/365/Default.aspx

National Federation of State High School Associations. (2011). Participation data. Retrieved from http://www.nfhs.org/Participation/

National Heart, Lung, and Blood Institute. (2003). *Facts about postmenopausal hormone therapy.* Retrieved from http://www.nhlbi.nih.gov/health/women/pht_facts.htm

National Institute of Arthritis and Musculoskeletal and Skin Diseases. (2009). *Osteoporosis: Peak bone mass in women.* Retrieved from http://www.niams.nih.gov/Health_Info/Bone/Osteoporosis/bone_mass.asp

National Institute of Arthritis and Musculoskeletal and Skin Diseases. (2010a). *Osteoarthritis.* Retrieved from http://www.niams.nih.gov/Health_Info/Osteoarthritis

National Institute of Arthritis and Musculoskeletal and Skin Diseases. (2010b). *Osteoporosis and arthritis: Two common but different conditions.* Retrieved from http://www.niams.nih.gov/Health_Info/Bone/Osteoporosis/Conditions_Behaviors/osteoporosis_arthritis.asp

National Institute of Arthritis and Musculoskeletal and Skin Diseases. (2010c). *Osteoporosis handout on health.* Retrieved from http://www.niams.nih.gov/Health_Info/Bone/Osteoporosis/osteoporosis_hoh.asp#5

National Institute of Arthritis and Musculoskeletal and Skin Diseases. (2010d). *Osteoporosis handout on health: Recommended calcium and vitamin D intakes.* Retrieved from http://www.niams.nih.gov/Health_Info/Bone/Osteoporosis/osteoporosis_hoh.asp#calcium

National Institute of Child Health and Human Development. (2004). *The NICHD community connection.* Washington, DC: Author.

National Institute of Child Health and Human Development Early Child Care Research Network. (1997). The effects of infant child care of infant–mother attachment security: Results of the NICHD Study of Early Child Care. *Child Development, 68,* 860–879.

National Institute of Child Health and Human Development Early Child Care Research Network. (2001). Child-care and family predictors of preschool attachment and stability from infancy. *Developmental Psychology, 37,* 847–862.

National Institute of Mental Health. (2010a). *Major depressive disorder among adults.* Retrieved from http://www.nimh.nih.gov/statistics/1MDD_ADULT.shtml

National Institute of Mental Health. (2010b). *Post-traumatic stress disorder (PTSD).* Retrieved from http://www.nimh.nih.gov/health/publications/post-traumatic-stress-disorder-ptsd/complete-index.shtml

National Institute of Neurological Disorders and Stroke. (2009). *Autism fact sheet* (NIH Publication No. 09-1877). Bethesda, MD: Author.

National Institute of Neurological Disorders and Stroke. (2010). *NINDS deep brain stimulation for Parkinson's disease information page.* Retrieved from http://www.ninds.nih.gov/disorders/deep_brain_stimulation/deep_brain_stimulation.htm

National Institute on Aging. (2010). *Hearing loss.* Retrieved from http://www.nia.nih.gov/HealthInformation/Publications/hearing.htm

National Institute on Alcohol Abuse and Alcoholism. (2002). *A call to action: Changing the culture of drinking at U.S. colleges. Final report of the Task Force on College Drinking* (NIH Publication No. 02–5010). Rockville, MD: Author.

National Institute on Alcohol Abuse and Alcoholism. (2007). *What colleges need to know now: An update on college drinking research.* Washington, DC: National Institutes of Health.

National Institute on Alcohol Abuse and Alcoholism. (2010). *Neuroscience: pathways to alcohol dependence.* Retrieved from http://pubs.niaaa.nih.gov/publications/AA77/AA77.htm

National Institutes of Health. (2000). *Osteoporosis prevention, diagnosis, and therapy: Consensus statement.* Retrieved from http://consensus.nih.gov/2000/2000Osteoporosis111html.htm

National Parkinson's Foundation. (2011a). *How is PD treated?* Retrieved from http://www.parkinson.org/Parkinson-s-Disease/Treatment

National Parkinson's Foundation. (2011b). *Parkinson's disease overview.* Retrieved from http://www.parkinson.org/parkinson-s-disease.aspx

National Radiological Protection Board. (2004). Review of the scientific evidence for limiting exposure to electromagnetic fields (0–300 GHz). *Documents of the NRPB, 15* (3).

Natsuaki, M. N., Biehl, M. C., & Ge, X. (2009). Trajectories of depressed mood from early adolescence to young adulthood: The effects of pubertal timing and adolescent dating. *Journal of Research on Adolescence, 19,* 47–74.

Nayernouri, T. (2011). Euthanasia, terminal illness and quality of life. *Archives of Iranian Medicine, 14,* 54–55. Retrieved from http://www.ams.ac.ir/aim/011141/0011.pdf

Neal, M. B., & Hammer, L. B. (2006). *Working couples caring for children and aging parents: Effects on work and well-being.* Mahwah, NJ: Erlbaum.

Neff, L. A., & Karney, B. R. (2005). To know you is to love you: The implications of global adoration and specific accuracy for marital relationships. *Journal of Personality and Social Psychology, 88,* 480–497.

Neft, N., & Levine, A. D. (1997). *Where women stand: An international report on the status of women in over 140 countries, 1997–1998.* New York: Random House.

Negash, S., Bennett, D. A., Wilson, R. S., Schneider, J. A., & Arnold, S. E. (2011). Cognition and neuropathology in aging: Multidimensional perspectives from the Rush Religious Orders Study and Rush Memory and Aging Project. *Current Alzheimer's Research, 8,* 336–340.

Neimeyer, R. (1997). Knowledge at the margins. *Forum Newsletter, 23*(2), 10.

Neisser, U., Boodoo, G., Bouchard, T. J., Boykin, A. W., Brody, N., Ceci, S. J., et al. (1996). Intelligence: Knowns and unknowns. *American Psychologist, 51,* 77–101.

Nell, V. (2002). Why young men drive dangerously: Implications for injury prevention. *Current Directions in Psychological Science, 11,* 75–79.

Nelson, K. (1973). Structure and strategy in learning to talk. *Monographs of the Society for Research in Child Development, 38* (Serial No. 149).

Nelson, L. J., Badger, S., & Wu, B. (2004). The influence of culture in emerging adulthood: Perspectives of Chinese college students. *International Journal of Behavioral Development, 28,* 26–36.

Nelson, M. A. (1996). Protective equipment. In O. Bar-Or (Ed.), *The child and adolescent athlete* (pp 214–223). Oxford, England: Blackwell.

Nerenberg, L. (2010). Elder abuse prevention: A review of the field. In J. C. Cavanaugh & C. K. Cavanaugh (Eds.), *Aging in America* (Vol. 3, pp. 53–80). Santa Barbara, CA: Praeger Perspectives.

Neugarten, B. L. (1969). Continuities and discontinuities of psychological issues into adult life. *Human Development, 12,* 121–130.

Neugarten, B. L., & Weinstein, K. K. (1964). The changing American grandparent. *Journal of Marriage and Family, 26,* 299–304.

Nevid, J. S., Rathus, S. A., & Greene, B. (2003). *Abnormal psychology in a changing world* (5th ed.). Upper Saddle River, NJ: Prentice Hall.

Newman, B., & Newman, P. (2007). *Theories of human development.* London: Psychology Press.

Newport, E. L. (1991). Contrasting conceptions of the critical period for language. In S. Carey & R. Gelman (Eds.), *The epigenesis of mind: Essays on biology and cognition* (pp. 111–130). Hillsdale, NJ: Erlbaum.

Newsom, J. T. (1999). Another side to caregiving: Negative reactions to being helped. *Current Directions in Psychological Science, 8,* 183–187.

Nimrod, G., & Hutchinson, S. (2010). Innovation among older adults with chronic health conditions. *Journal of Leisure Research, 42,* 1–23.

Nimrod, G., & Kleiber, D. A. (2007). Reconsidering change and continuity in later life: Toward an innovation theory of successful aging. *International Journal of Aging and Human Development, 65,* 1–22.

Nisbett, R. E., Aronson, J., Blair, C., Dickens, W., Flynn, J., Halpern, D. F., et al. (2012). Intelligence: New findings and theoretical developments. *American Psychologist, 67,* 130–159.

Nishida, T. K., & Lillard, A. S. (2007). The informative value of emotional expressions: "Social referencing" in mother–child pretense. *Developmental Science, 10,* 205–212.

Nistor, G. I., Totoiu, M. O., Haque, N., Carpenter, M. K., & Keirstead, H. S. (2005). Human embryonic stem cells differentiate into oligodendrocytes in high purity and myelinate after spinal cord transplantation. *Glia, 49,* 385–396.

Nord, M., Andrews, M., & Carlson, S. (2007). *Household food security in the United States, 2006.* Washington, DC: U.S. Department of Agriculture.

Norlander, B., & Eckhardt, C. (2005). Anger, hostility, and male perpetrators of intimate partner violence: A meta-analytic review. *Clinical Psychology Review, 25,* 119–152.

Nrugham, L., Larsson, B., & Sund, A. M. (2008). Predictors of suicidal acts across adolescence: Influences of familial, peer and individual factors. *Journal of Affective Disorders, 109,* 35–45.

Nurmsoo, E., & Bloom, P. (2008). Preschoolers' perspective taking in word learning: Do they blindly follow eye gaze? *Psychological Science, 19,* 211–215.

Nusbaum, L. E. (2010). *How the elder co-housing model of living affects residents' experience of autonomy: A self-determination theory perspective* (Doctoral dissertation, Wright Institute, Berkeley, CA). Retrieved from http://proquest.umi.com/pqdlink?Ver51&Exp502-05-2016&FMT57&DID52189312001&RQT5309&attempt51&cfc51

Oakhill, J. V., & Cain, K. E. (2004). The development of comprehension skills. In T. Nunes & P. E. Bryant (Eds.), *Handbook of children's literacy* (pp. 155–180). Dordrecht, the Netherlands: Kluwer.

O'Brien, C.-A., & Goldberg, A. (2000). Lesbians and gay men inside and outside families. In N. Mandell & A. Duffy (Eds.), *Canadian families: Diversity, conflict, and change* (2nd ed., pp. 115–145). Toronto: Harcourt Brace.

Oburu, P. O., & Palmérus, K. (2005). Stress related factors among primary and part-time caregiving grandmothers of Kenyan grandchildren. *International Journal of Aging and Human Development, 60,* 273–282.

O'Connor, T., Heron, J., Golding, J., Beveridge, M., & Glover, V. (2002). Maternal antenatal anxiety and children's behavioural/emotional problems at 4 years. *British Journal of Psychiatry, 180,* 502–508.

Odgers, C. L., Moffitt, T. E., Broadbent, J. M., Dickson, N., Hancox, R. J., Harrington, H., et al. (2008). Female and male antisocial trajectories: From childhood origins to adult outcomes. *Development and Psychopathology, 20,* 673–716.

O'Donoghue, M. (2005). White mothers negotiating race and ethnicity in the mothering of biracial, black–white adolescents. *Journal of Ethnic & Cultural Diversity in Social Work, 14,* 125–156.

Offer, D., Ostrov, E., Howard, K. I., & Atkinson, R. (1988). *The teenage world: Adolescents' self-image in ten countries.* New York: Plenum.

Office of Management and Budget. (2010). *Historical tables: Budget of the U.S. government, fiscal year 2011.* Retrieved from http://www.whitehouse.gov/sites/default/files/omb/budget/fy2011/assets/hist.pdf

Oh, E. S., Lee, J. H., Jeong, S.-H., Sohn, E. H., & Lee, A. Y. (2011). Comparisons of cognitive deterioration rates by dementia subtype. *Archives of Gerontology and Geriatrics, 53*(3), 320–322.

Ojanen, T., & Perry, D. G. (2007). Relational schemas and the developing self: Perceptions of mother and of self as joint predictors of early adolescents' self-esteem. *Developmental Psychology, 43,* 1474–1483.

Okagaki, L., & Sternberg, R. J. (1993). Parental beliefs and children's school performance. *Child Development, 64,* 36–56.

Okonkwo, O. C., Mielke, M. M., Griffith, H. R., Moghekar, A. R., O'Brien, R. J., Shaw, L. M., et al. (2011). Cerebrospinal fluid profiles and prospective course and outcome in patients with amnestic mild cognitive impairment. *Archives of Neurology, 68,* 113–119.

O'Leary, K. D. (1993). Through a psychological lens: Personality traits, personality disorders, and levels of violence. In R. J. Gelles & D. R. Loseke (Eds.), *Current controversies on family violence* (pp. 7–30). Newbury Park, CA: Sage.

Olinghouse, N. G. (2008). Student- and instruction-level predictors of narrative writing in third-grade students. *Reading and Writing, 21,* 3–26.

Olson, S. L., Sameroff, A. J., Kerr, D. C. R., Lopez, N. L., & Wellman, H. M. (2005). Developmental foundations of externalizing problems in young children: The role of effortful control. *Development and Psychopathology, 17,* 25–45.

Oltjenbruns, K. A. (2001). Developmental context of childhood: Grief and regrief phenomena. In M. S. Stroebe, R. O. Hansson, W. Stroebe, & H. Schut (Eds.), *Handbook of bereavement research: Consequences, coping, and care* (pp. 169–197). Washington, DC: American Psychological Association.

Oltjenbruns, K. A., & Balk, D. E. (2007). Life span issues and loss, grief, and mourning. In D. Balk, C. Wogrin, G. Thornton, & D. Meagher (Eds.), *Handbook of thanatology: The essential body of knowledge for the study of death, dying, and bereavement* (pp. 143–163). New York: Routledge/Taylor & Francis.

Omori, M., & Smith, D. T. (2009). The impact of occupational status on household chore hours among dual earner couples. *Sociation Today, 7.* Retrieved from http://www.ncsociology.org/sociationtoday/v71/chore.htm

Oncale v. Sundowner Offshore Services, 523 US 75 (1998).

O'Neill, D. K. (1996). Two-year-old children's sensitivity to a parent's knowledge state when making requests. *Child Development, 67,* 659–677.

Oregon Department of Human Services. (2012). *Oregon's Death with Dignity Act— 2011.* Retrieved from http://www.oregon.gov/DHS/ph/pas/docs/year13.pdf

Orentlicher, D. (2000). The implementation of Oregon's Death with Dignity Act: Reassuring, but more data are needed. *Psychology, Public Policy, and Law, 6,* 489–502.

Organisation for Economic Co-operation and Development. (2006). *Starting strong II: Early childhood education and care.* Paris: OECD.

O'Rourke, N., & Cappeliez, P. (2005). Marital satisfaction and self-deception: Reconstruction of relationship histories among older adults. *Social Behavior and Personality, 33,* 273–282.

Osgood, D. W., Ruth, G., Eccles, J. S., Jacobs, J. E., & Barber, B. L. (2005). Six paths to adulthood: Fast starters, parents without careers, educated partners, educated singles, working singles, and slow starters. In R. A. Settersten, Jr., F. F. Furstenberg, Jr., & R. G. Rumbaut (Eds.), *On the frontier of adulthood: Theory, research, and public policy* (pp. 320–355). Chicago: University of Chicago Press.

Oster-Aaland, L., Lewis, M. A., Neighbors, C., Vangsness, J., & Larimer, M. E. (2009). Alcohol poisoning among colleges students turning 21: Do they recognize the symptoms and how do they help? *Journal of Studies on Alcohol and Drugs* (Suppl. 16), 122–130.

Ostrov, J. M., & Godleski, S. A. (2010). Toward an integrated gender-linked model of aggression subtypes in early and middle childhood. *Psychological Review, 117,* 233–242.

Oswald, A. J., & Wu, S. (2010). Objective confirmation of subjective measures of human well-being: Evidence from the USA. *Science, 327,* 576–579.

Ottaway, A. J. (2010). The impact of parental divorce on the intimate relationships of adult offspring: A review of the literature. *Graduate Journal of Counseling Psychology,* 2(1), Article 5. Retrieved from http://epublications.marquette.edu/gjcp/vol2/iss1/5/

Owen, C. J. (2005). The empty nest transition: The relationship between attachment style and women's use of this period as a time for growth and change. *Dissertation Abstracts International. Section B. Sciences and Engineering,* 65(7-B), 3747.

Ozawa, M. N., & Yoon, H. S. (2002). The economic benefit of remarriage: Gender and class income. *Journal of Divorce & Remarriage, 36,* 21–39.

Paarlberg, K. M., Vingerhoets, A. J. J. M., Passchier, J., Dekker, G. A., & Van Geijn, H. P. (1995). Psychosocial factors and pregnancy outcome: A review with emphasis on methodological issues. *Journal of Psychosomatic Research, 39,* 563–595.

Palkovitz, R., & Palm, G. (2009). Transitions within fathering. *Fathering, 7,* 3–22.

Pankow, L. J., & Solotoroff, J. M. (2007). Biological aspects and theories of aging. In J. A. Blackburn & C. N. Dulmus (Eds.), *Handbook of gerontology: Evidence-based approaches to theory, practice, and policy* (pp. 19–56). Hoboken, NJ: Wiley.

Papa, A., & Litz, B. (2011). Grief. In W. T. O'Donohue & C. Draper (Eds.), *Stepped care and e-health: Practical applications to behavioral disorders* (pp. 223–245). New York: Springer.

Paquette, D. (2004). Theorizing the father–child relationship: Mechanisms and developmental outcomes. *Human Development, 47,* 193–219.

Paraita, H., Díaz, C., & Anllo-Vento, L. (2008). Processing of semantic relations in normal aging and Alzheimer's disease. *Archives of Clinical Neuropsychology, 23,* 33–46.

Parault, S. J., & Schwanenflugel, P. J. (2000). The development of conceptual categories of attention during the elementary school years. *Journal of Experimental Child Psychology, 75,* 245–262.

Parcel, G. S., Simons-Morton, B. G., O'Hara, N. M., Baranowksi, T., Kilbe, L. J., & Bee, D. E. (1989). School promotion of healthful diet and exercise behavior: An

integration of organizational change and social learning theory interventions. *Journal of School Health, 57,* 150–156.

Park, C. L. (2007). Religiousness/spirituality and health: A meaning systems perspective. *Journal of Behavioral Medicine, 30,* 319–328.

Park, D. C., Morrell, R. W., & Shifren, K. (Eds.). (1999). *Processing of medical information in aging patients: Cognitive and human factors perspectives.* Mahwah, NJ: Erlbaum.

Park, D. C., Smith, A. D., Lautenschlager, G., Earles, J. L., Frieski, D., Zwahr, M., & Gaines, C. L. (1996). Mediators of long-term memory performance across the life span. *Psychology and Aging, 11,* 621–637.

Park, G., Lubinski, D., & Benbow, C. P. (2008). Ability differences among people who have commensurate degrees matter for scientific creativity. *Psychological Science, 19,* 957–961.

Parke, R. D., & Buriel, R. (1998). Socialization in the family: Ethnic and ecological perspectives. In W. Damon (Ed.), *Handbook of child psychology* (5th ed., Vol. 3, pp. 463–552). New York: Wiley.

Parke, R. D., Coltrane, S., Duffy, S., Buriel, R., Dennis, J., Powers, J., et al. (2004). Economic stress, parenting, and child adjustment in Mexican American and European American families. *Child Development, 75,* 1632–1656.

Parke, R. D., & O'Neil, R. (2000). The influence of significant others on learning about relationships: From family to friends. In R. S. L. Mills & S. Duck (Eds.), *The developmental psychology of personal relationships* (pp. 15–47). New York: Wiley.

Parker, J. G., & Seal, J. (1996). Forming, losing, renewing, and replacing friendships: Applying temporal parameters to the assessment of children's friendship experiences. *Child Development, 67,* 2248–2268.

Parkman, A. M. (2007). *Smart marriage: Using your (business) head as well as your heart to find wedded bliss.* Westport, CT: Praeger.

Parritz, R. H. (1996). A descriptive analysis of toddler coping in challenging circumstances. *Infant Behavior and Development, 19,* 171–180.

Parrot, A., & Cummings, N. (2006). *Forsaken females: The global brutalization of women.* Lanham, MD: Rowman & Littlefield.

Parten, M. (1932). Social participation among preschool children. *Journal of Abnormal and Social Psychology, 27,* 243–269.

Pascalis, O., de Hann, M., & Nelson, C. A. (2002). Is face processing species-specific during the first year of life? *Science, 296,* 1321–1323.

Pascual, B., Aguardo, G., Sotillo, M., & Masdeu, J. C. (2008). Acquisition of mental state language in Spanish children: A longitudinal study of the relationship between the production of mental verbs and linguistic development. *Developmental Science, 11,* 454–466.

Patrick, S., Sells, J. N., Giordano, F. G., & Tollerud, T. R. (2007). Intimacy, differentiation, and personality variables as predictors of marital satisfaction. *The Family Journal, 15,* 359–367.

Patterson, G. R. (1980). Mothers: The unacknowledged victims. *Monographs of the Society for Research in Child Development, 45*(5, Serial No. 186).

Patterson, G. R. (2008). A comparison of models for interstate wars and for individual violence. *Perspectives on Psychological Science, 3,* 203–223.

Patterson, M. M., & Bigler, R. S. (2006). Preschool children's attention to environmental messages about groups: Social categorization and the origins of intergroup bias. *Child Development, 77,* 847–860.

Pauker, K., Ambady, N., & Apfelbaum, E. P. (2010). Race salience and essentialist thinking in racial stereotype development. *Child Development, 81,* 1799–1813.

Paxton, S. J., Eisenberg, M. E., & Neumark-Sztainer, D. (2006). Prospective predictors of body dissatisfaction in adolescent girls and boys: A five-year longitudinal study. *Developmental Psychology, 42,* 888–899.

Pearlin, L. I., Mullan, J. T., Semple, S. J., & Skaff, M. M. (1990). Caregiving and the stress process: An overview of concepts and their measures. *The Gerontologist, 30,* 583–594.

Pelphrey, K. A., Reznick, J. S., Davis Goldman, B., Sasson, N., Morrow, J., Donahoe, A., & Hodgson, K. (2004). Development of visuospatial memory in the second half of the first year. *Developmental Psychology, 40,* 836–851.

Peltola, M. J., Leppänen, J. M., Palokangas, T., & Hietanen, J. K. (2008). Fearful faces modulate looking duration and attention disengagement in 7-month-old infants. *Developmental Science, 11,* 60–68.

Pelucci, B., Hay, J. F., & Saffran, J. R. (2009). Statistical learning in a natural language by 8-month-old infants. *Child Development, 80,* 674–685.

Pennisi, E. (2005). Why do humans have so few genes? *Science, 309,* 80.

Penson, R. T. (2004). Bereavement across cultures. In R. J. Moore & D. Spiegel (Eds.), *Cancer, culture, and communication* (pp. 241–279). New York: Kluwer/Plenum.

Perkins, D. F., Jacobs, J. E., Barber, B. L., & Eccles, J. S. (2004). Childhood and adolescent sports participation as predictors of participation in sports and physical fitness activities during young adulthood. *Youth & Society, 35,* 495–520.

Perkins, H. W., Linkenbach, J. W., Lewis, M. A., & Neighbors, C. (2010). Effectiveness of social norms media marketing in reducing drinking and driving: A statewide campaign. *Addictive Behaviors, 35,* 866–874.

Perrone, K. M., Tschopp, M. K., Snyder, E. R., Boo, J. N., & Hyatt, C. (2010). Expectations and outcomes of academically talented students 10 and 20 years post–high school graduation. *Journal of Career Development, 36,* 291–309.

Perry, W. I. (1970). *Forms of intellectual and ethical development in the college years.* New York: Holt, Rinehart, & Winston.

Peters, A. M. (1995). Strategies in the acquisition of syntax. In P. Fletcher & B. MacWhinney (Eds.), *The handbook of child language* (pp. 462–483). Oxford, England: Blackwell.

Peterson, L. (1983). Role of donor competence, donor age, and peer presence on helping in an emergency. *Developmental Psychology, 19,* 873–880.

Pettit, G. S., Bates, J. E., & Dodge, K. A. (1997). Supportive parenting, ecological context, and children's adjustment: A seven-year longitudinal study. *Child Development, 68,* 908–923.

Pettito, L. A., Katerelos, M., Levy, B. G., Gauna, K., Tetreault, K., & Ferraro, V. (2001). Bilingual signed and spoken language acquisition from birth: Implications for the mechanisms underlying early bilingual language acquisition. *Journal of Child Language, 28,* 453–496.

Pharr, J. R., Moonie, S., & Bungum, T. J. (2012). The impact of unemployment on mental and physical health, access to health care, and health risk behaviors. *ISRN Public Health.* doi:10.5402/2012/483432

Phelps, J. A., Davis, J. O., & Schartz, K. M. (1997). Nature, nurture, and twin research strategies. *Current Directions in Psychological Science, 6,* 117–121.

Phelps, R. E., & Constantine, M. G. (2001). Hitting the roof: The impact of the glass-ceiling effect on the career development of African Americans. In W. B. Walsh, R. P. Bingham, M. T. Brown, C. M. Ward, & S. Osipow. (Eds.), *Career counseling for African Americans* (pp. 161–175). Mahwah, NJ: Erlbaum.

Phinney, J. (1989). Stage of ethnic identity in minority group adolescents. *Journal of Early Adolescence, 9,* 34–49.

Phinney, J. S. (2005). Ethnic identity development in minority adolescents. In C. B. Fisher & R. M. Lerner (Eds.), *Encyclopedia of applied developmental science* (Vol. 1, pp. 420–423). Thousand Oaks, CA: Sage.

Phipps, M. G., Rosengard, C., Weitzen, S., Meers, A., & Billinkoff, Z. (2008). Age group differences among pregnant adolescents: Sexual behavior, health habits, and contraceptive use. *Journal of Pediatric and Adolescent Gynecology, 21,* 9–15.

Piaget, J., & Inhelder, B. (1956). *The child's conception of space.* Boston: Routledge & Kegan Paul.

Piehler, T. F., & Dishion, T. J. (2007). Interpersonal dynamics within adolescent friendships: Dyadic mutuality, deviant talk, and patterns of antisocial behavior. *Child Development, 78,* 1611–1624.

Pienta, A. M., Hayward, M. D., & Jenkins, K. R. (2000). Health consequences of marriage for the retirement years. *Journal of Family Issues, 21,* 559–586.

Pierret, C. R. (2006). The "sandwich generation": Women caring for parents and children. *Monthly Labor Review, September.* Retrieved from http://www.bls.gov/opub/mlr/2006/09/art1full.pdf

Pillay, H., Kelly, K., & Tones, M. (2006). Career aspirations of older workers: An Australian study. *International Journal of Training and Development, 10,* 298–305.

Pincus, T., Callahan, L. F., & Burkhauser, R. V. (1987). Most chronic diseases are reported more frequently by individuals with fewer than 12 years of formal education in the age 18–64 United States population. *Journal of Chronic Diseases, 40,* 865–874.

Pinkhasov, R. M., Shteynshlyuger, A., Hakimian, P., Lindsay, G. K., Samadi, D. B., & Shabsigh, R. (2010). Are men shortchanged on health? Perspective on life expectancy, morbidity, and mortality in men and women in the United States. *International Journal of Clinical Practice, 64,* 465–474.

Pinto, K. M., & Coltrane, S. (2009). Division of labor in Mexican origin and Anglo families: Structure and culture. *Sex Roles, 60,* 482–495.

Piquet, B. J. (2007). That's what friends are for. *Dissertation Abstracts International. Section B. Sciences and Engineering, 67*(7-B), 4114.

Piscione, D. P. (2004). *The many faces of 21st century working women: A report to the Women's Bureau of the U.S. Department of Labor.* McLean, VA: Education Consortium.

Plomin, R., & Spinath, F. (2004). Intelligence: Genes, genetics, and genomics. *Journal of Personality and Social Psychology, 86,* 112–129.

Plunkett, K. (1996). *Connectionism and development: Neural networks and the study of change.* New York: Oxford University Press.

Polivka, L. (2010). Neoliberalism and the new politics of aging and retirement security. In J. C. Cavanaugh & C. K. Cavanaugh (Eds.), *Aging in America* (Vol. 3, pp. 160–202). Santa Barbara, CA: Praeger Perspectives.

Pollitt, E. (1995). Does breakfast make a difference in school? *Journal of the American Dietetic Association, 95,* 1134–1139.

Popenoe, D. (2009). Cohabitation, marriage, and child wellbeing: A cross-national perspective. *Society: Social Science and Public Policy, 46,* 429–436.

Popp, D., Laursen, B., Kerr, M., Stattin, H., & Burk, W. K. (2008). Modeling homophily over time with an actor–partner interdependence model. *Developmental Psychology, 44,* 1028–1039.

Porter, R. H., & Winberg, J. (1999). Unique salience of maternal breast odors for newborn infants. *Neuroscience & Biobehavioral Reviews, 23,* 439–449.

Poulin, F., & Chan, A. (2010). Friendship stability and change in childhood and adolescence. *Developmental Review, 30,* 257–272.

Power, T. L., & Smith, S. M. (2008). Predictors of fear of death and self-mortality: An Atlantic Canadian perspective. *Death Studies, 32,* 252–272.

Pratt, H. D. (2010). Perspectives from a non-traditional mentor. In C. A. Rayburn, F. L. Denmark, M. E. Reuder, & A. M. Austria (Eds.), *A handbook for women mentors: Transcending barriers of stereotype, race, and ethnicity* (pp. 223–232). Santa Barbara, CA: ABC-CLIO.

Pratt, M. W., Danso, H. A., Arnold, M. L., Norris, J. E., & Filyer, R. (2001). Adult generativity and the socialization of adolescents: Relations to mothers' and fathers' parenting beliefs, styles, and practices. *Journal of Personality, 69,* 89–120.

President's Council on Physical Fitness and Sports. (2004). Physical activity for children: Current patterns and guidelines. *Research Digest, 5*(2).

Pressley, M., & Hilden, K. (2006). Cognitive strategies. In W. Damon & R. M. Lerner (Eds.), *Handbook of child psychology* (6th ed., Vol. 2, pp. 511–556). Hoboken, NJ: Wiley.

Prinstein, M. J., & Cillessen, A. H. N. (2003). Forms and functions of adolescent peer aggression associated with high levels of peer status. *Merrill Palmer Quarterly, 49,* 310–342.

Prinstein, M. J., & La Greca, A. M. (2004). Childhood peer rejection and aggression as predictors of adolescent girls' externalizing and health risk behaviors: A 6-year longitudinal study. *Journal of Consulting and Clinical Psychology, 72,* 103–112.

Probert, B. (2005). "I just couldn't fit it in": Gender and unequal outcomes in academic careers. *Gender, Work & Organization, 12,* 50–72.

Pruchno, R. (1999). Raising grandchildren: The experiences of black and white grandmothers. *The Gerontologist, 39,* 209–221.

Pruett, M. K., Cowan, C. P., Cowan, P. A., & Diamond, J. S. (2012). Supporting father involvement in the context of separation and divorce. In K. Kuehnle & L. Drozd (Eds.), *Parenting plan evaluations: Applied research for the family court* (pp. 123–153). New York: Oxford University Press.

Pruett, M. K., Insabella, G. M., & Gustafson, K. (2005). The collaborative divorce project: A court-based intervention for separating parents with young children. *Family Court Review, 43,* 38–51.

Prus, S. G., Tfaily, R., & Lin, Z. (2010). Comparing racial and immigrant health status and health care access in late life in Canada and the United States. *Canadian Journal on Aging, 29,* 383–395.

Puhl, R. M., & Brownell, K. D. (2005). Bulimia nervosa. In C. B. Fisher & R. M. Lerner (Eds.), *Encyclopedia of applied developmental science* (Vol. 1, pp. 192–195). Thousand Oaks, CA: Sage.

Puhl, R. M., & Latner, J. D. (2007). Stigma, obesity, and the health of the nation's children. *Psychological Bulletin, 133,* 557–580.

Purcell, D., MacArthur, K. R., & Samblanet, S. (2010). Gender and the glass ceiling at work. *Sociology Compass, 4,* 705–717.

Pynoos, J., Caraviello, R., & Cicero, C. (2010). Housing in an aging America. In J. C. Cavanaugh & C. K. Cavanaugh (Eds.), *Aging in America* (Vol. 3, pp. 129–159). Santa Barbara, CA: Praeger Perspectives.

Qualls, S. H., & Layton, H. (2010). Mental health and adjustment. In J. C. Cavanaugh & C. K. Cavanaugh (Eds.), *Aging in America* (Vol. 2, pp. 171–187). Santa Barbara, CA: Praeger Perspectives.

Quillian, L., & Campbell, M. E. (2003). Beyond black and white: The present and future of multiracial friendship segregation. *American Sociological Review, 68,* 540–566.

Quinn, P. C., & Liben, L. S. (2008). A sex difference in mental rotation in young infants. *Psychological Science, 19,* 1067–1070.

Quirin, M., Loktyushin, A., Arndt, J., Küstermann, E., Lo, Y.-Y., Kuhl, J., et al. (2012). Existential neuroscience: A functional magnetic resonance imaging investigation of neural responses to reminders of one's mortality. *Social Cognitive and Affective Neuroscience, 7,* 193–198.

Racz, S. J., & McMahon, R. J. (2011). The relationship between parental knowledge and monitoring and child and adolescent conduct problems: A 10-year-update. *Clinical Child and Family Psychology Review, 14,* 377–398.

Radford, A. (1995). Phrase structure and functional categories. In P. Fletcher & B. MacWhinney (Eds.), *The handbook of child language* (pp. 483–507). Oxford, England: Blackwell.

Raedeke, T. D., & Smith, A. L. (2004). Coping resources and athlete burnout: An examination of stress mediated and moderation hypotheses. *Journal of Sport & Exercise Psychology, 26,* 525–541.

Ragins, B. R., Cotton, J. L., & Miller, J. S. (2000). Marginal mentoring: The effects of type of mentor, quality of relationship, and program design on work and career attitudes. *Academy of Management Journal, 43,* 1177–1194.

Raikes, H., Luze, G., Brooks-Gunn, J., Raikes, H., Pan, B. A., Tamis-LeMonda, C. S., et al. (2006). Mother–child bookreading in low-income families: Correlates and outcomes during the first three years of life. *Child Development, 77,* 924–953.

Rakic, P. (1995). Corticogenesis in human and nonhuman primates. In M. S. Gazzaniga (Ed.), *The cognitive neurosciences.* Cambridge, MA: MIT Press.

Rakison, D. H., & Hahn, E. R. (2004). The mechanisms of early categorization and induction: Smart or dumb infants? *Advances in Child Development and Behavior, 32,* 281–322.

Rakoczy, H. (2008). Taking fiction seriously: Young children understand the normative structure of joint pretense games. *Developmental Psychology, 44,* 1195–1201.

Ralph, L. J., & Brindis, C. D. (2010). Access to reproductive healthcare for adolescents: establishing healthy behaviors at a critical juncture in the lifecourse. *Current Opinion in Obstetrics and Gynecology, 22,* 369–374.

Ransjoe-Arvidson, A. B., Matthiesen, A. S., Lilja, G., Nissen, E., Widstroem, A. M., & Uvnaes-Moberg, K. (2001). Maternal analgesia during labor disturbs newborn behavior: Effects on breastfeeding, temperature, and crying. *Birth: Issues in Perinatal Care, 28,* 5–12.

Ranwez, S., Leidig, T., & Crampes, M. (2000). Formalization to improve lifelong learning. *Journal of Interactive Learning Research, 11,* 389–409.

Rape, Abuse, and Incest National Network. (2010). *Statistics.* Retrieved from http://www.rainn.org/statistics

Rapport, M. D. (1995). Attention-deficit hyperactivity disorder. In M. Hersen & R. T. Ammerman (Eds.), *Advanced abnormal child psychology.* Hillsdale, NJ: Erlbaum.

Raschick, M., & Ingersoll-Dayton, B. (2004). The costs and rewards of caregiving among aging spouses and adult children. *Family Relations, 53,* 317–325.

Rathunde, K. R., & Csikszentmihalyi, M. (1993). Undivided interest and the growth of talent: A longitudinal study of adolescents. *Journal of Youth and Adolescence, 22,* 385–405.

Rawlins, W. K. (2004). Friendships in later life. In J. F. Nussbaum & J. Coupland (Eds.), *Handbook of communication and aging research* (2nd ed., pp. 273–299). Mahwah, NJ: Erlbaum.

Rayner, K., Foorman, B. R., Perfetti, C. A., Pesetsky, D., & Seidenberg, M. S. (2001). How psychological science informs the teaching of reading. *Psychological Science in the Public Interest, 2,* 31–75.

Real, K., Mitnick, A. D., & Maloney, W. F. (2010). More similar than different: Millennials in the U.S. building trades. *Journal of Business and Psychology, 25,* 303–313.

Reesman, M. C., & Hogan, J. D. (2005). Substance use and abuse across the life span. In C. B. Fisher & R. M. Lerner (Eds.), *Encyclopedia of applied developmental science* (pp. 1069–1072). Thousand Oaks, CA: Sage.

Reich, P. A. (1986). *Language development.* Englewood Cliffs, NJ: Prentice Hall.

Reimer, M. S. (1996). "Sinking into the ground": The development and consequences of shame in adolescence. *Developmental Review, 16,* 321–363.

Reis, S. M., & Renzulli, J. S. (2010). Is there still a need for gifted education? An examination of current research. *Learning and Individual Differences, 20,* 308–317.

Remedios, J. D., Chasteen, A. L., & Packer, D. J. (2010). Sunny side up: The reliance on positive age stereotypes in descriptions of future older selves. *Self and Identity, 9,* 257–275.

Renaud, J., Berlim, M. T., McGirr, A., Tousignant, M., & Turecki, G. (2008). Current psychiatry morbidity, aggression/impulsivity, and personality dimensions in child and adolescent suicide: A case-control study. *Journal of Affective Disorders, 105,* 221–228.

Renshaw, K. D., Rodrigues, C., & Jones, D. H. (2008). Psychological symptoms and marital satisfaction in spouses of Operation Iraqi Freedom veterans: Relationships with spouses' perceptions of veterans' experiences and symptoms. *Journal of Family Psychology, 22,* 586–594.

Repacholi, B. M. (1998). Infants' use of attentional cues to identify the referent of another person's emotional expression. *Developmental Psychology, 34,* 1017–1025.

Reuter-Lorenz, P. A., & Park, D. C. (2010). Human neuroscience and the aging mind: A new look at old problems. *Journal of Gerontology: Psychological Sciences, 65B,* P405–P415.

Reville, B. (2011). Utilization of palliative care: Providers still hinder access. *Health Policy Newsletter, 24*(1). Retrieved from http://jdc.jefferson.edu/cgi/viewcontent.cgi?article51714&context5hpn

Reyes, H. L. M., Foshee, V. A., Bauer, D. J., & Ennett, S. T. (2011). The role of heavy alcohol use in the developmental process of desisting aggression during adolescence. *Journal of Abnormal Child Psychology, 39,* 239–250.

Reyna, V. F., & Farley, F. (2006). Risk and rationality in adolescent decision making. *Psychological Science in the Public Interest, 7,* 1–44.

Reynolds, A. J., & Robertson, D. L. (2003). School-based early intervention and later child maltreatment in the Chicago Longitudinal Study. *Child Development, 74,* 3–26.

Rhoades, G. K., Stanley, S. M., & Markman, H. J. (2009). Couples' reasons for cohabitation: Associations with individual well-being and relationship quality. *Journal of Family Issues, 30,* 233–258.

Rhoades, K. A. (2008). Children's responses to interparental conflict: A meta-analysis of their associations with child adjustment. *Child Development, 79,* 1942–1956.

Ribe, E. M., Heidt, L., Beaubier, N., & Troy, C. M. (2011). Molecular mechanisms of neuronal death. *Neurochemical Mechanisms in Disease, 1,* 17–47.

Ricciardelli, L. A., & McCabe, M. P. (2004). A biopsychosocial model of disordered eating and the pursuit of muscularity in adolescent boys. *Psychological Bulletin, 130,* 179–205.

Ricciuti, H. N. (1993). Nutrition and mental development. *Current Directions in Psychological Science, 2,* 43–46.

Rice, N. E., Lang, I. A., Henley, W., & Melzer, D. (2010). Common health predictors of early retirement: Findings from the English Longitudinal Study of Ageing. *Age and Ageing, 40,* 54–61.

Richmond, J., & Nelson, C. A. (2007). Accounting for change in declarative memory: A cognitive neuroscience perspective. *Developmental Review, 27,* 349–373.

Richters, J. E., Arnold, L. E., Jensen, P. S., Abikoff, H., Conners, C. K., & Greenhill, L. L., et al. (1995). NIMH collaborative multisite multimodal treatment study of children with ADHD: I. Background and rationale. *Journal of the American Academy of Child & Adolescent Psychiatry, 34,* 987–1000.

Rijken, A. J. (2009). *Happy families, high fertility? Childbearing choices in the context of family and partner relationships.* (Unpublished doctoral dissertation). University of Utrecht, Utrecht, the Netherlands.

Riley, L. D., & Bowen, C. (2005). The sandwich generation: Challenges and coping strategies of multigenerational family. *Counseling & Therapy for Couples & Families, 13,* 52–58.

Riley, M. W. (1979). Introduction. In M. W. Riley (Ed.), *Aging from birth to death: Interdisciplinary perspectives* (pp. 3–14). Boulder, CO: Westview Press.

Risacher, S. L., & Saykin, A. J. (2011). Neuroimaging of Alzheimer's disease, mild cognitive impairment, and other dementias. In R. A. Cohen & H. L. Sweet (Eds.), *Brain imaging in behavioral medicine and clinical neuroscience* (pp. 309–339). New York: Springer.

Roberson, E. D. (2011). Contemporary approaches to Alzheimer's disease and frontotemporal dementia. In E. D. Roberson (Ed.), *Alzheimer's disease and frontotemporal dementia: Methods and protocols* (pp. 1–9). New York: Humana Press.

Roberts, J. A. (2007). Developing an explanatory model of the chronicity of psychologically aggressive behavior among coupled gay and bisexual men. *Dissertation Abstracts International. Section A. Humanities and Social Sciences, 68*(2-A), 739.

Roberts, J. E., Burchinal, M., & Durham, M. (1999). Parents' report of vocabulary and grammatical development of African American preschoolers: Child and environmental associations. *Child Development, 70,* 92–106.

Roberts, R. E., Phinney, J. S., Masse, L. C., Chen, Y. R., Roberts, C. R., & Romero, A. (1999). The structure of ethnic identity of young adolescents from diverse ethnocultural groups. *Journal of Early Adolescence, 19,* 301–322.

Robertson, A. (2006). *Aging changes in the female reproductive system.* Retrieved from http://www.nlm.nih.gov/medlineplus/ency/article/004016.htm

Robertson, K., & Murachver, T. (2007). It takes two to tangle: Gender symmetry in intimate partner violence. *Basic and Applied Social Psychology, 29,* 109–118.

Robson, S. M., Hansson, R. O., Abalos, A., & Booth, M. (2006). Successful aging: Criteria for aging well in the workplace. *Journal of Career Development, 33,* 156–177.

Roby, A. C., & Kidd, E. (2008). The referential communication skills of children with imaginary companions. *Developmental Science, 11,* 531–540.

Roche, K. M., Ghazarian, S. R., Little, T. D., & Leventhal, T. (2011). Understanding links between punitive parenting and adolescent adjustment: The relevance of context and reciprocal associations. *Journal of Research on Adolescence, 21,* 448–460.

Rodeck, C. H., & Whittle, M. J. (Eds.). (2009). *Fetal medicine: Basic science and clinical practice.* London: Churchill Livingstone.

Rodrigue, K. M., Kennedy, K. M., & Park, D. C. (2009). Beta-amyloid deposition and the aging brain. *Neuropsychology Review, 19,* 436–450.

Roe, C. M., Fagan, A. M., Williams, M. M., Ghoshal, N., Aeschleman, M., Grant, E. A., et al. (2011). Improving CSF biomarker accuracy in predicting prevalent and incident Alzheimer disease. *Neurology, 76,* 501–510.

Roffwarg, H. P., Muzio, J. N., & Dement, W. C. (1966). Ontogenetic development of the human sleep–dream cycle. *Science, 152,* 604–619.

Rogers, S. D. (2010). Health promotion and chronic disease management. In J. C. Cavanaugh & C. K. Cavanaugh (Eds.), *Aging in America* (Vol. 2, pp. 57–80). Santa Barbara, CA: Praeger Perspectives.

Rogoff, B., Mistry, J., Goncu, A., & Mosier, C. (1993). Guided participation in cultural activity by toddlers and caregivers. *Monographs of the Society for Research in Child Development, 58* (Serial No. 236).

Rogosch, F. A., Cicchetti, D., Shields, A., & Toth, S. L. (1995). Parenting dysfunction in child maltreatment. In M. H. Bornstein (Ed.), *Handbook of parenting* (Vol. 4, pp. 127–159). Mahwah, NJ: Erlbaum.

Rönnqvist, L., & Domellöff, E. (2006). Quantitative assessment of right and left reaching movements in infants: A longitudinal study from 6 to 36 months. *Developmental Psychobiology, 48,* 444–459.

Roosevelt, F. D. (1935). *Statement on signing the Social Security Act.* Retrieved from http://docs.fdrlibrary.marist.edu/odssast.html

Roper, L. L. (2007). Air force single parent mothers and maternal separation anxiety. *Dissertation Abstracts International. Section A. Humanities and Social Sciences, 67*(11-A), 4349.

Roper v. Simmons, 543 U.S. 551 (2005).

Rose, A. J., & Asher, S. R. (1999). Children's goals and strategies in response to conflicts within a friendship. *Developmental Psychology, 35,* 69–79.

Rose, A. J., Carlson, W., & Waller, E. M. (2007). Prospective associations of co-rumination with friendship and emotional adjustment: Considering the socioemotional trade-offs of co-rumination. *Developmental Psychology, 43,* 1019–1031.

Rose, A. J., & Rudolph, K. D. (2006). A review of sex differences in peer relationship processes: Potential trade-offs for the emotional and behavioral development of girls and boys. *Psychological Bulletin, 132,* 98–131.

Rose, D. M., & Gordon, R. (2010). Retention practices for engineering and technical professionals in an Australian public agency. *Australian Journal of Public Administration, 69,* 314–325.

Rose, S. A., Feldman, J. F., & Jankowski, J. J. (2009). Information processing in toddlers: Continuity from infancy and persistence of preterm deficits. *Intelligence, 37,* 311–320.

Rose, S., & Zand, D. (2000). Lesbian dating and courtship from young adulthood to midlife. *Journal of Gay and Lesbian Social Services, 11,* 77–104.

Rosenbaum, J. L., Smith, J. R., & Zollfrank, B. C. C. (2011). Neonatal end-of-life spiritual support care. *Journal of Perinatal and Neonatal Nursing, 25,* 61–69.

Rosenblatt, P. C. (1996). Grief that does not end. In D. Klass, P. R. Silverman, & S. L. Nickman (Eds.), *Continuing bonds: New understandings of grief* (pp. 45–58). Washington, DC: Taylor & Francis.

Rosenblatt, P. C. (2001). A social constructivist perspective on cultural differences in grief. In M. S. Stroebe, R. O. Hansson, W. Stroebe, & H. Schut (Eds.), *Handbook of bereavement research: Consequences, coping, and care* (pp. 285–300). Washington, DC: American Psychological Association.

Rosengren, K. S., Gelman, S. A., Kalish, C., & McCormick, M. (1991). As time goes by: Children's early understanding of growth in animals. *Child Development, 62,* 1302–1320.

Rosso, B. D., Dekas, K. H., & Wrzesniewski, A. (2010). On the meaning of work: A theoretical integration and review. *Research in Organizational Behavior, 30,* 91–127.

Rostenstein, D., & Oster, H. (1997). Differential facial responses to four basic tastes in newborns. In P. Ekman & E. L. Rosenberg (Eds.), *What the face reveals: Basic and applied studies of spontaneous expression using the Facial Action Coding System (FACS). Series in affective science.* New York: Oxford University Press.

Roszko, E. (2010). Commemoration and the state: Memory and legitimacy in Vietnam. *Sojourn: Journal of Social Issues in Southeast Asia, 25,* 1–28.

Rothbart, M. K. (2007). Temperament, development, and personality. *Current Directions in Psychological Science, 16,* 207–212.

Rothbart, M. K., & Rueda, M. R. (2005). The development of effortful control. In U. Mayr, E. Awh, & S. W. Keele (Eds.), *Developing individuality in the human brain: A tribute to Michael I. Posner* (pp. 167–188). Washington, DC: American Psychological Association.

Rothbart, M. K., & Sheese, B. E. (2007). Temperament and emotion regulation. In J. J. Gross (Ed.), *Handbook of emotion regulation* (pp. 331–350). New York: Guilford.

Rothblum, E. D. (2009). An overview of same-sex couples in relationships: A research area still at sea. *Nebraska Symposium on Motivation, 54,* 113–139.

Rotherman-Borus, M. J., & Langabeer, K. A. (2001). Developmental trajectories of gay, lesbian, and bisexual youths. In A. R. D'Augelli & C. Patterson (Eds.), *Lesbian, gay, and bisexual identities among youth: Psychological perspectives* (pp. 97–128). New York: Oxford University Press.

Rovee-Collier, C. (1987). Learning and memory in infancy. In J. D. Osofsky (Ed.), *Handbook of infant development* (2nd ed., pp. 98–148). New York: Wiley.

Rovee-Collier, C. (1997). Dissociations in infant memory: Rethinking the development of implicit and explicit memory. *Psychological Review, 104,* 467–498.

Rovee-Collier, C. (1999). The development of infant memory. *Current Directions in Psychological Science, 8,* 80–85.

Rowe, M. M., & Sherlock, H. (2005). Stress and verbal abuse in nursing: Do burned out nurses eat their young? *Journal of Nursing Management, 13,* 242–248.

Roxburgh, S. (2002). Racing through life: The distribution of time pressures by roles and roles resources among full-time workers. *Journal of Family and Economic Issues, 23,* 121–145.

Rubin, K. H., Bukowski, W., & Parker, J. G. (1998). Peer interactions, relationships, and groups. In W. Damon (Ed.), *Handbook of child psychology* (5th ed., Vol. 3, pp. 619–700). New York: Wiley.

Rubin, K. H., Bukowski, W., & Parker, J. (2006). Peer interaction and social competence. In N. Eisenberg, W. Damon, & R. M. Lerner (Eds.), *Handbook of child psychology* (6th ed., Vol. 3, pp. 571–645). Hoboken, NJ: Wiley.

Rubin, K. H., Coplan, R. J., & Bowker, J. C. (2009). Social withdrawal in childhood. *Annual Review of Psychology, 60,* 141–171.

Rubin, K. H., Stewart, S., & Chen, X. (1995). Parents of aggressive and withdrawn children. In M. H. Bornstein (Ed.), *Handbook of parenting* (Vol. 1, pp. 255–284). Mahwah, NJ: Erlbaum.

Rubin, S. S. (1996). The wounded family: Bereaved parents and the impact of adult child loss. In D. Klass, P. R. Silverman, & S. L. Nickman (Eds.), *Continuing bonds: New understandings of grief* (pp. 217–232). Washington, DC: Taylor & Francis.

Rubin, S. S., & Malkinson, R. (2001). Parental response to child loss across the life cycle: Clinical and research perspectives. In M. S. Stroebe, R. O. Hansson, W. Stroebe, & H. Schut (Eds.), *Handbook of bereavement research: Consequences, coping, and care* (pp. 219-240). Washington, DC: American Psychological Association.

Ruble, D. N., Martin, C. L., & Berenbaum, S. A. (2006). Gender development. In N. Eisenberg, W. Damon, & R. M. Lerner (Eds.), *Handbook of child psychology* (6th ed., Vol. 3, pp. 858–932). Hoboken, NJ: Wiley.

Rudolph, K. D., Ladd, G., & Dinella, L. (2007). Gender differences in the interpersonal consequences of early-onset depressive symptoms. *Merrill-Palmer Quarterly, 53,* 461–488.

Rudolph, K. D., Troop-Gordon, W., & Flynn, M. (2009). Relational victimization predicts children's social-cognitive and self-regulatory responses in a challenging peer context. *Developmental Psychology, 45,* 1444–1454.

Ruppanner, L. E. (2010). Cross-national reports of housework: An investigation of the gender empowerment measure. *Social Science Research, 19,* 963–975.

Rushton, J. P., & Bons, T. A. (2005). Mate choice and friendship in twins. *Psychological Science, 16,* 555–559.

Russell, A., & Finnie, V. (1990). Preschool children's social status and maternal instructions to assist group entry. *Developmental Psychology, 26,* 603–611.

Russo, R. (Ed.). (2008). *A healing touch: True stories of life, death, and hospice.* Camden, ME: Down East Books.

Rutland, A., Killen, M., & Abrams, D. (2010). A new social-cognitive developmental perspective on prejudice: The interplay between morality and group identity. *Perspectives on Psychological Science, 5,* 279–291.

Rutter, M. (2007). Gene–environment interdependence. *Developmental Science, 10,* 12–18.

Rwampororo, R. K. (2001). Social support: Its mediation of gendered patterns in work–family stress and health for dual-earner couples. *Dissertation Abstract International. Section A. Humanities and Social Sciences, 61*(9-A), 3792.

Ryan, M. K., Haslam, S. A., & Kulich, C. (2010). Politics and the glass cliff: Evidence that women are preferentially selected to contest hard-to-win seats. *Psychology of Women Quarterly, 34,* 56–64.

Rye, M. S., Folck, C. D., Heim, T. A., Olszewski, B. T., & Traina, E. (2004). Forgiveness of an ex-spouse: How does it relate to mental health following a divorce? *Journal of Divorce & Remarriage, 41,* 31–51.

Rymer, R. (1993). *Genie.* New York: HarperCollins.

Sabia, S., Guéguen, A., Marmot, M. G., Shipley, M. J., Ankri, J., & Singh-Manoux, A. (2010). Does cognition predict mortality in midlife? Results from the Whitehall II cohort study. *Neurobiology of Aging, 31,* 688–695.

Saffran, J. R., Aslin, R. N., & Newport, E. L. (1996). Statistical learning by 8-month-old infants. *Science, 274,* 1926–1928.

Sagi, A., Koren-Karie, N., Gini, M., Ziv, Y., & Joels, T. (2002). Shedding further light on the effects of various types and quality of early child care on infant–mother attachment relationship: The Haifa study of early child care. *Child Development, 73,* 1166–1186.

Saginak, K. A., & Saginak, M. A. (2005). Balancing work and family: Equity, gender, and marital satisfaction. *The Family Journal, 13,* 162–166.

Sahin, E., & DePinho, R. A. (2010). Linking functional decline of telomeres, mitochondria and stem cells during ageing. *Nature, 464,* 520–528.

Sahni, R., Fifer, W. P., & Myers, M. M. (2007). Identifying infants at risk for sudden infant death syndrome. *Current Opinion in Pediatrics, 19,* 145–149.

Sakraida, T. J. (2005). Divorce transition differences of midlife women. *Issues in Mental Health Nursing, 26,* 225–249.

Salmivalli, C., & Isaacs, J. (2005). Prospective relations among victimization, rejection, friendlessness, and children's self- and peer-perceptions. *Child Development, 76,* 1161–1171.

Salovey, P., & Grewal, D. (2005). The science of emotional intelligence. *Current Directions in Psychological Science, 14,* 281–285.

Salthouse, T. A. (2000). Steps toward the explanation of adult age differences in cognition. In T. Perfect & E. Maylor (Eds.), *Theoretical debate in cognitive aging* (pp. 19–49). Oxford, England: Oxford University Press.

Salthouse, T. A. (2006). Mental exercise and mental aging. *Perspectives on Psychological Science, 1,* 68–87.

Salthouse, T. A. (2010a). Influence of age on practice effects in longitudinal neurocognitive change. *Neuropsychology, 24,* 563–572.

Salthouse, T. A. (2010b). *Major issues in cognitive aging.* New York: Oxford University Press.

Sandler, I. N., Wolchik, S. A., & Ayers, T. S. (2008). Resilience rather than recovery: A contextual framework on adaptation following bereavement. *Death Studies, 32,* 59–73.

Sangrador, J. L., & Yela, C. (2000). "What is beautiful is loved": Physical attractiveness in love relationships in a representative sample. *Social Behavior and Personality, 28,* 207–218.

Sangrigoli, S., Pallier, C., Argenti, A.-M., Ventureyra, V. A. G., & de Schonen, S. (2005). Reversibility of the other-race effect in face recognition during childhood. *Psychological Science, 16,* 440–444.

Sann, C., & Streri, A. (2007). Perception of object shape and texture in human newborns: Evidence from cross-modal transfer tasks. *Developmental Science, 10,* 399–410.

Saudino, K. J. (2009). Do different measures tap the same genetic influences? A multi-method study of activity level in young twins. *Developmental Science, 12,* 626–633.

Saudino, K. J., & Plomin, R. (2007). Why are hyperactivity and academic achievement related? *Child Development, 78,* 972–986.

Savage-Rumbaugh, E. S. (2001). *Apes, language, and the human mind.* New York: Oxford University Press.

Savani, K., Morris, M. W., Naidu, N. V. R., Kumas, S., & Berlia, N. V. (2011). Cultural conditioning: Understanding interpersonal accommodation in India and the United States in terms of the modal characteristics of interpersonal influence situations. *Journal of Personality and Social Psychology, 100,* 84–102.

Saxe, G. B. (1988). The mathematics of child street vendors. *Child Development, 59,* 1415–1425.

Saxon, S. V., & Etten, M. J. (1994). *Physical changes and aging* (3rd ed.). New York: Tiresias.

Scandura, T. A., & Williams, E. A. (2004). Mentoring and transformational leadership: The role of supervisory career mentoring. *Journal of Vocational Behavior, 65,* 448–468.

Scarr, S. (1992). Developmental theories for the 1990s: Development and individual differences. *Child Development, 63,* 1–19.

Scarr, S., & McCartney, K. (1983). How people make their own environments: A theory of genotype environment effects. *Child Development, 54,* 424–435.

Schaefer, D. R., Simpkins, S. D., Vest, A E., & Price, C. D. (2011). The contribution of extracurricular activities to adolescent friendships: New insights through social network analysis. *Developmental Psychology, 47,* 1141–1152.

Schaie, K. W., & Zanjani, F. (2006). Intellectual development across adulthood. In C. Hoare (Ed.), *Handbook of adult development and learning* (pp. 99–122). New York: Oxford University Press.

Scheibe, S., Kunzmann, U., & Baltes, P. B. (2007). Wisdom, life longings, and optimal development. In J. A. Blackburn & C. N. Dulmus (Eds.), *Handbook of gerontology: Evidence-based approaches to theory, practice, and policy* (pp. 117–142). Hoboken, NJ: Wiley.

Scheidt, R. J., & Schwarz, B. (2010). Environmental gerontology: A sampler of issues and applications. In J. C. Cavanaugh & C. K. Cavanaugh (Eds.), *Aging in America* (Vol. 1, pp. 156–176). Santa Barbara, CA: Praeger Perspectives.

Scherf, K. S., Behrmann, M., Humphreys, K., & Luna, B. (2007). Visual category-selectivity for faces, places and objects emerges along different developmental trajectories. *Developmental Science, 10,* F15–F30.

Schermerhorn, A. C., Chow, S., & Cummings, E. M. (2010). Developmental family processes and interparental conflict: Patterns of microlevel influences. *Developmental Psychology, 46,* 869–885.

Schlossberg, N. K. (2004). *Retire smart, retire happy: Finding your true path in life.* Washington, DC: American Psychological Association.

Schmeeckle, M., Giarusso, R., & Wang, Q. (1998, November). *When being a brother or sister is important to one's identity: Life stage and gender differences.* Paper presented at the annual meeting of the Gerontological Society, Philadelphia.

Schmidt, F. L., & Hunter, J. E. (1998). The validity and utility of selection methods in personnel psychology: Practical and theoretical implications of 85 years of research findings. *Psychological Bulletin, 124,* 262–274.

Schmidt, F. L., & Hunter, J. E. (2004). General mental ability in the world of work: Occupational attainment and job performance. *Journal of Personality and Social Psychology, 86,* 162–173.

Schmithorst, V. J., & Yuan, W. (2010). White matter development during adolescence as shown by diffusion MRI. *Brain & Cognition, 72,* 16–25.

Schmitt, D. P., Alcalay, L., Allensworth, M., Allik, J., Ault, L., Austers, I., et al. (2004). Patterns and universals of adult romantic attachment across 62 cultural regions: Are models of self and of other pancultural constructs? *Journal of Cross-Cultural Psychology, 35,* 367–402.

Schmitt, D. P., Youn, G., Bond, B., Brooks, S., Frye, H., Johnson, S., et al. (2009). When will I feel love? The effects of culture, personality, and gender on the psychological tendency to love. *Journal of Research in Personality, 43,* 830–846.

Schneider, B. A., Pichora-Fuller, K., & Daneman, M. (2010). Effects of senescent changes in audition and cognition on spoken language comprehension. In S. Gordon-Salant, R. D. Frisina, A. N. Popper, & R. R. Fay (Eds.), *The aging auditory system* (pp. 167–210). New York: Springer.

Schneider, E. L., & Davidson, L. (2003). Physical health and adult well-being. In the Center for Child Well-Being (Ed.), *Well-being: Positive development across the life course* (pp. 407–423). Mahwah, NJ: Erlbaum.

Schneider, W., & Bjorklund, D. F. (1998). Memory. In W. Damon (Ed.), *Handbook of child psychology* (5th ed., Vol. 2, pp. 467–521). New York: Wiley.

Schneider, W., & Pressley, M. (1997). *Memory development between 2 and 20* (2nd ed.). Mahwah, NJ: Erlbaum.

Schneiders, J., Nicolson, N. A., Berkhof, J., Feron, F. J., van Os, J., & deVries, M. W. (2006). Mood reactivity to daily negative events in early adolescence: Relationship to risk for psychopathology. *Developmental Psychology, 42,* 543–554.

Schott, W. (2010). *Going back part-time: Federal leave legislation and women's return to work.* Population Research and Policy Review, 31,1-30. Retrieved from http://www.sas.upenn.edu/~wschott/Schott-Part-time-return-052010.pdf

Schulman, E. A., & Hohler, A. D. (2012). The American Academy of Neurology position statement on abuse and violence. *Neurology, 78,* 433–435.

Schulte, H. A. (2006). Family of origin and sibling influence on the experience of social support in adult friendships. *Dissertation Abstracts International. Section B. Sciences and Engineering, 67*(6-B), 3510.

Schwartz, C. R., & Graf, N. L. (2009). Assortative matching among same-sex and different-sex couples in the United States. *Demographic Research, 21,* 843–878.

Schwarzer, G., Zauner, N., & Jovanovic, B. (2007). Evidence of a shift from featural to configural face processing in infancy. *Developmental Science, 10,* 452–463.

Schwarzer, R. (2008). Modeling health behavior change: How to predict and modify the adoption and maintenance of health behaviors. *Applied Psychology: An International Review, 57,* 1–29.

Segrin, C., Taylor, M. E., & Altman, J. (2005). Social cognitive mediators and relational outcomes associated with parental divorce. *Journal of Social and Personal Relationships, 22,* 361–377.

Seidl, A., & Johnson, E. L. (2006). Infants' word segmentation revisited: Edge alignment facilitates target extraction. *Developmental Science, 9,* 565–573.

Seifer, R., Schiller, M., Sameroff, A. J., Resnick, S., & Riordan, K. (1996). Attachment, maternal sensitivity, and infant temperament during the first year of life. *Developmental Psychology, 32,* 12–25.

Selman, R. L. (1980). *The growth of interpersonal understanding: Development and clinical analyses.* New York: Academic Press.

Selman, R. L. (1981). The child as a friendship philosopher: A case study in the growth of interpersonal understanding. In S. R. Asher & J. M. Gottman (Eds.), *The development of children's friendships.* Cambridge, England: Cambridge University Press.

Sénéchal, M., & LeFevre, J. (2002). Parental involvement in the development of children's reading skill: A five-year longitudinal study. *Child Development, 73,* 445–460.

Sénéchal, M., Thomas, E., & Monker, J. (1995). Individual differences in 4-year-old children's acquisition of vocabulary during storybook reading. *Journal of Educational Psychology, 87,* 218–229.

Serbin, L. A., Poulin-Dubois, D., Colburne, K. A., Sen, M. G., & Eichstedt, J. A. (2001). Gender stereotyping in infancy: Visual preferences for and knowledge of gender-stereotyped toys in the second year. *International Journal of Behavioral Development, 25,* 7–15.

Serbin, L. A., Powlishta, K. K., & Gulko, J. (1993). The development of sex typing in middle childhood. *Monographs of the Society for Research in Child Development, 58* (Serial No. 232).

Servaty-Seib, H. L., & Taub, D. J. (2010). Bereavement and college students: The role of counseling psychology. *The Counseling Psychologist, 38,* 947–975.

Seward, R. R., Yeatts, D. E., Amin, I., & DeWitt, A. (2006). Employment leave and fathers' involvement with children: According to mothers and fathers. *Men and Masculinities, 8,* 405–427.

Seyda, B. A., & Fitzsimons, A. M. (2010). Infant deaths. In C. A. Corr & D. A. Balk (Eds.), *Children's encounters with death, bereavement, and coping* (pp. 83–107). New York: Springer.

Seyfarth, R., & Cheney, D. (1996). Inside the mind of a monkey. In M. Bekoff & D. Jamieson (Eds.), *Readings in animal cognition* (pp. 337–343). Cambridge, MA: MIT Press.

Shalev, R. (1999). *Comparison of war–bereaved and motor vehicle accident–bereaved parents* (Unpublished master's thesis). University of Haifa, Haifa, Israel.

Shanahan, L., McHale, S. M., Crouter, A. C., & Osgood, D. (2007). Warmth with mothers and father from middle childhood to late adolescence: Within- and between-families comparisons. *Developmental Psychology, 43,* 551–563.

Shanahan, M. J., Elder, G. H., Burchinal, M., & Conger, R.-D. (1996a). Adolescent earnings and relationships with parents: The work–family nexus in urban and rural ecologies. In J. T. Mortimer & M. D. Finch (Eds.), *Adolescents, work, and family: An intergenerational developmental analysis.* Thousand Oaks, CA: Sage.

Shanahan, M. J., Elder, G. H., Burchinal, M., & Conger, R.-D. (1996b). Adolescent paid labor and relationships with parents: Early work–family linkages. *Child Development, 67,* 2183–2200.

Shapiro, S. (2007). Recent epidemiological evidence relevant to the clinical management of the menopause. *Climacteric, 10*(Suppl. 2), 2–15.

Share, D. L. (2008). Orthographic learning, phonological recoding, and self-teaching. In R. V. Kail (Ed.), *Advances in child development and behavior* (Vol. 36, pp. 31–84). San Diego, CA: Elsevier.

Shaw, S. S. (2007). Losing a parent twice. *American Journal of Alzheimer's Disease and Other Dementias, 21,* 389–390.

Shear, M. K., Simon, N., Wall, M., Zisook, S., Neimeyer, R., Duan, N., et al. (2011). Complicated grief and related bereavement issues for DSM-5. *Depression and Anxiety, 28,* 103–117.

Sherman, A. M., de Vries, B., & Lansford, J. E. (2000). Friendship in childhood and adulthood: Lessons across the life span. *International Journal of Aging and Human Development, 51,* 31–51.

Sherwin, S. (2011). Looking backwards, looking forward: Hope for *Bioethics'* next twenty-five years. *Bioethics, 25,* 75–82.

Sheu, H.-B., Lent, R. W., Brown, S. D., Miller, M. J., Hennessy, K. D., & Duffy, R. D. (2010). Testing the choice model of social cognitive career theory across Holland themes: A meta-analytic path analysis. *Journal of Vocational Behavior, 76,* 252–264.

Shih, P. C., & Jung, R. E. (2009). Gray matter correlates of fluid, crystallized, and spatial intelligence: Testing the P-FIT model. *Intelligence, 37,* 124–135.

Shoemaker, L. B., & Furman, W. (2009). Interpersonal influences on late adolescent girls' and boys' disordered eating. *Eating Behaviors, 10,* 97–106.

Shulman, S., & Kipnis, O. (2001). Adolescent romantic relationships: A look from the future. *Journal of Adolescence, 24,* 337–351.

Shutts, K., Banaji, M. R., & Spelke, E. S. (2010). Social categories guide young children's preferences for novel objects. *Developmental Science, 13,* 599–610.

Siddiqui, A. (1995). Object size as a determinant of grasping in infancy. *Journal of Genetic Psychology, 156,* 345–358.

Sidebotham, P., Heron, J., & the ALSPAC Study Team. (2003). Child maltreatment in the "children of the nineties": The role of the child. *Child Abuse and Neglect, 27,* 337–352.

Siegler, R. S. (1981). Developmental sequences within and between concepts. *Monographs of the Society for Research in Child Development, 46* (Serial No. 189).

Siegler, R. S. (1986). Unities in strategy choices across domains. In M. Perlmutter (Ed.), *Minnesota symposia on child development* (Vol. 19, pp. 1–48). Hillsdale, NJ: Erlbaum.

Siegler, R. S., & Alibali, M. W. (2004). *Children's thinking* (4th ed.). Upper Saddle River, NJ: Prentice Hall.

Silk, J. S., Morris, A. S., Kanaya, T., & Steinberg, L. D. (2003). Psychological control and autonomy granting: Opposite ends of a continuum or distinct constructs? *Journal of Research on Adolescence, 13,* 113–128.

Silverman, P. R., & Nickman, S. L. (1996). Children's construction of their dead parents. In D. Klass, P. R. Silverman, & S. L. Nickman (Eds.), *Continuing bonds: New understandings of grief* (pp. 73–86). Washington, DC: Taylor & Francis.

Silverman, W. K., La Greca, A. M., & Wasserstein, S. (1995). What do children worry about? Worries and their relations to anxiety. *Child Development, 66,* 671–686.

Simmons, R., & Blyth, D. (1987). *Moving into adolescence.* New York: Aldine de Gruyter.

Simons, D. J., & Keil, F. C. (1995). An abstract to concrete shift in the development of biological thought: The insides story. *Cognition, 56,* 129–163.

Simonton, D. K. (1997). Creative productivity: A predictive and explanatory model of career trajectories and landmarks. *Psychological Review, 104,* 66–89.

Simonton, D. K. (2007). Creativity: Specialised expertise or general cognitive processes? In M. J. Roberts (Ed.). *Integrating the mind: Domain general vs. domain specific processes in higher cognition* (pp. 351–367). New York: Psychology Press.

Simpson, E. L. (1974). Moral development research: A case study of scientific cultural bias. *Human Development, 17,* 81–106.

Sinclair, R. R., Sears, L. E., Zajack, M., & Probst, T. (2010). A multilevel model of economic stress and employee well-being. In J. Houdmont & S. Leka (Eds.), *Contemporary occupational health psychology: Global perspectives on research and practice* (Vol. 1, pp. 1–20). Malden, MA: Wiley-Blackwell.

Sinnott, J. D. (1994). New science models for teaching adults: Teaching as a dialogue with reality. In J. D. Sinnott (Ed.), *Interdisciplinary handbook of adult lifespan learning* (pp. 90–104). Westport, CT: Greenwood Press.

Sinnott, J. D. (1998). *The development of logic in adulthood: Postformal thought and its applications.* New York: Plenum.

Sinnott, J. D. (2009). Complex thought and construction of the self in the face of aging and death. *Journal of Adult Development, 16,* 155–165.

Skinner, B. F. (1957). *Verbal behavior.* New York: Appleton-Century-Crofts.

Skinner, E. A. (1985). Determinants of mother-sensitive and contingent-responsive behavior: The role of childbearing beliefs and socioeconomic status. In I. E. Sigel (Ed.), *Parental belief systems: The psychological consequences for children* (pp. 51–82). Hillsdale, NJ: Erlbaum.

Skouteris, H., McNaught, S., & Dissanayake, C. (2007). Mothers' transition back to work and infants' transition to child care: Does work-based child care make a difference? *Child Care in Practice, 13,* 33–47.

Slagboom, P. E., Beekman, M., Passtoors, W. M., Deelen, J., Vaarhorst, A. A. M., Boer, J. M., et al. (2011). Genomics of human longevity. *Philosophical Transactions of the Royal Society, 366,* 35–42.

Slobin, D. I. (1985). Cross-linguistic evidence for the language-making capacity. In D. I. Slobin (Ed.), *The cross-linguistic study of language acquisition* (Vol., 2 pp. 1157–1256). Hillsdale, NJ: Erlbaum.

Small, B. J., Hertzog, C., Hultsch, D. F., & Dixon, R. A. (2003). Stability and change in adult personality over 6 years: Findings from the Victoria longitudinal study. *Journal of Gerontology: Psychological Sciences, 58B,* P166–P176.

Smith, E. R., & Mackie, D. M. (2000). *Social psychology* (2nd ed.). Philadelphia: Psychology Press.

Smith, L. B. (2000). How to learn words: An associative crane. In R. Golinkoff & K. Hirsch-Pasek (Eds.), *Breaking the word learning barrier* (pp. 51–80). Oxford, England: Oxford University Press.

Smith, L. B. (2009). From fragments to geometric shape: Changes in visual object recognition between 18 and 24 months. *Current Directions in Psychological Science, 18,* 290–294.

Smith, R. E., & Smoll, F. L. (1996). The coach as the focus of research and intervention in youth sports. In F. L. Smoll & R. E. Smith (Eds.), *Children and youth in sport: A biopsychological perspective* (pp. 125–141). Dubuque, IA: Brown & Benchmark.

Smith, W. J., Howard, J. T., & Harrington, K. V. (2005). Essential formal mentor characteristics and functions in governmental and non-governmental organizations from the program administrator's and the mentor's perspective. *Public Personnel Management, 34,* 31–58.

Smits, I., Soenens, B., Vansteenkiste, M., Luyckx, K., & Goossens, L. (2010). Why do adolescents gather information or stick to parental norms? Examining autonomous and controlled motives behind adolescents' identity style. *Journal of Youth & Adolescence, 39,* 1343–1356.

Smoll, F. L., & Schutz, R. W. (1990). Quantifying gender differences in physical performance: A developmental perspective. *Developmental Psychology, 26,* 360–369.

Smyke, A. T., Zeanah, C. H., Fox, N. A., Nelson, C. A., & Guthrie, D. (2010). Placement in foster care enhances quality of attachment among young institutionalized children. *Child Development, 81,* 212–223.

Snedeker, B. (1982). *Hard knocks: Preparing youth for work.* Baltimore: Johns Hopkins University Press.

Snow, C. W. (1998). *Infant development* (2nd ed.). Upper Saddle River, NJ: Prentice Hall.

Snow, D. (2006). Regression and reorganization of intonation between 6 and 23 months. *Child Development, 77,* 281–296.

Snow, M. E., Jacklin, C. N., & Maccoby, E. E. (1983). Sex-of-child differences in father–child interaction at one year of age. *Child Development, 54,* 227–232.

Social Security Administration. (2011). *Annual statistical supplement, 2010.* Retrieved from http://www.ssa.gov/policy/docs/statcomps/supplement/

Sokol, R. J., Delaney-Black, V., & Nordstrom, B. (2003). Fetal alcohol spectrum disorder. *JAMA, 290,* 2996–2999.

Somerville, L. H., & Casey, B. J. (2010). Developmental neurobiology of cognitive control and motivational systems. *Current Opinion in Neurobiology, 20,* 236–241.

Son, S., & Bauer, J. W. (2010). Employed rural, low income, single mothers' family and work over time. *Journal of Family and Economic Issues, 31,* 107–120.

Spearman, C. (1904). "General intelligence" objectively determined and measured. *American Journal of Psychology, 15,* 201–293.

Spector, F., & Maurer, D. (2009). Synesthesia: A new approach to understanding the development of perception. *Developmental Psychology, 45,* 175–189.

Spector, P. E., Allen, T. D., Poelmans, S., Cooper, C. L., Bernin, P., Hart, P., et al. (2005). An international comparative study of work–family stress and occupational strain. In S. A. Y. Poelmans (Ed.), *Work and family: An international research perspective* (pp. 71–84). Mahwah, NJ: Erlbaum.

Spelke, E. S., & Kinzler, K. D. (2007). Core knowledge. *Developmental Science, 10,* 89–96.

Sperling, R. A., Aisen, P. S., Beckett, L. A., Dennett, D. A., Craft, S., Fagan, A. M., et al. (2011). Toward defining the preclinical stages of Alzheimer's disease: Recommendations from the National Institute on Aging–Alzheimer's Association workgroups on diagnostic guidelines for Alzheimer's disease. *Alzheimer's & Dementia: Journal of the Alzheimer's Association, 7,* 280–292.

Spirduso, W. W., Poon, L. W., & Chodzko-Zajko, W. (2008). Using resources and reserves in an exercise-cognition model. In W. W. Spirduso, L. W. Poon, & W. Chodzko-Zajko (Eds.), *Exercise and its mediating effects on cognition* (pp. 3–11). Champaign, IL: Human Kinetics.

Springer, K., & Keil, F. C. (1991). Early differentiation of causal mechanisms appropriate to biological and nonbiological kinds. *Child Development, 62,* 767–781.

Sprinzl, G. H., & Riechelmann, H. (2010). Current trends in treating hearing loss in elderly people: A review of the technology and treatment options. *Gerontology, 56,* 351–358.

Sritharan, R., Heilpern, K., Wilbur, C. J., & Gawronski, B. (2010). I think I like you: Spontaneous and deliberate evaluations of potential romantic partners in an online dating context. *European Journal of Social Psychology, 40,* 1062–1077.

Srivastava, S., John, O. P., Gosling, S. D., & Potter, J. (2003). Development of personality in early and middle adulthood: Set like plaster or persistent change? *Journal of Personality and Social Psychology, 84,* 1041–1053.

Sroufe, L. A., & Waters, E. (1976). The ontogenesis of smiling and laughter: A perspective on the organization of development in infancy. *Psychological Review, 83,* 173–189.

St. James-Roberts, I., & Plewis, I. (1996). Individual differences, daily fluctuations, and developmental changes in amounts of infant waking, fussing, crying, feeding, and sleeping. *Child Development, 67,* 2527–2540.

Staff, J., & Schulenberg, J. E. (2010). Millennials and the world of work: Experiences in paid work during adolescence. *Journal of Business and Psychology, 25,* 247–255.

Stafford, L., Kline, S. L., & Rankin, C. T. (2004). Married individuals, cohabiters, and cohabiters who marry: A longitudinal study of relational and individual well-being. *Journal of Social & Personal Relationships, 21,* 231–248.

Stanford v. Kentucky, 492 U.S. 361 (1989).

Stanovich, K. E., Toplak, M. E., & West, R. F. (2008). The development of rational thought: A taxonomy of heuristics and biases. In R. V. Kail (Ed.), *Advances in child development and behavior* (Vol. 36, pp. 251–285). San Diego, CA: Elsevier.

Starko, A. J. (1988). Effects of the revolving door identification model on creative productivity and self-efficacy. *Gifted Child Quarterly, 32,* 291–297.

Stauss, J. H. (1995). Reframing and refocusing American Indian family strengths. In C. K. Jacobson (Ed.), *American families: Issues in race and ethnicity* (pp. 105–118). New York: Garland.

Steele, C. M. (1997). A threat in the air: How stereotypes shape intellectual identity and performance. *American Psychologist, 52,* 613–629.

Steele, C. M., & Aronson, J. (1995). Stereotype threat and the intellectual test performance of African Americans. *Journal of Personality and Social Psychology, 69,* 797–811.

Steinberg, L. (1999). *Adolescence* (5th ed.). Boston: McGraw-Hill.

Steinberg, L. (2001). We know some things: Parent–adolescent relationships in retrospect and prospect. *Journal of Research on Adolescence, 11,* 1–19.

Steinberg, L., & Monahan, K. C. (2007). Age differences in resistance to peer influence. *Developmental Psychology, 43,* 1531–1543.

Steinberg, L., & Silk, J. (2002). Parenting adolescents. In M. H. Bornstein (Ed.), *Handbook of parenting* (2nd ed., Vol. 1, pp. 103–133). Mahwah, NJ: Erlbaum.

Steiner, J. E., Glaser, D., Hawilo, M. E., & Berridge, K. C. (2001). Comparative expression of hedonic impact: Affective reactions to taste by human infants and other primates. *Neuroscience & Biobehavioral Reviews, 25,* 53–74.

Stephan, Y., Fouquereau, E., & Fernandez, A. (2007). The relation between self-determination and retirement satisfaction among active retired individuals. *International Journal of Aging and Human Development, 66,* 329–345.

Stephens, M. A. P., & Clark, S. L. (1996). Interpersonal relationships in multi-generational families. In N. Vanzetti & S. Duck (Eds.), *A lifetime of relationships* (pp. 431–454). Pacific Grove, CA: Brooks/Cole.

Stephens, M. A. P., & Franks, M. M. (1999). Intergenerational relationships in later-life families: Adult daughters and sons as caregivers to aging parents. In J. C. Cavanaugh & S. K. Whitbourne (Eds.), *Gerontology: An interdisciplinary perspective* (pp. 329–354). New York: Oxford University Press.

Stephens, M. A. P., Townsend, A. L., Martire, L. M., & Druley, J. A. (2001). Balancing parent care with other roles: Interrole conflict of adult daughter caregivers. *Journal of Gerontology: Psychological Sciences, 56B,* P24–P34.

Sternberg, R. J. (1985). *Beyond IQ: A triarchic theory of human intelligence.* Cambridge, England: Cambridge University Press.

Sternberg, R. J. (1999). The theory of successful intelligence. *Review of General Psychology, 3,* 292–316.

Sternberg, R. J. (2003). Issues in the theory and measurement of successful intelligence: A reply to Brody. *Intelligence, 31,* 331–337.

Sternberg, R. J. (2006). A duplex theory of love. In R. J. Sternberg & K. Weis (Eds.), *The new psychology of love* (pp. 184–199). New Haven, CT: Yale University Press.

Sternberg, R. J. (2008). The triarchic theory of successful intelligence. In N. Salkind (Ed.), *Encyclopedia of educational psychology* (pp. 988–994). Thousand Oaks, CA: Sage.

Sternberg, R. J., & Grigorenko, E. L. (Eds.). (2004). *Culture and competence: Contexts of life success.* Washington, DC: American Psychological Association.

Sternberg, R. J., Grigorenko, E. L., & Kidd, K. K. (2005). Intelligence, race, and genetics. *American Psychologist, 60,* 46–59.

Sternberg, R. J., Jarvin, L., & Grigorenko, E. L. (2009). *Teaching for wisdom, intelligence, creativity, and success.* Thousand Oaks, CA: Corwin.

Sternberg, R. J., & Kaufman, J. C. (1998). Human abilities. *Annual Review of Psychology, 49,* 479–502.

Sternberg, R. J., & Lubart, T. I. (2001). Wisdom and creativity. In J. E. Birren & K. W. Schaie (Eds.), *Handbook of the psychology of aging* (5th ed., pp. 500–522). San Diego, CA: Academic Press.

Sterns, H. L., & Chang, B. (2010). Workforce issues and retirement. In J. C. Cavanaugh & C. K. Cavanaugh (Eds.), *Aging in America* (Vol. 3, pp. 81–105). Santa Barbara, CA: Praeger Perspectives.

Stevens, J., & Ward-Estes, J. (2006). Attention-deficit/hyperactivity disorder. In M. Hersen, J. C. Thomas, & R. T. Ammerman (Eds.), *Comprehensive handbook of personality and psychopathology* (Vol. 3, pp. 316–329). Hoboken, NJ: Wiley.

Stevens, N. L., & Van Tilburg, T. G. (2011). Cohort differences in having and retaining friends in personal networks in later life. *Journal of Social and Personal Relationships, 28,* 24–43.

Stevens, S. B., & Morris, T. L. (2007). College dating and social anxiety: Using the Internet as a means of connecting to others. *CyberPsychology & Behavior, 10,* 680–688.

Stevenson, H. W., & Stigler, J. W. (1992). *The learning gap.* New York: Summit Books.

Stewart, R. B., Mobley, L. A., Van Tuyl, S. S., & Salvador, W. A. (1987). The firstborn's adjustment to the birth of a sibling: A longitudinal assessment. *Child Development, 58,* 341–355.

Stice, E., & Shaw, H. (2004). Eating disorder prevention programs: A meta-analytic review. *Psychological Bulletin, 130,* 206–227.

Stifter, C. A., & Fox, N. A. (1990). Infant reactivity: Physiological correlates of newborn and 5-month temperament. *Developmental Psychology, 26,* 582–588.

Stiles, J., Reilly, J., Paul, B., & Moses, P. (2005). Cognitive development following early brain injury: Evidence for neural adaptation. *Trends in Cognitive Sciences, 9,* 136–143.

Stoner, S., O'Riley, A., & Edelstein, B. (2010). Assessment of mental health. In J. C. Cavanaugh & C. K. Cavanaugh (Eds.), *Aging in America* (Vol. 2, pp. 141–170). Santa Barbara, CA: Praeger Perspectives.

Stop Smoking. (2010). *Quit smoking even in old age: It's going to benefit.* Retrieved from http://www.stop-smoking-updates.com/quitsmoking/quitting-benefits/psychological-benefits/quit-smoking-even-in-old-age-its-going-to-benefit.htm

Strauss, W., & Howe, N. (2007). *Millennials go to college: Strategies for a new generation on campus* (2nd ed.). Ithaca, NY: Paramount.

Strayer, D. L., Drews, F. A., & Crouch, D. J. (2006). A comparison of the cell phone driver and the drunk driver. *Human Factors, 48,* 381–391.

Strayer, J., & Roberts, W. (2004). Children's anger, emotional expressiveness, and empathy: Relations with parents' empathy, emotional expressiveness, and parenting practices. *Social Development, 13,* 229–254.

Striano, T., Tomasello, M., & Rochat, P. (2001). Social and object support for early symbolic play. *Developmental Science, 4,* 442–455.

Stroebe, M. S., Boelen, P. A., van den Hout, M., Stroebe, W., Salemink, E., & van den Bout, J. (2007). Ruminative coping as avoidance: A reinterpretation of its function in adjustment to bereavement. *European Archives of Psychiatry and Clinical Neuroscience, 257,* 462–472.

Stroebe, M. S., & Schut, H. (2001). Models of coping with bereavement: A review. In M. S. Stroebe, R. O. Hansson, W. Stroebe, & H. Schut (Eds.), *Handbook of bereavement research: Consequences, coping, and care* (pp. 375–403). Washington, DC: American Psychological Association.

Stroebe, M. S., Schut, H., & Boerner, K. (2010). Continuing bonds in adaptation to bereavement: Toward theoretical integration. *Clinical Psychology Review, 30,* 259–268.

Stroebe, M. S., Schut, H., & Stroebe, W. (2007). Health outcomes of bereavement. *Lancet, 370,* 1960–1973.

Stroebe, W., Abakoumkin, G., & Stroebe, M. (2010). Beyond depression: Yearning for the loss of a loved one. *Omega: Journal of Death and Dying, 61,* 85–101.

Strough, J., & Berg, C. A. (2000). Goals as a mediator of gender differences in high-affiliation dyadic conversations. *Developmental Psychology, 36,* 117–125.

Stunkard, A. J., Sorensen, T. I. A., Hanis, C., Teasdale, T. W., Chakraborty, R., Schull, W. J., & Schulsinger, F. (1986). An adoption study of human obesity. *New England Journal of Medicine, 314,* 193–198.

Sturge-Apple, M. L., Davies, P. T., & Cummings, E. M. (2010). Typologies of family functioning and children's adjustment during the early school years. *Child Development, 81,* 1320–1335.

Sturge-Apple, M. L., Davies, P. T., Winter, M. A., Cummings, E. M., & Schermerhorn, A. (2008). Interparental conflict and children's school adjustment: The explanatory role of children's internal representations of interparental and parent–child relationships. *Developmental Psychology, 44,* 1678–1690.

Sturman, D. A., & Moghaddam, B. (2012). Striatum processes reward differently in adolescents versus adults. *Proceedings of the National Academy of Sciences, 109,* 1719–1724.

Subrahmanyam, K., Greenfield, P., Kraut, R., & Gross, E. (2001). The impact of computer use on children's and adolescents' development. *Journal of Applied Developmental Psychology, 22,* 7–30.

Sullivan, M. W., & Lewis, M. (2003). Contextual determinants of anger and other negative expressions in young infants. *Developmental Psychology, 39,* 693–705.

Sung, G., & Greer, D. (2011). The case for simplifying brain death criteria. *Neurology, 76,* 113–114.

Super, C. M., Herrera, M. G., & Mora, J. O. (1990). Long-term effects of food supplementation and psychosocial intervention on the physical growth of Colombian infants at risk of malnutrition. *Child Development, 61,* 29–49.

Super, D. E. (1976). *Career education and the meanings of work.* Washington, DC: U.S. Offices of Education.

Super, D. E. (1980). A life-span, life space approach to career development. *Journal of Vocational Behavior, 16,* 282–298.

Sussman, S., Pokhrel, P., Ashmore, R. D., & Brown, B. B. (2007). Adolescent peer group identification and characteristics: a review of the literature. *Addictive Behaviors, 32,* 1602–1627.

Sweeney, M. M. (2010). Remarriage and stepfamilies: Strategic sites for family scholarship in the 21st century. *Journal of Marriage and Family, 72,* 667–684.

Swinton, J., & Payne, R. (Eds.). (2009). *Living well and dying faithfully: Christian practices for end-of-life care.* Grand Rapids, MI: Eerdmans.

Tach, L., & Halpern-Meekin, S. (2009). How does premarital cohabitation affect trajectories of marital quality? *Journal of Marriage and the Family, 71,* 298–317.

Tager-Flusberg, H. (2007). Evaluating the theory-of-mind hypothesis of autism. *Current Directions in Psychological Science, 16,* 311–315.

Takata, K., Kitamura, Y., & Taniguchi, T. (2011). Pathological changes induced by amyloid-b in Alzheimer's disease. *Yakugaku Zasshi, 131,* 3–11.

Takeuchi, H., Taki, Y., Sassa, Y., Hashizume, H., Sekiguchi, A., Fukushima, A., et al. (2010). White matter structures associated with creativity: Evidence from diffusion tensor imaging. *NeuroImage, 51,* 11–18.

Tamayo, G. J., Broxson, A., Munsell, M., & Cohen, M. Z. (2010). Caring for the caregiver. *Oncology Nursing Forum, 37,* E50–E57.

Tamis-LeMonda, C. S., & Bornstein, M. H. (1996). Variation in children's exploratory, nonsymbolic, and symbolic play: An explanatory multidimensional framework. In C. Rovee-Collier & L. P. Lipsitt (Eds.), *Advances in infancy research* (Vol. 10, pp. 37–78). Norwood, NJ: Ablex.

Tamis-LeMonda, C. S., Shannon, J. D., Cabrera, N., & Lamb, M. E. (2004). Father and mothers at play with their 2- and 3-year-olds: Contributions to language and cognitive development. *Child Development, 75,* 1806–1820.

Tang, F., Morrow-Howell, N., & Choi, E. (2010). Why do older adult volunteers stop volunteering? *Ageing and Society, 30,* 859–878.

Tang, T. L. P., & McCollum, S. L. (1996). Sexual harassment in the workplace. *Public Personnel Management, 25,* 53–58.

Tanner, J. L., & Arnett, J. J. (2009). The emergence of emerging adulthood: The new life stage between adolescence and young adulthood. In A. Furlong (Ed.), *Handbook of youth and young adulthood: New perspectives and agendas.* London: Routledge.

Tanner, J. M. (1970). Physical growth. In P. H. Mussen (Ed.), *Carmichael's manual of child psychology* (3rd ed., pp. 77–155). New York: Wiley.

Tanner, J. M. (1990). *Fetus into man: Physical growth from conception to maturity* (2nd ed.). Cambridge, MA: Harvard University Press.

Tardif, T., Fletcher, P., Liang, W., Zhang, Z., Kaciroti, N., & Marchman, V. A. (2008). Baby's first 10 words. *Developmental Psychology, 44,* 929–938.

Taub, G. E., Hayes, B. G., Cunningham, W. R., & Sivo, S. A. (2001). Relative roles of cognitive ability and practical intelligence in the prediction of success. *Psychological Reports, 88,* 931–942.

Taumoepeau, M., & Ruffman, T. (2008). Stepping stones to others' minds: Maternal talk relates to child mental state language and emotion understanding at 15, 24, and 33 months. *Child Development, 79,* 284–302.

Taylor, J. L., O'Hara, R., Mumenthaler, M. S., Rosen, A. C., & Yesavage, J. A. (2005). Cognitive ability, expertise, and age differences in following air-traffic control instructions. *Psychology and Aging, 20,* 117–133.

Taylor, M., Carlson, S. M., Maring, B. L., Gerow, L., & Charley, C. M. (2004). The characteristics of fantasy in school-age children: Imaginary companions, impersonation, and social understanding. *Developmental Psychology, 40,* 1173–1187.

Taylor, R. J., Chatters, L. M., & Levin, J. (2004). *Religion in the lives of African Americans.* Thousand Oaks, CA: Sage.

Teichman, Y. (2001). The development of Israeli children's images of Jews and Arabs and their expression in human figure drawings. *Developmental Psychology, 37,* 749–761.

Tenenbaum, H. R., & Leaper, C. (2002). Are parents' gender schemas related to their children's gender-related cognitions? A meta-analysis. *Developmental Psychology, 38,* 615–630.

Terkel, S. (1974). *Working.* New York: Pantheon Books.

Terman, M. (1994). Light therapy. In M. H. Kryger, T. Roth, & W. C. Dement (Eds.), *Principles and practice of sleep medicine* (2nd ed., pp. 1012–1029). Philadelphia: W. B. Saunders.

Terracciano, A., McRae, R. R., & Costa, P. T., Jr. (2010). Intra-individual change in personality stability and age. *Journal of Research in Personality, 44,* 31–37.

Thelen, E., & Smith, L. B. (1998). Dynamic systems theories. In W. Damon (Ed.), *Handbook of child psychology* (5th ed., Vol. 1, pp. 563–634). New York: Wiley.

Thelen, E., Ulrich, B. D., & Jensen, J. L. (1989). The developmental origins of locomotion. In M. H. Woollacott & A. Shumway-Cook (Eds.), *Development of posture and gait across the lifespan.* Columbia, SC: University of South Carolina Press.

Therborn, G. (2010). Families in global perspective. In A. Giddens & P. W. Sutton (Eds.), *Sociology: Introductory readings* (3rd ed., pp. 119–123). Malden, MA: Polity Press.

Thiele, D. M., & Whelan, T. A. (2010). The relationship between grandparent satisfaction, meaning, and generativity. *International Journal of Aging and Human Development, 66,* 21–48.

Thiessen, E. D., Hill, E., & Saffran, J. R. (2005). Infant-directed speech facilitates word segmentation. *Infancy, 7,* 53–71.

Thiessen, E. D., & Saffran, J. R. (2003). When cues collide: Use of stress and statistical cues to word boundaries by 7- to 9-month-old infants. *Developmental Psychology, 39,* 706–716.

Thomas, J. W., Bol, L., Warkentin, R. W., Wilson, M., Strage, A., & Rohwer, W. D. (1993). Interrelationships among students' study activities, self-concept of academic ability, and achievement as a function of characteristics of high-school biology courses. *Applied Cognitive Psychology, 7,* 499–532.

Thomas, R., & Zimmer-Gembeck, M. J. (2011). Accumulating evidence for parent–child interaction therapy in the prevention of child maltreatment. *Child Development, 82,* 177–192.

Thompson v. Oklahoma, 487 U.S. 815 (1988).

Thompson, L. W., Gallagher-Thompson, D., Futterman, A., Gilewski, M. J., & Peterson, J. (1991). The effects of late-life spousal bereavement over a 30-month interval. *Psychology and Aging, 6,* 434–441.

Thompson, R. A. (2000). The legacy of early attachments. *Child Development, 71,* 145–152.

Thompson, R. A. (2006). The development of the person: Social understanding, relationships, conscience, self. In N. Eisenberg, W. Damon, & R. M. Lerner (Eds.), *Handbook of child psychology* (6th ed., Vol. 3, pp. 24–98). Hoboken, NJ: Wiley.

Thurstone, L. L., & Thurstone, T. G. (1941). *Factorial studies of intelligence.* Chicago: University of Chicago Press.

Toga, A. W., Thompson, P. M., & Sowell, E. R. (2006). Mapping brain maturation. *Trends in Neuroscience, 29,* 148–159.

Tolan, P. H., Gorman-Smith, D., & Henry, D. B. (2003). The developmental ecology of urban males' youth violence. *Developmental Psychology, 39,* 274–291.

Tomasello, M., Carpenter, M., & Liszkowski, U. (2007). A new look at infant pointing. *Child Development, 78,* 705–722.

Tomlinson, M., Cooper, P., & Murray, L. (2005). The mother–infant relationship and infant attachment in a South African peri-urban settlement. *Child Development, 76,* 1044–1054.

Toomey, R. B., Ryan, C., Diaz, R. M., Card, N. A., & Russell, S. T. (2010). Gender-nonconforming lesbian, gay, bisexual, and transgender youth: School victimization and young adult psychosocial adjustment. *Developmental Psychology, 46,* 1589–1589.

Tracy, B., Reid, R., & Graham, S. (2009). Teaching young students strategies for planning and drafting stories: The impact of self-regulated strategy development. *Journal of Educational Research, 102,* 323–331.

Trainor, L. J., Austin, C. M., & Desjardins, R. N. (2000). Is infant-directed speech prosody a result of the vocal expression of emotion? *Psychological Science, 11,* 188–195.

Treiman, R., & Kessler, B. (2003). The role of letter names in the acquisition of literacy. *Advances in Child Development and Behavior, 31,* 105–135.

Trim, R. S., Meehan, B. T., King, K. M., & Chassin, L. (2007). The relation between adolescent substance use and young adult internalizing symptoms: Findings from a high-risk longitudinal sample. *Psychology of Addictive Behaviors, 21,* 97–107.

Troseth, G. L., Pierroutsakos, S. L., & DeLoache, J. S. (2004). From the innocent to the intelligent eye: The early development of pictorial competence. In R. V. Kail (Ed.), *Advances in child development and behavior* (Vol. 32, pp. 1–35). New York: Academic Press.

Troutman, M., Nies, M. A., & Mavellia, H. (2011). Perceptions of successful aging in black older adults. *Journal of Psychosocial Nursing and Mental Health Services, 49*(1), 28–34.

Truong, K. D., & Sturm, R. (2009). Alcohol environments and disparities in exposure associated with adolescent drinking in California. *American Journal of Public Health, 99,* 264–270.

Trzesniewski, K. H., & Donnellan, M. B. (2010). Rethinking "Generation Me": A study of cohort effects from 1976–2006. *Perspective on Psychological Science, 5,* 58–75.

Tsao, T.-C. (2004). New models for future retirement: A study of college/university-linked retirement communities. *Dissertation Abstracts International. Section A. Humanities and Social Sciences, 64*(10-A), 3511.

Tsuno, N., & Homma, A. (2009). Aging in Asia—The Japan experience. *Ageing International, 34,* 1–14.

Tu, M. C.-H. (2007). Culture and job satisfaction: A comparative analysis between Taiwanese and Filipino caregivers working in Taiwan's long-term care industry (China). *Dissertation Abstracts International. Section A. Humanities and Social Sciences, 67*(9-A), 3488.

Turiel, E. (2006). The development of morality. In N. Eisenberg, W. Damon, & R. M. Lerner (Eds.), *Handbook of child psychology* (6th ed., Vol. 3, pp. 789–857). Hoboken, NJ: Wiley.

Turley, R. N. L. (2003). Are children of young mothers disadvantaged because of their mother's age or family background? *Child Development, 74,* 465–474.

Twenge, J. M., & Campbell, W. K. (2001). Age and birth cohort differences in self-esteem: A cross-temporal meta-analysis. *Personality and Social Psychology Review, 5,* 321–344.

Tynes, B. M. (2007). Role taking in online "classrooms": What adolescents are learning about race and ethnicity. *Developmental Psychology, 43,* 1312–1320.

U.S. Bureau of Labor Statistics. (2010a). *Employment Characteristics of Families survey.* Retrieved from http://www.bls.gov/news.release/famee.nr0.htm

U.S. Bureau of Labor Statistics. (2010b). *Labor force statistics from the Current Population Survey.* Retrieved from http://www.bls.gov/cps

U.S. Bureau of Labor Statistics. (2010c). *Women in the labor force: A databook* (2009 ed.). Retrieved from http://www.bls.gov/cps/wlf-intro-2009.htm

U.S. Bureau of Labor Statistics. (2010d). *Women's to men's earnings ratio by age, 2009.* Retrieved from http://www.bls.gov/opub/ted/2010/ted_20100708.htm

U.S. Census Bureau. (2010a). *The 2010 statistical abstract: PDF version.* Retrieved from http://www.census.gov/compendia/statab/2010edition.html

U.S. Census Bureau. (2010b). *Estimated median age at first marriage by sex: 1890 to the present.* Retrieved from http://search.census.gov/search?q5cache:aJo0LSIH0h0J:www.census.gov/population/socdemo/hh-fam/ms2.xls1median1age1first1marriage&output5xml_no_dtd&ie5UTF-8&client5default_frontend&proxystylesheet5default_frontend&site5census&access5p&oe5ISO-8859-1

U.S. Census Bureau. (2010c). *Facts for features: Grandparents Day: Sept. 12.* Retrieved from http://www.census.gov/newsroom/releases/archives/facts_for_features_special_editions/cb10-ff16.html

U.S. Census Bureau. (2011). *The 2011 statistical abstract.* Retrieved from http://www.census.gov/compendia/statab/

U.S. Department of Agriculture. (2010). *Expenditures on children by families, 2009.* Retrieved from http://www.cnpp.usda.gov/Publications/CRC/crc2009.pdf

U.S. Department of Agriculture. (2011). Choose MyPlate. Retrieved from http://choosemyplate.gov

U.S. Department of Health and Human Services. (1997). *Vital statistics of the United States, 1994* (Vol. 2, Pt. A). Hyattsville, MD: U.S. Public Health Service.

U.S. Department of Health and Human Services. (2000). *Reducing tobacco use: A report of the Surgeon General—Executive summary.* Atlanta, GA: U.S. Department of Health and Human Services, Centers for Disease Control and Prevention, National Center for Chronic Disease Prevention and Health Promotion, Office on Smoking and Health.

U.S. Department of Health and Human Services. (2001). *The Surgeon General's call to action to prevent and decrease overweight and obesity.* Rockville, MD: Author.

U.S. Department of Health and Human Services. (2008). *Physical activity guidelines for Americans.* Retrieved from http://www.health.gov/paguidelines/committeereport.aspx

U.S. Department of Health and Human Services. (2010a). *Child Maltreatment 2009.* Retrieved from http://www.acf.hhs.gov/programs/cb/stats_research/index.htm#can

U.S. Department of Health and Human Services. (2010b). *The Surgeon General's vision for a healthy and fit nation.* Rockville, MD: Author.

U.S. Department of Health and Human Services. (2012). *Nursing home quality initiatives.* Retrieved from http://www.cms.gov/Medicare/Quality-Initiatives-Patient-Assessment-Instruments/NursingHomeQualityInits/index.html

U.S. Department of Labor. (2000). *Report on the youth labor force.* Washington, DC: Author.

U.S. Department of Labor. (2010a). *Nontraditional occupations for women in 2009.* Retrieved from http://www.dol.gov/wb/factsheets/nontra2009.htm

U.S. Department of Labor. (2010b). *Women in the labor force: A databook* (2010 ed.). Retrieved from http://www.bls.gov/cps/wlftable6-2010.htm

U.S. Department of Labor. (2012). *Find It! By Audience — Job Seekers/Unemployed.* Retrieved from http://www.dol.gov/dol/audience/aud-unemployed.htm

Uhlenberg, P., & Cheuk, M. (2010). The significance of grandparents to grandchildren: An international perspective. In D. Dannefer & C. Phillipson (Eds.), *The Sage handbook of social gerontology* (pp. 447–458). Thousand Oaks, CA: Sage.

Umbel, V. M., Pearson, B. Z., Fernandez, M. C., & Oller, D.-K. (1992). Measuring bilingual children's receptive vocabularies. *Child Development, 63,* 1012–1020.

United Nations. (2005). *Demographic yearbook 2005.* Retrieved from http://unstats.un.org/unsd/demographic/products/dyb/dyb2005/Table25.pdf

United Nations. (2010a). *Divorces and crude divorce rates by urban/rural residence: 2004–2008.* Retrieved from http://unstats.un.org/unsd/demographic/products/dyb/dyb2008/Table25.pdf

United Nations. (2010b). *World population ageing 2009.* Retrieved from http://www.un.org/esa/population/publications/WPA2009/WPA2009-report.pdf

United Nations Children's Fund. (2006). *Progress for children: A report card on nutrition, 2000–2006.* New York: Author.

United Nations Children's Fund. (2007). *The state of the world's children, 2008.* New York: Author.

Vacco v. Quill, 521 US 793 (1997).

Vaish, A., Carpenter, M., & Tomasello, M. (2009). Sympathy through affective perspective taking and its relation to prosocial behavior in toddlers. *Developmental Psychology, 45,* 534–543.

Valkenburg, P. M., & Jochen, P. (2009). Social consequences of the Internet for adolescents: A decade of research. *Current Directions in Psychological Science, 18,* 1–5.

Valkenburg, P. M., & van der Voort, T. H. A. (1994). Influence of TV on daydreaming and creative imagination: A review of research. *Psychological Bulletin, 116,* 316–339.

Valkenburg, P. M., & van der Voort, T. H. A. (1995). The influence of television on children's daydreaming styles: A 1-year-panel study. *Communication Research, 22,* 267–287.

Vallerand, R. J. (2008). On the psychology of passion: In search of what makes people's lives most worth living. *Canadian Psychology, 49,* 1–13.

Vallerand, R. J., Paquet, Y., Philippe, F. L., & Charest, J. (2010). On the role of passion for work in burnout: A process model. *Journal of Personality, 78,* 289–312.

Van de Pol, J., Volman, M., & Beishuizen, J. (2010). Scaffolding in teacher-student interaction: A decade of research. *Educational Psychology Review, 22,* 271–296.

Van der Geest, S. (2004). Dying peacefully: Considering good death and bad death in Kwahu-Tafo, Ghana. *Social Science and Medicine, 58,* 899–911.

Van der Mark, I. L., van IJzendoorn, M. H., & Bakermans-Kranenburg, M. J. (2002). Development of empathy in girls during the second year of life: Associations with parenting, attachment, and temperament. *Social Development, 11,* 451–468.

Van Dierendonck, D., Garssen, B., & Visser, A. (2005). Burnout prevention through personal growth. *International Journal of Stress Management, 12,* 62–77.

Van Doorn, M. D., Branje, S. J. T., & Meeus, W. H. J. (2008). Conflict resolution in parent–adolescent relationships and adolescent delinquency. *Journal of Early Adolescence, 28,* 503–527.

Van Zalk, M., Herman, W., Kerr, M., Branje, S. J. T., Stattin, H., & Meeus, W. H. J. (2010). It takes three: Selection, influence, and de-selection processes of depression in adolescent friendship networks. *Developmental Psychology, 46,* 927–938.

vandenBerg, P., Neumark-Sztainer, D., & Wall, M. (2007). Steroid use among adolescents: Longitudinal findings from Project EAT. *Pediatrics, 119,* 476–486.

Vander Wal, J. S., & Thelen, M. H. (2000). Eating and body image concerns among obese and average-weight children. *Addictive Behaviors, 25,* 775–778.

Vazire, S., & Doris, J. M. (2009). Personality and personal control. *Journal of Research in Personality, 43,* 274–275.

Vazsonyi, A. T., & Snider, J. B. (2008). Mentoring, competencies, and adjustment in adolescents: American part-time employment and European apprenticeships. *International Journal of Behavioral Development, 32,* 46–55.

Veenstra, R., Lindenberg, S., Munniksma, A., & Dijkstra, J. K. (2010). The complex relation between bullying, victimization, acceptance, and rejection: Giving special attention to status, affection, and sex differences. *Child Development, 81,* 480–486.

Veenstra, R., Lindberg, S., Oldenhinkel, A. J., De Winter, A. F., Verhulst, F. C., & Ormel, J. (2005). Bullying and victimization in elementary schools: A comparison of bullies, victims, bully/victims, and uninvolved preadolescents. *Developmental Psychology, 41,* 672–682.

Vélez, C. E., Wolchik, S. A., Tein, J.-Y., & Sandler, I. (2011). Protecting children from the consequences of divorce: A longitudinal study of the effects of parenting on children's coping processes. *Child Development, 82,* 244–257.

Ventura, S. J., Abma, J. C., Mosher, W. D., & Henshaw, S. K. (2008). Estimated pregnancy rates by outcome for the United States, 1990–2004. *National Vital Statistics Reports, 56,* 1–26.

Verheijde, J. L. (2010). Commentary on the concept of brain death within the Catholic bioethical framework. *Christian Bioethics, 16,* 246–256.

Véronneau, M.-H., Vitaro, F., Brendgen, M., Dishion, T. J., & Tremblay, R. E. (2010). Transactional analysis of the reciprocal linkages between peer relationships and academic achievement from middle childhood to early adolescence. *Developmental Psychology, 46,* 773–790.

Verschaeve, L. (2009). Genetic damage in subjects exposed to radiofrequency radiation. *Mutation Research—Reviews in Mutation Research, 681,* 259–270.

Vestbo, J. (2011). Clinical diagnosis of COPD. In N. A. Hanania & A. Sharafkhaneh (Eds.), *COPD: A guide to diagnosis and clinical management* (pp. 21–31). New York: Springer.

Vieno, A., Nation, M., Pastore, M., & Santinello, M. (2009). Parenting and antisocial behavior: A model of the relationship between adolescent self-disclosure, parental closeness, parental control, and adolescent antisocial behavior. *Developmental Psychology, 45,* 1509–1519.

Visher, E. G., Visher, J. S., & Pasley, K. (2003). Remarriage families and stepparenting. In F. Walsh (Ed.), *Normal family processes* (pp. 153–175). New York: Guilford.

Vitiello, B., & Swedo, S. (2004). Antidepressant medications in children. *New England Journal of Medicine, 350,* 1489–1491.

Vitulano, L. A. (2005). Delinquency. In C. B. Fisher & R. M. Lerner (Eds.), *Encyclopedia of applied developmental science* (Vol. 1, pp. 327–328). Thousand Oaks, CA: Sage.

Von Bohlen und Halbach, O. (2010). Involvement of BDNF in age-dependent alterations in the hippocampus. *Frontiers in Aging Neuroscience, 2.* Retrieved from http://www.frontiersin.org/aging_neuroscience/10.3389/fnagi.2010.00036/full

Vorhees, C. V., & Mollnow, E. (1987). Behavior teratogenesis: Long-term influences on behavior. In J. D. Osofsky (Ed.), *Handbook of infant development* (2nd ed.). New York: Wiley.

Vygotsky, L. S. (1986). *Thought and language* (A. Kozulin, Trans.). Cambridge, MA: MIT Press. (Original work published in 1934)

Wachs, T. D., & Bates, J. E. (2001). Temperament. In G. Bremner & A. Fogel (Eds.), *Blackwell handbook of infant development* (pp. 465–501). Malden, MA: Blackwell.

Wachs, T. D., Black, M. M., & Engle, P. L. (2009). Maternal depression: A global threat to children's health, development, and behavior and to human rights. *Child Development Perspectives, 3,* 51–59.

Wadlington, W. (2005). Family law in America. *Family Court Review, 43,* 178–179.

Wahl, H.-W., & Oswald, F. (2010). Environmental perspectives on ageing. In D. Dannefer & C. Phillipson (Eds.), *The Sage handbook of social gerontology* (pp. 111–124). Thousand Oaks, CA: Sage.

Waites, C. (2009). Building on strengths: Intergenerational practice with African-American families. *Social Work, 54,* 278–287.

Wakschlag, L. S., Leventhal, B. L., Pine, D. S., Pickett, K. E., & Carter, A. S. (2006). Elucidating early mechanisms of developmental psychopathology: The case of prenatal smoking and disruptive behavior. *Child Development, 77,* 893–906.

Walberg, H. J. (1995). General practices. In G. Cawelti (Ed.), *Handbook of research on improving student achievement.* Arlington, VA: Educational Research Service.

Walker, A. C., & Balk, D. E. (2007). Bereavement rituals in the Muscogee Creek tribe. *Death Studies, 31,* 633–652.

Walker, L. E. A. (1984). *The battered woman syndrome.* New York: Springer.

Walker, L. J. (1980). Cognitive and perspective-taking prerequisites for moral development. *Child Development, 51,* 131–139.

Walker, L. J., & Taylor, J. H. (1991). Family interactions and the development of moral reasoning. *Child Development, 62,* 264–283.

Walker, P., Bremner, J. G., Mason, U., Spring, J., Mattock, K., Slater, A., et al. (2010). Preverbal infants' sensitivity to synaesthetic cross-modality correspondences. *Psychological Science, 21,* 21–25.

Wallerstein, J. S., & Lewis, J. M. (2004). The unexpected legacy of divorce: Report of a 25-year study. *Psychoanalytic Psychology, 21,* 353–370.

Walsh, J. L., Ward, L. M., Caruthers, A., & Merriweather, A. (2011). Awkward or amazing: Gender and age trends in first intercourse experiences. *Psychology of Women Quarterly, 35,* 59–71.

Walther, A. N. (1991). *Divorce hangover.* New York: Pocket Books.

Wang, H., & Wellman, B. (2010). Social connectivity in America: Changes in adult friendship network size from 2002 to 2007. *American Behavioral Scientist, 53,* 1148–1169.

Wang, Q., Pomerantz, E. M., & Chen, H. (2007). The role of parents' control in early adolescents' psychological functioning: A longitudinal investigation in the United States and China. *Child Development, 78,* 1592–1610.

Wang, S. S., & Brownell, K. D. (2005). Anorexia nervosa. In C. B. Fisher & R. M. Lerner (Eds.), *Encyclopedia of applied developmental science* (Vol. 1, pp. 83–85). Thousand Oaks, CA: Sage.

Wansink, B., & Sobal, J. (2007). Mindless eating: The 200 daily food decisions we overlook. *Environment and Behavior, 39,* 106–123.

Wanzer, S. H., & Glenmullen, J. (2007). *To die well: Your right to comfort, calm, and choice in the last days of life.* Cambridge, MA: Da Capo Press.

Warneken, F., & Tomasello, M. (2006). Altruistic helping in human infants and young chimpanzees. *Science, 311,* 1301–1303.

Warner, B., Altimier, L., & Crombleholme, T. M. (2007). Fetal surgery. *Newborn and Infant Nursing Reviews, 7,* 181–188.

Warner, E., Henderson-Wilson, C., & Andrew, F. (2010). *Flying the coop: Why is the move out of the home proving unsustainable?* Refereed papers presented at the 4th Australasian Housing Researchers Conference, University of New South Wales, Sydney, Australia. Retrieved from http://www.fbe.unsw.edu.au/cf/apnhr/papers/Attachments/Warner.pdf

Warnock, F., & Sandrin, D. (2004). Comprehensive description of newborn distress behavior in response to acute pain (newborn male circumcision). *Pain, 107,* 242–255.

Warren-Findlow, J., & Issel, I. M. (2010). Stress and coping in African American women with chronic heart disease: A cultural cognitive coping model. *Journal of Transcultural Nursing, 21,* 45–54.

Washington v. Glucksberg, 521 US 702 (1997).

Waterhouse, L. (2006). Multiple intelligences, the Mozart effect, and emotional intelligence: A critical review. *Educational Psychologist, 41,* 207–225.

Waters, E., & Cummings, E. M. (2000). A secure base from which to explore close relationships. *Child Development, 71,* 164–172.

Waters, H. S. (1980). "Class news": A single-subject longitudinal study of prose production and schema formation during childhood. *Journal of Verbal Learning and Verbal Behavior, 19,* 152–167.

Watts, F. (2007). Emotion regulation and religion. In J. J. Gross (Ed.), *Handbook of emotion regulation* (pp. 504–522). New York: Guilford.

Way, D. (2011). Dementia, delirium, and depression. In P. A. Fenstemacher & P. Winn (Eds.), *Long-term care medicine: A pocket guide* (pp. 225–245). New York: Springer.

Weaver, D. A. (2010). Widows and Social Security. *Social Security Bulletin, 70,* 89–109.

Webb, N. B. (2010a). Assessment of the bereaved child. In N. B. Webb (Ed.), *Helping bereaved children: A handbook for practitioners* (3rd ed., pp. 22–47). New York: Guilford.

Webb, N. B. (2010b). The child and death. In N. B. Webb (Ed.), *Helping bereaved children: A handbook for practitioners* (3rd ed., pp. 3–21). New York: Guilford.

Webb, S. J., Monk, C. S., & Nelson, C. A. (2001). Mechanisms of postnatal neurobiological development: Implications for human development. *Developmental Neuropsychology, 19,* 147–171.

Wechsler, H., Davenport, A., Dowdall, G., Moeykens, B., & Castillo, S. (1994). Health and behavioral consequences of binge drinking in college. *JAMA, 272,* 1672–1677.

Wegman, M. E. (1994). Annual summary of vital statistics—1993. *Pediatrics, 95,* 792–803.

Wegner, D. M., & Gold, D. G. (1995). Fanning old flames: Emotional and cognitive effects of suppressing thoughts of a past relationship. *Journal of Personality and Social Psychology, 68,* 782–792.

Weibel-Orlando, J. (1990). Grandparenting styles: Native American perspectives. In J. Sokolovsky (Ed.), *The cultural context of aging* (pp. 109–125). New York: Bergin & Garvey.

Weichold, K., & Silbereisen, R. K. (2005). Puberty. In C. B. Fisher & R. M. Lerner (Eds.), *Encyclopedia of applied developmental science* (Vol. 2, pp. 893–898). Thousand Oaks, CA: Sage.

Weinberg, M. K., Tronick, E. Z., Cohn, J. F., & Olson, K. L. (1999). Gender differences in emotional expressivity and self-regulation during early infancy. *Developmental Psychology, 35,* 175–188.

Weinstock, M. P., Neuman, Y., & Glassner, A. (2006). Identification of informal reasoning fallacies as a function of epistemological level, grade level, and cognitive ability. *Journal of Educational Psychology, 89,* 327–341.

Weisberg, D. S., & Bloom, P. (2009). Young children separate multiple pretend worlds. *Developmental Science, 12,* 699–705.

Weisgram, E. S., Bigler, R. S., & Liben, L. S. (2010). Gender, values, and occupational interests among children, adolescents, and adults. *Child Development, 81,* 778–796.

Weisner, T. S., & Wilson-Mitchell, J. E. (1990). Nonconventional family lifestyles and sex typing in six-year-olds. *Child Development, 61,* 1915–1933.

Weissman, M. D., & Kalish, C. W. (1999). The inheritance of desired characteristics: Children's view of the role of intention in parent–of spring resemblance. *Journal of Experimental Child Psychology, 73,* 245–265.

Weisz, J. R., McCarty, C. A., & Valeri, S. M. (2006). Effects of psychotherapy for depression in children and adolescents: A meta-analysis. *Psychological Bulletin, 132,* 132–149.

Wellman, H. M. (1993). Early understanding of mind: The normal case. In S. Baron-Cohen, H. Tager-Flusberg, & D. J. Cohen (Eds.), *Understanding other minds: Perspectives from autism.* Oxford, England: Oxford University Press.

Wellman, H. M., Cross, D., & Watson, J. (2001). Meta-analysis of theory-of-mind development: The truth about false belief. *Child Development, 72,* 655–684.

Wellman, H. M., & Gelman, S. A. (1998). Knowledge acquisition in foundational domains. In W. Damon (Ed.), *Handbook of child psychology* (5th ed., Vol. 2, pp. 523–573). New York: Wiley.

Wentworth, N., Benson, J. B., & Haith, M. M. (2000). The development of infants' reaches for stationary and moving targets. *Child Development, 71,* 576–601.

Wentzel, K. R., Filisetti, L., & Looney, L. (2007). Adolescent prosocial behavior: The role of self-processes and contextual cues. *Child Development, 78,* 895–910.

Werner, E. E. (1994). Overcoming the odds. *Journal of Developmental and Behavioral Pediatrics, 15,* 131–136.

Werner, E. E., & Smith, R. S. (1992). *Overcoming the odds: High risk children from birth to adulthood.* Ithaca, NY: Cornell University Press.

Werner, H. (1948). *Comparative psychology of mental development.* Chicago: Follet.

Wertsch, J. V., & Tulviste, P. (1992). L. S. Vygotsky and contemporary developmental psychology. *Developmental Psychology, 28,* 548–557.

West, M. D. (2010). Embryonic stem cells: Prospects of regenerative medicine for the treatment of human aging. In G. M. Fahy, M. D. West, L. S. Coles, & S. B. Harris (Eds.), *The future of aging* (pp. 451–487). New York: Springer.

Westbrook, L. A. (2002). The experience of mid-life women in the years after the deaths of their parents. *Dissertation Abstracts International. Section A. Humanities and Social Sciences, 62*(8-A), 2884.

Westerhof, G. J., Bohlmeijer, E., & Webster, J. D. (2010). Reminiscence and mental health: a review of recent progress in theory, research, and interventions. *Ageing and Society, 30,* 697–721.

Weymouth, P. L. (2005). A longitudinal look at the predictors of four types of retirement. *Dissertation Abstracts International. Section B. Sciences and Engineering, 65*(7-B), 3760.

Whalley, L. J., Fox, H. C., Deary, I. J., & Starr, J. M. (2005). Childhood IQ, smoking, and cognitive change from age 11 to 64 years. *Addictive Behaviors, 30,* 77–88.

Whitbourne, S. B., & Spiro, A., III. (2010). The intersection of physical and mental health in aging: Minding the gap? In J. C. Cavanaugh & C. K. Cavanaugh (Eds.), *Aging in America* (Vol. 2, pp. 119–140). Santa Barbara, CA: Praeger Perspectives.

Whitbourne, S. K. (1996). *The aging individual.* New York: Springer.

White, K. D. (2010). Note: Covenant marriage—An unnecessary second attempt at fault-based divorce. *Alabama Law Review, 61,* 869.

White, L., & Gilbreth, J. G. (2001). When children have two fathers: Effects of relationships with stepfathers and noncustodial fathers on adolescent outcomes. *Journal of Marriage and the Family, 63,* 155–167.

White, M. L., Peters, R., & Shim, S. M. (2011). Spirituality and spiritual self-care: Expanding self-care deficit nursing theory. *Nursing Science Quarterly, 24,* 48–56.

Whitehurst, G. J., & Vasta, R. (1975). Is language acquired through imitation? *Journal of Psycholinguistic Research, 4,* 37–59.

Whiting, B. B., & Edwards, P. E. (1988). *Children of different worlds.* Cambridge, MA: Harvard University Press.

Whiting, J. W. M., & Child, I. L. (1953). *Child training and personality: A cross-cultural study.* New Haven, CT: Yale University Press.

Whitney, L. D., & Ajmera, S. (2010). Nutrition and aging. In R. H. Robnett & W. C. Chop (Eds.), *Gerontology for the health care professional* (2nd ed., pp. 199–234). Sudbury, MA: Jones & Bartlett.

Whitty, M. T., & Buchanan, T. (2009). Looking for love in so many places: Characteristics of online daters and speed daters. *Interpersona: An International Journal on Personal Relationships, 3*(Suppl. 2). Retrieved from http://www.interpersona.org/pdf/interpersona3%28suppl.2%29.pdf#page564

Wicks-Nelson, R., & Israel, A. C. (2006). *Behavior disorders of childhood* (6th ed.). Upper Saddle River, NJ: Pearson Education.

Wilkinson, A. M., & Lynn, J. (2001). The end of life. In R. H. Binstock & L. K. George (Eds.), *Handbook of aging and the social sciences* (5th ed., pp. 444–461). San Diego, CA: Academic Press.

Williams, S. A. (2005). Jealousy in the cross-sex friendship. *Journal of Loss & Trauma, 10,* 471–485.

Williams, S. T., Conger, K. J., & Blozis, S. A. (2007). The development of interpersonal aggression during adolescence: The importance of parents, siblings, and family economics. *Child Development, 78,* 1526–1542.

Willinger, M. (1995). Sleep position and sudden infant death syndrome. *JAMA, 273,* 818–819.

Wilson, B. J. (2008). Media and children's aggression, fear, and altruism. *The Future of Children, 18,* 87–118.

Wilson, D. B. (2010). Meta-analysis. In A. R. Piquero & D. Wesiburd (Eds.), *Handbook of quantitative criminology* (Pt. 2, pp. 181–208). New York: Springer.

Wilson, G. T., Heffernan, K., & Black, C. M. D. (1996). Eating disorders. In E. J. Marsh & R. A. Barkley (Eds.), *Child psychopathology* (pp. 541–571). New York: Guilford.

Wilson, R. D. (2000). Amniocentesis and chorionic villus sampling. *Current Opinion in Obstetrics and Gynecology, 12,* 81–86.

Winecoff, A., LaBar, K. S. Madden, D. J., Cabeza, R., & Huettel, S. A. (2011). Cognitive and neural contributions to emotion regulation in aging. *Social Cognitive and Affective Neuroscience, 6,* 165–176.

Winner, E. (2000). Giftedness: Current theory and research. *Current Directions in Psychological Science, 9,* 153–156.

Witko, T. M. (2006). A framework for working with American Indian parents. In T. M. Witko (Ed.), *Mental health care for urban Indians: Clinical insights from Native practitioners* (pp. 155–171). Washington, DC: American Psychological Association.

Wojtowicz, A. E., & von Ranson, K. M. (2012). Weighing in on risk factors for body dissatisfaction: A one-year prospective study of middle-adolescent girls. *Body Image, 9,* 20–30.

Wolf, A. M. D., Wender, R. C., Etzioni, R. B., Thompson, I. M., D'Amico, A. V., Volk, R. J., et al. (2010). American Cancer Society guideline for the early detection of prostate cancer: 2010 update. *CA: A Cancer Journal for Clinicians, 60,* 70–98.

Wolfinger, N. H. (2007). Does the rebound effect exist? Time to remarriage and subsequent union stability. *Journal of Divorce & Remarriage, 46,* 9–20.

Wolraich, M. L., Lindgren, S. D., Stumbo, P. J., Stegink, L. D., Appelbaum, M. I., & Kiritsy, M. C. (1994). Effects of diets high in sucrose or aspartame on the behavior and cognitive performance of children. *New England Journal of Medicine, 330,* 301–307.

Womenshealth.gov. (2010). *Menopausal hormone therapy (MHT).* Retrieved from http://www.womenshealth.gov/menopause/symptom-relief-treatment/menopausal-hormone-therapy.cfm

Wong, P. T. P. (2008). Transformation of grief through meaning: Meaning-centered counseling for bereavement. In A. Tomer, G. T. Eliason, & P. T. P. Wong (Eds.), *Existential and spiritual issues in death attitudes* (pp. 375–396). Mahwah, NJ: Erlbaum.

Woodbridge, S. (2008). Sustaining families in the 21st century: The role of grandparents. *International Journal of Environmental, Cultural, Economic and Social Sustainability.* Retrieved from http://www98.griffith.edu.au/dspace/bitstream/10072/27417/1/50932_1.pdf

Woodgate, R. L. (2006). Living in a world without closure: Reality for parents who have experienced the death of a child. *Journal of Palliative Care, 22,* 75–82.

Woodward, A. L., & Markman, E. M. (1998). Early word learning. In W. Damon (Ed.), *Handbook of child psychology* (5th ed., Vol. 2, pp. 371–420). New York: Wiley.

Worden, W. (1991). *Grief counseling and grief therapy: A handbook for the mental health practitioner* (2nd ed.). New York: Springer.

World Health Organization. (2002). *Worldwide report on violence and health: Chapter 4. Violence by intimate partners.* Retrieved from http://www.who.int/violence_injury_prevention/violence/global_campaign/en/chap4.pdf

World Health Organization. (2010). *Why gender and health?* Retrieved from http://www.who.int/gender/genderandhealth/en/index.html

Worobey, J. (2005). Effects of malnutrition. In C. B. Fisher & R. M. Lerner (Eds.), *Encyclopedia of applied developmental science* (Vol. 2, pp. 673–676). Thousand Oaks, CA: Sage.

Wozniak, J. R., & Lim, K. O. (2006). Advances in white matter imaging: A review of in vivo magnetic resonance methodologies and their applicability to the study of development and aging. *Neuroscience & Biobehavioral Reviews, 30,* 762–774.

Wrenn, R. L. (1999). The grieving college student. In J. D. Davidson & K. J. Doka (Eds.), *Living with grief: At work, at school, at worship* (pp. 131–141). Levittown, PA: Brunner/Mazel.

Wright, J. C., Huston, A. C., Murphy, K. C., St. Peters, M., Pinon, M., Scantlin, R., et al. (2001). The relations of early television viewing to school readiness and vocabulary of children from low-income families: The Early Window Project. *Child Development, 72,* 1347–1366.

Wu, R., Mareschal, D., & Rakison, D. H. (2011). Attention to multiple cues during spontaneous object labeling. *Infancy, 16,* 545–556.

Wynn, K. (1992). Addition and subtraction by human infants. *Nature, 358,* 749–750.

Wynn, K. (1996). Infants' individuation and enumeration of actions. *Psychological Science, 7,* 164–169.

Xie, H., Li, Y., Boucher, S. M., Hutchins, B. C., & Cairns, B. D. (2006). What makes a girl (or a boy) popular (or unpopular)? African American children's perceptions and developmental differences. *Developmental Psychology, 42,* 599–612.

Xu, X., Ji, J., & Tung, Y. Y. (2000). Social and political assortative mating in urban China. *Journal of Family Issues, 21,* 47–77.

Xu, X., Zhu, F., O'Campo, P., Koenig, M. A., Mock, V., & Campbell, J. (2005). Prevalence of and risk factors for intimate partner violence in China. *American Journal of Public Health, 95,* 78–85.

Xu, Y., Farver, J. A., & Zhang, Z. (2009). Temperament, harsh and indulgent parenting, and Chinese children's proactive and reactive aggression. *Child Development, 80,* 244–258.

Yamini-Benjamin, Y. I. (2007). Moving toward a better understanding of black women's work adjustment: The role of perceived discrimination and self-efficacy in predicting job satisfaction and psychological distress in black women. *Dissertation Abstracts International. Section B. Sciences and Engineering, 67*(10-B), 6085.

Yancura, & Aldwin, C. (2010). Does psychological stress accelerate the aging process? In J. C. Cavanaugh & C. K. Cavanaugh (Eds.), *Aging in America* (Vol. 2, pp. 100–118). Santa Barbara, CA: Praeger Perspectives.

Yang, N., Chen, C. C., Choi, J., & Zou, Y. (2000). Sources of work–family conflict: A Sino–U.S. comparison of the effects of work and family. *Academy of Management Journal, 43,* 113–123.

Yap, M. B. H., Allen, N. B., & Ladouceur, C. D. (2008). Maternal socialization of positive affect: The impact of invalidation on adolescent emotion regulation and depressive symptomatology. *Child Development, 79,* 1415–1431.

Yárnoz-Yaben, S. (2010). Attachment style and adjustment to divorce. *Spanish Journal of Psychology, 13,* 210–219.

Yngvesson, B. (2010). *Belonging in an adopted world: Race, identity, and transnational adoption*. Chicago: University of Chicago Press.

Yoon, S. M. (2005). The characteristics and needs of Asian-American grandparent caregivers: A study of Chinese-American and Korean-American grandparents in New York City. *Journal of Gerontological Social Work, 44,* 75–94.

Young, S. K., Fox, N. A., & Zahn-Waxler, C. (1999). The relations between temperament and empathy in 2-year-olds. *Developmental Psychology, 35,* 1189–1197.

Youniss, J., McLellan, J. A., & Yates, M. (1999). Religion, community service, and identity in American youth. *Journal of Adolescence, 22,* 243–253.

Yu, T., & Adler-Baeder, F. (2007). The intergenerational transmission of relationship quality: The effects of parental remarriage quality on young adults' relationships. *Journal of Divorce & Remarriage, 47,* 87–102.

Yu, T., Pettit, G. S., Lansford, J. E., Dodge, K. A., & Bates, J. E. (2010). The interactive effects of marital conflict and divorce on parent–adult children's relationships. *Journal of Marriage and Family, 72,* 282–292.

Yuan, S., & Fisher, C. (2009). "Really? She blicked the baby?": Two-year-olds learn combinatorial facts about verbs by listening. *Psychological Science, 20,* 619–626.

Yumoto, C., Jacobson, S. W., & Jacobson, J. L. (2008). Fetal substance exposure and cumulative environmental risk in an African American cohort. *Child Development, 79,* 1761–1776.

Zacks, R. T., Hasher, L., & Li, K. Z. H. (2000). Human memory. In F. I. M. Craik & T. A. Salthouse (Eds.), *Handbook of aging and cognition* (2nd ed., pp. 293–357). Mahwah, NJ: Erlbaum.

Zafarullah, H. (2000). Through the brick wall and the glass ceiling: Women in the civil service in Bangladesh. *Gender, Work & Organization, 7,* 197–209.

Zahn-Waxler, C., Radke-Yarrow, M., Wagner, E., & Chapman, M. (1992). Development of concern for others. *Developmental Psychology, 28,* 126–136.

Zarrett, N., Fay, K., Li, Y., Carrano, J., Phelps, E., & Lerner, R. M. (2009). More than child's play: Variable- and pattern-centered approaches for examining effects of sports participation on youth development. *Developmental Psychology, 45,* 368–382.

Zaslow, M. J., & Hayes, C. D. (1986). Sex differences in children's responses to psychosocial stress: Toward a cross-context analysis. In M. E. Lamb, A. L. Brown, & B. Rogoff (Eds.), *Advances in developmental psychology* (Vol. 4, pp. 285–337). Hillsdale, NJ: Erlbaum.

Zelazo, P. D., & Cunningham, W. A. (2007). Executive function: Mechanisms underlying emotion regulation. In J. J. Gross (Ed.), *Handbook of emotion regulation* (pp. 135–158). New York: Guilford.

Zeng, Y., Gu, D., & George, L. K. (2011). Association of religious participation with mortality among Chinese old adults. *Research on Aging, 33,* 51–83.

Zhan, H. J. (2006). Joy and sorrow: Explaining Chinese caregivers' reward and stress. *Journal of Aging Studies, 20,* 27–38.

Zhang, B., Cartmill, C., & Ferrence, R. (2008). The role of spending money and drinking alcohol in adolescent smoking. *Addiction, 103,* 310–319.

Zhang, Y., Koerner, T., Miller, S., Grice-Patil, Z., Svec, A., Akbari, D., et al. (2011). Neural coding of formant-exaggerated speech in the infant brain. *Developmental Science, 14,* 566–581.

Zhou, Q., Eisenberg, N., Losoya, S. H., Fabes, R. A., Reiser, M., Guthrie, I. K., et al. (2002). The relations of parental warmth and positive expressiveness to children's empathy-related responding and social functioning: A longitudinal study. *Child Development, 73,* 893–915.

Zhou, Q., Wang, Y., Eisenberg, N., Wolchik, S., Tein, J.-W., & Deng, X. (2008). Relations of parenting and temperament to Chinese children's experience of negative life events, coping efficacy, and externalizing problems. *Child Development, 79,* 493–513.

Ziegler, J. C., Pech-Georgel, C., Dufau, S., & Grainger, J. (2010). Rapid processing of letters, digits, and symbols: What purely visual–attentional deficit in developmental dyslexia? *Developmental Science, 13,* F8–F14.

Zimiles, H., & Lee, V. E. (1991). Adolescent family structure and educational progress. *Developmental Psychology, 27,* 314–320.

Zimmer-Gembeck, M. J., & Helfand, M. (2008). Ten years of longitudinal research on U.S. adolescent sexual behavior: Developmental correlates of sexual intercourse, and the importance of age, gender and ethnic background. *Developmental Review, 28,* 153–224.

Zinar, S. (2000). The relative contributions of word identification skill and comprehension-monitoring behavior to reading comprehension ability. *Contemporary Educational Psychology, 25,* 363–377.

Zippel, K. S. (2006). *The politics of sexual harassment: A comparative study of the United States, the European Union, and Germany*. New York: Cambridge University Press.

Zmuda, J. M., Cauley, J. A., Kriska, A., Glynn, N. W., Gutai, J. P., & Kuller, L. H. (1997). Longitudinal relation between endogenous testosterone and cardiovascular disease risk factors in middle-aged men: A 13-year follow-up of former Multiple Risk Factors Intervention Trial participants. *American Journal of Epidemiology, 146,* 609–617.

Zukow-Goldring, P. (2002). Sibling caregiving. In M. H. Bornstein (Ed.), *Handbook of parenting* (2nd ed., Vol. 3, pp. 253–286). Mahwah, NJ: Erlbaum.

Name Index

DeLeeuw, J., 197
DeLoache, J. S., 97, 117, 135
DeLuca, S., 265–266, 280
DeLucia-Waack, J. L., 312
Delva, J., 182
Del Valle, J. F., 200
Dement, W. C., 66
Demir, A., 74
De Neys, W., 159
Deng, C. P., 319
Deng, X., 191
Denissen, J. J. A., 204, 243
Dennett, D. A., 402, 406
Dennis, J., 139
Dennis, T., 51
DePaulo, B. M., 299
DePinho, R. A., 384
Deptula, D. P., 201
Derdikman-Eiron, R., 256
De Schonen, S., 83
Desjardins, R. N., 112
Desmond, N., 307
Desrosiers, J., 424
Deutsch, A., 443, 444
Deutsch, D., 429
De Vries, B., 292
De Vries, H., 254
De Vries, M. W., 254–255
De Vries, R. E., 328
De Weerth, C., 69
Dewey, K. G., 69
De Winter, A. F., 205
DeWitt, A., 306
De Wolff, M. S., 131
Dey, J. G., 329, 340
De Zwaan, M., 224
Diamond, A., 247
Diamond, J. S., 312
Diaz, A., 307
Díaz, C., 395
Diaz, R. M., 247
Diaz Cintra, S., 45, 71
Dickens, B. M., 442, 443
Dickens, W., 165, 166, 279, 355, 442
Dickinson, G. E., 463
Dick-Read, G., 54
Dickson, D., 402, 406
Dickson, N., 256
Diego, M., 56
Diehl, M., 356
DiFonzo, J. H., 311–312
Dijkstra, J. K., 205
Dilworth-Anderson, P., 417
Dinella, L., 255
Dinsbach, A. A., 328
Dionea, G., 256
DiPietro, J. A., 44, 46
Dishion, T. J., 201, 203
Dissanayake, C., 337
Dixon, P., 306
Dixon, R.A., 360, 397
Dockstader, C., 228
Dodge, K. A., 138, 190, 199, 204, 256, 312
Dohnt, H., 224
Dolenszky, E., 200
Domellöff, E., 78
Dommaraju, P., 296
Donahue, P. J. D., 420
Donaldson, S. J., 182, 225
Dong, T., 202
Donnellan, M. B., 320
Donnelly, E.A., 410
D'Onofrio, B. M., 46, 51
Doohan, E.-A. M., 311
Doris, J. M., 285

Doskow, E., 309
Douch, R., 211
Douglas, E. M., 297
Dovey, T. M., 71
Dow, B., 424
Dowda, M., 182
Dowdall, G., 271
Downey, R. G., 176
Draghi-Lorenz, R., 133
Draper, F., 220–221
Drews, F. A., 48
Driscoll, A. K., 191
Drouet, V., 402, 404, 406
Druley, J. A., 368
Duan, N., 457
Dubinsky, R., 394
Dubois, B., 402, 406
Ducharme, F., 430
Duchene, M. S., 201
Duckworth, A. L., 165
Dufau, S., 174
Duff, K., 402, 404, 406
Duff, L. J., 181
Duffy, R. D., 319
Duffy, S., 139
Du Fort, G. G., 46
Dufour, M. C., 272
Dumas, J. A., 350
Duncan, G., 166, 198
Dunham, F., 116
Dunham, P. J., 116
Dunlosky, J., 395
Dunn, J., 88, 135, 193, 194, 195, 197
Dunn, J. F., 142
Dunn, M., 225
Dunson, D. B., 46
Dupuis, S., 308
Durham, M., 116
Durmysheva, Y., 397
Durr, J., 54
Dutton, W. H., 294–295
Dwyer, T., 67
Dyke, P. H., 267

E
Eagly, A. H., 146
Earles, J. L., 393
Earls, F. J., 256
Eastwick, P. W., 294
Eaton, D. K., 245
Eaton, J., 358
Ebberwein, C. A., 334
Ebersole, P., 348
Ebrahim, A. F., 441
Eby, L. T., 332
Eccles, J. S., 148, 182, 243
Eckhardt, C., 297
Eddleston, K. A., 321
Edelstein, B., 395, 396, 399, 400
Edwards, C. A., 202
Edwards, H., 460
Edwards, J. D., 393
Edwards, M. B., 460
Edwards, P. E., 145
Egan, S. K., 205, 247
Eichstedt, J. A., 144
Einspieler, C., 78
Eisenberg, M. E., 224
Eisenberg, N., 136, 140, 141, 142, 190, 191, 244
Eizenman, D. R., 82
Ekerdt, D. J., 419, 420
Elder, G. H., 221, 241, 252–253, 255
Elder, N., 45
Eley, T. C., 40, 255

Elkind, D., 241
Ellickson, P. L., 254
Elliott, D. B., 312
Elliott, J., 442
Ellis, B. J., 39
Ellis, J. W., 371
Ellis, S. J., 462
El Nokali, N. E., 177
Elovainio, M., 303
Else-Quest, N. M., 145
Emery, R. E., 221
Emick, M. A., 371
Engels, R. C. M. E., 201
Engle, P., 71
Engle, P. L., 55
Engle, S. M., 46
Ennett, S. T., 248, 249
Enslin, C., 321
Epel, E. S., 384
Epstein, L. H., 223, 224
Epstein, M., 320
Equal Employment Opportunity Commission, 330
Erickson, E., 363, 413–414
Ericsson, K. A., 181, 357, 358
Erikson, E., 10, 10, 128, 361
Erikson, E. H., 240, 244, 266–267, 268, 283
Ernst, M., 47
Eskritt, M., 160
Espinosa, M. P., 166
Esplin, P. W., 106
Etten, M. J., 351
Etzioni, R. B., 351
European Association of Palliative Care, 442
Evans, G. D., 306
Evans, J. A., 400
Evans, M. A., 174
Evans, N. J., 265–266
Evans, S. M., 148
Everaerts, D., 159
Everingham, C., 419
Eyler, F. D., 47

F
Faber, A. J., 313
Fabes, R. A., 136, 139, 140, 141, 142, 148, 190, 191
Fabricius, W. V., 196
Fagan, A. M., 402, 406
Faggiano, F., 254
Fagot, B. I., 148
Faith, M. S., 224
Falbo, T., 195
Fan, P.-L., 384
Fang, S., 191
Faraone, S. V., 172
Farley, F., 226
Farrant, B. M., 88
Farroni, T., 82
Farver, J. A., 256
Faucher, E. H., 448
Faux, A. L., 85
Favre, B., 269
Fay, K., 183
Fearon, R. M. P., 39, 131
Feddes, A. R., 201
Federal Bureau of Investigation, 256
Federal Interagency Forum on Aging-Related Statistics, 429, 430
Federal Interagency Forum on Child and Family Statistics, 226
Feldhusen, J. F., 168
Feldman, H. A., 402, 406

Feldman, K., 365
Feldman, R., 256
Feldstein, G., 301
Feng, D., 371
Feng, W. Y., 68
Feng, Z., 425
Fennell, C. T., 115
Fenson, L., 113
Ferdinand, R. F., 254
Fergusson, D. M., 46
Fernald, A., 135
Fernandez, A., 420
Fernandez, M. C., 115
Fernyhough, C., 110
Feron, F. J., 254–255
Ferrarini, T., 337
Ferraro, V., 115
Ferrence, R., 252
Ferreol-Barbey, M., 175
Fiej, J. A., 328
Field, M. J., 447
Field, T., 55, 56
Field, T. M., 120, 130
Fields, V., 420
Fierros, E., 183
Fiese, B. H., 284
Fifer, W. P., 67
Filyer, R., 361
Fincham, F. D., 304, 312, 313
Fingerman, K. L., 422
Fink, B., 176
Finkel, E. J., 294
Finnie, V., 139
Fischer, K. W., 133
Fisher, C., 115
Fisher, G. G., 400
Fisher, K., 390
Fisher, L. L., 349, 350, 351
Fisher-Borne, M., 297
FitzGerald, D. P., 211
Fitzsimons, A. M., 460
Fivush, R., 105
Flanagan, T., 198
Flanigan, C. M., 294
Flap, H., 294
Flavell, J. H., 122, 161
Fletcher, J., 88, 113
Flom, R., 85
Flory, K., 271
Flynn, H. K., 292
Flynn, J., 165, 166, 279, 355
Flynn, M., 205
Fogarty, K., 306
Folck, C. D., 311
Folkman, S., 352
Fontaine, R. G., 256
Fonzi, A., 201
Foorman, B. R., 174, 175
Forbes, D., 146
Forde, C., 419
Forehand, R., 254
Foreyt, J. P., 224
Forgatch, M., 197, 308
Forney, D. S., 265–266
Fortner, B. V., 448
Foshee, V. A., 248, 249
Foss, D.J., 357
Foster, E. M., 207
Foster, S. E., 254
Fouad, N.A., 320
Fouquereau, E., 420
Fowler, F., 191
Fowler, K. L., 449
Fox, H. C., 270
Fox, K. M., 404

Osgood, D., 147, 194, 195, 244, 366
Ostendorf, C. A., 391
Oster, H., 80
Oster-Aaland, L., 271
Ostrov, E., 244
Ostrov, J. M., 146, 204
Ostry, A., 193
Oswald, A. J., 414
Oswald, F., 410
Ott, B. R., 393
Ottaway, A. J., 312
Owsley, C., 393
Oyserman, D., 242
Ozawa, M. N., 312

P

Paarlberg, K. M., 45
Pachana, N. A., 393
Packer, D. J., 284
Paikoff, R., 246
Palermo, T. M., 224
Paley, B., 193
Palkovitz, R., 306
Pallier, C., 83
Palm, G., 306
Palmer, A. M., 355
Palmérus, K., 371
Palokangas, T., 135
Panegyres, P. K., 401
Pankow, L. J., 384
Papa, A., 454, 455, 456, 457
Paquet, Y., 324
Paquette, D., 130
Paquette, J. A., 204
Paraita, H., 395
Parault, S. J., 161
Parcel, G. S., 182
Pargament, K. I., 352
Park, C. L., 417
Park, D. C., 385, 386, 392, 393, 394, 395, 396, 406
Parke, R. D., 139, 192
Parker, J., 137, 202
Parker, J. G., 201, 203, 204
Parker, N., 370
Parkman, A. M., 303
Parra-Cordona, J. R., 431
Parritz, R. H., 136
Parrot, A., 298
Parsons, J. T., 301
Pascalis, O., 82, 84
Paschall, M. J., 271
Pascual, B., 88
Pasley, K., 196
Passchier, J., 45
Passtoors, W. M., 382, 384
Pastore, M., 256
Pate, R. R., 182
Pateman, B. C., 225
Patrick, J. H., 371
Patrick, S., 304
Patterson, G. R., 192, 256
Patterson, M. M., 210, 211
Pattie, A., 422
Patton, L. D., 265–266
Pauker, K., 211
Paul, B., 74
Paxton, S. J., 224
Payne, R., 443
Pearlin, L. I., 367
Pearson, B. Z., 115
Pearson, F., 308
Pech-Georgel, C., 174
Peel, E., 462
Peled, T., 198

Pell, T., 51
Peltola, M. J., 135
Pelucci, B., 112
Pence, K., 174
Penke, L., 385
Pennisi, E., 35
Penson, R. T., 440
Perez, A., 444
Perfetti, C. A., 174, 175
Perin, D., 176
Perkins, D. F., 182
Perkins, H. W., 286
Perrett, R., 419
Perrone, K. M., 320
Perry, D. G., 205, 243, 247
Perry, K. E., 175
Perry, W. I., 265–266
Pérusse, D., 146, 256
Pesetsky, D., 174, 175
Peters, A. M., 118
Peters, R., 417
Peterson, J., 461
Peterson, J. L., 145
Peterson, L., 141
Peterson, M., 293
Peterson, S. A., 360
Pethick, S. J., 113
Petitt, G. S., 138, 139, 140, 190, 256, 312
Petrill, S. A., 308
Pettito, L. A., 115
Pfeiffer, K. A., 182
Pfost, K. S., 325
Pharr, J. R., 334
Phelps, J., 183
Phelps, J. A., 38
Phelps, R. E., 328
Philippe, F. L., 324
Phillips, D., 166
Phinney, J., 242
Phipps, M. G., 247
Piaget, J., 11–12, *12*, 97, 158, 235, 241, 244
Pianka, P., 219
Pichora-Fuller, A., 390
Pickering, R. P., 272
Pickett, K. E., 47
Piehler, T. F., 201
Pienta, A. M., 423
Pierce, E. A., 52
Pierce, G. L., 384
Pierret, C. R., 336
Pierroutsakos, S. L., 117
Pierson, E., 325
Pike, A., 142
Pillay, H., 330
Pincus, T., 273
Pinderhughes, E. E., 256
Pine, D. S., 47
Pineda, A. Q., 255
Pinker, S., 118
Pinkhasov, R. M., 382
Pinon, M., 116
Pintello, D., 323
Pinto, K. M., 338
Piolat, A., 175
Piquet, B. J., 293
Piscione, D. P., 326
Pisoni, D. B., 80, 111
Platzman, K. A., 47, 51
Plaumann, M., 324
Plewis, I., 65, 66
Plienegger, J., 78
Plomin, R., 40, 142, 172
Plummer, D., 460
Plunkett, K., 103
Poelmans, S., 339

Pokhrel, P., 202
Polifka, J. E., 47
Polinder, S., 353
Polit, E. F., 195
Polivka, L., 432, 433, 434, 435
Pollak, S. D., 68
Pollitt, E., 181
Pomerantz, E. M., 191
Ponsonby, A. L., 67
Pontifex, M. B., 182
Poon, L. W., 360, 393
Pope, H. G., 225
Popenoe, D., 300
Popp, D., 201
Porter, R. H., 80
Poskiparta, E., 205
Post, L. A., 431
Potter, J., 360, 361, 362
Poulin, F., 200, 201
Poulin-Dubois, D., 144
Pourquette, C., 193
Power, T. L., 448
Powers, J., 139
Powlishta, K. K., 146
Prasada, S., 101
Pratt, H. D., 321
Pratt, M. W., 361
Prechtl, H. F. R., 78
President's Council on Physical Fitness and Sports, 182, 225
Pressley, M., 160, 175, 176, 228, 229
Prigerson, H. G., 457
Prinstein, M. J., 202, 203, 204
Probert, B., 325
Probst, T., 203
Pruchno, R., 371
Pruett, M. K., 311, 312
Prus, S.G., 391
Puhl, R. M., 223, 225
Pullen, P. C., 174
Pungello, E. P., 166
Punzalan, J. C., 301
Purcell, D., 328
Putnick, D. L., 46
Puybasset, M., 443, 445
Pynoos, J., 428, 429, 430, 431

Q

Qiu, W. Q., 400
Qualls, S. H., 400, 428
Quillian, L., 201
Quinn, P. C., 84, 145
Quirin, M., 448

R

Raab, G. M., 425
Racz, S. J., 190
Radford, A., 117
Radke-Yarrow, M., 140
Raedeke, T. D., 183
Raffaelli, M., 307
Ragins, B. R., 321
Ragsdale, B. L., 242
Rainer, S., 271
Rakic, P., 73
Rakison, D. H., 101, 114
Rakoczy, H., 138
Ralph, L. J., 247
Ram, N., 243
Ramakumar, S., 307
Ramey, C. T., 166
Ramineni, C., 177
Ramsay, D., 51
Ramsay, K., 68
Ranganathan, R., 77
Rankin, C. T., 300

Ranwez, S., 358
Rape, Abuse, and Incest National Network, 297
Rapee, R. M., 224
Rapport, M. D., 171
Raschick, M., 424
Rasmussen, F., 279
Rasmussen, H., 390
Rasmussen, R. L., 183
Rathouz, P. J., 46
Rathunde, K. R., 168
Rathus, S. A., 255
Rawlings, N. B., 418
Rawlins, W. K., 422
Rayner, K., 174, 175
Real, K., 326
Reddy, P., 461
Reddy, V., 133
Redman, T., 330
Reed, A., 82
Reeder, A. I., 252
Reese, E., 105, 106
Reesman, M. C., 254
Reichelmann, H., 389
Reid, R., 176
Reilly, J., 74
Reimer, M. S., 134
Reis, S. M., 168
Reiser, M., 136, 190, 191
Remedios, J. D., 284
Renaud, J., 255
Renn, K. A., 265–266
Renshaw, K. D., 304
Renshaw, P. D., 203
Renzulli, J. S., 168
Repacholi, B. M., 135
Resnick, S., 131
Reston, A. C., 224
Reuter-Lorenz, P.A., 385, 386, 392, 394, 395
Reville, B., 450
Reyes, H. L. M., 248
Reyna, V. F., 226
Reynolds, A. J., 213
Reznick, J. S., 113
Rhoades, G. K., 300
Rhoades, K. A., 193
Ribe, E.M., 385
Ricciardelli, L. A., 224
Ricciuti, H. N., 71
Rice, C., 54
Rice, N. E., 420
Richard, M. H., 242
Richmond, J., 105
Richters, J. E., 172
Riedmann, A., 299, 303, 308, 311
Riggins, R., 151
Riggs, D. W., 462
Riggs, M. L., 311
Rijken, A. J., 305–306
Rijsdijk, F., 255
Riksen-Walraven, J. M., 69
Riley, E. P., 47
Riley, M. W., 15
Riordan, K., 131
Risacher, S.L., 385, 404
Ritter, J., 254
Roberson, E.D., 401, 402
Roberts, B. W., 68
Roberts, C. R., 242
Roberts, J. A., 297
Roberts, J. E., 116, 151, 459
Roberts, R. E., 242
Roberts, W., 140
Robertson, A., 349

Subject Index

commitment, 266, 295, 311, 325
communicating results of research, 24–25
communication
   listening, 120
   of research results, 24–25
   online, 294–295
   speaking effectively, 120
   taking turns, 120
compensation, 10, 14–15
competence, 14, 101, 143, 161, 163, 250, 411
competence-environmental theory, 14, 411–413
complex emotions, 133–134
complicated or prolonged grief disorder, 457
complications, birth, 55–56
comprehension, reading, 175
computers, 207
conception, 42, 59
concrete-operational period, 158, 159
conflict, work-family, 338–339
conscientiousness, 360
consequences of attachment, 131
constancy, gender, 148
constricting actions, 139
content knowledge, 228–229
continuity theory, 410
continuity-discontinuity issue, 5–6
contraception, 246–247
control beliefs, 284–285
controversial children, 203–204
conventional level, 232
convergent thinking, 168
convoy, social, 422
cooing, 113
cooperative play, 139
coordinating skills, infants', 77
COPD (chronic obstructive pulmonary disease), 387
coping, 352–353
   with grief, 454, 455–457
   with stress, 352–353
core knowledge hypothesis, 100
corpus callosum, 72
correlation coefficient, 20
correlational studies, 20, 21
counting, learning, 107–108
covenant marriage, 311
creative ability, 163, 397
creative children, 168
cross-linking, 384
cross-sectional studies, 22
cross-sex friendships, 293
crowd, 202
crying, 65, 66
crystallization, 250
crystallized intelligence, 162, 277–279
culture. *see also* ethnicity
   abusive relationships, 298
   adoptive parents, 309
   caregiving for aging parents and, 368

couple-forming and, 295–296
emotional expression and, 134
generativity, 361, 363
identity and, 242
job satisfaction, 321–324
matchmaking and, 298
menopause, 349–351
multiple intelligences and, 164
parenting styles, 191–192
popular children, 203–204
role transitions, 265
role transitions marking adulthood and, 264–265
sexual harassment, 329–330
singlehood, 299
sociocultural forces, 7
custody, 196
CVA (cerebral vascular accident), 386–387
cytomegalovirus, 48

D
dating, 294–295
   adolescent, 245–249
   online, 294–295
   single parenthood and, 308
   speed, 294
   violence, 248–249
Death With Dignity Act, 443, 444, 450
death(s)
   adolescents and, 225–226, 255, 459
   alcohol-related, 271
   anxiety, 448–449
   childhood understanding of, 458–459
   clinical, 441
   contextual theory of, 448
   dealing with one's own, 446–448
   end-of-life intentions, 444–445
   ethical issues with, 442–445
   final scenarios and, 449–450
   grief process and, 453–457
   hospice and, 450–452
   legal and medical definitions, 441–442
   life-course approach to dying and, 446
   of one's child in young and middle adulthood, 460
   of one's child or grandchild in late life, 461
   of one's parent, 460
   of one's partner, 425, 454–455, 461–462
   sociocultural definitions of, 440
   suicide, 255, 443–444
   whole-brain, 441
   young adulthood and, 459–460
deductive reasoning, 159
delinquency, adolescent, 256–257

dementia, 401–405
   Alzheimer's disease, 387, 401–404
   vascular, 387
demographers, 378
demographics of aging, 378–380
dendrites, 72, 73
deoxyribonucleic acid (DNA), 35–36
dependent care dilemma, 335–337
dependent variables, 21
depression
   in adolescents, 254–255
   in late adulthood, 399–401
   postpartum, 55
   suicide and, 255
depth perception, 80–81
descriptions of others by children, 208–209
designs, research. *see* developmental research
developmental coaches, 320–321
developmental dyslexia, 169, 170–171
developmental research, 17–26
   applying results of, 25
   communicating results of, 24–25
   conducted ethically, 24
   designs for studying development, 22–23, 24
   general designs for, 20–22
   measurement in, 17–20
developmental theories, 9–17
   cognitive-developmental, 11–13
   definition of theory and, 9
   dynamic systems, 75
   ecological and systems perspective, 13–14
   learning theory, 10–11
   lifelong development perspective, 14–16
   psychodynamic theory, 10
   social learning, 11
diabetic retinopathy, 388
diagnosis and treatment, prenatal, 51–52
Dietary Guidelines for Americans, 274
diethylstilbestrol (DES), 50
differentiation, 77
direct instruction by parents, 192
disability
   children with, 169–171
   frailty in late life and, 426–428
discipline
   practices, 142
   prosocial behavior and, 140, 143
discontinuity and continuity, 5–6
discrimination and bias, 328–330
diseases, teratogenic, 48
disorganized attachment, 130–131
divergent thinking, 168

diversity of older adults, 378–380
divorce, 195–197. *see also* marriage
   collaborative, 311
   effects on children, 195–197, 311–312
   effects on the couple, 311
   single parenthood and, 308
   statistics, 310–311
dizygotic twins, 38
do not resuscitate (DNR) order, 445
dominance hierarchy, 202
dominant (alleles), 36, 37
Dora the Explorer (television program), 116
Down syndrome, 37, 37, 169
drugs
   for ADHD, 172
   for depression, 400
   for osteoporosis, 347
   for rheumatoid arthritis, 348
   for treating symptoms of menopause, 351
   teratogen, 47–48
   use by adolescents, 254
dual process model (DPM), 455, 457
dual-earner households, 338–339
durable power of attorney for health care, 444–445
dynamic systems theory, 75
dyslexia, developmental, 169, 170–171
dysphoria, 399

E
E-I-E-I-O model of memory, 396, 404
eating disorders, 224–225
ecological and systems perspective, 13–14
Eden Alternative, 430
edgework, 266
education. *see also* academic skills; learning
   effective schools and teachers and, 177–179
   level and health, 273
   marriage, 313
   part-time employment effect on, 252–253
   prejudice and, 211–212
   through video, 116
   worker retraining, 331–332
effortful control, 67
ego resilience, 364
egocentrism, 97–98, 99
   adolescent, 241
elaboration, 160
elder abuse and neglect, 431–432
electronic media, 116, 206–208
embryo, 43
emerging adulthood. *see also* young adulthood
   behavioral changes in, 266–267

college enrollment in,
265–266
establishing intimacy in,
266–267
growth, strength, and physical functioning in, 269
launching financial independence in, 267
role transitions marking,
264–265
emotional intelligence, 163
emotions
and well-being in late adulthood, 414–417
basic, 133, *134*
cultural differences in expression of, 134
emergence of complex,
133–134
experiencing and expressing,
133–134
integration logic and,
280–282
recognizing and using
others', 135
regulating, 135–136
sensitivity and gender, 146
using photographs to measure understanding of, 26
empathy, 140–141
employment. *see* work
empty nest, 365–366
enabling actions, 139
end-of-life
hospice and, 450–452
intentions, 444–445
issues, 449
environment
cues, infants, 77
hazards as teratogens, 48–49
heredity and, 38–41
intelligence and, 165–166
longevity and, 382
sensorimotor thinking and, 96
specialized brain growth and,
74
temperament and, 68
environmental press, 14
epigenetic principle, 10
episodic memory, 394
equal pay for equal work, 329, 340
equilibration, 95
Erikson's theory, 128–129,
413–414, 417
estrogen, 220, 349
ethical issues with death,
442–445
ethical research, 24
ethnic identity, 242
ethnicity. *see also* culture
diversity and parenting,
306–307
diversity of older adults and,
378–380
grandparenting and, 370–371
household labor division and,
337–338

identity and, 242
intelligence tests and, 166–167
longevity and, 382
occupational development,
327–328
eugenics, 59
European Americans
adolescent deaths, 225–226
birth of first child effect on
marriage and, 303
cohabitation among, 300
division of household labor
among, 338
divorce among, 310–311
family structure, 306
grandparenting by, 370
health, 273
intelligence testing and,
166–167
longevity, 382
occupational development
and, 328
older, 378–380
single parenthood among,
308
singlehood among, 299
European Association of Palliative Care, 442
euthanasia, 442–443
evolving gender roles, 149–150
exchange theory, 302
exercise. *see* physical fitness
exosystem, 13, *14*
experience
-expectant growth, 74
openness to, 360
experimental studies, 21
expertise development, 357–358
explicit memory, 394, *396*
expressive style, 116
extended family, 305
external aids, 396, *397*
extraversion, 360
extremely low birth weight, 56

F
fable, personal, 243
Facebook, 292
faces, perception of, 82–83, *84*
Fair Pay Act, 342
fallacies, identification of,
229–230
falls, 389–390
false-belief task, 87, *88*
families. *see also* children; marriage; parenting
child maltreatment and,
198–199
dependent care and,
335–337
dimensions and styles of parenting and, 190–194
dividing household chores
in, 338
dynamics and middle age,
365–372
extended, 305

in late life, 421–425
juggling multiple roles,
337–339
life cycle of, 305–309
nuclear, 305
parental role in, 306–309
relationships in, 190–199
siblings and, 194–195
work and, 335–339
familism, 307
Family and Medical Leave Act,
338
Family Lifestyles Project, 150
fast food, 224
fast mapping, 113–114
Fast Track, 256–257
fathers. *see also* males; parenting
age at birth of child, 306
divorced, 196, 311–312
father-infant relationships,
129–130
gender typing by, 146–148
step-, 196–197
fear
as basic emotion, 135
emergence of, 135–136
in adulthood, 285–286, 354
stranger wariness, 133
feedback from parents, 192
feeding, fine motor development
and, 75
females. *see also* gender; mothers
binge drinking and, 271
caring for aging parents,
366–367
dependent care and, 335–336
discrimination against,
328–329
eating disorders and, 224–225
equal pay for equal work, 329,
340
friendships, 293
intimacy and, 267
longevity, 382
menopause in, 349–351, 372
pubertal changes in, 218–222
reproductive changes in middle adulthood, 349–351
sexual harassment of, 329–330
sibling relationships and, 293
stereotypes of, 144
structural barriers for women
in work, 325
fertilization, 42
in vitro, 59
fetal alcohol spectrum disorder
(FAS), 47–48
fetal medicine, 52
filial obligation, 366
final scenarios, 449–450
financial independence, 267
fine motor skills, 75, 77–78, 181
firearms, 225–226
first words, 113–117
fitness. *see* physical fitness
Five-Factor model of personality,
359–361, *362*

fluid intelligence, 277–279
formal-operational period,
158–159
formula, 90
foster parents, 309
four-component model of grief,
455
frail older adults, 426–428
free radicals, 384
friendships
ABCDE model, 294
adult, 292–293
between parents and their
adult children, 365–366
children and, 200–202
cross-sex, 293
in late life, 422–423
sibling, 293
frontal cortex, 72, 219, *220*
functional health, 429
functional magnetic resonance
imaging (fMRI), 415
functional neuroimaging, 386

G
Gardner's theory of multiple
intelligences, 162,
163, 183
gays
adolescent sexual orientation,
247
couples, 300–301
death of a partner and, 462
in late life, 424
parenting by, 309
gender
-related differences, 144–146
-schema theory, 148–149
biological influences on gender role and identity, 149
constancy, 148
differences in motor skills,
181–182
differences in occupational
selection, 325–327
differences in play, 138–139
discrimination at work,
328–329
evolving roles, 149–150
friendships and, 293
identity, 148–149
intimacy and, 267
labeling, 148
longevity and, 382
retirement and, 419–420
stability, 148
stereotypes, 144, 150, 325
typing, 146–148
general designs for research,
20–22
generativity, 361, 363
genes, 35, *36. see also* heredity
Alzheimer's disease and,
402–404
biological theories of aging
and, 384
environment and, 39–40

genetic engineering and, 52
longevity and, 382
phenotypes associated with
single pairs of, *37*
risk, 403
genetic disorders, 45–46
chromosomal abnormalities,
34–37
genital herpes, *48,* 248
genital human papilloma virus,
248
genotypes, 38
germ disc, 42
gifted children, 168
Girl Scouts, 202
girls. *see* females
glass ceiling, 328–329
glass cliff, 328
glaucoma, 388
gonorrhea, *248*
grammatical development,
117–119
grammatical morphemes, 118
grandparenthood, 369–371, 461
grasping and reaching by infants,
77–78
Green House Project, 430
grief, 453–457
coping with, 455–457
process, 453–454
processing and avoidance,
456
prolonged grief disorder or
complicated, 457
reactions, 454–455
work, 454
grief-work-as-rumination
hypothesis, 455
groups, 202–203
growth
brain, 73–74
children, 69–71, *70,* 180–181
during puberty, 218–220
infants, 69–71
language, 116–117
of attachment, 129
guilt, 129, 135–136

H
habituation, 103
handedness, 78
Head Start, 166
health
changes in middle adulthood,
347–353
frailty in old age and,
426–428
functional, 429
immigrant status and, 391
in late adulthood, 384–391
nutrition and, 272–273
social, gender, and ethnic
issues in, 273–274
status and young adulthood,
269
stress and, 351–353
Healthy Marriage Initiative, 313

hearing, 79–80, *388,* 389
hearing, age-related changes in,
388–389
hemispheres, brain, 72
hepatitis B, 248
heredity. *see also* genes
depression and, 255
environment, and develop-
ment, 38–41
intelligence and, 165–166
longevity and, 382
mechanisms of, 34–37
prosocial behavior and, 141
temperament and, 68
heterocyclic antidepressants
(HCAs), 400
heterozygous (alleles), 36
heuristics, 229–230
hierarchy, dominance, 202
high-density lipoproteins (HDLs),
273
Hindu religion, 234, 417
Hispanic Americans. *see* Latino
Americans
historical context, 15
HIV (human immunodeficiency
virus), 248
Holland's personality-type
theory, 251
homogamy, 302
homozygous (alleles), 36
hope, 128
hormones
androgens, 220
estrogen, 220, 349
testosterone, 151, 220, 225, 353
hospice, 450–452
hostile aggression, 204
household, 428
household chores, division of,
337
housing options for older adults,
428–431
human development
basic forces in, 6–8
continuity and discontinuity
in, 5–6
defined, 4
nature and nurture in, 5
neuroscience and, 8–9
recurring issues in, 5–6
research, 17–26
theoretical perspectives on, *16*
universal and context-specific
development, 6
human immunodeficiency virus
(HIV), 248
hyperactivity, 171–173
hypoxia, 55

I
identity
establishing intimacy and,
266–267
ethnic, 242
evolving, 149–150
gender, 148–149

search for, 240–242
statuses, 241
illusion of invulnerability,
241–242
imaginary audience, 241
imitation, 11, 104–105
immigrant status and late adulthood, 391
impaired reading comprehension, 169, 170
implantation, 43
implementation, 250
implicit memory, 394, *396*
impulsivity, 172–173
in vitro fertilization, 59, 350
inattention, 172–173
incontinence, 401
independent variables, 21
infant-directed speech, 112
infants. *see also* childbirth;
children; newborns
attachment, 129
basic emotions, 133, *134*
cooing and babbling by, 113
emerging nervous system,
71–72
father-infant relationships,
129–130
fine motor skills, 75, 77–78
first words, 113–117
growth of the body, 69–71
information processing during,
103–108
integrating sensory information, 84–85
language exposure and,
111–112
locomotion, 75–77
mortality, 56–58
moving and grasping, 75–78
recognizing and using others'
emotions, 135
seeing by, 80–84
smelling, tasting, touching,
and hearing by, 79–80, *81*
theory of mind and, 87–88
videos for, 116–117
infatuation, 294
information processing. *see also*
cognitive development; intelligence
attention, 103–104
during adolescence, 227–231
general principles, 103–108
in late adulthood, 392–394
learning, 104–105
learning number skills and,
106–107
memory, 105–106
strategies for learning and
remembering, 160–161
theory, 12
working memory and, 228
initiative, 129
insecurity, occupational, 332–333
instrumental activities of daily
living (IADLs), 426–428, 430

instrumental aggression, 204
instrumental orientation, 232
integrating sensory information,
84–85
integration, 77
integrity *vs.* despair, 413–414
intellectual disability, 169
intelligence, 161. *see also* information processing
crystallized, 162, 277–279
emotional, 163
ethnicity and socioeconomic
status impact on testing,
166–167
fluid, 277–279
in adults, 275–282
mechanics of, 356–357
multiple, 162, *163,* 183
neuroscience and, 279
practical, 355–357, *356–357*
pragmatics of, 356
quotient (IQ), 164–165
testing, 164–167
theories of, 162–164
interindividual variability, 275
internal aids, 396
internal belief systems, 400
internal working model, 131
interpersonal norms, 232
interracial marriage, 307
intimacy, establishing, 266–267
IQ. *see* intelligence
irregular or rapid-eye-movement
(REM) sleep, 66
Islam, 298, 417

J
Japan, *58,* 113, 341, 368, 443
job satisfaction, 321–324. *see also*
work
joint and bone changes in middle
adulthood,
347–349, *351*
joint attention, 114
joint custody, 196
judgment, reflective, 280

K
Kaufman Assessment Battery for
Children, 167
kinetic cues, 80–81
kinkeeper, 365
knowledge-telling strategy, 176
knowledge-transforming strategy, 176
Kohlberg's theory of moral
reasoning, 232–233
beyond, 234
support for, 233–234
Kübler-Ross's theory on dying, 447

L
labeling, gender, 148
labor and delivery, 53–54. *see
also* childbirth
language, 111–121. *see also* learning; speech
bilingualism and, 115–116

verbal ability and gender, 145
vernix, 64
very low birth weight, 56
viability, age of, 44
video games, *206, 207*
vision, age-related changes in, 387–388
visual cliff, 80–81
visual expansion, 81
vitamin D, 349, 351, *352*
volunteering, 420, *421*
vulnerability-stress-adaptation model, 303
Vygotsky's theory, 13, 108–110

W
waking activity, 65
wariness of strangers, 133
wear-and-tear disease, 348
wear-and-tear theory, 384
Wechsler Intelligence Scale for Children IV (WISC-IV), 167, 273
well-being, 414–417
whole-brain death, 441
widowhood, 425, 454–455, 461–462
will, 128
wisdom, 397–398
withdrawal reflex, *65*
women. *see* females; mothers

Women's Health Initiative (WHI), 372
words
  -learning styles, 116
  as symbols, 113
  first, 113–117
  identifying, 112–113
  learning, 115–116
  mapping of, 113–114
  names, constraints on, 114
  recognizing, 174–175
work
  -family conflict, 338–339
  adolescents and, 249–253
  alienation and burnout in, 323–324
  bias and discrimination at, 328–330
  career development and, 250–251
  career plateauing at, 332
  coping with unemployment, 333–334
  equal pay for equal, 329, 340
  ethnicity and, 327–328
  family and, 335–339
  gender differences in occupational selection and, 325–327
  job satisfaction and, 321–324
  meaning of, 318

  occupational choice and, 318–319, 325
  occupational development and, 319–321, 326–327, 327–328
  occupational expectations and, 320
  occupational insecurity and, 332–333
  occupational transitions and, 331–334
  personality-type theory and, 251
  retirement and, 418–420, *421*
  retraining workers for, 331–332
  sexual harassment at, 329–330
  women and, 325–327
working memory, 228, 394
World Health Organization, 71, 276, 299
writing, 176–177

Y
young adulthood. *see also* emerging adulthood
  binge drinking in, 271, 286
  cognitive development in, 275–282
  creating scenarios and life stories in, 283

  death and, 459–460
  integrating emotion and logic in life problems in, 280–282
  lifestyle factors in, 269–273
  neuroscience research and intelligence in, 279
  personal control beliefs in, 284–285
  personality in, 282–285, 360–363
  physical development and health in, 269–274
  possible selves and, 283–284
  thinking in, 279–280

Z
zone of maximum comfort, 412
zone of maximum performance potential, 412
zone of proximal development, 109
zygote period, 42–43